C000102907

ISBN 978-0-282-88371-3
PIBN 10871248

EIGHTH ANNUAL REPORT

OF THE

BOARD OF REGENTS

OF THE

SMITHSONIAN INSTITUTION,

SHOWING

THE OPERATIONS, EXPENDITURES, AND CONDITION OF THE INSTITUTION UP TO JANUARY 1, 1854.

AND THE

PROCEEDINGS OF THE BOARD UP TO JULY 8, 1854.

WASHINGTON:
BEVERLEY TUCKER, SENATE PRINTER.
1854.

33d Congress, 1st Session. | [SENATE.] | Mis. Doc. No. 73.

LETTER

FROM THE

SECRETARY OF THE SMITHSONIAN INSTITUTION,

COMMUNICATING

The Annual Report of the Board of Regents.

July 25, 1854.—Ordered to be printed.
July 28, 1854.—Ordered that 10,000 additional copies be printed, 500 of which for the use of the Smithsonian Institution.

Smithsonian Institution, *July* 22, 1854.

Sir: I have the honor herewith to transmit to you the Annual Report of the Board of Regents of the Smithsonian Institution, and beg leave to request that you will present it to the Senate of the United States.

I have the honor to be, very respectfully, your obedient servant,

JOSEPH HENRY,
Secretary Smithsonian Institution.

Hon. David R. Atchison,
President of the Senate of the U. S.

OFFICERS OF THE SMITHSONIAN INSTITUTION.

FRANKLIN PIERCE, *Ex-officio* Presiding Officer of the Institution.
ROGER B. TANEY, Chancellor of the Institution.
JOSEPH HENRY, Secretary of the Institution.
CHARLES C. JEWETT, Assistant Secretary, in charge of the Library, up to July 10, 1854.
SPENCER F. BAIRD, Assistant Secretary, in charge of the Museum.

ALEXANDER D. BACHE,
JAMES A. PEARCE,
JOSEPH G. TOTTEN,
} Executive Committee.

RICHARD RUSH,
——— ———,
WM. H. ENGLISH,
JOSEPH HENRY,
} Building Committee.

W. W. SEATON, Treasurer.

REGENTS OF THE INSTITUTION.

——— ———, Vice President of the United States.
ROGER B. TANEY, Chief Justice of the United States.
JOHN T. TOWERS, Mayor of the City of Washington.
JAMES A. PEARCE, Member of the Senate of the United States.
JAMES M. MASON, Member of the Senate of the United States.
S. A. DOUGLAS, Member of the Senate of the United States.
W. H. ENGLISH, Member of the House of Representatives.
DAVID STUART, Member of the House of Representatives.
JAMES MEACHAM, Member of the House of Representatives.
RUFUS CHOATE, Citizen of Massachusetts.
GIDEON HAWLEY, Citizen of New York.
J. MACPHERSON BERRIEN, Citizen of Georgia.
RICHARD RUSH, Citizen of Pennsylvania.
ALEXANDER D. BACHE, Member of the National Institute, Washington.
JOSEPH G. TOTTEN, Member of the National Institute, Washington.

MEMBERS EX-OFFICIO OF THE INSTITUTION.

FRANKLIN PIERCE, President of the United States.
——— ———, Vice President of the United States.
WILLIAM L. MARCY, Secretary of State.
JAMES GUTHRIE, Secretary of the Treasury.
JEFFERSON DAVIS, Secretary of War.
JAMES C. DOBBIN, Secretary of the Navy.
JAMES CAMPBELL, Postmaster General.
CALEB CUSHING, Attorney General.
ROGER B. TANEY, Chief Justice of the United States.
CHARLES MASON, Commissioner of Patents.
JOHN T. TOWERS, Mayor of the City of Washington.

HONORARY MEMBERS.

ROBERT HARE.
WASHINGTON IRVING.
BENJAMIN SILLIMAN.
PARKER CLEAVELAND.

EIGHTH ANNUAL REPORT

OF THE

BOARD OF REGENTS

OF

THE SMITHSONIAN INSTITUTION,

SHOWING

The operations, expenditures, and condition of the Institution up to January 1, 1854, *and the proceedings of the Board up to July* 8, 1854.

To the Senate and House of Representatives:

In obedience to the act of Congress of August 10, 1846, establishing the Smithsonian Institution, the undersigned, in behalf of the Regents, submit to Congress, as a report of the operations, expenditures, and condition of the Institution, the following documents:

1. The Annual Report of the Secretary, giving an account of the operations of the Institution during the year 1853, including reports from the Assistant Secretaries, relative to the library, museum, &c.

2. Report of the Executive Committee, giving a general statement of the proceeds and disposition of the Smithsonian fund, and also an account of the expenditures for the year 1853.

3. Report of the Building Committee, relative to the progress made in 1853 in the erection of the Smithsonian edifice.

4. Proceedings of the Board of Regents and of the Establishment, up to July 2, 1854

5. Appendix.

Respectfully submitted.

ROGER B. TANEY, *Chancellor.*
JOSEPH HENRY, *Secretary.*

July 22, 1854.

REPORT OF THE SECRETARY.

To the Board of Regents of the Smithsonian Institution.

GENTLEMEN: Nothing of especial interest has occurred during the past year to mark an epoch in the history of the institution over which you preside. The several objects set forth in the plan of organization have been prosecuted as far as the funds which could be devoted to them would allow. A knowledge of the true character of the institution has been gradually extended, and it is a subject of gratification that the plan of operations is more highly appreciated the better it is understood. Every succeeding year which is added to the age of the institution will render it more stable, so long as it pursues undeviatingly the same course. All establishments, however, which are supported by bequests, intended to promote the public good, are necessarily subjected to the scrutiny of all who consider themselves personally interested in the trust. The managers are overwhelmed with suggestions, and subjected to illiberal criticisms, and unless they are firmly convinced of the propriety of their course, and have sufficient moral courage to pursue it notwithstanding opposition, there is danger of vacillation, and of an attempt to gain popularity by adopting measures not calculated to promote the desired end. It should, however, be recollected that opinions ought to be weighed rather than counted, and that nothing of importance can be accomplished either by an individual or an institution, except by constant and laborious exertion in one direction. In the beginning of this institution the plans best calculated to realize the liberal intentions of the donor were adopted after due deliberation, and have been constantly adhered to and developed as far as the requisitions of Congress and the limited income would allow. From the character of James Smithson and his pursuits there can be no reasonable doubt as to his intention in regard to the bequest. He was a man familiar with the precise language of exact science, and no other construction ought to be put upon the words of his will than that which a strict interpretation will allow. He leaves his property to found an establishment which shall bear his own name, and have for its object "the increase and diffusion of knowledge among men." It would evidently be incompatible with an enlarged and just interpretation of this will to confine its benefits exclusively to one people, and especially would it be unworthy the character of a great nation to accept the administration of a bequest intended for the good of mankind, and to apply it exclusively to its own use.

Nothing apparently can be further from the truth than the idea which was first prevalent in this country that Smithson left his money merely to diffuse practical knowledge among the people of the United States. On the contrary he intended this institution as a monument to his name which should be known of all men, and prized by the student of every branch of literature and science, which should not be restricted to merely spreading abroad the knowledge which already exists, but, above all, should be the means of enlarging the bounds of human thought. He was also too much of a philosopher to confine his bequest to the promotion of any one branch of literature or science, and therefore left the trust free to be applied to all.

His will recognizes a well established and very important distinction with regard to knowledge, viz. its increase and its diffusion. These, though frequently confounded, are very different processes, and each may exist independent of the other. While we rejoice that in our country, above all others, so much attention is paid to the diffusion of knowledge, truth compels us to say that comparatively little encouragement is given to its increase.

There is another division with regard to knowledge which Smithson does not embrace in his design, viz. the application of knowledge to useful purposes in the arts; and it was not necessary he should found an institution for this purpose. There are already in every civilized country establishments and patent laws for the encouragement of this department of mental industry. As soon as any branch of science can be brought to bear on the necessities, conveniences, or luxuries of life, it meets with encouragement and reward. Not so with the discovery of the incipient principles of science. The investigations which lead to these receive no fostering care from government, and are considered by the superficial observer as trifles unworthy the attention of those who place the supreme good in that which immediately administers to the physical necessities or luxuries of life.

If physical well being were alone the object of existence, every avenue of enjoyment should be explored to its utmost extent. But he who loves truth for its own sake, feels that its highest claims are lowered and its moral influence marred by being continually summoned to the bar of immediate and palpable utility. Smithson himself had no such narrow views. The prominent design of his bequest is the promotion of abstract science. It leaves to the teacher and the teeming press to diffuse popular knowledge, and to the Patent Office and the manufacturer to facilitate and reward the application of science to the useful arts. In this respect the Institution holds an otherwise unoccupied place in this country, and adopts two fundamental maxims in its policy: 1st, to do nothing with its funds which can be equally well done by other means; and, 2d, to produce results which, as far as possible, will benefit mankind in general. Any deviations from these maxims which the history of the Institution may exhibit, must be referred to the original requirements of the law of Congress authorizing its establishment, and not to the plan of active operations at first proposed in the programme, and which has constantly been kept in view from the beginning until the present time.

A miscellaneous and general library, museum, and gallery of art, though important in themselves, have from the first been considered by those who have critically examined the will of Smithson, to be too restricted in their operations and too local in their influence, to meet the comprehensive intentions of the testator; and the hope has been cherished that other means may ultimately be provided for the support of those objects, and that the whole income of the Smithsonian fund may be devoted to the more legitimate objects of the noble bequest.

I have been informed by the Commissioner of Patents that the space now occupied in the building of the Patent Office by the national museum, is imperatively required for the display of models; and he suggests that a part or the whole of the Smithsonian building shall be purchased for the deposit of this collection. If Congress will entirely relieve the Smithsonian fund from the expense of collecting and maintaining a museum, a large portion of the present building would be unnecessary, and the proposition to purchase a part or the whole of it might properly be entertained. The Smithsonian Institution, if required, would take the supervision of a government museum, and would turn over to it all the specimens collected after they had been examined and described. The importance of a collection at the seat of government to illustrate the physical geography, natural history, and ethnology of the United States, cannot be too highly estimated. But the support of such a collection ought not to be a burthen upon the Smithsonian fund.

It was stated in the last report that the plan of an equal division of the income between the library and museum on the one hand, and the lectures, the publications, and researches on the other, was found not to work well in practice. It leads to inharmonious action, and to a system of expenditure by no means compatible with proper economy or the limited income of the Smithsonian fund. The subject has, however, been referred to a special committee of the Regents, which I trust will give it due consideration, and report their views during the present session of the Board.

Publications.—During the past year no diminution has taken place in the objects of interest which have presented themselves for the assistance and patronage of the institution. The amount of publications has only been limited by the appropriation which could be devoted to this purpose.

1. The first memoir published during the past year is one by Dr. Joseph Leidy, Professor of Anatomy in the University of Pennsylvania, entitled, "The Ancient Fauna of Nebraska."

A considerable portion of the country between the Mississippi and the Rocky mountains consists of the more recent geological deposits, and particularly on the Upper Missouri there exists a tract of country known by the name of the Mauvaises Terres, or the Bad Lands; this at one time was probably the bottom of an immense lake, in which perished thousands of animals having no representatives at this time on the surface of the earth. It appears that the waters of this lake were removed by some convulsion of nature, that the sediment at its bottom became indurated, and that afterwards the whole country was traversed by an immense wave of water, which carried away the softer parts of the strata, and left standing the harder parts in a series of irregular prismatic and columnar masses frequently capped with irregular pyramids, and extending upwards to a height of from one to two hundred feet. "Viewed in the distance, these rocky piles in their endless succession assume the appearance of massive architectural structures, with all the accessories of buttresses, turrets, and tapering spires." The portion of the surface thus excavated forms a valley of ninety miles in length and thirty in breadth, which in its most depressed portion is about three hundred feet below the surface of the surrounding country. So thickly are the natural towers studded over the surface of this extraordinary region, that the traveller threads his way through deep confined passages, which resemble the narrow irregular streets and lanes of some of the old towns of the continent of Europe. At the foot of these columns, the remains of the ancient animals, which lived and breathed long before the advent of man upon the face of the earth, are found in such abundance as to form of this tract an extensive cemetery of vertebrated animals, rivalling, in the variety of its extinct species, the celebrated beds of the Paris basin.

This region having been brought to notice by a few fossil remains procured through the agents of the American Fur Company, an appropriation of about $200 for its exploration was made by the Smithsonian Institution to Mr. Thaddeus Culbertson, who was about to visit, on account of his health, the sources of the Missouri. The specimens of fossil remains which were thus procured, together with a collection subsequently presented to the Institution by Capt. Stewart Van Vliet, of the U. S. army, and several specimens kindly lent by Dr. Prout, of Missouri, were referred to Dr. Leidy for examination. In addition to these he had the use of a collection lent by Prof. O'Loghland, of Missouri, specimens belonging to the Academy of Natural Sciences, Philadelphia, and a collection made by Dr. Evans, at the instigation of Dr. D. Dale Owen, the whole embracing all the specimens which have yet been brought to the east from the Bad Lands. The bones are completely petrified, and their cavities filled with silicious matter. They are preserved in various degrees of integrity, some being beautifully perfect and others broken and imperfect, the latter having been evidently subjected to violence while imbedded in a soft mud. The animals belong to the classes mammalia and chelonia, or turtles. With a single exception, all the species of mammalia belong to the great order of ungulata or hoofed animals, of which there are seven species of four genera, which belong to the ruminantia, or cud-chewing animals; two species of one genus belonging to the paradigitata ordinaria, or even-toed animals; one species of the solipedia, or solid-hoofed animals; and four species of three genera belonging to the imparidigitata ordinaria, or uneven-toed animals.

The first specimen described belonged to a peculiar genus of ruminants which, among recent animals, is more nearly allied to the musk, and was probably hornless. The next is of a remarkable genus of ungulata representing a type which occupies a position in the wide physiological interval existing between recent ruminants and the anomalous fossil animal called the anoplotherium. Another genus is called oreodon, and constitutes one of the links necessary to fill up the very wide gap between existing ruminants and an exceedingly aberrant form of the same family now extinct. Another organic relic is that of an animal which combined the ruminant and carnivorous characteristics, of which there are several species. There are also two remarkable species of rhinoceros, differing from any remains of this animal found in other parts of the globe. The existing species of the rhinoceros are met with in Africa, Asia, and the islands of Java and Sumatra. Remains of extinct species have been found in Great Britain, the continent of Europe, Siberia, and the Himalayas; but no trace of this genus had previously been discovered in America. Another fossil remain belongs to the feline family, about a fifth smaller than the American panther, and is probably the most ancient known genus of this animal. Hundreds of fossil turtles are found in the "Bad Lands;" they belong to the genus testudo, of which five species are described in this paper.

The memoir occupies one hundred and twenty-six pages, and is illustrated by twenty-four plates, one of which is a folio. It has already been printed and copies distributed among working geologists. No copy-right is secured on the publications of the Institution; and it may be mentioned here, as an illustration of the manner in which the knowledge contained in the Smithsonian memoirs reaches the public generally in a popular form, that one of the figures of this paper has already been copied, and some of its materials given in a recent work on geology.

2. Another paper, the printing of which is nearly complete, is on the "Winds of the Northern Hemisphere," by Prof. James H. Coffin, of Lafayette College, Easton, Pennsylvania. It is the same which was mentioned in the Report for 1851. Its publication has been delayed in consequence of the difficulty experienced in finishing the maps and printing the tabular matter, and also on account of additions made to it by the author. It is a very elaborate memoir, of two hundred pages, consisting principally of tabular matter, and illustrated by thirteen maps. The most important results arrived at in this paper, are as follows: There exist in the northern hemisphere three great zones of wind, extending entirely around the earth, modified and, in some cases, partially interrupted by the configuration and character of the surface. The first of these is the trade wind, near the equator, blowing, when uninterrupted, from northeast to southwest. This belt is interrupted, however, in the Atlantic ocean, near the coast of Africa, upon the Mediterranean sea, and also in Barbary by the action of the Great Desert. The second is a belt of westerly wind, nearly two thousand miles in breadth, between latitude 35° and 60° north, and encircling the earth, the westerly direction being clearly defined in the middle of the belt, but gradually disappearing as we approach the limits on either side. North of this, there is another system of winds flowing southwardly from high northern latitudes, and gradually inclining towards the west as it moves into a latitude of greater easterly velocity.

Subsequent investigations have led Prof. Coffin to conclude that the lines which separate these systems are not parallels of latitude, but circles, having a common pole in about latitude 84° north, and longitude 105° west from Greenwich, and that the winds of high northern latitudes diverge or radiate from this point.

The principal cause of these phenomena is the greater heat of the sun between the tropics, which rarifies the air, and causes it to ascend into the higher regions; producing below a current from the pole towards the equator, and above a current in the opposite direction. The resulting motions to and from the equator are not in a north and south direction along the meridians, but are modified by the rotation of the earth: at the surface they deviate towards the west, and in the return current above towards the east. If the point mentioned by Prof. Coffin as the centre of the winds of the polar zone really exists, it is probably that of maximum cold; the air at this point would be condensed, and flow from it in radial lines in every direction along the surface of the earth. The paper is an important addition to meteorology, and has cost the author years of labor. The publication of it has also been very expensive, particularly on account of the maps and tables.

3. Another memoir accepted for publication is, "An Account of a Tornado that passed near New Harmony, Indiana, April 30, 1852, by John Chappelsmith."

The eastern portion of the North American continent is almost every year visited at different points by one or more tornadoes of frightful energy, but of exceedingly circumscribed limits; and it is almost an opprobrium to the science of this country that more reliable data have not been collected towards settling definitely the conditions of these remarkable phenomena, and for ascertaining their cause. For this purpose however, mere verbal descriptions of the effects are alone insufficient, there must be added to these accurate instrumental surveys, and, if possible, the indications of the barometer, thermometer, and hygrometer. The first accurate report of this kind was that by Prof. A. D. Bache, relative to a tornado which passed over the city of New Brunswick, in New Jersey, in 1834. A similar survey was made by Professor Eustis, of Harvard University, of the tornado of August 21, 1851, which passed near Cambridge.

We consider the present memoir as an exceedingly valuable addition to the stock of our knowledge on this subject. It gives not only all the collateral phenomena as far as they could be obtained, but presents a map of one square mile of the track on which are elaborately plotted the relative position and bearings of the prostrated trees. Some idea may be obtained of the enormous energy of this tornado from the statement of the author that " on a single square mile of the track, thousands of trees, many of them having a stem fifteen feet in circumference, were prostrated by a force acting simultaneously in opposite directions, and moving onward at the rate of a mile in a minute."

The author critically analyses the force at work, and arrives at the conclusion that the proximate cause of the phenomenon is an inward, upward, and onward moving column of air. Besides the map, the memoir is accompanied by diagrams and sketches to illustrate the character and effects of the tornado.

4. Another memoir is entitled "The Antiquities of Wisconsin, examined and surveyed by I. A. Lapham."

In the Report for 1851, it was mentioned that Mr. Lapham, an experienced engineer, had undertaken, under the direction of the American Antiquarian Society of Worcester, Massachusetts, to make explorations, surveys and drawings of the aboriginal antiquities of Wisconsin, and, to insure harmony of action in the cultivation of the wide field of research offered by the ancient monuments of this country, that the Antiquarian Society had agreed to present to the Smithsonian Institution the results of the labors of Mr. Lapham for publication, and to reserve its own funds for further explorations. Mr. Lapham's memoir has been completed, and, after having been examined and reported upon by a committee of the Antiquarian Society, has been presented to this Institution for publication. It consists of several hundred pages of manuscript, illustrated by sixty-three large drawings or plates adapted to the size of the Smithsonian Contributions, a map of the country, and ninety-seven figures or smaller designs, intended to be engraved on wood and interspersed with the text.

Elaborate works of defence, and such as are apparently designed for religious or sacrificial ceremonies, so numerous in other sections of the country, are seldom found in Wisconsin. In place of these, less elevated structures, though often on a scale of considerable horizontal extent, representing a variety of fanciful forms, abound along the sides of the streams and borders of the lakes. The figures are principally those of lizards, turtles, birds, bears, foxes, and men, and they appear to be confined within a limited territory between the Mississippi and Lake Michigan. It is very remarkable, says the committee, that none of the earlier travellers appear to have noticed the animal shape of the embankments; but this is accounted for by the extent and flatness of the works, and the difficulty of recognising them while covered with trees or a dense growth of other vegetation. Indeed, the surveyors who first attempted to plot them were sometimes surprised at the figures developed under their hands, and which could not have been perceived on the ground, unless from an elevated point of view.

The memoir of Mr. Lapham, with a few unimportant exceptions, includes an account of every known work or assemblage of works in this region, and the whole were carefully surveyed by himself or by competent individuals under his direction. On the map are laid down the relative position of the earth-works; and from this it appears that they lie chiefly along the course of streams and the borders of the interior lakes. Nearly the same forms are repeated in different localities, but with dissimilar arrangement, and often with slight, yet evidently intentional variation in figure. The works are enumerated as follows:

a. Tumuli of a conical shape and slight elevation.

b. Oblong mounds not more than three or four feet high, of regular width, extending in a straight line from twenty feet to several hundred, and even a thousand.

c. Embankments in crescent and serpentine forms.

d. Embankments tapering uniformly in width from one extremity to the other, and terminating in a point.

e. Similar tapering embankments, with two projections on one side, near the larger end, which are called lizards, and are very numerous.

f. The same general form, with projections on both sides at the larger end, and with a similar tapering tail, sometimes of exceedingly disproportionate length. These frequently present a striking resemblance to a turtle, and are known by the name of that animal.

g. Oblong embankments, with arms or wings extended on either side. These vary from simple crosses to figures of birds and men, the head being usually omitted.

h. Representations of animals of more definite outlines and better proportions: among these are bears, foxes, otters, &c., and upon the Wisconsin river, buffaloes. It is proved by numerous excavations that the works which resemble animals are destitute of relics; they are mere relievos or embossments on the surface of the earth, seldom exceeding four feet in height, and in some cases but a few inches. Mr. Lapham disclaims all intention of indulging a disposition to theorize or speculate on the origin or design of these remains, and declares his object to be merely the faithful performance of the offiee of surveyor, to study the facts, and to report them in as much detail as may be necessary, leaving to others the deductions which, in connexion with other information, may be drawn from them. In the opinion of the commission appointed by the society to examine the memoir, "Mr. Lapham has accomplished his task with great thoroughness and artistic skill; he seems to have explored the entire field, to have industriously delineated every object of interest, and to have omitted no detail of drawing or description which could conduce to a clear understanding of the matter of which he treats." The publication of this memoir, which will be alike creditable to the author, the Antiquarian Society, and this Institution, will furnish an interesting addition to the antiquities of this country, which cannot fail to be hailed with pleasure by the ethnologist.

5. Two botanical papers, furnished by Dr. John Torrey, of the New York Medical College, have been published during the past year. The first describes a new plant, to which the author has given the name of *Darlingtonia Californica*. It is a new pitcher-plant, which was first detected by Mr. W. D. Brackenridge, assistant botanist in the United States Exploring Expedition under Captain Wilkes. It has hitherto been found only near the Shasta mountain, on the Upper Sacramento. The specimens brought home by Mr. Brackenridge were without flowers or seed-vessels, so that the genus of the plant could not be determined, but it was taken for a new Sarracencia. After many years, the flowers were discovered by Dr. G. W. Hulse, and brought to Dr. Torrey, who has shown that the plant is an entirely new genus of the same small but very interesting natural order to which the Sarracencia belongs. He has bestowed upon it the name of Darlingtonia, in honor of Dr. William Darlington, of West Chester, Pennsylvania, author of several valuable botanical works. The genus formerly dedicated to this veteran botanist by De Candolle having been reduced to an older one, Dr. Torrey embraced the opportunity of restoring the name, and connecting it with one of the most remarkable plants of North America.

6. The second memoir by Dr. Torrey is an account of a new maritime shrubby plant, called "Batis Maritima," which grows on the shores of Key West, Jamaica, Cuba, and the neighboring parts of the continent. It has been known to botanists for more than one hundred and fifty years, yet, strange to say, it has not till now been correctly described, nor its place in the natural system determined with any cer-

tainty. Dr. Torrey considers it as the type of a distinct order, nearly allied to the empetraceæ, or crowberries.

Both memoirs are illustrated with plates, from beautiful drawings made by Sprague, at the expense of the institution.

7. The next memoir is a "Synopsis of the Marine Invertebrata of the Grand Manan, or the region about the Bay of Fundy, New Brunswick," by William Stimpson.

The island of Grand Manan, a part of the natural history of which this paper is intended to illustrate, lies at the mouth of the Bay of Fundy, and is surrounded by deep water, the bottom of which abounds in a variety of marine animals.

The memoir consists of a compend of observations made on the marine fauna of this region during a residence of three months in the summer of 1852, and also of a catalogue of the marine invertebrata found on the shores and in the adjacent waters.

Minute surveys of the marine animals of a given district are highly interesting; it is only by a comparison of the results of such examinations made at a series of points along a coast, that an accurate knowledge can be obtained of their distribution, and of the effects of external circumstances on their growth, habits, and economy. By such surveys we can ascertain whether a species may inhabit two distant localities without occurring in the intermediate space, a fact which has an important bearing on several interesting questions relative to geological changes. The author is a pupil of Professor Agassiz, and has been appointed one of the naturalists in the North Pacific Exploring Expedition, under Captain Ringgold.

The paper occupies 66 pages, and is illustrated by 37 lithographic figures.

8. A memoir has also been presented, and is now in the press, "On some new American species and localities of Microscopic Organisms," by Prof. J. W. Bailey, of West Point, New York.

Nearly two centuries have passed away since Leeuwenhoek, an eminent physician of Holland, discovered by means of the microscope a department of organized nature, consisting of bodies imperceptible to the unaided vision, and displaying active forms, so strange and varied in their appearance, that they excited a general curiosity. The discovery, in some of them, of organs of motion, convinced him of their animal character, and he gave to them the name of *animalcules*. They were afterwards called infusoria. Many opinions were entertained with regard to their character. Linnæus considered them as lifeless, oily particles, and their movements as altogether passive. We owe, however, to Prof. Ehrenberg, of Berlin, an extended series of observations on this subject, the results of which are, that the infusoria are organized bodies; the greater part, if not all, are animals; they exist in all quarters of the globe, as well on land as at the bottom of the sea, and their silicious and calcareous remains form, in this country, wide-spread fossil strata. At Andover, Massachusetts, there is a bed of these remains of fifteen feet in thickness, and underlying the city of Richmond, Virginia, one of twenty-eight feet. Professor Bailey has distinguished himself by researches in the same line, and has published on this subject a series of papers in Silliman's Journal, and in two memoirs in the Smithsonian Contributions. In the present memoir he has described new species of diatomaceæ, limnias, auliscus, peridinium, cothurnia, and monactinus; he has given the American localities of Amphitetras antediluviana, and tetragramma, and gives an account of the organic forms found in the Croton water, New York.

One of the species described forms a material resembling white clay, which occurs in a large deposit at Suisun bay, about thirty miles above San Francisco; and should, says Prof. Bailey, this fact meet the eye of any scientific traveller in California, it may induce him to furnish further information concerning the geological relations of this interesting deposit, and to collect a good supply of specimens for a more complete study.

It has been known to the New York microscopists, but not to the public generally, that the Croton water abounds in beautiful microscopic organisms, and particularly in diatomaceæ and desmidieæ. The author found in the sediment collected by means of a filter at the Astor House, more than fifty different species of these organisms. Of these the gallionella crotonensis is in the greatest abundance, and thousands of its fragments must be daily swallowed by those who use the unfiltered water. It is so abundant that Prof. Bailey suggests that it may yet prove of importance as a means of detecting the fraudulent dilution of various substances by this water.

This memoir is illustrated by a number of wood-cuts and thirty-eight elaborately drawn figures on a steel plate beautifully executed by J. E. Gavitt, an amateur naturalist and artist of Albany, New York.

9. During the past year the catalogue of Coleoptera by Frederick Ernst Melsheimer, M. D., mentioned in a previous Report, has been published and distributed. It forms an octavo volume of 174 pages.

At first sight it would appear that the study of insects is the most trivial and furthest removed of that of any part of creation from useful purposes; but independently of the interest which attaches to it as an exposition of animated nature, and an exhibition of organization and life in curiously diversified forms, there is scarcely any branch of natural history more intimately connected with the pursuits of the husbandman, the naval architect, and even those of the artist and the bibliographer, than entomology. It is the duty therefore of this Institution to afford every facility for the acquisition of this branch of knowledge, and to increase the number of those who make it their special study.

The coleoptera form one of the largest and most widely distributed class of insects; and on account of their boring habits, some of the species are highly destructive to timber. In order, however, to study them properly, it is necessary that the same species which exist in this country and in Europe may be identified, and that those which are new here may be separately described. The present memoir gives the names of all those which have been described, with references to the works where the descriptions may be found. Dr. Melsheimer has spent several years in the preparation of this work. It was referred for examination to Professor S. S. Haldeman and Dr. J. L. Le Conte, who reported in favor of its publication, and offered to superintend its printing and to bring it down to 1851. This they have done at the expense of much time and labor, and have thereby added materially to the usefulness of the catalogue.

10. A second edition of the Report on Recent Improvements in the Chemical Arts has been printed, and in due time an additional volume on this subject will be prepared.

11. The general interest which has been awakened by the recent application of electricity to purposes in the useful arts, and its recognised connexion with many important and mysterious phenomena of nature, led to the conclusion that an account of the recent discoveries in this branch of science would be highly prized by a large class of readers. In accordance with this view, a report by M. Müller, of Berlin, has been translated, and will be published as soon as the funds will allow of the expenditure. Stereotype copies of the original wood-cuts have been obtained from the author.

It will be especially interesting to the English reader, because it gives more particularly the researches which have been made in Germany, and which are consequently not readily accessible to the inhabitants of this country and Great Britain.

12. Catalogue of North American reptiles in the Museum of the Smithsonian Institution. Part I.—*Serpents.*—By S. F. Baird & C. Girard, pp. 188.—This work is intended to exhibit the nature and extent of the collection of North American reptiles in the museum of the Smithsonian Institution. According to the statement of Professor Baird, it contains full and original descriptions from authentic specimens of 119 species of serpents, of which sixty have been first described by the authors, and from specimens in the Smithsonian collection. All the well ascertained species of North American serpents are included in this catalogue, which thus serves as a complete manual on the subject. The great work by Dr. Holbrook on the reptiles of North America, published in 1842, enumerates 49 species, as being all that were known to him; a number less than half of those in the possession of the Smithsonian Institution.

The *phenomena of magnetism*, which a few years ago were only recognised as existing in iron, and in a slight degree in a few other metals, are now known to belong to all matter; and with those of electricity, with which they are intimately connected, either in the relation of effect and cause, or the concomitant effects of a more general principle, are probably displayed in every part of the material universe. Recent researches render it probable that the sun and moon exert a magnetic influence upon our earth. Were the study of this mysterious principle immediately connected with none of the physical wants of man, or with the arts of life, it would in itself be an object of high interest; but when we reflect how dependent upon it is the art of navigation, and how extensively it is employed in this country in tracing the divisions and boundaries of land, we are, from utilitarian considerations, induced to give it the most minute and laborious investigation.

It is now known that the magnetic needle is never at rest; that it is the subject of various changes, some depending upon the hour of the day, others upon the season of the year, others again upon longer periods of time.

It also varies in its direction at different places. Between the Atlantic and Pacific coast, or, for example, between Massachusetts bay and the mouth of the Columbia river, there is a variation of upwards of twenty-four degrees; but this variation is not constant even at the same place, but changes from year to year. With these changes it is necessary that the navigator should be familiar. It therefore becomes a matter of national importance that observations of these phenomena should be made at as many places and those as widely separated from each other as possible.

The Smithsonian Institution has endeavored to advance this branch of knowledge, by importing at different times, and at considerable expense, four entire sets of apparatus, besides separate instruments, for determining the direction and intensity of the magnetic force.

These instruments have been lent to observers, and in some cases sold to the government for the use of exploring parties, and have done, or are now doing, good service, in adding to the stock of facts which, by the process of induction, are to yield a knowledge of general laws.

It will be recollected that an appropriation was made at the last session of the Regents for supplying magnetic instruments to the Grinnell Expedition. These were procured from London, were given in charge to Dr. Kane, and, we trust, are at this time revealing to that intrepid explorer the fitful and mysterious changes of the magnetic force.

During the past year, a magnetic observatory has been erected within the grounds of the Smithsonian Institution. It principally consists, to insure an equable temperature, of an under-ground room, enclosed within two walls, between which a current of air is allowed to pass in order to prevent dampness. This observatory has been supplied with a set of apparatus for determining the continued variations in direction and intensity of terrestrial magnetism. By a very ingenious application of the photographic process, the invention of Mr. Brooks, of England, the instruments are made to record, on a sheet of sensitive paper moved by clock-work, their own motions.

First, to determine the variation of direction of the horizontal magnet: a steel bar, strongly magnetized, is suspended by several fibres of untwisted silk, so as to have perfect freedom of motion in the horizontal plane, and from a gas light, kept perpetually burning, a single ray of light is thrown upon a concave mirror permanently attached to the magnetic bar, and consequently partaking of its movements. This ray of light is reflected and brought to a focus at the surface of a revolving cylinder, moved by clock-work, on which the photographic paper is placed. When the magnet is at rest, the pencil of light is stationary, and consequently traces, on the moving paper, a simple straight line; but when the magnet is disturbed by terrestrial perturbations, its oscillations are recorded by the motion of the pencil of light in a curved or zigzag line.

To register the intensity of strength of the magnetic force, another bar magnet is suspended by two parallel silk threads about an inch apart, descending from two hooks fastened to the under side of a plate attached to the ceiling or some other support. The plate is then made to revolve through an arc of a circle until, by the force of torsion, the bar is deflected from a north and south to an east and west direction. It is thus kept in a state of equilibrium between the force of torsion of the threads, tending to turn its north end round still further to the south, and the magnetism of the earth, on the other hand, tending to bring it back to its north and south direction. If in this position the magnetism of the earth becomes stronger, it will prevail, and the north end of the needle will turn towards the north; if the magnetism of the earth diminishes in intensity, the force of torsion will prevail, and the same end will move towards the south. These motions, as in the case of the other magnet, are recorded by a beam of light on the paper surface of the revolving cylinder.

But beside the change of direction of the horizontal needle, a magnet so supported as to be free to take any position, in this latitude will arrange itself with its north end dipping down towards the horizon. The amount of this dip, or variation, varies also in different places, and at different times; and to record these changes a bar is supported, in the direction of the magnetic north and south, on two knife edges like the beam of a balance. Any change which takes place in the position of a magnet thus arranged, is recorded by a mirror attached to the prolongation of the axis on which the bar turns.

It is proposed to keep these instruments constantly in operation, for the purpose of comparing results with other observations of a similar character in different parts of the world; and also for the purpose of furnishing a standard to which the observations made at various points by the Coast Survey, and the different scientific explorations which are now in progress in the western portions of the United States, may be referred, and with which they may be compared.

This establishment ought to be supported by government; but as no provision has been made for it, and as the wants are pressing, in order to render more valuable the observations making in other countries as well as our own, the Smithsonian Institution, in connexion with the Coast Survey, has undertaken to commence it. In accordance, however, with the policy which has thus far governed the acts of the Institution, this observatory will be turned over to other hands as soon as other means are found for its support.

The other sets of magnetic instruments mentioned which have been imported by the Institution are intended to furnish portable magnetic observatories, in which the dip and the intensity are recorded by the pen from direct and personal observations.

Besides the facts which will be collected by the Coast Survey along our extended sea-board, those which the various exploring expeditions are furnishing, and those obtained by the instruments belonging to the Smithsonian Institution, a large number of records of observations exist as to the position of the magnetic needle in different parts of the United States in past times. A collection of these, and a comparison of them with more recent observations, would serve to throw light on the changes which have taken place in the course of years.

There is, also, on record in the Land Office, an extended series of observations which, though not made with great precision, will still be of value in delineating the general direction of the magnetic lines in different parts of the United States. Steps have been taken to collect all the existing materials relative to this subject, with the view of submitting them in due time to reduction and careful investigation.

Correspondence.—There is one part of the Smithsonian operations that attracts no public attention, though it is producing, it is believed, important results in the way of diffusing knowledge, and is attended, perhaps, with more labor than any other part. I allude to the scientific correspondence of the Institution. Scarcely a day passes in which communications are not received from persons in different parts of the country, containing accounts of discoveries, which are referred to the Institution, or asking questions relative to some branch of knowledge. The rule was early adopted to give respectful attention to every letter received, and this has been faithfully adhered to from the beginning up to the present time.

These communications relate to a great variety of subjects. Any topic which strongly excites the attention of the public at a given time, such as the announcement in the papers of a wonderful discovery, or an important invention which promises to introduce extensive changes in the useful arts, is sure to bring upon the Institution an increase of labor in the way of correspondence. The ordinary inquiries addressed to the Secretary relate to the principles of mechanics, electricity, magnetism, meteorology, names of specimens of plants, minerals, insects, and, in short, to all objects or phenomena of a remarkable or unusual character.

Requests are frequently made for lists of apparatus, for information as to the best books for the study of special subjects, hints for the organization of local societies, &c. Applications are also made for information by persons abroad relative to particular subjects respecting this country. When an immediate reply cannot be given to a question, the subject is referred, by letter, to some one of the Smithsonian co-laborers, to whose line of study it pertains; and the answer is transmitted to the inquirer, either under the name of the person who gives the information or under that of the institution, according to the circumstances of the case.

There is no country on the face of the earth in which knowledge is so generally diffused as in the United States, none in which there is more activity of mind or freedom of thought and discussion, and in which there is less regard to what should be considered as settled and well established principles. It will not therefore be surprising that the Institution should be called upon to answer a great number of communications intended to subvert the present system of science, and to establish new and visionary conceptions in its stead, and that numerous letters should be received pertaining to such subjects as the quadrature of the circle, the trisection of the angle, the invention of self-moving machines, the creation of power, the overthrow of the Newtonian system of gravitation, and the invention of new systems of the universe.

Many of these communications are of such a character that, at first sight, it might seem best to treat them with silent neglect; but the rule has been adopted to state candidly and respectfully the objections to such propositions, and to endeavor to convince their authors that their ground is untenable.

Though this course is in many cases attended with no beneficial results, still it is the only one which can be adopted with any hope of even partial good. In answering those who persist in declaring that the present received laws of mechanical action are erroneous, and that they have discovered new and more correct generalizations, they are requested to prove the truth of their assertions by predicting new and important phenomena, the existence of which may be immediately tested either by experiment or observation. It is not enough that the new system explains facts which we know, for this would be merely exhibiting old knowledge under a new form, but it should point out in the way of deduction new facts which have hitherto escaped the eye of the observer or the scrutiny of the experimenter.

It is to be regretted that so many minds of power and originality in our country should, from defective scientific training, be suffered to diverge so widely from the narrow path which alone leads to real advance in positive knowledge. Providence, however, seems in some measure to vindicate the equality of its distributions, by assigning to such a double measure of hope and self-esteem, which serves them instead of success and reputation.

The faithful discharge of the duty of the correspondence of the institution imposes a serious labor on the secretary and his assistants. Beside the correspondence above mentioned, there is added to their duties that which relates to the reception and publication of the memoirs; to the lectures; the letters sent forth by the Institution respecting particular branches of research; the answers to the almost innumerable inquires as to the character of the Institution, and applications for its publications; all the business matters which relate to the printing, engraving, binding, transportation, payment of accounts; and all the foreign correspondence relating to the exchanges of publications.

All the letters received are bound in volumes, and a copy of every answer is carefully preserved, the whole thus forming a permanent record of all the transactions of the Institution, as well as a history of the topics of scientific interest which have particularly occupied the public mind during any given period. The exposition of this labor, which has been increasing from year to year, will be a sufficient answer to the question which is sometimes asked as to what the officers of the Institution find to do.

Meteorology.—The general system of meteorology described in the last and previous reports has been continued, and though some changes have taken place among the observers, yet the number and efficiency of the corps have been kept up. New instruments have been gradually introduced, and constant improvement has taken place with the experience of each year in the precision and accuracy of the observations. Since the beginning of the system, a large amount of valuable matter relative to the meteorology of the United States has been collected; and the Institution has now commenced to reduce these observations, and to deduce from them the general laws which govern the climate of this country. It is believed that such results will be obtained as will justify the amount of expenditure of the Smithsonian fund which has been devoted to this purpose.

The reductions which had been made up to the close of the last session of the Regents were presented with the annual report to Congress, and were ordered to be printed. It has been found, however, that the tables cannot be presented in an octavo form, and that a special resolution of the Senate will be required to print them in a quarto volume.

An interesting part of the meteorological observations is now in process of reduction at Greenwich, free of expense to the Institution, by Captain Lefroy, late superintendent of the Toronto Observatory. He has undertaken this labor from a love of science, and has received some assistance in the way of clerk hire (as he informs me) from the fund placed in charge of the Royal Society by the British government for the promotion of science. The reduction will include not only all the observations collected by the Smithsonian Institution, but also those which can be obtained from every part of the earth during five years, beginning with 1848.

Among the questions proposed to be answered by Captain Lefroy in discussing the observations, are the following:

1. Does the aurora ever occur in low latitudes when it is wanting in higher ones?

2. Is it developed in continuous zones, or are there wide gaps in these zones; if the latter, have they any connexion with other atmospheric phenomena?

3. What are the ordinary diurnal laws of its development?

4. Can the facts be reconciled with any theory giving it a material objective existence, or is it an optical phenomenon?

5. Can the facts be reconciled with the zodiacal theory?

6. What are its geographical limits; and what causes their singular variation from day to day?

7. Are lines of equal frequency on the globe, or equal intensity, circles at all?

Definite answers to these questions would clear the ground for the establishment of a rational theory as to the cause of this phenomenon, the want of which, after all that has been said and written upon it, is an opprobrium to the science of the present century.

The results of Captain Lefroy's deductions will be presented in the form of a memoir to the Smithsonian Institution.

Propositions have been made during the past year to apply to government for aid in extending the meteorological system, or to transfer it from the Smithsonian Institution to the National Observatory, the Department of the Interior, or to an independent establishment supported by a direct appropriation from Congress.

In answer to these propositions the Secretary, in behalf of the Regents, has stated that it was not in accordance with the policy of the Institution to ask the aid of Congress for the purpose of carrying on any of its operations; but that it is consistent with its policy to relinquish any line of research which can be carried on equally well by other means. If, therefore, any of the plans proposed can be accomplished, the Institution will cheerfully relinquish this field, and devote its labors to other objects. The Institution has, however, already expended a large amount of money in collecting meteorological data, and it is due to the memory of the founder that full credit shall be given to his name for all the results which may be produced by the expenditure of the income of his bequest. This is one of the conditions on which the trust was accepted, and in case of any transfer of this kind it should be borne in mind. I may also remark, in the same connexion, that while full credit should be given to the officers and assistants for the faithfulness and efficiency with which they discharge their duties, they should not be allowed to publish, under their own names, results which have been collected and elaborated at the expense and under the direction of the Institution. The establishment of definite rules on this point, though a delicate matter, is one which requires attention.

According to the estimate of Mr. Blodget, who is still employed in reducing and discussing the observations, the whole number of meteorological observers now on the books as regular contributors, or as entitled to exchange for valuable series of observations sent, or for reports regularly made in previous years is (520) five hundred and twenty. The number added during the year 1853 to the list of previous observers, and who have returned observations for some portions of the year, is (119) one hundred and nineteen. The number of manuscript series of observations in detail, or in full summaries of means and extremes of the observed conditions for each month of the whole period observed, received during the year, is (75) seventy-five, covering an aggregate period of temperature observation of eight hundred and fifty years. About half these series also include observations of amount of rain. Of printed and published series a large number have been sent.

Exchanges.—The system of exchanges mentioned in the last and preceding Reports has been continued during the past year with unabated vigor and corresponding useful results. The records for 1853, as will be seen by a reference to Prof. Baird's report, show a large increase, both in transmission and receipts, over 1852. This part of the system of Smithsonian operations has everywhere received the commendation of those who have given it their attention or have participated in its benefits. The Institution is now the principal agent of scientific and literary communication between the old world and the new. Its system of exchange is established on a reliable basis, namely: that of the publications of the Institution itself. So long as the present plan of operations is continued, the Institution will annually distribute its Contributions, and will continue to receive in return the publications of all the literary and scientific societies of the world. The importance of such a system, with reference to the scientific character of our country, could scarcely be appreciated by those who are not familiar with the results which flow from an easy and certain intercommunication of this kind. Many of the most important contributions to science made in America have been unheard of in Europe, or have been so little known, or received so little attention, that they have been republished as new discoveries or claimed as the product of European research. By means of the Smithsonian system of exchange, the American author is enabled to place officially, as it were, a copy of his work in the hands of all those who are engaged in the same line of research, and to insure due credit to himself from the countenance and support of the Institution.

The packages transmitted during the past year amounted, in the aggregate, to 1,604. They weighed 12,220 pounds, and occupied nearly 400 cubic feet of space.

The receipts of works from abroad, in exchange for those sent out by the Institution, are much greater in value, as well as in number, than those of last year. The whole number of articles received for the library of the Institution during 1853, is 2,556. For other institutions, 1,052 packages have been received. The number of separate works which these contain is unknown.

The Museum.—Additions during the past year have been made to the museum from all branches of natural history and ethnology. They are principally derived from various portions of our own country, particularly from the region between the Mississippi river and the Pacific Ocean.

The Institution has taken the temporary charge of most of the collections of the various exploring expeditions which have been sent out during the past year. For a detailed account of the additions, I beg leave to refer to the accompanying report of Prof. Baird.

In accordance with the spirit which should pervade all parts of the Institution, much good may be done in the way of promoting natural history by distributing duplicate specimens among the cabinets of the country and recommending the establishment, by associations of teachers and others, of local collections, and by giving directions for conducting museums of this kind. The Institution, during the past year, has done good service in this way, and will continue and extend this means of diffusing knowledge.

Researches.—Though little has been done immediately by the Institution, since the date of the last Report, in the way of original research, yet it has rendered important aid to physical geography and natural history, by the facilities which it has afforded the several exploring parties which have been fitted out during the past year, for railway and boundary surveys, in the regions west of the Mississippi. The instruments have been compared, implements constructed, and practical instruction given in the art of observation and the means of preserving specimens.

The Secretary has devoted considerable time, as a member of commissions appointed by government, to scientific investigations. These duties, as well as those above mentioned, are performed entirely without remuneration; and the Institution is thus, in various ways, repaying, to a considerable extent, whatever expenditure the government has made on account of the Smithsonian bequest.

The Library.—The library during the past year has received an addition of 5,433 articles, the most valuable portion of which have been derived from the Smithsonian exchanges. The whole number of books, etc., now in the library is 25,856.

At its last session, Congress appropriated $3,000 to begin the preparation of a catalogue of its library on the Smithsonian plan proposed by Professor Jewett. This work has been successfully prosecuted since July last; and according to Professor Jewett's report, upwards of 6,000 volumes have been catalogued. This plan, the honor of the invention of which the Convention of Librarians has awarded to Professor Jewett, and which has been received with approbation by those well qualified to judge of its merits, is now in a fair way to be reduced to practice. The objects to be gained by adopting it are—

1. To avoid the necessity of preparing, composing, and correcting anew the titles once printed, when the library has received accessions; or the alternative of printing the titles of these accessions in supplements, which are very inconvenient appendages.

2. To prevent the repetition of the work of preparation of titles, composition, and correction of press, for copies of the same book in different libraries. The title once prepared and stereotyped remains at the Smithsonian Institution, to be used by any library having the same book.

3. To secure uniformity in the construction of catalogues, thus greatly facilitating the researches of the student.

For other facts and details, see Professor Jewett's report herewith submitted.

Lectures.—Lectures have been given as usual by a number of distinguished gentlemen on the following subjects:

A course of eight lectures by Dr. Robert Baird on "Modern Europe."

One lecture by Hon. Henry Barnard on "The School."

One lecture by Professor Stephen Alexander, of the College of New Jersey, on "Climate."

One lecture by Job R. Tyson, esq., of Philadelphia, "Patrick Henry.'

One lecture by Rev. Dr. C. C. Pise, "Charles Carrol, of Carrolton."

One lecture by Dr. E. K. Kane, U. S. N., "On the New Expedition in search of Sir John Franklin."

A course of five lectures by Professor A. Guyot on "The Harmonies of Nature and History."

A course of seven lectures by Dr. J. V. C. Smith, of Boston, on "Modern Egypt and its Institutions.

One lecture by George Sumner, esq., on "France."

Lectures were also delivered during the season, in the Smithsonian lecture room, to the Washington Young Men's Christian Association, Metropolitan Mechanics' Institute, and the Teachers Association.

We have concluded to adopt the plan of a continued course on a single subject extending through the entire season; and for this purpose Professor J. Lawrence Smith, of the University of Virginia, has been engaged to give a full course on chemistry during the present winter.

Meeting of the Establishment.—The Secretary was directed by the President of the United States to call a meeting of the members and honorary members of the "Smithsonian Institution," or, in other words, of the body which is generally known by the name of the "Establishment." I may mention that this body consists of the President of the United States, the Vice President, the Chief Justice, the Mayor of Washington, the several officers of the cabinet, (excepting the Secretary of the Interior, this department having been created since the passage of the act establishing the Institution,) the Commissioner of Patents, and such other persons as they may elect *honorary members*. This body met in the Smithsonian building on the 3d of May, 1853, and at a subsequent meeting adopted a set of by-laws, and elected Professor Parker Cleaveland, of Bowdoin College, Maine, an honorary member.

In accordance with the third section of the act of incorporation, a full account of the proceedings of the Establishment will be given in connection with the report of the proceedings of the Board of Regents.

Respectfully submitted,

JOSEPH HENRY,
Secretary Smithsonian Institution.

JANUARY, 1854.

REPORT OF THE ASSISTANT SECRETARY, IN CHARGE OF THE LIBRARY.

DECEMBER 31, 1853.

SIR: The following table exhibits the additions to the library during the year 1853, distinguishing the receipts by purchase, by donation and exchange, and by copy-right:

Sources.	Books.	Pamphlets and parts of vols.	Engravings.	Maps.	Music.	Drawings.	Other articles.	Totals.
By purchase	259	1,554	......	......	......	......	......	1,813
By donation and exchange	1,244	1,121	......	88	......	......	......	2,453
By copyright	505	181	14	8	448	......	11	1,167
	2,008	2,856	14	96	448	......	11	5,433

The whole number of books, pamphlets, maps, engravings, and other articles at present belonging to the library, is shown by the following table:

Sources.	Books.	Pamphlets and parts of vols.	Engravings.	Maps.	Music.	Drawings.	Other articles.	Totals.
By purchase	4,432	2,511	1,335	2	......	......	......	8,280
By donation and exchange	3,901	5,164	58	1,813	......	30	41	11,007
By copyright	2,809	420	38	59	2,274	9	97	5,706
By deposit	873	......	......	......	......	......	......	873
	12,015	8,095	1,431	1,874	2,274	39	138	25,866

The purchases during the year have been few and unimportant.

The receipts by exchange and donation have been numerous and valuable. A particular account of them is given by Professor Baird in his report upon the exchanges. It is not thought necessary, therefore, to dwell upon them here, further than to state, that many of the works thus received are of great value, from their intrinsic merit, and from the difficulty of procuring them through the ordinary channels of the book trade.

It is much to be regretted that no measures have yet been taken for the better regulation of the copy-right deposit. I have repeatedly called attention to the subject, and in my last two reports have expressed, at considerable length, views which I hoped might lead to a revision of the law. The interests of this Institution, of publishers, and of the literary public, require further legislation on this subject, and substantially such, it is believed, as was recommended in the reports alluded to.

Much inconvenience has been experienced from the delay in finishing the central building. The books stand in double rows, on most of the shelves, in the room where they are at present placed. Some of them have been injured, too, by exposure to dampness. It is impossible with the means provided to warm the room, and all who have been engaged in the library have suffered severely from colds contracted while working in it. It has been found necessary to remove many pamphlets and papers to the basement, where they are subject to injury, and where it is difficult to consult them. The labors of the library are doubled by the want of proper accommodations. On these accounts, it is much to be desired that the main library should be finished at as early a day as possible, in order that the books may be removed to a permanent, safe, and convenient lodgment.

Applications have been made to me during the year for the opening of the library in the evening, and some remarks on the subject have appeared in the newspapers. It was impossible to comply with these suggestions without employing an additional attendant. The present attendant is required to be on duty from daylight in the morning till five o'clock in the afternoon. It would be unjust to require services of him in the evening. Besides, no arrangements have been made for lighting the reading room, nor can they well be made till the building is finished. It has seemed necessary, therefore, to postpone, for the present, the further consideration of the subject; which I do, with the hope that it may hereafter be found practicable to extend the time for consulting the library, if desired by any considerable number of persons.

Another topic connected with the library, to which I wish to direct the attention of the Board of Regents, is the framing of a set of by-laws and regulations for the management of the library and the use of the books. I would also suggest the appointment of a standing committee upon the library. Such a committee becomes the more necessary as the library becomes of more importance, both from its extent and the character of its books, and as the time is near at hand for the completion of the building, and the permanent arrangement of the collection.

The reading-room has continued to be a place of great resort for citizens and strangers. The list of periodicals is extensive, and comprises many of the best scientific and literary journals of this country and of Europe.

It is proper for me here to call attention to the desirableness of completing the series of periodicals and of transactions and journals of learned societies. But very few of our sets are complete. Inquiries are daily made for back numbers which are wanting. As it is probable that we have received all or nearly all of the earlier publications of societies which they are able to supply, it seems advisable to furnish our agents in Europe with lists of the volumes which we possess, and authorize them to purchase, as opportunities may occur, the volumes that are wanting.

The "Notices of Public Libraries," prepared with considerable labor, and published three years ago by the Smithsonian Institution, is still almost daily called for, though about 6,000 copies, printed by Congress and by the Institution, have been distributed. Very few copies remain on hand. Since the book was published a large amount of additional matter has been received. There is a great demand for information of this kind, and it seems desirable to issue a new and enlarged edition of the Notices. It has been impossible for me, during the past year, to gain time for this work, from the daily duties of the library, and the unremitted labor which the superintendence of the catalogue system has imposed upon me.

The National Convention of Librarians and Bibliographers, which met in New York in September last, deserves to be particularly noticed in this report, on account of the frequent reference there made to the position and operations of the Smithsonian library, as well as on account of its importance to all libraries, and to the general interests of literature in this country. It was composed of more than eighty delegates, representing forty-seven libraries in all parts of the country, from Maine to California.

It is gratifying to know that the services of the Smithsonian Institution, in the department of bibliography, were fully recognised by this convention in the following resolution, which was unanimously adopted:

"*Resolved*, That the thanks of this convention be presented to the Board of Regents and officers of the Smithsonian Institution for their steady and effective efforts for the increase and diffusion of knowledge among men; and particularly for the measures which they have adopted for the encouragement and promotion of the public libraries of our country; and we have great pleasure in looking to that Institution as the central establishment of the United States for the furtherance of all such objects."

The convention also passed the following resolutions relative to the great central library of reference and research which it has been the intention of Congress to establish at the Smithsonian Institution:

"*Resolved*, That the establishment of a great central library for reference and research, while it is demanded by the condition of the United States as to general civilization and intellectual advancement, is especially interesting to this convention from the bearing it would have upon libraries throughout the country.

"*Resolved*, That we deem such an establishment as being eminently worthy of support from the national treasury; and that in no way can the government better promote the progress of learning through the whole country, than by placing a central national library under the administration of the Smithsonian Institution."

Among the topics which received particular attention at this convention was the preparation of a convenient manual as a guide to the organization of library societies, the collection of libraries, and their proper management. A committee was appointed to digest the plan of such a work. So impressed were the members of the convention with its importance, that "the business committee were requested to consider the expediency of memorializing Congress to procure the preparation of such a manual through the agency of the Smithsonian Institution."

Every week, and almost every day, applications are made at this Institution, by letter or by visitors, for information which a book of this kind would contain. The answers have to be many times repeated. I have consequently had the intention of preparing such a manual. The collections for the purpose are mostly made. The volume of statistics and descriptions of libraries was an important antecedent. The development of the catalogue system must also precede any systematic and well considered work of the kind. The period has now come for the fulfilment of this design, and I hope to be enabled and to be authorized to devote such time as may be necessary to its execution.

The library interest has become in this country one of rare magnitude and importance. Nothing can be done by the government, by this Institution, or by individuals here, which tends to promote the establishment or the efficiency of libraries, without being noticed and gratefully appreciated by all the intelligent and educated men of all parties and names, in every city and almost every village and hamlet throughout the land. Every city has its library, so has almost every village, and so have a large number of our common schools. Familiar as this fact is to many of us, it presents a new phase of society, and one indicative of mighty influences. The library is the necessary complement of the school. To teach children to read and then give them nothing to supply the desire awakened is mockery. It is reading rather than school-training which has produced the general intelligence of the American people. These libraries must be of various grades—the school and social library of popular English books of history, biography, and general literature for reading; the larger collections in cities for more general study and reference; and the great central library for learned investigations. These should all be linked and bound together in one voluntary yet harmonious system. Such is the general wish most emphatically expressed—a wish which the Smithsonian Institutioh may do much to cherish and to realize.

It now remains for me to speak of the progress which has been made during the year upon the catalogue system.

A new and greatly enlarged and improved edition of the report, containing an account of the system, rules for the preparation of catalogues, and (as examples under the rules) the catalogue of the bibliographical works in the Smithsonian library, has been prepared and stereotyped. An edition of a thousand copies, as far as to the examples, has been printed. The printers have since been employed upon the catalogue of the Library of Congress, and consequently the work upon the report has been suspended. It would require but a few weeks and an inconsiderable additional expenditure of money to complete this work. The calls for it are frequent, and I feel very desirous of being able to answer them at an early day. The book will probably contain about three hundred pages.

At the last session of the Board of Regents, a resolution was passed, requesting the Secretary of the Institution to call the attention of the joint Library Committee of Congress to the Smithsonian plan of cataloguing, and to the advantages—economical and literary—which would accrue to the Library of Congress and to other libraries, by their adoption of this plan. The committee examined the subject, and recommended to Congress an appropriation of three thousand dollars for commencing a catalogue. The work was begun in July last, and has proceeded most prosperously till the present time. Upwards of six thousand volumes have already been catalogued, and about one third of the appropriation remains unexpended. The consideration of the magnitude of the enterprise thus commenced, has led to great caution in adopting the rules establishing precedents. A great part of my time has necessarily been given to the work. Less will probably be required for the future.

I have so frequently and at so much length explained the details and the advantages of the system, that it is not necessary for me to dwell upon them at present, except very briefly.

The title of every work and of each distinct edition of every work is stereotyped upon a separate plate. The author's name also stands on a plate by itself. Each plate shows at a glance the heading to which it belongs. It is obvious that these plates may be placed together in alphabetical or other order, as may be desired. They are mounted on blocks for printing, like other stereotype plates.

The great ends to be gained and which will thus be secured, are:

1. To avoid the necessity of preparing, composing, and correcting anew the titles once printed, when the library has received accessions, or the alternative of printing the titles of these accessions in supplements, which are very inconvenient appendages.

2. To prevent the repetition of the work of preparation of titles, composition and correction of press, for copies of the same book in different libraries. The title, once prepared and stereotyped, remains at the Smithsonian Institution, to be used by any library having the same book.

3. To secure uniformity in the construction of catalogues, thus greatly facilitating the researches of the student.

It is obvious that the cost of the first catalogue will be greater than if it were not stereotyped. The work of preparation will also be more expensive; but the additional cost of the first edition will be more than saved in the first re-printing of the whole catalogue. It will be further understood that the sum paid by the first library is not only for its own benefit, but for that of every other library hereafter adopting the plan, so far as its books are the same. Congress is, therefore, now conferring a great boon upon other libraries, while at the same time it is taking the course the most economical for the procuring of its own catalogue.

It will be remembered that we had two classes of difficulties to meet, the one literary and the other mechanical. The theory of the system had first to be perfected in all its details. The practical application had then to be made. The time and money which have been expended in Europe in discussions connected with the subject of the best methods of cataloguing, indicate the difficulty of the theory. Practical stereotypers pronounced the scheme impracticable. A new mode of stereotyping, with a new material, had to be introduced, perfected, and applied for the purpose. There is no art so difficult of improvement as that of typography. These statements will indicate the mechanical difficulties which have been overcome.

It is gratifying to be able to state that the new process of stereotyping which we have adopted for this purpose is likely to be introduced into use on a large scale. The benefits which the Institution will thus have conferred upon the most perfect and most important of the arts, apart from the connexion of these improvements with the catalogue system, will not be the least among its achievements, as the efforts by which this end has been attained have not been the least of its labors.

Impressed as I was with the importance of the subject, and confident as I felt of its entire practicability in every particular, I was desirous that it should be fully discussed by librarians and practical bibliographers, as well as by printers, stereotypers, and experts in the typographical art. The convention to which I have alluded afforded a rare opportunity for this examination of our plans, and a fair and intelligent estimate of their value. I introduced the subject and invited discussion. It was manifest that those who were present had come together having formed various opinions as to the practicability of the scheme, though with but one sentiment as to its desirableness. The matter was discussed a whole day with freedom, and with the manifest desire to arrive at a just conclusion. I take great pleasure in quoting the following resolutions, which were unanimously adopted, as embodying the results of the long, careful, and interested examination:

"*Resolved*, That we have considered attentively the plan for constructing catalogues of libraries, and a general catalogue of the public libraries of the United States, by means of separate stereotype titles, originated and prepared by Prof. C. C. Jewett, and developed by him while librarian of the Smithsonian Institution. That we regard it as an object of high importance to the interests of our public libraries, and to the promotion of learning, and worthy to share in the funds of the Institution and the zealous exertions of its officers; the more so as it is an enterprise which cannot be successfully prosecuted, except under the guidance, protection, and pecuniary support of this central establishment for the increase and diffusion of knowledge.

"*Resolved*, That we have learned with pleasure that Congress, on the recommendation of the library committee, made an appropriation for the practical testing of the plan in its application to the Library of Congress, and that the work is now in successful progress.

"*Resolved*, That, as practical librarians and bibliographers, we take pride and satisfaction in the fact that a measure of so great literary utility has received the prompt and efficient support of our national legislature; and we would express the earnest hope that this support may be extended to it liberally, till its first great result in the complete stereotyped catalogue of the Library of Congress shall be attained."

We may reasonably congratulate ourselves upon the complete success of these plans up to the present point. They still need the fostering care of this Institution. As soon as the catalogue of the Library of

Congress shall be completed, other institutions, and even individuals, are ready to avail themselves of the scheme for procuring their catalogues. Its general adoption—the crowning point of all our efforts—seems, therefore, as sure as the completion of the first work.

It is manifest that appropriations will every year be necessary from the Smithsonian fund for the procuring of type, apparatus, and fixtures, as well as for filling any intervals that may occur in the continuity of the work. But it seems now quite certain that the system will ere long grow up into a large and self-supporting establishment, regulated by the combined libraries of the country.

Respectfully submitted.

C. C. JEWETT.

To JOSEPH HENRY, LL.D.,
Secretary of the Smithsonian Institution.

REPORT OF THE ASSISTANT SECRETARY IN CHARGE OF PUBLICATIONS, EXCHANGES, AND NATURAL HISTORY.

SIR: I herewith present to you the report of operations for the year 1853, in the departments assigned to my superintendence.

1. PUBLICATIONS.

During the year 1853, a much larger amount of matter has been printed and published by the Smithsonian Institution than in any year since the commencement of its operations. Two volumes of the quarto series have been completed, of which one has been distributed and the other is nearly ready. The following list contains the titles of the papers in these volumes.

List of Memoirs in Vol. V, Smithsonian Contributions.

1. Introduction; pp. 16.
2. A Flora and Fauna within living animals. By Joseph Leidy, M. D.; pp. 68, and ten plates.
3. Memoir on the Extinct Species of American Ox. By Joseph Leidy, M. D.; pp. 20, and five plates.
4. Anatomy of the Nervous System of *Rana Pipiens*. By Jeffries Wyman, M. D.; pp. 52, and two plates.
5. Nereis Boreali-Americana, or Contributions to the History of the Marine Algæ of North America. By William Henry Harvey, M. D., M. R. I. A; Part II. Rhodospermeæ; pp. 262, and twenty-four plates.
6. Plantæ Wrightianæ Texano-Neo-Mexicanæ; Part II, An Account of a Collection of Plants, made by Charles Wright, A. M., in Western Texas, New Mexico, and Sonora, in the years 1851 and 1852. By Asa Gray, M. D.; pp. 120, and four plates.

Vol. VI, Smithsonian Contributions.

1. Introduction; pp. 16.
2. Plantæ Fremontianæ, or Description of Plants collected in California by Col. J. C. Fremont. By John Torrey, F. L. S.; pp. 24, and ten plates.
3. Observations on the *Batis Maritima* of Linnæus. By John Torrey, F. L. S.; pp. 8, and one plate.
4. On the *Darlingtonia Californica*, a new Pitcher Plant from Northern California. By John Torrey, F. L. S.; pp. 8, and one plate.
5. Synopsis of the Marine Invertebrata of Grand Manan, or the Region about the Bay of Fundy. By William Stimpson, pp. 68, and three plates.
6. On the Winds of the Northern Hemisphere. By James H. Coffin, Professor of Mathematics and Natural Philosophy, in Lafayette College; pp. 200, and thirteen plates.

7. The Ancient Fauna of Nebraska, or a Description of Remains of Extinct Mammalia and Chelonia, from the Mauvaises Terres of Nebraska. By Joseph Leidy, M. D., Professor of Anatomy in the University of Pennsylvania; pp. 126, and twenty-five plates.
8. Occultations for 1853.

Volume V contains pages	538—plates	45
Volume VI contains pages	476—plates	53
Or an aggregate of quarto publications	1,014	98

Of these volumes, volume V has been distributed. Volume VI has not yet been bound up, but will be delivered and distributed early in 1854.

In addition to the above, several memoirs for the seventh volume are in hand, and the engravings nearly complete; among these are:

Chappellsmith, on the Tornado of Indiana.

Leidy, on the Extinct Sloths of North America.

Bailey, on New Microscopic Forms.

The octavo publications have also been of considerable extent, and are as follows:

Seventh Annual Report of the Board of Regents of the Smithsonian Institution, for 1852; pp. 96.

Report of the Secretary of the Smithsonian Institution, for 1852; pp. 31.

Catalogue of North American Reptiles in the Museum of the Smithsonian Institution. Part 1—Serpents. By S. F. Baird and C. Girard, pp. 188.

Catalogue of the described Coleoptera of the United States. By Frederick Ernst Melsheimer, M. D. Revised by S. S. Haldeman and J. L. Le Conte, pp. 190.

In addition to these a large number of circulars, relating to various subjects, has been printed.

2. Distributio n of Publications and Exchanges.

(a.) *Foreign Distributions and Exchanges.*

The records of foreign distributions and exchanges for the year 1853, show a large increase, both in transmissions and receipts, over 1852, thus exhibiting a steady enlargement of the sphere and extent of operations, gratifying to all who are interested in the speedy diffusion of knowledge throughout the world. As in past years, the Smithsonian Institution has been a most important medium of communication between the American scientific societies and their European correspondents.

The names of the institutions making use of the facilities afforded by the Smithsonian Institution, as well as the complete statistics of the whole business, will be found detailed in the accompanying tables.

The packages, amounting in the aggregate to 1,604, bearing 567 addresses, weighing 12,220 pounds, and occupying nearly 400 cubic feet of capacity, all left the Institution in May, and for a large number of these packages acknowledgments have already been received. The names of institutions receiving the Smithsonian Contributions to Knowledge, 258 in number, will be found in the table. Nearly 400, however, have received publications of some kind from the Institution; the total number of addresses, including those parcels sent by others, being 567, as already stated.

A.—Table exhibiting the statistics of printed matter sent abroad in 1852, by the Smithsonian Institution.

1. *Distributed by Dr. J. G. Flügel, Leipsic.*

Countries.	Addresses of principal packages.	Addresses enclosed in preceding.	Total.	Number of principal packages.	Packages enclosed from others.	Packages enclosed for others.	Total.	Weight in pounds.	Capacity in cub. ft.	Boxes.	Letters accompanying parcels.
Sweden........	7	7	.....	17	20	9	.....	....	...	...	.....
Norway........	4	1	.....	7	12	1	.....	....	...	...	.....
Iceland........	1	.....	.....	2	1	.....	.....	....	...	...	.....
Denmark........	7	4	.....	14	23	5	.....	....	...	...	.....
Russia........	15	6	.....	32	42	7	.....	....	...	...	.....
Holland........	12	3	.....	23	34	4	.....	....	...	...	.....
Germany........	85	58	.....	155	181	63	.....	....	...	...	.....
Belgium........	9	6	.....	18	34	8	.....	....	...	...	.....
Switzerland......	13	5	.....	19	49	6	.....	....	...	...	.....
Total.......	153	90	243	287	396	103	786	6,250	200	25	190

2. *Distributed by Hector Bossange, Paris.*

Countries.	Addresses of principal packages.	Addresses enclosed in preceding.	Total.	Number of principal packages.	Packages [illegible] from [illegible]	Packages [illegible] for others.	Total.	Weight in pounds.	Capacity in cub. ft	Boxes.	Letters accompanying parcels.
France..........	55	26	.....	80	102	29	.....	....	...	...	.....
Italy............	36	13	.....	43	56	15	.....	....	...	...	.....
Total.......	91	39	130	123	158	44	325	2,250	72	9	110

3. *Distributed through the Royal Society and the agency of Henry Stevens, London.*

Countries.	Addresses of principal packages.	Addresses enclosed in preceding.	Total.	Number of principal packages.	Packages enclosed from others.	Packages enclosed for others.	Total.	Weight in pounds.	Capacity in cub. ft.	Boxes.	Letters accompanying packages.
Portugal	1	1	......	2	6	1	......	......	......	......	......
Spain	4	2	......	6	9	2	......	......	......	......	......
United Kingdom	99	51	......	163	150	59	......	......	......	......	......
Australia	1	......	......	1	1	......	......	......	......	......	......
Total	105	54	159	172	166	62	400	2,786	90	7	140

4. *Distributed by others.*

Countries.	Addresses of principal packages.	Addresses enclosed in preceding.	Total.	Number of principal packages.	Packages enclosed from others.	Packages enclosed for others.	Total.	Weight in pounds.	Capacity in cub. ft.	Boxes.	Letters accompanying packages.
Old world	17	......	......	20	30	......	......	......	......	......	......
South America	16	2	......	23	18	2	......	......	......	......	......
Total	33	2	35	43	48	2	93	914	30	7	35

5. *General summary.*

Agents.	Addresses of principal packages.	Addresses enclosed in preceding.	Total.	Number of principal packages.	Packages enclosed from others.	Packages enclosed for others.	Total.	Weight in pounds.	Capacity in cub. ft.	Boxes.	Letters accompanying packages.
Dr. J. G. Flügel	153	90	243	287	396	103	786	6,250	200	25	190
H. Bossange	91	39	130	123	158	44	325	2,250	72	9	110
H. Stevens	105	54	159	172	166	62	400	2,786	90	7	140
Others	33	2	35	43	48	2	93	914	30	7	35
Total	382	185	567	625	768	211	1,604	12,200	392	48	475

B.—TABLE EXHIBITING THE NUMBER OF PIECES RECEIVED FROM THE DIFFERENT INSTITUTIONS IN THE UNITED STATES FOR DISTRIBUTION ABROAD.

Obtained by the Smithsonian Institution from various sources, but exclusive of its own publications		2,410
Boston Society of Natural History, Boston	54	
American Academy of Arts and Sciences, Boston	112	
American Journal of Science	35	
American Oriental Society, New Haven	33	
Academy of Natural Sciences, Philadelphia	186	
American Philosophical Society, Philadelphia	72	
U. S. Coast Survey	131	
Patent Office	100	
Typographical Bureau	30	
Indian Bureau	168	
Light House Board	5	
Secretary of the Navy	29	
J. Ross Browne	170	
Miscellaneous institutions and individuals	319	
		1,444
Total received		3,854

Most of the above consisted of single volumes; a number, however, were packages with several enclosures, which would probably bring the number of volumes to 4,000.

APPENDIX C.

List of Foreign Institutions in correspondence with the Smithsonian Institution.

SWEDEN.

Goteborg.—Kongl. Vetenskaps och Vitterhets Samhillet.
*Lund.—Kongl. Universitetet.
Observatory.
**Stockholm.*—Kongliga Svenska Vetenskaps Akademien.
Kongl. Landbruks-Akademien.
*Kongl. Vitterhets Historie och Antiquitets Akademien.
*Riksbiblioteket.
Svenska Akademien.
**Upsala.*—Kongliga Vetenskaps Societeten.
*Kongl. Universitetet.

Those marked * have received the fifth volume of "Contributions." The others have received separate memoirs and other publications.

NORWAY.

***Bergen.*—Bergen's Museum.
***Christiania.*—Det Kongelige Norske Universitet.
Observatory.
Physiographiske Forening.
Drontheim.—Det Kongel. Norske Videnskabernes Selskab.

ICELAND.

***Reykjavik.*—Islands Stiftisbokasafn.

DENMARK.

***Copenhagen.*—Kongelige Nordiske Oldskrift Selskab.
*Det Kongelige Danske Videnskabernes Selskab.
*Kongelige Bibliothek.
Königliches dänische Seecharten Archiv.
Observatory.
Skandinaviske Naturforskeres Forsamling.

RUSSIA.

Dorpat.—Gelehrte Estnische Gesellschaft zu Dorpat.
*Observatoire Impérial.
***Helsingfors.*—Societas Scientiarum Fennica.
***Kasan.*—University Library.
***Mittau.*—Kurländische Gesellschaft für Literatur und Kunst.
***Moscow.*—Société Impériale des Naturalistes de Moscou.
Pulkowa.—Observatoire Impérial.
***St. Petersburg.*—Académie Impériale des Sciences.
Depot of Naval Charts of Russia.
Geodetic Survey of Russia.
*Imperial Public Library.
*Kais. Russ. Mineralogische Gesellschaft.
*L'Etat Major du Corps des Ingénieurs des Mines de Russie.
*Observatoire Physique Central de Russie.
*Société Impériale d'Archéologie.

HOLLAND.

***Amsterdam.*—Académie Royale des Sciences à Amsterdam.
Genootschap Natura Artis Magistra.
Zoological Garden.
***Groningen.*—Academia Groningana.
***Haarlem.*—Hollandsche Maatschappij der Wetenschappen.
***Hague.*—Bibliothèque Royale.
Leyden.—Botanical Society of the Netherlands.
Musée d'Histoire Naturelle.
*University Library.

**Middelburg.*—Zeeuwsche Genootschap der Wetenschappen.
**Rotterdam.*—Bataafsch Genootschap der proefondervindelijke Wijsbegeerte te Rotterdam.
**Utrecht.*—Provinciaal Utrechtsch Genootschap van Kunsten en Wetenschappen.
Zwolle.—(Overyssel.)—Overysselsche Vereeniging tot Ontwikkeling van Provinciale Helvaart.

GERMANY.

**Altenburg.*—Naturforschende Gesellschaft.
Altona.—Geodetic Survey of Holstein.
Observatory.
Berlin.—Anstalt des topographischen Bureaus im general Stabe.
Deutsche Geologische Gesellschaft.
*Geographische Gesellschaft.
Gesellschaft für Erdkunde.
*Gesellschaft Naturforschender Freunde.
Gewerbe Institut.
Ingenieur Schule.
*Königliche Bibliothek.
Königliches Landes Œconomie Collegium.
*Königliches Museum.
*Königlich, Preussische Akademie der Wissenschaften zu Berlin.
Observatory.
Wiegman's Archiv für Naturgeschichte.
**Blankenberg.*—Naturwissenschaftlicher Verein des Harzes.
**Bonn.*—Naturhistorischer Verein des preussischen Rheinlandes und Westphalens.
Observatory
*University Library.
**Bremen.*—Stadt-Bibliothek.
**Breslau.*—Kaiserliche Leopoldinisch-Carolinische Akademie der Naturforscher.
**Dantzig.*—Naturforschende Gesellschaft.
Darmstadt.—Grossherzogliche Bibliothek.
Deidesheim.—Pollichia. Naturwissenschaftlicher Verein der bayerischen Pfalz.
**Dresden.*—King of Saxony.
*Königliche Bibliothek.
K. Sammlung für Kunst u. Wissenschaften.
Dusseldorf.—Gesellschaft Naturforschender Freunde Westphalens.
Emden.—Naturforschende Gesellschaft.
Erfurt.—Akademie Gemeinnütziger Wissenschaften.
**Erlangen.*—Königliche Universität.
**Frankfurt am Main.*—Senckenbergische Naturforschende Gesellschaft.
**Freiberg.*—Königlich-Sächsische Bergakademie.
**Freiburg.*—University Library.
**Giessen.*—University Library.
**Görlitz.*—Naturforschende Gesellschaft.
**Göttingen.*—Königliche Gesellschaft der Wissenschaften.

Göttingen.—*Königliche Universität.
Gotha.—Royal Library.
Grätz.—University Library.
Greifswald.—K. P. Staats u. Landwirthschaftl. Akademie Eldena.
*University Library.
Halle.—Deutsche Morgenländische Gesellschaft.
Naturforschende Gesellschaft.
*Naturwissenschaftlicher Verein in Halle.
Thüringisch-sächsischer Verein.
*University Library.
Hamburg.—Commerz Bibliothek.
Museum.
*Naturwissenschaftlicher Verein.
Observatory.
*Stadt-Bibliothek.
**Hannover.*—Königliche Bibliothek.
**Heidelberg.*—Grossherzoglich-Badische Universität.
**Innsbrück.*—University Library.
*Ferdinandeum.
**Jena.*—Grossherzogl. herzogl. sächs. Gesammt-Universität.
**Karlsruhe.*—Grossherzogliche Hofbibliothek.
**Kiel.*—Academia Christiana Albertina.
**Königsberg.*—Observatory.
University Library.
Kremsmünster.—Observatory.
Leipsic.—Dr. J. G. Flügel.
Fürstlich-Jablonowski'sche Gesellschaft.
*Königlich-Sächsische Gesellschaft der Wissenschaften.
*Stadt-Bibliothek.
University Library.
Mannheim.—Mannheimer Verein für Naturkunde.
**Marburg.*—Gesellschaft zur Beförderung der gesammten Naturwissenschaften.
*University Library.
**Meissen.*—Isis.
Merseburg.—Central Direction für die Provinz Sachsen.
**Munich.*—Königlich Bayerische Akademie der Wissenchaften.
*Königliche Hof und Staats-Bibliothek.
Observatory.
Polytechnic School.
Neu Wied.—Maximilian Prinz von Wied.
**Nürnberg.*—Naturhistorische Gesellschaft.
Olmütz.—University Library.
**Pesth.*—Ungarische Gelehrte Gesellschaft.
*University Library.
**Prag.*—Das Böhmische Museum.
K. K. patriotisch oekonomische Gesellschaft.
*K. K. Universität.
*Königlich-Böhmische Gesellschaft der Wissenschaften.
Regensburg.—K. Baierische Botanische Gesellschaft.
**Rostock.*—University Library.

**Stettin.*—Entomologischer Verein.
**Stuttgart.*—Königliche öffentliche Bibliothek.
Verein für Vaterländische Naturkunde.
Tharand.—Königliche Akademie für Forst u. Landwirthe.
**Tübingen.*—Königliche Universität.
**Vienna.*—Kaiserliche Akademie der Wissenschaften.
*K. K. Geologische Reichsanstalt.
*K. K. Hofbibliothek.
K. K. Hof-u. Staatsdruckerei.
K. K. Naturalien Kabinet.
*K. K. Orientalische Akademie.
Observatory.
*University Library.
Zoologisch-botanischer Verein.
**Würzburg.*—Physikalisch-medicinische Gesellschaft.
*University Library.
Württemberg.—Der Verein für Vaterländische Naturkunde in Württemberg.

SWITZERLAND.

**Basel.*—Die Gesellschaft fur Vaterländische Alterthümer in Basel.
College of Basel.
*Naturforschende Gesellschaft.
Bern.—College of Bern.
*Allgemeine Schweizerische Gesellschaft für die gesammten Naturwissenschaften.
*Naturforschende Gesellschaft.
**Genève.*—Bibliothèque de la ville de Genève.
Observatoire de Genève.
*Société de Physique et d'Histoire Naturelle de Genève.
Lausanne.—Société Vaudoise des Sciences Naturelles.
**Neuchatel.*—Société des Sciences Naturelles.
Zürich.—College of Zurich.
*Gesellschaft für vaterländische Alterthümer in Zürich.
*Naturforschende Gesellschaft in Zürich.

BELGIUM.

Antwerp.—Académie d'Archéologie.
Bruges.—Société des Sciences Naturelles.
**Bruxelles.*—Académie Royale des Sciences, des Lettres et des Beaux-Arts.
Bibliothèque Royale de Belgique.
*Observatoire Royal.
*City Library.
**Gand.*—Université de Gand.
**Liege.*—Société Royale des Sciences de Liège.
**Louvain.*—Université Catholique.
**Mons.*—Société des Sciences, des Arts et des Lettres, du Hainaut.

FRANCE.

Angers.—Société d'Agriculture, Sciences et Arts.
Angoulême.—Société d'Agriculture, Arts et Commerce.
Arras.—Société d'Arras.
Bayeux.—Société d'Agriculture, Sciences, Arts et Belles-Lettres.
Besançon.—Académie des Sciences, Belles-Lettres et Arts.
**Bordeaux.*—Académie Nationale des Sciences, Belles-Lettres et Arts.
 *Société Linnéenne de Bordeaux.
Brest.—Académie Navale.
**Caen.*—Académie des Sciences, Arts et Belles-Lettres.
 Société des Antiquaires de Normandie.
 Société Linnéenne de Normandie.
**Charente.*—Soc. d'Agriculture, Arts, et Commerce du Dép. de la Charente.
Cherbourg.—Société Académique de Cherbourg.
 Société des Sciences Naturelles de Cherbourg.
Clermont-Ferrand.—Académie des Sciences, Belles-Lettres et Arts de Clermont-Ferrand.
Dijon.—Académie des Sciences, Arts et Belles-Lettres de Dijon.
Evreux.—Société Libre d'Agriculture, Sciences, Arts et Belles-Lettres.
Le Mans.—Société d'Agriculture, Science et Arts.
Lille.—Société Nationale des Sciences, de l'Agriculture et des Arts.
**Lyon.*—Société Nationale de l'Agriculture, d'Histoire Naturelle et des Arts Utiles de Lyon.
 *Académie des Sciences, Belles-Lettres et Arts de Lyon.
 *Société Linnéenne de Lyon.
Marseilles.—Académie des Sciences, Lettres et Arts.
Mende.—Société d'Agriculture, Commerce, Sciences et Arts.
**Metz.*—Académie Nationale de Metz.
 Société d'Histoire Naturelle.
**Montpellier.*—Société Archéologique de Montpellier.
 Académie des Sciences et Lettres à Montpellier.
**Nimes.*—Académie du Gard.
**Orleans.*—Société des Sciences, Belles-Lettres et Arts d'Orléans.
**Paris.*—Bibliothèque de la Ville de Paris.
 *Bibliothèque du Jardin des Plantes.
 *Bibliothèque Impériale.
 Bureau des Longitudes.
 *Dépot des Cartes et Plans.
 *Ecole Nationale des Mines.
 *Institut de France.
 *Institut Historique de France.
 *Ministère de la Guerre.
 *Ministère de la Marine.
 *Ministère de l'Instruction publique et des Cultes.
 Observatoire.
 *Société des Antiquaires.
 *Société Asiatique.
 *Société de Géographie.
 Société de l'Ecole des Chartes.

Paris.—Société Entomologique.
*Société Ethnologique.
Société Française de Statistique Universelle.
*Société Géologique de France.
Société Impériale d'Horticulture de Paris.
Société Météorologique de France.
Société Nationale des Antiquaries de France.
Société Nationale et Centrale d'Agriculture.
Société Philomatique.
Reims.—Académie de Reims.
**Rouen.*—Académie des Sciences, Belles-Lettres et Arts de Rouen.
Saint-Quentin.—Société des Sciences, Arts, Belles-Lettres, et Agriculture.
**Strasbourg.*—Société des Sciences, Agriculture et Arts, du Bas Rhin.
*Académie des Sciences Naturelles.
Toulon.—Académie Navale.
**Toulouse.*—Académie des Sciences, Inscriptions et Belles-Lettres de Toulouse.
Tours.—Société d'Agriculture, des Sciences, d'Arts, et des Belles-Lettres.
Trevoux.—Société d'Agriculture, Sciences et Arts.
Troyes.—Société d'Agriculture, Sciences, Arts et Belles-Lettres.

ITALY.

**Bologna.*—Accademia delle Scienze dell' Istituto di Bologna.
Brescia.—Ateneo di Brescia.
Catania.—Accademia Gioenia di Scienze Naturali.
Chamberry.—Société Royale Académique de Savoie.
Florence.—Accademia del Cimento.
*Biblioteca Magliabecchiana.
Imperiale e Reale Museo di Fisica e Storia naturale di Firenze.
Observatory.
Genoa.—Accademia delle Scienze, Lettere, ed Arti.
Accademia Medico-chirurgica di Genova.
**Lucca.*—Reale Accademia Lucchese di Scienze, Lettere ed Arti.
**Milan.*—Biblioteca Brera.
*Imperiale Regio Istituto Lombardo di Scienze, Lettere ed Arti.
*Museo Civico.
Modena.—Observatory.
*Società Italiana delle Scienze.
Naples.—Accademia degli Aspiranti Naturalisti.
Observatory.
*Reale Accademia delle Scienze, e Belle Lettere.
**Palermo.*—Accademia Palermitana di Scienze e Lettere.
Observatory.
**Padua.*—Imperiale Regia Accademia di Scienze, Lettere ed Arti di Padova.
Pisa.—Accademia Valdarnese del Poggio.

**Pisa.*—University Library.
Ravenna.—Società Ravennate.
**Rome.*—Accademia Romana di Archeologia.
*Accademia Pontifica dei Nuovi Lincei.
*Biblioteca Vaticana.
British Academy of Fine Arts.
Correspondenza Scientifica in Roma.
Osservatorio Astronomico del Collegio Romano.
Siena.—Accademia delle Scienze.
**Turin.*—Accademia Reale delle Scienze.
**Venice.*—Biblioteca Marciana.
I. R. Istituto Veneto di Scienze, Lettere ed Arti.
Naval School.
**Verona.*—Accademia d'Agricoltura, Commercio ed Arti di Verona.

PORTUGAL.

**Lisbon.*—Academia Real dos Sciencias.

SPAIN.

**Madrid.*—Real Academia Española.
*Real Academia de Ciencias de Madrid.
*Real Academia de la Historia.
*Biblioteca Real.

GREAT BRITAIN AND IRELAND.

Bath.—Bath and West of England Agricultural Society.
Belfast.—Belfast Institution.
*Library of Queen's College.
*Natural History and Philosophical Society.
Berwick-on-Tweed.—Berwickshire Naturalists' Club.
**Cambridge.*—Cambridge Philosophical Society.
*Cambridge Observatory.
*University Library.
**Cork.*—Library of Queen's College.
Royal Cork Institution.
Dublin.—Botanical Society.
Dublin University Philosophical Society.
Geological Society of Dublin.
*Library of Trinity College.
*Royal Dublin Society.
Royal Irish Academy.
Edinburgh.—Botanical Society.
*Library of Faculty of Advocates.
Royal Institution for Encouragement of Fine Arts in Scotland
*Royal Observatory.
Royal Physical Society of Edinburgh.
*Royal Scottish Society of Arts.

**Edinburgh*.—Royal Society
*Society of Antiquaries of Scotland.
*University Library.
*Wernerian Society of Natural History.
**Galway*.—Library of Queen's College.
Glasgow.—Andersonian Institute.
*University Library.
**Greenwich*.—Royal Observatory.
**Leeds*.—Leeds Philosophical and Literary Society.
**Liverpool*.—Free Public Library, Museum and Gallery of Art, of the Town of Liverpool.
Historic Society of Lancashire and Cheshire.
Observatory.
Royal Institution.
London.—Aborigines Protection Society.
Annals and Magazine of Natural History.
*Archæological Institute of Great Britain and Ireland.
*Athenæum Club.
*Board of Admiralty.
*British Archæological Association.
*British Association for the Advancement of Science.
*British Museum.
*Chemical Society of London.
Department of Practical Art.
Entomological Society.
*Ethnological Society of London.
*Geological Society of London.
*Horticultural Society of London.
Institute of Actuaries.
*Institution of Civil Engineers.
*Library of Corporation of City of London.
*Library of Committee of Privy Council for Trade.
*Library of Eaton College.
*Library of the Hon. the East India Company.
*Library of the House of Commons.
*Linnæan Society.
*London Institution (Finsbury).
*London Library.
Meteorological Society.
*Microscopical Society.
*Museum of Practical Geology.
*Philological Society.
*Queen's Library.
*Royal Agricultural Society of England.
*Royal Asiatic Society.
Royal Astronomical Society.
*Royal College of Surgeons of England.
*Royal Geographical Society of London.
*Royal Institution of Great Britain.
Royal Society of Literature.
*Royal Society of London.

London.—*Society of Antiquaries of London.
*Society of Arts, Manufactures, and Commerce.
*Statistical Society of London.
Syro-Egyptian Society.
*Zoological Society of London.
**Manchester.*—Manchester Free Library and Museum.
*Literary and Philosophical Society of Manchester.
Maynooth.—College Library.
Newcastle-upon-Tyne.—Natural History Society of Northumberland, Durham, and Newcastle-upon-Tyne.
Oxford.—Ashmolean Society.
*Bodleian Library.
*Radcliffe Observatory.
Penzance.—Royal Cornwall Polytechnic Society.
*Royal Geological Society of Cornwall.
Salford.—Salford Borough Royal Museum and Library.
**St. Andrews.*—University Library.
**Woolwich.*—Military Academy.

GREECE.

**Athens.*—University Library.

TURKEY.

Constantinople.—Société Orientale de Constantinople.
*Library of the Sultan.

AFRICA.

**Grand Cairo.*—The Egyptian Society.
**Liberia.*—Government Library.
Mauritius.—Société d'Histoire Naturelle de l'Isle Maurice.

ASIA.

**Allahabad.*—Mission College.
**Batavia.*—Bataviaasche Genootschap van Konsten en Wetenschappen.
**Bombay.*—Royal Asiatic Society.
*Geographical Society.
**Calcutta.*—Asiatic Society.
Agricultural and Horticultural Society of India.
**Ceylon.*—Asiatic Society.
Batticotta Seminary.
**Hong Kong.*—Asiatic Society of China.
**Madras.*—Literary Society.
**Manilla.*—Royal Economical Society of the Phillipine Islands.

VAN DIEMEN'S LAND.

Launceton.—Launceton Library.
Hobarton.—Royal Society of Van Diemen's Land.

AMERICA.

**Bogota.*—Sociedad Economica de Amigos del Pais.
**Brazil.—Rio Janeiro.*—Imperial Brazilian Historical Society.
Royal Geological Society.
Sociedad auxiliadora de Industria Nacional.
**Caracas.*—Sociedad Economica de Amigos del Pais.
**Chili.—Santiago.*—Biblioteca Nacional.
Observatory of Santiago.
*University Library.
Demerara.—Queen's College.
**Guatemala.*—Sociedad Economica de Amigos del Pais.
**Habana.*—Real Sociedad Economica.
Mexico.—Mexico.—El Minerea.
El Museo Nacional.
Navy and War Tribunal.
*Sociedad Mexicana de Geografia y Estadistica.
Pueblo.—Colegio Palafoxano y de Pantaleon.
Vera Cruz.—Public Institute.

The receipts of works from abroad, in exchange for those sent out by the Smithsonian Institution, are much greater than those of last year. Many of these were of very great value, comprising a large number of more or less complete series of transactions and periodicals. For an enumeration of these, I would refer to the Report of the Assistant Secretary in charge of the Library.

D.—Table exhibiting the number of pieces received in exchange from abroad, in 1853.

Volumes.—Folio and quarto	511	
Octavo	929	
		1,440
Parts of volumes and Pamphlets.—Quarto	303	
Octavo	688	
		991
Maps and engravings		125
Total		2,556

E.—Table exhibiting the number of packages received for other American institutions, &c., in 1853.

Bowdoin College	6
Boston.—American Academy	26
Natural History Society	6
Bowditch Library	7
Cambridge.—Observatory	11
Botanic Garden	7
Harvard College	13
Astronomical Journal	9
Amherst.—Amherst College	8

Worcester.—Antiquarian Society	1
New Haven.—Journal of Science	14
American Oriental Society	7
Albany.—New York State Library	6
New York.—Lyceum of Natural History	13
Ethnological Society	3
Geographical Society	4
Philadelphia.—American Philosophical Society	39
Academy of Natural Sciences	25
Franklin Institute	2
Geological Survey of Pennsylvania	4
Washington.—National Observatory	28
Coast Survey	22
National Institute	6
Surgeon General	1
American Association	2
Congress Library	8
Astronomical Expedition to Chili	4
United States Patent Offiee	3
State Department	2
Georgetown.—Observatory	10
Miscellaneous, including libraries of States, minor institutions, &c.	755
	1,052

6. Domestic Exchanges.

The copies of Volume V. of Smithsonian Contributions to Knowledge intended for American institutions, were all sent off in May at the same time with those for foreign bodies. As heretofore, they were distributed through the following agents who have made no charge for their service: Messrs. J. P. Jewett & Co., Boston; George P. Putnam & Co., New York; Lippincott, Grambo & Co., Philadelphia; John Russell, Charleston; B. M. Norman, New Orleans; Dr. Geo. Engelmann, St. Louis; H. W. Derby, Cincinnati; and Jewett, Proctor & Worthington, Cleveland. Acknowledgments for nearly all have been already received.

NATURAL HISTORY.

Increase of the Museum.

The additions to the Museum during the year 1853 have been very extensive, covering the entire field of natural history and ethnology. Many of these consist of species altogether new to science; while others, though previously described, belong to forms of great rarity. The contributions to our knowledge of the geographical distribution of species have been of the most important character, the localities occurring as they do over the entire area of this country. A very large proportion of these localities are in the region between the Mississippi and the Pacific, many of them never before represented in natural history cabinets. This condition of things has been, in great measure, due to the labors of the various government parties organized for the survey of the boundary line between the United States and Mexico, and of the several routes for a Pacific railroad. Without a single exception, all these parties have been fitted out at the Smithsonian Institution with all necessary instruments and apparatus for natural history research, much of it contrived with special reference to the exigencies of the particular service involved. Full instructions were also supplied, by which persons without previous practice were enabled to master all the general principles required for making observations and collections of every kind.

In addition to the above official explorations, many of a more private character, and of greater or less extent, have been made by different persons, and transmitted to the Institution. The general result is to be seen in the large number of jars, kegs, boxes, and shelves filled with specimens of all kinds. From this it will be seen that the army has contributed a very large proportion of the whole receipts, affording a gratifying proof of the interest felt in the deposit at the metropolis, of complete collections of the natural history of North America.

Owing to the liberality of the officers of the various expeditions, and of the bureaus under whose charge they were fitted out, every facility was afforded in authorizing the necessary foree and funds to meet the wants of science as connected with these explorations. In this way the entire cost was defrayed by government, so that the Institution has been called upon only to make the necessary expenditures for government, and to give a general supervision to the whole.

Nor have the materials collected by the government parties been allowed to lie idle; on the contrary, they have been put, immediately on their arrival, into the hands of competent naturalists and skilful artists, for the elucidation and illustration necessary to fit them for appearing as a portion of the reports which the various parties have been called on to make.

I shall now proceed briefly to mention the general character of the additions to the Museum during the year, referring for particular information to the alphabetical list of donors subjoined. It is impossible at the present time to give an accurate enumeration of all the species received, especially as so many are entirely new. Every specimen, however, is labelled, as soon as it arrives, with the name of the donor and locality; and in the descriptive catalogues now in course of preparation, the complete account of the whole will be presented in a systematic form. The general history of the explorations, too, will be found to embrace more detail than can here be given.

Mammals.—During the past year many species of North American mammals have been received, embracing quite a notable proportion of the smaller forms from North America, especially the squirrels, spermophiles, and weasels. The Louisiana species have been received from Mr. Fairie; those of Wisconsin, from Dr. Hoy; of the Rocky mountain range, from the expedition of Governor Stevens; of the lower

Rio Grande, from Major Emory. Dr. O. W. Gibbs presented a musk deer, from Java, and Mr. Steenberg has contributed many of the species from Greenland and Scandinavia. The collections of Capt. Van Vliet and Lieut. Couch include many species from Mexico and Texas. Some valuable specimens from Minnesota were received from Mr. Cavileer and Dr. Head.

Birds.—The additions to this department have been very great, amounting to over 400 species, and more than 1,000 specimens. Of these 250 species are from the Rio Grande country, North Mexico, the Rocky mountains, and west of the Rocky mountains. Here, as well as among mammals, there have occurred some new species. Of remarkable perfection of preparation was a collection of 50 species of California birds, presented by Dr. Hermann; and the North Mexican series of Lieut. Couch have been of extraordinary magnitude and importance. Capt. Van Vliet, Mr. J. H. Clark and Mr. Arthur Schott under Major Emory, and Dr. Crawford, have gathered many valuable specimens in Texas. Species from Michigan have been received from the Rev. Chas. Fox; of Wisconsin, from Dr. Hoy and Mr. Barry; of Ohio, from Dr. Kirtland and Chas. Pease; of Louisiana, from Mr. Jas. Fairie.

Reptiles and Fishes.—As heretofore, owing to the particular attention invited to this department, the additions to the alcoholic collections have been most marked, especially of reptiles and fishes. Every portion of the country has been laid under contribution, and the additions to our knowledge of the distribution of species, as well as of their zoological character, have been of the greatest value. There is scarcely a State or Territory in the Union which has not sent a representation. The most marked results have been the addition to the Fauna of the United States of the dipsadians among serpents, and the characini, ants, the fresh water labroids, among fishes. Nearly two thousand glass jars have been filled with the specimens received, after being assorted; of which 200 were of serpents alone. The principal contributors have been Major Emory, Governor Stevens, Lieut. Whipple, Dr. Hammond, Dr. Jeffrey, Prof. Winchell, Drs. G. C. and B. F. Shumard, Dr. Hoy, Rev. A. C. Barry, Dr. Barratt, Mrs. Daniel, Major Rich, Capt. Van Vliet, James Fairie, S. F. Baird, Maj. Hagner, Maj. Sibley, Rev. Chas. Fox, Dr. Head, J. D. Sergeant, Mr. Kennicott, Mr. Dean, Capt. Atwood, Leo Lesquereaux, J. H. Richard, Prof. Agassiz, Capt. Farragut, D. B. Boden, &c.

Invertebrata.—Many valuable collections of invertebrata have been added during the year, the most important being a series from Grand Manan, from Mr. Wm. Stimpson, and illustrating his paper published in the Smithsonian Contributions to Knowledge. Others from the coast Massachusetts were sent by Capt. Atwood, and from Florida and the Gulf of Mexico by Dr. Hammond, Dr. Jeffrey, and Major Emory. Some interesting contributions have consisted of specimens of *Gordius* from the bodies of crickets and grasshoppers, contributed by Mr. Sanford and Mr. Eveleth.

Plants.—An extensive collection of plants of Alabama, was received from Prof. A. Winchell, to whom the Institution is indebted for valuable specimens in all departments of natural history. Dr. Ravenel has presented a suite of the Carolina fungi. Lieut. Whipple and Governor Stevens have sent in important collections from their fields of labor.

Minerals and Fossils.—In connexion with the survey of Gov. Stevens, Dr. Evans revisited the Mauvaises Terres last summer, and collected a large number of specimens of the fossil vertebrata of that region. These have been put into the hands of Dr. Leidy, who has detected the presence of some additional new species. Professor Winchell has sent quite a full series of the cretaceous and tertiary fossils of Alabama, and Major Emory the same from Texas. Many minerals have been received from Dr. Pendleton, of Georgia, and some Austrian stalactites from Mr. Dodge.

Ethnology.—Skulls of many tribes of Indians, as Lipans, Comanches, Apaches, Flat Heads, have been received from various sources; as also remains of works of art. An interesting contribution to this department is found in a specimen of the sculpture of the human foot in limestone by the early inhabitants of the country, and erroneously supposed to be an impression made while the stone was in a plastic state.

PRESENT CONDITION OF THE MUSEUM.

The collections belonging to or deposited with the Smithsonian Institution are at present scattered over the building in its various rooms. Much inconvenience is felt from the impracticability of arranging the specimens properly for examination and study. Everything is kept packed away in the smallest compass, and of course not easily referred to when needed for investigation. The alcoholic collections, however, have generally been accessible when required for use. When the new museum room is finished, which will be in the course of a few months, ample space will be afforded for the accommodation of all the specimens, although a considerable time must necessarily elapse before the cases can be put up, and the collections properly arranged.

At the present time the Institution may be said to possess one of the best general collections of specimens of North American natural history in the country, although in particular branches it may be greatly exceeded by several, both public and private. It is pre-eminently rich in the mammals, with their skulls and skeletons; and still more in the reptiles. As an illustration of this, it may be stated that the species of North American serpents alone amount to 130, of which 70 were never described before being received by the Institution. The enumeration by Dr. Holbrook of North American serpents, in 1842, consisted of 49. The other departments of reptiles have experienced nearly proportional increase. The collection of birds is second only to that of the Philadelphia Academy of Natural Sciences; of fishes only equalled by the private cabinet of Professor Agassiz; while in the various departments of invertebrata and of plants it holds much more than average rank. In fossil remains the collection is very rich, especially of the comparatively recent vertebrata of the various caverns throughout the country.

And, in connexion with this extent and importance of the Smithsonian museum, it may be well to call attention to the fact that it has been the work of but three years to raise this collection from nothing to the front rank among American cabinets, exceeding all perhaps in the number of new species first brought to light within its limits. Nor has effort been confined merely to the acquisition of specimens, but to their concentration in mass so as to supply all working naturalists with the materials of research. As already stated, applications for such assistance are constantly being received, and always met with all possible promptness; so that scarcely any natural history monograph or memoir of any extent has been published in this country within a year or two which has not been indebted in this way to the Institution. From the care, too, taken to keep separate all the localities, however near together, of any species, the collection affords information in reference to the geographical distribution of species of the very highest value.

WORK DONE IN NATURAL HISTORY.

The labor of unpacking and assorting collections as received, and labelling and recording the different specimens, has of course been very great, requiring much more time than the limited portion left after discharging the other duties assigned to me. In this, however, I have been assisted very greatly by Mr. Charles Girard, who has given much time and attention to this department, without any compensation for his services. By his help, I have been enabled to keep up with the details of labor necessary to give these collections their proper scientific value.

Much has been done during the year towards distributing duplicate specimens of the Smithsonian collection among the other cabinets of the country. In no way can the Institution be of more use in elevating the standard of natural science than in distributing carefully labelled suites of specimens to points where, from lack of libraries or other causes, the means of accurate identification are wanting. For remote regions of country, this mode of assistance is of especial benefit, and arrangements have already been entered into, in several cases, to receive miscellaneous collections and to return them properly labelled, with the addition of such other species as can conveniently be spared. Parties already in such connexion with the Smithsonian Institution, or about entering upon it, are found in New York, Ohio, Michigan, Wisconsin, Iowa, Illinois, Missouri, New Orleans, and North and South Carolina.

A collection of duplicates of North American serpents and Astaci has been presented to the Philadelphia Academy of Natural Sciences, including types of many new species published by the Institution. To the New York State Cabinet of Natural History was also sent a large collection of reptiles and fishcs of New York, embracing many species not previously received there.

The cataloguing of the collections of the Institution progresses as rapidly as my other duties will allow. One way in which a museum may be very useful to those unable to visit it personally, is by publishing catalogues of the specimens contained therein. If these exhibit original descriptions of the species, and especially if the list be made complete by enumerating also the species not contained in the collection, they become of great value to investigators, and may readily serve as manuals of science, attaining the rank of monographs. This has been done in the Catalogue of North American Serpents in the Museum of the Smithsonian Institution, published in Jannary, 1853, which, in a compact volume of one hundred and eighty-eight pages, contains full and original descriptions of one hundred and nineteen species—all belonging to the Institution, with the exception of five; and some of these, with many additional ones, have been received since that time. Similar catalogues of the other reptiles are in an advanced stage of progression, and will be ready for publication early in 1854.

In addition to the preparation of these catalogues, much has been done in the classification and description of the collections sent in by the various exploring expeditions. Considerable progress has been made towards the preparation of the several reports of the natural history of the United States and Mexican Boundary Survey, the survey of the North Pacific railroad route by Gov. Stevens, that of the Central route by Lieut. Whipple, that of the United States Astronomical Expedition to Chili by Lieut. Gillis, and several others. The preparation of many hundred sheets of drawings of new species for these reports has been carefully superintended. The reports prepared upon the natural history of the explorations by Capt. Sitgreaves and Capt. Marcy, have already been published by Congress. Some of these I now lay before you.

A large amount of valuable information relating to the descriptions, and the habits and manners of species, has been received during the year—much of it bearing directly upon important questions in science and rural economy. A very extensive correspondence has been required for the purpose of stimulating investigations and calling attention to the solution of particular problems. It is much to be regretted that the Institution has no medium of its own through which the information thus received can be promptly presented to the world. A monthly bulletin, of considerable size, could readily be filled with communications of this kind, as well as with brief notices and descriptions of collections received.

Registers of Periodical Phenomena.

The blank registers of periodical phenomena issued in the winter of 1852–'3, have been returned filled, and in connexion with those for the previous year, still in manuscript, form a body of information of the highest value. These will be carefully reduced, and published at an early period. A new edition having become necessary, a revision of the old lists of plants was carefully made by Drs. Torrey and Gray, and the revised form will be distributed in a few weeks. Instructions for making collections of microscopical organisms and infusoria have been added.

Assistance in the Museum.

As the time has already arrived when more attention and labor should be given to the collections of the Museum to make them fulfil all the purposes of instruction of which they are capable, it is very desirable that the Museum force should be increased. I have already adverted to the labor necessarily expended during the past year in merely unpacking and arranging the collections of new matter received. While the old specimens need a certain amount of care, new ones are being constantly added. I would, therefore, recommend that Mr. Girard be regularly employed by the Institution, at such salary as you may think suitable; and one other person in addition, to attend to the purely mechanical work required in the way of unpacking, washing bottles, tying on labels, cleaning specimens, &c. Such service as this could be obtained for about twenty-five dollars per month, and the help of both persons would be also available in other departments where it is imperatively required. This is especially the case in respect to the publications, exchanges, and transportation, where, as in the Museum operations, I have no regular assistance whatever.

Alphabetical list of donors to the Museum of the Smithsonian Institution.

Academy of Natural Sciences.—Skins of North American birds.

Prof. C. B. Adams.—Shells, &c., from Bermuda and St. Thomas.

Prof. L. Agassiz.—*Etheostoma* from Alabama and Missouri.

Capt. Atwood.—Fishes, crustacea, and radiata, from Provincetown, Mass.

Prof. A. D. Bache.—Surterbrand from Iceland.

Prof. S. F. Baird.—Twelve kegs, &c. of fishes, from Wisconsin, Michigan, Ohio, New York, and Canada.

Dr. J. B. Barratt.—Reptiles and fishes from South Carolina.

Dr. J. M. Bigelow.—Seeds from Texas and New Mexico.

Capt. Daniel Boden.—Specimens of lake trout and perch, from Otsego lake, New York.

J. S. Bowman.—Reptiles and fishes from the vicinity of Fort Kearney.

Major J. H. Carleton, U. S. A.—Specimen of *thelyphonus* from Santa Fé.

Charles Cavileer.—Mammals, &c., from Minnesota.

Robert Clarke.—Skulls of mammals and reptiles, in alcohol, from Essex county, N. J.

Prof. George H. Cook.—Living specimens of *Emys muhlenbergii*, from New York.

Dr. G. E. Cooper, U. S. A.—Skulls of Comanche and Lipan Indians.

Dr. J. G. Cooper.—Reptiles from California; skin of *Gymnotus electricus.*

Lt. D. N. Couch, U. S. A.—Very extensive collections of the vertebrata, with numerous insects and specimens of antiquities from Northern Mexico.

G. S. Cutting.—*Storeria dekayii* and *Chlorosoma vernalis*, from Middleboro', Mass.

Mrs. M. E. Daniel.—Reptiles from Anderson, S. C.

E. A. Dayton.—Skulls of beaver and fishes; (*Mustela canadensis;*) reptiles and fishes from the St. Lawrence river.

G. W. Dean.—Reptiles from Galveston, Texas.

Delaware County Institute, Pa.—Keg of fishes and reptiles; three hundred and eleven species of plants from Delaware county, Pa.

J. M. Dodge.—Stalactites from the cave of Adelsburg, Austria.

Rev. D. W. Eakins.—Limestone slab, with sculpture of human feet, from Verdigris river, Creek Nation.

Dr. George Engelmann.—Reptiles and fishes from St. Louis.

Samuel A. Eveleth.—*Gordius* taken from a cricket.

Jas. Fairie.—Shells of *Chelonura temminckii*, from Louisiana; Indian implements, reptiles, &c.

Capt. D. Farragut, U. S. N.—Fishes from Chesapeake bay.

Dr. E. Foreman.—*Unio hopetonensis* from Altamaha river.

Rev. Charles Fox.—Living specimens of *Eutænia;* fishes, reptiles, and mammals, from Michigan.

Dr. Julius Froebel.—Fossils from New Mexico.

Dr. Wolcott Gibbs.—Musk deer of Java, in the flesh.

B. R. Gifford.—Clays and concretions from Gay Head Bluffs, Martha's Vineyard.

Major Hagner, U. S. A.—*Siredon lichenoides*, from Fort Defiance, Navajo country.

C. F. Hammond.—Phosphate of lime, from Crown Point, N. Y.

Dr. J. F. Hammond.—Skin of *Crotalus adamanteus*, with fishes and reptiles, in alcohol, from Pensacola.

Dr. W. Hammond.—Skeletons and skulls from Fort Kearney.

Dr. J. F. Head.—Reptiles, fishes, and skulls of vertebrata, from Fort Ripley.

Dr. A. L. Hermann.—Skins of fifty species of birds, from California.

Dr. P. R. Hoy.—Fishes, reptiles, birds, and mammals, from Wisconsin.

Dr. R. W. Jeffrey.—Fishes and reptiles from Pensacola.

S. K. Jennings, jr.—Shed skin of *Masticophis flavigularis*, Texas.

Robert W. Kennicott.—Fishes and reptiles from Cook county, Illinois.

J. A. Lapham.—Shells from Wisconsin.

Leo Lesquereux.—Reptiles and fishes from Ohio.

Rev. Charles Mann.—Salamanders from Gloucester, Virginia.

Dr. Morrow.—Gold ore from Dorn's Mine, Abbeville, South Carolina.

Richard Nettle.—Fishes from the lower St. Lawrence.

Dr. E. C. Pendleton.—Minerals and shells from Georgia.

H. W. Ravenel.—Specimens of Carolina fungi.

W. H. Ravenel.—*Sceloporus undulatus*, South Carolina.

Major Wm. Rich.—Reptiles, fishes, &c., from the city of Mexico.

J. H. Richard.—Fishes from Pennsylvania.

E. S. Robinson.—Skin of *Crotalus adamanteus.*

Mr. Sabine.—Reptiles from California; skin of *Gymnotus electricus.*

S. N. Sanford.—*Gordius* taken from the body of a cricket.

Sir Robert Schomburgk.—Tertiary shells and ancient pottery from St. Domingo.

J. D. Sergeant.—Reptiles from Rock Island, Illinois.

Major E. S. Sibley, U. S. A.—Reptiles and insects from Fort Union, New Mexico.

Capt. Shiras, U. S. A.—Specimen of *mygale*, Texas.

Dr. B. F. Shumard.—Specimens of *amblyopsis*, *astacus*, and insects and reptiles, from the Mammoth Cave, Kentucky, and vicinity; fishes from Louisville, Kentucky; reptiles from Mississippi.

Dr. G. C. Shumard.—Reptiles and fishes from the Arkansas river.

Geo. Smith.—Living specimens of *Emys muhlenbergii*, from Delaware county, Pennsylvania.

Commodore Joseph Smith.—Specimens of woods used in ship-building; illustrations of growth and ravages of *teredo*. Prepared by Mr. Jarvis, inspector of Portsmouth yard.

J. M. Stanley.—Dress and war-club of Blackfoot chief.

Judge Augustus Steele.—Fishes, crustacea, and shells, from Atseena, Florida.

Schach Steenberg.—Skins and skeletons of mammals, fish and invertebrates, in alcohol; Greenland.

Wm. Stimpson.—Miscellaneous invertebrata from New England.

Capt. S. Van Vliet, U. S. A.—Skeleton of peccary; skins of birds; alcoholic specimens of reptiles, fishes, and crustacea, from the lower Rio Grande.

Col. B. L. C. Wailes.—Living tortoises, fossils, fishes, and reptiles, in alcohol, &c., from Mississippi.

Rev. Dr. Wheeler.—Lignite from Brandon, Vermont; *Osceola elapsoidea* from Florida.

Prof. Alexander Winchell.—Fossils, plants, reptiles, birds, &c., from Eutaw, Alabama; plants, fossils, and fishes, from Selma, Alabama.

Dr. S. Wylie Crawford, U. S. A.—Skin of *Cyrtonyx massena* from Texas.

List of Meteorological observers reporting to the Smithsonian Institution at the beginning of 1854, *compiled by Lorin Blodget.*

State.	Name.	Residence.
Nova Scotia	Henry Poole	Albion Mines, Pictou.
Canada	Dr. Chas. Smallwood	St. Martin's, near Montreal.
Maine	Rev. Samuel H. Merrill	Oldtown, Penobscot county.
	J. D. Parker	Steuben, Washington county.
	James G. Garland	Biddeford, York county.
	John J. Bell	Carmel, Penobscot county.
	Saml. A. Eveleth	Windham, Cumberland county.
	Joshua Bartlett	South Thomaston, Lincoln co.
	Geo. W. Burrows	Fryeburg, Oxford county.
	Wm. D. Dana	Perry, Washington county.
New Hampshire	Geo. B. Sawyer	Salmon Falls, Stafford county.
	Robt. C. Mack	Londonderry, Rockingham county.
	Dr. Wm. Prescott	Concord, Merrimack county.
	Hon. S. N. Bell	Manchester, Hillsborough county.
	Rev. L. W. Leonard	Exeter, Rockingham county.
	Albert A. Young Prof. Ira Young	Hanover, Grafton county.
Vermont	John K. Colby J. P. Fairbanks	St. Johnsbury, Caledonia county.
	Chas. A. J. Marsh	Craftsbury, Orleans county.
	D. Buckland	Brandon, Rutland county.
	D. Underwood	Castleton, Rutland county.
	Prof. Zadok Thompson	Burlington, Crittenden county.
Massachusetts	William Bacon	Richmond, Berkshire county.
	Prof. E. G. Snell	Amherst, Hampshire county.
	Dr. Ed. A. Smith	Worcester, Worcester county.
	Dr. H. C. Perkins	Newburyport, Essex county.
	Hon. John Brooks	Princeton, Worcester county.
	Dr. Jno. Geo. Metcalf	Mendon, Worcester county.
	Lucius C. Allen	Springfield, Hampden county.
	Samuel Rodman	New Bedford, Bristol county.
	Amasa Holcomb	Southwick, Hampden county.
	B. R. Gifford	Barnstable, Barnstable county.
	Henry Rice	North Attleboro', Bristol county.
	Hon. Wm. Mitchell	Nantucket.
Rhode Island	Henry C. Sheldon	North Scituate, Providence.
	Prof. A. Caswell	Providence.
Connecticut	Rev. Tryon Edwards, D. D.	New London, New London co'ty.
	Daniel Hunt	Pomfret, Windham county.
	James Rankin	Saybrook, Middlesex county.
	Dr. Ovid Plumb	Salisbury, Litchfield county.
New York*	Prof. Edward A. H. Allen	Troy, Rensselaer county.
	Thomas B. Arden	Beverly, Putnam county.
	Charles A. Avery	Seneca Falls, Seneca county.
	Prof. O. W. Morris	Institution for deaf and dumb, N. Y.
	C. Thurston Chase	Chatham, Columbia county.
	E. A. Dayton	Madrid, St. Lawrence county.
	E. W. Johnson	Canton, St. Lawrence county.
	Dr. P. O. Williams	Gouverneur, St. Lawrence county.
	J. H. Hart	Oswego, Oswego county.
	E. N. Byram	Sag Harbor, Suffolk county.
	C. S. Woodward	Beaver Brook, Sullivan county.
	Walker D. Yale	Houseville, Lewis county.

* New York Academy system in separate list.

LIST—Continued.

State.	Name.	Residence.
New York	John Bowman	Baldwinsville, Onondaga county.
	John Lefferts	Lodi, Seneca county.
	Elias O. Salisbury	Buffalo, Erie county.
	Laurens A. Langdon	Falconer, Chautauque county.
	Dr. Stillman Spooner	Wampsville, Oneida county.
	L. F. Munger	Albion, Orleans county.
	John F. Jenkins	North Salem, Westchester county.
New Jersey	Robert L. Cooke	Bloomfield, Essex county.
	Prof. Adolph Frost	Burlington, Burlington county.
	W. A. Whitehead	Newark, Essex county.
Pennsylvania	Dr. A. C. Blodget	Youngsville, Warren county.
	W. O. Blodget	Sugar Grove, Warren county.
	Samuel Brown	Bedford, Bedford county.
	John Comly	Byberry, Philadelphia county.
	Joseph Edwards	Lima, Delaware county.
	Dr. R. P. Stevens	Ceres, McKean county.
	Francis Schriener	Moss Grove, Crawford county.
	W. W. Wilson	Pittsburgh, Alleghany county.
	Prof. M. Jacobs	Gettysburgh, Adams county.
	Fenelon Darlington	Poçopson, Chester county.
	Ebenezer Hance	Morrisville, Bucks county.
	Dr. J. Heisely	Harrisburg, Dauphin county.
	Rev. D. J. Eyler	Waynesboro', Franklin county.
	J. R. Lowrie	Hollidaysburg, Blair county.
	Rev. J. Grier Ralston	Norristown, Montgomery county.
	Prof. J. A. Kirkpatrick	Philadelphia, Philadelphia county.
	Dr. Paul Swift	Haverford, Philadelphia county.
Maryland	Prof. Wm. Barr Miss H. M. Barr	Sykesville, Carroll county.
	Prof. L. H. Steiner	Baltimore, Baltimore county.
	Henry E. Hanshaw	Frederick, Frederick county.
Virginia	John W. Marvin	Winchester, Frederick county.
	Prof. Geo. R. Rosseter	Buffalo, Putnam county.
	Dr. Thomas Patton	Lewisburg, Greenbrier county.
	Benjamin Hallowell	Alexandria, Alexandria county.
	Prof. N. B. Webster	Portsmouth, Norfolk county.
	David Turner	Richmond, Henrico county.
	Lieut. R. F. Astrop	Crichton's store, Brunswick co'ty.
	Wm. S. Kern	Huntersville, Pocahontas county.
North Carolina	Rev. Frederick Fitzgerald	Jackson, Northampton county.
	Prof. James Phillips	Chapel Hill, Orange county.
South Carolina	Thornton Carpenter	Camden, Kershaw county.
Georgia	Dr. John F. Posey	Savannah, Chatham county.
	R. P. Gibson	Whitmarsh Island, Chatham co'ty.
	Prof. John Darby	Culloden, Monroe county.
	Dr. E. M. Pendleton	Sparta, Hancock county.
Florida	Dr. A. S. Baldwin	Jacksonville, Duvall county.
	Judge Aug. Steele	Cedar Keys, Levy county.
	John Newton	Knox Hill, Walton county.
	John Pearson, master navy yard	Pensacola, Escambia county.
Alabama	S. J. Cumming	Monroeville, Monroe county.
	Prof. H. Tutwiler	Havana, Greene county.
	Prof. M. Tuomey	Tuscaloosa, Tuscaloosa county.
	Benjamin F. Holley	Wetokaville, Talladega county.
Mississippi	Rev. E. Robinson	Garlandsville, Jasper county.

LIST—Continued.

State.	Name.	Residence.
Louisiana	Dr. E. H. Barton	New Orleans, Orleans county.
Texas	Dr. S. K. Jennings	Austin, Travis county.
	Prof. J. C. Ervendberg	New Weld, Comal county.
Tennessee	Commandant navy yard	Memphis, Shelby county.
	Prof. A. P. Stewart	Lebanon, Wilson county.
	W. M. Stewart	Glenwood, near Clarksville, Montgomery county.
	Prof. George Cooke	Knoxville, Knox county.
Kentucky	Dr. John Swain	Ballardsville, Oldham county.
	Rev. J. Miller	Millersburg, Bourbon county.
	O. Beatty	Danville, Boyle county.
	Lawrence Young	Springville, near Louisville, Jefferson county.
	A. H. Bixby	Pleasant Valley, Nicholas county.
	E. L. Bethune	Maysville, Mason county.
Ohio	Prof. R. S. Bosworth	College Hill, Hamilton county.
	L. Gronewez	Germantown, Montgomery co'ty.
	Rev. J. McD. Matthews	Hillsborough, Highland county.
	Geo. L. Crookham	Jackson C. H., Jackson county.
	J. G. F. Holston	Zanesville, Muskingum county.
	Prof. S. N. Sanford	Granville, Licking county.
	Prof. J. W. Andrews	Marietta, Washington county.
	F. A. Benton	Mt. Vernon, Knox county.
	E. Spooner	Keen, Coshocton county.
	Prof. J. H. Fairchild	Oberlin, Loraine county.
Michigan	Dr. Thomas Whelpey	Brest, Monroe county.
	L. Woodruff	Ann Arbor, Washtenaw county.
	Dr. M. K. Taylor	Brooklyn, Jackson county.
	Dr. W. M. Campbell	Battle Creek, Calhoun county.
	Jas. J. Strong	St. James, Beaver Island.
	Rev. Geo. Duffield, D. D.	Detroit, Wayne county.
Indiana	Prof. Jos. Tingley	Greencastle, Putnam county.
	W. W. Austin	Richmond, Wayne county.
	Dr. V. Kersey	Milton, Wayne county.
	Jno. Chappellsmith	New Harmony, Posey county.
Illinois	Dr. L. B. Mead	Augusta, Hancock county.
	Joel Hall	Athens, Menard county.
	Dr. John James	Upper Alton, Madison county.
	Dr. J. O. Harris	Ottawa, La Salle county.
	Prof. Wm. Coffin	Batavia, Kane county.
Missouri	Dr. Geo. Engelman	St. Louis, St. Louis county.
	O. H. P. Lear	Hannibal, Marion county.
Iowa	Dr. J. E. Ball	Keokuk, Lee county.
	Dr. Benj. F. Odell	Poulteney, Delaware county.
	Dr. E. C. Bidwell	Quasqueton, Buchanan county.
	D. E. Read	St. Mary's, Mills county.
	P. G. Parvin	Muscatine, Muscatine county.
	Dr. Asa Horr	Dubuque, Dubuque county.
Wisconsin	Dr. J. L. Pickard	Plattsville, Grant county.
	Prof. S. P. Lathrop	Beloit, Rock county.
	J. F. Willard	Janesville, Rock county.
	Thos. Gay, esq	Bellefontaine, Marquette county.
	Prof. S. H. Carpenter	Madison, Dane county.
	Edward S. Spencer	Summitt, Waukesha county.

LIST—Continued.

State.	Name.	Residence.
Minnesota	Rev. Elisha W. Carver	Red Lake, Pembina county.
	Rev. S. R. Riggs	Lac qui Parle, Dahkota county.
	Rev. D. B. Spencer	St. Josephs, Pembina county.

New York University system.

Name.	Station.
Prof. C. Dewey, D. D	Rochester, Monroe county.
Chas. A. Avery	Seneca Falls, Seneca county.
Dr. M. M. Bagg	Utica, Oneida county.
E. A. Dickinson	Jamestown, Chautauque county.
W. H. Gillespie	Mexico, Oswego county.
Charles J. Hazeltine	Cherry Valley, Otsego county.
Ira F. Hart	Elmira, Chemung county.
T. H. Bates	Booneville, Oneida county.
Prof. O. Root	Hamilton College, Oneida county.
W. E. Guest	Ogdensburg, St. Lawrence county.
John F. Jenkins	North Salem, Westchester county.
John Kruger	do do.
Prof. O. W. Morris	Institution for deaf and dumb, N. York city.
E. W. Johnson	Canton, St. Lawrence county.
W. C. Kenyon	Alfred, Alleghany county.
D. T. Mayhew	Lowville, Lewis county.
W. Root Adams	do do.
W. McLaren	Glen's Falls, Warren county.
Warren P. Adams	do do.
Samuel A. Law	Meredith, Delaware county.
Rev. W. D. Wilson	Geneva, Ontario county.
H. H. Poucher	Hudson, Columbia county.
Judge E. C. Reed	Homer, Cortland county.
John S. D. Taylor	Plattsburg, Clinton county.
John D. Watkins	Liberty, Sullivan county.
Frederick L. Hanford	do do.
J. H. Wines	East Hampton, Suffolk county.
Rev. Thomas M. Strong, D. D	Flatbush, Kings county.
J. O. Stratton	Oxford, Chenango county.
Charles H. Payson	Pompey, Onondaga county.
A. Porteus	Adirondack, Essex county.
F. B. Downes	Ithaca, Tompkins county.
H. H. Hall	Newburgh, Orange county.
C. W. Heywood	Rochester, Monroe county.
Lyman W. Conkey	Syracuse, Onondago county.
D. H. Cochran	Fredonia, Chautauque county.
Prof. George H. Cook	Albany, Albany county.
John N. Brinkerhoff	Union Hall, Jamaica, Queens county.

Observations transmitted in series or summaries.

State.	Name.	Residence.
Canada	Magnetic and meterological observatory	Toronto, Canada.
Indiana	Dr. Thomas Edmondson	Baltimore.
South Carolina	Rev. A. Glennie	Waccaman.
Florida	Wm. C. Dennis	Key West.
Missouri	Dr. George Engelman	St. Louis.
Iowa	E. H. A. Scheeper	Pella, Marion county.
California	Dr. J. H. Gibbons	San Francisco.
Bermuda	Surgeon Wellis	Centre Signal Station, Inland Island.
Montreal	J. H. Huguet Latour	
	Dr. Archibald Hall	
Central America	M. B. Halsted	Panama.
South America	Edward A. Hopkins	Ascension, Paraguay.

Observers commencing since January, 1854, *up to June* 1, 1854.

State.	Name.	Residence.
Massachusetts	Dr. James W. Robbins	Uxbridge, Worcester county.
	B. R. Gifford	Wood's Hole, Barnstable county.
	Albert Schlegel	Taunton, Bristol county
	Prof. P. A. Chadbourne	William's College, Williamstown.
Rhode Island	Samuel Powel	Newport, Newport county.
	Geo. Manchester	Portsmouth, Newport couuty.
Connecticut	T. S. Gold	West Cornwall, Litchfield county.
	Prof. John Johnston	Middletown, Middlesex county.
New York	Dr. E. M. Alba	Angelica, Alleghany county.
	John F. Jenkins	White Plains, West Chester.
	Warren P. Adams	Glen's Falls, Warren.
	Rev. W. D. Wilson	Geneva, Ontario county.
	Dr. Sanford B. Hunt	Buffalo, Erie county.
New Jersey	Prof. George H. Cook	New Brunswick, Middlesex co'ty.
Pennsylvania	J. R. Lowrie	Warrior's Mark, Huntingdon co.
	R. Weiser	Andersville, Perry county.
	Prof. Thickstun	Meadville, Crawford county.
Maryland	Rev. John P. Carter	Hagerstown, Washington county.
Virginia	Jed. Hotchiss	Bridgewater, Rockingham, county.
	A. Nettleton	Lynchburg, Campbell county.
North Carolina	J. Bryant Smith, M. D.	Lincolnton, Lincoln county.
South Carolina	Thornton Carpenter	Charleston, Charleston county.
	H. W. Ravenel	Aiken, Barnwell county.
Georgia	William Schley	Augusta, Richmond county.
	Prof. Wm. D. Williams	Madison, Morgan county.
Mississippi	Rev. J. Avery Shepherd	Lake Washington, Washington co.
	Wm. Henry Waddell	Grenada, Yalabusha county.
	Prof. L. Harper	Oxford, La Fayette county.
	A. R. Green	Jackson, Jackson county.

LIST—Continued.

State.	Name.	Residence.
Louisiana	Prof. W. P. Riddell	New Orleans, Orleans county.
Kentucky	A. H. Bixby	Lafayette, Christian county.
	J. D. Shane	Lexington, Fayette county.
Ohio	John Ingram	Savannah, Ashland county.
	D. G. W. Livesay	Gallipolis, Gallia county.
	Dr. J. P. Kirtland	East Rockport, Cuyahoga county.
	Edmund W. West	Huron, Erie county.
Michigan	Dr. S. F. Mitchell	East Saginaw, Saginaw county.
	Alfred E. Carrier	Grand Rapids, Kent county.
	Prof. Alexander Winchell	Ann Arbor, Washtenaw county.
Indiana	J. Knauer	Kendallville, Noble county.
	W. B. Coventing	do do.
	Daniel H. Roberts	New Garden, Wayne county.
Iowa	E. H. A. Scheeper	Pella, Marion county.
Wisconsin	G. Z. Livingston	Hudson, St. Croix county.
	J. A. Lapham	Milwaukie, Milwaukie county.
	Prof. Wm. Porter	Beloit, Rock county.
Minnesota	Rev. Solon W. Mauncey	Fort Ripley.
	Dr. C. L. Anderson	St. Anthony's Falls, Ramsey co'y.
Oregon	John D. Post	Oregon City.
California	Dr. J. H. Gibbons	San Francisco.

REPORT OF THE EXECUTIVE COMMITTEE.

The Executive Committee submit to the Board of Regents the following report, relative to the present state of the finances, and the expenditures during the year 1853.

They are happy to inform the Board that, after a strict examination of the accounts, they are enabled to present a very satisfactory statement of the present condition of the finances, and the result of the investigations as to the expenditures during the year.

The whole amount of the Smithsonian bequest, deposited in the treasury of the United States, (from which an annual income, at 6 per cent., is derived of $30,910 14,) is		$515,169 00
Amount of unexpended interest, reported last year as in charge of Messrs. Corcoran & Riggs	$208,800 00	
From which deduct amount expended on the building during the past year	29,391 98	
	179,408 02	
Of this it is proposed to expend the further sum of	29,408 02	
Which will leave to be added to the principal, according to the original proposition of Professor Bache		150,000 00
The whole fund will then be		665,169 00

Statement in relation to the expenditures of the Smithsonian Institution during the year 1853.

BUILDING, FURNITURE, FIXTURES, ETC.		
Pay on contracts	$25,500 00	
Pay of architects, superintendents, &c	1,580 70	
Magnetic observatory	1,578 28	
Expenses of building committee	77 00	
Miscellaneous, incidental to building	184 84	
Furniture, &c., for uses in common	354 05	
Furniture for library	117 11	
		$29,391 98
GENERAL EXPENSES.		
Expenses of Board of Regents	195 00	
Lighting and heating	646 47	
Postage	364 28	
Transportation	1,913 19	
Stationery	6 50	
General printing	894 19	
Apparatus	203 50	
Incidentals general	*3,352 42	
Watchman	367 00	
Salaries general	4,099 92	
		12,042 47
PUBLICATIONS, RESEARCHES, AND LECTURES.		
Smithsonian Contributions to Knowledge	8,160 04	
Reports on progress of knowledge	139 29	
Other publications	1,116 58	
Meteorology	2,346 51	
Pay of lecturers	783 00	
Illustrations and apparatus for lectures	661 84	
Attendance and lighting lectures, &c	445 40	
		13,652 66
LIBRARY, MUSEUM, AND GALLERY OF ART.		
Cost of books	841 75	
Stereotyping and printing	1,318 42	
Incidentals to library	1,581 02	
Salaries, library	2,499 96	
Explorations, museum	250 00	
Expense of collections, museum	240 04	
Incidentals, museum	229 71	
Salaries, museum	1,999 92	
		8,960 82
Total expenditures in 1853		64,047 93

* Including $948 34, charged for interest on over-drafts during the year.

The following is a general view of the receipts and expenditures for the year 1853:

RECEIPTS.		
Balance in the treasury, as per last report	$250 49	
Interest on the original fund for the year 1853	30,910 14	
Interest on the extra fund for the year 1853	10,440 00	
		$41,600 63
EXPENDITURES, EXCLUSIVE OF BUILDING.		
For items common to the objects of the Institution	12,042 47	
For publications, researches, and lectures	13,652 66	
For library, museum, and gallery of art	8,960 82	
Balance in the treasury	6,944 68	
		41,600 63

An appropriation of $30,000 was made at the last meeting of the Board of Regents, to be expended under the direction of the Executive Committee and the Secretary, for carrying on the operations of the Institution.

From the foregoing statement of accounts it will be seen that while the library and museum have had their share of the appropriation, the active operations have exceeded their part by upwards of $4,000. This excess has been caused, principally, by printing and preparing for the press a number of memoirs which are to form the volume of contributions for the year 1854.

Whatever may be the future distribution of the income, a greater expenditure than has been made for the library and museum, during the past year, could not, in the opinion of the committee, have been judicious.

The additions to the library and museum, the former of which were chiefly in return for the publications of the Institution under the system of exchanges, have been considerable and valuable. A particular estimate of these will be presented to the Board hereafter.

The Board are referred to the report of the Secretary, recently submitted, for a detailed account of the operations of the Institution during the past year. The committee think that these operations are in harmony with the law of Congress, with the objects of the founder of the Institution, and successfully carry out his idea of the increase and diffusion of knowledge.

After the present year, during which the building will probably be completed, the fund for annual expenditures will be somewhat enlarged, and increased benefits, it is hoped, will be realized.

J. A. PEARCE,
A. D. BACHE, } *Executive Committee.*
J. G. TOTTEN,

REPORT OF THE BUILDING COMMITTEE.

The Building Committee of the Smithsonian Institution beg leave to present to the Board of Regents the following report of their operations and expenditures during the year 1853:

It will be recollected by the Regents that the first plan of the Smithsonian building contemplated finishing the interior with wood and plaster, and that the Board subsequently adopted a resolution directing the wood-work to be removed and its place to be supplied with fire-proof materials.

In accordance with this resolution, the Building Committee directed plans and estimates to be made by Captain B. S. Alexander, of the United States corps of Engineers. These plans were laid before the Board at the last meeting, and approved; reserving, however, to the Building Committee the right to make any changes which they might think desirable during the progress of the work. Mr. Renwick having retired from the office of Architect, Captain Alexander was appointed in his place.

It will also be recollected by the Board, that shortly before the close of their last session, Mr. Gilbert Cameron, the former contractor, petitioned the Regents to be allowed to finish the building, alleging that, if he was not granted this privilege, his reputation as a builder would be injured; and also affirming that he was legally entitled to be allowed to complete the work, by the terms of his original contract, which the Board had never declared forfeited.

This subject was referred to the Building Committee, and legal advice was asked by them in reference to it, from J. M. Carlisle esq., who has acted for some years as counsel to the Board of Regents. His opinion was in favor of the claims of Mr. Cameron. The question was also submitted to P. R. Fendall, esq., United States district attorney, who coincided in opinion with Mr. Carlisle.

In accordance with these opinions, the committee concluded to let Mr. Cameron proceed with the work on the terms which he had previously submitted to them, and which was within the estimate which had been made by the architect.

Some delay unavoidably took place in arriving at this decision, and consequently the work was not commenced until June 13, 1853. Since then, however, it has been prosecuted with great vigor, and to the entire satisfaction of the Committee. The roof has been temporarily secured, the entire frame of wood work which occupied the interior removed, and a cellar excavated. A large brick sewer has been constructed through the middle of the building, and carried outward toward the canal, by which the cellar may be thoroughly drained and all waste water discharged. The foundation walls, piers, and arches, of a spacious and commodious basement, have been completed; the piers in the main story have been built, and the beams and arches of the floor for the rooms above finished. The brickwork of the upper story has also been completed; in short, the masonry from the foundation to the roof, and more than nine-tenths of the brickwork, have been finished. The principal part of the work yet remaining to be accomplished, according to the statement of the architect, may be classified as follows:

1. Finishing the necessary stairways for the lecture room and gallery.
2. Supporting the roof, so that the columns in the second story may be dispensed with.
3. Completing the interior finish, such as flooring, plastering, painting, &c.
4. Fitting up the lecture room with seats.

The Committee found great difficulty in deciding upon a proper position and plan of a lecture room, and, after much deliberation and frequent consultations, finally concluded to place it in the second story, in the middle of the main building, where the greatest width could be obtained.

The original plan contemplated the placing of the large lecture room on the first floor; but in this position it was impossible to procure a sufficient space, uninterrupted by large columns, which would materially interfere with the employment of the room for the purpose intended. In endeavoring to overcome this difficulty, it was at one time proposed to support the floor of the whole space of fifty feet in width, by means of heavy girders; but this being considered unsafe, the idea was abandoned. The only plan, therefore, at the option of the Committee for providing a suitable lecture room, was that which has been adopted. According to the present income and policy of the Institution, this is cheaper than any other plan proposed; and should the building ever be required for other purposes, such as an entire museum or library, the division walls could easily be removed, and the whole space reconverted into one large room. The plan adopted, therefore, makes the best provision for the present wants of the Institution, and can readily be adapted to any proposed change in the future application of the building. The whole of the first story has been thrown into one large room, with arrangements for dividing it, if necessary, by screens, into two apartments, with a central hall or wide passage between.

The Committee have kept constantly in view the idea of rendering the main building entirely fire-proof, and of constructing it in the most durable and substantial manner. This they have been enabled to accomplish through the constant supervision of Captain Alexander, who, as it appears to the Committee, has successfully evinced in this work a combination of practical skill and scientific knowledge.

From a comparison of the work done with that which remains to be accomplished, the architect is of opinion that, should nothing happen to prevent it, the building will be finished during the present year, and at a cost within the estimate; consequently, the $58,000, recommended to be set aside by the Executive Committee in their last report, together with a portion of the income of the past year, will be sufficient to defray all the expenses, and leave the $150,000 untouched. This refers, however, mainly to the completion of the building, and not to the furniture, which must be purchased by degrees out of the accruing interest on the above mentioned sum.

At the last session of the Board of Regents a resolution was adopted authorizing the erection of a small building for a Magnetic Observatory. This structure has been completed, and is now furnished with instruments, and will soon be in successful operation. It consists of a small room twelve feet by sixteen, under ground, enclosed by a nine inch brick wall, within which the instruments are placed. This room is surrounded by a rough stone wall, leaving a space of two feet in width on each side to permit a free circulation of air, for keeping the interior apartment dry. Above ground the structure is of wood, so finished as to correspond to some extent with the architecture of the Smithsonian Building, and consists principally of an entry and one room sixteen feet square, to serve as an office, and computing room for the observer. The whole cost of this building was $1,578 28. The entire expenditure on the building during the past year, exclusive of the magnetic observatory, is as follows:

Pay on contracts	$25,500 00
Architect and draughtsmen	1,580 70
Miscellaneous incidentals	261 84
Furniture	471 16
	27,813 70

Respectfully submitted,

RICHARD RUSH,
JOHN W. MAURY,
JOSEPH HENRY,
Executive Committee.

PROCEEDINGS

OF THE

BOARD OF REGENTS.

SEVENTH ANNUAL SESSION OF THE BOARD OF REGENTS.

[Continued from last Report.]

WASHINGTON, *March* 12, 1853.

The Board of Regents met this day at 10 o'clock, A. M. Present: Messrs. Colcock, Fitch, Mason, Maury, Totten, the Secretary, and W. W. Seaton, Treasurer.

The proceedings of the last meeting were read and approved.

The Secretary brought before the Board the subject of the disposition of the surplus fund, and stated that Messrs. Corcoran & Riggs had offered to allow interest at five per cent. if the deposit was continued with them.

Mr. Fitch offered the following resolution, which was adopted:

Resolved, That the surplus fund of $208,000 now on deposit with Corcoran & Riggs, be continued with them for twelve months, on their proposition to pay interest thereon at five per cent; provided, that a part thereof, not exceeding $58,000, may be withdrawn for building expenditures during the year, and that they deposit the same or equivalent securities to those now held therefor, to be approved by the Regents then in Washington and the Secretary.

Mr. Colcock offered the following resolution, which was adopted:

Resolved, That during the year 1853 the sum of thirty thousand dollars ($30,000) out of the Smithsonian income be, and is hereby, appropriated, to be expended under the direction of the Secretary, and with the advice of the Executive Committee, to defray the expenses of the Institution, and to carry out the several parts of the programme.

The Secretary brought before the Board the question of a new division of the income of the Institution, rendered necessary by the increase of the general expenses, of the addition to the sum contemplated for finishing the centre building for the library and collections, and other causes.

Mr. Fitch offered the following resolution, which was adopted:

Resolved, That the subject of the distribution of the income of the Institution in the manner contemplated by the original plan of organization, be referred to a Select Committee, to consist of Messrs. Pearce, Mason, Rush, Bache, Choate, Totten, and Maury, for a report at the next session of the Board of Regents of such changes, if any, as in their opinion are desirable; and that the same Committee be instructed to report fixed regulations relative to the reception of donations, &c.

General Totten offered the following resolution, which was adopted:

Resolved, That the Building Committee, and the Executive Committee jointly, be instructed to take into consideration and decide upon the propriety of making such alterations in the east wing of the Smithsonian building, as to convert it into a suitable dwelling for the Secretary, and that the Building Committee carry into effect the decision of the Joint Committee.

The Board then, on motion, adjourned *sine die*.

EIGHTH ANNUAL SESSION OF THE BOARD OF REGENTS.

WASHINGTON, *January* 4, 1854.

In accordance with a resolution of the Board of Regents of the Smithsonian Institution, fixing the time of the beginning of their annual meeting on the first Wednesday of January of each year, the Board met this day in the Regents' room.

Present: Messrs. English, Mason, Maury, Stuart, Totten, and the Secretary.

In the absence of the Chancellor, and on motion of Mr. Maury, Mr. Mason was called to the chair.

The Secretary informed the Board of the re-appointment of Mr. Meacham, of Vermont, and the appointment of Hon. Wm. H. English, of Indiana, and Hon. David Stuart, of Michigan, as Regents of the Smithsonian Institution on the part of the House of Representatives of the present Congress.

The Secretary stated that the accounts and reports of the Institution would be ready for presentation at the next meeting; whereupon, the Regents, after examining the building, adjourned to meet on Saturday, 14th January, at 10 o'clock, a. m.

WASHINGTON, *January* 14, 1854.

An adjourned meeting of the Board of Regents of the Smithsonian Institution, was held in the Smithsonian building on Saturday, January 14, at 10 o'clock, a. m.

Present: Messrs. Bache, English, Mason, Maury, Meacham, Pearce, Stuart, Taney, Totten, the Secretary, and W. W. Seaton, Esq., Treasurer.

The Chancellor, Hon. Roger B. Taney, took the chair.

The proceedings of the last meeting were read and approved.

The Secretary informed the Board that a meeting of the "Establishment" had been called by order of the President of the United States, in May last. The proceedings of the meeting were then read.

Mr. Maury, on the part of the Building Committee, submitted its report, which was read and adopted.

The Treasurer, W. W. Seaton, esq., presented the details of the expenditures during the year 1853; also a general statement of the finances; which were, on motion, referred to the Executive Committee.

The Secretary called the attention of the Board to the fact that a resolution had been adopted by the House of Representatives, appointing a Committee of nine to inquire into the expediency of withdrawing the Smithsonian fund from the Treasury of the United States, and investing it in some safe stocks.

On motion of Mr. Mason, the consideration of the subject was postponed until the Secretary should be called upon by the Committee of the House for information, and his report was presented to the Board.

The Secretary presented his report of the operations of the Institution for the year 1853, which was in part read.

On motion of Mr. Maury, it was

Resolved, That the vacancy existing in the Building Committee be filled by nomination of the Chair.

Whereupon, Mr. Wm. H. English was appointed.

The Board then adjourned to meet on Saturday, January 28, at 10 o'clock, a. m.

WASHINGTON, *January* 28, 1854.

An adjourned meeting of the Board of Regents was held on Saturday, January 28, 1854, at 10 o'clock, a. m. Present: Messrs. Bache, English, Maury, Meacham, Pearce, Stuart, Taney, Totten of the board, W. W. Seaton, esq., treasurer, and the Secretary:

The Chancellor took the chair.

The minutes of the last meeting were read and approved.

The Secretary stated to the board that honorable Joseph R. Chandler had offered to present to the House of Representatives, the petition of the board relative to funding the $150,000 of surplus income in the treasury of the United States, and to move that it might be referred to the committee which had been appointed by the House relative to the Smithsonian fund.

Whereupon, on motion of Mr. Pearce, the original memorial of the board to Congress was referred to the Executive Committee, with instructions to make such modifications in the wording of it as in their judgment might be rendered necessary by present circumstances.

A petition was presented from Gilbert Cameron, the contractor of the building, requesting the payment of the money due him, which had been kept back on account of a law suit between himself and one of the sub-contractors.

In reference to the same, Mr. Maury, on behalf of the Building Committee, presented a letter from J. M. Carlisle, esquire, attorney of the board, stating that the suit had been dismissed, and that the court had decided that the Board of Regents could not be sued. Mr. Maury also presented, on the part of the Building Committee, a letter from Joseph H. Bradley, esquire, requesting that the money be retained by the Board until the before mentioned law suit was finally decided.

On motion of Mr. Pearce, the subject was referred to a committee, with power to order the money to be paid in whole or in part, if in their judgment it was thought proper.

The chair appointed Messrs. Mason, Meacham and Totten, as the committee.

The Secretary laid before the board a bill from Henry Parish for a copy of Canina's work on architecture, purchased by James Renwick, junior, for the Institution in 1847, and now in the library, but which according to an accompanying letter from Mr. Renwick had never been paid.

On motion of Mr. Meacham, the Secretary was directed to settle the bill, provided on examining the accounts, no evidence could be found of its having been paid.

The Building Committee exhibited to the Board the drawings for the new lecture room.

The Secretary read the continuation of his report relative to the publications, correspondence, magnetism and meteorology.

A number of letters received since the last meeting, and the answers to them, were read to illustrate the character of the correspondence of the Institution.

Mr. Meacham offered the following resolution:

Resolved, That the Secretary and other officers of the Smithsonian Institution be directed to furnish the Board of Regents with estimates of appropriations necessary to be made in order to carry on the Institution the ensuing year, according to the laws for its organization.

After some discussion, the resolution was postponed for further discussion until the next meeting.

On motion, the board then adjourned to meet on Saturday, February 11, at 10 o'clock a. m.

WASHINGTON, *February* 11, 1854.

A quorum not being present, the board adjourned to meet on Saturday, February 18, at 10 o'clock a. m.

WASHINGTON, *February* 18, 1854.

An adjourned meeting of the Board of Regents of the Smithsonian Institution was held on Saturday, February 18, 1854, at 10 o'clock, a. m. Present: Messrs. Bache, English, Maury, Meacham, Pearce, Taney of the Board, and the Secretary:

The Chancellor took the chair.

The minutes of the last meeting were read and approved.

A communication was read by the Secretary, in reference to the Wynn estate, which, on motion of Mr. Pearce, was referred to Mr. Mason, to whom prior communications on the same subject had been referred.

A memorial was presented from Dr. S. Spooner of New York, offering to present to the Institution the original copper-plates of the Musée Francais and the Musée Royal, on condition that it would publish under his superintendence an edition of these works.

On motion of Mr. Pearce, the Secretary was directed, on the part of the Institution, respectfully to decline the proposition of Dr. Spooner, the Regents not considering themselves authorized to engage in such an enterprize.

The Secretary stated to the Board that Professor Wilson, of the English Commission to the Exhibition of the Industry of All Nations at New York, had presented to the Smithsonian Institution a set of models, casts, and drawings, to be used in teaching the arts of design.

The Secretary proposed to lend these to the Metropolitan Mechanics' Institute, of this city, for the use of its School of Design; which proposition was agreed to by the Board.

The Secretary read the correspondence between the Smithsonian Institution and the California Academy of Natural Sciences, in which the latter authorize the former to purchase a full set of meteorological and magnetic instruments for the use of the society; the means of defraying the expense of the purchase having been generously provided by its President, Dr. A. Randall.

A memoir on the "Europo American Physical Man" was laid before the Regents, which had been submitted to the Institution for publication since the last meeting of the Board.

Professor Bache presented a specimen of the photographic register of the motions of the magnetic needle, taken at the magnetic observatory of the Smithsonian Institution.

The Secretary informed the Board that the annual meeting of the United States Agricultural Society would be held on the 22d instant, in the Smithsonian Institution, and read the following extract from the address of the President of that Society:

"Our location at the national capital gives us peculiar facilities for intercommunication and for intercourse with members of Congress, representing all parts of our widely extended country. We may also secure many benefits from the Smithsonian Institution, whose objects are the general increase of knowledge and the promotion of science, objects so analogous to those of this Association as to give importance to the question whether reciprocal benefits might not be expected from closer relations. By the courtesy of this Institution we have been permitted to occupy their commodious apartments, and an inquiry should be made by our Executive officers, or a special committee, to ascertain what room or rooms can be obtained for the future accommodation of this Society. We need a public building, or offices in some existing edifice, for our Corresponding Secretary and Treasurer, for the preservation of our records, and of the agricultural seeds and products which are now in our possession, or may be hereafter required, and also for an agricultural library, museum, and cabinet."

On motion of Mr. Maury, the Secretary was authorized to offer such accommodations and facilities to the United States Agricultural Society as the Institution had at its disposal.

The continuation of the Secretary's report, relative to the Library, Museum, and Exchanges, was presented, but the reading was postponed till the next meeting.

The resolution offered by Mr. Meacham, at the last meeting of the Board, was then taken up for consideration.

Mr. Pearce moved to amend it by inserting the "Executive Committee and the Secretary," in place of the "Secretary and the other other officers of the Institution."

On motion of Mr. English, the resolution and amendment were referred to the Special Committee which was appointed at the last session on the distribution of the income of the Institution, consisting of Messrs. Pearce, Mason, Rush, Bache, Choate, Totten, and Maury.

As Mr. Choate had signified, in a letter to the Secretary, his inability to attend the meetings of this Committee, on motion of Mr. English, his place was filled by the appointment of Mr. Meacham.

The Board then adjourned to meet on Saturday, February 25, at 10 o'clock, a. m.

WASHINGTON, *February* 25, 1854.

An adjourned meeting of the Board of Regents of the Smithsonian Institution was held on Saturday, February 25, 1854, at 10 o'clock, a. m.

Present: Messrs. Douglas, English, Maury, Mason, Meacham, Pearce, Rush, Stuart, and the Secretary.

Hon. Stephen A. Douglas appointed from the Senate of the United States as a Regent of the Institution, to fill the vacancy occasioned by the expiration of the term of Hon. R. M. Charlton, appeared and took his seat in the Board.

In the absence of the Chancellor, Mr. Pearce was called to the chair.

The minutes of the last meeting were then read and approved.

The Secretary laid before the Board for inspection, the proof-sheets and illustrations of a memoir, by John Chappelsmith, on the Tornado which occurred near New Harmony, Indiana, in 1852.

The Secretary stated that, in accordance with the resolution of the Board at its last meeting, the use of the lecture room of the Institution had been given to the United States Agricultural Society, which had held its sessions there during the past week.

The continuation of the Report of the Secretary was read.

The Board then adjourned to meet on Saturday, March 4, 1854.

WASHINGTON, *March* 4, 1854.

A quorum not being present, the Board adjourned to meet on Saturday, March 11, 1854, at 10 o'clock, a. m.

WASHINGTON, *March* 11, 1854.

An adjourned meeting of the Board of Regents was held on Saturday, March 11, 1854, at 10 o'clock, a. m.

Present: Messrs. Bache, English, Maury, Mason, Meacham, Pearce, Totten, and the Secretary.

In the absence of the Chancellor, Mr. Pearce was called to the chair.

The minutes of the last meeting were read and approved.

The Report of the Executive Committee in relation to the finances and expenditures of the Institution, during the year 1853, was presented by the Chairman, Mr. Pearce.

On motion of Mr. Mason, the report was accepted.

The Committee to which was referred the resolution of Mr. Fitch, offered at the last session, and also the resolution offered by Mr. Meacham, at the meeting of the Board, January 28, 1854, reported the following resolution, and stated that a full report on the general snbject would be made hereafter:

Resolved, That the Executive Committee and the Secretary of the Institution be instructed to submit to the Board of Regents, at the commencement of each and every year, an estimate, in detail, of all sums which will be required for the expenditures of the current year, as a basis for specific appropriations to be made by the Board.

On motion, the resolution was adopted.

The Secretary stated to the Board that a memorial and resolution, relative to funding $150,000 in the Treasury of the United States, had been submitted by Hon. Joseph R. Chandler to the House of Representatives, and had been referred to the Committee previously appointed by the House to consider the expediency of withdrawing the Smithsonian fund from the Treasury of the United States and investing it in some safe stock.

The Special Committee to which was referred the subject of payment to Gilbert Cameron of the money due him which had been kept back on account of a lawsuit between him and one of the sub-contractors, reported that they had "examined the question referred to them, and were of the opinion that the balance due Gilbert Cameron should be paid to him, and direct accordingly."

The Secretary stated that, in accordance with this direction, he had paid Mr. Cameron $10,000, but had reserved a part of the money until the account could be critically examined.

A memorial from the American Philosophical Society to the Congress of the United States, praying "that the President of the United States should be authorized to enter into such correspondence with the government of Great Britain as may secure, in a reasonable time, a proper uniformity of coinage in the mode that may be found most discreet and convenient," was laid before the Board for its co-operation and approval.

On motion of Mr. Mason, the subject was referred to the Executive Committee.

A communication was read from Mr. J. R. Lambdin, President of the American Academy of Fine Arts, Philadelphia, recommending that the Smithsonian Institution should procure moulds from the best and most useful specimens of the collection in the British Museum, known as the Elgin Marbles, and that from these moulds, casts should be produced and sold at cost to such academies of art, &c., as may desire their possession.

On motion of Mr. Mason, this subject was referred to the Executive Committee.

The continuation of the Report of the Secretary in relation to the Museum, Exchanges, &c., was read.

The Board then adjourned to meet at the call of the Secretary.

SPECIAL MEETING.

WASHINGTON, *April* 29, 1854.

A special meeting of the Board of Regents of the Smithsonian Institution, called by the Secretary at the request of Messrs. Meacham, English and Stuart, was held on Saturday, April 29, 1854, at 10 o'clock. Present: Messrs. Bache, Douglas, Hawley, Maury, Meacham, Pearce, Taney, and the Secretary.

The Chancellor took the Chair. The minutes of the last meeting were read and approved.

Mr. Pearce, in behalf of the Executive Committee, presented the following estimate of the appropriations to be made for the year 1854.

"The Executive Committee recommend the following appropriations for the present year, from the income of the Institution:

For building	....	....	$7,000 00
For expenses of the meetings of the Board	....	$250 00	
For lighting and heating	....	600 00	
For postage	....	500 00	
For transportation and exchange	....	1,600 00	
For stationery	....	250 00	
For general printing	....	600 00	
For apparatus	....	350 00	
For incidentals general	....	835 00	
SALARIES GENERAL.			
Secretary	$3,500 00	....	
Clerk	1,000 00	....	
Book keeper	200 00	....	
Janitor	400 00	....	
Laborer	250 00	....	
Watchman	365 00	....	
Extra clerk hire	300 00	....	
		6,015 00	
			11,000 00
Smithsonian Contributions	....	6,000 00	
Reports on progress of knowledge	....	500 00	
Other publications	....	250 00	
Meteorology	....	3,000 00	
Computations	....	100 00	
Lectures	....	1,000 00	
			10,850 00
LIBRARY.			
Salary of Assistant Secretary	2,500 00	....	
Salaries of assistants in the Library—one at $600 and another at $540	1,140 00	....	
Purchase of books	1,800 00	....	
Incidentals	160 00	....	
Binding	250 00	....	
Stereotyping	150 00	....	
		6,000 00	
MUSEUM.			
Salary of Assistant Secretary	2,000 00	....	
Explorations	250 00	....	
Alcohol, &c	250 00	....	
Assistance or labor	100 00	....	
Apparatus	100 00	....	
Incidentals	100 00	....	
Catalogue	500 00	....	
Glass jars	250 00	....	
		3,550 00	
			9,550 00
Contingencies	....	....	100 00
			38,500 00

The Committee have not recommended an equal distribution between the active operations on the one hand, and the Library, Museum, &c., on the other, because the compromise resolutions which require such equality of distribution do not go into effect until the completion of the building."

J. A. PEARCE,
A. D. BACHE,
J. G. TOTTEN.
} *Executive Committee.*

On motion of Mr. Pearce, the above Report was laid upon the table.

The Secretary presented the following letter to the Board, in compliance with which he had called this special meeting:

WASHINGTON, *April* 13, 1854.

Prof. Jos. HENRY,
Secretary of the Smithsonian Institution.

In accordance with the provision of the third section of an act establishing the Institution, the undersigned request you to appoint a special meeting of the Regents on Saturday, the 29th inst., at 10 o'clock, a. m.

J. MEACHAM,
W. H. ENGLISH,
D. STUART.

Mr. Meacham then stated the reasons why he had requested this special meeting.

Mr. Pearce stated that the subject brought before the Board by Mr. Meacham, was now under consideration by a Special Committee appointed by the Regents, which would be ready to report at the next meeting.

On motion, the subject was postponed till the next meeting of the Board.

The Board then adjourned to meet on Saturday, May 13, at 10 o'clock, a. m.

WASHINGTON, *May* 13, 1854.

An adjourned meeting of the Board of Regents was held on Saturday, May 13, at 10 o'clock, a. m.

Present: Messrs. Bache, Hawley, Maury, Meacham, Pearce, Totten, and the Secretary.

The Chancellor being absent, Mr. Hawley was called to the chair.

The minutes of the last meeting were then read, and after correction, approved.

Letters from Hon. R. B. Taney, Chancellor of the Institution, and from Hon. Richard Rush, stating their inability to attend this meeting of the Board, were read by the Secretary.

Mr. Pearce, Chairman of the Special Committee on the resolutions of Messrs. Fitch and Meacham, stated that it was ready to report, but as it was considered desirable to have a full meeting of the Board when the subject should be discussed, he moved that the Board adjourn.

The Board then adjourned to meet on Saturday, 20th inst., at 10 o'clock, a. m.

WASHINGTON, *May* 20, 1854.

An adjourned meeting of the Board of Regents was held on Saturday, May 20th, at 10 o'clock, a. m.

Present: Messrs. Bache, Choate, Douglas, English, Hawley, Maury, Mason, Meacham, Pearce, Stuart, Totten, and the Secretary.

In the absence of the Chancellor, Mr. Hawley was called to the chair.

The minutes of the last meeting were read and approved.

Mr. Pearce, Chairman of the Special Committee appointed by the Board of Regents of the Smithsonian Institution, to which was referred the resolutions of Hon. Mr. Fitch and Hon. Mr. Meacham relative to the distribution of the income of the Smithsonian fund, etc., made the following report:*

The Committee who were directed to report whether it is desirable to make any changes in the distribution of the income of the Institution, in the manner contemplated by the original plan of organization, report as follows:

The distribution and application of the Smithsonian income should be made, so as to answer most effectually and beneficially the purposes for which the Institution was endowed and established. In making such distribution and application, the Regents should faithfully observe the requirements of the act of Congress establishing the Institution, and exercise no discretion but that which the law allows to them.

The purpose of the Institution is disclosed in the title of the act, in its preamble, and in its first section. The title is "An act to establish the Smithsonian Institution for the increase and diffusion of knowledge among men." The preamble states the bequest, by James Smithson, of all his property to the United States, to found at Washington, under the name of the Smithsonian Institution, "an establishment for the increase and diffusion of knowledge among men." It declares the acceptance of the trust, and "therefore for the faithful execution of the said trust according to the will of the liberal and enlightened donor," the first section constitutes an establishment by the name of the Smithsonian Institution "for the increase and diffusion of knowledge among men."

The fifth section enacts that the Regents shall cause to be erected "a suitable building of sufficient size, and with suitable rooms or halls for the reception and arrangement, upon a liberal scale, of objects of natural history, including a geological and mineralogical cabinet; also a chemical laboratory, a library, a gallery of art, and the necessary

---

* This committee consisted of the following Regents: Hon. J. A. Pearce, Hon. J. M. Mason, Hon. Richard Rush, Hon. John W. Maury, Gen. J. G. Totten, Prof. A. D. Bache, and the Hon. J. Meacham. The gentleman last named does not concur in this report.

lecture rooms," &c. This section points out certain means and instrumentalities by which the Institution is to "execute the trust" "according to the will of the liberal and enlightened donor." But it does not limit the Regents to these means and instrumentalities. A large discretion is elsewhere given to them to employ other means and instrumentalities "for the promotion of the purpose of the testator"—that is, "for the increase and diffusion of knowledge among men."

"The eighth section, in its last clause, directs an annual appropriation from the interest of the funds belonging to the Institution "not exceeding an average of $25,000 annually, for the gradual formation of a library composed of valuable works pertaining to all departments of human knowledge."

And the ninth section enacts that of "any other moneys which have accrued, or shall hereafter accrue, as interest upon the said Smithsonian fund, not herein appropriated, or not required for the purposes herein provided, the said managers [Regents] are hereby authorized to make such disposal as they shall deem best suited for the promotion of the purpose of the testator, anything herein contained to the contrary notwithstanding."

Let us see now, how far the Regents have complied with these requirements of the law.

They have caused to be erected a building, which is, in the judgment of the Board, suitable, of sufficient size, of plain and durable materials, with suitable rooms for the reception and arrangement, upon a liberal scale, of the objects mentioned in the fifth section of the act. The building, it is true, is not yet completed in all its parts. This has been the result, partly of design, and partly of accident. As the law specified no period within which the building should be completed, the time of its completion was necessarily within the discretion of the Regents. It was obvious that if they should not hurry its completion, but extend the work upon it through a series of years, they would save a large amount of accruing interest, which, when the building should be finished, might be added to the permanent fund, whereby the means of accomplishing the purposes of the testator would be largely increased. An additional reason for this was, that the structure, thus slowly and cautiously erected, would be more solid and permanent. This policy, therefore, was adopted, and it was determined that the building should be finished in five years. An accident, well known to the Board, and which in the end must prove to have been fortunate, required a change in the plan of a part of the edifice, and a larger expenditure of money. This cause has further delayed the completion of the building. But during the present year it will be finished on the liberal scale required by the law, and one hundred and fifty thousand dollars of accrued interest will be saved, to be added to the principal.

In the mean time, the Regents have made appropriations of money for the various objects specified in the fifth section of the act, by which and other means they have complied as well with the letter as the spirit of the law. A large and valuable collection of objects of natural history has been made, and for the most part, classified; a geological and mineralogical cabinet has been provided, and a chemical laboratory has been fitted up, in which researches and experiments have been made. The building contains an apartment intended for a gallery of art; and some works of art, a valuable collection of engravings, have been purchased.

A lecture room has been finished, and for several years lectures have been given at the expense of the Institution, on scientific and literary, abstruse and popular subjects, the admission to which has been free. A library of 12,000 volumes and 8,000 pamphlets and parts of volumes has been acquired by purchase, exchanges, and other means, containing many rare and valuable works pertaining to all branches of knowledge, such as are not to be found in general libraries, and are most highly prized by men of science and research.

This is a very good beginning according to the plan for the *gradual* formation of a library, which the act points out.

Of the entire amount expended from the commencement of the Institution, a little less than one-eighth has been given to researches and publications. The rest has been applied to the special objects mentioned in the act, and to the general expenses of the Institution.

In the act establishing the Institution, Congress carefully and wisely forbore to fix the amount or proportion of the annual income which should be appropriated to any of the objects mentioned in the fifth section. They did not even determine, or limit the sum which should be expended on the building, nor have they in any manner indicated that prominence should be given to any particular means or instrumentality for increasing and diffusing knowledge. All this they have left to the discretion of the Regents, to whom they entrusted the conduct of the Institution. They have, indeed, declared that annual appropriations should be made for the *gradual* formation of a library, and have provided that such appropriations shall not exceed $25,000 in the average.

This is nothing but a limitation upon the discretion of the Regents, and can by no rule of construction be considered as intimating the desire of Congress that such sum should be *annually* appropriated. The limitation, while it prevented the Regents from exceeding that sum, left them full discretion as to any amount within the limit. The interest on the Smithsonian Fund was about $30,000 per annum, and Congress could not but know that an appropriation of five-sixths of that amount per annum would leave a remainder entirely insufficient to defray the salaries and ordinary expenses of an Institution such as was designed by the act, and that nothing would be left for the care of collections, the lectures, and other means of promoting the purpose of the testator. In short, the act points out certain instrumentalities to be employed in the execution of the trust, created by, and for the purposes specified in the will of Smithson, and gives to the Managers or Regents authority to dispose of all the income not required for the purposes specified in the act, in such manner as they shall deem best suited for the promotion of the purpose of the testator. As Congress did not determine what portion of the income was to be applied to the purposes specified in the act, it follows that such determination is to be made by those to whom they intrusted the conduct of the business of the Institution; and thus the Regents are clearly invested with the power of determining how much of that income is required respectively for library, for museum, for lectures, or for any of the objects specified in the fifth section, and what disposition they will make of so much of the income as they do not think requisite to apply to these objects. So the Regents of 1847, who adopted the plan of organization, understood the law. So they reported to Congress. The Board of Regents, however its members have been changed from time to time, have always so understood it, and Congress, to whom they have annually and faithfully reported their proceedings, have never questioned the propriety of the construction.

In organizing the Institution, different opinions indeed were entertained by different members of the Board, as to the most effectual means of promoting the purpose of Smithson. The conflict of opinions resulted in the adoption of certain resolutions, which have been called the "compromise resolutions." These, while they recognize the intention of Congress, and the duty of the Regents, to provide for the accumulation of specimens of art and objects of natural history, and the gradual formation of a library; pertaining to all branches of knowledge, &c., also declare it to be expedient, and demanded by the will of Smithson, that in the plan of organization, the increase of knowledge by original research should form an essential feature; that for this end premiums should be offered for original papers containing positive additions to the sum of human knowledge, and that these and other suitable papers should be published in transactions of the Institution periodically, or occasionally, &c. The seventh of these resolutions is in these words:

"*Resolved*, That for the purpose of carrying into effect the two principal modes of executing the act and trust pointed out in the resolutions herewith submitted, the permanent appropriations out of the accruing interest shall, *so soon as the buildings are completed*, be annually, as follows; that is to say:

"*First.* For the formation of a library composed of valuable works pertaining to all departments of useful knowledge, and for the procuring, arranging, and preserving of the various collections of the Institution, as well of natural history, and objects of foreign and curious research, and of elegant art, as others, including salaries and all other general expenses connected with the same, excepting those of the first complete arrangement of all such collections and objects as now belong to the United States in the museum of the Institution, when completed, together with one-half of the salary of the Secretary, the sum of fifteen thousand dollars.

"*Secondly.* For the preparation and publication of transactions, reports, and all other publications of the Institution, including appropriations for original researches, and premiums for original papers; for the delivery of all lectures and payment of all lecturers, and for all general expenses connected with said lectures and publications, together with one-half of the salary of the Secretary, the remainder of the annually accruing interest; it being understood that all general and incidental expenses not specially connected with either of the above two great divisions of the plan of the Institution shall be equally divided between them."

It will be seen that this division of the income of the Institution between the two principal modes of executing the trust was to be made so soon as "*the buildings were completed*," and not before.

As the building is not completed, this division is not yet obligatory under the compromise resolutions. For some years the annual appropriations for the purposes of the Institution were specific, and were applied accordingly. But during the last two years they have been general, and a discretion has been exercised by the Secretary and the Executive Committee, which has resulted in applying to researches, publications, and lectures, an amount somewhat larger than that which has been applied to the library, museum, &c. But this is clearly no violation, as has been charged, of a compromise which is not by its very terms to go into effect until the completion of the building.

The commitee think it desirable that the appropriations should be specific, and have already so reported to the Board by a resolution submitted on the 11th of March, 1854; and at the last meeting of the Regents the Executive Committee submitted estimates of appropriations in detail for the present year.

Before expressing an opinion on *these resolutions*, the committee deem it their duty at this time to remark upon the plan which was discussed seven years ago, but which is now revived, of devoting the greater part of the income to the accumulation of a great library, thus either abandoning the active operations of research and publications, or so restricting this means of increasing and diffusing knowledge as to deprive it of all sensible value.

It has already been remarked that the language of the eighth section which directs the gradual formation of a library, is not mandatory as to the amount which shall be thus expended, and that the ninth section authorizes the Regents, after applying so much of the income as may be required for the purposes mentioned in the act, to dispose of the residue of the interest upon the Smithsonian fund in such manner "as they shall deem best suited for the promotion of the purpose of the testator, anything herein contained to the contrary notwithstanding." It is manifest, from what has been said before, that these sections of the law leave to the Regents a large discretion as to the amounts to be applied to the objects specified in the act, and in the choice of other means for promoting the purpose of the testator.

What, then, are the considerations which should govern them in rejecting this plan, which proposes a great library as the best and chief, if not the only, means of executing the trust created by the will of Smithson, and fulfilling their own duty under the law?

The "increase and diffusion of knowledge among men" are the great purposes of this munificent trust. To increase knowledge implies research, or new and active investigation, in some one or more of the departments of learning. To diffuse knowledge among men implies active measures for its distribution, so far as may be, among mankind.

Neither of these purposes could be accomplished or materially advanced by the accumulation of a great library at the city of Washington. This would be to gather within the walls of a building here those fruits of learning which had been reaped elsewhere. It would be the *hiving* of knowledge, not its increase and diffusion. It would be the collection of what philosophical inquirers, men of research, of observation, and of original thought had ascertained, conceived, or invented, and already published to the world. But it would not of itself add to the sum of human knowledge, it would not increase the stores of learning, but only bring them together. It would develop no new truths, reveal no hidden laws of nature, but only contain the record of what might be already known; so that in no proper sense could it be said to increase knowledge. Neither would it diffuse knowledge, except within a limited sphere. The Institution would necessarily be local, for although it might aid the few men of research residing in Washington, and such students and investigators as occasionally visited the city, it would fail to accomplish the more extensive purpose of the testator and of the law, since it could not be expected to draw hither the great body of such men. These must always be scattered over the country, engaged in pursuits which require their residence elsewhere, and with only occasional opportunities of aiding their inquiries by resort to the library of the Smithsonian Institution. While, therefore, a well selected library of valuable books pertaining to all departments of learning may well be one of the means employed by the Institution, its purpose requires other instrumentalities by which knowledge may be increased and diffused among men. We must never forget that both the will of Smithson and the act of Congress recognize that, as a *nation* is appointed the great dispenser of the fruits of his munificence, so these benefits are to be *universal*, and their recipients to be *men* everywhere and in all time.

If the language of the will had been "to increase and diffuse knowledge among *the people of the United States*," a library would be but a feeble and imperfect instrument as an active agent even for that limited purpose. The accumulation of books in the political centre of a great country, or even in the centre of population of a numerous people, would no doubt gratify the pride of the nation, and be attended with some profitable results. But such a library would not ensure mental activity to enquirers who should live remote from its locality, and its relation to all increase of knowledge would be merely incidental. It would have no effective operation in the thirty-one States which constitute the nation, or people of the Union, and instead of being diffusive in its nature, would be centralizing in its influence and passive in its character. Even if the will and the act of Congress were limited by the terms supposed, by no fair construction could the formation of a library be considered as an execution of the trust. But when we consider that the language of the will is not thus limited, and that the benefits of the bequest are intended for *mankind*, we cannot imagine how the establishment of a library could be considered as corresponding to the requisitions of a purpose so wide and liberal. That Smithson did not intend a library to be the prominent feature in the Institution contemplated by his bequest, may be inferred from the fact that his will did not mention it, when a single word would have been sufficient for this purpose.

And that Congress did not design to indicate a library as the principal object of the establishment which they founded by law to carry out the purpose of Smithson, will be made to appear by an examination of the enactment.

In the construction of a law of Congress, the opinions expressed in the speeches of some of those who voted for it cannot be taken as the opinion of all or even of the major part of them, but the act must be construed according to the general import and evident intention of all its parts.

If we can construe the law from its own provisions, it would be exceedingly unsafe and improper to interpret it by reference to the opinions of a portion only of those who voted for it, being the minor part of them. To do this would be to make the *opinions* of a few control the acts and intentions of the majority as expressed in the law, and in effeet to give to those few the law making owerpower. In the present case the evident intention was to carry out the pur ose of Smithson's will, name ly: "the increase and diffusion of knowledge among men."

The title of the act, its preamble and provisions, would have been palpably absurd, if their object had been only or chiefly to found a great library. To describe a library as an institution "for the increase and diffusion of knowledge among men," would be a preposterous abuse of terms. So, too, "to erect a suitable building of sufficient size, with suitable rooms or halls for the reception and arrangement, upon a liberal scale, of objects of natural history, geological, mineralogical, and botanical specimens, classed and arranged so as to facilitate the study of them, with a chemical laboratory, lecture rooms, &c.," as provided in sections 5 and 6, is wholly inconsistent with the idea of an institution, of which a library is to be the principal agent.

It is true that the eighth section of the act authorizes an application of an annual sum, not exceeding $25,000, for the gradual formation of a library. This is in great disproportion to the various objects before recited in the act, and if it had been mandatory, would have made the general authority and discretion given to the Regents in the ninth section, absurd and nugatory, and would indeed have equally defeated the other provisions before mentioned. Such an appropriation, if made, would establish a great library, but not such an institution as is indicated by the title of the bill, or warranted by its various provisions. Instead of a Secretary with assistants, it should have provided for a Librarian, with an assistant as secretary, and assistant librarians. Instead of providing for a building on a liberal scale, with suitable rooms or halls for a chemical laboratory, lecture rooms, &c., not indicating the library as of paramount importance, but according to the order of enumeration, placing it *after* other objects, the law would have declared it to be of primary importance, and designated the other objects as incidental or subsidiary to the Library. The act, in its various terms and provisions, does not seem to have been the result of plans entirely harmonious and consistent, but bears some marks of conflicting opinions; and the large discretion allowed in the ninth section appears to have been intended to give to the Regents the authority to reconcile and determine those difficulties which Congress could not avoid or provide for, to their own satisfaction.

Nothing, however, seems to be clearer than that the Legislature did not intend a public library to be the principal instrument of the Institution. The third section enacts that "the business of the Institution shall be conducted at the city of Washington by a Board of Regents." The terms of Smithson's will requires that Washington should be the locality of the Institution; but, if this section had reference to a public library, absorbing almost the whole interest of the fund, would such language have been employed? If a library at Washington was to be established, it was wholly unnecessary to provide that the business of the Institution should be conducted there, since the business of a library must be conducted where it is placed. The use of this langnage would seem to imply active transactions and not to refer to books. The application of $25,000 annually, (five-sixths of the whole income at the date of the act) to the purchase of books, would be inconsistent with, and subversive of the whole tenor of all that precedes the eighth section. Section ninth is singularly comprehensive, and appears to indicate a consciousness on the part of the framers of the bill, that its provisions might be proved by experience to be incongruous.

For this they provided the true remedy by investing the Regents with full power to use their judgment in the premises, subject only to the purpose of the will of Smithson, and so much of the law as was mandatory and peremptory, "all other provisions to the contrary, notwithstanding."

On the whole, therefore, the Committee think that neither the law nor the will of Smithson required the Regents to consider a great library as the paramount object of the Institution.

Its purpose requires means of exciting and sustaining research, of stimulating and directing original enquiries, the results of which constitute an increase of knowledge, and the publication of which diffuses it.

Scientific researches are often supposed by the uninformed to be of little or no real importance, and indeed are frequently ridiculed as barren of all practical utility. But nothing is more mistaken than this. The most valuable and productive of the arts of life, the most important and wonder-working inventions of modern times, owe their being and value to scientific investigations. By these have been discovered physical truths and laws, the intelligent application of which to practical inventions has given immense benefits to the world. The germs of these valuable improvements and inventions have been found and developed by scientific research, the original forms of which have often seemed to the many to be as idle and useless as they were curious. A proposition relating to the pendulum, which for many years remained only a curious theoretical relation, ultimately furnished a unit for the standard measures of States and nations. The discovery that a magnetic needle could be moved by a galvanic current, seemed for a long time more curious than useful, and yet it contained the germ of all that was afterwards developed in the telegraph. It has been well remarked that numerous applications and inventions always result from the discovery of a scientific principle, so that there are many Fultons for every Franklin.

There is no branch of industrial art which does not owe for the most part its improved processes to such investigations, although the artizans who employ them are often ignorant of their true source. Smithson, who was himself a man of science and research, and a contributor to the philosophical transactions of the Royal Society, well knew this. The members of Congress who framed the law were not ignorant of it, and the provisions for a chemical laboratory, and collections of natural history, proved that they looked to the prosecution of such inquiries under the auspices of the Smithsonian Institution.

Wisely, therefore, did the first Board of Regents propose, in order to INCREASE KNOWLEDGE—

First. To stimulate men of talent to make original researches, by offering suitable rewards for memoirs containing new truths, and to publish these and such other papers of suitable character as should be offered to the Institution.

Second. To cause particular researches to be made by competent persons.

And in order to DIFFUSE KNOWLEDGE—

First. "To publish occasionally a series of practical reports on the progress of the different branches of knowledge."

Second. "To publish occasionally separate treatises on subjects of general interest."

The results which have been produced by the Institution have received the approbation of the learned in every part of the civilized world, and fully justify the wisdom of the plan adopted by the Regents, and successfully carried into operation by the Secretary.

As a proof of this, we need only state the following facts given in the last report of the Regents to Congress.

"The Institution has promoted astronomy, by the aid furnished the researches which led to the discovery of the true orbit of the new planet Neptune, and the determination of the perturbations of this planet and the other bodies of the solar system, on account of their mutual attraction.. It has also aided the same branch of science by furnishing instruments and other facilities to the Chilian expedition, under Lieutenant Gillis; and by preparing and publishing an ephemeris of Neptune, which has been adopted by all the astronomers of the world.

"It has advanced geography, by providing the scientific traveller with annual lists of the occultations of the principal stars, by the moon, for the determination of longitude; by the preparation of tables for ascertaining heights with the barometer; and by the collection and publication of important facts relative to the topography of different parts of the country, particularly of the valley of the Mississippi.

"It has established an extended system of meteorology, consisting of a corps of several hundred intelligent observers, who are daily noteing the phases of the weather in every part of the continent of North America. It has imported standard instruments, constructed hundreds of compared thermometers, barometers, and psychrometers, and has furnished improved tables and directions for observing with these instruments the various changes of the atmosphere, as to temperature, pressure, moisture, &c. It has collected, and is collecting, from its observers, an extended series of facts which are yielding deductions of great interest in regard to the climate of this country and the meteorology of the globe.

"The Institution has advanced the science of geology, by its researches and original publications. It has made a preliminary exploration of the remarkable region on the upper Missouri river called the Bad Lands, and is now printing a descriptive memoir on the extraordinary remains which abound in that locality. It has assisted in explorations relative to the distribution in this country of the remains of microscopic animals found in immense quantities in different parts of the United States.

"It has made important contributions to botany, by means of the published results of explorations in Texas, New Mexico, and California; and by the preparation and publication of an extended memoir, illustrated with colored engravings, on the sea-plants of the coast of North America.

"It has published several important original papers on physiology, comparative anatomy, zoology, and different branches of descriptive natural history; and has prepared and printed, for distribution to travellers, a series of directions for collecting and preserving specimens.

"It has advanced terrestrial magnetism, by furnishing instruments for determining the elements of the magnetic force, to various exploring expeditions; and by publishing the results of observations made under its direction, at the expense of the government.

"It has collected and published the statistics of the libraries of the United States; and perfected a plan of stereotyping catalogues, which will render effective, as a combined whole, all the scattered libraries of the country.

"The Institution has also been instrumental in directing attention to American antiquities, and has awakened such an interest in the subject as will tend to the collection and study of all the facts which can be gathered relative to the ancient inhabitants of this continent. It has also rendered available for the purposes of the ethnologist and philanthropist the labors of our missionaries among the Dakotas, by publishing a volume on the language of this tribe of Indians, and has done good service to comparative philology by the distribution of directions for collecting Indian vocabularies.

"It has established an extended system of literary and scientific exchanges, both foreign and domestic, and annually transmits, between the most distant societies and individuals, hundreds of packages of valuable works. It has presented its own publications, free of expense, to all the first-class libraries of the world, and thus rendered them accessible, as far as possible, to all persons who are interested in their study. No restriction of copyright has been placed on their republication; and the truths which they contain are daily finding their way to the general public, through the labors of popular writers and teachers. The dis tribution of its publications and its system of exchanges has served not only to advance and diffuse knowledge, but also to increase the reputation, and, consequently, the influence of our country; to promote a kindly and sympathetic feeling between the New World and the Old—alike grateful to the philosopher and the philanthropist.

"These are the fruits of what is called the system of active operations of the Institution, and its power to produce other and continuous results is only limited by the amount of the income which can be appropriated to it, since each succeeding year has presented new and important fields for its cultivation. All the anticipations indulged with regard to it have been fully realized; and after an experience of six years, there can now be no doubt of the true policy of the Regents in regard to it."

Reports of a more popular character have been published, or are in preparation, which are well calculated to diffuse knowledge. Such is the report on the recent improvements in the chemical arts, by Messrs. Booth & Morfit, prepared and published under the direction of the Institution. The Secretary has said of it "that though chiefly intended to benefit the practical man, yet it will be found interesting to the general reader, as exhibiting the cotemporaneous advance of science and art, and the dependence of the latter upon the former for the improvemenr of its most important processes." Among the subjects of which it treats, may be mentioned fuel and furnaces, glass-making and pottery, cements, metals and their manufacture, chemicals, textile fabrics, mineral and organic manures. This work has been stereotyped, and besides those which are distributed on the plan of exchange, copies are offered for sale at the mere cost of printing, paper, and commission. Another report which is in preparation, on the forest trees of North America, giving their economical and ornamental uses and values, their history, mode of propagation, &c., &c., will supply to agriculturalists a work of great interest and importance which has long been a desideratum. Other reports have been prepared and will be ready for the press as soon as the funds can be appropriated for printing them.

The Committee need not repeat in detail all the parts of the plan of organization, but may mention that it included the exchange of the published transactions of the Institution, with those of literary and scientific societies and establishments; and provided for a museum and library, to consist of a complete collection of the transactions and proceedings of all the learned societies in the world, of the more important current periodical publications and of other works necessary to scientific investigations, thus employing the instrumentalities pointed out in the law, as means of increasing and diffusing knowledge, entirely consistent with, and necessary to, the plan of research and publication.

This plan is no longer experimental; it has been tested by experience; its success is acknowledged by all who are capable of forming a correct estimate of its results, and the Institution has every encouragement to pursue steadily its system of stimulating, assisting, and publishing research.

Whether the equal division of the income of the Institution, according to the plan of the compromise resolutions, should be observed after the completion of the building, is a question submitted to your Committee for report, and proper to be decided by the Board during the present year. The Committee think that while moderate appropriations should be annually made for the gradual increase of the library, and for other objects specified in the fifth section of the act establishing the Institution, so as to carry out in good faith the intention of Congress, it is not advisable to make the equal division of the income as proposed by the compromise resolutions.

The public generally, and even the Regents, most probably, do not know how small the funds of the Institution are in proportion to what is required of it, and the expense necessarily connected with so large a building.

The Secretary has stated in his Report that the general expenses, viz: meetings of the Regents and Committees, lighting and heating of the building, postage, transportation, stationery, general printing, apparatus, incidentals, and general salaries, have gradually increased, and will grow larger when the building shall be completed and entirely occupied. Last year these expenses amounted to $12,000. Besides this, the salaries of the assistants and pay of attendants in the library and museum are $5,740 per annum.

The salaries are as follows:

General Salaries.

That of the Secretary, (per annum,)			$3,500
Clerk			1,000
Book-keeper			200
Janitor			400
Laborer			250
Watchman			365
			5,715
Salary of assistant in charge of the library	$2,500		
An assistant to the assistant in the library	600		
Another assistant	540		
		$3,640	
Salary of assistant in charge of the museum		2,000	
Assistance and labor in museum		100	
			5,740
Total of permanent salaries at the present time			11,455

Together, the salaries and general expenses before mentioned amount to more than half the interest of the original fund, and to nearly half of the interest on that fund, augmented by $150,000 of accumulated interest, which the regents propose to add to it so as to make the permanent fund $665,000. The whole or the greater part of the interest on this addition to the original fund will be required during the present year for the building, and when that shall be finished, a considerable sum will be necessary to fit up and furnish the great central portion which is to be chiefly occupied by the library and museum. It may be assumed that not less $15,000 will be demanded for this purpose. But supposing the building to be completed and furnished, and the whole income at command for the operations of the Institution, and assuming that the salaries and general expenses will not increase, but remain as they were last year, at $17,740, there will be at the disposal of the Regents for all operations and purposes, including lectures, researches, publications, purchase of books for the library, binding, explorations for the benefit of the museum, apparatus, and the purchase of objects of art, a sum between $22,000 and $23,000. It will readily be perceived how inadequate this sum is to the rapid accumulation of a library, of collections for the museum and gallery of art, for lectures and those active operations which lead directly to the increase and diffusion of knowledge. Even this fund may be expected to be diminished by the greater expense which will attend the occupation of the entire building and the increased and constantly increasing collections.

The museum increases so rapidly by the deposit of Government collections, by donations, exchanges, and the receipt of specimens from special explorations aided by the Institution, that very small, if any, annual appropriations are required for it. But the expense of the care and exhibition of an increasing collection swells from year to year, while the Smithsonian funds are not so increased. The great object of the museum should be to furnish to men of science, eminent in their several departments, the means of advancing knowledge in these departments, by submitting specimens of new objects to their examination. If the expenditure could be borne, it would scarcely be desirable to increase the number of officers connected with the museum, so that the various branches of natural history might be fully represented, but considering the limited funds of the Smithsonian Institution, such an idea is not to be entertained.

On the contrary, the collections made should, in general, at all events, be referred for examination and description to the men most eminent in the country, and the results should be published in a manner worthy of their labors, by the Institution.

A larger but still a moderate appropriation for the library, varying as circumstances may require, should be annually made. It may be desirable, occasionally, to make larger investments in books, as when a library of special value and peculiar suitableness may be in the market, and within the means of the Institution. But this should be left to the discretion and sound judgment of the Regents at the time.

It is not believed to be advisable to accumulate in the Smithsonian Institution great masses of books, without reference to their peculiar character and value. What we want, and what the act of Congress contemplates, is not a collection of every thing which learned dulness and literary folly as well as real wisdom and sound science have put into print, a vast and unwieldly repertory, in which the trash as well as the precious may be found, but a library of *valuable* books pertaining to all departments of human knowledge. The exchanges will gradually furnish us with much that answers to this description, and moderate appropriations will supply, quite as rapidly as necessary, whatever besides may be requisite to constitute a valuable library of research in all departments of human knowledge. The library now consists of 12,005 volumes, besides 8,095 pamphlets and parts of volumes, and 1,874 maps, and 1,431 engravings.

In his report to the Secretary, of January, 1853, Professor Jewett stated that the library had nearly doubled in size during the year 1852, and that its greatest increase had been by exchanges. He said "they may be considered as the first fruits of a system of scientific and literary exchange, established and sustained by the Institution. They show, also, that the benefits derivable from its connexion with the system of active operations had not been over estimated.

"A considerable portion of the money expended in publications returns in the shape of books for the library. These again are constantly increasing the efficiency and interest of the publications. The value of the books received, by exchange, cannot be estimated by their number, or even their nominal price.

"They are works of the first importance to the scientific student, and which it is very difficult to procure by purchase, even with large funds at command."

Professor Baird estimated the value of the works thus received, during the year 1852, at from $4,000 to $5,000. If we estimate the future receipts from the system of exchange at half that sum annually, and suppose an appropriation in money of equal amount for the purchase of books, the growth of the library will be quite as rapid as was that of the library of Congress during the twenty-five years prior to the late fire, and its annual increase in value more than double that of the Congressional Library before the period mentioned. For several years before 1825, the ordinary appropriations of Congress for their library were not more than $2,000 per annum. Since that period they have been $5,000.

The Committee of Organization, in their report submitted in 1847, recommended such a selection of books as would "make the Smithsonian Library chiefly a supplemental one," and "to purchase for the most part valuable works which are not to be found elsewhere in the Union."

Of course this was not to be a universal rule, and not to exclude standard works of authority and reference. They particularly desired to see the library so supplied with important works on bibliography, so that it might become the centre of literary and bibliographical reference for the whole country. This desire has always been entertained by the Regents, and much has already been done towards this object. The collection of printed and manuscript catalogues has already been commenced with this view, and should be steadily followed up. It is believed that the appropriations suggested, together with the exchanges and occasional special appropriations, will, in a reasonable time, not only secure this object, but make the library the most important collection of valuable books, pertaining to all departments of knowledge, to be found in our country.

Suggestions have been made to the Committee of certain alterations in the organization of the Institution, which your Committee think not warranted by the letter and spirit of the law, and in conflict with the seventh section, which defines the duties and powers of the Secretary. That section admits of only one interpretation. Its terms are direct and explicit, and its objects are expressly and pointedly set forth. The entire property of the Institution is placed by it in the Secretary's hands, and he is distinctly constituted the responsible agent of the Board of Regents. He is "to make a fair and accurate record of all their proceedings," "to take charge of the building and property of the Institution," to discharge the duties of librarian and keeper of the museum. This language clearly shows the intention of the framers of the law to secure unity of action, to admit of no separate and independent departments, as is often the case in other institutions All the duties enumerated are devolved solely on the Secretary, and though other persons may be employed, they are merely *his* assistants, the offices being emphatically one. The Secretary alone is authorized to act, and if the business of the Institution demanded no more than the mind and labor of one man might be competent to perform, there would be no occasion for the employment of any one else.

The law is declaratory and positive in charging the Secretary with the enumerated duties, and therefore invests him and him alone with the corresponding powers. But as it must have been manifest that no Secretary could be able of himself to perform personally every thing required for the discharge of his enumerated duties, provision is made for aid to him, in the clause which says that he "may, with the consent of the board, employ assistants," &c.

The positions of the persons so employed are determined by the word which designates them in the clause authorising their employment. They are called "*assistants*." To whom? Not to the Regents, but to the Secretary. Their position is necessarily subordinate; and as their duties are those of assistants to their principal, they can no more be independent of him than they can be superior to him. This construction is so manifestly proper, that it would seem to require no argument to justify it. But if anything further were wanted, it may be found in the fact that the *Secretary* is to employ them in and about that very business with which *he* is charged and for which *he* alone is responsible. The character of this part of the section is permissive. He is not *required* to employ any one, but is permitted to employ persons to assist him, provided he satisfy the Board that their services are necessary as aids to him.

In another part of the same section provision is made for the payment and, if need be, the removal of the Secretary and his assistants, and in this connexion they are spoken of as officers, but by no ingenuity of construction can that word, in this connexion, be held to assign them special duties or confer any separate authority.

Thus careful has Congress been to provide an efficient system of operations which can only come from harmony of purpose and unity of action.

This view of the intention of Congress, so clearly expressed in the law, would be directly contradicted by the plan which has been suggested, of organizing the Institution definitely into several departments, placing at the head of these departments different assistants, establishing their relative positions, prescribing distinct duties for them, assigning certain shares of the income to be disbursed by them, and stating their authority, privileges, and remedies for infringement of their official rights, or of the interests entrusted to their care. All this would tend not to secure a loyal and harmonious co-operation, to a common end, of the assistants with the Secretary, but to encourage rivalry, to invite collision, to engender hostility, to destroy subordination, to distract the operations of the Institution, to impair its efficiency, and to destroy its usefulness.

The Committee are satisfied too, that the expenditures of the Institution would be unprofitably increased by organizing it into several departments, with authority to the head of each department to expend the money appropriated to it. The tendency would be to more subdivisions of duty, to an increase of assistants, by the introduction first of temporary and then of permanent employees, until, as the collections grew larger and the persons charged with their care became more numerous, the greater portion of the income would be absorbed in salaries. Thus the munificence intended to increase and diffuse knowledge among mankind, would be chiefly expended in salaries and official emoluments.

Already the Committee think it would be well to consider whether it might not be consistent with the proper working of the Institution to limit and reduce some of these expenses.

While the Committee desire to preserve and increase the library and museum, as already stated, they think it would be well to repeal the seventh resolution, passed by the Board of Regents on the 26th January, 1847, which has already been recited.

They recommend that, in future, the appropriations should be made without reference to any fixed rule of distribution or division between the different operations and objects of the Institution, and that the Board, while making specific appropriations, should apportion them according to their opinion of what is necessary and proper, giving to each object such sum as its intrinsic importance and a compliance in good faith with the law may seem to demand.

Thus they will be enabled to economize by postponing or limiting some operations and preferring others, by applying the funds to those objects which at the time appear most pressing, and which promise the most prompt, far-reaching, and beneficial action.

In conclusion, the Committee adopt the following remarks and recommendations, which they extract from a paper submitted to them by the Secretary, and desire that they may be considered as part of this report:

"If one-fourth of the whole income is devoted to the museum, additional assistants will be required for the care and management of the specimens, while the withdrawal of Prof. Baird from the publications and exchanges will require more help in that quarter.

"Besides the necessary expenditure for cases and furniture for the library, appropriations may be made for carrying on the catalogue system; for printing reports on libraries; for the publication of a library manual; for the preparation and publication of bibliographies; for completing sets of transactions, and the purchase of other books for the operations of the Institution; also for printing a catalogue or list of books in the library.

"In addition to the sum which will be necessarily required for the cases and furniture of the museum, a small sum may annually be appropriated for collecting particular desiderata in natural history, to be presented to other institutions as well as preserved in this; for purchasing instruments and models to illustrate particular branches of knowledge, or to assist in the prosecution of special lines of research, which may serve as samples to artizans in this country, or be used in investigations.

"Models may also be obtained for multiplying casts of the most celebrated specimens of ancient and modern art.

"Appropriations for all these objects cannot be made in the same year, but discretion, as I have said before, should be used as to the time when it would be the most advisable to make the expenditure in each particular case.

"As few operations as possible ought to be carried on in the building of the Institution. Printing, stereotyping, engraving, &c., can be done at a cheaper rate by contract; these require expensive superintendence; and workmen, as a general rule, cannot be expected to do as much for public institutions as for a private individual. Besides this, much time must be lost in the interval of the publication of the different articles, and when it is necessary, on account of the exhaustion of the appropriation, to stop for the year, this can only be done by disbanding the workmen, while the interest on the cost of the apparatus remains.

"These remarks also apply to calculations and reductions of observations, which, in many cases, can be distributed to professors in colleges, who, for a small addition to their salaries, will furnish results which could not be procured in the Institution for many times the same sum.

"The maxim stated in the programme, namely, that few individuals ought to be permanently supported by the Institution, should be constantly kept in view, and the greatest caution exercised in adding new members to the permanent corps.

"The Institution, in order to produce the greatest amount of useful effect with a given expenditure of income, must be a unit in plan and a unit in purpose. Each assistant must not merely have regard to the advancement of his own speciality, but the good of the whole, and though he may be assigned a specific duty, he should be ready and willing, at the call of the Secretary, to render service in any other. Without a system of government which will ensure this, not only the usefulness of the Institution will be greatly abridged, but its very existence jeoparded."

The committee submit to the Board the following resolutions:

Resolved, That the seventh resolution passed by the Board of Regents on the 26th of January, 1847, requiring an equal division of the income between the active operations and the museum and library, when the buildings are completed, be and it is hereby, repealed.

Resolved, That hereafter the annual appropriations shall be apportioned specifically among the different objects and operations of the Institution, in such manner as may, in the judgment of the Regents, be necessary and proper for each, according to its intrinsic importance, and a compliance in good faith with the law.

Respectfully submitted:

JAMES A. PEARCE, *Chairman*.

Mr. Mason offered the following resolution which was adopted:

Resolved, That the report of the Special Committee just made, be laid on the table for further consideration, and that the papers referred to in the report be communicated to the Board for their examination; and that said report, and such report of a minority of the Committee as may be made in the recess of the board, be printed.

On motion of Mr. English, the Board then adjourned, to meet on Saturday, the 8th of July, at 10 o'clock a. m.

WASHINGTON, *July* 8, 1854.

An adjourned meeting of the Board of Regents was held on Saturday, July 8, at 10 o'clock, a. m.

Present: Messrs. Bache, Douglas, English, Hawley, Mason, Pearce, Rush, Stuart, Totten, Towers, and the Secretary.

In the absence of the Chancellor, Mr. Hawley was called to the chair.

John T. Towers, esquire, mayor elect of the city of Washington, appeared and took the seat in the Board vacated by Mr. Maury, late mayor.

The Secretary laid before the Board the sixth volume of Smithsonian Contributions to Knowledge.

Mr. Mason, from the Select Committee on the resolutions of Messrs. Fitch and Meacham, offered the following resolution:

"The Secretary of the Institution and of this Board is, by the seventh section of the act 'to establish the Smithsonian Institution,' required to discharge the duties of 'Librarian and Keeper of the Museum,' having, with the consent of the Board of Regents, power to employ assistants, the better to enable him to discharge those duties; for a better construction whereof,

Be it resolved, That whilst power is reserved in the said section to the Board of Regents to remove both the Secretary and his assistants, in the opinion of the Board, power, nevertheless, remains with the Secretary to remove his said assistants."

Mr. English moved to amend the resolution by inserting the words "*with the consent of the Board of Regents*," after the words "power, nevertheless, remains with the *Secretary*."

Mr. Stuart moved that the consideration of Mr. Mason's resolution be postponed till the next meeting of the Board. On this question the yeas and nays were demanded.

Those voting in the affirmative:

YEAS.—Messrs. Douglas, English, Stuart, Towers—4.

NAYS.—Messrs. Bache, Hawley, Mason, Pearce, Totten—5.

So the motion was not carried.

The question was then taken on the amendment offered by Mr. English to Mr. Mason's resolution, and the yeas and nays taken:

YEAS.—Messrs. Douglas, English, Stuart, Towers—4.

NAYS.—Messrs. Bache, Hawley, Mason, Pearce, Totten—5.

So the amendment was lost.

Mr. Douglas moved a postponement of the subject for a week from next Friday.

The yeas and nays were taken on this motion:

YEAS.—Messrs. Douglas, English, Stuart, Towers—4.

NAYS.—Messrs. Bache, Hawley, Mason, Pearce, Totten—5.

So the motion was lost.

The question was then taken on Mr. Mason's resolution; which was adopted.

YEAS.—Messrs. Bache, Hawley, Mason, Pearce, Rush, Totten—6.

NAYS.—Messrs. Douglas, English, Stuart, Towers—4.

Mr. Stuart moved to postpone the consideration of the resolutions appended to the report of the Select Committee on the resolutions of Messrs. Fitch and Meacham, till the next annual session.

A division was called for—ayes 3, noes 6.

So the motion was lost.

Mr Douglas moved to postpone the consideration for two weeks.

A division was called for—ayes 4, noes 6.

So the motion was lost.

Mr. English moved that the Board adjourn.

This motion was withdrawn to allow the Chairman of the Executive Committee, Mr. Pearce, to bring forward the appropriations for the year recommended by the committee, and reported to the Board, April 29, 1854.

On motion, the appropriations, as reported by the Executive Committee, were adopted—ayes 7, noes 3.

The Secretary stated to the Board that he had employed Mr. Lorin Blodget to reduce and discuss the meteorological observations collected by the Smithsonian Institution, and that some misunderstanding had arisen between this gentleman and himself as to the adjustment of his claims in reference to the work, which he proposed to refer to the Executive Committee, and if necessary to a Commission of Examination, one of whom might be appointed by the Secretary, another by Mr. Blodget, and a third by the two persons so appointed; whereupon,

On motion of Mr. Mason, it was

Resolved, That the Executive Committee be authorized to investigate and settle the business presented to the Board by the Secretary.

Mr. English then renewed his motion to adjourn.

Adopted—ayes 6, noes 4.

The Board then adjourned *sine die.*

PROCEEDINGS OF THE ESTABLISHMENT.

WASHINGTON, *May* 3, 1853.

A meeting of the Smithsonian Institution, called by order of the President of the United States, was held this day, May 3, 1853, in the session hall of the Smithsonian building, at 11 o'clock, a. m.

Present: Franklin Pierce, President of the United States, *ex officio* President of the Smithsonian Institution; James Guthrie, Secretary of the Treasury; James C. Dobbin, Secretary of the Navy; James Campbell, Postmaster General; Caleb Cushing, Attorney General; John W. Maury, Mayor of Washington; Joseph Henry, Secretary of the Smithsonian Institution.

The Secretary gave an account of the operations of the Institution.

Less than half of the number of members being present, the meeting adjourned to meet on Tuesday, the 17th inst.

WASHINGTON, *May* 17, 1853.

An adjourned meeting of the Smithsonian Institution was held this day in the session hall of the Smithsonian building.

Present: Franklin Pierce, President of the United States; William L. Marcy, Secretary of State; James Guthrie, Secretary of the Treasury; Jefferson Davis, Secretary of War; James C. Dobbin, Secretary of the Navy; James Campbell, Postmaster General; Caleb Cushing, Attorney General; Charles Mason, Commissioner of Patents; John W. Maury, Mayor of Washington; Joseph Henry, Secretary of the Smithsonian Institution.

The President took the chair, and the minutes of the preceding meeting were read.

On motion, the President appointed a committee of five to draft a code of By-laws. The committee consisted of the following persons, to wit: Messrs Cushing, Dobbin, Maury, Davis, and the Secretary.

The committee, after due deliberation, reported through their chairman, Mr. Cushing, the following:

BY-LAWS OF THE SMITHSONIAN INSTITUTION.

SECTION 1. A stated annual meeting of the statute and honorary members of the Institution shall be held at the Hall of the Institution, in Washington, on the first Tuesday in May. Adjourned meetings may be held at such place and time as the members of the Institution at any meeting may order. Special meetings will be convened by direction of the President of the United States.

SEC. 2. Notice of all meetings of the Institution, whether stated, adjourned, or special, shall be given by the Secretary in writing, addressed to each member.

Sec. 3. The votes and proceedings of the Institution, with the names of the members present at each meeting, shall be recorded; and at the opening of every meeting the journal of the preceding meeting shall be read by the Secretary.

Sec. 4. A quorum of not less than six of the statute members shall be requisite for the transaction of any business except adjourning or obtaining the attendance of members.

Sec. 5 The Secretary shall at the stated annual meeting, make a general statement of the condition and affairs of the Institution during the past year.

Sec. 6. Honorary members, not exceeding one in each year, shall be elected by ballot, and by unanimous vote of the statute members: *Provided*, That no person shall be chosen without having been nominated at a previous meeting of the Institution.

Sec. 7. The rules of parliamentary proceedings, as received and practised in the Senate of the United States, shall govern the meetings of the Institution in all cases which are not inconsistent with the foregoing By-laws.

On motion, the report of the committee was adopted.

The Secretary presented an account of the organization and operations of the Institution, relative to the reception and publication of memoirs, researches, exchanges, the formation of catalogues of libraries; also an account of the state of the funds, and the policy with regard to the formation of collections, &c.

On motion of Mr. Davis, nominations were then received for the appointment of an honorary member of the Institution, to take place at a succeeding meeting.

On motion, the Institution adjourned to the first Monday in June ensuing, at 11 o'clock, a. m.

Washington, *June* 6, 1853.

An adjourned meeting of the Smithsonian Institution was held this day, June 6, 1853, in the session hall of the Smithsonian building.

Present: Franklin Pierce, President of the United States, *ex-officio* President of the Smithsonian Institution; James Guthrie, Secretary of the Treasury; William L. Marcy, Secretary of State; Jefferson Davis, Secretary of War; James Campbell, Postmaster General; Caleb Cushing, Attorney General; Charles Mason, Commissioner of Patents; Joseph Henry, Secretary of the Smithsonian Institution.

The President took the chair, and the minutes of the preceding meeting were read.

On motion, the Institution proceeded to ballot for the election of an honorary member.

Professor Parker Cleaveland was declared unanimously elected.

The advertisement of the Leopoldin Caroline Academy of Germany, relative to the Smithsonian Institution, was read by the Secretary.

The Institution then adjourned *sine die.*

The stated annual meeting of the Smithsonian Institution was held this day, May 2, 1854, at the hall of the Institution at 12 o'clock, m.

Present: Franklin Pierce, President of the United States; Hon. Wm. L. Marcy, Secretary of State; Hon. James Guthrie, Secretary of the Treasury; Hon. Jefferson Davis, Secretary of War; Hon. James C. Dobbin, Secretary of the Navy; Hon. Caleb Cushing, Attorney General; Hon. John W. Maury, Mayor of the city; Professor Robert Hare, honorary member; Professor Joseph Henry, Secretary of the Institution.

The President took the chair.

The minutes of the last annual meeting were read and approved.

On motion of Hon. Mr. Guthrie, the Institution proceeded to nominate candidates for election as honorary members.

Dr. Hare made some remarks respecting his apparatus, and the conditions on which it was presented to the Institution.

The Secretary explained the cause of the delay in completing the repairs, and in the proposed exhibition of the apparatus. This had been mainly due to an accident which happened to the building. A part of the interior gave way, and the Regents directed that the whole wood-work of the main building should be removed, and its place supplied with fire-proof materials. To meet the additional expense of this necessary change in the plan, the time of completing the edifice was extended, and funds which would have been devoted to other purposes were consequently given to this object. The building will, however, be completed in the course of the present year; a spacious room is now nearly ready to receive the apparatus, and due diligence on the part of the Institution will be made to finish the repairs of the articles, of which a considerable portion are now completed.

On motion the Institution then adjourned to the first Tuesday in June next (6th proximo.)

WASHINGTON, *June* 6, 1854.

An adjourned meeting of the Smithsonian Institution was held this day, June 6, 1854, in the hall of the Institution, at 12 o'clock, m.

Present: Hon. Wm. L. Marcy, Secretary of State; Hon. James Guthrie, Secretary of the Treasury; Hon. Caleb Cushing, Attorney General; Hon. Charles Mason, Commissioner of Patents; Prof. Joseph Henry, Secretary of the Institution.

There not being a legal quorum present, on motion of Mr. Cushing the Institution adjourned to meet on Saturday, July 15, 1854, at 12 o'clock, m.

WASHINGTON, *July* 15, 1854.

An adjourned meeting of the Smithsonian Institution was held this day, July 15, 1854, in the hall of the Institution, at 12 o'clock, m.

Present: Franklin Pierce, President of the United States; Hon. Wm. L. Marcy, Secretary of State; Hon. James Guthrie, Secretary of the Treasury; Hon. Jefferson Davis, Secretary of War; Hon. James C. Dobbin, Secretary of the Navy; Hon. James Campbell, Postmaster General; Hon. Caleb Cushing, Attorney General; Hon. Charles Mason, Commissioner of Patents.

The President took the chair. The minutes of the last meeting were read and approved.

The nominations previously made for honorary members were then read, and the Institution proceeded to ballot, but no choice was made.

On the second ballot no choice was made.

On motion, the election of an honorary member was postponed.

Ordered, That three persons be appointed a Committee of the Institution to confer with the Board of Regents as to suitable means of communication between the two bodies, and to report thereon at a subsequent meeting of the Institution.

The Secretary gave a general account of the affairs of the Institution; the condition of the building; the operations carried on during the past year; and a statement of the finances at the present time.

The President appointed Messrs. Cushing, Davis, and Mason as the committee of conference with the Board of Regents.

On motion of Mr. Campbell, the Institution adjourned to meet on the third Saturday (21st) of October next.

APPENDIX.

WILL OF SMITHSON.

I, James Smithson, son of Hugh, first Duke of Northumberland, and Elizabeth, heiress of the Hungerfords of Audley, and niece of Charles the Proud, Duke of Somerset, now residing in Bentinck street, Cavendish square, do this 23d day of October, 1826, make this my last will and testament

I bequeath the whole of my property of every nature and kind soever to my bankers, Messrs. Drummonds, of Charing Cross, in trust, to be disposed of in the following manner, and desire of my said executors to put my property under the management of the court of chancery.

To John Fitall, formerly my servant, but now employed in the London Docks, and residing at No. 27, Jubilee Place, North Mile End, Old Town, in consideration of his attachment and fidelity to me, and the long and great care he has taken of my effects, and my having done but very little for him, I give and bequeath the annuity or annual sum of £100 sterling for his life, to be paid to him quarterly, free from legacy duty and all other deductions, the first payment to be made to him at the expiration of three months after my death. I have at divers times lent sums of money to Henry Honori Juilly, formerly my servant, but now keeping the Hungerford Hotel, in the Rue Caumartin, at Paris, and for which sums of money I have undated bills or bonds signed by him. Now I will and direct that, if he desires it, these sums of money be let remain in his hands at an interest of five per cent. for five years after the date of the present will.

To Henry James Hungerford, my nephew, heretofore called Henry James Dickinson, son of my late brother, Lieutenant Colonel Henry Louis Dickinson, now residing with Mr. Auboin, at Bourg la Reine, near Paris, I give and bequeath for his life the whole of the income arising from my property, of every nature and kind whatever, after the payment of the above annuity, and, after the death of John Fitall, that annuity likewise, the payments to be at the time the interest or dividends become due on the stocks or other property from which the income arises.

Should the said Henry James Hungerford have a child or children, legitimate or illegitimate, I leave to such child or children, his or their heirs, executors, and assigns, after the death of his, her, or their father, the whole of my property of every kind, absolutely and forever, to be divided between them, if there is more than one, in the manner their father shall judge proper, and in case of his omitting to decide this, as the Lord Chancellor shall judge proper.

Should my nephew, Henry James Hungerford marry, I empower him to make a jointure.

In case of the death of my said nephew, without leaving a child or children, or of the death of the child or children he may have had, under the age of 21 years, or intestate, I then bequeath the whole of my property, subject to the annuity of £100 to John Fitall, and for the security and payment of which I mean stock to remain in this country, to the United States of America, to found at Washington, under the name of the Smithsonian Institution, an Establishment for the Increase and Diffusion of Knowledge among Men.

I think it proper here to state, that all the money which will be standing in the French five per cents. at my death, in the name of the father of my above mentioned nephew, Henry James Hungerford, and all that in my name, is the property of my said nephew, being what he inherited from his father, or what I have laid up for him from the savings upon his income.

JAMES SMITHSON. [L. S.]

Extract from a letter from Hon. RICHARD RUSH *to Hon. John Forsyth, Secretary of State.*

LONDON, *May* 12, 1838.

* * * * * * * *

"I have made inquiries, from time to time, in the hope of finding out something of the man, personally a stranger to our people, who has sought to benefit distant ages by founding, in the capital of the American Union, an institution (to describe it in his own simple and comprehensive language) for the increase and diffusion of knowledge among men. I have not heard a great deal. What I have heard, and may confide in, amounts to this: That he was, in fact, the natural son of the Duke of Northumberland; that his mother was a Mrs. Macie, of an ancient family in Wiltshire, of the name of Hungerford; that he was educated at Oxford, where he took an honorary degree in 1786; that he went under the name of James Lewis Macie until after a few years after he had left the university, when he took that of Smithson, ever after signing only James Smithson, as in his will; that he does not appear to have had any fixed home, living in lodgings when in London, and occasionally staying a year or two at a time in cities on the continent, as Paris, Berlin, Florence, Genoa, at which last he died; and, that the ample provision made for him by the Duke of Northumberland, with retired and simple habits, enabled him to accumulate the fortune which now passes to the United States. I have inquired if his political opinions or bias were supposed to be of a nature that led him to select the United States as the great trustee of his enlarged and philanthropic views. The reply has been, that his opinions, as far as known or inferred, were thought to favor monarchical rather than popular institutions; but that he interested himself little in questions of government, being devoted to science, and chiefly chemistry; that this had introduced him to the society of Cavendish, Wollaston, and others advantageously known to the Royal Society in London, of which body he was a member, and to the archives of which he made contributions; and that he also became acquainted, through his visits to the continent, with eminent chemists in France, Italy, and Germany. Finally, that he was a gentleman of feeble health, but always of courteous though reserved manners and conversation.

"Such I learn to have been some of the characteristics of the man whom generations to come may see cause to bless, and whose will may enrol his name with the benefactors of mankind."

NOTICE OF SMITHSON BY THE PRESIDENT OF THE ROYAL SOCIETY.

November 30th, 1829. Davies Gilbert, esq., President of the *Royal Society*, in his address to the society, mentions the death of Mr. Smithson as having occurred during the preceding year, or since the last annual meeting of the society, and remarks as follows:

"Mr Smithson has added eight (8) communications to our transactions. He was distinguished by the intimate friendship of Mr. Cavendish, and rivalled our most expert chemists in elegant analyses; but the latter part of his life has been passed abroad."—(See Philosophical Magazine, 2d series, vol. 7, p. 42.)

And again, in his address to *The Royal Society*, *November 30th*, 1830, Mr. Gilbert, in speaking of Mr Smithson, says:

"Of this gentleman I must be allowed to speak with affection. We were at Oxford together, of the same college, and our acquaintance continued to the time of his decease. Mr. Smithson, then called Macie, and an under graduate, had the reputation of excelling all other resident members of the university in the knowledge of chemistry. He was early honored by an intimate acquaintance with Mr. Cavendish; he was admitted into the Royal Society, *and soon after presented a paper on* the very curious concretion frequently found in the hollow of bambû canes, named *Tabasheer*. This he found to consist almost entirely of silex, existing in a manner similar to what Davy long afterwards discoved in the epidermis of reeds and grasses. Mr. Smithson enriched our transactions with seven other communications; a chemical analysis of some calamines; account of a discovery of native minium; on the composition and crystalization of certain sulphurets from Huel Boys, in Cornwall; on the composition of zeolite; on a substance procured from the elm tree called ulmine; on a saline substance from Mount Vesuvius; facts relative to the coloring matter of vegetables.

"He was the friend of Dr. Wollaston, and at the same time his rival in the manipulation and analysis of small quantities. Mr. Smithson frequently repeated an occurrence with much pleasure and exultation as exceeding anything that could be brought into competition with it, and this must apologise for my introducing what might otherwise be deemed an anecdote too light and trifling on such an occasion as the present.

"Mr. Smithson declared, that happening to observe a tear gliding down a lady's cheek, he endeavored to catch it on a crystal vessel, that one-half of the drop escaped, but having preserved the other half, he submitted it to re-agents, and detected what was then called microcosmic salt, with muriate of soda, and, I think, three or four more saline substances, held in solution.

"For many years past Mr. Smithson has resided abroad, principally, I believe, on account of his health; but he carried with him the esteem and regard of various private friends, and of a still larger number of persons who appreciated and admired his acquirements."—(See Philosophical Magazine, 2d series, vol. ix, p. 41.)

LIST OF PAPERS PRESENTED TO THE ROYAL SOCIETY BY JAMES SMITHSON.

1. "An Account of some Chemical Experiments on Tabasheer." Read July 7, 1791. By James Louis Macie, esq., F. R. S.—Philosophical Transactions, vol. 81, p. 368.
2. "A Chemical Analysis of some Calamines." Read November 18, 1802.—Philosophical Transactions, vol. 93, p. 12, and P. Magazine, vol. 14, p. 173.
3. "An Account of a Discovery of Native Minium." Read April 24, 1806.—Philosophical Transactions, vol. 96, p. 267, and P. Magazine, vol. 24, p. 274, and vol. 26, p. 114.
4. "On Quadruple and Binary Compounds, particularly Sulphurets." Read December 24, 1807, but not published in the P. Transactions.—Philosophical Magazine, vol. 29, p. 275.
5. "On the Composition of the Compound Sulphuret from Huel Boys, and an account of its crystals." Read January 28, 1808.—Philosophical Transactions, vol. 98, p. 55, and P. Magazine, vol. 29, p. 275.
6. "On the Composition of Zeolite." Read February 7, 1811.—Philosophical Transactions, vol. 101, p. 171, and P. Magazine, vol. 37, p. 152, and vol. 38, p. 30.
7. "On a substance from the Elm tree, called Ulmin." Read December 10, 1812.—Philosophical Transactions, vol. 103, p. 64, and P. Magazine, vol. 42, p. 204.
8. "On a saline substance from Mount Vesuvius." Read July 8, 1813.—Philosophical Transactions, vol. 103, p. 256, and P. Magazine, vol. 42, p. 425.
9. "A Few Facts Relative to the Coloring Matter of some Vegetables. Read December 18, 1817.—Philosophical Transactions, vol. 108, p. 110, and P. Magazine, vol. 57, p. 58.

CONTRIBUTIONS TO THE "ANNALS OF PHILOSOPHY," BY JAMES SMITHSON.

1. "On a Native Compound of Sulphuret of Lead and Arsenic." Paris, May 19, 1819, vol. 14, p. 96, 1819; and see vol. 16, p. 100.
2. "On Native Hydrous Aluminate of Lead, or Plomb Gomme.—Paris, May 28, 1819, vol 14, p. 31, 1819; and see vol. 16, p. 100.
3. "On a Fibrous Metallic Copper." Paris, March 17, 1820, vol. 16, p. 46, 1820.
4. "An Account of a Native Combination of Sulphate of Barium and Fluoride of Calcium." Paris, March 24, 1820; vol. 16, p. 48; 1820; and see vol 16, p. 100, for notices of 1 and 2, above.
5. "On some Capillary Metallic Tin forced through the pores of Cast Iron." Paris, February 17, 1821, vol. 17; new series, vol 1, p. 271, 1821.
6. "On the Detection of Very Minute Quantities of Arsenic and Mercury." Letter from Mr. Smithson, (not dated,) vol. 20; new series, vol. 4, p. 127, 1822.

7. "On Some Improvements of Lamps." Vol. 20, p. 363; new series, vol. 4, p. 127, 1822; and see Ann. de Chemie., vol. xli, p. 92, and Journal of Science and Art, vol. 28, p. 183.

8. "On the Crystaline form of ice." March 4, 1823.—Vol 21; new series, vol. 5, p. 340, 1823.

9. "A Means of discriminating between Sulphate of Barium and Strontium." April 2, 1823.—Vol. 21; new series, vol. 5, p. 359, 1823.

10. "On the Discovery of Acids in Mineral Substances." April 12, 1823.—Vol. 21; new series, vol. 5, p. 384, 1823.

11. "An Improved way of Making Coffee." June 4th, 1823.—Vol. 22; new series, vol. 6, p. 30, 1823.

12. "A Discovery of Chloride of Potassium in the Earth." (Not dated.) Vol. 22; new series, vol. 6, p. 258, 1823.

13. "A Method of Fixing Particles on the Sappare." October 24, 1823.—Vol. 22; new series, vol. 6, p. 412, 1823.

14. "On Some Compounds of Fluorine." January 2, 1824.—Vol. 23; new series, vol. 7, p. 100, 1824.

15. "An Examination of some Egyptian Colors." January 2, 1824. Vol. 23; new series, vol. 7, p. 115, 1824.

16. "Some Observations on Mr. Penn's theory concerning the formation of the Kirkdale Cave." June 10, 1824.—Vol. 24; new series, vol. 8, p. 50, 1824.

17. "A Note on a Letter from Dr. Black, describing a Very Sensible Balance."—Vol. 26; new series, vol 10, p. 52, 1825.

18. "A Method of Fixing Crayon Colors." London, August 23, 1825.—Vol. 26; new series, vol. 10, p. 236, 1825.

ACT OF CONGRESS ACCEPTING BEQUEST.

AN ACT to authorize and enable the President to assert and prosecute, with effect, the claim of the United States to the legacy bequeathed to them by James Smithson, late of London, deceased, to found at Washington, under the name of the Smithsonian Institution, an Establishment for the Increase and Diffusion of Knowledge among Men.

SEC. 1. *Be it enacted by the Senate and House of Representatives of the United States of America in Congress assembled,* That the President of the United States be, and he is hereby, authorized to constitute and appoint an agent or agents, to assert and prosecute for and in behalf of the United States, and in their name or otherwise, as may be advisable, in the Court of Chancery, or other proper tribunal of England, the right of the United States to the legacy bequeathed to them by the last will and testament of James Smithson, late of London, deceased, for the purpose of founding at Washington, under the name of the Smithsonian Institution, an Establishment for the Increase and Diffusion of Knowledge among Men; and to empower such agent or agents so appointed to receive and grant acquittances for all such sum or sums of money, or other funds, as may or shall be decreed or adjudged to the United States, for, or on account of said legacy.

SEC. 2. *And be it further enacted,* That the said agent or agents shall, before receiving any part of said legacy, give a bond or bonds, in the penal sum of five hundred thousand dollars, to the Treasurer of the United States and his successors in offiee, with good and sufficient securities to the satisfaction of the Secretary of the Treasury, for the faithful performance of the duties of the said agency, and for the faithful remittance to the Treasurer of the United States of all and every sum or sums of money or other funds which he or they may receive for payment in whole or in part of the said legacy. And the Treasurer of the United States is hereby authorized and required to keep safely all sums of money or other funds which may be received by him in virtue of the said bequest, and to account therefor separately from all other accounts of his office, and subject to such further disposal thereof as may be hereafter provided by Congress.

SEC. 3. *And be it further enacted,* That any and all sums of money and other funds which shall be received for or on account of the said legacy shall be applied, in such manner as Congress may hereafter direct, to the purpose of founding and endowing at Washington, under the name of the Smithsonian Institution, an Establishment for the Increase and Diffusion of Knowledge among Men, to which application of the said moneys and other funds the faith of the United States is hereby pledged.

SEC. 4. *And be it further enacted,* That, to the end that the claim to the said bequest may be prosecuted with effect, and the necessary expenses in prosecuting the same be defrayed, the President of the United States be, and he is hereby, authorized to apply to that purpose any sum not exceeding ten thousand dollars out of any moneys in the treasury not otherwise appropriated.

Approved July 1, 1836.

AN ACT TO ESTABLISH THE SMITHSONIAN INSTITUTION.

AN ACT to establish the "Smithsonian Institution," for the Increase and Diffusion of Knowledge among Men.

James Smithson, Esquire, of London, in the kingdom of Great Britain, having by his last will and testament given the whole of his property to the United States of America, to found at Washington, under the name of the Smithsonian Institution, an Establishment for the Increase and Diffusion of Knowledge among Men; and the United States having, by an act of Congress, received said property, and accepted said trust; therefore, for the faithful execution of said trust according to the will of the liberal and enlightened donor—

Be it enacted by the Senate and House of Representatives of the United States of America in Congress assembled, That the President and Vice-President of the United States, the Secretary of State, the Secretary of the Treasury, the Secretary of War, the Secretary of the Navy, the Postmaster General, the Attorney General, the Chief Justice, and the Commissioner of the Patent Office of the United States, and the Mayor of the City of Washington, during the time for which they shall hold their respective offices, and such other persons as they may elect honorary members, be, and they are hereby, constituted an "Establishment," by the name of the "Smithsonian Institution," for the Increase and Diffusion of Knowledge among Men; and by that name shall be known, and have perpetual succession, with the powers, limitations, and restrictions, hereinafter contained, and no other.

Sec. 2. *And be it further enacted*, That so much of the property of the said James Smithson as has been received in money, and paid into the Treasury of the United States, being the sum of five hundred and fifteen thousand one hundred and sixty-nine dollars, be lent to the United States Treasury, at six per cent. per annum interest from the first day of September, in the year one thousand eight hundred and thirty-eight, when the same was received into the said treasury; and that so much of the interest as may have accrued on said sum on the first day of July next, which will amount to the sum of two hundred and forty-two thousand one hundred and twenty-nine dollars, or so much thereof as shall, by the Board of Regents of the Institution, established by this act, be deemed necessary, be, and the same is hereby, appropriated for the erection of suitable buildings, and for other current incidental expenses of said Institution; and that six per cent. interest on the said trust fund—it being the said amount of five hundred and fifteen thousand one hundred and sixty-nine dollars received into the United States Treasury on the first of September, one thousand eight hundred and thirty-eight, payable, in half-yearly payments, on the first of January and July in each year—be, and the same is hereby, appropriated for the perpetual maintenance and support of said Institution; and all expenditures and appropriations to be made, from time to time, to the purposes of the Institution aforesaid, shall be exclusively from the accruing interest, and not from the principal of the said fund. *And be it further enacted*, That all the moneys and stocks which have been, or may hereafter be, received into the Treasury of the United States on account of the fund bequeathed by James Smithson, be, and the same hereby are, pledged to refund to the Treasury of the United States the sums hereby appropriated.

Sec. 3. *And be it further enacted*, That the business of the said Institution shall be conducted at the city of Washington by a Board of Regents by the name of the Regents of the "Smithsonian Institution," to be composed of the Vice-President of the United States, the Chief Justice of the United States, and the Mayor of the city of Washington, during the time for which they shall hold their respective offices; three members of the Senate, and three members of the House of Representatives; together with six other persons, other than members of Congress, two of whom shall be members of the National Institute in the city of Washington, and resident in the said city; and the other four thereof shall be inhabitants of States, and no two of them of the same State. And the Regents, to be selected as aforesaid, shall be appointed immediately after the passage of this act—the members of the Senate by the President thereof, the members of the House by the Speaker thereof, and the six other persons by joint resolution of the Senate and House of Representatives; and the members of the House so appointed shall serve until the fourth Wednesday in December, the second next after the passage of this act; and then, and biennially thereafter, on every alternate fourth Wednesday of December, a like number shall be appointed in the same manner, to serve until the fourth Wednesday in December, the second succeeding their appointment. And the senators so appointed shall serve during the term for which they shall hold, without re-election, their offiee as senators. And vacancies, occasioned by death, resignation, or otherwise, shall be filled as vacancies in committees are filled; and the other six members aforesaid shall serve, two for two years, two for four years, and two for six years; the terms of service, in the first place, to be determined by lot; but after the first term, then their regular term of service shall be six years; and new elections thereof shall be made by joint resolution of Congress; and vacancies occasioned by death, resignation, or otherwise, may be filled in like manner, by joint resolution of Congress. And the said Regents shall meet in the city of Washington on the first Monday of September next after the passage of this act, and organize by the election of one of their number as Chancellor, who shall be the presiding officer of said Board of Regents, by the name of the Chancellor of the "Smithsonian Institution," and a suitable person as Secretary of said Institution, who shall also be the Secretary of said Board of Regents; said Board shall also elect three of their own body as an Executive Committee, and said Regents shall then fix on the time for the regular meetings of said Board; and on application of any three of the Regents to the Secretary of the said Institution, it shall be his duty to appoint a special meeting of the Board of Regents, of which he shall give notice by letter to each of the members; and at any meeting of said Board, five shall constitute a quorum to do business. And each member of said Board shall be paid his necessary travelling and other actual expenses in attending meetings of the Board, which shall be audited by the Executive Committee, and recorded by the Secretary of said Board; but his services as Regent shall be gratuitous. And whenever money is required for the payment of the debts or performance of the contracts of the Institution, incurred or entered into in conformity with the provisions of this act, or for making the purchases and executing the objects authorized by this act, the Board of Regents, or the Executive Committee thereof, may certify to the Chancellor and Secretary of the Board that such sum of money is required; whereupon, they shall examine the same, and, if they shall approve thereof, shall certify the same to the proper officer of the treasury for payment. And the said Board shall submit to Congress, at each session thereof, a report of the operations, expenditures, and condition of the Institution.

SEC. 4. *And be it further enacted*, That after the Board of Regents shall have met, and become organized, it shall be their duty forthwith to proceed to select a suitable site for such building as may be necessary for the Institution; which ground may be taken and appropriated out of that part of the public ground in the city of Washington, lying between the Patent Office and Seventh street: *Provided*, The President of the United States, the Secretary of State, the Secretary of the Treasury, the Secretary of War, the Secretary of the Navy, and the Commissioner of the Patent Offiee, shall consent to the same; but if the persons last named shall not consent, then such location may be made upon any other of the public grounds within the city of Washington, belonging to the United States, which said Regents may select, by and with the consent of the persons herein named; and the said ground so selected shall be set out by proper metes and bounds, and a description of the same shall be made and recorded in a book to be provided for that purpose, and signed by the said Regents, or so many of them as may be convened at the time of their said organization; and such record, or a copy thereof, certified by the Chancellor and Secretary of the Board of Regents, shall be received in evidence in all courts of the extent and boundaries of the lands appropriated to the said Institution; and upon the making of such record, such site and lands shall be deemed and taken to be appropriated by force of this act to the said Institution.

Sec. 5. *And be it further enacted*, That, so soon as the Board of Regents shall have selected the said site, they shall cause to be erected a suitable building, of plain and durable materials and structure, without unnecessary ornament, and of sufficient size, and with suitable rooms, or halls, for the reception and arrangement, upon a liberal scale, of objects of natural history, including a geological and mineralogical cabinet; also a chemical laboratory, a library, a gallery of art, and the necessary lecture rooms; and the said Board shall have authority, by themselves, or by a committee of three of their members, to contract for the completion of such building, upon such plan as may be directed by the Board of Regents, and shall take sufficient security for the building and finishing the same according to the said plan, and in the time stipulated in such contract; and may so locate said building, if they shall deem it proper, as in appearance to form a wing to the Patent Oiffice building, and may so connect the same with the present hall of said Patent Office building, containing the National Cabinet of Curiosities, as to constitute the said hall in whole, or in part, the deposit for the cabinet of said Institution, if they deem it expedient to do so; provided said building shall be located upon said Patent Offiee lot, in the manner aforesaid: *Provided, however*, That the whole expense of building and enclosures aforesaid shall not exceed the amount of ——; which sum is hereby appropriated, payable out of money in the treasury not otherwise appropriated; together with such sum or sums out of the annual interest accruing to the Institution, as may, in any year, remain unexpended, after paying the current expenses of the Institution. And duplicates of all such contracts as may be made by the said Board of Regents shall be deposited with the Treasurer of the United States; and all claims on any contract made as aforesaid, shall be allowed and certified by the Board of Regents, or the Executive Committee thereof, as the case may be, and, being signed by the Chancellor and Secretary of the Board, shall be a sufficient voucher for settlement and payment at the Treasury of the United States. And the Board of Regents shall be authorized to employ such persons as they may deem necessary to superintend the erection of the building and fitting up the rooms of the Institution. And all laws for the protection of public property in the city of Washington, shall apply to, and be in force for, the protection of the lands, buildings, and other property of said Institution. And all moneys recovered by, or accruing to, the Institution, shall be paid into the Treasury of the United States to the credit of the Smithsonian bequest, and separately accounted for, as provided in the act approved July first, eighteen hundred and thirty-six, accepting said bequest.

Sec. 6. *And be it further enacted*, That, in proportion as suitable arrangements can be made for their reception, all objects of art and o foreign and curious research, and all objects of natural history, plants, and geological and mineralogical specimens belonging, or hereafter to belong, to the United States, which may be in the city of Washington, in whosesoever custody the same may be, shall be delivered to such persons as may be authorized by the Board of Regents to receive them, and shall be arranged in such order, and so classed, as best to facilitate the examination and study of them, in the building so as aforesaid to be erected for the Institution; and the Regents of said Institution shall afterwards, as new specimens in natural history, geology, or mineralogy, may be obtained for the museum of the Institution, by exchanges of duplicate specimens belonging to the Institution, (which they are hereby authorized to make,) or by donation, which they may receive, or otherwise, cause such new specimens to be also appropriately classed and arranged. And the minerals, books, manuscripts, and other property of James Smithson, which have been received by the Government of the United States, and are now placed in the Department of State, shall be removed to said Institution, and shall be preserved separate and apart from other property of the Institution.

Sec. 7. *And be it further enacted*, That the Secretary of the Board of Regents shall take charge of the building and property of said Institution, and shall, under their direction, make a fair and accurate record of all their proceedings, to be preserved in said Institution; and the said Secretary shall also discharge the duties of librarian and keeper of the museum, and may, with the consent of the Board of Regents, employ assistants; and the said officers shall receive for their services such sums as may be allowed by the Board of Regents, to be paid semi-annually on the first days of January and July; and the said officers shall be removable by the Board of Regents, whenever, in their judgment, the interests of the Institution require any of the said officers to be changed.

Sec. 8. *And be it further enacted*, That the members and honorary members of said Institution may hold such stated and special meetings, for the supervision of the affairs of said Institution and the advice and instruction of said Board of Regents, to be called in the manner provided for in the By-laws of said Institution, at which the President, and, in his absence, the Vice-President, of the United States shall preside. And the said Regents shall make, from the interest of said fund, an appropriation, not exceeding an average of twenty-five thousand dollars annually, for the gradual formation of a library composed of valuable works pertaining to all departments of human knowledge.

Sec. 9. *And be it further enacted*, That of any other moneys which have accrued, or shall hereafter accrue, as interest upon the said Smithsonian fund, not herein appropriated, or not required for the purposes herein provided, the said managers are hereby authorized to make such disposal as they shall deem best suited for the promotion of the purpose of the testator, anything herein contained to the contrary notwithstanding.

Sec. 10. *And be it further enacted*, That the author or proprietor of any book, map, chart, musical composition, print, cut, or engraving, for which a copyright shall be secured under the existing acts of Congress, or those which shall hereafter be enacted respecting copyrights, shall, within three months from the publication of said book, map, chart, musical composition, print, cut, or engraving, deliver, or cause to be delivered, one copy of the same to the Librarian of the Smithsonian Institution, and one copy to the Librarian of Congress Library, for the use of the said libraries.

SEC. 11. *And be it further enacted,* That there is reserved to Congress the right of altering, amending, adding to, or repealing any of the provisions of this act: *Provided,* That no contract, or individual right, made or acquired under such provisions, shall be thereby divested or impaired.

Approved August 10, 1846.

Construction of the "act establishing the SMITHSONIAN INSTITUTION," *by* HON. J. MC PHERSON BERRIEN, *one of the Regents.*

It will be argued at the outset, that the fund ought to be so administered as to give the fullest effect to the purposes of the donor; that the government of the United States, as the depositary of his confidence, has power to determine the mode of administration, and that its determination, so far as it extends, must guide and control the action of the Board of Regents. Beyond that limit, I suppose it will also be conceded that the Board has discretionary powers, acting as it does, under the constant supervision of Congress, which body has reserved to itself the right of modifying its grant of power, *ad libitum,* with the ordinary saving of individual rights.

We are then to look to the act of Congress to ascertain what Congress has directed, and what it has left at large. The act of 1846 creates what it denominates "an establishment" with a corporate name, invested with the powers, and subjected to the limitations and restrictions specified in the act. It directs the selection of a lot, and the erection of a building, with suitable arrangements for the classification and arrangement of the several objects specified in the 6th section. It places that building and those objects under the control of the Board of Regents. It requires them to make, from the interest of the fund, an appropriation *not exceeding* $25,000 annually, for the gradual formation of a library. Out of any other interest, moneys accrued or accruing, not therein appropriated, or not required for the purposes therein provided, the Board is authorized "to make such disposal as they shall deem best suited for the *promotion of the purpose of the testator*, anything therein contained to the contrary notwithstanding."

In my opinion, this places the whole income of the fund under the control of the Board of Regents. They must erect a building, suitably arranged to fulfil the purposes of Congress, but its cost is not limited. They must appoint a Secretary, but his salary is not specified. They must make an appropriation for the gradual formation of a library, of which the *maximum* only is provided, and then of all other moneys, accruing as interest, they may make such disposal as *they* shall *deem* best suited to promote the purposes of the donor; any former provision to the contrary notwithstanding.

Whether in the exercise of this discretionary power, the Board ought to look mainly to the gradual formation of a *library*, to the exclusion of other objects which they may deem better calculated to promote the purpose of Mr. Smithson, is a question which may be considered in a two-fold view.

We may inquire, 1. Whether there is anything in the act of Congress which requires this preference? I confine the inquiry to the *act itself*, and exclude the *expressed opinions of individuals* who participated in its enactment, as well as the *votes* of the two Houses *upon particular propositions* submitted while it was under discussion; the *first*, because it is *the act*, which *alone* expresses the *will* of the legislature, in the enactment of which different individuals may have concurred for very different reasons; the *second*, because a rejected proposition may have been voted down, not because it was deemed unwise or improper, but because it was considered unnecessary and superfluous; at all events, of those who reject it some may have been influenced by the former, and others by the latter consideration. The proceedings on this bill will help to illustrate this. The bill reported by the committee contained various specific provisions, as for a library, scientific collections, publications, &c., &c., &c. These were stricken out. Why? Because they were deemed inexpedient or improper? No; but because, since the act specified no amount which the Board was required to expend for a library, and left all the other accruing income, besides that which they determined to apply to this object, subject to their entire control, it would have been simply superfluous, as they were provided for by this general grant of power. I see nothing, therefore, in *the act of Congress* which requires the Board to give this preference to a library, to the exclusion of any other objects which they may deem more consonant to the purposes of the donor.

The remaining question is, 2. Have they erred in the exercise of the discretion confided to them? I think not. The purpose of the testator was two-fold.

The *increase* of knowledge *among men*.

Its *diffusion among men*.

It was not to enable the few persons who could have access to a library at Washington to master the knowledge *already existing* among men, but to *increase* the *sum* of that knowledge, and to give it a *world wide diffusion*. The first object might be attained by a library at Washington sufficiently comprehensive to embrace what is *now known* among men. The last can only be accomplished by the *labors of scientific men*, and their *diffusion* by the Board *throughout the civilized world*. But this subject is so well and thoroughly discussed by the committee, that I leave it with the simple expression of my entire concurrence in the reasoning and conclusion of their report. One other remark. Looking to the limited amount of the income, and to the expenditures, which Congress must have foreseen, I find it impossible to suppose that they could have contemplated any considerable expenditure for the library, since in thus providing for the acquirement by a *limited* portion of *our own people* of such knowledge as men *have hitherto attained*, they would have precluded all efforts for *its increase* and *diffu-*

sion throughout the world, and have thus defeated what seems to me to have been the most cherished wish of Mr. Smithson.

The only *official agents* provided by the acts of Congress are those specified in the third section, namely, the Board of Regents, the Chancellor, and the Executive Committee. By these it requires "the business of the said Institution to be conducted." Proceeding to define the duties of the *Secretary*, it constitutes him "librarian and keeper of the museum," charges him with the care of "the building and property of the Institution," and requires him, under the direction of the Board of Regents, "to make a fair and accurate statement of all their proceedings." Having thus traversed the whole circle of official duties, and aware that those assigned to the Secretary might become too onerous for a single individual, it authorized *him*, with the assent of the Board of Regents, to "employ assistants;" but such persons were, strictly speaking, not officers of *the Institution*, but, in the language of the act, *employés of the secretary*, or as the act expresses it, his "*assistants*," and in this sense only can the term "officers," used in the 7th section, when speaking of their liability to removal by the Board of Regents, be understood. The subordinate officers of the customs furnish a somewhat analogous case. They are appointed by the collector with the approbation of the Secretary of the Treasury. Now, the Secretary, as the official organ of the President, can remove both the collector and his subordinates, but this does not prevent the collector from removing them.

From what I have written, my opinion will be understood to be that the "assistants" *of the Secretary* are liable to removal by that officer and that such removal would be effective unless the Board, in the exercise of its controlling power over the Secretary, should think proper to interfere.

JOHN McPHERSON BERRIEN

Savannah, July, 1854.

Extract from an Address by the Secretary, on the Smithsonian Institution.

I propose answering in this lecture the following questions:

1. Who was James Smithson? and what was his character and pursuits?

2. What was his bequest? and what were its objects?

3. What plan has been adopted for carrying out the intention of the testator? and what fruit has this plan produced?

(1.) Smithson claimed to be of noble descent; and in his will declares himself the son of Hugh, first Duke of Northumberland, and of Elizabeth, niece of Charles the Proud, Duke of Somerset. He was educated at Oxford, and paid particular attention to the study of the physical sciences; was reputed to be the best chemist in the university, and was one of the first to adopt the method of minute analysis. As an example of his expertness in this line, it is mentioned that on one occasion he caught a tear as it was trickling down the face of a lady, lost half, examined the remainder, and discovered in it several salts. He made about thirty scientific communications to different societies, principally on chemistry, mineralogy, and geology. His scientific reputation was founded on these branches, though, from his writings, he appears to have studied and reflected upon almost every department of knowledge. He was of a sensitive, retiring disposition—passed most of his life on the Continent—was never married—appeared ambitious of making a name for himself, either by his own researches or by founding an institution for the promotion of science. He declares in writing, that though the best blood of England flows in his veins, this avails him not, for his name would live in the memory of men when the titles of the Northumberlands and the Percies are extinct or forgotten. He was cosmopolitan in his views, and declares that the man of science is of no country—the world is his country, and all men his countrymen. He purposed at one time to leave his money to the Royal Society of London for the promotion of science, but on account of a misunderstanding with the council of the society, he changed his mind and left it to his nephew; and, in case of the death of this relative, to the United States of America, to found the Institution which now bears his name.

(2.) In answer to the second question, I would state that the whole amount of money received from the bequest was $515,169; and besides this $25,000 was left in England, as the principal of an annuity given to the mother of the nephew of Smithson. This sum will also come to the Institution at the death of this person.

The government of the United States accepted the bequest, or, in other words, accepted the offiee of trustee, and Mr. Rush, of Pennsylvania, a gentleman who is still an active and efficient member of the Board of Regents, and one of the most ardent supporters of the Institution, was charged with the duty of prosecuting the claim. He remained in attendance on the English courts until the money was awarded to him. He brought it over in sovereigns—deposited it in the Mint of the United States, where it was re-coined into American eagles—thus becoming a part of the currency of the country. This money was afterwards lent to some of the new States, and a portion of it was lost; but it did not belong to the United States—it was the property of the Smithsonian Institution—and the government was bound in honor to restore it. Congress has acknowledged this by declaring that the money is still in the treasury of the nation, bearing interest at the rate of 6 per cent., annually producing a revenue of about thirty thousand dollars.

It may be stated in this place, that the principal remains perpetually in the treasury of the United States, and that nothing but the interest can be expended; not only has the original bequest been preserved, but a considerable addition has been made to the principal. At the time of the passing of the act establishing the Institution in 1846, the sum of $242,000 had accrued in interest, and this the Regents were authorized to expend on a building; but instead of appropriating this sum immediately to this purpose, they put it at interest, and deferred the completion of the building for several years, until $150,000 should be accumulated, the income of which might defray the expense of keeping the building, and the greater portion of the income of the original bequest be devoted to the objects for which it was designed. This policy has been rigidly adhered to, and the result is, that besides the original sum, and after all that has been devoted to the building, the grounds, and all other operations, there is now on hand $200,000 of accumulated interest. Of this sum $50,000 are to be appropriated to finishing the building, and the remainder is to be added to the principal. The funds have therefore been carefully husbanded.

The bequest, in the language of the testator, was, "*to found at Washington an establishment under the name of the Smithsonian Institution, for the increase and diffusion of knowledge among men.*"

According to this, the government of the United States is merely a trustee. The bequest is for the benefit of mankind, and any plan which does not recognise this provision of the will would be illiberal and unjust.

The Institution must bear and perpetuate the name of its founder; and hence its operations ought to be kept distinct from those of the government, and all the good which results from the expenditure of the fund should be accredited to the name of Smithson.

The object of the bequest is two-fold: first, to *increase;* and second, to *diffuse* knowledge among men. These two objects are entirely distinct, and ought not to be confounded with one another. The first is to enlarge the existing stock of knowledge by the addition of new truths; and the second to disseminate knowledge, thus enlarged, among men. The distinction is generally recognised by men of science, and in Europe different classes of scientific and other societies are founded upon it.

Again: the will makes no restriction in favor of any particular kind of knowledge, and hence all branches are entitled to a share of attention. Smithson was well aware that knowledge should not be viewed as existing in isolated parts, but as a whole, each portion of which throws light on all the other, and that the tendency of all is to improve the human mind, and to give it new sources of power and enjoyment. The most prevalent idea, however, in relation to the will, is that the money was intended exclusively for the diffusion of useful or immediately practical knowledge among the inhabitants of this country, but it contains nothing from which such an inference can be drawn. All knowledge is useful, and the higher the more important. From the enunciation of a single scientific truth may flow a hundred inventions, and the higher the truth the more important the deductions.

To effect the greatest good, the organization of the Institution should be such as to produce results which could not be attained by other means, and inasmuch as the bequest is for men in general, all merely local expenditures are violations of the will.

These views were not entertained at first, and great difficulties have been encountered in carrying them out. A number of literary men thought that a great library should be founded at Washington, and all the money expended on it. Others considered a museum the proper object, and another class thought the income should be devoted to the delivery of lectures throughout the country; while still another was of opinion that popular tracts should be published and distributed among the million. But all these views were advanced without a proper examination of the will, or a due consideration of the smallness of the income. The diffusion of tracts has been a favorite idea, but it must be recollected that a single report of the Patent Office costs the government three times as much as the whole income of the Smithsonian fund. A single pamphlet of ten pages could not annually be printed by the Institution, and distributed to all who would have a claim to it.

(3.) The next question is, by what plan can the several requisitions of the will be fulfilled.

This question was not fully settled by the act of Congress. It directed the formation of a Library, a Museum, a Gallery of Arts, Lectures, and a building on a liberal scale to accommodate these objects. One clause, however, gave the Regents the power, after the foregoing objects are provided for, to expend the remainder of the income in any way they may think fit for carrying out the design of the testator.

The objects specified in the act of Congress evidently does not come up to the idea of the testator, as deduced from a critical examination of his will. A library, a museum, a gallery of arts, though important in themselves, are local in their influence. I have from the beginning advocated this opinion on all occasions, and shall continue to advocate it whenever a suitable opportunity occurs.

The question, therefore, again recurs: what plan can be adopted in conformity with the terms of the bequest?

There are two. First—a number of men may be appointed by the Institution to make researches in the different branches of science, and to send accounts of their discoveries to all parts of the world. In this way, in the strictest sense of the terms, knowledge would be increased and diffused. But this plan is not compatible with the limited income of the Institution, and would offer many practical difficulties.

The other plan, and the one adopted, is to stimulate all persons in this country capable of advancing knowledge by original research, to labor in this line—to induce them to send the results to the Institution for examination and publication—and to assist all persons engaged in original investigations as far as the means of the Institution will allow; also to institute, at the expense and under the direction of the Institution, particular researches. This plan has been found eminently practicable, and by means of it the Institution has been enabled to produce results which have made it favorably known in every part of the civilized world. The communications are submitted to competent judges, who vouch for the value and truth of the discoveries. The publications which result from this plan are presented to all the first class libraries in the world; as well as to all colleges and well established public institutions in this country. The intention is to place the publications in such positions as will enable them to be seen by the greatest number of persons. In this way a knowledge of the discoveries are diffused among men as widely as the income will allow.

No copyright is taken for the memoirs, and the writers of popular books are at liberty to use them in the compilation of their works. The knowledge which they contain is thus in time still more generally diffused. In other countries, institutions for the promotion of the discovery of new truths, and the publication of the results, are endowed by the government; but there are no institutions for this purpose here, and hence men of science labor under great disadvantages. The higher the value of a work of science, the fewer do its readers become. If writers wish to make money by their labors, they must publish novels.

The Principia of Newton did not pay for itself, and yet in the present day every one shares in the benefits accruing from it.

Another part of the plan is to publish reports on scientific subjects, and to spread them as widely as the state of the funds will allow.

Note.—For an account of what has actually been accomplished, see the several reports of the Secretary.

REPORTS OF THE SECRETARY OF THE SMITHSONIAN INSTITUTION, FROM 1847 TO 1853.

To make the operations of the Institution more generally known, it has been thought advisable to append to this Report, for reprinting, the several Annual Reports of the Secretary. They give a connected history of all the operations of the Institution, from its organization to the end of the year 1852. These Reports exhibit the fact that very little change has been made in the plan of active operations originally adopted, and that all the anticipations which were entertained in regard to it have been fully realized.

FIRST REPORT.*

Report of the Secretary of the Smithsonian Institution to the Board of Regents, December 8, 1847.

GENTLEMEN: A statement of the financial condition of the Smithsonian Institution, and of the progress made in the erection of the building, having been presented to your Board by the Committees charged with the care of these objects, it becomes my duty, as Secretary of the Institution, to give an account of what has been done relative to the development of the plan of organization, and of the steps which have been taken in the way of carrying it into operation.

In accordance with my instructions, I consulted with men of eminence in the different branches of literature and science, relative to the details of the plan of organization, and arranged the various suggestions offered, in the form of the accompanying programme. This, after having been submitted to a number of persons in whose knowledge and judgment I have confidence, is now presented to the Board, with the concurrence of the Committee on Organization, for consideration and provisional adoption. I regret that my engagements have been such as to render it impossible for me to call upon many persons whose counsel would have been valuable, but I hope hereafter to avail myself of their advice in behalf of the Institution. I also regret that I could not give the names of those whose suggestions have been adopted in the programme; the impossibility of rendering justice to all, has prevented my attempting this. Many of the suggestions have been offered by different persons, independently of each other; and, indeed, the general plan of the increase and diffusion of knowledge, as adopted by the Board, is such as would naturally arise in the mind of any person conversant with the history of physical science, and with the means usually employed for its extension and diffusion.

The introduction to the programme contains a series of propositions, suggested by a critical examination of the will of Smithson, to serve as a guide in judging of the fitness of any proposed plan for carrying out the design of the testator. The first section of the programme gives the details of the plan proposed for the increase and diffusion of knowledge by means of publication and original researches. The second section furnishes the details, so far as they can be made out at the present time, of the formation of a library, and a collection of objects of nature and art. These two plans combined, embrace the general propositions adopted by the Board of Regents at their last meeting, as the basis of future operations. It is intended in the proposed plan to har-

* The first report of the Secretary was given in the second report of the Regents to Congress, hence the number of the former is one less than that of the latter.

monize the two modes of increasing and diffusing knowledge, and to give to the Institution the widest influence compatible with its limited income. That all the propositions will meet with general approval cannot be expected; and that this organization is the best that could be devised is neither asserted nor believed. To produce *a priori* a plan of organization which shall be found to succeed perfectly in practice, and require no amendment, would be difficult under the most favorable circumstances, and becomes almost impossible where conflicting opinions are to be harmonized, and the definite requirements of the act establishing the Institution are to be observed. It is not intended that the details of the organization, as given in the programme, should be permanently adopted without careful trial; they are rather presented as suggestions to be adopted provisionally, and to be carried into operation gradually and cautiously, with such changes, from time to time, as experience may dictate.

PROGRAMME OF ORGANIZATION OF THE SMITHSONIAN INSTITUTION.

[Presented to the Board of Regents, December 8, 1847.]

INTRODUCTION.

General considerations which should serve as a guide in adopting a plan of organization.

1. WILL OF SMITHSON. The property is bequeathed to the United States of America, "to found at Washington, under the name of the Smithsonian Institution, an establishment for the increase and diffusion of knowledge among men."

2. The bequest is for the benefit of mankind. The government of the United States is merely a trustee to carry out the design of the testator.

3. The Institution is not a national establishment, as is frequently supposed, but the establishment of an individual, and is to bear and perpetuate his name.

4. The objects of the Institution are—1st, to increase, and 2d, to diffuse, knowledge among men.

5. These two objects should not be confounded with one another. The first is to increase the existing stock of knowledge by the addition of new truths; and the second to disseminate knowledge, thus increased, among men.

6. The will makes no restriction in favor of any particular kind of knowledge; hence all branches are entitled to a share of attention.

7. Knowledge can be increased by different methods of facilitating and promoting the discovery of new truths, and can be most efficiently diffused among men by means of the press.

8. To effect the greatest amount of good, the organization should be such as to enable the Institution to produce results in the way of increasing and diffusing knowledge, which cannot be produced by the existing institutions in our country.

9. The organization should also be such as can be adopted provisionally, can be easily reduced to practice, receive modifications, or be abandoned, in whole or in part, without a sacrifice of the funds.

10. In order to make up for the loss of time occasioned by the delay of eight years in establishing the Institution, a considerable portion of the interest which has accrued should be added to the principal.

11. In proportion to the wide field of knowledge to be cultivated, the funds are small. Economy should therefore be consulted in the construction of the building; and not only should the first cost of the edifice be considered, but also the continual expense of keeping it in repair, and of the support of the establishment necessarily connected with it. There should also be but few individuals permanently supported by the Institution.

12. The plan and dimensions of the building should be determined by the plan of the organization, and not the converse.

13. It should be recollected that mankind in general are to be benefited by the bequest, and that, therefore, all unnecessary expenditure on local objects would be a perversion of the trust.

14. Besides the foregoing considerations, deduced immediately from the will of Smithson, regard must be had to certain requirements of the act of Congress establishing the Institution. These are a library, a museum, and a gallery of art, with a building on a liberal scale to contain them.

SECTION I.

Plan of organization of the Institution, in accordance with the foregoing deductions from the will of Smithson.

To Increase Knowledge. It is proposed—

1. To stimulate men of talent to make original researches, by offering suitable rewards for memoirs containing new truths; and,

2. To appropriate annually a portion of the income for particular researches, under the direction of suitable persons.

To Diffuse Knowledge. It is proposed—

1. To publish a series of periodical reports on the progress of the different branches of knowledge; and,

2. To publish occasionally separate treatises on subjects of general interest.

DETAILS OF THE PLAN TO INCREASE KNOWLEDGE.

I. *By stimulating researches.*

1. Rewards, consisting of money, medals, &c., offered for original memoirs on all branches of knowledge.

2. The memoirs thus obtained to be published in a series of volumes, in a quarto form, and entitled "Smithsonian Contributions to Knowledge."

3. No memoir, on subjects of physical science, to be accepted for publication, which does not furnish a positive addition to human knowledge resting on original research; and all unverified speculations to be rejected.

4. Each memoir presented to the Institution to be submitted for examination to a commission of persons of reputation for learning in the

branch to which the memoir pertains, and to be accepted for publication only in case the report of this commission is favorable.

5. The commission to be chosen by the officers of the Institution, and the name of the author, as far as practicable, concealed, unless a favorable decision be made.

6. The volumes of the memoirs to be exchanged for the transactions of literary and scientific societies, and copies to be given to all the colleges and principal libraries in this country. One part of the remaining copies may be offered for sale; and the other carefully preserved, to form complete sets of the volumes, to supply the demand from new institutions.

7. An abstract, or popular account, of the contents of these memoirs to be given to the public, through the annual report of the Regents to Congress.

II. *By appropriating a portion of the income, annually, to special objects of research, under the direction of suitable persons.*

1. The objects, and the amount appropriated, to be recommended by counsellors of the Institution.

2. Appropriations in different years to different objects; so that, in course of time, each branch of knowledge may receive a share.

3. The results obtained from these appropriations to be published, with the memoirs before mentioned, in the volumes of the Smithsonian Contributions to Knowledge.

4. Examples of objects for which appropriations may be made:

(1.) System of extended meteorological observations, for solving the problem of American storms.

(2.) Explorations in descriptive natural history, and geological, magnetical, and topographical surveys, to collect materials for the formation of a Physical Atlas of the United States.

(3.) Solution of experimental problems, such as a new determination of the weight of the earth, of the velocity of electricity and of light; chemical analyses of soils and plants; collection and publication of articles of science, accumulated in the offices of government.

(4.) Institution of statistical inquiries with reference to physical, moral, and political subjects.

(5.) Historical researches, and accurate surveys of places celebrated in American history.

(6.) Ethnological researches, particularly with reference to the different races of men in North America; also, explorations and accurate surveys of the mounds and other remains of the ancient people of our country.

DETAILS OF THE PLAN FOR DIFFUSING KNOWLEDGE.

I. *By the publication of a series of reports, giving an account of the new discoveries in science, and of the changes made from year to year in all branches of knowledge not strictly professional.*

1. These reports will diffuse a kind of knowledge generally interesting, but which, at present, is inaccessible to the public. Some of the

reports may be published annually, others at longer intervals, as the income of the Institution, or the changes in the branches of knowledge, may indicate.

2. The reports are to be prepared by collaborators eminent in the different branches of knowledge.

3. Each collaborator to be furnished with the journals and publications, domestic and foreign, necessary to the compilation of his report; to be paid a certain sum for his labors, and to be named on the title page of the report.

4. The reports to be published in separate parts, so that persons interested in a particular branch can procure the parts relating to it, without purchasing the whole.

5. These reports may be presented to Congress, for partial distribution; the remaining copies to be given to literary and scientific institutions, and sold to individuals for a moderate price.

The following are some of the subjects which may be embraced in the reports:

I. PHYSICAL CLASS.

1. Physics, including astronomy, natural philosophy, chemistry, and meteorology.
2. Natural history, including botany, zoology, geology, &c.
3. Agriculture.
4. Application of science to arts.

II. MORAL AND POLITICAL CLASS.

5. Ethnology, including particular history, comparative philology, antiquities, &c.
6. Statistics and political economy.
7. Mental and moral philosophy.
8. A survey of the political events of the world; penal reform, &c.

III. LITERATURE AND THE FINE ARTS.

9. Modern literature.
10. The fine arts, and their application to the useful arts.
11. Bibliography.
12. Obituary notices of distinguished individuals.

II. *By the publication of separate treatises on subjects of general interest.*

1. These treatises may occasionally consist of valuable memoirs translated from foreign languages, or of articles prepared under the direction of the Institution, or procured by offering premiums for the best exposition of a given subject.

2. The treatises should in all cases be submitted to a commission of competent judges previous to their publication.

3. As examples of these treatises, expositions may be obtained of the present state of the several branches of knowledge mentioned in the table of reports. Also of the following subjects, suggested by the Com-

mittee on Organization, viz.: the statistics of labor, the productive arts of life, public instruction, &c.

SECTION II.

Plan of organization, in accordance with the terms of the resolutions of the Board of Regents, providing for the two modes of increasing and diffusing knowledge.

1. The act of Congress establishing the Institution contemplated the formation of a library and a museum; and the Board of Regents, including these objects in the plan of organization, resolved to divide the income into two equal parts.

2. One part to be appropriated to increase and diffuse knowledge by means of publications and researches, agreeably to the scheme before given. The other part to be appropriated to the formation of a library and a collection of objects of nature and of art.

3. These two plans are not incompatible with one another.

4. To carry out the plan before described, a library will be required, consisting, 1st, of a complete collection of the transactions and proceedings of all the learned societies in the world; 2d, of the more important current periodical publications, and other works necessary in preparing the periodical reports.

5. The Institution should make special collections, particularly of objects to verify its own publications.

6. Also a collection of instruments of research in all branches of experimental science.

7. With reference to the collection of books other than those mentioned above, catalogues of all the different libraries in the United States should be procured, in order that the valuable books first purchased may be such as are not to be found in the United States.

8. Also catalogues of memoirs, and of books in foreign libraries, and other materials, should be collected for rendering the Institution a centre of bibliographical knowledge, whence the student may be directed to any work which he may require.

9. It is believed that the collections in Natural History will increase by donation, as rapidly as the income of the Institution can make provision for their reception; and therefore it will seldom be necessary to purchase any articles of this kind.

10. Attempts should be made to procure for the Gallery of Arts casts of the most celebrated articles of ancient and modern sculpture.

11. The arts may be encouraged by providing a room, free of expense, for the exhibition of the objects of the Art-Union, and other similar societies.

12. A small appropriation should annually be made for models of antiquities, such as those of the remains of ancient temples, &c.

13. For the present, or until the building is fully completed, besides the Secretary, no permanent assistant will be required, except one, to act as Librarian.

14. The duty of the Secretary will be the general superintendence with the advice of the Chancellor and other members of the establish

ment, of the literary and scientific operations of the Institution; to give to the Regents annually an account of all the transactions, of the memoirs which have been received for publication, and of the researches which have been made; and to edit, with the assistance of the Librarian, the publications of the Institution.

15. The duty of the Assistant Secretary, acting as Librarian, will be, for the present, to assist in taking charge of the collections, to select and purchase, under the direction of the Secretary and a committee of the Board, books and catalogues, and to procure the information before mentioned; to give information on plans of libraries, and to assist the Secretary in editing the publications of the Institution, and in the other duties of his offiee.

16. The Secretary and his assistants, during the session of Congress, will be required to illustrate new discoveries in sciences, and to exhibit new objects of art; also distinguished individuals should be invited to give lectures on subjects of general interest.

17. When the building is completed, and when, in accordance with the act of Congress, the charge of the National Museum is given to the Smithsonian Institution, other assistants will be required.

Explanations and illustrations of the programme.

Though the leading propositions of the programme have been fully discussed by the Board, yet it will be important to offer some remarks in explanation and illustration of them in their present connexion.

That the Institution is not a national establishment, in the sense in which institutions dependent on the government for support are so, must be evident, when it is recollected that the money was not absolutely given to the United States, but intrusted to it for a special object, namely: the establishment of an institution for the benefit of men, to bear the name of the donor, and, consequently, to reflect upon his memory the honor of all the good which may be accomplished by means of the bequest. The operations of the Smithsonian Institution ought, therefore, to be mingled as little as possible with those of the government, and its funds should be applied exclusively and faithfully to the increase and diffusion of knowledge among men.

That the bequest is intended for the benefit of men in general, and that its influence ought not to be restricted to a single district, or even nation, may be inferred not only from the words of the will, but also from the character of Smithson himself; and I beg leave to quote, from a scrap of paper in his own hand, the following sentiment bearing on this point: "The man of science has no country; the world is his country—all men his countrymen." The origin of the funds, the bequest of a foreigner, should also preclude the adoption of a plan which does not, in the words of Mr. Adams, "spread the benefits to be derived from the Institution not only over the whole surface of this Union, but throughout the civilized world." "Mr. Smithson's reason for fixing the seat of his Institution at Washington obviously was, that *there* is the seat of government of the United States, and *there* the Congress by whose legislation, and the Executive through whose agency, the trust committed to the honor, intelligence, and good faith of the nation, is to be fulfilled." The centre of operations being permanently fixed at Washington, the character of this city for literature and science will be the more highly exalted in proportion as the influence of the Institution is more widely diffused.

That the terms *increase* and *diffusion* of knowledge are logically distinct, and should be literally interpreted with reference to the will, must be evident when we reflect that they are used in a definite sense, and not as mere synonymes, by all who are engaged in the pursuits to which Smithson devoted his life. In England there are two classes of institutions, founded on the two ideas conveyed by these terms. The Royal Society, the Astronomical, the Geological, the Statistical, the Antiquarian Societies, all have for their object the increase of knowledge, while the London Institution, the Mechanics' Institution, the Surry Institution, the Society for the Diffusion of Religious Knowledge, the Society for the Diffusion of Useful Knowledge, are all intended to diffuse or disseminate knowledge among men. In our own country, also, the same distinction is observed in the use of the terms by men of science. Our colleges, academies, and common schools, are recognised as institutions partially intended for the diffusion of knowledge, while the express object of some of our scientific societies is the promotion of the discovery of new truths.

The will makes no restriction in favor of any particular kind of knowledge; though propositions have been frequently made for devoting the funds exclusively to the promotion of certain branches of science having more immediate application to the practical arts of life, and the adoption of these propositions has been urged on the ground of the conformity of such objects to the pursuits of Smithson: but an examination of his writings will show that he excluded from his own studies no branch of general knowledge, and that he was fully impressed with the important philosophical fact, that all subjects of human thought relate to one great system of truth. To restrict, therefore, the operations of the Institution to a single science or art, would do injustice to the character of the donor, as well as to the cause of general knowledge. If preference is to be given to any branches of research, it should be to the higher, and apparently more abstract; to the discovery of new principles, rather than of isolated facts. And this is true even in a practical point of view. Agriculture would have forever remained an empirical art, had it not been for the light shed upon it by the atomic theory of chemistry; and incomparably more is to be expected as to its future advancement from the perfection of the microscope, than from improvements in the ordinary instruments of husbandry.

The plan of increasing and diffusing knowledge, presented in the first section of the programme, will be found in strict accordance with the several propositions deduced from the will of Smithson, and given in the Introduction. It embraces, as a leading feature, the design of interesting the greatest number of individuals in the operations of the Institution, and of spreading its influence as widely as possible. It forms an active organization, exciting all to make original researches who are gifted with the necessary power, and diffusing a kind of knowledge, now only accessible to the few, among all those who are willing to receive it. In this country, though many excel in the application of science to the practical arts of life, few devote themselves to the continued labor and patient thought necessary to the discovery and developement of new truths. The principal cause of this want of attention to original research is the want, not of proper means, but of proper encouragement. The publication of original memoirs and periodical reports, as contemplated by the programme, will act as a powerful stimulus on the latent talent of our country, by placing in bold relief the real laborers in the field of original research, while it will afford the best materials for the use of those engaged in the diffusion of knowledge.

The advantages which will accrue from the plan of publishing the volumes of the Smithsonian Contributions to Knowledge are various. In the first place, it will serve to render the name of the founder favorably known wherever literature and science are cultivated, and to keep it in continual remembrance with each succeeding volume, as long as knowledge is valued. A single new truth, first given to the world through these volumes, will forever stamp their character as a work of reference. The Contributions will thus form the most befitting monument to perpetuate the name of one whose life was devoted to the increase of knowledge, and whose ruling passion, strong in death, prompted the noble bequest intended to facilitate the labors of others in the same pursuit.

Again, the publication of a series of volumes of original memoirs will afford to the Institution the most ready means of entering into friendly relations and correspondence with all the learned societies in the world, and of enriching its library with their current transactions and proceedings. But perhaps the most important effect of the plan will be that of giving to the world many valuable memoirs, which, on account of the expense of the illustrations, could not be otherwise published. Every one who adds new and important truths to the existing stock of knowledge, must be, of necessity, to a certain degree, in advance of his age. Hence the number of readers and purchasers of a work is often in the inverse ratio of its intrinsic value; and consequently, authors of the highest rank of merit are frequently deterred from giving their productions to the world on account of the pecuniary loss to which the publication would subject them. When our lamented countryman, Bowditch, contemplated publishing his commentary on La Place, he assembled his family and informed them that the execution of this design would sacrifice one third of his fortune, and that it was proper his heirs should be consulted on a subject which so nearly concerned them. The answer was worthy of the children of such a father: "We value," said they, "your reputation more than your money." Fortunately, in this instance, the means of making such a sacrifice existed; otherwise one of the proudest monuments of American science could not have been given to the world. In the majority of cases, however, those who are most capable of extending human knowledge are least able to incur the expense of the publication. Wilson, the American ornithologist, states, in a letter to Michaux, that he has sacrificed everything to publish his work: "I have issued," he says, "six volumes, and am engaged on the seventh; but as yet I have not received a single cent of the proceeds." In an address on the subject of natural history, by one of our most active cultivators of this branch of knowledge, we find the following remarks, which are directly in point: "Few are acquainted with the fact that from the small number of scientific works sold, and the great expense of plates, our naturalists not only are not paid for their labors, but suffer pecuniary loss from their publications. Several works on different branches of zoology, now in the course of publication, will leave their authors losers by an aggregate of $15,000. I do not include in this estimate works already finished—one, for instance, the best contribution to the natural history of man extant, the publication of which will occasion its accomplished author a loss of several thousand dollars. A naturalist is extremely fortunate if he can dispose of 200 copies of an illustrated work, and the number of copies printed rarely exceeds 250." It may be said that these authors have their reward in the reputation which they thus purchase; but reputation should be the result of the talents and labor expended in the production of a work, and should not in the least depend upon the fact that the author is able to make a pecuniary sacrifice in giving the account of his discoveries to the public.

Besides the advantage to the author of having his memoir published in the Smithsonian Contributions free of expense, his labors will be given to the world with the stamp of approval of a commission of learned men; and his merits will be generally made known through the reports of the Institution. Though the premiums offered may be small, yet they will have considerable effect in producing original articles. Fifty or a hundred dollars awarded to the author of an original paper, will, in many instances, suffice to supply the books, or to pay for the materials, or the manual labor required, in prosecuting the research.

There is one proposition of the programme which has given rise to much discussion, and which, therefore, requires particular explanation: I allude to that which excludes from the contributions all papers consisting merely of unverified speculations on subjects of physical science. The object of this proposition is to obviate the endless difficulties which would occur in rejecting papers of an unphilosophical character; and though it may in some cases exclude an interesting communication, yet the strict observance of it will be found of so much practical importance that it cannot be dispensed with. It has been supposed, from the adoption of this proposition, that we are disposed to undervalue abstract speculations: on the contrary, we know that all the advances in true science—namely, a knowledge of the laws of phenomena, are made by provisionally adopting well conditioned hypotheses, the product of the imagination, and subsequently verifying them by an appeal to experiment and observation. Every new hypothesis of scientific value must not only furnish an exact explanation of known facts, but must also enable us to predict, in kind and quantity, the phenomena which will be exhibited under any given combination of circumstances. Thus, in the case of the undulatory hypothesis of light, it was inferred, as a logical consequence, that if the supposition were true that light consisted of waves of an ethereal medium, then two rays of light, like two waves of water under certain conditions, should annihilate each other, and darkness be produced.

The experiment was tried, and the anticipated result was obtained. It is this exact agreement of the deduction with the actual result of experience that constitutes the verification of an hypothesis, and which alone entitles it to the name of a theory, and to a place in the transactions of a scientific institution. It must be recollected that it is much easier to speculate than to investigate, and that very few of all the hypotheses imagined are capable of standing the test of scientific verification.

For the practical working of the plan for obtaining the character of a memoir, and the precaution taken before it is accepted for publication, I would refer to the correspondence, given in a subsequent part of this report, relative to the memoir now in process of publication by the Institution. As it is not our intention to interfere with the proceedings of other institutions, but to co-operate with them, so far as our respective operations are compatible, communications may be referred to learned societies for inspection, as in the case of the above mentioned memoir, and abstracts of them given to the world through the bulletins of these societies, while the details of the memoirs and their expensive illustrations are published in the volumes of the Smithsonian Contributions. The officers of several learned societies in this country have expressed a willingness to co-operate in this way.

Since original research is the most direct way of increasing knowledge, it can scarcely be doubted that a part of the income of the bequest should be appropriated to this purpose, provided suitable persons can be found, and their labors be directed to proper objects. The number, however, of those who are capable of discovering scientific principles is comparatively small; like the poet, they are "born, not made," and, like him, must be left to choose their own subject, and wait the fitting time of inspiration. In case a person of this class has fallen on a vein of discovery, and is pursuing it with success, the better plan will be to grant him a small sum of money to carry on his investigations, provided they are considered worthy of assistance by competent judges. This will have the double effect of encouraging him in the pursuit, and of facilitating his progress. The Institution, however, need not depend upon cases of this kind, even if they were more numerous than they are, for the application of its funds in the line of original research. There are large fields of observation and experiment, the cultivation of which, though it may afford no prospect of the discovery of a principle, can hardly fail to produce results of importance both in a practical and theoretic point of view. As an illustration of this remark, I may mention the case of the investigations made a few years ago by a committee of the Franklin Institute, of Philadelphia. The Secretary of the Treasury of the United States placed at the disposal of this society a sum of money, for the purpose of making experiments with reference to the cause of the explosion of steam boilers. A committee of the society was chosen for this purpose, which adopted the ingenious plan of writing to all persons in the United States engaged in the application of steam, and particularly to those who had observed the explosion of a steam boiler. In this way opinions and suggestions in great variety, as to the cause of explosions, were obtained. The most plausible of these were submitted to the test of experiment: the results obtained were highly important, and are to be found favorably mentioned in every systematic work on the subject of steam which has appeared, in any language, within the last few years. New and important facts were established; and, what was almost of as much consequence, errors which had usurped the place of truth were dethroned.

In the programme, examples are given of a few subjects of original research to which the attention of the Institution may be turned. I will mention one in this place, which, in connexion with the contents of our first memoir, may deserve immediate attention. I allude to a small appropriation made annually for researches with reference to the remains of the ancient inhabitants of our country. This is a highly interesting field, and what is done in regard to it should be done quickly. Every year the progress of civilization is obliterating the ancient mounds, cities and villages are rising on the spots they have so long occupied undisturbed, and the distinctive marks of these remains are every year becoming less and less legible.

In carrying out the spirit of the plan adopted, namely, that of affecting men in general by the operations of the Institution, it is evident that the principal means of diffusing knowledge must be the *press*. Though lectures should be given in the city in which Smithson has seen fit to direct the establishment of his Institution, yet, as a plan of general diffusion of knowledge, the system of lectures would be entirely inadequate; every village in our extended country would have a right to demand a share of the benefit, and the income of the Institution would be insufficient to supply a thousandth part of the demand. It is also evident that the knowledge diffused should, if possible, not only embrace all branches of general interest, so that each reader might find a subject suited to his taste, but also that it should differ in kind and quality from that which can be readily obtained through the cheap publications of the day. These requisites will be fully complied with in the publications of the series of reports proposed in the programme. A series of periodicals of this kind, posting up all the discoveries in science from time to time, and giving a well digested account of all the important changes in the different branches of knowledge, is a desideratum in the English language. The idea is borrowed from a partial plan of this kind in operation in Sweden and Germany; and for an example of what the work should be, I would refer to the annual report to the Swedish Academy of its perpetual secretary, Berzelius, on physical science. The reports can be so prepared as to be highly interesting to the general reader, and at the same time of great importance to the exclusive cultivator of a particular branch of knowledge. Full references should be given, in foot-notes, to the page, number, or volume of the work from which the information was obtained, and where a more detailed account can be found. It is scarcely necessary to remark, that the preparation of these reports should be entrusted only to persons profoundly acquainted with the subjects to which they relate, namely: to those who are devoted to particular branches, while they possess a knowledge of general principles. Sufficient explanations should be introduced to render the report intelligible to the general reader, without destroying its scientific character. Occasionally reports may be obtained from abroad—as, for example, accounts of the progress of certain branches of knowledge in foreign countries—and these may be translated, if necessary, and incorporated into other reports, by some competent person in this country.

Besides the reports on the progress of knowledge, the programme proposes to publish occasionally brief treatises on particular subjects. There are always subjects of general interest, of which brief expositions would be of much value. The preparation of these, however, should be intrusted to none but persons of character and reputation, and should be subjected to a revision by competent and responsible judges before they are given to the public. They may be presented in the form of reports on the existing state of knowledge relative to a given subject, and may sometimes consist of memoirs and expositions of particular branches of literature and science, translated from foreign languages. The reports and treatises of the Institution, sold at a price barely sufficient to pay the expense of printing, will find their way into every school in our country, and will be used not as first lessons for the pupil, but as sources of reliable information for the teacher.

The second section of the programme gives, so far as they have been made out, the details of the part of the plan of organization directed by the act of Congress establishing the Institution. The two plans, namely, that of publication and original research, and that of collections of objects of nature and art, are not incompatible, and may be carried on harmoniously with each other. The only effect which they will have on one another is that of limiting the operation of each, on account of the funds given to the other. Still, with a judicious application, and an economical expenditure of the income, and particularly by rigidly observing the plan of finance suggested by Dr. Bache, in the construction of the building, much good may be effected in each of the two branches of the Institution. To carry on the operations of the first, a working library will be required, consisting of the past volumes of the transactions and proceedings of all the learned societies in every language. These are the original sources from which the most important principles of the positive knowledge of our day have been drawn. We shall also require a collection of the most important current literature and science for the use of the collaborators of the reports; most of these, however, will be procured in exchange for the publications of the Institution, and therefore will draw but little from the library fund. For other suggestions relative to the details of the library, I would refer you to the annexed communication from Professor Jewett, Assistant Secretary, acting as librarian.

The collections of the Institution, as far as possible, should consist of such articles as are not elsewhere to be found in this country, so that the visitors at Washington may see new objects, and the spirit of the plan be kept up, of interesting the greatest possible number of individuals. A perfect collection of all objects of nature and of art, if such could be obtained and deposited in one place, would form a museum of the highest interest; but the portion of the income of the bequest which can be devoted to the increase and maintenance of the museum will be too small to warrant any attempt towards an indiscriminate collection. It is hoped that in due time other means may be found of establishing and supporting a general collection of objects of nature and art at the seat of the general government, with funds not derived from the Smithsonian bequest. For the present, it should be the object of the Institution to confine the application of the funds, first, to such collections as will tend to facilitate the study of the memoirs which may be published in the Contributions, and to establish their correctness; secondly, to the purchase of such objects as are not generally known in this country, in the way of art, and the illustration of antiquities, such as models of buildings, &c.; and, thirdly, to the formation of a collection of instruments of physical research, which will be required both in the illustration of new physical truths, and in the scientific investigations undertaken by the Institution.

Much popular interest may be awakened in favor of the Institution at Washington, by throwing the rooms of the building open, on stated evenings during the session of Congress, for literary and scientific assemblies, after the manner of the weekly meetings of the Royal Institution in London. At these meetings, without the formality of a regular lecture, new truths in science may be illustrated, and new objects of art exhibited. Besides these, courses of lectures may be given on particular subjects by the officers of the Institution, or by distinguished individuals invited for the purpose.

Commencement of the operations of the Institution.

I was authorized, in connexion with the Committee on Organization, to commence the publication of the Smithsonian Contributions to Knowledge, and to receive any memoir which might be presented on any subject, provided it was found, on examination, to furnish an interesting addition to the sum of human knowledge, resting on original research. The first memoir presented, and found to be of the character prescribed by the resolution of the Board, was one on the remains of the ancient inhabitants of the North American continent. It contains the result of several years' labor in the survey and exploration of the mounds and earthworks of the Mississippi valley, and will furnish a highly interesting addition to the antiquities of our country, which could not have been given to the world but for the timely aid extended to it by this Institution. The memoir was referred to the American Ethnological Society, with a request that a committee of its members might be appointed to examine and report on its character, as to fitness for publication in the Smithsonian Contributions to Knowledge. On the favorable report of this committee, and on the responsibility of the society, the memoir has been accepted for publication. The following correspondence will serve to give an account of the work, and to illustrate the manner in which it is proposed to submit the papers which may be presented for publication to a commission of competent judges.

CORRESPONDENCE RELATIVE TO THE ACCEPTANCE FOR PUBLICATION OF THE ETHNOLOGICAL MEMOIR OF MESSRS. SQUIER AND DAVIS.

From Messrs. Squier and Davis to the Secretary of the Smithsonian Institution.

CHILLICOTHE, O., *May* 15, 1847.

DEAR SIR: It is proposed in the recognised plan of organization of the Smithsonian Institution, of which you are the executive officer, to publish, under the title of "*Smithsonian Contributions to Knowledge*," such original papers and memoirs "as shall constitute valuable additions to the sum of human knowledge." Under the belief that it falls legitimately within the scope of the above plan, the undersigned herewith submit for acceptance and publication, subject to the prescribed rules of the Institution, a MS. memoir, entitled, "ANCIENT MONUMENTS OF THE MISSISSIPPI VALLEY, *comprising the results of Extensive Original Surveys and Explorations:* by E. G. SQUIER and E. H. DAVIS." The extent of these investigations, and their general character, are sufficiently indicated in the prefatory remarks to the volume.

With high consideration, we are truly yours,

E. GEO. SQUIER,
E. H. DAVIS.

JOSEPH HENRY, Esq.,
Secretary Smithsonian Institution.

From the Secretary of the Smithsonian Institution to the President of the American Ethnological Society.

WASHINGTON, *June* 2, 1847.

DEAR SIR: I am authorized by the Regents of the Smithsonian Institution to publish, in the numbers of the "*Smithsonian Contributions to Knowledge*," any memoir which may be presented for this purpose, provided that, on careful examination by a commission of competent judges, the memoir shall be found to furnish a new and interesting addition to knowledge, resting on original research. The accompanying memoir, entitled "*Ancient Monuments of the Mississippi Valley*," *&c.*, having been presented for publication, I beg leave to refer the same, through you, to the American Ethnological Society, with a request that a committee of the members may be appointed to examine and report on its character, in reference to the particulars above mentioned. If the report of the committee is favorable, the memoir will be accepted for publication; full confidence being placed in the ability of the committee to judge of the character of the article, and in their caution in making up their opinion.

I have the honor to be, very respectfully, your obedient servant,

JOSEPH HENRY,
Secretary Smithsonian Institution.

Hon. ALBERT GALLATIN,
President American Ethnological Society.

Extracts of a letter from the President of the American Ethnological Society to the Secretary of the Smithsonian Institution.

NEW YORK, *June* 12, 1847.

"DEAR SIR: I have the honor to enclose a copy of the proceedings and resolutions of the New York Ethnological Society upon the MS. work on American antiquities, by Messrs. E. G. Squier and E. H. Davis, submitted with your letter of the 2d inst.

"I approve entirely of the resolutions and recommendations of the society.

* * * * * * * * * * *

"Whatever may be the intrinsic value of the remains of former times which are found in the United States, it is necessary that they should at least be correctly described, and that existing gross errors should be corrected; and I repeat my conviction that, though ardent, Messrs. Squier and Davis are animated by that thorough love of truth which renders their researches worthy of entire confidence.

* * * * * * * * * * *

"I have the honor to be, &c.,

"ALBERT GALLATIN.

"Prof. J. HENRY,

"*Secretary of Smithsonian Institution.*"

At a regular meeting of the American Ethnological Society, held at the house of the Hon. ALBERT GALLATIN, on the evening of the 4th of June, the president laid before the members a communication from Professor J. HENRY, Secretary of the Smithsonian Institution, transmitting, for the examination and opinion of the society, a MS. work on the Ancient Aboriginal Monuments of the United States. On motion, the letter and accompanying MS. were referred to a committee consisting of EDWARD ROBINSON, D. D., JOHN R. BARTLETT, Professor W. W. TURNER, SAMUEL G. MORTON, M. D., and Hon GEORGE P. MARSH, to report upon the same. At a subsequent meeting of the society, this committee submitted the following report and resolutions, which were unanimously accepted and adopted:

REPORT.

The committee of the American Ethnological Society, to which was referred the communication of the Secretary of the Smithsonian Institution, transmitting a manuscript work, entitled "ANCIENT MONUMENTS OF THE MISSISSIPPI VALLEY, *comprising the results of Extensive Original Surveys and Explorations,*" by E. G. SQUIER and E. H. DAVIS, beg leave to report that:

They have examined the work in question, and regard it not only as a new and interesting, but as an eminently valuable addition to our stock of knowledge on a subject little understood, but in which is felt a deep and constantly increasing interest, both in our country and abroad. In their judgment, the work is worthy of the subject, and highly creditable to the authors. Its chief features are, a scientific arrangement, simplicity, and directness of statement, and legitimate deduction from facts, while there is no attempt at mere speculation or theory. If published, it will be an enduring monument to connect the names of the investigators in honorable and lasting remembrance with the great subject of American Archæology.

The existence and progress of these investigations were made known to the society by correspondence early in the year 1846; and in June of that year specimens of the relics recovered, accompanied by numerous maps and plans of ancient earthworks and sectional views of the mounds from which the remains were taken, were laid before the society by Mr. Squier in person. These excited deep interest and surprise in all who saw them; and the society immediately took measures to encourage further investigation, and secure the publication, under its own auspices, of the important results already obtained. A few months later, the chairman of the present committee, being in Ohio, was enabled through the kindness of Messrs. Squier and Davis, to visit several of the more important monuments in the immediate vicinity of Chillicothe, and, among these, "Mound City," so called, from which very many of the minor relics and specimens were procured. He was struck with the accuracy of the plans and drawings, as well as of the accounts which had been laid before the society, and bears full testimony to the fidelity and integrity with which the process of investigation and delineation has been conducted.

During the last and present season the researches of these gentlemen have been actively prosecuted and widely extended, and the above work, largely illustrated, comprising the results, has been prepared. These results are so numerous and important, and consequently such is the extent and magnitude of the work itself, as to put its publication beyond any means which the society can command. Under these circumstances, your committee learn with pleasure that preliminary arrangements have been made for its publication by the Smithsonian Institution among its "Contributions to Knowledge." It can only be a matter of sincere gratification to this society to see that which it cannot itself accomplish for the history and antiquities of our country taken up and carried out under such favorable auspices; and they cannot but rejoice that an opportunity is thus afforded to that noble Institution of opening its high career by fostering scientific researches into the interesting problems connected with the ante-Columbian history and aboriginal monuments of our own country.

In view of these facts, your committee would recommend the adoption of the following resolutions by the society:

Resolved, That this society regard the researches of Messrs. Squier and Davis as of very great importance in American Archæology, and as casting much light upon our aboriginal antiquities, especially upon the character and habits of the earliest races which had their seat in the Mississippi valley.

Resolved, That we regard the work prepared upon this subject as one of great general interest, and as worthy to be adopted for publication by the Smithsonian Institution, both as resting on original researches, and as affording remarkable illustrations of the history of the American continent.

Your committee would also append to this report the accompanying letters from Samuel G. Morton, M. D., of Philadelphia, and Hon. George P. Marsh, of Vermont, both members of this society, and joint members of this committee.

All of which is respectfully submitted.

EDWARD ROBINSON,
JOHN R. BARTLETT, } *Committee.*
W. W. TURNER,

NEW YORK, *June*, 1847.

NEW YORK, *June* 9, 1847.

I have examined with much interest and attention the manuscripts, drawings, and ancient relics in the possession of Mr. E. G. Squier, and am happy to say that my previous impressions concerning the value of the researches of that gentleman and his associate are fully confirmed. It is fortunate for the cause of American Archæology that the first systematic attempt at its elucidation should have been conceived and executed in so truly philosophical a spirit; and rich as this age already is in antiquarian lore, it has, I think, received few more important contributions than that which the enlightened and generous zeal of these two private gentlemen is about to confer upon it. The Smithsonian collections could not begin with a more appropriate or creditable essay; and I hope that every facility may be afforded to the authors in bringing before the public the results of their honorable labors in as suitable a form and with as little delay as possible.

GEO. P. MARSH.

PHILADELPHIA, *June* 8, 1847.

As a member of the committee of the American Ethnological Society, appointed to report on the memoir on American Archæology, by Messrs. E. G. Squier and E. H. Davis, I have great pleasure in saying, that after a careful and repeated inspection of the materials in the hands of those gentlemen, I am convinced they constitute by far the most important contribution to the Archæology of the United States, that has ever been offered to the public. The number and accuracy of their plans, sketches, &c., have both interested and surprised me, and it is gratifying to learn that the preliminary arrangements have been made for their publication under the honorable auspices of the Smithsonian Institution.

SAML. GEORGE MORTON.

The memoirs of Messrs. Squier and Davis will occupy the greater portion, if not the whole, of the first volume of the Contributions. The illustrations will consist of fifty-five quarto plates of the mounds, earth-works, and maps of the adjacent country; also, of about two hundred wood-cuts, principally delineations of the various articles found in the mounds. Those who consider no branch of knowledge of any value but such as relates to the immediate gratification of our physical wants, have objected to the acceptance of this memoir as one of the first publications of the Institution; but it must be recollected that the will of Smithson makes no restriction in favor of any particular kind of knowledge, and that each branch is, therefore, entitled to a share of his bequest. The ethnological memoir of Messrs. Squier and Davis was the first, of the proper character, presented for publication, and hence it was entitled to the first place in the series of Smithsonian Contributions. Beside this, it furnishes an addition to a branch of knowledge which is at this time occupying the attention of a large class of minds, and which cannot fail to be interesting to every intelligent person who would learn something of the changes to which man has been subjected.

It is proposed to insert in one of the volumes of the Contributions a sketch of the life of Smithson. The materials for this have been collected from the several volumes of the Transactions of the Royal Society, and the scientific journals of the beginning of the present and the latter part of the last century. The first volume will be published as soon as the wood-cuts and plates, now in the course of preparation, are finished.

Besides the memoirs before mentioned, a number of others have been presented, some of which, though apparently of interest, and the product of thought and labor, were not of the character required by the resolution of the Board, and these have either been returned to their authors, or are in the possession of the Secretary. A number of others have also been provisionally adopted, or are in the course of preparation. Some of these are on the most abstruse parts of physical science, and all will do honor to the intellectual character of our country. Though the number of original memoirs which will be found worthy of a place in the Contributions will probably not be large, yet it will, perhaps, be best to set apart a definite portion of the income of the bequest—as, for example, at present three or four thousand dollars annually—to defray the expense of this part of the plan of increasing knowledge. A considerable portion, however, of the sum thus expended will be returned to the Institution in the form of additions to its library. I may also suggest, in this place, the propriety of the adoption by the Board of a resolution inviting all engaged in original research to send the results of their labors for publication in the Smithsonian Contributions.

The Board also directed me to commence the collection of apparatus; and I accordingly sent orders to Europe, to the amount of twelve hundred dollars, for the purchase of such articles as could not be procured in the United States. Most of the instruments have been received, and will be found of importance not only in the way of original research, but also in illustrating some of the most interesting and recent phenomena of physical science, as well as serving as samples for imitation to the artists of this country. It was thought that these articles would be admitted free of duty, and a petition to this effect was presented to the Secretary of the Treasury; but—though this officer is well known to be much interested in the prosperity of the Institution—such is the nature of the law that the duty could not be remitted.

There is an article of apparatus which, within a few years past, has opened almost a new world of research in the phenomena of life and organization, the use of which is now indispensable in advancing our knowledge of physiology and its kindred branches of science. I allude to the achromatic microscope, to increase the power of which the artists of Germany, France, and England have vied with each other. On account of the small number of persons who are capable of constructing the proper lenses, the best specimens of this instrument are very scarce in this country, and can be procured only at a great expense. Under these circumstances, it was a matter of much interest to learn, from a source which could be relied on, that an individual in the interior of the State of New York had successfully devoted himself to the study of the microscope, and that he was able to produce instruments of this kind which would compete with the best of those constructed in Europe. In order to do justice to the talents and labors of this person, as well as to furnish the Institution with a valuable instrument of research, I requested him to construct a microscope, to be paid for out of the funds for the purchase of apparatus, provided that a commission, appointed by myself, should find it capable of producing certain effects. This proposition was accepted, and the result will probably be given to the Board at the next meeting.

Preparations have also been made for instituting various lines of physical research. Among the subjects mentioned by way of example in the programme for the application of the funds of the Institution is terrestrial magnetism. I need scarcely say that this is a subject of high interest not only in a theoretical point of view, but also in its direct reference to navigation and the various geodetical operations of civil and military life. A resolution of Congress authorizing the exploration of the mineral lands adjacent to the great lakes has given to us the means of advancing this branch of knowledge with but little expenditure of the funds of the Institution. The Secretary of the Treasury readily agreed to the proposition that there should be added to the mineralogical and geological surveys of these regions, determinations of the dip, the variation, and the intensity of the magnetic forces, provided that the Smithsonian Institution would furnish one set of the instruments, and take charge of the direction of the observations, and of reducing and publishing them. In the survey of the mineral lands in the vicinity of Lake Michigan, under Dr. Jackson; Dr. Locke, of Cincinnati, has been employed with his own apparatus; and, to make provision for the survey in Wisconsin, preliminary steps have been taken to procure other instruments from London.

Another subject of research mentioned in the programme, and which has been urged upon the immediate attention of the Institution, is that of an extensive system of meteorological observations, particularly with reference to the phenomena of American storms. Of late years, in our country, more additions have been made to meteorology than to any other branch of physical science. Several important generalizations have been arrived at, and definite theories proposed, which now enable us to direct our attention, with scientific precision, to such points of observation as cannot fail to reward us with new and interesting results. It is proposed to organise a system of observations which shall extend as far as possible over the North American continent; and, in order to do this, it will be necessary to engage the co-operation of the British government. I have accordingly addressed a letter to Lieutenant Colonel Sabine, Corresponding Secretary of the Royal Society, who assures me that, as soon as the plan is fully matured for this country, there will be no difficulty in establishing a system of corresponding observations in the British provinces. I have also addressed letters to several gentlemen distinguished for their attainments in meteorology, asking for suggestions as to the plan of observation; and I beg leave to refer the Board to the accompanying report of Professor Loomis, of New York University, and also to the communication of Professor Espy, received in answer. The former contains an exposition of the advantages which may be derived from the study of meteorology, and what has been done in this branch of science in this country, and what encouragement there is for the further prosecution of the same subject, together with a general plan of operations. The present time appears to be peculiarly auspicious for commencing an enterprise of the proposed kind. The citizens of the United States are now scattered over every part of the southern and western portion of North America, and the extended lines of telegraph will furnish a ready means of warning the more northern and eastern observers to be on the watch for the first appearance of an advancing storm.

All which is respectfully submitted.

JOSEPH HENRY, *Secretary.*

To the REGENTS *of the Smithsonian Institution.*

REPORT

OF THE

COMMITTEE OF THE AMERICAN ACADEMY OF ARTS AND SCIENCES,

APPOINTED TO

CONSIDER THE PLAN PROPOSED FOR THE ORGANIZATION OF THE SMITHSONIAN INSTITUTION.

SUBMITTED TO THE ACADEMY, DECEMBER 7, 1847.

The Committee of the American Academy of Arts and Sciences, to whom was referred a letter of Professor Henry, of the 30th September, together with the *programme* of the organization of the Smithsonian Institution accompanying the said letter, have had the same under consideration, and beg leave to submit the following report:

Professor Henry is understood to be desirous of ascertaining the opinions of the scientific bodies of the country on the subject of the proposed organization of the Smithsonian Institution; and the free expression of their views is invited by him.

The interesting nature and high importance of this foundation, and the novel and peculiar circumstances attending its establishment, make it highly expedient, in the opinion of the committee, that every step taken in its organization should be deliberately considered. They think it no more than just to express their satisfaction, that the control of the infant establishment has been placed in the hands of a Board of Regents of the highest intelligence, respectability, and weight of character; and in the wise selection made of the officers on whom the active executive duties of the Institution will devolve, the committee perceive a satisfactory pledge as far as they are concerned.

Prof. Henry's *programme* commences with "General considerations which should serve as a guide in adopting the plan of organization." He points out the nature of the bequest as made to the United States for the purpose of founding at Washington, under the name of the Smithsonian Institution, an establishment for the increase and diffusion of knowledge among men. The bequest is accordingly for the benefit of mankind. The government of the United States is but a trustee to carry out this noble design. Even the people of the United States are interested only so far as they constitute one of the great families of the human race.

The objects of the Institution are twofold: first, the increase; and second, the diffusion of knowledge; objects which, although frequently in a vague way confounded with each other, (inasmuch as it often happens that knowledge is diffused by the same acts which increase it,) are nevertheless logically distinct, and require to be separately regarded. No particular kind of knowledge is specified by the founder as entitled to preference; all branches are entitled to a share of attention; and the order and degree in which they are cultivated must be decided by a wise regard to means and circumstances. Knowledge may be increased by various modes of encouraging and facilitating the discovery of new truths; it is diffused chiefly, though not exclusively, through the instrumentality of the press. The organization should be such as to produce results not within the province of the existing institutions of the country. It was, for instance, evidently not the design of the liberal founder to establish a collegiate institution or a place of education; nor would it be wise to appropriate his bequest for such an object, already sufficiently attained by the ordinary resources of public and private liberality. Considering the novelty of the undertaking, it would be manifestly unwise to stake too much on the success of the first efforts. The organization should be such as to admit of changes and modifications under the light of experience. As several years have elapsed since the fund came into the possession of the United States, it seems no more than equitable that a considerable portion of the accruing interest should be added to the principal, to make up for the loss of time. The committee consider this suggestion as perfectly reasonable, and trust it will receive the favorable consideration of Congress. Liberal as is the original bequest, the sum is but small compared with the great objects to be accomplished. This consideration suggests the absolute necessity of economy in any outlay on buildings and fixtures; in reference to which a prudent regard must be had, not merely to the first cost, but to the future expenses of repairs, and the support of the establishment. Great care must be taken not to multiply the number of persons to be permanently supported by the Institution. A clear and settled idea of its organization and mode of operation must precede the adoption of a plan of building; lest after the completion of a costly edifice it should be found nearly or quite useless, or worse than useless, by forcing a character upon the Institution which would not otherwise have been given it. All view to mere local ornament or advantage should be discarded at the outset, in the management of a trust created for the benefit of mankind.

Such, very slightly expanded in a few of the propositions, are the general considerations proposed by Professor Henry as guides in adopting a plan of organization. They command the entire assent of the committee, and none of them more so than those which refer to the necessity of strict economy in the expenditure of the fund on a building, and the exclusion of undue regard to local ornament. It would not be difficult to point to a memorable instance in which the most munificent bequest ever made for the purposes of education has been rendered comparatively unavailing, in a sister city of the Union, by the total disregard of these wise principles. It is an additional reason for observing them, that the attempt to erect a highly imposing building for local ornament will not only crush in the bud all hope of fulfilling the ulterior objects of the bequest, but will be almost sure to fail of a satisfactory result, as far as the edifice itself is concerned.

The Secretary's plan of organization in reference to the increase of knowledge is so accurately digested and so thoroughly condensed, that the committee think it would be best to quote his own words:

"To INCREASE KNOWLEDGE, it is proposed—

"1st. To stimulate men of talent to make original researches, by offering suitable rewards for memoirs containing new truths; and

"2d. To appropriate annually a portion of the income for particular researches under the direction of suitable persons."

These methods of *increasing knowledge* are further unfolded in the following "detail of the plan" for that purpose:

"I. *By stimulating researches.*

"1st. Rewards, consisting of money, medals, &c., offered for original memoirs on all branches of knowledge.

"2d. The memoirs thus obtained to be published in a series of volumes in a quarto form, and entitled 'Smithsonian Contributions to Knowledge.'

"3d. No memoir on subjects of physical science to be accepted for publication which does not furnish a positive addition to human knowledge; and all unverified speculation to be rejected.

"4th. Each memoir presented to the Institution to be submitted for examination to a committee of persons of reputation for learning in the branch to which the memoir pertains, and to be accepted for publication only in case the report is favorable.

"5th. The commission to be chosen by the officers of the Institution, and the name of the author, as far as practicable, concealed until a favorable decision shall have been made.

"6th. The volumes of the memoirs to be exchanged for the transactions of all literary and scientific societies, and copies to be given to all the colleges and principal libraries in this country. One part of the remaining copies may be offered for sale, and the other carefully preserved to form complete sets of the work to supply the demand from new institutions.

"7th. An abstract or popular account of the contents of these memoirs should be given to the public through the annual report of the Regents to Congress.

"II. *By appropriating a portion of the income annually to special objects of research, under the direction of suitable persons.*

"1st. The objects and the amounts appropriated to be recommended by counsellors of the Institution.

"2d. Appropriation in different years to different objects, so that in course of time each branch of knowledge may receive a share.

"3d. The results obtained from these appropriations to be published with the memoirs before mentioned, in the volumes of the Smithsonian Contributions to Knowledge.

"4th. Examples of objects for which appropriations may be made:

"(1.) System of extended meteorological observations, for solving the problem of American storms.

"(2.) Geological, magnetical, and topographical surveys, to collect materials for a physical atlas of the United States.

"(3.) Solution of experimental problems, such as weighing the earth, new determination of the velocity of electricity and light, chemical analyses of soils and plants, collection and publication of articles of science accumulated in the offices of the government.

"(4.) Institution of statistical inquiries, with reference to physical, moral, and political subjeets.

"(5.) Historical researches and accurate surveys of places celebrated in history.

"(6.) Ethnological researches, particularly with reference to the present races of men in North America; also explorations and accurate surveys of the mounds and other remains of the ancient people of our country."

The committee have made this long extract from Professor Henry's *programme* in order to give to the Academy an adequate idea of the proposed plan, as far as it refers to the first branch, or the *increase of knowledge*. It has, in some of its features, been already adopted. It is already announced that one voluminous memoir, copiously illustrated by engravings, is already on its passage through the press, under the auspices of the Smithsonian Institution. The committee refer to an elaborate memoir, by Messrs. Squier and Davis, on the aboriginal mounds discovered in large numbers in various parts of the United States, and especially in the region northwest of the Ohio. This memoir was accepted on the favorable report of the Ethnological Society of New York, to which it had been referred by the Secretary of the Institution, and in whose Transactions an abridgment of it has appeared. It is also understood that a memoir on one of the most interesting subjects which engages the attention of geometers and mathematicians at the present moment, viz., the planet Neptune, has been invited by the Secretary from one of our own members.

While the committee would deprecate all attempts unduly to stimulate the increase of knowledge, as sure to prove abortive, and to result at best in the publication of crude investigations, they believe it quite possible to remove some of the obstructions to its progress. Narrow circumstances are too apt to be the lot of genius when devoted to scientific pursuits; and the necessity of providing for personal and domestic wants too often absorbs the time and faculties of those who might, if relieved from cares of this kind, have adorned their age and benefited mankind. To such men a moderate pecuniary advantage derived from a successful investigation might be of vast importance. The efficacy of market upon production is not limited to the creations of physical labor. It is seen in the history of science and literature of every age and country. Invention in the mechanical arts and skill in practical science are well paid in this country, and how great is the harvest! The extraordinary effect even of an honorary inducement is seen in the case of the medal offered by the King of Denmark for the discovery of Telescopic Comets. On these principles it may be hoped that by offering a moderate pecuniary compensation for researches of real merit, valuable contributions to knowledge will be produced; while their publication will tend directly to the diffusion of knowledge.

An encouragement somewhat similar toward the promotion of the increase of knowledge would be afforded by another part of the proposed operations, that of providing the requisite apparatus and implements, and especially books, to be placed in the hands of those engaged in particular lines of investigation. In this way it is not unlikely that a considerable amount of talent may be rendered effective, which at present is condemned to inactivity, from local position unfavorable to scientific research.

It is not the purpose of the committee to engage in minute criticism of the details of the *programme;* but it may not be out of place to suggest a doubt of the practicability or expediency of carrying into rigid execution, "the rejection of all unverified speculations," as proposed in the third paragraph of the first section above cited; while it is obviously advisable to discountenance all theoretical speculations not directly built upon observation, it might be too much to exact, in all cases, that these speculations should have been actually verified. No small portion of modern geology is an ingenious structure of speculative generalizations. The undulatory theory of light can hardly claim any other character. The nebular theory, though proposed and illustrated by the highest astronomical talent of the past and present generation, is rapidly sinking from the domain of accredited speculations. It may be doubted even whether M. Le Verrier's brilliant memoirs on the perturbations of Uranus would not, as published before the discovery of Neptune, have fallen within this principle of rejection rigorously applied. Upon the whole, the committee think very favorably of all parts of the plan for increasing knowledge; and feel no doubt that it would afford important encouragement to scientific pursuits. To suppose that it will create an era in science, or throw into the shade the ordinary educational and intellectual influences at work in the country, would be extravagant. It is enough and all that can be expected, if it be a rational plan for appropriating moderate means towards the attainment of a desirable end.

To fulfil the other object of the trust, viz. to "diffuse knowledge," the Secretary proposes to publish "A Series of Reports, giving an account of the new discoveries in science, and of the changes made from year to year in all branches of knowledge not strictly professional." These reports are to be prepared by collaborators, most eminent in their several departments, who are to receive a compensation for their labors; the collaborators to be furnished with all the journals and other publications necessary to the preparation of their reports.

The following enumeration of the proposed subjects of these reports will afford the Academy a full conception of this part of the plan.

I. *Physical class.*

1. Physics, including Astronomy, Natural Philosophy, Chemistry, and Meteorology.
2. Natural History, including Botany, Zoology, and Geology.
3. Agriculture.
4. Application of Science to Art.

II. *Moral and Political class.*

5. Ethnology, including particular History, comparative Philology, Antiquities, &c.
6. Statistics and Political Economy.
7. Mental and Moral Philosophy.
8. A Survey of the Political Events of the World, Penal Reform, &c.

III. *Literature and the Fine Arts.*

9. Modern Literature.
10. The Fine Arts, and their application to the Useful Arts.
11. Bibliography.
12. Obituary notices of distinguished individuals.

Another branch of the plan for the diffusion of knowledge contemplates the offer of premiums for the best essays on given subjects.

The publications of the Institution, of whatever form, are proposed to be presented to all the colleges, and to the principal libraries and scientific institutions throughout the country, and to be exchanged for the transactions of all scientific and literary societies throughout the world; thus laying the foundation of a valuable library. An adequate number are to be preserved to supply the future demand of new institutions, and the remainder are to be placed on sale at a price so low as to render them generally accessible.

For carrying out the plan thus sketched for increasing and diffusing knowledge, the Regents propose to appropriate one half of the income of their fund. The remainder is to be expended in the formation and maintenance of *a library, a collection of instruments of research in all branches of experimental science, and a museum.*

This partition of the income of the fund is stated to be "a compromise between the two modes of increasing and diffusing knowledge."

A library is one of the objects contemplated in the act of Congress establishing the Board for the management of the trust. It is requisite for carrying out the plan above proposed. At the same time, it will be observed that the distribution, by exchange, of the publications, which that scheme of operations will call into existence, will rapidly provide the Institution, without further expense, with the class of works, often of a costly character, which are most directly important as the means of advancing and diffusing positive knowledge. It is accordingly in these that the Secretary proposes to lay the foundations of the library, forming, 1. A complete collection of the transactions and proceedings of all the learned societies in the world; and, 2. A similar collection of all the current periodical publications, and other works necessary in preparing the contemplated periodical reports.

In the next place, it is proposed to procure by preference those books which are not found in the other public libraries of the United States; regarding the want of them as one of more urgency to be supplied than that of a symmetrical and proportionate collection of books in all the departments of science. Such a library as the plan proposes may be fairly regarded as an important instrument for the increase and diffusion of knowledge.

The collection of scientific apparatus and instruments of research is no less needful in the furtherance of the above mentioned plan, which, as it proposes to aid individuals in the prosecution of important researches, may often do so most effectually by the loan of the instruments required for a particular investigation. They will also be needed, especially at Washington, for carrying out, under the most advantageous circumstances, the various experimental investigations in Physics already pursued by the Secretary with such credit to himself, and such honor to the scientific character of the country.

The Smithsonian Institution is also to be entrusted with the conservation of a National Museum, Congress having, by a clause in the Act of Incorporation, devolved upon it the charge of the immense collections belonging to the public, of which those brought home by Captain Wilkes from the Exploring Expedition form the greater portion, but which are daily increasing from many other sources. These collections, when a proper and convenient place shall have been prepared for their reception and preservation, are likely to accumulate with still greater rapidity in time to come.

While there is an obvious propriety and convenience in thus entrusting the care of the public collections to the officers of the Smithsonian Institution, it will not, the Committee trust, be forgotten by Congress that the income of the Smithsonian bequest—moderate at best, and consecrated to an object distinct as it is elevated—ought not to be burdened with the cost of constructing an edifice for the reception and exhibition of the public collections, or of their preservation and care. These objects would alone absorb a considerable portion of the fund. If drawn upon to carry them into effect, its efficiency for any other purpose will be seriously diminished, if not altogether destroyed.

The plan also contemplates a museum of the fine arts as well as a scientific apparatus. It proposes to procure "casts of the most celebrated articles of ancient and modern sculpture" and "models of antiquities." While it is undoubtedly true that a gallery of this description would find an appropriate place in an establishment devoted to the increase and diffusion of knowledge in its broadest sense, the Committee cannot but hope that the *immediate* execution of this part of the plan will not be attempted; but that it will be deferred till other objects of more decided utility have been provided for, and until a surplus of unappropriated funds shall have accrued.

The Academy will perceive that the most novel and important feature of the plan is that which proposes to insure the publication of memoirs and treatises on important subjects of investigation, and to offer pecuniary encouragement to men of talent and attainment to engage in scientific research. It is believed that no Institution in the country effects either of these objects to any great extent. The nearest approach to it is the practice of the Academy and other Philosophical Societies, of publishing the memoirs accepted by them. These, however, can rarely be works of great compass. No systematic plan of compensation for the preparation of works of scientific research is known by the Committee to have been attempted in this or any other country. It can scarcely be doubted that an important impulse would be given by the Institution, in this way, to the cultivation of scientific pursuits: while the extensive and widely ramified system of distribution and exchange by which the publications are to be distributed throughout the United States and the world, would secure them a circulation which works of science could scarcely attain in any other way.

It is an obvious characteristic of this mode of applying the funds of the Institution, that its influence would operate most widely throughout the country; that locality would be of comparatively little importance as far as this influence is concerned; and that the Union would become, so to say, in this respect, a great school of mutual instruction.

The Committee would remark in conclusion, that in a plan of operations of this kind, very much depends upon the activity and intelligence with which it is administered. The characters of the Board of Regents are a sufficient warrant for the prudence and good judgment which will watch over the general interests of the foundation; while the reputation of the Secretary and his assistant, the librarian, is so well established in their respective departments, as to render any tribute from the Committee entirely superfluous.

All which is respectfully submitted by the Committee.

EDWARD EVERETT,
JARED SPARKS,
BENJAMIN PEIRCE,
HENRY W. LONGFELLOW,
ASA GRAY.

DECEMBER 4, 1847.

Read at a meeting of the Academy held December 7, 1847, and accepted.

Ordered to be communicated to the Secretary of the Smithsonian Institution.

O. W. HOLMES,
Recording Secretary.

SECOND ANNUAL REPORT

Of the Secretary of the Smithsonian Institution, giving an account of the operations of the year 1848. *Presented December* 13, 1849.

GENTLEMEN: By a resolution of the Board of Regents, at their last annual meeting, I was charged with the execution of the details of the programme which had been provisionally adopted, and was directed to report annually to the Board the progress made in the execution of the duty assigned to me. In accordance with this resolution, I present the following statement of the operations of the past year.

The programme of the plan of organization of the Institution has been submitted to a number of literary and scientific societies, and in every case has received their unqualified approbation. The principal officers of these societies have expressed a willingness to co-operate with the Smithsonian Institution in carrying out the plans which have been adopted, and it is confidently believed, that as soon as these are fully developed and brought into practical operation, they will meet with general approval.

It was recommended in my last report that the details of the plan should be adopted provisionally, and should be carried into operation gradually and cautiously, with such changes, from time to time, as experience might dictate. The Institution is not one of a day, but is designed to endure as long as our government shall exist; and it is therefore peculiarly important that in the beginning we should proceed carefully and not attempt to produce immediate effects at the expense of permanent usefulness. The process of increasing knowledge is an extremely slow one, and the value of the results of this part of the plan cannot be properly realized until some years have elapsed. Independently of these considerations, the financial arrangements adopted by the Board of Regents are such as to prevent the full operation of the Institution until after three years from next March; up to that time more than one half of the income is to be devoted to the erection of the building, and indirectly to the increase of the permanent fund.

It will be recollected that the programme embraces—

1st. The plan of publishing original memoirs on all branches of knowledge, in a series of quarto volumes.

2d. The institution of original researches under the direction of competent persons.

3d. The publication of a series of reports from year to year, giving an account of the progress of the different branches of knowledge.

4th. The formation of a library and a museum of objects of nature and art.

Publication of original memoirs.

The first volume of the Smithsonian Contributions to Knowledge has been published and partially distributed. It consists of a single memoir on the Ancient Monuments of the Mississippi Valley, comprising the results of extensive original surveys and explorations by E. G. Squier, A. M., and E. H. Davis, M. D. It is illustrated by forty-eight lithographic plates, and by two hundred and seven wood engravings. The mechanical execution of the volume will bear comparison with that of any publication ever issued from the American press.

In the publication of the first volume of the Contributions, the question occurred as to the propriety of securing the copyright to the Institution. I had not an opportunity of conferring with the Executive Committee on this point, and was therefore obliged to settle it on my own responsibility. I concluded that it would be more in accordance with the spirit of the Institution to decide against the copyright. The knowledge which the Smithsonian Institution may be instrumental in presenting to the world should be free to all who are capable of using it. The republication of our papers ought to be considered as an evidence of their importance, and should be encouraged rather than prohibited.

The first memoir occupies an entire volume, and this accidental circumstance has given rise to a misconception of the plan. It has been supposed that each volume of the Smithsonian Contributions is, in like manner, to consist of a separate treatise on a particular subject selected with a view to popular interest. But such is not the case; each volume will generally contain a number of separate memoirs, on different branches of knowledge, similar to the usual published transactions of learned societies. The only reason why the first volume is occupied with a subject of general interest rather than one on some more abstruse branch of science is, that the memoir it contains was the *first* which was presented of the character prescribed by the plan. No preference is to be given to any branch of knowledge. The only questions to be asked, in considering the acceptance of a memoir, are, whether it is a positive addition to knowledge, resting on original research, and of sufficient importance to merit a place in the Smithsonian Contributions.

The rules adopted for the acceptance of a memoir are the same as those generally followed by learned societies. The memoir is surrendered by the author to the Institution, and no additions or alterations are allowed to be made after it has been submitted to the commission appointed to examine it, unless by their consent. A certain number of copies is presented to the author for distribution, with the privilege of striking off, at his own expense, additional copies for sale; which in most cases, particularly when the memoir is of popular interest, will be all the remuneration expected by the author.

From what has been said, it will be evident that the papers published in the Contributions cannot generally be of a popular nature. The popular effects to be produced by the Institution are principally those which may be attained by the reports on the progress of the different branches of knowledge, and by the occasional publications in connexion with these of separate treatises on some subject of special interest.

Applications have been made for the first volume of the Contributions from many academies and private institutions; and were our means sufficient, we would be pleased to supply all demands of this kind. But this is obviously impossible, for they alone would exhaust all the income of the Institution.

Preparations have been made for the publication of the second volume of the Contributions, and a sufficient number of memoirs have been already accepted, or are in preparation, to furnish the materials. Five of these are on astronomical subjects, and afford as important additions to this science as have ever been made to it in this country. Two of them relate to investigations on the new planet Neptune, which are only second in value to the original discovery of this distant member of our system. Abstracts of these have been given to the world, and have been received with general approbation. A third is a determination of the zodiac of the asteroids, or the zone in the heavens to which the positions of these small planets are confined. This paper is of much practical importance in facilitating the researches now in progress in different parts of the world relative to the nature of these fragments (as they would seem to be) of a large planet between Jupiter and Mars. It may be at once determined, by an inspection of the table annexed to this paper, whether any star mapped in an old catalogue, and now no longer to be found in the same place, can possibly be one of the asteroids. A fourth paper is an account of a new comet, the discovery of which by an American lady is one of the first additions to science of this kind, so far as I am informed, ever made in this country. The fifth memoir is an account of the Georgetown Observatory, the instruments with which it is furnished, the mode of using them which has been adopted, and the results of the observations which have been made. An important paper is also in process of preparation for the same volume on the gigantic fossil cetacean remains which are found in the southern and western States of the Union.

Other papers are in progress which partake of the character of original researches, since they are, in part, at least, prepared at the expense and under the direction of the Smithsonian Institution. They will be mentioned under the next head.

In a few cases, memoirs have been presented which, though exhibiting research and considerable originality, are not of a character to warrant their adoption as parts of our volumes of Contributions to positive knowledge. The rule given in the programme has been rigidly adhered to, viz. to decline accepting any paper on physical science which consists merely of an unverified hypothesis, however ingenious and plausible such an hypothesis may be. A law of nature is not susceptible of a logical demonstration, like that of a proposition of geometry, but is proved by its fitness to explain old, and to predict new, phenomena. The verification of an hypothesis, as we have stated in the last report, consists in deducing consequences from it, and ascertaining, by a direct appeal to observation or experiment, the truth or falsity of these deductions. Any paper, therefore, on material science which does not contain original experiments and observations cannot be admitted as a part of the Contributions to Knowledge. The rule we have adopted is in accordance with the practice of cautious investigators. The law of universal gravitation existed for several years in the mind of Newton as a well conditioned hypothesis before it was given to the world as a verified and established theory. Besides this, the rules of logic which are employed in discussing the questions of ordinary life are not applicable to the precision of scientific inquiry. The materials in this case, to borrow an expression of an author of celebrity, "must be weighed in the scale of the assayer, and not, like the mixed commodities of the market, on the weight-bridge of common opinion and general usage."

It has been objected to our publishing original memoirs, that in so doing we are merely performing the duties of a learned society. The answer is, that the learned societies in this country have not the means, except in a very limited degree, of publishing memoirs which require expensive illustrations, much less of assisting to defray the cost of the investigations by which the results have been obtained. The real workingmen in the line of original research hail this part of the plan as a new era in the history of American science. The assistance which the Institution will thus render to original research will occupy the place of the governmental patronage of other countries, and will enable true genius, wherever found, to place its productions before the world free of cost, and in a manner most favorable for securing due attention and proper appreciation.

From our experience thus far, I am convinced that, circumscribed as is the class of memoirs accepted by the Institution, we shall have no want of materials to fill at least one quarto volume a year. There has been in our country within the last few years a remarkable increase in the attention given to original research, not only in material science, but in every branch of knowledge susceptible of addition. And this is evinced by the character and variety of the papers which have been presented for publication. The wide difference between the increase of knowledge and its diffusion, is beginning to be seen and appreciated, and the time is not far distant when we shall be as distinguished for our additions to science as for its diffusion and application. The revolutions of Europe are not only sending to our shores the choicest specimens of art, but also men of reputation and skill in scientific investigation. Besides this, the present state of France is attended with such an interruption of the ordinary means of scientific publication, that the manuscript volumes on natural history of one of the most distinguished professors of the Jardin des Plantes are offered to us for publication in the Smithsonian Contributions for no remuneration, save a few copies for distribution among friends. Were the Institution fully in operation I should not hesitate, in accordance with the liberality which should characterize an establishment founded on the bequest of a foreigner, to recommend the adoption of these memoirs for publication at the expense of the Institution, and perhaps we might now distribute them through several of our volumes and finish the publication of them in the course of a few years.

Original researches.

The second part of the plan consists in instituting original researches, the results of which are to be published, with the other memoirs, in the volumes of the Smithsonian Contributions. Under this head may be first mentioned the publication of the tables ordered at the last meeting of the Board, for facilitating the calculation of the time of appearance of occultations of the fixed stars by the moon. The object of these tables is to assist in the accurate determination of the longitude of important places on the continent of North America, and their value has been attested by the recommendation of some of the most distinguished astronomers of this country. The accurate establishment of the longitude of any place renders it a landmark to the surveyor, the geographer, and the astronomer, and furnishes a most important element in determining its relative position on the map of the country. The observation of occultations affords one of the most ready means of solving this most difficult practical problem. The tables were calculated at the expense and under the direction of the Institution, and were sent to all persons known to be interested in practical astronomy, with a request that the observations which might be made in connexion with them might be sent to the Institution for computation, or published in some accessible journal. These tables have been so well received by astronomers, that, with the concurrence of the Executive Committee, I have ventured to order the computation of a set of the same kind on a more extensive scale for the year 1849. Copies of these will be sent to United States officers on the coast of Oregon and California, and will be distributed among all the other observers in this country. They will be found of much practical importance to the corps engaged by the general government in establishing the boundary lines of our new possessions. It is hoped that the remuneration allowed for the labor of computing these tables will not be considered extravagant, when it is mentioned that it has occupied the whole time of Mr. Downes for nearly six months, at the rate of eight hours a day.

With the concurrence of the Executive Committee, I have also published an ephemeris of the planet Neptune, or in other words, a table indicating its position in the heavens during each day of the present year, by which those interested in astronomy are enabled readily to find the place of the new planet in the heavens, or the direction in which the telescope must be pointed in order to observe it. Copies of this have been sent to all the principal astronomers in the world, and it has received the highest commendation. It was calculated by Mr. S. C. Walker from the orbit deduced by himself, a full account of which forms one of the papers of the second volume of the Contributions. It is the first accurate ephemeris which has ever appeared of this newly discovered member of our solar system.

An appropriation of one thousand dollars was made at the last meeting of the Board for the commencement of a series of meteorological observations, particularly with reference to the phenomena of American storms. According to the estimate of Prof. Loomis, appended to my last report, three thousand dollars will be required for the purpose of reducing this part of our plan to practice. It is hoped that one thousand dollars in addition will be appropriated this year, and an equal sum the next, so that, at the end of that time, we shall be prepared for full operation. At the last session of Congress an appropriation was made for meteorology under the direction of the Secretary of the Navy; and in order that the observations thus established may not interfere with those undertaken by the Smithsonian Institution, that officer has directed Professor Espy to co-operate with the Secretary of the Institution.

It is contemplated to establish three classes of observers among those who are disposed to join in this enterprise. One class, without instruments, to observe the face of the sky as to its clearness, the extent of cloud, the direction and force of wind, the beginning and ending of rain, snow, &c. A second class, furnished with thermometers, who, besides making the observations above mentioned, will record variations of temperature. The third class, furnished with full sets of instruments, to observe all the elements at present deemed important in the science of meteorology. It is believed that much valuable information may be obtained in this way with reference to the extent, duration, and passage of storms over the country, though the observer may be possessed of no other apparatus than a simple wind-vane.

With the instruments owned by private individuals, with those at the several military stations, and with the supply of the deficiency by the funds of the Smithsonian Institution, it is believed that observations can be instituted at important points over the whole United States, and that, with the observations which we can procure from Mexico and the British possessions of North America, data will be furnished for important additions to our knowledge of meteorological phenomena. As a beginning to this extended system, six sets of instruments have been forwarded to the coast of Oregon and California, for the purpose of establishing periodical observations on the western side of the Rocky mountains. Also, a set has been forwarded to Bent's Fort, and another to Santa Fé. Circulars have been prepared and will shortly be issued for the purpose of ascertaining the number and locality of all those who, with or without instruments, are willing to join in the enterprise. I am indebted to Prof. Coffin, of Lafayette College, for a list of all persons, as far as they are known, who have heretofore been accustomed to make meteorological observations in North America, which will be of much importance in our future investigations relative to this subject.

As a part of the system of meteorology, it is proposed to employ, as far as our funds will permit, the magnetic telegraph in the investigation of atmospherical phenomena. By this means, not only notice of the approach of a storm may be given to distant observers, but also attention may be directed to particular phenomena, which can only be properly studied by the simultaneous observations of persons widely separated from each other. For example, the several phases presented by a thunderstorm, or by the aurora borealis, may be telegraphed to a distance, and the synchronous appearances compared and recorded in stations far removed from each other. Also, by the same means, a single observatory, at which constant observations are made during the whole 24 hours, may give notice to all persons along the telegraphic lines, of the occurrence of interesting meteorological phenomena, and thus simultaneous observations be secured. The advantage to agriculture and commerce to be derived from a knowledge of the approach of a storm, by means of the telegraph, has been frequently referred to of late in the public journals. And this, we think, is a subject deserving the attention of the general government.

Under the head of researches, I may mention that several papers are in preparation, under the direction and partly at the expense of the Institution. The first of these relates to a series of valuable observations on the temperature and velocity of the Gulf stream, the author of which the science of our country was called to mourn while he was engaged in an important public service. The observations are now in progress of reduction, and the results will furnish an interesting memoir for the next volume of our Contributions.

The drawings and engravings of a paper on the botany of Oregon are also in progress; and as a small advance has been made to assist in completing these, the memoir will fall under the head of original researches, in part conducted by the Institution.

In the last report, it was mentioned that a magnetic survey of the mineral regions of the northern lakes had been added to the geological and mineralogical survey, the results of which were to be submitted to the Smithsonian Institution. An appropriation was made by the Secretary of the Treasury during the past summer for a continuation of this survey; but on account of the lateness of the season at which the arrangement was made, the person to whom the work was entrusted was not enabled to engage in it this year. Operations, however, will probably be commenced as soon as practicable, next spring.

There is in the Land Office a large collection of facts relative to the variation of the compass, which have been derived from the observations of the public surveyors, who are directed in all cases to note the variation of the needle from the true meridian, at the several stations of their surveys. The observations are made with an instrument called the solar compass, which probably gives the variation at each place within a quarter of a degree of the truth. The number of these observations, it is believed, will make up in a considerable degree for their want of greater precision; and from the whole, the lines of declination may be determined with considerable accuracy. The Secretary of the Treasury has liberally directed that all the matter relating to this subject in the Land Ofhee may be placed at my disposal, and Mr. Wilson has undertaken to present the whole in a series of maps, the publication of which in the Contributions cannot fail to be received as an interesting addition to terrestrial magnetism.

Among the objects of research enumerated in the programme, is the analysis of soils and plants; but it is the policy of the Smithsonian Institution, in order to employ its funds most effectually in the way of increasing and diffusing knowledge, not to engage in any operation which could be as well if not better carried on under the direction and with the funds of another institution. In accordance with this, an arrangement has been made with the Commissioner of Patents that the two Institutions may not interfere with each other; and as, at the request of Mr. Burke, an appropriation has been made by Congress for a series of experiments on the above-mentioned subjects, the Smithsonian Institution will, therefore, for the present abandon this field of research for others less effectually occupied.

I may also mention in this connexion, that the Smithsonian Institution has been the means of starting an important literary enterprise, intended to facilitate the study of the history and literature of our country. Mr. Henry Stevens, who has been engaged for a number of years as the agent in this country of the British Museum, and other European libraries, has commenced the preparation of a bibliographical work, comprising a description of all books relative to, or published in, America prior to the year 1700, and indicating not only the contents and value of the books, but also the principal libraries in this and other countries where they are to be found. The preparation of a work of this kind will be in accordance with that part of our plan which contemplates rendering the Institution a centre of bibliographical knowledge, and will have a direct influence in promoting the objects of the various historical societies which are now established in almost every State of the Union, and in bringing the Institution into friendly relations with them. A certificate has been given to Mr. Stevens to the effect that this work, if found, by a commission to whom it shall be referred, properly executed, will be accepted for publication as part of the Smithsonian Contributions to Knowledge. Assured by this certificate that the work will be properly executed, a number of gentlemen and institutions, whose libraries will be examined and referred to, have liberally subscribed to defray the necessary expense of its preparation. With this encouragement, Mr. Stevens has started for Europe to commence investigations in foreign libraries. To satisfy ourselves as to the importance of a work of this kind, a circular letter was addressed to a number of individuals distinguished for their knowledge of such subjects, and the answer in all cases was highly favorable to the scheme. Some of these answers I have given in the appendix, together with the details of the plan of the work as proposed by Mr. Stevens.

At the last session of Congress an appropriation of $5,000 was made, on motion of Mr. Stanton, for a series of astronomical observations in the southern hemisphere, for the purpose of a new determination of the parallax of the planets, and consequently of their distance from the sun, by simultaneous observations on the planets Venus and Mars, made at places situated north and south of the equator. This appropriation has been found inadequate to furnish all the instruments required; and inasmuch as the expedition should not be undertaken unless the observers are provided with all the aids which the latest improvements in modern science can furnish, and since, to wait for an additional appropriation from Congress would cause the delay of a whole year, Lieutenant Gilliss has applied to the Institution to purchase and lend to him an achromatic telescope, which, if not paid for by an additional appropriation from the government, will, after its return from the south, form part of the apparatus of the Institution. This instrument will cost about $2,000, to be paid for at the end of three years. The Executive Committee, to whom I applied for counsel on this subject, agreed with me in opinion, that this was a proper occasion for the application of the funds of the Institution to the promotion of science. The instrument has accordingly been ordered to be constructed by an American artist, and to be accepted only in case its performance shall meet the approval of a commission of practical astronomers appointed to examine it.

The position on the coast of Chili, to be occupied by the southern observers, is peculiarly favorable to the study of the facts connected with one of the most mysterious and interesting phenomena of terrestrial physics—namely, the earthquake. Lieutenant Gilliss has been requested to give particular attention to this subject, and for the purpose of facilitating his inquiries a seismometer, or instrument for measuring the intensity and direction of the *earthwave*, has been ordered at the expense of the Institution, to be placed in charge of the expedition during its absence. The cost of this instrument is not yet ascertained; it will, however, not exceed one hundred and fifty dollars.

I think it highly probable that these instruments will be paid for by the general government. The liberal spirit which dictated the original appropriation will, I doubt not, complete the outfit by the addition of a sum sufficient to defray all the necessary expenses.*

Under the head of original researches, I may call to the Regents the fact of my having been directed to continue my own investigations on physical science, and to report occasionally to the Board my progress therein. In the course of last year, I found an opportunity while at Princeton, to commence a series of investigations on radiant heat, which apparently produced some results of interest, but which my subsequent engagements have prevented me from fully developing. I was also directed to cause to be made a series of experiments on the economical value of building material. It will give me much pleasure to obey this instruction of the Board as soon as a place in the Smithsonian building and the necessary apparatus are procured for properly conducting the research.

Reports on the progress of knowledge.

The Smithsonian Contributions are intended to consist of entirely original additions to the sum of human knowledge, and are to be principally exchanged for the transactions of learned societies, and to be distributed among public institutions. The Reports, on the other hand, are to be of a more popular kind, and are intended for as wide a distribution as the funds of the Institution or the means of publishing them may permit. They will give an account of the progress of the different branches of knowledge in every part of the world, and will supply a desideratum in English literature.

The objects of the Smithsonian Institution are not educational. The press in our country already teems with elementary works on the different branches of knowledge, and to expend our funds in adding to these, would be to dissipate them without perceptible effect. Neither do we believe that the distribution of penny magazines, or tracts on the rudiments of science, can ever supersede the labors of the school-master. As a general rule, knowledge presented in a fragmentary form, can only be useful to minds well stored with general principles, to which the isolated facts may be referred; and knowledge, both fragmentary and diluted, is almost worthless, even in the way of popular distribution. The elementary principles of science may be systematically taught to a certain extent in common schools, and the reports we intend to publish will be found of value to the teacher, and through him to the pupil, as well as interesting to the general reader. While these reports are rendered as free as possible from technical terms, they will treat of

* Since writing this report, the appropriation has been made by Congress.

subjects requiring attention and thought to understand them. We think it better that they should be above rather than below the average intelligence of the country; that they should start from a given epoch, and in most cases should be preceded by a brief exposition of the previous state of each subject.

Arrangements have been made for commencing some of these preliminary reports, as well as reports on the state of our knowledge of special subjects; among these are—

1. A report on the present state of chemistry as applied to agriculture.
2. A report on the forest-trees of North America, giving their economical uses, their mode of propagation, and their history.
3. A report on the present state of our knowledge of lightning and the best means of guarding against accidents from its effects.
4. A report on the late discoveries in astronomy.
5. A report on meteorological instruments, with practical observations and directions with reference to the use of them.

In connexion with this last report, I may mention that a proposition has been made to the Institution by Professor Guyot, of the University of Neufchatel, relative to the importance of commencing at this epoch, and at the beginning of the labors of the Smithsonian Institution, the adoption of the centigrade scale of the thermometer. This is a subject, indeed, worthy of the attention of the Regents. It should, however, be discussed with caution, and be decided only after due deliberation.

The first idea of reports on the progress of knowledge, with which we are acquainted, is due to the Emperor Napoleon, who called upon the French Academy of Sciences, to present him with accounts of the progress of the different branches of knowledge within a given period. Until within the last few years the only regular reports of the kind were those presented to the Swedish Academy. Since that time, however, a series of annual reports on chemistry have been commenced by an association of gentlemen in France, and also a series on the different branches of material science, by the Physical Society of Berlin. The several numbers of the latter are now in progress of translation, in order to furnish in part the materials for the reports to be prepared for the Smithsonian Institution during the coming year.

Although comparatively little has been done in our country in the way of original research, yet it might be important that the Institution should call for the preparation of a report on the history of the progress of original science in America down to the end of the present half century. This report would exhibit a constant increase in the number and importance of the researches made in our country, and might be found of much service in giving due credit to the labors of those who have been really engaged in the advance of knowledge among us. A report of this kind, however, would require the association of a number of persons combining literary with scientific attainments.

Occasional publication of separate treatises on subjects of general interest.

This part of the plan of organization requires to be carried into operation with much caution. It is liable to much abuse, unless the publication be restricted to a well defined range, viz: to scientific reports on the present state of knowledge of a given subject, to precede the periodical reports; to translations from foreign languages of papers of general interest; and occasionally, perhaps, the exposition of a subject on which, at a particular time, popular knowledge is required. We should be careful not to establish a precedent which may lead us into difficulty, in the way of declining the publication of works which may be presented to us. Scarcely a week passes in which the Institution is not requested to publish some essay or compilation, and the funds which can be devoted to all our publications would not suffice for one half of those offered of this kind. The only work of this class which has yet been attempted by the Institution, is one entitled, "Hints on Public Architecture," under the direction of the Building Committee. Although the Secretary's name was mentioned in the resolution authorizing the publication of this treatise, yet he has thus far had no connexion with it. The publication was authorized before the details of the plan of organization were fully settled. It was at first intended merely as a report of the Building Committee, giving an account of the plans submitted, and the one adopted for the Smithsonian building, together with a report of the investigations of the committee with regard to the materials of construction, &c. It was afterwards changed into the form of a regular treatise, in order that it might be referred to a commission of persons chosen to examine it, and that, the Institution might thus be relieved from the responsibility of pronouncing upon its fitness for publication. I think it important that, besides the preface of this work, a full account of its origin should be given in an introductory advertisement.

Library.

During the past year the library has continued to increase by donations, and by the books which have been deposited by publishers, in accordance with the 10th section of the act establishing the Institution. The requirements of this act are, however, not strictly observed by all publishers; and I would direct the attention of the Board to a special report of the Assistant Secretary with reference to this point. The whole subject will probably come before Congress during its present session.

Professor Jewett, the Assistant Secretary, has been industriously engaged during the past year in procuring statistics of the libraries of the United States, and in digesting plans for the details of the library of the Institution, and I beg leave to refer you to the able and interesting report of the results of his labors, herewith submitted. A considerable portion of the copies of the Smithsonian Contributions will be presented to public institutions which publish transactions, and which are able to present us in return with additions to our library. The volume now in process of distribution has been preceded by a circular requesting exchanges of the works of all institutions which issue transactions and catalogues of all libraries to which the Contributions may be sent.

Preparation for lecturing.

The plan of organization contemplates a series of free lectures, particularly during the session of Congress. These will be commenced as soon as the building is ready for the purpose. This part of the plan also cannot be put into full operation until after the building is completed. A number of gentlemen have consented to favor us with their services. Men of talents, however, cannot be expected to leave their homes and subject themselves to the expense of visiting Washington, and to the trouble of preparing a course of lectures, without a proper remuneration. It will be necessary, therefore, that an annual appropriation be made for this purpose. The amount, however, must necessarily be small until the building is completed, or until all the interest of the fund can be devoted to the primary objects of the Institution. Besides this, the lecture-room in the east wing, now finished, will scarcely hold more than five hundred persons, while the one in the main building is intended to accommodate twice as many.

Donation.

Dr. Robert Hare, of Philadelphia, having resigned the chair of chemistry in the University of Pennsylvania, which he had filled with honor to himself and his country for nearly thirty years, has presented to the Smithsonian Institution the instruments of research and illustration, collected and used by himself during his long and successful scientific career. Many of these instruments are the invention of the donor, are connected with his reputation, and belong to the history of the science of our day. The gift is important, not only on account of its intrinsic value, but also as establishing a precedent of liberality, which we trust will be frequently observed by others, as well as being an expression of Dr. Hare's approbation of the plan and confidence in the stability of the Institution. A number of other donations have been received, of which a list, with the names of the donors, will be given in a subsequent report.

In view of what has been stated in the foregoing report, the Secretary trusts that the Board of Regents will be satisfied, if ever they had any doubts on the subject, that the plan adopted is one well calculated to carry out the benevolent intentions of the donor, of increasing and diffusing knowledge among men; and that a satisfactory answer has been given to the question frequently asked, namely, When is the Institution to begin? It will be seen that it has commenced the most importa part of its operations, and the results are now in progress of dissemination in every part of the civilized world.

Respectfully submitted,

JOSEPH HENRY,
Secretary of the Smithsonian Institution.

THIRD ANNUAL REPORT

Of the Secretary of the Smithsonian Institution, for the year 1849.

To the Board of Regents of the Smithsonian Institution:

GENTLEMEN: In accordance with the resolution that the Secretary shall present at each annual meeting of the Board of Regents an account of the operations of the Institution during the past year, I respectfully submit the following.

Agreeably to the scheme of finance adopted by the Board, the greater portion of all the income of the Smithsonian fund is at present devoted to the erection of the building; and until this is paid for, the money which can be appropriated to the active operations of the Institution will be comparatively small, not only small in proportion to the demands made upon it, but small in reference to the results which the public generally expect it to produce. It is believed, however, that a proper consideration of the facts presented in the following report will warrant the conclusion, that the Institution, during the past year, has been gradually extending its sphere of usefulness, and successfully bringing into operation the different parts of its plan of organization.

It will be recollected that the several propositions of the programme were adopted provisionally, and it is gratifying to be able to state that experience thus far has indicated no important changes. The general plan has continued to receive the approbation of the enlightened public both in this country and in Europe, and to increase general confidence in the power of the Institution to confer important benefits on our country and the world.

In presenting the different operations of the Institution, I shall adopt, as in my last report, the principal divisions of the programme:

1st. Publication of memoirs in quarto volumes, consisting of positive additions to knowledge.

2d. Institution of original researches, under the direction of competent persons.

3d. The publication of a series of reports, giving the present state and progress of different branches of knowledge.

4th. Formation of a library and museum of objects of nature and art.

5th. Lectures.

Publication of Memoirs.

Agreeably to the plan of the Institution, these memoirs are intended to embody the results of researches which could not otherwise be readily published, and are to be distributed to societies, public libraries, and other institutions. An account of the first memoir was given in the last report. It relates to the ancient monuments of the Mississippi valley, and occupies an entire volume. It has been presented, as far as opportunity would permit, to the principal literary and scientific societies of the world, to all the colleges and larger libraries of this country, and has everywhere been received with much commendation. All the societies from which we have as yet heard, have declared their willingness to co-operate with the Institution, and to give us their publications in exchange, from which source our library has already been enriched with valuable additions.

It is to be regretted that our means would not permit us to distribute the first volume more liberally than we have done, and that the price put upon the copies offered for sale has placed them beyond the reach of many persons desirous of obtaining them. This arose from the fact, that in order to remunerate the authors for the expense and labor bestowed on the memoir, they were allowed to strike off from the types and plates of the Institution an edition to be sold for their own benefit. To avoid risk of loss, the edition was a small one, and the price put at ten dollars. An occurrence of this kind will not happen again; for, although it would be desirable to pay authors for their contributions, yet it is now found that materials will be offered, free of all cost, more than sufficient to exhaust the portion of the income which can be devoted to publications.

In printing the future volumes it will be advisable to strike off an extra number of copies for sale on account of the Institution, and to dispose of those for little more than the mere cost of press-work and paper.

The second volume of Contributions is now in the press, and will consist of a number of memoirs which have been submitted to competent judges and found worthy of a place in the Smithsonian publications. In this volume we have adopted the plan of printing each memoir with a separate title and paging. The object of this is to enable us to distribute extra copies of each memoir separately, and also to furnish the author with a number of copies regularly paged for his own use. It will likewise enable us to classify the memoirs according to subjects.

The following is a brief account of the memoirs contained in the second volume, so far as they have been reported on by the commissioners to whom they have been submitted:

1. *A memoir on the planet Neptune, by Sears C. Walker.*—An abstract of this memoir has been published in the proceedings of the American Philosophical Society, and has received the approbation of the scientific world. It presents the several steps of the discovery of an orbit which has enabled Mr. Walker to compute the place of the new planet with as much precision as that of any of the planets which have been known from the earliest times.* Starting from the observations of the motion of the planet during a period of about four months, Mr. Walker calculated an empirical orbit, which enabled him to trace its path among the stars of the celestial vault through its whole revolution of 166 years. He was thus enabled to carry its position backward until it fell among a cluster of stars accurately mapped by Lalande towards the close of the last century; and, after a minute and critical investigation, he was led to conclude that one of the stars observed by Lalande on the night of May

* It is proper to state that a part of the researches given in this memoir was made during the author's connexion with the National Observatory, under the direction of Lieutenant Maury. An account of these will probably soon be published in the next volume of the records of operations of this observatory.

10, 1795, was the planet Neptune. This conclusion was rendered almost certainty by the observation, made on the first clear night, that all the stars in the cluster above mentioned were found in place, except the one previously fixed upon as the new planet. Some hesitation was created, however, by noting that the missing star in Lalande's maps was marked as doubtful. In order to settle this difficulty, the original manuscript of the astronomer deposited in the Observatory of Paris was referred to. It was then found that Lalande had twice observed the same star; and not finding the right ascension and declination each time the same, and not dreaming it was a planet, he selected one of the observations for publication, marking the position indicated doubtful. The planet had moved during the interval of observation, and thus produced the discrepancy. By allowing for the movement during the time elapsed, the two observations precisely agree. There could, therefore, be no longer any doubt that this star, observed and mapped fifty years ago as a fixed star, was in reality the planet Neptune. Mr. Walker, availing himself of this discovery, had now a series of observations embracing not a few months of the motion of the planet, but which carried it back fifty years. From these data he was enabled to deduce a pure elliptical orbit, or one which the body would describe were there no other planets in the system. This orbit has been investigated by another of our countrymen in a series of profound and beautiful researches, adding much to our knowledge both of Neptune and Uranus. I allude to the labors of Professor Peirce, of Cambridge.

It is well known that the planet Neptune was discovered by mathematical deductions from the perturbations observed in Uranus, and that Leverrier and Adams, the independent authors of this discovery, not only pointed out the direction in which the unseen planet was to be found, but also, from *a priori* considerations, gave the dimensions, form, and position of the orbit it describes around the sun. The direction indicated was the true one, but the elements of the orbit were widely different from those subsequently found to belong to the actual orbit of the planet. Professor Peirce submitted the data used by Leverrier and Adams to a new and critical examination, and succeeded in discovering the cause of their error, and of verifying the conclusions of Mr. Walker. He afterwards proceeded to consider the inverse problem, viz: that of deducing the perturbations which Neptune ought to produce in the planet Uranus. His final results gave a perfect explanation of all the anomalies in the motions of Uranus, and furnished the data, for the first time since its discovery in 1781, for correct tables for determining its position in the heavens. Professor Peirce also investigated the action of all the other planets on Neptune, and his results enabled Mr. Walker, by applying them to his elliptical orbit, to compare the actual with the calculated place of the planet. This led to a further correction of the elliptical orbit, and a more perfect table of calculated places. In this way, by a series of profound and beautiful investigations, alternately combining the data of observation with theoretical considerations, these two astronomers have perfected our knowledge of the motion of the most distant planets of our system, and furnished the means of giving their past and future position through all time. The details of Mr. Peirce's paper have not yet been prepared for the press.

They will probably be given in due time to the world as a part of the Smithsonian Contributions.

The investigations mentioned in the foregoing account have been attended with very laborious arithmetical calculations. A small appropriation has been made to defray, in part, the expense of these. Indeed, without the aid thus given, the discoveries we have related would scarcely have been made—at least at this time, and in our country.

2. The next memoir is *An account of the discovery of a Comet by Miss Maria Mitchell, of Nantucket*, with its approximate orbit, calculated by herself. The honor of this discovery has been duly awarded to the author. A medal has been presented to her by the King of Denmark, and the comet itself is now known to astronomers in every part of the world by her name. From the peculiarities of the case, the Executive Committee recommended that a small premium be presented to Miss Mitchell.

3. The third memoir is *On a new method of solving Cubic Equations, by Professor Strong, of New Brunswick, New Jersey* ; a purely mathematical paper, which has been pronounced an interesting addition to that branch of science.

4. The fourth memoir is *A contribution to the Physical Geography of the United States.* It presents a section, from actual surveys, of the descent of the bed of the Ohio river from its source, in the State of New York, to its mouth, on the Mississippi. By a series of observations and elaborate calculations, the author exhibits the amount of water which passed down the river during a period of eleven years prior to 1849. This, compared with the amount of rain which fell during the same time on the surface drained by the river, gives a series of interesting results in reference to evaporation.

It also contains a proposition for improving the navigation of the Ohio, founded upon data given in the preceding part of the memoir. Whatever may be the result of the plan here proposed, this memoir has been recommended for publication as a valuable addition to the physical geography of the United States. The author is Charles Ellet, jr., the celebrated engineer of the wire bridges over the Niagara and Ohio rivers. Another memoir is promised by the same author, which will be a continuation of the same subject.

5. The fifth memoir is contributed by Dr. Robert Hare, of Philadelphia, and is intended to elucidate the remarkable phenomena exhibited at the great fire in the city of New York on the 19th of July, 1845, during which two hundred and thirty houses were destroyed, containing merchandise amounting in value to sixty-two millions of dollars. "A series of detonations, successively increasing in loudness, were followed by a final explosion, which tore in pieces the building in which it took place, threw down several houses in its vicinity, and forced in the fronts of the houses on the opposite side of the street." These effects were attributed to gunpowder, though the owner of the building in which the explosion occurred declared that none of this article was present, but that the house contained a large quantity of nitre, in connexion with merchandise of a combustible nature.

This memoir contains a series of investigations relative to the explosions which may be produced by heated nitre in connexion with carbonaceous matters. The author shows, by numerous experiments, that explosions of a violent kind can be produced by forcibly bringing into contact at a high temperature, nitre, and substances of an inflammable character. It also contains several new experiments on the combustion of gunpowder under different circumstances.

6. The sixth memoir is *On the Ancient Monuments of the State of New York, by E. G. Squier*, and may be regarded as a continuation of the memoir by Squier and Davis on the ancient monuments of the Mississippi valley. The expense of the explorations which form the basis of this memoir was two hundred dollars, one half of which was defrayed by the members of the Historical Society of New York, and the remainder by this Institution.

7. Another memoir is by Professor Secchi, a young Italian of much ingenuity and learning, a member of Georgetown College. It consists of a new mathematical investigation of the reciprocal action of two galvanic currents on each other, and of the action of a current on the pole of a magnet. It begins with the assumption that the force between the elements of the currents and the magnet is inversely as the square of the distance, and directly as the sine of the inclination, and then presents the mathematical inferences which legitimately flow from these data. The deductions are of such a nature that the author has been able to verify them by means of well devised experiments, and the results accord as nearly with the deductions as the complex nature of the subject will admit. The investigations involve the mathematical theory of the galvanometer, and the experiments furnish much interesting and useful information, aside from the principal object of the memoir, particularly on the comparative value of different kinds of galvanic batteries.

8. The next paper is by Professor Louis Agassiz, of Harvard University, and is entitled *The Classification of Insects upon Embryological Data*. It gives an account of a series of new and interesting facts observed by the author relative to the metamorphosis of insects, which have an important bearing on general questions in zoology, and which will probably lead to the arrangement of these animals according to a new system of classification, founded upon more definite principles than those heretofore adopted.

9. The next is a memoir by Dr. R. W. Gibbes, on the *Mosasaurus* and some new allied genera of the gigantic lizards which formerly inhabited our planet, and of which the remains are now found in different parts of the United States, particularly in the marl beds of various parts of the country. This is an interesting addition to palæontology, and has received a favorable report from the commission to whom it was referred.

Researches.

The programme of organization contemplates the establishment of researches, under the direction of suitable persons, the expense to be borne in whole or in part by the Institution. In the last report it was mentioned that a telescope and other apparatus had been ordered for Lieutenant Gilliss in his astronomical expedition to Chili, and that, without this assistance, the expedition would have been delayed a year. I am now, however, happy to state that the expense of these instruments has since been paid by an appropriation of Congress; and the Institution has thus been the means of promoting the objects of the expedition without any expenditure of its income. Certain improvements in astronomical instruments, however, have been made since the departure of Lieutenant Gilliss which would much facilitate his observations, and enable him to do much more with his small number of assistants; and it may be well for the Institution to furnish him with instruments of this kind.

Under the head of researches it may also be mentioned that, during the past year, we have caused to be computed, at the expense of the Institution, an ephemeris of Neptune, giving the position of the planet in the heavens from August 4, 1846, to February 4, 1848, and also in the last half years of 1848 and 1849. This ephemeris is based on the orbit of Neptune established by Mr. Walker and corrected by the perturbations of the planet Neptune by the action of Jupiter, Saturn, and Uranus, as deduced from the mathematical investigations of Professor Peirce, of Harvard University.

We have distributed copies of this ephemeris to all persons known to us who are interested in practical astronomy, not only in this country but in Europe. It has been received with high commendation, and is found to give the actual place of the planet in the heavens within the limits of a few tenths of a second of arc; indeed, the coincidence of the calculated and observed places is so marked, that, were the actual planet of the heavens and that of the ephemeris to be considered as a double star, they would have so close a proximity that no telescope yet constructed could separate them.

Occultations for 1850.

A set of tables in continuation of those mentioned in the last and preceding report for facilitating the calculation of the appearance of occultations of fixed stars by the moon during the year 1850 has been prepared by Mr. Downes, of Philadelphia, and published by the Institution. At the last session of Congress an appropriation was made for establishing a Nautical Almanac, which will furnish, among other aids to astronomical observation, sets of tables of the kind just mentioned. Lieutenant Davis, of the United States navy, to whom the superintendence of this national work has been entrusted, recommended that the expense of the preparation of the tables for 1850 should be defrayed from the appropriation for the Almanac; and this recommendation has been concurred in by the Secretary of the Navy. The Institution has, therefore, been called upon merely to pay for the printing and distribution of the tables, and thus again enabled, with a small outlay of its funds, to afford important facilities for the advance of science.

Meteorology.

Under the general head of researches we may also give an account of the progress made in establishing the system of meteorological observations proposed in the preceding reports. Circulars describing the plan of operation were distributed to the several parts of the Union through members of Congress at the last session, and the results fully equalled our anticipations. From localities widely separated from each other, and distributed over the greater portion of the United States, about one hundred and fifty monthly returns are now regularly received. To carry on this system efficiently, much labor is necessarily required in the way of correspondence; but it bids fair to furnish the Institution with a wide field of usefulness in bringing it into communication with individuals who, though secluded in position, are desirous of improving themselves, as well as of promoting general knowledge. The correspondence we have thus established, and which we hope to extend, through the aid of the members of the present Congress, will enable us to acquire definite information on a variety of subjects besides those which relate to meteorology. We have already accumulated in this way a mass of curious and instructive information, which we hope, in the progress of the development of the plan of the Institution, to digest and present to the public.

We would mention in this connexion that two of our meteorological correspondents have proposed the collection of statistics of diseases, including the rise, progress, and decline of epidemics. This is a subject we would commend to the American Medical Association. The Smithsonian Institution could assist in an enterprise of this kind by receiving the information which is attainable, and collating it, under the direction of a committee of gentlemen belonging to the medical profession.

It will be recollected that our plan of meteorological observations embraces three classes of observers—one to record the changes in the aspect of the sky, the direction of the wind, beginning and ending of rain, snow, &c.; another, in addition, to give an account of the changes of temperature indicated by the thermometer; and a third, furnished with a full set of instruments for recording the most important atmospheric changes. The importance of the information which may be derived from a careful record of the weather without instruments can scarcely be realized by persons who have given but little attention to the subject. The place of origin, direction, velocity of motion of a storm, as well as the direction and velocity of the wind which composes it, whether gyratory or inward and upward, may all be determined by a sufficient amount of data of the kind we have mentioned. Also, a careful record of the observations of meteors seen by individuals from different positions would furnish interesting data for determining the elevation and velocity of these mysterious visitors.

There are other data which can only be obtained by the use of accurate instruments; fortunately, however, a comparatively small number of observers are sufficient for determining these. The instruments should be of the best possible construction, placed in important situations, and observed at suitable times and with undeviating regularity by competent observers. Few persons are acquainted with the difficulty of procuring accurate meteorological instruments. The ordinary thermometers for sale in the shops frequently differ several degrees from each other, particularly at the higher and the lower temperatures, and even the same thermometer is liable, for a time after its construction, to undergo a change in the size of the bulb, and thus to derange the accuracy of the scale. An accurate barometer is another instrument which cannot readily be obtained, unless at too great a price for the means of ordinary observers. The common weather glasses, sold under the name of barometers, though they may be of use in indicating variations of atmospheric pressure, and thus assist in furnishing data for determining the progress of aerial waves, are inapplicable to the precise and accurate observations necessary to determine the minute changes of atmospheric pressure, or to ascertain the height of places above the level of the sea.

Considerable pains have been taken during the past year to ascertain the best form of a barometer, which could be procured at a reasonable cost; and, after considerable inquiry and comparison of different instruments, we have at length decided upon one, with an adjustable cistern and enclosed in a brass case, which may be transported to a distance, and will serve as well for a mountain barometer as for indicating meteorological changes. For the construction of these instruments, we have employed Mr. James Green, formerly of Baltimore, now of New York; and in order that the instruments furnished by him to ourselves, or sold to our observers, may be comparable with each other, we have procured a standard barometer from London, with which each instrument, previously numbered, is accurately compared, and the record carefully preserved. We have also decided upon the forms of rain and snow guages and wind vanes, and have ordered a number of these to be constructed by Benjamin Pike & Son, Broadway, New York.

It is the policy of the Institution to do as much with its funds as possible, and to call in aid from every quarter whence it may be obtained. With reference to the system of meteorology, I am happy to inform the Board that we have received assistance from a number of sources from which it could scarcely have been expected at the commencement of the scheme. The last Congress appropriated two thousand dollars for meteorology, to be expended under the direction of the Navy Department. It was understood that Professor Espy was to be engaged in the investigations to be made in accordance with this appropriation, and, in order that his labors might co-operate with those of the Institution, the late Secretary of the Navy directed him to apply to me for instructions. During the past year he has been engaged in directing observations and making preparation for a series of experiments having an important bearing on the explanation of meteorological phenomena. It is understood that the remainder of this appropriation, after paying the salary of Mr. Espy, will be expended in defraying incidental expenses, such as printing, engraving, &c.

The Regents of the University of the State of New York, in 1825, organized a system of meteorology, which has continued ever since, and which has added many interesting facts to the stock of scientific knowledge. In order to extend the usefulness of this system, the Regents of the University have lately resolved to reorganize the whole, and to supply the observers with accurate and well compared instruments. This work has been intrusted to Dr. T. Romeyn Beck and one of our Regents, Gideon Hawley, esq., both of Albany. They have adopted the same system and instruments as those of the Smithsonian Institution, and have agreed to co-operate fully with us in the observation of the general and particular phenomena of meteorology. A similar movement has been made in the legislature of Massachusetts for the establishment of a system of observations; and it is hoped that the other States of the Union will follow these examples. We are also happy to state that the medical department of the army, under the direction of Surgeon General Lawson, has signified its willingness to unite with us in the same system, and to furnish the new military posts with instruments constructed on the same plan, and compared with the Smithsonian standard. We hope, therefore, within the coming year, that there will be established at least fifty stations in different parts of North America, furnished with accurate instruments of this kind.

During the past summer I visited Canada, principally for the purpose of examining the meteorological instruments and the method of using them employed at the Observatory of Toronto. Captain Lefroy, the director of this institution, afforded me every facility for acquiring the desired information. He also furnished me with a list of military posts in Canada at which observations may be made, and gave assurance of the hearty co-operation in our labors of the officers attached to these posts. We have also a prospect of procuring permanent observations from Bermuda, some of the West India islands, and from Central America.

From all these statements, it will be seen we are in a fair way of establishing a general system of meteorology, extending over a great portion of North America, including many stations furnished with compared instruments referred to the same standard. When fully organized, it will constitute one of the most important systems ever instituted; but to bring it fully into operation will require a judicious expenditure of all the funds at our disposal for this purpose. At the last session of the Board one thousand dollars were appropriated for meteorological purposes, the greater portion of which has been expended for instruments, among which are those to serve as standards; an equal sum, at least, will be required for the next year.

In connexion with the regular meteorological system, successful applications have been made to the presidents of a number of telegraph lines to allow us, at a certain period of the day, the use of their wires for the transmission of meteorological intelligence. We propose to furnish the most important offices along the lines with sets of instruments, and to give the operators special instructions for the observation of particular phenomena. It is hoped by this means to obtain results not otherwise accessible. Instruments for this purpose are now in process of construction, and as soon as they are completed the transmission of observations will commence.

The establishment of the extended system of meteorology which we have just described is a work of time and labor, the correspondence alone being sufficient constantly to occupy the time of one person; and the adjustment of the several parts of the plan has required more time than my other engagements would permit me to devote to it.

Magnetic Observations.

A set of magnetic apparatus was ordered from London for the purpose of determining the lines of magnetic intensity, declination, and inclination. These are intrusted to Colonel Emory, of the Boundary Commission, and in his possession they will probably be made to do good service in the cause of science. As soon as the funds will admit of the appropriation, it would be advisable to purchase several sets of instruments of the same kind, to be placed in the hands of the scientific explorers of our new territories, and for determining the principal magnetic lines across the United States.

Physical Geography.

Another subject of much interest connected with the physical geography of our country is the collection of the statistics of all railway and canal explorations which have been made in various parts of the United States and Canada. This information, at present in the possession of individuals, is of little value, and, unless collected by some public institution, will soon be lost to the world. Surveys of this kind furnish the most exact data for the determination of what may be called the mountain bases, or general water-sheds of the surface; and no portion of the world of the same extent has been so thoroughly traversed with these explorations as the United States. Connected with these, sketches should be made of the principal mountain ranges, barometrical measurements of the higher peaks, with geological sections of the strata through which the public works are carried. For the purpose of commencing this collection, we have addressed letters to all persons within our knowledge who possess information of this kind, requesting memoirs from them containing results of their own measurements and observations. By this means we hope to present a series of papers of the same character as that of Mr. Ellet, and thus furnish materials for a more accurate physical map of North America, as well as the means, in connexion with our operations in meteorology, for a more exact study of our climate.

During the past year Professor Guyot has made a barometrical exploration of the mountain system of New Hampshire, and he purposes to devote a portion of each year to investigations of this kind.

Natural History.

Our new possessions in Oregon, California, and Mexico offer interesting fields for scientific inquiry, particularly in the line of natural history; and Dr. Gray, of Cambridge, and Dr. Engleman, of St. Louis, aided by several scientific gentlemen interested in this branch of science, have sent a number of collectors to develop the resources of those regions, particularly so far as the botany is concerned.

Among these, Mr. Charles Wright has been engaged to make explorations during the past year in New Mexico, at the expense of a subscription by individuals and institutions. He has just returned laden with a valuable collection of plants, seeds, &c., which are to be divided among those who defrayed the expense. In behalf of the Smithsonian Institution $150 was subscribed towards this enterprise, and for this we are entitled to a full set of all the objects collected. These are to be submitted to Dr. Gray, of Cambridge, to be described in a memoir by him, and to be published in the Smithsonian Contributions. Mr. Wright is expected to start on another expedition early in the spring, for the purpose of making explorations in natural history in the regions around El Paso; and it will be well for the Smithsonian Institution to further assist this laudable enterprise with another subscription of an equal amount.

We have also purchased, for the sum of $20, a set of the plants collected by Mr. Fendler in the vicinity of Santa Fé during the year 1847. This adventurous explorer, under the direction of the gentleman previously mentioned, is now engaged in investigating the botany of the great valley of the Salt Lake, and it is proposed further to assist him by the purchase of a set of the collections he may obtain. By co-operating in this way with individuals and institutions we are enabled, at a small expense, materially to advance the cause of science.

Ancient Monuments.

Another object, the prosecution of which falls particularly within the province of the Institution, is that of obtaining descriptions of the ancient monuments of North America. Circulars have been sent to gentlemen in various parts of the country, requesting them to furnish surveys and explorations of mounds, and other ancient works, which are reputed to exist in their vicinity. To facilitate these investigations, we have requested the authors of the first volume to draw up, from the results of their experience, a set of instructions for the proper examination and description of works of this kind. The same subject has also been placed before several historical societies, established in places where mounds are known to exist. In connexion with this subject, we cannot too highly commend the policy of the new Territory of Minnesota, which, among the first of its acts, has established a Historical Society, to gather up the record of events as they occur, and thus to preserve the unappreciated facts of the present—destined to become history in the future. An important and interesting part of the labors of such societies would be the survey and exploration of the ancient monuments which might be found in their vicinity. Brief accounts of these might be published in the proceedings of the societies, while detailed descriptions and drawings could be given to the world at the expense and through the transactions of the Smithsonian Institution.

The publication of our first volume has awakened a lively interest in this subject, and we have received accounts of various locations of mounds and other ancient works in different parts of the country which were previously unknown. A gentleman, well qualified for the task, is now engaged in preparing for us an ethnological chart indicating the relative positions, as far as they are known, of all the monuments of this kind. This chart may be improved from time to time, and will be the means of eliciting important additional information. Indeed this whole subject should be prosecuted by the Institution, until all accessible information has been collected. The Smithsonian Institution owes this to the world. The work should be done quickly; for the plough, as well as the elements, are every year rendering less visible the outlines and distinctive forms of these remnants of the arts and policy of the ancient inhabitants of this continent.

Bibliographia Americana.

In the last report an account is given of the preparation of a work on the bibliography of America, by Henry Stevens, of Vermont. This work, it will be recollected, is to contain a brief account of every book published in, or relating to, North America, prior to 1700, with references to the different libraries in this and other countries in which these works are to be found. The Institution agreed to publish this work at its own expense, provided, on examination by a commission of competent judges, it is found properly executed. Mr. Stevens is now engaged in the British Museum cataloguing all the works embraced in this plan, and informs me that he is making good progress in his enterprise.

Reports on the Progress of Knowledge.

Of the reports on the progress of knowledge proposed in the plan of organization, none have as yet been published, though several of those mentioned in my report of last year have been completed, or are very nearly ready for the press. The appropriations, however, for the last year were not found sufficient for carrying out further this part of the plan.

The most important report now in progress is that on the forest-trees of North America, by Dr. Gray, Professor of Botany in Harvard University. It is intended in this work to give figures from original drawings of the flowers, leaves, fruit, &c., of each principal species in the United States proper, for the most part of the size of nature, and so executed as to furnish colored or uncolored copies—the first being intended to give an adequate idea of the species, and the second for greater cheapness and more general diffusion.

This work will be completed in three parts, in octavo, with an atlas of quarto plates—the first part to be published next spring. A portion of this will be occupied with an introductory dissertation giving the present state of our knowledge, divested as much as possible of all unnecessary technical terms—of the anatomy, morphology, and physiology of the tree—tracing its growth from the embryo to its full development and reproduction in the formation of fruit and seed. This will be illustrated by drawings from original dissections under the microscope, and sketches made, in every instance, from nature. As the work will be adapted to general comprehension, it will be of interest to the popular as well as the scientific reader.

Report on the history of the discovery of the planet Neptune.—The first part of a report on recent discoveries in astronomy has been completed, and is ready for the press. This is written by Dr. B. A. Gould, of

Cambridge, editor of the American Astronomical Journal. Copious references to authorities are given in foot-notes, which will render the work interesting to the professed astronomer as well as to the less advanced student.

A report has been prepared by Professor Guyot, late of the University of Neufchatel, on the construction and use of meteorological instruments, more particularly designed for distribution among our meteorological observers. This gentleman is now engaged, at the expense of the Regents of the University of the State of New York, in establishing a new system of meteorology, and in instructing the observers in the use of the instruments; for which service he is well adapted by his experience in a similar undertaking in Switzerland.

The report on the application of chemistry to agriculture is also nearly ready for the press. This is by Dr. Lewis C. Beck, of Rutgers College, New Jersey.

Collections.

Apparatus.—The plan of organization also contemplates the formation of a museum of physical instruments, which may be used for experimental illustration and original research, and may serve as models to workmen as well as to illustrate the general progress of inventions in this line.

The munificent donation of Dr. Hare has enabled us to commence this collection with very flattering prospects. It now contains, besides the articles of Dr. Hare, instruments for the illustration of the principles of light, heat, and sound, procured from Paris, and a full set of pneumatic instruments, of superior size and workmanship, constructed expressly for the Institution by Mr. Chamberlain, of Boston; also, a number of chemical articles purchased during the last year; a set o magnetical instruments, already noticed; a standard barometer and thermometers, and other meteorological instruments, procured from Europe. It is proper that I mention, in this place, that we are indebted to Professor Snell, of Amherst, for superintending the construc tion of a set of very ingenious instruments devised by himself for th illustration of wave motion. It is believed that the collection of instru ments of research will, in due time, not only form a feature of grea interest, but that it will surpass in extent similar collections in othe countries.

It is intended to publish a descriptive catalogue of all the instru ments, for the use of visitors; and it may be advisable to illustrate thi by wood-cuts, particularly as we have had presented to us all the woo engravings employed by Dr. Hare in describing his apparatus.

It is not in accordance with the plan of organization to confine th instruments of observation to the immediate use of the officers of th institution but to suffer them to be employed, under certain restrictions by others who are possessed of the requisite degree of skill. Thi practice may be attended in some cases with loss, and the breakage o instruments; but the expenditure which may be incurred on this accoun will probably be more than compensated by the advance to knowledg resulting from the adoption of the plan.

A small appropriation has been made for collections in natural history during the past year; and, under the direction of a distinguished young naturalist, upwards of ten thousand specimens of vertebrated animals, principally reptiles and fishes, have been obtained. Many of these are rare specimens from unexplored parts of our country, and a considerable number of them consists of undescribed species. They furnish the materials for an interesting series of memoirs on physiology, embryology, and comparative anatomy. The whole cost of making this collection did not exceed $140. We are convinced, from the important results obtained by this small expenditure, that a most valuable working collection of objects of the natural history of North America can be obtained at a very moderate outlay of funds.

Library.

During the past year the process of developing the plan of the library, as given in the programme, has been carried out by Professor Jewett as far as the funds which could be devoted to the purpose would allow.

Considerable progress has been made in the plan of forming a general catalogue of all the important libraries in the United States; and Professor Jewett has wisely commenced the preparation of a catalogue of all the books to be found in the different libraries in the city of Washington, including those of the several departments of the government; and in this way he will be enabled to exhibit the importance of catalogues of this kind.

He has also devoted much time to the continuation of his researches relative to the statistics of libraries in this country, and for an account in detail of his valuable labors in this line I must refer to his report herewith transmitted. I will also direct attention to some important suggestions in his report on the subject of the deposit of books for securing copyright, and the establishment of a bulletin.

Museum.

The formation of a museum of objects of nature and of art requires much caution. With a given income to be appropriated to the purpose, a time must come when the cost of keeping the objects will just equal the amount of the appropriation; after this no further increase can take place. Also, the tendency of an Institution of this kind, unless guarded against, will be to expend its funds on a heterogenous collection of objects of mere curiosity; whereas the plan presented in the programme contemplates complete definite collections arranged for scientific purposes, rather than for popular display.

In this connexion there is one point which I beg to present to the consideration of the Board as one of much importance, and which, if possible, should be decided at this meeting, because on it will depend the arrangement of that part of the building devoted to natural history. I allude to the acceptance of the museum of the Exploring Expedition.

By the law incorporating this Institution, "all objects of art and of foreign and curious research, and all objects of natural history, plants, and geological and mineralogical specimens belonging to or hereafter to belong to the United States, which may be in the city of Washington, in whosesoever custody the same may be, shall be delivered to such persons as may be authorized by the Board of Regents to receive them."

This law evidently gives to the Smithsonian Institution the museum in the Patent Office, the conservatory of plants, and all specimens of nature and art to be found in the several offices and departments of the government. The act, however, cannot be construed as rendering it obligatory on the Regents to take charge of these articles, if, in their opinion, it is not for the best interests of the Institution that they should do so. Though one of the reasons urged upon the Regents for the immediate erection of so large a building was the necessity of providing accommodation for this museum, I have been, from the first, of the opinion that it is inexpedient to accept it.

This museum was collected at the expense of the government, and should be preserved as a memento of the science and energy of our navy, and as a means of illustrating and verifying the magnificent volumes which comprise the history of that expedition. If the Regents accept this museum, it must be merged in the Smithsonian collections. It could not be the intention of Congress that an Institution founded by the liberality of a foreigner, and to which he has affixed his own name, should be charged with the keeping of a separate museum, the property of the United States. Besides this, the extensive museum of the Patent Office would immediately fill the space allotted for collections of this kind in the Smithsonian edifice, and in a short time another appropriation would be required for the erection of another building. Moreover, all the objects of interest of this collection have been described and figured in the volumes of the expedition, and the small portion of our funds which can be devoted to a museum may be better employed in collecting new objects, such as have not yet been studied, than in preserving those from which the harvest of discovery has already been fully gathered.

The answer made to some of these objections has usually been, that the government would grant an annual appropriation for the support of the museum of the Exploring Expedition. But this would be equally objectionable; since it would annually bring the Institution before Congress as a supplicant for government patronage, and ultimately subject it to political influence and control.

After an experience of three years, I am fully convinced that the true policy of the Institution is to ask nothing from Congress except the safe-keeping of its funds, to mingle its operations as little as possible with those of the general government, and to adhere in all cases to its own distinct organization, while it co-operates with other institutions in the way of promoting knowledge; and on the other hand, that it is desirable that Congress should place as few restrictions on the Institution as possible, consistent with a judicious expenditure of the income, and that this be judged of by a proper estimate of the results produced.

Lectures.

At the last meeting of the board an appropriation of five hundred dollars was made to defray the expense of lectures to be given before the Smithsonian Institution, a part of which only is expended. The first course, in accordance with this part of the plan of organization, was by Professor Koeppen, of Denmark, on Modern Athens. These lectures were illustrated by a number of large drawings, for the use of which the Institution is indebted to the Lowell Institute, of Boston. A second course was delivered by Dr. Hitchcock, President of Amherst College, on geology, in the lecture-room of the east wing of the Smithsonian building; and both courses were attended by large and apparently interested audiences. The results of these lectures indicate that much good may be effected in Washington by this means of communicating knowledge. No city, perhaps, of the same number of inhabitants, contains so many intelligent and well educated persons desirous of obtaining information; and no point in our country is so favorably situated for the dissemination of opinions, by means of lectures, as the political centre of the American Union. Invitations have been given to a number of distinguished gentlemen in different parts of the United States to favor us with courses of lectures during the present session of Congress, and in almost every case the invitation has been accepted. It is intended to extend these invitations so as to call here in succession all who have distinguished themselves in literature or science. We shall not seek mere popular lecturers, whose chief recommendation is fluency of speech, or powers of rhetorical declamation, but chiefly those who are entitled, from their standing and acquirements, to speak with authority on the subjects of their discourse, and whose character will tend to give due importance to their communications. It is to be regretted that the amount of funds which can be devoted to this object is not as great as could be wished. It is hoped, however, that many persons will consider the opportunity of visiting Washington, and the compliment paid by the invitation, as in part a remuneration for the labor and time which their lectures may cost. But in all cases, sufficient should be allowed to defray all necessary expenses, and, as soon as the state of the funds will permit, to reward liberally, rather than otherwise, those who are called to assist the Institution in this way. I forbear to publish the names of those who have consented to lecture, lest they should be accidentally prevented from filling their engagement, and the public thus be disappointed.

To facilitate the approach to the building, at the time of these lectures, the walks were temporarily improved, at a considerable expense to the Institution. It is hoped that the authorities of the city of Washington will cause bridges to be erected across the canal, and walks to be constructed through the public grounds, to facilitate the approach to the building, and that the Institution will not be expected to provide accommodations of this kind.

Building.

The east wing of the building was taken possession of by the Secretary in April last, and has since been constantly occupied. The west wing is now finished, and it is contemplated to occupy it temporarily as a library until the portion of the main building intended for this purpose is completed.

The plan of the Smithsonian building was designed by the architect, and recommended to the Board by a committee of the Regents, before the programme of organization was adopted. It is not strange, therefore, when the building came to be occupied, that changes in the internal arrangement should be deemed advisable which would better adapt it to the wants of the Institution. Such changes, at my suggestion, have been made; and for the propriety of these I am responsible. They are principally, however, those of simplification, and in themselves add nothing to the cost of the edifice. An increased expense, however, will arise out of the furnishing of new rooms which have been acquired by the alterations.

All of which is respectfully submitted.

JOSEPH HENRY,
Secretary of the Smithsonian Institution.

FOURTH ANNUAL REPORT

Of the Secretary of the Smithsonian Institution, for the year 1850.

To the Board of Regents of the Smithsonian Institution:

GENTLEMEN: During the past year the several parts of the plan of organization have been prosecuted as efficiently as the portion of the income which could be devoted to them would permit. The financial affairs are in a prosperous condition, and though the funds are burthened with the erection of a costly building, and the expenditures trammelled by restrictions growing out of the requisitions of the charter of incorporation, yet the results thus far obtained, are such as satisfactorily to prove that the Institution is doing good service in the way of promoting and diffusing knowledge.

Though the programme of organization has been given in two of the annual reports and extensively published in the newspapers, its character does not appear to be as widely known and as properly appreciated as could be desired. Indeed it will be necessary at intervals to republish the terms of the bequest, and also the general principles of the plan which has been adopted, in order that the public may not only be informed of what the Institution is accomplishing, but also reminded of what ought reasonably to be expected from its operations. Moreover, there is a tendency in the management of public institutions to lose sight of the object for which they were established, and hence it becomes important frequently to advert to the principles by which they ought to be governed. I beg leave, therefore, as introductory to this report, briefly to recapitulate some of the propositions of the programme of organization, and to state some of the facts connected with its adoption.

SMITHSON left his property, in case of the death of his nephew, to whom it was first bequeathed, "to found at Washington, under the name of the Smithsonian Institution, an establishment for the increase and diffusion of knowledge among men." These are the only words of the testator to serve as a guide to the adoption of a plan for the execution of his benevolent design. They are found, however, when attentively considered to admit of legitimate deductions sufficiently definite and comprehensive.

1. The bequest is made to the United States, in trust for the good of *mankind.*

2. The objects of the Institution are two-fold; first, to increase, second, to diffuse knowledge; objects which, though often confounded with each other, are logically distinct and ought to be separately regarded. The first is the enlargement of the existing stock of knowledge by the discovery of new truths, and the second is the dissemination of these and other truths among men.

3. No particular kind of knowledge is designated; hence a liberal interpretation of the bequest will include no part of the great domain of

science and literature from the degree of attention its importance may demand.

4. Since mankind are to be benefited by the bequest, any unnecessary expenditure on merely local objects would not be in accordance with the proper administration of the trust.

5. Though the funds are generally considered large, and much is expected of them, they are really small in proportion to the demands made upon them. The annual income of the bequest is less than half the cost of the publication of a single yearly report of the Patent Offiee.

6. In order, therefore, that the limited income may effect the greatest amount of good, it should be expended in doing that which cannot be done as well by other means.

These views, which have commanded the assent of all unprejudiced and reflecting persons who have studied the subject, have been the guiding principles in all cases in which I have had any power of direction; and I am happy to say they are fully adopted by the present directors and officers of the Institution.

To carry out the design of the testator, various plans were proposed; but most of these were founded on an imperfect apprehension of the terms of the Will. The great majority of them contemplated merely the diffusion of popular information, and neglected the first and the most prominent requisition of the bequest, namely, the "increase of knowledge." The only plan in strict conformity with the terms of the Will, and which especially commended itself to men of science, a class to which Smithson himself belonged, was that of an active living organization, intended principally to promote the discovery and diffusion of new truths by instituting original researches, under the direction of suitable persons, in History, Antiquities, Ethnology, and the various branches of Physical Science. and by publishing and distributing among libraries and other public institutions, accounts of the results which might thus be obtained, as well as of those of the labors of men of talent which could not otherwise be given to the world.

This plan, which was probably in the mind of the donor when he gave expression to the few but comprehensive words which indicate the objects of the bequest, is found from our experience to be eminently practical. It requires no costly building or expensive permanent establishment. Its operations, limited only by the amount of the income, are such as to affect the condition of man wherever literature and science are cultivated, while it tends in this country to give an impulse to original thought, which, amidst the strife of politics, and the inordinate pursuit of wealth, is of all things most desirable.

It was with the hope of being able to assist in the practical development of this plan, that I was induced to accept the appointment of principal executive officer of the Institution. Many unforeseen obstacles, however, presented themselves to its full adoption; and its advocates soon found, in contending with opposing views and adverse interests, a wide difference between what, in their opinion, ought to be done and what they could actually accomplish.

The plan was novel and by many considered entirely chimerical; indeed it could not be properly appreciated except by those who had been devoted to original research. Besides this, the law of Congress incorporating the Institution, while it did not forbid the expenditure of a part of the income for other objects, authorized the formation of a Library, a Museum and a Gallery of Art, and the erection of a building, on a liberal scale, for their accommodation. It was, indeed, the opinion of many that the whole income ought to be expended on these objects. The Regents did not consider themselves at liberty to disregard the indications of Congress, and the opinion expressed in favor of collections; and after much discussion it was finally concluded to divide the income into two equal parts, and, after deducting the general expenses, to devote one half to the active operations set forth in the plan just described; and the other, to the formation of a Library, a Museum and a Gallery of Art.

It was evident, however, that the small income of the original bequest, though in itself sufficient to do much good in the way of active operation, was inadequate to carry out this more extended plan—to maintain the staff of attendants, and to defray other contingent expenses incidental to a large establishment of this kind. Besides the Secretary and an assistant to attend to the general operations, two principal assistants would be required, one to take charge of the Library and the other of the Museum of Natural History; and to these sufficient salaries must be given, to secure the services of men of the first reputation and talents in their respective lines. It, therefore, became absolutely necessary that the income should be increased; and in order to do this, it was proposed to save the greater part of the $242,000 of accrued interest which Congress had authorized to be expended in a building, by erecting, at a cost not to exceed $50,000, the nucleus of an edifice, which could be expanded as the wants of the Institution might require, and to add the remainder to the principal.

Unfortunately, however, for this proposition, Congress had presented to the Institution the great museum of the Exploring Expedition; and a majority of the Regents, supposing it necessary to make immediate provision for the accommodation of this gift, had taken preliminary steps, previous to my appointment, to construct a large building, and indeed a majority of the committee, to which the matter was referred, had determined to adopt the plan of the present edifice. Strenuous opposition was, however, made to this; and as a compromise, it was finally agreed to draw from the United States treasury $250,000 of accrued interest, and instead of expending this immediately in completing the plan of the proposed building, to invest it in treasury notes, then at par, and to finish the building in the course of five years, in part out of the interest of these notes, in part out of the sale of a portion of them, and also in part out of a portion of the annual interest accruing on the original bequest. It was estimated that in this way, at the end of five years, besides devoting $250,000 to the building, the annual income of the Institution would be increased from $30,000 to nearly $40,000, a sum sufficient to carry out all the provisions of the programme.

After the resolutions relative to the division of the income, between collections on the one hand and active operations on the other, had been adopted, and the plan of finance as to the building had been settled, I was requested to confer with persons of literary and scientific reputation, and to digest into the form of a general programme the several resolutions of the Board. In the programme which was thus produced and afterwards adopted, it is attempted to harmonize the different propositions of the Board, and to render them all, library, collections, &c., as far as possible, subservient to a living, active organization. Though a valuable library will in time be accumulated, by donation and the exchange of the publications of the Institution, the design at first is to purchase only such books as are immediately necessary in the other operations of the Institution, or which cannot be procured in this country; and the Librarian is required to perform other duties than those which pertain to the office of an ordinary collector and curator of books. He is directed to report on plans of libraries, and the best method of managing them; to collect the statistics of the libraries of the United States; to make a general catalogue as far as possible of all the books in this country, and to procure all the information necessary for rendering the Institution a centre of bibliographical knowledge. Instead of attempting to form a miscellaneous collection of objects of nature and art, it is proposed to collect only those which will yield a harvest of new results, and to preserve principally such as are not found in other collections, or will serve to illustrate and verify the Smithsonian publications.

The tendency of an Institution in which collections form a prominent object, is constantly towards a stationary condition; with a given income, the time must inevitably come when the expenditures necessary to accommodate the articles with house room and attendance will just equal the receipts. There is indeed no plan by which the funds of an institution may be more inefficiently expended, than that of filling a costly building with an indiscriminate collection of objects of curiosity, and giving these in charge to a set of inactive curators. Happily, the programme of organization and the system of expenditure which the Regents have adopted, if rigidly adhered to, will prevent this state of things, and happily the spirit of the present directors and officers who are to give the initial form to the character of the Institution, is in accordance with as active operations as the state of the funds and requisitions of Congress will allow.

It is to be regretted that Congress did not leave the entire choice of the plan of organization to those who were to be entrusted with the management of the bequest, and that, instead of the plan of a costly building, there had not been adopted the nucleus of a more simple edifice, which could have been modified to meet the wants which experience might indicate.

The original estimate for the building, furniture, and improvement of the grounds was $250,000; and could the actual cost have been confined to this sum, all the results anticipated from the scheme of finance which had been adopted would have been realized at the end of five years. During the past year, however, it has been found necessary, for the better protection of the collections, to order the fire-proofing of the interior of the edifice, at an increased expense of $44,000. This additional draft on the funds can only be met by extending the time for the completion of the building; and even this will require the appropriation of a portion of the income which ought to be devoted to other purposes. The active operations will suffer most by this draft on the income, since it will be made for the better accommodation of the library and the museum.

It must not be inferred, from the foregoing account, that the affairs of the Institution are in an unfavorable condition; on the contrary, though they are not in every respect what could be wished, still, under the circumstances I have mentioned, they are much better than could have been anticipated. The funds are in a very prosperous state, and all the obstacles in the way of the usefulness of the establishment, may, by judicious management, in time be removed. The opposition which was made to the building, led to the adoption of the plan of finance to which I have heretofore adverted, and from this has been realized much more than could have been expected.

After all the expenditures which have been made on the building, grounds, publications, researches, purchase of books and apparatus, not only is the original bequest untouched, but there is now on hand upwards of $200,000 of accrued interest. This will be sufficient to finish the exterior of the building, including all the towers, the interior of the wings, ranges, and a part of the interior of the main edifice; which will afford sufficient accommodation for some years to come, and leave $150,000 to be added to the principal.

This result has been produced by a rigid adherence to the determination of increasing the annual income; and in accordance with this, and in obedience to the direction of the Board of Regents, a petition has been presented to Congress, asking that $150,000 may be taken from the Institution and placed in the treasury of the United States, on the same terms as those of the acceptance of the original bequest, never to be expended, and yielding a perpetual interest of six per cent.

If this petition be granted, all the funds will be permanently and safely invested, and the original income will be increased from $30,000 to nearly $40,000. Out of this, beside carrying on the more important object of the plan, it is proposed to appropriate yearly a small sum for the gradual completion of the interior of the building.

The great importance of a small addition to the income will be evident, when it is recollected that a definite sum is annually required to defray the necessary expenses of the establishment, and that after this has been provided, every addition will tend to produce a greater proportional amount of useful effect. The proposed increase will be sufficient to pay all the salaries of the officers, and leave the original income in a great measure free to be applied to the objects contemplated in the plan.

At the last meeting of the Board, Professor Baird, of Dickinson College, Pennsylvania, a gentleman distinguished for his attainments in science, was appointed an Assistant Secretary in the department of natural history. His appointment was made at this time more particularly in order that his services might be secured to take charge of the publications, and that we might avail ourselves of the ample experience which he had gained in this line. He entered on his duties in July last, and besides being actively engaged in organizing the department of natural history, he has rendered important service in conducting our foreign exchanges and attending to the business of the press.

This addition to our force was absolutely necessary to a more efficient discharge of the duties which devolve on us. No person, except from actual experience, can form an idea of the amount of labor required for the transaction of the ordinary business. The correspondence alone is sufficient to occupy two persons continually during the usual office hours.

During the past year one half of the whole income has been appropriated to the building; and after deducting the general expenses, the remainder has been equally divided between the two great classes of objects designated in the plan. The portion of the income after these divisions, which could be devoted to any one object, has been necessarily small; for example, all that could be expended for researches, publications, and lectures, and indeed for every thing of which the public at a distance could take immediate cognizance, has not exceeded $4,500, and yet out of this sum we have been expected to produce results for which the whole income would be entirely inadequate. I trust, however, that a proper consideration of the facts presented in the remainder of this report, will show that much has been done in proportion to the means at our command.

Publication of Original Memoirs.

The important aid which can be rendered to the promotion of knowledge by the publication, and in some cases by assistance in the preparation of important memoirs, is now beyond all question. Experience has thus far abundantly shown that much more matter of the most valuable character will be presented for publication, free of all charge, than the portion of the income devoted to this object will allow us to publish. Indeed, there is now on hand, or in preparation, more material of this kind than we shall be able, with our limited income, to give to the world in two or three years. In view of this fact, I cannot repress the expression of regret which I have always felt, that the restrictions arising from the requisitions of Congress do not permit a greater expenditure for this most important object. It is chiefly by the publications of the Institution that its fame is to be spread through the world, and the monument most befitting the name of Smithson erected to his memory.

Most of the distinguished foreign literary and scientific societies have placed the Institution on their list of exchange, and in many instances have presented not only the current volume of their transactions, but also full sets of the preceding volumes. We have reason to believe that before the expiration of another year, we shall receive in exchange the transactions of nearly all the learned societies of the world, and that the Institution will be recognised by them as an active co-operator in the promotion of knowledge. Professor Baird has furnished a list of the literary and scientific societies to which the quarto volumes have been presented.

The following Memoirs, an account of which was given in my last report, have been printed, or are now in press:

1. Researches relative to the planet Neptune; by S. C. Walker.
2. Contributions to the Physical Geography of the United States; by Charles Ellet, Jr.

3. Memoir on the Explosiveness of Nitre; by Dr. Robert Hare.

4. On the Aboriginal Monuments of the State of New York; by E. G. Squier.

5. Memoir on the Reciprocal Action of two Galvanic Currents; by A. Secchi, of Georgetown College.

6. On the Classification of Insects, from Embryological Data; by Professor Louis Agassiz.

7. Monograph of Mosasaurus and the allied Genera; by Dr. R. W. Gibbes.

Besides these, several other papers not described in my last report havè been printed, and are ready for separate distribution. The first of these I shall mention is by Professor Lieber, of the College of South Carolina, on the vocal sounds of Laura Bridgman, the blind and deaf mute, whose mind, apparently forever consigned to darkness, has been almost miraculously enlightened, by the sagacity, ingenuity, and perseverance of Dr. Howe.

There is, perhaps, at this time, no living human being who offers to the psychologist so attractive an object of study as this individual; and hence every observation relative to her peculiar habits is of great interest. Dr. Lieber has, from year to year, during his summer vacations, been in the habit of visiting Laura Bridgman, and on one occasion spent three months in her immediate neighborhood for the purpose of studying the sounds which she utters as indicative of ideas. These sounds consist principally of such as she volutarily adopted to designate different individuals. The results of the observations given in this paper are accompanied by a series of philosophical deductions and suggestions which cannot fail to interest the psychologist and physiologist. This memoir is illustrated by an engraved *fac simile* of a letter from Laura Bridgman's own hand.

The next paper is by Professor Bailey of West Point. This gentleman has rendered himself favorably known to the world of science by his researches on minute animals and plants, which, though mostly unseen by the naked eye, are found as widely distributed, and as permanent and definite in character, as the largest organized objects in nature. This paper gives the results of a series of microscopic observations which the author made during his sojourn in the southern part of the United States, whither he was ordered last winter on account of his health. It designates numerous localities of microscopic animals and plants, and furnishes lists of the species found in each. It also contains a series of tables presenting a number of species with the different localities where each was found. The species so classed include those of the Desmidiæ, Diatomaceæ, Infusoriæ, and Algæ. Following these is a deseription of numerous other species, most of which are represented by lithographic figures.

Among the interesting facts arrived at by the author, are the discovery of an extensive stratum of fossil infusoriæ near Tampa Bay, Florida; the existence of infusoriæ in the rice fields of the south; and the demonstration of the cosmopolite character of many microscopic objects hitherto believed to exist only in Europe.

Another paper by the same author, but presented to the Institution by Professor Bache, Superintendent of the U. S. Coast Survey, has reference to a microscopic examination of soundings along the eastern coast of the United States; samples of all the materials brought up by the sounding apparatus of the Coast Survey having been carefully preserved by Professor Bache in bottles, and so arranged as to present, as it were, the surface geology of the bottom of the sea within a certain distance from the shore. Specimens of these were given to Professor Bailey for microscopic examination, and the results are presented in this paper. It exhibits the fact of a high development of minute organic forms, mainly of Polythalamia, in all deep soundings, varying from fifty-one to ninety fathoms, occurring in an abundance similar to that in which analogous fossil forms are found in the marls under the city of Charleston. It also shows that each locality has its predominant species, by means of which alone the region whence they were taken may be indicated. Many of the conclusions derived are of much interest to the mariner, the geologist, and the naturalist. The paper closes with a brief description of the genera and species referred to, embracing several that are new, the whole accompanied by numerous figures.

In connexion with the foregoing may be mentioned a paper by Mr. Charles Girard, entitled "A Monograph of the Fresh water Cottoids of North America," which has been accepted, and will soon be published. The species of fish called *Cottus gobio*, was supposed to be common to Europe and America, and thus to form an exception to a general rule in regard to the fresh water species of the two continents. It has been discovered by Mr. Girard and others, that the European species, as described by Linnæus, is really composed of several, and that while none of these are found in North America, we have actually a number of species peculiar to this country. The memoir contains elaborate descriptions of the known species as well as of several new ones, together with copious notes on their scientific history, their geographical distribution, affinities with each other and with foreign species, anatomical structure, &c.,—the whole illustrated by appropriate figures. It is worthy of remark, that most of the hitherto undescribed species presented in this memoir were collected by Professor Baird, and now form a part of the Smithsonian collection.

Another memoir, now in course of preparation, is one which will of itself occupy a considerable portion of one of the quarto volumes of the Smithsonian Contributions. It affords an interesting illustration of the working of the plan of organization in the way of eliciting important scientific knowledge which would not otherwise be produced, or, if produced, could not be given to the world through any other channel.

This memoir consists of a description of the marine plants, or Algæ, which are found along the eastern and southern coasts of the United States, and which are deserving of attention, not only on account of their beauty, variety, and the illustrations they present of the growth and development of vegetable forms, but also on account of their economical value with reference to agriculture and the chemical arts. This volume is in the course of preparation by Professor Harvey, of the University of Dublin, Ireland, a gentleman who is recognised as the first authority in this branch of botany. He was induced to visit this country by an invitation to lecture on the Algæ before the Lowell Institute, and by the opportunity thus offered him of studying his favorite branch of science in a new region. After completing his lectures, he made a collection of the marine plants of our coast, and offered to furnish drawings of the genera and species, with detailed descriptions free of all cost, provided the Institution would bear the expense of publication.

Upon the warm recommendation of some of the principal botanists of the country, the liberal offer of Professor Harvey was accepted, and he is now engaged in making with his own hand the drawings on stone. The preparation of the work, besides the time expended in collecting the specimens, will occupy two or three years. This voluntary contribution to knowledge from a man of science may surprise those whose minds are not liberalized by philosophical pursuits, and who cannot conceive any object in labor unconnected with pecuniary gain.

To assist in defraying the heavy expense of the publication of this work, it is proposed to color the plates of a part of the edition, and to offer copies for sale. The work will also be issued in parts, so as to distribute the cost through several years.

In addition to the foregoing, an appendix—added to Mr. Squier's paper on the ancient monuments of New York—has been printed. Also, there has been such an urgent demand for copies of Mr. Ellet's paper on the physical geography of the Mississippi Valley, that it has been thought advisable to reprint it and distribute the whole of the first edition among all persons to whom a knowledge of its contents would be of peculiar importance.

The several papers which have been described in this and the preceding Report will, when collected together, form the contents of the second and part of the third volume.

The plan adopted of printing each memoir with a separate title and paging has been found to answer a good purpose. There is no delay in printing one paper on account of the engraving of the plates of another; and long before a volume can be completed, a separate memoir may be widely circulated among those most interested in its perusal. As an example of this, I may mention that one of the papers which forms part of the second volume of the Contributions has already been reprinted in the London and Edinburg Journal, with due credit given to the Institution.

Reports on the Progress of Knowledge.

The income of the Institution as yet has not been sufficient for fully reducing to practice this part of the plan of organization. The preparation of these reports can only be intrusted to those who are familiar with the subjects, and well skilled in the art of composition, and the services of such persons cannot be obtained without an adequate remuneration. Of the several reports mentioned at the last meeting of the Board but one has been published, viz: that on the discovery of the planet Neptune, by Dr. B. A. Gould, of Cambridge, editor of the Astronomical Journal. It has been stereotyped, and copies distributed amongst all our meteorological observers and other persons in the country known to us as being actively engaged in promoting the science of astronomy.

The preparation of the report on the Forest-Trees of North America, though delayed in consequence of the absence of the author, Dr. Gray, of Harvard University, on a visit to Europe, is still in progress. The illustrations are in the hands of the artists, and the first part will probably be published during the present year. The cost of this report, on account of the elaborate illustrations, will be greater than was at first anticipated; consequently the publication of the entire work must necessarily be spread over a number of years. It is believed, however, that a considerable part of the expense will be repaid to the Institution by the sale of copies at a small advance on the original cost.

The other reports on the Progress of Knowledge mentioned in my last communication to the Regents are ready for the press, and will be published, in whole or in part, during the present year.

The Report on the statistics of Libraries of the United States, prepared by Professor Jewett, has been ordered to be printed by Congress, as an appendix to the Regents' Report. A sufficient number of extra copies will be presented to the Institution, for distribution to all the libraries from which statistical information was received. It forms a volume of about two hundred and twenty-five pages, and will, I am sure, be considered an important contribution to bibliographical statistics.

Distribution of Publications.

We have found considerable difficulty in deciding upon the rules to be observed in the distribution of the Smithsonian publications. It is evident that, from the small portion of the income which can be devoted to this object, the distribution must be circumscribed. Fifteen hundred copies of each memoir have been printed; but this number, though all that the income could furnish, has not been found sufficient to meet a tenth part of the demand. It should be recollected that, though these memoirs consist of the results of new investigations of the highest importance to the well-being of man, in extending the bounds of his knowledge of the universe of mind and matter, yet they are not generally of such a character as to be immediately appreciated by the popular mind, and, indeed, they are better adapted to instruct the teacher than to interest the general reader. They should, therefore, be distributed in such a way as most readily to meet the eye of those who will make the best use of them in diffusing a knowledge of their contents.

The following rules have been adopted for the distribution of the quarto volumes of collections of memoirs:

1. They are to be presented to all Learned Societies which publish transactions and give copies of these in exchange to the Institution.
2. To all Foreign Libraries of the first class, provided they give in exchange their catalogues, or other publications, or an equivalent from their duplicate volumes.
3. To all Colleges in actual operation in this country, provided they furnish in return meteorological observations, catalogues of their libraries and of their students, and all other publications issued by them relative to their organization and history.

4. To all States and Territories; provided they give in return, copies of all documents published under their authority.

5. To all incorporated Public Libraries in this country, not included in either of the foregoing classes, containing more than seven thousand volumes; and to smaller Libraries, where a whole State or large district would be otherwise left unsupplied.

The author of each memoir receives, as his only compensation, a certain number of copies, to distribute among his friends, or to present to individuals who may be occupied in the same line of research. In this way single memoirs are distributed to individuals, and especially to those who are most actively engaged in promoting discoveries. Copies of the reports, and also in some cases of particular memoirs, are sent to our meteorological observers. Besides these, we have placed on the list the more prominent Academies and Lyceums, as recipients of the minor publications. It is also intended, in order to benefit the public more generally, to place on sale copies of memoirs and reports; though on account of the number required for the supply of Institutions, we have not, as yet, been able to carry this plan into effect.

No copyright has been taken for the Smithsonian publications; they are therefore free to be used by the compilers of books, and in this way they are beginning to reach the general reader and to produce a beneficial effect on the public mind.

Meteorology.

The system of meteorology under the direction of the Smithsonian Institution has, during the last year, made good progress. And though the whole number of stations has not been much increased, yet the character of the instruments adopted, and consequently the value of the observations, has been improved both in precision and variety.

This system is intended to embrace, as far as possible, the whole extent of North America, and to consist of three classes of observers. One class, without instruments, to record the changes in the aspect of the sky, the direction of the wind, the beginning and ending of rain, the appearance of the aurora, &c. Another, in addition to the foregoing, to give an account of the changes of temperature, as indicated by the thermometer. A third class, furnished with full sets of instruments, to record all changes deemed important in the study of meteorology.

To carry on this system, the Institution has received or expects to receive assistance from the following sources:

1. From the small appropriation made by Congress, to be expended under the direction of the Navy Department.

2. From the appropriations made by different States of the Union.

3. From the observations made under the direction of the Medical Department of the United States army.

4. From the officers of her Majesty's service in different parts of the British possessions in North America.

5. From observations made by institutions and individuals, in different parts of the continent, who report immediately to the Smithsonian Institution.

A small appropriation has been made by Congress for two years past, to be expended under the direction of the Navy Department for meteorological purposes; and Professor Espy, engaged under the act making this appropriation, has been directed to co-operate with the Institution, in promotion of the common object. Besides the aid which we have received from Professor Espy's knowledge of this subject, the general system has been benefited in the use of instruments purchased by the surplus of the appropriation, after paying the salary of the director and other expenses.

During the last year, Professor Espy has been engaged in a series of interesting experiments on the variations of temperature produced by a sudden change in the density of atmospheric air. The results obtained are important additions to science, and directly applicable to meteorology. The experiments were made in one of the rooms of the Smithsonian Institution, and with articles of apparatus belonging to the collection which constituted the liberal donation of Dr. Hare. An account of these investigations will be given in a report to the Secretary of the Navy.

It was mentioned in the last Report that the Regents of the University of the State of New York, in 1849, made a liberal appropriation of funds for the re-organization of the meteorological system of observations established in 1825; and that Dr. T. Romeyn Beck and the Hon. Gideon Hawley, to whom the enterprise was entrusted, had adopted the forms and the instruments prepared under the direction of the Smithsonian Institution. Another appropriation has been made, for 1850; and the system has been carried, during the past year, into successful operation by Professor Guyot, late of Neufchatel, in Switzerland. This gentleman, who has established a wide reputation as a meteorological observer by his labors in his own country, was recommended to Dr. Beck and Mr. Hawley by this Institution, and employed by them to superintend the fitting up of the instruments in their places, to instruct the observers in the minute details of their duty, and to determine the topographical character and elevation above the sea of each station.

The whole number of stations which have been established in the State of New York is thirty-eight, including those which have been furnished with instruments by the Smithsonian Institution, and the Adirondack station by the liberality of Archibald McIntyre, esq., of Albany. This number gives one station to twelve hundred and seventy square miles, or about one in each square of thirty-five and a half miles on a side. These stations are at very different heights above the level of the sea. They were selected in conference with Dr. Beck, Professor Guyot, and myself. The State is naturally divided into the following topographical regions, namely:

1. The Southern or maritime region.

2. The Eastern, or region of the Highlands and Catskill mountains, with the valleys of the Hudson and Mohawk rivers.

3. The Northern, or region of the Adirondack mountains, isolated by the deep valleys of the Mohawk, Lake Champlain, the St. Lawrence, and Lake Ontario.

4. The Western, or region of the western plateau, with the small lakes and sources of the rivers.

5. The region of the great lakes, Erie and Ontario.

I regret to state that no efficient steps have as yet been taken to organize the system of Massachusetts, for which an appropriation was made by the legislature, at its last session. I have lately written to Governor Briggs, urging immediate action, and offering, on the part of the Institution, to render any assistance in our power towards furthering so laudable an enterprise. No answer has yet been received.*

The observations made at the different military stations, under the direction of the Medical Department of the United States army, have been partially re-organized, and a number of new stations and several of the old ones furnished with improved Smithsonian instruments. The head of the Medical Department of the army, Dr. Lawson, has assigned the general direction of the system of observations to Dr. Mower, of New York, to whom we are indebted for the valuable aid which this extended set of observations furnishes the general system. The immediate superintendence of the reduction of these observations is in charge of Dr. Wotherspoon, to whose zeal and scientific abilities the cause of meteorology bids fair to be much indebted.

The most important service the Smithsonian Institution has rendered to meteorology during the past year, has been the general introduction into the country of a more accurate set of instruments at a reasonable price. The set consists of a barometer, thermometer, hygrometer, wind vane, and snow and rain guage.

The barometer is made by James Green, No. 422 Broadway, New York, under the direction of the Institution. It has a glass cistern with an adjustable bottom enclosed in a brass cylinder. The barometer tube is also enclosed in a brass cylinder, which carries the vernier. The whole is suspended freely, from a ring at the top, so as to adjust itself to the vertical position. The bulb of the attached thermometer is enclosed in a brass envelope communicating with the interior of the brass tube, so as to be in the same condition with the mercury, and to indicate truly its temperature. Each instrument made according to this pattern is numbered and accurately compared with a standard. In the comparisons made by Professor Guyot, a standard Fortin barometer, by Ernst, of Paris, was employed; also a standard English barometer, by Newman, of London, belonging to this Institution. These instruments, for greater certainty, have been compared with the standard of the Cambridge Observatory, and of Columbia College, both by Newman; also with the standard of the Observatory of Toronto, Upper Canada.

The results of these examinations prove the barometers made by Mr. Green, according to the plan adopted by the Smithsonian Institution, to be trustworthy instruments.

The thermometers are by the same maker; and those intended for the State of New York were compared with a standard by Bunten, of Paris, and with another by Troughton & Simms, of London. Those found to differ more than a given quantity from the standards were rejected.

---

* A letter has since been received, and the system placed under the direction of this Institution.

The instruments for indicating the variation of the hygrometrical condition of the atmosphere, consist of two thermometers, of the same dimensions, accurately graduated. The bulb of one of these is enveloped in a covering of muslin moistened with water, and that of the other is naked.

The rain and snow guages, and also the wind vanes, are made under the direction of the Institution, by Messrs. Pike & Son, 166 Broadway, New York. The rain guage is an inverted cone of sheet zinc, of which the area of the base is exactly one hundred square inches. This cone or funnel terminates in a tube which carries the water into a receiving vessel. The water which has fallen is measured by pouring it from the guage into a cylinder, so graduated as to indicate hundredths of inches. A smaller cylinder is also provided, which gives thousandths of inches, and may serve, in case of accident, as a substitute for the larger cylinder. The rain gauge is placed in a cask sunk in the earth, with its month near the level of the ground.

The snow gauge is a cylinder of zinc of the same diameter as the mouth of the rain guage. The measurement is made by pressing its mouth downward to the bottom of the snow, where it has fallen on a level surface, then carefully inverting it, retaining the snow, by passing under it a thin plate of metal. The snow is afterwards melted, and the water produced is measured in one of the graduated glass cylinders of the rain guage.

The wind vane is a thin sheet of metal, (it might be of wood,) about three feet long, carefully balanced by a ball of lead, and attached to the top of a long wooden rod, which descends along the wall of the building to the sill of the observer's window. It terminates in the centre of a fixed dial-plate, and its movements indicate the direction of the wind by a pointer attached to the rod.

The observer is by this arrangement enabled to determine the course of the wind, by looking down on the dial-plate, through the glass of the window, without exposing himself to the storm.

Besides the full sets of instruments furnished by the State of New York, from the appropriation of the regents of the University, the Smithsonian Institution has furnished a number of sets to important stations; and, in order that they might be more widely disseminated, we have directed Mr. Green to dispose of sets, to individuals, at a reduced price, on condition that they will give us copies of the results of their observations; the remainder of the cost being paid by this Institution. A number of persons have availed themselves of this privilege.

To accompany the instruments, and for the use of those who take part in the Smithsonian system of meteorological observations, a series of minute directions, prepared by Professor Guyot, has been printed by the Institution. It occupies forty octavo pages, with wood-cut representations of the instruments, and is accompanied by two lithographic engravings, to illustrate the different forms of clouds, and to facilitate their notation in the journals, in accordance with the nomenclature adopted by meteorologists. A set of tables has also been furnished for correcting the barometrical observations, on account of variation of temperature. A set of hygrometrical tables, to be used with the wet and dry bulb thermometers, and a set for the calculation of heights by the barometer, will be prepared.

We may also mention, in connexion with this subject, that a series of preliminary experiments have been made, in the laboratory of this Institution, for the purpose of constructing, from direct observation, a scale of boiling temperatures, corresponding to different degrees of rarefaction of the air. With a thermometer, each degree of which occupies one inch in length of the scale, the variations of the boiling point corresponding to a slight change in altitude are found to be more perceptible than those in the length of the barometrical column.

A series of experiments has also been made for testing the performance of the aneroid barometer under extremes of atmospheric pressure. The instrument, as usually constructed, has not been found, from these experiments, very reliable though it may be improved, and thus serve as an indicator of minute atmospheric changes. I think, however, it will not answer for the determination of changes of atmospheric pressure of considerable magnitude.

For the better comprehending the relative position of the several places of observation, now embraced in our system of meteorology, an outline map of North America has been constructed, by Prof. Foreman. This map is intended also to be used for presenting the successive phases of the sky over the whole country, at different points of time, as far as reported; and we have been waiting for its completion, to commence a series of investigations, with the materials now on hand, relative to the progress of storms.

A valuable collection of returns relative to the aurora, has been received in accordance with the special instructions which we have issued for the observation of this interesting phenomenon. These are to be placed in the hands of Captain Lefroy, of the Toronto Observatory, and incorporated with observations of a similar kind which he has collected in the British possessions of North America. An account in full of the whole series will be presented by Captain Lefroy, to be published in the Smithsonian Contributions.

The meteorological correspondence is under the charge of Professor Foreman. This is found not only to involve considerable labor in the way of arranging the regular returns and sending the required blanks and directions, but also in the discussion of questions on almost every branch of science propounded by the meteorological observers, which we think it our duty in all cases to treat with respect, and to answer to the best of our knowledge.

Researches, &c.

Explorations.—The programme of organization contemplates the institution of researches in Natural History, Geology, &c.; and, though the state of the funds would permit of little being done in this line, yet we have made a beginning. Besides the assistance rendered to the exploration of the botany of New Mexico, by the purchase of sets of plants from Mr. Wright and Mr. Fendler, as mentioned in my last Report, a small sum was appropriated, to defray the cost of transportation of the articles which might be collected by Mr. Thaddeus Culbertson, in the region of the Upper Missouri. This gentleman, a graduate of the institutions at Princeton, had purposed to visit the remote regions above mentioned for the benefit of his health, and was provided by Professor Baird with minute directions as to the preservation of specimens and the objects which should particularly engage his attention. His journey was undertaken, and executed, under particularly favorable circumstances for exploration. He was accompanied by his brother, Mr. Alexander Culbertson, for many years connected with the American Fur Company, who was familiar with the whole country, and had himself sent valuable specimens of fossil mammalians to the Philadelphia Academy of Natural Sciences.

Mr. Culbertson first visited an interesting locality called the *Mauvaises Terres*, or Bad Lands, where his brother had previously found the remains of the fossils sent to the Academy. He afterwards ascended the Missouri, to a point several hundred miles above Fort Union. He returned in August last in renewed health to gladden the hearts of his parents and friends, with the prospect of long life and usefulness; but though he had withstood the privations and exposures of the wilderness, he sank under an attack of a prevalent disease and died after a few weeks' illness.

He left a journal of all the important events of his tour, which is thought of sufficient importance to be appended to this Report.

For a particular account of the interesting specimens which he procured, many of which are new and undescribed, I must refer to the appended report of Professor Baird. A part of the specimens, those of the fossil remains, have been referred to Dr. Leidy, of Philadelphia, who will present the result of his investigations relative to them, for publication in one of the volumes of the Smithsonian Contributions.

A small appropriation has also been made to defray in part the expense of exploration, relative to the erosions of the surface of the earth, especially by rivers, and for investigations relative to terraces and ancient sea-beaches, under the direction of President Hitchcock. An abstract of these investigations, as far as they have been made, has been received by the Institution; and a full account of the whole, it is expected, will soon be ready for publication.

An exploration for the increase of the Smithsonian collection, particularly in fishes and reptiles, of which our knowledge is most imperfect, was undertaken by Professor Baird, accompanied by a number of young gentlemen, his former pupils. The result of this expedition, which cost the Institution little more than the price of materials and transportation, was a large number of specimens, including numerous species before unknown to science.

Experiments.—A series of experiments has been made, during the past year, under the direction of Professor Jewett, to test the value of a new plan of stereotyping. If the result of these experiments be favorable, it is proposed to purchase the right to use the invention, for the purposes of the Institution. Should the invention be found to possess the character to which it appears entitled, it will not only be of much importance to the Institution, but to the world; and we shall have done good service to the cause of knowledge, by giving it our countenance and assistance. Professor Jewett has found it especially applicable to his system of stereotyping catalogues of libraries, by separate titles; and in this way it will certainly be of great value, even shonld it fail in other respects to realize the sanguine expectations of its inventor.

The result of the experiments will be submitted to a commission of persons properly qualified to judge of its merits; and if their report be favorable, a small sum will be allowed for the use of it.

Besides the experiments mentioned under the head of meteorology, made by Mr. Espy, on the cold produced by the rarefaction of air, Dr. Hare, of Philadelphia, is employing articles of apparatus belonging to the Institution, in a series of researches on the phenomena exhibited in the air and in a vacuum by rubbing silicious minerals against each other. The results of these experiments, with the drawings of the apparatus employed, he intends to present to the Institution in the form of a memoir for the Smithsonian Contributions to Knowledge.

Computations.

Occultations for 1851.—For the purpose of facilitating the accurate determination of geographical points in the United States, a list of occultations and the co-ordinates of reductions for the years 1848, 1849, and 1850, was prepared and published at the expense of the Smithsonian Institution. Congress has since ordered the publication of an American Nantical Almanac; and as lists of occulations will form a part of this ephemeris, Mr. Preston, late Secretary of the Navy, directed that the expense of computing these tables for 1850 should be defrayed from the appropriation for the Almanac, provided the printing and distribution were at the expense of the Smithsonian Institution. The same course has been authorized by Mr. Graham, the present Secretary of the Navy.

Copies of these tables, computed by John Downes, of Philadelphia, have been sent to all persons known to the Institution, who would probably make use of them in the way of improving our knowledge of the geography of this country. They have been furnished particularly to officers of the United States army, and other persons engaged in exploring our new possessions and determining their boundaries. All persons, to whom these tables were presented, have been requested to send the result of their observations, made in connexion with the use of them, to this Institution, or to publish them in some accessible journal.

Ephemeris of Neptune.—It was stated, in the last Report, that the orbit of the planet Neptune, established by the researches of Mr. Walker, and comprised in his memoir published by the Institution, gives the data for calculating an ephemeris or tables of the daily position of this planet, rivalling in precision the tables for any of the older planets. Sets of these tables were computed and published for 1848 and 1849, at the expense of the Smithsonian Institution; but those for 1850 and 1851 have been computed under the direction of Lieutenant Davis, superintendent of the Nautical Almanac, and at the expense of the appropriation under his charge, while the expense of printing the tables has been borne by this Institution.

These tables are corrected for the perturbing influence of the planets Jupiter, Saturn, and Uranus, by deductions from mathematical investigations of Professor Peirce, of Harvard University. They have been used in following the motion of Neptune, by all the principal astronomers of the world, and have everywhere received the highest commendation, reflecting honor on the Institution, and on the science of the country.

Museum.

The act of Congress authorizing the establishment of the Smithsonian Institution contemplates the formation of a Museum of Natural History. It would not, however, be in accordance with the spirit of the organization, to expend the income in the reproduction of collections of objects which are to be found in every museum of the country. Natural history can be much more effectually promoted by special collections of new objects; by appropriations for original explorations and researches; and above all, by assistance in the preparation of the necessary drawings, and by presenting to the world, in a proper form, the labors of naturalists. In conformity with these views, it has been resolved to confine the collections, principally, to objects of a special character, or to such as may lead to the discovery of new truths, or which may serve to verify or disprove existing or proposed scientific generalizations. A number of special collections, important in this point of view, are mentioned by Professor Agassiz, in the Appendix to my last Report; and, for a more enlarged statement relating to the same subject, I would refer naturalists to the accompanying report by Professor Baird, to whom the charge of the collections of natural history has been confided.

A considerable number of specimens in mineralogy, geology, and botany, had been received previous to Professor Baird's connexion with the Institution; and since he has entered upon his duties, a large addition has been made to the stock, by the deposit of his own cabinet, and by donations from various sources.

The collection is principally rich in undescribed species of fishes and reptiles; and especial care will be taken, by Professor Baird, to enhance its value, by procuring, in all cases, as far as practicable, such specimens as may help to solve questions of scientific interest. The collection has been arranged in one of the rooms of the basement story, so as to be available to the student in this branch of science, and has already done service in this way, by furnishing the facts given in one of the memoirs of the Smithsonian Contributions. Though letters are constantly received requesting the Institution to purchase collections of plants, minerals, and other objects of natural history, yet we have declined, in all cases, to avail ourselves of opportunities of this kind to increase the cabinet. Experience has, thus far, shown that specimens of all kinds will accumulate, from donations and exchange, as rapidly as they can be accommodated with room, and properly arranged.

I have given, in my last report, the reasons why it is not thought advisable, on the part of the Institution, to accept the gift, proffered by Congress, of the great museum of the Exploring Expedition, and I have no reason to change my opinion on that point.

For a detailed account of the specimens forming the Smithsonian collection, I refer to Professor Baird's report, herewith submitted.

American Antiquities.

During the past year, we have received information of the locality of a number of mounds, and other remains of ancient art, in different parts of the United States. A gentleman is now engaged in the examination of the mounds of Western Virginia, with the intention of presenting the results of his labors for publication in the Smithsonian Contributions.

The survey of the mineral land in the vicinity of Lake Superior has disclosed the site of an ancient copper mine, whence, in all probability, the copper of the ornaments, instruments, &c., found in the mounds, was derived. The remains of the implements, and of the ore, as left by the ancient miners, are exhibited in place, and afford an interesting illustration of the state of arts among the mound-builders. The geological surveyors have promised to make accurate measurements and drawings of everything of interest connected with these works, and to present them, with suitable descriptions, to the Institution, for publication.

Mr. E. G. Squier, during his sojourn in Central America, as Chargé d'affaires of the United States, made some interesting explorations relative to the antiquities of that country, and has sent to this Institution five large stone idols and several smaller objects, as the beginning of an ethnological museum. For the cost of shipment and transportation of the three larger idols by way of Cape Horn, the Institution is indebted to the liberality of B. Blanco, esq., of New York.

For some remarks relative to the importance of forming an ethnological museum, I beg to refer to a paper by Mr. Squier, given in the Appendix to this Report.

Apparatus and instruments of research.

It is a part of the plan of the Institution to appropriate a small portion of the funds to the purchase of sets of instruments for physical research, to be used by the officers of the Institution, and, under certain restrictions, by other persons. In accordance with this purpose, I was requested, by the Board of Regents, to procure an astronomical clock, with the electro-magnetic registering apparatus, to be lent to Lieutenant Gillis during the continuance of his astronomical labors in Chili. The clock has been imported from Germany, and is now in the hands of the instrument maker, to receive the registering attachments. The whole will be sent to Chili, as soon as the apparatus is completed. I regret that the difficulty of procuring the services of suitable workmen has delayed so long the completion of these instruments.

A communication from Lieutenant Gillis, informs us that the Chilian government has resolved to establish a permanent national observatory at Santiago, and that it will purchase the instruments above mentioned. The Institution will therefore again, as in the case, mentioned in a former Report, of the purchase of a telescope for the same expedition, be the means of promoting science without an expenditure of its income.

The apparatus for determining the elements of terrestrial magnetism, mentioned in my last Report, as having been lent to Colonel Emory, has been delivered to Colonel Graham, to be used on the Mexican Boundary Survey. To replace these, the Institution has received permission to order another set, from London, at the expense of the government; and thus, by an addition to the number of instruments of this kind, the means of promoting the science of terrestrial magnetism, in this country, will be increased.

The purchase of standard meteorological apparatus, and also the instruments which have been distributed to different important stations, throughout the country, is a part of the same plan.

During the past year a considerable portion of the apparatus constituting the liberal donation of Dr. Hare, of Philadelphia, has been repaired and fitted up; and we hope, during the present season, to complete the repairs of the remainder, and to place the whole in a proper position for exhibition and use.

Library.

It has been stated, that the programme of organization is intended to harmonize the several requisitions of Congress, and the resolutions of the Board of Regents, with a system of active operations, the influence of which shall be as widely extended as practicable. Though almost every one will admit the value of libraries, and the importance of colleeting in this country as great a variety of books as possible, yet it may well be doubted whether the accumulation of a large number of books which are to be found in almost every library of the country, is, in the present state of the funds, to be expected or aimed at. It is believed that a portion of the income devoted to the library, may be more efficiently expended in the promotion of the desired ends by other means, and hence, it was resolved to make special collections of books; particularly to procure such as are not in the country, and also, in order to render more available those which are now in our libraries, to prepare, as far as practicable, a general catalogue of all the books they contain.

In accordance with these views, Professor Jewett has devised a plan of facilitating the publication of catalogues of libraries, which bids fair to be of much importance to the literature of the country. This plan has been submitted for examination to a commission of gentlemen well acquainted with the subject, and we have received from them a very favorable report recommending its adoption.

The propositions submitted to the commission for examination, were as follows:

1. A plan for stereotyping catalogues of libraries by separate movable titles; and

2. A set of general rules, to be recommended for adoption, by the different libraries of the United States, in the preparation of their catalognes.

For a full account of Professor Jewett's plan, and of the advantages anticipated from it, I must refer to his report herewith submitted. I may, however, briefly allude to the leading principle of the plan, which is to stereotype the titles of books on separate movable blocks. These blocks once prepared, and kept in a central depository, may be used for the printing of new editions of the catalogues for which they were originally made, allowing the interposition of additional titles in their proper order; as well as for the printing of all other catalogues containing the same titles. The collection of the stereotype blocks of the titles of the several libraries will thus form the stereotyped titles of a general catalogue of all the libraries. They will lend themselves to the construction of bibliographies of particular branches of knowledge, and will admit of being arranged alphabetically, chronologically, or in classes, in accordance with any required system.

These blocks are not to be made in advance of a demand for their use. They are to be gradually accumulated, by an arrangement, which, imposing only a temporary and light burden upon the funds of this Institution, will effect the great public object desired, at the same time that it diminishes to but a fraction of the present cost the expenses of publishing catalogues, and secures the construction of them upon a uniform and approved system.

The details of a plan so comprehensive may well be supposed to be difficult of adjustment, and not capable of being clearly described within the limits of a few paragraphs. These, however, have been fully considered by a competent tribunal; and the plan has received commendation and promises of co-operation, from some of the principal institutions of the country.

During the last year, the library has continued to increase by donation, by receipts under the copyright law, by exchanges for the publications of the Institution, and by purchase. It now numbers, in all, nearly ten thousand separate articles, and bids fair, from the same sources, to become a very valuable collection.

Though one half of the annual interest is to be expended on the library and the museum, the portion of the income which can be devoted to the former will, in my opinion, never be sufficient, without extraneous aid, to collect and support a miscellaneous library of the first class. Indeed, all the income would scarcely suffice for this purpose. Still, by means of exchanges, donations, and purchases, a library of great value may be collected and sustained; and this, with the constantly increasing library of Congress, the libraries of the Departments, and that of Georgetown College, will furnish a collection of books not unworthy of the capital of this nation.

From the report of Professor Jewett, it will be seen that a Gallery of Art has been commenced, and that it is already in possession of a valuable collection of engravings.

In this connexion, I may mention that at the last annual meeting of the Board a letter was presented from the Hon. Abbott Lawrence, informing the Regents that a portrait of Smithson had been offered through him for sale to the Institution. This portrait, which was in the possession of the widow of John Fitall, a servant of Smithson, mentioned in his will, was purchased for thirty guineas, and is now in the Gallery of Art. It represents the founder of this Institution, in the costume of a student of Oxford, and was probably painted when he was not more than twenty years of age. There is, also, in the possession of the Institution a medallion of Smithson, in copper, taken in after life. It is from this that the head on the title-page of the Smithsonian publications has been copied.

Lectures.

During the past session of Congress a series of popular lectures has been given to the citizens of this place and strangers, in the lecture room of the Smithsonian building. These lectures, were delivered by gentlemen distinguished for their standing, and for their attainments in literature and science, who were invited for this purpose. The interest in these lectures has been sustained to a wonderful degree. They have been attended from the first by large audiences; and the results thus far indicate that considerable good may be derived from the diffusion of knowledge in this way, in a central position like Washington, where persons from every part of the Union are found. Although the lectures appear to the public one of the most prominent objects of the Institution, and although they are attended with much trouble and considerable expense, they really form the least important feature of the plan adopted. So long, however, as there is a prospect of doing good by means of them, it is due to the city in which the Institution is located that they should be continued.

Much complaint has been made on account of the size of the lecture room. It is certainly too small to accommodate all who have wished to attend. We have, however, endeavored, in several instances, to obviate this difficulty, by procuring a repetition of the lectures; but this plan is attended with additional expense, and cannot, in all cases, be adopted. Should large audiences continue, it may be well to provide a larger lecture room in the main building, and, by removing the seats from the present lecture room, convert it into a museum of apparatus. This change, if thought advisable, can be made at very little, if any, additional expense; since the present wood-work of the interior of the main building is to give place to a fire-proof structure, which will admit of being arranged as a lecture room. Indeed, the original plan contemplated a room of this kind in the main building; but the arrangement of it was such as to seat scarcely more than the room at present used.

Many enquiries are made as to the publication of these lectures. In some cases, reports of them have been given in the newspapers, and it will be advisable to extend this practice to all; but the publication, in a separate form, of lectures, which in many cases are not written out, and not intended by their authors as additions to knowledge, would be attended with much expense and little useful effect. The Institution, in several instances, is doing better service, by publishing in full the original researches on which the lectures are based. The papers of Professor Agassiz, of Professor Harvey, and of Lieutenant Davis, are of this character, and will be given to the world through the Smithsonian Contributions.

The following is a list of the Titles of Lectures given before the Institution during the last session of Congress, with the names of the distinguished gentlemen by whom they were delivered:

A single lecture on Holland, by the Rev. Dr. George W. Bethune, of Brooklyn, New York.

A course of lectures on the Relations of Time and Space, the Vastness of the Visible Creation, and the Primordial Arrangement of Existing Systems; by Professor Stephen Alexander, of Princeton, New Jersey.

A course of lectures on Science applied to Agriculture; by Professor J. F. W. Johnston, of the University of Durham, England.

Two lectures, one on the Tendencies of Modern Science, and the other on the Spirit of the Age; by the Rt. Rev. Bishop Alonzo Potter, of Pennsylvania.

One lecture on the Ability of the Individual to Promote Knowledge; by the Rev. John Hall, of Trenton, New Jersey.

A course of lectures on the Unity of the plan of the Animal Creation; by Professor Louis Agassiz, of Cambridge, Massachusetts.

A course of lectures on the Tides of the Ocean and their Geological Relations; by Lieutenant Charles Henry Davis, of the United States navy.

A course of lectures on Marine Algæ or Sea Weeds, and also on the Morphology of the Vegetable Kingdom; by Professor William H. Harvey, of the University of Dublin, Ireland.

Two lectures, one on the Origin and Growth of the Union during the Colonial Period, and the other on some points of the History and Peculiarities of the English Language; by Professor Henry Reed, of the University of Pennsylvania.

A course of lectures on the Chemical Operations of Nature; by Professor Lewis C. Beck, of Rutgers College, New Jersey.

The first part of a general course, giving an exposition of the Dynamical Phenomena of Geology; by Professor Henry D. Rogers, of Boston.

Whatever may have been the effect of these lectures in the way of diffusing knowledge, it is evident, from the character of the men by whom they were delivered, that they presented truths intended to elevate and improve the moral and intellectual condition of the hearers.

All of which is respectfully submitted:

JOSEPH HENRY,
Secretary of the Smithsonian Institution.

FIFTH ANNUAL REPORT

Of the Secretary of the Smithsonian Institution, for the year 1851.

To the Board of Regents of the Smithsonian Institution:

GENTLEMEN: Besides the care of all the property of the Institution, and the responsibility of the direction of its operations, under the control of the Regents, the Secretary is required to give an account, at their annual session, of the condition of the Institution, and of its transactions during the preceding year.

In the discharge of this duty on the present occasion, I am happy to inform the Regents, that the Institution under their care is still in a prosperons condition, and that since their last meeting it has continued silently, but effectually, to enlarge the sphere of its influence and usefulness, and to elicit from every part of the civilized world commendations, not only of the plan of organization it has adopted, but also of the results it has produced.

In my last Report I gave a brief account of the means employed to increase the income, so that in addition to the requirements of Congress in regard to the formation of a library and a museum, and the erection of a building on a liberal scale, operations of a more active character could be incorporated into the plan of organization.

During the past year the same policy has been observed; and though the officers of the Institution have been subjected to the inconvenience of transacting business in an unfinished building, and in rooms not intended for the purpose, yet this has been considered of minor importance in comparison with the saving of the funds. Every dollar now expended on the building lessens the amount of accruing interest, and diminishes the means of producing results which are to affect the world at large; hence the importance of an adherence to the plan of finishing it by degrees. Since the last session of the Board, it has, therefore, not been thought advisable to urge the contractor to a rapid completion of his work, and all the expenditures on account of the building have been made from the accrued interest of the current year, and from a portion of that of the year preceding. There is, consequently, still on hand the two hundred thousand dollars of accumulated interest mentioned in the last and preceding reports. Of this, it will be recollected, $50,000 are to be applied towards finishing the building, and the remainder to be invested as part of the principal.

The importance of increasing the funds and of gradually developing the operations embraced in the programme, was set forth in the last report. The Institution, it is to be hoped, is not one of a day, but is to endure as long as our government shall last; it is therefore necessary, in the beginning, that we should constantly look to the future, and guard against the temptation, to which we are continually exposed, of expanding too rapidly.

By a resolution of the board, at their session in 1849, the Secretary was directed to petition Congress to take from the Institution $150,000, and such other sums, not exceeding in all $200,000, as may have been or shall be received in accruing interest or otherwise, upon the same terms as those on which the original bequest had been accepted. This petition was referred to a committee and favorably reported upon; but unfortunately the press of business prevented Congress from acting upon it at their last session. The petition will again be renewed; and it is believed that so reasonable a request will meet with a favorable reception. It is, however, thought important that the amount should be increased, and that the sum of $250,000 be inserted in the petition. instead of that named in the resolution.

In addition to the $150,000 which the Regents thus seek to invest, there is still a portion of the original legacy remaining in England, as the principal of an annuity settled upon Madame De la Batut, the mother of the nephew of Smithson, to whom the property was originally bequeathed. Besides this, I am informed, upon good authority, that the Institution is the contingent legatee of an estate of considerable magnitude, depending on the demise without issue of a single individual. We may also reasonably expect that if the affairs of the Institution are properly conducted, and its funds judiciously husbanded or properly expended on the legitimate objects of the bequest, other trusts will be committed to its care. It therefore becomes important that the limit should be at least $250,000, so that the whole sum, including the original bequest, shall amount to a little more than $750,000. There can surely be no just grounds of fear that the income of this sum will be devoted to improper uses, so long as it is an essential part of the plan to produce fruits, the value of which can be judged by all who are capable of appreciating the advance of knowledge. This request is also in accordance with the policy adopted by the Institution of asking nothing from Congress but the safe keeping of its funds, and the appointment to its Board of Regents of gentlemen of intelligence and high moral principles.

The government has thus far liberally fulfilled the obligations which it imposed upon itself in accepting the trust. Not only has the original sum been permanently invested in the treasury of the United States, but interest has been allowed from the time of receiving the funds. Congress has also made several donations to the Institution, which, though they will not prove as valuable to us as could be wished, indicate a liberal intention. The first gift was the great museum of the Exploring Expedition, for the accommodation of which the larger portion of the present building was originally intended; the second was a grant of nineteen acres of land surrounding the building of the Institution; the third, a copy of every book published in the United States for which a copyright might be granted; the fourth and last gift was that of all the plates, manuscripts, &c., of the Exploring Expedition, for the purpose of publishing a new edition for distribution.

These donations, though made with kindly feelings and in a spirit of liberality, have proved singularly unprofitable. The maintenance of the museum of the Exploring Expedition would subject the Institution to an annual expense which would materially interfere with more important operations. After expending several thousand dollars on the improvement of the grounds, it has been deemed best to return them to the charge of the general government. Wete the copyright act fully complied with, perhaps some benefit might accrue from it to the Institution; but in the manner in which it is at present observed, the expense of postage and of clerk hire in recording the titles and furnishing the certificates of deposit, has more than equalled the value to us of all the books received. Lastly, it has been estimated that the publication of a new edition of the expensive volumes of the results of the Exploring Expedition would cost at least fifty thousand dollars. Fortunately, it has not been considered obligatory on the Institution, except in the case of the copyright law, to accept these gifts.

Publication of Memoirs.

Since the adoption of the plan of organization, nearly fifty original memoirs, purporting to be additions to the sum of human knowledge, have been presented to the Institution for publication. Though a number of these have been returned to their authors, principally on account of not falling within the restricted class of communications accepted for publication, yet they have generally been productions of much merit, and have evinced a surprising activity of mind, and manifest a growing attention in this country to original research. The probable success of this part of the plan of organization was not overrated; for, were the whole income of the Institution devoted alone to publishing the results of the labors of men of literature and of science, which otherwise would never see the light, it could be profitably expended. In this respect, the Smithsonian bequest supplies the wants which in Europe are met by richly endowed academies and national societies.

It will be recollected that each memoir is printed separately, and with a separate title and paging, so that it can be distributed to persons most interested in its perusal as soon as it comes from the press, without waiting for the completion of the volume to which it belongs. In this way, the author is enabled to present a full account of his discoveries to the world with the least possible delay; while, by the rules of the Institution, he is allowed to publish an abstract of his paper in the proceedings of the American Association for the Advancement of Science, or in those of any other properly organized society.

The number of copies of the Smithsonian Contributions distributed is greater than that of the transactions of any scientific or literary society; and therefore the Institution offers the best medium to be found for diffusing a knowledge of scientific discoveries.

Every memoir published by the Institution is issued with the stamp of approval of a commission of competent judges: and in order to secure a cautious and candid opinion, the name of the author, and those of the examiners, are not made known to each other unless a favorable report is given; and, in this case, the names of the commission are printed, as vouchers for the character of the memoir, on the reverse of the title-page.

This plan secures an untrammelled expression of opinion, while it induces caution on account of the responsibility which it involves.

Besides deciding on the fitness of original memoirs for publication, the Institution is continually applied to for information relative to almost every department of literature and science. Respectful attention is always given to these applications; and when the desired answer does not fall within the line of study of any officer of the Institution, it is sought for from those in whose knowledge and judgment we have full confidence. No inconsiderable portion of time is occupied in giving the information involved in the answers to these inquiries; but I am happy to inform the Board that in this service, as well as in that of examining memoirs, we have received the co-operation of a considerable number of the most distinguished individuals in our country, and in scarcely a single case has application for assistance in this way been refused. By the operation of the plan adopted, the Institution can command the talents and the learning of the world, and with a small corps of permanent officers, or a sufficient clerical force, can discharge the duty of an association to which subjects relative to all branches of knowledge can be referred.

There is one class of requests which, by a resolution of the Board of Regents, we are directed to refuse, viz: those for the examination and approval of the innumerable inventions by which the ingenious and enterprising seek to better their own condition and that of the public. Were it not for this resolution, originally proposed by General Cass, we would be overwhelmed with applications of this kind, and have forced upon us the business of the Patent Office. Besides this, the principal object of the organization is the discovery of new truths, rather than the application of known principles to useful purposes. Not that we would undervalue the labors of the inventor; but because practical knowledge has a marketable value which always insures its cultivation, provided the higher philosophical truths on which it is founded are sufficiently developed and made known.

The idea is still very generally entertained that Smithson bequeathed his property to this country for the diffusion of useful knowledge among the people, and that his intention would be best consulted by the expenditure of all the income in the publication and general distribution of tracts on practical subjects. The adoption of this plan would be to dissipate the funds without beneficial effect. A single report of the Patent Office costs, in some instances, more than three times the income of the Smithsonian fund, which itself would be insufficient for the general diffusion of a single octavo page of printed matter. The property, however, was not left to the inhabitants of the United States, but to the government, in trust for the good of man; and not merely for the dissemination or diffusion of knowledge, but, first of all, for creating, originating, increasing it. Furthermore, Smithson does not confine his bequest to the promotion of *useful* knowledge alone, in the lower sense of the term, but includes all knowledge in his liberal and philosophical design. The true, the beautiful, as well as the immediately practical, are all entitled to a share of attention. All knowledge is profitable; profitable in its ennobling effect on the character, in the pleasure it imparts in its acquisition, as well as in the power it gives over the operations of mind and of matter. All knowledge is useful; every part of this complex system of nature is connected with every other. Nothing is isolated. The discovery of to-day, which appears unconnected with any useful process, may, in the course of a few years, become the fruitful source of a thousand inventions.

That the encouragement of the discovery of new truths, the publication of original memoirs, and the establishment of new researches, are in conformity with the design of Smithson, is not only manifest from the terms of his will. but also from the fact, which has lately come to our knowledge, that he at first left his property to the Royal Society of London, for the very object embraced in this part of the plan. And what prouder monument could any man desire than the perpetual association of his name with a series of new truths? This building and all its contents may be destroyed; but the volumes of the Smithsonian Contributions, distributed as they are among a thousand libraries, are as wide-spread and lasting as civilization itself.

During the past year a number of memoirs have been accepted for publication, and are either in the press or are waiting the drawings to illustrate them, now in the hands of the engraver. It is the duty of the Secretary, in accordance with the original plan of the Institution, to give a popular account of these memoirs in his annual Report.

1. The first is a memoir by Dr. Asa Gray, professor of botany in Harvard University, consisting of an account of a collection of plants made by Mr. Charles Wright, in an expedition from Texas to El Paso, in the summer and autumn of 1849.

It was stated in my Report for that year that one hundred and fifty dollars had been subscribed on the part of the Institution toward the outfit of Mr. Wright, and that the plants collected by him would be submitted to Dr. Gray for examination and description. The memoir now mentioned is the result of this arrangement, though it also contains notices of plants gathered by other collectors in adjacent regions, especially by Dr. Wislizenus in the valley of the Rio Grande and Chihuahua, and by the lamented Dr. Gregg in the same district, and in the northern part of Mexico. This memoir is a good exposition of the character of the vegetation, and consequently of the climate, of the regions traversed.

Specimens of all the plants obtained by Mr. Wright belong to this Institution; and these, with sets collected by Fendler and Lindheimer, form the nucleus of an important and authentic North American herbarium.

2. Another paper on botany is by Dr. John Torrey, of the college of New Jersey, Princeton. It gives illustrations of the botany of California, and describes a number of new and interesting plants discovered by Colonel Frémont in his different explorations in that country.

Some of the plants collected by this intrepid traveller have been described in the appendix to his first and second report, but many are still unpublished. Of the collections made during his third expedition no descriptions have been given, except that two or three of the new plants were briefly characterized by Dr. Gray, in order to secure priority of discovery.

In the memoir presented to the Institution, Dr. Torrey has given descriptions of a number of genera of new and remarkable plants, all collected by Colonel Frémont in the passes and on the sides of the Sierra Nevada. With regard to this publication Dr. Torrey remarks, that he had hoped that arrangements would have been made by the government of the United States for the publication of a general account of the botany of California; but as there is no immediate prospect of such a work being undertaken, this memoir, on some of the more interesting genera discovered by Colonel Frémont, has been prepared for the Smithsonian Institution.

The drawings to illustrate this paper have been made, at the expense of the Institution, by Mr. Isaac Sprague, of Cambridge, who, in the opinion of Dr. Torrey, ranks among the best botanical draughtsmen of our day.

3. The next paper presents the results of a series of observations made in the years 1845–6–7, to determine the dip, inclination, and intensity of the magnetic force in several parts of the United States, by John Locke, M. D., professor of chemistry in the Medical College of Ohio. The results presented in this paper are a continuation of a series derived from observations begun in 1837, and prosecuted annually for ten years. The first parts of the series have been published in the Transactions of the American Philosophical Society, and have been incorporated by Colonel Sabine in his contributions to Terrestrial Magnetism. A part of the observations given in this memoir were made at the expense and under the direction of the United States Coast Survey. Another portion was made in accordance with the direction of the Hon. Robert J. Walker, late Secretary of the Treasury, as a part of the investigations instituted for the exploration of the mineral lands belonging to the general government. This paper has been examined by competent judges, and recommended for publication in the Smithsonian Contributions, as an important addition to knowledge.

4. A paper has also been presented for publication by the executors of the late Dr. Troost, of Nashville. It consists of descriptions and drawings of a very numerous family of extinct zoophytes, to which the organic remains, called the stone lily, belongs. The vicinity of Nashville appears to be a remarkable locality for these remains; and the paper of Professor Troost describes several hundred species, of which two only have living representatives.

The memoir, however, is not in a condition to be published without revision, and additions to bring it up to the state of knowledge at the present time. This labor has been gratuitously undertaken by Professor Agassiz, of Cambridge, and Professor James Hall, of Albany. The collection of specimens from which the drawings were made is now in the possession of these gentlemen, and the memoir will be published as soon as the corrections and additions are made.

5. The next memoir is on the Winds of the Northern Hemisphere, by Professor James Coffin. The design of this communication, in the words of the author, is "to answer the following questions, viz:

"*a*. What is the average direction in which the lower strata of the air moves over different regions of the northern hemisphere?

"*b*. What is the rate of progress in the mean direction as compared with the total distance travelled by the wind?

"*c*. What modifications do the mean direction and rate of progress undergo in the different months of the year?

"*d*. What is the direction of the deflecting forces that cause these modifications?

"*e.* What is the average relative force and velocity of winds from several points of the compass?

"*f.* How will the introduction or omission of the latter element affect the answer of the preceding questions?"

The data used in answering these questions have been collected with great labor, and consist of observations made at no less than five hundred and seventy-six different stations on land, and a large number taken during numerous voyages at sea. The field of observation includes a zone which extends from the equator to near the parallel of 85° of north latitude, and occupies a period, taken in the aggregate, of 2,800 years.

Several of the foregoing questions have been answered approximately by other writers, but never, it is believed, from as extensive an induction as is presented in this memoir.

This paper is illustrated by a number of maps and diagrams, which render its publication very expensive. It was presented to the Institution more than a year ago, but the appropriation for printing was not sufficient to allow of its publication at that time.

6. The Institution has also commenced the publication of an extended memoir, consisting of a grammar and lexicon of the Dakota language, the results of the joint labors during eighteen years of the Dakota mission, assisted by the most intelligent natives of this tribe of Indians. The whole has been arranged and placed in its present form by the Rev. S. R. Riggs, of the American Board of Missions.

This work was prepared under the auspices of the Historical Society of Minnesota, and recommended by this association to the favorable attention of the Smithsonian Institution. It is designed to meet the requirements of the missionary in his labor of diffusing the light of religion and civilization among one of the most numerous and important tribes of Indians in the country. It also forms an interesting addition to ethnology, which will be highly prized by all devoted to this branch of knowledge.

A language is not originally a thing of man's device, or the result of conventional art, but the spontaneous production of human instinct, modified by the mental character, the physical conditions, and other peculiarities of the people or tribe among which it had its origin, or by whom it is used. It is subject to definite laws of formation and development, and is intimately connected with the history of the migrations and affiliations of the people by whom it is spoken, and hence becomes an object of interest to the student of the natural history of man.

In accordance with the policy of not expending the Smithsonian fund in doing with it what could be equally well done by other means, this memoir was first referred to the Bureau of Indian Affairs, with the hope that it might be adopted as a part of the materials of the volumes published under the direction of that bureau; but this was not found practicable, and the task was therefore undertaken by the Institution.

The memoir will occupy an entire volume, and would have been too much for our present income, had not about one third of the whole cost of publication been promised by subscription from the members of the Historical Society of Minnesota and the American Board of Missions. The latter institution defrays the expenses of Mr. Riggs while he is engaged in superintending the passage of the work through the press. It is a pleasant circumstance that in this instance, as well as in many others, the organization of the Institution enables it to co-operate with other institutions, and to assist them in their labors of promoting knowledge.

This memoir, which is now in the press, was referred for critical examination to Professor Felton, of Cambridge, Massachusetts, and to Professor Turner, of New York. The latter has furnished us with a report on the importance of collecting information relative to the different dialects now in use among the Indians.

7. Dr. Joseph Leidy, of Philadelphia, has prepared a memoir for the Institution, accompanied by numerous illustrations, entitled "A Flora and Fauna within living Animals." It is an elaborate history of a most remarkable series of plants, in many cases accompanied by parasitic animals, found growing, as an ordinary or natural condition, within the interior of the bodies of living animals. In some of the latter, it is stated, growing plants are never absent; and in a species of insects, viz: *Papulus Cornutus*, a forest of vegetation is always found covering the inner surface of the *ventriculus* or second stomach.

The plants of course are Cryptogamic, and are algoid in their character. Some are as long as half an inch, but usually they are very much smaller. They grow attached to the mucous membrane of the cavities in which they are found, and occasionally from the exterior covering of worms infesting the same cavities. Several genera and species of these plants are characterized under the names of *Euterobryus elegans*, *E. attennatus*, *Arthromitus cristatus*, *Cladophytum comatum*, and *Corynocladus radiatus*.

The mode of growth and reproduction of several of the species has been carefully traced and fully illustrated by figures.

The researches are prefaced by some observations on the laws of parasitic life in general, which are presented in a highly philosophical manner, and entirely free from hypothesis—the whole forming one of the most remarkable papers on physiology which has ever been produced by our countrymen.

8. Lieutenant Charles Henry Davis, United States navy, Superintendent of the American Nautical Almanac, has presented a memoir on the dynamic effects of the tides.

This memoir is a continuation of one presented by the author to the American Academy a few years ago, and is of much interest, not only in a scientific point of view, as connected with important geological changes, but also on account of its practical bearings upon the transformations which are constantly going on at the entrance of rivers, channels, and in the formation of headlands and promontories. Were our globe a perfect spheroid of revolution, surrounded by water of uniform depth, the tides of the ocean would consist of nearly perpendicular undulations of the particles of the liquid, and a mere translation of form, without a transference of matter. But, in the ease of a globe of irregular surface, covered with water of varying depth, the oscillations of the ocean must constantly produce currents in definite directions, which tend continually to change the position of the moveable materials which are found at the bottom of the sea, particularly as we approach land. A part of the force of the particles of water forming the sinking swell of the wave, in the ease of an obstruction to their free descent by a diminished depth, is expended in producing a current along the inclined plane of the surface leading to the shore.

Lieutenant Davis has entered with much ardor upon this new field of research, and after an examination of various parts of the shore of the United States, through a series of years, in which he was engaged on the Coast Survey, has succeeded in developing the laws of action which give rise to the changes before mentioned.

He finds that the tendency of the flood-tide is to transport the matter from the bottom of the ocean and deposit it on land. He is enabled to explain the character of the alluvial formations, to account for their peculiar shape, their comparative sizes, their accumulation, and to prediet the results of certain combinations of circumstances on their future changes. The particular object of this memoir is to inquire into the mechanical operations of the tides, and the uses they may have served in the general economy of the globe in arranging the loose materials of the earth's crust.

Smithsonian Reports and other publications.

Since the last meeting of the Board of Regents, the report of Professor Jewett on the Public Libraries of the United States has been published and widely distributed. It is impossible to collect at once full and reliable accounts of all the libraries of the country, and this report is intended merely as a beginning, to be followed by others on the same subject. It has been sent to all the libraries of the United States, with the request that its deficiencies may be pointed out and additional materials furnished to render it more perfect. The great interest which is felt in this work is manifested by the amount of statistical information which has already been received in return for this volume.

A report has also been published on the Recent Improvements in the Chemical Arts. It is compiled from articles which have appeared during the last ten years in the various journals of science and the arts in the English, French, and German languages. Though this report is chiefly intended to benefit the practical man, yet it will be found interesting to the general reader, as exhibiting the contemporaneous advance of science and art, and the dependence of the latter on the former for the improvement of its most important processes.

The accounts given in the teport alluded to do not consist of descriptions of methods which have been merely proposed and published without practical verification. On the contrary, care has been taken to select such as have been actually tried, or such as offer great probability of success from the well established principles on which they are based.

The preparation of this report was entrusted to Professor James C. Booth, assayer of the United States Mint at Philadelphia, who associated with himself Mr. Campbell Morfit, of Baltimore. The work has been executed in a manner highly creditable to the authors, and will, I doubt not, prove very acceptable to the public. Notes will be made of the new inventions of the same class, as they appear in the journals, so that in the course of a few years another report of a similar kind, or one which may be considered a continuation of this, can be published.

Copies, at the mere cost of printing, paper, and commission, are offered for sale. The matter has been stereotyped, in order to supply all the demand, and to reproduce this member of the series, should the subject be continued.

The progress of the elaborate report on the Forest-trees of North America, mentioned in the last two Reports, was for some time arrested by the absence of the author, Dr. Gray, in Europe. He has now, however, returned, and will resume the preparation of the drawings, as soon as the funds of the Institution will admit of the expenditure. This work has proved a more expensive undertaking than was at first anticipated, and can only be finished on the original plan, by extending the time of its publication over several years. It will form a valuable contribution to the botany and economical and ornamental arts of our country.

Dr. F. G. Melsheimer, of Dover, Pennsylvania, has presented to the Institution a catalogue of the coleopterous insects of North America, with references to the principal places of description. This has been put to press, but progresses slowly on account of the great care necessary in correcting the proofs. When printed, it will be of great service to the cause of American entomology.

Besides the reports, other works are in progress, among which may be mentioned a small volume by Professor Baird, consisting of practical directions for the collection and preservation of specimens of natural history. This will be illustrated with numerous figures, and issued as soon as the engravings can be procured. A part of the letter-press has been finished. It is especially designed for the use of travellers and officers of the army and navy who may be inclined to make collections for the Smithsonian Institution, but will be of general interest to the cultivators of natural history.

A volume of tables of use in meteorology and other branches of scientific observations, has been prepared, under the direction and at the expense of the Institution, by Professor Arnold Guyot. The following are the contents of this volume, viz:

1. Thermometrical tables for the conversion of the scales of different thermometers into each other.

2. Hygrometrical tables giving the elastic force of vapor, the relative humidity, &c.

3. Barometrical tables for the comparisons of different scales, reduction of observations to the freezing-point, and correction for capillary action.

4. Hypsometrical tables for calculating altitudes by the barometer, and by the difference of the boiling-point.

5. Tables of the corrections to be applied to the monthly means to obtain the true mean.

6. A set of miscellaneous tables frequently required in physical investigations.

These tables supply a desideratum in the English language, and will doubtless be highly prized by all engaged in physical research. It is proposed to extend their number so as to include a wider range of objects, and to publish them in parts to suit different purposes. Copies will be distributed with the quarto volumes of our publications, and sent to meteorological observers. The tables have been stereotyped, and may therefore be offered for sale at a low rate.

Since the date of the last Report, a number of separate memoirs have been bound together so as to form the second volume of the series of Smithsonian Contributions. The memoirs, an account of which has just been given, will be ready for distribution during 1852.

The second volume has been forwarded to all the colleges and other institutions specified in the rules adopted for the distribution of the Smithsonian publications in this country, and to all the first class libraries and principal literary and scientific societies abroad. Through the liberality of the members of the Senate of the United States and its officers, we have been enabled to send to our foreign correspondents, in addition to our own publications, copies of reports to Congress, and other works published at the expense of government. In return, the Institution has received a series of flattering acknowledgments and valuable presents, not only of the current numbers of transactions, but in several instances of entire sets of all the volumes.

The promotion of knowledge is much retarded by the difficulties experienced in the way of a free intercourse between scientific and literary societies in different parts of the world. In carrying on the exchange of the Smithsonian volumes, it was necessary to appoint a number of agents. Some of these are American consuls, and other respectable individuals, who have undertaken in most cases to transact the business free of all charge, and in others for but little more than the actual expense incurred. These agencies being established, other exchanges could be carried on through them and our means of conveyance, at the slight additional expense owing to the small increase of weight; and we have accordingly offered the privilege of sending and receiving small packages through our agency to institutions of learning, and in some cases to individuals, who choose to avail themselves of it. The offer has been accepted by a number of institutions; and the result cannot fail to prove highly beneficial, by promoting a more ready communion between the literature and science of this country and the world abroad.

As a part of the same system, application was made through Sir Henry Bulwer, the British minister at Washington, for a remission of duties on packages intended for Great Britain; and we are informed that a permanent arrangement will probably be made, through the agency of the Royal Society, for the free passage through the English custom-house of all packages from this Institution.

The Smithsonian exchanges are under the special charge of Professor Baird, who has been unwearied in his exertions to collect proper materials, and to reduce the whole to such order as will combine security with rapidity of transmission.

The system of exchange here described has no connexion with that established between national governments by Mr. Vattemare. It is merely an extension of one which has been in operation on a small scale for nearly half a century between the American Philosophical Society and the American Academy on this side of the Atlantic, and the several scientific societies on the other.

Ancient Monuments.

The success of the first memoir published by the Smithsonian Institution has awakened much attention to American antiquities, and a number of communications have been submitted on this subject. Among these is one by Mr. William Pidgeon, of Virginia, who has spent a number of years in the exploration of mounds, and other ancient remains, on the upper branches of the Mississippi.

The results of his labors are of a very interesting character, though the facts contained in his memoir are too much mingled with the traditions received by him from the Indians, and with his own hypotheses, to be accepted as a part of the Smithsonian Contributions. After repeated conversations with Mr. Pidgeon, I was clearly of the opinion that his researches ought to be given to the public in some way, in order that his statements might receive due attention, and be corroborated or disproved by other explorers; and I am pleased to be able to state that a gentleman of Washington has undertaken to arrange and edit these researches, and that they will be published in a separate volume for the benefit of the authors.

We have also received communications relative to mounds from Mr. Charles Whittlesey, of Ohio, from Mr. Titian R. Peale, of Washington, and Mr. William E. Guest, of Ogdensburg, New York. The first of these may be considered as supplementary to the memoir of Messrs. Squier and Davis, describing works omitted in their survey. The second gives a plan and description of the mounds which formerly existed on the present site of St. Louis, Missouri, made during the visit of Major Long's party in 1849 to that country, on their way to the Rocky mountains. This sketch is now interesting on account of the fact that, in the rapid progress of improvement, these mounds have been nearly obliterated, and that they can only be preserved to science, as they existed more than thirty years ago, by this publication.

The third is an account, with drawings, of ancient works at Preseot, in Canada West. The great size of the remains of trees which occupy the ground, evince the long time which must have elapsed since these works were constructed, and the entire absence of stone pipes and arrow heads has induced the belief that they are of a higher antiquity than those in the Ohio valley.

The last two contributions will form a single memoir, the plates for which are partially completed.

But the most interesting circumstance connected with the study of the ancient remains of this country is a recent action of the American Antiquarian Society of Worcester, Massachusetts. This institution was founded in 1812 by the zeal and liberality of Isaiah Thomas, for the purpose of collecting and preserving such manuscripts, pamphlets, and other articles as relate to the history of this country, and for the exploration and publication of its antiquities. It was at the expense of this society that the original researches of Mr. Atwater, on the mounds of the Ohio valley, were first published; and during the last two years the condition of its funds has again enabled it to take the field, and to direct its attention to the remarkable antiquities in the State of Wisconsin.

These antiquities, it is well known, consist of representations, on a gigantic scale, of birds, beasts, and fishes; and though many of them have been surveyed, and accounts of them given in the memoir of Messrs. Squier and Davis, comparatively few of those which are said to exist have been explored or delineated. For this reason, the council of the society have engaged Mr. I. A. Lapham, an experienced engineer, to make the explorations and surveys and drawings of these mounds. He has been engaged in these operations for two seasons, and is now employed in making up an account of his labors.

To insure harmony of action in the cultivation of the wide field of research offered in the investigations of the ancient monuments of this country, the Antiquarian Society has agreed to present to the Smithsonian Institution the results of the explorations of Mr. Lapham for publication, and to reserve its limited funds for further explorations. The memoirs will be examined and revised by the society, and will be published under its auspices in the Smithsonian Contributions.

This arrangement is another pleasing evidence of the feeling with which the efforts of this Institution are regarded, and the willingness with which other institutions co-operate with it in the important work of promoting original knowledge.

Explorations, Researches, &c.

During the last year several minor explorations have been made in the line of natural history, partly at the expense of the Institution. The sum of fifty dollars was appropriated to Professor C. B. Adams, of Amherst College, to pay in part his expenses while making collections in the West Indies and Panama. For the sum advanced, an ample return has been made in new and rare specimens. Professor Baird and Mr. Charles Girard have also made explorations which have added to the collections of the Institution at a cost little beyond that of the expense of transportation.

In this connexion I may mention that Professor Baird has contributed the report on the vertebrate animals collected by Captain Stansbury in his expedition to the Salt Lake region, and facilities have been given at the Institution to a number of persons making scientific reports to Congress.

A series of experiments also have been made in our laboratory by a commission appointed by government to examine the stone proposed for the extension of the Capitol. It is believed that the Institution may, in the aid it affords the government in scientific operations, more than repay all the obligation imposed by the acceptance of the Smithsonian trust.

It was mentioned in the last report that the specimens which were procured by Mr. Culbertson from the Upper Missouri, had been referred to Dr. Joseph Leidy, of Philadelphia, for examination. He has since made a report giving a brief statement of the results of his investigation. From this report it appears that the specimens are of much scientific interest, showing, as they do, for the first time, the existence in this country of an eocene deposite, rivaling in the number of its species of extinct animals the celebrated basin of Paris.

Occultations.

It has been mentioned in the preceding reports, that lists of occulations, and tables of reductions, have been published, from 1848 to 1851, inclusive. The cost of the computation of these tables, as well as that of their publication for the past two years, was borne by the Institution, but since then Congress has ordered the establishment of an American Nautical Almanac; and as these tables will form a part of this ephemeris, Mr. Preston, the late Secretary of the Navy, directed that the expense of the computation should be defrayed from the appropriation for the Almanac, the printing and distribution to be at the charge of the Institution. A similar order has been given by the Hon. Wm. A. Graham, the present Secretary of the Navy, relative to the tables for 1851 and 1852.

The tables for 1852 are much extended by the introduction of occultations visible in every part of the earth. The form is also somewhat altered, in order better to adapt it to the arrangement to be adopted by the Nautical Almanac.

The primary object of these tables is to facilitate the accurate determination of the longitude of places within the territory of the United States; and in this respect they have done good service, especially in the hands of the officers of the Coast Survey, and the explorers and surveyors of our new possessions on the coast of the Pacific. Their extension will render them useful to geographers in every part of the world. They have been computed, for the present and the last two years, under the direction of Lieut. Davis, the accomplished superintendent of the American Nautical Almánac. As soon as this work, which will be an honor to the country, is ready to be issued, the publication will be relinquished by the Smithsonian Institution.

We observe again, in this case, the policy of not expending the funds of the Institution in doing what other means can accomplish.

It will be recollected that Mr. Sears C. Walker, astronomical assistant of the United States Coast Survey, prepared for the Smithsonian Transactions a memoir containing a determination of the true orbit of the planet Neptune, and that from this orbit, and the mathematical investigations of Professor Peirce, an ephemeris of Neptune was compiled. The ephemeris was prepared for the years 1848 and 1849, under the direction and at the expense of this Institution; but for the years 1850, '51, '52, it was computed under the superintendence of Lieutennat Davis, and at the expense of the appropriation for the Nantical Almanac, while the cost of printing and of the distribution has been defrayed by the Institution.

The ephemeris has been generally adopted by the principal astronomers of the world; and Professor Airy, the astronomer royal of Great Britain, has undertaken the labor, in his last volume of Greenwich Observations, of critically comparing his observations on the planet in the heavens with the predictions of the Smithsonian ephemeris. From these comparisons it is found that the ephemeris gives the position of the planet with a degree of precision not inferior to that with which the places of the planets longest known are calculated. The labors, therefore, of Mr. Walker on the elements, and Professor Peirce on the theory of the planet Neptune, have been crowned with complete success. It is proposed hereafter to collect all the observations which may have been made on the planet, and compare them with the ephemeris, in order, if necessary, still further to correct the orbit

Meteorology.

The general system of meteorology now in operation in this country, and described in the last Report, has during the past year been continued and gradually extended. The instruments constructed under the direction of the Institution, with the aid of Professor Guyot, have been further improved, and some slight changes, indicated by experience, have been made to render them more convenient to the practical observer; and they may now be considered not only equal in accuracy to the instruments of the best construction from abroad, but in some respects superior. They are furnished with the means of ready adjustment to the standard instruments; and being in every instance accurately compared before they are used, and the error corrected, the labor of inserting a correction in the journal is avoided. New efforts have also been made to obtain a still more accurate comparison between the standard barometer of this country and those of the more important European observatories. For this purpose a second standard barometer by Newman, compared with the standard of the Royal Society, and a barometer by Ernst, compared with the standard of the Paris Observatory, were ordered at the expense of the Institution. By a long series of comparisons between these two instruments and others at Cambridge, (Massachusetts,) Toronto, (Canada West,) and Washington city, the object sought has, it is believed, been obtained. The thermometers also, constructed by Mr. Green, of New York, for the Institution, have been compared with European standards; and an important step has thus been made towards obtaining reliable results as to the absolute meteorological elements of the different parts of this continent.

It was stated in the last Report that the regents of the University of New York had made an appropriation for supplying thirty-three academies in that State with instruments, and had given the establishment of the whole system in charge to this Institution. The State of Massachusetts has also made a similar appropriation and arrangement. During the past year the instruments for this State have been constructed, and a part of the stations established under the care of Professor Guyot.

At the last meeting of the American Association, a report was made, and a series of resolutions adopted, for extending the system of observations with the same instruments to other parts of this continent. These resolutions directed the committee to memorialize Congress for aid in extending the system under the direction of this Institution; to request the Secretary of the Treasury to provide for making observations at the several light-houses to be established on the coast of California; to ask the surgeon-general to establish new stations at important points; to memorialize the other States of the Union to follow the example of New York and Massachusetts, and also the Canadian government to co-operate in the same enterprize.

What may be the result of the labors of the members of the committee to which this duty is entrusted, it is impossible to say. They can scarcely fail, however, to awaken a more general interest in the enterprise, and to receive a favorable response to some of the requests.

Since the date of the last Report, the system particularly intended to investigate the nature of American storms, immediately under the care of this Institution, has been continued and improved, both in the number of the stations, and, in some degree, in the character of the instruments. An appropriation was made to furnish a larger number of stations than previously with barometers and thermometers, by distributing these instruments, in some cases entirely at the expense of the Institution, and in others by selling them to the observers at half their original cost; but the demand was so great, and the loss by breakage in transmitting the instruments so frequent, that the appropriations were soon exhausted, and until we can afford to devote a large sum to the object, and employ a special agent to transport the articles to their destination, it will be inadvisable to attempt anything more in this way.

Though the instruments employed by these observers in some cases cannot be relied on for giving absolute results, yet they serve a good purpose in determining changes of pressure and temperature; and the returns give all the varying phases of the sky.

Thus far, the returns which have been received from this system have been arranged in folio volumes; and a beginning has been made in the way of deducing general conclusions from them, which may test the value of the observations and lead to their improvement, by suggesting other objects of inquiry. The results already obtained give promise of interesting and valuable additions to our knowledge of the nature of the storms which traverse this continent during the winter seasons, and will probably serve to settle definitely several theoretical questions of much interest to the meteorologist.

The meteorological correspondence of the Institution is principally attended to by Professor Foreman, and the labor which this involves is sufficient to occupy the greater portion of his time. The letters received from this class of coöperators are not confined to the subject of meteorology, but include the whole domain of physical science. We consider it, as before observed, a duty in all such cases to give any information required; and if this is not in the possession of the officers connected with the Institution, it is procured from other sources.

For the details as to the management of the meteorological affairs of the Institution, see Professor Foreman's report on this subject.

Library and Collections.

It will be recollected that the income of the Institution was, by a compromise alluded to in a former Report, to be divided into two equal parts, one part to be devoted to the formation of a museum, a library, and a gallery of art, and the other to publications, researches, and other active operations. The terms of this compromise have been rigidly adhered to, as will be seen by a reference to the general statement of accounts given in the last Report. Up to the date of the appointment of Professor Baird, in July, 1850, the part of the income devoted to the collections was expended on the library, or on objects pertaining to it. Since that time, a portion has been devoted to the museum.

It is proper to remark that this compromise was founded upon another, namely, that the cost of the building and furniture should be limited to two hundred and fifty thousand dollars. But in order to the better security of the collections, the Regents have since found it necessary to add, in round numbers, fifty thousand dollars to this sum, which must of course diminish the income which would otherwise have been devoted to the active operations.

It is evident that one spirit, if possible, should pervade the whole organization, and that the same policy should be adopted with reference to all parts of the plan. Among the maxims which have been acted upon, that of occupying ground untenanted by other institutions, and of doing nothing with the funds which can be equally well accomplished by other means, has commended itself to the intelligent and reflecting portion of the public; and it has always appeared to me that this is as applicable to the formation of collections of books and specimens, as to the publications and other operations of the Institution.

With reference to the library, the idea ought never to be entertained that the portion of the limited income of the Smithsonian fund which can be devoted to the purchase of books will ever be sufficient to meet the wants of the American scholar. On the contrary, it is the duty of this Institution to increase those wants by pointing out new fields for exploration, and by stimulating other researches than those which are now cultivated. It is a part of that duty to make the value of libraries more generally known, and their want in this country more generally felt; to show in what branches of knowledge our libraries are most deficient; to point out the means by which those deficiencies can be supplied; to instruct the public in the best methods of procuring, arranging, cataloguing, and preserving books; to give information as to the best form and construction of library buildings; in short, to do all which was originally intended in the plan, of rendering the Institution a centre of bibliographical knowledge, to which the American scholar can refer for all information relative to books in general, and particularly to those in our own country. The libraries of the country must be supplied by the country itself: by the general government; by the State governments; by cities, towns, and villages; and by wealthy and liberal individuals. It is to be hoped that in the restoration of the Library of Congress, a foundation will be laid for a collection of books worthy of a government whose perpetuity principally depends on the intelligence of the people.

The proper management of books, and general instruction as to their use, are matters perhaps of more importance than their accumulation in any one place. It is estimated that about twenty thousand volumes, including pamphlets, purporting to be additions to the sum of human knowledge, are published annually; and unless this mass be properly arranged, and the means furnished by which its contents may be ascertained, literature and science will be overwhelmed by their own unwieldy bulk. The pile will begin to totter under its own weight, and all the additions we may heap upon it will tend to add to the extension of the base, without increasing the elevation and dignity of the edifice.

One of the most important means of facilitating the use of libraries, particularly with reference to science, is well digested indexes of subjects, not merely referring to volumes or books, but to memoirs, papers, and parts of scientific transactions and systematic works. As an example of this, I would refer to the admirably arranged and valuable catalogue of books relating to Natural Philosophy and the Mechanical Arts, by Dr. Young. "If my library were on fire," said a celebrated author, "and I could save but one scientific book, it would be Dr. Young's catalogue." This work comes down to 1807; and I know of no richer gift which could be bestowed upon the science of our own day than the continuation of this catalogue to the present time. Every one who is desirous of enlarging the bounds of human knowledge should, in justice to himself, as well as to the public, be acquainted with what has previously been done in the same line, and this he will only be enabled to accomplish by the use of indexes of the kind above-mentioned.

The most important operation during the past year relative to the library, is the progress made by Professor Jewett in completing his plan of stereotyping catalogues with separate titles, described in the last Report.

To reduce this plan to practice, a series of original experiments were required, involving the expenditure of much time and labor. For this purpose, in preference to the usual method of stereotyping, a new one, invented by Mr. Josiah Warren, of Indiana, has been adopted on the recommendation of a committee to whom it was referred for examination. It is a fact well known to inventors, that however simple the theoretical plan of effecting a desired object may appear, a series of unforeseen difficulties must often be encountered in the details, before the idea can be realized in actual results. These difficulties, in the present case, it is believed, have been overcome; and the plan is now ready to be applied to the formation of a general and uniform catalogue of the libraries of the country. The course proposed is first to proceed with the catalogue of the library of the Institution, in accordance with the rules recommended by the commission appointed to report on this subject. This, stereotyped by the new process, may be distributed as a model for the other libraries which may adopt the plan. After all parts of the plan have thus been thoroughly tried, it will be desirable to commence on some large collection. The late accident which has happened to the Library of Congress will induce the necessity of a new catalogue, and it is hoped that a liberal and enlightened policy will lead to the adoption of the Smithsonian plan. This will not only enable the government to issue, at a trifling expense, a new catalogue every year, with all the additions in their proper place, but also to assist in giving to the country an improved system of cataloguing, and facilitate the production of a general catalogue of all the libraries of the country.

Since the publication of the account of Mr. Jewett's plan of forming general catalogues, the invention has been claimed separately by two individuals in Europe. It is true, the want of such a plan has long been felt, and a general idea may have been conceived as to how it might be accomplished; but no attempts have been made to reduce it to practice, and indeed had they been made, they could not have succeeded, and would have done injury to the cause. The conditions necessary to success never before existed, and a premature attempt always tends to lessen public confidence in an enterprise, when the proper time for its actual accomplishment arrives. Besides this, there is a wide difference between the mere suggesting the possibility of a plan, and actually overcoming the difficulties which arise at every step in reducing it to practice.

With reference to the copyright law, something ought to be done to put the whole matter on a better footing. I repeat the assertion before made, that this law, as it now exists, imposes a tax on the Institution, without an adequate return. The great majority of the books received are such as are found in almost every public and private library; with very few exceptions they would never be purchased by the Institution, and are consequently dear at any price, even that of shelf-room and attendance, not to mention cost of transportation and of furnishing the certificates.

Granting the proposition that it is important that a copy of every book originally published in this country should be somewhere preserved, it does not follow that the Smithsonian fund ought to be burdened with the expense of this charge.

If they should be preserved, it becomes the duty of Congress to provide for their care, as much as it does for that of the models of the Patent Office; and no good reason can be assigned why the one should not be imposed upon the Institution as well as the other. Indeed, models are a species of books intended to convey ideas which printing cannot impart.

The objection to the present arrangement may be obviated by adopting the suggestion of Professor Jewett, that but one copy, instead of three, of each book, be sent to Washington for deposit, and that in place of the other two copies, a small fee be paid to the Institution, sufficient to defray all expenses; the maxim again being applied of not expending the funds in doing that which can and ought to be done by other means.

By reference to the report of the Librarian, it will be seen that the collection of books has continued to be increased by purchase, by copyright, and by exchange. From the last-mentioned source the Institution is obtaining a most valuable series of books of the highest interest to the scientific student, consisting principally of the transactions and proceedings of learned societies. In a few years, it is believed, as complete a collection of these will be gathered as it is possible to obtain.

The museum is to consist, according to the law of Congress, and the terms of the compromise, of "objects of art, of foreign and curions research, and of natural history, of plants and geological and mineralogical specimens." It would, however, be unwise in the Institution to attempt the formation of full collections of all these objects, or, in other words, to form an establishment similar to that of the British Museum. The whole income devoted to this object would be entirely inadequate. The portion of the main building appropriated to the museum consists of a single room, two hundred feet long by fifty feet wide. This space may be entirely filled in the course of three years, without the purchase of a single article, if the means be adopted which present themselves at the seat of government for making collections. But when this space is filled, the accumulation of specimens must cease, or an addition be made to the building, which, to harmonize with the present edifice, would involve a large expenditure. The question then arises, from what source is this money to be obtained? It cannot be derived from the annual income of the capital, for this would cripple the more important operations. It may be said that Congress will furnish the means; but this is relying on a very uncertain source, and the policy of applying to Congress for any aid is doubtful.

Furthermore, a promiscuous collection, embracing full sets of the objects above specified, is unnecessary in carrying out the plan of organization of the Institution.

For example, the organic remains brought from the upper Missouri by Culbertson, have been examined and reported on by Dr. Leidy, of Philadelphia, in that city; and the plants from California and Mexico have been referred to Dr. Torrey at Princeton, and to Dr. Gray at Cambridge. In this way, not only has the learning of these gentlemen been brought into requisition, but also their special cabinets rendered subservient to our use. The co-operation of the learning and talent, as well as the use of the libraries and collections of the whole country, is an essential feature of the plan, and ought not to be lost sight of.

I would, however, distinctly disavow the intention of underrating the importance of collections in themselves. On the contrary, it ought to be the duty of the Smithsonian Institution to point out the means by which they may be made, and to aid in the work, to the extent of its ability, by embracing all opportunities which may offer for procuring specimens for distribution, and by facilitating exchange and assisting explorations.

Though the formation of a general collection is neither within the means nor the province of the Institution, it is an object which ought to engage the attention of Congress. A general museum appears to be a necessary establishment at the seat of government of every civilized nation. The navy, the army, and the whole corps of commercial and diplomatic agents in foreign countries, all consider it their duty to send to the seat of government of their own nation every object which may serve to improve or to interest the people. Indeed the government of the United States has already formed the nucleus of such a museum in the collections now in the Patent Offiee. An establishment of this kind can only be supported by government; and the proposition ought never to be encouraged of putting this duty on the limited, though liberal bequest of a foreigner. The Smithsonian Institution will readily take the supervision of an establishment of this kind, and give plans for its organization and arrangement, provided it be requested to do so, and the means for effecting the object be liberally supplied.

I make these remarks with reference to the collections, because I am fully impressed with the fact that the tendency of the Institution will be to a statical condition, in which the income will be absorbed in the support and accommodation of objects of a doubtful or contingent value. There is even danger in receiving donations from individuals. The articles may be valuable in part, but may consist also of much which the Institution cannot well afford to keep. Besides this, it is extremely difficult to discharge, acceptably, the duty of the curator of property thus acquired. Since the house-room and the income of the Institution for the accommodation and support of collections are limited, great care must be exercised in the choice of the articles, and preference given to those which are of importance in determining problems of interest, and which give promise of the ready production of new and interesting results.

For a detailed account of the additions to the museum during the past year, and the present state of the collections, I must refer to Professor Baird's report herewith presented.

In an appendix to this will be found a list of the donations, with the names of the donors alphabetically arranged. These consist principally of specimens not generally found in other collections; and though they may not be very attractive to ordinary visitors, the student of natural history will find in them much of interest.

The circular prepared by Professor Baird, describing the method of collecting and preparing specimens, and indicating objects especially desirable, has proved effective in procuring important contributions.

Among the objects which should be collected and preserved with care, are the remains of the specimens of the arts of the aboriginal inhabitants of this country, the contents of mounds, and the stone implements found on the surface of the earth. The implements and industrial products of the present tribes of Indians should also be gathered as the materials for the advance of the new and interesting science of ethnology. Of the contents of mounds, but a limited amount of specimens exist; and as these are not, like the spontaneous productions of nature, constantly in the process of reproduction, every article should be diligently sought for, and carefully preserved. Some additions have been made to the collections in this line.

The museum of natural history, besides plants and minerals, numbers eighteen hundred and fifty jars, containing specimens in spirits of mammalia, reptiles, fishes, articulata, mollusca, and radiata, amounting in all to twenty-five hundred species. Besides these, there are about nine hundred specimens of skulls and skeletons, and three thousand of skins of European and American birds.

Lectures.

In accordance with the suggestion contained in the act of incorporation of the Institution, courses of lectures have been given during the past year in the lecture-room of the Smithsonian building, and the reports of these lectures are generally copied in the public papers throughout the Union. Though the plan of diffusing knowledge by means of lectures is too restricted in its influence to meet fully the liberal views of the Smithsonian bequest, yet there is no place in the

United States where such means will have a tendency to affect more minds and do more good than in the city of Washington. Persons from all parts of the country assemble here during the sessions of Congress. It was supposed, at first, that the interest in these lectures would soon die away; but the experience of three years has indicated no tendency of this kind. This is in part owing to the constant influx of strangers and change of inhabitants. Besides this, there is in this city, in proportion to the whole number of inhabitants, a large number of intelligent persons, with moderate salaries, who gladly avail themselves of the means of improvement offered by the gratuitous lectures of the Institution.

As an evidence of the high appreciation of the advantages which these lectures afford the citizens of Washington, I may mention that the corporation of the city has ordered, since the last meeting of the board, a bridge to be constructed over the canal at Tenth street, for the special accommodation of those who attend the evening instruction given at the Institution. This bridge, with a well-drained and well-lighted path across the public grounds, will afford a direct and comfortable approach to the building from a central point on Pennsylvania avenue.

In my last Report I mentioned the fact that much complaint had been made through the public papers on account of the size of the lecture-room. It was the original intention of the Regents to construct a lecture-room in the main building, though, according to the plan proposed, the number of persons it would hold would scarcely have been greater than that now accommodated. This plan, however, was thought to be unsafe, because it was not proposed to make the interior fire-proof; but since an opposite course has been resolved upon, a large lecture-room may with safety be constructed in the main building, and the present lecture-room, having temporarily served the purpose, may be applied to other uses.

The proper construction of a lecture-room is, however, a problem of great difficulty, which in the present instance will be much enhanced by the form and peculiarities of the building. It must be well adapted to sight, to sound, to ventilation, and warming. A room might be constructed which would seat five thousand persons; but we know of none such, in every part of which an ordinary speaker can be distinctly heard. Too much must, therefore, not be expected with reference to the new lecture-room, though every endeavor will be made to render it as perfect as the conditions to which it is unavoidably subjected will allow.

The selection of the lecturers, and the arrangement of the courses, have been found, in some cases, an unpleasant and perplexing duty. The gentlemen invited, as a general rule, have been men of high standing, and have been chosen on account of their reputation and moral worth, rather than with reference to their proficiency in the art of rhetoric. It is not the aim of the Institution in these lectures merely to please the ear, but to impart important truths which may be valued for their own sake.

Many applications have been made for the use of the lecture-room of the Institution for pay lectures and exhibitions of a private character;

but these have in all cases been refused. The use of the room has, however, on several occasions been given to the faculty of Columbian College, and also for the meetings of the Teachers' Association of the District of Columbia. The organization of this association took place in the Smithsonian building in 1850, and its meetings have been regularly held in the lecture-room from that time to the present. It is believed that the spirit of the will of Smithson is properly consulted in giving encouragement and rendering facilities to these meetings. The association has been kept up with much spirit, and I am sure that much good has resulted from the organization. It has served to cherish a feeling of harmony among the teachers, and to awaken a spirit of improvement relative to education and general knowledge.

The following is a list of the titles of lectures given before the Institution during the last session of Congress, with the names of the gentlemen by whom they were delivered:

A course of six lectures on History as a science, and a single one on Poetry, by Dr. Samuel H. Cox, of Brooklyn, New York.

Two lectures on Induction and Association, by Dr. John Ludlow, Provost of the University of Pennsylvania.

A course of five lectures on Entomology, and one on the Alps, by Rev. Dr. John G. Morris, of Baltimore, Maryland.

Two lectures on the History and the Forms of the English Language, by Professor W. C. Fowler, of Amherst, Massachusetts.

One lecture on the Architecture of the Middle Ages, by Dr. A. H. Vinton, of Boston.

Two lectures by Professor S. S. Haldeman, of Columbia, Pennsylvania, on the Mechanism of Speech, and its bearing upon the natural history of the human race.

Two lectures on Geology, by Dr. Benjamin Silliman, sr., of Yale College, New Haven.

JOSEPH HENRY,
Secretary of the Smithsonian Institution.

SIXTH ANNUAL REPORT

Of the Secretary of the Smithsonian Institution, for the year 1852.

To the Board of Regents of the Smithsonian Institution:

GENTLEMEN: The object of the Annual Report of the Secretary is not only to present to the Regents an account of the transactions of the period which elapses between their successive sessions, but also to make such suggestions as may be important to the future management of the affairs of the Institution, and to state such facts in reference to it as may be interesting to the public, or which may furnish a connected history of its transactions.

Since the beginning of the Institution no change has taken place in the policy originally adopted with reference to the system of active operations. The details of this plan were well considered, and its importance as the only means of properly carrying out the intention of the donor were fully understood at the first. The theory of the plan was expressed in a few propositions, which have been constantly kept in view, and acted upon as far as the law of Congress and other restrictions would permit.

This plan, although prosecuted under very unfavorable circumstances, has produced results such as to render the name of the Institution favorably known wherever science and literature are cultivated, and to connect it indissolubly with the history of the progress of knowledge in our times. As a proof of this we need only state the following facts:

The Institution has promoted astronomy, by the aid furnished the researches which led to the discovery of the true orbit of the new planet Neptune, and the determination of the perturbations of this planet and the other bodies of the solar system, on account of their mutual attraction. It has also aided the same branch of science by furnishing instruments and other facilities to the Chilian expedition, under Lieut. Gilliss; and by preparing and publishing an ephemeris of Neptune, which has been adopted by all the astronomers of the world.

It has advanced geography, by providing the scientific traveller with annual lists of the occultations of the principal stars; by the moon, for the determination of longitude; by the preparation of tables for ascertaining heights with the barometer; and by the collection and publication of important facts relative to the topography of different parts of the country, particularly of the valley of the Mississippi.

It has established an extended system of meteorological investigation, consisting of several hundred intelligent observers, whoare daily noting the phases of the weather in every part of the continent of North America. It has imported standard instruments, constructed hundreds of compared thermometers, barometers, and psychrometers, and has furnished improved tables and directions for observing with these instruments the various changes of the atmosphere, as to temperature, pressure, moisture, &c. It has collected, and is collecting, from its observers, an extended series of facts, which are yielding deductions of great interest in regard to the climate of this country and the meteorology of the globe.

The Institution has advanced the science of geology, by its researches and original publications. It has made a preliminary exploration of the remarkable region on the upper Missouri river called the "Bad Lands," and is now printing a descriptive memoir on the extraordinary fossil remains which abound in that locality. It has assisted in explorations relative to the distribution in this country of the remains of microscopic animals found in immense quantities in different parts of the United States.

It has made important contributions to botany, by means of the published results of explorations in Texas, New Mexico, and California, and by the preparation and publication of an extended memoir, illustrated with colored engravings, on the sea-plants of the coast of North America.

It has published several important original papers on physiology, comparative anatomy, zoology, and different branches of descriptive natural history; and has prepared and printed, for distribution to travellers, a series of Directions for collecting and preserving specimens.

It has advanced the science of terrestrial magnetism, by furnishing instruments for determining the elements of the magnetic force, to various exploring expeditions; and by publishing the results of observations made under its direction, at the expense of the government.

It has collected and published the statistics of the libraries of the United States, and perfected a plan of stereotyping catalogues, which will render effective, as a combined whole, all the scattered libraries of the country.

The Institution has been instrumental in directing attention to American antiquities, and has awakened such an interest in the subject as will tend to the collection and study of all the facts which can be gathered relative to the ancient inhabitants of this continent. It has also rendered available for the purposes of the ethnologist and philanthropist the labors of our missionaries among the Dakotas, by publishing a volume on the language of this tribe of Indians; and has done good service to comparative philology by the distribution of directions for collecting Indian vocabularies.

It has established an extended system of literary and scientific exchanges, both foreign and domestic, and annually transmits between the most distant societies and individuals, hundreds of packages of valuable works. It has presented its own publications, free of expense, to all the first-class libraries of the world, and thus rendered them accessible, as far as possible, to all persons who are interested in their study. No restriction of copyright has been placed on their republication; and the truths which they contain are daily finding their way to the general public, through the labors of popular writers and teachers. The distribution of its publications and its system of exchanges have served not only to advance and diffuse knowledge, but also to increase the reputation, and, consequently, the influence of our country; to promote a kindly and sympathetic feeling between the New World and Old—alike grateful to the philosopher and the philanthropist.

These are the fruits of what is called the system of active operations of the Institution, and its power to produce other and continuous results is only limited by the amount of the income which can be appropriated to it, since each succeeding year has presented new and important fields for its cultivation. All the anticipations indulged with regard to it have been fully realized; and, after an experience of six years, there can now be no doubt of the true policy of the Regents in regard to it.

I am well aware, however, that the idea is entertained by some that the system of active operations, though at present in a flourishing condition, cannot continue to be the prominent object of attention; and that under another set of directors, other counsels will prevail and other measures be adopted, and that what has been done in establishing this system will ultimately be undone. It is true, there is cause of fear that the policy in this respect may be changed; for the system we are here considering requires constant exertion, and is little suited to the tastes and habits of those who seek place and position from mere personal considerations. There is cause to fear, also, from the experience of the past, that the general expenses of a large building, the support of the establishment necessarily connected with it, and the cost of collecting, preserving, and exhibiting specimens of nature and art, will so increase as to paralyze the spirit of activity. Furthermore, the proposition is frequently urged upon the Regents, by persons who have not duly considered the will of Smithson, or who fail to appreciate the importance of the present plan, that a large portion of the income should be devoted to the diffusion of a knowledge of some popular branch of practical art; and there may be some fear that a timid policy on the part of the friends of the Institution will lead them to favor such a plan.

To obviate these tendencies, it is the duty of the present Regents, if they are convinced that the policy of active operations is the true one, to endeavor to correct, as far as possible, the errors which may have been committed in the beginning, and to give the Institution such an impulse in the proper direction, that it cannot deviate from it without immediately arresting the attention of the enlightened public, both at home and abroad, who will not fail to demand, authoritatively, a sufficient reason for the change.

A promise has been made to all persons in this country, engaged in original researches, and who are capable of furnishing additions to the sum of human knowledge, that the result of their labors shall continue to be presented to the world through the Smithsonian publications. The honor of the Institution is also pledged to the scientific and literary societies from which it has received exchanges, in this and other countries, that it will continue to send to them at least an annual volume of Contributions, of a character similar to those with which they have already been presented. It is on this condition that the library has been so richly favored, not only with the current volumes of transactions, but also, in many cases, from the oldest societies, with full sets of all the previous volumes of their series of publications. Besides this, the libraries of all the colleges and literary and philosophical societies of this country are supplied with full sets of the Smithsonian Transactions;

and in this way a foretaste has been given of the fruit of the operations, which will tend, in some degree, to insure their continuance.

But if, notwithstanding all this, the Institution is destined to a change of policy, what has been well done in the line we are advocating can never be undone. The new truths developed by the researches originated by the Institution, and recorded in its publications; the effect of its exchanges with foreign countries; and the results of the cataloguing system, can never be obliterated; they will endure through all coming time. Should the government of the United States be dissolved, and the Smithsonian fund dissipated to the winds, the "Smithsonian Contributions to Knowledge" will still be found in the principal libraries of the world, a perpetual monument of the wisdom and liberality of the founder of the Institution, and of the faithfulness of those who first directed its affairs.

Whatever, therefore, may be the future condition of the Institution, the true policy, for the present, is to devote its energies to the system of active operations. All other objects should be subordinate to this, and be in no wise suffered to diminish the good which it is capable of producing. It should be prosecuted with discretion, but with vigor; the results will be its vindication.

It was stated in the last Report that the Institution had been the contingent legatee of a considerable amount of property. During the past year the facts with reference to this bequest have been investigated, and it appears that Mr. Wynn, of Brooklyn, N. Y., deceased, left a legacy to his wife, and the greater part of his property, valued at $75,000, to his daughter, a child six years old, with the condition that at the death of this daughter without issue, the property should come to the Smithsonian Institution. In making this bequest Mr. Wynn says, in his will: "I know no benevolent institution more useful and appropriate than the Smithsonian Institution at Washington."

This circumstance is highly gratifying to the friends of the Institution, not because it offers a remote possibility of an increase of the funds, but on account of the evidence it affords of the liberal views of the deceased, and of his confidence in the proper management and importance of the Smithsonian bequest. The will of Mr. Wynn induces us to believe that the right administration of the Smithsonian fund will cause similar examples of liberality on the part of wealthy individuals of our country; and in this point of view the responsibility which rests on those who have the direction of the affairs of this Institution is greater than that with reference to the good which the income itself may immediately accomplish.

Though it is scarcely to be expected that many unconditional bequests will be made, yet the example of Smithson may induce the founding of other institutions which may serve to perpetuate other names, and increase the blessings which may flow from such judicious liberality. Man is a sympathetic being; and it is not impossible that Smithson himself may have caught the first idea of his benevolent design from the example of our countryman, Count Rumford, the principal founder of the Royal Institution of London.

Bequests for special purposes, bearing the names of the testators, are not incongruous with the plan of this Institution. Lectureships on particular subjects, annual reports on special branches of knowledge, provision for certain lines of research, and libraries for general use or special reference, may be founded under the name of those who bestow the funds, and be placed under the direction of, and incorporated with, the Smithsonian Institution. The charge, however, of such bequests ought not to be accepted unless they are sufficient in themselves to meet the expenses of the object contemplated by them, and would not encumber or impede the legitimate operations of the Institution. For example: were a library of a hundred thousand volumes offered, it would be unwise to accept it were it not accompanied by the funds necessary to the erection of a building and to the proper support of the collection.

In July, 1850, a new system of accounts was introduced, which has been continued to the present time. According to this system, every payment is made by an order of the Secretary on the Treasurer, who, in turn, gives his check on Messrs. Corcoran & Riggs, with whom the semi-annual interest and the other income of the Institution are deposited. As often as once a quarter all the bills are examined and referred to their appropriate classes, in presence of all the officers of the Institution. After the accounts are posted, they are referred to the Executive Committee for final examination.

By a reference to the report of the Executive Committee, it will be seen that the funds are in a good condition, and that, although during the past year $14,047 have been paid on the building, there is still on hand, after all the expenditures for publications and other purposes, besides the original bequest, upwards of $200,000 of accrued interest. It is to be regretted that Congress has not yet acted on the petition requesting the perpetual funding of $150,000 of the last-mentioned sum. It is highly important that this money should be permanently invested as a part of the principal, so that it can neither be lost nor expended. There are no other means of effectually accomplishing this result except by funding it in the treasury of the United States. The proposition should be pressed upon Congress, though there may be, at present, no very certain prospect of success; for, if the petition be refused, and the money be afterwards lost by improper investment or injudicious expenditure, the responsibility would, in part, rest with the government.

The charge of this fund, and of all the disbursements, is attended with much solicitude. It involves a degree of responsibility which, to a person unaccustomed to large financial transactions, is very onerous. I beg leave, however, in this place, to mention the obligation which the Institution is under to W. W. Corcoran, Esq., for the aid which he has, in all cases, afforded in the management of the funds, and the judicious advice which he has always given relative to their investment.

From the report of the Building Committee it appears that the contract for finishing the interior of the wings and ranges, and the rooms of the towers, has been completed. The whole interior of the main building, comprising a rectangular space of two hundred feet long, fifty wide, and about sixty high, remains to be finished with fire-proof materials. It is proposed to divide this space into two stories and a basement; these stories to be devoted to the library, the museum, and a large and convenient lecture-room.

The business of the Institution would be much facilitated were this part of the building completed. Since Congress has authorized the establishment of a library and museum, it will be well to place all the objects of interest to the public in the main building, and make this exclusively the show part of the establishment, devoting the wings and ranges, and rooms of the towers, to the business operations and other purposes of the Institution. In the present condition of affairs there is no part of the edifice to which the public has not access, and, consequently, business has to be transacted amidst constant interruptions. The loss of time and effective life to which all are exposed who occupy a position of notoriety in the city of Washington, is truly lamentable; and where this is increased by facility of access to gratify mere curiosity, the evil becomes scarcely endurable. Progress in business, under such circumstances, can only be made by an encroachment on the hours usually allotted to rest, and that, too, at the expense of wasted energies and shortened days.

Publications.

During the past year the following memoirs, described in the previous Reports, have been collected into volumes and distributed to public institutions in this country and abroad:

1. Observations on Terrestrial Magnetism.
2. Researches on Electrical Rheometry.
3. Contributions to the Natural History of the Fresh-water Fishes of North America.
4. First part of the Marine Algæ of the coast of the United States.
5. Plantæ Wrightianæ Texano-Neo-Mexicanæ, Part I.
6. Law of Deposit of the Flood Tide, its dynamical action and offiee.
7. Description of Ancient Works in Ohio.
8. Occultations visible in the United States during the year 1852.
9. A Grammar and Dictionary of the Dakota language.

The memoir last mentioned occupies an entire volume, the fourth of the Smithsonian series of Contributions. The other memoirs are contained in the third volume of the same series.

The remaining memoirs, described in the last Report, are still in the press, the printing of them having been delayed by the exhaustion of the appropriation for the year, and by several necessary corrections. A sufficient number of papers will, however, be printed in the course of a few months, with the new appropriation, to complete the fifth volume of Contributions; and if the means prove sufficient, we can readily issue the sixth volume during the present year.

The result of the plan of publication has fully realized the anticipations which were entertained of its usefulness. It supplies the food it feeds upon. The appearance in the Contributions of a memoir on any subject immediately directs attention to that subject, and induces other laborers to engage in the same field of exploration. This is particularly manifest in the interest awakened with regard to the antiquities of our country, and to the language of the Indian tribes, by the publications of the Institution on these subjects.

The following is an account of the memoirs received since the date of the last Report:

1. Contributions to the History of the Marine Algæ of North America.—By Dr. W. H. Harvey: Part II.

In the Report for 1850, an account was given of the acceptance for publication of an extended and expensive memoir of the Marine Algæ of the eastern and southern coasts of the United States, by Prof. Harvey, of the University of Dublin. The first part of this memoir was published last spring, and has found much favor with the botanical world, as well as with the inhabitants and visitors of our sea-board. The second part of the same memoir is now printed, and will be ready for distribution in the course of a few weeks. It is illustrated by twenty-four plates, and comprises 240 pages of printed matter.

The common name of the class of plants which forms the subject of this memoir, viz: sea-weeds, has subjected the Institution to the charge of expending its funds on trifling and unworthy objects; and as the same objection may be made to many of the papers forming the series of Smithsonian Contributions, a few words in vindication of researches of this character may not be inappropriate.

Nothing in the whole system of nature is isolated or unimportant. The fall of a leaf and the motion of a planet are governed by the same laws. The structure of a lichen and the formation of an oak are equally the result of definite plans. It is in the study of objects, considered trivial and unworthy of notice by the casual observer, that genius finds the most important and interesting phenomena. It was in the investigation of the varying colors of the soap-bubble that Newton detected the remarkable fact of the fits of easy reflection and easy refraction presented by a ray of light in its passage through space, and upon which he established the fundamental principle of the present generalization of the undulatory theory of light. Smithson himself, the founder of this Institution, considered the analysis of a tear as nowise unworthy of his peculiar chemical skill; and well might he so consider it; for the knowledge of the composition of every secretion of the body is of importance, in a physiological point of view, as well as in the preservation of health and the cure of disease. The study of the cause of the spasmodic muscular contraction of a frog, when brought into contact with two pieces of metal, revealed to Galvani the first facts of the branch of science which now bears his name. The microscopic organization of animals and plants is replete with the highest instruction; and, surely, in the language of one of the fathers of modern physical science, "nothing can be unworthy of being investigated by man which was thought worthy of being created by God."

These remarks are particularly applicable to the study of the lower classes of the organic creation. Nature everywhere exhibits economy of means in attaining the most complex and diversified ends. Every result is produced in the simplest manner when viewed in relation to the whole design. All parts of organized beings, whether plants or animals, are formed of a few elementary structures, variously transformed and combined. To obtain a knowledge of the plan and process of organization, we must begin with the most simple combinations, precisely as we would do in the study of mathematical analyses, in which the student commences with the least complicated formulæ, and gradually proceeds to those of a more involved character. It is for this reason that the study of the algæ, or sea-weeds, is of special interest to the physiologist. The framework of every vegetable is built up of cells or little membranous sacks. All vegetable structures, whether wood, bark, or leaves, are formed of aggregations of these cells, differently moulded and united. As we pass along the series of organized forms, we may descend from those of a higher to those of a lower complexity, until, in the class of algæ, we arrive at plants of which the whole body is composed of a few cells strung together; and finally at others, the simplest of organized bodies, whose entire framework is a single cell. Now, it is only by a critical study of these rudimentary forms, and by tracing them into their complex combinations, that man can ever hope to arrive at a knowledge of the laws of organization. We might speak of the importance of a knowledge of the algæ in their application to agriculture and the chemical arts; but what we have here stated will be a sufficient reason for their study, independent of all minor considerations.

2. The next memoir consists of an account of a series of researches in the comparative anatomy of the frog, by Dr. Jeffries Wyman, of Cambridge, Massachusetts.

The whole animal kingdom may in one sense be considered as the different development of four separate plans of organization, giving rise to four different classes of animals, viz: the Radiata, the Articulata, Mollusca, and Vertebrata. Whatever discovery is made with regard to the organization of any of the species belonging to any one of these classes, tends to throw light on the organization of the whole class; and it is only by the careful study of all the different animals of a class, and a comparison of their analogous parts, that we can arrive at a knowledge of the general laws which control the development of the whole. Thus the study of human anatomy is the basis of the investigation of the anatomy of all animals with a back-bone; and conversely, the anatomy of any animal of this class tends to throw light on that of man.

Dr. Wyman's paper gives an account of a series of elaborate investigations of the nervous system of a very common, but, in a physiological point of view, highly interesting animal.

The following are the several points of the memoir:

(1.) An anatomical description of the more important parts of the nervous system.

(2.) Comparisons between them and the corresponding organs of other animals, both higher and lower in the scale.

(3.) The metamorphoses which they undergo, especially the spinal chord and some of the cranial nerves, showing the existence of a more complete analogy between the immature condition of Batrachian reptiles and the class of fishes, than has hitherto been noticed.

(4.) An application of the facts observed in connexion with the cranial nerves to the philosophical anatomy of the nervous system, showing what is believed to be the true nature of the special sense nerves, as contrasted with other cranial or the true spinal nerves, and the conformity of the other cranial nerves to the common spinal type.

3. The next communication has the following title: "Plantæ Wrightianæ Texano-Neo-Mexicanæ, Part II.—By Dr. Asa Gray, Professor of Botany in Harvard University."

It has been stated in two of the preceding Reports that a small appropriation was made for botanical explorations in Texas and New Mexico, and that the results had been placed in the hands of Dr. Gray for scientific investigation. The first memoir on this subject was described in the last Report. It has been printed, and copies distributed to all the working botanists in this country and Europe. It also forms a part of the third volume of the "Smithsonian Contributions."

The object of the present memoir is to give a scientific account of the collections made by Mr. Wright, under the direction of Col. J. D. Graham, U. S. Topographical Engineers, and Major W. H. Emory, of the Boundary Commission, in New Mexico and in Eastern Texas, during the summer and autumn of 1851, and the spring and early part of the summer of 1852.

The description of the plants from this region was previously carried as far as the order *Compositæ*. In the present paper Dr. Gray gives a similar account of the recent collections up to the same point, and reserves the other portions of these collections made by Mr. Wright, with the remainder of the undescribed plants of Fendler and Lindheimer, to be described in a general memoir. One portion of the collection was made from July to November, from El Paso to the Copper Mines of Santa Rita del Cobre, in the southwestern part of New Mexico; and thence into the northern part of the Mexican State of Sonora, as far as Santa Cruz, returning to the Copper Mines by way of Guadalupe Pass, and thence back to El Paso. The plants obtained during this tour are of exceeding interest, and comprise a larger portion of new species than any other collection that has fallen into Dr. Gray's hands. Another portion was obtained in the vicinity of El Paso and the rancho of Frontera, and down the Rio Grande for sixty or seventy miles; also, up the valley of the river as far as Camp Fillmore, and thence into the Organ mountains, which bound the valley on the east. Another collection was made in a hasty excursion to Lake St. Marie and Lake Guztman, in Chihuahua. These several collections afford many novelties, no botanist having previously explored this region at the same season of the year.

It is expected that a full account of the topography and productions of this country will be given in the reports of Colonel Graham and Major Emory.

The interest which attaches to the results of explorations of this kind is not confined to the botanist, but extends to the physical geographer and the political economist. An accurate description of the botany of a region is a sure guide to a knowledge of its power of producing and sustaining vegetable and animal life, and consequently of its value in a commercial and political point of view.

4. Dr. Leidy, of Philadelphia, has presented a memoir on the extinct species of the ox of America. In this paper he indicates the former

existence of four species of the ox, which were probably contemporaneous with the *Mastadon* and the *Megalonyx*. Fossil remains of these animals have been frequently found in the United States, and descriptions of them are scattered through various works; but no approach has before been made to a correct view of the number and character of the species. The present existing species of ox are found indigenous in every part of the world except South America and Australia, and this is the more remarkable, because the domestic ox introduced into the former country by Europeans exists in immense herds on the pampas in a wild state. There is a similar fact with regard to the horse. America, at the period of its discovery, possessed no indigenous quadruped of this kind, though the climate is highly favorable to its existence, and the remains of two extinct species are frequently found. Two of the species of ox described by Dr. Leidy belong to the genus Bison, and one of these is of gigantic size. The other two species belong to a new genus called *Bootherium.*

5. Another memoir presented by the same author forms an interesting addition to our knowledge of the extinct gigantic sloth tribe of North America. It comprises a description of remains of the *Megalonyx*, *Mylodon*, *Megatherium*, and of a new genus called *Eriptodon.*

The scientific world is indebted for the first account of the remains of a large extinct quadruped of the sloth tribe to President Jefferson. Fragments of the bones of this animal were found in a saltpetre cave in Greenbrier county, Virginia. They were regarded with little or no interest by the persons who first observed them, and, as they encumbered the saltpetre bed, would probably have been thrown out and suffered to decay, had not the news of their existence reached the ears of the distinguished individual before mentioned. Though devoted to politics, he was too much of a philosopher not to see in these mouldering fragments of a skeleton objects of high interest connected with the past history of our globe. He described them in a memoir published in the Transactions of the American Philosophical Society at Philadelphia in 1797, and gave to the animal to which they belong the name of *Megalonyx*, or the great claw. The materials in his possession, however, were too scanty to allow of his determining the true character of the quadruped. Dr. Wistar, of Philadelphia, suspected the animal to have been a gigantic sloth; and this opinion was confirmed by Cuvier, from the ample materials for comparison at his command. The original bones described by Jefferson are preserved in the collection of the Philosophical Society; but, besides these, Dr. Leidy had access to specimens of the remains of the same animal, found in different parts of the United States. From the study of these he has been enabled to throw much additional light upon the characters of the *Megalonyx*. He considers that the only remains of this animal yet known are those found in the United States, and satisfactorily proves that the lower jaw of an extinct quadruped, discovered by Dr. Darwin in South America, and referred by naturalists to the *Megalonyx* of Jefferson, does not belong to an animal of the same genus.

The remains of the *Mylodon*, or gigantic sloth, were first discovered by Darwin in his researches in the southern part of South America. Remains of another species found in North America were described by Dr. Harlan, but were erroneously referred to the *Megalonyx.* Dr. Leidy, in his memoir, describes the collection of the remains of this animal belonging to the New York Lyceum.

The *Megatherium*, which is the largest of all the extinct sloth tribe, when full grown, was more than fourteen feet long, including the tail, and eight feet high. It was first discovered in South America, but has since been found in Georgia; and it was from this locality, the only one in the United States yet known, that the remains described by Dr. Leidy were obtained.

The fourth and new genus of American sloths, called the *Eriptodon* by the author, is established upon a peculiar form of teeth which belonged to an animal of about the size of the *Megalonyx*, the bones of which were also found in Georgia.

Dr. Hays, one of the commission to which this memoir was submitted, remarks in his report, that "the author has not only made valuable additions to our knowledge of an interesting tribe of animals, but has also collected and arranged the facts previously known so as to throw new light on the subject, and to render his memoir an important starting-point for future investigators."

Grammar of the Choctaw language.

The publication of the volume on the Dakota language, described in the last Report, has called forth another important memoir on comparative philology, namely, a Grammar of the Choctaw language, by the Rev. Harvey Byington, for thirty years a missionary among the Indians.

It was referred for examination to Professor Felton, of Cambridge, and to Professor Gibbs, of Yale College, both of whom pronounced it an important addition to ethnology, and warmly recommended its publication. The work was afterwards placed in the hands of Professor W. W. Turner, formerly Professor of Hebrew in the New York Theological Seminary, now librarian of the United States Patent Office. Previous to sending it to the press, the author, after numerous interviews with Professor Turner, concluded that his memoir was susceptible of so much improvement by a further study of the language, that he asked leave to withdraw it for a time. This request was of course granted, and Mr. Byington has returned to his missionary labors, and will again present the work after it has received the desired improvements.

Reports and other minor publications.

Since the date of the last Report to the Regents, the following articles have been printed and partially distributed:

1. Directions for making Collections in Natural History. This is a pamphlet of twenty-four pages, by Professor Baird, and is much called for by the correspondents of the Institution.

2. A work by Professor Jewett, containing an exposition of the system adopted by the Smithsonian Institution for constructing catalogues of libraries, by means of separate stereotype titles, with rules for the

guidance of librarians, and examples for illustration. This work is comprised in seventy-eight pages, and though not large, it has been produced at the expense of much time and labor.

3. A second emission of the Report on the Recent Improvements in the Chemical Arts has been printed, and in part distributed. This work is stereotyped, and therefore copies can be supplied at any time, at a comparatively small cost.

4. A Description of the Portraits of the North American Indians in the gallery of the Smithsonian Institution, by the painter of the portraits, J. M. Stanley, esq. This is a pamphlet of seventy-six pages, and contains brief sketches of the characters and incidents in the history of forty-three different tribes of Indians.

5. The first part of the collection of tables to facilitate meteorological and other calculations, by Professor Guyot: this was mentioned in the last Report, and has been stereotyped and distributed. It is a very acceptable present to the meteorological observers of the Institution, and other persons engaged in scientific investigations.

Several reports on different subjects are in progress of preparation; but the appropriation for this part of the programme of operations is at present so small, that the completion of them has not been urged upon the authors. The first part of the report on forest trees, by Dr. Gray, of Cambridge, will be ready for the press the latter part of the present or begining of the next year.

Distribution of publications and exchanges.

Copies of the Smithsonian Contributions to Knowledge are sent to all the first-class libraries and literary and scientific societies of the world, and in return the Institution receives an equivalent in Transactions and other publications. After the printing of the first volume of Contributions was completed, a copy of it and of the programme of organization were sent to the principal foreign literary and scientific institutions, with the request that they would exchange publications, on the condition that a volume of equal importance should be presented to them annually. At first the number of responses to this proposition was small; but since the character of the Institution has become known and appreciated, the works received in exchange have rapidly increased in number and importance. The whole number of articles received during 1852 is four thousand seven hundred and forty-four, which is more than three times that of all the previous years. The publications received in many cases consist of entire sets of Transactions, the earlier volumes of which are out of print, and cannot be purchased. They are of use in carrying on the various investigations of the Institution, and of value to the country as works of reference. They ought not to be considered as donations to the library, but as the products of the active operations, which the Institution is at liberty to dispose of in the manner best suited to further its designs. The principal object, however, of the distribution of the Smithsonian volumes, is not to procure a large library in exchange, but to diffuse among men a knowledge of the new truths discovered by the agency of the Smithsonian fund. The worth and importance of the Institution is not to be estimated by what it accumulates within the walls of its building, but by what it sends forth to the world. Its great mission is to facilitate the use of all the implements of research, and to diffuse the knowledge which this use may develope. The Smithsonian publications are sent to some institutions abroad, and to the great majority of those at home, without any return except, in some cases, that of co-operation in meteorological and other observations. Applications for these publications have now become so numerous that the edition printed will supply but a part of the demand, and it becomes a difficult matter to select the places which will best subserve the purpose of rendering them accessible to the greatest number of persons who would be benefited by their perusal.

In connexion with the distribution of its own publications, the Institution has adopted an arrangement to establish and promote a more general exchange of literary and scientific productions between this and other countries. For this purpose it receives packages from societies and individuals in the different parts of the United States, and transmits them to England or the continent, and through its agents distributes them to the parties for whom they are intended. It also receives the articles sent in return, and forwards them to those to whom they are addressed. To facilitate this operation, the packages to the Institution are addressed to the Collector of Customs in New York, and by him, on the certificate of the Secretary, admitted free of duty, and without the delay of an examination.

In carrying out this plan, the Institution is much indebted to the liberal course adopted by the government of Great Britain, and to the ready co-operation of the Royal Society of London. All packages intended for Great Britain, for some parts of the continent, and the East Indies, are directed to the care of the Royal Society, and on the certificate of its president, are, by a special order of the government, admitted duty free, and without the delay and risk of inspection. The packages are afterwards distributed by the agent of the Institution, or by those of the Society.

This system of exchange does not stop here. The Royal Society has adopted the same plan with reference to Great Britain and all other parts of the world; and the Smithsonian Institution, in turn, becomes an agent in receiving and distributing all packages which the Society desires to send to this country. A general system of international communication, first started by this Institution for the distribution of its own publications, has thus been established, which will tend to render the results of the labors of each country in the line of literature and science common to all, and to produce a community of interest and of relations of the highest importance to the advancement of knowledge, and of kindly feeling "among men."

The results of the operations of the system of foreign exchanges during the year 1852 are exceedingly gratifying. The whole number of packages sent out, including the Smithsonian publications, is 572, containing 9,195 articles, and weighing 9,855 pounds. There have been received, in addition to the 4,745 articles for this Institution, 637 packages, containing an unknown number of volumes, for other institutions in this country. The details of the business of the exchanges are intrusted to Professor Baird; and I would refer, for a particular statement of all the facts connected with it, to his report, herewith submitted.

The planet Neptune.

It has been mentioned in the last annual reports that Mr. S. C. Walker, of the U. S. Coast Survey, prepared, at the expense of the Smithsonian Institution, a memoir containing an exposition of the elements of the true orbit of the planet Neptune, and that from this orbit and the mathematical investigation of Professor Peirce, of Cambridge, an ephemeris of Neptune had been deduced, which has been accepted by all the astronomers of the world, as the only certain guide to the position of the planet. This ephemeris was prepared for 1848 and 1849, at the expense of the Institution; but since the last-mentioned date it has been calculated at the expense of the appropriation for the Nautical Almanac, while the cost of printing and distribution has been defrayed by the Institution. The same arrangement will continue for the ephemeris of 1853 and 1854, after which the whole will be transferred to the Nautical Almanac.

Occultations.

The moon, in her passage eastward around the earth, continually passes between us and the fixed stars or planets which lie in her path, and obscures them from our view. The instant of the disappearance of a star behind the moon, or the occultation of a star, as the phenomenon is called, can be noted by observers widely separated from each other, and hence this phenomenon becomes a ready means of determining the difference of longitude between two places. The employment of occultations for fixing geographical positions is easy, and leads to accuracy in the results. The telescope may be of moderate size, and requires no accurate adjustment; the position assigned it may be such as to suit the convenience of the observer. The frequent occurrence of occultations renders the use of them of great importance to the travelling observer; and the publication of lists of these, and of tables for their reduction, is essential to the improvement of geography. They are of particular value in this country on account of the frequent exploring and surveying expeditions now carried on by our government and our people, and to be continued for an indefinite time in the extensive territory of the West, and the newly acquired possessions of the Southwest. Tables of occultations for 1849 and 1850 were prepared and published at the expense of this Institution; but for subsequent years the expense of their preparation has been defrayed by the appropriation for the Nautical Almanac, under the direction of Lieutenant Davis, while the composition and press-work are still at the expense of the Institution. As soon as the Nautical Almanac is fully commenced, the publication of these tables will be entirely relinquished to this enterprise of the government.

Up to 1850 the tables published were of occultations visible in the United States. Since, however, the preparation of the tables has been in charge of the director of the Nautical Almanac, the list has been so extended as to make it useful to geographers in general as well as to those of the United States. This extension was rendered important on account of the surveys undertaken by our government in other parts of the globe. Also, a table has been added, giving the correction of the latitude due to the oblate spheroidal figure of the earth.

When we consider the character and condition of the vast continent of North America, which it belongs to us chiefly to reduce to a habitable and civilized state, we shall perceive that the practical scientific explorer has no higher duty than to settle the geography, the magnetism, the natural history, and the climate, of these regions.

Researches.

At the session of the Regents, in 1849, an appropriation was made to supply Lieutenant Gilliss with a telescope for his expedition to Chili, to aid him in his observations for a new determination of the distance of the inferior planets, and, consequently, of the actual distances of the several members of the solar system. A subsequent appropriation was made for the purchase of an astronomical clock for the same purpose. The first appropriation was repaid to the Institution by a grant from Congress to cover the expenses of the expedition, and the second will also be reimbursed by the purchase of the clock and all the other instruments by the Chilian government, for the permanent establishment of an observatory in that country.

By these operations, the Institution has been the means of rendering essential aid to science, without, in the end, diminishing the amount of its income. Lieutenant Gilliss, after voluntarily exiling himself from his family and his country for four years, has returned with a rich harvest of materials in astronomy, meteorology, magnetism, and natural history, in the reduction, generalization, and description of which the Institution may also furnish important aid.

The sum of one hundred and fifty dollars has been advanced to Prof. C. B. Adams, of Amherst College, to defray in part the expense of an exploration of the molluscs of the West Indies. This subject is intimately connected with the geological changes which have taken place on the surface of our globe; and it was with particular reference to this point that Professor Adams undertook these researches. This is his second expedition to the same regions; and in both instances the Smithsonian Institution has seconded his proposition, and warmly recommended it to the favorable consideration of the trustees of Amherst College. A small sum appropriated in this way, though not enough in itself to produce much effect, is still sufficient to complete the amount to be raised, and thus serve to determine the commencement of the enterprise.

Meteorology.

The general system of observations relative to the meteorology of the continent of North America, described in the previous Reports, has been continued and extended. It consists at present of the following classes, viz:

1. The Smithsonian system proper, made up of voluntary observers in different parts of the United States, who report immediately to the Institution.

2. The system of observations of the University of the State of New York, re-established under the direction of this Institution, and supported by the State of New York.

3. The system of observations established under the direction of this Institution, by the State of Massachusetts.

4 The extended system of observations made at the several military posts of the United States, under the direction of the Surgeon General of the army.

5. Separate series of observations by exploring and surveying parties, in some cases directed, and in part furnished with instruments, by this Institution.

6. Meteorological records from British America, consisting of observations made at the various posts of the Hudson's Bay Company, and at the residence of private individuals in Canada.

In the first three of these classes there are about two hundred observers distributed over the entire continent. In the older States they are very thickly distributed, and they are entirely wanting in none. Texas, Arkansas, the Indian Territory, Missouri, Iowa, and Minnesota, have each competent and reliable observers reporting directly to the Smithsonian Institution, in addition to those at the military posts, which are in the same regions.

Further westward, and more widely separated, the observers at the military posts, and those of surveying and exploring parties, continue the connexion of the system to the Pacific coast, where the number of military posts is greater, and private observers are again found.

The New York system embraces twenty-five academies as stations, all furnished with new and reliable instruments at the expense of the State.

In Massachusetts twelve stations are furnished in like manner, of which eight have reported.

In 1852 ninety-seven military posts reported meteorological observations, and for 1853 the number will be greater rather than less.

The whole number of stations and observers available in making the deductions for 1852 was three hundred and fifty; and this number, either reporting directly to the Institution or furnishing their observations for its use, may be relied upon for the eurrent year.

Besides the observations derived from this general system, a large collection has been procured from individuals in different parts of the country, who have kept records of the weather, in some cases for many years. This collection was obtained by issuing a circular from the Institution, requesting copies of any records which might have been kept relative to the climate of this country. The amount of information received in answer to this circular was far greater than was expected, and much more valuable matter was thus called forth than was previously known to exist.

In order that the materials procured from the aforementioned sources may be rendered available for scientific or practical purposes, it is necessary that they should be reduced, discussed, and arranged for publication. This work was commenced at the close of 1851, and has been prosecuted with considerable vigor during the past year. It was given by me in charge to Mr. Lorin Blodget, of Western New York, who has engaged in the work with much ardor, has devoted to it his whole time and attention, and has evinced an unusual degree of talent for investigations of this character.

The results which have thus far been obtained are of interest to the science of meteorology, and valuable to the practical arts of life. The following is a descriptive list of the deductions presented in a tabular form:

Temperature Tables.

1. Tables of general mean temperature for a series of years, embracing a summary of the annual means for the years 1849, 1850, 1851, and 1852, with a general summary of reliable observations of mean temperature on the North American continent.
2. Tables of mean temperature for each month, season, and year, for 1849, 1850, 1851, and 1852, embracing 273 stations in 1849; 284 in 1850; 300 in 1851; and 396 in 1852.
3. Tables of mean temperature at each observed hour for the same periods and the same stations.
4. Tables of the monthly extremes of temperature, with the range above and below the monthly mean, for the same periods and the same stations.
5. Collection of tables of temperature at different stations, observed for a series of years.
6. Miscellaneous tables of temperature, not conforming entirely to either of the above divisions.

The first class of tables embraces six hundred and seventy stations, distributed over the entire continent, from the West Indies and Mexico to the Polar seas.

The second class has a more limited range, and is generally confined to the United States and its territories, as observed by the military system, and that of the Smithsonian Institution, with a few stations in Canada and the British possessions on this continent.

The third class of tables is nearly the same in extent with the preceding, and for three complete years, viz:—1850, 1851, and 1852.

The fourth class is of the same extent and time.

The fifth is a climatic arrangement of tables from various stations, extending in continuous series over periods varying from five to sixty years.

Tables of Precipitation.

1. Tables of distribution of precipitation in rain and melted snow for each month, season, and year, for 1849, 1850, 1851, and 1852.
2. General tables of precipitation for a series of years, containing the results of the preceding tables, with a general summary of all reliable and accessible observation of fall of rain on the North American continent. These tables give results from about four hundred stations, principally in the United States, its Territories. and the West Indies.

3. Irregular tables and single series, extending over long periods, and where reliable observations have been made.

A series of charts has been constructed to exhibit the distribution of temperature on the North American continent, by isothermal lines; and also another series, illustrative of the distribution of precipitation for each month, season, and year of 1850, 1851, and 1852, and for the periods given in the general tables. It is proposed to present these results to Congress as a part of the Annual Report of the Regents, and as the first fruit of the labors of the Smithsonian Institution on the subject of meteorology.

Catalogue of Libraries.

In addition to the preparation of the work previously mentioned, Professor Jewett has continued his experiments on the new process of stereotyping, to be used in his system of cataloguing. Much difficulty and delay have been experienced in the prosecution of these experiments, on account of the want of workmen to construct the peculiar apparatus required. The services of an ingenious and skilful artisan have, however, been secured; and the process is now brought to such a state that it can be applied with certainty, and abridgment of labor, to produce the best specimens of typography.

The system of catalogues described in previous Reports, though future experience may suggest other improvements, is now apparently perfect in all its details. A stereotyping office has been established in the basement of the west wing of the Smithsonian building, and the Institution is ready to commence the formation of a general catalogue of the principal libraries of the United States. The commission to which the catalogue system was referred, recommended that measures be taken to procure the preparation and printing of the catalogue of the Library of Congress. The cost of the first collection of stereotype titles can be best borne by this library, and it will be the first to reap the benefit of this invention. The stereotype blocks of the titles can be preserved in the Institution, and a new catalogue annually furnished at a small expense, with all the additions inserted in their proper places. The same titles will be employed in printing the catalogues of other libraries, and the new titles which may be prepared for these will, in turn, be used for the Library of Congress.

I beg leave to commend this subject to the immediate consideration of the Board of Regents. The whole plan is in perfect harmony with the active operations, and has always received my cordial commendation. The Institution has incurred the expense of reducing it to practice, so far as it depends on mechanical arrangements; and it now only requires to be applied, to realize all the benefits which have been anticipated in regard to it, to do honor to the Institution and to confer deserved reputation on its author.*

---

* NOTE.—Since this report was presented to the Board of Regents, Congress has appropriated three thousand dollars to commence the catalogue of its library on the stereotype plan, under the direction of the Smithsonian Institution.

Library.

During the last year the library has received important additions from the books presented in exchange for the volumes of the Smithsonian Contributions and other publications. The whole value of the works thus received during the year, according to the estimate of Professor Baird, is not less than from four to five thousand dollars. From this source alone a highly interesting and valuable collection of books, pertaining to all branches of positive knowledge, will, in time, be obtained. The reputation which the publications of the Institution have given it abroad, has induced individuals to present a number of valuable works to the library. For an account of the whole, I must refer to the report of Professor Jewett, herewith submitted. The library has also been increased by the purchase of such books as were required in the operations of the Institution, and with a series of scientific and other periodicals.

The copyright law is still in existence, and the library has received, during the past year, the usual number of articles from this source. The remark, however, may again be made with truth, that the action of this law, as it now exists, imposes a burden on the Institution from which it should be relieved.

The whole number of articles, according to the report of Professor Jewett, now in the library, is twenty-one thousand seven hundred.

Museum of Natural History.

The additions to the collection in natural history, under the persevering efforts of Professor Baird, have increased in a compound ratio over those of previous years. Large additions will also be made by the exploring expeditions which are about to leave for the different parts of this continent and distant seas; but the expense of preparing and transporting these, it is hoped, will be defrayed by the general government. For a detailed account of the number and variety of the specimens collected, I must refer to Professor Baird's report accompanying this communication.

Gallery of Art.

Besides a library, a museum, and lectures, the act of Congress establishing the Smithsonian Institution directed the formation of a gallery of art. The only articles belonging to the Institution which have been yet collected in accordance with the last-mentioned regulation of Congress, are the valuable series of engravings by the old masters, decribed in a previous Report. One of the original propositions of the programme is that of encouraging art, by providing a suitable room for the exhibition of pictures free of expense to the artist. In accordance with this, the large room in the west wing will be devoted to this purpose. It now contains a very interesting series of portraits, mostly full-size, of one hundred and fifty-two North American Indians, with sketches of the scenery of the country they inhabit, deposited by the artist who painted them, Mr. J. M. Stanley These portraits were all taken from life, and are accurate representations of the peculiar features of prominent individuals of forty-three different tribes, inhabiting the southwestern prairies, New Mexico, California, and Oregon. The faithfulness of the likenesses has been attested by a number of intelligent persons who have visited the gallery, and have immediately recognised among the portraits those of the individuals with whom they have been personally acquainted. The artist expended in the work of obtaining these pictures ten years of his life, and perseveringly devoted himself to his task in the face of difficultics and dangers which enthusiam in the pursuit could alone enable him to encounter. The Institution has published a descriptive catalogue of these portaits, which are of interest to the ethnologist as representatives of the peculiar physiognomy, as well as of many of the customs, of the natives of this continent.

Lectures of the Institution.

Public lectures have become one of the characteristics of the day, and next to the press, perhaps, tend, more than any other means of diffusing knowledge, to impress the public mind. The liberal price paid by the Lowell Institute, and some of the associations in our large cities, induces men of reputation to devote themselves to the preparation of popular lectures. In some parts of the country a number of adjacent cities or villages enter into an arrangement by which the same lecture may be repeated, in succession, at each place; and in this way the amount paid becomes sufficient to call forth the best talent. A plan of this kind has been adopted by the Athenæum of Richmond, Virginia, with reference to the lectures before the Smithsonian Institution, the effect of which has been mutually beneficial. Popular lectures appear better adapted to present literary and historical facts, and to give information relative to subjects of art and of morals, than to impart a knowledge of scientific principles. These require more attention and continuous thought than can be generally expected from a promiscuous audience. Hence the scientific lecturer frequently aims at a brilliant display of experiments, rather than to impress the mind with general principles.

Local lectures are too limited in their influence to meet a proper interpretation of the will of Smithson; yet they were ordered by Congress, and are calculated to do more good in this city than in any other part of the Union.

In selecting lecturers, the consideration of mere popular effect has not been regarded. The persons chosen have been such as to give weight to the lecture, and to reflect credit on the Institution. The object has been to give instruction rather than amusement—to improve the public taste rather than to elicit popular applause. The Institution, to be respected, must maintain a dignified character, and seek rather to direct public opinion than to obtain popularity by an opposite course.

The moral effect which the lectures have on the city of Washington cannot be otherwise than beneficial. When the weather is favorable, the room is every evening crowded before the hour of commencement with an intelligent audience. The lecturers have generally been persons from a distance, who have expressed surprise to find such a large and respectful attendance in a city which is commonly thought to be exclusively devoted to politics and amusement. The plan of inviting gentlemen of reputation and influence from a distance renders the Smithsonian operations familiar to those best qualified to appreciate their value, and best able to give a correct account of the character of the Institution in their own districts of country, as well as to vindicate its claims to the confidence and friendly regard of the public. The results of this course, and the distribution of the volumes of Contributions to colleges and other institutions, it is hoped, will so establish the Institution in the good opinion of the intelligent and influential part of the community, that it may bid defiance to the assaults of those who are ignorant of its true character, or are disappointed in not sharing its honors without the talents or the industry to win them.

The following is a list of the titles of lectures given during the last session of Congress, with the names of the gentlemen by whom they were delivered:

A course of three lectures by Dr. E. K. Kane, U. S. N., on Arctic Exploration.

A course of three lectures by President Mark Hopkins, of Williams College, on Method applied to Investigation.

A course of four lectures by Prof. W. B. Rogers, of the University of Virginia, on the Phases of the Atmosphere.

A course of twelve lectures by Dr. Benjamin Silliman, sen., of Yale College, on Geology.

A course of two lectures by Prof. C. C. Felton, of Harvard University, on Greek Literature.

One lecture, by Job R. Tyson, esq., of Philadelphia: Queen Elizabeth and Oliver Cromwell, their characters and times, contrasted and compared.

A course of six lectures by Dr. B. A. Gould, jr., of Cambridge, on the Recent Progress of Astronomy.

A course of six lectures by Prof. Louis Agassiz, of Cambridge, on the Foundation of Symmetry in the Animal Kingdom.

A course of six lectures by Prof. B. Silliman, jr., on the four ancient elements—Earth, Air, Fire, and Water.

Omitted from previous report: A course of twelve lectures by Dr. Henry Goadby, on the Structure and Functions of Insects.

In the last Report to the Regents some general remarks were made relative to the library and museum, and nothing has since occurred to change the opinions then expressed. On the contrary, the experience of another year has tended to confirm these opinions, and to clearly exhibit the fact that it will be impossible to continue with the present income some of the most important operations, and rigidly adhere to the resolution of the Regents of 1847, to devote one half of the whole income to the library and museum, besides all the expenditures still required on the building for the accommodation of these objects. By a reference to the annual reports of the Executive Committee, it will be seen that the general incidental expenses have continually increased from year to year; and it is evident that they must continue to increase in a geometrical ratio, on account of the greater repairs which, in time, will be required on the building. After deducting from the income the cost of repairs, lighting, and heating; of messenger, attendants, and watchmen; of stationery, transportation, and postage; after dividing the remainder by two, and deducting from the quotient the expense of the public lectures, the final sum to be devoted to the most important, and, indeed, the only legitimate object of the bequest, is exceedingly small.

The attempt has, however, been made in good faith to carry out the resolution of February, 1847; and if items which may properly be charged to the library and collections were added to this side of the account, the balance up to the present date would be in favor of the active operations. But the plan has not been found to work well in practice. The income is too small properly to support more than one system of operations, and therefore the attempt to establish and sustain three departments, with separate ends and separate interests, must lead to inharmonious action, and consequently to diminished usefulness.

However proper such a division of the income might have been in the beginning, in order to harmonize conflicting opinions, and to submit with proper caution the several proposed schemes to a judicious trial, the same considerations do not now exist for its continuance; changes have since occurred which materially alter the conditions on which the resolution was founded. The plan of active operations was not at first fully understood even by the literary men of the country. It was considered chimerical, and incapable of being continued for any length of time; and hence it was thought important to provide for the means of falling back upon a library and collections. The experience of six years has, however, established its practicability and importance, and it is now considered by the great majority of intelligent persons who have studied the subject, the only direct means of realizing the intention of the donor. Again: the building was to have been finished in five years, and the income after this was to be increased by the interest on the remaining surplus fund; but the Regents have found it necessary, for the better security of the library and museum, to add fifty thousand dollars to the cost of the edifice; and ten years will have elapsed from the beginning, instead of five, before any income from the surplus fund will be available. This additional expense is not incurred for the active operations, and the question may be asked whether they ought to bear any part of this additional burden. Furthermore, at the time the division was made, it was thought obligatory on the part of the Institution to support the great museum of the Exploring Expedition; but the Regents have since concluded that it is not advisable to take charge of this collection; and Congress, by its appropriation for the enlargement of the Patent Office, concurred in the opinion expressed in the Senate by the Hon. Jefferson Davis, that it was a gift which ought not to be pressed upon the Institution. The inquiry may also, in this case, be made, whether it is advisable in the present state of the funds, and the wants of the active operations, to expend any considerable portion of the income in the production of a collection of objects of nature and art. Again: the active operations are procuring annually for the library, by exchange, a large number of valuable books, which, in time, of themselves will form a rare and valuable collection; and even if the division of the income is to be continued, a sum equal in amount to the price of these books ought to be charged to the library, and an equal amount credited to the active operations.

Though a large library connected with the Institution would be valuable in itself, and convenient to those who are in the immediate vicinity of the Smithsonian building, yet, as has been said before, it is not essential to the active operations. It would be of comparatively little importance to the greater number of the co-laborers of the Institution, who are found in every part of the United States, and are not confined even within these limits. The author of the great work on the American Algæ, now publishing in the Smithsonian Contributions, is a resident member of Trinity College, Dublin; and very few of the authors of the Smithsonian memoirs reside in Washington. The libraries, therefore, of the whole country, and in some cases of other countries, are at the service of the Institution, and employed for its purposes.

Similar remarks apply to the museum. It is not the intention of the Institution to attempt to examine and describe within the walls of its own building all the objects which may be referred to it. To accomplish this, a corps of naturalists, each learned in his own branch, would be required, at an expense which the whole income would be inadequate to meet. In the present state of knowledge, that profound attainment necessary to advance science can be made by an individual, however gifted, only in one or two narrow lines; and hence several members are required to complete a single class in any of the learned academies of Europe: therefore the plan which was once proposed, of establishing on the Smithsonian fund an academy of associated members, was entirely incompatible with the limited income of the Institution. The more feasible and far less expensive organization was adopted, of referring, for investigation, all scientific questions of importance, as well as objects of natural history, to persons of reputation and learning in different parts of the United States, and perhaps, in some cases, in foreign countries. By the operation of this plan, which has been found eminently practicable, the collections, as well as the libraries of the whole country, are rendered subservient to the use of the Institution.

There can be but little doubt that, in due time, ample provision will be made for a library and museum at the capital of this Union worthy of a government whose perpetuity depends upon the virtue and intelligence of the people. It is, therefore, unwise to hamper the more important objects of this Institution, by attempting to anticipate results which will be eventually produced without the expenditure of its means.

The prominent idea embraced in the Smithsonian organization, is that of co-operation and concerted action with all institutions and individuals engaged in the promotion of knowledge. Its design is not to monopolize any part of the wide fields of nature or of art, but to invite all to partake in the pleasure and honor of their cultivation. It seeks not to encroach upon ground occupied by other institutions, but to expend the funds in doing that which cannot be as well done by other means. It gives to the words of Smithson their most liberal interpretation, and "*increases and diffuses knowledge among men*" by promoting the discovery of new truths, and by disseminating these in every part of the civilized world.

Respectfully submitted,

JOSEPH HENRY,

Secretary Smithsonian Institution.

INDEX.

Page.

Ability of the Individual to Promote Knowledge, Lecture on 207
Aboriginal Monuments of New York 191
Academy of Arts and Sciences, Report of 148
Accounts, new system of, introduced 235
Achromatic Microscope ordered 146
Achromatic Telescope purchased 163
Active Operations, results of 252, 231
Act of Congress accepting Bequest of Smithson 111
Act of Congress establishing the Smithsonian Institution 112
Adams, John Quincy, Words of, respecting Plan 133
Adams, Prof. C. B., Appropriation to 245
Adams, C. B., Exploration by 220
Address on Smithsonian Institution 120
Advantages of Publications 135
Africa, Institutions in 49
Agassiz, Prof. L., Memoir by 172
Agassiz, Prof. L., Lectures by 251, 207
Agassiz, Prof. L., Troost's Memoir 213
Agricultural Society, use of rooms granted to 76
Agriculture, Application of Chemistry to 180
Air, Earth, Fire, Water, Lectures on 251
Airy, Prof., Accuracy of Ephemeris of Neptune 221
Alexander, Capt. B. S., appointed Architect 69
Alexander, Prof. S., Lectures by 207, 27
Alps, The, Lecture on 230
American Antiquarian Society 219, 14
American Antiquities 219, 203, 178, 172, 140, 14
American Association, Committee of, on Extending Meteorological System 222
American Board of Missions 214
American Medical Association 174
American Philosophical Society 239, 218, 213
American Sloths 240
Analysis of Soils and Plants 162
Ancient Monuments 219, 203, 178, 172, 140, 14
Aneroid Barometer, Experiments on 199
Annals of Philosophy, Contributions to, by Smithson 110
Antiquities of Wisconsin 220, 14
Apparatus 180, 145
Appendix 105
Appropriations for 1854 .... 99, 79
Architecture of the Middle Ages, Lecture on 230
Arctic Exploration, Lectures on 251

Page.
Asia, Institutions in........ 49
Association, Lecture on........ 230
Astronomical Clock........ 203
Astronomical Instruments for Chili........ 203, 173
Astronomy, Promotion of, by the Institution........ 231
Astronomy, Recent Progress of, Lectures on........ 251
Atchison, Hon. D. R., Letter to........ 3
Atwater, Mr., on Mounds of Ohio Valley........ 219
Aurora........ 199, 24
Bache, Prof., Paper presented by........ 191
Bailey, Prof. J. W........ 191, 17
Baird, Dr. Robert, Lectures by........ 27
Baird, Prof. S. F., appointed Assistant........ 224, 189
Baird, Prof. S. F., Directions for Collecting Specimens of Natural History by........ 217
Baird, Prof. S. F., Explorations by........ 220, 200
Baird, Prof. S. F., in charge of Exchanges........ 218
Baird, S. F., Report of, for 1853........ 36
Baird and Girard, Catalogue of Serpents........ 19
Barometers, by Ernst and Newman........ 197
Barnard, Henry, Lectures by........ 27
Bartlett, John R., Report on Squier & Davis........ 144
Batis Maritima........ 16
Batut, Madame de la........ 209
Beck, Prof. Lewis C., Lecture by........ 207
Beck, Prof. Lewis C., Report by........ 180
Beck, T. Romeyn, Meteorological System of New York........ 175
Belgium, Institutions in........ 44
Bermuda, Meteorological Observations from........ 176
Berrien, Hon. J. M., Construction of the Act by........ 117
Berzelius, Report of, on Physical Science........ 138
Bethune, Rev. Dr. G. W., Lecture by........ 207
Bibliographia Americana........ 179, 163
Birds, received 1853........ 53
Blanco, B., Liberality of........ 203
Blodget, Lorin........ 247, 99, 25
Booth, Prof. J. C........ 216
Booth and Morfit, Report on Chemical Arts, by........ 242, 216, 19
Bossange, Hector, Distribution of Publications by........ 38
Botany of California........ 212
Botany, Promotion of, by the Institution........ 232
Bowditch, Anecdote of........ 135
Brackenridge, W. D........ 16
Bridgman, Laura, Vocal Sounds of........ 191
Briggs, Governor........ 197
Building, Changes in........ 184
Building Committee, Summary of Report for 1852........ 235
Building Committee, Report of, for 1853........ 69
Bulwer, Sir Henry........ 218
Byington, Rev. Harvey, Choctaw Grammar by........ 241
By-Laws of the Smithsonian Institution........ 100
California Academy of Natural Sciences........ 76
Cameron, Gilbert, Balance due, paid........ 78

Page.

Cameron, Gilbert, Petition from........ 74
Canada, Visit of Secretary to........ 176
Carlisle, J. M., Counsel for the Board........ 69
Carroll, Charles, of Carrollton, Lecture on........ 27
Cass, Gen., Resolution of........ 211
Catalogue of Apparatus........ 180
Catalogue of Books in Washington........ 181
Catalogues of Libraries........ 248, 204
Catalogue of Library of Congress........ 248, 27
Catalogue of North American Reptiles........ 19
Catalogue System, Advantages of........ 241, 33
Centigrade Scale proposed to be adopted........ 165
Central America, Meteorological Observations from........ 176
Chamberlain, Mr., Pneumatic Instruments by........ 180
Chandler, Joseph R., Chairman of Committee on Smithsonian Institution in House of Representatives........ 78
Chappellsmith, Jno., Account of a Tornado........ 14
Chemical Arts, Recent Improvements in........ 242, 216, 19
Chemical Operations of Nature, Lectures on........ 207
Chemistry, Application of, to Agriculture........ 180
Chilian Government established Observatory at Santiago........ 203
Chili, Astronomical Expedition to........ 245, 203, 172, 163
Choctaw Language, Grammar of........ 241
Classification of Insects upon Embryological Data........ 172
Cleaveland, Prof. Parker, elected Honorary Member........ 101
Climate, Lectures on........ 27
Coast Survey, Observations made by........ 213
Coast Survey connected with Smithsonian Institution in Magnetic Observations........ 21
Coffin, Professor J. H., Winds of the Northern Hemisphere........ 213, 13
Coleoptera, Catalogue of........ 217, 18
Collections in Natural History........ 253, 249, 227, 202, 181, 177, 51, 26
Comet, Discovery of, by Miss Mitchell........ 171
Commencement of Operations of the Institution........ 140
Commissioner of Patents, Arrangement with........ 162
Commission on Catalogue System........ 204
Committee of Conference with Board of Regents........ 103
Committee on By-Laws........ 100
Communication of Chancellor and Secretary........ 7
Comparative Anatomy of the Frog........ 238
Comparative Anatomy, promotion of, by the Institution........ 232
Compatibility of two plans........ 139
Compromise, rigidly adhered to........ 224
Congress, act of, accepting bequest of Smithson........ 111
Congress, act of, establishing the Institution........ 112
Congress, appropriation by, to commence Catalogue of its Library........ 248, 27
Construction of the act of establishment, by Mr. Berrien........ 117
Contribution to the Physical Geography of the United States........ 171
Convention of Librarians........ 31
Copyright Law, change in, necessary........ 226
Copyright, none taken on Smithsonian Publications........ 195
Corcoran & Riggs, deposit with........ 72
Corcoran, W. W........ 235

	Page.
Correspondence, nature and extent of	22
Correspondence relative to acceptance of Squier & DaVis's work	141
Cost of publishing Scientific works	136
Cox, Dr. Samuel H., Lectures by	230
Cromwell and Queen Elizabeth, Lectures on	251
Croton Water, microscopic organisms in	18
Cuba, Institutions in	50
Cubic Equations, new method of solving	171
Culbertson, Alexander	200
Culbertson, Thaddeus	227, 220, 199, 12
Dakota Language, Grammar and Dictionary of	214
Darlington, Dr. William	16
Darlingtonia Californica	16
Darwin, Dr., Researches by	239
DaVis, Hon. Jefferson, Opinion respecting Museum of Exploring Expedition	252
DaVis, Lieutenant C. H., Lectures by	207
DaVis, Lieutenant C. H., Memoir on the Tides, by	215
Denmark, Institutions in	41
Derby, H. W., Agent	51
Description of Ancient Works in Ohio	236
Diffusing Knowledge, means of	138, 130
Directions for Collection and Preservation of specimens of Natural History	241, 217
Distribution of publications	242, 194, 37
Domestic Exchanges	51
Donation from Dr. Hare	180, 167
Donors to Museum	57
Downes, John, Occultations for 1849, by	160
Downes, John, Occultations for 1850, by	173
Downes, John, Occultations for 1851, by	201
Dynamical Phenomena of Geology, Lectures on	207
Dynamic effects of the Tides	215
Earth, Air, Fire, Water, Lectures on	251
Earthquake, Instrument for measuring	164
Ehrenberg, Professor	17
Eighth Annual Report presented	3
Electrical Rheometry	236, 172
Electricity, recent discoVeries in	19
Elgin Marbles, Moulds from, proposed	78
Ellet, Charles, Jr	171
Emory, Major W H	204, 177
Engelman, Dr. George, Agent	51
English Language, History of, Lecture on	230
EngraVings, Valuable Collection of, procured	205
Entomology, Lecture on	230
Ephemeris of Neptune	221, 201, 173, 160
Erosions of the Surface of the Earth	200
Espy, Professor	196, 175, 161, 147
Establishment, Members of	6
Establishment, meetings of	109
Estimates to be made by Executive Committee and Secretary	78
Ethnology	232, 228, 219, 203, 178, 172, 140, 54, 14
Ethnological Chart	178

Page.
Ethnological Society, Report of, on Squier and Davis's Memoir.................. 141
Europo-American Physical Man, Memoir on.................................. 76
Everett, Edw., Report on Programme.. 155
Examples of Objects for which appropriations may be made..................... 130
Exchange, Advantages of Smithsonian System of.............................. 25
Exchanges.. 232, 218, 37, 25
Executive Committee, Report of, 1853....................................... 66
Executive Committee to settle claims of L. Blodget............................ 99
Expenditures during 1853.. 67
Experiments in Stereotyping.. 200
Experiments on Building Material.. 220
Experiments on the Cause of Explosion of Steam-boilers........................ 137
Explanations and Illustrations of the Programme.............................. 133
Explorations.. 245, 220, 199, 181, 52
Exploration by Prof. Baird... 200
Exploring Expedition, Museum of.. 182
Explosiveness of Nitre... 171
Exposition of System of Cataloguing...................................... 241, 32
Extinct species of Fossil Ox.. 239
Extra copies of Report ordered.. 3
Extract from an Address by the Secretary.................................... 120
Felton, Prof. C. C., lectures by.. 251
Felton, Prof. C. C., Memoir examined by..................................... 215
Felton, Prof. C. C., Recommendation of Choctaw Grammar....................... 241
Fendler, Mr., Plants collected by... 212, 128
Fifth Report of the Secretary.. 208
Fire, Water, Air, Earth, Lectures on... 251
First Report of the Secretary, December, 1847................................ 127
Fishes received, 1853... 53
Fitall, Jno., Widow of.. 205
Fitch, Hon. G. N., Resolution on Income...................................... 72
Fitch, Hon. G. N., Resolution on Surplus Fund................................ 72
Flora and Fauna within living animals.. 215
Flügel, Dr. J. G., Distribution of Publications by............................ 38
Foreign Distribution and Exchange... 37
Foreign Institutions in Correspondence....................................... 40
Foreman, Prof. E., Outline Map by... 199
Foreman, Prof. E., Meteorological Correspondence, by.......................... 223
Forest Trees, Report on... 217, 179
Forsyth, Hon. Jno., Letter to, from Richard Rush.............................. 108
Fossils received 1853... 54
Foundation of Symmetry in the Animal Kingdom, Lectures on..................... 251
Four Ancient Elements, Lectures on... 251
Fowler, W. C., Lectures by.. 230
Fourth Report of the Secretary.. 185
France, Institutions in... 45
France, Lectures on... 27
Frémont, Col., Plants discovered by.. 212
French Academy of Science... 165
Fruits of the Active Operations.. 231
Funds, General Statement of.. 235, 66
Gallatin, A., letter from... 142

Page.
Gallatin, A., letter to, from Prof. Henry........ 141
Gallery of Art........ 249, 205
General considerations in adopting plan of organization........ 128
General Expenses, Remarks on........ 251
Geography, promotion of, by the Institution........ 231
Geology, Lectures on........ 251, 230, 183
Geology, promotion of, by the Institution........ 232
Germany, Institutions in........ 42
Gibbs's, Prof., recommendation of Choctaw Grammar........ 241
Gibbes, R. W., Memoir by........ 172
Gilbert, Davies, Notice of Smithson, by........ 109
Gilliss, Lieut. J. M........ 245, 203, 163
Girard, Chas., Catalogue of Serpents by........ 19
Girard, Chas., Exploration by........ 220
Girard, Chas., Memoir by........ 192
Gould, B. A., Lectures by........ 251
Gould, B. A., History of discovery of Planet Neptune........ 179
Graham, Col., Apparatus delivered to........ 204
Grammar of the Choctaw language........ 241
Grand Manan, Marine Invertebrata of........ 17
Gray, Dr. Asa, Plantæ Wrightianæ........ 238, 212
Gray, Dr. Asa, Plants referred to........ 227
Gray, Dr. Asa, Report on Forest Trees, by........ 242, 217, 194, 179
Gray, Dr. Asa, Report on Programme, by........ 155
Great Britain and Ireland, Institutions in........ 47
Greece, Institutions in........ 49
Gregg, Dr., Collections by........ 212
Greek Literature, Lectures on........ 251
Green, James, Meteorological Instruments made by........ 197, 175
Guatemala, Institutions in........ 50
Guest, W. E., on Mounds........ 219
Guyot, Prof. A., Barometrical Exploration by........ 177
Guyot, Prof. A., Lectures by........ 27
Guyot, Prof. A., Meteorological Tables........ 242, 217
Guyot, Prof. A., Proposition made by........ 165
Guyot, Prof. A., Report on Meteorological Instruments........ 180
Haldeman, Prof. S. S., Coleoptera........ 18
Haldeman, Prof. S. S., Lectures by........ 230
Hall, Prof. James, Troost's Memoir........ 213
Hall, Rev. Jno., Lecture by........ 207
Hare, Dr. Robt., Apparatus of, repaired........ 204
Hare, Dr. Robt., Donation from........ 180, 167
Hare, Dr. Robt., Experiments of........ 201
Hare, Dr. Robt., Memoir by........ 171
Hare, Dr. Robt., Remarks respecting Apparatus of........ 102
Harlan, Dr., Species described by........ 241
Harmonies of Nature and History, Lectures on........ 27
Harvey, Prof. W. H., Lecture by........ 207
Harvey, Prof. W. H., Marine Algæ........ 237, 192
Hawley, Gideon........ 175
Hays, Dr., Opinion of Memoir on Extinct Sloth........ 241
Henry, Patrick, Lecture on........ 27

Page.
Henry, Prof. Jos., Letter from, to Hon. Albert Gallatin........................ 141
Henry, Prof. Jos. See Secretary..
Herbarium, North American.. 212
Hints on Public Architecture.. 166
Historical Society of Minnesota.. 214, 178
Historical Society of New York... 172
History as a Science, Lecture on....................................... 230
History and Peculiarities of the English Language, Lectures on................. 207
Hitchcock, President Edward, Investigations by.......................... 200
Hitchcock, President Edward, Lectures by............................... 183
Holbrook, Dr., on Reptiles... 19
Holland, Institutions in... 41
Holland, Lecture on... 207
Honorary Members, List of.. 6
Honorary Member, Nominations for...................................... 102, 101
Hopkins, President Mark, Lectures by................................... 251
Howe, Dr. S. G.. 191
Hulse, Dr. G. W... 16
Hygrometer described.. 198
Iceland, Institutions in... 41
Increase and Diffusion logically distinct.............................. 134
Increase and Diffusion of Knowledge, plans for......................... 129
Increase of general expenses... 251
Induction, Lecture on.. 230
Institutions for the Diffusion of Knowledge............................ 134
Institution for the Increase of Knowledge.............................. 134
Instruments for Meteorological Observers.......................... 197, 175, 174
Interruptions to Business.. 236
Invertebrata received, 1853.. 53
Italy, Institutions in... 46
Jackson, Dr., Survey of Mineral Lands.................................. 146
Jefferson, President, first account of Extinct Sloth, by............... 239
Jewett, C. C., Report for 1853... 29
Jewett, J. P. & Co., Agents.. 51
Jewett, Proctor, & Worthington, Agents................................. 51
Johnson, Professor J. F. W., Lecture by................................ 207
Kane, Dr. E. K., Lectures by... 251, 27
Koeppen, Professor, Lectures by.. 183
Lalande.. 169
Lambdin, J. R., Letter from, on Moulds from Elgin Marbles............... 78
Land Office, series of Magnetic Observations in........................ 22
Lapham, I. A., Antiquities of Wisconsin................................ 14
Lapham, I. A., Survey of Mounds, by.................................... 220
Law of Deposit of the Flood-Tide....................................... 215
Lawrence, Hon. Abbot... 205
Lawson, Surgeon General Thomas... 176
Le Conte, Dr. J. L., Coleoptera.. 18
Lecture Room... 206
Lectures.................................... 250, 228, 206, 183, 27
Leeuwenhoek.. 17
Lefroy, Captain J. H., Aurora.. 176, 24
Leidy, Dr. Joseph, Ancient Fauna of Nebraska........................... 11

Page.
Leidy, Dr. Joseph, Extinct Species of Ox.. 239
Leidy, Dr. Joseph, Flora and Fauna.. 215
Leidy, Dr. Joseph, organic remains, sent to.. 227
Leidy, Dr. Joseph, Report on Specimens from Nebraska........................ 220
Leopoldin Caroline Academy 101
Letter from three Regents calling special meeting.............................. 80
Letter to the President of the Senate.. 3
Leverrier, Planet Neptune.. 170
Libraries, Report on.. 216
Lieber, Professor.. 191
Library.................................... 253, 249, 248, 223, 204, 181, 166, 29, 26
Lindheimer.. 212
Lippincott, Grambo, & Co., Agents.. 51
Literary and Scientific Assemblies, rooms thrown open for..................... 140
Locke, Dr., Employed in Survey of Mineral Lands 146
Locke, John.. 213
London and Edinburgh Journal.. 193
Longfellow, H. W., Report on Programme.................................... 155
Loomis, Prof., Estimate of Expenses for Meteorological System.................. 160
Loomis, Prof., Exposition of Advantages from Study of Meteorology............ 147
Lowell Institute.. 250, 192, 183
Ludlow, Dr. Jno., Lectures by.. 230
Macie, James Lewis, Original name of Smithson.............................. 108
Magnetic Force, Dip, Inclination, and Intensity of.............................. 213
Magnetic Instruments, Description of.. 20
Magnetic Instruments purchased.. 204
Magnetic Observatory.. 21,20
Magnetism 232, 204, 176, 162, 19
Mammals received 1853 52
Marine Algæ.. 237, 192
Marine Algæ, Lectures on.. 207
Marine Invertebrata of Grand Manan.. 17
Marsh, Geo. P., Report on Squier & Davis.. 144
Mason, Hon. J. M., Resolution on Powers of Secretary........................ 98
Massachusetts Meteorological System.. 222, 197
Mauvaises Terres.. 200, 11
McIntyre, Archibald.. 196
Meacham, Hon. J., Appointed on Special Committee........................... 77
Meacham, Hon. J., Resolution on Estimates.................................... 75
Mechanism of Speech, Lecture on.. 230
Meeting of the Establishment.. 27
Melsheimer, F. G., Coleoptera.. 217, 18
Memorial on Uniform Coinage.. 78
Memorial to Congress on Surplus Fund.. 78
Meteorological Correspondence.. 199
Meteorological Instruments.. 223, 222, 197
Meteorological Observers, Jan. 1, 1854.. 60
Meteorological Observers, commencing since 1st Jan., 1854...................... 64
Meteorological System of New York (established 1825) 196, 175
Meteorological Tables.. 217
Meteorology, Promotion of, by the Institution.................................. 231
Meteorology, System of.. 245, 222, 195, 174, 23

	Page.
Method applied to Investigation, Lectures on	251
Metropolitan Mechanics' Institute, Models lent to	76
Metropolitan Mechanics' Institute Lectures	27
Mexico, Institutions in	50
Microscopic Examination of Soundings	192
Microscopic Organisms, New Forms of	17
Minerals received 1853	54
Minnesota, Historical Society of	214
Mitchell, Miss Maria	171
Modern Athens, Lecture on	183
Modern Egypt and its Institutions, Lectures on	27
Modern Europe, Lectures on	27
Monograph of the Fresh Water Cottoids	192
Monograph of Mosasaurus	191, 172
Morfit, Campbell	216
Morphology of the Vegetable Kingdom, Lectures on	207
Morris, Dr. Jno. G., Lectures by	230
Morton, Samuel G., Report on Squier & Davis	144
Mosasaurus, Monograph of	191, 172
Mounds of Western Virginia	203
Mower, Dr., Valuable Aid from	197
Müller, M., Work on Electricity	19
Museum	253, 249, 226, 202, 181, 56, 54, 51, 26
Museum of Exploring Expedition	182
National Museum, Importance of	227
Natural History, Promotion of, by the Institution	232
Natural History, Work done in	55
Nautical Almanac	244, 221, 201, 173
Neptune, Ephemeris of	221, 201, 173, 169
Neptune, History of Discovery of Planet	179
Neptune, Memoir on the Planet	169
New Expedition in Search of Sir John Franklin, Lecture on	27
New York Meteorological System	222, 196
New York Meteorological Observers	63
Nitre, Explosion of	171
Norman, B. M., Agent	51
Norway, Institutions in	41
Notices of Public Libraries in the United States	216, 194, 31
Objections to publishing memoirs answered	159
Observations in Series or Summaries	64
Observers, Classes of	174
Observers, List of Meteorological	60
Occultations, Description of	244
Occultations for 1850	173
Occultations for 1851	201
Occultations for 1852	222
Octavo publications for 1853	37
Officers of the Institution	5
Original Researches	245, 220, 199, 172, 159, 26
Original Research, Encouragement to	137
Origin and Growth of the Union during the Colonial Period, Lectures on	207
Papers presented to Royal Society by Smithson	110

Page.
Papers referred to in Report of Select Committee, to be communicated to the Board 97
Parish, Henry, Bill for Canina's Architecture 75
Peale, Titian R., Mounds at St. Louis 219
Pearce, Hon. J. A., Report of 81
Peirce, Benj., Report on Programme 155
Peirce, Prof. B., Planet Neptune 244, 222, 202, 170
Phases of the Atmosphere, Lectures on 251
Photographic Register of Motions of the Magnetic Needle 76, 20
Physical Geography of United States 177, 171
Physical Society of Berlin 165
Physiology, Promotion of, by the Institution 232
Pidgeon, Wm., Exploration of Mounds by 219
Pike, B., and Sons, Instrument Makers 198, 175
Pise, Rev. C. C., Lectures by 27
Plan of Organization 129
Planet Neptune 244, 221, 201, 169, 160
Plantæ Fremontianæ 212
Plantæ Wrightianæ 239, 236
Plants received 1853 53
Poetry, Lecture on 230
Policy in Accepting Donations 209
Portraits of North American Indians in Smithsonian Institution 242
Portugal, Institutions in 47
Potter, Rev. Alonzo, Lecture by 207
Primordial Arrangement of Existing Systems, Lecture on 207
Proceedings of the Board of Regents 72
Programme of Organization 128
Programme of Organization, Report of Committee of American Academy on 148
Prominent idea of Smithsonian Operations 253
Publications, Advantages of 135
Publications 236, 210, 190, 168, 156, 36, 11
Purchases of Objects of Natural History not to be made 202
Putnam, Geo. P., and Co., Agents 51
Queen Elizabeth and Oliver Cromwell, Lectures on 251
Radiant Heat, Investigations on 163
Rain and Snow Gauges 198
Receipts during 1853 67
Receipts by Exchange, 1853 50
Received for American Institutions, &c 50
Received from American Institutions for distribution abroad 40
Reciprocal Action of two Galvanic Currents 191
Recent Improvements in the Chemical Arts 242, 216, 19
Recent Progress of Astronomy, Lectures on 251
Reed, Prof. Henry, Lecture by 207
Regents of the Institution, List of 5
Regents of the Institution, Proceedings of 72
Regents of University of New York 175
Registers of Periodical Phenomena 56
Relations of Time and Space, Lectures on 207
Removal of Assistants by Secretary authorized by Board 98
Removal of Assistants, J. M. Berrien's Opinion on 119

Page.
Report of American Ethnological Society........ 142
Report of Building Committee........ 69
Report of Executive Committee........ 66
Report of Committee of American Academy of Arts and Sciences on the Programme of Organization........ 148
Reports of the Secretary from 1847 to 1853........ 125
Report of the Secretary for 1848........ 156
Report of the Secretary for 1849........ 168
Report of the Secretary for 1850........ 185
Report of the Secretary for 1851........ 208
Report of the Secretary for 1852........ 231
Report of the Secretary for 1853........ 9
Report of Select Committee ordered to be printed........ 97
Report of Select Committee on Estimates........ 78
Report of Select Committee on Resolutions of Messrs. Fitch and Meacham........ 81
Report on Forest Trees........ 242, 217, 194, 179
Report on Libraries........ 216, 194, 31
Reports on Progress of Knowledge........ 241, 216, 193, 179, 164, 138, 19
Reptiles receiVed 1853........ 53
Researches........ 245, 220, 199, 172, 159, 26
Resolution of February, 1847, carried out........ 252
Resolutions submitted by Select Committee........ 97
Richmond Athenæum, Arrangement by, respecting Lecturers........ 250
Riggs, Rev S. R., Dakota Grammar by........ 214
Robinson, Edward, Report on Squier and Davis........ 144
Rogers, Prof. H. D., Lecture by........ 207
Rogers, Prof. W. B., Lectuies by........ 251
Royal Society, Co-operation with........ 243
Royal Society, Publications Distributed by........ 39
Royal Society, Papers presented to, by Smithson........ 109
Royal Society, Remarks of President of........ 109
Rules for Acceptance of Memoirs........ 156
Rules for Distribution of Smithsonian Publications........ 194
Rumford, Count, Founder of Royal Institution........ 234
Rush, Hon. R., Letter to Hon. Jno. Forsyth, from........ 108
Russell, Jno., Agent........ 51
Russia, Institutions in........ 41
Sabine Colonel, Terrestrial Magnetism........ 213
Sabine Colonel, Correspondence with, on Meteorology........ 146
Santiago, Observatory at........ 203
School, Lecture on The,........ 27
Science Applied to Agriculture, Lectures on........ 207
Secchi, Prof. A., Memoir by........ 191, 172
Second Report of the Secretary........ 156
Secretary, Reports of........ 231, 208, 185, 168, 156, 127, 125, 9
Seismometer, ordered for Lieut. Gilliss........ 164
Serpents, Catalogue of, in Smithsonian Museum........ 19
Silliman, Prof. B., Jr., Lectures by........ 251
Silliman, Prof. B., Sr., Lecture by........ 251, 230
Sixth Report of the Secretary........ 231
Sloth Tribe of North America........ 240
Smith, Prof. J. Lawrence, Lectures by........ 27

Page.
Smithson, Account of, by Richard Rush........ 108
Smithson, Medallion of........ 206
Smithson, Notice of, by DaVies Gilbert........ 109
Smithson, Portrait of........ 205
Smithson, Will of........ 107
Smithsonian Contributions........ 56
Smithsonian Contributions, Distribution of Vol. V........ 40
Smithsonian Institution, Act Establishing........ 112
Smithsonian Institution, Address on........ 120
Smithsonian System of Exchanges........ 218
Snell, Prof., Illustration of WaVe Motion........ 180
South America, Institutions in........ 50
Spain, Institutions in........ 47
Sparks, Jared, Report on Programme........ 155
Special Committee on Distribution of Income, &c., appointed........ 72
Special Committee, Report of........ 81
Special meeting of the Board........ 79
Spirit of the Age, Lecture on........ 207
Spooner, Dr. S., Proposition respecting publication of Musée Français, &c........ 75
Sprague, Isaac, Botanical Draughtsman........ 213
Squier, E. G., Memoir by........ 172, 141
Squier, E. G., Idols from........ 203
Standard Meteorological Instruments........ 222, 197
Stanley's Indian Gallery, account of........ 249, 242
Statement of Finances, end of year 1853........ 66
Stansbury, Captain, Report on Animals collected by........ 220
Statistics of Diseases........ 174
SteVens, Henry........ 179, 163, 39
Stimpson, William, Marine InVertebrata of Grand Manan........ 17
Strong, Professor, New Method of solving Cubic Equations, by........ 171
Subjects which may be embraced in the Reports........ 131
Sumner, George, Lecture by........ 27
Sweden, Institutions in........ 40
Swedish Academy, Reports of........ 165
Switzerland, Institutions in........ 44
Tables of Precipitation........ 247
Tables to facilitate Meteorological Calculations........ 242
Teachers' Association Lectures........ 27
Telegraph lines used for Meteorological Intelligence........ 176
Temperature Tables........ 247
Tendencies of Modern Science, Lecture on........ 207
Terrestrial Magnetism........ 232, 213, 204
Thermometers, by Bunten, Troughton & Simms........ 197
Third Report of the Secretary........ 168
Thomas, Isaiah, Antiquarian Society founded by........ 219
Tides of the Ocean, and their Geological Relations, Lectures on........ 207
Topographical Regions of State of New York........ 196
Tornado, Account of New Harmony........ 14
Toronto, ObserVatory at........ 176
Torrey, Dr. John, Batis Maritima........ 16
Torrey, Dr. John, Darlingtonia Californica........ 16
Torrey, Dr. John, Plantæ Fremontianæ........ 212

Page.
Torrey, Dr. John, Plants referred to........ 227
Totten, General, Resolution on alteration of East Wing........ 73
Tracts on Practical Subjects........ 211
Treasurer, Report of........ 73
Treatises on Particular Subjects........ 165, 139, 131
Troost, Dr., Memoir by........ 213
True policy of the Institution........ 234
Turkey, Institutions in........ 49
Turner, Professor W. W., Choctaw Grammar examined by........ 241
Turner, Professor W. W., Dakota Grammar examined by........ 215
Turner, Professor W. W. Report on Squier & Davis........ 144
Tyson, Job R., Lectures by........ 251, 27
Unity of the Plan of the Animal Creation, Lectures on........ 207
Unverified Speculations excluded from the Contributions........ 136
Value of Works received by Exchange........ 249
Van Dieman's Land, Institutions in........ 49
Variation of the Needle........ 20
Vastness of the Visible Creation, Lectures on........ 207
Vattemare, M., System of Exchange........ 218
Vindication of Researches and Memoirs........ 237
Vinton, Dr. A. H., Lectures by........ 230
Walker, Hon. Robert J., Observations directed by........ 213
Walker, Sears C........ 244, 221, 169
Warren, Josiah, New Method of Stereotyping........ 225
Water, Earth, Air, Fire, Lectures on........ 251
West India Islands, Meteorological Observations from........ 176
Whittlesey, Charles........ 236, 219
Wilkes, Com., Plants collected by Exploring Expedition under........ 16
Will of Smithson........ 107
Winds of the Northern Hemisphere........ 213
Wilson, Prof., of England, Models, &c., from........ 76
Wilson, American Ornithologist, Letter to Michaux........ 135
Wind Vanes........ 198
Wisconsin, Antiquities of........ 220, 14
Wistar, Dr., Gigantic Sloth........ 239
Wislizenus, Dr., Plants gathered by........ 212
Wotherspoon, Dr., Reduction of Meteorological Observations, by........ 197
Wright, Charles, Explorations........ 212, 177
Wyman, Dr. Jeffries, Anatomy of the Frog, by........ 238
Wynn Estate, Communications respecting........ 75
Wynn, Mr., account of Bequest of........ 234
Young, Dr., Index to Natural Philosophy, by........ 225
Young Men's Christian Association, Lectures........ 27
Zoology, Promotion of, by the Institution........ 232
Zoophytes, Troost's Memoir on........ 213

NINTH ANNUAL REPORT

OF THE

BOARD OF REGENTS

OF THE

SMITHSONIAN INSTITUTION,

SHOWING THE

OPERATIONS, EXPENDITURES, AND CONDITION OF THE INSTITUTION
UP TO JANUARY 1, 1855.

AND THE

PROCEEDINGS OF THE BOARD UP TO FEBRUARY 24, 1855.

WASHINGTON:
BEVERLEY TUCKER, SENATE PRINTER
1855.

33d Congress, } SENATE. { Mis. Doc.
2d Session. } { No. 24.

LETTER

OF THE

SECRETARY OF THE SMITHSONIAN INSTITUTION,

COMMUNICATING

The Ninth Annual Report of the Board of Regents of that Institution.

March 1, 1855.—Read and ordered to be printed—motion to print 10,000 additional copies referred to Committee on Printing.
March 2, 1855.—Ordered that 10,000 additional copies be printed, 2,500 of which be for the use of the Smithsonian Institution.

Smithsonian Institution,
Washington, February 28, 1855.

Sir: In behalf of the Board of Regents, I have the honor to submit to the Senate of the United States, the Ninth Annual Report of the operations, expenditures, and condition of the Smithsonian Institution.

I have the honor to be, very respectfully, your obedient servant,

JOSEPH HENRY,
Secretary Smithsonian Institution.

Hon. Jesse D. Bright,
President of the Senate.

NINTH ANNUAL REPORT

OF THE

BOARD OF REGENTS

OF THE

SMITHSONIAN INSTITUTION,

SHOWING THE

OPERATIONS, EXPENDITURES, AND CONDITION OF THE INSTITUTION UP TO JANUARY 1, 1855, AND THE PROCEEDINGS OF THE BOARD UP TO FEBRUARY 24, 1855.

To the Senate and House of Representatives:

In obedience to the act of Congress of August 10, 1846, establishing the Smithsonian Institution, the undersigned, in behalf of the Regents, submit to Congress, as a Report of the operations, expenditures, and condition of the Institution, the following documents:

1. The Annual Report of the Secretary, giving an account of the operations of the Institution during the year 1854.

2. Report of the Executive Committee, giving a general statement of the proceeds and disposition of the Smithsonian fund, and also an account of the expenditures for the year 1854.

3. Report of the Building Committee, relative to the progress made in 1854 in the erection of the Smithsonian edifice.

4. Proceedings of the Board of Regents up to February 24, 1855.

5. Appendix.

Respectfully submitted.

ROGER B. TANEY, *Chancellor.*
JOSEPH HENRY, *Secretary.*

FEBRUARY 28, 1855.

OFFICERS OF THE SMITHSONIAN INSTITUTION.

FRANKLIN PIERCE, *Ex officio* Presiding Officer of the Institution.
ROGER B. TANEY, Chancellor of the Institution.
JOSEPH HENRY, Secretary of the Institution.
SPENCER F. BAIRD, Assistant Secretary.
W. W. SEATON, Treasurer.
WILLIAM J. RHEES, General Assistant.

ALEXANDER D. BACHE, JAMES A. PEARCE, JOSEPH G. TOTTEN,	Executive Committee.
RICHARD RUSH, WILLIAM H. ENGLISH. JOHN T. TOWERS, JOSEPH HENRY,	Building Committee.

REGENTS OF THE INSTITUTION.

—— ——, Vice President of the United States.
ROGER B. TANEY, Chief Justice of the United States.
JOHN T. TOWERS, Mayor of the city of Washington.
JAMES A. PEARCE, member of the Senate of the United States.
JAMES M. MASON, member of the Senate of the United States.
S. A. DOUGLAS, member of the Senate of the United States.
W. H. ENGLISH, member of the House of Representatives.
DAVID STUART, member of the House of Representatives.
JAMES MEACHAM, member of the House of Representatives.
GIDEON HAWLEY, citizen of New York.
J. MACPHERSON BERRIEN, citizen of Georgia.
RICHARD RUSH, citizen of Pennsylvania.
ALEXANDER D. BACHE, member of the National Institute, Washington.
JOSEPH G. TOTTEN, member of the National Institute, Washington.

MEMBERS EX OFFICIO OF THE INSTITUTION.

FRANKLIN PIERCE, President of the United States.
——— ———, Vice President of the United States.
WILLIAM L. MARCY, Secretary of State.
JAMES GUTHRIE, Secretary of the Treasury.
JEFFERSON DAVIS, Secretary of War.
JAMES C. DOBBIN, Secretary of the Navy.
JAMES CAMPBELL, Postmaster General.
CALEB CUSHING, Attorney General.
ROGER B. TANEY, Chief Justice of the United States.
CHARLES MASON, Commissioner of Patents.
JOHN T. TOWERS, Mayor of the city of Washington

HONORARY MEMBERS.

ROBERT HARE.
WASHINGTON IRVING.
BENJAMIN SILLIMAN.
PARKER CLEAVELAND.

REPORT OF THE SECRETARY.

To the Board of Regents of the Smithsonian Institution:

GENTLEMEN: It again becomes my duty to present to your honorable Board the Annual Report of the present condition of the Smithsonian Institution, and of its operations during the year 1854.

In this report I shall follow the course adopted in the previous ones, namely, to state such facts as may appear to be necessary to a connected history of the Institution, and to offer such suggestions as may seem important in reference to its future management.

At no period since the commencement of the Institution has it attracted more attention, or given rise to more discussion, than during the past year; but, thanks to the liberality of Congress, who ordered the printing of twenty thousand extra copies of the last report, to which were appended all the preceding reports of the secretary, together with sundry other documents, ample means have been afforded the reading public to become acquainted with the will of Smithson, his pursuits in life, with the law of Congress establishing the Institution, and with all the acts of the Regents in the discharge of their duty.

That the disposition of a bequest of so novel a character, the intention of which was so briefly though comprehensively expressed, should give rise to a diversity of opinion, or that the act of Congress in reference to it, which received repeated amendments, and was passed, after a discussion of several years, by a small majority, should be differently construed, is not surprising.

In the language of Mr. Adams: "A British subject, of noble birth and ample fortune, desiring to bequeath his estate to the purpose of increasing and diffusing knowledge throughout the whole community of civilized man, selected for the repository of his trust, with confidence unqualified, the United States of America. In the commission of every trust there is an implied tribute to the integrity and intelligence of the trustee; there is, also, an implied call for the faithful exercise of those properties to the fulfilment of the purposes of the trust. The tribute and the call acquire additional force and energy when the trust is committed for performance after the decease of him by whom it is confided, and when he no longer exists to witness or constrain the effective fulfilment of his design. The magnitude of the trust, and the extent of confidence bestowed in the committal of it, do but enlarge and aggravate the obligation which it carries with it. The weight of duty imposed is in proportion to the honor conferred by confidence without reserve."

"The principal purpose of Mr. Smithson was, evidently, the discovery of new truths, the invention of new means for the enlargement of human power, and not the mere communication of knowledge already possessed. In this point of view the bequest assumes an interest of the highest order, peculiar to itself, most happily adapted to the character of our republican institutions, and destined, if administered in the spirit in which it was bestowed, to command the grateful acclamations of future ages." No restriction is made as to any kind of knowledge; but it is knowledge, the source of all human wisdom and beneficent power, which is to be increased and diffused; "knowledge, which as far transcends the postulated lever of Archemides, as the universe transcends this speck of earth upon its face; knowledge, the attribute of Omnipotence, of which man alone, in the physical and material world, is permitted to participate." Let not, then, any branch or department of human knowledge be excluded from its equitable share of this benefaction. Again, no nation, community, or class of men, is designated as the special recipient of this bounty; and it would be inconsistent with the self-respect of a great confederated nation to receive, from the hands of a foreigner, a liberal fund for the increase and diffusion of knowledge throughout the world of man, and to apply it exclusively to its own purposes.

The Regents, at their first session, conscious of the importance and magnitude of the trust confided to them, and of the responsibilities which devolved upon them, gave to the whole subject attentive and laborious consideration. They were impressed with the fact that the object of the law was to carry out the will of Smithson, and if there were any doubtful points, it was their duty to construe them with a view to this object. In conformity with this a plan was adopted, which, while it fulfilled all the requirements of the law, was in strict accordance with a logical interpretation of the will of the donor. This plan, after seven years' experience, has been found to realize all the hopes and anticipations which were entertained in regard to it by its most sanguine advocates; and, though it was adopted provisionally, to be changed or modified as circumstances might indicate, yet no essential alteration has been considered necessary by those best acquainted with its operations. It is true that it is not, perhaps, in all respects, the simplest plan which could have been designed for carrying out the will of the testator; and had the Regents been entirely unrestricted, they would probably have devoted a less portion of the income to local objects; but, under all the conditions of the problem, it is believed that it was the best which could have been adopted to produce the desired result. And it may not be too much to say, that the present condition of the Institution, as to general reputation and financial prosperity, is much more favorable than experience in the management of public trusts would reasonably have led us to anticipate.

All the requirements of the act of Congress, in the opinion of the Regents, have been faithfully and fully observed. Liberal provision has been made for the accommodation of a library, a museum, and a gallery of art, with lecture rooms and a laboratory, in the construction of a building which has cost $300,000. A *library* has been commenced and means devised for its continual extension, which will soon form the best special collection of valuable works pertaining to all branches of positive knowledge to be found in this country. The books which it now contains, if estimated by the prices paid for those which have been purchased, may be valued at not less than $40,000. A *museum*, the most complete of any in existence in several branches of the natural history of the North American continent, has been collected, which has been valued at $30,000. A valuable and extensive cabinet of *apparatus*, consisting of instruments of illustration and research, has been formed. A beginning has also been made of a *gallery of art*, consisting of a choice collection of specimens of engravings by the old masters.

Not only have the objects specified by Congress received due attention, but also by a series of *active operations* the influence of the Institution has been extended to almost every part of our own and foreign countries. The publications, the exchanges, and the researches which have been instituted and prosecuted by the Institution, have indissolubly connected the name of SMITHSON with the progress of knowledge in our day.

In accomplishing these objects the funds have not been exhausted, nor have debts been incurred. On the contrary, by strict adherence to a well devised system of finance, not only does the fund originally bequeathed by SMITHSON remain undiminished in the Treasury of the United States, but there is now on hand nearly $140,000 of unexpended income to be added to the principal.

In other words, the funds and property are now estimated at double the amount of the original bequest.

The plan of increasing and diffusing knowledge by means of researches and publications is in strict accordance with the will of Smithson. It embraces as a leading feature the design of interesting the greatest number of individuals in the operations of the Institution, and of extending its influence as widely as possible. It supplies a want which has long been felt in this country, and offers a greater inducement to profound study by rendering the products of original research more available than any other plan heretofore proposed. Every one who makes a discovery in any department of knowledge must of necessity be somewhat in advance of the reading public, at least in the special branch to which his discovery pertains; and therefore the number of readers, and consequently of purchasers of a work giving an account of these discoveries will be comparatively small. "I have frequently congratulated myself," says one of our collaborators, "upon living at a time when an Institution exists in our country which would publish discoveries and original investigations or positive additions to knowledge, without expense to the author. What would not poor Morton have done had he been able in this way to publish his researches, whereas his single work on *Crania Americana* was given to the world at the loss of several thousand dollars."

The Institution does much more than ordinary societies in the way of stimulating research. It not only gives to the world with the stamp of its approval the various papers which constitute its contributions to knowledge, but in a large number of cases it furnishes materials and pecuniary means for carrying on the investigations. The aid which it affords in this way, though small in amount, is sufficient to determine whether an investigation shall be prosecuted to a successful termination or abandoned almost at its very commencement.

It was at first proposed to offer premiums for original memoirs on different branches of knowledge; but it has been found by experience that the inducements held out by the offer of publication free of expense under the sanction of the Institution, and the assistance which is occasionally afforded, will produce more material of the first quality than will exhaust the small portion of the income which can be devoted to researches and publication.

In first proposing the system of literary exchanges which is now extended over every part of the civilized world, a promise was made to all the foreign societies which should send their transactions to the Smithsonian library that, on the part of the Institution, at least one quarto volume of original contributions to knowledge would annually be given in return. The experience of seven years has rendered it evident that this promise can be fully redeemed. Indeed, were the funds sufficient, two large volumes might be published in the same time.

The seventh volume is nearly completed, and will be ready for distribution in the course of a few weeks. It will contain a number of memoirs, the largest of which are on the subject of American antiquities. An account of one of these, viz., that on the *Effigy Mounds* of Wisconsin, was given in the last report.

A number of memoirs have been examined and accepted for publication since the date of the last report.

1. A paper has been prepared at the special request of the Institution, by S. F. Haven, esq., librarian of the American Antiquarian Society, Worcester, Massachusetts, which will form a part of the seventh volume.

Its intention is to give a retrospective view of the progress of knowledge and opinions relative to the whole subject of American antiquities. For this purpose the author has, in the first place, presented a summary of the opinions of early writers upon the question of the origin and sources of the native population of this country, and in this connexion has noticed some of the more prominent writers of later date who have sustained one or other of the ancient hypotheses.

In the second place he has considered the accounts of the early Spanish and French adventurers, and the reports of the Jesuit missionaries, who first became acquainted with the inhabitants in their native condition, so far as those accounts have a bearing on the origin and uses of the earth-works of this country.

In the third place he has sought to ascertain the names of the early explorers who examined and described any of these ancient remains, and to give the extent of their investigations.

He has next followed the succession of observations and speculations of different periods down to the present time; and, lastly, he has given a concise *resumé* of the facts which have thus far been established.

These are, 1st. The nature and extent of the aboriginal monuments in the United States east of the Rocky mountains;

2d. Their location relatively to one another and to different portions of the country;

3d. Their affinities to the works of existing or recently extinct tribes.

The memoir is intended to have a bibliographical character, so far as this could be effected without interrupting the continuity of the narrative. It will be found important, not only in pointing out what has been done and thought on this interesting subject, but also in indicating definite points of further research.

The preparation of this article has cost the author no small amount of labor. The information was principally to be found in publications which, in their day, had but a limited circulation; and now, even, when known to exist, are not easily found. It may be interesting to mention that there have been several periods during which attention has been particularly directed to the aboriginal remains of this country, and between them intervals of time in which they excited comparatively no interest. Before the war of the revolution, investigations had been commenced, which were of course suspended or terminated by that event. After peace was restored and military stations were established in the interior, and settlements began to be extended beyond the Ohio, accounts of remarkable works were published in the miscellaneous periodicals of the day. The officers of the army were the principal explorers; but two of the most active of these, General Parson and General Heart, were removed by death; and as the mounds became more familiar to the settlers, the interest in them comparatively declined. After the war of 1812, they again became the object of inquiry, which resulted in the publication of Mr. Atwater's researches under the auspices of the American Antiquarian Society. Since then, though occasional articles appeared, no important additions were made to our knowledge in regard to them until the publication of the first volume of the Smithsonian Contributions. The reputation acquired by this work has induced a number of other laborers to enter the field, which, we trust, will soon be fully explored. Indeed, it is believed that samples of nearly every variety of earth-work to be found within the limits of the territory of the United States, east of the Rocky mountains, have been figured in the publications of the Institution. It is intended, however, to continue to collect all the information which may be obtained, and in due time to publish a map of the relative position of all the works which are found to exist, at least within the limits of the United States.

The Institution from the first has given particular attention to antiquities, philology, and other branches of the new and interesting department of knowledge called ethnology, which relates to the natural history of man in his physical, moral, intellectual, and æsthetical characteristics. It is a common ground, in the cultivation of which lovers of literature and science are equally interested. The works we have thus far published on these subjects have elicited the highest commendations, and the Smithsonian Contributions are now generally referred to as containing important materials for their elucidation.

2. Some years ago an artist of considerable merit and great accuracy, Mr. Sawkins, visited the celebrated remains of ancient architecture at Mitla, in the State of Oajaca, Mexico. Mr. Sawkins made careful drawings of the ruins by means of a *camera lucida*, and recorded his observations upon the spot. Within a few months these drawings and memoranda have come into the possession of Mr. Brantz Mayer, of Baltimore, whose writings upon Mexico and its antiquities have been very largely circulated in this country during the last six or seven years. Mr. Mayer considered Mr. Sawkins's sketches and observations

as of so much value to the aboriginal history of our continent, and especially in completing the links of civilization between North and South America, that he prepared a brief memoir upon Zapotec remains, which the Institution has considered it advisable to publish with the drawings. We are happy to believe that this contribution will in some degree supply a deficiency which has been often acknowledged in regard to remains on the western slopes of the Mexican Cordillera.

3. Another memoir presented to the Institution is on the *Recent secular visitation of the Aurora Borealis*, by Professor Denison Olmsted, of Yale College. This paper partakes more largely of a hypothetical character than most of those which have been accepted for publication. The facts, however, which it contains are considered so important and so well deserving of permanent record, that they outweigh this objection.

On the evening of the 27th of August, 1828, after a long absence of any striking appearances of the aurora borealis, there commenced a series of exhibitions which increased in frequency and magnificence for the six following years, arrived at a maximum during the years 1835,–'6,–'7, and after that period regularly declined in number and intensity until November, 1848, when, according to the author, the series appeared to come to a close. The occurrence, however, of three remarkable exhibitions of the aurora during September, 1851, and of another of the first class as late as February, 1852, indicate that the close was not as abrupt as was at first supposed, but still there was a diminution in the number of brilliant exhibitions after 1848. Professor Olmsted, in this memoir, gives the history of the foregoing series of auroras, which, in his opinion, are the most remarkable which have ever occurred since the first recorded observations. The author first refers the several varieties of the aurora to six different forms, viz: 1. Auroral light; 2. Arches; 3. Streamers; 4. Coronas; 5. Waves; 6. Auroral clouds; and afterwards distributes these different forms into four distinct classes. The first is characterized by the presence of three out of four of the most prominent varieties, viz: arches, streamers, coronas, and waves.

The second class is formed of a combination of two or more of the leading characteristics of the first class.

The third class consists of the presence of only one of the rarer characteristics, either streamers or an arch, or irregular coruscations.

Class fourth consists of the most ordinary form of the aurora, as mere northern twilight or a few streamers.

From the year 1780 to 1827 striking exhibitions of the aurora were seldom observed, although, probably, a greater or less number of the inferior descriptions of those of the third and fourth classes occurred every year in our own latitude, and a still greater number in the regions nearer the poles. But aged persons who witnessed the displays of 1827, 1835, 1836, and 1837, testify that they were similar to such as occurred in their youth from 1760 to 1781. Strange sights were described as having been seen in the air during the old French war, which closed in 1763. From 1781 none of equal intensity had occurred for nearly half a century; the splendid arch, therefore, and other striking accompaniments of the aurora of 1827 took us by surprise, and were viewed with wonder by nearly all the existing generation. Immediately after this great aurora, exhibitions of the phenomenon became more frequent. From 1827 to 1848, 885 appearances of the aurora are given in the records referred to by the author. Of these, 12 were of the first class, 45 of the second, 161 of the third, and 667 of the fourth.

The author places the middle of the period about 1837; and by subtracting from this 65 years, he arrives at the middle of another visitation. The duration of the period he considers to be a little more than 20 years. The middle of the next period of brilliancy, if this assumption be correct, will be about the beginning of the next century. Whatever may be the truth of this conclusion, the description of a large number of auroras which he has collected, given either from the records of others or from his own observations, renders his communication valuable. He does not adopt the hypothesis of the electrical origin of this meteor, but considers it connected with the phenomena of the zodiacal light. The most conclusive proof, however, of the truth of the former hypothesis is found in the fact of the disturbance of the magnetic needle, when delicately suspended, during the appearance of the aurora, and the actual transmission of currents of electricity along the lines of telegraphs which extend in a north and south direction. The last fact has been reported separately to us by different individuals belonging to the Smithsonian corps of observers.

Though no complete explanation has been given of all the facts of the aurora, yet the most plausible hypothesis is that which attributes the phenomena to electricity generated principally in the torrid zone by evaporation. By this process the earth is rendered negative, and the vapor which ascends into the upper atmosphere highly positive. It is thence transferred towards the poles by the return trade winds, and descends to the earth to restore the equilibrium. A current of electricity is thus constantly passing from the poles to the equator during the appearance of the aurora; and hence, according to this view, the disturbance of the needle.

As an appendix to this paper, Peter Force, esq., of this city, has presented to the Institution an extended series of notices of the aurora collected from all the publications in which they occur, from about 1827 to the present year, arranged in order of time and of latitude. This will be a valuable contribution of facts towards a definite determination of the law and physical cause of these mysterious meteorological phenomena.

It would scarcely be complimentary to the general intelligence of the public of the United States, if I were again to attempt to vindicate the importance of investigations like that of the aurora; and it may be a sufficient answer to those who would question it, to say that they are such as particularly occupied the attention of Smithson himself, and that they must, consequently, be included as a part of that knowledge which it was the intention of his bequest to increase and diffuse among men.

4. The next paper is on the Tangencies of circles and spheres, by Major B. Alvord, of the United States army. It consists in the solution of a series of problems which have at different times exercised the ingenuity and skill of the geometer. It was referred separately for examination to Professor Lewis R. Gibbes, of Charleston, South

Carolina, and Professor A. E. Church, of West Point. In the language of one of the examiners: "The solutions of the problems relating to the circles, though not entirely original, are yet brought more directly to depend upon the fundamental principle of tangency as enunciated by the author, and are more elegant, than those given in any works with which I am acquainted. The paper also presents the only clear and complete explanation of the number of solutions and of the various positions of the tangent circles (and spheres) in each case that I have seen. I have not been able to find heretofore any complete solutions of all the problems relating to the sphere. Those of the author of the memoir are accurate, and easy to be understood by any person familiar with the elements of solid and descriptive geometry, and I think their publication will furnish a valuable addition to geometrical knowledge.'

It is a fact not without interest, that an officer of the army is enabled, while discharging his duty at a distant post of the frontier of our country, to concentrate his thoughts, and exercise his talents, on so abstruse a part of pure mathematics. The paper will be illustrated by three engraved plates in quarto.

5. A dictionary of the Chippewa language has been offered to the Smithsonian Institution for publication by the Rev. S. A. Belcourt, a missionary among the Indians of British America. He has devoted 23 years to the study of this language. He urges its adoption by the Institution on the ground that in all probability this work, which, to use his own language, "has cost me so many years of labor and nights of thought, and which, in my humble opinion, will be valuable to science and philanthropy, especially to philology, will forever be lost; and who would undertake a work of such magnitude after learning the fate of this?"

The language of the Ojibewas, according to the author, is the parent of all the dialects existing from the mouth of the St. Lawrence north and following the 27th parallel to the source of the Missouri. Were the present funds of the Institution sufficient for the purpose we should not hesitate to accept this work, and we are not entirely without hope that some means may be procured independent of the Institution to defray a considerable portion of the expense of its publication.

Correspondence.—During the past year the Institution has received a large number of communications asking information on a variety of subjects, particularly in regard to the solution of scientific questions, the names and characters of objects of natural history, and the analysis of soils, minerals, and other materials which pertain to the industrial resources of the country. Answers have in all cases been given to these inquiries, either directly by the officers of the Institution, or by reports from the Smithsonian colaborers. Very frequently certificates are requested as to the value of certain minerals, with a view to bring them into market; but in these cases the inquirers are referred to certain reliable analytical chemists, who make a business of operations of this kind. The information procured and given at the expense of the Institution is such as relates to the general diffusion of knowledge, and not to that which may immediately tend to advance the pecuniary interest of individuals. Requests are often also made to have experiments instituted for testing proposed applications of science to the arts; and provided these can be tried with the apparatus of the Institution, and the results which may flow from them are to be given to the public without the restriction of a patent, the request is granted.

Explorations, Researches, &c.—(1.) About the beginning of the year 1853, Lieutenant D. N. Couch, U. S. A., communicated to the Smithsonian Institution a proposition to make at his own expense a scientific exploration in the States of Mexico, adjoining the lower Rio Grande. After this proposition was duly considered, and the details of the plan arranged, it was commended by me in a letter to the Secretary of War, and a request made that Lieutenant Couch might have leave of absence for the purpose of carrying out his design. The request was granted, and this young officer soon after embarked on his expedition. He was furnished with instructions and apparatus by the Institution, and his attention was especially directed to the existence in Mexico of a valuable collection of manuscripts and specimens in natural history, of which information had been communicated to us. He was requested to examine and report as to its character. He found the manuscripts to contain a large amount of historical and geographical information, chiefly pertaining to the States of the old republic which lay between the Sabine and Sierra Madre, and a series of maps and results of topographical and meteorological observations. The collections in natural history consisted of specimens in botany, zoology, mineralogy, &c.

These collections were made by Luis Berlandier, a native of Switzerland, and a member of the Academy of Geneva. He came to Mexico in 1826, for the purpose of making a scientific examination of that country. Soon after his arrival he was appointed one of the Boundary Commission organized by the then new republic, with the object of defining the boundaries, extent, resources, &c., &c., of the northern or frontier States. This position gave him unusual facilities for observation and investigation relative to the character of the country, and for making collections of its natural history. He, however, never returned to his native country, but married and settled in Mexico, and continued his researches until the period of his death in 1851. Lieutenant Couch purchased the whole collection from the widow of the deceased, and transmitted it immediately to the Institution, which bore the expense of transportation. It contains matter which would be valuable to the general government, and which it is hoped will be purchased, and a sufficient sum paid to reimburse the cost of procuring it. In the appendix will be found a catalogue of the manuscripts.

Lieutenant Couch himself collected a large number of specimens in natural history, which were presented to the Institution, and have already been examined and described. Among the specimens of mineralogy is a remarkable meteorite, weighing upwards of 250 pounds, portions of which have been analyzed by Professor J. Lawrence Smith, in our laboratory, and by Dr. Genth, in Philadelphia.

The scientific explorations in natural history, made under the auspices of the Smithsonian Institution during 1854, were those of Dr. Hoy, Mr. Barry, and Professor Baird. That of Dr. Hay was made in western Missouri and Kansas, and occupied about a month; during which he gathered together large collections of North American vertebrata, and forwarded them to the Institution. Mr. Barry took northern Wisconsin for the field of his labors, and spent several months in traversing the State, penetrating into various regions scarcely visited before by the white man. Several lakes and streams, not on the map, were discovered, and named by him. His most important results consisted in very full series of fishes from many localities. Professor Baird spent six weeks on the coast of New Jersey, at Beesley's Point, collecting specimens, and studying the habits of the marine fishes of the neighborhood. Thence he proceeded to several places on Long Island, especially to Greenport and Riverhead; and afterwards made explorations at various points on and near the Hudson river, as far north as Sing Sing. Full series of fishes and crustacea were procured at all these places, and sent to the Smithsonian Institution.

(2.) *Terrestrial Magnetism.*—The observatory established at the joint expense of the Coast Survey and the Institution, described in the last report, for determining the changes in the different elements of the magnetic force, has not yet been fully supplied with all the necessary instruments. This has been occasioned by the illness of Mr. Brooks, of England, the inventor, who has not been able to furnish the apparatus for recording the variations in the dip and intensity. The only part of the system which has been in partial operation, is that of the variation or declination instrument; and in this, the glass cylinder which supports the sensitive paper, and which is needed to render the record more perfect, is wanting.

An attempt was made to supply this deficiency by means of a copper cylinder, coated with gold by the electrotype process. It was found, however, that the porosity of the gold allowed the acid to act upon the copper below, and thus to produce stains upon the paper. It is hoped this observatory will be fully equipped in the course of the present spring, and that a continued record will hereafter be kept up.

It was mentioned in the last report, that a set of instruments had been furnished the Grinnell expedition under command of Dr. Kane. No intelligence, however, has yet been received from this expedition; but should our most anxious hopes be realized in reference to this enterprise, we doubt not a series of results will be obtained which will well repay the cost of the instruments. If not, the Institution should receive some degree of commendation for aiding in an undertaking which reflects so much honor on the intelligence and liberality of one of our citizens, and the gallantry and enterprise of a young officer of our navy.

Four complete sets of instruments have been constructed in London for the Institution; three of these have been purchased by the general government, and have been employed in the different surveying expeditions. The fourth has been lent, in succession, to different individuals, for the purpose of accumulating magnetic observations in different parts of the United States.

A simple instrument for determining the minute changes in the direction of the magnetic needle, devised by Mr. J. E. Hilgard of the United States Coast Survey, is now in the process of construction, under the direction of this Institution, for the Academy of Natural Sciences, California. The cost of this instrument is defrayed by the liberality of the President of the Academy, Dr. A. Randall.

Observations continued for a certain time at different periods along the coast of the Pacific, and compared with the photographic records obtained by the apparatus in this Institution, would afford interesting results as to the simultaneous perturbations of the magnetic force at distant places on the same continent.

Under the head of magnetism, it may be mentioned that a complete set of apparatus has been obtained from Ruhmkorff, of Paris, for exhibiting the facts of the new branch of science called dia-magnetism. A few years ago, but four metals were known to possess magnetic properties, namely, iron, nickel, cobalt, and manganese. It is now known that all bodies exhibit analogous phenomena when placed under the inductive influence of powerful magnets; but they are not all similarly affected. All bodies may, however, be divided into two classes: one in which polarity is developed at the extremities of a bar of the substance, as in the case of iron, and hence called simple magnetic bodies; and the other class, in which the polarity is transverse to the length of the bar, and the substance is hence called *dia-magnetic*. The simple repetition of these experiments in this country is of importance, and the apparatus may serve as a model for imitation to our ingenious artists.

(3.) On the 26th of last May, the central track of an annular eclipse passed over the northern part of the United States. The eclipse itself was visible over almost the entire area of the North American continent; and as no obscuration of the sun of equal magnitude would again occur in this country until 1865, it was important that all the facilities possible should be afforded for observing its different epochs and phases, as well as the concurring phenomena. For this purpose, in conjunction with the superintendent of the Nautical Almanac, a large map, exhibiting the times of beginning and ending, and the amount of obscuration and phases of the eclipse for every part of the United States, Canada, and Mexico, together with tables and explanations, were prepared and distributed to all the observers in correspondence with the Smithsonian Institution. A set of minute instructions, published under the direction of the American Association for the Advancement of Science, was also presented to the same persons. Unfortunately, the weather proved cloudy over a considerable portion of the space covered by the central part of the shadow, though a number of interesting observations were made. The expense of the map and tables were defrayed jointly by this Institution and by the appropriation for the Nautical Almanac.

The results of the observations, so far as they have been reported, have been published in the Astronomical Journal, edited by Dr. B. A. Gould, jr., Cambridge, Massachusetts. They are illustrated by photographic impressions of the sun, made under the direction of Professor Bartlett, at West Point, and also by others, made under the direction of Professor S. Alexander, of Princeton, New Jersey. The expense of these was borne by the Institution, for which full credit has been given.

I may mention in this connexion that Professor Coffin, of Lafayette College, Pennsylvania, has presented to the Smithsonian Collections an interesting map, on which are delineated the paths or central tracks of all the great solar eclipses of the nineteenth century which traverse the

United States. These are nine in number. Seven of them have passed; the first of the remaining two will occur in October, 1865, and the other in August, 1869.

There are but two journals exclusively devoted to astronomy now in existence. The first is published at the expense of the King of Denmark, and the second in Cambridge, Massachusetts, by Dr. B. A. Gould, jr. The latter is intended to give the earliest intelligence of astronomical discoveries—particularly those made in our own country. At the last meeting of the British Association, the president commended this publication, and expressed a wish that it might be continued. I regret, however, to say that though no branch of science is cultivated with more ardor and success at the present time in the United States than astronomy, yet this work, so essential to its continued progress, is very inadequately sustained. Not only the labor of conducting it has devolved upon the editor, but also a considerable portion of the expense of its publication. The Smithsonian Institution has, from the first, subscribed for a number of copies, to be distributed among its foreign correspondents, and, rather than suffer so meritorious a work, which does so much service to the cause of science and credit to our country, to be discontinued, it might be well to enlarge the subscription. It is to be hoped that, in due time, donations and bequests will be made by liberal individuals for the support of scientific enterprises of this character.

It is gratifying to learn that $10,000 of the Appleton bequest have been devoted to the publications of the American Academy, and an equal sum to those of the Historical Society of Massachusetts; and we may venture to ask whether there are not, in this country, wealthy individuals who can properly appreciate the importance of the labors of Dr. Gould, and establish his journal on a permanent foundation.

(4.) *The laboratory of the Institution,* during the past year, has been used by Professor J. Lawrence Smith in the examination of American minerals; and, on behalf of the Treasury Department, in investigations relative to the different kinds of molasses imported into this country. He also made a series of analyses of meteorites, among which were fourteen specimens belonging to the cabinet of James Smithson, the founder of this Institution.

An extensive series of experiments have been made during the last year, and are still in progress at the Institution, under the direction of a commission appointed by the Secretary of War, consisting of General Totten, Professor Bache, and myself, for testing the materials employed in the extension of the capitol. For the purpose of these investigations, we have employed the beautiful and ingenious machine invented by Major Wade, late of the United States army, which is so contrived as to give in pounds per square inch of the material, the resistance to crushing, to twisting, and to longitudinal and transverse fracture. The materials have been selected and prepared under the direction of Captain Meigs, superintendent of the capitol extension; and the details of the manipulations and calculations have been entrusted to Mr. William Shippen.

The commission has taken advantage of this opportunity to extend the experiments to a number and variety of other building materials submitted to them from different parts of the United States; and they hope to be allowed to extend their inquiries until they also embrace the comparative strength of the most important articles used in the arts. For example, it is of great practical importance to know the relative and absolute strength of cordage, and the various textile fabrics manufactured by different processes from the raw materials produced in different countries. No complete series of experiments has ever been made upon the strength of the varieties of American timber. Enquiries, however, of this kind involve much labor and considerable expense, and can only be properly carried on by the aid of the government

(5.) *Meteorology.*—During the past year valuable additions have continued to be made to our meteorological collections. Though changes have taken place in the individuals, the number of the observers reporting immediately to the Institution is about the same as that given in the last report. A considerable number of full sets of standard instruments, made under our direction by Mr. James Green, of New York city,* have been procured by observers, and the character of the meteorological returns has consequently continued gradually to improve in completeness and precision. The records we have collected now form a copious store of valuable materials for the solution of many interesting problems relative to the meteorology of this country, which have been resorted to by several original investigators for data necessary to their researches. But to render these materials more generally available for the advancement of science, it is desirable to reduce them to tabular forms, and to publish them in as much detail as our funds will allow. In this way the greatest number of persons will have an opportunity of submitting them to the inductive process, by which general laws are deduced from particular facts. There is no part of physical science in which so much is to be done, even in the way of partial generalization, as in meteorology; and hence the importance of engaging as many minds as possible in its investigation.

It is the policy of the Institution to furnish all the means in its possession to aid scientific research, and not to hoard up its treasures or confine their use to those who may be immediately connected with the establishment, or who may be supported by its funds. *Co-operation*, and not *monopoly*, is the motto which indicates the spirit of the Smithsonian operations. It is with this view that I have been anxious to have the materials in our possession reduced to a form for publication; and, indeed, it has been a source of much solicitude that we have not been able before this time to present to the observers the means by which they could compare the results of their records with those of others in different districts. Few persons, however, are aware of the labor, chiefly of a mechanical character, required to tabulate materials of this kind, and the cost of printing them in sufficient fullness of detail to render them generally applicable to scientific or economical purposes. Besides this, I regret to inform the Board that our attempts in the line of reduction have thus far not been successful. I employed for this purpose a person who seemed to possess all the requisite qualifications, and who engaged in the work with commendable industry and apparent

* No. 422 Broadway, New York.

enthusiasm; but, I am sorry to have to say that before the work was completed, he set up such claims to a personal right of property in it, and to a control over the manner in which it should be prepared and published, as were entirely incompatible with the rights of the Institution, and with a due regard to its reputation. I was, therefore, obliged, after many attempts to induce an opposite course, to place the work in other hands. The reductions are now entrusted to Professor COFFIN, of Lafayette College, Pennsylvania, the author of the memoir on the winds of the North American continent; and from his established reputation for scrupulous exactness and punctuality, as well as for intellectual and moral qualities, we may confidently expect to have at least one part of the work ready for the press before the next session of the Board of Regents.

The materials collected consist of two classes, viz: one which includes all the records of observations published in books and periodicals, or contained in manuscripts which have been lent us for reduction; and the other consists of the current observations, which now embrace all the returns we have received for several years past. The reduction of the first class, on which we have expended much money, was, I supposed, nearly ready for the press; but, on examination, it has been found necessary to subject the whole to a careful revision, in order to correct the errors in it which a critical examination has brought to light.

It may be well to state, for the information of the public, that the appropriation which was made for the purchase of instruments to distribute among observers has been exhausted, and that the experiment was not as successful as could have been wished. A considerable number of the instruments were broken, and but comparatively few returns have been received. It does not, therefore, appear advisable to renew the appropriation with the portion of our income which can at present be devoted to meteorology.

Blank forms are furnished liberally to individuals who may desire to record the changes of the weather, or the progress of periodical phenomena.

In order to prevent difficulties similar to those which have heretofore occurred, it is important to state that all communications on the subject of meteorology—and, indeed, on the general business of the establishment, should be addressed to the "Secretary of the Institution." He alone is responsible to the Regents; and it is, therefore, necessary that he should have full knowledge and control of the correspondence.

EXCHANGES.—The system of international exchange has been conducted with very important results during the last year. The additions to the library from this source exceed considerably, in number, those of any previous year; amounting, in the aggregate, to over three thousand volumes and parts of volumes. Many of these consist of expensive works published by governments or institutions in Europe, and such as are not found in any other library in this country. It will not be extravagant to estimate the value of these returns at three thousand dollars; since most of them are the current volumes of the year, and bear the high price of scientific periodicals.

As mentioned in previous reports, the Smithsonian Institution acts as the principal medium of communication between the scientific and literary associations of the old and the new world. During the past year the number of the societies availing themselves of the facilities thus offered has largely increased, including, among others, nearly all the State agricultural societies of America, publishing transactions. This result has been produced by a circular which was issued by the Institution, early in the spring of last year, to make known more generally the system of exchange. Copious returns are being constantly received for the societies; and an intercourse is thus established which cannot fail to produce important results, both in an intellectual and moral point of view.

The governments of England and France have for some time admitted the packages of the Institution free of duty and without examination. A request for a similar favor was made to the Prussian government, during the past year, and it has been liberally granted by the commissioners of the Zollverein. There is, therefore, no port to which the Smithsonian parcels are shipped where duties are charged on them—a certified invoice of contents by the secretary being sufficient to pass them through the custom-house free of duty. On the other hand, all packages addressed to the Institution, arriving at the ports of the United States, are admitted, without detention, duty free. This system of exchange is, therefore, the most extensive and efficient which has ever been established in any country. Its effect on the character and reputation of our own country can scarcely be too highly estimated; while its influence, though silent, is felt in every part of the globe where literature and science are cultivated.

Library.—A difficulty which occurred between the librarian and myself has led to his separation from the Institution; and, since the 10th of last July, I have given the library, as far as my multiplied duties would allow, my personal supervision. With the assistance of Professor Baird and others, means have been devised for improving its condition and for rendering it more available for consultation. At present it is not thought advisable to appoint a special bibliographer, but to endeavor to conduct the business of the library by means of the assistants now employed, and by such temporary help as may be found necessary. An assistant has been employed to make a catalogue of all the books received by exchange, and to prepare the volumes and parts of volumes for binding. The list is now complete and will be appended to the next report to Congress, for the purpose of pointing out to our correspondents the deficiencies in the sets of transactions, and thus affording the opportunity to supply them. What we cannot procure in this way we shall endeavor to supply by purchase.

I have also directed that the statistics of the library should be kept, namely, the number of different persons who come to read, and the number and character of the books they call for. During the last six months 150 different individuals have read or consulted 742 books in the library; of these 400 were works of light literature, belonging to the copyright deposit. During the same period 2,576 names were entered in the registry of visitors. The principal value of the library has been to the officers of the Institution, and to other persons engaged in research connected with the Smithsonian publications. These, during the period above-mentioned, have drawn out of the library 450 volumes, principally of a scientific character.

The reading room of the library receives the leading periodicals of this country and Great Britain, together with a number from France, Germany, &c.; and, therefore, offers desirable facilities for the reading community of Washington, and for those who visit the seat of government, to keep up with the general progress of knowledge; while by means of the more profound transactions of learned societies the student is afforded the opportunity of becoming acquainted with the advances made in special branches of literature and science.

Very erroneous ideas have been entertained as to the amount which has been expended on the library. It is true the whole sum directly paid for books has not exceeded $14,139 16; but this does not include the binding, the transportation, the superintendence, and all the other expenses connected with an establishment of this kind. Neither does it exhibit the value of the books procured by exchanging the publications of the Institution for the current volumes of learned societies, or the cost in clerk hire and postage of the books received from the copyright system. The whole expenditure on the library and operations connected with libraries, including a proportional part of the general expenses since the beginning of the Institution, is $71,429 45. To this should be added at least $130,000 for the cost of the part of the building devoted to the library, and we shall then have an expenditure of the income of the Smithsonian bequest on the library and objects immediately connected with it of about $200,000.

In the original programme of organization, a proposition was introduced by Professor Bache to render the Institution a centre of bibliographical knowledge, to which students in every part of the country could apply, by letter or otherwise, for information as to what books existed on a particular subject, and in what libraries they could be found. For this purpose a large number of works on bibliography have been obtained, and efforts have been made to procure copies of all the catalogues of libraries in this country. To facilitate the answers to enquiries relative to the places where particular books could be found, it was proposed to secure three copies of each catalogue, one to be preserved in its original form, and the other two to be cut up, in order that the titles on each side of a leaf could be pasted on cards, and the whole arranged in drawers so as to form a general catalogue. Considerable progress was at one time made in this work, and several thousand cards were prepared by a bookbinder.

It was, however, stopped in order to prosecute the system proposed by Professor Jewett, namely, that of forming a general catalogue of libraries by means of stereotyping separate titles. It appears to me, however, that the first plan ought to be carried out as far as possible, particularly in regard to collecting catalogues; and these should not be confined to those of the libraries of the United States, but embrace, as far as practicable, those of the libraries of Europe. It may happen that an extract may be required by a student from a book not to be found in this country, and that this can be effected through the correspondence of the Institution, provided the location of the work in Europe is known.

About three years ago a series of experiments were undertaken at the expense and under the direction of the Institution for improving and applying a new method of stereotyping. The right to use the process was purchased of the original inventor, but it was not found in a condition to be applied, particularly to stereotyping catalogues, and in order to improve it an artizan from Boston was employed under the immediate direction of the librarian. The experiments were successful, and the improved process has been employed by Mr. John C. Rives in printing the Congressional Globe. I was anxious that it should be generally applied, in order that the art might not depend on the contingency of the life or will of a single individual. Besides this, should the process be generally introduced, the use of it for the Institution could be more cheaply procured by contract than by attempting to do our own work by a separate establishment in the building. I have, however, just learned that a patent has been applied for, in the name of the artizan before mentioned, for the very improvements which were made at the expense of the Smithsonian fund. This act, though it may be in accordance with the usages of employees under the government, is not, in my judgment, compatible with the liberal spirit of the will of Smithson. While due credit and proper remuneration should be given to any employee for his labors, the results should redound to the reputation of the Institution and to the general good of the public. This remark is also especially applicable to the claims set up by an employee in the meteorological department.

During the past year the process of cataloguing the Congressional library in accordance with the plan adopted by this Institution has been carried on under the direction of Professor Jillson, of Brown University. The whole number of titles catalogued has been 9,654, and of volumes 21,805. The stereotyping of the titles has been suspended for the present, in order to give the workmen who have been engaged on it an opportunity of applying the new art to the printing of the Congressional Globe. It is hoped that an additional appropriation will be made during the present session of Congress sufficient to complete the whole catalogue. We shall then have the statistics necessary to ascertain the cost of preparation of a catalogue of this kind, and the means necessary to give definite information, in reference to it, to the principal libraries of the country.

The edition of Notices of the Public Libraries in the United States, published by the Institution in 1851, is exhausted; and it will be necessary during the present year to collect the materials for a new and enlarged edition. A circular* for this purpose will be issued as soon as possible, and it is hoped that the work will be prepared in time to be submitted to Congress with the annual report for 1855. I have entrusted the duty of collecting the materials for this purpose to Mr. William J. Rhees, who now occupies the place formerly filled by Dr. Foreman, the latter having been appointed to the position of examiner in the Patent Office.

The purchases, though few in number, are of considerable value; and the additions from the system of exchange, as has before been stated, have increased in importance. The articles received on account of the copyright law were more numerous last year than the year before, but not more valuable. 848 separate pieces of music

*A circular distributed by the Institution is given in the Appendix to this Report.

have been received, for each of which two separate manuscript copies of every word of the title page was required. From this single fact it is evident that the operation of the present copyright law does not confer a material benefit upon the Institution, unless it be as a means of swelling the number of articles annually added to the library, which would appear to be at present a matter of some popular importance. It would be well to ask Congress, at least, to relieve the Institution from the burden imposed upon it by the additional postage to which we are constantly subjected on this account.*

The additions to the library during the year 1854 are shown by the following table:

	Books.	Pamphlets and parts of vols.	Engravings.	Maps.	Music.	Drawings.	Other articles.	Total.
Purchase	529	391	......	......	......	......	......	920
Donation and exchange	920	2,397	1	323	......	1	......	3,642
Copyright	441	203	16	28	848	5	69	1,610
Deposit	......	......	......	......	......	......	......	......
Total	1,890	2,991	17	351	848	6	69	6,172

If we add these to the number given in the report of the librarian last year, we shall have the following—

Aggregate to 1855.

	Books.	Pamphlets and parts of vols.	Engravings.	Maps.	Music.	Drawings.	Other articles.	Total.
Purchase	4,961	2,902	1,335	2	......	......	......	9,200
Donation and exchange	4,821	7,561	59	2,136	......	31	41	14,649
Copyright	3,250	623	54	87	3,122	14	166	7,316
Deposit	873	......	......	......	......	......	......	873
Total	13,905	11,086	1,448	2,225	3,122	45	207	32,038

*Since this was written, Congress has passed an act allowing all copyright publications to be sent to the Institution *free of postage* through the mail. A circular sent to all the publishers in the United States on this subject will be found in the Appendix.

MUSEUM AND COLLECTIONS.—(1.) The principal object of the Smithsonian collection of specimens is to present a full illustration of the natural history of North America. The income is not sufficient to collect and support a miscellaneous museum to illustrate all the branches of the physical geography of the globe. Such an establishment can only be sustained by the general government. Were the Institution to embrace all the opportunities which are afforded it to collect specimens, the cost of transportation alone would soon absorb the greater portion of the sum which can be devoted to this branch of the general plan of operations. We are, therefore, obliged to limit our exertions, and to direct them to objects which are more immediately necessary in facilitating certain definite lines of research, and to leave to other institutions the collection of such materials as may be required to make up the complement of specimens necessary to represent the mineral and organic products of our continent.

During the last year, the additions to the museum have been more numerous and valuable than in any previous period of the same extent. Much has been done by parties aided more or less by the Institution, and much by persons in an individual and independent capacity.

The Institution has taken charge of the arrangement and preservation of all the specimens obtained by the various expeditions of the government; but, as these embrace all objects of natural history, they would scarcely fall within the plan of a special museum. The principal aim, therefore, in taking charge of all the specimens is not to swell the Smithsonian collection, but to preserve them from destruction, and to render them immediately available to science, with the hope that Congress will, at some future day, make a liberal appropriation to support a national collection, of which these will form the nucleus.

In order to carry out the general policy of the Institution, a liberal distribution of the duplicate specimens should be made to societies and other establishments in this country and abroad. During the past year something has been done in this line; and when the collections are properly arranged, and the number of duplicates ascertained, the system of distribution may be so extended as materially to affect the progress of natural history in this country and the world. But the amount of good which may be done in this way must again be limited by the portion of the income which can be expended for this purpose; due regard being had to the claims of all branches of knowledge, of which this is but one.

The primary object of the establishment being kept constantly in view, the specimens in all cases will be open to the use of individuals who may desire to increase knowledge by original research; and the only condition which will be required to be strictly observed is that full credit be given to the Institution for the facilities which it may afford.

No branch of the operations of the Institution can be carried on without the expenditure of a greater amount of labor than might, at first sight, appear to be necessary. Some idea of that required to attend to the specimens added to the museum may be obtained from the fact that over 360 different lots, consisting of barrels, kegs, cans, boxes,

&c., besides many single specimens, have been received during the last year. All these had to be assorted, labelled, and recorded in books, and in most instances duplicate lists sent to the donors. In the case of smaller animals, large numbers of extra specimens are generally collected, to serve for anatomical investigation, or for distribution and exchange.

(2.) *Achromatic Microscope.*—In the first report of the Secretary it was mentioned that an individual, in the interior of the State of New York, had successfully devoted himself to the study and construction of the microscope, and was able to produce specimens of this instrument which would compete with the best of those constructed in Europe; and that, to do justice to the talents and labor of this person, Mr. Spencer had been requested to construct a microscope of the first quality, to be paid for by the Institution, if a commission appointed to examine it should find it capable of producing certain effects. The artist made a number of instruments which fully satisfied the conditions required by the agreement, but which still fell short of the ideal standard of perfection which existed in his own mind.

He has, however, at length completed a microscope, the performance of which far exceeds that which was anticipated when the proposition was made; and the Institution has thus not only secured a valuable instrument of research, but has assisted in developing the talents and making more generally known the skill of a native artist of surpassing merit. I may mention that Mr. Spencer has associated with himself Professor Eaton, of Troy, New York; and they are now able to supply the increasing demand in this country for this invaluable means of research which, within the last few years, has opened a new world to the physiologist and botanist, as well as to the investigator of inorganic matter.

(3.) *Gallery of Art.*—The Stanley collection of Indian portraits still remains deposited in the west wing of the building. They were removed, however, for a short time for exhibition at the Maryland Institute, Baltimore, and the State Agricultural Fair at Richmond, Virginia. They have constantly excited much interest, and it will be a subject of great regret if means cannot be procured to preserve entire a series of portraits which has been produced at so much labor and cost, and which is so faithful a representation of the peculiar physiognomy and costume of the different tribes of Indians now found within the boundaries of the territories of the United States. Mr. Stanley was engaged as the artist of the Pacific railroad survey under Governor Stevens, and has thus had an opportunity of adding much to his material for enlarging the collection. Since it was first deposited in the Institution he has also added to it portraits of several individuals belonging to the Indian delegations which, within the last two years, have visited Washington.

(4.) Professor Wilson, of the British Commission, appointed to attend the Exhibition at the New York Crystal Palace, presented to the Institution, in behalf of the London Society of Arts, a collection of models, drawings and instruments, to facilitate instruction in the art of design. In order to render these immediately useful, they were lent to the School of Design, which has been established in this city by the Metropolitan

Mechanics' Institute, under the charge of Professor Whitaker; and they are still in possession of this society, and are not only valuable on account of the immediate use to which they are applied, but also in serving as patterns for imitation for other schools of a similar character.

The Institution possesses, as has been stated in a previous report, a valuable collection of engravings by the first masters; but these have, from the first, been deposited in drawers, and have therefore not been accessible to the general visitor. It may be well, if the expense is not too great, to have them placed in groups, under glass, in large frames, and thus exhibited to all.

Building.—The main building of the Smithsonian Institution is at length completed. During the last six years, the wings, the connecting ranges, and the apartments in the southern tower, have alone been occupied. The unfinished condition of the edifice has undoubtedly produced an unfavorable impression on the numerous strangers who visit the city of Washington. The object, however, of the delay, as has been repeatedly stated in previous reports, was, first, that a more permanent building, and one better adapted to the uses of the Institution, might be provided; and secondly, that funds might be saved from the accruing interest to furnish an additional income sufficient at least to defray the annual expense of so large and costly an edifice. Both these objects have been attained. The interior of the building, instead of being constructed of wood and plaster, as was originally intended, has been finished with fire-proof materials; and improvements have been made in the plan first adopted which render the edifice better suited to the purposes for which it was intended. The first story consists of one room 200 feet long and 50 feet wide, which can be divided by a screen into two apartments, one of which may be devoted to the library and the other to the museum. The second story is divided into three spaces, the middle one of which is occupied by the great lecture room, capable of containing 2,000 persons, and constructed on acoustic and optical principles. It is believed that this room is the most perfect of its kind in this country, and that it will serve as a model for apartments of a similar character. The spaces adjoining the lecture room east and west form rooms each fifty feet square, which may contain cases around the walls for apparatus and other collections of objects of art, and at the same time serve for meetings of societies or for lectures to smaller audiences on special subjects. On the north side of the lecture room, in the front towers, are rooms intended for the preparation of the experimental illustrations of lectures, but which may be used as committee rooms, while the large lecture room serves for the more public addresses and exhibitions.

The object kept in view in all the changes which have been made in the original design of the building is its adaptation to purposes of general interest, and particularly to the accommodation of conventions and associations intended to promote knowledge or improve the arts of life.

During the past year a number of societies have availed themselves of the facilities afforded by the Institution, and have held their sessions in the Smithsonian building. The first was the United States Agricultural Society, which continued its session for three days, with lectures in the evening. It was attended by delegates from almost every part of the United States, and has published a journal of its proceedings, in which due credit is given to the Institution.

The second was the American Association for the Advancement of Science, which met the last of April and continued in session until about the 10th of May. Special preparation was made for this association; and although the building was still in an unfinished state, it is believed the members were well satisfied with their accommodation, as well as the hospitality and attention they received from the President and officers of the general government.

The third was the Association of Medical Superintendents of Hospitals for the Insane, which continued in session several days. The subjects discussed were not only of much importance relative to the treatment of diseases of the mind, but also of interest to the psychologist. Some, too, were of a practical character, connected with the general economy and management of public institutions. The subjects of heating and ventilating were fully discussed.

The fourth was the meeting of the American Association for the Advancement of Education, which has just closed its session. The Smithsonian Institution is thus assisting to render the city of Washington a centre of literary and scientific association, which may serve to diversify its character as the political metropolis of the nation.

Lectures.—In conformity with the law of Congress, a series of lectures was given during the winter of 1853–'4, and the experiment was made of establishing a full course on a single subject, namely, of chemistry. This was given by Dr. J. Lawrence Smith, late of the University of Virginia, and now professor of chemistry in the Louisville Medical College. The interest in all the lectures was fully sustained until the last.

A number of lectures were also given before the Mechanic's Institute and the Young Men's Christian Association in the Smithsonian lecture room.

The following is a list of the lectures given, with the names of the gentlemen by whom they were delivered.

A course of three lectures by Benjamin Hallowell, of Alexandria, Virginia.

1st. The general principles of astronomy, with the movements and consequent phenomena of the bodies of the solar system.

2d lecture. The sun, Neptune, the asteroids, and comets.

3d lecture. Fixed stars, nebulæ, and stellar systems.

A course of three lectures by Professor C. W. Hackley, of Columbia College, New York. Subject: History of institutions of learning and science.

A course of two lectures by W. Gilmore Simms, esq., of Charleston, South Carolina. Subject: The moral character of Hamlet. Also two lectures for the Young Men's Christian Association, on poetry and the practical.

One lecture by Professor W. J. Whitaker, of Massachusetts. Subject: Method of teaching the art of design.

A course of three lectures by Park Benjamin, of New York. Subjects: 1st. Fashion; 2d. Americanisms; 3d. Intellectual and social amusements.

One lecture by W. G. Dix, of Cambridge, Massachusetts. Subject: The Andes and Ecuador.

A course of twenty-two lectures by Professor J. Lawrence Smith, of the University of Virginia.

1st. The importance of the study of chemistry, and its close connexion with the progress of the arts and manufactures of the present age; also general notice of the nature of bodies, more especially gaseous bodies.

2d. The elements of the atmosphere: oxygen, nitrogen, and ozone, or oxygen in its allotropic condition.

3d. The physical properties of the atmosphere: its weight, color, elasticity, &c.

4th. The compounds of nitrogen and oxygen.

5th. Sulphur and some of its compounds.

6th. Sulphuric acid and its applications. Phosphorus and phosphoric acid.

7th. Chlorine, its applications in the arts and its combination with oxygen. Iodine and its uses, with a notice of its application in the photographic art.

8th. Some of the compounds of chlorine and iodine, bromine, hydrogen, and its application to æronautics.

9th. Compounds of oxygen and hydrogen; the oxyhydrogen blowpipe and the Drummond light; water in several of its relations.

10th. Combinations of hydrogen with nitrogen, sulphur, phosphorus, and chlorine.

11th. Carbon under its various forms of diamond, charcoal, and mineral coal; the combinations of carbon and oxygen.

12th. The agency of carbonic acid in forming incrustations of carbonate of lime; the respiration of plants and animals; the formation of coal-beds and the composition of coals; carbonic oxide and some of the compounds of carbon.

13th. Compounds of carbon and hydrogen; explosions in coal mines; Sir Humphrey Davy's lamp; combustion.

14th. On the phenomena of combustion and ebullition.

15th. On the phenomena of illumination, with an exhibition of every variety of illumination, from a candle to the electric light.

16th. On the phenomena of illumination, with illustration of every form of artificial illumination; an account of the construction and principle of the Fresnel light used in light-houses.

17th. On the ebullition and congelation of water, with a short account of the application of the vapor of water as a motive power.

18th. The conversion of water into steam; its application as a motive power, with some remarks on the explosion of boilers; an account of some of the vapors and gases proposed as substitutes for steam as motive power.

19th. General properties of the metals; potash and soda, with an account of their applications to the arts of glass and soap making, &c.

20th. On the compounds of lime, alumina, and silica, with their applications.

21st. On some of the properties of gold, silver, mercury, and lead, with the manner of their occurrence in nature.

22d. On the properties of copper and iron, with the manner of their occurrence in nature; on meteoric iron and meteorites.

From the foregoing account of the transactions of the past year, it must be evident to every intelligent and unprejudiced person that the Institution has perseveringly continued its course of usefulness, and that, although some of its operations are not of a character to attract public attention or elicit popular applause, yet they are eminently productive of the benevolent results intended by the bestower of the bequest. From the report of the Executive Committee, it will be seen that the funds are still in a good condition; although, on account of unforeseen difficulties in the completion of the building, and of the unexpected rise in the price of labor and material, a larger draft has been made upon the extra fund than was intended. This can be made up, however, if thought necessary, in the course of a few years, by means of the interest which will accrue from the same fund.

It is evident that the collections of books and specimens have increased as rapidly as is consistent with the best interests of the Institution. Every addition to these collections increases the cost of attendance and supervision, and therefore must, with a fixed income, tend to diminish the power of acquisition; and when it is recollected that the Institution is, theoretically at least, to be perpetual, it will be evident that we should be more solicitous in regard to the quality of articles than to their number or quantity. Though these views may not commend themselves to all, I believe they will be found to meet the approval of a large majority of the intelligent community.

In order to preserve the continuity of the history of the Institution in the annual reports of the secretary, it is necessary to allude to the fact that during the past year internal difficulties and changes have occurred which have given rise to a series of attacks on the policy and management of the Institution; but however painful occurrences of this kind may be to those immediately concerned, yet they seem almost inevitable in the first organization of an establishment where precedence is wanting, and where experience furnishes no instruction. They had their origin in the want of a definite recognition of the responsibilities and consequently of the powers of the secretary.

It is evident there can be no efficient action in an Institution of this character without entire harmony of views and unity of purpose, and these can only be secured by one executive head. The Regents have settled this principle, and thus removed all cause of future difficulty of a similar character.

JOSEPH HENRY,
Secretary of the Smithsonian Institution.

JANUARY, 1855.

APPENDIX TO THE REPORT OF THE SECRETARY.

REPORT OF THE ASSISTANT SECRETARY.

SIR: I beg leave to present herewith a report for the year 1854 of operations in such departments of the Smithsonian Institution as have been particularly entrusted by you to my care.

Respectfully submitted,

SPENCER F. BAIRD,
Assistant Secretary.

To JOSEPH HENRY, L.L. D.,
Secretary of the Smithsonian Institution.

1. PUBLICATIONS.

The sixth volume of Smithsonian Contributions to Knowledge, although for the most part printed in 1853, was not published and distributed until the present year. The seventh volume, to consist mainly of Lapham's Memoir on the Ancient Remains of Wisconsin, is in hand, though delayed somewhat by the failure of the contractor to supply paper. The plates, over sixty in number, are nearly all lithographed and printed, and the numerous wood-cuts engraved. The paper, by Professor Bailey, on new microscopic organisms, with one steel plate, has been printed and distributed to microscopists in advance of its appearance in the full volume.

The octavo publications during the year are as follows:

Eighth annual report of the Board of Regents of the Smithsonian Institution, pp. 310.

On the construction of catalogues of libraries, and of a general catalogue. Second edition, pp. 96.

Directions for collecting, preserving, and transporting specimens of natural history, prepared for the use of the Smithsonian Institution. Second edition, pp. 28.

List of foreign institutions in correspondence with the Smithsonian Institution, pp. 20.

List of domestic institutions in correspondence with the Smithsonian Institution, pp. 16.

a—FOREIGN EXCHANGES.

The following table exhibits the statistics of the sixth transmission of packages to Europe, made by the Institution in June, 1854.

The circular issued by the Institution early in the spring, offering its services to the scientific societies of the country, in the transmission of packages to Europe, was eagerly responded to by a large number. The rules requiring that all parcels be delivered free of cost in Washington, that each one be legibly addressed with the name of the donor, and that a separate invoice be sent by mail, or apart from the packages, were pretty generally complied with. It is to be regretted, however, that the last named regulation was not observed in some instances, thus greatly increasing the labor of the officers in charge, by rendering it necessary to make a transcript of the titles from the bundles themselves.

Such publications as were sent without specific addresses were distributed as appropriately as the information in possession of the Institution allowed.

The boxes containing the pa[illegible]a[illegible] enumerated in the list, left the Institution towards the end of June, and, having been shipped by packet, did not reach their European ports until some time in September. They were immediately unpacked by the agents of the Institution, and the parcels distributed, with the accompanying circulars, to their respective addresses. Acknowledgments for many of them have already been received.

A.—Table showing the amount of printed matter sent abroad in 1854 by the Smithsonian Institution.

1. *Distributed by Dr. J. G. Flügel, Leipsic.*

COUNTRIES.	Addresses of principal packages.	Addresses enclosed in the preceding.	Total of addresses.	Number of principal packages.	Packages enclosed from American institutions.	Packages enclosed from other parties.	Total of packages.	Weight of boxes.	Number of boxes.
Sweden	8	19	......	15	41	22	......	......	....
Norway	3	2	......	5	13	3	......	......	....
Iceland	1	......	......	2	7	......	......	......	....
Denmark	4	11	......	9	33	13	......	......	....
Russia	16	9	......	29	73	13	......	......	....
Holland	9	11	......	19	61	14	......	......	....
Germany	97	110	......	142	209	112	......	......	....
Switzerland	11	17	......	18	42	21	......	......	....
Belgium	9	12	......	13	45	16	......	......	....
Total	158	191	349	252	524	214	990	4,875	22

2. *Distributed by Hector Bossange, Paris.*

COUNTRIES.	Addresses of principal packages.	Addresses enclosed in the preceding.	Total of addresses.	Number of principal packages.	Packages enclosed from American institutions.	Packages enclosed from other parties.	Total of packages.	Weight of boxes.	Number of boxes.
France	64	47	......	80	148	47	......	......	....
Italy	28	24	......	37	69	27	......	......	....
Portugal	1	......	......	2	14	......	......	......	....
Spain	4	......	......	5	20	......	......	......	....
Total	97	71	168	124	251	74	449	1,884	6

3. *Distributed through the Royal Society and Henry Stevens, London.*

COUNTRIES.	Addresses of principal packages.	Addresses enclosed in the preceding.	Total of addresses.	Number of principal packages.	Packages enclosed from American institutions.	Packages enclosed from other parties.	Total of packages.	Weight of boxes.	Number of boxes.
Great Britain and Ireland...	93	98	191	109	206	108	423	2,013	5

4. *Distributed by other parties.*

COUNTRIES.	Addresses of principal packages.	Addresses enclosed in the preceding.	Total of addresses.	Number of principal packages.	Packages enclosed from American institutions.	Packages enclosed from other parties.	Total of packages.	Weight of boxes.	Number of boxes.
Rest of old world..........	18	2	......	19	45	2	......	......	....
South America.............	9	......	......	22	26	......	......	......	....
Total...................	27	2	29	41	71	2	114	1,019	5
Grand total...........	375	362	737	526	1,052	398	1,976	9,791	38

The number of foreign institutions to which full series of Smithsonian publications were sent for 1854 amounted to 263, or five more than the previous year. The list is necessarily subject to considerable variation, new names being added, and others taken off for non-compliance with the regulations of the Institution, or other causes. An acknowledgment of the reception of one package is imperatively required before another is sent, and in the failure to meet this rule, some first class institutions are dropped for one or two years, or until the omission is rectified.

There is no port to which the Smithsonian parcels are shipped where any duties are charged on them, a certified invoice of contents from the Institution being sufficient to carry them through the custom-houses free of duty.

Receipt of books by exchange.—The additions to the library of the Smithsonian Institution, by its exchanges, have been very marked during the year. Attention was called in the last report to the very great increase in our foreign exchanges, in consequence of the extension of the list of recipients of Smithsonian publications. During 1854, the works received have been fully equal in value to those of 1853, containing actually a larger number of pieces, and binding up to a greater number of volumes. The following table exhibits the record of this department. The discrepancy between this record and that of the library is owing to the fact that the latter included donations from individuals and other sources in this country, which the former did not, and that some separate sheets of maps were all bound together before being placed in the library:

B.—TABLE EXHIBITING THE NUMBER OF PIECES RECEIVED IN EXCHANGE DURING 1854.

Volumes.—Folio and quarto	271	
Octavo	655	
		926
Parts of Volumes and Pamphlets.—Folio and quarto	447	
Octavo	1,021	
		1,468
Maps and Engravings		434
Total		2,828

As was to be expected, a large proportion of receipts by exchanges consisted of the publications of learned societies, many of which, in addition to their current volumes, have sent their back series, either in whole or part. This department of the library is rapidly becoming more and more complete, and is believed even now to exceed that of any other library in the country. The catalogue now in preparation of the publications of societies and periodicals belcnging to the Institution will furnish a ready means of indicating what are the desiderata of this nature.

In addition, however, to returns from societies, the receipts from public libraries and universities of duplicates from their shelves have been very numerous, and consisting, as they usually do, of important scientific works, have proved highly acceptable. Owing to the constant communication kept up with the principal men of science at home and abroad, and the transmission to them of such publications of the Smithsonian Institution as related to their specialities, very many valuable memoirs and works have been received in return from this source

In the very great number of large donations received during the year it has been found impossible to give a particular enumeration ot them without encroaching too much in the space allotted to me. This is, however, less necessary, as the catalogues now in preparation, and shortly to be printed, will convey full information on the subject.

The following tables contain a statement of the packages received from the various sources specificed, for distribution in Europe as well as those received from Europe for this country:

C.—TABLE OF PACKAGES FROM AMERICAN INSTITUTIONS FOR DISTRIBUTION ABROAD.

Cambridge.—Nautical Almanac	35
Boston.—American Academy of Arts and Sciences	133
Boston Society of Natural History	42
New Haven.—American Journal of Science	47
New York.—New York Lyceum of Natural History	99
American Ethnological Society	19
Philadelphia.—Academy of Natural Sciences	136
American Philosophical Society	116
Philadelphia College of Pharmacy	9
Washington.—United States Patent Office	150
National Observatory	111
Light-honse Board	15
New Orleans.—New Orleans Academy of Natural Sciences	300
Columbus, Ohio.—Ohio Board of Agriculture	21
Detroit, Michigan.—Michigan State Agricultural Society	200
Madison, Wisconsin.—Wisconsin State Agricultural Society	143
San Francisco, California.—Geological Survey of California	60
Santiago, Chile.—Observatory of Chili	48
From miscellaneous sources, including individuals, &c	1,132
Total received	2,816

D.—TABLE OF PACKAGES RECEIVED FROM EUROPE FOR DISTRIBUTION TO VARIOUS SOCIETIES IN AMERICA.

Canada.—Various Societies	3
Boston.—American Academy of Arts and Sciences	50
Natural History Society	26
Bowditch Library	5
Cambridge.—Observatory	7
Botanic Garden	3
Harvard University	13
Astronomical Journal	12
American Association	13
Worcester.—Antiquarian Society	1
New Haven.—American Journal of Science	37
American Oriental Society	5
Albany.—New York State Library	10
New York.—New York Lyceum of Natural History	11
American Ethnological Society	1
Geographical and Statistical Society	3
American Institute	5
West Point.—United States Military Academy	1
Philadelphia.—American Philosophical Society	47
Academy of Natural Sciences	40
Franklin Institute	1
Geological Survey of Pennsylvania	5

Washington.—	President of the United States	1
	State Department	3
	United States Patent Office	12
	Congress Library	7
	Coast Survey	6
	National Observatory	30
	National Institute	3
	Commissioner of Indian Affairs	1
	United States Naval Astronomical Expedition, Chili	15
Georgetown, District of Columbia.—	Georgetown College	6
Chicago, Illinois.—	Mechanics' Institute	5
Colleges in different places		19
Various State libraries		37
Miscellaneous societies and individuals		543
Total		987

In concluding this portion of my report, I would beg to call your attention to the zeal and fidelity with which the agents of the Institution in London, Leipsic, and Paris, have discharged their duties. The thanks of the Institution are most especially due to Dr. J. G. Flügel, of Leipsic, whose efforts in the great cause of tightening the bonds of union between the literary and scientific men and institutions of the two worlds are beyond all praise.

3.—Domestic Exchanges.

The copies of volume 6 of Smithsonian Contributions were distributed early in the summer, through the agents of the Institution in different cities of the Union, as follows: Messrs. J. P. Jewett & Co., Boston; Geo. P. Putnam & Co., New York; Lippincott, Grambo & Co., Philadelphia; John Russell, Charleston; B. M. Norman, New Orleans; Dr. Geo. Engelmann, St. Louis; H. W. Derby, Cincinnati; and Jewett, Proctor & Worthington, Cleveland. The services of these gentlemen, involving considerable expense of time and trouble, have, in every instance, been given without charge.

4.—Museum.

a—*Increase of the Museum.*

During no period in the history of the Institution have the receipts of specimens been so numerous, or valuable, as in the year 1854. Contributions have been steadily flowing in from widely remote regions, many of which had been previously but little known. Expeditions, both public and private, individuals and societies, have all aided in gathering together what is now confidently believed to be the most valuable collection in the world of many divisions of the natural history of North America. Much has been done by parties aided directly to a greater or less extent by the Smithsonian Institution, and much by persons acting in an individual and independent capacity. The most important additions have, however, been received from the various government expeditions mentioned hereafter. Many officers of the army, as heretofore, have forwarded more or less complete collections, made in the neighborhood of the posts at which they have been stationed.

The government expeditions by which collections have been made are as follows:

United States Mexican Boundary Commission, under the scientific direction of Major Emory, United States army; General Robert B. Campbell, commissioner. The region illustrated by the collections received consisted of the Rio Grande, from Eagle Pass to its mouth. Under the present organization of the commission, with Major Emory acting as commissioner in addition to his former duties, there is reason to hope for new results of the most important character.

Survey of route for railroad to the Pacific—

A. Northern route, under Governor I. I. Stevens. Region traversed extending from Fort Benton, on the Missouri, to the Pacific ocean.

B. Parallel of 38°, under Lieutenant E. G. Beckwith. From the Arkansas, by way of Fort Massachusetts and Salt Lake, to San Francisco.

C. Parallel of 35°, under Lieutenant Whipple. From Fort Smith, on the Arkansas, via Albuquerque, Zuñi, San Francisco mountains, and the Mohave, to San Francisco.

D. Partial route, under Lieutenant R. S. Williamson. Extending from San Francisco to the Mohave, and Tejon Pass to camp Yuma.

E. Parallel of 32°, under Lieutenant J. G. Parke. Extending from camp Yuma via Tueson to El Paso.

F. Parallel of 32°, under Captain J. Pope. From El Paso, across the head of the Brazos and Colorado, to Preston in Texas.

Exploration of the coast of California, by Lieutenant W. P. Trowbridge, United States army.

Exploration of the La Plata and its tributaries, by Lieutenant Page, United States navy.

A more particular account of these several expeditions will be found in the article on scientific explorations.

From these different expeditions a large number of collections have been received, embracing material of the first importance and interest. Full reports are in preparation, and will be presented to Congress for publication with the other results of the explorations, and with such amount of illustrations as circumstances may require or authorize.

Among the more private explorations, from which results of the greatest importance have been received, are those of Dr. P. R. Hoy, in Missouri; Reverend A. C. Barry, in Wisconsin; Gustavus Wurdemann, in Louisiana; Lieutenant H. G. Wright, at Garden Key, Florida; Robert Kennicott, northern Illinois; Dr. L. A. Edwards, Fort Towson, &c.; together with my own, on the Jersey coast. Further accounts of these will be hereafter given.

In view of the vast multitude of objects received during the year, it is manifestly impossible to give full details respecting them; and I can here only refer to this subject in the most general manner, taking up the collections in the following order:

Mammals.—A specimen of the so-called Sampson fox, a peculiar variety of the red fox, or *Vulpes fulvus*, was received from Dr. Ackley and Dr. Kirtland, of Cleveland. Various kinds of *Sorex*, and other small mammals, from Reverend Chas. Fox, of Grosse Isle, Michigan.* The fœtus of a whale, from the arctic regions, was presented by Lieutenant Maury. The fresh skin and horns of a fallow deer (*Cervus dama*), and elk (*Elaphus canadensis*,) by Colonel Tuley, of Clarke county, Virginia, whose extensive park contains many fine specimens of these species. A pair of living wild cats (*Lynx rufus*,) were sent by Dr. Evans through Dr. D. D. Owen. The most important additions, however, have been received from Lieutenant Trowbridge, collected on the Pacific coast, including skins of deer, wolves, foxes, hares, lynxes, &c., with many small mammals. In this collection are several new species of bare.

Birds.—A very large collection of the birds of California was received from Lieutenant Trowbridge, embracing nearly all of the larger aquatic species of the coast, and another from Mr. Cutts. A collection of over 100 skins, from Gustavus Wurdemann, at Calcasieu, Louisiana, included several very rare and new species. Dr. Brewer presented some specimens from Wisconsin, and Mr. William M. Penrose an albino blackbird from near Carlisle, Pennsylvania.

Reptiles and fishes.—As usual, it is in this department that the additions have been greatest. The species of Wisconsin have been received from Dr. Hoy and Mr. Barry; of New Jersey and New York, from Mr. Brevoort and myself; of Mississippi, from Colonel Wailes and Reverend Benjamin Chase; of California, from Dr. Newberry, Mr. Bowman, and Lieutenant Trowbridge; of Illinois, from Mr. J. D. Sergeant, Robert Kennicott, and Mr. Harris; of South Carolina, from Professor Holmes, Mrs. Daniel, and Dr. Barker; of North Carolina, from Mr. Bridger, Mr. McNair, and Mr. Lineback; of Louisiana, from Mr. Wurdemann; of Missouri, from Dr. Hoy, Dr. Engelmann, and Mr. Lear; of Alabama, from Mr. Edgeworth; of Minnesota, from Mr. Riggs; of Tennessee, from Professors Owen and Johnson; of Chihuahua, from Mr. Potts; of Gulf of Mexico, from Lieutenant Wright; of Surinam, from Dr. Wyman; of Brazil, from Mr. Austin; of Trinidad and Key West, from Professor W. H. Thomas; of Africa, from Dr. Steele; together with many others. My limited space will not allow me to go into details respecting these collections beyond stating that those of Lieutenant Trowbridge are the most important, adding, as they do, some fifty new species of fishes alone to the North American fauna. Collections of reptiles deposited by Dr. Webb, who procured them in northern Mexico, New Mexico, and Texas, are likewise very valuable.

Quite a large number of living reptiles—snakes, lizards, turtles, &c., were received during the year, but, owing to the want of means for their proper preservation, few survived. Among those, however, at present in apparent good health, may be mentioned a northern rattlesnake *(Crotalus durissus)* from Virginia; the black massasauga, *(Crotalophorus massasauga,)* sent from Ohio by Dr. Kirtland; six specimens of *C. tergeminus*, Say, or prairie rattle, from Illinois, by Robert

* To this gentleman the Institution has been under very great obligations for numerous specimens illustrating the zoology of Michigan, accompanied, usually, by copious notes on the habits and peculiarities of the species. It is with profound regret that I have to record his death by cholera during the past summer.

Kennicott; two young alligators from Professor Forshey, Texas; a snapping turtle, (*Chelonura serpentina*) from Mississippi, and various others. Another season will, however, find us better prepared for a great variety of species already promised. Few collections of living animals excite more interest in the spectator than those of reptiles, while the habits of many species, at present unknown, can only be ascertained by their study in captivity. None admit of such confined accommodations, or require so little attendance and food.

Invertebrata.—Marine invertebrata of Jersey, were collected by myself, and of Louisiana by Mr. Wurdemann. A highly interesting and valuable collection made by Mr. Jarvis, inspector of timber in the Portsmouth navy yard, and presented by Commodore Smith, chief of the Bureau of Docks and Yards, illustrates well the growth of the teredo and barnacle, with the real or pretended artificial methods of preventing their ravages. From the experiments of Mr. Jarvis, however, it would seem to be proved conclusively that the white zinc paint, made by the New Jersey Company, as long as the surface covered by it remains unbroken, forms as effectual a protection to a ship's bottom as copper sheathing itself. Nearly all the alcoholic collections received included specimens of astaci and insects from different parts of North America.

Fossils.—Many valuable collections of fossil remains have been received. An interesting series from the vicinity of Satow was forwarded by the Rev. L. Vortisch; Mr. G. Lambert, of Mons, presented a series of carboniferous fossils of Belgium; specimens from Texas were sent in by Lieutenant J. G. Benton, United States army, and by Dr. Julius Froebel; from Panama by Dr. E. L. Berthoud; from Illinois by Dr. Stevens; from North Carolina by Mr. Bridger. A complete set of minerals and fossils of the remarkable brown-coal beds of Brandon, Vermont, was received from David Buckland. Sharks teeth and mastodon bones of Florida, from Captain Casey, United States army; fossil-wood of California, from Mr. Langton, and infusorial earth of Monterey, from Major Barnard.

Minerals.—A valuable collection of specimens illustrating the materials of which some of the principal public buildings in Europe are constructed, gathered by Mr. Evans, was deposited in his name by Lieutenant Gillis, and minerals of New Mexico and Texas were received from Lieutenant Colonel J. K. Mansfield, United States army, and Dr. Froebel; opal of Mexico from Mr. Rogers. A series illustrating the auriferous deposites of Bridgewater, Vermont, was presented by Mr. Cunningham.

Plants.—Some very large collections of plants of the Rocky Mountains and the regions west were brought in by the exploring expeditions. Others were sent from Texas by Dr. Ervendburg, from Minnesota by Mr. Riggs, from Madagascar by Messrs. Cotheal, &c. A very large leaf of the Talipot tree was presented by Commodore Aulick.

Antiquities.—Various specimens of Indian remains in North America have been received during the year from various sources, as also an ancient Peruvian vase from Talcahuana.

b—*Work done in the Museum.*

The labor of receiving, unpacking, and assorting the specimens received during the year has been very great, occupying a large share of my time as well as that of Mr. Girard.

Some idea of the labor involved may be obtained from the fact that in 1854 there were received 35 kegs and barrels, 26 cans, 175 jars, 94 boxes, and 32 packages, all containing a greater or less number of specimens, giving an aggregate of over 350 different lots, without including numerous specimens received singly. All these had to be assorted or repacked, labelled by localities, at least, and recorded in the proper books, and in most cases duplicate lists sent to the donors. We have, however, succeeded without other than mechanical aid in accomplishing all that was immediately necessary to be done, leaving very few arrears for the ensuing year.

Considerable progress has, likewise, been made in the determinations and descriptions of the collections themselves. A number of reports upon the vertebrata of the several explorations, both of the Pacific railroad survey, and of the United States navy astronomical expedition, under Lieutenant Gillis, have been either completed by Mr. Girard and myself or are in an advanced state of progress. The series of descriptive systematic catalogues of the collections has been extended by the preparation of an elaborate account of the North American toads by Mr. Girard, and of the frogs and tree frogs by myself; these are entirely finished and ready for press, and will make a volume nearly as large as the catalogue of North American serpents. Full descriptions of the families, genera, and species of all inhabiting North America (including about 20 new ones) are given, and analytic and exhaustive methods applied to the species. Such catalogues, forming as they do so many manuals in North American zoology, extend the benefits of the museum far beyond its walls. The demand, indeed, for them is so great, from all parts of the world, that of the catalogue of serpents two editions of 1,000 copies each have been called for and distributed.

A good deal of time has also been taken up in the preparation of specimens for examination, cleaning skeletons and skulls, dissecting, &c., while the selection, labelling, packing, and recording of the collections sent from the Institution have created no inconsiderable amount of labor.

In connxtion with the subject of the work done in the museum, it may, perhaps, be proper to refer to the article in the appendix containing the result of my observations on the habits and peculiarities of the fishes of the Jersey coast, as made in the summer, together with descriptions of the colors from life of such species as are apt to fade in spirits.

c—*The present Condition of the Museum.*

The paragraph upon the work done in the Museum covers to some extent the subject of the present heading. No change has been made in the places of deposit of the specimens owing to the very recent period at which the new hall intended to receive the collections was completed, and this year, it is earnestly hoped, will not pass without an improvement in this respect. The new hall is quite large enough to contain all the collections hitherto made, as well as such others belonging to the government as may be assigned to it. No single room in the country is, perhaps, equal to it in capacity or adaptation to its purposes, as, by the proposed arrangement, it is capable of receiving twice as large a surface of cases as the old Patent Offiee hall, and three times that of the Academy of Natural Sciences of Philadelphia. In this room, then, there will be abundant opportunity to arrange all the collections which have been made or may be expected for some time to come in the order best suited to the wants of the student and most interesting to the casual visitor. In the mean time, under the conditions of the past year, everything has been done to render the collections as available and accessible as circumstances would allow; all the North American mammalia, amounting to over 500 specimens in skins, have been arranged systematically in drawers of dust and insects-proof walnut cases. The birds have been similarly treated, while the reptiles and fishes (each species from each locality in a separate jar) have been assorted as systematically as the over crowding of the present confined space would allow. During the year several thousand jars have been filled with alcholic specimens, which are illy accommodated on shelves, nearly every square inch of which was occupied at the beginning of the year. The shells of mollusca with the minerals and fossils, have generally been repacked after entry and stored away for the present, requiring as they do a less vigilant supervision. This has, to a certain extent, likewise been done with the plants.

d—*Distribution of Collections.*

In accordance with the spirit of the Institution, quite a large number of specimens, in sets varying in magnitude, have been distributed during the past year to various institutions and individuals desiring them for purposes of special investigation. Some of these may be looked upon in the light of returns for similar favors received or promised, but they have generally been furnished without reference to an equivalent of any kind. As the facilities of the Institution for receiving and properly arranging its collections increase and the duplicates are ascertained, by a proper examination of the specimens, this system of distribution may be carried to an extent that shall materially affect the progress of science throughout this country and the world.

To the investigator who has heretofore been obliged to spend the best years of his life in collecting together the materials of his labor, gathered amid toils and privations to which, in the end, he may be forced to succumb, the advantage of finding all he needs ready to his hand, and in greater extent and variety than he could singly hope to obtain, are beyond all calculation. For this reason it is that the accumulation of a large amount of duplicate material becomes necessary, in addition to the complete series of specimens to be retained on the shelves.

Among the more important collections thus distributed may be mentioned one of 145 species of North American birds, in 199 specimens, to the Swedish Academy of Sciences at Stockholm, in return for a very valuable collection of skins and skeletons of north European mammalia; 97 species and 160 specimens of North American birds to Mr. F. Sturm, of Nürnburg, in return for collection of birds, &c., from central Europe; 104 lots of fishes and invertebrates to Professor Agassiz, of Cambridge, in return for numerous donations of duplicates from his pre-eminently valuable collection; fishes of Massachusetts to Dr. D. H. Storer, of Boston, to assist him in the preparation of his memoir on the fishes of the State; numerous birds and quadrupeds, both European and North American, to the Philadelphia Academy of Natural Sciences; eggs of American birds to Dr. T. M. Brewer, for his work on North American oology; large numbers of North American coleoptera to Dr. Leconte, for his memoirs on this department of entomology, &c. The list is capable of considerable extension, but there is enough to show how the Institution has endeavored to co-operate with all societies and individuals, engaged in special investigations, requiring materials additional to those already in their possession.

It will, however, be sufficiently evident that the Smithsonian Institution cannot indiscriminately undertake systematic exchange of specimens with other parties—with individuals especially. The force of the natural history department is not now sufficient for this, and may never be. To the mere collector, as distinguished from the investigator, it will not be expedient to distribute specimens to any considerable extent, as the disposable stock may be reduced so low as to render it difficult or impossible to do proper justice to the student. While, however, the Institution cannot undertake the mere business of exchange with individuals, unless in exceptional cases, and even with institutions, it can do and has done much to facilitate such exchange between other parties. Scarcely a week passes without the communication of information of the readiness or desire of exchange in particular departments on the part of different individuals or associations. All notifications or applications of the kind are systematically recorded in the proper books and duly referred to when occasion requires.

LIST OF THE PRINCIPAL DONATIONS TO THE MUSEUM OF THE SMITHSONIAN INSTITUTION DURING 1854.

Professor E. B. Andrews.—Keg of fishes from the Ohio river.

Commodore J. Aulick, U. S. N.—Leaf of Talipot palm (*Corypha umbracaulifera*) from Ceylon.

Joseph B. Austin.—Jar of reptiles from Para.

Spencer F. Baird.—Two kegs and one hundred jars of fishes, and invertebrates, with skins of birds, skulls and teeth of sharks and rays; from Beesley's Point, Cape May county, New Jersey. One keg of fishes from Greenport and Riverhead, Long Island. One keg of fishes from the fresh and brackish waters about Sing-Sing, New York. One keg of fishes from the Hackensack river and Sparkill, Rockland county, New York.

Dr. S. W. Barker.—Living specimens of *Nerodia erythrogaster*, *Heterodon niger*, *Ophibolus getulus*, and *Elaps fulvus* from South Carolina.

Major J. G. Barnard, U. S. A.—Infusorial earth from Monterey, California.

Rev. A. C. Barry.—Keg of fishes from southern Wisconsin; two kegs of mammals, reptiles, fishes, &c., from northern Wisconsin.

Lieutenant J. G. Benton, U. S. A.—Box of fossils from San Antonio, Texas.

Dr. E. L. Berthoud.—Fossils from the isthmus of Panama. Indian relics and fishes from Bourbon county, Kentucky.

J. S. Bowman and S. M. Bowman.—Fishes and reptiles collected on the route from Salt Lake city to Marysville, California.

C. C. Brevoort.—Fresh specimens of *Esox fasciatus* from Long Island. Fresh specimens of trout and hake from New York. Fishes, in alcohol, from the vicinity of Brooklyn, New York.

T. M. Brewer, M. D.—Skins of birds from Dane county, Wisconsin.

J. L. Bridger.—Stand containing a series of tertiary fossils, with living serpents, *Farancia abacurus*, and two birds, *Ortyx Virginianus*, from Edgcombe county, North Carolina.

David Buckland.—Box of minerals and fossils from the brown coal deposit of Brandon, Vermont.

Captain Casey, U. S. A.—Fossil teeth of mastodon and sharks from Florida.

Rev. Benjamin Chase.—Stuffed *Sternothaerus* from Concordia lake, Louisiana.

Captain Chatten.—Specimens, in alcohol, of *Ophidium marginatum* from Beesley's point, New Jersey.

Charleston College, S. C.—Duplicates of a collection of Batrachia.

Messrs. Cothcal & Co., New York.—Specimens of seeds of silk cotton; leaves, fruit, and manufactured cloth from the Rafar palm, Madagascar. Model of Madagascar canoe.

John P. Cunningham.—Box of minerals illustrating the auriferous deposits of Vermont.

R. D. Cutts.—Skins of thirty species of birds from San Francisco county, California.

Mrs. M. E. Daniel.—Can of reptiles and fishes from Anderson, South Carolina.

Edward T. Denig.—Reptiles and fishes from Fort Union, Nebraska.

T. J. Dryer.—Specimens of minerals from the summit of Mount Hood, Oregon.

J. Eckels, (United States consul, Talcahuana.)—Peruvian vase and ear of corn, disintered near Talcahuana.

A. E. Edgeworth.—Can of reptiles and fishes, with dried plants, shells, &c., from Marengo county, Alabama.

Dr. L. A. Edwards, U. S. A.—One box of fossils, one bale of plants, ten jars of reptiles and insects, and various heads and feet of birds, from Fort Towson, Arkansas.

Dr. George Engelmann.—One barrel fishes, reptiles, and mammals from St. Louis.

L. C. Ervendburg.—Package of seeds of Texas plants.

Dr. J. Evans and Dr. D. D. Owen.—Two living wild cats, (*Lynx rufus*,) from the Upper Missouri.

Dr. Julius Froebel.—Box of fossils and minerals from Texas and New Mexico.

Professor Charles Fox.—Skin of shrew, (*Sorex dekayi.*)

Lieutenant J. M. Gilliss, U. S. N.—Specimens of building materials collected in Europe, by W. W. Evans. Deposited.

John Greiner.—Specimens of *Phrynosoma*, in alcohol, from Santa Fé.

Dr. A. M. Grinnan.—Collection of plants from near Fredericksburg, Virginia. Can of reptiles and fish from Madison, Virginia.

J. O. Harris.—Fossils, insects, fishes, and reptiles, from Ottawa, Illinois.

Dr. Henderson, U. S. N.—Jar of fishes from Columbia county, Pennsylvania.

Mrs. Mary Hereford.—Bones of *Zeuglodon*, from a marl bed in Calvert county, Maryland.

Dr. Hereford.—Living specimens of *Leptophis æstivus*, from Prince George's, Maryland.

Dr. P. R. Hoy.—Fishes from southern Wisconsin; keg of fishes, reptiles, and mammals, from Illinois and Missouri; two kegs of fishes and reptiles from western Missouri; reptiles from Mansfield county, Ohio.

Rev. Thomas R. Hunt.—Red shale, with teeth of fishes, from northern Pennsylvania.

R. W. Kennicott.—Two jars of reptiles, fishes, &c., from northern Illinois; box containing six living *Crotalophorus tergeminus*, and other species of serpent, with other reptiles, from northern Illinois.

Dr. W. S. King, U. S. A.—Skins of chaparal cock, (*Geococcyx Mexicanus*,) from San Diego, California.

C. F. Kirtland.—Keg of fishes from Yellow creek, Ohio.

Professor J. P. Kirtland and Dr. Ackley.—Fresh specimen of Sampson fox, (*Vulpes fulvus*,) from Cleveland, Ohio.

Prof. J. P. Kirtland.—Four living specimens of *Crotalophorus massassanga*.

G. Lambert.—Fossils and rocks from Belgium.

W. F. Langton.—Fossil wood and sulphuret of iron, from the Minnesota mines in California.

O. H. P. Lear.—Fishes from Marion county, Missouri.

Major John Le Conte.—Jar of reptiles from Liberty county, Georgia; skin of *Sorex* from Georgia.

J. C. Lineback.—Can of reptiles and fishes from Salem, North Carolina.

Marshall McDonald.—Living specimen of *Scotophis Alleghaniensis*, Alleghany black snake, from Hampshire county, Virginia.

Lieutenant A. McRae, United States navy.—Scorpions and crustaceans from Panama.

J. C. McNair.—Eight jars of reptiles and fishes from Summerville, North Carolina.

R. C. Mack.—Specimens of Zanzibar copal, enclosing an insect and a lizard.

Rev. Charles Mann and *Masters George and William Mann.*—Salamander *(Amblystoma opacum)* with eggs taken in February, 1854. Can of fishes and reptiles from Gloucester county, Virginia.

Colonel J. K. Mansfield, United States Army.—Box of minerals and fossils, collected between Fort Atkinson and Santa Fé, New Mexico.

Hon. George P. Marsh.—Keg of fishes and reptiles with shells, &c., from Palestine, Syria, &c.

Lieutenant M. F. Maury, United States Navy.—Fœtus of right whale, and portion of the skin of sperm whale of 75 barrels, from the North Atlantic.

Professor O. W. Morris.—Young *Menopoma* just excluded from the egg, Holston river, Tennessee.

W. E. Moore.—Skin of humming bird, from the Island of Juan Fernandez.

Dr. J. S. Newberry.—Jar of reptiles from Bodega, California (deposited.)

Professor R. Owen.—Keg of reptiles and fishes from Tennessee.

William M. Penrose.—Skin of albino female of *Agelaius phoeniceus*, shot near Carlisle, Pennsylvania.

Charles Pillichody.—Two cans of fishes from Mobile, Alabama.

John Potts.—Skins of mammalia and reptiles in alcohol, from New Mexico. Skins of *Lepus artemisia* and of several birds, with a can of reptiles and fishes, from Chihuahua.

Alfred L. Riggs.—Can of reptiles and fishes, from Lac qui Parle, Minnesota.

Jeremiah Rogers.—Precious opal from Mexico.

Hon. Sion H. Rogers.—Fossil bone from Roanoke, North Carolina.

Sir R. Schomburgh.—Land shells, from Guiana.

J. D. Sergeant.—Specimens of *Pityophis* and *Eutænia*, from Illinois.

Dr. G. G. Shumard.—Five cans of fishes, one can of reptiles and two boxes of insects, from Fort Smith, Arkansas.

Captain E. K. Smith, U. S. A.—Fishes and reptiles, from St. Augustine, Florida.

Commodore Smith, U. S. N.—Series of specimens illustrating the experiments of Mr. John Jarvis, inspector of timber, navy yard, Portsmouth, Virginia, on the growth and ravages of teredo and barnacle, and means of protection against them.

Dr. Thomas L. Steele.—Four jars of reptiles and fishes, with one *Pteropus*, from Cape Palmas, west Africa.

Dr. R. P. Stevens.—Box of fossils and shells, from Illinois.

Professor W. H. B. Thomas.—Jar of reptiles, from Trindad, and one from Key West, Florida. Skin of *Scalops breweri.*

Lieutenant W. P. Trowbridge, U. S. A.—One keg and can of reptiles and fishes, with two boxes of skins of birds and mammals, skeletons, shells, &c., from San Diego, Monterey, and Presidio, California.

Colonel Joseph Tuley.—Skins and horns of male fallow deer, *Cervus dama*, and elk, *Elaphus canadensis*, from his park in Clarke county, Virginia.

Pfarrer L. Vortisch.—Collections of minerals, fossils, and antiquities, from Satow, Germany.

Colonel B. L. C. Wailes.—Three kegs of fishes, from Mississisippi. Keg of reptiles and fishes, from Washington, Mississippi.

Dr. T. H. Webb.—Reptiles, mammals, insects, &c., from California, New Mexico, and Texas. (Deposited.)

Lieutenant H. G. Wright, U. S. A.—Keg of fishes, from Fort Jefferson, Garden Key, Florida.

Gustavus Wurdemann.—Fishes, reptiles, and invertebrates, from Aransas, Texas, and New Orleans. Box of bird skins, and ten jars of reptiles, fishes, &c., from Calcasieu, Louisiana. Six jars of fishes, &c., from Fort Morgan, Mobile, Alabama. Reptiles, fishes, and invertebrates, Brazos, Texas. Fishes, reptiles, and invertebrates in alcohol, with skins of birds and mammals, from Aransas, Texas.

Dr. J. Wyman.—Can of fishes and reptiles, from Surinam and Guiana.

List of Meteorological Stations and Observers.

State.	Name of observer.	Residence.	County.
Nova Scotia	Henry Poole	Albion Mines	Pictou.
	A. T. S. Stuart	Wolfville, Acadia College.	
Canada	Dr. Charles Smallwood	St. Martin's, near Montreal.	
Maine	George B. Barrows	Fryeburg	Oxford.
	Joshua Bartlett	South Thomaston	Lincoln.
	John J. Bell	Carmel	Penobscot.
	William D. Dana	Perry	Washington.
	Samuel A. Eveleth	Windham	Cumberland.
	Rev. S. H. Merrill	Bluehill	Hancock.
	J. D. Parker	Steuben	Washington.
New Hampshire	Samuel N. Bell	Manchester	Hillsborough.
	Rev. L. W. Leonard	Exeter	Rockingham.
	R. C. Mack	Londonderry	Rockingham.
	Dr. William Prescott	Concord	Merrimack.
	George B. Sawyer	Salmon Falls	Stafford.
	Henry E. Sawyer	Great Falls	Stafford.
	Albert A. Young } Prof. Ira Young }	Hanover	Grafton.
Vermont	D. Buckland	Brandon	Rutland.
	James K. Colby } J. P. Fairbanks }	St. Johnsbury	Caledonia.
	Charles A. J. Marsh } James A. Paddock }	Craftsbury	Orleans.
	D. Underwood	Castleton	Rutland.
	Zadock Thompson	Burlington	Crittenden.
Massachusetts	Lucius C. Allin	Springfield	Hampden.
	William Bacon	Richmond	Berkshire.
	John Brooks	Princeton	Worcester.
	Marshal Conant	Bridgewater	Plymouth.
	Prof. P. A. Chadbourne	Williamstown	Berkshire.
	Emerson Davis	Westfield	Hampden.
	B. R. Gifford	Wood's Hole	Barnstable.
	Amasa Holcomb	Southwick	Hampden.
	George Chandler, M. D.	Worcester	Worcester.
	D. J. Holmes } James Orton }	Williamstown	Berkshire.
	Hon. Wm. Mitchell	Nantucket	Nantucket.
	R. D. Mussey	Rockport	Essex.
	Dr. J. Geo. Metcalf	Mendon	Worcester.
	Dr. H. C. Perkins	Newburyport	Essex.
	Henry Rice	North Attleboro'	Bristol.
	Samuel Rodman	New Bedford	Bristol.
	Dr. James Robbins	Uxbridge	Worcester.
	Prof. E. S. Snell	Amherst	Hampshire.
	Dr. E. A. Smith	Worcester	Worcester.
	Albert Schlegel	Taunton	Bristol.
Rhode Island	Prof. A. Caswell	Providence	Providence.
	George Manchester	Portsmouth	Newport.
	Samuel Powel	Newport	Newport.
	Henry C. Sheldon	North Scituate	Providence.
Connecticut	Rev. T. Edwards	New London	New London.
	T. S. Gold	West Cornwall	Litchfield.
	D. Hunt	Pomfret	Windham.
	Prof. J. Johnston	Middletown	Middlesex.
	Dr. Ovid Plumb	Salisbury	Litchfield.
	James Rankin	Saybrook	Middlesex.
New York	E. M. Alba	Angelica	Alleghany.
	Edward A. H. Allen	Troy	Rensselaer.
	Thomas B. Arden	Beverly	Putnam.
	Warren P. Adams	Glen's Falls	Warren.
	Charles A. Avery	Seneca Falls	Seneca.
	John Bowman	Baldwinsville	Onondaga.
	S. De Witt Bloodgood	New York	New York.

METEOROLOGICAL LIST—Continued.

State.	Name of observer.	Residence.	County.
New York—Con	Eph. N. Byram	Sag Harbor	Suffolk.
	J. Everett Breed	Smithville	Jefferson.
	C. Thurston Chase	Chatham	Columbia.
	E. A. Dayton	Madrid	St. Lawrence.
	J. S. Gibbons	New York	New York.
	W. E. Guest	Ogdensburg	St. Lawrence.
	J. Caroll House	Lowville	Lewis.
	J. H. Hart	Oswego	Oswego.
	Dr. S. B. Hunt	Buffalo	Erie.
	E. W. Johnson	Canton	St. Lawrence.
	John Lefferts	Lodi	Seneca.
	L. A. Langdon	Falconer	Chautauque.
	Charles A. Lee	Peekskill	Westchester.
	Capt. W. S. Malcom	Oswego	Oswego.
	L. F. Munger	Le Roy	Genessee.
	Prof. D. J. Pratt	Fredonia	Chautauque.
	Dr. J. W. Smith	East Franklin	Delaware.
	Elias O. Salisbury	Buffalo	Erie.
	Dr. H. P. Sartwell	Penn Yan	Yates.
	Rev. Thomas H. Strong	Flatbush	Kings.
	Stillman Spooner	Wampsville	Madison.
	C. S. Woodward	Beaver Brook	Sullivan.
	P. O. Williams	Gouverneur	St. Lawrence.
	Walter D. Yale	Houseville	Lewis.
New Jersey	Robert L. Cooke	Bloomfield	Essex.
	Prof. Geo. H. Cook	New Brunswick	Middlesex.
	Rev. Ad. Frost	Burlington	Burlington.
	E. T. Mack	New Brunswick	Middlesex.
	W. A. Whitehead	Newark	Essex.
Pennsylvania	Samuel Brown	Bedford	Bedford.
	W. O. Blodget	Sugar Grove	Warren.
	Dr. A. C. Blodget	Youngsville	Warren.
	John Comly	Byberry	Philadelphia.
	D. S. Deering	Brookville	Jefferson.
	Fenelon Darlington	Pocopson	Chester.
	Joseph Edwards	Chromedale	Delaware.
	Rev. D. J. Eyler	Waynesboro'	Franklin.
	John Heisely	Harrisburg	Dauphin.
	Ebenezer Hance	Morrisville	Bucks.
	O. T. Hobbs	Randolph	Crawford.
	John Hughes	Pottsville	Schuylkill.
	M. Jacobs	Gettysburg	Adams.
	Prof. J. A. Kirkpatrick	Philadelphia	Philadelphia.
	J. R. Lowrie	Warrior's Mark	Huntington.
	Rev. J. Grier Ralston	Norristown	Montgomery.
	Paul Swift	Haverford	Philadelphia.
	Francis Schreiner	Moss Grove	Crawford.
	Dr. H. Smyser	Pittsburgh	Alleghany.
	Dr. R. P. Stephens	Ceres	McKean.
	T. H. Thickstun	Meadville	Crawford.
	A. D. Weir	Freeport	Armstrong.
	W. W. Wilson	Pittsburgh	Alleghany.
	R. Weiser	Andersville	Perry.
Delaware	Prof. W. A. Crawford	Newark	New Castle.
	J. P. Walker	Dover	Kent.
Maryland	Prof. William Baer; Miss H. M. Baer	Sykesville	Carroll.
	Rev. John P. Carter	Hagerstown	Washington.
	Henry E. Hanshaw	Frederick	Frederick.
	Benj. O. Lowndes	Blenheim	Prince George's.
	Prof. Jas. F. Maguire	New Windsor	Carroll.
Virginia	Lieut. R. F. Astrop	Crichton's Store	Brunswick.
	Samuel Couch	Ashland	Putnam.
	Benj. Hallowell	Alexandria	Alexandria.

METEOROLOGICAL LIST—Continued.

State.	Name of observer.	Residence.	County.
Virginia—Continued.	Jed. Hotchkiss	Bridgewater	Rockingham.
	Samuel X. Jackson	Leesburg	Loudon.
	William S. Kern	Huntersville	Pocahontas.
	Charles J. Meriwether	Montcalm	Albemarle.
	J. W. Marvin	Winchester	Frederick.
	A. Nettleton	Lynchburg	Campbell.
	Thomas Patton	Lewisburg	Greenbier.
	Prof. Geo. R. Rosseter	Buffalo	Putnam.
	David Turner	Richmond	Henrico.
	Prof. N. B. Webster	Portsmouth	Norfolk.
North Carolina	Rev. Fred. Fitzgerald	Jackson	Northampton.
	Dan. Morelle	Thornbury	Northampton.
	Prof. Jas. Phillips	Chapel Hill	Orange.
	Dr. J. Bryant Smith	Lincolnton	Lincoln.
South Carolina	Thornton Carpenter	Camden	Kershaw.
	Alex. Glennie	Waccaman	All Saints Parish.
	H. W. Ravenel	Aiken	Barnwell.
	J. A. Young	Camden	Kershaw.
Georgia	R. T. Gibson	Whitemarsh Island	Chatham.
	William Haines	Augusta	Richmond.
	John F. Posey	Savannah	Chatham.
	Dr. E. M. Pendleton	Sparta	Hancock.
	William Schley	Augusta	Richmond.
	Prof. Wm. D. Williams	Madison	Morgan.
Florida	Dr. A. S. Baldwin	Jacksonville	Duval.
	W. C. Dennis	Key West	Monroe.
	John Newton	Orange Hill	Washington.
	John Pearson	Pensacola	Escambia.
	Aug. Steele	Cedar Keys	Levy.
Alabama	George Benagh	Tuscaloosa	Tuscaloosa.
	S. J. Cumming	Monroeville	Monroe.
	Prof. John Darby	Auburn	Macon.
	Ben. F. Holley	Wetokaville	T[illegible]dega.
	R. T. Meriwether	McMath's P. O.	Tuscaloosa.
	H. Tutwiler	Green Springs	Green.
	Prof. M. Tuomey	Tuscaloosa	Tuscaloosa.
Mississippi	A. R. Green	Jackson	Jackson.
	Prof. L. Harper	Oxford	Lafayette.
	Rev. E. S. Robinson	Garlandsville	Jasper.
	Wm. Henry Waddell	Grenada	Yalabusha.
Louisiana	Dr. E. H. Barton	New Orleans	Orleans.
	Prof. W. P. Riddel	Jackson	St. James Parish.
Texas	Prof. L. C. Ervendberg	New Wied	Comal.
	J. W. Glenn	Austin	Travis.
	Dr. S. K. Jennings	Austin	Travis.
Tennessee	Dr. Robert T. Carver	Friendship	Dyer.
	George Cooke, Prof. L. Griswold	Knoxville	Knox.
	Jas. Higgins	Memphis	Shelby.
	Prof. Hamilton	Trenton	Gibson.
	Prof. Ben. C. Jillson	Lebanon	Wilson.
	W. M. Stewart	Glenwood	Montgomery.
	Prof. A. P. Stewart	Lebanon	Wilson.
Kentucky	O. Beatty	Danville	Boyle.
	E. L. Berthoud	Maysville	Mason.
	Rev. J. Miller, Rev. G. S. Savage	Millersburg	Bourbon.
	L. G. Ray	Paris	Bourbon.
	Dr. John Swain	Ballardsville	Oldham.
	J. D. Shane	Lexington	Fayette.
	Mrs. Lawrence Young	Springdale	Jefferson.
Ohio	Prof. J. W. Andrews	Marietta	Washington.
	Prof. G. M. Barber	Berea	Cuyahoga.
	R. S. Bosworth	College Hill	Hamilton.
	F. A. Benton	Mount Vernon	Knox.

METEOROLOGICAL LIST—Continued.

State.	Name of observer.	Residence.	County.
Ohio—Continued....	Geo. L. Crookham......	Jackson, C. H......	Jackson.
	Miss Ardelia Cunningham	Unionville..........	Lake.
	Jacob N. Desellem......	Richmond..........	Jefferson.
	Lewis M. Dayton.......	Newark............	Licking.
	J. H. Fairchild..........	Oberlin............	Loraine.
	L. Groneweg...........	Germantown.......	Montgomery.
	G. A. Hyde............	Norwalk...........	Huron.
	F. Hollenbeck..........	Perrysburg.........	Wood.
	Dr. J. G. F. Holston....	Zanesville..........	Muskingum.
	F. W. Hurtt...........	Cincinnati..........	Hamilton.
	Dr. John Ingram........	Savannah..........	Ashland.
	Dr. J. P. Kirtland......	East Rockport......	Cuyahoga.
	G. W. Livezay.........	Gallipolis..........	Gallia.
	John F. Lukens.........	Zanesfield..........	Logan.
	J. McD. Mathews.......	Hillsboro'..........	Highland.
	G. S. Ormsby..........	College Hill........	Hamilton.
	Prof. S. N. Sanford.....	Granville...........	Licking.
	Robert Shields..........	Bellcentre..........	Logan.
	E. Spooner.............	Keen..............	Coshocton.
	Edmund West..........	Huron.............	Erie.
Michigan...........	William Campbell.......	Battle Creek........	Calhoun.
	Alfred E. Currier........	Grand Rapids.......	Kent.
	Rev. Geo. Duffield......	Detroit.............	Wayne.
	Dr. S F. Mitchell.......	East Saginaw.......	Saginaw.
	Capt. A. D. Perkins.....	Monroe............	Monroe.
	H. R. Schetterly........	Grand Traverse.....	Michilimackinac.
	L. H. Streng...........	Saugatuck..........	Alleghany.
	J. J. Strang............	St. James...........	Michilimackinac.
	Dr. M. V. Taylor.......	Brooklyn...........	Jackson.
	Miss Octavia C. Walker.	Cooper.............	Kalmazoo.
	Dr. Thomas Whelpley...	Brest...............	Monroe.
	Lorin Woodruff.........	Ann Arbor.......	Washtenaw.
	A. Winchell............	Ann Arbor.......	Washtenaw.
Indiana..............	W. W. Austin..........	Richmond..........	Wayne.
	C. Barnes..............	Madison...........	Jefferson.
	A. H. Bixby............	Lafayette...........	Tippecanoe.
	J. Chappelsmith.........	New Harmony......	Posey.
	W. B. Coventry.........	Kendallville........	Noble.
	Dr. V. Kersey..........	Milton.............	Wayne.
	J. Knauer..............	Kendallville........	Noble.
	H. Peters...............	Lafayette...........	Tippecanoe.
	D. H. Roberts..........	New Garden........	Wayne.
	Prof. Joseph Tingley....	Greencastle.........	Putnam.
Illinois..............	Prof. W. Coffin.........	Batavia............	Kane.
	L. G. Edgerly..........	Granville...........	Putnam.
	John Grant.............	Manchester.........	Scott.
	Joel Hall...............	Athens.............	Menard.
	Dr. J. A. Harris........	Ottawa.............	La Salle.
	Dr. John James.........	Upper Alton........	Madison.
	Dr. S. B. Mead.........	Augusta............	Hancock.
Missouri............	Fred. Behmer..........	Fort Pierre.........	
	Dr. Engelmann.........	St. Louis...........	St. Louis.
	O. H. P. Lear..........	Dry Ridge..........	Marion.
Iowa...............	Miss Ida E. Ball........	Keokuk............	Lee.
	E. C. Bidwell...........	Quasqueton.........	Buchanan.
	Dr. Asa Horr...........	Dubuque...........	Dubuque.
	Daniel McCready.......	Fort Madison.......	Lee.
	Benjamin F. Odell......	Poultney...........	Delaware.
	Rev. Joshua Phelps......	Alexander College...	Dubuque.
	P. G. Parvin...........	Muscatine..........	Muscatine.
	E. H. A. Scheeper......	Pella...............	Marion.
Wisconsin..........	Miss M. E. Baker......	Ceresca............	Fond du Lac.
	Thomas Gay...........	Belle Fontaine......	Marquette.
	L. A. Lapham..........	Milwaukie..........	Milwaukie.
	Prof. S. P. Lathrop......	Beloit..............	Rock.

METEOROLOGICAL LIST—Continued.

State.	Name of observer.	Residence.	County.
Wisconsin—Contin'd.	G. F. Livingston	Hudson	St. Croix.
	Dr. J. L. Pickard	Platteville	Grant.
	J. McQuigg W. Porter	Beloit	Rock.
	S. H. Carpenter J. W. Sterling	Madison	Dane.
	Edward S. Spencer	Summit	Waukesha.
	J. F. Willard	Janesville	Rock.
	Carl Winkler	Milwaukie	Milwaukie.
Minnesota	C. F. Anderson	St. Anthony's Falls	Ramsey.
	Rev. Elisha W. Carver	Red Lake	Pembina.
	A. O. Kellum	St. Joseph	Pembina.
	Rev. S. W. Mauncey	Fort Ripley	
	S. R. & A. L. Riggs	Lac qui parle	Dahkota.
	David B. Spencer	St. Joseph	Pembina.
California	Dr. H. Gibbons	San Francisco	San Francisco.
	Dr. F. W. Hatch	Sacramento	Sacramento.
	Rev. J. A. Shepherd	San Francisco	San Francisco.
Nebraska	D. E. Reed	Bellevieu	
Paraguay	E. A. Hopkins	Ascension	

Meteorological observers—New York University system.

Name.	Residence.	County.
M. R. Batchelder	Fredonia	Chautauque.
John N. Brinkerhoff	Union Hall, Jamaica	Queen's.
Prof. Chester Dewey	Rochester	Monroe.
John Felt, jr	Liberty	Sullivan.
W. H. Gillespie	Mexico	Oswego.
Ira F. Hart	Elmira	Chemung.
John F. Jenkins	White Plains	Westchester.
Mrs. M. T. Lobdell	North Salem	Westchester.
A. W. Morehouse	Spencertown	Columbia.
Prof. O. W. Morris	Institute for Deaf and Dumb	New York city.
Prof. David Murray	Albany	Albany.
Edw. C. Reed	Horner	Cortland.
Prof. O. Root	Clinton	Oneida.
J. O. Stratton	Oxford	Chenango.
Jos. W. Taylor	Plattsburg	Clinton.
Rev. R. D. Van Kleek	Flatbush	King's.
Prof. W. D. Wilson	Geneva	Ontario.

ALPHABETICAL LIST OF METEOROLOGICAL OBSERVERS.

Name.	Residence.	State.
Adams, Warren P	Glen's Falls	New York.
Alba, E. M	Angelica	New York.
Allen, Edw. A. H	Troy	New York.
Allin, Lucius C	Springfield	Massachusetts.
Anderson, C. F	St. Anthony's Falls	Minnesota.
Andrews, Prof. J. W	Marietta	Ohio.
Arden, Thos. B	Beverly	New York.
Astrop, Lieut. R. F	Crichton's store	Virginia.
Austin, W. W	Richmond	Indiana.
Avery, Chas. A	Seneca Falls	New York.
Bacon, Wm	Richmond	Massachusetts.
Baer, Miss H. M	Sykesville	Maryland.
Baer, Prof. Wm	Sykesville	Maryland.
Baker, Miss M. E	Ceresca	Wisconsin.
Baldwin, Dr. A. S	Jacksonville	Florida.
Ball, Miss Ida E	Keokuk	Iowa.
Barber, Prof. G. M	Berea	Ohio.
Barnes, C	Madison	Indiana.
Barrows, Geo. B	Fryeburg	Maine.
Bartlett, Joshua	South Thomaston	Maine.
Barton, Dr. E. H	New Orleans	Louisiana.
Batchelder, M. R	Fredonia	New York.
Beatty, O	Danville	Kentucky.
Behmer, F	Fort Pierre	Missouri.
Bell, John J	Carmel	Maine.
Bell, Samuel N	Manchester	New Hampshire.
Benagh, George	Tuscaloosa	Alabama.
Benton, F. A	Mount Vernon	Ohio.
Berthoud, E. L	Maysville	Kentucky.
Bidwell, E. C	Quasqueton	Iowa.
Bixby, A. H	Lafayette	Indiana.
Blodget, Dr. A. C	Youngsville	Pennsylvania.
Blodget, W. O	Sugar Grove	Pennsylvania.
Bloodgood, S. De Witt	New York	New York.
Bosworth, R. S	College Hill	Ohio.
Bowman, John	Baldwinsville	New York.
Breed, J. Everett	Smithville	New York.
Brinkerhoff, John N	Union Hall, Jamaica	New York.
Brooks, John	Princeton	Massachusetts.
Brown, Samuel	Bedford	Pennsylvania.
Buckland, D	Brandon	Vermont.
Byram, E. N	Sag Harbor	New York.
Campbell, Wm	Battle Creek	Michigan.
Carpenter, S. H	Madison	Wisconsin.
Carpenter, Thornton	Camden	South Carolina.
Carter, Rev. Jno. P	Hagerstown	Maryland.
Carver, Rev. E. W	Red Lake	Minnesota.
Carver, Dr. Robt. T	Friendship	Tennesse.
Caswell, Prof. A	Providence	Rhode Island.
Chadbourne, Prof. P. A	Williamstown	Massachusetts.
Chandler, Dr. George	Worcester	Massachusetts.
Chappelsmith, John	New Harmony	Indiana.
Chase, C. Thurston	Chatham	New York.
Coffin, Prof. W	Batavia	Illinois.
Colby, Jas. K	St. Johnsbury	Vermont.
Comly, John	Byberry	Pennsylvania.
Conant, Marshal	Bridgewater	Massachusetts.
Cooke, George	Knoxville	Tennessee.
Cooke, Robert L	Bloomfield	New Jersey.
Cook, Prof. George H	New Brunswick	New Jersey.
Couch, Samuel	Ashland	Virginia.
Coventry, W. B	Utica	New York.
Crawford, Prof. W. A	Newark	Delaware.

METEOROLOGICAL LIST—Continued.

Name.	Residence.	State.
Crookham, George L	Jackson	Ohio.
Cumming, S. J	Monroeville	Alabama.
Cunningham, Miss A	Unionville	Ohio.
Currier, Alfred E	Grand Rapids	Michigan.
Dana, William D	Perry	Maine.
Darby, Prof. John	Auburn	Alabama.
Darlington, Fenelon	Pocopson	Pennsylvania.
Davis, Emerson	Westfield	Massachusetts.
Dayton, E. A	Madrid	New York.
Dayton, Lewis M	Newark	Ohio.
Deering, D. S	Brookville	Pennsylvania.
Dennis, W. C	Key West	Florida.
Desellem, Jacob N	Richmond	Ohio.
Dewey, Professor Chester	Rochester	New York.
Duffield, Rev. George	Detroit	Michigan.
Edgerly, L. G	Granville	Illinois.
Edwards, Joseph	Chromedale	Pennsylvania.
Edwards, Rev. T	New London	Connecticut.
Engelmann, Dr	St. Louis	Missouri.
Ervendburg, Prof. L. C	New Wied	Texas.
Eveleth, Samuel A	Windham	Maine.
Eyler, Rev. D. J	Waynesboro'	Pennsylvania.
Fairbanks, J. P	St. Johnsbury	Vermont.
Fairchild, J. H	Oberlin	Ohio.
Felt, John	Liberty	New York.
Fitzgerald, Rev. F	Jackson	North Carolina.
Frost, Rev. A	Burlington	New Jersey.
Gay, Thomas	Bellefontaine	Wisconsin.
Gibbons, Dr. H	San Francisco	California.
Gibbons, J. S	New York	New York.
Gibson, R. T	Whitemarsh Island	Georgia.
Gifford, R. R	Wood's Hole	Massachusetts.
Gillespie, W. H	Mexico	New York.
Glennie, Alexander	Waccaman	South Carolina.
Glenn, J. W	Austin	Texas.
Gold, T. S	West Cornwall	Connecticut.
Grant, John	Manchester	Illinois.
Green, A. R	Jackson	Mississippi.
Griswold, Prof. L	Knoxville	Tennessee.
Groneweg, L	Germantown	Ohio.
Guest, W. E	Ogdensburg	New York.
Haines, William	Augusta	Georgia.
Hall, Joel	Athens	Illinois.
Hallowell, Benjamin	Alexandria	Virginia.
Hamilton, Professor	Trenton	Tennessee.
Hance, Ebenezer	Morrisville	Pennsylvania.
Hanshaw, Henry E	Frederick	Maryland.
Harper, Prof. L	Oxford	Mississippi
Harris, Dr. J. O	Ottawa	Illinois.
Hart, Ira F	Elmira	New York
Hart, J. H	Oswego	New York.
Hatch, Dr F. W	Sacramento	California.
Heisley, John	Harrisburg	Pennsylvania.
Higgins, James	Memphis	Tennessee.
Hobbs, O. T	Randolph	Pennsylvania.
Holcomb, Amasa	Southwick	Massachusetts
Hollenbeck, F	Perrysburg	Ohio.
Holley, B. F	Wetokaville	Alabama.
Holmes, D. J	Williamstown	Massachusetts
Holston, Dr. J. G. F	Zanesville	Ohio.
Hopkins, E. A	Ascension	Paraguay.

METEOROLOGICAL LIST—Continued.

Name.	Residence.	State.
Horr, Dr. Asa	Dubuque	Iowa.
Hotchkiss, Jed	Bridgewater	Virginia.
House, J. Carroll	Lowville	New York.
Hughes, John	Pottsville	Pennsylvania.
Hunt, D	Pomfret	Connecticut.
Hunt, Dr. S. B	Buffalo	New York.
Hurtt, F. W	Cincinnati	Ohio.
Hyde, G. A	Norwalk	Ohio.
Ingram, Dr. John	Savannah	Ohio.
Jackson, Samuel X	Leesburg	Virginia.
Jacobs, M	Gettysburg	Pennsylvania.
James, Dr. John	Upper Alton	Illinois.
Jenkins, J. F	White Plains	New York.
Jennings, Dr. S. K	Austin	Texas.
Jillson, Professor B. C	Lebanon	Tennessee.
Johnson, E. W	Canton	New York.
Johnston, Professor J	Middletown	Connecticut.
Kellum, O. A	St. Joseph's	Minnesota.
Kersey, Dr. V	Milton	Indiana.
Kirkpatrick, Prof. J. A	Philadelphia	Pennsylvania.
Kirkland, Dr. J. P	East Rockport	Ohio.
Knauer, J	Kendallville	Indiana.
Langdon, L. A	Falconer	New York.
Lapham, I. A	Milwaukie	Wisconsin.
Lathrop, Prof. S. P	Beloit	Wisconsin.
Lear, O. H. P	Dry Ridge	Missouri.
Lee, Charles A	Peekskill	New York.
Lefferts, John	Lodi	New York.
Leonard, Rev. L. W	Exeter	New Hampshire.
Livezay, G. W	Gallipolis	Ohio.
Livingston, G. Z	Hudson	Wisconsin.
Lobdell, Mrs. Mary J	Salem Centre	New York.
Lowndes, B. O	Blenheim	Maryland.
Lowrie, J. R	Warrior's Mark	Pennsylvania.
Lukens, John F	Zanesville	Ohio.
Mack, E. T	New Brunswick	New Jersey.
Mack, R. C	Londonderry	New Hampshire
Maguire, Prof. J. F	New Windsor	Maryland.
Malcom, Captain W. S	Oswego	New York.
Manchester, George	Portsmouth	Rhode Island.
Marsh, Charles A. J	Craftsbury	Vermont.
Marvin, J. W	Winchester	Virginia.
Mauncey, Rev. S. W	Fort Ripley	Minnesota.
Matthews, J. McD	Hillsboro'	Ohio.
McCready, D	Fort Madison	Iowa.
McQuigg, J	Beloit	Wisconsin.
Mead, Dr. S. B	Augusta	Illinois.
Meriwether, Charles J	Montcalm	Virginia.
Meriwether, R. T	McMath's	Alabama.
Merrill, Rev. S. H	Bluehill	Maine.
Metcalf, Dr. J. G	Mendon	Massachusetts.
Miller, Rev. J	Millersburg	Kentucky.
Mitchell, Dr. S. K	East Saginaw	Michigan.
Mitchell, Hon. Wm	Nantucket	Massachusetts.
Morehouse, A. W	Spencertown	New York.
Morelle, D	Thornbury	North Carolina.
Morris, Prof. O. W	New York	New York.
Munger, L. F	Le Roy	New York.
Murray, Prof. David	Albany	New York.
Mussey, R. D	Rockport	Massachusetts.

METEOROLOGICAL LIST—Continued.

Name.	Residence.	State.
Nettleton, A	Lynchburg	Virginia.
Newton, Jno	Orange Hill	Florida.
Newton, W. H	Fond du Lac	Minnesota.
Odell, B. F	Poultney	Iowa.
Ormsby, J. S	College Hill	Ohio.
Orton, Jas	Williamstown	Massachusetts
Paddock, Jas. A	Craftsbury	Vermont.
Parker, J. D	Steuben	Maine.
Parvin, T. S	Muscatine	Iowa.
Patton, Thos	Lewisburg	Virginia.
Pearson, Jno	Pensacola	Florida.
Pendleton, Dr. E. M	Sparta	Georgia.
Perkins, Capt. A. D	Monroe	Michigan.
Perkins, Dr. H. C	Newburyport	Massachusetts.
Peters, H	Lafayette	Indiana.
Phelps, Rev. Joshua	Alexander College	Iowa.
Phillips, Prof. Jas	Chapel Hill	North Carolina.
Pickard, Dr. J. L	Plattsville	Wisconsin.
Plumbe, Dr. Ovid	Salisbury	Connecticut.
Poole, Henry	Albion Mines	Nova Scotia.
Porter, W	Beloit	Wisconsin.
Posey, John F	Savannah	Georgia.
Powel, Sam'l	Newport	Rhode Island.
Pratt, Prof. D. J	Fredonia	New York.
Prescott, Dr. Wm	Concord	New Hampshire.
Ralston, Rev. J. G	Norristown	Pennsylvania.
Rankin, James	Saybrook	Connecticut.
Ravenel, H. W	Aiken	South Carolina.
Ray, L. G	Paris	Kentucky.
Reed, D. E	Belleview	Nebraska Territory.
Reed, Edward C	Homer	New York.
Rice, Henry	North Attleboro'	Massachusetts.
Riddle, Professor W. P	Jackson	Louisiana.
Riggs, S. R. and A. L	Lac qui Parle	Minnesota.
Robbins, Dr. James	Uxbridge	Massachusetts.
Robinson, Rev. E. S	Garlandsville	Mississippi.
Rodman, Samuel	New Bedford	Massachusetts.
Root, Professor O	Clinton	New York.
Rosseter, Professor Geo. R	Buffalo	Virginia.
Salisbury, Elias O	Buffalo	New York.
Sanford, Professor S. N	Granville	Ohio.
Sartwell, Dr. H. P	Penn Yan	New York.
Savage, Rev. G. S	Millersburg	New York.
Sawyer, George B	Salmon Falls	New Hampshire.
Sawyer, Henry E	Great Falls	New Hampshire.
Scheeper, E. H. A	Pella	Iowa.
Schetterly, H. R	Grand Traverse	Michigan.
Schlegel, Albert	Taunton	Massachusetts.
Schley, William	Augusta	Georgia.
Schreiner, Francis	Moss Grove	Pennsylvania.
Shane, J. D	Lexington	Kentucky.
Sheldon, Henry C	North Scituate	Rhode Island.
Shepherd, Rev. J. A	San Francisco	California.
Shields, Robert	Bellecentre	Ohio.
Skeen, William	Huntersville	Virginia.
Smallwood, Dr. Charles	St. Martin's	Canada.
Smith, Dr. E. A	Worcester	Massachusetts.
Smith, Dr. J. Bryant	Lincolnton	North Carolina.
Smith, Dr. J. W	East Franklin	New York.
Smyser, Dr. H	Pittsburg	Pennsylvania.
Snell, Professor E. S	Amherst	Massachusetts.
Spencer, David B	St. Joseph	Minnesota.

METEOROLOGICAL LIST—Continued.

Name.	Residence.	State.
Spencer, Edward S	Summit	Wisconsin.
Spooner, E	Keen	Ohio.
Spooner, Stillman	Wampsville	New York.
Steele, Augustus	Cedar Keys	Florida.
Sterling, J. W	Madison	Wisconsin.
Stevens, Dr. R. P	Ceres	Pennsylvania.
Stewart, Prof. A. P	Lebanon	Tennessee.
Stewart, W. M	Greenwood	Tennessee.
Strang, J. J	St. James	Michigan.
Stratton, J. O	Oxford	New York.
Strong, L. H	Saugatuck	Michigan.
Strong, Rev. T. H	Flatbush	New York.
Stuart, A. P. S	Wolfville	Nova Scotia.
Swain, Dr. John	Ballardsville	Kentucky.
Swift, Paul	Haverford	Pennsylvania.
Taylor, Jos. W	Plattsburg	New York.
Taylor, Dr. M. K	Brooklyn	Michigan.
Thickstun, T	Meadville	Pennsylvania.
Thompson, Zadock	Burlington	Vermont.
Tingley, Prof. Jas	Greencastle	Indiana.
Tuomey, Prof. M	Tuscaloosa	Alabama.
Turner, David	Richmond	Virginia.
Tutwiler, H	Green Springs	Alabama.
Underwood, D	Castleton	Vermont.
Van Kleek, Rev. R. D	Flatbush	New York.
Waddell, Wm. H	Grenada	Mississippi.
Walker, Miss Octavia C	Cooper	Michigan.
Walker, J. P	Dover	Delaware.
Webster, Prof. N. B	Portsmouth	New Hampshire.
Weir, A. D	Freeport	Pennsylvania.
Weiser, R	Andersville	Pennsylvania.
West, Edmund	Huron	Ohio.
Whelpley, Dr. Thos	Brest	Michigan.
Whitehead, W. A	Newark	New Jersey.
Willard, J. F	Janesville	Wisconsin.
Williams, P. O	Gouverneur	New York.
Williams, Prof. W. D	Madison	Georgia.
Wilson, Prof. W. D	Geneva	New York.
Wilson, W. W	Pittsburg	Pennsylvania.
Winchell, A	Ann Arbor	Michigan.
Winkler, Carl	Milwaukie	Wisconsin.
Woodruff, Lum	Ann Arbor	Michigan.
Woodward, C. S	Beaver Brook	New York.
Yale, Walter D	Houseville	New York.
Young, Albert A	Hanover	New Hampshire.
Young, J. A	Camden	South Carolina.
Young, Mrs. Lawrence	Springdale	Kentucky.
Young, Prof. Ira	Hanover	New Hampshire.

REPORT OF THE EXECUTIVE COMMITTEE.

ADOPTED JANUARY 15, 1855.

The Executive Committee submit to the Board of Regents the following report relative to the present state of the finances, and the expenditures during the year 1854.

The whole amount of the Smithsonian bequest, deposited in the treasury of the United States (from which an annual income, at 6 per cent., is derived of $30,910 14) is		$515,169 00
Amount of unexpended interest, reported last year as in charge of Messrs. Corcoran and Riggs	$179,408 02	
From which deduct amount passed by them to the credit of the treasurer, to meet payments on building during 1854	54,408 02	
	125,000 00	
Balance in the treasury, January 1, 1855	14,159 59	
		139,159 59
		$654,328 59

The following is a general view of the receipts and expenditures for the year 1854, exclusive of amount drawn from Corcoran and Riggs on account of the building.

RECEIPTS.

Balance in the treasury, as per last report	$6,944 68	
Interest on the original fund for the year 1854	30,910 21	
Interest on the extra fund for the year 1854	7,276 39	
		$45,131 28

EXPENDITURES.

For items common to the objects of the Institution	$12,752 00	
For publications, researches, and lectures	8,094 38	
For library, museum, and gallery of art	9,512 19	
For building purposes—difference between the amount expended and the amount withdrawn from Corcoran and Riggs	613 12	
Balance in the treasury	14,159 59	
		$45,131 28

Detailed statement of the expenditures during 1854.

BUILDING, FURNITURE, FIXTURES, ETC.		
Pay on contracts	$52,280 00	
Pay of architect and draftsman	1,237 00	
Miscellaneous incidental to building	495 13	
Magnetic observatory	18 77	
Furniture, &c., for uses in common	938 12	
Furniture, &c., for library	52 12	
		$55,021 14
GENERAL EXPENSES.		
Expenses of Board of Regents, &c	467 71	
Lighting and heating	887 30	
Postage	467 67	
Transportation and exchanges	1,644 43	
Stationery	662 50	
General printing	1,094 22	
Apparatus	427 26	
Incidentals general, including salary of clerk, book-keeper, janitor, watchman, laborer, extra clerk hire	3,600 99	
Salary of Secretary	3,499 92	
		12,752 00
PUBLICATIONS, RESEARCHES, AND LECTURES.		
Smithsonian Contributions to Knowledge	3,773 96	
Reports on progress of knowledge	83 84	
Other publications	917 89	
Meteorology	2,203 38	
Investigations	10 00	
Pay of lectures	895 00	
Illustrations and apparatus for lectures	156 37	
Attendance and lighting lectures, &c	53 94	
		8,094 38
LIBRARY, MUSEUM, AND GALLERY OF ART.		
Cost of books	2,166 50	
General catalogue	151 35	
Stereotyping and printing	551 71	
Incidentals, library, including salary of two assistants, and binding	2,329 55	
Salary of Assistant Secretary	1,319 43	
Explorations, museum	250 00	
Expenses of collections, museum	157 19	
Incidentals, including alcohol, &c., assistance and labor, apparatus, catalogue, glass jars, &c	536 54	
Salary of Assistant Secretary	1,999 92	
Incidentals, gallery of art	50 00	
		9,512 19
Total expenditures in 1854	....	85,379 71

In the appropriations made, April, 1854, for the year the estimated income of the Institution was $38,500—[the actual income was $38,186 60]—of this sum $7,000 was devoted to the building and the remaining $31,500 to the operations of the Institution.

The first mentioned sum (7,000) is included in the balance in the treasury, the whole of which may be appropriated during the present year to the building.

The whole expenditure on the operations of the Institution was $30,358 57, which is $1,141 83 less than was appropriated.

The appropriation was not made until one-third of the year had passed, and this, with the unusual expenditure occasioned by a call of a special meeting of the Board, and the extra clerk hire and printing on account of the various reports, rendered it impossible to apportion the disbursements in exact conformity to the estimates. They will be found, however, approximately to agree—those for publications, &c., being less, and those for library, museum, &c., more.

On account of the additions which the building committee have found it necessary to make to the contract for the better security and adaptation of the building, the extra fund has been reduced to $140,000, instead of $150,000, as was formerly contemplated. It is probable a further reduction will be required to pay the amount still due on the contract, and for other purposes connected with the building, but this should not be allowed to diminish the extra fund below $125,000.

The following table presents a general exhibit of all the receipts and expenditures on account of the Smithsonian fund, from the beginning of the Institution until the first of January, 1855.

General statement of the expenditures of the Smithsonian Institution.

	To Dec. 31, 1847.	Year 1848.	Year 1849.	Year 1850.	Year 1851.	Year 1852.	Year 1853.	Year 1854.	Aggregate.
1. *Building, furniture, and fixtures, grounds.*	Dolls. Cts.	Dolls. Cts.	Dolls. Cts.	Dolls. Cts.	Dolls. Cts.	Dolls. Cts.	Dolls. Cts.	Dolls. Cts.	Dolls. Cts.
Pay on contracts for building	22,899 00	48,810 00	50,300 00	24,000 00	22,000 00	10,000 00	25,500 00	52,280 00	255,780 00
Pay of architects, superintendents, &c.	3,482 76	2,949 86	3,124 12	2,459 42	2,214 45	1,839 83	1,580 70	1,237 00	18,888 14
Expenses of building committee	1,338 85	17 24	....	6 00	43 53	7 50	77 00	....	1,490 12
Experiments, &c. on building materials	488 13	62 00	15 50	....	....	....	....	....	565 63
Examination of quarries	250 76	....	....	....	....	....	....	....	250 76
Premiums paid for plans	1,250 00	....	....	....	....	....	....	....	1,250 00
Miscellaneous, incidental to building	509 63	1,738 65	1,980 18	1,868 05	62 07	1,198 64	184 84	495 13	8,037 19
Magnetic observatory	....	....	....	....	....	....	1,578 28	18 77	1,597 05
Furniture and fixtures for uses in common	....	....	1,717 52	892 93	657 06	682 94	354 05	938 12	5,242 62
Do.......do....for publications	....	....	....	....	21 00	....	....	....	21 00
Do.......do....for lectures	....	....	25 00	166 50	149 99	....	....	....	341 49
Do.......do....for library	....	....	347 00	545 80	255 22	265 15	117 11	52 12	1,582 40
Do.......do....for museum	....	....	....	....	52 68	3 56	....	....	56 24
Do.......do....for gallery of art	....	....	....	....	....	....	....	....	....
Grounds	1,293 50	109 88	727 17	1,615 96	515 54	49 45	....	....	4,311 50
	31,503 63	53,687 63	58,236 49	31,554 66	25,971 54	14,047 07	29,391 98	55,021 14	299,414 14
2. *General expenses.*									
Expenses of regents and committees	3,323 45	114 25	84 25	216 12	291 20	267 18	195 00	467 71	4,959 16
Lighting and heating	....	....	378 95	58 50	486 35	399 70	646 47	887 30	2,857 27
Postage	60 06	65 76	307 36	183 05	370 78	472 07	364 28	467 67	2,291 03
Transportation	36 96	85 92	266 19	517 55	851 43	1,827 91	1,913 19	1,644 43	7,143 58
Stationery	7 02	63 11	85 46	231 85	419 96	222 38	6 50	662 50	1,698 78
General Printing	294 63	68 50	199 00	134 25	1,159 06	350 42	894 19	1,094 22	4,194 27
Apparatus	1,546 47	412 71	1,799 90	899 92	148 69	844 88	203 50	427 26	6,283 33
Incidentals general	1,947 75	1,337 03	1,847 33	1,441 72	1,878 43	2,821 34	3,352 42	....	14,626 02
Salaries	1,014 49	4,265 20	4,811 58	4,548 48	3,799 92	4,299 92	4,099 92	6,733 91	33,573 42
Watchmen	....	....	....	....	....	....	367 00	367 00	734 00
	8,230 83	6,412 48	9,780 02	8,231 44	9,405 82	11,505 80	12,042 47	12,752 00	78,360 86

3. Publications, researches, and lectures.									
Smithsonian Contributions	756 00	2,956 87	2,082 87	3,662 36	3,211 76	5,736 74	8,160 04	3,773 96	30,340 60
Reports on progress of knowledge			444 00	935 91	473 82	1,616 75	139 29	83 84	3,693 61
Other publications			152 54	585 98	100 00	1,007 86	1 116 58	917 89	3,880 85
Meteorology			814 00	1,256 66	394 50	2,079 88	2,346 51	2,203 38	9,094 93
Computations		525 00	225 00		300 00				1,050 00
Investigations		100 00	50 00	90 00	110 00	75 00		10 00	435 00
Pay of lecturers			275 00	1,521 05	635 00	1,385 00	783 00	895 00	5,494 05
Illustrations and apparatus for lectures				92 22	316 49	230 13	661 84	156 37	1,457 05
Attendance and lighting for.....do		80 00	118 62	38 50	36 75	93 12	445 40	53 94	866 33
Salaries, publications, &c			150 00	1,000 00	900 00				2,050 00
	756 00	3,661 87	4,312 03	9,182 68	6,478 32	12,224 48	13,652 66	8,094 38	58,362 42
4. Library, museum, and gallery of art.									
Cost of books	545 99	365 86	2,878 14	4,225 25	2,016 90	1,098 77	841 75	2,166 50	14,139 16
General catalogue			591 58	284 97	174 88	377 25		151 35	1,580 03
Copyright	35 00		41 66	156 00		52 00			284 66
[illegible]ls to library		600 00	790 72	833 24	1,402 01	1,196 48	1,581 02		6,403 47
Salaries to library		750 00	2,499 98	1,999 92	1,999 92	2,499 96	2,499 96	3,648 98	15,898 72
Explorations, museum				150 00	50 00		250 00	250 00	700 00
Expenses of collections for museum			184 50	543 00	183 03	215 57	240 04	157 19	1,523 33
Cost of transportation for....do				103 00					103 00
Incidentals for.............do				20 00	512 06	563 01	229 71	536 54	1,861 32
Salaries for.............do				750 00	1,500 00	1,999 94	1,999 92	1,999 92	7,249 78
Purchases for gallery of art				173 30	10 00				183 30
Incidentals for..do.....do			11 25	100 00	6 00			50 00	167 25
Stereotyping						1,305 28	1,318 42	551 71	3,174 41
	580 99	1,715 86	6,997 83	9,338 68	7,854 80	9,308 26	8,960 82	9,512 19	54,269 43
	41,071 45	65,477 84	79,326 37	58,307 46	49,710 48	47,085 61	64,047 93	85,379 71	490,406 85

DR. *Fund account of*

RECEIPTS.

1846.				
July	1	To James Smithson, net proceeds of his bequest....		$515,169 00
		To interest thereon to date, paid by the United States.		242,129 00
Sept.	10	To H. W. Hilliard, Regent, over payment returned.		90
1847.				
Jan.	1	To interest on assumed debt, 1st July to 31st December, 1846, first half year....................		15,455 07
July	5	To interest on assumed debt, to 1st July, 1847, second half year..............................		15,455 07
Oct.	21	To interest on $250,000 treasury notes, to 17th August, six months............................		7,500 00
Nov.	26	To proceeds of treasury notes sold, viz: Amount of notes..	$10,000 00	
		To interest to day of sale......................	121 67	
				10,121 67
				805,830 71
1848.				
Jan.	1	To proceeds of Professor Henry's Lectures at Princeton..		1,000 00
	15	To interest on assumed debt, to 1st January, 1848, third half year		15,455 00
April	1	To interest on $240,000 treasury notes, to 17th February, 1848, six months.........................		7,200 00
	4	To George M. Dallas, chancellor, premium paid for $7,000 treasury notes		105 00
		To $7,000 treasury notes, deposit to credit of Wm. W. Seaton, chairman..............................		95 00
May	10	To proceeds of treasury notes, viz: Amount of notes.	7,000 00	
		To premium thereon...............................	140 00	
		To interest to day of sale........................	45 50	
				7,185 50
July	7	To interest on assumed debt, to 1st July, 1848, fourth half year		15,455 00
Aug.	17	To interest on $240,000 treasury notes, to 17th August, six months................................		7,200 00
	24	To proceeds of treasury notes, viz: Amount of notes.	5,000 00	
		Premium $200 00		
		Less commission.................. 12 50		
			187 50	
		To interest to day of sale........................	5 00	
				5,192 50
Oct.	16	To proceeds of treasury notes, viz: Amount of notes.	9,000 00	
		Premium $270 00		
		Less commission.................. 11 25		
			258 75	
		To interest to day of sale.........................	85 50	
				9,344 25
				68,232 25
1849.				
Jan.	5	To interest on assumed debt, fifth half year........		15,455 14
Feb.	17	To treasury notes, this amount redeemed and funded in United States six per cent. stock...............		226,000 00
	28	To interest on treasury notes, $226,000, to 17th February, six months..............................		6,780 00
April	17	To United States six er cent. stock sold, viz: Amount of stock....p.........................	16,000 00	
		Premium........................ $1,600 00		
		Less commission................ 20 00		
			1,560 00	
				17,560 00
July	2	To interest on $210,000 stock, from 17th February to 30th June, 1849..........................		4,614 24
	5	To interest on assumed debt, sixth half year........		15,455 07

the Smithsonian Institution. CR.

EXPENDITURES.

1846.			
July	1	By the United States—assumed debt	$515,169 00
Sept.	6	By Wm. W. Seaton, chairman Executive Committee—	
		From treasury United States	2,000 00
	10	Repaid by Mr. Hilliard	90
Dec.	21	From treasury United States	2,000 00
1847.			
Feb.	17	By treasury notes, proceeds of warrants on treasury United States.	250,000 00
	25	By Wm. W. Seaton, chairman Executive Committee—	
		From treasury United States	3,584 07
July	8	Second half year, interest on assumed debt	15,455 07
Oct.	21	Six months' interest on $250,000 treasury notes	7,500 00
Nov.	26	Proceeds of $10,000 notes sold	10,121 67
			805,830 71
1848.			
Jan.	1	By Professor Joseph Henry, Secretary, on account of his salary	1,000 00
	15	By Wm. W. Seaton, chairman Executive Committee, third half year's interest	15,455 00
April	1	By treasury notes, investment of so much interest on notes received this day	7,000 00
		By George M. Dallas, chancellor, balance of said interest	200 00
	4	By Wm. W. Seaton, chairman Executive Committee, deposited by Mr. Dallas	95 00
May	10	Proceeds of notes sold	7,185 50
July	5	Fourth half year's interest	15,455 00
Aug.	2	Interest on treasury notes due 17th August	7,200 00
	24	Proceeds of notes sold	5,192 50
Oct.	16	Proceeds of notes sold	9,344 25
		By profit and loss, premium paid for $7,000 treasury notes	105 00
			68,232 25
1849.			
Jan.	9	By Wm. W. Seaton, chairman Executive Committee, fifth half year's interest	15,450 14
Feb.	17	By United States six per cent. stock, loan of 1847	226,005 00
	28	By Wm. W. Seaton, chairman Executive Committee, interest on treasury notes, 17th February	6,780 00
April	17	Proceeds of stock sold	17,560 00
July	2	Interest on stock to 30th June	4,614 24
	7	Sixth half year's interest	15,455 07
Oct.	20	Proceeds of stock sold	11,287 50

DR. *Fund account of*

RECEIPTS.

1849.				
Oct.	20	To United States six per cent. stock sold, viz:		
		Amount of stock	$10,000 00	
		Premium $1,312 50		
		Less commission 25 00		
			1,287 50	
				$11,287 50
				297,151 95
1850.				
Jan.	2	To interest on $200,000 six per cent. stock, to 1st of January, six months		6,000 00
	4	To interest on assumed debt, seventh half year		15,455 07
July	2	To interest on $200,000 six per cent. stock, to 30th June, six months		6,000 00
	9	To interest on assumed debt, eighth half year		15,455 07
	27	To United States six per cent. stock sold, viz:		
		Amount of stock	10,000 00	
		Premium $1,400 00		
		Less commission 25 00		
			1,375 00	
				11,375 00
Sept.	19	To United States six per cent. stock sold, viz:		
		Amount of stock	10,000 00	
		To premium	1,600 00	
				11,600 00
Dec.	28	To Washington monument, office furniture sold to that society		50 71
	31	To interest on $180,000 six per cent. stock, to 31st December, six months		5,400 00
				71,335 85
1851.				
Jan.	20	To interest on assumed debt, ninth half year	....	15,455 07
July	7	To interest on $180,000 six per cent. stock to June 30, six months	....	5,400 00
	16	To interest on assumed debt, tenth half year	....	15,455 07
				36,310 14
1852.				
Jan.	7	To interest on $180,000 six per cent. stock to December 31, six months	....	5,400 00
	20	To interest on assumed debt, tenth half year	....	15,455 07
	26	To proceeds of six per cent. stock sold, viz: Amount of stock	180,000 00	
		Premium thereon	28,800 00	
				208,800 00
July	2	To interest on assumed debt, half year	....	15,455 07
Dec.	27	To repayment by J. Wyman on account of Smithsonian Contributions	....	5 00
	31	To interest on $208,800 from January 26 to September 11, at five per cent	....	6,554 00
	31	To interest on $208,800 from September 11 to December 31, at four per cent	....	2,575 20
				254,244 34
1853.				
Jan.	11	To interest on assumed debt, half year	....	15,455 07
Feb.	11	To repayment on account of apparatus	....	294 63
March	31	To repayment on account of Smithsonian Contributions	....	74 00
June	30	To interest on $208,800 from January 1 to June 30, at five per cent	....	5,220 00

the Smithsonian Institution. Cr.

EXPENDITURES.

Date	Item	Amount
		297,151 95
1850.		
Jan. 2	By Wm. W. Seaton, chairman Executive Committee, interest on stock to 1st January	$6,000 00
4	Seventh half year's interest	15,455 07
July 2	By Wm. W. Seaton, treasurer, interest on stock to 30th June	6,000 00
9	Eighth half year's interest	15,455 07
27	Proceeds of stock sold	11,375 00
Sept. 19	Proceeds of stock sold	11,600 00
Dec. 28	Furniture sold on account of pay of architects, &c	50 71
31	Interest on stock to 31st December, 1850	5,400 00
		71,335 85
1851.		
Jan. 20	By W. W. Seaton, treasurer, half year's interest	15,455 07
July 7	By W. W. Seaton, treasurer, interest on stock to June 30	5,400 00
16	By W. W. Seaton, treasurer, half year's interest	15,455 07
		36,310 14
1852.		
Jan. 7	By W. W. Seaton, treasurer, interest on stock to December 31	5,400 00
20	By W. W. Seaton, treasurer, half year's interest	15,455 07
26	By Corcoran & Riggs, amount in their hands, on interest	208,800 00
July 2	By W. W. Seaton, treasurer, half year's interest	15,455 07
Dec. 27	By W. W. Seaton, treasurer, repayment by Wyman	5 00
31	By W. W. Seaton, treasurer, interest paid by Corcoran & Riggs	6,554 00
31	......do..............do..........do.................do.......	2,575 20
		254,244 34
1853.		
Jan. 11	By W. W. Seaton, treasurer	15,455 07
Feb. 11	......do..............do	294 63
March 31	......do..............do	74 00
June 30	......do..............do	5,220 00
July 2	......do..............do	15,455 07
Dec. 7	......do..............do	40 00

DR. *Fund account of*

RECEIPTS.

1853.			
July 2	To interest on assumed debt, half year	....	$15,455 07
Dec. 7	To repayment on account of Smithsonian Contributions	....	40 00
31	To interest on $208,800, at five per cent., from July 1 to December 31	....	5,220 00
			41,758 77
1854.			
Jan. 12	To interest on assumed debt from July 1 to December 31, 1853	....	15,455 07
18	To Corcoran & Riggs, on account of funds in their hands	....	48,800 00
April 1	To Corcoran & Riggs, on account of funds in their hands	....	10,000 00
July 14	To interest on assumed debt from January 1 to June 30, 1854	....	15,455 07
21	To Corcoran & Riggs, interest to June 30, 1854, on funds in their hands	....	3,875 00
Aug. 7	To Corcoran & Riggs, on account of funds in their hands	....	10,000 00
Sept. 25	To Corcoran & Riggs, on account of funds in their hands	....	5,000 00
Nov. 2	To Corcoran & Riggs, on account of funds in their hands	....	10,000 00
Dec. 30	To Corcoran & Riggs, interest to December 31, 1854, on funds in their hands	....	3,401 39
	REPAYMENTS.		
Jan. 4	To sale of clock, on account of apparatus	....	400 00
14	To Minnesota Historical Society, on account of Smithsonian Contributions	....	20 00
March 13	To Coast Survey offiee, on account of apparatus	....	560 92
	To Coast Survey office, on account of transportation	....	12 27
17	To J. M. Gilliss, Navy Department, on account of transportation	....	16 62
July 29	To G. P. Putnam, sale of books, on account of Smithsonian Contributions	....	143 69
			123,140 03

the Smithsonian Institution. CR.

EXPENDITURES.

1853.			
Dec.	31	By W. W. Seaton, treasurer	$5,220 00
			41,758 77
1854.			
Jan.	12	By W. W. Seaton, treasurer	15,455 07
	18	.....do.............do.	48,800 00
April	1	.....do.............do.	10,000 00
July	14	.....do.............do.	15,455 07
	21	.....do.............do.	3,875 00
Aug.	7	.....do.............do.	10,000 00
Sept.	25	.....do.............do.	5,000 00
Nov.	2	.....do.............do.	10,000 00
Dec.	30	.....do.............do.	3,401 39
Jan.	4	.....do.............do.	400 00
	14	.....do.............do.	20 00
March	13	.....do.............do.	560 92
	13	.....do.............do.	12 27
	17	.....do.............do.	16 62
July	29	.....do.............do.	143 69
			123,140 03

The committee, after conferring with the secretary, submit the following estimates for appropriations for the year 1855:

BUILDING, FURNITURE, ETC.		
Pay on contracts	$8,000 00	
Pay of architects, &c	500 00	
Incidental expenses to building	500 00	
Furniture and fixtures	1,000 00	
Magnetic observatory	20 00	
		$10,020 00
GENERAL EXPENSES.		
Meetings of Board	600 00	
Lighting and heating	850 00	
Postage	500 00	
Transportation and exchange	1,600 00	
Stationery	350 00	
General printing	250 00	
Apparatus	500 00	
Incidentals general	600 00	
Salaries—Secretary	3,500 00	
Clerk	1,200 00	
Book-keeper	200 00	
Janitor	400 00	
Laborer	250 00	
Watchman	365 00	
Extra clerk hire	200 00	
		11,365 00
PUBLICATIONS, LECTURES, ETC.		
Smithsonian Contributions	4,500 00	
Reports on progress of knowledge	2,000 00	
Other publications	500 00	
Meteorology	2,000 00	
Computations, researches, and investigations	500 00	
Lectures	1,000 00	
		10,500 00
LIBRARY, MUSEUM, AND GALLERY OF ART.		
Library—		
Pay of assistants	2,000 00	
Cost of books and binding	3,500 00	
Incidentals to library, cases, &c	1,000 00	
Stereotyping system	100 00	
	6,600 00	
Museum—		
Salary—Assistant secretary	2,000 00	
Explorations	200 00	
Alcohol, glass jars, &c	350 00	
Assistance and labor	100 00	
Incidentals, cases, &c	1,000 00	
Catalogue	250 00	
	3,900 00	
		10,500 00
Contingencies		100 00
		42,485 00

Respectfully submitted.

J. A. PEARCE,
A. D. BACHE,
J. G. TOTTEN,
Executive Committee.

JANUARY, 1855.

REPORT OF THE BUILDING COMMITTEE.

The building committee of the Smithsonian Institution presents the following report of their operations and expenditures during the year 1854.

It was stated in the last report that the work of completing the building was commenced by Mr. Gilbert Cameron, the original contractor, under the direction of Capt. Alexander, of the engineer corps, on the 13th of June, 1853. It has been uninterruptedly prosecuted from that time to the present, and the committee are now pleased to inform the Board that the main or centre building is finished, with the exception of a few and unimportant additions.

It was, however, discovered, in the progress of the work, that many changes and additions would be required, in the plan adopted, for the better security and adaptation of the building, which would involve an additional expense; but in the present state of the Institution, and in consideration of the long delay in finishing the edifice, the committee thought it best to press on the work.

The main building, which is 200 feet long, 50 feet wide, and 60 feet from the basement floor to the upper ceiling, is divided into three stories. The first story consists of the basement, separated into two large rooms, and the space between them for the heating apparatus. The two apartments are intended for store rooms and other purposes connected with the mechanical operations of the Institution.

The second story consists of one large room, 200 feet long, 50 feet wide, and 25 feet high, the ceiling of which is supported by two rows of columns extending the whole length; at the middle of the space corresponding to the principal entrances, are two wing walls, by which, with the addition of screens, the whole space may be divided into two large rooms, with a hall extending across the building between them. This story may be used for a library or a museum, or for both, as the wants of the Institution may require. It is finished in a simple but chaste style, and has received general commendation. Indeed it is, perhaps, in appearance, one of the most imposing rooms in this country, apart from adaptation to its purposes.

The floor through the middle part is formed of cut stone, that of the other parts is of wood, which, resting on the arches beneath, without space between to contain air, is considered sufficiently fire-proof, and not subject to dampness from the variation of temperature and humidity of the atmosphere.

The upper story is divided into three apartments without pillars, a lecture room of about 100 feet in length in the middle, and two rooms, each 50 feet square, on either side. These rooms are intended for collections. The one on the west may be connected with the library, and that on the east with the museum. The latter has been fitted up with cases in which to deposit the collection of apparatus presented to the Institution by Dr. Hare, the other with a separate case to contain the personal effects of James Smithson. The lecture room, the optical and acoustic properties of which are probably unsurpassed by any apartment intended for the same purpose in the United States, occupies one-half of the upper story of the main building, besides a portion of the front and rear towers; its precise length is 96 feet, and extreme width 62 feet. It will comfortably seat 1,500 persons, and, when crowded, will contain upwards of 2,000. The apartments on each side of the lecture room, besides being fitted up with cases for books, specimens, or apparatus, can be used for meetings of associations, while large assemblies for public discussions can be accommodated in the lecture room.

The whole arrangement of the upper part of the building is made with a view to afford facilities for meetings of large associations which have for their object the promotion, diffusion, or application of knowledge. If at any time the space now occupied by the lecture room should be required for other purposes, the seats and gallery may be removed and the partition walls which are unconnected with the roof may be taken down and the whole upper story converted into one large hall. Besides the main building just finished, the whole edifice consists of two wings, two connecting ranges, and a front and rear projection at the middle on which towers are erected.

The whole amount paid on account of the building, the grounds, and furniture is $299,414 14. The amount paid during the past year is $55,021 14, of which $13,000 is on the work previously done under the direction of the former architect. In order to secure the faithful performance of the work, fifteen per cent. has been withheld from the monthly payments until the whole should be finished. The sum which, on this account, is still due to the contractor, has not yet definitely been ascertained. According to an addendum to the original contract, the Regents were at liberty to make any changes in the building or in the time of its completion which they might deem necessary, and the contractor should receive pro rata, according to the prices agreed upon, for work so executed, and reasonable compensation for damages which might be sustained.

The following letter from the architect will give additional information:

WASHINGTON, D. C., *December* 30, 1854.

GENTLEMEN: I have the honor to report to you that the work on your building has been prosecuted during the past year without intermission, and that the central portion of it is now nearly completed.

There are some small matters yet to be attended to, and a few trifling repairs and alterations yet to be made in the other parts of the building. These can all be completed in a few weeks.

I am happy to state that the building has been completed without any accident, either to the workmen employed, or to the building itself, and that in my opinion, every part of the work has been substantially done.

I have devoted much study to the plans which have been executed, and given the work my personal supervision nearly every day.

An examination of the rooms of the central building will impress one with the idea of great simplicity. There is not much ornament, but still enough, as I think, to enable the building to do its duty with grace and dignity.

The lower hall is equally adapted to the purposes of a museum or a library. The lecture room is the best which it was possible to make within the walls of the building, and now that it has been completed, I am happy in being enabled to state that were it to be made over again, I would not alter any of its essential features.

I would not be doing justice to Professor Henry were I not to acknowledge the great assistance I have received from him in arranging the details of this room. I am free to confess that during the progress of the work he has given me suggestions which have materially improved my plans.

It will be seen by an examination of the payments which have been made to the contractor, that the cost of completing the building considerably exceeds the estimates which I prepared before the work was begun. This is due in part to the rise in the prices of materials and labor, but principally to the execution of many improvements which were not originally contemplated, but which it was thought best to make during the prosecution of the work. These improvements were the sewers for drainage; the cisterns for supplying water; the substitution of stone for iron stairs; the making of new sashes for many of the windows; the strengthening and in part re-construction of the roof of the main building, putting in copper gutter, and leaders on the towers, besides other alterations and additions tending to swell the cost of the work.

Hoping that my efforts to improve your building will meet you approbation, as well as that of the Board of Regents,

I am, gentlemen, very respectfully, your obedient servant,

B. S. ALEXANDER,
Architect Smithsonian Institution.

To the Building Committee of the Smithsonian Institution.

A full statement of the amount due the contractor cannot be given until a more precise estimate of all the items of work done under the direction of the architect has been made.

Respectfully submitted,

RICHARD RUSH,
WILLIAM H. ENGLISH,
JOSEPH HENRY,
Building Committee.

JOURNAL OF PROCEEDINGS

OF THE

BOARD OF REGENTS

OF

THE SMITHSONIAN INSTITUTION.

NINTH ANNUAL SESSION.

WEDNESDAY, January 3, 1855.

In accordance with a resolution of the Board of Regents of the Smithsonian Institution, fixing the time of the beginning of their annual meeting on the first Wednesday of January of each year, the Board met this day in the Regents' room.

Present: Messrs. Bache, Berrien, Douglas, Mason, Pearce, Rush, Towers, and the Secretary.

In the absence of the Chancellor Mr. Pearce was called to the chair.

The Secretary informed the Board of the re-election by joint resolution of Congress of Hon. Rufus Choate, of Massachusetts, and Hon. Gideon Hawley, of New York, as regents of the Smithsonian Institution for six years ensuing.

On motion of Mr. Mason the Board adjourned to meet on Friday, January 12, at 10 o'clock, a. m., and the Secretary was requested to inform the absent members of the Board that the report of the Select Committee on the distribution of the income would then be taken up for consideration.

FRIDAY, January 12, 1855.

An adjourned meeting of the Board of Regents of the Smithsonian Institution was held on Friday, January 12, at 10 o'clock a. m.

Present: The Chancellor, Roger B. Taney, Messrs. Bache, Berrien, Choate, Douglas, English, Hawley, Mason, Meacham, Pearce, Rush, Stuart, Totten, Towers, Professor Henry, Secretary, and Mr. Seaton, Treasurer.

The minutes of the last meeting were read and approved.

A communication from J. W. Simonton, Washington editor of the New York Daily Times, and S. Thayer, of the New York Evening Post, asking permission to attend the meetings of the Board to report its proceedings, was read.

Mr. Meacham moved that the request be granted, which was lost.

The order of the day being the consideration of the report and resolutions of the Select Committee on the distribution of the income, the first resolution was read, namely:

Resolved, That the seventh resolution passed by the Board of Regents on the 26th of January, 1847, requiring an equal division of the income between the active operations and the museum and library when the buildings are completed, be and it is hereby repealed.

Remarks were made by Messrs. Choate, Pearce, Douglas, and Berrien.

On motion of Mr. Mason the yeas and nays were ordered.

The question was then taken on the adoption of the first resolution as follows:

YEAS.—The Chancellor, Roger B. Taney, Messrs. Bache, Berrien, Hawley, Mason, Pearce, Rush, and Totten—8.

NAYS.—Messrs. Choate, Douglas, English, Meacham, Stuart, and Towers—6.

The second resolution was then read:

Resolved. That hereafter the annual appropriations shall be apportioned specifically among the different objects and operations of the Institution in such manner as may, in the judgment of the regents, be necessary and proper for each, according to its intrinsic importance, and a compliance in good faith with the law.

The question being taken on this resolution it was adopted.

YEAS.—The Chancellor, Roger B. Taney, Messrs. Bache, Berrien, Hawley, Mason, Pearce, Rush, Totten, Towers—9.

NAYS.—Messrs. Choate, Douglas, English, Meacham, and Stuart—5.

Mr. Meacham then offered the following resolution, which was the first reported by him in his minority report, namely:

Resolved, That a compliance in good faith with the letter and spirit of the charter of the Smithsonian Institution, requires that a large proportion of the income of the Institution should be appropriated "for the gradual formation of a library composed of valuable works pertaining to all departments of human knowledge."

The question being taken on this resolution it was lost.

YEAS.—Messrs. Choate, Douglas, Meacham, and Stuart—4.

NAYS.—The Chancellor, Roger B. Taney, Messrs. Bache, Berrien, English, Hawley, Mason, Rush, Pearce, and Totten—9.

Mr. Meacham's second resolution was then read, namely:

Resolved, That the expenditures for the library shall be made under the direction of a "library committee" of three members, to be annually elected by the Board of Regents from members not upon the Executive Committee, or upon other committees which may be appointed to superintend the affairs of other departments or objects of the Institution.

The question being taken on this resolution it was lost.

YEAS.—Messrs. Choate, Douglas, and Meacham—3.

NAYS.—The Chancellor, Roger B. Taney, Messrs. Bache, Berrien, English, Hawley, Mason, Pearce, Rush, Stuart, and Totten—10.

On motion of Mr. Pearce the following resolution was adopted.

Resolved, That a committee of three be appointed by the Chancellor to confer with a Committee of the Establishment as to suitable means of communication between the two bodies, and to report thereon at a subsequent meeting of the regents.

The Chancellor appointed Messrs. Mason, Douglas, and Totten.

A communication from Gilbert A. Cameron was read; which, on motion, was referred to the Building Committee.

The Treasurer then made a statement of the condition of the finances of the Institution; which was referred to the Executive Committee.

The Board then adjourned to meet on Saturday, 13th January, at 10 o'clock.

SATURDAY, JANUARY 13, 1855.

An adjourned meeting of the Board of Regents of the Smithsonian Institution was held on Saturday, January 13, at ten o'clock, a. m.

Present: The Chancellor, Roger B. Taney, Messrs. Bache, Berrien, Choate, English, Hawley, Mason, Meacham, Pearce, Rush, Totten.

The minutes of the last meeting were read and approved.

Mr. Pearce, in behalf of the Executive Committee, presented the estimate of appropriations for the year 1855, which, on his motion, was laid on the table for the present.

Mr. Pearce, in behalf of the Executive Committee, presented the following report in relation to the case of Mr. Blodget, which had been referred to that committee by the Board.

REPORT.

At a meeting of the Board of Regents held Saturday, July 8, 1854, the Executive Committee was authorized to investigate and settle the business presented to the Board by the Secretary, in reference to the adjustment of the claims of Mr. Lorin Blodget.

The committee having investigated the matter referred to them, presents the following report in part

Mr. Blodget was employed by the Secretary of the Institution to aid him by such labors in relation to the meteorological observations under the direction of the Smithsonian Institution as the Secretary might assign. The rates of compensation for these services were fixed from time to time by the same officer, and Mr. Blodget is entitled to no other compensation than that paid to him. His footing in the Institution was simply that of a temporary employé of the Secretary, in whose hands rested the determination of his duties, pay, and duration of service. Employed and paid for these services in connexion with the meteorological operations, the fruit of his labors belong exclusively to the Institution.

In addition to these payments the committee is prepared on receiving satisfactory statements or vouchers from Mr. Blodget of reasonable expenses incurred during any journeys he may have made with the consent of the Secretary for objects connected with his duties in meteorology in the Institution, to refund the amount, as also any moneys which may appear to the satisfaction of the committee to have been paid out by him and not already repaid for clerical or other services connected with the meteorological observations of the Smithsonian Institution, and for which an equivalent advantage has been recived.

J. A. PEARCE,
JOS. G. TOTTEN, } *Executive Committee.*
A. D. BACHE,

Communications and a memorial from Mr. Blodget to the Board were then read and ordered to lie on the table.

The report of the Executive Committee was then adopted unanimously.

It being stated to the Board by Mr. Choate on behalf of Mr. C. C. Jewett that he did not design, for reasons stated by him, to ask the action of the regents at their present meeting on his memorial of the 3d July last, communicated to the Board through the Secretary, Mr. Mason moved that the said paper be returned by the Secretary to Mr. Jewett.

On motion the memorial to the Board was then read.

Mr. Choate then requested permission in behalf of Mr. Jewett to withdraw the memorial, which was granted.

The Secretary then stated to the Board that he had deemed it his duty since its last session to remove Mr. Charles C. Jewett from the office of assistant to the Secretary. He deeply regretted the necessity which he had been under to exercise this authority, declared to be vested in him by the Board, and for the present he rested his reasons for the act on the character of a paper submitted by Mr. Jewett to the select committee on the distribution of the income, and upon the opinion in regard to that paper expressed by the committee to which it was submitted.

Mr. Pearce offered the following:

The Secretary having stated to the Board that since the last meeting of the Regents in 1854 he had removed Mr. Jewett, under the authority declared to be vested in him by the resolution of July 8, 1854.

Resolved, That while the Board regret the necessity of Mr. Jewett's removal, they approve of the act of the Secretary.

Resolved, That this approval by the Board is not deemed by them to be essential to the validity of the act of the Secretary in so removing Mr. Jewett.

The Board then adjourned to meet on Monday, January 15, at ten o'clock.

MONDAY, January 15, 1855.

The Board of Regents met to-day at ten o'clock.

Present: The Chancellor, Roger B. Taney, Messrs. Bache, Berrien, Douglas, Hawley, Mason, Pearce, Rush, Towers and Totten.

The Chancellor, took the chair, and the minutes of the last meeting were read and approved.

Mr. Pearce's resolutions offered at the last meeting on Saturday were then taken up.

The question being taken on the first resolution, it was adopted. Yeas.—The Chancellor, Roger B. Taney, Messrs. Bache, Berrien, Hawley, Mason, Pearce, Rush, Totten—8.

Nays.—Messrs. Douglas, Towers—2.

The second resolution was then taken up and adopted.

Yeas.—The Chancellor, Roger B. Taney, Messrs. Bache, Berrien, Hawley, Mason, Pearce, Rush, Totten—8.

Nays.—Messrs. Douglas, Towers—2.

On motion of Mr. Rush, Mr. John T. Towers was elected to fill the vacancy in the Building Committee.

The report of the Executive Committee, making estimates of appropriations for the year 1855, &c., was then taken up and adopted.

On motion of General Totten, the following resolution was adopted:

Resolved, That in case the sum required for the completion of the Smithsonian building should exceed the amount appropriated for the same, that the Building Committee have authority to pay for any unavoidable excess out of funds on deposit to the credit of the Institution.

The report of the Building Committee was then read, and on motion adopted.

A memorial and printed pamphlet from John Lord, of Portland, Maine, was read and ordered to lie on the table.

The Board then adjourned to meet on Saturday, January 27, at ten o'clock a. m.

WASHINGTON, *January* 27, 1855.

An adjourned meeting of the Board of Regents of the Smithsonian Institution was held on Saturday, January 27, 1855, in the regents' room.

Present: The Chancellor, Roger B. Taney, Messrs. Bache, Pearce, Stuart, Towers, Totten.

The minutes of the last meeting were read and approved.

The following communication was read:

HOUSE OF REPRESENTATIVES,
Washington, January 26, 1855.

SIR: I am instructed by the special committee of the House of Representatives, raised in conformity with the accompanying resolution, to request you to inform the Board of Regents of the Smithsonian Institution that the committee is ready to proceed to the discharge of its duties—and that any communication the Board may think proper to make will be most respectfully entertained.

The committee will meet on Thursday, February 1, at half past 7 o'clock, p. m., in the rooms of the Hon. W. H. Wittee, at the National Hotel.

The presence of an authorized representation of the Board, during the investigation of the matters referred to the committee, would aid us in the performance of the duty imposed by the order of the House of Representatives.

Very respectfully, your obedient servant,
CHARLES W. UPHAM, *Chairman.*

Professor Jos. HENRY,
Secretary of the Smithsonian Institution.

Copy of resolution of House enclosed.

IN THE HOUSE OF REPRESENTATIVES U. S.—*January* 17, 1855.

On motion of Mr. Meacham,

Resolved, That the letter of Hon. Rufus Choate, resigning his place as Regent of the Smithsonian Institution, be referred to a select committee of five, and printed; and that said committee be directed to inquire and report to this House whether the Smithsonian Institution has been managed, and its funds expended, in accordance with the law establishing the Institution; and whether any additional legislation be necessary to carry out the designs of its founders, and that said committee have power to send for persons and papers.

The Speaker thereupon appointed Mr. Upham, of Massachusetts; Mr. Witte, of Pennsylvania; Mr. Taylor, of Tennessee; Mr. Wells, of Wisconsin; and Mr. Puryear, of North Carolina, the said committee.

On motion of Mr. Pearce, it was—

Resolved, That a committee of five be appointed by the Chancellor to represent the Board of Regents before the committee of the House of Representatives.

The Chancellor appointed Messrs. Pearce, Mason, Bache, Rush, and the Secretary, as the committee.

The Secretary laid before the Board his annual report.

Communications, and a bill of charges from Lorin Blodget, were read, and, on motion of Mr. Stuart, referred to the Executive Committee.

Communication from G. Cameron, the contractor for the building, was read, and referred to the Building Committee.

Communication from J. M. Stanley, artist, offering to dispose of his Indian Gallery, was read, and, after remarks, on motion it was—

Resolved, That the Secretary be instructed respectfully to decline the offer made to the Board by Mr. Stanley.

A communication relative to the Geographical and Commercial Gazette was read, and referred to the Executive Committee.

The Board then adjourned to meet on Saturday, February 10, at 10 o'clock, a. m.

WASHINGTON, *February* 10, 1855.

Present: Messrs. Bache, Mason, Pearce, Totten, and the Secretary

There being no quorum, adjourned to Saturday, February 17.

WASHINGTON, *February* 17, 1855.

Messrs. English, Pearce, Totten, Towers, and the Secretary present. There being no quorum, adjourned to meet on Saturday, February 24.

WASHINGTON, *February* 24, 1855.

An adjourned meeting of the Board of Regents was held on Saturday, February 24, 1855, at 10 o'clock a. m.

Present: The Chancellor, Roger B. Taney, Messrs. Bache, Douglas, English, Pearce, Totten, Seaton, treasurer, and the Secretary.

A report entitled "Report of the Hon. James Meacham, of the special committee of the Board of Regents of the Smithsonian Institution, on the distribution of the income of the Smithsonian fund," &c., was presented, and on motion laid on the table.

On motion of Mr. English, the following resolution was adopted:

Resolved, That three persons be appointed a committee of finance, who shall inquire into the safety and propriety of the present investment of the funds of the Institution, not in the Treasury of the United States, and who shall have the authority to withdraw the said fund from the present place of deposit, and invest them otherwise in the name of the regents of the Institution.

The chancellor appointed Messrs. English, Pearce and Mason as the committee.

The following report was read:

The committee to whom was referred the resolution of the "establishment," proposing a conference by committee with the Board of Regents, for the purpose of determining the mode of communication between the establishment and the Board of Regents, submit the following report:

That they have met and conferred with the committee appointed for that purpose by the establishment, and have, after consultation, agreed upon the following resolutions, to be reported by the committees to their respective constituencies, and the committee recommend that they be adopted by the Board of Regents, and made a part of the by-laws.

1. The general communication between the Institution and the Board of Regents shall be made through their common secretary.

2. The secretary will regularly communicate to each body all such acts of either as may concern the other respectively, or may require their joint action.

3. When either body may desire any special communication with the other, it will propose a conference by committee.

All which is respectfully submitted.

J. M. MASON, *Chairman.*

JANUARY, 1855.

The report of the committee was approved.

The following resolution was offered by Mr. Douglas, and adopted by the Board:

Resolved, That all correspondence of this Institution with any person or society shall be conducted by the Secretary, and no assistant or employee shall write or receive any official letter or communication pertaining to the affairs of the Institution, except under the authority and by the direction of the Secretary, and all such correspondence shall be duly registered and recorded in such manner as the Secretary shall direct.

The Board then adjourned to meet at the call of the Secretary.

APPENDIX

TO THE

REPORT OF THE REGENTS

OF THE

SMITHSONIAN INSTITUTION.

Report on American Explorations in the years 1853 *and* 1854. *By S. F. Baird, Assistant Secretary of the Smithsonian Institution.*

The report on this subject for 1853, though ready for publication at the time of printing the last Annual Report of the Smithsonian Institution, was kept back until the present year, as most of the expeditions mentioned in it were still in the field at the close of 1853, and of many no definite intelligence had been received. Nearly all of these have, however, returned; and their officers are now busily engaged in preparing their reports. I therefore shall present the principal events for 1853 and 1854 in one narrative, without always distinguishing those of each year.

The number of important scientific explorations embraced in this period, mark it conspicuously in the history of American discovery. Most of these are due to the appropriation for the survey of the China seas and Behring's Straits, and that for a survey of the several routes for a railroad to the Pacific, (although many more private expeditions were set on foot,) in addition to the regular operations of the United States and Mexican Boundary Survey, whose labors during the past years were in continuation of those commenced before. Many reports of explorations, commenced or completed prior to 1853, have been published during this period, and will be noticed in their proper places.

With scarcely an exception, every expedition of any magnitude has received more or less aid from the Smithsonian Institution. This has consisted in the supplying of instructions for making observations and collections in meteorology and natural history, and of information as to particular desiderata; in the preparation, in part, of the meteorological, magnetical, and natural history outfit, including the selection and purchase of the necessary apparatus and instruments; in the nomination and training of persons to fill important positions in the scientific corps; in the reception of the collections made, and their reference to individuals competent to report upon them; and in employing skillful and trained artists to make accurate delineations of the new or unfigured species. Much of the apparatus supplied to the different parties was invented or adapted by the Institution for this special purpose, and used for the first time, with results surpassing the most sanguine expectations

I shall now proceed to present such facts as may be necessary to a full understanding of the history and progress of these several expeditions, considering first those having North America for their field.

United States and Mexican Boundary Survey.

The operations on the eastern end of the boundary line, as originally established, were brought to a successful termination towards the end of 1853, by the energy and skill of Major Emory, and all the parties returned to Washington by the beginning of 1854. After the purchase of a portion of Sonora from Mexico, it became necessary to make a new survey of the Mexican boundary; and Major Emory having been appointed commissioner, he completed his preparations in a very short time, and proceeded to the field of his labors, arriving at El Paso, the initial point, the beginning of December, 1854. From this point he will proceed westward, expecting to meet half-way the sub-party of Lieutenant Michler, who starts eastward from Fort Yuma. Major Emory is accompanied by Dr. Kennerly as surgeon and naturalist, from whom much may be expected in the development of the natural history of the country, with the facilities which Major Emory has always furnished to the scientific corps of his several explorations. The natural history collections brought back from the lower Rio Grande, by Major Emory, were very extensive and important.

Survey of routes for a Railroad to the Pacific.

Just before the adjournment of Congress, in March, 1853, an appropriation of $150,000 was made, to defray the expenses of the survey of various routes along which it was supposed that a railroad, extending between the Mississippi river and the Pacific, might be constructed. By virtue of the authority committed to him by Congress, the Secretary of War proceeded to organize six parties, for the exploration of four main routes leading to the Pacific; and of these, Gov. I. I. Stevens, Lieutenant R. S. Williamson, Captain Gunnison, Lieutenant A. W. Whipple, and, at a later period, Lieutenant J. G. Parke and Captain J. Pope, were severally placed in command. All these parties were abundantly provided with the apparatus and instructions, written or printed, necessary to enable them to make copious collections in natural history, and observations in physical science. Each party (excepting the two last, which were not so fully organized) went accompanied by a surgeon, zoölogist, botanist, mineralogist, geologist, and a civil engineer; though, occasionally, the same person united several of these functions. The parties set out for their several labors in the following order and organization.

1. *Northern route under Governor I. I. Stevens.*

This portion of the survey was first in the field and most extensive in its organization. It was placed under command of Governor I. I. Stevens, lately of the corps of the United States engineers, and assistant in charge of the Coast Survey, who had been appointed governor of the new Territory of Washington, and was now about proceeding to the field of his duties. The survey was divided into two main bodies, one to proceed towards the Rocky mountains from the east, the other to cross the isthmus and start in from the Pacific side to meet the former. Each of these parties was again subdivided into sub-parties, the progress and superintendence of which is as follows :

Governor Stevens, with the main party, proceeded from St. Paul, on the 8th of June, 1853, westward to Fort Union, a trading post belonging to the American Fur Company, situated at the mouth of the Yellow Stone river; thence up the Missouri river to the mouth of Milk river; and up the valley of Milk river, nearly due west, to Fort Benton, another trading post of the American Fur Company near the Falls of the Missouri, where they arrived September 1.

From Fort Benton Governor Stevens crossed to the mission of St. Mary's; thence, by the Cœur d'Alene, to Fort Colville; thence to Fort Vancouver and Olympia.

Lieutenant Saxton started from Fort Vancouver, and proceeded up the Columbia river, by water, as far as the Dalles; from the Dalles, up the valley of the Columbia, by land, to Walla-walla, a trading post occupied by the Hudson's Bay Company; thence in a northeasterly direction to the western extremity of Kalispe lake, crossing Lewis's fork of the Columbia, forty miles from Walla-walla, and Clarke's fork, near the outlet of Kalispe lake; thence along the northern shore of this lake and Clarke's fork of the Columbia, in a southeasterly direction, recrossing the river near the mouth of the Bitter Root, one of its branches; and thence nearly due south to the Flathead village of St. Mary's, situated on the St. Mary's fork of the Bitter Root, thirty miles south of the mouth of the Hellgate river. He proceeded up the valley of the Hellgate or Blackfoot river and the Foospinney, one of its branches, to the Blackfoot pass in the Rocky mountains. This pass is situated about ninety miles from Fort Benton, near the sources of the Teton and Medicine rivers. He crossed the mountains through this pass, and met Governor Stevens and his party at Fort Benton. From Fort Benton he went down the Missouri river to St. Louis—in a keel-boat as far as Fort Leavenworth.

Lieutenant Donelson, with the main party, passed over Lieutenant Saxton's route from Fort Benton to Fort Vancouver. Dr. Suckley went down the river, from St. Mary's valley, in a canoe, from the Flathead village to Fort Colville. Captain McClellan explored the country on both sides of the Cascade range northward from Vancouver; he met Governor Stevens's parties at Fort Colville, and then continued his expedition as far north as our northern boundary line. Lieutenant Mullen went from Fort Benton to St. Mary's village by the Jefferson fork of Missouri. He remained at St. Mary's village during the winter, continuing his explorations as far north as the Flathead lake, and southward to Fort Hall. After continuing in the mountains for nearly a year, he returned to Olympia in the winter of 1854–'55. Lieutenant Macfeely returned from St. Mary's village to Fort Vancouver by the southern Nez Percé trail down the valley of Kooskooskie and Little Salmon rivers. Mr. Tinkham, civil engineer, accompanied Governor Stevens's party as far as St. Mary's village, and recrossed the Rocky mountains to Fort

Benton, and surveyed the Marias pass, situated to the north of the Blackfoot or Cadot's pass, and proceeded to Olympia, Washington Territory, by a new route through some pass in the Cascade mountains. Lieutenant Grover was to make an accurate survey of the Missouri river from the Falls to the mouth of the Yellow Stone, and then across the Rocky mountains, in mid-winter on snow shoes, by the route Lieutenant Saxton followed. His object was to test the climate in the mountains during the most unfavorable season of the year. Mr. Doty was left at Fort Benton to make meteorological and other observations during the winter. He remained until the autumn of 1854, when he proceeded to Washington Territory, and joined Governor Stevens.

Most of these parties were provided with the means of making observations and collections in natural and physical science, and all have faithfully carried out their instructions.

Dr. Suckley, surgeon and naturalist to the main party, accompanied Governor Stevens as far as the Flathead village, and thence down the river, as described.

Dr. J. G. Cooper acted in the same capacity in connexion with Captain McClellan's expedition. Both these gentlemen, aided by the officers and assistants of the command, were occupied the whole time in making extensive collections of the highest interest. Lieutenant Donelson, with the party under his command, in proceeding up the Missouri to Fort Union, spared no exertion to accomplish the same object, and gathered a large collection of plants and of specimens in alcohol.

Dr. Evans, United States geologist for Oregon, accompanied by Dr. B. F. Shumard, visited the Mauvaises Terres of Nebraska, in connexion with Governor Stevens's exploration, and collected a very extensive series of the fossil mammals and chelonians of that region, embracing several species not previously found by him. He arrived in Oregon late in 1853, and has since been engaged in completing his regular explorations of the geology of Oregon and Washington, with very important results.

Since the completion of the survey, Dr. Suckley and Dr. Cooper have continued their explorations most energetically. The former spent several months at Steilacoom, on Puget's Sound, as United States surgeon of the post, and then went to the Dalles, from which point he accompanied a party sent to Fort Boisé, to chastise some Indians. Dr. Cooper has been most of his time at Shoal-water bay. Both of these gentlemen have collected and sent home, from their respective stations, very valuable and extensive series of animals and plants, with important notes on their habits and peculiarities.

2. *Survey of the route near the 38th parallel, under the late Captain Gunnison, and continued by Lieutenant Beckwith.*

The party of Captain J. W. Gunnison originally consisted of himself in command, Lieutenant E. G. Beckwith, commissary and quartermaster; R. N. Kern, topographer and draughtsman; J. H. Peters and T. L. Homans, assistant engineers; Dr. Scheel, surgeon and mineralogist; F. Kreutzfeldt, botanist and draughtsman; together with an escort of thirty men, commanded by Captain Morris, United States rifles. The party was organized at camp Shawnee Reservation, on the 20th of June, and proceeded up the Sandy Hill fork of the Kansas, and then across to the Arkansas, and up to the Abispah. After exploring this region, they crossed over on the Trincheres, and next to the Huerfano, thence across the mountains to the head of the Sangre del Cristo Pass, and down the valley of this stream to Fort Massachusetts. From this point they passed up the valley of San Luis, through Cooachotope pass, and down to Grand river of the Colorado; along it, past the Uncompagre and Aoonakara. Beyond this they struck the old Spanish trail, and after crossing Green river left it and passed through Wahsatch pass, for Sevier river, and down this river nearly to Sevier lake. While exploring the regions about this lake, nearly the whole of the scientific corps, consisting of Captain Gunnison, Mr. Kern, Mr. Kreutzfeldt, and several other persons, were surprised by a party of the Pah Utahs, on the morning of the 26th of October, 1853, and all put to death. Science has much to deplore in the loss of these gentlemen, all so well known previously for their intrepid zeal as explorers: Captain Gunnison, in connexion with Captain Stansbury's survey of Great Salt Lake; and Mr. Kern as the companion of Colonel Frémont, Captain Simpson, Captain Sitgreaves, Lt. Parke, and others. Mr. Kreutzfeldt was also a member of the memorable party of Colonel Frémont, which met with such sad disasters in the region of his latest exploration.

Most of the instruments and papers of the party were captured by the Indians, but afterwards given up; and the command devolving on Lieutenant Beckwith, he spent the winter at Salt Lake city, and in the spring of 1854 proceeded across to California by a new route. He returned in September, and is now engaged in completing his report. He brought with him a valuable collection of specimens.

3. *Survey of the route near the 35th parallel of latitude, under Lieutenant Whipple.*

The third railroad party was commanded by Lieutenant A. W. Whipple, formerly connected with the survey of the Mexican boundary. His party consisted of Lieutenant J. C. Ives, principal assistant; Dr. J. M. Bigelow, surgeon and botanist; Jules Marcou, geologist; Dr. C. B. R. Kennerly, surgeon and zoölogist; H. B. Möllhausen, topographer and artist; Hugh Campbell, astronomer; Albert H. Campbell, engineer; together with Messrs. White, Garner, Hutton, Sherburne, and Parke. Lieutenant Ives, with Dr. Kennerly and Mr. Hugh Campbell, were detailed to go by Indianola and San Antonio, to El Paso, for the purpose of securing certain instruments left there, after which they joined Lieutenant Whipple at Albuquerque. The main party went from Fort Smith mainly up the Canadian, and across the Llano Estacado, to Anton Chico. Here it divided, Mr. Albert Campbell, with the main party, proceeding directly to Albuquerque, *via* Laguna; Lieutenant Whipple pursuing a somewhat different route; and all the parties, including that of Lieutenant Ives, meeting at Albuquerque, on the 26th of October. From Albuquerque they went over to the Little Colorado, *via* the Pueblo of Zuñi; next by way of the San Francisco mountains to Bill Williams's fork; down this stream to the Colorado, then up the Mohave, and across to San Francisco. The party returned to the United States in April, 1854, with the exception of Dr. Bigelow, the botanist, who remained a few months longer exploring the Sierra Nevada.

The collections in every department were very large, and included many new and rare species.

4. *Survey of the several partial routes on the Pacific side under Lieutenant Williamson.*

The fourth of the principal government parties for the survey of the Pacific railroad route is that of Lieutenant R. S. Williamson, accompanied by Lieutenant J. G. Parke as assistant, William P. Blake as geologist, and Dr. A. L. Heermann as surgeon and naturalist, together with a skillful artist and civil engineer. The escort was commanded by Lieutenant Stoneman. The party started from San Francisco and passed up the San Joaquin and Tulare valley, and explored the region about Walker's Pass, and along the Mohave over to the Colorado. They also examined the Tejon Pass, the Canada de las Uvas, the Cajon, the Gorgona and Caliente passes of the coast range. Lieutenant Williamson returned in the latter part of 1854, and is now engaged in preparing his report, to include notices of many interesting collections in natural history.

5. *Survey near the 32d parallel of latitude, western end, under Lieutenant Parke.*

After the completion of the survey of Lieutenant Williamson, Lieutenant Parke, accompanied by Lieutenant Stoneman and Dr. Heermann, started from San Diego in January, 1854, and proceeded by way of Warner's Ranch to camp Yuma at the mouth of the Gila, and thence up this river to the Pima and Maricopa villages, thence to Tucson, Fort Webster, Doña Ana and Trentera. This point was reached on the 24th of March, the entire distance from San Diego having been traversed with wagons in about sixty days. Here the exploration terminated, and the party proceeded rapidly home *via* San Antonio, reaching Washington in May, 1854.

In October, 1854, Lieutenant Parke again returned to California for the purpose of making further surveys. He was accompanied by Mr. Albert H. Campbell, civil engineer; Dr. Antisele, surgeon and geologist; H. Campbell, G. G. Garner, and N. H. Hutton, assistants. Lieutenant Parke will organize his expedition at Benicia, with all possible dispatch, and proceed to explore the Salinas river, from the Bay of Monterey to its sources, with a view of fiuding a practicable passage through the coast range into the Mohave basin, or into the valley of Los Angeles. Further examinations will also be made of the Mohave river, in the vicinity of the Colorado, on Lieutenant Whipple's route. Returning thence, this party will start from San Diego and go across to El Paso, on the Rio Grande, by the route south of the Gila.

6. *Survey near the 32d parallel of latitude, eastern end, under Captain John Pope.*

Captain Pope, accompanied by Lieutenant Garrard, Captain Taflin, and Dr. Diffenderfer, with an escort under the command of Lieutenant Marshall, left El Paso on the 20th of February, for Preston, Texas, for the purpose of completing the survey of the 32d parallel, prosecuted at the western end by Lieutenant Parke. The line followed was nearly straight except through the Guadalupe mountains. The Pecos was passed near the mouth of Delaware creek, and the Llano Estacado traversed for a distance of one hundred and twenty-five miles. From this the party proceeded *via* head waters of Brazos and Colorado, arriving in Preston about the middle of May. The natural history collections made were very extensive and valuable, including, as they did, a portion of those gathered by Dr. T. C. Henry, U. S. A., in New Mexico, during a period of several years. Captain Pope has since returned to the Llano Estacado, for the purpose of experimenting upon Artesian borings in the desert. He is accompanied by Dr. G. G. Shumard, as surgeon and geologist, well known in connexion with explorations by Captain Marcy.

Exploration of Colonel Frémont.

In order to test the depth of winter snow along the central route traversed by Captain Gunnison and Messrs. Beale and Heap, Colonel Frémont started late in the season, and on the 25th of November was still below the mouth of the Huerfano. Entering the mountain region on the Huerfano on the 3d of December, he emerged from it, and reached the Little Salt settlement on the 9th of February, having found but four inches of snow in the Coochetope Pass on the 14th of December. From Parowan he proceeded to San Francisco, and has since then been engaged in preparing a report on the results of his trip.

Expedition of Messrs. Beale and Heap.

Lieutenant E. F. Beale, superintendent of Indian affairs in California, about to return to the scenes of his philanthropic labors among the Indians, in the vicinity of Tejon Pass, embraced the occasion to make the journey over land by the central route. He was in company with Mr. G. H. Heap. They left Westport, Missouri, on the 6th of May, and proceeded to Fort Atkinson on the Arkansas, crossing the head waters of the Osage and the Neosho. From this point they passed up the Arkansas to the Huerfano, and proceeded to the Mormon settlements near Little Salt lake and the vegas of Santa Clara, very nearly on the route pursued by Captain Gunnison, excepting that they went up the Huerfano instead of the Abispah. From the vegas they pursued the old Spanish trail leading from Abiquiu across the desert of the Mohave, and thence to Los Angeles, where they arrived on the 22d of August, making a distance of 1,852 miles from Westport in 100 days. Some of the party had travelled 715 miles more in going to Taos and back, in consequence of the loss of stores. The party was at one time in imminent danger of collision with the same band of Indians that afterwards massacred Captain Gunnison.

J. Soulé Bowman.

Mr. Bowman left Kansas the 20th of May, 1853, on his journey to California, and travelling up the Kansas river crossed it at the Baptist mission, and proceeded to Salt Lake city, *via* Fort Kearney and Fort Laramie. Leaving Salt Lake city on the 29th of July, he proceeded to Humboldt river, passing down its north side to the sink. From the sink he took the Truckee river route, and thence, by Beckwith's cut off to Bidwell's bar and Marysville. Shortly after his arrival in San Francisco he was attacked with the typhoid fever, which carried him off in a few days. Mr. Bowman's untimely end is greatly to be lamented, not only as a citizen, relative, and friend, but as a man of science. For many years he has embraced every opportunity for making collections in natural history, even under the most unfavorable circumstances.

In a previous report I have referred to a collection made for the Institution by Mr. Bowman. Those gathered by him during the trip just referred to were of much greater extent, embracing quite a full series of fishes and reptiles from a previously unexplored region—many new to science and all in excellent condition. These were received in April, 1854, through the kind assistance of his brother, S. M. Bowman, of San Francisco, and of Lieutenant Whipple.

Exploration of the Brazos, by Captain R. B. Marcy.

Captain Marcy, having completed and published his report of an exploration of Red river in 1852, was detailed in 1854 to select and survey certain lands in Texas, donated by that State for the benefit of the Indian tribes included within her limits. He accordingly left New York for this purpose in May, and proceeded to Fort Belknap, near which the reservation is situated. Accompanied and assisted by Major Neighbors, Indian agent, he performed the duty assigned him, and from interviews with the chiefs of the southern Comanches, found that these Indians were not averse to the idea of settling down permanently and cultivating the soil.

In the course of the summer Captain Marcy visited the head waters of the Brazos and the Big Witchita, a region previously untrodden by the white man. During his entire trip he was accompanied by Dr. G. G. Shumard, as surgeon and naturalist, who made extensive and valuable collections and observations, which will be embodied in the report of Captain Marcy.

Lieutenant D. N. Couch.

In the winter of 1852–'53, Lieutenant Couch, of the United States artillery, under leave of absence from the War Department, left Washington for the purpose of making explorations in the natural history and geography of Mexico. After a short stay at Brownsville, accompanied by several servants, he crossed the river into Mexico, and went first to Monterey in New Leon. Here he spent some time in examining the Sierras south and west of that city, and thence proceeded to Parras in Coahuila, 185 miles west of Monterey. He went next to the plains of the lower Bolson de Mapimi, Durango, visiting there the celebrated Durango caves. Owing to the desertion of some of his attendants, he was unable to extend his journey further west, and retracing his steps he explored the salt plain of Alamo de Parras before returning to the United States by his original route.

During the whole of this journey Lieutenant Couch gathered copious collections in all departments of zoology, and made a large number of original notes upon the habits of the species. Many new species were obtained by him, and important discoveries made respecting the geographical distribution of others. A portion of the results thus secured have been published by Lieutenant Couch, and others may shortly be expected.

When in Matamoras Lieutenant Couch purchased the entire collection of notes and specimens left by Doctor L. Berlandier. This was the result of many years of labor in the province of Tamaulipas, and proved to be of extraordinary value.

Count Cypriani.

According to Mr. Heap, Count Cypriani, ex-Governor of Leghorn, left Westport in May, 1853, for a trip to California, *via* Fort Laramie and the South Pass, Great Salt Lake, and Carson's Valley. His party consisted of eleven scientific men and a sufficient escort, well provided with all means of scientific research. No information has yet been received of the further movements of this party.

Explorations of S. F. Baird.

By authority of the Secretary of the Smithsonian Institution, Mr. Baird, during the summer of 1853, proceeded in company with Dr. J. P. Kirtland, of Cleveland, to Racine, Wisconsin, where they spent a week in exploring the streams and prairies in its vicinity, with the assistance of Dr. P. R. Hoy and Rev. A. C. Barry, well known naturalists, resident in that place; and with them next visited the interior of the State, spending some time at Madison, and returning *via* Milwaukie. Dr. Kirtland and Mr. Baird next visited Ohio, spending some days at Elyria, and a week at Poland, Ohio. From Poland they went to Detroit, where they were joined by Professor Charles Fox and Dr. Davenport, with whom they visited Ann Arbor and Port Huron, exploring, in addition, a considerable extent of Detroit river. Mr. Baird next went alone to Montreal, and down the river below Quebec, then back again to Lake Champlain. The principal result of this trip covering over 5,000 miles, was the acquisition of very full sets of the fishes of the lake basin over a water line of about 1,500 miles, serving to develope important facts in regard to their geographical distribution. A complete series of the fishes of Ohio, as described by Dr. Kirtland in his "Fishes of the Ohio," was also secured from the original localities.

and identified on the spot by this distinguished naturalist. The entire collection of fishes and other alcoholic specimens filled twelve kegs and large cans. In 1854, Mr. Baird visited the coast of New Jersey, and spent six weeks in the vicinity of Beeseley's Point, at the mouth of Great Egg Harbor river, studying the habits and collecting specimens of the marine species. A full account of the results of this trip will be found in the present report. Additional explorations of similar character, were made at Greenport and River-head, Long Island, as also near Piermont and Sing Sing, on the Hudson river. At Piermont he had the valuable aid of Mr. John G. Bell, of New York, in collecting full series of the fish of the Hackensack and Sparkill, embracing several species new to the State, and others heretofore only found in that locality.

Exploration in Western Missouri and Kansas, by Dr. P. R. Hoy.

Dr. Hoy, well known as an ardent and successful naturalist of Racine, Wisconsin, left that place on the 4th of April, 1854, for a natural history excursion to Missouri. Stopping at various points to make collections, he reached St. Louis on the 12th, and next day proceeded up the Missouri river. After a short stay at Boonville, Cooper county, Missouri, he went on to Lexington, Missouri, and from this point made various excursions, some of them into Kansas; after remaining in this region some time, Dr. Hoy returned to Racine in June. Availing himself of every opportunity to add to his collections, Dr. Hoy gathered together many species of birds, reptiles, and fishes; among the latter quite a number new to science. One hundred and fifty-two species of birds were observed, or obtained by him above Boonville alone, some of them not previously known to occur so far to the east. His alcoholic collections have been sent to the Institution, and prove to be of great interest.

Exploration of Northern Wisconsin, in 1854, *by Rev. A. C. Barry.*

Mr. Barry left Racine on the 10th of May, 1854, for his trip through northern Wisconsin, and reached Oshkosh, *via* Sheboygan and Fond du Lac, on the 13th. His route thence was up the Fox, to Lake Butte des Morts; thence up the Wolf, to the junction of the Waupacca; thence to the mouth of the Embarras, and across the country to the Wisconsin, striking the river at Plover Portage. From this point he passed down the Wisconsin river, examining the country and streams on both sides as far as Richland city; returning by way of Dodgeville, Madison, Palmyra, East Troy, and Rochester, to Racine, where he arrived towards the end of June. In the course of his journey, Mr. Barry made copious notes of his observations, which will be hereafter presented to the Institution. The numerous collections of fishes and reptiles made by him have already been received, and were gathered principally in the following localities:

Lake Winnebago, Lake Butte des Morts, Waupacca river, Little Waupacca, Embarras river, Spring brook, Baird's lake, Wisconsin river, Lemmonwier river, Yellow river, Bear creek, Pine river, Green creek, Little Plover, Big Plover, and Carp lake.

Exploration and Survey of the China Seas and Behring's Straits.

In the summer of 1852, Congress made an appropriation of $125,000 for "building or purchase of suitable vessels and for prosecuting a survey and reconnoisance for naval and commercial purposes, of such parts of Behring Straits of the North Pacific ocean and the China seas as are frequented by American whale ships, and by trading vessels in their routes between the United States and China." The act was passed at too late a period in the year to allow any action beyond the organization of the party, and the commencement of preparations for departure. The command of the expedition was entrusted by the Secretary of the Navy, Hon. John P. Kennedy, to Captain C. Ringgold, an officer of much experience in the duties required, from his connexion with the United States exploring expedition under Captain Wilkes. The necessary vessels were procured and equipped in the most substantial manner, and fitted out with all the instruments required for making observations in astronomy, hydrography, magnetism, meteorology, together with the most complete equipment of natural history apparatus ever taken to sea. The expedition was fortunate in securing the services of Mr. William Stimpson as principal zoologist, and Mr. Charles Wright as botanist, both of them gentlemen well known for successful prosecution of their respective departments in former explorations. Mr. F. H. Storer went out as chemist and taxidermist, and E. M. Kern, the intrepid companion of Frémont and Sitgreaves, as artist and photographer. Many of the naval officers on board expected to lend efficient aid in the natural history department as well as in the physical, to which they are more especially assigned.

The squadron, as finally organized, consisted of the following vessels:

1. *The sloop Vincennes*, bearing the flag of Commander Ringgold, with Lieutenant Rolando as lieutenant commanding and executive officer; Lieutenant J. M. Brooke, acting lieutenant and assistant astronomer; William B. Boggs, purser and artist; Frederick D. Stuart, secretary and draughtsman; William Stimpson, zoologist to expedition; F. H. Storer, chemist and taxidermist, and Edward M. Kern, photographer and artist.

2. *Steamer John Hancock*, Lieutenant John Rodgers in command; Charles Wright, botanist to expedition, and A. H. Ames, assistant naturalist.

3. *Brig Porpoise*, Alonzo B. Davis, Lieutenant Commanding.

4. *Schooner Fennimore Cooper*, acting Lieutenant Commanding H. R. Stevens.

5. *Store ship John P. Kennedy*, Lieutenant Commanding Napoleon Collins.

These vessels left Norfolk in June, 1853, and went to St. Simon's bay, Cape of Good Hope, and after a short stay, proceeded to Hong Kong, China. The sloop of war Vincennes, Commander C. Ringgold, and the brig Porpoise, Lieutenant Commanding A. B. Davis, by the way of Van Dieman's Land, through the Coral seas, passing the Caroline and Ladrone and Bashee islands, arriving at Hong Kong on the 17th of March; the steamer John Hancock, Lieutenant Commanding John Rodgers, the store ship John P. Kennedy, Lieutenant Commanding N. Collins, and the tender Fennimore Cooper, Lieutenant Commanding H. K. Stevens, by the way of the Straits of Sunda and Gasper, the Carimata and Billeton passages, and the Sooloo sea. Their arrival at Hong Kong was reported by Commander Ringgold early in June, 1854.

During the absence of Commodore Perry, with the greater part of the East India squadron, at Japan, the civil war raging in China, and particularly in the vicinity of Canton, so alarmed American citizens holding valuable property in that region, that Commodore Ringgold considered it proper to suspend temporarily the special duties to which he was assigned, and render protection to his exposed countrymen; so that he failed to accomplish a large portion of the surveys that had been planned for the year.

The expedition has, however, again resumed its scientific duties with important results. Several large collections in natural history have been sent home, and others are on the way. Captain Ringgold having returned to the United States, the squadron is in command of Captain Rodgers.

Exploration of the Parana and its tributaries, by the steamer Water Witch.

This surveying steamer, under Lieutenant Commanding Thomas J. Page, left Washington in January, 1853, for the Parana, having as an object the survey of this great river and its principal tributaries. Captain Page was provided with a complete outfit of apparatus for natural history collections, together with a skilful horticulturist, whose business is the gathering of live specimens of the most interesting plants. A good many valuable seeds have already been sent home. The vessel arrived at Buenos Ayres on the 25th of May, but was detained for some time in consequence of the internal dissensions of the country, and the necessity of protecting the interests of American citizens; and it was not until the 7th of November that Captain Page was permitted to leave Ascension to proceed up the river. A small steamer of very light draught, was taken out by the Water Witch, in order to pursue the exploration into waters too shallow for the larger vessel. This vessel has been engaged since her arrival in Paraguay in making the intended explorations, as well as in protecting American interests in that quarter, and the collections made and sent home have added much to our knowledge of the natural history of the country.

Expedition of Lieutenant MacRae, United States Navy.

At the termination of the observations of the United States naval astronomical expedition in Chile, Lieutenant MacRae was instructed by Lieutenant Gilliss to cross the Uspallata pass of the Andes, and the pampas of the Argentine confederation, for the purpose of ascertaining the law of decrease of magnetical intensity with elevation, the atmospheric condition of the higher Andes, the geography of the principally travelled route between Mendoza and Buenos Ayres, and other important facts interesting to men of science. He succeeded in making observations for all the magnetic elements at stations differing in elevation 3,000 feet, both ascending and descending the Cordilleras, and at each 100 miles in crossing the pampas. Having accidentally broken his barometer and injured his chronometer, shortly after leaving Mendoza, Lieutenant MacRae, as soon as he arrived in the United States, volunteered to return at his own expense for the purpose of completing observations which the loss of these instruments prevented him from doing on his first trip. Permission being granted by the Navy Department, he again embarked for South America, reached Mendoza from Buenos Ayres in time to observe the solar eclipse of November 30, 1853; twice crossed the Portillo pass at an elevation of 14,319 feet; again passed over the Cumbre and Uspallata passes, 12,656 feet; and finally returned to the United States in March, 1854.

Lieutenant MacRae made such collections in natural history as his limited opportunities allowed; among them a new species of the curious genus *Trichomycterus.* He also procured several fine specimens of *Cavia australis.*

The report of his journeys will be found embodied in the first volume of the report of the United States naval astronomical expedition.

Japan Expedition.

Although not specially an exploring party, yet the magnitude of the squadron sent out under charge of Commodore Perry, and the importance of the interests committed to his charge, render a brief notice necessary in this place. The principal object of the expedition was to form a treaty with the emperor of Japan for the protection of American interests in and about the island, as well as to look after these interests generally in that quarter of the globe. The squadron, under command of Commodore Perry, consisted of the steamers Mississippi, Powhatan, and Susquehanna; the sloops of war Macedonia, Plymouth, Saratoga, and Vandalia; and the store ships Supply, Southampton, and Lexington. With a portion of this fleet Commodore Perry arrived at Jeddo bay on the 8th of July, and, after a brief interview with one of the ministers of state, left, to return in the spring of 1854. Of the happy results of this renewed visit, and of the treaty made with such important bearings on commerce and humanity, I need not here speak, as they are well known to every one. Commodore Perry has returned to the United States, bringing with him copious journals of the voyage, with numerous drawings, and many collections illustrating the natural products and manufactures of Japan. Collections of plants, seeds, reptiles, and fishes, of much interest, were also made by Dr. James Morrow, agriculturist to the expedition.

Brig Dolphin.

Lieutenant O. H. Berryman, in command of the brig Dolphin, has been engaged in a continuation of his previous labors and those of Lieutenant Lee of sounding the depths of the Atlantic Ocean, in connexion with the researches of Lieutenant Maury on the winds and currents of the ocean. His results have been of the highest interest to science, as well as of very great practical value to the navigator. The report by Lieutenant Lee of his observations while in command of the Dolphin has recently been published by Congress.

Arctic Expedition under Doctor Kane.

The brig Advance which with her consort, the Rescue, had joined in 1850 the band of searchers for the long lost Sir John Franklin, was again fitted out and commissioned for a renewed effort in that direction, under command of Dr. E. K. Kane, the intrepid surgeon and annalist of the first or the Grinnell expedition. The Advance, liberally lent for the purpose by her owner, Mr. Henry Grinnell, was provided with all the means necessary for resisting the vigor of an arctic winter, and for making various deeply interesting observations in natural and physical science in the polar regions. The Smithsonian Institution furnished a complete set of magnetical apparatus, besides fitting out the entire natural history equipment; and the funds necessary for the general expenses were supplied by Mr. Grinnell and by private subscriptions. Doctor Kane intended to have particular attention paid to the Acalephæ and crustacea of the arctic seas, as well as to the collection of skeletons of cetaceans and pinnipedians. Mr. Henry Goodfellow has charge of the natural history department; Dr. I. I. Hayes is surgeon, and Augustus Sontag, astronomer. The entire force consisted of but seventeen men. Dr. Kane proposed to visit Uppernavik, and there procure the necessary dogs and Eskimos for an overland journey, to be fully provided with these as well as with suitable dresses of furs, &c. His intention was to go directly to Smith's Sound at the foot of Baffin's bay, and, passing up the Sound to as great a distance as possible, seek a secure harbor for the winter. He then expected to take his sledge-boats, and with seven men, besides the Eskimos, proceed by land or water, as the case might require, in a direction due north as far as circumstances would allow.

The vessel left New York on the 31st of May, and the latest dates from Dr. Kane were from Uppernavik to July 20, 1853. He had succeeded in obtaining what he needed for his onward march, and expected to start immediately for the north.

Since then nothing has been heard from him, and Congress has authorized an expedition for his succor.

Exploration of the coast of Western Africa, by Lieutenant W. F. Lynch, United States Navy.

Commander W. F. Lynch, United States navy, who left the United States in November, 1852, on a reconnoissance of the coast of western Africa, preparatory to a more extended exploration at some subsequent period, returned on the 1st of May, 1853, having been busily engaged, during the greater part of the interval, in prosecuting the object of his mission. He examined a large portion of the coast of Liberia, and went up a number of the rivers. He suffered much from the sickness which is so constant an attendant of the white man on that coast, and which caused an abrupt termination of his labors. He recommends that any future exploring party should consist almost entirely of citizens of Liberia, organized under the flag of the United States; and that the whites should ride out the fever at Monrovia, on account of the existence of suitable accommodations there. The proper rendezvous for the inland march he considers to be Millsburg, at the head of navigation of the St. Paul's, whence the route should extend *via* Boporah, an important native town, to the range separating the tributaries of the Niger from those which flow into the Atlantic. That range attained, it is to be followed to the parallel of Cape Palmas, and thence to the sea. A full report of the exploration of Commander Lynch is presented in the annual report of the Secretary of the Navy for the first session of the thirty-third Congress.

Darien Ship Canal Expedition.

A survey of the Isthmus of Darien, in reference to the project of uniting the waters of the Atlantic and Pacific by a ship canal, was undertaken under the joint auspices of the English, French, and American governments.

The English expedition sailed for the Isthmus on the 17th of December, 1853, and arrived at Caledonia bay on the 19th of January. It consisted of the brig Espiegle and the survey schooner Scorpion, the former having on board Mr. Gisborne, Dr. Cullen, and Messrs. Forde and Bennett, with four assistant engineers, on the part of the Atlantic and Pacific Junction company, and of Lieutenant Singer, R. E., and staff, in behalf of the British government. The French steamer Chimère joined them, at the same time, with a scientific corps. The United States sloop-of-war Cyane, under Captain Hollins, had reached Caledonia bay on the 8th of January; and, after some preparation, a party under command of Lieutenant Strain, of the United States navy, started out to make the transit. Losing their way, and suffering greatly for want of proper food and water, a number perished, and it was only through the aid of an English party from the Virago that Lieutenant Strain and a few of his men were saved from destruction. The British steamer Virago, Captain Preevorst, attempted the transit from the Pacific side, and reached a point commanding a view of the Atlantic. From the facts gathered by the different parties, it appears conclusively that a canal is impracticable in the region where that survey was made.

Exploration of the Valley of the Amazon.

Messrs. Herndon and Gibbon, of the United States navy, after completing the survey of the valley of the Amazon, returned some time ago, and have published their general report. This contains much that is entertaining and novel, and several large editions have already been called for by Congress.

Exploration by Mr. Scrope.

In December, 1852, Mr. Thomas H. Scrope, an enterprising young gentleman of New York, left Para in a steamer for the town of Loretto, on the Peruvian Amazon, about 3,000 miles from Para. He took with him everything necessary to make collections in natural history, and has signified his intention of spending as much time as possible in gathering specimens of the animals and plants of that little known region. Nothing has since been heard from him.

Dr. Thomas Steele.

Dr. Thomas Steele, a missionary of the American Colonization Society, left in the packet Shirley, in November, 1853, for Cape Palmas. He intended there to make such collections as were indicated to him as of particular interest, for which purpose a quantity of alcohol was sent out to him by the Smithsonian Institution. Some important collections were sent home by him, and it is with much regret that we are informed of his recent death by fever.

REPORTS OF EXPLORATIONS PUBLISHED IN 1853, 1854.

A—Government Reports.

Captain L. Sitgreaves, U. S. A.—Report of an Expedition down the Zuñi and Colorado rivers, by Captain L. Sitgreaves, United States Topographical Engineers, accompanied by maps, views, sketches, and illustrations. Washington: Robert Armstrong, public printer, 1853. Public document, 32d Congress, 2d session, Senate executive No. 59, one volume 8vo., pp. 198, 78 plates, and one map. An edition was also published by the House.

This report is principally occupied by an account of the natural history of the region traversed by Captain Sitgreaves in this and a previous exploration. The mammals and birds are by Dr. Woodhouse, surgeon and naturalist to the expedition: the reptiles by Dr. Edward Hallowell; the fishes by S. F. Baird and C. Girard; and the plants by Dr. Torrey. Six new species are described of North American mammals, five of birds, eighteen of reptiles, three of fishes, and ten of plants.

Captain R. B. Marcy, U. S. A.—Exploration of the Red river of Louisiana, in the year 1852, by Randolph B. Marcy, captain 5th infantry, United States army, assisted by George B. McClellan, Brevet Captain, United States Engineers, with reports of the natural history of the country, and numerous illustrations. Washington: Robert Armstrong, public printer, 1853, two vols. 8vo., pp. 320, 66 plates and two maps. 32d Congress, 2d session, Senate executive No. 54.

This report includes sub-reports on the minerals, by Professor C. U. Shepard; on the geology of the expedition, by President Hitchcock and George G. Shumard, M. D.; on the palæontology, by B. F. Shumard, M. D.; on the mammals, by Captain Marcy; the reptiles and fisbcs, by S. F. Baird, and C. Girard; the shells, by Professor C. B. Adams and G. G. Shumard; the orthoptera, arachnida, and myriapoda, by C. Girard; the plants, by Dr. Torrey; and the ethnology by Captain Marcy and Professor W. W. Turner. Fourteen new species of fossils are described, five of reptiles, five of fishes, ten of orthoptera, arachnida and myriapoda, and three of plants, all of which are figured. Dr. G. G. Shumard acted as surgeon and naturalist, and the collections were made principally by him and Captain McClellan.

Lieutenants Herndon and Gibbon, U. S. N.—Exploration of the valley of the Amazon, made under direction of the Navy Department, by William Lewis Herndon and Lardner Gibbon, lieutenants, United States navy.

Part 1. By Lieutenant Herndon, 2 vols. 8vo. Washington: Robert Armstrong, public printer, 1853, pp. 418, 16 plates and three maps. 32d Congress, 2d session, Senate executive No. 36.

Part 2. By Lieutenant Gibbon, 2 vols. 8vo. Washington: Robert Armstrong, public printer.

Some interesting collections in natural history were made by these gentlemen, but not published in their reports.

Lieutenant S. P. Lee, U. S. N.—Report and charts of the cruise of the United States brig Dolphin, made under direction of the Navy Department, by Lieutenant Lee, 2 vols .8vo. Washington: Beverley Tucker, printer to the Senate, 1854. 15 charts and one map. 33d Congress, 1st session, Senate executive No. 59.

Captain W. F. Lynch, U. S. N.—Official report of a mission to Africa in 1852, 1853; pp. 329—366 of the report of the Secretary of the Navy, in President's message for 33d Congress, 1st session. Part III, 1853.

Professor A. D. Bache.—Report of the Superintendent of the Coast Survey, showing the progress of the survey during the year 1852. One vol., 4to. Washington: Robert Armstrong, public printer, 1853. Pp. 184 and 37 plates.

Professor A. D. Bache.—Report of the Superintendent of the Coast Survey, showing the progress of the survey during the year 1853. One vol., 4to. Washington: Robert Armstrong, public printer. Pp. 278, and 54 plates.

H. R. Schoolcraft, LL. D.—Information respecting the History, Condition and Prospects of the Indian tribes of the United States; collected and prepared under the direction of the Bureau of Indian Affairs per act of Congress of March 3, 1847, by Henry R. Schoolcraft. Illustrated by S. Eastman, Capt. U. S. A. Published by authority of Congress ———. Part III, 4to., 1853, pp. 636 and 45 plates. Part IV, 4to., 1854, pp. 668 and 41 plates.

These volumes, in addition to the subjects specially covered by the title, contain valuable journals of expeditions by officers of the United States army and others, at various periods of time.

Pacific Railroad Surveys.—Letter from the Secretary of War transmitting reports of surveys, &c., of railroad routes to the Pacific ocean, made February 6, 1854. 8vo., pp. 118. 33d Congress, 1st session, Ex. doc. No. 46.

This contains the partial reports from the several expeditions, all of them still in the field at the date of the report.

Report upon the northern Pacific railroad exploration and survey, by Gov. I. I. Stevens, made June 30, 1854. Pp. 548.

Report of explorations for a railway route near the 35th parallel of latitude from the Mississippi river to the Pacific ocean, by Lieut. A.W. Whipple, corps of topographical engineers, made July 31, 1854. 8vo., pp. 154.

Report of Explorations for that portion of a Railway Route near the 32d parallel of latitude, lying between Doña Ana on the Rio Grande, and the Pima village on the Gila, by Lieut. Jno. G. Parke, U. S. A., of corps topographical engineers. Made August 22, 1854. 8vo., pp. 32.

The above are all the railroad reports published in 1854, the remainder not being finished till 1855. The maps accompanying the reports were not finished in 1854.

B—Private reports.

Dr. E. K. Kane, U. S. N.—The United States Grinnell Expedition in search of Sir John Franklin. A personal narrative. By Elisha Kent Kane, M. D., U. S. N. New York: Harper and Bros. 1 vol., 8vo. 1853.

John R. Bartlett.—Personal narrative of Explorations and Incidents in Texas, New Mexico, California, Sonora, and Chihuahua, connected with the United States and Mexican Boundary Commission in 1850–'53. By John Russell Bartlett, United States Commissioner during that period; with maps and illustrations. 2 vols., 8vo., 1854. New York: D. Appleton & Co.

G. H. Heap.—Central route to the Pacific, from the valley of the Mississippi to California. Journal of the expedition of E. F. Beale, Superintendent of Indian Affairs in California, and Gwinn Harris Heap, from Missouri to California, in 1853. By Gwinn Harris Heap. Philadelphia: Lippincott, Grambo, & Co. 1 vol., 8vo. 1854. With map and illustrations.

Lieut. J. G. Strain, U. S. N.—Report of the Darien expedition. Harper's Magazine for March, April, and May, 1855.

REPORTS ORDERED BY CONGRESS, AND TO BE PUBLISHED.

Lieut. J. M. Gilliss, U. S. N.—Report of the United States naval astronomical expedition in Chile. This report will occupy several volumes quarto, and contain much matter on the natural history of the country.

Commodore M. C. Perry, U. S. N.—Report of the Japan expedition.

Captain C. Ringgold, U. S. N.—Report of the Expedition for the exploration of the China seas and Behring's straits.

Reports of the several parties for survey of railroad routes from the Mississippi river to the Pacific ocean. These will embrace the government expeditions under Gov. I. I. Stevens, Lieut. A. W. Whipple, Lieut. E. G. Beckwith, Lieut. R. S. Williamson, Lieut. J. G. Parke and Capt. J. Pope, with the private ones of Col. J. C. Frémont and Mr. Lander.

A. B. Gray.—Report and map of surveys in New Mexico, &c.

Professor A. D. Bache.—Report of the superintendent of the United States Coast Survey during the year 1854.

H. R Schoolcraft, LL. D.—History and Statistics of the Indian tribes of the United States. Parts V and VI. The sixth and last part is to contain an abstract or synopsis of the whole work.

CONCLUDING REMARKS.

The record of explorations for the year will be incomplete without brief reference to the numerous researches and collections made at different points in North America, the results of which have come to the knowledge of the Institution. Few have any conception of the amount of quiet investigation in natural history now going on in this country, principally by persons laboriously engaged in other duties and using only scattered intervals of leisure. The records of the Institution almost daily receive entries of contributions of facts and specimens of natural history from such sources.

Some general remarks and notices on this subject will be found detailed in the report on additions to the museum in 1854. I would, however, make a particular reference to the labors of Lieutenant W. P. Trowbridge, United States army, who, while successfully prosecuting his duty as tidal observer on the Pacific coast, in connexion with the United States Coast Survey, has employed his leisure moments in forming one of the largest collections of natural history ever made in this country. In this he has been zealously aided by Messrs. Cassidy, Szabo, and others, members of his parties.

Mr. R. D. Cutts, likewise connected with the Coast Survey, has also made some interesting collections on the coast of California and transmitted them to the Institution; and a gentleman of the same branch of the public service, Mr. Gustavus Wurdemann, has supplied one of the fullest series of the animals of the Louisiana gulf coast ever received by the Institution. It is a subject of profound congratulation that while exhausting every department of physical research in connexion with the survey of our coast, the distinguished superintendent encourages his assistants to pay all possible attention to the various branches of natural science, recognising fully their connexion with those more immediately belonging to the survey. One effect has been the gathering together of vast materials illustrating the marine infusoria and microscopic shells of our coast, which have already been examined with important hydrographical results.

LECTURES

DELIVERED BEFORE THE SMITHSONIAN INSTITUTION.

No. I.—THE CAMEL.

BY HON. GEO. P. MARSH.

The first command addressed to man by his Creator, and substantially repeated to the second great progenitor of our race, not only charged him to subdue the earth, but gave him dominion over all terrestrial creatures, whether animate or inanimate, and thus predicted and prescribed the subjugation of the entire organic and inorganic world to human control and human use.

Man is yet far from having achieved the fulfilment of this grand mission. He has, indeed, surveyed the greater part of his vast domain; marked the outline of its solid and its fluid surface, and approximately measured their areas and determined their relative elevation; pierced its superficial strata, and detected the order of their historical succession; reduced to their primal elements its rocks, its soils, its waters, and its atmosphere, and even soared above its canopy of cloud. He has traced, through the void of space, its movements of rotation, revolution, and translation; resolved the seeming circles of its attendant satellite into strangely tortuous paths of progression; investigated its relations of density, attraction, and motion, to other visible and invisible cosmical orbs; and unfolded the laws of those mysterious allied agencies, heat, light, electricity, and magnetism, whose sphere of influence seems commensurate with that of creation. But, notwithstanding these triumphs, earth is not yet all his own; and millions of leagues of her surface still lie uninhabited, unenjoyed, and unsubdued—yielding neither food, nor clothing, nor shelter to man, or even to the humbler tribes of animal or vegetable life, which, in other ways, minister to his necessities or his convenience.

In like manner, man has studied the biography, and the relations of affinity or dependence, of the infinitely varied contemporaneous forms of organic life; traced the history of myriads of species of both plants and animals, which had ceased to be before the Creator breathed into *his* nostrils the breath of life; and demonstrated the past and present existence of numerous tribes of organic beings, too minute to be individually cognizable by any of the unaided senses, and yet largely influencing our own animal economy, and even composing no unimportant part of the crust of the solid globe; but of the vegetables that clothe and diversify its soil, of the animated creatures that float in its atmosphere, enliven its surface, or cleave its waters, but comparatively few have as yet been rendered in any way subservient to human use, fewer still domesticated and made the permanent and regular denizens of his fields or companions of his household.

The efforts of civilized man towards the fulfilment of this great command have been directed almost exclusively to the conquest of inorganic nature, by the utilization of minerals; by contriving methods for availing himself of the mechanical powers and of natural forces, simply or in cunning combinations; by cutting narrow paths for facilitating travel and transport between distant regions; and by devising means of traversing with certainty and speed the trackless and troubled ocean.

The proper savage smelts no ores, and employs those metals only which natural processes have reduced. He binds the blocks of which he rears his temples with no cement of artificial stone. He drains no swamps, cuts no roads, excavates no canals, turns no mills by power of water or of wind, and asks from inorganic nature no other gifts than those which she spontaneously offers, to supply his wants and multiply his enjoyments.

On the other hand, the very dawn of social life, in those stages of human existence which quite precede all true civilization, demands, as an indispensable condition, not the mere usufruct of the spontaneous productions of organic nature, but the complete appropriation and domestication of many species of both plants and animals. Man begins by subjugating, and thereby preserving, those organic forms which are at once best suited to satisfy his natural wants, and, like himself, least fitted for a self-sustaining, independent existence;* and he is to end by extending his conquests over the more widely dissimilar, remote, and refractory products of creative nature. We accordingly owe to our primeval, untutored ancestors, the discovery, the domestication, the acclimation of our cereal grains, our edible roots, our improved fruits, as well as the subjugation of our domestic animals; while civilized man has scarcely reclaimed a plant of spontaneous growth, or added a newly tamed animal to the flocks and herds of the pastoral ages. Indeed, so remote is the period to which these noble triumphs of intelligent humanity over brute and vegetable nature belong, that we know not their history or their epochs; and if we believe them to be in fact human conquests, and not rather special birth-day gifts from the hand of the Creator, we must admit that cultivation and domestication have so completely metamorphosed and diversified the forms and products, and modified the habits, and even, so to speak, the inborn instincts of both vegetables and animals, that but the fewest of our household beasts and our familiar plants can be certainly identified with the primitive stock. Most of these, it is probable, no longer occur in their wild state and original form; and it is questionable whether they are even capable of continued existence without the fostering care of man.

In both these great divisions of organic life there are some species

* It is not the domestic animals alone whose existence is perpetuated by the protective, though often unconscious, agency of man. In the depths of our northern forests the voice of the song-bird, or of the smaller quadrupeds, is but seldom heard. It is in the fields tilled by human husbandry that they find the most abundant nutriment, and the surest retreat from bird and beast of prey. The vast flights of the wild pigeon are found, not in the remote, primitive woodlands, but along the borders of the pioneer settlements; and, upon our western frontier, it is observed that the deer often multiply for a time after the coming in of the whites, because the civilized huntsman destroys or scares away the wolf, the great natural enemy of the weaker quadrupeds.

peculiarly suited to the uses of man as a migratory animal. The bread stuffs of the old world, and, in a less degree, our only American cereal, Indian corn, the pulse, the cucurbitaceous plants, and the edible roots of our gardens, as well as the horse, the dog, the sheep, and the swine, seem almost exempted from subjection to climatic laws. While, therefore, a degree of latitude, a few hundred feet of elevation, a trifling difference in soil, or in the amount of atmospheric humidity, oppose impassable barriers to the diffusion of most wild plants and animals, the domesticated species I have enumerated follow man in his widest wanderings, and make his resting-place their home, whether he dwells on a continent or an island, at the level of the sea or on the margin of Alpine snows, beneath the equator or among the frosts of the polar circle.

Others, again, of the domesticated families of the organic world seem, like the untamed tribes, inexorably confined within prescribed geographical bounds, and incapable of propagation or growth beyond their original limits; while others still, though comparatively independent of climate and of soil, are nevertheless so specially fitted to certain conditions of surface, and certain modes of human life, to the maintenance of which they are themselves indispensable, that even the infidel finds, in these mutual adaptations, proofs of the existence and beneficent agency of a self-conscious and intelligent creative power.

Among the animated organisms of this latter class, the camel is, doubtless, the most important and remarkable. The Ship of the Desert has navigated the pathless sand-oceans of Gobi and the Sahara, and thus not only extended the humanizing influences of commerce and civilization alike over the naked and barbarous African and the fur-clad Siberian savage, but, by discovering the hidden wells of the waste and the islands of verdure that surround them, has made permanently habitable vast regions not otherwise penetrable by man. The "howling wilderness" now harbors and nourishes numerous tribes in more or less advanced stages of culture; and the services of that quadruped, on which Rebekah journeyed to meet her spouse, and which, though neglected and despised by the polished Egyptian, constituted a principal item in the rural wealth of the father of Joseph, are as indispensable to these races, as are those of any other animal to man in any condition of society.

The camel lives and thrives in the tropics; through almost the whole breadth of the northern temperate zone; and is even met beyond Lake Baikal in conjunction with the reindeer, with which, among some of the northern tribes, he has exchanged offices, the deer serving as a beast of the saddle, while the camel is employed only for draught or burden.* But his appropriate home is the desert, and it is here alone that he acquires his true significance and value, his remarkable powers being the necessary condition and sole means by which man has in any degree extended his dominion over the Libyan and the Arabian wildernesses.

In presence of the improvements of more advanced stages of society, the camel diminishes in numbers and finally gives place to other animals better suited to the wants and the caprices of higher civilization. Upon good roads, other beasts of draught and burden are upon the whole more serviceable, or, to speak more accurately, more acceptable to the

* Ritter, Erdkunde XIII, 662—667.

tastes of cultivated nations; and the ungainly camel shares in the contempt with which the humble ass, the mule, and even the ox, are regarded by the polished and the proud. Besides this, both the products and the restraints of proper agriculture are unfavorable to his full development and physical perfection. When the soil is enclosed and subjugated, and the coarse herbage and shrubbery of spontaneous growth are superseded by artificial vegetation, he misses the pungent and aromatic juices which flavor the sun-burnt grasses and wild arborescent plants that form his accustomed and appropriate diet; the confinement of fence, and hedge, and stall are repugnant to his roving propensities and prejudical to his health, and he is as much out of place in civilized life as the Bedouin or the Tartar. Hence the attempts to introduce him into Spain, Italy, and other European countries have either wholly failed, or met with very indifferent success; and though he still abounds in Bessarabia, the Crimea, and all the southeastern provinces of Russia. yet the rural improvements which the German colonists have introduced into those regions have tended to reduce his numbers. When the wandering Tartar becomes stationary, encloses his possessions, and converts the desert steppe into arable ground, his camels retreat before the horse, the ox, and the sheep, and retire to the wastes beyond the Don and the Volga. So essentially nomade indeed is the camel in his habits, that the Arab himself dismisses him as soon as he acquires a fixed habitation. The oases of the desert are generally without this animal, and he is not possessed by the Fellahheen of the Sinaitic peninsula, by the inhabitants of Sinah or the oasis of Jupiter Ammon, or by those who cultivate the valleys of Mount Seir.

Of the primitive races of man, known to ancient sacred and profane history, but one, the Bedouin Arab, has retained unchanged his original mode of life. It is the camel alone, whose remarkable properties, by making habitable by man regions inaccessible to the improvements of civilization, has preserved to our own times that second act of the great drama of social life, the patriarchal condition. The Arab in all his changes of faith, heathen, christian, mussulman, has remained himself immutable; and the student of biblical antiquity must thank the camel for the lively illustrations of scripture history presented by the camp of the Ishmaelite sheikh, who is proud of his kindred with the patient Job, and who boasts himself the lineal descendant of Ibrahim el Khaleel, or Abraham "the friend" of God.

Naturalists divide the camel into two species, the *Camelus dromedarius*, or one-humped camel of Arabia and Africa, and the *Camelus Bactrianus*, or two-humped camel of northern Asia.* It has been suspected that the camel of the Sahara is distinct from that of more northern Africa,

* These geographical limitations, if not strictly accurate are nevertheless sufficiently so for general purposes. Although Höst (Efterrettninger om Marokos, 270) saw the two-humped camel at Morocco, and individuals of this species are sometimes met in Syria, yet it is pretty certain that he is not bred in Africa, or in the warmer regions of the Asiatic continent, but properly belongs to northern latitudes. The one-humped camel has a wider range. He is found among the Kirghises, and in Tartary, and the highlands of central Asia; he seems to bear the cold almost as well as the Bactrian, but he has neither the speed nor the powers of endurance which characterize the dromedary of the African and Arabian deserts. Although neither species probably now exists in a wild state, yet there is good reason to believe that the Bactrian was found wild at no very remote period in the desert of Gobi, where this variety probably originated. Humboldt, Ansichten der Natur, I, 88.

which is pretty certainly of the Arabian stock, and of comparatively late introduction into that continent;* but this conjecture does not appear to be supported by any direct historical or physiological evidence. The scientific specific designation of the one-humped camel is not well chosen. The term *dromas*, as applied to the camel by the ancients, was not used to indicate a *specific* difference. The *camelus dromas* was what the proper *dromedary* is now, that is, simply a *running*, or swift camel, used chiefly or altogether for the saddle; and he might be, as he may be still, of either species, Bactrian or Arabian. In fact, any light-built, easy-paced, and swift-footed camel, of whatever species or variety, is a dromedary; though there are certain breeds, in which the slender head, tall short body, small hump, clean limbs, and generally livelier color, which characterizes the stock, have become hereditary, just as similar peculiarities of form are perpetuated in the thorough-bred hunter and race-horse. In popular phraseology, the term dromedary has been to a considerable extent applied to designate a camel with two humps, from an erroneous supposition that the swift riding-camel (deloul al heiri or maberry of the Arabs, haguin or hedjin of the Egyptians) was of that species. This mistake appears to have originated in a misinterpretation of a passage of Aristotle by Solinus and Theodore Gaza; and the error, though exposed and corrected by Gesner, three hundred years ago, and by almost every naturalist who has since described the animal, continues to influence the language, and mislead the popular opinion of the nineteenth century.

The varieties comprehended under each of the two species are numerous; but they do not differ from each other in size, in form, or in speed, more widely than the breeds of the common horse. Indeed the anatomical differences between the Arabian and the Bactrian camel are so slight, that some naturalists have maintained their specific identity; and it appears to be certain that the common physiological test of specific difference, the incapacity, namely, of the cross to propagate, does not hold good as applied to this animal.† The skeletons of the two species are distinguishable, if at all, only by a slight difference of proportion; and the visceral structure being the same in both, the only foundation for a specific distinction appears to be in the number of humps. In the living animal, the species are readily distinguished by their outward peculiarity; and besides their obvious difference, the Bactrian is shorter limbed and much more hairy than the Arabian camel.

---

*Minutoli thinks he recognises the head of the camel among the figures upon an obelisk at Luxor. Upon the walls of some of the smaller apartments of the great temple of Karnac are carved heads, which certainly appear to me to resemble that of this animal more closely than of any other quadruped; and St John (Adventures in the Libyan Desert, Chap. XII) says he found the camel among the sculptures of the temple at the oasis of Jupiter Ammon. But modern Egyptologists consider some of these figures to represent the head of the lion, others that of the giraffe, and it is certain that no part of the skeleton of the camel has been met with in the catacombs. Although it appears from Strabo, that the tribes of the desert anciently employed the camel in the transport of merchandise between Captos and Berenice, as they do now between Cairo and Suez, yet there is abundant evidence to show that this animal was not used by the proper Egyptians before the time of the Ptolemies, nor does it appear to have been known upon the Barbary coast until a much later period. See Ritter's essay, Ueber die geographische Verbreitung des Kameels, Erdkunde XIII, where this question, and almost all others belonging to the geographical distribution of the camel, are discussed with the usual learning and ability of that great writer.

† Ritter, Erdkunde XIII, 659.

Some writers describe the Bactrian as upon the whole smaller and weaker than the Arabian; but as others state the contrary, the difference in this respect is probably not great. It seems well settled that in countries where the two species exist together, the cross, though inferior to the dromedary in speed, is found to be a more powerful, and for general purposes a more serviceable animal than either of the unmixed races, as possessing in a good degree the most valuable properties of both.*

The general anatomy of the camel is the same as that of other ruminants; but the bump, the horizontal posture of the head, the direction of the eye, the power of closing the nostril, the callosities upon the breast and legs, the spreading and cushioned foot, and above all the curious structure of the stomach, to which he owes his most valuable property, the power of long abstinence from water, distinguish him from all other quadrupeds. The hump is simply a flesby, or rather fatty, protuberance upon the back, like that of the bison, unsupported by any special bony process, and it is least developed in the highest bred animals, so that the maherry of the Sahara is popularly described as being without that appendage. The fullness of the protuberance, however, depends much upon the condition of the animal. The state of the hump is a test constantly referred to in the sale or hire of the camel, and the jockeys resort to various contrivances to give it an unnatural plumpness and solidity.† When the camel has been, for a length of time, full fed, and subjected to moderate labor only, the hump assumes a greater plumpness of form and hardness of texture; but if ill kept or overworked, the fat of the hump is absorbed, and the protuberance becomes flaccid, and is sometimes even reduced to little more than its skin. It seems to serve as a repository of nutriment, and the absorption of its substance into the general system appears to be one of the special arrangements by which the camel is so admirably fitted for the life of privation to which he is destined.‡

The head of the camel, especially of those of the Bisharye and Ababdeh breeds, is carried high and nearly horizontal; and this circumstance, with the length and curvature of the neck, and the outline of the arched back, creates so strong a general resemblance between this quadruped and the ostrich, that the latter is called by the Arabs the camel-bird. The eye is projecting, sheltered above by a very salient bony arch, and its axis is nearly parallel to that of the head, though with a slight inclination towards it anteriorly. From this conformation of the organ, the sight of the animal is habitually directed rather downwards than forward, to the ground upon which he is just about to tread than to the distance. It is, in a great degree, to this structure, as I believe, that his remarkable sure-footedness is to be attributed. The eye always scans the surface where the foot is next to be placed; and in moving about among the scattered luggage and

*See a valuable paper, extracted from the notes of General Harlan, in the Report of the American Patent Office for 1853, Agriculture, p. 61. According to Ritter, Erdkunde XIII, 646, and the authorities there cited, the word Booghdee, used by General Harlan to designate the cross between the Bactrian and Arabian, means the young male Bactrian. General Harlan's testimony in favor of the strength and power of endurance of the mixed breed is exceedingly strong; but he appears to undervalue the pure Bactrian, which is certainly found extremely serviceable in European and Asiatic Russia, both for draught and burden, and in those countries, at least, is almost wholly exempt from disease. Fraser, Khorasan, 273.

†Tavernier: Voyages, I. 132. ‡Carbuccia, 10.

furniture of a camp, he rarely treads on the smallest article. The nostrils are fringed with long hairs, and provided with sphincters, which enable the animal to close them, and thus to exclude insects and the sand with which the desert winds are so often charged, while the hairs, to a considerable extent, perform the same office during the occasional partial opening of the apertures, required for respiration. The Bedouins understand the value of a wide nostril as well as a Newmarket jockey, and they frequently slit the nose of the animal in such a way as to give each aperture the form of a Y. The slitting of the nostrils is a common preparation for a race, and I once saw this absurd operation performed upon a dozen young dromedaries, which were to contend for the prize on the following day.

The camel is provided with seven callosities, which receive the shock of his fall in lying down for repose, or at the command of his master for the convenience of mounting or dismounting, or of loading and unloading, and the weight of the body is supported by them when at rest. One of these is upon the breast nearly between the fore legs, two upon each of the fore, and one upon each of the binder legs. The callosities upon the breast and at the knees are evidently organic, as they consist of a horny substance and are found in the fœtus. The others appear to be a mere thickening of the skin, and they may be the effect of friction and pressure. The full development of the callosities is one of the "points" of a good maherry, and it ought to be accompanied with a slender barrel, so that in the recumbent posture the belly shall scarcely touch the ground.

In lying down the animal throws himself slightly forward, and first bending one fore leg, poises himself for an instant, and then falls suddenly upon the callosities at the knees; he now advances the hind feet a little and drops upon the gambrel joint; the callus upon the breast is brought to the ground by a third descent, and those upon the upper and forward part of the hind leg by a fourth. Each of these movements, (which are renewed in rising,) and especially the first, is attended with a considerable shock; and the inexperienced rider is very apt to be thrown over the camel's head, unless he steadies himself by holding fast to the saddle pins. The Arabs slide down from and climb up to the saddle, without making the animal kneel, or even stopping him, and any active man may readily learn to do the same, but Europeans seldom practice this method. The French soldiers in Algeria use a long stirrup with two *steps* to mount by, and a loop upon a lance, such as were used by some ancient mounted troops, or attached to a musket, might answer the same purpose.

The foot of the camel is equally adapted to treading upon yielding sand and to climbing the rugged rock, which, in all extensive deserts, forms a much larger proportion of the surface than accumulations of sand. The surface of the wilderness is in general a hard, compact, gravelly soil, or composed of loose stones or bare rocks, and wherever it is not too hard for wear, or too soft permanently to retain impressions, the valleys pursued by the caravans are furrowed with paths which have been thousands of years in wearing. These tracks are 15 or 18 miles wide, and four or five inches deep, running generally parallel to each other at a couple of yards apart, and now and then intertersecting each other. An Arabian poem, older than the time of Mohammed, compares these paths to the stripes of a parti-colored cloak; and the Arabian traveller of the present day finds the same resemblance between the face of the desert and the "many colored coat" of its more opulent inhabitants.

The foot is composed of two long toes united by and resting upon an elastic cushion with a tough and horny sole or facing. The foot spreads upon touching the ground, somewhat like that of the moose and reindeer, and affords a broader support to the weight of the animal than almost any other quadruped is provided with. The camel, therefore, sinks less in the sand than any other large animal; but he nevertheless instinctively avoids it, as a horse does a puddle, and prefers any other surface except mud, loose rolling pebbles, and sharp pointed rocks.* The sole, though of a horny texture, is sufficiently yielding to allow the cushion of the foot to accommodate itself to the inequalities of a rocky surface,† and the camel climbs with facility ascents so steep and rugged, or even so slippery, as to be scaled with difficulty by any other domestic animal. The limestone ledges in the northern portion of the lesser Arabian peninsula are often worn to a glassy smoothness by primitive water currents, or by the attrition of the desert sands, yet the camel traverses them in all directions with entire security. Observing a caravan climb a long ascent of this description in Arabia Petrea, I had the curiosity to measure the inclination of the rock, and found the angle with the horizon to be fifteen degrees. The surface was everywhere almost as slippery as polished marble, and the length of the slope exceeded half a mile; but the whole caravan of more than fifty camels surmounted it without any accident. The northern slope of the pass of Negabad, on the eastern arm of the Red sea, appears to me even steeper than that I have just described, and the path is as rugged and the zigzags as short as those of almost any of the mule routes over the Alps, but it is constantly crossed by loaded caravans without difficulty. But these are trifles compared with the performances of camels in Algeria, as stated by the French officers. According to an official report to the war department of France in 1844, in the expedition to Milianeh, camels carrying burdens of 250 kilogrammes (550 pounds) climbed without accident slopes rising at an angle of 45 degrees, and readily traversed every route practicable by mules.‡

This structure of the foot gives the animal a peculiarly noiseless tread. The thunder which at a distance announces the approach of a troop of cavalry, does not herald the advance of a caravan; and even his rider hears but the faint rustling of the sand or the small pebbles displaced by the foot, as they roll back to the cavity left by the tracks of the animal. The regularity of his step and their gentle, purling sound, excite a peculiarly drowsy influence in the silence of the

* Denham and Clapperton's Travels, I, chap. 3, do. p. 169. Pietro della Valle complains that his camel, though the freshest and strongest in the caravan, fell in the soft sand "more than seven times in one day."

† The sole seems entirely impenetrable to thorns, and the camel treads with impunity on the strong sharp spines with which the fallen branches of the desert acacias are thickly armed.

‡ Carbuccia: Du Dromadaire, pp. 8, 169.

wilderness, which not even the danger of a fall enables the inexperienced traveller always to resist.

In mud the footing of the camel is insecure. The hind legs are little separated down to the gambrel joint, but from this point they diverge at a considerable angle, so that the ancient poem I have before quoted compares the hinder feet to two water buckets borne upon a yoke, and the increased breadth of base thus acquired contributes much to the sure-footedness of the camel on dry ground.

Upon a wet and slippery soil, on the contrary, the liability of the foot to slide is increased by this arrangement; and in case of such an accident, as the foot usually slides laterally, the hip joint is often dislocated or so badly wrenched that the animal is unable to rise with his burden and proceed upon his journey.* It is commonly said that the camel never rises after falling under his load, and that he immediately perishes under such circumstances. I have myself witnessed instances to the contrary, although I have no doubt that where the fall is from exhaustion the death of the animal is nearly certain. Where the mud is merely a thin layer of wet earth over a rocky or other very hard surface, the camel passes over it without much risk; and I have repeatedly seen caravans travel at their ordinary pace and with entire confidence and security over pavements covered with several inches of snow and soft mud.

The camel readily fords rivers with gravelly or pebbly bottoms, and I have seen them wade around headlands in the Red sea, in water three or four feet deep; but the passage of streams with soft bottoms, or with deep water, by camels is always a matter of great difficulty. It is almost impossible to train them to enter a ferry boat, or to lie quietly in crossing rivers by this mode of conveyance; and though they float readily, yet they are bad swimmers, the roundness of the barrel and the height of the head and hump above the line of flotation exposing them constantly to the danger of losing their balance and rolling over upon the side, in which case they are sure to be lost. For this reason it is common to lash the head to the gunwale of a boat, or to support it by some other contrivance in crossing deep waters.†

But the most interesting and important anatomical peculiarity of the camel is that curious structure by which he is enabled to take in at once and retain, by a special arrangement, a sufficient quantity of water to supply the wants of the animal economy for several days. It was conjectured by Cuvier, and it is believed by some more recent naturalists, that the stomach of the camel is not only able to retain for many days water swallowed by the animal, but that it possesses the further power of secreting a special fluid for moistening the fauces and viscera, and mingling with the food in rumination, in some such way as some fish are able to keep the skin moist for some time after they are taken from the water, by the exudation of a fluid secreted for that purpose. It is even said that the fluid found in the water-sack, after the death of the camel, possesses chemical properties which prove it to be an

* According to General Harlan, (Patent Office Report, 1853,) the hind legs are sometimes hobbled above the gambrel joint to prevent their spreading.

† Denham and Clapperton, II, pp. 80, 212. Father Huc, I, chap. 6. Lyon's Travels, p. 124.

animal secretion; but it does not appear that this fact has been established to the satisfaction of the physiological chemist.*

It is not easy to explain the structure of the stomach without drawings, and it must suffice to say that, according to Sir Everard Home, it consists, like that of other ruminants, of four cavities. The first of these performs the functions of both the first and second in the horned ruminants; the second is simply a receptacle for water; the use of the third is not ascertained; and the office of the fourth is the same as that of the corresponding stomach in other animals having four gastric cavities.†

Thus by means of the nutriment supplied by the absorption of the hump, and the fluid preserved in, and, perhaps, also secreted by, the water-sack, the camel is able to travel several days without any new supplies of food or water. The period of abstinence depends upon the breed, training, and habits of the particular animal, the season and temperature, and the amount of labor demanded of him.

With respect to food, there is no doubt that the camel often endures two, three,‡ and even more days of entire privation; but long abstinence is seldom necessary, because, although there is one well attested instance of the existence of a tract of desert frequently crossed by caravans, six days' journey in width, and absolutely without a particle of vegetation,§ yet there are few portions of the Libyan or Arabian deserts where more or less of the shrubs on which the camel feeds do not occur at very much shorter intervals.

According to Denham, the African camel is prepared for long journeys by having balls of dough crammed down his throat, while, on the contrary, Father Huc, a much less reliable authority, declares that the Bactrian is hardened by several days of previous abstinence. Under ordinary circumstances, the camel is not fed at all, even on very long journeys, but is left to snatch his food as he can during the march of the caravan, or gather it more leisurely while it halts. In a journey of seven weeks which I made with these animals in Arabia Petræ in the months of May and June, but a single camel of the caravan received any food from his driver. This was a fine large animal bred by the Ababdeh Arabs, which was fed every evening with from a pint to a quart of beans.

When herbage and browse are altogether wanting, a small quantity of beans, a few handfulls of dates or even date-stones, a ball or two of dough of barley-meal, millet, or other grain, weighing from one to three pounds, or a small supply of some dry vegetable are given each camel daily. According to Edrisi, they are sometimes fed with dried fish. Denham says they are fond of bones, and Riley even declares that he sometimes saw them fed with charcoal. The favorite food of the camel consists of the leaves, branches, and seed-pods of the acacias and other prickly trees or shrubs, of thistles, and of the saline plants so common

* According to Carbuccia, the fluid in the water-sack remains undamaged and drinkable several days after the death of the camel.—Du Dromadaire, 12.

† The gall bladder is wanting in the camel, and no trace of the biliary secretion has been found upon dissection.—Plinii Hist. Nat. XI, 74; Carbuccia, 103.

‡ Carbuccia, 10.

§ Denham and Clapperton, I, c. 3.

in the desert; and every vegetable zone is found to furnish some plant specially suited to his nutriment, while, in case of necessity, he scarcely refuses any green thing.* His powerful jaws and teeth enable him to grind and masticate branches of the hardest wood as thick as the huger. His palate is lined with a very hard cartilage; and the inside of the lip, the tongue, and the gums are protected by a skin almost equally impenetrable. The lips are, nevertheless, very flexible, and the upper labrum is divided. In feeding on the acacia or other prickly plants, he retracts and partially inverts the lips, grasps the twigs with the tongue and jaws, and thus crops and chews the thorniest shrubs with impunity.

The camels domesticated in Tuscany, which, though degenerated by a residence of centuries in the moist climate and alluvial soil of the lower Arno, are of the Arabian stock, neglect the green and tender cultivated grasses, but devour with avidity the leaves and smaller branches of the oak and the alder, and the hard dry stems of the thorn, the thistle, and the broom. The working camels at the grand duke's farm, near Pisa, are sheltered and fed on hay during the winter, but the rest of the herd remain in the open air, and subsist on twigs and withered shrubs through the cold season.

The Bactrian camel has the same fondness for saline plants as his African congener; but he feeds also upon the leaves, twigs, and bark of deciduous trees, the coarsest grasses, thistles, reeds, rushes, weeds, straw, and, in short, upon such vegetable diet as is rejected by almost every other domestic quadruped.

The statements of travellers differ very considerably in regard to the quantity of solid food required by the camel. My own observation would lead me to think it extremely small. As I have already stated, he is usually not fed at all; and in travelling his only opportunity of gathering his food is between the evening halt and sunset, when he returns to the camp, with such scattering mouthfuls as he can snatch upon the march. The vegetation of the desert is usually so sparse that the quantity of nutritious food which can be collected after the day's journey is performed must be very inconsiderable; and though upon starting in the morning the animal shows signs of hunger, and much annoys his rider by suddenly stopping or starting aside to crop a tempting thorn twig or thistle, yet in an hour or two his appetite is satisfied, and he performs the rest of his task without seeming to crave food. I was assured by the keeper of the herd at Pisa, that when fed entirely on hay, the camel consumed little more than half as much as the horse; while, on the other hand, a correspondent in the Crimea informs me that the Bactrian camel requires at least fifty pounds of hay per day in winter, and another in Bessarabia estimates the daily winter supply of hay and straw at seventy pounds. Pattenger states that the camels in Beloochistan receive about fifteen pounds of meal daily, besides grass and shrubs, and he adds the singular fact that the Belooches give these animals considerable quantities of opium with their food; but most travellers state that when fed at all, the camel receives five

* Carbuccia, page 10, says that the camel never touches the "aloe;" but an official report, at page 182 of the same volume, enumerates the "cactus" among the wild vegetables consumed by him.

or six pounds of meal at most. The power of the camel to abstain from water is much more frequently and severely tested than his ability to dispense with food. The testimony of travellers, as well as of native observers on this subject varies widely; but their discrepancies can generally be explained by difference of breed, of season, or the greater or less succulence of the solid food consumed by the animal.

The most extraordinary statements I have seen are those of the official reports of the French officers attached to the dromedary corps in Algeria. One of these reports declares that the camels of the corps employed in the expedition of El Aghouat did not drink from February to May, though the weather was very hot; and General Carbuccia, the commander of the corps, positively states that the Algerine camel under no circumstances drinks oftener than once in seven days.* Although many travellers have related cases of very long privation, while the animal had daily access to an abundant supply of green succulent food, yet that excellent observer Russell mentions an instance of fifteen days abstinence as altogether unprecedented; and I have been able to find but one other well authenticated case, which is that mentioned by Denham and Clapperton,† of so long an abstinence as eight days, when the animal fed mostly on dry food. Most travellers concur in saying that under such circumstances the extreme limit of endurance of the Arabian camel, whose powers in that respect are much greater than those of the Bactrian or other northern breeds, does not exceed five or six days. The longest period of complete privation I have personally witnessed was four days in very hot weather, and upon withered fodder; and I have always observed that the camel drank as often as he had an opportunity. In most countries where the animal is used, it is said he can dispense with drinking twice as long as the horse under the same circumstances. This I doubt not is a very near general approximation to the truth.‡ These facts, however wonderful, are by no means so extraordinary or incredible as they may at first sight appear. The domestic ox, when supplied with abundance of green fodder, seldom inclines to drink. Persons familiar with sheep husbandry know that in rich pastures that animal thrives very well for many weeks in the hottest summers, without any water but that which falls in the shape of dew; and if I mistake not, Captain Stansbury's mules travelled two whole days along the margin of Salt Lake, without food or water.

It is not the mere power of abstinence alone that so eminently fits the camel for travelling the steppe and the desert. His preference for the brackish and even saline waters which almost exclusively occur in those regions, and which are often so highly impregnated with mineral substances as to be rejected by most other quadrupeds, is a property almost as valuable. Russell even states that he prefers sea-water to

* Carbuccia, 10, 11, 89, 204.

† Denham and Clapperton, I. c. 3.

‡ The quantity of water swallowed by the camel, after long privation, is very great. I have seen one empty at a draught three goat skins, holding not less than seven gallons each; and Riley speaks of even much greater quantities. The camel smells, or by some other sense detects water at the distance of a mile or more; and the uncontrolled violence with which he rushes to the well to satisfy his thirst is one of the greatest inconveniences, not to say dangers, of desert travel.

fresh; but this is not confirmed by other authorities, and I have seen them, when parched with thirst, rush to the sea, wade into it, and turn from it with evident disappointment on finding the water salt.

The rate of travel of the burden camel is exceedingly uniform, and varies little in the different species and breeds of the animal. Rennelle, Robinson, and other inquirers, have very carefully investigated this subject, with a view to the use of the camel's pace in geography as a measure of distance. His speed is naturally modified by the nature of the ground, but as all irregularities of this sort are usually compensated in long journeys, it may be safely averaged at two miles and one third per hour. Over a smooth and level surface, I have found his ordinary length of step to be six feet, and the number of steps of each foot thirty-seven to the minute. This gives a speed of two miles fifty-two hundredths to the hour, under the most favorable circumstances; but upon rougher ground it was proportionately retarded, and I believe Robinson's estimate to be a very exact average.

The length of the caravan day's journey, when there is no special motive for haste, is regulated by the distance between wells and pasture grounds; but it is seldom less than ten, and more frequently twelve or fourteen hours, and in most countries the entire day's journey is accomplished without a halt. Averaging the hours of travel at twelve, the distance performed would be twenty-eight miles, and this rate may be kept up any number of days in succession.

This is the estimate for animals with full burdens, and left to their natural gait; but in case of emergency, and especially under lighter loads and fleeter camels, both the rate of travel and the length of the day's journey may be very much increased.

Bergmann states the ordinary day's journey of the loaded Bactrian camel at forty miles, and without burden at from fifty to sixty-five miles; and my correspondents in Bessarabia and the Crimea agree in stating that upon a good dry road a pair of Bactrians will draw a load of 3,000 to 4,000 pounds a distance of fifty miles without eating, drinking, or halting. These authorities, which I believe are entirely reliable, show that for transportation the Bactrian camel is superior to the Arabian; and it appears that when properly trained he is also capable of attaining a considerable speed under the saddle, though in this respect he cannot compete with the Arabian dromedary. Some of the Arab accounts of the fleetness of the maherry are no doubt fables, and one may well question whether Johnson's story of the dromedary that bore his master on an errand of love from Morocco to Mogador and back, a distance of 200 miles, in a single day, is not exaggerated. But the numerous well authenticated evidences of this animal's great speed and power of endurance, leave no doubt that in the union of these two qualities he far surpasses the horse, as well as all other domestic quadrupeds.

Mehemet Ali, when hastening to his capital to accomplish the destruction of the Mamelukes, rode without changing his camel, from Suez to Cairo, a distance of eighty-four miles, in twelve hours. A French officer in the service of the Pasha performed the same feat in thirteen hours, and two gentlemen of my acquaintance have accomplished it in less than seventeen. Laborde travelled the distance in the same time, and afterwards rode the same dromedary from a point opposite Cairo to Alexandria, a distance of about one hundred and fifty miles, in thirty-four hours. But the most extraordinary well authenticated performance of the dromedary is that recorded by the accurate Burckhardt, under whose personal observation it fell. In this instance the animal carried its rider one hundred and fifteen miles in eleven hours, including twenty minutes spent in crossing and recrossing the Nile. Upon longer journeys the daily rate of the best dromedaries, though not equal to these instances, is still extraordinary. A French officer of high rank and character in the Egyptian service, assured me that he had ridden a favorite dromedary ninety miles in a single day, and five hundred miles in ten. Mails have been carried from Bagdad to Damascus, upon the same animals, four hundred and eighty-two miles, in seven days; and on one occasion, by means of regular relays, Mehemet Ali sent an express to Ibrahim Pasha, from Cairo to Antioch, five hundred and sixty miles, in five days and a half. But the most remarkable long journey on record is that of Col. Chesney, of the British army, who rode with three companions, and without change of camel, from Basrah to Damascus, a distance of nine hundred and sixty miles, in nineteen days and three or four hours, thus averaging fifty miles per day, the animals having no food but such as they gathered for themselves during the halts of the party.

The gaits of the dromedary are all properly paces or ambles; though in racing I have seen them break into an irregular gallop, as they also do for a short distance when hotly pursued by cavalry, and they then outstrip the horse.* The motion of the burden camel and the slow walk of the dromedary are necessarily violent, from the great length of step, and at first very wearisome to the rider; but a few days' practice accustoms him to this rough exercise, and he performs his day's journey with as little exhaustion as upon horseback. The quicker movements of the dromedary, at his average pace of five or five and a half miles an hour are much easier and less fatiguing than his walk, and a day's journey of fifty or sixty miles at this pace is an easy achievement. At much more rapid rates, however, the motion becomes again intolerably violent, and an inexperienced rider fiuds it almost impossible to cling to the saddle, or even to catch his breath, though at the ordinary speed the seat is more secure than on horseback.

The burden of the ordinary camel varies with the age of the animal, his breed, and training, and it ranges from three hundred and fifty or four hundred pounds for the lighter and more delicate of the Arabian camels, to twelve, and for moderate distances even fifteen hundred pounds for those bred by the Turcomans in Asia Minor. From six to eight hundred pounds would be a safe average, according to the weight of the animal and the smoothness or ruggedness of the route; and with the smallest of these loads the ordinary camel would easily surmount any mountain passes practicable to other beasts of burden. The weight of the pack-saddle, which is considerable, is excluded in these estimates. In some parts of the East the Arabian camel is employed as a beast of draught, and is even harnessed to the plough. I have seen

* Carbuccia, 16, 77. Bergmann *apud* Ritter, XIII, 691.

them employed for transporting heavy stone on carts in Egypt, and they have been not unfrequently used for drawing heavy ordnance. In general, however, the Arabian camel is employed altogether as a beast of burden. In Bessarabia the Bactrian camel is used for the plough and for draught, while in the Crimea he is used for draught alone, and is seldom or never ridden in either of those provinces. Throughout Chinese and independent Tartary, however, as well as in Siberia, the Bactrian camel, though sometimes harnessed to wheel carriages, is much more generally employed for the saddle or burden; and the prejudice which has extensively prevailed that the configuration and sensitiveness of the bumps forbids the use of the pack-saddle for this species, appears to be without foundation.

In whatever mode the camel is employed, his harness is very simple. In some regions he is guided by a plain halter, in others the septum or one of the alæ of the nose is pierced, an iron ring inserted, and to this is attached a cord to serve as a bridle; and in the military service it has been found convenient to use the halter and this rude bridle in conjunction.* In the burden caravans the camels are not unfrequently tied head to tail, in files of about seven animals, the driver riding ahead upon a donkey or a camel, and the last camel in the file carrying a bell, so that the driver may be advertised by the ear if the chain by any accident is broken.

The pack-saddle, whether for riding or for burden, is made by stuffing a bag seven or eight feet long with straw or grass, doubling it and sewing the ends together. This forms an oblong ring, which is furnished with a rope crupper and placed upon the back so as to enclose the hump. Upon this cushion rests a frame consisting of two pairs of flat sticks meeting at top like a chevron or pair of rafters, and connected at bottom by a couple of sticks two or three feet long, secured to the others by thongs. The pad soon fits itself to the shape of the back and sides, and the frame nestles into the pad, while the hump rising in the centre of the whole apparatus keeps everything in place, so that no girdle, or at most a loose rope, is needed to confine the saddle. The load stowed in sacks, or better still in rope nettings, is balanced across the saddle, and the water-skins are suspended beneath.

The gear of the dromedary is somewhat lighter, but of the same fashion. The wooden frame is more neatly made, the uprights being curved outwards and uniting at top in two conical pummels, one before and one behind, six or eight inches high, and perhaps two in diameter at the base, covered with figured brass plate or otherwise decorated, and terminating in a knob. Over the saddle is thrown a large pair of saddle-bags of striped goat's-hair cloth, ornamented with fringes and cowrie shells, and upon this are laid blankets, cushions and carpets, and perhaps a gay housing over all. The rider is perched at the summit of this pyramid, directly over or perhaps a little in advance of the hump; and his stirrups, if he uses them, his water-bottle, his gun, a smaller pair of saddle-bags or a carpet-bag, or any other convenience he may choose, are hung to the pommels. In riding the maherry, how-

* Carbuccia, 44, 45, 50, 51, 133. According to Erman and Father Huc, the Northern Tartars pierce the septum of the nose and insert a piece of wood or bone, to which they attach the reins of the bridle.

ever, the wilder tribes sit on a small saddle placed upon the shoulders, in front of the hump, and sustain themselves in their seat by crossing the ankles over the neck.*

As the camel lies down to receive and discharge his burden, he is very quickly and conveniently loaded and unloaded; the latter operation generally consisting simply in loosing a knot of the cord by which the packages are slung across the saddle, and the camel then immediately rises and goes in search of pasture. On returning to the camp at veening he lies down between the packages; and if these consist of merchandize or other articles not requiring to be opened at night, the driver has only to knot the cord again, and the animal is ready for the march. The pack-saddle is very rarely removed; and as the camel very seldom stretches himself on his side or attempts to roll, the saddle is never lost.

For draught he is simply yoked to the pole of the wagon, just as the ox is with us, and requires no other gearing. This extreme simplicity and economy of harness has, with trifling modifications, been carried into the military service by the French in Algeria, and wherever else the camel has been employed in war, and is found to answer all purposes as completely as the costly furniture with which we supply our cavalry. Every soldier may be his own saddler, and he requires no material but bagging, straw or grass, a little cordage, and a few small sticks, which may be found wherever there is any arborescent vegetation, to extemporize at an hour's warning the complete equipage of his beast.

The training of the camel commences when he is quite young, and, as his *manège* is very simple, it is soon completed. At the close of his third or early in his fourth year he is in his full strength, and the period of his service begins earlier and lasts longer than that of the horse. In Algeria he never attains a greater age than thirty years, and he is fit for labor for about fifteen or twenty years. In Syria and Asia Minor his ordinary life and service is ten years longer; while in the Crimea, as I am assured by a Russian officer of great experience in the use of the animal, the Bactrian sometimes lives to a hundred, and, upon an average, to sixty or seventy; though another correspondent in Bessarabia states the ordinary term of his life at thirty-five years.

The average height of the Arabian camels I have measured was nineteen hands, or six feet four inches, to the top of the hump, the head being an inch or two higher. The tallest I have used measured seven feet and seven feet three inches respectively. The very powerful Turcoman camel is somewhat lower than the Arabian, and the height of the Bactrian is stated at from six to eight feet, his weight at one third more than that of the ox, which in the Crimea is estimated at nine hundred pounds, making the weight of the camel twelve hundred; and I was informed at Pisa that the camels of the grand duke's stables sometimes weighed fourteen hundred pounds.

The swift dromedary varies much in size. Layard mentions a deloul (the name of this variety in the Syrian desert) from the Nedjd, where very fine animals are raised, which was little taller than an Arab horse;† and all the true Arabian dromedaries I have met were very

* Lyon's Travels, 114. † Layard: New Researches, 332.

small. The hedjin, a dromedary of the upper Nile, on the contrary, is much taller, frequently, I am sure, not much below eight feet; and the maberry of the great desert is taller still. Lyon speaks of a Tibboo maberry of seven feet eight inches as small; and on one occasion a dromedary of this variety, measuring not less than nine feet and a half, was brought to the camp of Captain Denham.*

The most common colors of the camel are mouse, drab, and fawn; but black and white animals occur, and a very delicate and pleasing rose tint is not uncommon among the high-bred dromedaries of the greater Arabian peninsula.

The milk of the camel is a very favorite drink in all countries where the animal is used, and it is highly salubrious and nutritious. Some tribes possessing large herds live wholly upon it during a great part of the year, and it is very frequently given to favorite horses, which are extremely fond of it.† My own curiosity never led me to taste it, but the ladies of my party drank it constantly for many weeks, and found it both agreeable and refreshing; though, when the pasturage was particularly dry and spicy, they thought it rather too highly flavored with the aromatic savors with which, as poets sing, even the air is charged in Araby the blest. The quantity given in the desert without green food is small, certainly not exceeding a quart; but the Bactrian camel, which enjoys in general a more succulent diet, yields twice as much.

The utility of the camel does not cease with his life. His flesh, especially the hump and heart, is a favorite food among all camel-drivers, and when the animal is in good case it is described as little inferior to beef; but in the desert the camel is seldom killed until it is almost ready to die of exhaustion, and European travellers have found it in that condition tough and ill-tasted. The skin varies in thickness and strength with the breed, and is found of all qualities from that of the horse to the toughness and solidity of sole leather. Athough I have seen camels regularly sheared, yet, in general, the hair is wrenched off by hand at the time of shedding the coat. In southern latitudes the quantity is small, and the fibre short and coarse; but the Bactrian yields a fleece weighing ten pounds, of longer and finer fibre; and there are varieties in the basin of the Caspian with long silky hair scarcely inferior in quality and value to the wool of the Cashmere and Thibet goat. These breeds would be well worth introducing for the fleece alone.‡ The tallow is hard and firm, and for candles scarcely inferior to spermaceti or wax,§ and the bones would, no doubt, be found of value in the arts.

The Arab holds the camel and the date-palm to have been formed out of the same clay as our common father Adam, and to have proceeded more immediately from the hand of the Creator than any other quadruped or tree; and he believes he shall meet them again in Para-

---

* Lyon: Travels in Africa, 313. † Denham and Clapperton, I, 169.

‡ Father Huc. (American edition,) I. chap. 9, Ritter XIII, 676, 654. Erman, Reisen, I. 198, speaks of the camel's hair shawls brought to the fair of Nishnei Novgorod from Bokhara as of the most extraordinary fineness and beauty. They are made of the hair or rather wool combed from the belly of the animal, and spun into yarn as fine as human hair, and are sold at higher prices than the most delicate Cashmeres.

§ Carbuccia, 82—Ritter XIII, 692.

dise. Mohammed proclaimed his dispensation from the back of a camel, and was translated to Paradise by the same conveyance.

The camel alone is permitted to carry the sacred veil to Mecca, and he serves as the pulpit from which the Cadi preaches at Mount Ararat the annual sermon to the pilgrims to that holy spot. Notwithstanding these high claims, the Arab seldom pets his dromedary as he does his horse.

Beyond an occasional handful of food, and a dressing of the snows of the extreme north, he is never housed or otherwise sheltered in any of the wide range of climates through which he roves. To the extremest heat of an African sun the Arabian camel is utterly indifferent; and the Bactrian braves, without shrinking, the chilling frosts and the icy blasts of northern Siberia. I have often watched the camel's habits in this respect in the desert, and though we sometimes encamped near palms and other trees, or where he would readily have found a shelter beneath the cool shadow of a rock, I could never discover that, even under the most glaring light and scorching heat, he at all preferred the shade to the sun.

The camel, though less vicious than the horse, is not altogether so patient an animal as he is generally represented. His anger is indeed not easily excited, but when once thoroughly irritated, he long remembers the injury which has provoked him, and the "camel's temper" is a proverbial expression used by the Arabs to denote a vindictive and unforgiving disposition.* Although he sometimes strikes with the fore foot, yet the hoof being unarmed, his blows are feeble, and his only dangerous weapon is his teeth. These are used with powerful effect in the barbarous fights which are sometimes got up as spectacles, but it is only under certain special circumstances, which are easily avoided, that he attacks his driver.

His only ordinary manifestation of discontent is the harsh and ill-natured growl he sets up whenever he is approached to be loaded or mounted, and especially when any attempt is made to overcharge him. In the stillness of the desert the growl of a caravan, preparing for the morning's march, is heard for miles around; though the true maberry seldom growls, and it is said there are breeds which have entirely lost this disagreeable peculiarity; yet, in general, silent as is the march of a burden caravan, its halts are very unmistakeably announced to all wanderers within a long distance of its track. So harsh indeed is the growl of the camel, that Father Huc gravely declares that his camel-driver, on one occasion, put a pack of wolves to flight by tweaking his camel's nose till he roared again.†

The Arabs habitually travel much by night, and this not, as has been supposed, for the sake of the guidance of the stars, which they seldom need, but partly to avoid the greater heat of the day, and more especially to allow the camel, which never feeds by night, the day-

*Höst, an accurate observer, says, (Efterretninger om Marokos, 269,) that the Sultan of Morocco had camels trained to act as executioners, and all writers concur in representing the male as dangerous during the rutting season. According to Carbuccia, pp. 7, 8, 83, this paroxyism is calmed by tarring the head of the camel, or permanently prevented by a simple process attended with little inconvenience, and no danger to the animal.

†Father Huc, I, chap. 3.

light for gathering his food.* It is common to start from midnight to two o'clock, and to march, without halting, ten, fifteen, or sometimes twenty hours, after which the camp is formed; and if it is not yet dark, the camels are turned out to graze till sunset, when they return to the camp, are hobbled, by tying up one of the folded fore legs, and ruminate and sleep to the hour of departure. Although so long a day's journey without pause is fatiguing to the rider, yet, except with light dromedaries, experience is in favor of the practice. To halt without unloading the camels would afford them no relief, but fatigue them the more by practically lengthening their day's work; and if they are unloaded and allowed to wander in search of food, the time lost in colleeting them and rearranging their burdens would bring the caravan too late to the camping ground. Where, however, the party, as is the case with military expeditions of a few days' length, is unaccompanied by burden camels, and the dromedaries are loaded with only the equipage, water, and provisions of their riders, the hours of travel and repose can, without inconvenience, be arranged and varied to suit the exigencies of the occasion.

The question of the practicability and advantages of introducing the camel into the United States for military and other purposes, is one of much interest and importance; and I hope I shall be pardoned if I prolong a discourse, which I fear has proved but a dry one, for the sake of suggesting some considerations upon a topic to which I have devoted some attention, both at home and abroad.

Among those who are practically familiar with the habits and properties of the camel, and who have studied the physical conditions of our territory west of the Mississippi, there is, I believe, little or no difference of opinion on the subject; and I am persuaded that the ultimate success of judicious and persevering effort is certain, and will be attended with most important advantages. At the same time, it must not be concealed that, as much depends on a point that nothing but experience can determine,—the selection, namely, of the particular breeds best adapted to our climate, soil, and other local conditions,—the result of a first experiment, unless tried on a liberal scale, and with animals of more than a single variety, is extremely uncertain. The question must be considered under two aspects: the one regarding the camel as simply a beast of burden; the other, his value as an animal of war. But even if it is conceded, which I by no means admit, that the organization of a proper mounted dromedary corps is impracticable or inexpedient, it does not, by any means, follow that the camel may not be of great value in the commissariat, and in all that belongs to the mere movement of bodies of men, as well as in the independent transportation of military stores and all the munitions of war.

The first question to be discussed is the adaptation of any variety of either species to the climate and soil of any portion of our territory. So far as mere extremes of temperature are concerned, it is quite certain that we have nowhere, west of the Mississippi, fiercer or more long-continued heats, more parched deserts, or wastes more destitute of vegetation, than those of the regions where the Arabian camel is

* Fraser, Khorasan, 379.

found in his highest perfection; and the Bactrian thrives in climates as severe as even the coldest portion of our northeastern territory.

There is, however, it must be admitted, one point of difference between our general climate and that of the eastern continent which has an unfavorable bearing on the question. I refer to the greater moisture of our atmosphere and the greater frequency of rains during the summer season. In general, the countries where the camel thrives have a proper dry season, little or no rain falling during the summer months. But to this rule there are exceptions. The valley of the lower Danube has summer rains, and a very wet autumn, winter, and spring; and many northern Asiatic districts are subject to similar climatic conditions. But the objection, whatever may be its force, seems to apply merely to the proportion of the year during which the animal can labor, and not to its influence upon his constitution; because, it appears that in the cold and damp Russian provinces the camel is less subject to disease, and attains a greater longevity, than in any other part of the world; and it is remarkable that in the Crimea, at least as I am informed, he is little used in the hottest and driest season, because the heat is found too great for that variety, and his services are most valuable in winter.

On alluvial and other soft soils caravans using the camel will, no doubt, be obliged to halt during rains and until the ground is dry; but upon all other surfaces, one or other of the species may be used without regard to weather or season; and as none of the passes of the Rocky mountains are more rugged or steeper than those of Arabia or Tartary, there is every probability that he may be advantageously employed over all the known routes between the Mississippi and the Pacific coast.

In reference to the special properties of the different varieties it may be observed that, although, as we have already seen, the Arabian camel traverses the roughest routes and climbs exceedingly steep ascents, yet the Bactrian and the cross between the two species are even better fitted for sealing difficult mountain passes. This difference is, probably, partly due to habit and training; but the greater elongation of the toe of these breeds, which sometimes projects beyond the cushioned sole and forms a sort of claw, undoubtedly somewhat facilitates climbing by giving a grasp to the foot-hold, for which reason the Bactrian anciently was, and sometimes still is, called the mountain camel.

My Russian correspondents, to whom I have so often referred, say that the Bactrian is chiefly used for winter transportation, and that his feet require no protection, but, to use their own words, are so formed that he travels well not only on frozen ground, but upon ice and snow. Timkowski saw caravans of this breed cross a glacier; and Bergmann says that, in winter, the Calmucks prefer them to horses for the saddle, because their long legs enable them to wade through deeper snows, and adds that they bear severe cold better than the horse, the ox, or the sheep.

Father Huc and Pallas give similar accounts of the power of the Bactrian camel; and Pallas adds that he is used not only in deep snows and half-frozen morasses, but that he fords rapid torrents, and, with a little training, even swims well.

In the month of February, Erman saw, at Kiachta, on the Russo-Chinese frontier, herds of camels in the open air, feeding on withered and frozen wild vegetables, at a temperature of 25 degrees below zero of Fahrenheit, and remarks that they fear neither the severe winter of Siberia nor the parching summer heats of the sand-wastes of the desert of Gobi. The alternation of thaw and frost alone, says he, is dangerous to them, in consequence of the icy crust formed under such circumstances, which wounds their feet and limbs.

So numerous is the camel in these frozen realms, that almost the whole commerce between Russia and China, by way of Kiachta, is carried on by means of them; and they transport merchandise over the whole of the vast distance between Orenburg on the Ural, and Petropawlowsk on the peninsula of Kamtschatka. In the month of October, Timkowski met on the desert of Gobi, in latitude 46°, and at the height of 2,500 feet above the sea, a herd of 20,000 camels; the Russian expedition against Khiva and Bokhara, in 1840, employed more than an equal number; and Berghaus estimates the number of camels in European Russia at not less than 100,000.

So far, then, as climate and soil are concerned, it may be regarded as quite certain that the Bactrian camel can sustain any exposure to which he would be subjected in our trans-Mississippian territory; and there is no reason to doubt that the mezquit, acacia, and other shrubs, and the saline plants known to exist in many of those regions, would furnish him an appropriate and acceptable nutriment.

I cannot speak with equal confidence of the ability of the Arabian camel, and especially of the maberry of the desert, to bear corresponding trials. All high-bred animals are delicate, and impatient of exposure to great extremes and sudden changes; and although Denham and Clapperton speak of hard frosts in latitude 13° north, and Lyon records a temperature four degrees below the freezing point, in districts constantly traversed by the maberry, yet the finest and fleetest animals will not bear the winter climate of Algiers.* But, although we may not be able to breed dromedaries of a speed equal to the most extraordinary performances I have described, there is no reason to doubt that the more common animal, which will travel eight or ten hours a day at five miles an hour, for many days in succession, and with greater speed for a shorter period, can be bred and used with advantage throughout our southwestern territories, and on all the more southern passes of the mountains which divide the valley of the Mississippi from the Pacific slope, as well as throughout the State of California.

The ancient Asiatics, and, at a later period, the Romans, made a very extensive use of the dromedary in war, not only for the transportation of men and munitions, but as technical cavalry in actual combat; and they are still employed in Persia, Bokhara, and Tartary, for military purposes, and especially for the conveyance of light pieces of artillery, which are mounted between the humps, and used in that position, the camel kneeling while the gun is loaded, aimed, and fired. In modern European armies they have hardly been employed, except by Napoleon, in transporting the baggage of his army in the Syrian cam-

* Carbuccia, 4.

paign, in his celebrated dromedary regiment; and, more recently, by the army of occupation in Algeria. Upon the march from Egypt to Syria, the baggage, the camp equipage, and the sick,* of an army of 15,000 men, were transported solely by camels.

It is remarkable that the military archives of France furnish little or no information, beyond the mere number of the corps, respecting the dromedary regiment of the army of Egypt, the historical documents belonging to the subject having been chiefly lost or suppressed; and all we know concerning it is derived from an imperfect and erroneous account in the great work on Egypt, and a late paper by Gourard, one of the savans who accompanied the expedition. Without entering into minute detail, it must suffice to say that this regiment, which numbered something less than 500 men, was organized in the main like a regiment of cavalry, and performed the same general service, with the most brilliant success. Although the men were taken from the infantry, a very short time was required to teach them the new discipline and drill, and the animals were habituated to the necessary evolutions in an incredibly short space of time. The services rendered by the corps were of a most important character, and its performances, according to Prélat, were quite unprecedented in military annals. This officer states that the ordinary march of the regiment was thirty French leagues, or about seventy-five miles, *without a halt;* and that a detachment belonging to it marched six hundred miles in eight days. These latter extraordinary statements rest on the testimony of a single individual, and though the corps was composed wholly of picked animals and picked men, and animated by the energy of a Bonaparte, it is very difficult to yield them full credence.

The experiments in Algeria, though satisfactory to the officers charged with them, whose reports seem entirely conclusive upon the value and economy of the camel as an animal of war, have been attended with less brilliant results. The prejudices of the officers and men against the use of this awkward and ungraceful animal in the regular service have proved very difficult to overcome. The peculiar organization of the French commissariat has interposed serious pecuniary obstacles, and the government has always seemed disinclined to consider this question in a spirit of liberality and candor. It is, however, proved that the use of the dromedary contributes in a most important degree to the economy, the celerity, and the efficiency of military movements in desert regions; and I cannot doubt that it would prove a most powerful auxiliary in all measures tending to keep in check the hostile Indians on the frontier, as well as in maintaining the military and postal communication between our Pacific territory and the east.

There are few more imposing spectacles than a body of armed men advancing under the quick pace of the trained dromedary; and this sight, with the ability of the animal to climb ascents impracticable to

---

* For the transportation of the *wounded* the camel is not so suitable, on account of the roughness of his motion; but, for even these, the *tachtirawan*, or litter borne by two camels, would probably answer. Invalids often travel, as I have witnessed, in a *cajava*, or, as it is sometimes called, a *mahafa*. This consists of a pair of boxes or frames, properly with a canvass sacking, five feet long, two wide, and two deep, slung across the pack-saddle, and protected by an awning. A strong camel will carry two persons in this way.

horses, and thus to transport mountain howitzers, light artillery, stores, and other military matériel into the heart of the mountains, would strike with a salutary terror the Comanches, Lipans, and other savage tribes upon our borders.

The habits of these Indians much resemble those of the nomade Arabs, and the introduction of the camel among them would modify their modes of life as much as the use of the horse has done. For a time, indeed, the possession of this animal would only increase their powers of mischief; but it might in the long run prove the means of raising them to that state of semi-civilized life of which alone their native wastes seem susceptible. The products of the camel, with wool, skin, and flesh, would prove of inestimable value to these tribes, which otherwise are likely soon to perish with the buffalo and other large game animals; and the profit of transportation across our inland desert might have the same effect in reclaiming these barbarians which it has had upon the Arabs of the Siniatic peninsula.

Among the advantages of the camel for military purposes, may be mentioned the economy of his original cost, as compared with the horse or mule, when once introduced and fairly domesticated;* the simplicity and cheapness of his saddle and other furniture, which every soldier can manufacture for himself; the exemption from the trouble and expense of providing for his sustenance, driving, sheltering, or shoeing him; his great docility, his general freedom from disease,† his longevity, the magnitude of his burden, and the great celerity of his movements, his extraordinary fearlessness,‡ the safety of his rider, whether from falls§ or the viciousness of the animal, the economical value of his flesh, and the applicability to many military purposes of his hair and his skin, the resources which in extreme cases the milk might furnish, and finally his great powers of abstinence from both food and drink.‖

---

* The price of the camel is exceedingly low in all countries where he is bred. Except for the highest breed, maherries, it nowhere, except in the Crimea, exceeds fifty dollars, and is in general considerably below this sum. The reason of this is that it costs nothing to breed the animal. The dam continues to labor during the whole period of gestation, (which runs according to climate, from eleven, or in some cases, ten to twelve months,) and even the dropping of a foal scarcely delays her march. (Denham and Clapperton, I. c. 3, Ritter XIII, 610.) The young requires no care and little training, and is already serviceable in his third year.

† According to the concurrent testimony of all observers, no domestic animal is so free from disease as the camel. General Harlan's statement, that he is more liable to maladies than the horse, is unsupported by any other writer, and it must rest on some local peculiarity of climate or of breed. My correspondents in southern Russia describe the Bactrian as almost completely exempt from all ailments. In Algeria the camel suffers much from the sting, or more properly the oviposition of an insect; and it might be important, in importing the animal from that country, to select a season when he is free from the egg and the larvæ, in order to avoid introducing the insect with the camel.

‡ Carbuccia, 25, 168.

§ The security of the seat, though at once *felt* by all who have mounted the camel, seems hardly reconcilable with the violence of his motion, and is not easily explained; but nothing is more rare than a fall from his back. Every oriental traveller can testify that the Arabs often sleep upon their camels when on the march, and Colonel Chesney (Expedition to the Euphrates, II, 671) and Layard give curious accounts of the preparation and even cooking of food on the backs of the camels by the Arab women, during forced marches. They even contrive to milk the milch animals without halting.

‖ The use of the camel has enabled the corps which have employed it in Algeria to dispense altogether with a baggage train, as the animal can transport a very considerable burden, in addition to the soldier and his accoutrements, at a much more rapid rate than the ordinary march of a column of infantry or artillery.

I may add another advantage, which will be appreciated by all who know the difficulty of conducting a caravan of mules or horses across the plains. I mean the security from stampedes and other nocturnal alarms and losses. The dromedary is a much less timid animal than the horse or mule, and he is not sufficiently gregarious in his habits to be readily influenced by a panic terror. The mode by which he is confined at night furnishes a complete security against escapes from fright or other causes. As he lies down, he folds the forelegs under the body. The Arab passes a loop around one or both of the folded limbs, above the knee, and secures the end of the cord around the neck. When both legs are thus shackled, the camel can rise only to the knee: if one only is hobbled, he rises with difficulty, and moves very slowly; and if an Indian were to cut the loop, and thus free the animal, and even succeed in mounting him, he would not be able, without a previous practice, which he has not the means of acquiring, to put him up to such a speed as to elude pursuit.* There is another point which I have never heard insisted on, but which has often struck me with some force in riding the camel. I mean the greater range of vision which, in a level country, the greater elevation of the seat gives the rider. The eye of a horseman is upon an average scarcely eight feet above the ground. Upon the dromedary it is two feet higher, and commands a wider range accordingly.

To all these advantages I am aware of no drawbacks but the expense of introducing the animal and experimenting with him, and the difficulty of accustoming horses to the sight of him. The first objection is too trifling to be debated in a case of so much importance; and though the latter has been found formidable in Tuscany, and according to Father Huc, even in Tartary, where the camel has been very long in use, yet it is of no great force as applied to the sparsely populated regions of the Far West, and as the multiplication of the animal would be gradual and slow, it is not likely that any great or general evil would flow from this source.

The facts I have recited seem to me abundantly to warrant the conclusion that at the least the experiment is worth trying, and it is highly desirable that it should be tested on a scale large enough and varied enough to embrace all the chances of success.†

For transportation, the choice would lie between the Turcoman camel of northeastern Asia Minor and the Bactrian. The former might easily be procured at Aleppo, and shipped at Alexandretta, or perhaps better at Trebizond, on the Black sea. The Bactrian, which seems

* The only serious inconvenience attending the use of the camel in marching through a country inhabited by hostile Indians, is the necessity of allowing him to wander in search of food; but as he habitually returns to camp before sunset, of his own accord, and never feeds, and very seldom stirs during the night, he would require to be watched only for a couple of hours during the whole twenty-four.

† Very full information on the military qualities and the hygiene of the Arabian camel, upon the dromedary regiment of the army of Egypt, and the use of this animal in war by the ancients, may be found in the work of Carbuccia I have so often cited, and the papers of Gourard appended to it. The title is: Du Dromadaire comme bête de somme, et comme animal de guerre; par le Général G. L. Carbuccia. Paris, 1853. The appropriation made by Congress for introducing the camel ($30,000) will prove hardly sufficient, it is to be feared, for trying the experiment on a sufficiently liberal scale; and it is therefore doubly important that advantage should be taken of the knowledge acquired by the French in their African possessions.

on the whole the more promising animal, might most readily be obtained at Odessa, or in the Crimea; but, as the camels of those provinces are trained only for draught, it would be more advisable to procure them from the Calmucs, in the neighborhood of the Caspian, where they are used for burden and for the saddle, and, according to Bergmann, possess great speed, and they could be shipped at some of the ports of the sea of Azow, or they might perhaps, with even greater convenience, be bought at Petropawlowsk, on the Pacific, at the season of the visit of the caravans, and landed in California.

The dromedaries should be brought from Algeria rather than from Egypt, because they are there accustomed to much severer winters, a moister climate, and a rougher country; and the experience of the French military service in the use of them might be of great value in aiding in the selection of the breeds or individual animals, as well as in furnishing patterns of the best harness and gearing. The number of each ought to be at least sufficient for the organization of a small regular corps, to be trained in the use of them, and the officers should be provided with all the information which can be gathered from Asiatic and European experience on the subject.

"If," says General Marey Monge, "cavalry had been unknown in France, and we, seeing the great advantages derived from it by the Arabs, had now for the first time attempted to introduce it into our military service, we should have had a thousand difficulties to overcome. Objections would have been made on the score of kicks and bites, errors would have been committed in the choice of saddles and bridles, the horses would have met with accidents or contracted ailments from our want of experience and ignorance of farriery; in the first engagements, our mounted men would have been thrown or run away with, they would have been clumsy in managing their arms on horseback, and probably been roughly handled by the superior skill of the Arab horsemen. A party would have been formed against the innovators, who would themselves have become disgusted, and the attempt to introduce mounted corps would perhaps have been abandoned; but if, in spite of accidents, mistakes, and losses, we had persevered, we should have ended by forming what we have now, an efficient and excellent cavalry."

This argument is as valid with us as it was in Algeria; and if the experiment shall be tried in the United States without success, it will probably fail for reasons as specious but as inconclusive as those which General Monge supposes against the introduction of cavalry into the French military service.

Note.—A late writer in the Révue Orientale, 1280, says: "I knew in Egypt a camel driver who had bought a dromedary belonging to a sherif of Mecca, deceased, at Cairo. This animal often made the trip between the latter city and Suez, going and returning in twenty-four hours, thus travelling a distance of sixty leagues in a single day." [The performance of the dromedary is rather understated. The actual distance between Cairo and Suez is *eighty-four* English miles, and the animal must consequently have accomplished one hundred and sixty-eight miles in twenty-four hours. He remained four hours at Suez for rest, and therefore travelled at the rate of eight miles and four tenths per hour.]

LECTURES.

No. II.—ON THE NATURE AND CURE OF THE BITE OF SERPENTS AND THE WOUNDS OF POISONED ARROWS.

BY DR. DAVID BRAINARD, OF CHICAGO, ILLINOIS.

Among the many points in which the science of the present day surpasses the knowledge of past centuries, there is none more conspicuous than that which relates to the nature, the effects, and the means of deteeting poisonous substances.

To be convinced of this we have only to cast a glance at the state of society in the latter part of the sixteenth century, the time of Charles IX and Henry III, of France.

At that period Italian manners and customs had been introduced into France by Catharine de Medici, and with them the knowledge of those poisons whose use, in Italy, had rendered the names of certain families pre-eminent in the annals of infamy.

The most-distinguished surgeon of the sixteenth century, Ambroise Paré, has left us, in his works, a very curious account of the means resorted to by the Italian perfumers to convey poisons in a manner which should not be suspected.

Paré was the surgeon of Charles IX, and, being a Protestant, was saved from the massacre of St. Bartholomew, concealed in the cabinet of the king in the palace of the Louvre, at the time when the signal for the slaughter was sounded.

The object of the monarch in saving his life was to have the benefit of his superior skill as a surgeon, and especially in the art of detecting poisons and counteracting their effects.

Paré states that poisons are, "by the artifices and sublimations of the wicked traitors, poisoners, and perfumers," deprived of their bitter taste, and even rendered agreeable to the palate, while they are so concentrated as to prove fatal in a short time, and so subtle as to defy the efforts of the most skillful to detect them.

In relating the case of Pope Clement, who was poisoned by the vapors of a torch, he says that flowers and odors of any kind were often used to convey the fatal influence; and that every prelate, beneficed clergyman, or other person whose wealth or rank promised advantage to any who might compass his death, lived in constant dread of poison.

A whole chapter of his work on medicine and surgery is devoted to the means of guarding against being poisoned. He advises the avoiding of all sauces, and especially those which are sweet, salted, or in any way pungent; and, in like manner, being thirsty, not to drink in large draughts, or to eat greedily, but to consider well the taste of what is eaten or drunk. "Moreover, we should eat," says he, "those things which break the force of venoms before each repast, and particularly a fat soup made of good meat," and only take wine or other drinks after having eaten. He counsels taking in the morning mithirstate or theriaca, with a little good wine or malvoisie, or the leaves of rue with a nut and dried figs, which, he adds, "are remedies of singular efficiency." And "let not those who have a suspicion of having been poisoned, sleep; for the force of the venom is sometimes so great, so contrary to nature, that it exerts its power, and its effect in the body is like that of fire in dried straw."

"The true way to avoid poisoned perfumes," he adds, in concluding, "is never to smell them; to fly such perfumers as you would the plague, drive them out of the kingdom of France, and send them among Turks and infidels."

Modern science has revealed the nature of these poisons so subtle, so mysterious, and so dreaded.

The torch of chemistry has explored the secret chambers of those "wicked poisoners and perfumers."

Armed with its light the law is enabled to cast a shield around every individual, and give to the humblest a consciousness of safety which, in former times, the most powerful could not enjoy.

But science in this respect is not yet perfect. There are still substances mysterious, subtle, and dangerous, for which neither tests nor antidotes have been discovered. Many of the savage tribes of America possess the art, unknown to civilized man, of imbuing their weapons with a substance so deadly that a slight wound from one of them is dangerous, if not fatal.

The venom of serpents, the smallest drop of which brought in contact with the blood in the system is fatal, cannot be distinguished by chemical tests from the most harmless mucus or saliva.

There is reason to believe that this venom is sometimes employed by man; that he arms himself with the substance bestowed by Providence on the serpent for its defence, and uses it for the purpose of procuring subsistence or satisfying his destructive instincts.

Of the serpents which are furnished with this poison, the most common and dangerous is the crotalus, or rattlesnake, several varieties of which are found in the western and southern States of the Union, where they constitute an object of dread, and a source of danger to the first settlers of the country.

The rattlesnake derives its name from the peculiar structure of its tail, on which are arranged a number of rings called the rattle, with which a sound is made not unlike the buzzing of the wings of certain insects. The number of these rings increases with its age; but it is not certain that they correctly indicate the number of years it has lived.

The rattle is generally sounded whenever the serpent is angry, so that those familiar with the noise may avoid the danger; but in many instances the wound is inflicted without any warning being given.

The rattle itself is to be regarded as a means of defence in addition to the fangs and venom; for the peculiar note which it produces is terrifying to most animals, and they shrink from it with instinctive fear.

It seems to have been regarded by some of the aboriginal inhabitants of America as highly ornamental, for it is one of the objects which the natives of central America have most frequently represented in the carvings of stone with which they decorated the front of their temples.

The apparatus by which this serpent inflicts a wound and deposits the venom within it, excels in delicacy and perfection any instrument for inoculation which human ingenuity has as yet been able to devise.

It consists of moveable fangs or teeth placed one or more on either side of the mouth beneath the upper jaw.

They are exceedingly sharp, curved, and move upon a hinge, so that, when in a state of repose, they lie with the point backwards, almost covered by the membrane of the mouth. The fang is perforated at its root by a canal which terminates near the point in a groove.

It is through this that the venom is ejected so as to be thrown, not upon the surface, but deposited at the bottom of the wound.

When about to strike, the fangs are raised so as to project directly forward, and the serpent coils himself so that, in the act of straightening, the head is thrust with great force a distance of about half his length. At the moment when the fang is most perfectly projected, the same muscle which elevates it presses also on the sac which contains the venom and ejects it, through the canal of the tooth, with force; so that, if the object is not attained, it is thrown to a certain distance, and may be seen falling in drops.

If the object aimed at is attained, as soon as the the teeth are inserted they are turned backward and drawn through the flesh like hooks to lacerate it. Indeed it often happens that the animal bitten, by a sudden movement draws the serpent after him, or that the fangs themselves are left in the wound.

The serpent, too, with the subtle instinct of his nature, as soon as the wound is inflicted, coils himself so as to resist being moved and thus inflicts a severe injury.

Nature, as if this weapon were indispensable to the species, has provided in the most ample manner for its indefinite reproduction when accidentally removed or shed at stated periods.

There exists at the side of the principal teeth in use, several others in different stages of development, which, in case any are shed or removed, grow and supply their place.

The gland which forms the venom corresponds to the largest of the salivary glands in man. The duct through which it is discharged is enlarged so as to form a reservoir capable of containing several drops, which may be kept in reserve.

That the saliva of one class of animals should contain the most concentrated venom, while that of others is the mildest of fluids, presents a contrast of the strongest character; but a certain analogy can be traced even in this instance, for in all animals when rabid, the saliva becomes poisonous, and in many, as in men, it sometimes assumes a certain degree of activity which renders it dangerous from the effect of anger alone.

The venom of the rattlesnake is a fluid of the consistence and color of olive oil; it has a peculiar and disagreeable odor, and is said to have a pungent taste.

There is no chemical test by which it is distinguished, nor are any peculiar appearances to be observed in it by the most powerful microscope.

It may be swallowed without danger. All the venom which could be extracted from several serpents mixed with water and poured into the mouth of a young bird in the nest when it opened its beak for food, did it no injury.

Persons bitten by serpents generally experience, as the first effect, an intense pain in the part wounded—vertigo, nausea, fainting, and coldness.

If the venom has been inoculated directly into a vein, these symptoms terminate in death in a short time. If not, the part swells, becomes discolored, spotted over the surface of the member, and sometimes over the entire body.

The swelling is sometimes very great, extending over a large surface; but the heat and inflammatory reaction which accompany it are of a low grade.

If the amount of venom which has been deposited be small, or the wound has been properly treated, the swelling after having reached a certain point slowly subsides, but the part affected remains for a long time indurated. It has even been supposed that the extraordinary enlargement known under the name of elephantiasis is in many cases a remote effect of this wound.

As soon as the swelling commences to subside, another danger threatens the patient, viz: passive hemorrhage. The constitutional effects of the poison are such that they produce a dissolved state of the blood like that which exists in scurvy. Hence bleeding is liable to occur from the mouth, lungs, bowels, ulcerated surfaces, or the slightest wounds, or from all these at a time.

In a case which occurred in the Illinois general hospital, the blood which flowed from the gums was found so entirely destitute of fibrine, the principle upon which the coagulation depends, that no trace of it could be detected under the microscope. At this state the breath exhales a fetid odor, which is not only sickening at the moment, but which is said to have produced serious illness in those exposed for a length of time to its influence.

Bites which occur about the face are much more dangerous than those upon the extremities.

This discoloration results from the dissolved state of the blood which gives rise to hemorrhage, mortification, and death.

Nevertheless, the bite even of the most venomous species of serpents is not invariably nor even generally fatal.

There are seasons when they are inactive and inflict but a slight wound. The venom is at times much less virulent than at others, or it may have been exhausted by repeated bites. Small serpents have not sufficient force to penetrate the skin, and bites where the skin is thick or covered with clothing are least dangerous.

On the other hand if the serpent be old, of large size, and the bite occur in the commencement of summer, the danger is very great.

There is reason to believe that the poison used by the Indian tribes on their arrows, is, in many cases, nothing else than the venom of the serpent preserved in a peculiar manner.

Mr. Schomburgh himself says that the belief, that animal poisons entered into its composition was so rooted in Guiana, that on the occasion of his second visit, in 1837, he was unable to eradicate it.

Messrs. Bernard and Felouze, in a memoir presented to the Academy of Sciences at Paris, in 1850, express the opinion that it acts in the manner of a venom, that is an animal poison. They state that M. Goudot, who furnished them with the specimen they employed, had resided many years in South America, and was fully aware of the method of its preparation, and that he assured them that the poison of the most venomous serpents constantly entered into its composition.

He even described the manner of taking the serpents, and extracting the poison.

An intelligent traveller in California informs me that the Digger Indians in that State possess the art of poisoning their arrows, and that the substance which they use for the purpose is well known to be obtained from the rattlesnake.

Dr. George Johnson, of St. Louis, also told me that several tribes of Indians on the Rio Grande employ the venom of the serpent for this purpose, and that there is a species known to them which have the vesicles receiving the venom so large as to contain a quantity sufficient to poison a great number of arrows.

An intelligent missionary, who had resided many years in the East Indies, states that the traditional account of the method of preparing the woorara of that country is, that the venom of serpents is mixed with it to form the most active part.

This substance called woorara, curare, corare, tiennas, has been variously described by different travellers as being of an animal or a vegetable nature, or a mixture of the two. Sir Walter Raleigh is said to have been the first who heard of its existence; but certain missionaries in South America gave at an early day an account of its effects, but so mingled with fanciful details as to deprive it of most of its value as authority.

At the commencement of the present century, Humboldt gave a detailed account of its manufacture, stating that it is prepared by heat from the bark of a certain vine called by the natives on the bank of the Amazon, *bejuco de menacure* mixed with the juice of certain other plants to give it consistence.

De le Condamine states that it is an extract made by heat from the juices of divers plants, about 30 in number, and that the bejuco is one of them.

Robert H. Schomburgk* confirms in most respects the account given by Humboldt. He named the vine from which it is obtained, *Strychnos toxifera.*

The Reverend Thomas Yond, who resided as a missionary in English Guiana, describes its mode of preparation very minutely. He states that two species of Strychnos and six other species of plants enter into its composition.

Mr. Schomburgk treats as entirely fabulous the accounts of the employment of animal substances, such as poisonous ants or the venom of serpents, in its preparation; and most English writers seem to consider it certain that it owes its activity to strychnine.

On the other hand Boussingault and Roulin, (Annales de Chimie, September, 1828,) who made an analysis of it, state that it does not contain strychnine but a vegetable principle very different from it.

Its effects on the system sufficiently indicate that its action does not

* Annals and Magazine of Natural History, vol. VII, p. 407.

depend on strychnine. It affects the brain, producing fainting, insensibility, and paralysis; while strychnine acts upon the spinal marrow, producing convulsions but leaving the consciousness intact.

When injected into the veins, even in the minutest quantity, it kills in a few seconds, while a much larger quantity of strychnine is required to cause death when thus administered.

Mr. Charles Waterton, in his Wanderings in South America, states that in addition to the woorara vine, the natives employ in its compositiou the black and red ant and the fangs of serpents, which, he adds, they invariably extract and preserve whenever occasion is presented.

From a chemical analysis of this substance which I had made, though not completed, but which has revealed formic acid and a protean compound among its constituents, I am enabled to state with great certainty that a.imal substances enter to a certain extent at least into its composition.

Humboldt, in his voyage to the equinoctial regions of South America, states that Indians, who had been wounded by poisoned arrows, described to him the effects as identical with those of the bite of serpents.

These effects, as noticed in experiments on animals and birds, seem to me to bear the closest analogy with those of the venom of serpents, if they are not identical.

The fact that the woorara is, like the poison of serpents, innocuous when swallowed, strongly militates against the opinion that it is strychnine, or, indeed, any vegetable alkaloid. As usually met with, the kind which is brought from South America is contained in small gourds, over the internal surface of which it is spread. On being detached it presents a dark color, has a resinous fracture, a bitter taste, is readily mixed with water, but imperfectly dissolved by it. Its appearance is the same when mixed with alcohol; but both these fluids dissolve the active principle of it. The solution is acid. If the quantity of water used be small, the mixture has a ropy, tenacious consistence. The solution is coagulated by the nitrate of silver, and by the solution of iodine and iodide of potash in distilled water, and, when treated with the latter solution, neither the part coagulated nor the fluid expressed from it retains its poisonous quality. It does not effervesce with acids. Its aqueous solution is not coagulated by heat, and boiling does not impair its activity.

The manner in which poisonous substances act in producing their effects has long been regarded as one of the most difficult subjects in the wide range of nature. So long as the doctrines of astrology prevailed, they were supposed to derive their properties from the malign influence of the stars.

Ambroise Paré, certainly one of the most enlightened men of his time, was governed by the then prevailing doctrine when he said: "Poisons which act by a specific nature do not produce their effects because they are hot, or cold, or dry, or of an excessive humidity, but because they have that peculiar property of the celestial influences which is contrary to human nature."

In the infancy of toxicology the effect of nearly all poisons was referred to sympathy.

When they were applied to wounds, and the heart ceased to act, it was said to be from a sympathetic affection, conveyed in some mysterious manner by the nerves.

The statement that any such impression is conveyed is as purely gratuitous as was the explanation of the pressure of the atmosphere by the simple expression, "nature abhors a vacuum."

Since the experiments of Magendie, in 1809, on the subject of absorption, it has generally been admitted that most poisons produce their effect on the system by being absorbed and carried into the circulation, and that they exert their influence by virtue of their peculiar properties.

Conia digitaline and nicotine destroy the action of the heart; strychnia acts upon the spinal marrow; opium, the woorara, and poison of serpents on the brain.

Now, although the absorption of poisons, and their presence physically in the blood and organs, is a most important fact,—one, indeed, upon which the whole science of toxicology reposes,—it is not to be imagined for a moment that it affords the slightest explanation of their mode of action.

The question still remains, whether they act by being applied to the sentient extremities of the nerves, or in some other manner not yet understood.

Liebig has offered the explanation, that the poison by some chemical change is converted into the substance of brain, which is thereby rendered unfit to support vital energy.

This hypothesis is entirely gratuitous, improbable, and, in view of the rapid action of many substances on the brain, impossible.

Fontana was much nearer the truth when about a century ago he attributed death from the poison of the viper to the effect produced on the blood. He was of the opinion that, injected into the veins of animals, it caused coagulation of the blood, which arrested the circulation. He made more than six thousand experiments with vipers, repeated and varied in every possible way. In regard to the coagulation of the blood in this case, I am not able to deny that it may occur, as I have not experimented with vipers; but I am sure it is the reverse of what takes place from the bite of the rattlesnake, for it is uniformly found dissolved after death from this cause, and incapable of coagulating to the same extent as in health. I am also certain that a change does occur in the form of the globules of blood in pigeons and frogs poisoned by woorara and the bite of the rattlesnake.

If the wing of a bat or the web of a frog's foot be subjected during life to observation beneath the focus of a microscope, innumerable small bodies are seen hurrying along the arteries, towards their extremities, traversing the small, hair-like vessels called capillaries, and returning towards the heart by the veins.

These bodies are the blood globules. They vary in form in different classes of animals, being circular and flattened in men, and ovoid in birds and frogs.

The integrity of these globules is essential to life; for whenever they become altered, they adhere to the sides of the vessels and to one another, and can no longer traverse the capillaries.

The theory that poisons alter the form of the globules, so as to render them unfit for circulation, is not a new one, for Fontana alludes to it, but says he had not been able to detect in them any change.

This arose, no doubt, from the imperfect instruments employed, and from the deficient means of examination. Fontana claimed to have invented the microscope, but only used a single lens, and examined blood in considerable quantities.

By using the most perfect microscope, and examining the blood of frogs and of pigeons, in which the globules are ovoid and of large size, I have been able to discover that, after poisoning by serpent bite or the woorara, their form is constantly altered, so that, instead of being of a distinct and regular outline, they are found irregular, indented, and partially disintegrated.

Those taken from the capillaries are most, those from the heart and large vessels least affected; but even of the former only a small portion of the whole number will be found changed, as death takes place before all have time to become mutually affected.

When death occurs quickly from the effect of the bite of the rattlesnake or from the woorara, it is, in my view, from these substances being absorbed, and acting upon the blood by altering the form of the globules, so as to render them unfit for circulation, whereby they are arrested in the capillary vessels of the brain, and thus destroy its action.

There are doubtless other changes produced on the circulating fluid besides this of the globules.

The late Dr. J. W. Burnett, of Boston, noticed that when blood obtained by pricking his finger was mingled with the venom of the rattlesnake, the globules ceased to run together, as they naturally do.

But I think the change of the globules which I have detected is of itself quite sufficient to account for the sudden effects even of the most violent poisons.

The belief that some substances cause death by their effect upon the blood seems to have prevailed long before it was expressed by Fontana.

Shakspeare, with that intuitive perception of truth characteristic of his writings, has adopted it in his account of the killing of the king, when the ghost thus describes to Hamlet the effects of the poison:

"Sleeping within mine orchard,
My custom always in the afternoon,
Upon my secure hour thy uncle stole,
With juice of cursed hebanon in a vial,
And in the porches of mine ears did pour
The leperous distilment, whose effect
Bears such an enmity to the blood of man
That, swift as quicksilver, it courses through
The natural gates and alleys of the body,
And, with a sudden vigor, it doth posset
And curd, like eager droppings into milk,
The thin and wholesome blood; so did it mine,
And a most instant tetter marked about,
Most lazar like, with vile and loathsome crust,
All my smooth body."

We arrive now at the consideration of the second part of our subject, the treatment of poisoning by serpent bite, and the woorara.

According to the division of scientific studies most commonly adopted, the pursuit of science for itself, pure science as it is called, ranks above any practical application of it, however important and useful this latter may be, though I regard it important in proportion as it has capacities for useful application.

One might indeed devote himself to the pursuit of some of the natural sciences for the inherent pleasure which it affords.

But the study of the venom of serpents and its effects would be surrounded by few attractions, were it not that the knowledge thus acquired may be made available for the relief of some of the severest accidents to which man is subject.

The experiments upon birds and animals required to carry out these researches are painful, and can only be justified by the benefit which results from their performance.

In this country there is fortunately less occasion than in some others for defending the study of the practical applications of science, as the genius of the people, and their habits, tend to practical results rather than abstract researches. It is indeed possible that to many scientific men of our country the classic fable of Atalanta, who, in turning aside to seize the golden apple, lost the prize of the race, may not be inapplicable.

In reference to the venom of the rattlesnake there is much need that further investigations should be instituted.

It is a substance for which, as I have already said, no antidote has hitherto been known, and concerning the nature of which no adequate researches have ever been made.

What is required is a series of experiments in regard to it similar to those which Fontana performed with the viper.

The treatment resorted to for serpent bites varies in different countries, that remedy being generally selected which tradition or accident may have suggested; and it would be a waste of time to enumerate all those inert or deleterious articles whose use has been recommended even in books of medicine and surgery. It may suffice to say, under this head, that scarcely any substance can be named so inert as not to have been recommended, or so disgusting as not to have been employed; nor is any practice so absurd as not to have found favor with the profession.

Among them may be mentioned burying the member bitten in fresh earth, thrusting it into the entrails of animals, or even putting the whole body of the patient into an ox laid open for the purpose—practices which, as they are either cooling or sweating, are not destitute of plausible reasons in their favor.

Arsenic, in the form of the Tanjore pill, has been extensively used by British practitioners both in the East and West Indies; but although many successful cases were cited in its favor, it has fallen into disuse.

Among intelligent physicians of the present day the treatment consists in washing the part, sucking it, or applying cups, to extract the poison, using caustic for the purpose of destroying it, while stimulants, such as ammonia and alcohol, are administered internally.

Of these means, washing, applying ligatures upon the members, and cupping, are those alone whose utility has been well established by reason and experience.

That the removal of as much as possible of the venom from the wound is useful, is self-evident, and sucking it for this purpose seems to have been an instinctive act; for not only does tradition relate that it was in use in ancient times and among savage nations, but history informs us that it has been resorted to more recently. Among the notable instances of which may be mentioned that of Queen Eleanor, wife of Edward I, who, it is stated, sucked the wound which her husband received from a poisoned dagger in the war of the Crusades, thereby preserving his life.

The application of ligatures around a member bitten, as it retards absorption, has the same effect as introducing the poison in divided doses, and at longer intervals of time. In this way quantities might safely be received, which, if carried at once into the blood, would prove quickly fatal.

Cupping-glasses exhausted over the wound act in the same manner, with the additional advantage, that by drawing fluids from the part they may remove at least a portion of the venom.

The value of these means has been tested by numerous experiments upon various animals and with different classes of poisons.

Of the applications resorted to, aqua ammonia is that mostly relied upon. But Fontana found that mixing it with the venom of vipers only hastened death. He also found that alcohol, oil, the mineral acids, and alkalies, (except caustic potash, which instantly destroys the tissues,) nitrate of silver, incisions in the part, and even amputating the member bitten, did not prevent a fatal termination.

In my experiments with the rattlesnake I have found that mixing the venom with alcohol, oil of turpentine, nitrate of silver in solution, or ammonia, did not diminish its activity.

The solutions of soda and potash have no effect in retarding its action, unless sufficiently strong to destroy the tissues by acting as a caustic.

My friend, Dr. J. C. Morfit, who aided me in my experiments, tried liquor potassæ, a solution of bicarb. of soda, tincture of arnica, and ammonia in water. The result of my observation is, that to the present time no substance has been found in any degree capable of neutralizing the venom of the serpent or the woorara, without destroying the part bitten, except the solution of iodine, and iodide of potassium, in water. Of the virtues of this solution I shall have occasion to speak hereafter.

Alcohol taken internally to intoxication has at the present time the reputation of counteracting the effects of the venom of the rattlesnake.

The evidence in its favor is scarcely sufficient to justify the confidence reposed in it, as the following facts will show:

1st. The venom, when mixed with alcohol, is rapidly fatal if inoculated.

2d. Alcohol introduced into the stomach of birds or animals bitten hastens death.

3d. Persons bitten by rattlesnakes when in a state of intoxication are not, on that account, secure.

I have authentic information of several cases in which the bite of that serpent proved rapidly fatal on intoxicated persons. I think it certain, however, that the effect of alcohol taken in this way is beneficial rather than injurious; but this is not my belief in regard to ammonia, which I think calculated to favor the action of the poison rather than retard it.

Among the substances in popular use in the western States of the Union, I ought not to omit to speak of the sulphate of alumina or alum. This and other astringents are principally useful in that stage of the affection when hemorrhages are liable to occur, and they may then be employed with advantage both as internal remedies and local applications.

It may be expected that I should here speak of those plants which, under the name of rattlesnake weeds or roots, possess, in the popular belief, a specific virtue against the bite of this serpent. The plant known under this name in many parts of the west is a species of *Liatris*, having a broad leaf with spines along the edges. It has a pungent aromatic taste, and is a diffusible stimulant of moderate force. The manner in which it is generally used is by beating it up into a poultice and placing it upon the part, and also taking an infusion as a drink. It has no specific virtues as an antidote, as I have known deaths to occur after its use; but as a stimulant it may be, in some degree, useful.

There are many other plants, also, reputed to possess similar virtues, among which may be mentioned *Eryngium aquaticum*, or button-snake root; several species of *Impatiens*, or jewel weed; the *Eupatorium perfoliatum*, or boneset; the *Scrophularia*, the *Scutellaria*, the *Plantago*, and probably many others; of all of which it is sufficient to say, that there is no conclusive evidence to justify their being regarded in the light of specifics, though, like the *Liatris*, they may be more or less useful in certain cases.

As remedies are by some deemed important from having been used by the Indians, it may be mentioned that the *Impatiens*, or jewel weed, is said to be often employed by them. A medical officer of the army informs me that the common nettle applied as a poultice, and taken in infusion, is a favorite treatment among the Cherokees. For this, as for hydrophobia and most diseases, there are secret remedies, possessing, according to report, the most instantaneous and marvellous power of neutralizing the action of the poison.

There exists, according to popular belief, a tree whose smallest branch or leaf has the effect if placed before a serpent of rendering him so timid and fearful that he will neither bite nor resent the roughest treatment, nor can he live in the region where it grows. The leaves possess the power (according to the same vague report) when beaten up and placed on the bitten part of instantly causing the pain to cease; so that the patient, like one touched by a hand of miraculous power, is straightway cured. The tree which is reported to possess such virtue is nothing else than a species of *Fraxinus*, or common ash. It is certain that it has none of the powers ascribed to it, either on the actions of the serpent or the effects of its venom.

Having made many experiments, with a view of determining the action of various substances on the venom of the rattlesnake and on the woorara, I have found but one which, in any degree, neutralizes it without destroying the tissues of the part.

The solution of iodine and iodide of potassium in water possesses the power, when properly used, of invariably retarding death, if it does not prevent it. The manner in which the experiments were conducted with the woorara, was, in the first place, to ascertain the quantit required to cause death.

In general I found $\frac{1}{5}$ of a grain to kill a pigeon in five minutes, when injected under the skin.

2. I then mixed the same quantity with 20 drops of a solution of iodine and iodide of potassium, of the strength of 10 grains of the former and 30 of the latter to the ounce of distilled water, and injected it under the skin of the pigeon. It produced no sensible effect.

3. I threw the poison under the skin of the pigeon, and applying a cupping glass lightly on the part, injected the solution of iodine through the same canula. No symptom of poisoning followed.

4. I covered a deep wound of the muscle in a pigeon with a paste made of the woorara and water. The bird died in five minutes.

5. I repeated the same experiment, but washed the wound with the solution of iodine. There was no bad effect.

These experiments have been repeated by myself alone, and, in connexion with others, more than a hundred times with the same results. I feel confident, therefore, that their accuracy cannot be called in question, and that, in regard to the woorara, it is quite safe to affirm that the solution of iodine neutralizes its action. In making this statement, I would by no means be understood as asserting that it does so in all circumstances and in all proportions. The circumstances which prevent its doing so are the introduction of the poison in such a situation that the solution cannot reach it, or so directly into the circulation that it has not time to act upon it. In most cases of wound neither of these conditions is likely to occur.

According to the experiments which I have made for the purpose of determining the proportion of iodine required to neutralize the poison, it appears that one third of a grain of woorara is perfectly neutralized by one eighth of a grain of iodine.

The treatment of the bite of the serpent is more difficult to determine by experiment than that of the wounds poisoned by woorara. The bite itself is often profound, penetrating so deeply that applications cannot be made to the bottom of it without inflicting an additional injury, which, in itself, would be dangerous to small animals. On the other hand, if the venom be first extracted from the serpent, and then inoculated, its action is uncertain. Much of what appears to be venom is, probably, only saliva, which serves as a vehicle, and is with difficulty distinguished from it. Nevertheless, I have succeeded in saving more than half the birds bitten, and in greatly prolonging life in those which died.

The manner in which these experiments are conducted is as follows:

The bite having been inflicted on a given part, by having the serpent properly confined, immediately apply a cupping glass lightly upon the point, then insert a fine trochar beneath the cupping glass, under the skin, and, while the air is being exhausted, press the solution of iodine into the tissues of the part with a small syringe adapted to the canula of the trochar. The cupping glass is retained upon the wound until the solution has had time to disseminate itself, and become mixed with the poison.

In case of a superficial wound, when the treatment could be applied immediately, nothing more would be required than to wash it with the solution.

As pigeons, upon which these experiments were made, are more easily affected than mammals, the antidote which succeeds with them more certainly succeeds in case of the bite on man.

The principle on which the iodine operates in counteracting the effect of these poisons, is most probably from its antiseptic properties.

They belong to a class described by Orfila under the name of putrefactive poisons, characterized by being innocuous, or of little activity, when swallowed, but causing wounds upon which they are applied to run rapidly into mortification.

Iodine, like chlorine, has the effect of counteracting this change; preventing the discoloration which results from such wounds, and the alteration of the blood to which they give rise, while it possesses over chlorine the additional advantage of not causing inflammation or mortification, when injected under the skin and disseminated in the tissues.

The practice of injecting it into the parts, instead of applying it upon the surface, is founded upon the principle, now well established in toxicology, that an antidote, to be effectual, must not only be introduced into the system, but brought in contact with the poison where it physically exists.

Now for all inoculated poisons it is clear that to comply with this condition the antidote must also be inoculated; that is, introduced into the same tissues, and take its course through the same vessels which the poison has to traverse, to reach the vital organs.

When the poison is inoculated and the antidote swallowed, or applied on the surface, it is impossible that they could be brought in contact in more than the minutest proportions.

Used in this way, the iodine also favors the production of adhesive inflammation, whereby lymph is effused and coagulated around the wound, absorption retarded, and the disease rendered less diffusive. In this respect iodine, injected under the skin, is more efficient than blisters or cauterization with the nitrate of silver, which can only act superficially.

Although I have advanced the theory that iodine is an antidote to septic poisons, by virtue of its anti-putrescent properties, I would not, by any means, be understood as limiting its effects to this method of action. On the contrary, I believe it is, to a certain extent, an antidote for some poisons pertaining to other classes.

Donné found it to counteract the action of strychnia to a great degree; and I have observed that it has a very considerable power as an antidote to prussic acid, an action which its analogy to chlorine would lead us to expect, as chlorine is well known to prevent the effects of this acid.

The plan of treatment which I recommend for the bite of serpents and wounds from poisoned arrows, is—

1st. To wash the part with a solution of iodine and iodide of potassium, and apply cupping-glasses over the wound, or ligatures around the member, so as to prevent absorption.

2d. If the wound be deep, or if absorption has already taken place,

I recommend injecting the solution under the skin, beneath the cupping-glass, and disseminating it by friction about the wound.

This recommendation is founded upon the result of over one hundred experiments with the woorara, and about sixty with the rattlesnake, made upon pigeons, dogs, cats, rabbits, and guinea-pigs.

This treatment can be combined with the administration, internally, of such remedies as may be thought most useful; and among these alcohol, in some form, taken freely is, in the present state of our knowledge, to be preferred.

LECTURES.

No. III.—THE ZONE OF SMALL PLANETS BETWEEN MARS AND JUPITER.

BY PROFESSOR ELIAS LOOMIS, OF THE UNIVERSITY OF NEW YORK.

Seventy-five years since, the only planets known to men of science were the same which were known to the Chaldean shepherds thousands of years ago. Between the orbit of Mars and that of Jupiter there occurs an interval of no less than three hundred and fifty millions of miles, in which no planet was known to exist before the commencement of the present century. Nearly three centuries ago the immortal Kepler had pointed out something like a regular progression in the distance of the planets as far as Mars, which was broken in the case of Jupiter. Being unable to reconcile the actual state of the planetary system with any theory he could form respecting it, he hazarded the conjecture that a planet really existed between the orbits of Mars and Jupiter, and that its smallness alone prevented it from being visible to astronomers. But Kepler himself soon rejected this idea as improbable, and it does not appear to have received any favor from the astronomers of that time.

An astronomer of Florence, by the name of Sizzi, took decided ground against all such innovations of doctrine. He maintained that since there are only seven apertures in the head—two eyes, two ears, two nostrils, and one mouth—and since there are only seven metals, and seven days in the weeks, so there can be only seven planets. These seven planets, according to the ancient systems of astronomy, were Saturn, Jupiter, Mars, the Sun, Venus, Mercury, and the Moon.

In 1772, Professor Bode, of Berlin, first announced the singular relation between the distances of the planets from the sun, which has since been distinguished by the name of Bode's law. This law exhibited in a striking light the abrupt leap from Mars to Jupiter, and suggested the probability of a planet revolving in the intermediate region. This conjecture was rendered still more plausible by the discovery in 1781 of the planet Uranus, whose distance from the sun was found to conform nearly with the law of Bode. In Germany, especially, a strong impression had been produced that a planet really existed between Mars and Jupiter, and the Baron de Zach went so far as to compute the orbit of the ideal planet, the elements of which he published in the Berlin Almanac. In the year 1800, several astronomers, of whom the Baron was one, formed an association, whose object was to effect the discovery of the unseen body. For this purpose the zodiac was divided into twenty-four zones, one of which was to be explored by each astronomer. Soon after the formation of this society the planet was discovered, but not by any of those astronomers who were engaged expressly in searching for it. Piazzi, the celebrated Italian astronomer, while engaged in constructing his great catalogue of stars, was induced carefully to examine, several nights in succession, a part of the constellation Taurus, in which Wollaston, by mistake, had assigned the position of a star which did not really exist. On the first of January, 1801, Piazzi observed a small star which, on the following evening, appeared to have changed its place. On the third, he repeated his observations, and he now felt assured that the star had a retrograde motion in the zodiac. He continued to observe the star until the 11th of February, when he was seized with an illness which interrupted his labors. After the planet had approached too near the sun to admit of further observations for that season, Piazzi communicated to astronomers all his observations. Professor Gauss found that they might all be satisfied by an elliptic orbit, of which he computed the elements. The planet was re-discovered on the 31st of December, almost exactly in the place which had been predicted by Gauss; and it received the name of Ceres.

The distance of Ceres from the sun was found to be almost exactly the same as had been assigned by Bode's law. In this respect, therefore, the newly discovered planet harmonized with the other bodies of the system to which it belonged. The new planet was, however, excessively minute, its diameter, according to Herschel's measurements, amounting to only one hundred and sixty-one miles.

The discovery of this planet was soon followed by another of a similar nature. Dr. Olbers, while engaged in searching for Ceres, had carefully studied the positions of all the small stars lying near her path. On the 28th of March, 1802, after observing Ceres, he swept over the vicinity with an instrument termed a "comet seeker," and was astonished to find a star of the seventh magnitude in a position where he was sure no star had been visible the preceding month. In less than three hours, he found that its place had changed. On the following evening he looked again for his star, and found that its motion was unquestionable. The elements of its orbit were soon determined by Professor Gauss, who found that its distance from the sun was nearly the same as that of Ceres; and it received the name of Pallas.

A comparison of the relative magnitudes of the planetary orbits had suggested the existence of an unknown planet revolving between Mars and Jupiter. Instead of one planet, however, two had been discovered. Olbers remarked that there was a point where the orbits of these two bodies approached very near each other; and he conjectured that they might possibly be the fragments of a larger planet, which had been split in pieces by some tremendous catastrophe; and he intimated that there might be many more fragments which had not yet been discovered. He also inferred that, according to this theory, the orbits of all the fragments would have two common points of intersection situated in opposite parts of the heavens, through which every fragment must pass in the course of each revolution. He therefore proposed every month to search carefully the two points of the heavens in which the orbits of Ceres and Pallas were found to intersect each other. The speedy discovery of a third planet tended to confirm the truth of this hypothesis.

On the 1st of September, 1804, Professor Harding discovered a small star very near the place where Olbers had asserted that the fragments of the shattered planet must all pass. On the evening of the fourth he found that the star had changed its place. This planet was named Juno. Its orbit was computed by Gauss, who found its distance from the sun to coincide nearly with those of Ceres and Pallas.

Stimulated by this new discovery, Olbers continued with unwearied assiduity to explore the two regions of the heavens already referred to, and, after three years of laborious search, his perseverance was crowned with success. On the 29th of March, 1807, he discovered a small star in a place where none had been found in his previous examinations. He soon satisfied himself that this object was a planet; and it received the name of Vesta. The elements of the orbit were determined by Gauss, who found its distance from the sun to be a little less than that of Ceres, Pallas, or Juno.

Dr. Olbers continued his systematic examination of the heavens until 1816, but was rewarded by no further planetary discoveries.

In 1825, a fresh impulse was given to researches of this nature by the resolution of the Berlin Academy, to procure the construction of a series of charts showing the position of all stars down to the ninth magnitude situated within fifteen degrees of the equator. Only about two thirds of the charts contemplated in this great undertaking have yet been executed.

After the discovery of Vesta, succeeded a long interval of thirty-eight years, during which the excitement created by these first discoveries subsided, and the search for new planets was generally abandoned.

At length, in 1845, a fifth asteroid was announced by an observer hitherto unknown to fame, Hencke, of Germany. In 1847, the same observer announced a sixth asteroid, and from this time numerous observers in every part of Europe devoted much of their time, while some devoted nearly all of their energies to the search for planetary bodies; and discoveries at once multiplied with astonishing rapidity. Three new asteroids were discovered in 1847, one in 1848, one in 1849, three in 1850, two in 1851, eight in 1852, four in 1853, and six have been announced during the year 1854, making at the present time a total of thirty-three. Of these thirty-three ten were first discovered by Mr. Hind, of London; seven by Dr. Gasparis, of Naples; three by Luther, of Bilk; while Dr. Olbers, of Bremen, Hencke, of Driesen, Chacornac, of Paris, and Goldsmith, also of Paris, have each of them discovered two asteroids; and Piazzi, Harding, Graham, Marth, and finally Ferguson, of our own National Observatory, have each discovered one. Moreover, in several instances, the same planet has been independently discovered by more than one astronomer.

In scarcely a single instance could these discoveries be termed the result of accident. They have been the result of a laborious search expressly undertaken for the discovery of these bodies. Mr. Hind, who has been the most successful explorer in this field, nearly ten years ago commenced comparing the Berlin charts with the heavens, and began to map down for himself the stars in other regions of the ecliptic, which did not fall within the limits of the Berlin charts. Any discrepancy between the stars on the maps and the stars in the heavens was carefully scrutinized; so that if a new star presumed to show itself within the limits of the charts, it was at once pounced upon as an unlicensed wanderer.

The discoveries of Gasparis were also made partly by comparing the Berlin maps with the heavens, and partly by a series of observations in zones of declination, made for the express purpose of finding new planets. Nearly all the asteroids have been discovered by a systematic comparison of the visible state of the heavens, with the state as recorded in charts.

The rapid discovery of twenty-nine new asteroids, after a barren interval of almost forty years from the discovery of Vesta, is calculated to excite surprise; but it is explained by the diminutive size of the new planets, and the great increase in the number of observers, as well as the use of more powerful instruments. Vesta appears like a star of the sixth magnitude, Pallas of the seventh, while Ceres and Juno are of the eighth. Of the twenty-nine asteroids more recently discovered, none of them, with perhaps two exceptions, are larger than the ninth magnitude, while several are as small as the tenth, and one or two scarcely, if ever, rise so high as the tenth magnitude. The reason that Olbers was not more successful in his search was that he employed a telescope of too feeble power, and did not extend his examination beyond stars of the eighth magnitude.

Some may conclude that the number of asteroids already known is so great that the discovery of additional ones is a matter of no interest, and is unworthy the attention of astronomers. I regard the question in a very different light. If only one planet had hitherto been discovered between Mars and Jupiter, our idea of the simplicity and perfection of the solar system would have been satisfied; and there might have been found ingenious minds attempting to prove by a priori reasoning, that no other planets could possibly exist, unless beyond the limits of the orbit of Neptune. But our theory of the solar system, although apparently simple, would not have been the *true* theory. Every new discovery shows the solar system to be more complex than we had supposed; and unless we prefer error (provided it has a show of simplicity) to truth, when it appears to our view complex, we shall value every new discovery in the solar system, because it promises to conduct us nearer to the true theory of the universe. Every new asteroid which is discovered is a new fact to be explained. It presents a new test by which every theory is to be tried. The true philosopher, instead of regarding the rapidly increasing number of asteroids with indifference, will watch each new discovery with growing interest, in the hope that it may furnish the key to the true theory of the solar system.

The existence of thirty-three planets revolving round the sun, at distances closely allied to each other, and differing from all the other planets in their diminutive size, is one of the most singular phenomena in our solar system. This fact will appear the more striking if we draw a diagram representing the orbits of all the known planets in their proper proportions. We shall find that while the orbits of Mercury, Venus, the earth, and Mars are quite detached from each other, and the orbits of Jupiter, Saturn, Uranus, and Neptune are separated by intervals which the imagination can scarcely grasp; between Mars and Jupiter is a cluster of bodies whose orbits are so interlaced as to suggest the apprehension of frequent and inevitable collision. The orbit of Fortuna approaches the orbit of Metis within less than the moon's distance from the earth, while the orbit of Massilia approaches almost equally near to the orbit of Astræa, and the orbit of Lutetia to that of Juno.

It is evident then that these thirty-three small planets sustain to each other a relation different from that of the other members of the solar system. We see a family likeness running through the entire group; and it naturally suggests the idea of a common origin. This idea, as has been already stated, occurred to the mind of Olbers after the discovery of the second asteroid, and led to his celebrated theory, that all these bodies originally constituted a single planet, which had been broken into fragments by the operation of some internal force. Have we any means of testing the soundness of this theory?

If the earth should be broken into fragments by the operation of some internal force, (such for example as that which causes the eruption of a volcano,) the fragments might be projected in various directions, and with very unequal velocities, but each would describe an ellipse, of which the sun would occupy one of the foci; if we except the extreme but possible case of a fragment projected with such a velocity as to carry it beyond the limit of the sun's attraction. If we leave out of view the disturbance arising from the mutual attraction of the planets, which produces only minute effects, each fragment would continue to describe the same ellipse in its successive revolutions about the sun; in other words, these ellipses *would all have a common point of intersection.* The same conclusion must hold true for the asteroids, according to the theory of Olbers. The question, of course, arises, have the orbits of the asteroids a common point of intersection? A single glance at a diagram of these orbits will settle this question in the negative. But it is replied that the orbits of the planets are disturbed by their mutual attraction: these orbits should *originally* have had a common point of intersection; but at each revolution they suffer a slight displacement, until in the lapse of time the position of the orbits has become so completely changed as to leave scarcely a trace of their original intersection. Is such a result possible? A few simple considerations will satisfy us that if the orbits of the asteroids ever had a common point of intersection, such a result must have belonged to a period of time indefinitely remote.

The line in which the plane of a planet's orbit intersects some other plane, selected for common reference, is called technically the line of the *nodes.* If the asteroid orbits ever had a common point of intersection, all the nodal lines upon one of the orbits must have coincided. Now, as two of the asteroid orbits are inclined less than one degree to the earth's orbit, we will, for greater convenience, employ the latter as the plane of reference. On referring to a table of the planetary elements, we see that the ascending nodes of the asteroids are distributed, though unequally, through the four quadrants of the circle. Ten of them lie in the first quadrant, twelve in the second quadrant, seven in the third, and four in the fourth. The nodes of all the planetary orbits are in constant motion; but the motion for a single year is extremely small. The annual motion of the node of Mercury is ten seconds; that of Venus is twenty seconds; Mars twenty-five seconds, &c. The most rapid motion found in the nodes of any of the asteroid orbits, as far as the computation has been made, is about fifty seconds a year. If we suppose the nodal lines of all these orbits to move steadily toward each other, it would require, in some of them, a motion of fifty seconds a year, continued for more than six thousand years, to bring them to a coincidence.

It must also be observed, that not only must the nodes of all the asteroids coincide, but the distance of the planets from the sun must be the same at that instant. Now, the distances of these bodies from the sun, when at their nodes, differ by more than a hundred millions of miles; so that, to bring them all together, requires something more than a change in the position of the nodes. We may bring about a coincidence in the case of some of the asteroids, by supposing the longer diameter of the elliptic orbit to change its position, without disturbing the plane of the orbit. Such a change does really take place in the case of every planetary orbit, but with none of the larger planets does it exceed twenty seconds a year. In the case of one of the asteroid orbits, this motion has been found to amount to seventy seconds a year; but, even with this motion, it would require the lapse of five thousand years to bring about an intersection in the case of many of the asteroid orbits. When, now, it is remembered that, in order to give a common point of intersection to these thirty-one orbits, all the nodal lines must coincide, and, at the same instant, all the distances from the sun must be equal to each other, we must be prepared to admit that such an occurrence could only have taken place myriads of years ago.

The preceding difficulties, however, are small, in comparison with another which remains to be stated. The orbit of Hygeia completely encloses the orbit of Flora, and, indeed, several other orbits, and would still enclose them, although the greater diameter of each of them were revolved through an entire circumference—since the least distance of Hygeia from the sun exceeds the greatest distance of Flora. The same is true of Themis, as compared with Flora, and several other orbits. The least distance of Hygeia from the sun exceeds the greatest distance of Flora by more than *twenty-five millions of miles*. In order to render an intersection of these orbits possible, we must suppose a great variation of the eccentricity. But the change of eccentricity of the planetary orbits is exceedingly slow, and the present rate of increase of the eccentricity of Vesta must be continued *twenty-seven thousand years*, to render the aphelion distance of that planet equal to the perihelion distance of Hygeia. Moreover, the eccentricity of the orbit of Vesta is now *increasing*, which implies that in past ages the interval between Vesta and Hygeia must have been greater than it is at present; whence the conclusion appears irresistible, that the orbits of Vesta and Hygeia cannot have intersected for *several myriads of years*. When the secular variations of the elements of each of the asteroids have been computed, astronomers will be able to assign a limit of time, beyond which the intersection of all the asteroid orbits must have occurred, if, indeed, such an intersection ever took place. The discovery of many of these bodies is so recent that, as yet, there has not been sufficient time for such a computation; but, from what we already know, we hazard little in venturing the opinion, that when this computation shall be made, it will appear that, if the asteroid planets ever composed a single body which exploded, as Olbers supposed, such explosion must have occurred *myriads of years ago.* Indeed, the discovery of such a host of asteroids seems to have stripped the theory of Olbers of nearly all the plausibility it possessed when it was originally proposed; and it would seem hardly less reasonable to suppose that the earth and Venus originally constituted but one body, than to admit the same for the thirty-three asteroids.

But, if we reject the theory of Olbers, what do we conclude? That the asteroids bear no special relationship to each other? Do they not all clearly indicate a family resemblance? And, if so, how do we account for this relationship?

There are several reasons for believing in some peculiar relationship between the asteroids.

1. Unlike the other planets of our system, they are all of diminutive size—the largest of them hardly exceeding one or two hundred miles in diameter. M. Leverrier, after a close examination of the nature and amount of the influences exerted by the entire group of asteroids upon the planets Mars and the earth, has arrived at the conclusion that the sum total of the matter constituting the small planets between Mars and Jupiter, including undiscovered as well as known asteroids, *cannot exceed about one fourth of the mass of the earth.*

2. The asteroids, in their position, occupy a zone entirely distinct from the other planets of the solar system. Between the orbits of Jupiter and Saturn, as well as between Saturn and Uranus, is an immense interval, furnishing space enough for a host of little bodies to circulate around the sun; but in not a solitary instance has any such body been found, except between Mars and Jupiter. Some may attempt to account for this circumstance, by saying that astronomers have long been watching exclusively this portion of space, and have left all other regions entirely unexplored. An exploration conducted upon such a principle is simply a physical impossibility. If there were a small planet between the earth and Mars, it would have stood the same chance of detection, in the explorations of the past ten years, as if it were situated between Mars and Jupiter; and, indeed, it would have stood a better chance of detection, inasmuch as it would appear of greater brightness on account of its proximity to us. If there were a small planet circulating between Jupiter and Saturn, it would have stood the same chance of detection as if it had been placed this side of Jupiter, except that it would appear somewhat fainter on account of its increased distance. The fact that we have discovered thirty-three small planets between Mars and Jupiter, and not a solitary one in any other portion of the solar system, points to something *special* in this region of the heavens. In other words, we have discovered *a limited zone* of little planetary bodies, and have not been able to discover a single body of the same class situated out of this zone.

3. The orbits of these little bodies present some special peculiarities.

The ascending nodes of the orbits are not distributed uniformly through the zodiac. The ascending nodes of twenty-two orbits are included within the space of 180 degrees; while only eleven are left for the remaining 180 degrees of the zodiac. A similar remark applies to the position of the perihelia. In the first half of the zodiac we find twenty-five perihelia, while only eight remain for the other half of the circumference. We could not have anticipated any such bias in the orbits if they had always been entirely independent of each other.

4. But the most striking peculiarity of these orbits is, that they all lock into one another like the links of a chain, so that if the orbits are supposed to be represented materially as hoops, they all hang together as one system. The orbits of Hygeia and Themis being the largest of all the orbits, completely enclose nearly all of them, and lock into but a small number; while the orbits of Massilia, Astræa, Pallas, &c., look into nearly all of the orbits, so that if we take hold of the orbit of Hygeia, which we fancy to be a material hoop, it will support the orbits of Iris, Thalia, Calliope, and two or three others, while these in turn lock into and support all the rest. Indeed, if we seize hold of any orbit at random, it will drag all the other orbits along with it. This feature, by itself, sufficiently distinguishes the asteroid orbits from all the other orbits of the solar system.

If we reject the theory that these asteroids were originally united in one solid body, it seems, nevertheless, difficult to avoid the conclusion that similar causes have operated in determining the orbits of this zone of planets. It is impossible to assign any cause for these resemblances without adopting some theory respecting the origin of the solar system. The theory of gradual condensation, as developed by Laplace in the nebular hypothesis, affords at least a plausible explanation of these phenomena.

Laplace supposes that the matter composing the bodies of our solar system, originally existed in the condition of an immense nebula, extending beyond the limits of the most distant planet—that this nebulous mass had an exceedingly elevated temperature, and a slow rotation on its axis—that the nebula gradually cooled; and as it contracted in dimensions, its velocity of rotation, according to the principles of mechanics, increased, until the centrifugal force arising from the rotation, became equal to the attraction of the central mass for the exterior zone, when this zone necessarily became detached from the central mass. As the central mass continued to contract in its dimensions, and its velocity of rotation continued to increase, the centrifugal force again became equal to the attraction of the central mass for the exterior zone, and a second zone was detached. Thus a number of zones of nebulous matter were successively detached until, by gradual condensation, the central mass became of comparatively small dimensions and great density.

The zones thus successively detached would form concentric rings of vapor, all revolving in the same direction round the sun. If the particles of each ring continued to condense without separating from each other, they would ultimately form a liquid or a solid ring. But generally each ring of vapor would break up into separate masses, revolving about the sun with velocities slightly different from each other. These masses would assume a spheroidal form: that is, they would form planets in the state of vapor. If one of these masses were large enough to attract each of the others in succession to itself, the ring of vapor would be converted into a single spheroidal mass of vapor, and we should have a single planet of great mass for each zone of vapor detached. But if no one of these masses had a preponderating size, they would all continue to revolve about the sun in independent orbits, and would form a zone of little planets such as we have actually discovered between Mars and Jupiter.

With regard to the actual number of bodies belonging to this zone of planets, we can do little more than hazard a plausible conjecture. Already we have one asteroid of the sixth magnitude, one of the seventh, four of the eighth, eighteen of the ninth, and nine of the tenth or eleventh. It would require four hundred bodies as large as the largest of the asteroids, to make a body one fourth of the size of the earth; and, according to Leverrier, the sum of all the asteroids cannot exceed this limit. When we consider the shortness of the period during which stars below the eighth magnitude have been systematically observed, we see room for the discovery of several more planets of the ninth magnitude, and perhaps three or four hundred more of inferior dimensions.

With such a wonderful field of probable discovery inviting the explorations of astronomers, may we not hope that the enterprize of America will claim its share of the labor of this research? The rapid progress which the last few years have witnessed in our country, both in the facilities for observation, and in the number of active observers, is one of the most encouraging signs of the times. It is scarcely a quarter of a century since the first telescope, exceeding those of a portable size, was imported into the United States; and the introduction of meridional instruments of the large class is of still more recent date. Now we have one telescope which acknowledges no superior; and we have several which would be esteemed worthy of a place in the finest observatories of Europe. We have also numerous meridional instruments of dimensions adequate to be employed in original research. These instruments have not been permitted to remain unemployed. At the Observatory in this city, and also at Cambridge, extensive catalogues of stars are now in progress; while nearly every known member of our solar system has been repeatedly and carefully observed. These observations are all permanently recorded by a simple touch of the finger upon a key which closes an electric circuit—a method recently introduced at Greenwich Observatory, and known everywhere throughout Europe by the distinctive name of the American method.

Numerous, important, and striking discoveries have been the result of this astronomical activity. A host of comets have been independently discovered on this side of the Atlantic; and among them three, at least, were observed here before they were seen in Europe. The two nebulæ which have been longest and best known, and which have attracted the wondering gaze of every astronomer since the invention of the telescope, were never adequately figured until an American eye saw them, and an American pencil depicted them. The planet Saturn, which, for many years, was made the subject of special study by the elder Herschel, with his wonderful means of observation, first revealed to American scrutiny a new ring, and an eighth satellite. The novel spectacle of a comet divided into two nearly equal portions was first witnessed by American eyes; and an American observer has added one to the long list of planetary discoveries.

It is gratifying to reflect that while the great powers of Europe are contending in mortal strife, and misery marks the progress of their arms, the astronomers of England are allies not only to the astronomers of France, but to those of America, of Germany, and of Russia also. The triumphs of science are bloodless and do not endanger the peace of nations. Let the New World contend with the Old in a generous emulation—not for the conquest of disputed principalities or fortified cities—but for a holier and a nobler conquest—the conquest of the skies.

LECTURE III.

THE AMERICAN FIRE-ALARM TELEGRAPH.

BY WILLIAM F. CHANNING, M. D., OF BOSTON, MASSACHUSETTS.

There are few positions more imposing than to stand at the capital of a country like our own, made up of confederated States, each State made up of confederated counties, each county perhaps made up of confederated townships; every part, from the least to the greatest, conspiring to form an organized whole—one nation, one people. From such a centre it is natural to look abroad over the fair land, at territories and commonwealths, at cities and hamlets, whose interests and national life are thus interwoven into one, and to ask what are the laws and what the means of organization by which civilization attains these her great ends? It is natural, from such a point of view, to inquire into the general laws of relation by which parts are intelligently bound together to form a composite whole for some end of use or beauty, that is, the laws of relation by which every organization, every mechanism, in the high sense of that word, is formed. The material universe, with its majestic movements of suns, stars, planets, light, heat, winds, tides, seasons, is such a mechanism, actuated ever by the infinite Power, shaped and guided by the infinite Wisdom, animated by the infinite Love. The power which went forth at creation established the universe, with all its beauty and capacity, by the intelligent combination of outward parts. By the marriage of elementary atoms, by the joining of lesser unities to form greater, in accordance with a principle of absolute order and harmony, nature took her perfect form. With this type of creation ever before us, the manifestation of God in his works, let not the word mechanism, if it effects only the humblest organization of material elements, appear to us low or unworthy. Whoever, in practical science, attains a result of human use, by the intelligent combination of outward parts, emulates, in his degree, the creative wisdom, which, in the language of an apocryphal writer, hath made all things by number, measure, and weight.

In the organization of states and municipalities, the object or end in view, the formative principle, is some ideal of human life and society, some thought or aspiration for freedom, justice, brotherhood; but the embodiment of these is an outward frame-work of civilization, the highest mechanism to which human thought and human hands have ever been applied, requiring the perfect relation of parts, and methods of communication and intercourse arranged and governed by an absolute law of order. It is here that Science becomes the great instrument of Civilization.

In the early history of this country, the thirteen colonies stretched along the sea-coast, and commerce joined their interests and established a common circulation between them. The sailing vessel—the clipper-schooner—then measured the possible rate of intercourse and capacity of co-operation between those States. A languid life existed; a weak Confederacy in the outset was formed, proportioned to their outward means of communication and organization. A few centuries earlier than this, before navigation and other arts of locomotion had made much progress, each settlement on the coast would have been the centre of a small jurisdiction, with still less power of co-operation or union with its neighbors; science would have slept; events would have been slow; the human mind, for the most part, stagnant; civilization in abeyance; man isolated in industry and social sympathy from his fellow man.

At the time of the formation of the American Constitution our fathers looked with anxiety at what seemed to them an immense territory, though now but a small fraction of this republic, and asked if veins and arteries could ever ramify through this body politic, and interfuse the whole system with a common life-blood. To increase the difficulty and danger, new territory was added, new States in the interior of the country came in; but, at the same time, the genius of civilization and the providence of God gave to us the realization of the dream of the poet in the invention of the steamboat. A new means of relating men to each other, of combining their industry, of introducing the era of peace and good will upon earth, was discovered. Wherever the great rivers penetrated the heart of the continent, there quick communication could be had with the centres of government, industry, and commerce throughout the land.

A few years later, and our population, with the instinct of freedom, spread still further over the prairies and into the wilderness. The nation was again outgrowing its means of intercommunication and common life, when the railroad and steam-car were invented, and again the continuance of the commonwealth became possible; the confederated republic had a new lease of life by virtue of the application of science to civilization.

Still later our empire spread to the Pacific and stretched three thousand miles across the American continent. Different oceans washed its two shores. Our faces on the Atlantic coast were turned eastward, our brothers on the Pacific looked westward, and the Rocky mountains rose between. By steamboat or railroad, weeks must now intervene in the communication between distant parts of this mighty organization of confederated municipalities and States. The veins and arteries were provided, but the living nation had yet no nervous system to flash communication from one part to another, and to combine the whole into an organized body, which might, in its capacity for future expansion, include the whole race, and inhabit the whole earth. Before this time of need had fully arrived, the electric telegraph received its most important development, and was introduced into America.

The electric telegraph is thus the nervous system of this nation and of modern society, by no figure of speech, by no distant analogy. Its wires spread like nerves over the surface of the land, interlinking distant parts, and making possible a perpetually higher co-operation among men, and higher social forms than have hitherto existed. By means of its life-like functions the social body becomes a living whole, and each of its new applications marks a step in the organization of human life.

We are thus conducted to the result of the highest philosophy: that society, in its form of organization, is human, and that it presents in its progressive development continually higher analogies with the laws of individual being. In passing from these general principles to scientific detail, in the illustration of the municipal fire-telegraph, we shall find some of these analogies presenting themselves in still more definite and striking forms, thereby setting their seal of confirmation on the natural arrangement of the system of telegraphic organization, which is the special subject of the lecture this evening.

Soon after the first introduction of the electric telegraph into this country, I conceived the idea of the municipal telegraph, as distinguished from the common form of telegraph connecting distant places. The telegraph, as you know, usually consists of a galvanic battery or generator of electricity in one city or town, and insulated wires or electrical conductors going out thence and proceeding to a register or telegraphic instrument in another city or town, which instrument indicates every electrical wave or impulse that is sent over the wires from the distant extremity of the line. This requires that there shall always be what is called a "circuit" of electrical conductors—that is, that the electric current shall have the opportunity of going out from one pole of the battery, through one conductor to the distant register, and returning through another conductor to the other pole of the battery. When this "circuit" is completed, an electrical wave or current immediately begins to pass through the conductors, though they may be hundreds of miles in length; and when the "circuit" is broken anywhere, it ceases to pass. All telegraphic signalizing is thus effected by alternately completing and breaking the circuit at suitable intervals.

The municipal telegraph, while it employs the same essential conditions, adopts a very different arrangement. Its function is not to conneot distant towns or independent centres of life and activity with each other, but it is to organize a single city or town so as to bring every subordinate part into relation with its centre of government and direction. Its purpose is to multiply points of communication, to cover the surface of the municipal body as thickly, if you please, with telegraphic signalizing points as the surface of the human body is covered with nervous extremities or papillæ, the whole being intelligently connected into a system by which the municipal body shall understand itself in every part, and shall have a common life and vital functions for its own essential purposes.

The common telegraph is *linear*—it is a "line" of telegraph. The municipal telegraph is the application of the telegraph to a *surface*, making it cover a space with telegraphic nerves and papillæ as thickly as required, to furnish a complete organization. The common telegraph connects *distant* points, as its very name implies, the more distant the better to illustrate its character. The municipal telegraph contemplates the linking together of a multitude of *near* points, the nearer the better to illustrate the peculiarity of the system. The common telegraph connects two independent centres of life and activity. The municipal telegraph connects a multitude of subordinate points with one centre, and makes the position of those points dependent upon the centre and the needs of the system.

The occurrence of a fire in a city is one of the exigencies in which rapid and intelligent co-operation is necessary between the members of the municipal body. As our warehouses, manufactories, and public buildings are constructed, the extent of a conflagration depends to a great extent upon whether it is reached by the fire department within a short time or not. The first ten minutes in directing the alarm is worth hours afterwards. In organizing a system of fire alarms it becomes, therefore, necessary that every locality in a city shall have the means in its immediate neighborhood of notifying the existence of a fire. In order that this may be done systematically and under organic direction, it is necessary that this notification should be sent, in the first instance, to a common centre, which will naturally be at the city hall; and it is further necessary that the means should exist of giving thence an *instantaneous*, *definite*, and *public* alarm of fire.

The first requisite for a fire telegraph is certainly in its means of communication. What, then, are the safeguards of the municipal telegraph by which its indications may be made always reliable, and by which interruption, by accident or design, may be rendered improbable or impossible? These are the use of strong well-insulated wires, carried over the houses and attached to lofty and well selected buildings; the use of duplicate wires, following different routes, between all the stations, so that if one wire is broken from any cause, another and distant wire may still continue the circuit; and the dispensing entirely with the use of the ground as any part of the circuit, as used in common telegraph lines. Instead, also, of using, in a municipal telegraph, one great circuit which should traverse a whole city, a number of lesser circuits may be used, radiating from the centre, like the petals of a flower; so that if one circuit should be interrupted, all the others would still be intact and operative. These safeguards prove sufficient in practice to make the municipal telegraph the most certain means of communication which has yet been devised, under all conditions of weather and season.

In June, 1845, nearly ten years ago, I first published a notice of the fire-alarm telegraph, involving, essentially, the principles and safeguards upon which it has since been constructed. No definite action was taken upon it until 1848, when the subject was brought before the city government of Boston by the mayor, and two machines for striking the city bells from a distance, by means of the telegraph, were constructed under direction of Moses G. Farmer, esq., one of the ablest and most ingenious telegraphic engineers in the country.* One of these machines was placed in the belfry of the Boston city hall and connected with the line of telegraph extending to New York. Under these circumstances the operator in New York, by tapping on his finger-key, struck the bell on the city hall a number of times, and, according to the newspapers of that day, thus originated a false alarm of fire in Boston. This was the first illustration of the capacities of the fire-alarm telegraph.

The matter slept, however, till 1851, when I brought the system

* These original machines were exhibited, with other apparatus, in delivering this lecture; but for the sake of connexion, reference to the experimental illustrations will be excluded from this written report.

formally, and with specific plans, before the city government of Boston, and urged their action as due to science and to the public interest. This city government, unlike many others, induced only by the statement of scientific truth, voted ten thousand dollars to test a system wholly untried, and without precedent in the world. The mechanism and construction were placed in the hands of Moses G. Farmer, esq., and in 1852 were brought by him into thorough and successful operation. The American fire-alarm telegraph, in its development as a practical system of organization, tested now for nearly three years, should thus always be ascribed to Mr. Farmer equally with myself.

It has been stated that the conditions of the fire-alarm telegraph require that information should, in the first place, come in from any part of the circumference or surface of a city to its centre, and that thence an alarm should go out in a definite form to the public. The organization of a city under the system is as follows:

From the central station, at the city hall, go out wires over the house-tops, visiting every part of the city, and returning again. These are the *signal circuits*, by which the existence of a fire is signalized from any part of the surface of the city to the centre. Strung on these circuits, or connected with them, are numerous *signal boxes*, or signalizing points, of which there may be one at the corner of every square. These are cast-iron, cottage-shaped boxes, attached to the sides of the houses, communicating, by means of wires enclosed in a wrought-iron gas-pipe, with the signal circuit overhead. On the door of each signal-box the number of the fire district, and also the number of the box or station itself, in its district, are marked, and the place in the neighborhood where the key-holder may be found is also prominently notified. On opening the door of the signal-box a crank is seen. When this is turned it communicates to the centre the number of the fire district and of the box, and nothing else. Repeated turns give a repetition of the same signal. By this means any child or ignorant person who can turn a coffee-mill can signalize an alarm from his own neighborhood with unerring certainty.

Connected with the signal circuits at the central office, where they all converge, are a little alarm-bell and a register, which notifies and records the alarm received from the signal-box. The galvanic battery which supplies all the signal circuits is also placed at the central station. If a fire occurs near signal-box or station 5, in district 3, and the crank of that box is turned, the watchman or operator at the central station will immediately be notified by the little bell, and will read at once on his register the telegraphic characters which signify district 3, station 5. The characters used in the fire telegraph are a group of dots to indicate the district number—as three dots for district 3, and a group of dots and lines to indicate, by arbitrary characters, the station number. Thus a line and two dots may indicate station 5. These alternate on the record, and are repeated as often as the crank is turned.

The register used at the central station is generally the Morse register; which I recommend, in connexion with the system, as being most in harmony with its principle of operation.

We have traced the alarm of fire from a signal-box into the central station. How shall the alarm be given from that centre to the public? From the central station proceed also several circuits of wires, called alarm circuits, which go to the various fire-bells throughout the city, and which are connected with striking machines similar in character to the striking machinery of a clock, but *liberated by telegraph*. The operator at the central station is enabled, by the mere touch of his finger upon a key, to throw all the striking machines into simultaneous action, and thus give instantaneous public alarm.

By what precise mechanism is this effected at the alarm-bell stations? The heavy hammers may be raised above the bells by any force which can be conveniently applied, as by a weight which may be wound up by hand. But in all cities where the water is confined under pressure in the mains, it will supply, by means of the eccentric water engine, known familiarly under the name of the "water meter," the power necessary to wield the heavy hammers with the greatest facility. But how are hammers of one or two hundred pounds weight to be tripped by telegraph? To effect this readily Mr. Farmer invented his electro-magnetic escapement, one of the most beautiful and original of recent mechanical applications. In this escapement the electro-magnet, when it becomes charged by the galvanic influence received from the central station, attracts the little piece of soft iron or armature in front of it, which supports a small lever poised nearly vertically, and weighted with a little ball at its upper end. This lever and ball, when tripped by the withdrawal of the armature, acquires sufficient momentum to strike up the *detent* of the train of wheels which, in their revolution, raise the hammer and then allow it to fall. A single blow of the hammer follows each electrical impulse sent from the central station, and the revolution of the train of wheels raises also the falling lever into its place and catches it again on the armature lever, ready to be disengaged or tripped for another blow.

At the central station, connected with the alarm circuit, is a galvanic battery and an instrument for completing the circuit of that battery, called the district keyboard. This is constructed with several keys, corresponding to the numbers of the fire districts in the city. If you depress any of these the machinery inside commences to move, and the circuit is completed at such intervals as to strike and repeat on the distant alarm bells the district number represented by that key with suitable pauses between.

We supposed that the operator at the central station received the signal of fire from district 3, station 5. He now places his finger on the key of district 3, in the keyboard. Instantly all the alarm bells in the city begin to strike synchronously the district number *three*, and continue, no matter what their number or what the weight of their hammers, so long as that single finger rests on that key.

But the operator has a finger key before him connected with the signal circuits, by which he can answer back and strike a little electro-magnet, armature, and bell, enclosed in each signal box. He has received a signal of fire from district 3, station 5. While his hand rests on the key of district 3 he taps occasionally *five* times on the return key of the signal circuits, which I have just described. The little bell in each signal box, at the corner of every square, strikes *five*. The fireman listens to the public alarm bells and gets from them the number of the district; he runs by the nearest signal box and listens a moment to gather the station number from its little signal bell, and he now knows that the fire is at district three, station five. He directs his own motions and his engine, from the start, to within, perhaps, one hundred yards of the fire.

No other system has ever attempted to localize a fire more precisely than by the district number; and in some cities, like New York, the districts may be two miles long.

In all previous systems there has been a delay, first in getting an alarm from the fire to the bells, and, second, in finding the place of the fire in the district after the alarm was given, and reaching it by the shortest route. By the fire telegraph both district and station are publicly notified; the one by the alarm bells, the other by the signal boxes.

Let us now consider for a moment the analogy between the municipal organization thus described and the nervous organization of the individual. A coal of fire falls upon my hand; one of the nervous extremities, or papillæ, the "signal box" of the part, sends instantly its own special signal, by means of a nerve of sensation or signal wire to the brain, where the existence and locality of the lesion is at once recognized. An act of intelligence and volition ensues. The watchman of the central station, or brain, does his part. An impulse to motion is sent out over the proper motor nerves, or alarm wires, and muscles are called into play in a suitable manner to remove the cause of injury, just as the electro-magnetic muscles and iron limbs in the bell towers are thrown into suitable and related action to the original cause and place of alarm.

The telegraph, in its common form, communicating intelligence between distant places, performs the function of the *sensitive* nerves of the human body. In the fire telegraph it is made to act for the first time in its *motor* function, or to produce effects of power at a distance; and this is also connected with the sensitive function, through a brain or central station, which is the reservoir of electric or nervous power for the whole system. We have thus an "excito-motory" system, in which the intelligence and volition of the operator at the central station come in to connect sensitive and motor functions, as they would in the case of the individual.

The conditions of municipal organization absolutely compelled the relation of circuits which has been described. The analogy with the laws of individual life was not perceived until after the system was evolved, and it came then as a confirmation of the correspondence of the system to natural law, and of the necessity of the arrangement as a means of order.

I should not be precluded from saying in this place, what historic truth at this time requires, that the development of the "motor function" of electricity, or of the means by which electro-magnetic power can be exerted at a distance, is due to the early experiments of the Secretary of this Institution, Professor Henry, whose discoveries in electro-magnetism and especially of the quantity and intensity of the magnet in 1830, laid the foundation for all subsequent forms of the electro-magnetic telegraph, and made subsequent steps comparatively easy. In the publication of these experiments, the induction of the electric telegraph as thenceforth possible was distinctly made by him; and at a period not much. later, weights were released and bells rung by him at a distance by electric influence transmitted through long conductors.

In Boston, where the fire-alarm telegraph has been in successful operation for nearly three years, a star of wires is seen radiating from the top of the city building. These are the signal circuits connecting into one system forty-six signal boxes scattered over the city, and the alarm circuits connecting twenty-four belfries on church, school and engine houses. A few large bells would be preferable to this multiplicity of smaller ones, but this whole number are struck by the touch of a single man's finger in the central station. For the sake of economy in battery power, the district keyboard is so arranged as to throw the battery on the four alarm circuits separately, but in rapid succession at each blow. Practically, the bells strike together or as much so as is desirable. At night, sometimes out of the profoundest stillness, the district number will suddenly strike upon the ear in a chime of perhaps eight or ten bells, their sound coming in one after the other in proportion to their distance from the ear, but always in an invariable succession at each blow. Then the alarm ceases and the whole city is as suddenly silent.

The operator at the central station is sometimes able to throw the bells on, and tap back to the signal boxes before the originator of the alarm has ceased to turn his crank in the immediate neighborhood of the fire. As soon as the bells strike, groups of persons will be seen clustering round each signal box to listen to the tapping of the station number, and it is soon known to the whole fire department exactly where the alarm originated.

The battery employed on the Boston signal circuits is Farmer's protected Grove's battery, which keeps in action several weeks or even months without being replenished. Instead of a galvanic battery on the alarm circuits, a large magneto-electric machine has been recently substituted, which is driven by a water meter, and which furnishes the electric current by which the bells are rung.

The heaviest hammer in the system at Boston weighs one hundred pounds, and it is wielded by the Cochituate water at an expense of only one gallon for each blow, and tripped by telegraph from a distance of two miles. By virtue of the electric current and the pent up water, this bell, and others associated with it, might be rung in measured strokes from the beginning to the end of the year by the pressure of a single man's finger in a distant room.

All of the stations in Boston are provided with "lightning catchers" or ground conductors for atmospheric or induced electricity. Hence an incidental protection from lightning commensurate with the extent of the network of wires above is obtained for the city. When these ground conductors have been temporarily removed from the alarm-bell stations, a flash of lightning has been occasionally followed by a single blow from one or more of the bells. But where the lightning catchers have been in place, they have proved sufficient, except in rare instances, to divert atmospheric or induced currents from the electro-magnets to the ground. No practical or serious inconvenience has resulted from this source. But it has occasionally been a matter of curiosity and interest to hear the lightning thus tolling the alarm bell.

The total loss by fire under the telegraph fire-alarm system, according to the accurate "Report of the Boston Fire Department for the year 1854," was only $150,772, or less than one dollar for every inhabitant; a loss which, for its small amount in so compact and wealthy a city, cannot be paralleled in America.

Out of 195 alarms of fire in Boston in 1854, *twelve* are recorded as false; but at least *six* of these were from supposed fires, leaving only *six* unaccounted for. The whole number of alarms and the proportion of false alarms have been greatly diminished by the system. Science can make no contribution to civilization without the requisite social conditions. The trust of the fire telegraph system, in this case was placed in the hands of the citizens, and it has yielded to them its full fruits without abuse. This may deserve perhaps to be chronicled as an instance of well rewarded confidence in the sobriety and capacity for self-government of the American people. The signal box, which is the sensitive extremity of the system, may be protected by various methods according to social requirements. In Boston it has been guarded by putting it in the most public place and exposing it to the fullest light.

The fire-alarm telegraph contains also the elements of a perfect police system. In addition to the crank for alarm, every signal box is provided with a finger key, by means of which communications in the ordinary telegraphic method can be sent to the central station, and an answer can be returned from the centre and read by sound from the little bell in the signal box.

The mechanism of the fire telegraph is arranged and disposed for the purpose of preserving wealth, the fruit of human industry and of nature's bounty, from destruction. It therefore accomplishes an end of human use. But more than this, it is a higher system of municipal organization than any which has heretofore been proposed or adopted. In it the New World has taken a step in the forms of civilization in advance of the Old.

LECTURE V.

BY PROFESSOR HENRY REED, OF THE UNIVERSITY OF PENNSYLVANIA.

[The publication of these lectures will awaken in the sympathizing hearts of many of their readers a painful reminiscence of the loss in the Arctic of their amiable and gifted author.]

THE UNION.

FIRST LECTURE.

The subject upon which I propose to address you is the growth of the American Union during the colonial era of our history. In treating such a subject, at the present time, it is my desire to say, in the first place, that I shall purposely forbear speaking of the Union as it now exists, with its manifold and countless blessings, its present estate, and its prospects. It is the retrospect which I intend to turn to, and in that retrospect there is abundance both of admonition and encouragement for all after time, much to inspire a thoughtful loyalty to the Union, and a deep sense of responsibility for each generation coming to live within that Union, and to transmit it unimpaired to posterity, such as it has grown to be, not by man's will or sagacity, but by the providential government of the world, which may be traced in the history of our race.

In speaking of history as making manifest such providential government of the world, I do but recognise and follow one of the highest principles which we owe to the improved culture of historical science in the present century. That improvement is not alone in more laborious and dutiful habits of research, in the more studious use of original documents, but in a truer philosophy of history, not such as in a former age, arrogating the title of philosophy, contracted its vision within the scant range of scepticism, but a philosophy which reverently traces on the annals of the human race marks of more than human agency—an overruling Providence. As in that which is especially denominated "*sacred* history" the purposes of the Creator are expressly revealed, so in that which is styled, in contradistinction, "*profane* history," as purposes of the same Creator must needs exist, the thoughtful student may gain at least some glimpses of them, and yet refrain all the while from rash interpretation of the Divine will in the guidance and government of man and of the races of man to whom the earth is parcelled out.

It becomes more practicable to trace the providential purposes when we look over long tracts of time. The history of Rome, for instance, with its twelve centuries of growth, and decay, and ruin—in one point of view, what is it but a purposeless record of strife, external and internal—conquest and the domestic feud of patrician and plebian—

and ended, at last, like an unsubstantial pageant, leaving no influence behind it; but, in another point of view, it becomes a more intelligible memorial of the life of a nation that had a destiny to fulfil, an appointed work to do—to build up a system of law which should enter into modern European and American jurisprudence, and with its strong Pagan power to pave a path for Christianity to travel into the vast regions which at one time were included within Roman dominion.

Now, turning to American history, and especially that portion of it which is devoted to the Union, it is possible, I believe, to place the events in such combinations, to discover in them such a concurrent tendency, as to leave no room to question that those events were controlled as the secondary causes of the results to which form was given in our system of government. From the latter part of the last century—from the year of the adoption of the Constitution of the United States of America, with its primary purpose of forming *a more perfect union*, back into the century of English colonization, back still earlier to the years of discovery, and even earlier yet to those remote centuries in which, many generations before Columbus or Cabot, European eyes, we may believe, beheld this continent for the first time—throughout that long tract of time there is, I do not fear to say, a tendency more or less visible towards the future results, and not least among those results towards this Union. That tendency may be traced both in what was frustrated and in what has been achieved; so that all things seem to lead to this result, the predominance in North America of one European race, and that race the race which speaks the English tongue. I thus entitle it for the want of a better and briefer name. The title "*Anglo-Saxon*" is hardly adequate or expressive enough for a breed of men in whose veins there runs the mingled current of Saxon and Norman blood, perhaps of ancient British, Celtic, Roman, and Danish blood. From the earliest time in which intercourse began between the eastern and western hemispheres down to our own day, the great movement has been the extension of what may be called *Saxondom*—a part of that larger movement, not confined to North America, but extending to southern Africa, to India from Ceylon to its northern mountains, and to Australia and the islands in the distant seas—the movement which is carrying the language and the laws of our race widely over the earth.

My present purpose is to look at this movement as it has a connexion with American history, and especially with the Union; and, without attempting in any way to make historical facts bend to hypothesis, to show that the history of discovery, the history of colonization and of colonial government, all establish this historical truth, that the work of laying the foundation of a great political system in North America was reserved for the race that speaks the English language, by whatever name we may choose to call that race; further, that, in order to develop so essential a part of that system as the union of a federal republic, the work was reserved for the English race at a particular period of their history in the mother country. Thus it is to remote causes that we are to trace that political power which animates a government extending from the lakes to the Gulf of Mexico, and from the Atlantic to the Pacific.

It seems to me that there is no consideration better calculated to deepen in the mind of every reflecting citizen a reverence for the Union than a just sense of its origin; and that is to be acquired by the studious asking and answering of this question, How was this Union formed? Has the origin of the Union a date—a day or a year? Can we find its epoch—as of independence, or of the confederation, or of the Constitution? Was it done in convention? Did men come together by some delegated authority and deliberate in solemn council, and ordain a Union? Never. It was the work of time, the natural consequence of events, a growth from circumstances, or whatever other phrase may be used as a substitute for an express acknowledgment of a Providence in the destinies of mankind. It is not possible to trace the Union to any premeditated plan, the idea of any one man, or the concert of any body of men. You can find no authority to pronounce it the direct product of human foresight, of political wisdom and experience. You cannot point to any day in our history, and say that on such a day Union existed, and on the day before there was nothing of the kind. In truth the Union was not made, *it grew*. It grew as the tree grows, planting its roots deeper and deeper, and lifting its branches stronger and stronger and higher and higher, its vital forces coursing upward and outward to its lightest leaf. The Union grew as the forest grows, and the seed was not sown by man's hand. This element of government is at the same time an element of national character. It is part of the life of Saxon liberty, and it came with the Saxon race to be developed and expanded in a land which seems to have been reserved to be the Saxon's heritage.

Whatever may have been accomplished when European enterprise began its work on this continent with those long unknown or forgotten discoveries of the Scandinavian navigators, who, 500 years before Columbus, were the first to behold these western shores, those obscure voyages left no abiding influence here. The Northman had no distinct destiny here; and idle as it would be now to speculate on such a future as there might have been if Scandinavian discovery had been followed by conquest and settlement, one cannot help thinking how fruitless would have been the strife between the savage *native* races and the fierce uncivilized barbarians of the northern seas. This land was not meant for the Northman's home. The voyages of the eleventh and twelfth centuries passed away, leaving no trace behind them, and, what was more important, leaving the land open to the enterprise of other and distant generations who had a destiny here.

When, in the fifteenth century, the south of Europe was stirred by the spirit of maritime adventure, and Portugal took the lead in it, the enterprise of that kingdom found a southern and not a western direction, in the voyages along the western coast of Africa, planned by that remarkable personage, Prince Henry (a Plantagenet by the mother's side, let me say in passing.) This land was not given to the race of Portugal first, though they were among modern discoverers.

When Spain slowly followed the career of which the neighboring kingdom had set the example, and when Columbus had nearly crossed the Atlantic, steering due westward to the continent of North America, then only a few days' sail distant, a flight of birds, as is familiarly remembered from the well known story, were seen winging their way across the course of the vessels, and the great navigator following those pilots of the air southwestward, lost the continent, and the power of Spain was planted only on the islands. As a flight of birds gave, according to the legend, augury for the first doings of Rome's history, so in another way it has a place in our earliest annals. Again, on his second voyage, the path of Columbus lay among the islands; and when the papal power was invoked to determine the disputes between Spain and Portugal, respecting their rights of discovery, and Alexander VI adjudged his famous partition, which seems to appropriate to these two contending powers all that was discovered, and all that was to be discovered in the new world—soon after this exercise of power, (more than human by one less than human in the crimes that have made the name of Borgia infamous,) soon after, the sovereign of a country which held slacker allegiance to Rome, gave the commission to the Cabots, and that authority, which has been well styled "the oldest American State paper," set the Saxon foot upon this soil, the first of European feet to touch the continent. The land was not meant, either by claim of discovery or by papal gift, to be the Spaniards' home. The two small English vessels which had cleared from Bristol, "with authority to sail to all parts of the east, west, and north, under the royal banners and ensigns, to discover countries of the heathen, unknown to Christians, to set up the king's banner there, to occupy and possess, as his subjects, such places as they could subdue, with rule and jurisdiction," coasting along perhaps some thirty degrees of latitude, from Labrador to Virginia, gave to an English race their title here. Thus early, within a very few years after the beginning of western discovery in the fifteenth century, was laid the foundation of future dominion; for whatever other European races might thereafter seek a home on this portion of the continent, it would be only for such partial or temporary occupation as would sooner or later be absorbed in the occupations by that race which was then, in that era, the first to touch the mainland. It was thus that the way was prepared to make the country the heritage of that race which speaks the English tongue, a race in whose institutions the name of PEOPLE was never lost, whether in their furthest antiquity in the forests of Germany, or under Saxon, Danish, or Norman rule, after their migration to Britain, whether under the kingly confederacy of the Saxon, or under the power of the strongest Norman sovereigns, Plantagenet or Tudor; so that, with the popular element ever present, every political struggle has been either to regain something lost, or to expand and improve some ancient right.

In studying the originating influences of our institutions, political and judicial, there can be no question, I believe, but that the first influence is to be sought in the character of the race. Powers and habits of thought and feeling come to us with our blood, and extend to all who come within the range of their influence. We have but expanded what the Saxon began more than a thousand years ago, before, indeed, the races of the north had a history of their own or a place in the history of the more civilized south. The influence of race is most obvious when we think of the inheritance of the common law, or such a special tradition, from unknown origin, as the trial by jury. My present purpose is to trace the agency of the same principle, I mean the influence of race, where it is less apparent, in that part of our political system which is expressed by the term "the Union," and then to follow it onward through the processes of colonization and the course of colonial government.

The question to be considered is, what element was there in the Anglo-Saxon character and institutions, which, being transplanted to this country, and being left to freer and more unrestrained action, would facilitate the formation of a federal government, of a Union? Such an element is to be found in *the tendency to local self-government*, which is characteristic of the race, and is conspicuous in the history of their institutions. This is a tendency the very reverse of that which is described by such terms as "*centralization*" or "*consolidation*." Saxon freedom has, no doubt, been held chiefly on the tenure of this principle, that the central power of the State has always recognised a great variety of local powers. Even with regard to metropolitan influences, how obvious is it that London has never been to England what Paris has been and is to France, whether royal, imperial, or republican France. It has been justly said that "centralization and active life pervading the whole body are hard to reconcile; he who should do this perfectly would have established a perfect government. * * It seems to be a law that life cannot long go on in a multitude of minute parts without union; nay, even without something of that very centralization which yet, if not well watched, is so apt to destroy the parts by absorbing their life into its own; there must be a heart in the political as in the natural body to supply the extremities continually with fresh blood."—(*Arnold.*)

Now, throughout the whole history of our race—the race that speaks the English tongue here and in England, during the three score years of our Constitution, during the brief existence of the confederation, during the contentional colonial period between 1763 and 1776, and during the earlier colonial times, or, in the mother-country, during the various eras of the history of the race there—it has been the combination of these two principles—the principle of *centralization* and the principle of *local independence*—that has distinguished the race, that has made its power, its safety, and its freedom. Political strength and health have been in the just distribution and harmony of these powers, having an archetype, it may be said, in the tranquil and perpetual harmony of the solar system—the noiseless on-goings of the stars. In the political system of the Saxon—royal or republican—the danger has ever been in any excess of either the centripetal force on the one hand, or the centrifugal on the other. Whatever variations there may have been from time to time, this may, I believe, safely be pronounced the great Saxon characteristic—a habit of local government, exercised in a certain subordination, or rather relation, to a central government. And further, it would not be difficult to discover in such distribution of power in local institutions much of the discipline, the training for more expanded opportunities of government, which has helped onward what appears to be the destiny of the race. Observe how, after the Saxon occupation of Britain, the conquered territory, small comparatively in extent, was divided into several petty kingdoms—those loosely compacted kingly commonwealths which were to form the heptarchy; and again, how each of these was parcelled out into those various divisions, the counties, shires, hundreds, tithings, and other partitions, the origin of which perplex the antiquarian. The old Saxon spirit of local independence and authority animated the local institutions, assemblies, tribunals of various kinds, with an energy that never could have been developed under a strongly controlling central power.

When the Norman conqueror sought to complete the subjugation of England, by introducing the laws and institutions of his own country, and a rigorous establishment of the feudal system, all this Saxon variety of law, of usage, of manners, and of men, was a perpetual hindrance, which it was part of the conquest to do away with. The conqueror's strong hand was laid on the free diversities which the Saxon had been used to of old, for conquest, dominion, empire, demanded more of a submissive uniformity; and accordingly, as an instance of it, we find the conqueror introducing, for the administration of justice, an office unknown to the Saxon—the offiee of chief justiciar. The biographer of the English Chief Justices remarks, in the opening sentence of his work:

"The offiee of Chief Justice, or Chief Justiciar, was introduced into England by William the Conqueror, from Normandy, where it had long existed. The functions of such an officer would have ill accorded with the notions of our Anglo-Saxon ancestors, who had a great antipathy to centralization, and prided themselves upon enjoying the rights and the advantages of self-government.

* * * "In Normandy, the interference of the supreme government was much more active than in England; and there existed an officer called CHIEF JUSTICIAR, who superintended the administration of justice over the whole dukedom, and on whom, according to the manners of the age, both military and civil powers of great magnitude were conferred." Lord Campbell adds in a note: "It is curious to observe that, notwithstanding the sweeping change of laws and institutions introduced at the conquest, the characteristic difference between Frenchmen and Englishmen, in the management of local affairs, still exists after the lapse of so many centuries; and that, while with us parish vestries, town councils, and county sessions are the organs of the petty confederated republics into which England is parcelled out, in France, whether the form of government be nominally monarchical or republican, no one can alter the direction of a road, build a bridge, or open a mine, without the authority of the 'Ministre des Ponts et Chaussées.' In Ireland, there being much more Celtic than Anglo-Saxon blood, no self-reliance is felt, and a disposition prevails to throw everything upon the government."

This Saxon characteristic is to be discovered not only in the number but also in the diversity of local institutions, arising from diversity of character and traditional influences. Although in the course of time—many centuries—such diversities have been smoothed down by many assimilating processes, perhaps no country on the face of the earth, within so narrow a space, presents so great variety of customs as England continues to do. Habits, manners, the tenure of land, rules of inheritance, display a free variety strongly contrasted with the servile uniformity of governments with stronger controlling central powers. Usages which appertain to the North Briton are unknown to the South Briton—the man of Kent, or Cornwall, or Wales. The cities and towns have a variety of municipal power and privilege resting on the authority of immemorial usage.

The origin of all this diversity, in which there has been developed so much of practical power, is to be traced to the same cause which has transmitted it to America—the mode in which the land was occupied by the successive races who came to its shores. The Roman conquerors and colonists, the continued migrations of the Saxons, the abiding incursions of the Danes, the conquest by the Norman, each brought and left an influence, a set of laws or customs at the least; and in the after ages, no tyranny was strong enough or senseless enough, no revolution was rash enough, to attempt that worst of all revolutionary havoc, total obliteration of the past, the absolute subjugation of local variety and independence.

Such diversity may possibly offend the merely speculative mind, which is apt to crave that which is squared and levelled to a more theoretic exactness and completeness; but it is the power which has been disciplined by such diversity, and the freedom that accompanies it, which has spread the race over the earth, and has engendered our Union. It is well known that in material nature, in the lower orders of creation, considerable *uniformity* is met with; but that the higher we ascend, the more diversity is found. A great modern historical philosopher adopted, as a leading principle in his science, this truth, that "as in organic beings the most perfect life is that which animates the greatest variety of numbers, so among States that is the most perfect in which a number of institutions originally distinct, being organized each after its kind into centres of national life, form a complete whole."

Now I believe that it is possible to show that during the whole of our colonial era, during what may be called the *primitive* period of our political institutions, the whole course of events tended to the establishment of this principle thus philosophically stated by Niebuhr. I mean to say explicitly, that the providential government of the doings of men on this portion of the world, and with reference to this portion of the world, from the discovery of it onwards to the adoption of the Constitution of the United States, has led on to what has been described as the highest form of political life, a republican system including the principle of distributed local government, in the parlance familiar to us, "a Federal Republic," or in the philosophical language of the historian whom I just quoted, "a complete whole, formed of a number of institutions," originally distinct, organized each after its kind into centres of life. I am aware that it may sound presumptuous to speak confidently of the purposes of the providential government over the world, or over portions of it, or over the movements of this or that race. But when the principle of a providential government of the human race is recognised, as it must be by every mind whose belief has advanced beyond the confines of absolute atheism, and also, during a long course of years, near three hundred years in the case to which I wish to apply the principle, you can trace a correspondence between the events on such a period and a final result, I do not know why we need fear to affirm that those events were providentially controlled and guided to that result. This conviction is further strengthened when we can perceive beyond such result adequate consequences, can see how that result was in the future to be productive of good. The evidence of such consequences is in the knowledge that the form of government which alone renders popular institutions compatible with extent of territory, is that form which has its origin in this ancient element of Saxon local self-government. Who can question that it is such a political system that has expanded this republic from its primitive circumscription to its present extent, so that that which at first reached not far beyond the sound of the Atlantic, became enlarged beyond the mountains; then beyond the Mississippi; and now, having crossed the second great mountain range of the continent, has on its other border the sound of the earth's other great ocean. I know of no grander traditional influence to be observed in history, than this simple Saxon characteristic element and the mighty issues of it now manifest around us, the connexion between this principle of local government obscurely recognised in the ancient fatherland of the Saxon, carried thence to England to be combined with the central power of a constitutional monarchy, and now a living principle here, helping, by the harmony of state rights and federal energy, to extend and perpetuate the republic.

On an occasion like the present, I do not propose to attempt to enter into the details of American colonization, or to dwell upon the familiar story of our early history, but rather to use them only so far as it may be necessary to illustrate the principle I have endeavored to set forth. A rapid review of colonial events, brought into a new connexion and concentered on one principle, will, I hope answer the purpose of maintaining the historical argument which I desire to submit to you. There is perhaps nothing in our early history which now appears more remarkable to us than the long delay on the part of the English government, or the English people, in making use of the title which the right of discovery had given them to the soil of America. It presents a curious blank, near a century before any attempt was made to occupy or to colonize the newly discovered land, and more than a century before a permanent settlement was accomplished.

It has been remarked, that the only immediate result of Cabot's voyage and discovery of the continent, was the importation into England from America of the first turkeys that had ever been seen in Europe. Such was the beginning of the immense commerce between England and America. For a long time the right of discovery seemed a barren title; and it is a noticeable fact that while it was the first of the Tudor kings whose commission authorized Cabot to set up the English banner here, it was the last of the Tudor sovereigns who sought to make her title here a reality by planting English homes; and indeed the whole dynasty passed away without anything permanent being achieved. Doubtless, the delay was salutary, was propitious for the future; and perhaps we can conceive how it was so when we recall the character of that Tudor dominion and the spirit of that age. It was not the temper of that dynasty to give the colonial free-agency (it might almost be called independence) which was to prove the germ of republican nationality. It was not the spirit of that age to ask for such large power of local government as by a later generation was quietly assumed and exercised. The ancient Saxon element of local self-government could not well have been transplanted here, while the strong rule of the Tudor was centralizing so much about the throne; and therefore, (I speak of it as an inference in the logic of history,) the whole sixteenth century passed away and the land was still the natives'; for when the year 1600 came, there was not an English family, no English man or woman, on this continent, unless perchance there was wandering somewhere some survivor of Raleigh's lost colony.

It would be vain now to speculate upon the influence which might have been exercised on the destinies of our country if that which was the perishable colonization of the 16th century had been permanent. But a knowledge of what was attempted, and of the manner of it, serves to show that it would have been different in character, and therefore in its influences from the later colonization.

When, in 1578, Sir Humphrey Gilbert obtained from Queen Elizabeth letters patent, authorizing him to discover and colonize remote and heathen lands—the first grant of the kind ever made by an English sovereign—there was conferred upon him almost a monopoly of the right of colonization, with privileges and authorities for the government of his designed colonies of almost indefinite extent, and with a prohibition upon all persons attempting to settle within two hundred leagues of any place which Sir Humphrey Gilbert or his associates should occupy during the space of six years. While we may deplore the adverse fortunes of this brave voyager—his baffled enterprises and the pious heroism of his dark perishing in the mid-Atlantic—it is not to be lamented that a scheme of colonization so vice-regal in its character; should not have been accomplished. The same comment may be made on the grant to Sir Walter Raleigh—which was of prerogatives and jurisdiction no less ample—to end, after repeated efforts and the well known expeditions which he sent out to the new world, in disappointment and a name; for all that has proved perpetual from those enterprises is the word "*Virginia*"—a title given, for a considerable time, to an almost indefinite region of America.

Let me here take occasion to state that some recent investigations of the State records in England, and particularly a hitherto unnoticed entry on the close-roll of the 24th of Elizabeth, have established the fact that another illustrious public man of those times—Sir Philip Sidney—had turned his earnest and active mind to American discovery, and probably contemplated a voyage in his own persou to the western hemisphere. That he did so as early as 1582—which was earlier than the voyages equipped by Raleigh—is a fact, the evidence of which has but very lately been discovered, and was published, for the first time, only in the month of February, 1850. It appears that Sidney obtained from Sir Humphrey Gilbert, under the Queen's patent to him, a right to discover and take possession of three millions of acres in America. The grant was large enough to be almost indefinite, and is another instance to illustrate the policy of colonization which prevailed in that generation.

Although Sidney's meditated enterprise was relinquished, it is pleasing to find associated with the early plans of American colonization the name of one who has left so matchless a memory—the scholar, statesman, poet, the friend of poets, the soldier whose early death was mourned by a nation—a death memorable with its last deed of heroic charity, when putting away the cup of water from his own lips, burning as they were with the thirst of a bleeding death, he gave it to a wounded soldier with those famous words, eloquent in their simplicity, "*Thy necessity is yet greater than mine.*"

Permit me to extend this digression a little further to notice an American allusion which occurs in the English literature of the same period in which Sir Philip Sidney flourished. When, in 1590, Spenser gave to the world the first part of "*The Fairy Queen,*" he dedicated that wondrous allegory to "The most high, mighty, and magnificent Empresse, renouned for pietie, virtue, and all gracious government, Elizabeth, by the grace of God, Queen of England, France, and Ireland, and VIRGINIA." Yes, there stands the name of that honored State—then, as it were, the name of British America; and while there is many a reason for the lofty spirit of her sons, the pulse of their pride may beat higher at the sight of the record of the "Ancient Dominion" on the first page of one of the immortal poems of our language.

To return to my subject. It can readily be perceived that such schemes of colonization as were planned during the reign of Elizabeth—Sir Humphrey Gilbert's, Sir Philip Sidney's, Sir Walter Raleigh's—could hardly have resulted otherwise than in the establishment of vast feudal principalities, to continue under rulers who would have been no less than viceroys, or to be resumed under the immediate sovereignty of the throne. Such occupation of the land could scarce have led on, by any natural sequence and series of events, to a popular government—still less to a political system in which the element of "Union" would exist. There would not have been enough of partition. There would not have been enough of either the spirit or the privilege of distinct and separate colonization—the establishment of communities independent of each other, destined in a later age to grow so naturally into Union. Colonization then would have been too much like that of France in Canada—something far more regular and uniform, and imposing in appearance as an affair of State; but fraught with no such momentous power of development as was latent in the freer Saxon method. There would have been far less of that "*wise and salutary neglect*" which Mr. Burke spoke of when, in his speech on conciliation with America, he said: "The colonies, in general, owe little or nothing to any care of ours. They are not squeezed into this happy form by the constraints of watchful and suspicious government; but through a wise and salutary neglect, a generous nature has been suffered to take her own way to perfection." It was, indeed, "a wise neglect." But let me add that it was a wisdom which cannot, with accuracy, be predicated of a passive, negative, neglectful State policy, but of the providential guidance of the race by which there was bestowed upon them the freedom of self-discipline, of political power and expansion. It sounds like a paradox and a contradiction; but it is an obvious truth that the first element of union is separation—distinctiveness of existence and of character. The history of union begins not with *unity*, but with the creation of such separate existences as in the future may, by some process of assimilation and connexion, become united but not consolidated—forming a complete whole, the portions of which do not lose their distinct organization.

Passing onward from the perishable colonization of Queen Elizabeth's times to that colonization which proved permanent, it is apparent that it did take that form, and direction, and character, the natural though distant results of which are to be seen in what is now around us. This holds good of the whole period of English colonization in America, from James the First to George the Second—a century and a quarter; from the arrival of the first permanent colony in Virginia, and the building of Jamestown, (1607,) down to Oglethorpe's settlement of Georgia, in 1732.

The grant to Sir Walter Raleigh having become void by his attainder, British America was again in the King's gift—and that King the first of the Stuarts. Now, although the notions of royal prerogative which were cherished by the Stuarts were as high as those of the Tudors, still the relative position of the sovereign was changed, for the progress of constitutional government had developed new sentiments of allegiance and new powers of resistance. The seventeenth century, which, in fact, may be called the century of American colonization, for it comprehends nearly all of it, was more propitious than the previous century to the planting of colonies destined to grow to a republic. The process of partition now began—giving scope therefor to the ancient Saxon principle of local government. It was at first, as is well known, a simple twofold partition; for when king James the First granted the patent for the territory stretching from the 34th to the 45th degree of latitude, he divided it between the two companies, the Southern or London company, and the Northern or Plymouth company. By virtue of these grants, and the settlements under them, the country was parcelled out into two great divisions, soon known by the familiar designations of Virginia for the former, and New England for the latter.

I do not propose on an occasion like this to trace the detailed series of grants and settlement: it is enough for the present to remark that the course of colonization was a continued process of partition; so that in 1732, at the time of the Georgia settlement, the strip of territory along the coast of the Atlantic, which then formed British America, was divided into the *thirteen colonies*—a colonial system fashioned into thirteen distinct political communities.

This was not merely *territorial* partition; political and social varieties distinguished the colonies. This was a consequence of what was a remarkable peculiarity in the English settlement of America, that colonization was *individual* enterprise, receiving the sanction but not the support or assistance of the government. No colony in the seventeenth century, to which period they nearly all belonged, had any direct aid from king or parliament. The solitary exception occurred in a parliamentary grant of aid to the Georgia colony. Colonization which was individual enterprise partook of the variety of individual character and motive—of the different and even conflicting principles, civil and ecclesiastical, which were dominant or depressed at different periods of the seventeenth century. This, it seems to me, is well worthy of notice, that no century of English history, either earlier or later, was so calculated to give character—and varied character, too—to the colonies, as that century which was the century of colonization—the seventeenth. It was an age in which the activity of the nation, theretofore busy in other directions, was turned to questions of government. The thoughts of men were anxious and occupied—not with questions respecting the succession of this or that branch of a royal family, but with the principles that lie at the very foundation of government, the limits of power, and the rights and duties of the subject. It was an age—better than any other in the annals of the mother-country—fitted to send along with the sons who left her to seek a distant home the dutiful spirit of loyalty, willing obedience to law, and the dutiful spirit of freedom—the two great principles of constitutional government. There was political variety, as well as social; for the colonial governments, although all bearing a resemblance to the government of the mother-country, had those distinctive characteristics by which they are classified into the Royal, the Proprietary, and the Charter governments.

It seems strange that the colonial policy of one kingdom should admit of such a diversity, that in some the king's control was perpetually present; in others it was transferred to lords-proprietary, subjects to whom was given the half-kingly power of palatines; and in others so free were the charters that the people, for a long time after the royal authority was wholly abrogated by independence, asked no change in them. Strange as such colonial diversity appears, it was far more favorable to the future results than any uniform system of colonial government.

I have endeavored to show that a principle, which may safely be said to be a characteristic of our race, in all regions of the earth, has been brought hither to become a great element in our national system; and, further, that throughout the whole period of discovery and colon zation, whatever was adverse to that principle was checked or frustrated; while, on the other hand, the tendency of events was to the steady development of that principle—the creation of the materials for *Union.*

In the next lecture I propose to consider the process by which those materials were brought together, without the loss of their distinctive character, as component parts of the Union.

THE UNION.

SECOND LECTURE.

Having considered, at the close of my last lecture, the partition of British America into the several colonial governments, I propose now to ask your attention to the events and influences which combined without consolidating them—in other words, the formation, or, more properly, the *growth of the Union*. For this process there were needed two powers of an opposing nature—a centralizing and a repulsive power—the former to give connexion, the latter to preserve the distinctive local organization.

Let me remark, by way of introduction, that in studying the history of the Union the mind is peculiarly exposed to that unconscious delusion, so frequent in historical studies, which consists in allowing notions and impressions of the present time to enter inappropriately into our estimate of the past. It is thus that we often deceive ourselves with unperceived anachronisms. The complicated frame-work of our political system has been for more than half a century acquiring strength and solidity by the actual working of the system and by the imperceptible processes of time. There are the countless interchanges arising from an active commercial spirit, the progress of the arts is speeding and facilitating intercourse to an extent never dreamed of in the olden time, there are the thousands of social affinities of interest and affection by which fellowship is created and confirmed between various and remote sections of the country. Conceive for an instant the possibility of a knowledge of the written intercommunication, on any one day, transmitted by the agency of the post office or the electric telegraph, what a story it would tell of strong and incalculable affinity—political, commercial, social—of community of traffic and of feeling, precious and far-reaching! So habitually familiar to us is all this, that when we turn to an early era of our history we are apt, unawares, to carry our present associations back where they do not belong. Familiar as we are in our day and generation with the recurrence and easy gathering of conventions, composed of delegates from all parts of the Union, for every variety of purpose—ecclesiastical and political, scientific, educational, commercial, agricultural, and fanatical—we are prone to underrate the difficulties of intercourse in former times of more laborious travelling. In the early colonial period the colonies took little heed of each other. There was interdependence between a colony and the mother-country, but not between one colony and another. This was, perhaps, a consequence of the policy which was restriction on the commerce and manufactures of the colonies. It was, in a great measure, in accordance, too, with the feelings of the colonists, for *Old* England long had a place in their hearts; but what was *New* England to Virginia, or Virginia to New England? "*Home*" was the significant and endearing title which continued to be applied, with a permanence of habit that is remarkable, to the mother-country. When the news of the great fire in London, in 1666, reached Massachusetts, subscriptions of money were made throughout the colony for the relief of the sufferers.

It appears, too, both from documentary history and from private correspondence, how limited was the intercourse between the inhabitants of the different colonies. In the biographies of men whose movements are of sufficient consequence to be traced and recorded, but few instances of the kind can be collected. Washington, in 1756, travelled as far eastward as Boston, and in the next year he visited Philadelphia; but both these visits were occasioned by peculiar demands of a public nature connected with the old French war—the first, for the purpose of a personal interview with the commander-in-chief, General Shirley; the second, to attend a conference of governors and officers, summoned by Lord Loudoun. These are, I believe, the only occasions, before the beginning of the Revolution, when he attended the Congress of 1774, that Washington went to the northern or middle provinces. Mr. Quincy's visit to the middle and southern colonies, immediately before the Revolution, was (as is obvious from the record of it) an undertaking of quite an unusual character; in 1773, writing home from Charleston, he speaks of "this *distant shore*." No other instance occurs now to my recollection, except a visit to Boston of two of the Philadelphia patriots—John Dickinson and Joseph Reed—a few years before the war of independence. Even as late as the meeting of the first general Congress—that, I mean, of 1774—there is much, it appears to me, in the private letters and other contemporary evidence of that period which shows that when the delegates to that Congress assembled they came together very much as strangers to each other personally, and representing, too, communities strange to each other but finding more congeniality than they had anticipated.

In thus noticing individual intercourse, as illustrative of the times, there is one case, indeed, which I have not spoken of, because it is clearly *exceptional*, and must so be considered in judging of the personal intercommunication during the colonial period. I refer to the case of Dr. Franklin. Boston-born and Philadelphia-bred he had, no doubt, in consequence a less provincial feeling, a more expanded sense of citizenship, which was favored too by the course and opportunities of his remarkable career, his personal activity, and his official positions. No man had so much to do with various colonies; for, not to speak of his wanderings in boyhood, we find him, under his appointment in 1753 as Postmaster General for America, travelling in his one-horse wagon from Pennsylvania into New England. Again, in conference with delegates from seven of the colonies at the Albany Congress of 1754, busy at Boston with Governor Shirley, at Philadelphia with a Massachusetts commissioner, and all in quick succession; in Maryland acting as a sort of unofficial quartermaster for General Braddock; at a later period of colonial history, in England, uniting the agencies of Pennsylvania, Massachusetts, and Georgia. Now, although undoubtedly the formation of the Union is to be traced to causes of deeper import than any individual influences, I cannot but think that such various and extended intercourse as Dr. Franklin's must have aided in no small degree in bringing about that community of civic feeling which at length took the shape of political union. Sagacious, practical, affable, a man of the people in the best sense of the term, led by official duties hither and thither through the land, brought into business relations with the highest and the humblest functionaries, governors and generals and village postmasters, Franklin cannot but be regarded as an instrument imperceptibly and unconsciously doing the work of union. His case was, however, an exception to the ordinary intercourse among the inhabitants of the several colonies, and as an exception proving what we are apt to lose sight of, that the formation of the Union was a slow, a laborious, and reluctant process. *Happily* so, for thus it gained a strength which no hasty or premature coalition ever could have acquired. The period of transition from the original state of political severalty to the present political combination may be described as a space of time not shorter than a century and a half, making the computation from the first distinct effort at union, the original suggestion in 1637 of that little local coalition styled "The New England Confederacy," down to the Declaration of Independence, or, if a later date be preferred, when in 1789 the Union was made "*more perfect*" by the adoption of the present Constitution. During this long period the processes of combination were going on silently, imperceptibly, seldom thought of, and never fully appreciated; advances sometimes made, and then the cause retrograding; the power of attraction prevailing at one time, and the power of repulsion at another; connexion at one period looked to for security, and again shunned and resisted as concealing danger.

It is not without interest to observe that there was nothing in the physical character of the country, with all its variety of soil and climate, which presented impediments in the formation of the Union. There was no natural frontier at any part of the territory occupied by the settlements which were for a long time limited to the country extending from New Hampshire to Georgia, and bounded by the ocean and the first great range of mountains.

Rivers flowing north and south are thought to be most influential upon civilization, perhaps by connecting the climate and soil of different latitudes. When our territory was expanded to receive the whole valley of the Mississippi, we can look back to the long and difficult negotiations respecting the navigation of that river, when its banks were held by different powers, as indicating that Nature fitted it for a great highway for *one* people, and to bind them strongly together for ever.

No bay or river interposed a dangerous or difficult navigation; indeed, the great rivers, the Delaware, the Susquehannah, the Hudson, and the Connecticut, each flowing through the territory of several colonies, served by their free navigation to facilitate the intercourse of the colonists. There was no such mountain intersection as would cut off by a natural barrier one portion of the country from another, such as has been observed in Italy, where only a few years ago a Neapolitan naturalist, making an excursion to one of the highest of the central Apennines, found medicinal plants growing in the greatest profusion which the Neapolitans were regularly in the habit of importing from other countries, as no one suspected their existence within their own kingdom.

Looking to the physical character of the continent in relation to the subject of social and political union, I may allude to another consideration as affecting our national progress and permanence. It has been observed by a distinguished French naturalist that mountain ranges which run east and west establish much more striking differences with regard to the dwellers on the opposite sides than those ranges which extend north and south, a statement confirmed by observation through the history of mankind. The Scandinavian Alps have not prevented the countries on both sides being occupied by a people of common descent, while the feeble barrier of the Cheviot hills and the Highlands has served to keep the Anglo-Saxon and the Celt apart even in a period of advanced civilization. The Spaniards and the Italians differ more from their neighbors across the mountains extending east and west than the former from the Portuguese, or the Piedmontese from the Provençals. Of this physical law of civilization and the destiny of races the most remarkable illustration is perhaps to be found in the separation, which continued through so many centuries of ancient history, of the races that occupied the northern coasts of the Mediterranean and the races that dwelt in Central Europe. There is no more remarkable fact in the history of mankind; and the barrier which so wondrously preserved this separation between populous nations comparatively so near to each other, was that east and west mountain range, which extends from the western extremity of the Pyrennees, at the shores of the Atlantic eastward, to the shores of the Caspian. It was a partition that remained unbroken by either the southern or the northern race, with rare and only partial exceptions, until at length the time arrived for those vast irruptions by which a new civilization was to take the place of the ancient and the Roman. The application of this law of Nature to our own race occupying this continent is manifest, and it is of momentous interest in connexion with the origin, the extension, and the perpetuity of the Union. The mountain ranges, great and small, extend in a northwardly and southwardly direction, but none in that direction which seems to have a power for partition over the races of men. It is only *conventional* lines running east and west that perplex the nation.

The physical character of the territory occupied by these colonies which where to become the thirteen United States, was favorable to the establishment of Union. Further, it may be regarded as favorable to the same result that during the colonial period no addition of territory took place which might have introduced an incongruous element, unmanageble material to be brought into union. In making this remark, I have especially in my thoughts the failure of Cromwell's plan for securing his then recent conquest of Jamaica by co-operation with Massachusetts in planting a New England colony there. The Protector's proffered gift of a West India island was declined by the practical good sense of the general court of the colony; and thus the community which was destined to grow in compact strength on their own soil was saved from being parted into two communities with the ocean between them. The interview between Cromwell and Leveret, the agent of the colony, as narrated by the latter in his despatch to Governor Endicott, (December 20, 1656,) is curiously characteristic on the one hand of that intense and deep policy which is part of the mystery of the Protector's character, and on the other, of the keen, clear-sighted, common sense of the representative of the colony:

"At my presenting," writes Leverett, "your letter of the 1st of December, 1656, to his Highness, he was pleased to inquire of New England's condition, and what news as to the business of Jamaica; to which I gave answer according to the advice received. By his resent thereof, together with what I had from him the 18th November, he manifested a very strong desire in him for some leading and considerable company of New England men to go thither; for at that time he was pleased to express that he did apprehend the people of New England had as a clear a call to transport themselves from thence to Jamaica, as they had from England to New England, in order to their bettering their outward condition, God having promised his people should be the head and not the tail; besides that design hath its tendency to the overthrow of the man of sin; and withal was pleased to add, that though the people had been sickly, yet it was said to be a climacterical year; that others had been to view the place, as Nevis people, who, upon liking, were gone down; and Christopher's people were upon motion; and he hoped by what intelligence he had from Captain Gookin, that some considerable numbers would go from New England. His Highness was pleased to hear me in what I objected. As to the bettering our outward condition, though we had not any among us that had to boast, as some particulars in other plantations, of raising themselves to great estates, yet take the body of the people, and all things considered, they lived more comfortably like Englishmen than any of the rest of the plantations. To which his Highness replied that they were more industrious, what then would they be in a better country? To which I added, that there were now in New England produced to bespeak us a Commonwealth greater than in all the English plantations besides; the which his Highness granted. I objecting, the contrariety of spirits, principles, manners, and customs of the people of New England, to them that were at the island or on any other plantations that could remove thither, so not like to cement; his Highness replied that were there considerable persons that would remove from thence, they should have the government in their hands, and be strengthened with the authority of England, who might be capable of giving check to the ill and vicious manners of all."—(Hutchinson's History, Vol. I, p. 176.)

We need not now speculate what might have been the effect; a people who had this consciousness of *much that bespake them a commonwealth*, had they been tempted away from their own stern clime and soil to dwell in a tropical island; but of this we may be assured, when we look forward to the subsequent career of that people, that it was happily provided that they should remain compact at home.

In like manner at a later period of our history, all the efforts which at the beginning of the revolutionary struggle were made to bring the other British provinces into co-operation with the thirteen colonies proved utterly ineffectual. It will be remembered, that when the first general Congress met in 1774 and deliberated on plans of peaceful resistance to the obnoxious policy of the mother-country, it was a matter of solicitude to increase and fortify that resistance by enlarging the sphere of it. It must be borne in mind that all that was then aimed at was colonial redress; to that, and not to independence did the first Congress direct its thoughts, its words, its action. The events of that time followed in such quick succession, leading so rapidly on to independence, and now seen to be so rapidly connected with such a result, that we are apt to forget that independent existence as a nation was not, for some time after the contest began, aimed at, or even desired. The heart of the people felt and avowed a sincere and natural reluctance to break away from an ancient allegiance. Thus contemplating a continuance of the colonial condition and not looking beyond it, the desire was to render colonial resistance as effective as possible, by bringing as large an amount of it as possible to bear on the ministry and parliament. Accordingly repeated exertions were made to induce all the colonies to make common cause. The Congress, composed at first of the delegations of twelve colonies, from New Hampshire to South Carolina, appealed to the other colonies, Nova Scotia, St. Johns, and earnestly and urgently to Canada. The addresses to these British provinces fill a large space in the journal of the first Congress. The hope was that all British America might be brought to think, feel, and to act in unison in a cause then regarded as a temporary one, simply colonial redress, the restoration of a former colonial policy with which the colonist was content.

And here let me remark in passing that this attempted policy of general colonial co-operation appears to me to explain both the use and the disuse of a term which for several years was a very familiar one, but afterwards became obsolete in our political vocabulary and for a long time has had only a historical significance. I refer to the word "*continental*" as employed both formally and familiarly in the titles "the *continental* Congress," "the *continental* Army," and in a phrase of less agreeable association "the *continental* Currency." The term was an appropriate one when it was meditated to make the colonial resistance co-extensive with the British communities on the continent; and such was the plan when the word came into use, and it passed into disuse when it was at length ascertained that such enlarged co-operation was not to be accomplished, but that out of the conflict there was to arise a new nationality not co-extensive with the continental extent of British power in America.

The second Congress, I mean that of 1775, clung to the same hope and the same policy of colonial combination on the most enlarged scale; and this feeling continued even after the beginning of hostilities. Again did Congress address to the non-participant provinces elaborate appeals and invitations; again did they communicate arguments to Canada to demonstrate the hidden perils of the Quebec bill, to show the superiority of the common law over the civil law, to expound religious toleration, persuading the French Canadian that Roman Catholic and Protestant might dwell together securely and harmoniously as in the cantons of Switzerland.

Nay, further, the Congress indulged the expectation of even more than cis-Atlantic opposition, for it sent its voice from Philadelphia across the sea to the people of Ireland. In the earliest scheme of confederation—that submitted to Congress by Dr. Franklin, in July, 1775—one of the articles expressly provided for the admission of Ireland, the West India islands, Quebec, St. Johns, Nova Scotia, Bermudas, and East and West Floridas into the "Association," which was then relied upon as a means of colonial redress.

Besides the appeals and the invitations addressed to the Canadians, there was a hope that a successful invasion of Canada might bring the population there into that support of the common colonial cause for which the other means had failed. Accordingly, the expedition under Montgomery, in the winter of 1775–'6 had a purpose additional to mere conquest—that of gaining the support and the assistance of their fellow-colonists.

Still clinging to this object, Congress resorted to one other and the last attempt—an embassy to speak in person to the Canadian—the commission composed of Dr. Franklin, Charles Carrol, and Samuel Chase, taking with them for their coadjutors a Roman Catholic priest, the Rev. John Carrol, (afterwards archbishop of Baltimore,) and equally pacific agents, a printer and a French translator.

All these efforts—addresses made and made again, invasion, the embassy of commissioners—all proved utterly unavailing in bringing to those early Congresses any co-operation from other British provinces. The addresses were not responded to, probably were hardly heeded; the military expeditions failed, and the commissioners found no audience. The printer who accompanied Dr. Franklin and the other commissioners proved of no avail, in consequence of an unanticipated but fatal obstacle, and that was that reading was a very rare accomplishment with the French Canadian population. Quebec was not more impregnable to Montgomery than were the minds of the Canadians to Franklin and a printing-press.

These schemes for more extended colonial combination—began in 1774, continued during 1775 and into 1776—all came to naught; and now we can see, what was not visible to those who conceived those schemes, how happy it was that they *did* come to naught. I do not mean to question or to disparage the sagacity of those colonial statesmen, who during three years persevered in those schemes and the various methods of accomplishing them. Judged with relation to the objects aimed at, those schemes were wise and patriotic; but the objects were only *colonial* opposition, and the combination which was contemplated was only to be a temporary one, to cease whenever the colonial grievances should cease. But in God's government over the destinies of the race and country other and greater results were in reserve,—independence, nationality, union,—and considered with relation to such results, I repeat it was most happy that all attempts to bring about Canadian combination proved absolutely fruitless. It was only eleven years before, let it be remembered, that Canada had been transferred, by conquest and the treaty of Paris, from French to British dominion. A province so recently foreign in laws, in language, in the various social elements, must needs have proved an incongruous, if not a discordant member in such a union as was on the eve of completion between the thirteen colonies. The very fact that it was necessary for Congress to cause the addresses to Canada to be translated into French, is of itself enough to show how little congeniality there would have been for the perpetual purpose of union. When, therefore, Canadian sympathy and co operation were invoked, "a wiser spirit" was at work to make that invocation of no effect.

While the addition of these incongruous materials was happily prevented, it must not be forgotten that the portion of the continent which was to be the soil of the Union already included within its bounds, indeed in its very centre, elements equally foreign and unsuited to natural combination; for almost contemporaneous with the settlement of Virginia and of New England, in the first quarter of the seventeenth century, Hudson's voyage had created the claim of Holland, and the grant by the States General to the Dutch West India Company planted their settlement along the banks of the Hudson. Thus was introduced into the very heart of the land a hostile element, for England and Holland were at strife in the East Indian commercial settlements, in which region, the massacre of the English traders, at Amboyna, occurred about the same period.

Another occupation, foreign, but less antagonistic, was that which connects with American history the name of one of the wisest and noblest of Europe's continental kings, statesman, and soldier, Gustavus Adolphus, of Sweden; a company of whose subjects settled, it will be remembered, on the banks of the Delaware.

Settlements such as these, by two of the great European powers, and on most important sections of the continent, were unpropitious to any progress of union among the British colonies, for the foreign and unfriendly occupation was interposed between the northern and the southern settlements, an occupation held too by one of these foreign powers for well nigh half a century, and during all that time ambitious of larger colonial dominion, and actively aggressive.

For the removal of these impediments to our union, there was needed the strong control of conquest. In one respect that process was simplified, as if the course of things was so guided as to leave behind as little as possible of the ill blood and rankling recollections of conquest. There was engendered no animosity between the Swedes and the English colonists; for it was Holland that did the work of conquest, and subjugated the little Swedish colony on the banks of the Delaware.

For England, there was, therefore, left only one colonial adversary; and the adverse element of a foreign occupation of a considerable and important part of the continent was done away by the result of the war between England and Holland; the treaty of Breda, and the final cession of the territory, thus establishing English colonial dominion in uninterrupted occupation of the whole extent of the country, which was thereafter to be in union.

It would, perhaps, not be easy now to measure the sense of repugnance which survived in the minds of the conquered Dutch colonists; the natural reluctance at the transfer, by conquest, of their allegiance; the compulsory identification with a people who had other laws and usages, and another language: but whatever these feelings may have been, they met soon with what must have been a most unlooked for alleviation in the course of events in Europe; for it was only twelve years after the Dutch colonists in America passed under British dominion, that their native country, Holland, gave a sovereign to Great Britain, and thus the throne of their conquerors was filled by one of their countrymen, him who had been their Stadtholder, their Prince of Orange. Thus British rule became less of foreign rule to them; and thus the revolution of 1688 may be referred to as having contributed a harmonizing influence to the progress of the American union.

The Dutch dominion in America, adverse as it was to union in one respect, by parting the northern from the southern English colonies, in another respect exerted an influence favorable to colonial combination. It was not only the presence of hostile Indian tribes on the New England frontier, but it was also the neighborhood of the Dutch, "that prompted the first effort of colonial union; that of the united colonies of New England" which had its beginning in 1643, the first "confederacy," the first time the word "confederacy" was used in America. It was the first of these combinations, serving to show how it was a sense of common danger, the sense of strength and security in united action, which, by slow and safe gradations, was to bring the several colonies into union, disclosing, from time to time, how natural it would be for the sentiment of social union, which all the while, no doubt, however unrecognised at the time, was growing strong, to be converted into *political* union; how the sense of brotherhood, of a community of citizenship would imperceptibly prepare itself to assume political form and consistency.

I cannot pause to comment on that early confederacy, its principles, its system, and its uses. It purported to be "a *perpetual* league of friendship and amity," and it contained provision for its enlargement by the admission of other colonies into confederacy with the four colonies who were the contracting parties. Limited as this confederacy was in the number of its members, cautiously restricted as it was in its powers, and close and pressing as the dangers were, five years were consumed in the planning of it; *perpetual* as it professed to be, it lasted no more than about forty years; no other colony was added to it, and as the dangers which suggested it passed away, the confederacy lost its interest, and when its existence ceased incidentally with the abrogation of the New England charters, in the reign of James II, no effort was made to renew it. The old Saxon principle of distinctive local government was at work even within the narrow circuit of these kindred Puritan colonies, and no adequate motive for union presented itself. There are traces of mutual jealousies there; especially was there jealousy of the centralizing authority of Massachusetts. This feeling was manifest in the solicitude on the part of the Plymouth colony to preserve its separate existence. It breaks out in the bitter humor of a not very felicitous pun on the Bay colony, in a despatch from the Plymouth agent to the Plymouth governor, when, writing from London in 1691, he says: "All the frame of Heaven moves upon one axis, and the whole of New England's interest seems designed to be loaden on one bottom, and her particular motion to be concentric to the Massachusetts tropic. You know who are wont to trot after the bay horse."—(Wiswall to Hinckly, Nov. 5, 1691. Hutch. I, 365.)

In the New England confederacy, unanimity in religious creed was an essential principle of political concord, an impediment to the progress of union, if the confederacy had continued, for admission was refused to their dissenting fellow-colonists of Rhode Island. The Puritan clergy who went to Virginia were ejected for non-conformity; and it was only about twenty years before William Penn obtained the charter for Pennsylvania, and came with his Quaker followers, that the "*Friends*" who ventured into New England were scourged under the law against "vagabond Quakers," and the sterner penalty of death inflicted.

If at an early period sectarian animosity was burning lines of division between the colonists, the now tolerant christianity of a later time contributed largely to the more accordant results of blending the communities together. Each christian society was at length enabled peacefully to commune with its own brotherhood in other sections of the country, and thus ecclesiastical sympathy became one of the means by which the way was prepared for civil and political sympathies. The inhabitants of different and distant colonies became members of one household in their faith, thus learning, perhaps, how they might become members of one political family. Among the churches of the church of England in the colonies, no ecclesiastical union in one collective representative assembly was formed until after the peace of 1783. The Presbyterians, feeling the want of ecclesiastical combination, as appears from a circular letter of the ministers and elders at Philadelphia, began in 1764 to take measures to effect a union of their scattered forces.

I turn now to another and very different influence of union, which is to be discovered in the military colonial combinations. On repeated occasions the authorities of the colonies—governors and commissioners—were brought into connexion for conference respecting hostilities, offensive as well as defensive. It was upon such an occasion, in 1690, at New York, that the word "*Congress*" first has a place in our history. But, besides such occasional conferences, the colonists were brought together in joint military service, to know each other the better thereby. This kind of association may be traced as an influence of union, more or less operative on different occasions from the times of what were called "King William's war," and "Queen Anne's war," at the close of the seventeenth and at the beginning of the eighteenth century, down to the peace of Paris, in 1763, at the end of the old French war. The colonies contributed their respective sums of money to the general cost of the war, and troops levied in the different colonies served together in the several early attempts on Canada, in the expedition against Cape Breton and the capture of Louisburg, and upon what was the first foreign service of the colonists, (I mean foreign beyond the continent,) Vernon's disastrous expeditions against Carthagena and Cuba. The associated service in the old French war was the latest discipline of the kind to prepare the colonies for the war of the revolution.

While such influences and others of a more imperceptible nature, which I cannot now pause to discuss, were working propitiously for union, there was a counter-agency produced by the indications of a desire on the part of the British government to adopt a different colonial policy, to substitute for "that wise and salutary neglect," which Mr. Burke afterwards commended, a more active control. In carrying out such a policy there would be needed more of union, not spontaneous, voluntary colonial union, but compulsory union, by the imperial power on the other side of the Atlantic. It was at the close of the seventeenth century that William the Third formed the standing Council of the Lords Commissioners for Trade and Plantations, vested with new and centralizing powers of superintendence. There had been in the more arbitrary reign of James the Second indications of the same policy of more active colonial control; and it made itself manifest in the new methods of colonial administration, their policy and their plans, in one instance nothing less than a recommendation that "all the English colonies of North America be reduced (reduced, such was the word) under one government and one viceroy." The consequence of all this was, that union began to present itself to the thoughts of the colonists in the obnoxious light of a means of increasing the ascendancy of the royal prerogative; and they watched with perpetual vigilance every approach to combined action, to union avowedly or covertly compulsory, as something that was fatal to colonial rights.

The ancient Saxon element of distributed power was quickened into renewed activity during a long period of apprehension. When, in consequence of the suggestion of the Board of Trade and of the colonial secretary, the Albany convention was held in 1754, with its delegations from seven colonies, extending as far south as Maryland, the plan of union proposed by that Congress was, as is well known, rejected; although the war with France was imminent, and although the author of the plan was Franklin himself, a delegate from Pennsylvania. The several colonial assemblies detected too much of prerogative in the scheme of union, which had the singular fate of proving also unsatisfactory in England, because of the opposite objection of too little prerogative. Franklin was discouraged in his hopes of colonial confederation; and one of his correspondents said to him, writing from Boston, in 1754: "However necessary a union may be for the mutual safety and preservation of these colonies, it is certain it will never take place unless we are forced to it by the supreme authority of the nation."

It was by the action of the supreme power of the nation that union did take place, but not in the way contemplated when those words were used. When the new and obnoxious colonial policy took the well defined shape of the Stamp Act, union, which had been dreaded when the proposal came in any form from the British government, was instinctively resorted to as a means of defence and security, and the delegations of nine colonies, as far south as South Carolina, met in the Congress of 1765.

When, nine years later, the power of the British government struck, with the Boston Port Bill, at one single point, the sentiment of union was discovered to be strong enough and quick enough to make common cause with almost instantaneous rapidity, and twelve colonies (soon afterwards to reach the full complement of the old thirteen) assembled by their delegations in the Congress of 1774. When it is considered that those delegations were chosen in various ways, with much of irregularity, of necessity, I know of nothing so remarkable in the history of representation as the meeting of those fifty-two men in a room of a building familiar to Philadelphians as the Carpenters' Hall, locking the doors, enjoining secresy on the members, and all the while the people from New Hampshire to Georgia waiting quietly, willingly, resolutely, prepared to do, I will not say the *bidding* of that

Congress, but to accept the conclusions of that Congress as the voice of the nation. What higher proof could there be of the unknown strength of union? I say the *unknown* strength of the sentiment of union, because that Congress contemplated nothing more than "*association*" (as it was termed) in a policy of non-importation and non-exportation. When the Congress of 1774 adjourned, it was a *contingent* adjournment, leaving it to be determined by the course events might take whether the colonies would again be found acting in concert. The plan of confederation proposed by Franklin in 1775 looked to no duration beyond the continuance of the obnoxious acts of Parliament; and even after the war began, and the continental army was formed, perpetuity of union appears not to have formed part of the plan of operations. It was not until the wearied patience of the people was worn out, and the aggrieved sense of freedom driven to the last resort, that the coalition of the colonies began to assume the aspect of permanence. Then, and not till then, it became apparent what had long been the tendency of things touching the relation between those distinct communities. Together they had sought redress for their grievances; together they had declared their rights; they appealed, petitioned, remonstrated together; and when they encountered the same repulse and the same disappointment, they "*associated*" under solemn pledges, "the sacred ties of virtue, honor, and love of country," for a combined pacific resistance. At length, when all had failed, and they saw that the hour had come for the last appeal, they bowed down together in "public humiliation, fasting, and prayer," and, with hearts thus fortified, they stood prepared to face the common danger. It was one war to all. Blood was soon shed; and that blood, poured out for the common cause of all, was the seal of union. Further, when hostilities had been continued for more than a year, and it became manifest that the war was ineffectual as a means of mere colonial redress, the process which established national existence was at the same time the consummation of union. The colonies, which found themselves in a state of revolutionary anarchy, instead of hurrying to separate action, deliberately sought the advice of the whole country as it might be given by Congress. They sought and they followed that guidance. This was union. When the final and formal act of independence came, it was done by all and for all. That was union. Therefore, there is, I think, no proposition in our constitutional history clearer, simpler, truer than this, that *Union is our country*.

In conclusion, permit me to say, that I fear I have exposed myself to some condemnation for rashness in attempting to treat so large a subject within such limited space. I have had it most at heart to show how, during a very long period of time, there has been a tendency of events proving a providential purpose in the establishment of the Union. However the feelings of men may differ in respect for antiquity, what mind can refuse to recognise a claim for all that can be given of thoughtful, affectionate, and dutiful loyalty to that which for our good was achieved by more than human agency working through centuries. For the *Constitution* of the United States you may carry your debt of gratitude to the memory of that assembly of sages and statesmen who in convention constructed the Constitution. The debt of gratitude for

Independence may be paid to that other assembly of wise and good men who declared it. But for the UNION, our thanksgiving must be laid at the foot of the throne of God; and therefore treason to the Union cannot be conceived of but as a crime which heaps upon the traitor an accumulated guilt of thankless impiety. I speak it with reverence and with humility, and with thoughtfulness in the words I use, when I say that this Union of ours was the work of God.

LECTURES.

VI.—ON METEOROLOGY.

BY ROBERT RUSSELL, ESQ.,* OF SCOTLAND.

First Lecture.

To study the peculiarities of the atmospheric changes in North America, and the effects of the climate on agriculture, are the principal objects for which I have visited this part of the world. I am much gratified to find so large a number of meteorological observers scattered over all parts of this vast continent, contributing so materially to the advancement of science.

Since I have had an opportunity of studying the meteorology of the United States, I have been much impressed with the limited area of the field for investigations within the British islands. It now appears as a mere handbreadth, in comparison to the wide territory over which you are prosecuting your inquiries into the causes of atmospheric disturbauces.

Your government has done considerable for the support of meteorology. It has accumulated at the National Observatory, under the direction of Lieutenant Maury, an invaluable collection of facts relative to the sea. It has established observations at each of its military posts, and has secured the services of Professor Espy, who has done more for theoretical meteorology, in my opinion, than any other living man.

But I must confess that I would have turned my face to the Old World somewhat unsatisfied, if I had not had, through the politeness of the Secretary, an opportunity to examine the meteorological records collected within the walls of this Institution, and, through them, to become acquainted with the peculiarities of your climate; and to trace out the nature and extent of some of the atmospheric disturbances which had attracted my attention during my tour.

In this short course of lectures I shall not enter upon those questions which relate to general meteorology, but shall confiue myself principally to the analogies which seem to subsist between the action of atmospheric agents in Europe and in North America, and point out a few facts which demand more extended observations for their solution.

*NOTE.—The author of these lectures came to this country with letters of introduction from Sir David Brewster, Professor Airy, and other distinguished cultivators of science in Great Britain. The Smithsonian meteorological records were opened for his investigation, and other facilities extended him for the prosecution of his studies. Without intending to endorse the peculiar views which he may have advanced, we may say that his lectures contain facts and suggestions fully worthy of attention. J. H.

To comprehend the nature of the changes which the atmosphere undergoes, the elementary principles of meteorological science must be understood; but I do not intend to enter more minutely into these than will enable those who have not devoted much attention to the subject to comprehend the more important truths.

The nature of the atmosphere was long involved in obscurity. Its properties could not be ascertained till chemistry and other branches of natural science were considerably advanced. Air has so little color that it is almost invisible, and offers so little resistance to motion, that it was considered by the school of Aristotle imponderable. This opinion was entertained for many centuries afterwards, until the invention of the barometer, by Toricelli, in 1640, and the discovery of the fact pointed out by Pascal, that the barometer stands lower on the top of a mountain than at its base, left no doubt remaining that air was possessed of weight, and, consequently, that the atmosphere exerted a great pressure.

If a glass tube, three feet in length, be filled with mercury, and its open end inverted in a basin of the same liquid, the mercury in the tube will stand, at the level of the sea, nearly 30 inches higher than the surface of that in the basin. This column of mercury, which, if its section is a square inch, weighs nearly 15 pounds, is balanced by a column of air of the same section and extending to the top of the atmosphere. The pressure of the atmosphere is, therefore, equal to that of an ocean of mercury of 30 inches deep, or to a pressure on each square inch of surface of about 15 pounds. Moreover, mercury is 13½ times heavier than water, and 10,500 times heavier than dry air at the surface of the earth; hence the pressure of the atmosphere is equal to that of an ocean of water of about 33 feet deep, or an ocean of air, of equal density throughout, of 27,000 feet high.

That the atmosphere should press on the surface of the earth, and on all parts of our bodies, with a weight of 15 pounds to the square inch, is, at first sight, a very perplexing fact; but it is fully illustrated by the familiar and analogous pressure of water. The diver who descends below the surface of the sea is pressed on all sides by the superincumbent weight of water, and, instead of being incommoded by this, is rendered more buoyant. The particles of the air are of extreme tenuity and of almost perfect mobility, and therefore offer no resistance to bodies moving among them. On these accounts the weight of the air, and the great pressure of the atmosphere, remained so long concealed.

For a long time after the discovery of the pressure of the atmosphere, the world remained in ignorance of its chemical and mechanical constitution. The analysis of air was, however, one of the first triumphs of modern chemistry. Rutherford discovered hydrogen, one of its components, in 1772; and, two years after, Priestly and Shiel, independently of each other, discovered the other principal ingredient, namely, oxygen.

Dry air is composed of 77 parts nitrogen, 23 oxygen, by weight; 79 parts nitrogen, 21 oxygen, by volume; carbonic acid, 1.1000 by weight; ammonia, only a trace. The atmosphere also contains a certain amount of moisture. This is the only component which is liable to much change in its quantity. It varies from two per cent. to an inappreciable portion.

Again, the chemical composition of air had been established several years before its mechanical character was fully made out. The sages of Egypt and of Greece disputed about the constitution of matter; but their speculations, however ingenious, led to no definite results. At the end of the last century many valuable facts had been accumulated on this point; but no great law had been proposed to link these facts together before JOHN DALTON applied the atomic theory of the constitution of matter to explain the mechanical phenomena of the atmosphere.

Dalton did much for chemical science, and is justly regarded as the father of meteorology. He was gifted with gigantic powers of mind, and, in other respects, possessed a noble character.

Modern science regards matter as made up of atoms endowed with attracting and repelling force. In the case of a solid or liquid, these two forces are in equilibrium—the atoms are held at a distance from each other, and do not fill all the space enclosed within their boundaries. If a solid or liquid is subjected to pressure, the atoms are made to approach each other, and the repulsion is increased; so that, when the pressure is removed, the atoms fly back to their original position. If, on the contrary, we attempt to draw a solid apart, the attraction comes into operation, and offers a resistance which is called cohesion. In the case of aeriform substances, the repulsion entirely preponderates. Dalton gave to this theory a definite form, and applied it to the phenomena of the atmosphere.

All our conceptions of the constitution of substances, in regard to their solid, liquid, or aeriform states, are more or less intimately associated with the atomic constitution of matter in its relations to heat. Thus, the action of heat converts a solid into a liquid, by giving mobility to its atoms. The action of heat converts a liquid into an elastic vapor, or gas, by imparting a repulsive force to its atoms. Indeed, in regard to gases, the repulsive force and heat are often looked upon as identical, and we shall consider them to be so. The elastic properties of gas, steam, or vapor, are, then, owing to the mutual repulsion of the atoms, in consequence of the action of heat. This view, arising naturally out of the atomic constitution of matter, gives an explanation of the mechanism of gases no less simple than consistent.

To illustrate this principle one fact will suffice. If water is converted into steam under the ordinary pressure of the atmosphere, a cubic inch is transformed into about a cubic foot of vapor. The atoms of water are, therefore, twelve times further apart in the case of steam than they are in that of the liquid. The action of heat has had the effect of putting every atom in a state of repulsion with regard to its fellows—every one tends to fly from the other with as much force as if each was under the influence of a powerful spring. The intensity of the repulsion of the atoms constitutes the force of the steam. The elastic properties of the gases of the atmosphere are also owing to the mutual repulsion of their atoms, though the repulsion is much more permanent in this case than in that of steam. No cold or pressure has yet been found sufficient to reduce nitrogen or oxygen to a liquid form.

The bulk of gas is increased by heat, which must not be looked upon as increasing the size of the atoms, but only as increasing the repulsive force between them. The repulsive or expansive force is measured by the weight which it can support. In the atmosphere, the expansive force of a portion of air, or its elasticity, is exactly balanced by the gravity of all the air above it. The weight of the atoms, from the top to the bottom of the atmosphere, amounts, as we have said before, to about fifteen pounds on each square inch; the elastic or repulsive force which keeps the atoms apart is exactly equal to this amount. Gravity and elasticity are so equally poised, and the atoms move so freely amongst each other, that the air is in a state of the most delicate balance that can be imagined.

The expansive property of gases is a remarkable phenomenon in physics. We have no means of ascertaining its limits, but we know if the whole air was exhausted from this room, a single cubic inch of either oxygen or nitrogen would, if admitted into so large a vacuum, instantly occupy every part of it, and still press, though with diminished force, against the walls for further expansion. The repulsive force which exists among the atoms, though greatly weakened, would not be exhausted.

The law which regulates the density and elasticity of gases was discovered about half a century after Toricelli invented the barometer. Mariotte found, by experiment, "That the density and elasticity of atmospheric air are directly, but the space it occupies inversely, as the force of compression." That is to say, if you exhausted the air from the receiver of an air-pump until the barometer stood at fifteen inches, the pressure or elasticity of the air would only be half of what it was before the experiment. It would take two cubic inches of air in this state of rarity to weigh as much as one did when the barometer was at thirty inches; or, in other words, one half of the atoms being removed, the remaining half are further apart, since they still occupy the same space. The number of atoms being reduced one half, if the temperature is the same, their repulsive force is also reduced in the same ratio, and, therefore, the repulsion of the particles of any gas increases as the cube root of the distance between them diminishes. The repulsion between the atom at the very top of the atmosphere and those below it is so much weakened by separation that it is precisely equal to the weight.

From the simple fact that the repulsion of the atoms of gases varies as the number of atoms contained in a given space, it follows that the elasticity and density of a gas are as the pressure directly, that the volume is as the pressure inversely, and that, consequently, the one can be deduced from the other by the simple rule of proportion. This law holds true in regard to the most minute additions of weight, and we have the full assurance of reason, founded on experiment, other things being equal, that the distance which separates every atom of air from the top to the bottom of the atmosphere decreases as we descend; in short, each atom is nearer the atom immediately below it than the one above. The various strata of the atmosphere thus in some measure resembles fleeces of wool or loose balls of cotton piled upon each other. The wool or cotton is more compressed, and therefore more dense, in proportion to the weight it bears; it is most so next the bottom, and least so at the top. The air, in the same way, is more rare as we ascend to greater heights, the atoms being farther apart, and their repulsive force diminished. In consequence of the great capabilities of gases for expanding with diminished pressure, the atmosphere, instead of being only about five miles in height, as it would be if of equal density with the lowest stratum, (?) is really upwards of fifty miles high.

The atmosphere is not only in a most delicate state of balance in respect to elasticity and pressure, but it is no less so in respect to the amount of heat contained in its different strata. The expansive force of gases, or the repulsion which exists among their atoms, seems, as we have already stated, to be identical with heat. When air, at the temperature of freezing water, is condensed in the hollow globe of an air-gun, an immense amount of heat becomes sensible. Tinder, it is well known, can be lighted with a single stroke of a condensing syringe. In the rarefied gas a large amount of heat is stored away and inappreciable by our instruments or senses, which is again given out by compression.

The intimate connexion subsisting between heat and the expansion of gases is most beautifully seen in the atmosphere. As already stated, the atoms of air as we ascend are at greater distances from each other. If the distance between any two atoms is diminished, they give out heat or render it sensible; whereas, if we increase the distance between them, they store it away. The upper strata are sensibly colder than the lower, not because the atoms have less heat, but because the heat is diffused through a larger space when the atoms are farther apart. One pound of air at the level of the sea, within the tropics, may be said to contain no more heat than the same weight at the top of the highest mountain perpetually covered with snow. It is for this reason that the same wind which is warm in the valley becomes colder as it ascends the sides of the mountain. The diminishing pressure allows the air to expand and store away its heat. It is, therefore, not the snow on the top of mountains which cools the air, but it is the rarity of the air which keeps the snow itself from melting. As a general law, the decrease of temperature amounts to 1° Fahrenheit for every 300 feet in perpendicular height.

A variation in the amount of heat affects the volume of a gas as sensibly as a variation in the pressure. An addition of heat increases the repulsive force of the atoms, and thus expands the volume. All gases, reckoning from the freezing point of water, expand nearly the 480th part of their bulk for every degree of temperature; or, in other words, if one cubic foot of air had its temperature raised 480° above the freezing point, its elastic force would be doubled, or it would tend to expand to twice its former bulk.

If a number of atoms of air in the lower stratum receives a greater amount of heat than those in the vicinity, they will repel each other to a greater distance apart than they were before they were heated, and will have a tendency to ascend, on the same principle that a piece of cork rises in water.

On these undisputed data Dalton founded his two famous conditions of atmospheric equilibrium, which are now regarded as the true basis on which all atmospheric disturbances are to be studied. First, that the atmosphere can only remain in a state of rest or equilibrium when the barometer stands at the same height at the level of the sea in all parts of the globe, because the aerial envelope has a tendency like water to seek its equilibrium. Second, that the atmosphere must every where have the same temperature at the level of the sea, and that its various strata as we ascend must have a temperature corresponding to their position—that is, that every atom, from the top to the bottom of the atmosphere, must possess the same absolute amount of heat.

A number of natural agencies are at work to disturb the equilibrium of the atmosphere, and to give rise to aerial currents; among them the most important is the difference of temperature in different parts of the earth. The air within the tropics, constantly heated by the rays of an almost perpendicular sun, is rendered lighter, and is pushed upward by the heavier air north and south of this region. A current in this direction from each pole is thus produced at the surface of the earth, while an opposite current towards each pole is generated by the rarefied air which rises above the heated belt, and flows backward like water seeking its equilibrium. These currents, on account of the rotation of the earth, are not along the meridian, but those at the surface take a westerly direction, while those above flow in an easterly course. This is the origin of the trade winds at the surface of the earth, and of the great westerly current which is almost constantly moving in the upper strata over the middle and northern portions of the United States. That such a current does prevail over the regions mentioned is clearly proved by Professor Coffin's admirable report on the winds of the northern hemisphere, published in the Smithsonian Contributions to Knowledge. The phenomenon of the constancy of this upper current early attracted my notice in my tour through this country, and I learn from the records that it is the same all the year. The fact of the existence of this current is referred to by President Dwight, in his History of New England, to explain some atmospheric phenomena; and, indeed, it is one of the keys to a knowledge of the peculiarities of the meteorology of this country.

To understand some of the peculiar actions which occur in the lower strata of the atmosphere, it is necessary for us to consider a little more attentively the effect which sometimes takes place when a large area is slowly heated and the air above it gradually expanded. In this case the heated air, increasing its volume and resting on the surface of the earth, pushes up the air above it, and thus retains it in a state of unstable equilibrium. This condition was observed by the French savans as existing over the heated sand of the desert, and giving rise to the mirage. It was also observed by Colonel Sykes, on the plains of Hindostan, and is quite common in all latitudes.

This is a very unstable condition of the atmosphere, and is constantly liable to be overturned; yet its philosophy is not difficult to comprehend. When the atoms of air in the lower stratum are gradually and equally heated, all have a tendency to rise, and the cold atoms above have a tendency to descend. But as there is not room for all to descend and all to ascend at the same time, there is little downward or upward motion.

This is a very simple principle, but it is the only one which enables us to comprehend how a dead calm often exists immediately before violent storms, and even before the tremendous hurricanes of the West India islands. A large amount of power is in this way held in reserve ready to be developed under various circumstances. We shall mention some phenomena as illustrations which are produced in this way.

The unstable condition of the air, which results from the undue heat of the lower stratum, produces those great whirlwinds of dust and sand in the deserts of Arabia and Africa. The air flows in beneath, and revolves as it ascends, carrying loose material with it. Humboldt, when crossing over the great plains of South America during the hot season, recorded a curious instance of the effect of the sun's rays on the surface of the ground when the air was calm: "In the Mesa de Paja," says that illustrious traveller, "we entered the basin of the Llanos. The sun was almost at its zenith; the earth, wherever it appeared sterile and destitute of vegetation, was at the temperature of 86° to 90° F.; not a breath of wind was felt at the height at which we were on our mules; yet in the midst of this apparent calm whirls of dust incessantly arose, driven on by these small currents of air which glide only over the surface of the ground, and are occasioned by the difference of temperature between the naked sand and the spots covered with grass."—(Personal Narrative, Vol. 1.) The land and the sea breezes observed in warm countries are caused by somewhat similar agencies. The land in the day time becomes heated to a much greater degree than the sea; the air over the former expands and flows away above, while the comparatively cold air from the sea rushes over the land. This is exactly reversed at night, the air over the sea being slightly warmer than over the land—the breeze is from the latter. All are agreed as to the general cause of this phenomenon, but I am inclined to think the particular mode of action has not received that attention which it deserves. As I shall have occasion to show that the action of the sea breeze in Great Britain apparently furnishes us with the true principle upon which certain violent disturbances sometimes take place over one half of Europe, I shall be a little particular in describing the exact mode of action. And I am not singular in opinion that a modification of the same principle applies to some of the storms of the United States. On a recent visit to Cuba I had an opportunity to study some well defined instances of land and sea breezes. I was particularly interested in the former, because I was less familiar with them from personal observation; for while the sea breeze is common in summer on the east coast of Scotland, the land breeze is very rare. Hugh Miller has given a description of the sea breeze in his work entitled "My School and Schoolmasters," as it occurs on the Cromarty coast, which is well worth a perusal by those who take an interest in such matters.

The particular summer sea breeze of North Britain, so far as I have had an opportunity of observing, only occurs when an upper current is flowing from a westerly quarter. This condition seems to be essential to its action. The breeze is always strongest on the coast, it gradually moderates as it passes into the interior, and finally dies away long before it reaches the west coast. The manner in which the sea breeze loses its force shows that it is gradually absorbed into the upper current, and that it does not rise in one vertical column, but that there is a constant ascension and absorption going on over the whole extent agitated by the breeze. By way of exemplification, and to render my exposition more clear, I shall direct your attention to the action which takes place between soft and salt water, at the mouths of large rivers. Captain King observed a current of salt water running up the mouth of the Santa Cruz, beneath the fresh water. In this case we cannot for a moment imagine that the salt water rises in a body at any particular spot, and returns as salt water to the sea; but only that the salt under current is gradually absorbed into the fresh stream above, at every point as far as the salt water extends.

Now suppose the sea breeze has a depth of 2,000 feet, and extends 50 miles into the interior of the country; it will not rise in a vertical column of 2,000 feet in width, but will be gradually absorbed, by rising in small portions into the upper current along the whole distance traversed. The greater depth of salt water at the mouth of the river corresponds to the greater velocity of the air on reaching the land. The spot where the breeze is not felt has its counterpart in that point of the bed of the river where the salt water ceases to flow against the stream. The deep upper current from the southwest, which overlies the shallow sea breeze, performs the part of the large body of fresh water of the river, to which the other phenomena are merely secondary. The power which propels the salt water up the bed of the river is the difference in the weight of the fresh and salt water. In the sea breeze, the air over the surface of the land is lighter than that over the sea at the same elevation; and it is this difference in the weight of the two columns of air which, in this case, is the propelling power. If the barometer was sufficiently delicate, the rate of motion of the breeze might be calculated with considerable precision.

The heat of the sun materially affects the force of the winds at the earth's surface in all parts of the world. The still air of evening is well known to be in striking contrast with the breeze of midday. During the night the air cools more rapidly next the ground than at a greater elevation. The ascending currents cease with the heat of the sun, and friction soon induces a calm.

At the meeting of the British Association for the Advancement of Science the year before last, I took occasion, in illustrating the action of one class of storms which agitate the atmosphere of Europe, to point out the fact that the sun, during the summer months, in North Britain, had the effect to reverse the motion of a thin stratum of air at the surface of the ground; while, *during the day*, a north current constantly flowed above and a south current flowed below, *during the night* the latter was reversed. I have found similar phenomena to prevail in the United States. For some days, in Charleston, last January, I observed that the wind was south during the heat of the day, and north in the morning. I cannot stop now to discuss the cause of this phenomenon, though it is exceedingly interesting in a scientific point of view. But there is an analogous effect produced, upon a grand scale, east of the Rocky mountains, over the United States, as well as the British Possessions, that requires to be noticed in this place. It has been most satisfactorily made out by Professor Coffin, that southerly winds, in North America, are much more common in summer than in winter; the following are his reductions:

Region	Month	North winds	South to W.S.W.
Between lat. 32° and 33°, 9 stations, 8 year's average: S. Carolina, Georgia, Alabama, and Mississippi.	Jan.,	N. winds, 3.06.	— S. to W.S.W. 7.77 days.
	July,	N. winds, 1.83.	— S. to W S.W. 10.16 days.
Delaware, Maryland, and Eastern Virginia.	Jan.,	N. winds, 2.81.	— S to W.S.W. 6.29 days.
	July,	N. winds, 1.05	— S. to W.S.W. 13.00 days.
New England States south of latitude 45°, 49 stations, 5 years.	Jan.,	N. winds, 3.55.	— S. to W.S.W. 6.60 days.
	July,	N. winds, 1.44.	— S. to W.S.W. 15.74 days.
Between 45° and 50° latitude: Iowa, Wisconsin, Michigan, Canada, and Maine, 10 stations, 17 years.	Jan.,	N. winds, 4.17.	— S. to W.S.W. 5.73 days.
	July,	N. winds, 1.83.	— S. to W.S.W. 10.77 days.
Total north wind		19.74	Total south wind. 76.06

I quite concur in the opinion, first entertained by Volney, that the summer south winds of the United States are chiefly supplied from the trade winds of the tropics. To this wind is to be ascribed the amazing fertility of the climate for sugar, cotton, Indian corn, and tobacco. The isthmus which connects North and South America is too high to allow the trade winds to cross into the Pacific ocean; and in summer they appear to be frequently directed northwards by this great natural wall, and find their way across the Gulf of Mexico, and spread out as a surface current loaded with moisture over the Mississippi valley and the eastern seaboard States. If the isthmus which connects the two continents had been sufficiently low to allow the trade winds to cross into the Pacific, the valley of the Mississippi would have had, in all probability, a much less productive summer climate, resembling that of the south of Europe or the north of Africa.

I may here mention that there is only an extremely limited area in Europe which has sufficient summer rains, with the requisite temperature, to grow Indian corn, and that there are no cotton or sugar regions. The summers of Spain, except on the northwest of the country, are usually so very dry that little Indian corn can be grown without artificial watering. The productive powers of the soil are almost entirely centred in the valleys, which are irrigated by the melting of the snow of the mountains.

The summers of Italy are also too dry, and the melting of the snow on the Alps is essential to the fertility of Lombardy. The largest and best region for Indian corn in Europe is in the south and east of France. Mr. Marsh, in his introductory lecture here, told us that for three months rain did not fall in summer at Constantinople. In Palestine, "rain in summer" is still as rare as the "snow in harvest." In the valley of the lower Nile, a shower of rain is a remarkable phenomenon; the overflowings of the river serve for the growth of wheat, but no Indian corn or millet can be had without laborious irrigation; accordingly, fifty thousand oxen are employed in summer to draw water for this purpose. In upper Egypt no crops of any kind are obtained without the same appliance; and during a low current in the river the peasants are obliged to raise the water upwards of forty feet. When we reflect on these facts, the great fertility of the summer climate of North America, east of the Rocky Mountains, is very surprising. The aridity of the Mediterranean shores is owing to the prevalence of northerly winds; while the fertility of the United States is owing to the prevalence of those from the south. This statement is amply supported by Professor Coffin's researches in the Smithsonian Contributions.

The warm surface wind which sets in from the Gulf of Mexico over the United States, is not only the great source of fertility, but is also the great disturbing element of the atmosphere at all seasons of the year. During the warm season, in this country, when the wind changes to north or northwest, the sky becomes peculiarly transparent and blue in color. I have frequently had occasion, in my tour through Canada and the United States, to observe that the lower south and southwest wind begins to blow, as in Great Britain, shortly after the sun heats the air at the surface of the ground, and that the sky soon loses its peculiar transparency. One point in regard to this surface wind from the south deserves special notice. I allude to the fact that it is often at rest or very sluggish during the night, and most active during the maximum heat of the day. This vast surface wind which spreads over the region east of the Rocky Mountains, and over the Gulf of Mexico, is therefore daily put put in motion by the heat of the sun. The short time which I have been able to devote to this subject leads me to believe that the breeze begins to stir at an earlier hour in the day in the higher latitudes, and that it is gradually propagated to the south. The sun rising earlier the farther we advance northward is probably the cause of this phenomenon.

Mr. Thom, in his work on the "Nature and Course of Storms," p. 255, informs us that south and southwest winds prevail during summer over the projecting shoulder of South America, at Guiana; and I was informed by the sugar-planters that in Cuba south winds are common during the rainy season, namely, May, June, July, and August. Mr. Phelps, also, in a recent communication to the meteorological department of the Smithsonian Institution, mentions the fact that at Fort Brown, on the Rio Grande, the "prevailing winds are from the south, or probably a point or two to the east of south. This, he says, is more particularly the case during spring and the earlier part of summer, when they are usually pretty constant, especially during the day time, blowing at the rate of fourteen miles an hour, or five degrees of latitude per day. But Professor Coffin's report, already alluded to, gives us the best view of this great aerial current, which flows over the Mississippi valley, as well as along the Atlantic slope.

The two great systems of atmospheric currents, viz: the lower and warm surface wind from the south, and the cold and dry current flowing constantly in the upper regions from the west, are intimately associated with all the changes of the weather in the United States. But before we attempt to trace the nature of these changes we must direct attention to another element of meteorology, which we have as yet almost left out of view, viz: the elastic and invisible vapor of water contained in the air, and which plays so important a part in almost all atmospheric changes.

Science, as we have seen, was long perplexed with the problem of the manner in which water existed in the air; sometimes entirely invisible, at others obscuring the heavens with clouds, or falling as rain or snow. For the solution of this question, we are also indebted to John Dalton, who gave an explanation of the matter, no less simple than consistent and ingenious. He at the same time opened up a new view of the mechanism of mixed gases, gave us new ideas of the constitution of the atmosphere, and enabled us to comprehend the agency which "divides the waters of the firmament from the fountains of the deep." The hygrometry of the atmosphere will be considered in our next lecture.

METEOROLOGY.

Second Lecture.

That water placed in an open vessel over a fire does not have its temperature raised above 212 degrees, however great the heat may be, and that the steam produced is no warmer, is among the first of the wonders which arrests the attention of the student entering upon the field of physical science. The heat of the fire is absorbed in the production of the steam. .The atoms of water are made to repel each other. A cubic inch of this liquid converted into steam at 212 degrees, at the ordinary pressure of the atmosphere, has its bulk increased nearly 1,700 times. The elasticity of the steam thus produced is equal to the weight of a perpendicular column of 30 inches of mercury. This must appear quite evident when we consider how steam is formed. It rises from the bottom of the vessel which contains the water, in bubbles, and can only be rapidly formed when the repulsion of the atoms is able to resist the whole weight of the incumbent atmosphere.

Dalton, however, discovered that vapor is formed at all temperatures; that the boiling point of water and the elasticity of the vapor are entirely regulated by heat and pressure. This he proved by allowing a small quantity of water to ascend to the top of the mercury in a common barometer tube, where it produced vapor, the elasticity or pressure of which could be exactly measured by the height of the column, as the heat was increased or diminished. This simple experiment showed that the connexion between the temperature, density, and elasticity of steam is subject to the same physical law which regulates the density and elasticity of the permanent gases. The following exhibits a few cases of steam at different temperatures, with the corresponding force and weight:

Temp.		force	in inches;	weight of cubic foot,	grains.
Temp.	0°;	force 0.068	in inches;	weight of cubic foot, 0.856	grains.
	20°	" 0.140	"	" 1.688	"
	40°	" 0.280	"	" 3.239	"
	60°	" 0.560	"	6.222	
	80°	" 1.060	"	" 11.333	"
	212°	" 30. 00	"	" 257.218	"

In fact, after allowing for the difference of the temperature in steam, according to the law which holds in reference to other gases, the pressure of steam at any low temperature being given, the weight of a cubic foot of steam can be calculated by the simple rule of proportion.

Steam or vapor, at all temperatures, may be considered as water containing a definite amount of heat. A pound of steam at 212° contains very little more caloric than a pound of vapor at 32°. This is proved by the fact that steam, at any temperature, when condensed, is capable of raising the temperature of its own weight of water more than 1,000°. If a cubic foot of steam at 32°, weighing 2.539 grains, were subjected to pressure, and none of the heat evolved during the condensation lost, a small volume of steam at 212° would be produced. But a cubic foot of steam at 32° could not exist in the atmosphere by itself, as it would be subjected to a pressure of 30 inches of mercury, whereas it could bear no more than one-fifth of an inch. Hence a difficulty arose amongst chemists in regard to the manner in which water existed in the invisible form in the atmosphere at all temperatures, and under all pressures. There was also some difficulty in accounting for the manner in which the mixture of the different gases took place.

It has been found that air brought down from the tops of the highest mountains, and from the greatest elevation reached by aeronauts, is nearly the same in composition as at the surface of the earth. This fact was rather perplexing, because the different gases of the atmosphere have not the same specific gravity. A cubic foot of oxygen weighed more than one of nitrogen, while one of carbonic acid was 50 per cent. heavier than either.

Common air	1.0000
Carbonic acid	1.5240
Nitrogen	0.9760
Oxygen	1.1026
Steam 212°	0.6235

The carbonic acid being the heaviest gas, it should chiefly occupy the lower stratum of the atmosphere; and the nitrogen the top. Dalton, to reconcile a variety of phenomena with each other, added a new proposition to the theory of the atomic constitution of the mixed gases—namely, that the atoms of oxygen do not repel the atoms of nitrogen, but only those of their own kind. That the one gas is as a vacuum to the other. On this principle the most complete mixture of gases is explained, the atoms of one gas by their mutual repulsion are forced apart as is in void space, and thus diffused among those of another. At the last lecture we mentioned that if this room were completely exhausted of air, and a cubic inch of hydrogen introduced, it would instantly expand and fill the whole space. Now, the same thing would happen if a cubic inch of hydrogen were introduced into the room filled with air. The process would be much slower, but the mutual repulsion of the atoms of hydrogen would still be in as active operation as it was in the vacuum, and would still cause them to separate until they pressed against the walls of the room with as much force as if there were no air in it.

Not only has the truth of this law been verified, but the diffusive velocity of the various gases ascertained by actual measurement. This velocity is inversely as the density of the gases; in other words, the lighter the gas the greater its rapidity of diffusion. The vapor of water, or steam, is subject to the same law; and this is the solution of the difficulty we mentioned as to its capability of existing in the atmosphere at all temperatures. In accordance with this law, the atoms of water, as well as those of the several gases which compose the atmosphere, are as far separate from the atoms of their own kind as they would be if each alone occupied the space. The pressure of the compound atmosphere is therefore made up of the joint pressures of the individual gases.

Strictly speaking, vapor is not condensed by the pressure of air, but by diminution of temperature; and the amount of moisture which can exist at any time in the atmosphere depends upon the amount of heat. Air saturated with moisture may be likened to a vessel filled with round shot or sand. The spaces between the atoms of the permanent gases are occupied by the atoms of steam, in the same way as water fills up the vacant spaces between the shot or sand. The atoms of water are at a distance when steam at any temperature is by itself, and they can possess no greater repulsive force than is due to the temperature of the evaporating surface. Pressure applied to the atoms will cause condensation, if the heat arising from this act is lost. This is the same in the moistest atmosphere—the atoms of water are at a distance, and their repulsive or diffusive force is the cause of their remaining invisible. Evaporation, therefore, in the atmosphere at a given temperature, can only take place when the atoms of water are removed as far from those on the evaporating surface as they would be in pure steam at the same given temperature.

Air is said to be saturated with moisture when as many atoms of vapor are contained in it as would exist in a vacuum at the same temperature. The atoms of air merely fill up the interstices of the elastic vapor of water, or the converse. If the temperature be diminished, the repulsion of the atoms will not be sufficient to support so great a pressure, and a part of the vapor will be condensed into water. The reduced temperature at which this condensation begins to take place is called the dew point, or point of precipitation.

The elastic force of vapor would ultimately cause it to rise to the top of the atmosphere by virtue of this repulsive or diffusive property, if it were not checked by other causes. At one time meteorologists attributed many atmospheric phenomena to the great activity of the diffusive power of the vapor of water; but we are indebted to Professor Espy for showing that this has been very much overrated, and other agents are the more active causes.

The air has its temperature raised during the day by the direct heat from the sun and contact with the earth, and loses the greater part of this heat during the night by radiation into space. The ground radiating heat much faster than air in a clear, calm night, is generally cooled down below the point of precipitation of the vapor, and thus condensation of moisture is produced and dew formed. This effect of radiation has a most beneficial influence on vegetation. The formation of dew is regulated by a very simple law, viz: that *the dewed surface is always colder than the air in contact with it.* In the same way the dew-point of the air is ascertained by cooling down any body until moisture is formed upon it. Several hygrometers have been formed on this principle.

The amount of moisture in the atmosphere has a great influence in modifying the heating power of the sun's rays, as well as in the radiation of heat during the night into space. We often find two days in summer equally free from clouds and equally calm, while the one may be oppressively warm, and the other comparatively cool. This does not arise from a difference in the power of the sun's rays, but from the quantity of moisture in the atmosphere.

The influence of moisture in tempering the sun's rays is a remarkable fact and well worthy of further investigation. When the dew point is high, or, in other words, when the air is filled with moisture, the radiation from the earth is prevented, and the temperature of the night remains almost as high as that of the day; when the dew point is low, the sun's rays pass, without absorption, to the earth, and impart little of their heat directly to the air. The medium dew points are, therefore, most favorable to extreme heat in the atmosphere, and the greater heat beyond the tropics is probably owing to this cause.

The fact that the amount of moisture in the air regulates the temperature of the nights has not received the attention which it deserves. I shall hereafter show that the hygrometrical condition of the atmophere throws a very considerable amount of light on the action of North American and European storms; and therefore I am more anxious to draw your particular attention to the relation between the dew point of the vapor of the air and the night temperatures, because this is the only means which I have of indicating the hygrometrical conditions connected with the storms of the United States.

It seems to be a law which holds in general over the world that the temperature of the air at sunrise during calm nights, at a certain distance from the ground, falls a little below the dew point of the air during the preceding day. The mean temperature of the air at sunrise, therefore, approximates very closely to the mean dew point. The great amount of moisture in the air within the tropics is the cause of the warm and brilliant nights. Radiation from the air and ground, under these conditions, seems to lose its power. On the other hand, travellers in all parts of the world inform us, incidentally, as to the connection between dry air and cold nights. Mr. Inglis, in his travels through Spain, relates that he was oppressed by the hot rays of the sun in the valley of Granada while the hoar frost was lying white in the shade. Eastern travellers in the deserts often complain of the broiling heat of the air during the day, and of its chill temperature at night. Beautiful allusions to the same law are also found in Scripture; many of you will recollect that one of the greatest hardships which Jacob experienced while he tended Laban's flocks was, that through the "drought by day and the frosts by night sleep departed from his eyes." On the other hand, the moisture from the Atlantic in summer allows the air to retain its heat in the valley of Chamouni, in Switzerland, so that grapes ripen in the immediate proximity of the glaciers which descend from the Alps. At Bergen, in Norway, the same element allows the cherry-tree to mature its fruit where you can pluck it and throw the stones upon the broad mass of ice which slowly descends from the mountains.

Those days during summer in the United States on which the sky is very transparent are rather deficient in moisture. The air is then somewhat bracing, as the sun does not have the power of heating it up to a high degree. The great changes in the weather which take place at all seasons over the United States, and the very cold winters in comparision to those of Europe, are intimately associated with the hygrometric condition of the atmosphere, which we must now consider.

Why are the winters so cold at Washington in the 38° of latitude, the same as that of Lisbon, in Portugal, where the orange-trees are now in blossom? This is owing to the great prevalence of west and northwest winds, which are very dry, and sweep over the vast territory from Canada to Florida, and are converted into the northern of Cuba and the coast along the Gulf of Mexico. President Dwight, a most accurate observer, in his Travels and History of New England describes the character and effect of the winds so accurately, that I will quote two short passages. He says, "In 1787 the west wind began to blow about the 20th November, and continued its progress with only four short interruptions until the 20th of the following March—somewhat more than 100 days. During the whole time the weather for the season was very cold." Also, "in 1780 the wind blew from the west more than six weeks without any intermission, and during the whole of this time the weather was so cold that snow did not dissolve sufficiently to give drops from the southern eaves of houses." So long as the westerly wind continues to blow in winter there is no cessation of your cold, and so long as it continues to flow in a broad regular stream in summer there is no end to your drought. President Dwight maintains that the west and northwest wind is merely the descent of the upper current which flows so regularly right across the Rocky Mountains. Whoever will take the trouble to examine the meteorological observations within the Smithsonian Institution, I am inclined to think, will come to the same conclusion. If the south wind was as common in winter as in summer, and if there was no descent of this upper current, your winters might be as mild as those of Portugal, which are tempered by the moist wind from the southern Atlantic.

The question naturally arises, why is the west wind so extremely cold? The answer is, simply, because in crossing the Rocky Mountains it is robbed of its moisture; and becoming so dry that the sun pours down his rays of heat; in vain neither the air by day nor the ground by night can retain them; they fly off into space. The principle on which air is dried in passing over high mountains is a very simp e one, if we merely bear in mind that air expands under diminished pressure and becomes colder by the heat being diffused over a greater space. Professor Espy has very ably investigated this subject on theoretical grounds. But, as our space is exceedingly limited, I shall merely adduce some examples by way of illustration. Mr. Walsh made an ascent in a balloon on the 26th August, 1852, from Kew Gardens, in England. The barometer stood at 30 inches, and the dew point was 61°; or, in other words, the air contained 6,06 grains of water in every cubic foot. At the height of 18,370 feet the barometer stood at 15 inches, temperature of air 70, dew point 2°8, or equivalent to 0.8 grain of water in a cubic foot. But at this elevation the air being expanded by the diminished pressure, two cubic feet will only weigh about as much as one did at the surface of the earth. Two cubic feet, therefore, would contain 1.6 grains of water. Now, it will be evident, if this upper air was to descend to the surface of the earth, it would have its temperature raised by coming under increased pressure; but its dew point, as will be seen by inspecting a table, would be no higher than 23°, instead of 61°; the radiation during one night would, therefore, cool down the air at the surface of the earth to this temperature. The dry upper current coming over the Rocky Mountains often descends to the earth in winter, and is the cause of the severe weather at that season in the country east of these mountains. The great westerly current of air from the Pacific in passing over the Rocky Mountains, and in ascending their westerly slopes, becomes colder by expansion, and, consequently, deposits its moisture. It is true the heat liberated by the condensation of the vapor will tend to elevate the temperature of the air on the top and at the foot of the mountain above its nominal point; but this effect is counteracted, as we have said, by the increased freedom the dry air gives to the radiation of heat from the surface of the earth and the lower stratum of air, particularly when it is spread over a wide extent of radiating surface. The descent, therefore, of the dry and upper current of westerly winds to the surface of the earth is, I think, the principal cause of the sudden and extreme changes of weather in this clime. President Dwight states that in the month of July, 1804, considerable snow fell at Salem, in New England, and that a severe frost was experienced in different parts of the same country. In all parts of the world where moist winds, or those from the ocean, blow over high ranges of mountains, they deposit their moisture in the form of rain and snow on the windward slopes. This is the case on the coast range of Oregon and California, and also on the slopes opposite the prevailing moist winds in South America.

In England not more than 23 inches of water falls annually in some of the level eastern counties during the year, while nearly 200 inches occasionally fall on the western side of the mountains of Cumberland. The west wisds of Norway are remarkably mild and rainy for such a high latitude, while the same winds in Sweden are comparatively cold; the air, in losing its moisture on the high chain of mountains, loses its power of retaining the large amount of latent heat extricated by the condensation of vapor.

The production of cold through expansion is the cause of clouds resting on the tops of mountains when they should apparently be borne away on the breeze. The precipitation of vapor as the air rises on the one side, and the evaporation of it as the air descends on the other, is the true cause of the phenomenon. The formation of clouds in the sky and precipitation of moisture are chiefly produced, as Mr. Espy has demonstrated, by the ascent of comparatively moist and warm air from below. The expansion produces cold, and of course the precipitation of moisture into clouds and rain. The cumulus clouds of summer are thus formed by ascending currents of moist air. The condensation of the vapor extricates a large amount of latent heat, which expands the air within the cloud, and thus produces an increased buoyancy. Before thunder-storms the air is usually moist and oppressive, the perspiration from the skin is checked by the moisture, and feels warmer on this account than it really is. The temperature within this cloud being higher than that on the outside in consequence of the evolution of latent heat, the passage of a thunder-cloud over any place almost invariably disturbs the air at the surface of the ground. The extrication of heat is a motive power which constantly causes the air to ascend in the front of the storm as the cloud drifts along in the upper current. Squalls are produced in the same way. Professor Espy, in his Report on Meteorology, says: "Low clouds are constantly forming in the front of squalls by the upward motion of the moist air as fast as their hinder parts are swept down by the falling rain, and thus they appear constantly just in front of the squall, for it is only in front that there is an up-moving column of air from below."

We shall enter a little more particularly into this subject, to show the analogy between these isolated disturbances arising from the formation of cloud and precipitation of rain and the land and sea breezes, hurricanes of the West India islands, thunder storms of America and Europe, and also some of the great snow and rain storms of both continents.

In Humboldt's celebrated voyage from Europe to South America he relates that, on reaching the latitudes of the trades, the "wind fell gradually the further we receded from the African coast; it was sometimes smooth water for several hours, and these short calms were regularly interrupted. Black, thick clouds, marked by strong outlines, rose in the east, and it seemed as if a squall would have forced us to haul our top-sails; but the breeze freshened anew, there fell large drops of rain, and the storm dispersed. Meanwhile it was curious to observe the effects of several black, isolated, and very low clouds which passed the zenith. We felt the force of the wind augment or diminish progressively according as small bodies of vesicular vapor approached or receded. It is by the help of these squalls, which alternate with dead calms, that the passage from the Canary islands to the Antilles or southern coast of America is made in the months of June and July."

From this description we gather that there was an upper current prevailing from the east, in which the clouds drifted, bearing them over the calm air resting on the ocean. The air in front of the cloud is disturbed as soon as the cloud approaches, and a violent squall prevails so long as it is overhead. This shows the intimate connexion between the upper and lower currents of the atmosphere when clouds are passing.

Unless clouds were constantly replenished by vapor from below, it is physically impossible that they could continue to throw down such great quantities of rain over long tracts of country as they are sometimes known to do. At no time, even within the tropics, is the air over one spot capable of precipitating more than three inches of rain.

In the squalls described by Humboldt we observe that there was calm both before and after the passage of the cloud. The motion of the air at the surface of the sea is much the same as if the whole portion of it under the cloud were in a state of vertical rotation around a horizontal axis. You will perceive that there is a resemblance in the motion of the air under isolated storm-clouds to that of the air in land

and sea breezes. The latent caloric evolved by the condensation of vapor is the moving power in this class of phenomena, and the difference between the temperature of the land and the sea is the disturbing force in the other. I have frequently attempted to show that many of the European storms were to be ascribed to a modification of these principles. Since reaching Washington it has been pointed out to me by Professor Henry that Professor Mitchell, of North Carolina, gave in Silliman's Journal a similar explanation of some of the American storms as far back as 1831. I had never seen this paper, and was a little surprised to find so great a similarity in our views, more especially as he had actually selected the same passages I have quoted from Humboldt as a common starting-point. But I have since found that Volney more than half a century ago accounts for one American snow-storm on the same principle.

I must, in the first place, draw your attention to a feature which appears to be common to the hurricanes of the West India Islands, and to the local squalls in the region of the trade winds, viz: that there is usually a calm before these terrific disturbances of the atmosphere. All who have examined these meteors are of opinion that the current above is from the southeast, and bears the hurricane clouds over the still and highly heated air; this being surcharged with moisture is in a most unstable state of equilibrium, which is liable to be overturned by the slightest cause that conspires to produce an up-moving volumn of air. To illustrate this I will merely read to you Captain Marryatt's graphic description of the coming on of a West Indian hurricane as given in "Peter Simple:" "What a hot day this has been; not a cat's paw upon the water, and the sky all of a mist. Only look at the sun, how he goes down, puffed out to three times his size, as if he were in a terrible passion. I suspect we shall have a land breeze off strong. The heat was excessive and unaccountable, not the slightest breath of wind moved in the heavens or below; no clouds to be seen, and the stars were obscured by a sort of mist: there appeared a total stagnation in the elements. We had not pulled long before a low moaning was heard in the atmosphere, now here, now there, and we appeared to be pulling through solid darkness; I looked, and dark as it was, it appeared as if a sort of black wall was sweeping along right towards us. The moaning gradually increased to a stunning roar, and then at once it broke upon us with a noise to which no thunder can bear comparison. The sea was perfectly level, but boiling and covered with a white foam, so that we appeared in the night to be floating on milk."

Professor Mitchell, in the paper to which I have already referred, expresses the opinion that thunder storms must be much less grand and imposing in Europe than in America, because poets have not considered them worthy of particular attention. Shakspeare, however, has not neglected our thunder storms, and with his usual philosophical discrimination has portrayed some of their more important peculiarities:

"We often see, against some storm,
A silence in the heavens, the rack stand still,
The bold winds speechless, and the orb below
As hush as death: anon the dreadful thunder
Doth rend the region."—*Hamlet.*

The formation and progress of thunder storms are very peculiar in this country. We have already alluded to the frequency of south and southwest winds over the United States in summer. These currents, derived, as we have said, from the trade winds of the tropics, contain a large amount of moisture, and are the source of the great fertility of the Mississippi valley. Extensive rains and thunder storms only occur after the south wind has prevailed for some time. I am inclined to believe that this vast aerial current, which flows below the upper westerly current, is much deeper in the southern than in the northern States. Mr. Phelps's observations, near the mouth of the Rio Grande, show that in his district the thunder clouds drift in the southeast current; and I have been informed that they follow the same direction in Louisiana and Alabama. But in the higher latitudes, as for example that of Washington, the thunder clouds all move in the direction of the upper current from a point or two north or south of west. The moisture which forms these clouds is no doubt derived from the lower stratum, whose upper surface is exposed to the erosion of the upper current, constantly sweeping a portion away towards the Atlantic. The action of the lower moist current rising into the upper and forming cloud, and perhaps part of the upper descending, is no doubt the principal propelling power of the surface wind. President Dwight gives a very good description of the thunder storms of New England, and refers to points which should be specially borne in mind. On one occasion he says: "The meridional line upon which I stood was crossed by the storm several miles to the south. During the whole day the wind had blown from the south, and continued to blow in the same direction on the surface throughout the afternoon, without a moment's intermission. But had the wind," says he, "which carried the cloud when it passed over the meridian swept the surface, the wind for a time, at least, must have been entirely stopped. This, however, was not the fact even for a moment." On another occasion, in 1809, a "thunder storm passed over New Haven, from the northwest, with great rapidity. It continued, as I judge, from an hour to an hour and a half. But though the clouds moved rapidly to the *southeast*, a *southwest* wind blew the whole of that day and *while the thunder storm was overhead with great violence.*"

The increase in the strength of the southwest wind, as the clouds drifted overhead from the northwest, shows that the lower and upper currents mixed together; that as in the case of the squall mentioned by Humboldt, a part of the lower stratum of air rising formed cloud, and that a part of the upper stratum descending to the earth was carried away by the prevailing surface wind from the southwest. This propelling power, I think, cannot be doubted in thunder storms; but I imagine the same principle must be taken into account as a source of motion to the southwest surface winds whenever clouds form in the sky and drift in the upper current. Thunder squalls drifting from the west, as I am also informed by Professor Espy, often draw in the stratum of air from the east immediately above the earth's surface; while the falling rain under the clouds forces the air outwards towards the east, and it rises immediately before the rain, carrying up dust and other materials. A slight westerly breeze then usually springs up and follows the cloud just a little in the rear.

In fact, from the very irregular nature of the winds of the lower stratum, we must in general look for a local cause of propulsion, on the same principle that the motion of the air at the surface of the earth, during the day in summer, with clear and dry weather, is constantly varied by the heat of the sun at every spot over which the breeze passes. As soon as the warm southerly wind begins to blow as a general surface current over the United States, the conditions necessary to the production of a storm already exist. The southerly wind, often veering about very irregularly, will then frequently continue in the same direction, until the whole country from the Gulf of Mexico to Canada is covered with a comparatively hot and moist stratum of air. Under these circumstances a crisis must ensue, when the upper current from the Rocky Mountains resumes its sway at the surface of the earth. In winter it often sweeps the stratum of moist air from over the United States into the Atlantic, and completely changes the character of the weather in a very short time. In summer the changes are generally much less marked; for Professor Coffin's researches show that the northerly winds then lose their power. At this season the process usually takes place in a gradual manner. Thunder clouds, drifting in the upper current, as described by Professor Dwight, shower down their watery contents over the land, and thus enable Indian corn to be successfully cultivated over a surface of country vastly greater than in any other part of the world. How these effects are brought about, involves the whole question of the action of storms east of the Rocky Mountains. We shall leave, however, the further discussion of this for the present, and conclude this lecture by one example, showing the scale upon which thunder storms are sometimes developed much about the same time over a vast area of country. I am only sorry that my time has not permitted me to analyze this storm in all its details.

During the first days of last September the wind was mostly from the south; the weather became excessively hot and oppressive; the newspapers in all parts of the country were recording the high temperatures; when, on the 6th, thunder storms took place nearly simultaneously in Iowa, Illinois, Indiana, Ohio, Pennsylvania, New York, East and West Canada, and the New England States. Large quantities of rain fell in various parts of the country, as the storms were in several places somewhat locally developed. At some points the northwest upper current reached the surface of the earth for a time, the southwest wind again blowing as before, until a general change of wind to the northwest prevailed, and caused a great fall in the temperature. At Saratoga the thermometer stood at 96° in the shade on the afternoon of the 6th, and at 46° on the morning of the 9th at Rochester. It is a fact worthy of attention that a severe storm, amounting to a hurricane, swept the southeastern coast of the United States just about the time that this great change was taking place in the north and west. It is certainly well worthy the investigation of American meteorologists to ascertain whether any connexion exists between the weather in the northwestern States and the hurricanes of the West Indian islands, for in this instance the coincidence of phenomena was quite remarkable. As will be seen from our next lecture, great changes occurring in the northwest are rapidly propagated to the southeast in the case of winter storms.

METEOROLOGY.

Third Lecture.

When northwest winds prevail over the United States in winter, the air is very dry and cold; so long as the wind remains in this quarter there is no termination to the cold weather. It does not moderate, at least the thermometer does not rise, until the moisture is increased. I suppose it is admitted by meteorologists that the cold spells of weather in the United States are first felt in the west and northwest, and gradually extend over the country to the southeast. This direction, it will be observed, corresponds very nearly with the course of the current, which is so constant in the upper stratum of the atmosphere in this region. But it is a curious fact, well worthy of the attention of meteorologists, that the warm and moist surface air which precedes storms and cold weather travels also from northwest to southeast; at all events, it apparently does so. Sometimes a belt of moist air, several hundred miles in breadth, and extending from the mouth of the Mississippi to the lakes, and probably much further north, seems to advance from the west, while there is very cold weather both behind and in front of it. The storms of February, 1842, described by Professor Loomis in the Transactions of the American Philosophical Society, were of this character. On the morning of the 10th November last, similar phenomena were presented: the eastern portion of the Mississippi valley, and all the States south of the lakes and west of the Alleghany range, were under the influence of a comparatively moist and warm stratum of air, at the very moment that the temperature was about 20° lower from latitude 35° to 45° on the Atlantic seaboard, and between the same parallel of latitude in the western States west of longitude 92°. By the night of the 10th November, the weather became very moist and warm in the Atlantic seaboard States, more so than it had been in Ohio the previous day.

The moisture which was found in the broad band could not originally have come from the west, northwest, or north, because these winds are always exceedingly dry; nor could it have come from the Atlantic ocean, because the weather remains cold on the coasts when it is much warmer in Ohio. Indeed the storm was at hand before the east wind set in, and this is a usual occurrence. There can be but little doubt, therefore, that this moisture is originally derived from the Gulf of Mexico, and that it is spread over the middle and eastern portion of the United States by the southerly current, which, as we have before remarked, is, in our opinion, a deflected portion of the trade winds.

In a former lecture, I pointed out the fact, abundantly proved by Professor Coffin, that these southerly winds prevail more in *summer* than in *winter;* and an important point here suggests itself for future discussion. I think it very probable that a broad band of southerly winds, extending across the country from Florida to Texas, may flow northward and gradually diffuse itself as a surface current over the valley of the Mississippi and the seaboard States. The sun heating the earth more at the north, during the longer days, assists in the propulsion of this current. The higher portions of this lower current are in contact with the under surface of the cold upper current from the west, and in the mingling of the two the moisture of the former is precipitated into clouds or rain. In some cases the lower current may thus be gradually absorbed into the upper one, and this action may take place over a considerable portion of the country, producing an extended cloudiness and perhaps a general fall of rain without violent atmospheric disturbance.

In winter, the propulsion of the southerly winds is not favored by the heat of the sun; at this season, therefore, they do not extend to so great a breadth as in summer, and only flow over the northern regions in streams, forming narrow belts of warm and moist air, to which we have just adverted. This warm current is often bounded by cold air, on the east and the west. The cold air on both sides is drifting from west to east, the warm current between (flowing from south and southwest) is also carried laterally to the east; and hence, the moist and warm weather of winter has an apparent motion from west to cast.

Our inquiries relative to this point lead us to believe that the south and southwest winds in winter may begin to blow over Texas and the high ground a little to the east of the slopes of the Rocky Mountains, and cause a rise of temperature to the west of the Mississippi, when the northwest wind is still blowing dry, cold, and clear, over the whole of the middle and eastern States.

This, however, does not continue long; the west, northwest, and north winds soon descend between the western edge of the southern current and the mountains, and gradually force the former eastwards. On these occasions the north or northwest wind is the predominant one, which, rushing along the slopes of the mountains to the south, forms the well known northers from Vera Cruz to Cuba. According to this view, the norther should be felt sooner at the former place than at the latter. This much is certain, that almost every cold spell of weather which is experienced in the United States during winter is propagated to Cuba in the form of a norther, which, though the thermometer seldom sinks it below 55° at sunrise, is disagreeably felt by the inhabitants of the island.*

* Since this lecture was written, I have had occasion to examine an interesting series of "Queries and Strictures," by Dr. Hare, in regard to Mr. Espy's Meteorological Report. The view which we have taken of the northers in the Gulf of Mexico will, as far as it goes, answer in the affirmative Dr. Hare's 20th query, page 5:

"Whether northers are not consequent to the displacement of the warmer air lying on the Gulf by the colder air of the territory of the United States north or northeast (northwest?) of the Gulf, to whatever cause that displacement may be due?"

Among the number of interesting points suggested by Dr. Hare for discussion, an answer to the following queries we consider would contribute much to the advancement of the meteorology of the United States:

"5th. Wherefore, in one of Mr. Espy's generalizations, he alleges that storms travel from *west* towards the east during the five winter months, instead of alleging that they travel from northwest to southeast, consistently with the observations of Loomis, above mentioned?"

"7th. Whether there is not another distinct kind of storm, long known and universally recognised as the 'northeaster,' or 'northeastern gale,' which has been distinguished from the southeaster, so called by its direction, its longer endurance, lesser violence, and by its not being usually followed, after a brief lull, by a northwester, nor any violent wind in a direction directly opposite to that in which it blew at the beginning of the storm?"

On no question has there been more discussion among meteorologists than that in regard to the cause of the fluctuations in the height of the barometer, especially during storms. John Dalton made the following remarks on this subject more than sixty years ago; and they are well worthy of consideration in the present day, particularly since we possess better opportunities of ascertaining their truth:

1. "The barometer," says Dalton, "has little variation within the tropics; while within the northern temperate zone, and doubtless within the southern also, its range increases in going from the equator. The mean annual range at Paris, for twenty years, was 1½ inches; the greatest range, or difference between the highest and lowest observations, for the same term, was 2 inches. At Kendal, the mean range for five years was 2.13 inches, the greatest range was 2.65 inches. In Sweden and Russia the range is still greater.

2. "In the temperate zones the range and fluctuations of the barometer are always greater in winter than in summer.

3. "The rise and fall of the barometer are not local, or confined to a small district of country, but extend over a considerable part of the globe, a space of two or three thousand miles in circuit, at least.

4. "It appears that the mean state of the barometer is rather lower than higher in winter than in summer, though a stratum of air on the earth's surface always weighs more in the former season than the latter.

5. "F. Laval made observations for ten days together upon the top of St. Pilen, a mountain near Marseilles, which is 960 yards high, and found that when the barometer varied 2¾ lines at Marseilles it varied 1¾ inches upon St. Pilen. Now had it been a law that the whole atmosphere rises and falls with the barometer, the fluctuations in any elevated barometer would be to those of another barometer below it nearly as the absolute heights of the mercurial column in each, which in these instances were far from being so. Hence, then, it may be inferred that the fluctuations of the barometer are occasioned chiefly by a variation in the density of the lower regions of the air, and not by an alternate elevation and depression of the whole superincumbent atmosphere."

I am quite aware that some of the deductions of Dalton require to be a little modified. His first proposition, however, that the range of the barometer increases in going from the equator towards the poles, is amply borne out as a general law by observations in this country as well as in Europe.

His fifth proposition is also correct, viz: that the fluctuations of the barometer are occasioned chiefly by a variation in the density of the lower regions of the air, and not by changes in the whole superincumbent atmosphere. To illustrate this, I will state a hypothetical case. In the balloon ascent made by Mr. Walsh, alluded to in a previous lecture, it was found that the barometer stood at 15 inches at the height of 18,370 feet. If the whole air below this elevation had been occupied by hydrogen gas, which is much lighter than common air, being only about one fifteenth of its weight at the same pressure, this lighter gas, possessing as much elasticity as common air, would be able to bear up the upper stratum of the atmosphere, weighing 15 inches of mercury; but at the surface of the earth the barometer would fall about 14 inches below its ordinary height. Now it is easily seen that if the warm and light wind from the southward, which blows with so much regularity in summer, were as light as hydrogen gas, with the same elasticity, it would cause an immense fall of the barometer along the whole of the Mississippi valley when it displaced the cold air which has come over the Rocky Mountains. The southerly winds from the Gulf of Mexico are much warmer and lighter than those which have poured down the eastern slopes of the Rocky Mountains, and been cooled by radiation on the plains to the east. Consequently when they displace these colder winds in the valley of the Mississippi, a fall of the barometer ought, to a certain extent, to take place. I am, therefore, of the opinion that the fact of the displacement of the warm and moist current from the Gulf by the colder air from the west and northwest is sufficient to account for the fluctuations of the barometer, in a great many instances, in places to the west of the Alleghany chain of mountains.

Professor Espy informs me that he has traced a central line of minimum pressure, which precedes the eastern storms on the Atlantic coast first in the western States. This line is of great length from north to south; and from an examination of his charts of the weather, in his Report on Meteorology, I was at once struck with the fact that its direction corresponds with the trough of the Mississippi valley, and with the course of the moist winds from the Gulf of Mexico. In Europe, I have often been enabled to trace the connexion between the fluctuations of the barometer and changes in the temperature and moisture of the air; but I have never found the connexions so regular and intimate as in the Mississippi valley, which is more removed from influences which tend to disturb this action.

In my last lecture I showed that the temperature of the air at sunrise is, as a general rule, a close approximation to the dew point. A high dew point, or, in other words, a large amount of vapor, has the effect, as we have before said, of maintaining the warmth of the air during the night.

The observations collected by the Smithsonian Institution give the temperature at 7, A. M., and 9, P. M. As a rise or fall in the temperature at these hours may be considered as indicating an increase or decrease in the amount of moisture in the air, and as the fluctuations of the barometer are also given for the same hours, I have, therefore, in the diagrams, [figures 1, 2, 3, 4,] shown the connexion which exists between the heat and moisture of the air and the changes in the pressure.

I have compared the temperature taken at 7, A. M., and 9, P. M., leaving out the day temperature altogether. The temperature at these hours, as I have stated, is a close approximation to the dew point. And this fact, which, as a general rule, holds true, especially in autumn, is the only means I possess to ascertain the hygrometrical state of the air during the storms of this country. The amount of vapor is an essential element in the investigation of atmospheric disturbances, and hence even an approximate estimate of the quantity is important.

The following curves of temperature and pressure of the atmosphere for 7, A. M., and 9, P. M., from the 7th to the 16th of November inclusive, are intended to illustrate the connexion between the moisture, temperature, and pressure, during a storm :

No. 1—*Curve of temperature and pressure for Tuscaloosa, Alabama. Latitude* 33° 12′ *N.*; *Longitude* 87° 12′ *W.*

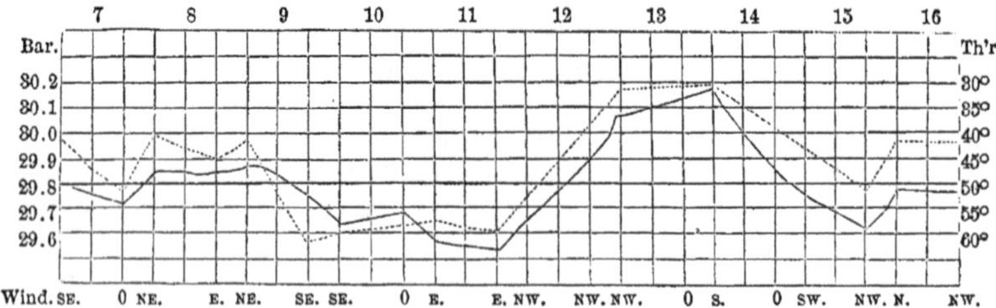

No. 2—*Curve of temperature and pressure for New Weid, Texas. Latitude* 29° 42′ *N.*; *Longitude* 97° 0′ *W.*

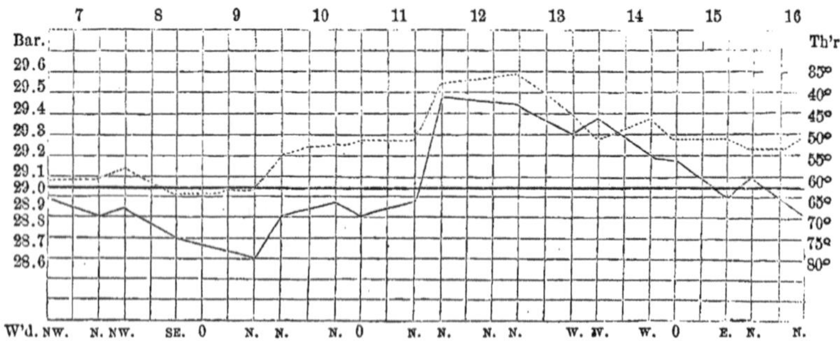

No. 3—*Curve of temperature and pressure for Milwaukie, Wisconsin. Latitude* 43° 3′ *N.*; *Longitude* 87° 57′ *W.*

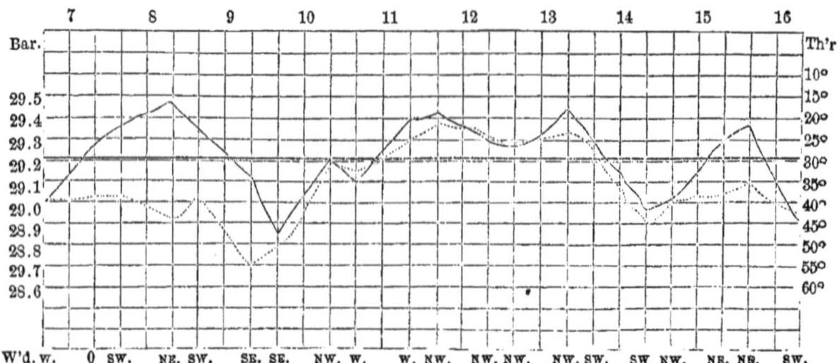

No. 4—*Curve of temperature and pressure for Steuben, Washington county, Maine. Latitude 44° 44′ N.; Longitude 67° 50′ W.*

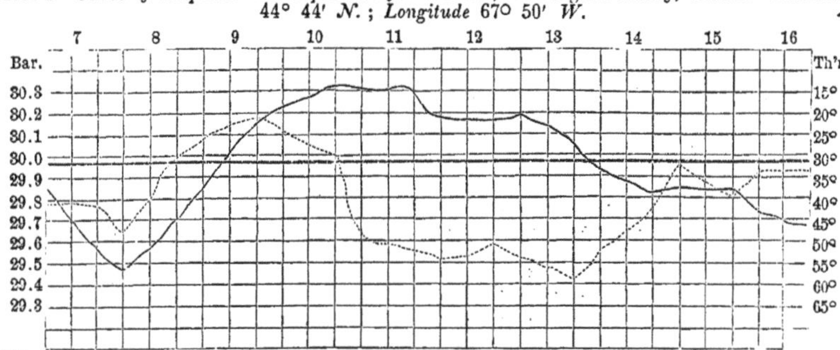

The continuous line represents the changes of the barometer, and the dotted line those of the thermometer. The figures on the left-hand margin of the wood-cut indicate heights of the barometer in intervals of one-tenth of an inch, and those on the right hand side, of the thermometer in intervals of five degrees of Fahrenheit's scale.

The figures along the upper margin indicate the days of the month during which the storm continued, and the letters along the lower the direction of the wind during the same time.

In order to exhibit more strikingly the relation of the temperature, moisture, and pressure, the dotted line is inverted so as to represent the highest point of the thermometer by the lowest point of the curve. With this arrangement the two curves in the first three figures are nearly parallel, showing that in the middle regions of the United States the abnormal depressions of the barometer are attended with a rise in the thermometer and consequently an increase of moisture, while in the eastern States, as illustrated by figure 4, the result is almost entirely opposite—the increase of temperature is accompanied with a rise in the barometer.

If we suppose that a south wind, of 10,000 feet in height, with a temperature of 70°, occupies the Mississippi valley, and the upper current from the west flows across its surface, in ordinary circumstances this stratum of air would weigh a little more than nine inches of mercury. Now, if we further suppose a cold northwest wind, having its dew point or morning temperature down to 30°, to displace the warmer current, by crowding it to the east and occupying its place, as ten thousand feet of air at this low temperature weighs 1-12th more, or ¾ inch of mercury, this denser and colder column will cause a rise in the barometer to that extent. Now, if a decrease of temperature of 40° causes a rise of ¾ inch of mercury, a decrease of 5° would cause a rise of nearly 1-10th inch. This effect would be produced without taking into account the changes which might take place during storms in the upper strata of the atmosphere.

I have compared the fluctuations of the barometer at 7, A. M., and 9, P. M., with the changes in the temperature at these hours from the 7th to 16th November last, in the States of Maine, Vermont, New York, Michigan, Wisconsin, North Carolina, Kentucky, Missouri, East Florida, Alabama, Texas, and also at Washington. By making 5° of temper-

.ature correspond with 1-10th inch of mercury in the barometer, I find some very interesting results are brought out. In all the States south and west of the Alleghany range, the parallelism between the changes in the barometer and the changes in temperature are much greater than I anticipated. See figures Nos. 1, 2 and 3.

Some remarkable exceptions, however, occur, in which a rise of temperature is accompanied with a rise of the barometer. These exceptions are found to the east of the Alleghanies and the mountains of New England, where the curves of temperature and pressure of the air entirely lose the regularity which they possess in the southern and western States. The changes of the barometer before storms in the northeastern States appear to be very peculiar, at least I am acquainted with nothing like them in Europe. When the mercury rises a little above 30 inches in Great Britain, the index of the barometer points to "set fair," and an eastern storm rarely comes on before the mercury begins to sink. When the mercury is above 30 inches in Maine, during winter or autumn, a storm is often at hand, and the barometer does not fall before the weather gets colder and drier. An examination of the weather, from the 7th to 16th November last, (see figure 4,) apparently shows that the indications of the barometer, as a weather prophet, must be interpreted by a contrary rule to that which is observed in the western States and in England. The probable cause of this will be afterwards adverted to. I shall now proceed to give you an account of a general storm, which will serve to illustrate the principles I have stated:

The weather on the 12th November, 1854, presented a curious picture of extremes over the United States. The northwest wind was advancing like an extended wall, from Iowa to Texas, and clearing the whole country of its moisture. By looking at the following table of temperature for that day, we shall see the progress which it had made at the time mentioned:

Iowa, Poultney	11°	7, A. M.
Wisconsin, Madison	19°	"
Missouri, St. Louis	26°	"
Mississippi, Oxford	34°	9, P. M.
Texas, New Wied	36°	"

On the morning of the 12th the first killing frost was felt in Louisiana, and over Michigan, the northern parts of Illinois, Indiana, and Ohio, the ground was covered for the first time with snow. In these States the northwest wind was flowing beneath the colder edges of the southwest stream from the Gulf, forcing it to ascend and precipitate part of its moisture in the form of snow. As the under current rose it was caught by the upper current, and, as in the case of thunder storms, it was swept off towards the east. This at least seemed to be the process at Indianapolis, where, on the 12th, four inches of dry snow fell, while the lower wind from the north and northwest was overlaid by a current bearing clouds from the southwest. On the morning of the 13th, at the same place, the wind set in from the west.

On looking at the meteorological chart for the morning of the 12th, we perceive at a glance that the temperature gradually rises from Iowa to Maine, from Missouri to Savannah, and from Texas to Florida. The eastern seaboard States now experienced the southwest stream of moist and hot air—hotter and moister than it was in the west, because while this moveable current is gradually borne to the east its temperature is higher from having been blowing longer from a warmer quarter—on the same principle that an ordinary south wind in summer is warmer the second day it blows than on the first. The temperatures on the east coast are in very striking contrast to what they are on the west of the Mississippi.

Florida,	wind	SW.,	temperature	70°,	rainy.
Savannah,	"	SE.,	"	64°,	rainy.
North Carolina, Thornbury,	"	E.,	"	60°,	rainy.
Washington,	"	W.,	"	48°,	rainy.
New York,	"	WNE.,	"	53°,	rainy.
Maine, Steuben,	"	SW.,	"	54°,	rainy.

The weather remained moist and warm on the 13th in the Atlantic States, but the cold air was rapidly advancing from the northwest. By the morning of the 14th it had swept the whole of the southwest current into the Atlantic and brought cold and clear weather. In Florida the temperature of 70° on the morning of the 12th was changed to the freezing by the 14th; frosts also occurred on the same day in Georgia, South Carolina, North Carolina, Virginia, Pennsylvania, and New York. It is worthy of observation that at the very time the northwest wind was making its cold felt from Florida to New York, the south wind, or a modification of it, had already set in over Texas, and raised the temperature 15°, and its influence was afterwards also felt as far north as St. Louis, in Missouri. This was merely the first stage of preparation for another atmospheric disturbance which was to run a similar course.

Striking changes in the temperature of the weather are produced in autumn by the colder wind from the west descending and bearing the moister stream before it; when this hot stream is extended along the Atlantic coast it in all probability becomes the vehicle of the hurricanes which proceed from the West Indian islands. A severe hurricane, having its course along the Florida coast, desolated the rice grounds on the Charles and Savannah rivers on the 8th September last; but a thunder storm, extending over the greater portion of the northern States, began on the 6th and travelled from northwest to southeast, causing a great atmospheric disturbance and lowering of the temperature.

We have only space to say a few words on the barometer during the storm of the 12th. Though rain and snow fell over an immense area that day, and the wind blew with great force in the Atlantic States, still the barometer was above the mean in the morning from Maine, in the east, to Wisconsin, in the west. In this section it is probable that the northwest current, overlying the whole storm, did not sweep away the ascending moist currents with sufficient rapidity, and hence the accumulation of air causing the barometer to rise before storms on the east coast. The Alleghany range must, so far, favor this accumulation by retarding or hindering the freer action of the winds from the west. When the air has a high temperature in summer, the increased pressure before storms is, I believe, not so much observed. In this storm, also,

I find no traces of accumulation of air in Florida, where the curves of pressure and moisture coincide very accurately, as much so as they do throughout the Mississippi valley. The following reductions exhibit the state of the barometer over three sections of the United States. The figures show the difference of the pressure above or below the mean for the month, in hundredths of an inch:

First Section.

Maine...........	at 7 A. M.	....	+ .23 inches.
Vermont.........	" "	....	+ .21 "
New York (State).	" "	....	+ .33 "
Michigan........	" "	....	+ .16
Wisconsin.......	" "	....	+ .21 "

Second Section.

North Carolina....	at 7 A. M.	....	0 mean.
Kentucky.........	" "	....	— .17 inches.
Missouri.........	" "	....	+ .12 "

Third Section.

East Florida......	at 7 A. M.	....	— .18 inches.
Alabama..........	" "	....	— .17 "
Texas............	" "	....	+ .41 "

During the weather from the 7th to the 16th of November, the fluctuations of the barometer in the southern and western States do not seem to have been greater than could be ascribed to the changes of temperature. The great fall of the barometer in tropical storms, and the tornadoes of the United States, seem to me to admit of no other explanation than that given by Professor Espy, viz: an inward ascending column of air becoming much lighter from the extrication of latent caloric.

In regard to the winds, during the progress of this storm, only two systems are well developed. The northwest winds, on the 10th, were observed both in the rear and front, while the southwest current occupied the middle. The east wind is so partially developed, that we must regard it merely as an eddy in the more general system which embraces it. We cannot expect to find much regularity in the course of any set of winds, because this can only take place with an invariable temperature. Inequality of local temperature is the principal cause of the irregularity of the arrows which represent the direction of the wind on the meteorological chart.

On the 12th, the weather was very wet and stormy along the Atlantic States, and much rain also fell in the Ohio valley. Snow fell over a considerable area immediately to the south of the lakes.

We shall now very briefly trace the peculiarities of the weather and storms of Europe. The east wind very seldom blows over a large area of the United States, unless during storms. In northern Europe the case is very different: dry and cold winds are very common in spring, and, at this season, not only is the surface wind from the east, but the current in the higher regions is also from the same quarter. It usually bears cirrous clouds, thus showing the great height to which it extends in the atmosphere. So long as the east wind blows as an undivided current in winter, the weather is intensely cold in England. Coming over ranges of mountains and a long stretch of land, it is something like the west wind of the United States—as long as it is continuous, the cold is unabated; when the same wind prevails in summer the whole country is parched with drought; but when the surface east wind is overlaid by a current from the southwest, then the east wind becomes excessively wet and disagreeable. An east wind in Scotland is very rarely stormy either in summer or autumn, unless it has an upper current from the southwest. This upper current from the ocean supplies the moisture which is precipitated by the lower wind. After long periods of dry summer weather in Scotland, the barometer begins to fall several days before the rain storm comes on. The first symptoms of change are, usually, cirrous clouds floating in the upper regions of the atmosphere, and indicating a greater saturation going on above. Cumulous clouds at length form, and drift from southwest to northeast, often directly against the lower wind. A thunder storm begins the rainy season; and so long as the upper current continues, the east wind is rainy or moist.

The fall of the barometer, it would appear, arises from a warm and moist stratum of air taking the place of a colder one above; on the same principle as a moister and warmer one depresses the barometer in the Mississippi valley. For this reason the barometer is very much consulted as an indicator of changes in the weather in Great Britain.

The summer rain-storms often extend over a large area in Europe. I have traced the northeast wind blowing, as a broad current, from the Alps to the south of Scotland, while rain was falling over the greater part of this space.

The winter storms are also regulated by the same principles. When there is no upper current from the west, the east wind remains dry and cold; but when the southwest upper current begins to blow, it becomes wet and stormy, and almost all the great falls of snow in winter take place under these conditions. The barometer does not give as long a warning of an approaching storm in winter as it does in summer, but there is invariably a fall in the mercury before the storm comes on. To illustrate the character of our winter storms the following example is given:

During the month of December, 1853, the wind was, in general, east in England, not only at the surface of the ground but at great elevations in the atmosphere. The barometer was high and steady for that winter month. The rivers from the north to the south of the island were more ice-bound than they had been for 15 years.

On the 1st of January, 1854, the weather was very cold over Great Britain, as well as the northwest of Europe. There was no storm that day, and the temperature of the air did not differ much from Sandwich, in Orkney, to Brussels, in Belgium.

	Wind.	Temperature. Max.	Min.
Sandwich Manse, Orkney	NW	28°	28°
Keleoliess, Fife	NW	34°	12°
Highfield, Nottingham	WNW	32°	14°
Liverpool, Lancashire	NNW	36°	= 27°

Holkham, Norfolk	W.	38°	= 20°
Helsten, Cornwall	NW.	41°	34°
St. Aubin, Jersey	NW.	35°	32°
Versailles, France	NW., calm	32°	24°
Brussels, Belgium	SW., calm	29°	24°
Heligoland, Denmark	N., stormy	...	

A disturbing element was, however, after a short time introduced; at Jersey the wind set in from the westsouthwest on the morning of the 2d, and a thaw commenced; the wind was high from this quarter at night, with heavy rain. A current also set in from the southwest, both at Versailles and Brussels, with snow falling more or less during the whole day. At Helsten, near Land's End in Cornwall, the wind was northeast, and 7-10th inch rain fell in the night; but it is quite evident that this rain, thrown down by the northeast wind, must have been derived from the upper current from the southwest, as the air still remained dry and frosty at Bath, on the west, and at Holkham, on the east. This supposition is rendered highly probable, from the fact that the upper stratum of clouds was from the southwest. It was some time before the storm was developed in the eastern counties.

The wind seems to have begun to blow very briskly from an easterly quarter over the south of England on the 3d, with much snow at night. An inch of rain fell that day in Jersey, with a squally wind from the cast. The temperature remained low and the sky clear in Scotland and the north of England. The wind was from an easterly quarter that day at Paris, Brussels, and off the coast of Denmark. The southwest upper current, still prevailing, saturated the air all over England and the south of Scotland, and a violent storm of snow on the 4th was the result, which extended over a large portion of the west of Europe, the wind being easterly at almost all the different stations. It is curious to observe that no snow or rain fell at Helsten, near Land's End, on the 4th, the point to which all the wind on the east coast was blown; which shows that it must have been absorbed in some way before reaching the west coast. In Scotland the wind, on the 4th of January, was quite as violent as in the south of England; but very little snow fell on the eastern coast. A deep snow fell, with a strong northeast wind, at the temperature of 32°. The wind was excessively cold and dry in Aberdeen, being as low as + 9° max. — 6° min. The upper current had not influenced it sufficiently to raise the thermometer above these low temperatures. During this very low temperature in Aberdeenshire, the northeast wind was about 23° higher in Belfast. This difference of temperature is vastly greater than in the case of a sea breeze, and might alone account for the violent gale on the Irish coast.

The disturbance of the equilibrium of the atmosphere in this and our other winter storms seems to be occasioned, first, by a flowing away of part of the cold upper current, and a warmer and lighter air taking its place; and, second, by the denser air below flowing towards the warm and moist air over the ocean, which causes the saturated air to rise to a greater elevation, and condense its moisture. The condensed vapor, by the extrication of its caloric, favors ascending currents, which are gradually absorbed into the upper current and carried towards the earth. I have already mentioned that no snow or rain fell at Land's End while the day was nearly calm, and at the same time a violent hurricane, with much snow, was apparently blowing right towards this very locality. But this case exactly resembles the action of the sea breeze—the northeast wind being gradually absorbed into the upper current along the whole area over which it blows. The warming influence of the southwest upper current is well illustrated by the fact, stated to me by Mr. Moyle, that snow did not cover the ground for an hour last winter, though much fell with the northeast wind not far to the eastward of his place.

Though the storm had begun at Heligoland on the afternoon of the 5th, it did not reach Aberdeenshire on the 4th. The northeast winds were quite dry beyond this county; and the sky at Sandwich, in Orkney, was bright, and the air quite calm. Notwithstanding the prevalence of the easterly winds, we find that the temperature is advanced from west to east, especially along the western coast of Europe; and on the 6th, the upper current seems to have so completely worn away the lower current, that the wind was from the southwest on that day from Cornwall to Belgium. But in the north of England and over Scotland the lower current increased in depth, and for a time checked the warm upper current, or drove it back, and restored cold weather. All places under the influence of the southwest wind had their temperature raised, while those under the northeast had it depressed. This will be shown by the following table of temperature and direction of the wind:

Helsten,	S. W.	minimum	36°	Orkney	E.	minimum	23½°
Jersey,	S. S. W.	"	38°	Aberdeen	calm	"	10°
Paris,	S. W.	"	35°	Fifeshire	E.	"	30°
Brussels,	S. W.	"	34°	Liverpool	S. E.	"	30°

This may be taken as an example of our eastern storms. They are preceded by a fall of the barometer, but the manner in which they terminate has nothing of that regularity which distinguishes your storms. Very often the southwest wind blows as a deep current, and produces moist and warm weather in the depth of winter. The lower eastern wind, which is often very stormy, must be regarded as a mere surface stream, which is usually absorbed by the deeper upper current.

Now, I think it is very probable that an action similar to that of our northeastern storms is sometimes developed over the United States and in Canada. While I was sailing down the St. Lawrence, in the beginning of last October, a strong head wind prevailed from the northeast, at the same time that the clouds at no great height were drifting from the southwest. At Quebec, I also observed the same phenomenon; and, according to Professor Mitchell, of North Carolina, northeast storms are sometimes developed over large portions of the United States when the clouds are from the opposite quarter. I have had no opportunities since I have been in this country to examine the northeast rain storms, which appear to be more frequent in the New England States than to the south. But I suspect we must always bear in mind that an upper current flows from the west quarter even when the lower northeast wind and middle southwest current are prevailing.

There is another class of storms of very common occurrence in Great

Britain, during the continuance of which there are very rarely any east winds. There is also this peculiarity about them, that they seldom give warning of their approach by any fall in the barometer; indeed, it often shows a pressure above the mean just before they commence. The wind springs up from the southwest, and blows as a broad stream over the whole island, and in almost all these storms an upper current prevails from the northwest, which descends before the termination of the disturbance, and at once brings cold and dry weather. This particular form of atmospheric disturbance occurs at all seasons of the year, sometimes as a very gentle breeze, and often as storms of the most violent character. The changes of the wind are from southwest to northwest, crossing due west at once, and at this time blowing with their greatest violence. But our limits forbid us to enter further into this subject.

In the course of these lectures it has been my wish to state as clearly and distinctly as possible the general principles on which nearly all meteorologists are agreed, and to avoid, as far as might be, the discussions of points in reference to which there is less harmony of opinion. I have been anxious to place before you what I consider to be the distinctive features of the storms of North America and of Europe. I am quite aware that the topic would have furnished materials for a much greater number of lectures, but a mere outline was all that could be properly attempted in the time allotted. I have presented the phenomena in the connexion in which they now represent themselves to my mind. I may, however, have reason to modify my present views of American storms when I have found leisure to arrange and discuss more thoroughly the ample materials I have collected in my tour. But, whatever may be the change in this respect, I shall always retain a lively and constant impression of the kindness, the hospitality, and the liberality which I have everywhere met with in my travels through this favored land.

APPENDIX TO MR. RUSSELL'S LECTURES, BY THE SECRETARY OF THE SMITHSONIAN INSTITUTION.

As an appendix to Mr. Russell's lectures, we give the following tables, showing the mean diurnal variations of the temperature, moisture, pressure, &c., of the air. The principal series are from observations made at Greenwich, near London, under the direction of Mr. Glaishier. The tables for Bombay are from the observations of Dr. Buist, those for Philadelphia are from the valuable series made under the direction of Professor Bache at Girard College.

By a comparison of the quantities given, it will be seen that all the changes are connected with and depend upon the position of the sun in the heavens, or, in other words, upon the amount of solar heat received at the different hours of the day. The numbers given in the series for Greenwich are deduced from the observations continued for several years, comprising more than 20,000 individual records, and, therefore, abnormal variations are eliminated, and the special changes due to constant causes are exhibited in their true values.

Table I gives the mean diurnal variation of the temperature of the air in the shade at intervals of two hours, from 2 o'clock in the morning until the end of the 24 hours. It will be seen by this table that on the average the coldest period of the day is a little before sunrise, and that the temperature of the air remains nearly stationary from about 4 o'clock until near 6 o'clock in the morning, that it then gradually rises until 2 p. m., when it reaches its maximum, and then declines. The first rays of the sun are probably expended in vaporizing the dew and moisture at the surface of the earth, and as this process renders a large portion of heat latent the air does not increase very rapidly in temperature.

TABLE I.

MEAN DIURNAL VARIATION OF TEMPERATURE AT GREENWICH.

2 A. M.	4 A. M.	6 A. M.	8 A. M.	10 A. M.	NOON.	2 P. M.	4 P. M.	6 P. M.	8 P. M.	10 P. M.	12 NIGHT.
45° 4'	44° 8'	44° 8'	46° 9'	50° 4'	53° 6'	55° 1'	54° 5'	52° 3'	49° 5'	47° 5'	46° 3'

— Minimum. + Maximum.

TABLE II.

MEAN DIURNAL VARIATION OF THE WEIGHT OF WATER IN A CUBIC FOOT OF AIR AT GREENWICH.

2 A. M.	4 A. M.	6 A. M.	8 A. M.	10 A. M.	NOON.	2 P. M.	4 P. M.	6 P. M.	8 P. M.	10 P. M.	12 NIGHT.
GR. 3.52	GR. 3.49	GR. 3.51	GR. 3.64	GR. 3.78	GR. 3.88	GR. 3.92	GR. 3.89	GR. 3.79	GR. 3.71	GR. 3.63	GR. 3.58

— Minimum. + Maximum.

Table No. II gives the mean diurnal variation of the absolute weight in grains of moisture in a cubic foot of the air, as determined by a series of calculations from the record of the observations of the wet and dry bulb thermometer.

It will be seen by a comparison of table No. II with table No. I that as the temperature increases, the amount of water which exists in the air as vapor also increases. The two elements heat and moisture mutually influence each other as to the quantity present in the atmosphere at a given time. With an increase of elevation of the sun above the horizon its rays pass to the earth through the atmosphere less obliquely and impinge more perpendicularly on the surface. This produces an increased amount of vapor, with an increased elastic force, which enables the air in turn to absorb and retain a larger quantity of heat.

The maximum quantity of moisture is at 2 p. m. The increase in weight is from about 3½ grains to near 4 grains.

This table, however, does not give the amount of vapor which the air could hold if sufficient moisture were present to entirely saturate it. Indeed the air is very seldom fully saturated, and in order to begin to precipitate the vapor it contains into water, it is generally necessary to lower the temperature quite a number of degrees. The point of temperature at which the moisture begins to settle—for example, on the surface of a bright tin cup partly filled with water which is slowly cooled down by gradually adding ice water—is called the *dew point.* The greater number of degrees the water is obliged to be lowered before dew begins to be deposited, or the greater the difference between the temperature of the air and the dew point the greater is the dryness of the air, or the greater is the tendency of vapor to exhale from the skin and from all bodies containing moisture.

Table No. III gives the mean diurnal variation in the dew point.

TABLE III.

MEAN DIURNAL VARIATION OF THE DEW POINT AT GREENWICH.

2 A. M.	4 A. M.	6 A. M.	8 A. M.	10 A. M.	NOON.	2 P. M.	4 P. M.	6 P. M.	8 P. M.	10 P. M.	12 NIGHT.
43° 1′	42° 9′	42° 9′	44° 0′	45° 2′	46° 2′	46° 5′	46° 3′	45° 6′	44° 7′	44° 1′	43° 6′
	— Minimum.					+ Maximum.					

If we subtract the numbers in this table from those in Table No. 1, we shall have approximately the relative dryness, or evaporating power of the air; this is given in No. IV.

TABLE IV.

MEAN DIURNAL VARIATION OF DRYNESS, (APPROXIMATELY,) AT GREENWICH.

2 A. M.	4 A. M.	6 A. M.	8 A. M.	10 A. M.	NOON.	2 P. M.	4 P. M.	6 P. M.	8 P. M.	10 P. M.	12 NIGHT
2° 3′	1° 9′	1° 9′	2° 9′	5° 2′	7° 4′	8° 6′	8° 2′	6° 7′	4° 8′	3° 4	2° 7′
	— Minimum.					+ Maximum.					

From this it appears that the minimum dryness or greatest dampness of the air also occurs at four o'clock in the morning, and the maximum dryness at two o'clock in the afternoon.

The degree of humidity, however, of the air, may be more definitely expressed by the result of a more laborious process, namely, by dividing the weight of water in the air at a given time by the whole quantity the air could hold if it were saturated. By making the necessary calculation, and considering the point of saturation as unity, we shall have the following table:

TABLE V.

MEAN DIURNAL VARIATION OF THE HUMIDITY OF THE AIR AT GREENWICH

2 A. M.	4 A. M.	6 A. M.	8 A. M.	10 A. M.	NOON	2 P. M.	4 P. M.	6 P. M.	8 P. M.	10 P. M.	12 NIGHT.
0.926	0.934	0.938	0.906	0.843	0.783	0.753	0.761	0.800	0.851	0.891	0.914
	+ Maximum.					— Minimum.					

When the quantity of water is in the least degree greater than the atmosphere can contain at a given temperature, condensation takes place, which may be either in the form of fogs or dew in the lower strata or clouds, and rain in the upper. The formation of clouds will therefore depend on the amount of moisture in the atmosphere. This is shown by

TABLE VI.

MEAN DIURNAL VARIATION OF THE CLOUDINESS OF THE ATMOSPHERE AT GREENWICH.

2 A. M.	4 A. M.	6 A. M.	8 A. M.	10 A. M.	NOON.	2 P. M.	4 P. M.	6 P. M.	8 P. M.	10 P. M.	12 NIGHT.
.65	.67	.69	.70	.71	.71	.71	.69	.66	.62	.60	.61
					+ Maximum.					— Minimum.	

The actual weight of a given portion of the air is also affected by the variation of temperature. This is shown in the following table, in which the minimum of weight occurs at the hour of maximum temperature.

TABLE VII.

MEAN DIURNAL VARIATION OF THE WEIGHT OF A CUBIC FOOT OF AIR AT GREENWICH.

2 A. M.	4 A. M	6 A. M.	8 A. M.	10 A. M.	NOON.	2 P. M.	4 P. M.	6 P. M.	8 P. M.	10 P. M.	12 NIGHT.
Gr. 541.7	Gr. 542.2	Gr. 542.2	Gr. 540.1	Gr. 536.3	Gr. 532.9	Gr. 531.0	Gr. 531.5	Gr. 533.9	Gr. 537.2	Gr. 539.4	Gr. 540.6
	+ Maximum.					— Minimum.					

The next table, which gives the variation of the barometer, shows that the indications of this instrument are not precisely the same as those obtained by actually weighing a portion of air. The table exhibits two maxima and two mimima in the course of the twenty-four hours.

TABLE VIII.

MEAN DIURNAL VARIATION OF ATMOSPHERIC PRESSURE AT GREENWICH.

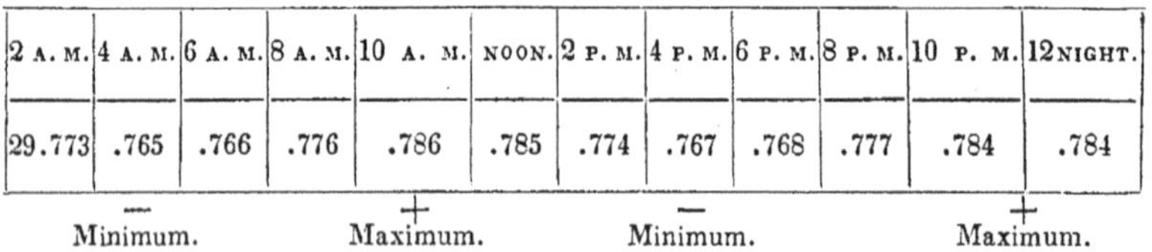

2 A. M.	4 A. M.	6 A. M.	8 A. M.	10 A. M.	NOON.	2 P. M.	4 P. M.	6 P. M.	8 P. M.	10 P. M.	12 NIGHT.
29.773	.765	.766	.776	.786	.785	.774	.767	.768	.777	.784	.784

— Minimum. + Maximum. — Minimum. + Maximum.

At first sight, it might appear that the weight and pressure, or in other words the density and pressure, ought to vary together, but a little reflection will make it plain that an increase of pressure on a portion of the surface of the earth may be counteracted by a variation of temperature. The height of the barometer indicates the weight of a column of air, extending to the top of the atmosphere; now, this column may be unduly heated at one point, as we ascend, and unduly cooled at another, and while the absolute weight of a portion of the air at any point of the column may vary, the pressure of the whole column may remain the same, or the converse. It is probable, however, that the variation of the weight which is found at the surface does not extend to a great elevation, and that when it is not indicated by the barometer it is because the change is too small to be noted by that instrument.

The fact that the barometer exhibits two maxima and two minima in the course of the twenty-four hours has given rise to much speculation as to its cause. The most common explanation is, that it is due to the joint action of the variation of the temperature and moisture. In the morning, the moisture rising into the atmosphere increases the weight of the air more than the heat diminishes it by expansion, while at about ten o'clock, a. m., the effect of heat overbalances that of vapor, and again as the sun begins to decline, the weight of the latter predominates. Mr. Espy attributes the daily oscillations of the barometer to the upward and downward motion of the particles of air and moisture as they are separated or approximated by the change of temperature. The particles weigh more while the rate of separation is increasing, and less while it is diminishing. This is a true cause, but we are not certain that it is a sufficient one. Whatever may be the cause of the daily oscillations of the barometer, we know the effect is nearly the same in parts of the earth most widely separated.

The diurnal variation of the pressure of the wind is also intimately connected with the variation of the temperature and weight of the air; this is shown by the following table, which gives the sums of the pressure upon a square foot in pounds avoirdupois at each hour of the 24. The numbers are those given by Osler's self-registering anemometer.

TABLE IX.

MEAN DIURNAL VARIATION OF THE PRESSURE OF THE WIND AT GREENWICH.

1 A. M.	2 A. M.	3 A. M.	4 A. M.	5 A. M.	6 A. M.	7 A. M.	8 A. M.	9 A. M.	10 A. M.	11 A. M.	NOON.
603¼	584¼	546	558½	575	585¾	650¾	781	906¾	1.008¾	1.204½	1.360
		— Minimum.									

1 P. M.	2 P. M.	3 P. M.	4 P. M.	5 P. M.	6 P. M.	7 P. M.	8 P. M.	9 P. M.	10 P. M.	11 P. M.	12 NIGHT.
1.405¼	1.415¼	1.323¼	1.187	1.032½	874	721	649¼	649¾	634	650½	642¼
	+ Maximum.										

For the purpose of comparison, and to illustrate the fact that the diurnal variations of the meteorological elements follow the same general law in the parts of the earth the most widely separated, the following tables are given from observations made at Bombay:

TABLE X.

MEAN DIURNAL VARIATION OF TEMPERATURE AT BOMBAY, 1843.

2 A. M.	4 A. M.	6 A. M.	8 A. M.	10 A. M.	NOON.	2 P. M.	4 P. M.	6 P. M.	8 P. M.	10 P. M.	12 NIGHT.
79° 4′	78° 9′	78° 4′	79° 6′	81° 8′	83° 2′	84° 1′	83° 9′	82° 3′	81° 2′	80° 3′	79° 8′
		— Minimum.				+ Maximum.					

The minimum temperature in this table occurs at 6 a. m., and the maximum at 2 p. m.

TABLE XI.

MEAN DIURNAL VARIATION OF TENSION OF VAPOR AT BOMBAY, 1843.

2 A. M.	4 A. M.	6 A. M.	8 A. M.	10 A. M.	NOON.	2 P. M.	4 P. M.	6 P. M.	8 P. M.	10 P. M.	12 NIGHT.
0.766	0.761	0.750	0.766	0.771	0.778	0.795	0.800	0.802	0.801	0.780	0.775
		— Minimum.						+ Maximum.			

According to this table the tension or elastic force of vapor at Bombay arrives at its minimum at 6 a. m., and its maximum not until 6 p. m. This difference in the time of the maximum and minumum at Bombay and Greenwich probably arises from the tropical position of the former.

TABLE XII.

MEAN DIURNAL VARIATION OF THE BAROMETER AT BOMBAY, 1843.

2 A. M.	4 A. M.	6 A. M.	8 A. M.	10 A. M.	NOON.	2 P. M.	4 P. M.	6 P. M.	8 P. M.	10 P. M.	12 NIGHT.
In. 29.786	In. 29.778	In. 29.805	In. 29.840	In. 29.852	In. 29.817	In. 29.776	In. 29.755	In. 29.774	In. 29.806	In. 29.825	In. 29.809
— Minimum.				+ Maximum.			— Minimum.			+ Maximum.	

This table exhibits, as in the case of that for Greenwich, two maxima and two minima.

The following tables exhibit the mean diurnal variations in the meteorological elements at Girard College, Philadelphia. They present the result of the observations for each hour of the 24.

TABLE XIII.

MEAN DIURNAL VARIATION OF THE TEMPERATURE OF THE AIR AT PHILADELPHIA.

Computed from the observations made in 1842, *and from the* 1*st July*, 1843, *to the* 1*st July*, 1845.

1 A. M.	2 A. M.	3 A. M.	4 A. M.	5 A. M.	6 A. M.	7 A. M.	8 A. M.	9 A. M.	10 A. M.	11 A. M.	NOON.
48.2	47.8	47.3	46.8	46.6	47.0	48.1	50.1	52.1	54.1	55.7	56.8
				— Minimum.							

1 P. M.	2 P. M.	3 P. M.	4 P. M.	5 P. M.	6 P. M.	7 P. M.	8 P. M.	9 P. M.	10 P. M.	11 P. M.	12 NIGHT.
57.9	58.6	58.9	58.7	57.7	56.0	54.1	52.5	51.0	50.2	49.4	48.7
		+ Maximum.									

By comparing table XIII with table I, it appears that the diurnal variation of temperature, at Greenwich and Philadelphia, is nearly the same. The minimum occurs a little earlier at the latter, and the maximum a little later.

TABLE XIV.

MEAN DIURNAL VARIATION OF THE DEW-POINT AT PHILADELPHIA.

Computed from the observations made from the 1st July, 1843, to 1st July, 1845.

1 A. M.	2 A. M.	3 A. M.	4 A. M.	5 A. M.	6 A. M.	7 A. M.	8 A. M.	9 A. M.	10 A. M.	11 A. M.	NOON.
42.0	41.7	41.4	41.1	41.1	41.4	42.0	42.9	43.7	44.1	44.3	44.5

Minimum.

1 P. M.	2 P. M.	3 P. M.	4 P. M.	5 P. M.	6 P. M.	7 P. M.	8 P. M.	9 P. M.	10 P. M.	11 P. M.	12 NIGHT.
44.7	44.6	44.5	44.1	43.7	43.7	43.6	43.3	43.1	42.9	42.7	42.3

+
Maximum.

The variations of the figures, in table XIV and table III, also follow the same general law.

TABLE XV.

MEAN DIURNAL VARIATION OF DRYNESS, (APPROXIMATELY,) AT PHILADELPHIA.

Computed from the observations made from July 1, 1843, to July 1, 1845.

1 A. M.	2 A. M.	3 A. M.	4 A. M.	5 A. M.	6 A. M.	7 A. M.	8 A. M.	9 A. M.	10 A. M.	11 A. M.	NOON.
6.1	6.2	5.7	5.6	5.3	5.4	6.0	6.9	8.2	10.0	11.3	12.3

Minimum.

1 P. M.	2 P. M.	3 P. M.	4 P. M.	5 P. M.	6 P. M.	7 P. M.	8 P. M.	9 P. M.	10 P. M.	11 P. M.	12 NIGHT.
13.3	14.1	14.5	14.8	14.2	12.6	10.7	9.4	8.3	7.4	6.8	6.4

+
Maximum.

From table XV, it does not appear that Mr. Russell's rule, for ascertaining the dew point from the minimum temperature, holds true in Philadelphia. Table No. IV, gives a much nearer approximation, and, in moist seasons, the same will probably be the case in this country, particularly at the south. By comparing the quantities given in table No. XV, with those in table No. IV, it will be seen that the relative dryness of Philadelphia is much greater than that of London or Greenwich.

TABLE XVI.

MEAN DIURNAL VARIATION OF THE CALCULATED FORCE OF VAPOR AT PHILADELPHIA.

Computed from the observations made in 1842, *and from July* 1, 1843, *to July* 1, 1845.

1 A. M.	2 A. M.	3 A. M.	4 A. M.	5 A. M.	6 A. M.	7 A. M.	8 A. M.	9 A. M.	10 A. M.	11 A. M.	NOON.
.344	.341	.334	.335	.333	.336	.343	.351	.359	.363	.365	.369

— Minimum.

1 P. M.	2 P. M.	3 P. M.	4 P. M.	5 P. M.	6 P. M.	7 P. M.	8 P. M.	9 P. M.	10 P. M.	11 P. M.	12 NIGHT.
.371	.375	.375	.373	.376	.376	.372	.364	.358	.353	.350	.348

\+ Maximum.

TABLE XVII.

MEAN DIURNAL VARIATION OF ATMOSPHERIC PRESSURE, BAROMETER REDUCED, AT PHILADA.

Computed from the observations made in 1842, *and from July* 1, 1843, *to July* 1, 1845.

1 A. M.	2. A M.	3 A. M.	4 A. M.	5 A. M.	6 A. M.	7 A. M.	8 A. M.	9 A. M.	10 A. M.	11 A. M.	NOON.
29.938	29.936	29.933	29.935	29.941	29.951	29.960	29.966	29.969	29.967	29.958	29.944

— Minimum. + Maximum.

1 P. M.	2 P. M.	3 P. M.	4 P. M.	5 P. M.	6 P. M.	7 P. M.	8 P. M.	9 P. M.	10 A. M.	11 A. M.	12 NIGHT.
29.927	29.916	29.910	29.909	29.911	29.918	29.927	29.935	29.943	29.946	29.949	29.941

— Minimum. + Maximum.

Table XVII shows two maxima and two minima in the height of the barometer, which correspond very nearly in time with those of table VIII for Greenwich.

TABLE XVIII.

MEAN DIURNAL VARIATION OF THE FORCE OF WIND, IN POUNDS, AT PHILADELPHIA.

Computed from the observations made in 1843 and 1844.

1 A. M.	2 A. M.	3 A. M.	4 A. M.	5 A. M.	6 A. M.	7 A. M.	8 A. M.	9 A. M.	10 A. M.	11 A. M.	NOON.
.50	.50	.52	.53	.51	.47	.47	.56	.64	.80	.88	.98
			+ Maximum.		— Minimum.						

1 P. M.	2 P. M.	3 P. M.	4 P. M.	5 P. M.	6 P. M.	7 P. M.	8 P. M	9 P. M.	10 P. M.	11 P. M.	12 NIGHT.
1.02	1.03	1.03	.98	.82	.61	.59	.50	.51	.52	.50	.47
	+ Maximum.										— Minimum.

Table XVIII, compared with table IX, exhibits a greater mean pressure of the wind at Greenwich than at Philadelphia. The maximum intensity, during the whole 24 hours is, in both tables, at 2 P. M.

TABLE XIX.

MEAN DIURNAL VARIATION OF THE SKY COVERED BY CLOUDS, AT PHILADELPHIA.

Computed from the observations made from the 1st July, 1843, to 1st July, 1845.

1 A. M.	2 A. M	3 A. M.	4 A. M.	5 A. M.	6 A. M.	7 A. M.	8 A. M.	9 A. M.	10 A. M.	11 A. M.	NOON.
.60	.61	.61	.65	.70	.74	.79	.86	.83	.85	.86	.88
— Minimum.											

1 P. M.	2 P. M.	3 P. M.	4 P. M.	5 P. M.	6 P. M.	7 P. M.	8 P. M.	9 P. M.	10 P. M.	11 P. M.	12 NIGHT.
.88	.89	.87	.88	.83	.80	.74	.69	65	.64	.65	.63
	+ Maximum.										

Tables XIX and VI exhibit nearly the same variation in the time of greatest and least cloudiness at Greenwich and Philadelphia.

EXTRACTS

FROM THE

SCIENTIFIC CORRESPONDENCE

OF THE

SMITHSONIAN INSTITUTION.

On Mr. John Wise's observations and inferences respecting the phenomena of a thunder storm, to which he was exposed during an ærial voyage, made by means of a balloon, June 3, 1852, from Portsmouth, Ohio.

BY DR. ROBERT HARE.

1. I have read with great interest the account published by Mr. Wise, a well known æronaut, of his balloon ascension during a thunder storm. This heroic excursion should awaken much attention in the scientific world, as opening a new and fruitful avenue to meteorological research in the immediate theatre of the stormy commotions of the atmosphere. The query "*Cui bono?*" can no longer be reasonably put to those who, like Wise, have been thought *unwisely* to have subjected themselves to risk in the sterile field of æronautic adventure.

2. The fact that this ærial voyage is the one hundred and thirty-first of those of which this veteran æronaut has survived the perils, indicates that they have not been so perilous in reality as in appearance; nor, so far as can be judged from the facts furnished by Wise's letter, does the unusual circumstance of a cotemporaneous thunder storm appear to add to the danger. Moreover, this practically safe result is just such as an attentive consultation of the well ascertained laws of electricity would justify. It is quite consistent with those laws that the æronaut, seated in his car, suspended by silken cords from a silken globe, should be more secure than persons simultaneously situated on terra firma beneath the clouds by which the balloon is surrounded. Supported as described, in the non-conducting air, by a non-conducting apparatus, an animal must be too well insulated to become the means of an electrical discharge, whether from the clouds to the earth, or

from one cloud to another. Neither the diameter nor length of the human frame would be sufficiently great, in proportion to the interval to be percurred, to cause a discharge of lightning to deviate much from any route which it otherwise would pursue, in order to employ that frame as a part of its circuit in the discharge.

3. There would be more risk of suffering by a dynamic inductive shock. This shock is exemplified when persons are stunned while near one who is directly struck. Yet while enveloped in a thunder cloud, the æronaut could not be injured by any discharge, whether between that cloud and another or between it and the earth.

4. The most intense electrical excitement, as imparted by a powerful machine to an animal supported by an insulated stool, produces no serious discomfort, so long as no spark is taken from any particular spot. The destructive violence of electricity is only displayed during transition, as when a comparatively slender body is made the medium of reciprocal neutralization to oppositely excited surfaces.

5. Under this view of the case, it is to be hoped that Mr. Wise may prove the pioneer in a new career of observation, and that encouraged and instructed by his example, a succession of scientific observers may visit the region of clouds during thunder gusts and gales.

6. The greatest source of danger is the violence of the winds, which when high must make it difficult to quit the terrestrial surface, or to descend upon it with safety. The velocity of the wind, *however great*, would have no more influence upon a balloon floating in it aloft, than the orbitual movement of our planet upon the bodies resting upon its surface.

7. As, agreeably to the narrative of Mr. Wise, the ascension commenced at half-past five, p. m., it is inconceivable how a landing could have been effected at nearly one hundred miles from the place of starting, especially as in the fifth paragraph of his synopsis he alleges that he was in the margin of the third storm noticed, twenty-five minutes. It is to be presumed that there is an erratum as respects the time, either of the commencement or of the termination of his voyage.

8. Presuming, however, that the observations of Mr. Wise are reliable as respects certain phenomena which bear upon the theory of storms, I will endeavor to show that they are quite consistent with the idea that electricity is a principal agent in the generation of storms.

9. Mr. Wise gives the following synopsis of the observations made during his aerial voyage:

"1st. Thunder storms have two plates of clouds; the upper of these discharging the contents, whatever they may be, whether rain, hail, or snow, into the lower.

"2d. Sheet lightning, of an orange color, undulates silently between the upper and lower strata of clouds, with a waving motion.

"3d. Discharges of electricity take place from the lower cloud. By discharges are meant thunder and lightning.

"4th. The distance between the upper and lower cloud was not less than two thousand feet, by eye measurement.

"5th. The current uprising from the terrestrial surface was not continued higher than the lower cloud, and was rising and whirling, while I was in the margin of the storm, during twenty-five minutes.

"6th. The storm was much wider below than above and diverging at least twenty-five degrees from a perpendicular line.

"7th. The deposition of rain and hail was thicker about the centre of the storm.

"8th. Under the shadow of the upper cloud it is very cold, and in the lower cloud quite warm. The upper cloud was moved by the current which always moves from west to east."

To these allegations Mr. Wise might have added the following, as they are merely a repetition of facts alleged in his narration:

9th. A balloon, instead of being borne ahead by the current of air in which it floats, may be so approximated to the cloud as to be involved in the "outskirts of its rain," and be made to "rock by its whirling motion."

10th. A third cloud may be formed by the rushing together of two others, seen previously in opposite quarters, and remote from each other.

11th. The gas in a balloon may be so acted upon by the electric medium around it, as to acquire an augmentation of volume equivalent to calorific expansion.

10. The existence of two "plates," or strata, of clouds, as stated in paragraph 1st of the above synopsis, I have for some time considered as the usual concomitant of rainy weather. When, agreeably to the observations of Dalton, on which Espy founded his theory of storms, the vapor in an ascending mass of air is condensed, by the rarifaction and consequent increase of calorific capacity, which the air acquires on attaining the elevated region usually occupied by the clouds, this increase of capacity enables it to rob the aqueous vapor associated with it of heat; but by these means becoming warmer than if this vapor were not present, it consequently acquires an ascensional power; but by admixture with a larger portion of air, the warmth and moisture are again absorbed in the state of vapor, so that the clouds thus created below a certain level are reabsorbed at a higher level, producing a cold proportionally as great as the heat resulting from its condensation. This may be called the level of absorption, while the level at which they are created may be called the level of condensation. Between these levels the clouds, in fine weather, seem to float as if they were persistent, when, in reality, they are no more of this character than the fog which surmounts the escape-pipe of a steam-boiler when letting off steam.

11. Yet the moisture which escapes from permanent condensation at the first level at which this process takes place, by reaching a higher level, may be a second time condensed, by which a second stratum of clouds, as much colder as the associated air is rarer, may be generated. The process of reabsorption which had previously taken place immediately above the lower stratum, can now only take place immediately above the upper stratum, and, in consequence of the greater refrigeration, must proceed with proportionally less rapidity. Consequently the

absorption now no longer compensates for the condensation, and the excess must be precipitated as rain, hail, or snow.

12. That the upper stratum should be colder than the lower one, as alleged in the synopsis, is explained: first, by the difference of the altitude; secondly, the evaporation going on from the upper one must rob it of heat by a process from which the other stratum is protected by its presence; thirdly, radiation by the same superiority of altitude goes on copiously from the upper stratum, while this, by its interposition, checks radiation from the lower stratum.

13. The formation of clouds within the space occupied by the upper stratum must prove the air associated with those clouds to be saturated with moisture. Hence the clouds formed in any subjacent stratum cannot be absorbed within the interval between the strata, and must, of course, be more likely to accumulate so as to produce rain.

14. That the upper stratum should be so overcharged with electricity as to give it out in "sheet lightning," undulations, or aurora boreal corruscations, is perfectly consistent with the suggestion which I have advanced respecting the existence of three concentric spaces occupied severally by our globe—the denser non-conducting part of the atmosphere, and the rarified medium beyond that last mentioned, which is sufficiently rare to form a conductor or coating, the terrestrial surface performing a similar part within, the atmospheric electric existing intermediately.

15. The frequency of the aurora boreal corruscations and flashes is no doubt the consequence of discharges from one part of the exterior concentric space to another, especially when proceeding from either the arctic and antarctic regions to those of intermediate latitudes.

16. It is well known that ice, when very cold and, consequently, dry, performs the part of an electric no less than glass. The friction of globules, as existing in the fog produced by escaping steam, has been inferred by Faraday to be a competent source for the torrents of electricity generated by a high steam; and it is not improbable that the friction between wind and the terrestrial surface may induce opposite states in the stratum of air bounded by that surface and the stratum occupied by the earth, and that occupying the space above the region of the clouds.

17. The discharges of lightning are the means of equalization between these spaces. Observation shows that the higher regions of the atmosphere are equally surcharged with electricity so as to prove dangerous to travellers among the Sierras or table lands of the Andes. Hence the upper stratum of clouds is liable to be surcharged with electricity oppositely to the earth. But whatever electrifies the inner terrestrial coating must produce a proportional opposite excitement in the outer one.

18. When an upper stratum of clouds, such as Mr. Wise describes as the "cloud cap," is highly electrified by corruscations from the outer concentric space, as above supposed, it is consistent that it should attract the oppositely electrified air in the vicinity of the terrestrial surface. This air must at the same time undergo dilatation like that to which the gas in Wise's balloon was subjected, and must, of course, be repelled by the similarly electrified earth. Calorific expansion may

co operate, and thus an ascensional power be generated sufficient to make it rise to the region of the clouds, where rarefaction so increases the calorific capacity of the air, that it robs the aqueous vapor, existing in the air, of its heat, and thus condenses it into a cloud. Meanwhile the heat involved by the vapor in condensing keeps the temperature higher than if the moisture were not present, and, according to Espy, should be productive of an upward force competent to produce a tornado. But according to Wise's statements, the uprising current does not reach the upper stratum of clouds.

19. In the fifth paragraph of his synopsis it is alleged not to be continued higher than the lower cloud; but in his narrative he alleges that when "the balloon was half way down between the cloud and the lower stratum, the uprising current arrested the descent" and was rising and whirling as he was in the margin of the storm.

20. The fact that the balloon, instead of being carried ahead by the current in which the "thunder gust," first noticed by our voyager, floated, was carried towards it so as to be "involved in the outskirts of its rain," and to be affected by its motion, can only be ascribed to centripetal currents; and the whirl might be the natural consequence of the conflicting concurrence of such currents. The rising of the air in the axis of the whirl would require that there should be inblowing currents to supply the deficit created by this upward blast. It is difficult to comprehend why the balloon was not drawn into the vortex and carried round with it.

21. I have never seen nor heard any evidence justifying the idea that an ordinary thunder gust involves the existence of a whirling motion about a vertical axis. The rushing together of two thunder gusts, or clouds, to form a third, as stated in the narrative, and noticed in the 9th paragraph of the synopsis, indicates the existence of two currents rushing towards an intermediate space, where a whirl might contingently ensue, a result which is quite consistent with the inblowing theory, agreeably to which whirling is an incidental consequence, not a cause nor an essential feature of storms. In these respects Wise's observations are irreconcilable with the rotatory theory, which assumes the whole of the theatre of stormy reaction to whirl about a common axis. Agreeably to this idea, the two thunder gusts, instead of rushing towards each other, would have to be carried further apart by a centrifugal motion, and the air, instead of rising about the axis, would have been drawn downward to supply the centrifugal currents.

22. The persistence of the upper stratum, or "cloud cap," as this stratum is designated in the narrative, is inconsistent with the Espyan hypothesis, which requires that in every thunder gust, no less than in a tornado, that the whole mass of air, of which the commotions constitute the storm, should be turned inside out, by an upward blast produced by the heat arising from condensing vapor. Of course, this force could not come into existence below the level at which the condensation commences, in other words, that of the lower stratum of clouds, and could not continue to operate further than the inferior level of the upper stratum. Any buoyancy thus created would tend to carry up the "cloud cap," while it could have no effect at any level below

that at which the increase of temperature should commence, as I have proved, both experimentally and theoretically.

23. Supposing the electrical charge in the upper stratum to be the main agent in the phenomena, it would be consistent that its influence should be exercised more widely, as the air acted upon should be further off, since distance enlarges the sphere as it lessens the force of the attraction.

24. This seems to explain the widening of the stormy mass affected towards its base, as stated in the sixth paragraph of the synopsis.

25. Agreeably to the seventh allegation of the synopsis, the greatest deposition of rain took place towards the interior or central part of the stormy mass, while, according to Espy, the moisture ascends over the focal area, and descends on one or more sides. But Mr. Wise was not well situated to form an accurate estimate in this respect. Until the facts are better examined or confirmed, it were better to postpone the examination of this question.

26. The ninth paragraph is added by me, being founded on the allegations of Mr. Wise in the fourth, fifth, and sixth paragraphs of his narrative.

27. It must be evident that by the narrator the words thunder storm, or thunder gust, are used as synonymous with a stratum of thunder clouds; so that when he informs us that two tremendous thunder storms were approaching each other rapidly beneath him, it is evidently intended to convey the idea of two great thunder clouds coming together so as to form one.

28. This is not the first time that the coming together of two thunder clouds has been alleged to happen. In the report on the tornado of Chenay, by Peltier, such an approximation is stated to have preceded the formation of the meteor. Evidently they could not be brought together by charges of electricity unless those charges were of an opposite kind; but if they were of an opposite kind, the union of the clouds would have caused reciprocal neutralization, so far as their charges were equivalent. This result would have been inconsistent with that augmentation of electrical energy consequent to their uniting, which is in both cases alleged to have ensued. The only explanation which I can suggest, consistently with the laws of electrical reaction, is, that these masses of vapor were both neutral, and that they were both attracted simultaneously by the upper stratum of clouds, designated by Mr. Wise as the "cloud cap," and charged therefrom as soon as they attained sufficient proximity so as to form one cloud.

29. The last paragraph of synopsis was added by me upon the inference of the narrator that his balloon acquired an ascensional power which awakened surprise, and respecting which, on reflection and consideration, he came to the conclusion that "*the electrical medium*" *in which he was floating was* acting on the gas and attenuating it."

30. In concluding an essay entitled "Additional objections to Redfield's theory of storms," published in Silliman's Journal about the year 1843, as well as on various other occasions, and especially in my two strictures on Espy's report, I have advanced that æriform particles, when existing in a mass of air electrified, either vitriously or resinously, must repel each other more than when they are in a normal

state; and, consequently, the mass which they constitute must be dilated proportionably to the intensity of the charge. Moreover, a mass so electrified must be repelled by the earth proportionably to the charge, so that in this way a diminution of barometrical pressure and atmospheric density may ensue.

31. But, according to Dalton's observations, the temperature being constant, the quantity of moisture in the air is as the space occupied by it, since it is the capacity of the space, not that of the air, which regulates the proportion of moisture associated with the latter.

32. It follows that when by electrical repulsion the air is dilated it will have an increase of its capacity for moisture, proportional to its dilatation, and when the electricity causing the increase of capacity is discharged the moisture must precipitate.

33. And further, when two masses of air, oppositely electrified, coalesce proportionably to the neutralization, moisture must be deposited.

34. Such masses must acquire by a reaction with the earth, and an ascensional tendency arising from repulsion between them and the terrestrial surface. Mr. Wise's observations respecting the influence of the electric medium upon the gas within his balloon, by which it was so attenuated as to create a surprising ascensional power, is altogether confirmatory of my inferences.

35. It appears that Mr. Wise was enabled to vary the direction of his sailing by varying the altitude at which he floated. Hence, as there are always two currents during gales, it would be possible for an aerial navigator to determine his course by his elevation, as Mr. Wise appears to have done. In a northeastern gale he might first use one current in order to go to a sufficient distance, and then use the other to return.

CORRESPONDENCE.

THE CLIMATE OF SAN FRANCISCO.

BY DR. H. GIBBONS.

No. 1.—GENERAL REMARKS.

Since the 1st of December, 1850, I have kept a record of observations on the weather in this city, of which I propose to give you a summary, for the especial benefit of distant enquirers. It may be well to observe, that while the climate of the western coast of North America possesses some peculiar features, that of San Francisco and the immediate vicinity differs from every other place on the coast, and is, in some respects, the most extraordinary climate in the world. This is owing to the peculiar position of the city, having the ocean on one side, and on the other a vast bay, extending north and south near a hundred miles, and separated from the ocean by a mountain wall, except at the break where the city is located, and where the bay communicates with the sea by a narrow strait. On the coast, a trade-wind from the northwest blows almost constantly, in the summer season especially, and a strong ocean current flows in the same direction.

The thermometrical observations forming the basis of the following summary were made three times a day, viz: about sunrise, which is the coldest period; at noon, or after, being the warmest period; and at eleven in the evening. In computing the mean temperature for the month, I have used two observations only, the extremes at sunrise and at mid-day; experience having shown that the mean thus calculated is very near the true temperature for the twenty-four hours.

In the Atlantic States, the warmest period of the day in winter is from one to two o'clock, and in summer from two to three. In San Francisco the same rule holds in winter but not in summer; for the sea breeze, which springs up about noon, or soon after, instantly depresses the temperature, so that the warmest time of the day, from May to August, inclusive, is an hour or two earlier than in winter.

For the want of proper care in the location of the thermometer, many of the observations which are thrown into print lose much of their value. The greatest error is commonly at mid-day, when the instrument is exposed to reflection from buildings and other objects on which the sun is shining. Every such object acts as a mirror, and tends to elevate the column of mercury above the proper mark for the air. The thermometer should, therefore, be excluded, not only from the direct, but also from the reflected heat of the sun, and it should at the same time be exposed to a free circulation of air; hence, to obtain a proper location is often very difficult. The figures in my observations will be found lower, in many instances, than those obtained by other observers, in consequence of the care exercised in this respect. In making the morning observation, I use a self-registering thermometer, which is certain to give the minimum temperature.

The summary, which I will now present, gives the mean for each month at or before sunrise, when it is the coldest, or at noon, when it is warmest, and at eleven in the evening; the mean temperature of the month, computed from two daily observations; also, the warmest and the coldest mornings in each month, and the warmest and coldest days at noon, with the range of the thermometer. It embraces a period of fourteen months—from December, 1850, to January, 1852, inclusive.

DECEMBER, 1850.—Sunrise 43.29 degrees Farenheit; noon 54.13; 11 p. m. 45.39. Monthly temperature 48.71. Coldest morning 28, warmest morning, 54; coldest noon 38, warmest noon 64; range 36.

JANUARY, 1851.—Sunrise 41.68; noon 56.94; 11 p. m. 44.90. Monthly temperature 49.31. Coldest morning 30, warmest morning 56; coldest noon 50, warmest noon 64; range 34.

FEBRUARY, 1851.—Sunrise 41.97; noon 60.03; 11 p. m. 43.64. Monthly temperature 51. Coldest morning 33, warmest morning 52; coldest noon 55, warmest noon 71; range 38.

MARCH, 1851.—Sunrise 44; noon 63.68; 11 p. m. 44.84. Monthly temperature 53.84. Coldest morning 34, warmest morning 50; coldest noon 53, warmest noon 74; range 40.

APRIL, 1851.—Sunrise 48.20; noon 67.27; 11 p. m. 49.80. Monthly temperature 57.73. Coldest morning 42, warmest morning 56; coldest noon 57, warmest noon 84; range 42.

MAY, 1851.—Sunrise 49.58; noon 64.32; 11 p. m. 50.42. Monthly temperature 55.95. Coldest morning 45, warmest morning 54; coldest noon 57, warmest noon 71; range 26.

JUNE, 1851.—Sunrise 50.90; noon 66.73; 11 p. m. 51.80. Monthly temperature 58.81. Coldest morning 49, warmest morning 56; coldest noon 60, warmest noon 78; range 29.

JULY, 1851.—Sunrise 51.50; noon 64.32; 11 p. m. 52.10. Monthly temperature 57.91. Coldest morning 47, warmest morning 54; coldest noon 60, warmest noon 73; range 26.

AUGUST, 1851.—Sunrise 54.97; noon 69.45; 11 p. m. 56.06. Monthly temperature 62.21. Coldest morning 50, warmest morning 66; coldest noon 63, warmest noon 82; range 32.

SEPTEMBER, 1851.—Sunrise 53.97; noon 69.27; 11 p. m. 54.20. Monthly temperature 61.62. Coldest morning 50, warmest morning 63; coldest noon 64, warmest noon 75; range 25.

OCTOBER, 1851.—Sunrise 53.36; noon 70.42; 11 p. m. 55.45. Monthly temperature 61.89. Coldest morning 47, warmest morning 60; coldest noon 60, warmest noon 83; range 36.

NOVEMBER, 1851.—Sunrise 48.93; noon 63.60; 11 p. m. 51.90. Monthly temperature 56.26. Coldest morning 41, warmest morning 57; coldest noon 52, warmest noon 73; range 32.

DECEMBER, 1851.—Sunrise 46.10; noon 56.55; 11 p. m. 48.26. Monthly temperature 51.32. Coldest morning 35, warmest morning 58; coldest noon 51, warmest noon 61; range 26.

JANUARY, 1852.—Sunrise 44.61; noon 56.97; 11 p. m. 49.39. Monthly temperature 50.79. Coldest morning 35, warmest morning 52; coldest noon 50, warmest noon 64; range 29.

For the year 1851: Sunrise 48.76; noon 64.38; 11 p. m. 50.28.

Yearly temperature 56.57. Coldest morning (January 17th) 30, warmest morning (August 18th) 66; coldest noon (January 9th) 50, warmest noon (April 28th) 84; range 54.

The average yearly temperature at Philadelphia is 51.50. Two degrees south of Philadelphia, in the latitude of San Francisco, it is near 54. It follows that the yearly temperature at this point of the Pacific coast is not much higher than on the Atlantic border. The vicinity of the Golden Gate is much colder in summer than any other point on the Pacific coast south of the Columbia river, owing to the almost incessant sea breezes, induced by the geographical features of the region round about.

The most striking peculiarity of the climate of San Francisco is its uniform temperature. There are no extremes of heat or cold. The warmest day in the year was the 28th of April, when the mercury reached 84; next to this was the 19th of October, 83. On the 18th of August it was 82, but this was *the only day in the three summer months* when it rose above 79! The thermometer was at or above 80 only on nine days in the year, six of which were in October. At Philadelphia, it reaches this point on from sixty to eighty days in the year.

Only once in the year did the mercury sink to the freezing point, and it was below 40 only on twenty-five mornings. At Philadelphia, it falls to the freezing point or lower about 100 times in the year.

The coldest day in the year, at noon, was 50. This is about equal to the *warmest* weather in the three winter months at Philadelphia. There, the months of January and February sometimes pass without one day as warm as this.

The warmest month in the year, at sunrise, was August, then September, then October. July, which is decidedly the hottest month in most other climates, was the fourth on the list, being considerably colder than October.

The warmest month at noonday was October; then August, September, April and June, in the order named. July comes in with May, being the sixth on the list, and only a trifle warmer at noonday than March and November.

At 11 p. m. August was the warmest, and next comes October and September, before July, which is but a trifle warmer at this hour than November. November was warmer in the evening than June.

The lowest temperature in the year being 30°, and the highest 84°, it follows that the range of the thermometer was 54°. On the Atlantic border, in the same latitude, the range is nearly 100°. At Philadelphia the greatest cold is 10° below zero, and the greatest heat 94°—making a range of 104°. At San Francisco, in December, 1850, the thermometer was one morning as low as 28°, and did not rise above 38° at noon, so that ice remained in the shade all day. This was regarded as an extraordinary degree of cold. Up to the present date, February 25, 1852, the extreme cold of the winter has been 35°, and it is probable the coldest weather is past.

January is the coldest month of the year in the Atlantic States, and February a trifle warmer. The same is true of San Francisco, judging from the past year. The temperature of January, at Philadelphia, is about 30½°, and that of July, the warmest month, 73½°; difference

43°. The difference between January and August, the coldest and warmest months at San Francisco, was not quite 13°!

To facilitate comparison, I insert the mean temperature for a series of years of the several months at Philadelphia: January, 30½°; February, 31¾°; March, 40°; April, 50°; May, 60½°; June, 69°; July, 73½°; August, 71½°; September, 64°; October, 53°; November, 42½°; December, 33¾°. By observing that one degree of latitude makes about one degree of difference in temperature in the Atlantic States, the reader may easily compute, from these data, the mean temperature at any given place. For example, if the place be two degrees north of Philadelphia, you will find its mean temperature by deducting two from the temperature at Philadelphia; if south, by adding.

The coldest month in 1851, at San Francisco, (viz: January,) was 9° warmer than the average of the coldest month at Philadelphia; while August, the warmest month at San Francisco, was 11° *colder* than the average of July, the warmest month at Philadelphia.

At San Francisco, the temperature falls more rapidly in the afternoon and evening than in the Atlantic States, but less rapidly during the night. From 11 P. M. to sunrise, the mercury at Philadelphia falls four or five degrees on the average, while at San Francisco the difference was less than two degrees, and in four of the months less than one degree; except in the winter, when the change is similar in this respect at the two points. In November, December, and January, at San Francisco, the thermometer falls from two to three and a half degrees between 11 P. M. and sunrise. The same is true precisely of Philadelphia. But while at Philadelphia in all the other months the fall during the same period of the night is twice as great, it is less than half as much at the former place. In other words, the temperature falls in the night, after 11 P. M., four times as much at Philadelphia as at San Francisco, from February to September inclusive.

In the summer months there is scarcely any change of temperature in the night. The early morning is sometimes clear, sometimes cloudy, and always calm. A few hours after sunrise the clouds break away, and the sun shines forth cheerfully and delightfully. Towards noon, or most frequently about 1 o'clock, the sea breeze sets in and the weather is completely changed. From 60° to 65° the mercury drops forthwith to near 50°, long before sunset, and remains almost motionless till next morning. This is the order of things in three days out of four in June, July, and August. May and September exhibit something of the same character, the sea winds establishing themselves in the former and declining in the latter month. This subject will be more fully investigated under the head of winds.

The remarkable uniformity of temperature at San Francisco may be further illustrated by taking note of the number of days in the year which give the same degree. The most frequent temperature at sunrise was 53°, the mercury standing at that point on forty-five mornings. The most frequent at noon was 64°, forty-two days showing that temperature. Referring to my journal kept at Philadelphia, I happened to open at the year 1839, which exhibits a fair representation of the climate there. I find the most frequent temperatures at sunrise were 52° and 68°, but that the mercury stood at each of these points on fourteen mornings only. The greatest number of days in the year coinciding in temperature at noon was sixteen, with the thermometer at 68°.

At San Francisco, in the year 1851, there were one hundred and sixty-one mornings with the temperature from 50° to 54° inclusive. At Philadelphia the greatest number of mornings within the like range of the thermometer, in the year 1839, was but forty-six. At the former place there were two hundred and nineteen days within a range of 5° at noon, while the greatest number within that range at Philadelphia was but sixty.

It is not uncommon for the thermometer at noon to stand almost at the same point day after day, for one or two weeks. March, April, and October, were the most irregular months in this respect, being interspersed with a great proportion of warm days. But no other month of the year elapsed without exhibiting one or two weeks continuously when the mercury varied only 5°. From the 12th to the 26th February, (15 days,) the lowest mark at noonday was 55°, and the highest 60°. From the 2d to the 16th of June, (15 days,) the lowest was 65°, and the highest 70°. From the 1st to the 13th of July, (13 days,) the lowest was 61°, and the highest 65°; and from the 17th to the 27th of the same month, the lowest was 60°, and the highest 65°. In the first 13 days of August, the lowest was 63°, and the highest 65°—a variation of only 2°. From the 13th to the 21st of September, the lowest was 65°, and the highest 66°—only 1° of variation in nine days.—From the 2d to the 11th of November, (10 days,) the range was between 62° and 67°; and from the 14th to the 24th, (11 days,) between 60° and 65°. From December 8th to the 24th, (15 days,) the variation was from 54° to 58°—only 4°.

The sudden fluctuations of temperature incident to the climate of the Atlantic States are unknown here. We have none of those angry outbreaks from the northwest, which change summer to winter in a few hours. But the diurnal depressions of temperature in the afternoon are considerable. The average fall of the thermometer from noon to 11 P. M., for the whole year, is at Philadelphia 11°; at San Francisco 14°. The change at the latter place is the more striking, from its greater rapidity. In the season of the sea breezes, a few hours will reduce the temperature fifteen, twenty, and on some of the warmest days, twenty-five degrees; and this change is effected long before sunset. Under the head of *winds*, this subject will be more fully examined.

Comparing one day with that succeeding, the difference is never great. The greatest difference during the year at noon, between two adjoining days, was 21°. Turning to the table for 1839, at Philadelphia, in the month of March alone, three instances are found exceeding this: the differences being in one case 29°, in the second 33°, and in the third 35°. Though no other month was equal to March in this respect, yet there were several other examples during the year which exceeded the extreme at San Francisco.

As regards the influence of the seasons on vegetation, the common order is reversed. The entire absence of rain in the summer months parches the soil, and reduces it almost to the barrenness of a northern winter. The cold sea winds of the summer solstice defy the almost vertical sun, and call for flannels and overcoats. When the winds cease, as they do in September and October, comes a delightful Indian summer. In November and December the early rains fall, and the temperature being moderate, vegetation starts forth, and midwinter finds the earth clad in lively green and spangled with countless flowers. The spring opens with genial warmth, but just as the April sun begins to give promise of summer heat, its rays are shorn of their power by the winds and mists of the Pacific.

These remarks apply only to a small portion of the State of California. Beyond the influence of the Bay of San Francisco and its outlet, the sea winds are scarcely perceptible, even near the ocean. In a subsequent chapter, I will present the results of my observations on the winds, clouds, rain, and other phenomena of the climate, as noticed at San Francisco, together with some notes on the climate of other portions of the State, and also its general relations to health.

NO. 2.—WINDS.

In a former article I gave the result of my observations on Temperature. The present chapter refers to the Winds.

The course of the wind is noted in my journal by three daily entries, viz: forenoon, afternoon and evening. Should the wind change during either of these periods, as it very often does, especially in the forenoon, the change is marked, and taken into account in the summing up. With these explanations, the reader will have no difficulty in comprehending the following table, which shows the winds of each month of the year, and the total of the year:

1852.	N.	NE.	E.	SE.	S.	SW.	W.	NW.
January	35	2	1	14	7	7	21	6
February	18	5	2	6	9	13	15	16
March	7	2	1	8	4	14	34	23
April	3	5	1	4	7	13	45	12
May	1	1	1	2	4	11	65	8
June	1	1	1	1	5	14	62	5
July	0	0	1	2	1	14	74	1
August	0	1	1	1	6	11	72	1
September	1	0	0	2	2	11	72	2
October	8	3	3	6	6	2	54	11
November	10	4	2	8	15	12	30	9
December	15	9	3	12	24	7	13	10
	99	33	17	66	90	129	557	104

The direction of the coast is nearly NW. and SE., or about one point north of NW., and one point south of SE. Hence the winds from NW. to S., inclusive, blow from the ocean, and those from N. to SE. from the land. The former greatly preponderate, exhibiting an aggregate of 880 observations, to 215 of the latter. That is to say, the winds blew from the ocean semi-circle more than three-fourths of the year.

It is still more striking that the winds came from due west, or rather from the octant corresponding to that point, more than half the year; the summing up of that column being 557 against 538 from all other points, embracing seven eighths of the compass.

Observe the remarkable contrast between the columns of west and east winds, the latter presenting only 17 observations in the year! It is a well ascertained fact that westerly winds predominate in the temperate latitudes of the northern hemisphere, on both continents. But I cannot discover that in any other spot on the globe the winds blow from one octant 186 days, and from the opposite octant only six days in the year.

Dividing the year into four seasons, January, February and December being classed as the winter months, we have the following result:

	N.	NE.	E.	SE.	S.	SW.	W.	NW.
Spring..........	11	8	3	14	15	38	144	43
Summer........	1	2	3	4	12	39	208	7
Autumn........	19	7	5	16	33	25	156	22
Winter..........	68	16	6	32	40	27	49	32

Thus it appears that the proportion of land winds to sea winds, in the several months, was as follows:

January,	land winds,	52	observations;	sea winds,	41	observations.
February,	do	31	do	do	53	do.
March,	do	18	do	do	75	do.
April,	do	13	do	do	77	do.
May,	do	5	do	do	88	do.
June,	do	4	do	do	86	do.
July,	do	3	do	do	90	do.
August,	do	3	do	do	90	do.
September	do	3	do	do	87	do.
October,	do	20	do	do	73	do.
November,	do	24	do	do	66	do.
December,	do	39	do	do	54	do.

Grouping the months into seasons, and reducing the observations to days, three observations representing one entire day, we find in the—

Spring,	land winds,	12	days,	sea winds,	80	days.
Summer,	do	3	do	do	89	do.
Autumn,	do	16	do	do	75	do.
Winter,	do	41	do	do	49	do.
Total,		72			293	

In every month of the year the sea winds exceed the land winds, except January, when the reverse occurred. In January, 1852, the land winds were 61, and the sea winds 32. In February, however, the former were but 27, and the latter 60. In December, 1850, the land winds exceeded the sea winds by one observation, the figures standing 47 to 46.

By casting the eye over the tables, one is struck with the progressive increase of the sea winds after the month of January, and the almost entire absence of the opposite winds from May to September, inclusive—the land winds in these five months occupying only six days.

The winds from north and east are always dry, and in winter cool.

They are nearly always attended with a sky of cloudless blue. Those from northwest to southwest are cold and chilling at all seasons, and in summer loaded with the ocean mists. But they do not often produce rain. The coast winds from south and southeast are most conducive to rain, and they are always warm. The course of the winds in relation to rain will be considered under the head of rains.

The force of the winds at different periods of the day, and from different points of the compass, is a subject of some interest. It is represented by figures—0 indicating calm or nearly calm, 1 a light breeze, 2 a moderate breeze, 3 a strong breeze or wind, 4 a high wind, and 5 a very high wind. The observations occupy three columns, for the forenoon, afternoon, and evening. The mean of each of these columns for every month is given in the following table, and the fourth column contains the mean of the three observations, collectively, for each month.

	Forenoon.	Afternoon.	Evening.	Mean.
January	1.21	1.45	.66	1.11
February	1.45	1.93	1.07	1.48
March	1.68	2.24	1.40	1.77
April	1.55	2.32	1.33	1.73
May	1.77	2.61	1.61	2.00
June	1.85	2.80	1.92	2.19
July	1.66	2.97	2.19	2.27
August	1.45	2.66	1.77	1.96
September	1.48	2.38	1.28	1.71
October	.87	2.05	.87	1.26
November	.85	1.22	.70	.92
December	1.37	1.32	1.07	1.25
1851	1.43	2.16	1.32	1.64

The reader will perceive that the average force of the wind in the afternoon was greater than in the forenoon, in every month of the year except December. By referring to my Philadelphia tables, I find there is no uniformity in this respect, the morning winds being stronger in some months, and the afternoon winds in others.

The evening winds were uniformly lighter than the afternoon, and lighter than those of the forenoon, except in the three summer months, when they were decidedly stronger than in the forenoon. At Philadelphia the evening winds sum up lower in strength than those of the forenoon or afternoon, in every month, without exception.

The table shows a remarkable progressive increase in the force of the atmospheric currents from January to July, the latter being the most windy month of the year; and then a decrease till November, the calmest month. At Philadelphia there is no such regularity. Autumn is the calmest season at both places, but summer comes next in the Atlantic States, then winter, and lastly spring, which is the windiest season on the eastern side of the continent.

From May to September, inclusive, there is more wind at San Francisco than at Philadelphia; but in the remaining five months, from October to April, there is less.

Not only in regard to time do the winds from the western semicircle greatly preponderate, but also in force. The land winds are often very light and transient, not affecting an ordinary vane. Besides, many of the observations placed in this column in my journal are due to the influence of the bay, from which a gentle current—really a sea breeze—frequently flows upon the city for a brief period in the forenoon, before the general current from the ocean sets in from the opposite quarter. These bay currents are strictly local; and on the opposite side of the bay they take the opposite direction, and swell the proportion of sea winds in that location.

The following table is a summary of three daily observations, continued through the year 1851, showing the direction of the atmospheric currrents, with reference to their comparative force.

	N. & N.W.	E. & N.E.	S. & S.E.	W. & S.W.
Nearly calm	49	24	49	30
Light breeze	86	39	88	146
Breeze	69	5	36	335
Wind	20	0	13	191
High wind	2	0	2	29
Very high wind	0	0	3	1

Thus it appears that the wind was very high only on three days in the year. Much as is said of the violence of the wind at this place, I have never yet witnessed a wind in California equal to that which frequently attends a thunder-gust or an easterly storm of the highest grade in the Atlantic States.

From the east quarter of the compass the current did not rise beyond a moderate breeze in the entire year, and only for five observations did it reach that degree of force. As we recede from that limit, either northward or southward, the winds increase both in frequency and strength. But it is not until we pass the north point on one hand, and the southeast point on the other, that they are high. Of the twenty observations above noted as "winds" from the north and northwest, seventeen were from northwest, and only three from north. The two high winds under the same head were from northwest. So in regard to the thirteen winds, three high winds, and two very high winds, in the column headed south and southeast; a small proportion were from due southeast, the mass of them coming from south-southeast and south. The high winds of winter, when such occur, are from this quarter, and bring rain. The high winds of summer are always westerly, and without rain.

In the course of the year there were 169 windy days. On 123 of this number, the wind did not rise till after the sun had crossed the meridian, and it continued after sunset on 57 only. There were but 20 days in the year windy at sunrise.

The sea breeze of summer, which forms the most striking trait of the climate of San Francisco, demands something more than a passing notice, and will be reserved for another chapter, together with the subjects of clouds, rains, electrical phenomena, &c.

No. 3.—THE SEA BREEZE.

The tables contained in my last number exhibit the great excess of sea winds over land winds in every month of the year 1851, excepting January, when the excess was in favor of land winds. In this respect, the month of January in the present year corresponds with the last. December, 1850, shows a very slight preponderance of land winds. From these data I infer the general rule, that the westerly or sea winds predominate in every month except January and December, and that the latter month varies in this respect, being sometimes on the one side and sometimes on the other.

I have already stated that the westerly winds increase, both in frequency and in force, from February to July, and then begin to fall off very gradually. The precise relation of sea to land winds, in each month, as to frequency, is shown by computing their per centage of the whole number of observations. The result for the year 1851 is as follows:

January, sea winds	44	per cent.
February, do.	63	do.
March, do.	81	do.
April do.	86	do.
May, do.	95	do.
June, do.	96	do.
July, do.	97	do.
August, do.	97	do.
September, do.	96	do.
October, do.	78	do.
November, do.	73	do.
December, do.	38	do.
To which may be added—		
December, 1850, sea breeze	49	do.
January, 1852, do.	34	do.
February, 1852, do.	69	do.

Whatever may be the direction of the wind in the forenoon, in the spring, summer, and autumn months, it almost invariably works round towards the west in the afternoon. So constant is this phenomenon, that in the seven months from April to October, inclusive, there were but three days on which it missed, namely, on the 8th of April, the 18th of May, and the 27th of August. And these three days were all rainy, with the wind from the south or south-southwest.

The sea winds are moderate in the spring until the month of May, when they begin to give trouble. In June they increase in force, reaching their greatest violence about the beginning of July. In August they begin to decline in force, though not in constancy. In September they continue steady, though moderate; and in October they lose their annoying qualities, and become gentle and agreeable.

The sea winds of summer are commonly supposed to come from the northwest. But this is a great error, arising, no doubt, from the fact that our citizens have mostly been accustomed to cold winds, in the

Atlantic States, from that quarter. In the early spring they sometimes proceed from north of west. As the season advances they depart entirely from this course, and are almost invariably from south of west. From May to September, a period of five months, the direction of the afternoon sea breeze was north of west on twelve days only; and even on these occasions it was mostly within one point of west. The prevailing direction was west southwest.

I have reason to believe that the wind off the coast, at sea, during the period referred to, is more northwardly than on land, and that it is deflected from that course about the bay of San Francisco. Such, at least, is the account given by the captains of vessels navigating the coast.

There was a decided sea breeze on 23 days in March, 17 days in April, 22 days in May, 24 days in June, every day in July and August, 28 days in September, 30 days in October, and 8 in November.

The number of afternoons that might be described as *windy* was, in February 8, March 16, April 15, May 18, June 24, July 29, August 23, September 19, October 8, November 2. On the 162 days thus noted, the mornings were seldom windy, the wind rising above a moderate breeze in the forenoon on 34 days only. In May there were 5 days windy at sunrise, and 1 in June; but not one in the months of April, July, August, September, and October.

The sea breeze generally rises to its height soon after noon-day, mostly between one and two o'clock, but sometimes not till three or four. It commonly falls about sunset, or soon after. Sometimes it continues till midnight. In the early part of the season it is apt to set in earlier and continue later. There were 8 windy evenings in May, 11 in June, 11 in July, 5 in August, and none in September.

The idea of mist and vapor is commonly associated with these winds; but the sky is clear, or partially so, more than half the time There were 6 cloudy mornings in May, 11 in June, 16 in July, 21 in August, and 22 in September. About 9 or 10 o'clock, the clouds mostly broke away rapidly, a light breeze springing up at the same time. Several hours of very pleasant weather occurred towards noon, almost every day. The sun shone forth with genial warmth, the mercury rising generally from about 50 at sunrise, to 60 or 65 at noon; but when the sun had reached the zenith, the wind rapidly increased, coming down in gusts from the hills, which separate the city from the ocean, and often bringing with it clouds of mist. But the dampness is never sufficient to prevent the elevation of clouds of dust and sand, which sport through the streets in the most lively manner. The mercury falls suddenly, and long before sunset it fixes itself within a few degrees above 50, where it sticks pertinaciously till next morning; often not moving a hair's breadth for twelve hours. Many times I have examined the instrument on suspicion that some defect had fixed the column immovably. The chilling temperature adds to the effect of sand and dust. Persons who have business out of doors are seen buttoning up their coats or overcoats, and rubbing industriously at the various apertures about the face as they hurry through the streets, in the worst possible humor. Such weather, at the summer solstice, with an almost vertical sun, is pronounced "perfectly ridiculous."

The mist often increases towards evening, and, when the wind falls, remains all night in the shape of a heavy fog. Sometimes, when the sun has been shining brightly, the mist comes in from the ocean in one great wave, and suddenly submerges the landscape. In a few minutes it may vanish, and give place to the cheerful sunshine. In short, there is no conceivable admixture of wind, dust, cloud, fog, and sunshine that is not constantly on hand during the summer at San Francisco. Not unfrequently you are tantalized with a rainbow at sunset. Once I saw a solar rainbow before night in the east, and soon afterwards another bow, in the west, made by the moon.

I have already noticed the almost constant prevalence of the west and southwest currents. As the sea breezes become established, the entire absence of winds from north and northwest is remarkable. In the month of May, and in the beginning of June, there were a few light breezes from that quarter. But from the 13th of June until near the middle of October, a period of four months, there is not a solitary observation noted in my record, even of the lightest or most transient wind, from north or northwest. I think it probable that the same cannot be said of any other spot on the globe, in the north temperate zone.

The uniformity of the summer weather is occasionally broken by the intervention of a few warm and pleasant days, when the wind is not high enough to convert summer into winter. Under these circumstances the thermometer mounts to 70 or 75. In the latter spring and early autumn months it is warmer. But as soon as the "summer" has fairly set in, flannels and firewood are in almost constant demand, at least until August.

No one but an actual observer can appreciate the utter impotency of an almost vertical sun during a brisk sea breeze. The rays of the sun have scarcely more warmth than moon beams. Instead of raising the thermometer 30 or 40 degrees, they seldom produce more than ten degrees of elevation in the sweep of the wind.

Such is the "summer" at San Francisco. Everybody complains of the chilly winds, the mist, and the dust. If you have nothing to do but sit in the house, you are perfectly comfortable. Even for out-door employment or exercise, the mornings are almost invariably pleasant. The evenings are generally too cool to sit without fire, and the nights are never too warm to dispense with blankets. For the purpose of rest and sleep, the night in California is perfectly luxurious all the year through. With sprinkled streets, the afternoons will lose much of their bad character at San Francisco.

It might be inferred that a climate such as I have described is unfavorable to health, especially with persons liable to diseases of the chest. But the fact is just the reverse. The tone and vigor given to the animal frame by the uninterruptedly bracing temperature, appear to raise it above the control of inherent tendencies to pulmonic disorders. I believe the humid and saline condition of the atmosphere co-operates in the benefit. But I shall consider this subject more fully under a distinct head.

In all other parts of California, except the region about the Bay of San Francisco, the summer is very different. Along the coast are mists and sea breezes, but the winds are moderate and not so chilling.

Inland, they do not extend beyond the barrier of hills which skirt the coast. A distance of fifty miles in any direction from San Francisco brings you into a different climate. In a southeast course, towards San José, you escape the winds and fogs of summer by travelling twenty or thirty miles. Even in Contra Costa, directly across the bay, they are less severe, though the trees show, by their semi-prostrate attitudes, the direction of the prevailing atmospheric currents.

The general principles on which depend the diurnal currents of air, which set in from sea to land, are well known. The land being more heated than the ocean by the sun's rays, the superincumbent heated air rises in a steady column. Its place must be supplied from some quarter, and the colder and denser air of the ocean accordingly flows in, constituting a sea breeze. Independently of this, we have the universal westerly current, coinciding in its course and tending to add strength and constancy to the sea breeze, while the topographical features of the Bay of San Francisco, and the region of country bordering on it, enhance the effect. These several causes combined will explain the extraordinary constancy and force of the westerly winds at this point.

The importance of these winds, in connexion with the climate of San Francisco, has led me to dilate much more than I intended in taking up the subject. There are other incidents of the climate yet to be considered.

No. 4.—RAIN, STORMS, CLOUDS, AND MISTS.

Mining and agriculture, the leading interests of California, are intimately connected with the distribution of rains. The absence of rain during one portion of the year, and its profuse supply during the remaining period, a phenomenon which maintains through a great extent of the western coast of the American continent, gives the subject additional interest as connected with meteorological science. These considerations induce me to enter into some details which may prove beneficial, although they may possibly not be so interesting to every class of readers. The prevailing idea of mists and fogs, and the relation of the climate to health, furnish additional reasons for some degree of minuteness in the investigation.

The subjoined table presents the following details, for each month, from December, 1850, to March, 1852, inclusive of both months.

1st. column. The number of days on which rain fell.

2d. The quantity of rain in inches.

3d and 4th. The proportion of clear and cloudy weather.

5th. The number of days clear, or nearly so, from sunrise to sunset.

6th. The number of days entirely cloudy, from morning to night.

7th, 8th, and 9th. The number of days misty in the forenoon, in the afternoon, and in the evening.

Months.	Days of rain.	Inches.	Proportion clear days.	Proportion cloudy days.	Whole days clear.	Whole days cloudy.	Misty, a. m.	Misty, p. m.	Misty eve.
1850.									
December.......	4	1.15	22	9	17	3	4	2	2
1851.									
January.........	4	0.65	24	7	12	1	8	3	5
February........	4	0.35	23	5	14	1	4	1	2
March..........	9	1.88	20	11	9	3	2	1	1
April...........	8	1.14	20	10	10	3	3	1	1
May............	3	0.69	23	8	15	1	0	0	2
June............	0		20	10	10	1	0	3	6
July............	0		20	11	9	0	1	6	19
August	1	0.02	21	10	10	1	0	2	9
September......	2	1.00	23	7	7	0	2	1	2
October.........	2	0.18	26	5	15	0	2	1	3
November.......	5	2.14	23	7	13	2	2	2	4
December.......	15	7.07	19	12	10	5	1	0	0
1852.									
January.........	4	0.58	23	8	13	0	6	1	2
February........	4	0.12	21	8	5	2	5	0	0
March..........	14	6.40	19	12	9	4	2	0	0

It appears that the quantity of rain in the year 1851 was a small fraction over 15 inches. The annual quantity in the Atlantic States varies from 35 to 60 inches, with an average of about 45 inches. The driest season there gives more than double the amount exhibited in the foregoing table. So small a quantity as 15 inches falling in one year would be a terrible calamity to our Atlantic neighbors. It would involve the entire country in embarrassment, bankruptcy, and famine.

The winter of 1850–'51 was remarkably dry. Throwing it aside, and taking the year from the 1st of April, 1851, to the 1st of April, 1852, so as to include the rains of the following winter, we have 19.84 inches. I presume this figure is not very far from the mean of a series of years. But it is still much below the annual supply east of the Rocky Mountains.

It is well known that tropical countries have the most abundant rains, and that the quantity diminishes as you go northward. This is the general rule. On examining the records in my possession, scattered through a variety of publications, the smallest annual fall of water that I can find distributed in the Atlantic States or in the valley of the Mississippi, is at Burlington, Vermont, on the eastern border of Lake Champlain. The mean for a series of 13 years was 32.24 inches, and the least quantity in any one year was 26.35 inches, in 1849. In making these statements, the snow reduced to water is always included.

According to my own register, kept in Wilmington, Delaware, from 1827 to 1843, and at Philadelphia from that time till 1850, the least annual fall of water was 38.70 inches, in 1837, and the greatest 66.87 inches, in 1831.

The latter is an extraordinary supply for the middle States, but it is exceeded in the southern and southwestern sections of the country. It appears by a table published in the reports of the Patent Office, that there fell in Union county, Arkansas, latitude 33° 18′ north and longitude 16° west of Washington, in the year 1850, not less than 81.37 inches. And this is not the maximum quantity in the southern tier of States.

Whether the rains in other parts of the State correspond in quantity with those of San Francisco, I am unable to say. I have taken measures to obtain exact information concerning this and other departments of the meteorology of California. But the only data of importance at present in my hand, consist of a journal for 1850 and 1851, kindly furnished me by Dr. R. V. Abbott, of the United States army, kept by him at Camp Far West, in the northern part of the State, latitude 39° 20′ north, longitude 121° 18′ west from Greenwich. From this record is taken the following account of the rain in each month of those years:

	1850.		1851.	
January	6.71	inches.	2.06	inches.
February	60	"	1.16	"
March	5.56	"	3.44	"
April	1.40	"	3.06	"
May	0.00	"	0.86	"
June	0.00	"	0.00	"
July	0.00	"	0.00	"
August	0.00	"	0.00	"
September	2.00	"	0.30	"
October	0.00	"	0.10	"
November	2.10	"	1.86	"
December	2.00	"	6.63	"
Total	20.37		19.57	

Thus it appears that the quantity which fell in San Francisco, in the year ending April 1, 1852, and which I have assumed as the probable annual mean, viz: 19.34 inches, corresponds very nearly with the annual supply for two years at Camp Far West.

In the two winters, or rainy seasons, embraced in my table, there were but four days on each of which the quantity reached one inch, viz: November 8, 1851, 1.50 inches; December 22, 1851, 2 inches; March 6, 1852, 1.20 inches; and March 8, 1852, 1.15 inches. These quantities bear no comparison with the rains of the Atlantic States. In almost every month of the year there are rains in that region from 1 to 3 inches in depth. The greatest quantity in a day at San Francisco was 2 inches. The heaviest rains at Wilmington, in each year, from 1830 to 1840, were as follows: 1830, 2.70 inches; 1831, 3.00; 1832 2; 1833, 3.35; 1834, 5.10; 1835, 2.70; 1836, 3.80; 1837, 2; 1838, 3.60; 1839, 3; and in 1840, 6.75 inches.

The last noted rain, in 1840, was nearly equal to the greatest monthly fall at San Francisco. That of 1834, being upwards of five inches, fell in the space of two hours. Compared with deluges such as these, the rains of California are but gentle showers.

The winter of 1849–'50, according to the representations of those who then resided here, was a season of continual ourpourings, not excelled since the forty days and forty nights of primeval times. They tell us the water came down not in drops but in streams, and that the streets of the city were converted into flowing rivers and fathomless quag-mires. The tubs and casks that were left out at night were always found full and overflowing next morning. Unfortunately, there was no rain-guage to verify these statements. Doubtless the rains were copious at that time, probably much more so than since. But the doleful traditions respecting them may be referred in part to the absence of comfortable defences against the elements. The early settlers had to reside in tents, or beneath cribriform roofs, and tread in unplanked and submerged paths. These circumstances magnified and multiplied the falling drops, and penetrated the sufferers with indelible hydropathic impressions. Hence the rainy winter of 1849–'50 is uniformly dwelt on with great pathos and eloquence by those who endured it.

The question may arise, whether the floods that occurred in March, 1852, did not require a larger supply of rain than fell at San Francisco. But those who have not investigated the subject can form no adequate idea of the immense quantity of water requisite to make an inch of rain. Let us suppose the river Sacramento to drain a surface of one thousand square miles, and the channel at Sacramento to be 200 yards wide. Through this channel let one inch of rain be required to drain off in 24 hours, with a current of four miles an hour. It is easily calculated that one inch of rain, falling on a surface of one thousand square miles, would, under such circumstances, raise the river eight feet and keep it at that height 24 hours.

The presence of a few inches of snow, with the subjacent earth frozen, so as to prevent it from imbibing, will greatly enhance the diluvial effects of even a moderate rain. The snow, first absorbs the water and retains it until fully saturated, and then the entire mass rapidly liquifies and flows off. This was the case in the freshets that were precipitated from the mountains and hills of California in March last. One of the most destructive floods that ever occurred in eastern Pennsylvania was occasioned by a warm rain of less than two inches, which fell when the ground was frozen and covered with three or four inches of snow.

It is one striking feature of the winter of California, that when the weather puts on its rainy habit, the rain continues every day for an indefinite period; and when it ceases, there is an entire absence of rain for a long time. Thus, after three days of rain in the first week of December, 1851, the sky was perfectly clear for 13 days. Then, beginning with the 19th, rain fell every day for 13 days, or until the end of the month. After this it continued clear for nearly two months, there being but four slight rains in January, and two in February, until the 28th of the latter month, when the rainy diathesis again developed, and rain fell daily for 12 days. After the 10th of March, there were but four rains for more than a month.

There appear to be two rainy seasons, rather than one—something like the early and later rains of Palestine. The one takes place in the latter part of November or December, when the sea winds relinquish their sway, and the other in March, when they are about to resume their authority. Between those periods there is an interregnum of dry weather.

By adding together the number of rainy days in December 1850 and '51, and so of the corresponding months of the two seasons, the two rainy periods and the intervening period of drought are rendered more conspicuous.

December	1850 and '51.	Days of rain, 19,	quantity	8.23	inches.
January	1851 and '52.	" 8,	"	1.23	"
February	1851 and '52.	" 8,	"	0.47	"
March	1851 and '52.	" 23,	"	8.28	"

Thus in the four months embracing the early and later periods in the two seasons, there were 42 days of rain, and 16½ inches, while in the four intermediate months there were only 16 days of rain, and rather less than one inch and three quarters!

Dr. Abbott's journal, at Camp Far West, exhibits the same thing, though to a less extent. In that locality the early rains were continued into January. But February was a dry month. That the rule is general from year to year, the data are not sufficiently extended to warrant me in declaring; but the facts evidently tend to that conclusion. I am informed that the month of February was dry, in the memorable winter of 1849–'50, at San Francisco.

There were 53 days of rain in 1851, at San Francisco, and at Camp Far West, 62 in 1850, and 68 in 1851. In the Atlantic States the average number of days of rain in the year is about 100.

The average quantity of water for each day of rain at San Francisco, during the period embraced by the table, was about one fourth of an inch. At Camp Far West it was something more. The average in the Atlantic States is about twice that amount.

The rains in California are extremely irregular, falling almost invariably in showers. A settled and uniform fall of rain for twenty-four hours, or for even twelve hours, would be a strange occurrence. The southeast storms are the longest, but they seldom last many hours; or at least the rain does not, though the wind may continue. It seldom rains for two consecutive minutes with uniform rapidity. Often, in the space of one minute, there are several distinct showers. The sun breaks forth frequently in the midst of a shower, and directly the sky is almost clear. Presently, when you have no suspicion, you hear the rain on the roof with the suddenness of a shower-bath. These extemporaneous outpourings come from the west, and are always transient.

The night is more favorable to rain than the day. No matter how dense the clouds, how fair the wind, and how resolute the barometer in its promise of falling weather, the sun rarely fails to break up the arrangements towards noon, and to tumble the dense vapor into confused masses. I am informed by Robert Lammont, Esq., who was engaged in grading the streets of the city in the pluvious winter aforesaid, that the men in his employ were forced to suspend their labors for only four entire days in the whole time.

The entire season, with all its rains, is really delightful. It is not winter, but spring. The grass starts, and the flowers begin to blow on the hills as soon as the early rains have moistened the soil. In January nature wears her green uniform, studded with floral jewels. As spring advances the blossoms increase in variety and profusion, until their yellow carpeting shows on the hills at the distance of five miles. With the drought of June comes the winter of vegetation.

I have something more to say in regard to the course of the winds and clouds during rain, and on the subject of mists and dews.

No. 5.—RAIN, STORMS, CLOUDS, AND MISTS.

In my last article I inquired whether moderate rains, such as have fallen at San Francisco, would be adequate to the production of the floods of last March; and I stated that a single inch of rain, poured into the river from a surface of 1,000 square miles, and forming a current of four miles an hour, would raise the river at Sacramento to eight feet, and keep it at that height 24 hours. When we consider that the Sacramento really drains something like 15,000 square miles, before reaching the city, we find no difficulty in accounting for the freshets without supposing an extraordinary fall of water. In the five days from the 5th to the 9th of March, there fell five inches of water at San Francisco. Suppose the same quantity throughout the State, and four fifths of it to sink into the earth, the remaining fifth, equal to one inch, running off, and requiring an entire week in the drainage. With a channel at Sacramento 200 yards wide, and a current of four miles an hour, the river would be raised *seventeen feet*, and kept at that height a whole week! With these data in mind, there is no difficulty in comprehending the great effects of even moderate rains in producing freshets, especially when the melting snows add to the supply.

The table contained in my last article shows that the number of days entirely or nearly clear, from sunrise to sunset, in the year 1851, was 134. This is not very different from the Atlantic States. At Philadelphia the number varies from 100 to 140, with an average of 125.

Owing to the many days that are partly clear, the number entirely clear does not present a criterion of the proportion of clear weather. By taking also into consideration the days that were clear in part, we find, as the table exhibits, the proportion of clear weather to cloudy, in the year, to be 262 to 103. The ratio at Philadelphia is about 220 to 145. The sky is therefore less clouded at San Francisco than on the Atlantic border.

I have already noticed the inconstant character of the clouds, the sky being seldom completely clouded for 12 hours, even in the rainiest period. The number of days in the year entirely cloudy, from the rising to the setting of the sun, was 18. At Philadelphia 50 is a very low number, and there are often 75. Seldom does any month of the year elapse in the Atlantic States without one or more days perfectly cloudy. At San Francisco there were but three such days in the six months from May to October. On most of the 18 days set down as entirely cloudy, the clouds were at times sufficiently broken to render the sun visible. It is an extraordinary circumstance for the sun to make his day's journey without showing his face.

The chilling mists of summer, conspiring with the wind and dust, leave on one's mind impressions not the most agreeable or evanescent;

but, after all, the weather is not so misty as might be supposed. By referring to the table given in my last paper, the misty weather appears to have been distributed as follows, in the four seasons of the year:

Winter...........	13	mornings,	5	afternoons,	7	evenings.
Spring...........	9	do.	3	do.	4	do.
Summer...........	1	do.	11	do.	34	do.
Autumn...........	6	do.	4	do.	9	do.

It should be noticed that the mornings were seldom misty for more than an hour or two after sunrise, and the afternoons not often misty throughout. The mist generally comes in detached clouds, driven by the wind, and sometimes in a universal stratum. Nearly always it gravitates sensibly towards the earth, in the form of a very fine rain, occasionally wetting the surface.

In the entire year there was mist on 27 mornings, 21 afternoons, and 45 evenings. At Philadelphia the average is about 20 mornings, 5 afternoons, and 10 evenings.

The tendency to the production of mist reaches its height in July. There were 19 foggy evenings in that month. The winter months, however, were most productive of mist *in the morning*. In the summer months there was but one foggy morning.

I now come to speak of the direction of the wind and clouds during the rains. In the sixteen months ending with March, 1852, and consequently embracing the greater part of two rainy seasons, there were 79 days on which rain fell, with the wind as follows:

East 0, northeast 2, north 2, northwest 6, west 8, southwest 17, south 20, southeast 24.

Or, the classification may stand thus:

East and northeast....................................	2
North and northwest....................................	8
West and southwest....................................	25
South and southeast....................................	44

Thus, from east and northeast, emphatically the rainy quarter in the Atlantic States, there was scarcely any rain. More than half the rains came from south and southeast. The rainiest point is in a direct line with the southern coast, or about south-southeast.

The easterly storms, which form so prominent a feature of the Atlantic climate, are unknown here. There is nothing that bears a resemblance to them. The rains from southeast are often attended by high gales, which extend over a large portion of the western coast of North America, and inflict some injury on shipping. But these gales are less violent than the most severe easterly storms of the Atlantic coast.

The direction of the cloud producing the rain is often of greater importance than that of the lower atmospheric current. There are mostly two strata of clouds, the lower concurring with the wind on the earth's surface, and seldom supplying rain, and the higher, which is the true rain-cloud, varying in its course from the lower, and sometimes having the very opposite direction.

In the 67 rains which furnished an opportunity of observing the upper cloud, its course was as follows:

Northeast	1
North and northwest	7
West	16
Southwest	23
South	14
Southeast	6

These results concur with observations made in the Atlantic States, showing that the higher strata of atmosphere which sweep northward from the equatorial region, saturated with aqueous vapor, are the principal source of rain in the temperate latitudes.

In the following table is recorded the number of days in each month on which clouds were observed in the lower and higher strata of atmosphere, the first column referring to the lower clouds, and the second to the higher. In the other columns is noted the direction of the higher clouds, as far as observed. The direction of the lower clouds, which mostly move with the wind near the earth's surface, is omitted.

Months.	Low.	High.	N.	N. E.	E.	S. E.	S.	S. W.	W.	N. W.
1850.										
December	17	23	......	......	......	4	4	......	2	......
1851.										
January	15	29	......	......	......	......	3	8	10	......
February	19	21	......	......	......	......	3	1	1	7
March	24	28	......	......	......	......	4	8	8	3
April	24	22	1	2	......	2	......	15	1	1
May	26	24	......	1	2	......	3	8	......	2
June	26	15	......	......	2	3	......	3	1	2
July	28	8	......	......	......	1	1	4	......	1
August	28	17	......	......	......	......	2	14	......	......
September	29	14	......	......	......	......	1	8	4	......
October	20	24	......	......	......	......	7	6	3	5
November	20	27	4	......	1	1	3	2	4	7
December	19	31	......	2	......	5	5	7	4	7
1852.										
January	22	29	3	1	......	4	1	7	7	1
February	21	27	2	4	1	1	4	......	10	3
March	28	26	......	1	......	......	4	11	4	2
Total	......	......	10	11	6	21	44	112	49	41

The higher cloud was, in the majority of cases, a light cirrhus, often very partial, or seen only in the horizon, and composed probably of congealed vapor, at an elevation of two or three miles. In other cases it was a cũro-cumulus, or a nimboid-cumulus. In almost every month of the year, even during the dry season, the clouds put on the appearance of rain and then vanish. It is evident that the phenomena which produce rains in other climates are present in this, but not quite in sufficient degree to accomplish the result, except during the rainy season, and then only by paroxysms, with intervening periods of drought.

The table shows the presence of an upper cloud on 260 days of the year 1851, and a lower cloud on 278 days. The lower cloud was deficient most frequently in the rainy season, but present almost daily in the dry season. The upper cloud was most wanting in the dry season, especially in July.

The higher currents of the atmosphere, as indicated by the clouds, pursue the same general course as in the Atlantic States. They show the prevalence of an almost constant stream from the tropical regions, traceable to the action of the sun, which beats and rarefies the air within the tropics, and causes it to ascend and pour over towards the poles. Starting northward, the current comes over portions of the earth having a slower rotary motion, and is thus deflected from a due north course, becoming a southwesterly instead of a south current.

No. 6.—REVIEW OF THE WEATHER FOR THE YEAR 1853.

The first part of January was cloudy and rainy, but after the 11th the weather was mostly clear and charming, only one rain occurring in the last two weeks. The lowest temperature was 41, and the highest 62. The mean at sunrise was 47½ and at noon 56½. The prevailing winds were very light from north and northwest. There were nine days entirely clear and four days entirely cloudy. January, 1852, was colder, having five mornings below 41; January, 1851, was much colder, having thirteen mornings below that point. Both these months were dry, scarcely any rain falling. But the first two weeks of January, 1852, were rainy; the remainder of the month dry. Sacramento city was drowned on the first of the month. In January, 1851, there was three-quarters inch of rain; 1852, half inch; and 1853, four inches.

February, for the first three weeks, the weather was superb. Up to the 21st there were no less than seventeen days entirely clear. In the last week there were four rainy days, but in the whole month only one day was entirely cloudy. The temperature was delightful, the means at sunrise and noon being 48 and 60. The coldest morning 42, and the warmest noon 67. The prevailing winds were from north, northwest and west, and most light. The hills were covered with flowers. In February, 1852, there were four mornings colder than in this month, and in 1851, thirteen colder mornings. February appears to be always a dry month. In 1851 there was one-third inch of rain; in 1852, half inch; in 1853, one inch.

March was mostly a pleasant month, with several moderate rains towards the middle, and three days of heavy rain in the last week. The prevailing winds were from west, northwest, and north, with an increasing tendency to west, and increasing force. The minimum temperature was 41, and the maximum 77; mean at sunrise 49½, and at noon 62. The first week of the month was very warm. On the 15th, Mount Diablo was covered with snow, as mostly happens towards the end of March. There is commonly considerable rain in this month. In the dry winter of 1851 there was two inches; in 1852, six and a half inches; in 1853, five inches.

April was a pleasant month, with winds generally from west and northwest, and frequent light sea breezes. Temperature agreeable, varying from 46 to 56 at sunrise, and from 59 to 75 at noon; means at sunrise and noon 52 and 65. The heaviest rain for several years fell on the night of the 16th, viz: upwards of three inches in twelve hours. The only thunder of the season occurred during this rain. April mostly gives us some days of rainy weather. In 1851 an inch of rain fell; in 1852, only quarter of an inch; in 1853, five inches. The coldest morning was 46. In 1851 there were five colder mornings, and in 1852 eighteen. Dry and cold weather go together in our winters.

May was generally warm and pleasant; the coldest morning being 47 and the warmest 62, while the coldest noon was 61 and the warmest 81. The means at sunrise and noon were 53½ and 68. The wind settled in the western quarter, and increased in force, though not offensively high. There were several slight rains, with a large portion of cloudy and broken weather. The clouds always give their parting blessing in May. In 1851, there fell three fourths inch of rain; in 1852, one third inch; and in 1853, one third inch.

June was uncommonly warm; the mercury ranging from 49 to 60 at sunrise, and from 60 to 84 at noon. The sea winds were constant, but not often fraught with mist. The sky was unusually clear for summer.

The weather of July was uniform; varying in temperature at sunrise from 50 to 55, and at noon from 63 to 78. The means at sunrise and noon were 52½ and 68. Cloudy and misty weather prevailed, and there were but four days of clear sky from sunrise to sunset.

August was a cloudy and misty month; but less so than July. Its temperature also was very uniform, ranging at sunrise from 51 to 56 and at noon from 63 to 76. The means at sunrise and noon were 53 and 67. The sea winds, though constant, were not often high.

In the three summer months of 1851, there were four misty mornings and 33 misty evenings; in 1852, 7 mornings and 27 evenings; and in 1853, 15 mornings and 36 evenings misty.

September was rather pleasant, affording one or two days really hot. The morning extremes were 50 and 60, and the noon extremes 63 and 88. The sea winds continued their daily visits with diminished force; and there was much cloudy and broken weather, with two small rains near the middle of the month. The means at sunrise and noon were 55 and 70. September usually brings a day or two of light rain. One inch fell in 1851, a few drops only in 1852, and the eighth of an inch in 1853.

October was, as usual, warmer than several of the previous months. The coldest morning was 49 and the warmest 64; the coldest noon 60 and the warmest 85. The means at sunrise and noon were 54½ and 71. During this month the sea winds began to give out. The sky was generally fair; and one slight rain fell, amounting to 1-10 inch. In October, 1851, there was 2-10th inch; and in 1852, three fourths inch.

November placed the usual embargo on the sea winds. The temperature was moderate—a few slight frosts occurring. The coldest morning was 44 and the warmest 59; the coldest noon 55 and the warmest 73. The means at sunrise and noon were 51 and 63. There was much cloudy weather, with occasional moderate rains. The prevailing winds were from west and south. The first southeasterly storm, in '51, was on the 8th; in '52, on the 13th; and in '53, on the 16th. Quantity of rain in the three years, respectively, 2 inches, 5½ inches, and 1½ inches.

December was more pleasant than common. The coldest morning was 40 and the warmest 54; the coldest noon 50 and the warmest 69. The means at sunrise and noon were 46½ and 57½. Hoar frosts were frequent; but the cold was not sufficient to injure vegetation. A copious rain fell on the 10th, and several light rains at other times. Prevailing winds from north, northwest, northeast, and south. Thunder was heard on the 10th, for the second time in the year. In December '50, there fell 1 inch of rain; '51, 7 inches; '52, 12 inches—the greatest quantity in any one month for three years and more; in '53, 2 inches.

The summing up for the year 1853 exhibits a mean temperature of 51⅓ at sunrise, and 65 at noon, which is warmer by two degrees than either 1851 or 1852. The lowest point reached by the mercury was 40—or eight degrees above the freezing point. The extreme of heat was 88. In 1852, the extremes were 35 and 98; in 1851, 30 and 84; and in December, 1850, the thermometer fell as low as 28. The amount of rain in each month of 1853 was, in round numbers, as follows: January, on eight days, 4 inches; February, four days, 1 inch; March, six days, 5 inches; April, eight days, 5 inches; May, three days, ⅓ inch; June, July, and August, none; September, two days, ⅛ inch; October, one day, 1-10 inch; November, eight days, 1½ inches; December, six days, 2 inches; making, in the year, forty-four days on which rain fell, to the depth of 19 inches. In 1851, there was rain on fifty-three days—quantity, 15 inches; in 1852, on sixty days—quantity, 25½ inches. From the first of January, 1853, to the dry season, the quantity was 16½ inches; and from the dry season to the end of the year, 3½ inches. The last rain of the spring was May 24th, and the first of the autumn was September 15th. The hills began to look green in the last week of November, and at the close of the year at least thirty species of plants were in bloom around the city, some of them the lingering flowers of summer, and a few the products of a new growth. There were two small specimens of thunder during the year, none of the aurora borealis, and a considerable sprinkling of meteors in the second week of August, and also in the fourth week of November.

No. 7.—THE WEATHER OF FEBRUARY, 1854.

The subjoined figures will enable the reader to compare this month with the corresponding months of 1851, 1852, and 1853:

	1851.	1852.	1853.	1854.
Mean temperature at sunrise	41.97	45.69	48.18	47.93
Mean temperature at noon	60.03	60.41	60.07	59.21
Mean temperature at 10 o'clock p. m.	43.64	49.59	51.00	49.07
Monthly temperature	51.00	53.05	54.13	53.57
Maximum	71.00	65.00	67.00	69.00
Minimum	33.00	40.00	42.00	38.00
Range	38.00	25.00	25.00	31.00
Clear, (proportion,)	23 days.	21 days.	22 days.	15 days.
Cloudy, (proportion,)	5 days.	8 days.	6 days.	13 days.
Whole days clear	14 days.	5 days.	17 days.	5 days.
Rain on	4 days.	4 days.	4 days.	13 days.
Quantity	0.35 inch.	0.12 inch.	1.16 inch.	8.41 inch.
North and northwest winds	9 days.	6 days.	10 days.	8 days.
Northeast and east winds	2 days.	3 days.	1 day.	2 days.
South and southeast winds	5 days.	4 days.	8 days,	8 days.
Southwest and west winds	12 days.	16 days.	9 days.	10 days.
High winds	0 days.	0 days.	0 days.	1 day.

The temperature of the month was about the medium standard. At sunrise it was not nearly so cold as 1851, but at noon it was rather below either of the other years, owing to the large number of cloudy and rainy days, which are apt to be cool at noon. On three or four mornings there were slight frosts. In the middle of the month, and again on the 28th, the coast mountains were seen covered with snow, as they mostly are when the rains at this point are accompanied with a temperature below 50. The most extraordinary feature of the month was the quantity of rain. February is usually a dry month, but this year it was the exact reverse. In February, 1851, the quantity was 0.35 inches; February, 1852, 0.12 inches; February, 1853, 1.16 inches; making in three months an aggregate of 1.63 inches, or less than one-fifth of the supply for the month just past. In the three years just mentioned, the greatest monthly supplies of rain were as follows: December, 1851, 7.07 inches; March, 1852, 6.40 inches; November, 1852, 5.31 inches; December, 1852, 11.90 inches; April, 1853, 5.05 inches. Thus it appears that February of the present year exceeded any other month in that period, except December, 1852.

Up to the first of March, the quantity of rain since the dry season was 16.26 inches. At the same date in 1851, the quantity was 3.40 inches; in 1852, 11.11 inches; and in 1853, 23.28 inches. The rains of this winter, therefore, though much greater than those of 1851 and 1852, have been but little over two-thirds of last winter's supply at this date. Subsequent to this date in 1851, and before the dry season, rain fell on twenty days, quantity 3.71 inches; in 1852, on eighteen days, 6.89 inches; in 1853, on seventeen days, 10.18 inches. From these data we may infer that our rains are by no means at an end.

Owing to the cold and wet weather, vegetation is very backward, having scarcely moved since the first of January. On the 15th of February, 1852, I found sixteen species of plants in bloom on the hills west of the city; and on the 22d I gathered forty-three species on a walk to the fort at the entrance of the bay. Last year, also, the country was covered with flowers in February. But this spring scarcely a flower has made its appearance. The spring of 1851 was equally backward, on account both of cold and of drought.

No. 8.—THE CLIMATE OF SAN FRANCISCO FOR THE YEAR 1854.

The year began with very fine weather. On the fifth was a severe norther, which damaged the shipping in the harbor. A few cold mornings followed, and on the 12th the rains set in. From that date to the 24th, rain fell on nine days to the depth of four and a quarter inches. The rains were cold and several times accompanied with hail, and snow covered the distant mountains. The coldest weather on my record was at this time. On the 19th, 20th, and 21st, the thermometer stood at 31, 25, and 31. At noon on the 20th it rose no higher than 37. The mud was frozen solid so as to bear the heaviest wagons. Of course, the oldest inhabitant had never seen the like. In December, 1850, it was nearly as cold, the mercury then falling to 27. The month wound up with a few very warm days. The mean temperature at sunrise was 42.26, at 9 A. M. 45.71, at noon 54.23, at 10 P. M. 45.26, being the coldest month on my book; that is, since the winter of 1849–'50. The greatest heat was 69, and the extreme of cold 25. The prevailing winds were north, northeast, and northwest.

It should be mentioned, as a rare phenomenon, that hail fell on the morning of the 15th so as to cover the ground and to lay for an hour. In the winter of 1849–'50 the ground was covered with hail or snow in like manner.

February was rather warm. The mean at sunrise was 47.93, at 9 A. M. 50.86, at noon 59.21, and at 10 P. M. 49.07. The extreme of heat was 69, of cold 38. Rain fell on no less than thirteen days, and in the quantity of 8.41 inches—the greatest quantity in any month on my record, excepting December, 1852, when there was nearly twelve inches. This is the more remarkable as February is usually a dry month. On the 12th, hail fell in a heavy shower so copiously that it could be gathered by the bucketfull where it collected from the roofs. The prevailing winds were from west, south, northwest, and north, in the order named as to frequency. Our high wind occurred from south-southeast.

March was of moderate temperature. The mean at sunrise was 47.23, at 9 A. M. 52.06, at noon 60.97, at 10 P. M. 49.45. The extreme of heat was 72, of cold 38. Rain fell on ten days 3.17 inches—a moderate supply for March. Most of the rain was during a cold storm on the 13th, 14th, and 15th, the wind blowing moderately part of the time from northeast, which is a rare direction for a rain wind. The westerly winds increased in frequency, as usual in this month. Those from south, northwest, and north, divided among them one half the month. There were no high winds.

The warmest April on my book was that of 1854. The mean at sunrise was 51.10, 9 A. M. 59.83, noon 68.43, 10 P. M. 52.90. The extreme heat was 83, of cold 45. Rain on 6 days, 3.31 inches, nearly two inches of which fell on the 28th,—the last rain of the season. The sea breeze came nearly every day, though with moderate force. On 10 days the winds were from other quarters than west. During this month the hills and fields assumed the gorgeous array of flowers which marks a California landscape in the spring.

May was a very unpleasant month, cold and windy, often cloudy and threatening rain. On one day only was there rain, and then but two-hundredths of an inch, in the form of mist. The mean temperature at sunrise was 48.95, at 9 A. M. 59.00, at noon 64.61, at 10 P. M. 50.68—being three degrees below April. The mercury rose no higher than 73, and the lowest extreme was 43. There were light frosts on several mornings, and vegetation advanced tardily. Potatoes of the season's growth appeared in the market on the Ist. A hail storm occurred at Sacramento on the 6th. The winds were westerly on 25 days. On 8 days they were high.

June, also, was a cold month, rather below April in temperature. Mean at sunrise 50.10, 9 A. M. 61.83, noon 66.80, 10 P. M. 51.50. The warmest day was 74, and the coldest morning 47. There was an unusual tendency to rain, and several times a few large drops deigned to violate the law of the season. On the 17th it rained moderately for two hours, four-tenths of an inch collecting in the guage. On the 13th was a heavy storm of rain and hail in Utah. On 23 days the wind was west, and on four northwest. It was high on eight days.

July was rather above the average temperature. The means were, at sunrise 51.87, 9 A. M. 63.94, noon 70.65, 10 P. M. 54.16. In the three years preceding, the mercury had not reached 80 in July, but in this year it was at or above 80 on four days, and on one day as high as 87, which is near the extreme heat of our climate. The lowest extreme was 46. The first week was beautifully clear, but afterwards there was scarcely a morning or evening without cloud and mist. The wind was constantly west, and on six days it was high.

August was a trifle below the average temperature. Mean at sunrise 52.42, 9 A. M. 62.39, noon 68.29, 10 P. M. 53.81. There were two days above 80, the highest being 85. The minimum temperature was 50. Almost every afternoon was windy, and though the wind was high on one day only, yet the weather was about as unpleasant as our summer climate can afford. The mornings were generally cloudy and the evenings misty. A light shower of rain fell on the 27th. At Los Angeles and San Diego it rained heavily on the 20th and 21st, and on the Trinity river there was a thunder storm on the 26th, with heavy rain and snow on the mountain peaks.

September, commonly the warmest month in the year, was nearly as cold as August. Mean at sunrise 53.30, 9 A. M. 61.43, noon 67.73, 10 P. M. 54.40. There were two warm days, on one of which the mercury rose to 87. The greatest depression was 46. Cloudy mornings and misty evenings prevailed, and the sea breeze blew with great constancy and with more force than usual in September. This month seldom passes without rain, but on the present occasion the only rain was a trifling shower on the 15th. There was a heavy rain at Los Angeles about the same time.

The weather of October was generally agreeable. Mean temperature at sunrise, 53.32; 9 A. M., 60.97; noon, 68.13; 10 P. M., 55.42. There were three days above 80, the warmest being 83. The minimum temperature was 46. It was the warmest month of the year, except July. The winds were light, and distributed to west, northwest, north, and south, the first predominating. The most extraordinary feature of the month was its frequent rains. Rain fell on no less than 10 days; quantity 2.12 inches. The first rain was on the 4th. At Marysville the ground was covered with hail on the 23d. At the close of the month the hills around the city began to look green, and the wise men predicted a very rainy winter.

The climate of November was very fine. Mean at sunrise, 50.67; 9 A. M., 55.97; noon, 65.13; 10 P. M., 53.00. The extremes were 72 and 47. The mornings ranged from 47 to 55, and the noondays from 58 to 72. The winds were from west, northwest, and north, and gentle as zephyrs. The sky was almost uninterruptedly clear. A single rain fell, amounting to four tenths of an inch; and the wise men reversed their prediction and promised a very dry winter instead of a wet one.

December furnished a continuation of the fine weather of November, with a decline of temperature corresponding to the season. Mean at sunrise, 47.03; 9 A. M., 51.32; noon, 60.65; 10 P. M., 49.39. There were a number of slight frosts, and ice formed in favorable situations, though the minimum temperature was 38. The warmest day was 71. The most gentle breezes prevailed from north, northeast, and northwest. There were 15 days entirely clear. A trifling rain, .08 inches, fell on the 3d, and no more until the 31st, when a rain storm set in, which was quickly handed over to the new year, leaving three tenths of an inch to December.

The mean temperature of the whole year sums up as follows: Sunrise, 49.68; 9 A. M., 57.11; noon, 64.57; 10 P. M., 51.76. The mean of the sunrise and noon observations gives the figure for the year, 57.13. The temperature for 1851, deduced in the same way, was 56.57; 1852, 56.53; and 1853, 58.51. The year 1853 appears to have been unusually warm. Taking 1854 as a fair representation of the climate of San Francisco, it follows that our climate is two or three degrees warmer than that of the corresponding latitude on the Atlantic coast, though it does not exhibit the extremes either of heat or cold incident to the latter.

The extreme of heat in 1854 was 87. There were only twelve days in the year at or above 80, of which one was in April, four in July, two in August, two in September, and three in October. In 1851 there were nine days at or above 80; in 1852, thirteen; and in 1853, eleven.

The extreme of cold was 25. There were three days in the year when the mercury fell to the freezing point, all in January. In 1851, the thermometer fell to the freezing point on one day only; in 1852, 35 was the lowest depression; and in 1853, it did not sink below 40.

The warmest month in the year was July, then October, then September, then August, then April, and June stands the sixth in order, and only two degrees above November. In neither of the three years preceding was July the warmest month. In 1851 the warmest months occurred in the following order: August, October, September, June, July, April. In 1852: September, July, August, June, October, November. In 1853: October, September, June, May, July, August. To the daily visitations of the cold ocean wind in the summer is owing this great variation from the order of the months as to comparative temperature in other climates.

January was the coldest month, then February, then December, and next March. In other years, December sometimes takes the precedence of January. February, which in the Atlantic States is often the coldest month in the year, is not so here.

Rain fell on 54 days in the year, 22.12 inches in depth. This is our average supply, though only half the quantity that falls in the Atlantic States. In 1853, the quantity was 19.03 inches; in 1852, 25.60 inches; and in 1851, only 15.12 inches. The old inhabitants tell of occasional seasons when scarcely any rain has fallen, and when the cattle have perished from want. Such very dry seasons are said to recur at intervals of eight or ten years.

The greatest amount of rain was in February, next comes January, next April, then March. This differs from the ordinary arrangement. Taking the last four years into view, December gives the most rain, and March comes next, while the intervening months are comparatively dry. In fact, we have the early rains, beginning in November and continuing through December into the early part of January; and the later rains, beginning in March, and continuing at times through April.

Lightning is seen at San Francisco on an average three or four times a year, and thunder is heard less frequently. On the 15th January, flashes of lightning were observed in the evening, during a cold rain storm from the south; and on the 22d February, under similar circumstances, lightning was again noticed. But no thunder was audible in either case; nor was there any further exhibition of atmospheric electricity during the year. There was thunder three times in 1851, five times in 1852, and twice in 1853.

No exhibition of auroral light was observed in the year. Since my residence here, from August, 1850, I have seen the aurora borealis only on two occasions, once in January and once in February, in the year 1852.

There was no unusual display of shooting stars during the year. In September, 1851, in August, 1852, and in August, 1853, they were numerous for several nights in succession.

Earthquake shocks were distinctly felt on the mornings of the 9th of January and 21st of October.

Abstract of Meteorological Observations for Sacramento, California, latitude 38° 34′ 42″ *north, longitude* 121° 40′ 5″ *west; elevation above the level of the sea* 30 *feet; for the year ending March* 31, 1854. *By Thomas M. Logan, M. D.*

1853–'54.	April.	May.	June.	July.	Aug.	Sept.	Oct.	Nov.	Dec.	Jan.	Feb.	March.	Mean.
Barometer.													
Maximum	30.38	30.28	30.20	30.20	30.05	30.10	30.40	30.45	30.45	30.45	30.40	30.40	30.45
Minimum	29.88	29.88	28.88	29.95	29.85	29.90	29.90	29.30	29.70	29.70	29.70	29.85	28.88
Mean	30.13	30.09	29.79	30.06	30.30	29.85	30.15	30.05	30.13	29.11	30.17	29.05	29.97
Thermometer.													
Maximum	76	78	97	93	93	95	88	72	64	59	62	68	97
Minimum	50	54	58	62	58	54	58	46	32	19	38	37	19
Mean	61	68	77	75	71	76	73	53	48	43	51	53	62
													Total.
Clear days	16	19	27	25	22	28	26	13	21	19	10	13	239
Cloudy days	7	6	2	2	8	1	4	10	6	5	5	9	66
Rainy days	7	6	1	4	..	1	1	6	4	7	13	9	59
Days of Wind.													
North wind	3	2	3	..	..	..	1	..	2	4	3	4	22
Northwest wind	8	7	13	4	1	9	23	13	16	16	10	8	128
West wind	1	..	..	..	..	..	1	..	1	1	1	2	7
Southwest wind	7	10	7	2	3	5	3	4	2	1	1	5	50
South wind	3	4	4	1	2	4	1	5	1	3	1	8	37
Southeast wind	7	7	3	24	25	9	2	5	2	5	6	1	96
East wind	1	1	..	..	..	1	..	3	2	..	4	1	11
Northeast wind	..	..	..	..	..	2	..	..	4	1	4	2	13

REMARKS.—By clear days is meant that no clouds were visible at the times of observation; by cloudy, that some were visible; and by rainy days, that some rain fell then, without reference to quantity. Not being provided in time with a suitable pluviometer, the quantity of rain cannot be put down in figures. The greatest amount that fell at any one period was on the 22d February, after raining forty-eight hours without intermission. The last rain of the past season occurred on the 20th May, 1853. There was a slight sprinkle afterwards on the 26th June, and on the 17th and 21st July. The first rains of the present season occurred on the 15th September and 10th October. The regular rainy season, however, did not set in until the 14th November. About the middle of January the coast-range of mountains presented the novel appearance of being covered with snow. The degree of cold during this month was unprecedented. Not having a thermometrograph, the minimum, which generally occurs shortly before sunrise, may not have been obtained. Sutter lake was frozen over on the 6th and on the 21st of January, and remained so all the day of the 22d. This degree of cold is one of those extraordinary occurrences which is sometimes experienced in the most equable and genial climates. Thus, for instance, in 1507 the harbor of Marseilles was frozen over its whole extent; for which a cold of at least 0.4° was requisite. Again, in 1709, the Gulf of Venice, and harbors of Marseilles, Genoa, and Cette, were frozen over. Such irregular occurrences are caused by the long prevalence of particular winds, and should not be taken into computation in making an estimate of the mean annual temperature of any place. Notwithstanding, however, even the past extraordinary winter, we find the mean annual temperature of Sacramento vieing with the land of the olive and the vine. An isothermal line drawn across our continent, from this point, would deviate as many degrees to the south as from the western to the eastern side of the old continent.

Meteorological table for Sacramento, California, for the year ending March 31, 1855. *By Thomas M. Logan, M. D.*

1854–'55.	April.	May.	June.	July.	August.	Sept'r.	October.	Nov.	Dec.	Jan.	Feb.	March.	Mean.
Barometer.	Inch.	Inch.	Inch.	Inch.	Inch.	Inch.	Inch.	Inch.	Inch.	Inch.	Inch.	Inch.	Inch.
Maximum	30.45	30.28	30.22	30.13	30.20	30.20	30.20	30.35	30.26	30.34	30.11	30.04	30.45
Minimum	29.85	29.	29.90	29.85	29.80	29.85	29.83	30.05	29.68	29.44	29.50	29.52	29.
Mean	30.04	30.02	30.03	30.08	30.05	30.04	30.13	30.21	29.69	29.95	29.78	29.72	29.98
Thermometer.	°	°	°	°	°	°	°	°	°	°	°	°	°
Maximum	78.	77.	90.	101.50	99.	90.	90.	72.	68.	62.	70.	76.	101.50
Minimum	49.	48.	49.	50.75	52.	48.	49.	44.	29.	27.	32.	41.	27.
Mean	60.	62.	67.	80.63	69.47	65.05	60.01	55.05	47.93	43.71	52.50	54.82	59.84
Dew Point.	°	°	°	°	°	°	°	°	°	°	°	°	°
Maximum	......	......	......	68.	62.50	55.	55.	49.50	49.	44.50	51.50	59.	68.
Minimum	......	......	......	45.50	43.	40.50	32.	34.	25.50	30.	18.	32.	18.
Mean	......	......	......	61.59	50.22	48.20	45.40	42.65	39.	38.08	41.37	45.13	34.30
Number of—													Total.
Clear days	9	23	20	27	25	26	12	20	19	8	16	10	215
Cloudy days	12	4	7	4	5	3	10	8	9	18	3	13	96
Rainy days	9	4	2	......	1	1	9	2	3	5	9	8	54*
Inches of rain	1.50	0.21	0.31	......	$0.0\frac{1}{2}$	sprinkle.	1.01	0.65	1.15	2.67	3.46	4.20	$15.16\frac{1}{2}$
Days of—													
North wind	1	1	$\frac{1}{3}$	$2\frac{2}{3}$	$\frac{2}{3}$	$1\frac{2}{3}$	$2\frac{1}{3}$	$6\frac{2}{3}$	3	$2\frac{1}{3}$	$4\frac{1}{3}$	2	28
Northwest wind	10	6	6	4	$2\frac{1}{3}$	2	$7\frac{2}{3}$	$12\frac{2}{3}$	$17\frac{2}{3}$	13	10	$10\frac{2}{3}$	102
West wind	1	1	$\frac{1}{3}$	$11\frac{1}{3}$	1	$3\frac{1}{3}$	$\frac{2}{3}$	$1\frac{1}{3}$	$\frac{1}{3}$	$\frac{2}{3}$	......	1	22
Southwest wind	8	$8\frac{1}{3}$	$7\frac{2}{3}$	$7\frac{2}{3}$	8	$10\frac{1}{3}$	8	$3\frac{1}{3}$	......	3	5	5	$74\frac{1}{3}$
South wind	5	$8\frac{2}{3}$	10	5	8	5	$3\frac{1}{3}$	......	1	$1\frac{2}{3}$	2	$3\frac{2}{3}$	$53\frac{1}{3}$
Southeast wind	3	$3\frac{2}{3}$	$3\frac{2}{3}$	......	$10\frac{2}{3}$	7	$7\frac{2}{3}$	$2\frac{1}{3}$	$4\frac{1}{3}$	$6\frac{1}{3}$	6	8	$62\frac{2}{3}$
East wind	$\frac{1}{3}$	$1\frac{1}{3}$	1	......	$\frac{1}{3}$	$\frac{2}{3}$	$\frac{1}{3}$	1	3	$1\frac{1}{3}$	$\frac{1}{3}$	$\frac{1}{3}$	10
Northeast wind	$1\frac{2}{3}$	1	1	$\frac{1}{3}$	......	......	1	$2\frac{2}{3}$	$1\frac{2}{3}$	$2\frac{2}{3}$	$\frac{1}{3}$	$\frac{1}{3}$	$10\frac{2}{3}$

REMARKS.—By clear days is meant that no clouds were visible at the times of observation; by cloudy, that some were visible; and by rainy days, that some rain fell, without reference to quantity. The heaviest rain of the year commenced falling at noon, on the 27th February, and continued without intermission until 10, P. M., of the 28th, measuring 2.10 inches. The last rain of the past season occurred on the 17th June, 1854, and amounted to 0.20 inches. The first rain of the present season was on the 4th October, when 0.14 inches fell. Thus far the present has been a comparatively dry season. The Sacramento river remained at a very low stage until 15th March, when it rose 20 feet 2½ inches above low-water mark; since which time it has been gradually falling. The 13th July was the hottest day experienced during the year, and, indeed, since the settlement of the country. The thermometer was observed, in some less favored situations than ours, at 107°, at the hottest time of the day. The mean temperature of the hottest part of the day for the week ending July 15th was 97°. The night of the 16th August was the hottest as yet noticed in the country; the thermometer standing at 82° at 10 o'clock, P. M., and 70° at sunrise. The weather during the whole winter was mild, dry, and pleasant; and the spring opened early. On the 1st February, the cowslip was observed in profuse blossom on the surrounding plains; on the 15th, the wild violet; on the 20th, the peach tree; and on the 23d, the willow (*salix nigra*) and the nemophila, a small indigenous blue flower.

Meteorological Observations at Sacramento, California, lat. 38° 34′ 42″ *north, long.* 121° 40′ 05″.

BY F. W. HATCH, M. D.

The observations with the thermometer and barometer, and record of the winds, embrace a period of ten months, from June, 1854; and those of the psychrometer, the period embraced between August, 1854, and March, 1855, inclusive. The means of the thermometer are calculated from four daily observations, viz: at sunrise, (for which the minimum is used, at noon,) at sunset, and 10 P. M.; those of the barometer, from three daily readings, at sunrise, noon, and 10 P. M; and the same number for the psychrometer, but at different hours, viz: at or near sunrise, 3 P. M., and 10 P. M. The course of the wind is given four times daily, corresponding with the observations of the thermometer, and will serve to show the influence of the wind, both upon the elevation of the barometer and the humidity of the atmosphere. A long and patient examination and system of comparison, upon this subject, has convinced me of the almost perfect uniformity of a high barometer and a northerly wind, (north or northwest,) and the reverse condition with a south or southeast wind. There are some exceptions to this rule, and in our northwest gales the barometer often falls low; but what I have stated is the *ordinary* course under *ordinary* conditions. The source of these winds in the mountains of Oregon, and of the others (south, southeast, and southwest) from the Pacific, will, moreover, account for their respective influence upon the humidity of the atmosphere.

Not less evident is the relation of the winds to temperature, especially in the summer months. It is common, at this season, for the wind, after sunrise, to change to a northerly direction, and to continue in this quarter for a greater or less length of time, varying from a few hours to a period of the day as late as 3 or 4 P. M. In their passage over the burning plains of the interior, and by contact with the heated air, they have acquired, before they reach here, an elevated temperature, and are dry and occasionally hot. This state of things is, however, mostly succeeded by a delightful breeze from the ocean in the afternoon, when both the temperature and the humidity of the atmosphere undergo a rapid transition. These facts would be more clearly denoted by an examination of the daily record, and especially by a separate observation in the forenoon, than by the *means* which I send, inasmuch as the northerly wind of the morning is frequently unnoticed in my *regular tables*, from the fact of its prevalence only between the hours of sunrise and noon. The above is a correct view of the ordinary course of the wind in the summer season. In the winter, on the contrary, the north wind prevails more, and comes to us in all its original freshness and coolness.

TABLE No. 1.—*Of daily and monthly means of the Barometer at Sacramento, Cal., from four daily observations from June,* 1854, *to March,* 1855, *inclusive.*

Days.	1854, June.	July.	August.	September.	October.	November.	December.	1855, Jan'ry.	February.	March.
	Inches.	Inches.	Inches.	Inches.	Inches.	Inches.	Inches.	Inches.	Inches.	Inches.
1	30.026	29.850	30.023	29.880	30.036	30.123	30.086	29.553	29.903	30.156
2	30.080	29.960	30.036	29.840	30.036	30.160	29.936	29.963	30.020	30.110
3	30.050	29.953	29.940	29.866	29.880	30.263	29.986	29.916	30.206	30.146
4	29.980	29.870	29.973	29.910	29.790	30.223	30.080	29.683	30.236	30.080
5	29.940	29.833	30.003	29.866	29.880	30.130	30.156	30.010	30.076	30.040
6	29.973	29.830	29.993	29.860	30.016	30.036	30.22	30.283	29.943	29.956
7	30.130	29.875	30.026	29.910	29.973	29.983	30.203	30.260	30.070	30.066
8	30.006	30.003	29.893	30.033	29.830	30.003	30.156	30.240	30.160	30.060
9	29.943	30.060	29.883	29.983	29.866	30.036	30.216	30.273	30.250	29.983
10	29.923	30.046	30.033	29.930	29.920	30.106	30.41	30.273	30.093	29.923
11	29.913	30.036	30.046	29.923	29.966	30.090	30.406	30.110	30.216	29.916
12	29.933	29.963	29.976	29.940	29.930	30.073	30.29	30.076	30.203	29.770
13	29.873	29.873	29.960	29.980	30.090	30.056	30.276	30.246	30.150	29.733
14	29.863	29.856	29.990	29.966	30.083	30.146	30.206	30.230	30.183	29.840
15	29.883	29.846	30.006	30.040	29.983	30.113	30.123	30.156	30.216	30.020
16	29.936	29.833	29.926	30.026	29.950	30.053	30.05	30.116	30.203	30.163
17	29.973	29.903	29.833	29.986	29.926	30.020	30.06	30.130	30.290	30.130
18	29.950	30.003	29.753	29.956	30.013	29.943	30.236	30.103	30.176	30.130
19	29.916	30.003	29.816	29.983	30.003	30.046	30.233	30.126	29.770	30.133
20	29.926	29.993	29.820	29.946	30.086	30.083	30.17	30.226	29.690	30.130
21	29.946	29.996	29.823	29.940	30.110	30.013	30.126	30.253	29.826	30.083
22	29.993	30.010	29.956	30.010	30.016	30.056	30.106	30.210	29.880	30.100
23	29.986	29.976	29.980	30.083	29.860	30.133	30.163	30.153	29.883	30.100
24	29.976	29.933	29.933	29.970	29.840	30.150	30.12	30.080	30.010	30.090
25	29.983	29.916	29.896	29.873	30.040	30.150	30.096	30.016	30.056	30.013
26	29.973	29.943	29.953	29.923	30.006	30.103	30.14	30.053	29.993	29.896
27	29.980	29.966	30.086	29.886	30.116	30.130	30.313	29.953	29.963	29.856
28	30.043	29.960	30.026	29.820	30.150	30.056	30.276	29.910	29.843	29.940
29	29.963	29.890	29.950	29.783	30.193	29.956	30.10	29.756	......	29.986
30	29.683	29.876	29.970	29.880	30.196	30.000	29.99	29.903	......	29.906
31	......	29.983	29.920	......	30.226	......	29.833	29.966	......	29.720
Monthly means	29.946	29.926	29.949	29.944	30.003	30.075	30.157	30.072	30.054	30.006

Days.	1854, June.	July.	August.	September.	October.	November.	December.	1855, Jan'ry.	February.	March.
	°	°	°	°	°	°	°	°	°	°
1	58.87	69.12	64.33	66.50	74.62	51.00	57.75	49.00	53.62	58.75
2	61.75	68.75	67.87	65.00	76.00	56.75	56.50	41.50	55.12	58.25
3	65.62	74.00	72.75	61.12	76.50	57.00	52.62	43.50	56.00	58.75
4	68.12	78.50	65.87	63.75	69.00	57.62	54.00	43.50	55.25	58.00
5	59.50	78.12	65.25	65.12	65.50	59.75	51.00	34.50	55.25	56.125
6	56.25	74.62	68.62	63.00	65.50	60.50	48.75	34.25	53.75	59.75
7	62.00	78.00	70.00	63.12	65.50	55.50	46.25	40.25	56.50	61.25
8	67.00	78.50	78.50	63.50	66.50	52.75	47.00	43.50	54.87	59.00
9	74.25	77.25	74.75	62.25	62.87	56.37	44.25	44.87	56.00	57.125
10	78.25	78.00	69.75	62.25	63.50	53.62	44.87	45.00	51.75	51.50
11	71.50	77.75	76.50	60.00	64.75	55.62	44.75	44.50	50.25	51.50
12	62.87	81.12	74.25	60.25	61.25	57.62	45.37	42.50	51.75	50.875
13	67.75	86.37	72.00	61.37	57.50	54.50	46.00	41.50	54.50	53.25
14	70.87	83.87	72.00	60.75	58.00	54.37	47.50	39.75	56.50	49.375
15	68.37	78.75	77.00	60.87	60.00	55.00	47.37	38.25	58.00	46.75
16	68.87	72.00	85.00	66.25	62.25	56.87	46.25	39.50	57.00	45.50
17	62.87	69.50	84.50	72.00	61.00	57.37	49.62	39.75	54.00	49.75
18	66.25	64.75	72.75	75.25	59.00	57.00	49.12	43.37	54.37	57.25
19	71.00	65.75	71.75	78.75	58.75	58.50	46.12	46.37	48.00	58.25
20	69.87	64.25	74.62	68.50	66.50	55.75	45.75	41.75	45.25	55.75
21	64.25	67.37	73.00	67.50	65.75	55.75	45.62	42.50	45.50	58.25
22	62.50	71.75	64.00	68.50	65.00	59.87	51.87	44.62	46.87	60.75
23	66.12	78.00	69.37	71.25	61.75	60.75	51.37	45.50	47.25	64.00
24	65.25	83.00	68.12	72.50	56.25	60.75	53.50	50.75	47.00	64.125
25	66.75	76.00	64.37	68.75	58.25	60.25	54.50	53.25	51.50	63.00
26	66.50	75.75	65.50	69.37	58.00	60.87	49.25	52.00	53.87	62.00
27	69.56	76.00	62.75	71.25	56.25	59.50	44.50	51.57	54.25	57.50
28	67.75	75.50	69.00	68.62	58.50	58.50	43.25	50.75	57.00	56.25
29	67.00	75.25	64.75	66.75	58.50	51.50	42.00	51.25	.....	59.25
30	72.37	71.75	66.75	68.75	59.50	53.00	43.75	50.75	.....	57.75
31	.....	67.00	70.87	.....	57.75	.....	49.75	56.87	.....	55.50
Monthly means	66.86	75.70	70.33	65.26	62.56	56.78	48.42	44.74	52.82	56.62

Meteorological observations at Sacramento, California.

Date.	Thermometer—four daily observations.												Barometer.		
	Daily temperature.				Maximum extremes.				Minimum extremes.						
	Sunrise.	Noon.	Sunset.	10 P. M.	Sunrise.	Noon.	Sunset.	10 P. M.	Sunrise.	Noon.	Sunset.	10 P. M.	Snrise.	Noon.	10 P. M.
1854.	*														
June	54.04	76.03	72.05	65.33	66.00	87.00	84.00	78.00	46.00	67.00	62.00	50.00	29.96	29.95	29.93
July	61.25	88.74	80.17	74.88	73.00	97.50	92.00	83.00	51.50	72.00	67.00	61.00	29.90	29.95	29.92
August	55.90	81.90	76.25	67.25	69.00	96.00	95.00	84.00	49.50	72.00	68.00	58.00	29.95	29.95	29.93
September	51.38	76.33	70.63	62.70	61.00	86.00	87.00	72.00	47.00	68.00	64.00	55.00	29.93	29.97	29.92
October	51.32	71.03	68.25	59.67	62.00	88.00	86.00	75.00	46.00	62.00	60.00	52.00	30.00	30.00	30.00
November	44.21	65.25	63.13	54.53	52.00	70.00	69.00	61.00	39.50	58.00	57.00	46.00	30.09	30.06	30.07
[illegible]r.	37.25	55.12	53.90	47.41	52.00	66.00	54.00	57.00	28.00	50.00	50.00	36.00	30.16	30.16	30.13

* The minimum observation is used for the sunrise column.

Meteorological observations at Sacramento, California.

Date.	Attached thermometer.			Thermometrograph.			Extremes of month.				Hygrometer, 12 M.*					
											Dew point.			Moisture.		
	Sunrise.	Noon.	10 P. M.	Mean maximum.	Mean minimum.	Mean range.	Maximum.	Date.	Minimum.	Date.	Maximum.	Minimum.	Mean.	Maximum.	Minimum.	Mean.
1854.																
June..........	66.70	75.00	72.70	81.05	54.04	26.97	95.50	10th	46.00	2d	65.00	41.00	54.36	.802	.354	.537
July...........	63.00	63.00	80.87	91.32	81.25	30.22	103.00	13th	51.50	20th	68.50	43.00	60.53	.849	.243	.507
August	73.42	75.35	77.52	87.00	55.90	31.09	102.00	16th	49.50	2d	68.00	45.00	57.11	.609	.254	.460
September	68.63	70.73	73.33	81.85	51.38	29.83	94.00	19th	47.00	16th	60.50	44.00	53.31	.691	.252	.493
October........	68.83	70.83	73.00	73.83	52.38	21.54	93.00	2d	46.00	14 & 27	63.00	31.00	52.19	.905	.206	.568
November	62.16	65.20	65.80	68.13	44.21	23.85	74.00	1st & 6th	39.50	10th	50.97	26.96	44.99	.686	.306	.494
December......	56.03	62.58	61.54	59.04	37.25	21.79	69.00	1st & 17	28.00	30th	48.00	25.9	36.99	.813	.293	.539

* Daniel's hygrometer used until September; since then the swinging thermometer, as recommended by Professor Espy. The moisture tables were calculated from Dalton's tables of the force of vapor, while using Daniel's hygometer; and after that, from the *tension* tables of *Auguste*.

Meteorological observations at Sacramento, California.

Date.	Wind. Four daily observations. (The figures refer to the number of observations.)																								WEATHER.														
	North to East.				East to South.				South to West.				West to North.				Sensible breeze to moderate wind.				Moderate to violent wind.				Clear, or mostly clear.				Cloudy, or mostly cloudy.				Clear all day, or mostly clear.	Cloudy all day, or mostly cloudy.	Rain.		Fog.	
	Sunrise.	Noon.	Sunset.	10 P. M.	Sunrise.	Noon.	Sunset.	10 P. M.	Sunrise.	Noon.	Sunset.	10 P. M.	Sunrise.	Noon.	Sunset.	10 P. M.	Sunrise.	Noon.	Sunset.	10 P. M.	Sunrise.	Noon.	Sunset.	10 P. M.	Sunrise.	Noon.	Sunset.	10 P. M.	Sunrise.	Noon.	Sunset.	19 P. M.			Days.	Inches,	Days.	Inches.
1854.																																				*		
June .	0	0	0	0	21	10	21	20	7	10	7	9	2	10	2	1	26	23	24	28	4	7	6	2	19	25	26	28	11	5	4	2	19	2	3	......	4	......
July . .	0	0	0	0	20	9	19	20	8	13	10	9	3	9	2	2	28	28	27	26	8	3	4	5	26	27	30	30	5	4	1	1	23	0	0	......	0	......
Aug . .	0	0	0	0	25	12	17	16	5	14	12	15	1	5	2	0	27	24	25	26	4	7	6	5	28	30	29	30	3	1	2	1	28	0	1	......	2	......
Sept . .	0	1	0	0	21	15	17	20	9	11	11	10	0	3	2	0	27	25	25	22	3	5	5	8	25	28	26	30	5	2	4	0	18	0	1	Sp'kle	2	......
Oct . . .	0	2	0	0	20	16	16	14	5	6	7	12	6	7	8	5	28	26	28	28	3	5	3	3	17	20	16	25	14	11	15	6	8	4	10	1.02	5	......
Nov . .	3	3	4	3	9	10	7	9	4	2	5	6	14	15	14	12	28	26	27	29	2	4	3	1	24	27	25	27	6	6	5	3	20	2	4	0.67	7	0.0163
Dec . . .	0	4	1	1	13	9	15	15	1	8	2	2	17	15	13	13	28	23	28	29	8	8	3	2	18	19	22	23	13	12	9	8	11	5	5	2.20	11	0.1243

* Had no rain-gauge until October.

Table of daily means of Psychrometer, with direction of wind, at Sacramento, Cal.

1854.	Wind. Direction.
June. 1	SSE; S; SW; SSW.
2	SSW; SSE; S; S.
3	SE; S; S; SSW.
4	SE all dy.
5	SE; S; SSE; SE.
6	SE all day.
7	SW; SE; SSW.
8	SSW; NW; S; SSE.
9	SSE; NW; NNW; NNW.
10	NW; WNW; SSE, SSE.
11	SE; S; SE; SE.
12	SSE all day.
13	SSW; NW; SSE; SSE.
14	S; SW; SSE; SE.
15	SE; SW; SE; SE.
16	SE; SSW; S; SSE.
17	SE; NW; SE; SW.
18	SW; NW; SE; SE.
19	SE; NW; SSE SSE.
20	SE all day.
21	do
22	do
23	SE; SSW; SE; SE.
24	SS; SSE; SW; SW.
25	WNNW; SW; SW.
26	WNW; NW; S; S.
27	SSW; SW; SSW; SSE
28	SE all day.
29	do
30	SE; S; SSE; SSE.

1854.	Wind. Direction.*
July. 1	S; S; SSE; SE.
2	" " " "
3	SE; WNW; SSE; SE.
4	SE; NW; SE; S.
5	SE; S; SE; SE.
6	NW all day.
7	" " "
8	NW; WNW; SE; S.
9	S; SW; SSE; S.
10	SE; S; SSW; SE.
11	SW; S; SE; SE.
12	S; N in forenoon; W; SSE; SE.
13	SE, SW; SE; SE.
14	S; NW; S; S.
15	SW; NW in forenoon; SW; SW; SE.
16	SE; S; S; S.
17	SE all day.
18	do
19	do
20	do
21	do
22	do
23	S; WNW; S; S.
24	SE; NW; SE; SE.
25	SE; SE; S; SE.
26	SE; S; S; SE.
27	SE all day.
28	do
29	do
30	SE; SSW; SSE; S.
31	SE; SE; SE; S.

1854.	Mean. D. B.	Mean. W. B.	Wind.
Aug. 1	63.66	56.33	SE; SSW; SE; SE
2	70.40	61.33	SE. SW; SSE; SE.
3	74.	65.	SE; S SE, SE.
4	67.33	58.66	SE; SSW; SE; SE.
5	65.66	59.66	SE; S; SE; S.
6	68.66	60.66	SE all day.
7	71.	65.	SE; SW; S; S.
8	78.33	64.66	do
9	75.33	62.33	S; SE; S; S.
10	69.66	61.33	SE all day.
11	71.66	63.33	do
12	75.	62.33	SE; W; S; S.
13	72.	63.	SE; S; S; S.
14	72.33	60.66	SE; SSW; SSE: SE.
15	77.	62.66	SE; S; S; S.
16	84.66	66.	S; WNW; S; S.
17	83.33	68.	SE all day.
18	73.33	61.66	do
19	71.33	61.	S; S; S; SE.
20	73.66	63.33	SE all day.
21	72.66	6.	do
22	63.66	57.33	do
23	68.66	58.	S; SSE; S; S.
24	67.66	57.66	SE; W; SE; SSE.
25	63.33	56.	S; SSE; SE; S.
26	63.66	54.66	SE; S; SE; SE.
27	61.66	54.	SE; SW; SW; SW;
28	66.33	55.38	NW; W; W; S.
29	64.33	57.66	SE all day.
30	65.66	56.66	SE; W; W; S.
31	68.66	62.33	SE; S; S; S.

1854.	Mean. D. B.	Mean. W. B.	Wind.
Sept. 1	65.33	57.66	SE all day.
2	63.	56.33	S; SSW SE; SE.
3	60.66	55.33	SE all day.
4	62.66	55.66	S; SW; S: S.
5	64.	56.33	SE; SSW S, SSE.
6	63.	56.66	SE; S; S; SE.
7	62.66	55.66	S; S; SE SE.
8	63.33	56.66	SE; SE, S; S.
9	62.33	55.66	SSE all day.
10	62.33	55.33	do
11	60.	54.66	S; SE; S; S.
12	59.66	54.66	S; SSE, SE; SE.
13	60.66	54.33	S; SSE; SSE; SE.
14	60.	54.	SE; S; S; S.
15	60.33	55.33	SE all day.
16	66.66	57.33	
17	71.	59.33	
18	77.	62.33	
19	67.	62.	SW; S.
20	67.66	59.33	SE all day.
21	66.	58.	do
22	67.66	59.66	do
23	67.33	59.66	SE; WNW; SW; SW.
24	69.	57.33	SW; W; S; S.
25	68.	56.66	SE all day.
26	62.33	58.66	SE; SSE; S; S;
27	70.	58.33	SE; N; NW; S.
28	66.66	58.33	SSE; SW; SE; SE.
29	66.	57.	SEE all day.
30	66.66	56.66	SE; WNW; WNW; SW.

* Psychrometrical observations not commenced before the 1st of August.

Table of daily means of Psychrometer, with direction of wind, at Sacramento, Cal.

Oct.	Mean D. B.	Mean W. B.	Wind.	Nov.	Mean D. B.	Mean W. B.	Wind.	Dec.	Mean D. B.	Mean W. B.	Wind.
1	74.	58.33	NNW; N; W; W.	1	57.	50.	NW all day.	1	57.	48.33	SW; NW; NW; NW.
2	74.33	60.66	SW; SW; W; SW.	2	55.	47.66	SE; SE; SW; SW.	2	58.33	49.	NW; NW; SE; SE.
3	75.66	61.66	SW all day.	3	52.66	49.66	SW; W; NNW; SE.	3	54.33	51.66	SE; SW; WSW; WSW.
4	67.66	59.33	SE all day.	4	55.66	49.33	SSE all day.	4	55.	50.66	NW all day.
5	64.66	58.	do.	5	57.66	51.33	do.	5	51.33	48.66	SE; NE; N; N.
6	65.	59.	do.	6	58.66	50.66	SE all day.	6	48.66	46.	NW; N; SE; SE.
7	64.33	57.66	S; WNW.	7	54.66	46.33	SE; SE; S; S.	7	46.66	44.33	W; WNW; WNW.
8	72.33	56.66	NNW; NW; SSE; S.	8	53.	48.33	SW all day.	8	47.33	42.	SSE; W; SE; SE.
9	64.	58.66	SE all day.	9	55.33	46.	SE; W; NW; NW.	9	42.66	40.33	SE; SE; S; S.
10	61.66	55.66	SE; SSE; SW; S.	10	51.33	47.	N all day.	10	44.66	41.33	NW all day.
11	60.33	57.33	SE all day.	11	54.33	48.66	do.	11	44.	38.66	do.
12	61.66	59.	S; S; SSW; SE.	12	56.66	48.	NW; W; W.	12	45.	40.66	do.
13	58.	53.	SE; NE; S; S.	13	53.	48.	SW; SSE; SSE; SSE.	13	44.66	41.33	do.
14	56.33	49.66	W; N; NW; SW.	14	54.	48.33	SE; NW; WNW; WNW	14	47.	41.66	do.
15	58.	51.33	NW; NW; SW; SW.	15	54.33	46.66	W all day.	15	46.33	41.33	do.
16	59.66	53.66	SE all day.	16	55.	48.33	NW; W; W; W.	16	45.66	41.33	do.
17	60.	53.33	do.	17	56.	48.66	NW all day.	17	49.66	42.33	NW; N; SE; SE.
18	57.66	51.66	SE; S; SE; SE.	18	55.	51.	NE; SSE; NE; S.	18	51.33	43.66	W; SE; SE; SE.
19	58.	51.66	SE all day.	19	58.66	53.	NW all day.	19	46.66	40.	SE all day.
20	62.66	56.33	SE; SE; S; S.	20	54.	51.	NW; SE; SE; SE.	20	44.66	43.	do.
21	65.	58.33	SSE all day.	21	55.33	52.66	SE; SW; S; S.	21	45.66	41.	SSE all day.
22	64.33	58.33	SE SSE ;SW; SW.	22	59.66	55.66	SE; SE; SW; SW.	22	52.	45.33	SE all day.
23	59.66	54.66	SSE all day.	23	59.	53.66	SW; SE; SE; SE.	23	51.	45.33	do.
24	54.	52.33	do.	24	59.	53.	NW all day.	24	53.66	47.66	do.
25	57.	52.33	SE all day.	25	59.33	52.66	NW; N; N; N.	25	55.	51.33	SE; S; SSE; SE.
26	57.66	53.66	do.	26	60.66	53.33	NW all day.	26	48.66	44.66	SE; SW; SSE; SSE.
27	55.	50.66	SSE; NW; W; SW.	27	58.	52.	do.	27	43.33	37.33	WNW; N; NW; NW.
28	57.66	52.	SW; SE; SSE; SE.	28	57.33	51.33	do.	28	42.33	37.33	NNW all day.
29	57.33	50.	SE; NW; NW; NW.	29	51.	43.66	WNW; NW; NW; SSE.	29	37.66	35.66	NNW; NW; NW; SE.
30	60.66	50.	NW all day.	30	53.33	47.33	NW; NW; SE; SE.	30	43.33	39.	NW; W; SSE; S.
31	57.66	50.	do.					31	48.66	46.	SE all day.

Table of daily means of Psychrometer, with directions of wind, at Sacramento, Cal.

1855.	Mean D. B.	Mean W. B.	Wind.	1855.	Mean D. B.	Mean W. B.	Wind.	1855.	Mean D. B.	Mean W. B.	Wind.
Jan.				Feb.				Mar.			
1	50.	46.33	S; SW; [illegible] NW.	1	54.	47.66	N; S; SW; N.	1	58.66	53.66	SE; S; S; SW.
2	42.66	39.	WSW; SE; SE; SE.	2	54.33	49.	N NW; NW; NE; NE.	2	57.66	53.	SE; S; S; S.
3	43.66	41.66	SE all day.	3	55.66	48.66	[illegible]; NW; S [illegible]W.	3	59.	55.33	S; SSE; [illegible]NW.
4	43.66	41.33	S; SW; SW; SW.	4	56.66	50.33	W; N; SE; ENE.	4	58.33	53.	W; S; S; SE.
5	35.33	33.	SE all day.	5	54.	49.33	WNW; N; N; WSW.	5	57.33	56.	E S S S.;
6	34.33	31.	Do.	6	55.33	51.	N; S; SE; SE.	6	60.66	59.	S; SE; S; S.
7	39.33	35.66	[illegible]; W.	7	54.33	51.	SSE; S; S; SSW.	7	62.	58.66	S; SE; SE; SE.
8	44.66	40.33	NW all day.	8	55.66	52.66	S all day.	8	57.66	56.33	ESE ;S S S.;
9	45.66	43.66	NW; NW; N; SE.	9	53.66	50.33	S; WSW; WSW; NE.	9	51.66	50.66	S S ;S [illegible]W.
10	45.	42.33	SE; NE; SE; SE.	10	52.	49.33	SSE all day.	10	51.66	47.	NE; WNW; W; SE.
11	45.66	43.	[illegible]; NW; [illegible] W.	11	50.33	46.66	E; NNW; NW; NNW.	11	51.33	46.66	[illegible]W; S; E.
12	43.66	41.66	N; N; SE; E.	12	51.33	46.33	SSW; S; NNW; NNW.	12	52.33	50.66	S; S; SSE; SE.
13	40.33	38.	NW; ESE; SE; SE.	13	52.66	49.66	[illegible]W; WSW.	13	54.33	50.	S all day.
14	39.33	37.66	SE; NW; NW; SE.	14	56.	52.	SSE ;S; S; [illegible] W.	14	49.	47.	SSE all day.
15	39.	36.66	SSE; NE; SW; SE.	15	57.33	49.66	NW all day.	15	47.	42.	[illegible]ay.
16	39.66	37.	SE; SSE; ESE; SE.	16	57.	46.	Do.	16	44.33	36.66	[illegible]; SE; E.
17	40.33	39.	NW; N; SE; SE.	17	51.	46.33	NW; NW; NE; N.	17	50.66	44.	N; NNW; NW; NW.
18	43.33	42.	S; SE; SE; N.	18	55.66	46.33	SE; [illegible]N.	18	58.	53.33	N; N; NW; NW.
19	47.	44.	SSE all day.	19	48.33	38.33	NNW; [illegible]; NW.	19	59.	52.33	NW all day.
20	41.33	39.33	[illegible]; NW; W.	20	45.33	37.66	NW; NNW; NW; NNW.	20	55.33	53.33	NW; NW; NW; SW.
21	42.33	37.66	WSW; WSW; NNW; NNW	21	44.66	38.33	N; SE; SSW; SSW.	21	59.	52.33	NE; NW; NW; NNE.
22	44.66	39.	NW; NNE; NNE; NW.	22	46.66	42.	SSE; S SSE SE.;	22	62.	57.33	NNW; NNW; NW; N.
23	47.33	43.66	SSE; SSE; ENE; E.	23	47.33	43.33	SSW; SSW; N; WNW.	23	64.66	56.66	NE; SSE; ESE; [illegible].
24	51.	46.33	NW; N; NNE; SE.	24	45.66	40.33	NNW; W; N; NNE.	24	64.33	59.	NW; N; NE; NE.
25	53.	47.	SW; NE; NW; [illegible] W.	25	52.	46.66	NNW; SSE; NW; NW.	25	64.	57.33	NE; NW; SE; SE.
26	51.66	46.33	NW; N; N; WNW.	26	55.33	52.33	SE; SE; NE; [illegible] W.	26	61.66	54.66	E; N; N; SE.
27	50.	44.	NW; NNW; E; SE.	27	55.	53.	NW ESE S S.;	27	58.33	53.	S; S; SSE; S.
28	49.	43.	NW; N; NE; W.	28	57.66	56.33	SE; S; SE; SE.	28	57.66	53.33	SE; [illegible]; SSE; SSE.
29	51.33	46.33	NW; NNE; SSE; ENE.					29	58.33	53.33	SSE ;SW; S; NE.
30	50.66	47.66	[illegible]NNW; N NE; NW.					30	58.33	55.	SE; SE; SSE; S.
31	56.66	52.33	N; SE; N; NNW.					31	57.	54.	S; SSE; S; SSE.

REMARKS CONTRIBUTING TO THE PHYSICAL GEOGRAPHY OF THE NORTH AMERICAN CONTINENT.

BY JULIUS FROEBEL.

SAN FRANCISCO, *December* 8, 1854.

Since the annexation of California our geographical knowledge of the western half of our continent has made a progress the rate of which is unsurpassed in the history of geography, and almost equals the fastness of California life itself, by which it has been produced. In every direction the great wilderness of the western table-lands, and of the continental slope along the Gila and Colorado, together with the adjoining portion of Sonora, is traversed by engineers, by cattle traders, emigrants, prospecting miners, and bold adventurers, who all contribute in daily augmenting our store of topographical details concerning these vast regions. But while this store is accumulating, it cannot be expected that travellers, who have to pay attention to some particular and more or less immediate interest, should trouble themselves with geographical questions of a more general character. Thus some misconceptions in our general ideas of the physical structure of our continent, produced by some former and premature generalizations of systematic geography, are still propagated by maps and books, as well as Congressional railroad speeches, and the influence of these errors on different branches of science, as well as on common life, is important enough to make it worth while to correct them. I am referring here to the prevailing notions of the geographical system of our continent, or the manner in which its mountain chains and table lands are generally believed to be arranged and connected, or separated. As this arrangement, together with the geological constitution of the soil, form the principal conditions of the local deviations of climate and of the distribution of organic life, it is easy to conceive how the most interesting chapters of physical geography must be affected by any prevailing misconception in that respect.

A correct knowledge of the whole system of elevations and depressions of the surface of a country can only be the result of a complete and careful topographical survey and subsequent representation. To execute such a task over a large continent, like that of North America, can only be the work of generations. Even the most advanced States of Europe, small as they are in extent, and almost unlimited as the power of their governments is to expend money for such a purpose, have only lately succeeded in possessing good topographical maps of their territories. But while thus we must resign to our grandchildren the satisfaction of having a clear and correct conception of the ups and downs of the continent we inhabit, we are under the necessity, for our own present wants, to form an approximate idea. Insufficient as the number of our observations must be, and discontented as they are in a great measure, we must try to fill up the *lacunæ* of our knowledge by generalizations and ideal connexions. It is natural that, in so doing, we should be exposed to error; but we shall keep our mistakes within the narrowest possible limits, if we proceed by the way of simple inductions, and refuse to submit to premature theories. No doubt the propensity of the human mind to bring isolated facts into an ideal connexion originates in our highest intellectual faculty, by which alone we are able to discover the general laws which govern the endless variety of cases. But there is scarcely one science which has not been led astray from time to time by this same propensity, and no science, perhaps, more so than geology, of which orography, or the knowledge of the external form of the dry surface of our globe, may, in some respects, be said to be a chapter, while physical geography in general is its descriptive department.

Among the many mistaken notions still prevalent on that subject, is the opinion that the principal systems of water-courses or the great river basins and continental depressions must be divided by mountain chains. In America this is not more true than in any other part of the world. But great and important as is the number of well known facts which prove that the less striking differences of level followed by the water-courses of a country may be independent of the system of real mountain chains, both being very often the results of two entirely different series of causes, still these facts are regarded as mere exceptions to a general rule, and, wherever positive observations are wanting, geographers continue to fill up the blanks in our maps according to that supposition. Thus, to separate the Pacific from the Atlantic slope, and especially from that towards the Mexican Gulf, the Rocky Mountains have been brought into an imaginary connexion with the Sierra Madre of Mexico, and this latter chain has been forced on our maps to take a direction which it does not take in reality. I have often heard the name of the former unhesitatingly extended to the latter by Americans living in northern Mexico, though there is an interval of several hundred miles in longitude and latitude between their nearest points. A generalization even of a bolder character is sometimes made, when the Sierra Madre and the Rocky Mountains together are said to be the continuation of the "Cordilleras" of South America. But the system of the Andes does not continue through the Isthmus of Darien; and the hills of the Isthmus of Panama have little to do with them. These hills, again, are not connected with the mountains and table lands of upper Mosquitia, of Honduras, and Guatemala, nor with the volcanic cones which rise in isolated beauty from the plains of Nicaragua and San Salvador.

It may be observed that these interruptions of continuity are not important enough to affect a general view of the subject, and it may be conceded that this is true. Certainly we may speak with all propriety of the mountains and table lands of the western side of the new world as of one great system following the course of its western coast from Terra del Fuego to the northern Polar ocean, and separated by wide tracts of flat and, comparatively speaking, low country, from the groups and chains which occupy certain sections of the eastern side of both the northern and southern continents. But this is only repeating a fact almost too general and simple to be much dwelt upon. It being once known, as it is, to everybody, the special arrangement of the numerous subordinate members becomes the object of investigation, and it is this object we have here in view.

In this investigation the question is not only whether certain groups or chains of mountains are really connected or separated, but what other relations may exist between them, relations that may be of high interest to the geologist and meteorologist, or to those who are studying the laws of the distribution and diversity of vegetable, animal, and human life. Mountains, though separated by intervening space, may be the productions of simultaneous and connected geological processes, or, by taking corresponding situations in reference to the whole geographical structure of their respective regions, may form corresponding parts in the system of natural circumstances and conditions, so that one may be said to be the *equivalent* of the other in one or the other of the different series of causes and effects which constitute the great organism of nature. Thus we may not only ask whether the Rocky Mountains are connected with the Sierra Madre or not, but we may, if the latter be the case, put the question whether the one must not be considered, at least, as the *equivalent* of the other. This question, indeed, has been raised by the geologists of this country in respect to the different chains of our own system of mountains. It has become an interesting question of geology and physical geography, whether the peninsular chain of Lower California is the southern equivalent of the Sierra Nevada, or is that of our coast range, and whether the so-called San Bernardino chain is corresponding to any of the three, or has its own independent character and existence.

Since Elie de Beaumont has drawn the attention of geologists to certain relations which appear to exist between the bearings of mountain chains and the geological periods of their respective upheavals, it has been asserted that such questions should be decided; and that the classifications and nomenclature of geography should be regulated by the facts which constitute geological character, and not by those of mere outward form. But it is easy to show that, by subjecting the whole matter to the domination of a mere scientific principle, we yield to the claims of one science at the cost of the equally just claims of another, as well as of every-day utility. Thus, for example, it is a well established fact of geology, that different sections of the Alps are to be referred to very different geological epochs, while each of these sections has its geological equivalents in certain more or less distant parts of the world. Still it is in the interest of climatology and of the study of the distribution of plants and animals, as it is in that of common life and of human history, to adhere to the old and natural way of viewing and naming, by which the Alps are considered as one mountain chain, which has nothing to do with certain mountains or hills in Spain, in Scandinavia, and in Greece. It is an equally well established fact, that the hills in the south of England and a certain section of the Caucasus, that the Thuringian forest in Germany and certain mountains in Greece, that one section of the Pyrenees and a certain section of the Alps, are to be referred respectively to the same geological periods. Still no sensible man, unless he is considering the matter expressly under a geological point of view, would say that these mountains respectively belong to each other. Even not to augment the sufferings of schoolmasters and schoolboys, we should abstain from innovations which would oblige them to become good geologists before they could understand, the one what he is teaching, the other what he is learning. The outward forms of the surface of our globe should be considered independently of the system of geological periods and mineral masses. The knowledge of each, though there is an intimate connexion between the two, has its own peculiar interest, and the claims of the geologist in that respect have no better foundation than those of the botanist who would propose to give different names to two sections of the same chain of mountains, because one is covered with pine trees, the other with oak.

After these preliminary remarks, intended to clear the subject of some confused notions in respect to its general principles, I may pass over to a statement of facts, which shall be mostly such as have fallen under my own observation.

1. The great chain of the Rocky Mountains divides, in the neighborhood of the origin of the Rio Grande, into two ranges, of which one runs along the eastern, the other along the western side of that river, down to about the latitude of Santa Fé.

Every one who has travelled from the Missouri river to the capital of New Mexico, is well aware of the fact that the latter part of the road, from Las Vegas to its termination, turns round the southern promontory of the *eastern range.* To the north he leaves steep, high, and mostly snow-covered mountains, while the elevations to the south are of two kinds, but both different in character from the great chain to the north. Some there are, it is true, which have been caused by plutonic eruptions, and the upheaval of metamorphic and sedimentary masses; but they are merely little isolated groups, or ridges, such as the Placer, Sandilla, and Manzana mountains. The rest are either mere declivities, or detached portions of the general table land. This latter, at an average altitude of nearly 7,000 feet above the sea, turns round that same southern promontory, from the eastern to the southwestern side of the great chain, and, running out here in a projecting corner to the westward, reaches the very borders of the valley of the Rio Grande, where, at many places, the traveller has a view over its edges down into the valley near Albuquerque. The little groups and ridges just mentioned have entirely the general character of the numerous mountains which, like the islands of an archipelago, are scattered all over the high plains of western Texas and Mexico. If, nevertheless, they be considered as the southern continuations, or representatives, of the Rocky Mountains, which in a certain sense they really are, it should be in view of the correspondence of the natural arrangement of elevations in that section of country to the western terminal range, which, south of Santa Fé, appears to pass over to the eastern side of the river, following, in this way, the general south-by-east course of the system.

2. Whoever has travelled from El Paso to California by the Gila route knows that, following Cook's route in its southern bend, he has to pass over several mountain spurs; but that, choosing the straight line of a more northern track, called Leroux's route, he passes from the Rio

Grande to the Gila, near the Pima villages, without the necessity of surmounting a single real mountain-chain. In general, there is no doubt that, if the traveller were not bound to touch the few watering places, and to avoid difficulties of another character, he could keep off from mountains altogether. If, therefore, the *western terminal range* of the Rocky Mountains should reach so far south as the origin of the Gila river, it certainly does not pass over to the south of that locality. It is, however, much more likely that the road from Albuquerque to Zuñi, and, perhaps, even the old Spanish trail from Santa Fé, by Abiquiu and the head waters of the San Juan river, to Los Angeles, turns round the real southern promontory of the western terminal range.

It is true that further south, in the neighborhood of Socorro, in about 34° of latitude, mountains of considerable elevation, and steep, Alpine forms, stand on the western side of the Rio Grande. They appear, however, to be separated from the Rocky Mountains by a wide interval of flat and open country, which has been made use of for the passage of several routes. This section of country I do not know from personal observation, except from what I could see in coming down the Rio Grande. Now, even conceding that reasons might be found to consider the mountains near Socorro as a continuation of the western terminal range of the Rocky Mountains, still they would not form a connexion with the Sierra Madre, because such a connexion cannot be found further south. Between Valverde and Santa Barbara the same group of mountains form those impassable narrows of the valley of the Rio Grande, which compel the traveller to leave the river and traverse, for ninety miles, the ill-reputed desert of the *Jornada del Muerto*, or "dead man's journey," the south-eastern portions of the group thus proving to stand on the eastern side of the Rio Grande.

3. The mountains which here obstruct the valley, those further north which rise in picturesque forms from the western side of the river near Socorro, together with the Copper Mine Mountains, and the little group of Ben Moor, appear to belong, in reality, to a central and separate system, in which the Gila river takes its origin, and which might be called the Upper Gila mountains. Its centre appears to be the *Sierra Blanca*, so called, not from being covered with eternal snow, as might be supposed, but from the white color of its rocks. In a deep and narrow cañon of the southern portion of the system I observed white masses of a porphyritic or trachytic formation, with transitions into pearlstone.

It has been pretended that the real connecting link between the Rocky Mountains and the Sierra Madre is formed by a chain called the Sierra de los Mimbres. But the traveller in the section of country where it should exist will look in vain for such a chain. The name, indeed, is only applied to the restricted and subordinate mountain locality on the southern verge of the Upper Gila Mountains, so called from the Rio de los Mimbres, a small creek which, during the dry season, is lost in the plain, but is said to continue its course so far south as to reach the Laguna de Santa Maria, a lake situated west by south of El Paso. *Mimbre* is the Mexican name of a beautiful bignoniaceous shrub (a *Chilopsis*) exclusively growing in the alluvial beds of sand and pebbles of little intermittent streams. The little creek, therefore, has its name from the shrub; and the mountain locality in which the creek has its origin, near the now deserted Fort Webster, obtains its appellation from the creek—a fact which shows its subordinate character.

4. After having approximately defined the southern extremity of the Rocky Mountains, I have now to follow the course of those detached groups and ridges which, in a certain sense, to be explained hereafter, may be called its southern equivalent. I have already stated that, if such an equivalent exists, it is to be looked for on the *eastern* and *not* on the western side of the Rio Grande. The traveller coming from San Antonio de Bejar, on his way to El Paso or to the Presidio del Norte, has to pass these mountains, which, situated west of the Pecos river, mark a step from a lower to a higher section of the plateau of western Texas. In steep and singular forms, of a character entirely different from the hills formed by declivities and detached portions of table land, as common in western Texas as they are on the head waters of the Pecos and the Canadian, these groups and ridges of plutonic and metamorphic masses, formed by a combination of upheavals and eruptions, emerge from the high surrounding plains.

On the road to the Presidio del Norte they are passed in the *Puerto del Paisano*, on the road to El Paso, in the *Puerto de las Limpias*, or "Wild Rose" Pass, two localities of the most striking character of wild and romantic mountain scenery—particularly the latter of the two, where the walls of immense porphyritic eruptions are separated into innumerable strange shapes of needles, spires, columns, and spheroids. South of the Presidio del Norte, in the neighborhood of San Carlos, this line of mountains strikes again the Rio Grande, passing from the eastern to the western side of the river without changing its general direction, the river forming here a great eastern bend, in a long, deep, narrow, and impassable gorge, through which, in a series of rapids, it pours down from the elevated country of its upper and middle course into the deep country of the Mexican gulf. On its western side, then, the line of mountains bordering the *Bolson de Mapimi* to the east runs further south through the States of Coahuila, Nuevo Leon, San Luis Potosi, and Vera Cruz, where it forms the eastern margin of the plateau of Anahuac.

5. I come now to speak of the *Sierra Madre*. This denomination has been the cause of many geographical misunderstandings and misconstructions. It has been understood as a real proper name, while it is but an appellative, meaning the mother chain of mountains—*i. e.*, the principal chain of a country in general, just as the Mexicans call *acequia madre* the principal channel of a system of irrigation. Thus the name may occur in different localities without thereby authorizing geographers to conclude that all the mountain chains which have received that denomination belong to one and the same system. It may, therefore, really be as some maps have it—I do not know from what source—that a certain chain *east* of Durango, belonging to the line of ridges which passes over from Texas to Mexico, is known under the name of Sierra Madre, too. But it is certain, and every one who has travelled across Mexico in that latitude knows it, that the Sierra Madre, in the sense generally adopted in the country, is *not east* but *is west* of Durango, and is passed by the road from that city to Mazatlan. Of a mountain chain in New Mexico called Sierra Madre, and pretended to be situated on the west-

ern side of the Rio Grande, I have never heard. But if the name should occur there, too, as some maps likewise have it, I am almost sure that it has only been used by some Mexican theorist who wanted to convey a general idea of the geography of his country according to his own fancy—that it is not, therefore, a commonly employed term there—and under no consideration could even a fact contrary to this conviction prove any connexion of the Rocky Mountains with the Sierra Madre proper, which, following the direction of the Pacific coast of Mexico, borders the interior table-land of that country towards the low country of Michoacan, Jalisco, Sinaloa, and Sonora. If such a conclusion could be allowed to be drawn from a mere name, it would certainly be as justifiable to prove a connexion, or at least a relation, of the Sierra Madre proper to that chain of mountains which our geologists now call the *San Bernardino chain*, but which the old Californians likewise know under the name of Sierra Madre.

Now as to the Sierra Madre proper, there is a singularity in the natural structure of this marginal chain, which, though by no means uncommon in other similar chains in different parts of the world, is one of the principal causes of the misconstructions of our maps in respect to western and northern Mexico. Nearly all the more considerable rivers which empty into the Gulf of California have their origin on the high plains of the interior table-land—that is to say, on the eastern side of the Sierra Madre—and, bursting through deep and narrow gorges or rents, cross the chain at right angles before they come down on a lower terrace of the country, and ultimately into the "*tierra caliente*" of the coast. This fact is to be seen in the most striking manner on the road from Chihuahua to the rich mining place of Batoseágachic, where the traveller passes, without any ascent, from the high plateau on the eastern side of the Sierra down into the deep country on its western side, through one of these openings; the road coming out on the latter side at an elevation of several thousand feet above the lower country, where he may see the orange and banana, while he is still in the region of the pine-trees and of a northern climate. The water-course at the bottom of the transversal gorge is tributary to the Rio del Fuerte, which empties into the gulf somewhat south of the Rio Yaqui. One of the two principal branches of this latter river, the Rio de Papigóchic or Conception, shows a similar phenomenon. For nearly a hundred miles it runs along the eastern side of the sierra in a northerly direction, through the beautiful savannas of the western table-land of Chihuahua, passing many fine little towns, until at last it makes a sudden turn to the west, enters a gap in the mountains so narrow that it is scarcely perceptible in the landscape, and through it dashes down into the deep country on the western side of the chain. One of these two passages must be had in view by the projectors of the railroad from El Paso or the Presidio del Norte to Guaymas, for which Santa Anna has lately given a concession. As geographers, however, have not understood this character of the chain, they have placed it so far to the east of its real situation as to get it on the eastern side of the origin of the rivers of Sonora and Sinaloa.

At the same time there are some reasons to suspect that the astronomical positions of the interior of these two States are likewise too far east; by which circumstance, if my supposition, suggested chiefly by the comparison of distances on both sides of the mountain chain, should prove just, the sierra, even keeping its relative situation, would be brought nearer to the line of direction of the Rocky Mountains than it comes in reality, and by the combinations of the two errors the disfigurations of our maps appear to have been doubled. Thus, while the southern terminal ranges of the Rocky Mountains have been laid down too far west, the northern terminal ranges of the Sierra Madre have been laid down too far east, and both have been brought nearer to each other than they really are.

6. Of the latter ranges, the extreme northern spurs, situated south of the middle and lower Gila, are passed by Cook's route on the trail between the Guadalupe pass and Fort Yuma. Near the latter place, or the junction of the Gila and Colorado, the Coast Range of Sonora and Sinaloa, which forms the western foot of the whole Sierra Madre system—a system which, throughout its whole extension, is formed by parallel ranges—has its northern termination. Beyond the Gila and Colorado, however, its direction is continued by a chain of mountains which the traveller on his way through the desert, between the latter river and Carizo creek, has at some distance to his right hand. At a very acute angle it converges with the chain which comes from the peninsula of Lower California, till at last it falls in with it, the San Bernardino peak forming, as I have been assured by persons who have been on the spot, the point of junction. Thus the extreme northwestern spur of the Sierra Madre constitutes what has been called by geologists the San Bernardino range, but has been known to the old Californians under that same name of Sierra Madre, as I have already stated. If, therefore, the Sierra Madre has a northern equivalent, we have to look for it not in the Rocky Mountains but in the Sierra Nevada system. But the real meaning of all these relations will receive more light from their connexion with the more general structure of the western half of our continent, of which, therefore, I shall try to give a few outlines.

This western half is known to be composed of a great longitudinal basin, extending, in a direction corresponding to the Pacific coast, from the Isthmus of Tehuantepec to the polar region. Through the greater part of its extent it is confined between an eastern and western marginal chain of mountains. The greater part of its surface has an elevation which gives it the character of a table land, and by its marginal chains it is separated from an eastern and a western lateral terrace.

In California and Oregon, Utah and New Mexico, and in the countries farther to the north, the two marginal chains are clearly and conspicuously marked by nature. The eastern one is formed by the Rocky Mountains, the western one by the Sierra Nevada, Cascade Mountains, and their more northern equivalents. In Mexico, the western chain is constituted by the Sierra Nevada, and is likewise clearly traced by nature; but the eastern one, composed of that line of detached and irregular groups and ridges which crosses the Rio Grande from east to west at the narrows and rapids of San Carlos, is less conspicuous, and may be entirely overlooked by those who are not sufficiently informed about the matter. Nevertheless, as already stated, if the Rocky Mountains have a southern equivalent, it must be recognised in the mountains of western Texas, Coahuila, Nuevo Leon, San Luis Potosi, and Vera

Cruz; and if the Sierra Madre has a northern equivalent, it must be recognised in the Sierra Nevada, the Cascade Mountains, and their more northern continuations: because the first line forms the eastern, the second line the western borders of the great longitudinal basin of our western interior, the whole construction being thus under the rule of a strict physico-geographical analogy.

8. Though in respect to its prevailing elevation, this great basin may be called a plateau or table-land, still it has considerable differences of altitude, and three great slopes—not to speak of similar phenomena of a minor importance—which form transitions from the inner and higher to the outer and lower countries: that of the Rio Grande, that of the Colorado and Gila, and that of the Columbia—the former breaking through the western marginal chain.

Between the middle part of the valley of the Rio Grande and the middle part of the valley of the Gila, the country is less elevated than to the north and south of that line. The level of *Lake Guzman*, situated west-southwest of El Paso, is, according to Mr. Schuchart, even lower than that of the Rio Grande at El Paso. *Lake Santa Maria* must have about the same level. Into this latter lake the *Rio Mimbres*, which comes from the north, is said to empty in time of copious rains; while from the south the *Rio de Santa Maria*, emptying into the same lake, rushes down from the central plains of Chihuahua. A line traced from these two lakes to the *Dry Lagoon* of Cook's route, forms a northwestern continuation of this depression of the table-land; and from the latter place the middle part of the Gila may be reached without overcoming any considerable elevation, which, however, would be found to exist to the north as well as to the south of that line. The upper Gila runs in a narrow part of the higher country north of it; and though its bottom may be even lower than the level of the open country along the general line of depression, still that does not form an objection against the general construction, as it has neither an opening to the Rio Grande nor is it accessible much higher up than where the road from Tucson first strikes it. If Cook's wagon route, in taking from *Dry Lagoon* a southwestern course to the Guadalupe pass, deviates to the south of our line, it is because it follows a series of fine watering and pasture-places, situated just between the mountains of the highest section of country, which contains the origin of the southern affluents of the Gila and of the northern river of Sonora.

9. Thus it would appear that an ocean of a level not much higher than the Rio Grande near El Paso would separate Mexico from the rest of North America.

But an ocean of that level—setting aside the more important changes it would produce in the form of our continent—would cover the Colorado desert, and, extending over the deep mountain passes southeast of Los Angeles, would gain the Pacific here, and make an island of Lower California.

It is very possible that such a state of things has really once existed. The nearly horizontal strata of the cretaceous formation of Texas appear to enter in a western direction and unconformable superposition between elevations of other sedimentary rocks and granite, syenitic, porphyritic, and trachytic mountains, which must have already existed when, and must have been above the surface of the ocean in which the cretaceous strata were deposited. Strata of that formation, in unconformable superposition, appear to exist at several places between upheaved and eruptive tracts of country, in northern Chihuahua and Sonora. And if a closer geological investigation should really prove that, a little south of the upper and coinciding with the lower Gila, a branch of the ocean should once have formed a strait across what is now forming our present continent, we might say that some hundred thousand years ago the natural line of a railroad, which in our days should connect the eastern and western side of that continent, was already traced by nature.

It is an interesting fact that the desert north of the Lower Colorado, which is in the western continuation of that old range of lower country, is, even now, perhaps, the lowest spot of the American continent—as, according to recent measurements, it is in part even somewhat under the level of the ocean. While travelling through that country, I was struck by certain phenomena connected with the periodical filling and drying of what has been called *New River*, and of the several lagoons connected with it. The immense mud deposits of *Little Lagoon*, which I have examined, prove the former existence of long and uninterrupted periods in which the water of the Colorado entered the desert and kept the bed of New River, together with the basins of this lagoon, full; while the existence of mezquit trees, now killed by its water, from which the upper parts of their trunks and branches emerge in a dead state, proves that other uninterrupted periods have passed when the water of the Colorado did not enter the desert. Now, it has been asserted that these fluctuations are the consequence of the more copious or more scanty rains in the countries drained by the Colorado and its tributaries; but the fluctuations appear to have been of such an extent in time and level, that the cause assigned to them appears to me to be inadequate to the effect, and I am more inclined to believe that the phenomenon is, at least in part, produced by fluctuations of the ground in consequence of the action of subterranean forces. There is a large solfatara even now in action at the northern side of the Lower Colorado.

10. But to return to my strictly geographical object: It follows from the foregoing statements and remarks that the great longitudinal basin which constitutes the inner part of the western section of our continent, is divided, by a depression of soil which runs from the Middle Rio Grande to the Middle Gila, into a northern and a southern table-land, the former being that of New Mexico, Utah, Upper Oregon, and other more northern countries—the latter that of Mexico in its present confines, as they have been fixed by the Gadsden purchase. At the same time it can be seen how great an error it is, affecting the whole physical geography of the continent, to bring the Sierra Madre into connexion with the Rocky mountains. It makes the western marginal chain of the southern to be the continuation of the eastern marginal chain of the northern half of the great longitudinal basin, separating analogous and confounding heterogenous phenomena of orography, of climatology, and of the distribution of vegetable and animal life. Those who have studied the climate, and the flora and fauna of these regions, will find that I am right in my assertions.

MISCELLANEOUS CORRESPONDENCE

ON

NATURAL HISTORY.

Some Remarks on the Natural History of Beaver Islands, Michigan.

BY JAMES J. STRANG.

SAINT JAMES, BEAVER ISLAND, *December* 7, 1853.

Secretary of Smithsonian Institution:

I have prepared for your use the following lists of animals, plants, &c., found upon the "Beaver Islands," in Lake Michigan, which I beg to submit to you. I am aware that these lists are quite imperfect, but hope they will serve some useful purpose until better can be prepared.

Truly and sincerely, yours,

JAMES J. STRANG.

DOMESTIC ANIMALS.

Horses, oxen, sheep, swine, dogs, cats.

WILD ANIMALS.

Foxes, red, quite numerous.

Foxes, black, scarce; silver grey, very rare. Some hunters assert that these are the same variety, the colour only distinguishing the sex. The silver grey is the most valuable fur in market, a single skin being priced at more than fifty dollars.

Hare, or rabbit. Two species, large and small.

Chipmunk, or red ground-squirrel.

Otter, very scarce.

The beaver are extinct. Caribou, or reindeer, range as far south as here, but visit the islands only on the ice, and very rarely. Elk are found on the east shore, and bears on both. American deer are found as near as Green Bay and Manistee river, *piloting civilization.*

BIRDS.

Geese, brant, duck (numerous varieties), loons, gulls (two varieties), crows, hawks, (several varieties), woodcock, pigeons, blackbird, robin, redheaded woodpecker, snipe, snowbird, pewee.

FISHES.

In some of the small streams on the mainland "brook trout" are found in abundance. Most of the streams are destitute of them, but abound in other fish, the names of which I do not know.

The small lakes within the islands, as well as the mainland, are well stocked with fish, of which perch, suckers, and bass, are the most abundant.

In lake Michigan, among and around the islands, are sturgeon, pike, pickerel, siskowit, trout, whitefish, herring, suckers, perch, ling or lawyers.

STURGEON, (*Aupenscr.*)—I have been able to learn very little of the habits of the sturgeon. While the shoal channels among the islands are frozen, the tribe of Indians residing on Garden Island depend much upon them for subsistence. They are usually taken with spears, in from one to four fathoms water.

The quality of the flesh is very fine. Properly cooked, it can scarcely be distinguished from veal cutlet. They also make from them considerable quantities of lamp-oil, quite superior to that furnished by contractors for the light-houses.

The mode of taking them is as follows: The fishermen go onto the ice at the favorite resorts of the sturgeon, and cut holes through the ice about one foot in diameter. By the side of the hole they put down a small quantity of hemlock or cedar brush, (either of which is an antidote to frost.)

On the brush the fisherman lies down, with his head over the hole, covering himself entirely with his blanket, so as to keep out all light, except what reflects up from the water. He is provided with a spear of great strength, usually consisting of but one tine, with three or four barbs on *one* side. The spear-handle is thirty or forty feet long, and of heavy wood, so that it will penetrate the water with a slight effort. The spear is not made fast to the handle, but slightly pressed into a mitre in the end of it; so that the first motion of the fish will take the spear out of the handle. But the spear is connected to the handle by a strong cord several fathoms in length. The reason for this is, that the struggles of the fish would break a very strong spear handle if the spear was fastened. But, by this arrangement, the fish spends his strength in pulling upon the cord, without being able to get loose.

It is supposed the fish congregate around the holes in the ice to breathe the fresh air. The fisherman watches their coming, and seizing the first favorable opportunity, seldom fails of taking one if within twenty or thirty feet. The sturgeon are exceedingly shy. They are not sought in the summer, and very seldom taken in seeking other fish.

I have never learned the weight of sturgeon in this region. They are usually from four to seven feet long—and are of value simply as winter subsistence for the Indians.

Pike and Pickerel.—I can communicate nothing reliable concerning pike and pickerel. They are taken in small quantities for market; but none of the fishermen have been able to give me any information as to their habits. It is even disputed among fishermen whether they are not one and the same variety of fish, though, I think, without any good reason.

SISKOWIT, (*Salmo siskowit.*)—Siskowit abound principally in Lake Superior, where the best quality are taken. But they are taken in limited quantities in Lake Michigan. Fishermen generally suppose they are a mule between trout and white-fish. and their appearance favors this opinion. But they are very abundant in parts of Lake Superior where the quantity of white-fish and trout is not large, and in various parts of Lakes Huron and Michigan. Where white-fish and trout are always found together, no siskowit are found; which is hardly consistent with the theory that they are produced by a crossing of the two. Five minutes' intelligent observation at the spawning season would dispel the doubt, but I can find no person who has made it.

The siskowit is the fattest of all fish, and yet has no unpleasant or oily odor. It is valued in market above all the fish of the lakes. But there is a species of white-meated trout, of indifferent quality, so greatly resembling siskowit that it is frequently sold under that name, by which means the siskowit is undervalued, except where well known.

Mackinac Trout (*Salmo amethystus*).—The trout of this region have a world-wide fame, under the name of Mackinac trout. There is no good reason for the use of this local name, as they are found from Dunkirk, on Lake Erie, to Fond du Lac, on Lake Superior, and Milwaukee, on Lake Michigan, and I presume through a much wider region. What relation they bear to the trout of other regions I am unable to determine.

The trout are great eaters, and subsist principally on other fish. They are always pursuing white-fish and herring, and are not unfrequently caught in the nets while stealing white-fish from them.

Indians take them in the winter with spears, in the same manner as the sturgeon; also, in the same manner, with snatch-hooks instead of spears, using an artificial decoy fish, but no bait.

Trout are taken for market by trolling, with snatch-hooks, set hooks, gill-nets, and seines.

The apparatus for snatching trout can hardly be described as "a stick and a string, with a worm at one end and a fool at the other." A trout hook is made of steel wire, from one fourth to three eighths of an inch in diameter, is weighted with about two pounds of lead, in the shape of two cones with the bases joined, through which the shank passes lengthwise. The line is a cotton one of the strength of a bed cord, usually from three to six hundred feet in length. In fishing through the ice, the moment a bite is felt the fisherman throws the line over his shoulder, and runs with all his might, in a direct line, till the fish is on the ice. When in a boat, he allows the fish to run with the hook, occasionally pulling lightly, till the captive's strength is exhausted, and then pulls him in. As high as eighteen barrels have been snatched in one week by two persons; but four barrels a week is very good fishing.

Of trolling and set-hooking I could add nothing to what is generally known, except that the apparatus corresponds in strength with that used in snatching. Seining and gill-netting will be described under the head of whitefish.

I think the average weight of trout caught in seines and gill-nets (after dressing) is not above four pounds. Those caught with hooks are a trifle heavier. But individuals weighing fifteen pounds are common, and they have been taken of above fifty pounds weight.

Their spawning season is in autumn, about the first of November; but individuals are found with mature spawn several months earlier. I have thought it possible that they spawn more than once a year.

WHITEFISH *(Coregonus)*.—The whitefish are the most abundant, and, as an article of commerce, the most valuable fish of this region. Fifty thousand barrels per annum are taken among the Beaver Islands, and the quantity is rapidly increasing. As an article of food they are preferred to the trout, and inferior only to siskowit. Indians occasionally take them through the ice with spears. But they are only caught in quantities with seines and gill-nets.

Seines of all sizes are used in the usual manner. The seining begins soon after the disappearance of the ice in the spring, and lasts from one to three weeks, when various kinds of fish are taken, suckers being most abundant, but whitefish are taken in large quantities. The spawning season makes about three weeks of whitefish seining in November.

Fishing is principally done with gill-nets. The season begins from the middle of May to the forepart of June, according to the warmth of the weather, and usually ends the first week in December.

Gill-nets are usually about five or six feet wide, and twenty rods long. If designed for trout the meshes are four inches, for whitefish three and a half, and for herring three inches. When set for fishing, one edge is weighted with stones and the other buoyed up with cedar floats, so that they maintain a vertical position. From six to twelve nets are bridled together and called a gang.

When the nets are prepared for setting, the fisherman takes them to some favorite resort of the fish, usually a feeding or spawning place, and first sinks a stone anchor to the bottom and makes fast to it a buoy with a flag-staff and flag attached; then fastening the end of the gang to a buoy by a line long enough to reach the bottom, he rows or sails his boat in the direction he wishes to place the nets, paying out the nets as the boat moves till he gets to the end, when he fastens to it another buoy and flag by a line long enough to drop the net to the bottom.

The nets are usually left in the water three days, when they are lifted, the fish taken out, stones and floats taken off, and the nets dried, repaired, and prepared for setting again. Twenty fish to a net is a good yield, but as many as one hundred are sometimes taken.

Whitefish come into the shoals in the spring (for what purpose I have been unable to learn); hence the spring seining. The first gilling is usually in from two to five fathoms water. As the season advances they retire to deeper water, till by the first of September they are found in from fifty to one hundred and fifty fathoms water. Indeed, off Fox Island nets have been set with success in water fourteen hundred feet deep. The largest fish come from the deep water.

The spawning season begins in November, and terminates in December. This year (1853) it commenced November 11, and is apparently just closing (December 7). The spawning season is indicated by the fish leaving deep water and appearing in immense numbers on rocky shoals. The first day they appear upon the shoals the nets take all males, apparently well stocked with milt. The second day a few females appear among them, plump with spawn. The proportion of females increases till after a week or ten days, when they are two, three, and four times as many as the males, after which the females slowly disappear, and the males last leave the spawning ground.

The best opinion seems to be that the males precede the females only to prepare the ground, especially as they at that time assume an extraordinary roughness of the scales, and employ themselves constantly in scraping up gravel on which the spawn is subsequently deposited. Some, however, believe that the mere inclination to milt causes them to seek the proper positions without reference to the presence or absence of females. Others still are of opinion that they preceed only to wait for the females, and do not commence milting till the spawning commences. The males have been accused of lingering on the spawing ground to feast on the spawn; but this is contrary to nature, and, undoubtedly, a slander. The most careful observers assure me they are employed in *covering up the spawn*.

Seining during the spawning season is the most productive of all fishing. Twenty barrels with a seine one hundred rods long is a common haul. One hundred and forty-seven barrels have been taken at a single haul. But there are very few places adapted to it. The only situation adapted to it is a smooth sand or shingle beach, a bottom free from rocks and surrounded by rocky reefs.

HERRING (*Coregonus*).—Herring are taken in the same manner as whitefish; also in gill nets, set under the ice in winter. They are usually the first taken in the spring. I have not been able to learn their spawning season; and their habits have been very little observed. When heavy winds prevail, they seek shelter in quiet bays, and in the lee of the various islands. Flocks of gulls hover over them continually, and carnivorous fish pursue them wherever they go, even into the nets. They are killed by a very slight touch. Indeed, they seem to be the prey of everything that eats fish.

The average weight of dressed herring is not above one pound. They are usually pickled in the same manner as whitefish, and not unfrequently sold under that name, but are too small to be desirable. When scalded and smoked, after the Scotch mode, they are equal to any ever found in market, and are remarkable for fatness. Labor is too dear to justify saving them in this manner.

I have never compared them anatomically with salt-water herring, and therefore do not know whether these are genuine herring. But from flavor and general appearance, I presume they are. [They are entirely different.—S. F. B.]

Herring, whitefish, and trout, are found of several varieties, differing materially in their qualities, and something in their appearance and habits. But we have no names for the several varieties, and their peculiarities have not been noted.

SUCKERS (*Catastomus*).—The lake suckers, though similar to the fish of the same name in most of the western rivers, are very superior in quality for eating. For this reason, and to avoid the ill repute of the name "*sucker*," they are usually sold under the name of "lake shad," a name founded merely on caprice, and used for purposes of fraud. They are not supposed to bear any resemblance to the shad.

Suckers are usually taken with seines, early in the spring, at the mouths of rivers and brooks. They frequent particular shores and shoals in June, but whether for spawning or some other purpose, I have been unable to learn; they are there taken with seines in great quantities. Suckers are sometimes taken for manure alone.

PERCH.—Perch abound in all the waters of this region, except mere brooks, and are in constant use fresh, but are never preserved in any way. I find no man who has observed their habits in any respect. They are taken with hooks and spears with so much facility, that children hook them with pins, and spear them with sharpened rods.

BASS.—Bass, of two or three varieties, are found in one of the lakes within this island; I presume they abound in others. No notice has been taken of their habits, and I can get no information concerning them from those who fish for them every year. They are taken both winter and summer.

LING or LAWYERS (*Lota*).—These are a valueless fish, taken in small numbers. They will live twenty-four hours out of water. No amount of boiling will make the flesh tender. If exposed it will not rot, but only dries up like an oxhide. The Indians eat the livers only.

SUNFISH (*Pomotis*).—Sunfish abound in all the small lakes. Nothing is noted of them. I cannot get even an intelligent description of them, though they are frequently caught for food.

GENERAL REMARKS.—Trout subsist on all kinds of fish. They are a voracious fish of prey, seizing and devouring, so far as we can learn, every other kind, even their own. Herring are their constant prey. Whitefish of two pounds weight have been found within the belly of the trout. Small trout are sometimes found in them. Whitefish in gill-nets are gnawed and torn by them, and in this operation the largest trout are frequently themselves tangled in the meshes of the nets and taken. It is supposed they seek the spawn of other kinds of fish, and that the whitefish seek rocky shores to avoid them; and in support of this theory it is alleged, among other things, that when the whitefish are spawning nets set a little further out catch trout. Possibly, however, this may arise from the habit of the trout of spawning in a little deeper water.

Whitefish subsist on a kind of worm of the same structure as the leech. Probably it may be a leech, but white and semi-translucent for want of red blood to prey upon. Also upon the seed of a kind of seaweed, or submarine moss, which exists in great abundance in all the deep waters of this region. On inquiry of a dozen intelligent fishermen I can hear of but one instance of a whitefish being found with fish in his belly.

Throughout the fishing region there are vast submarine meadows, rising almost to the dignity of forests. Probably most of the fish subsist on this growth, and a few only by prey. If this is the case, the supply of fish will ever be regulated by the productiveness of these fish-meadows; for so numerous are the spawn, that no conceivable amount of catching can sensibly diminish the stock of fish. The usual spawn of a female is between fifty and one hundred thousand.

Whitefish are only found in very pure water. In channels of the greatest depth, where steamboats are constantly passing and occasionally throwing over ashes and litter, the whitefish disappear.

Where fishing is extensively carried on, many nets are lost by the lines parting, and the buoys and flags going loose. The nets remain at the bottom continually catching fish, which remain and perish. Other nets, with fish in them, are broken up by storms and left scattered about the bottom. The effect of this is to drive off the fish and destroy the fisheries. But no amount of fishing, where these calamities were avoided, has ever sensibly diminished their productiveness.

SPAWNING GROUNDS.—In passing over the lake in the fishing region, when the surface is perfectly unruffled, the man of science is surprised to see the bottom *regularly paved with large stones*. Careful observation shows that, naturally, the bottom was strewn with boulders, varying in weight from such as can be lifted with one hand to mountain masses of detached rock.

Selecting some convenient point with a large boulder as a nucleus, the others *have been rolled together*, so as to form a compact pavement, in some instances, of many acres in extent without a single blank space. In doing this work all the other ground is cleared of rock, except here and there a boulder of several tons weight. Throughout these pavements a few large boulders remain scattered as by the hand of nature. But, except them, the smallest rocks are in the centre of each pavement, gradually enlarging as you approach the circumference, till the outside courses are only perceptibly less than the scattered boulders which remain unmoved. There is an entire absence of all mathematical arrangement, but in its kind no work of man can be more perfect.

The islands of this region are an upheaval, and in several places these pavements are now above water and can be examined to advantage, and there can be no mistake as to their structure. They are found in the greatest depths that the eye can penetrate. Some are a few rods and others many acres in extent; and the vacant spots intervening are (except occasionally an immense boulder) as thoroughly cleared of every kind of stone as a well-kept lawn. They present only the appearance of clean washed sand.

Fish, when spawning, are observed to place small stones and pebbles in this same order, and all are agreed that these are spawning grounds. When it is considered that the ponderability of stone in water diminishes as the depth increases, it may not be deemed incredible that the present known species of fish have made these pavements for spawning grounds. I will not, however, speculate further, but submit the fact for the consideration of those more capable of judging.

A thousand avocations and duties constantly pressing upon me have prevented my giving the attention to these subjects that I would be pleased to. But if the few facts I have been able to obtain, and this hurried communication, prepared in haste (with many others) in the few hours that the last steamboat of the season lies in this harbor, is of any value, I shall be quite happy to continue to correspond, and to continue, as far as possible, to make observations for that purpose.

On the habits of the Black Bass of the Ohio, (Grystes fusciatus.)

BY JOHN EOFF, ESQ., OF WHEELING.

"On my return from a small hunting expedition to the head waters of Sand creek, Jackson County, Virginia, I found your kind letter of November 26; and, in order to comply best with your wishes and views therein expressed, I will give you such a description of one particular species of fish, (which I consider the most valuable, on account of their quality as a pan-fish and their quantity,) in our western streams, viz: the bass, (called by the early settlers in the western country, yellow, or black perch). They are a remarkably active and voracious fish, with a large and hard mouth, and vary in size, according to their age, from three quarters of a pound to three pounds, and occasionally have been caught to weigh as high as six pounds or seven pounds. Their food, when small, appears to be all kinds of insects, (flies, worms, &c.); when larger, though not entirely leaving off their earlier habits, their principal food is the smaller fish of other kinds. In the winter season they retire to deep and still water, and apparently hide under rocks, logs, &c., and remain there until the 1st of April, when they come out and begin to ascend the streams, apparently to find a convenient place for spawning, which commences about the 15th of May, varying some little according to the warmth of the season, &c. When that event is about taking place, they appear to separate into pairs, male and female, and hunt out some retired place, or nook, where the water is about eighteen inches deep, and still, but adjoining deeper water, to which they can escape if alarmed; they there commence making their nests, that is, washing all the mud, &c., off the bottom, so as to leave it perfectly clean, in a circular form, the diameter of the circle (or nest) being about twice the length of the fish; after which the female begins depositing her eggs, which appear to become glued to the bottom, or small stones, in rows, after the deposit has taken place. She remains night and day, either on her nest, or swimming round about it, apparently guarding the eggs, and driving every other smaller fish away. This watching or guarding continues until the eggs are what is called *hatched*, which occurs in from eight to ten days, according to the temperature of the water. The young fish at first remain near the bottom, and appear like a gauze veil floating. In two or three days they gradually rise and spread, the old one leaves them, they separate, and each one shifts for itself, *i. e.*, hides under leaves, small sticks, and stones.

I, as yet, have had no positive means of determining the precise time for a young bass to arrive at *maturity*, but suppose it to be three years, from the following facts. In the spring of the year (April) you may find large numbers of young bass about two or two and a half inches in length, rather in company with other minnows; in the following autumn and fall of the year you will find very few of that size, but congregating together, and alone you will find a number from three to four inches in length; while during the same fall you may catch young bass of about eight inches long, with the formation of the young egg within them, preparatory for spawning the following spring. In the spawning season you will find a large number of nests of small bass, the bass being ten or eleven inches long, which I have always concluded were three years old. Hence, from the above facts, you will perceive that the bass of our western country are valuable, and, at the same time, can be easier transferred, and in greater quantities, from one stream to another, than almost any other fish. All that is necessary to supply a pond with any quantity, would be to examine their nests at the time they are spawning, and to pick up the small gravel out of their nests, with the eggs attached thereto, and put them in a bucket of water, and place them in your pond, in such a position that smaller fish could not devour the eggs; and in a short time they would hatch, and the young ones would help themselves. Or, to secure a larger quantity in a short time, wait until the young are hatched, and are in innumerable quantities, suspended over the nest; then, with a piece of gauze net, dip them up and empty them in a vessel containing as much pure water as will sustain them until you can convey them to your pond; and then, as I before observed, they can support themselves, while young, on insects, &c. Or, early in April or May, if you are fond of angling, you can go to a stream in which there are plenty, and in catching fifteen or twenty, will almost always get nearly one half the number smaller ones. Put these into your pond unhurt; and, as they have not spawned that season, they will soon stock the water. Then all that remains to be done is to supply your pond with other small fish, minnows, &c., for food for the large bass, and they will increase in quantity just in proportion to their supply of food. Hence I am satisfied that if a farmer would convert one acre of his land into a pond, well supplied with fresh water, that acre would raise and support more fish yearly (the value of which would be more,) than any other two acres cultivated in any other manner—the expense of cultivating deducted from each.

Mr. William Shriver, a gentleman of this place, and son of the late David Shriver, esq., of Cumberland, Maryland, thinking the Potomac river admirably suited to the cultivation of the bass, has commenced the laudable undertaking of stocking that river with them; he has already taken, this last season, some twenty or more in a live box, in the water tank on the locomotive, and placed them in the canal basin at Cumberland, where we are in hopes they will expand and do well, and be a nucleus from which the stock will soon spread.

Some Remarks on the Natural History of the country about Fort Ripley, Minnesota.

BY J. F. HEAD, SURGEON U. S. ARMY.

Communicated by the Surgeon General of the United States Army.

[Extract.]

* * * The mammalia most frequently found are the prairie and large gray wolf, (*Canis latrans and C. occidentalis,*) the former very abundant; the red deer, (*Cervus virginianus,*) not very numerous; the ground squirrel, (*Sciurus striatus,*) field mouse, (*Mus leucopus?*) weazel, (*Mustela erminea,*) muskrat, (*Fiber zibethicus,*) badger, (*Meles labradoria,*) and porcupine, (*Hystrix dorsata,*) and occasionally the otter, (*Lutra braziliensis,*) marten, (*Mustela martes,*) mink, (*M. lutreola,*) skunk, (*Mephietis amer.,*) lynx, (*Lynx canadensis,*) and red fox, (*Canis fulvus.*) Other varieties of fox are taken somewhat further north, (*C. decussatus, C. argentatus, and C. cinereo-argentatus,*) and may inhabit this neighborhood. The black bear, (*Ursus americanus,*) though found in the surrounding country, has never been seen in the immediate vicinity of the post. The moose (*Cervus alces*) and carabou (*C. turandus*) are said to be occasionally seen at about one hundred and fifty miles north, and the elk (*C. canadensis*) on the prairies thirty or forty miles west of this place. The gray squirrel (*Sciurus carolinensis*) is not found in any part of the territory. The buffalo (*Bison americanus*) does not approach within one or two hundred miles. In the autumn of 1848 the varying hare, (*Lepus americanus,*) vulgo "white rabbit," was very abundant, but during the following year (*the winter of which was not unusually severe*) they almost completely disappeared from a region for many miles around this point. Many of the Indians, who depend much on these animals for subsistence during the winter, were consequently reduced to actual starvation.

Of birds the following species have been identified: The golden eagle, (*Falco fulvus,*) bald eagle, (*F. leucocephalus,*) owl, (*Strix virginiana,*) meadow lark, (*Sturnus ludovicianus,*) red-winged and cow blackbirds, (*Icterus phœniceus and I. pecoris,*) crow blackbird, (*Quiscalus versicolor,* raven, (*Corvus corax,*) crow, (*C. americanus,*) blue jay, (*C. cristatus,*) chickadee, (*Parus atricapillus,*) cedar bird, (*Bombycilla carolinensis,*) king bird, (*Muscicapa tyrannus,*) pewee, (*M. fusca,*) thrush, (*Turdus rufus,*) robin, (*T. migratorius,*) yellow bird, (*Sylvia æstiva?*) blue bird, (*Sialia wilsonii,*) (rare,) snow bunting, (*Emberiza nivalis,*) wood-peckers, (*Picus auratus, P. erythrocephalus, P. pubescens,* king-fisher, (*Alcedo alcyon,*) swallow, (*Hirundo rufa,*) whipper-will and night-hawk, (*Caprimulgus vociferus. C. virg.,*) pigeon, (*Columba migratoria,*) "pheasant," or "partridge," (*Tetrao umbellus,*) grouse, (*T. cupido,*) *golden plover, (*Charadrius pluvialis,*) killdeer, (*Ch. vociferus,*) crane, (*Grus canadensis,*)

* This bird, at first rather rare, but now rapidly multiplying in this vicinity, differs somewhat in plumage, and perhaps in its habits, from the descriptions of *T. cupido*. It is possibly *T. phasianellus*. Never having examined other species before coming to this station, and possessing neither a plate nor a good description of the latter bird when specimens were procurable, I am at present unable to determine the question.

green heron, (*Ardea virescens,*) curlew, (*Numenius longirostris,*) sand-pipers, (*Tringæ,*) yellow-feet, (*Totanus vociferus,*) smaller do., (*T. flavipes,* (peet-weet,) (*T. macularius,*) upland plover, (*T. bartramii?*) snipe, (*Scolapax wilsonii,*) a few woodcock, (*Sc. minor,*) rail, (*Rallus,*) coot, (*Fulica americana,*) horned grebe, (*Podiceps cornutus,*) terus, (*Sterna,* several species,) goose, (*Anser canadensis,*) brant, (*A. bernicla,*) loon, (*Colymbus glacialis,*) *Mergus merganser, M. cucullatus.* Ducks of the following species, and doubtless others not identified: the golden-eye, (*Fuligula clangula,*) scaup duck, or blue-bill, (*F. marila,*) buffel-head, (*F. albeola,*) dusky duck, (*Anus obscura,*) mallard, (*A. boschas,*) summer duck, (*Anus sponsa,*) and teal (*A. discors and A. crecca*). The ducks* pass this point nearly in the order of the above enumeration, on their way northward, the first appearing about the middle of April, and return nearly in an inverse order late in August and early in September. A few individuals of nearly all the above-mentioned species appear to breed in this latitude, as does also occasionally the Canada goose. Lingering for a few weeks about the rice-lakes in this vicinity, where they acquire a fine condition and flavor, they continue their course to the south in October and November, by the middle of which month the last of the migratory tribes have disappeared; and the grouse having retired into the recesses of the forest, the raven, blue jay, and snow bunting are left apparently the sole feathered inhabitants of this desolate region.

The *reptiles* have scarcely been noted. Of serpents, the only species seen are the common "garter snake," (*Coluber sirtalis,*) and a species of adder. The rattle-snake, if ever met above the falls of St. Anthony, must be very rare. Two are reported to have been killed at Sac Rapids, about 50 miles south of this place.

The *fish* most abundant in the Mississippi at this point, and in the neighboring streams and small lakes, (which appear to be least scantily supplied with them,) are the "glass-eye," Ohio "salmon," or pike perch, (*Lucioperca americana,*) lake bass, (*Grystes nigricans?*) and rock bass, (*Centrarchus æneus?*) or species much resembling them; yellow perch, (*Perca flavescens,*) of small size and somewhat rare; a large species of sun-fish, (*Pomotis appendix,*) pike weighing from one to eight pounds, (*Esox vittatus?*) small cat-fish, (*Pimelodus,*) and a variety of suckers, &c., (*Cyprinidae*). The gar-pike (*Lepidosteus*) has never been seen, nor are any of the salmonidæ found in the streams falling into the Mississippi north of the Falls of St. Anthony. A species of whitefish, called by the Indians tulabie, (a Coregonus?) is taken, however, in some of the lakes nearer to the sources of this river. A large pike, specifically distinct from that above mentioned, and weighing from eight to forty pounds, is occasionally taken here, and more frequently in the river Minnesota. Two specimens captured here weighed, respectively, 18 or 20 pounds. The only one examined seems to differ both from *E. boreus* and *E. estor*.

The entomologist would find a wide field for research in this region. Insect life here appears to compensate for its brevity by its astonishing activity. During the short summer, the woods and prairies swarm

*The canvass-back duck and red-head (*F. valisneria and F. ferina*) have never been observed here, though both are frequently met at Fort Snelling.

with insects, among the most noticeable of which are the mosquito, the large "horse-fly," and the "black fly"—a small dipterous insect with black body and white legs. The last two species inflict almost inconceivable torture on the domestic animals, effectually keeping in poor condition those turned out to graze, and obliging the farmer regularly to make a large smoke at night to windward of his cattle yard. The mosquitos are said to be more abundant here during June and July than in the swamps of Louisiana, and are a most serious annoyance, both by day and night, to those whose pursuits call them abroad. The honey-bee is unknown here, but is reported to have appeared in the southern portion of the Territory within a few years. * *

On the habits of the Gopher of Illinois (Geomys bursarius).

BY J. B. PARVIN, ILLINOIS COLLEGE.

I send to the Institution a young gopher, a little more than half grown, which I hope will reach you in safety. If he arrives alive, take a flour barrel and fill it half full of moist earth, potatoes, corn, or beets, at the bottom, for food, and he will dig down and help himself, if the earth is compact, so that he can make a hole in it without its caving in upon him. I have never seen them drink; but it will be well to set a dish of water where he can come out on the top of the earth and drink it. Keep the barrel covered loosely, but so that he cannot climb out; and set it on a floor or plank, so that if he should get out he need not get easily into the ground. His habits of digging and eating you will see only by careful watching in the barrel. He uses his paws and his pouches to carry both dirt and food. He digs long holes in the ground, extending sometimes for rods or even miles, about two feet below the surface, and at suitable distances makes side cuts, at an angle of about 45°, running from the longitudinal main track up to the surface. Through these side cuts he carries up the dirt from the trunk below, as long as he finds it convenient to retain it, in his pouches—then he turns back and fills this side cut full of quite hard earth down to his main trenches, and then makes another and another side cut further on—filling all these up and stopping every crevice where light or air can enter, so that his abode, when finished, is one long winding passage, wholly excluded from all light and air, from one to three or four, perhaps more feet under ground—generally about two feet, except in places where it is made deeper to deposite food in piles, or to procure water. In these subterranean passages he lives at all times, and gathers food, roots, &c., in summer, and stores them in large deep holes for winter. He is never seen above ground except in the rare cases when food becomes scarce in one field, or for some other cause he prefers another; then he will sometimes condescend to walk a part of the way above ground, rather than persevere in his migration by digging below, and then for most part only in the night. Whether they live in droves or families, or only in pairs, is uncertain; but if two strange gophers are put together, they at once attack each other, and the victor devours his antagonist. I cannot, therefore, send you a pair at once, as I promised; and this is the first and only one I have seen this summer, except one killed and mangled in taking, so thoroughly did my boys wage their war of extermination on them last year. I will watch for more in the spring, if wanted. I have not time now for a more particular description, but will answer in future any questions desired. You are aware of its mischievous destruction of hedges and fruit-trees, as also of clover and all root crops.

On the habits of a species of Salamander, (Amblystoma opacum.) Bd.

BY THE REV. CHARLES MANN.

GLOUCESTER C. H., *Virginia.*

One of my sons requests me to say that, in all the cases in which he had found the Salamander with *eggs*, the latter were under the animals, both male and female being curled up over them. From the number found in this way, there can be little doubt of the eggs having been laid by the animals. This was the case with the specimen sent. The first specimen obtained a year ago with eggs, which he could find no means of sending you, and the one sent, *were* found in November. He says, he has seen them in the summer with eggs. The localities are the beds of *small ponds* in the woods, which in rainy seasons have water in them, but were dry when he obtained these. I sent a younger son, the other day, to get other specimens; and he returned saying he found but one pair, and they ran into the water (the late rains having partially filled the pond). These had hatched, and had several young. The nests of the one sent, and of others previously taken, were in a small hollow in the surface of the earth, deeply covered with leaves, and under which were tunnels extending in various directions. In these hollows the animals were, as I have said, curled up over their eggs. My son has been too much otherwise engaged to look for other specimens as yet, but will search for more and send them on if he succeeds in getting them. The specimens I mentioned in my letter were more interesting, because the eggs contained the embryos, as I supposed, near the period of hatching. Not knowing how to keep them, I put them in a box of sand; the old ones escaped, and the eggs dried up. The other varieties were found in a spring branch. We are fully assured they are oviparous; the old opinion of the young taking refuge in the stomach of the mother, may or may not be true. Of the common lizard, we have more than once found the eggs with perfectly formed animals in them, on one occasion so formed, that the young one ran away on the covering of the egg being cut.

My sons request me to send you some more Salamanders. A large one with one hundred and eight eggs under it was found in December. The young animals were so far matured that they were in motion as soon as released from the covering. The largest specimen was found near a pond, say twenty or thirty feet from it, and tunnels, like those of mole hills, extended from the nest in every direction under the leaves, as if the animals had been in search of food. No *small ones* have been *found out of the water,* except the very small ones which we send you, and these have come from the broken eggs.

On the Amblystoma luridum, a Salamander inhabiting Wisconsin.

BY P. R. HOY, M. D., OF RACINE, WISCONSIN.

Characteristics: Back bluish-black, with light amber spots; tail compressed, larger than the body; length 11 inches.

Description: Body robust, smooth, and shiny; head large; snout rounded; eye moderately prominent; neck short, with a distinct cervical fold; nostril small, sub-lateral; mouth opening beyond the eyes; tail sub-quadrangular at its origin, then becomes compressed laterally, moderately arched, and terminated in an obtuse point, rounded on the upper and under edges, with a notch above just below the vent. A vertebral furrow at the termination of the body and origin of the tail. Legs stout, anterior four toed, the posterior five toed, and two fifths larger.

Color: Above, back, tail, head, and extremities bluish-black, with reddish reflection, and spotted with pale amber; mouth and circle round the eye reddish lemon; flanks with a row of large oblong orange spots slightly varied with lemon yellow. Below, abdomen slate-blue, spotted irregularly with pale lemon and orange; tail, inside of legs and feet, thickly punctate with black, toes all tipped with the same; throat and chin orange, irregularly sprinkled with crimson points.

Length	11.00
Head and body to centre of vent	5.25
Tail	5.75
Head, length to gular fold	1.20
" breadth between the eyes	0.72
" just back of the eyes	1.00
" breadth between the nostrils	0.40
Tail, breadth at vent	0.80
" " one inch below	0.95
" " at the vent	0.35
Hind-leg, including longest toe	1.75
Fore-leg, " " "	1.30
Longest toe of hind-foot	0.43
Longest toe of fore-foot	0.26

Their motion on land is slow, but they swim with activity. They resent any insult offered to their mouth or eyes by quick and repeated strokes with their ample tails. I have met with but two individuals of this fine reptile, which were found about my cellar after a wet night.—(The first October 20, 1849, and the last November 1, 1850.) They are nocturnal, and, probably, only quit the water in the fall in order to seek some *congenial* winter quarters.

DIARY

Of an excursion to the ruins of Abó, Quarra, and Gran Quivira, in New Mexico, under the command of

MAJOR JAMES HENRY CARLETON, U. S. A.

WEDNESDAY, *December* 14, 1853.

A squadron of cavalry, formed of company "H," first dragoons, commanded by First Lieutenant Samuel D. Sturgis, and company "K," first dragoons, commanded by Brevet Major James Henry Carleton, in all one hundred strong, with one 12-pounder mountain howitzer, left Albuquerque, at eleven o'clock this morning, as an expedition to explore the country around the ruins of Gran Quivira, New Mexico, and for other objects connected with the bands of Apache Indians who often infest that portion of the territory.

Our route, for the first forty miles, lies down the left bank of the Rio Grande. This part of the country has often been described. Its principal features are easily named. The Rio Grande, at this point, averages about one hundred yards in width, and not more than eighteen inches in depth. Its waters are turbid, like those of the Kanzas. Its bottom and banks are composed of sand. The valley along the river is very level, and usually not over two feet higher than the surface of the water. In some places it is more than two miles broad. It has a great deal of sand mixed with the soil; but it is remarkably fertile. From this valley a second bottom, or table-land, extends, by a gradual ascent, back to the mountains on either hand. This table-land is destitute of water and uncommonly sterile. The lower level, which skirts the river, and which is irrigated from it, is the source of nearly all the agricultural wealth of New Mexico.

A storm of rain which came on yesterday continued, almost without intermission, for the whole of last night and until late this forenoon; the roads are, therefore, very muddy. In consequence of the beaviness of the travelling, the squadron was encamped near the residence of an American gentleman, named Baird, seven miles 694 yards below Albuquerque. Here we are able to obtain wood and hay; but we are obliged to send across the Rio Grande to purchase corn.

THURSDAY, *December* 15, 1853.

About four o'clock this morning it commenced snowing, with a piercing wind from the north. Our poor horses, exposed to the inclemency of the storm, were soon chilled and trembling with the cold. By eight o'clock the weather began to moderate; but we had snow-squalls, from different points of the compass, for the whole forenoon. Before we reached a little hamlet, called Valencia, fourteen miles 265 yards from our camp of yesterday, we encountered a shower of rain and sleet. As in this place we could get two *corrals*, wherein our horses could be partially sheltered, it was decided that we should encamp here for the night. The weather seems singularly unpropitious for an expedition. It is said to be quite unusual to have these storms in New Mexico at this season of the year. To-night, however, at nine o'clock, the clouds have all left the heavens, and we have promise of a fair day to-morrow.

Three Mexican citizens of respectability, a Mr. Chavis and two of his sons-in-law, came to our camp this evening, and informed Major Carleton that it was their intention to establish a colony of settlers at a point east of a range of mountains known as the Sierra Blanca, and along some streams affluent to the Pecos, called *the Seven Rivers;* that they proposed going with this command as far as Gran Quivira; and that from that point to the Seven Rivers they desired to be furnished with an escort of dragoons. They were told that they could accompany the expedition as far as Gran Quivira, but that no escort would be given beyond that point. They were informed that Brevet Lieutenant Colonel Chandler, of the army, was about to proceed from near Doña Ana, with three companies, directly to the country in the neighborhood of the Seven Rivers, and, if they wished to do so, they could have the advantage of his protection. Mr. Chavis concluded to go by the way of Gran Quivira, at all hazards; and to proceed across the country, from that point, even without an escort. The truth doubtless is, the old gentleman fancies that the purpose for which this squadron is going into that country is to search for a great amount of treasures which are said to be buried beneath the ruins there, and he hopes he may be able to obtain a share of them.

FRIDAY, *December* 16, 1853.

The weather became very cold last night; all the ponds of water extending up and down the valley are frozen over, and the ground is hard and resounds loudly at the tread of the column. The sand-bars along the river seem to be covered with geese, ducks, and brant, which have been driven by the ice from the lagoons and sloughs. They are so tame they hardly fly at our approach.

We arrived at a little town, called Casa Colorada, about four o'clock this afternoon. This place is thirty-nine miles 537 yards from Albuquerque. Here our road leaves the river for the mountains toward the east. As it will take two days to march to Manzana, the next and last point where we can procure any corn, we are encamped for the night; and shall here buy, and haul in our wagons to-morrow, the forage our animals will require to that town.

The citizens of Casa Colorada gave a ball this evening in honor of our coming. The sudden arrival amongst them of so many armed men is a matter of great astonishment.

The result of our observations, as regards the general appearance of the inhabitants of the country, made during these first forty miles of our march, may be stated in a few words. The dirty little villages through which we have passed, as well as those we have seen in the distance, have generally turned out their inhabitants *en masse* to get a sight at us. This gave us a sight at them. Had we been painters it would doubtless have been an interesting one; for men, women, children—motley assemblages—exhibited themselves to us in groupes picturesque, as well as in crowds grotesque. Some blanketed, with sombreros and cigarritos; some with whitewashed and some with scarlet-dyed faces, some with rebosos, some nearly naked, some on house-tops shading their eyes with their hand, and some peering through chinks and crannies in the mud walls of their dwellings; but all curious as to whence we came and whither we were going. The national expression of *Quien sabe* appeared deeply written on every face. In no rancho or village have we seen a solitary indication of industry, cleanliness, or thrift since we left Albuquerque; and it may be remarked, parenthetically, that we have yet to see, in that town, the first evidence of these cardinal virtues. Indolence, squalid poverty, filth, and utter ignorance of everything beyond their corn-fields and acequias, seem to particularly characterize the inhabitants who are settled along the east bank of the river. We have seen nothing denoting energy on the part of any one, save that shown by the old man Chavis and his two sons-in-law. On the contrary, we could but observe amongst them what seemed to be a universal proclivity for rags, dirt, and filthiness, in all things; with sheer laziness and listlessness marking their every movement and all that they do. It may be said that the people whom we saw were of the lower order; but we were justified in coming to that conclusion from not seeing any of a better class.

SATURDAY, *December* 17, 1853.

We started this morning at eight o'clock. For about two miles our road lay up a gradually inclined plane, where we found ourselves on an almost level *mesa* that stretched, uninterruptedly, eastward to the base of those mountains which commence at the Sandia Peak and extend towards the south below El Paso del Norte.

This plain is sandy and entirely destitute of water. We saw several herds of cattle grazing upon it; but, so far as we could observe, there was very scanty pasture. Our guide, a Mexican, informed us that these herds are driven to the Rio Grande for water only once in two days. We saw but a solitary flock of antelopes, numbering some ten or twelve. This was midway between the river and the mountains.

The scenery, viewed from elevated points on this plain, was very beautiful. The Socorro and the Ciboletta ranges of mountains, and the distant peaks of others toward the north, were covered with snow, and gleamed in the sun with dazzling splendor. The long Sierras towards which we were now moving were also clothed in a winter-robe of white. They bounded the whole eastern horizon. Their tall summits and jagged outline, like a fringed edge, standing sharp and clearly defined against the morning sky, glowed in the light as if burnished with silver. While towards us, along their whole western slope—which descended toward the plain as a coast towards the ocean—the valleys and precipices reposed in cold blue shadows, chilly enough to make the beholder shudder in looking upon them.

Just before arriving at the foot of these mountains, we found a pond of water four hundred yards to the right of the road. Our guide informed us that in the dry season no water can be obtained at this place.

There are here two passes through the mountains; the one on the left hand going eastward, leading through a difficult *cañon*, is practicable only as a bridle path; the one on the right hand affords every natural facility for making a most excellent road for wagons.

These passes are known, in the language of the country, as *Los Puertos de Abó.* The summit of the right band pass is nineteen miles and sixty-three yards from Casa Colorada, and lies east 20° south from that town. The road for this whole distance is by far the finest we had seen in New Mexico, and is not surpassed, in any point of excellence, by the celebrated shell road at New Orleans.

The first outcropping of stone which we observed as we approached the mountains was of quartz, trap, and greenstone. These are surmounted by numerous strata of fossiliferous limestone, of good quality. These strata in some places are hundreds of feet in thickness. This latter formation prevails exclusively at the summit of the pass.

There is no timber of any kind to be met with until you come near the top of the mountains; the growth then is entirely of dwarfish piñon and stunted cedar.

We encountered snow half way up the pass. The scene presented by the column winding its circuitous route to the summit, with parts of it lost to view behind some jutting crag, or just emerging into sight from some deep gorge—the foreground filled with the dragoons moving upon different turns of the road, the sun glancing brightly on their appointments—the towering snow-clad peaks on either hand—the back ground the valley of the Rio Grande, with the distant mountains in the northwest marking with a serrated line the far off horizon—was a picture whose beauty will not easily be forgotten.

The general direction of the chain of mountains stretching northward of the pass toward Sandia Peak is north 10° west. The first elevated peaks southward of Sandia are called *La Tetilla;* the next *La Sierra de la Manzana;* then come *Los Puertos de Abó;* and then the high range still further south which is known as *La Sierra del Palo Duro.*

From the summit of the pass for the first two or three miles the road is very circuitous. It then has an easy gradual descent for about three miles further, when you come to a deep cañon which lies entirely to the left, but in sight of the road, and at a distance from it of six or eight hundred yards. There, in the cañon, good sweet water is always found. This place is called *Agua de Juan Lujan.* Near this, but a few hundred yards further east, we passed a large spring of salt water. It is known by the Mexicans who travel the road as *La Salada.* Passing this, we next encountered, for some three or four miles, *mesas* of dark chocolate-colored sandstone, through which we wound our way to a point where the roads forked. We took that which leads to the left hand. In less than half a mile, our road lying up the dry bed of a wet-weather creek, we came to a fine streamlet of fresh water. This was fringed by a beautiful grove of cotton wood. At the distance of four hundred yards, after we struck the water. we came to the RUINS OF ABÓ. Here we are encamped for the night.

At this time, when so many surveys are making from different points along the Mississippi toward the Pacific, with a view of ascertaining the best route for a railroad track, perhaps the suggestion may be of value that the Pass of Abó offers advantages in this respect which may not be found in any of the other passes through these mountains. They are certainly of sufficient consideration to make it an object to have this pass thoroughly explored before others shall be adopted. By directing the route from Anton Chico, on the Pecos river, immediately past the Ruins of Abó, and thence through the cañon by which the bridle-path lies that has already been spoken of, the open plain in the great valley of the Rio Grande can be reached without tunnelling a rod, and with no more difficulty as to the blasting of rocks and grading down of acclivities, than has been encountered on any of the ordinary railroads in the United States. Let the road be directed across the plain so as to pass the Rio Grande at the mouth of the Puerco river, thence up the valley of that river to its west branch, and up the valley of that branch to Laguna; thence to Zuñi, and from that point by the route which the indefatigable Whipple will without a doubt find, to the shores of the Pacific. These suggestions may possibly be of practical utility to those who are engaged in by far the greatest enterprise of modern times.

The RUINS OF ABÓ consist of a large church, and the vestiges of many other buildings, which are now but little else than long heaps of stones, with here and there portions of walls projecting above the surrounding rubbish. There is yet standing enough of the church to give one a knowledge of the form and magnitude of the building when in its prime. The ground plan of this structure is in the form of a cross, its longitudinal direction being within ten degrees of the magnetic meridian. It was, perhaps, situated exactly upon that meridian when the building was erected—the variation of the compass accounting for the present difference. The great entrance was in the southern end. From thence to the head of the cross, where the altar was doubtless situated, it is one hundred and thirty-two feet, inside. This, the nave of the church, is thirty-two feet in width. The short arm of the cross, or what in cathedrals is called the transept, is forty-one feet in length and twenty-three in breadth. The transept is sixty-six feet from the doorway. These measurements were made with a tape-line in a very high wind. The round numbers in feet are, therefore, only given, without noting the fractional parts of a foot.

The walls are of great thickness, and their height is, at this day, in over half the structure, all of fifty feet. The upper edge of these walls is cut into battlements. The church, as well as the neighboring buildings now in ruins about it, was built of a stratified, dark red sandstone, such as crops out along the creek and makes its appearance on the sides of the surrounding hills. The pieces of stone do not average over two and a half inches in thickness, and are not generally over one foot in length. Each piece is of the form it had when it was broken from its native bed. We saw not a single dressed stone about the ruins. These stones are laid in mortar made of the ordinary soil from the ground immediately at hand. The roof of the church was evidently supported by beams and covered with earth, as in the churches still occupied as places of worship throughout New Mexico. We saw no signs of an arch, nor any indication that those who planned and built the church at Abó were at all acquainted with architecture as a science. The walls over the doors and windows, so far as we could observe, had been supported by beams of wood. When these had become destroyed, those stones which were liberated above had dropped down; so that now, over each window there is a rude sort of Gothic arch, owing its form, not to design, but to accident. The wood-work of the church was evidently destroyed by being burnt. Wherever in the walls portions of beams still remain they are found charred and blackened by fire.

The form of the church alone, proves it to have been designed by Christians. Perhaps the workmen employed in its construction were Indians. We saw a distinct mark of an axe in one of the pieces of timber, which is imbedded in the east wall of the church some six feet from the ground. Saws also were doubtless used, but we discovered no marks of them. The stick of timber marked with the axe, and some beams that supported a landing at the head of the stairway which is made in the west wall, were the only pieces of wood about the ruins which were not burned so much over their surface as to obliterate all marks of tools.

The extent of an exterior wall, which, from the appearance of the present heaps of stones, once surrounded the church and the town, was about nine hundred and forty-two feet north and south, with an average width east and west, of say four hundred and fifty feet. A large population must have occupied this town and its neighborhood, if one were to judge of the number of people by the size of the church built to accommodate them at their devotions.

We saw few, if any, unmistakeable signs that the ground had been cultivated in the vicinity of these ruins. Nor is there any good arable land, so far as we could observe, at any point nearer the Rio Grande; for uplands to be arable, in the climate of New Mexico, must be so situated as to be capable of irrigation. The stream of water at Abó is in a deep ravine. It is very inconsiderable in point of size, and loses itself in the sand in less than five hundred yards below the springs which feed it. The adjacent country is rolling and broken, and covered with piñon and cedar. The underlying rocks are secondary red sandstone. The summits of the mesas and neighboring eminences are composed of grey limestone filled with marine fossils.

It was nearly night when we reached Abó. There was a keen freezing gale from the northwest, and the whole appearance of the country was cheerless, wintry, and desolate. The tall ruins, standing there in solitude, had an aspect of sadness and gloom. They did not seem to be the remains of an edifice dedicated to peaceful, religious purposes, a place for prayer, but rather as a monument of crime, and ruthlessness, and violence. The cold wind when at its height appeared to roar and howl through the roofless pile like an angry demon. But when at times it died away, a low sigh seemed to breathe along the crumbling battlements; and then it was that the noise of the distant brook rose upon the ear like a wail.

In the mystery that envelopes everything connected with these ruins—as to when, and why, and by whom, they were erected; and how, and when, and why, abandoned—there is much food for very interesting speculation. Until that mystery is penetrated so that all these questions can be answered without leaving a doubt, Abó belongs to the region of romance and fancy; and it will be for the poet and the painter to restore to its original beauty this venerable temple, to rebuild its altars, and to exhibit again unto us its robed priests, its burning censers, its kneeling worshippers.

SUNDAY, *December* 18, 1853.

It took us until half past nine o'clock this morning to complete our examination of the ruins. We then marched over a rolling and, in places, broken country twelve miles 760 yards, and in a general direction of N. 12° E. For the whole of this distance the country is covered with groves of cedar and piñon trees. We then came to the *Ruins of Quarrá.* These appear to be similar to those of Abó, whether regarded with a view to their evident antiquity, the skill exhibited in their construction, their preservation at the present time, or the material of which they are built. They too are situated upon a small stream of water that soon disappears in the earth.

The church at Quarrá is not so long by thirty feet as that at Abó. We found one room here, probably one of the cloisters attached to the church, which was in a good state of preservation. The beams that supported the roof were blackened by age. They were square and smooth, and supported under each end by shorter pieces of wood carved into regularly curved lines and scrolls, like similar supports which we had seen at the ends of beams in houses of the better class in Old Mexico. The earth upon the roof was sustained by small straight poles, well finished and laid in herring bone fashion upon these beams. In this room there is also a fire-place precisely like those found in the Mexican houses at the present day.

We had heard that in a stone panel inserted in the front end of the church at Quarrá we should find emblazoned the *fleur-de-lis*, the ancient armorial bearings of France; and many therefore supposed that possibly this church had been erected by French Catholics who had come as missionaries across the country from the direction of New Orleans. But we saw no panel, no fleur-de-lis, and no stone of any kind, that bore marks of a chisel or of a hammer. Every piece in the church, in the cloisters, and in the debris of a neighboring village, was in the same rough form which it had when it was broken from the quarry.

The course from Quarrá to the town of Manzana is, W. 35° N.; the distance is four miles 1,145 yards. We now find ourselves at a very great elevation. The whole country is clad in a winter garb. The high Sierra de las Manzanas, and the towering pyramidal peaks called Las Tetillas, gleam with a depth, it is said, of more than two feet of snow.

The town of Manzana is situated at the base of the Sierra of that name, and a small rivulet which, in running eastward to the open plains, soon sinks into the ground. Several dams are constructed along this rivulet, to collect and retain the water for purposes of irrigation. The town is built partly of logs set on end *jacal* fashion, with the interstices filled with mortar, and with roofs covered with earth, and partly of *adobes*. It sports a very dilapidated church, erected, it would seem, as a practical antithesis to the morals of the inhabitants; for Manzana enjoys pre-eminently the wide-spread notoriety of being the resort of more murderers, robbers, common thieves, scoundrels, and vile abandoned women than can be found in any other town of the same size in New Mexico, which is saying a good deal about Manzana. Fortunately it contains but few inhabitants, not more than five or six hundred at most. It is not an old town. When the first settlers came here they found two groves of apple-trees, one just above the site now occupied by the town, and one just below. Tradition says these trees were planted at the time Abó and Quarrá were inhabited; and yet, tradition has lost all trace of when that time was. It is said the Catholic church of New Mexico claims that they were planted by some priests, but admits that it has no records or authentic traditions about the ruins we have visited. Her claim, however, that *some* priests did this at *some* period or other, is good enough to authorize her to farm out these two orchards yearly, as we were informed, to the highest bidder. Two of the largest trees in the lower grove were found to be respectively eight feet and six feet in circumference. The largest was hollow —a mere shell of an inch or two in thickness. These trees have a venerable appearance. They have never been pruned, and have, therefore, grown gnarled and scraggy. Many of them are much smaller than those which were measured. They have grown, doubtless, from seeds which have fallen from the older ones. How long this process of self-planting has been kept up, of course, no one can know. Apple-trees are not indigenous to New Mexico. Assuming it to be true, however, that the largest of these trees were planted at the period referred to, then the ruins of Abó and Quarrá are more than two centuries old.

These two groves, or rather these two clumps of trees, are not standing regularly in rows and orchard-like; on the contrary, they are crowded together in the most irregular and natural manner.

The name of this town, and of the towering Sierra to the west of it, was adopted from finding these orchards here; *Manzana* being the Spanish for apple, and *Manzano* the botanical name in that language for apple-tree. The name of the town is spelt indiscriminately in both ways throughout New Mexico.

Immediately about Manzana, and up the slope towards the high mountains west of the town, there is a pine forest many miles in extent, of most excellent timber for boards and for building purposes. Some twenty-five or thirty miles in an easterly direction there is a large salt lake, which has no outlet. This lake, supplies nearly the whole of the upper portion of the territory with salt. There are fine roads leading towards it from different directions. We were informed that the bottom of the lake is covered with a sheet of solid salt, which, in the dry season, is some three or four inches in thickness. When the rainy season sets in, filling the lake with fresh water drained from the surrounding prairies, this sheet of salt is said to dissolve down to half this thickness. We were not prepared to examine and visit this lake. It lies directly off our route, and has neither wood nor fresh water within many miles of it. The proper time to go to it would be during the rainy season and when there is grass.

We had procured orders from the vicar general of New Mexico for what corn we should require at Manzana—corn which had been paid in by the peasantry as tithes *(diezmos)* to the Catholic church. When we arrived there, we found that the corn belonging to the church was some six or eight miles off, at another village, called Torreon. So we were forced to buy on credit what forage we required.

Here we learned that a small party of Texans had recently been at the ruins of Gran Quivira in search of treasures. Whilst there they sent an Apache Indian in to Manzana for some articles they wanted. An American named Fry, a hunter, who lives at Manzana, went out to the ruins in company with two Mexicans to see these Texans; when he reached there he found them gone. He ascertained while he was gone that there was no water to be found at a pond where our Mexican guide expected we should find it, as it had dried up; and that unless we found another small pond some six or eight miles from that, and which our guide knew nothing about, we should be obliged to go without any, for he said there was probably no snow about the ruins, as about Manzana, which we could melt. So Fry was employed to pilot us to this pond, as, failing to find it, we could obtain no water nearer to Gran Quivira than at the little stream at Quarrá, which is a distance of thirty-five miles.

MONDAY, *December* 19, 1853.

This morning we loaded the wagons with all the corn they would hold; but it did not amount to over two days' feed, as our other supplies had to be taken along besides. In addition to this the dragoons put into their haversacks enough for their horses for one night. We started about ten o'clock in the morning and retraced our steps toward Abó, to a point on the road known as *arroyo de la Cienega*—a dry bed of a wet-weather stream. This is nearly two miles below Quarrá. Here we left the beaten track and took a course across the country in the direction of E. 40° S. After travelling some six miles we struck an Indian trail which leads from Manzana to the country of the Mescalero Apaches. This we followed in the same general direction to some holes in the rocky bed of another wet-weather stream called *Las Aguachas.* These often contain water enough for a small party with animals, but we found them quite dry. One, only, had a small cake of ice, but no water. They are 13 miles 1,022 yards from where we left the road. The country for this distance is quite barren. It has but little grass, but is covered with the tall branching cactus, and with scattered clumps of piñon and cedar-trees. On our right hand, for the last third of this distance, we have had a mesa covered with timber to its summit, which is called *La Mesa de los Tumanes.* It is improperly laid down upon the maps as a Sierra, or mountain range. It runs from west to east, commencing a few miles south of Abó and ending in a point on the plains about fifteen miles east of Las Aguachas, where we cross over it by ascending gradually through an open prairie, which can easily be seen from the place where we left the road below Quarrá.

The stone that crops out at Las Aguachas is a remarkably fine sandstone, suitable for grindstones and whetstones. The best is at the upper end of the ravine where the last pool of water would be found in the wet season.

When we reached this point it was nearly night. A cold piercing wind was blowing, and it was yet some miles to the place where we hoped to find water. The wagons were some two or three miles behind; Major Carleton pushed on with the squadron, having Fry for a guide, to find the pond before dark; leaving Lieutenant Sturgis with twelve men at Las Aguachas, to wait for the wagons, and then follow with them on the trail. The Mexican guide stayed with the lieutenant, that he might track the squadron after night should set in. After travelling a little over five miles, the squadron arrived at the water. It was found in a deep hollow in the open prairie. The pond is not over eighty or one hundred yards in diameter, and might easily be missed after dark even by one acquainted with its locality. The water is fresh and sweet. This pond is nearly a mile from timber. It lies immediately off against the mouth of a pass through the Mesa de los Tumanes, and is known to the shepherds as *La Laguna de la Puerta*, the Lake of the Pass. Here we made holes in the ice, and, having watered all the horses, moved up into the pass, where we found wood in abundance, and very good protection from the cold wind. We soon had large fires burning, which served as a beacon to the lieutenant, who was behind bringing up the wagons. Shortly after dark he arrived. One of the wagons was immediately unloaded and sent with the water-kegs to the lake; the men taking lanterns to see to get the water through the ice. By ten o'clock at night our horses were groomed and fed, the men had had their suppers, and large piles of piñon wood were blazing the whole length of the camp, giving it a cheerful and picturesque appearance.

This camp is twenty-five miles and 90 yards from Manzana.

TUESDAY, *December* 20, 1853.

As we knew it would be quite impossible to march to Gran Quivira and make the necessary observations there and back to the laguna in one day, it was decided to rest this forenoon, and to fill the kegs and India rubber water-tanks with water, and then to march to the ruins in the afternoon; to encamp near them to-night; to employ the forenoon of to-morrow in their examination; and then to return to-morrow evening to this place. In this way our animals would not be without wate more than a day and a half. We accordingly broke up our camp about half-past twelve o'clock. After we had filled our kegs and tanks at the laguna, we ascended a high ridge for a mile or more, when our guide pointed out to us what he said was the great church or cathedral, at Gran Quivira. It was in an air line all of thirteen miles distant, and yet we could see it distinctly with the naked eye. We could have seen it easily when five or six miles further off, had there been no obstruction to the view; a proof of the remarkable clearness of the atmosphere in this elevated region. It lies S. 5° E by the compass from Laguna de la Puerta, and served for a land-mark towards which to direct our march. Our course was a very straight one; for the country, which is an open rolling prairie, offered no impediment to our moving in a right line. The weather changed to be very cold during the afternoon; when near sunset a fierce wind arose from the direction of the snow-clad mountains in the west, and a cold vapor like a cloud came over the country, enveloping everything in a dense fog, and covering men and horses with a hoar frost. It was feared that the gale would change into one of those dreadful winter northers which are sometimes experienced in this country, and which are so fatal to men and animals when exposed to their fury on the open prairie. So the direction of the march was changed, that we might get the shelter of the timber on the slope of the Mesa de los Tumanes, which stretched along our right at a distance of not more than three or four miles. This we struck very opportunely, just as night was setting in. We soon had large fires blazing, and all our horses well blanketed and picketed on the leeward side of them, to get the benefit of the heated air and of the eddy in the wind from the long line of tents. In this way they were kept from suffering, although the night was uncommonly cold and inclement.

So still another day has passed away, and the ruins are not yet reached. Quivira would seem always to have been a difficult place to arrive at. We find in Castañeda's history of the expedition into this country made by Francisco Vasques de Coronado, in 1540, '41, and '42, that that general was forty-eight days in hunting for it, starting from some point between the Rio Grande and the Gila river. All the way from Albuquerque we have asked the people of the country where the ruins were situated? How they looked? Who built them? &c., &c. To all these questions we could seldom get a more definite reply than *Quien sabe?* It seemed as if the genii who, in the Eastern tale at least, are said to guard the depositories of great treasures, were determined to make the existence of such a place as Gran Quivira as much of a problem to us as to the Mexicans themselves. We had seen, before the fog set in, an edifice in the distance, which had seemed to move away as we approached it, like the weird lakes of water in a mirage. But to-morrow, at all events, will decide for us whether that edifice be a Fata Morgana or not.

WEDNESDAY, *December* 21, 1853.

At daybreak this morning every tree and spire of grass, and even the blankets upon our horses, were covered with ice. The trees seemed as if every twig was made of frosted silver. The wind had gone down, and overhead the sky was clear; but a heavy bank of fog extended all along the east, obstructing our view of the Sierra de las Gallinas, which bounds the horizon in that direction. It was long ere the approaching sun waded up through so dense a veil.

Soon after we left camp we again saw the cathedral of Gran Quivira; but in surmounting one eminence after another as we moved along over a rolling country, the ruins, phantom like, seemed to recede before us the same as yesterday. When we first saw them this morning they appeared to be about a mile and a half distant, when in reality they were more than five miles off. The last three of these five miles' travel was over nothing but a succession of sand hills covered with a tall coarse grass, with two or three heads on each stalk, which seemed to be peculiar to this place. The horses sank more than fetlock-deep into the soft yielding sand; while it was with great difficulty that the mules, at a snail's pace, drew the wagons along.

At eleven o'clock in the forenoon we came to the last high ridge on the point of which the ruins are situated. This ridge is composed of dark blue compact limestone, which crops out in several places along its slopes. The ascent is quite abrupt on every hand, except towards the east; the ridge is prolonged in that direction for several miles. We all felt rejoiced that finally we had reached a place about which so much had been written, and yet so little had really been known.

Whatever may have been the grandeur and magnificence of that place in ages long past, its present appearance and condition are easily described.

We found the ruins of Gran Quivira to consist of the remains of a large church, or cathedral, with a monastery attached to it; a smaller church or chapel; and the ruins of a town extending nine hundred feet in a direction east and west, and three hundred feet north and south. All these buildings had been constructed of the dark blue limestone which is found in the vicinity.

The cathedral, which we had seen from Laguna de la Puerta, is one hundred and forty feet long outside, with the walls nearly six feet in thickness. It stands longitudinally W. 15° S., with the great entrance in the eastern end. The altar was in the western end. Like the churches at Abó and Quarrá, it is constructed in the form of a cross. From the doorway at the foot of the cross to the transept, it is eighty-four feet seven inches; across the transept it is twenty-one feet six inches; and from thence to the head of the cross it is twenty-two feet seven inches; making the total length, inside, one hundred and twenty-eight feet eight inches. The width of the nave is twenty-seven feet; the length, inside of the short arm of the cross, is thirty-six feet. A gallery extended along the body of the cathedral for the first twenty-four feet. Some of the beams which sustained it, and the remains of two of the pillars that stood along under the end of it which was nearest to the altar, are still here; the beams in a tolerably good state of preservation—the pillars very much decayed; they are of pine wood, and are very elaborately carved. There is also what, perhaps, might be termed an entablature supporting each side of the gallery, and deeply embedded in the main wall of the church; this is twenty-four feet long by, say, eighteen inches or two feet in width; it is carved very beautifully, indeed, and exhibits not only great skill in the use of various kinds of tools, but exquisite taste on the part of the workmen in the construction of the figures. These beams and entablatures would be an ornament to any edifice even at the present day. We have cut one of the beams into three parts, to take back with us. The entablatures are so deeply set in the walls that we are unable to procure a piece of them. The beams are square, and are carved on three sides; the floor of the gallery rested on the fourth side.

The stone of which the cathedral was built was not hewn, nor even roughly dressed; but the smoothest side of each piece was laid to the surface with great care. We saw no one piece in all the ruins which was over a foot in length. The mortar was made from the ordinary soil found upon the spot; it affords but a poor cement to resist the action of the elements and the ordinary ravages of time.

The walls of the cathedral are now about thirty feet in height. It was estimated, from the great quantity of stones which have fallen down, forming a sort of talus both within the walls and outside of them, that, originally, this building was all of fifty feet in height. There is a small room to the right as you enter the cathedral, and another room, which is very large, and which communicates with the main body of the building by a door at the left of the transept. There was also communication between this large room and the monastery, or system of cloisters, which are attached to the cathedral. The chapel is one hundred and thirty feet from the cathedral. This building is one hundred and eighteen feet long, outside, and thirty-two in width; its walls are three feet eight inches in thickness; it is apparently in a better state of preservation than the cathedral, but yet none of the former wood-work remains in it.

A short distance from the chapel there is an enclosure, which we supposed was the ancient cemetery.

The remains of the town are but heaps of stones, with here and there some evidences of narrow streets running nearly east and west, and north and south. Through these stones pieces of beams and sticks of wood are seen to project; these indicate, by moss and otherwise, that they are of very great antiquity; they are bleached white by the weather, and are deeply gnawed by the tooth of time.

We saw some deep pits, which were circular, and walled around like wells; we believed them to be the remains of cisterns—they were not deep enough for wells; some have concluded that they were *estufas.* Two hundred and ninety feet north of the cathedral there are evident traces of an *estanque*; this, as well as the cisterns, was probably made to collect the rain-water which ran from the different buildings.

Toward the east we saw a well defined road, which kept the ridge for a few hundred yards, and then turned off toward the southeast, where all further vestiges of it are lost in the sand. Where it is the most plainly marked along the summit of the ridge some large cedar trees are growing directly in the middle of it; these trees look to be very old indeed.

In every direction about the ruins we found great quantities of broken pottery, many specimens of which we have collected to take to Albuquerque. Some of it is handsomely marked and well glazed. We also found several stones which were evidently once used as *matates.* These matates are in use to this day, to rub boiled corn upon until it becomes a kind of dough, suitable to be kneaded into cakes called *tortillas.* We have selected two, which we shall take home with us. These prove to us that the ancient inhabitants of Gran Quivira knew the use of corn as an article of food.

There is no sign that the ground in the vicinity has ever been cultivated, and no mark whatever of irrigating ditches. Indeed, an acequia, or open aqueduct, could not, it is believed, have brought water to the Gran Quivira, for the point occupied by the town appears to be considerably higher than the surrounding country.

We were informed by men at Manzana who had been *pastores* in their youth, and had herded sheep in this region of country, that there is a fine bold spring of water at the base of the Sierra de las Gallinas, about fifteen miles from the ruins, and that they had heard that water once ran in an aqueduct from that spring to the Gran Quivira. This could hardly have been possible, unless the aqueduct was a closed pipe; because, from appearances, the country intervening between those two points is considerably lower than either of them.

We saw no indications that there had ever been such an aqueduct, nor did we see any sign that wells had been digged in the neighborhood. From every feature of the country, both within and without the surrounding sand-hills, we could but be lost in conjecture as to the method adopted by the inhabitants to obtain even water to drink, let alone for purposes of irrigation, unless they were supplied by some spring or stream that has long since disappeared. The nearest point where water can always be obtained *now*, is the spring which the *pastores* spoke of as being at the base of the Sierra de las Gallinas, fifteen miles away. The Laguna de la Puerta is 14 miles 773 yards from Gran Quivira, in nearly a direct line; but this is said to become entirely dry in seasons of great drought.

As at Abó and Quarrá, we were surprised at not finding, in the cathedral and chapel, some of the doorways and windows surmounted by an arch. Had they been so, originally, these buildings would be in a better state of preservation. The beams across windows and doors, in giving way to the weight above as they became decayed, made a fair beginning towards letting down the whole superstructure.

Mr. Gregg, in speaking of the ancient ruins of New Mexico, says: "The most remarkable of these are *La Gran Quivira*. This appears to have been a considerable city, larger and richer by far than the capital of New Mexico has ever been. Many walls, particularly those of churches, still stand erect amid the desolation that surrounds them, as if their sacredness had been a shield against which time dealt his blows in vain. The style of architecture is altogether superior to any thing at present to be found in New Mexico. What is more extraordinary still is, that there is no water within less than some ten miles of the ruins; yet we find several stone cisterns, and remains of aqueducts, eight or ten miles in length, leading from the neighboring mountains, from whence water was no doubt conveyed. And as there seem to be no indications whatever of the inhabitants having ever been engaged in agricultural pursuits, what could have induced the rearing of a city in such an arid woodless plain as this, except the proximity of some valuable mine, it is difficult to imagine. From the peculiar character of the place, and the remains of cisterns still existing, the object of pursuit, in this case, would seem to have been a *placer*—a name applied to mines of gold-dust intermingled with the earth. Other mines have, no doubt, been worked in the adjacent mountains, as many spacious pits are found, such as are usually dug in pursuit of ores of silver; and it is stated that in several places heaps of scoriæ are found.

"By some persons these ruins have been supposed to be the remains of an ancient pueblo, or aboriginal city. This is not probable; for, though the relics of aboriginal temples might possibly be mistaken for those of Catholic churches, yet it is not presumed that the Spanish coat of arms would be found sculptured and painted upon their façades, as is the case in more than one instance. The most rational accounts represent this to have been a wealthy Spanish city, before the general massacre of 1680, in which calamity the inhabitants perished,—all except one, as the story goes,—and that their immense treasures were buried in the ruins. Some credulous adventurers have lately visited the spot in search of these long-lost coffers, but as yet (1845) none have been found."

There is no indication that the escutcheon of Spain was ever sculptured or painted on any façade about the ruins; and the facts, as regards the style of architecture and the remains of an aqueduct, do not, as is shown by this journal, agree with his statement. Mr. Gregg must have described the appearance of this place from what he heard about it; for on all those subjects of which he wrote from personal observation he is most excellent authority.

Pedro de Castañeda accompanied Francisco Vasquez de Coronada in his great expedition to the north in search of gold. He wrote a history of the campaign. General Vasquez de Coronada arrived in a country which was called *Quivira*, in the month of June, 1542. *If* the present ruins of Gran Quivira are in a region identical with the Quivira then visited, it may be of interest to state what Castañeda says of it and of its inhabitants:

"Up to that point the whole country is only one plain; at Quivira, mountains begin to be perceived. From what was seen, it appears to be a well peopled country. The plants and fruits greatly resemble those of Spain: plums, grapes, nuts, mulberries, rye, grass, oats, pennyroyal, origanum, and flax, which the natives do not cultivate, because they do not understand the use of it. Their manners and customs are the same as those of the Teyas; and the villages resemble those of New Spain. The houses are round, and have no walls; the stories are like lofts; the roofs are of straw. The inhabitants sleep under the roofs; and there they keep what they possess."

The manners and customs of the Teyas, to which he likens those of the people of Quivira, are described as follows:

"These natives are called Querechos and Teyas. They live under tents of buffalo skins tanned, and subsist by the chase of these animals. These nomadic Indians are braver than those of the villages; they are taller, and more inured to war. They have great troops of dogs, which carry their baggage; they secure it on the backs of these animals by means of a girth and a little pack-saddle. When the load becomes deranged, the dogs begin to bark to warn their master to adjust it. These Indians live on raw meat, and drink blood; but they do not eat human flesh. Far from being evil, they are very gentle, and very faithful in their friendships. They can make themselves very well understood by signs. They cut meat in very thin slices, and dry it in the sun; they reduce it afterwards to a powder, to preserve it. A single handful thrown into a pot answers for a meal, for it swells greatly.

They prepare it with the fat which they preserve when they kill a buffalo. They carry around the neck a great intestine filled with blood, which they drink when thirsty. If they open a buffalo, they squeeze the masticated grass which is found in the stomach, and drink the juice which runs out; they say that this is the whole substance of the belly. They open a buffalo at the back, and divide it at the joints, by means of a piece of pebble attached to the end of a stick, with as much facility as if they used a knife of the best steel."

The present ruins are not the remains of the round houses with roofs of straw, which Castañeda describes as the dwellings of the inhabitants of Quivira, three hundred and twelve years ago; and if they had had in those days instruments to shape and carve these beautiful beams and pillars, and entablatures, they would hardly have used pebbles at the ends of sticks in cutting up the buffaloes which they had killed. Besides, the matates we have found are almost positive proof that the people who once resided here ate as food tortillas made of corn; while, from Castañeda's account, one is obliged to believe that the inhabitants of the country which he calls Quivira lived entirely upon the flesh of the buffalo, as the Comanches do at the present day.

Castañeda says likewise that: "The Indians of the country had neither gold or silver, and were not acquainted with the precious metals. The Cacique wore on his breast a plate of copper, which he held in the greatest esteem."

Many have supposed that the ancient Aztecs built the edifices at Gran Quivira, Abó and Quarrá, during their migration from Aztlan toward Anahuac; and that the ruins now found in the Navajo country, and the *Casas Grandes* which are still to be seen along the Gila river, were built by the same people and at about the same period of time. Captain Johnson, of the first dragoons, visited the ruins of the Gila river in November, 1846; from his description of one of the Casa Grande, the largest and best of any he saw, we can discover no point of resemblance between it and these now before us. Captain Johnson says: "After marching six miles, still passing plains which had once been occupied, we saw to our left the *Casa de Montezuma*. I rode to it, and found the remains of the walls of four buildings, and the piles of earth showing where many others had been. One of the buildings is still quite complete, as a ruin. The others had all crumbled but a few pieces of low, broken wall. The large Casa was fifty feet by forty, and had been four stories high; but the floors and roof had long since been burnt out. The charred ends of the cedar joists were still in the wall. I examined them, and found that they had not been cut with a steel instrument. The joists were round sticks, There were four entrances, north, south, east, and west; the doors are about four feet by two. The rooms had the same arrangement on each story. There was no sign of a fireplace in the building, The lower story was filled with rubbish; and above, it was open to the sky. The walls were four feet thick at the bottom, and had a curved inclination inwards to the top. The house was built of a sort of white earth with pebbles, probably containing lime, which abounded on the ground adjacent; and the surface still remained firm, although it was evident they (the walls) had been exposed to great heat from the fire. Some of the rooms did not open to all the rest, but had a hole a foot in diameter to look through. In other places were smaller holes." Clavigero, the historian, believes that this great movement of the Aztecs from the north towards the south commenced about the year of our Lord 1160, and that Casas Grandes were built by them at various halts which they made in their circuitous journey towards the valley of Mexico. It has been shown that in 1542 there were no buildings of the size and character of the Casas Grandes, or such as are found here now, in all the country called Quivira, which Castañeda visited and described. So one must conclude that, so far as the Aztecs are concerned, whatever they may have had to do with the building of the edifices either in the Navajo country, or on the Gila, or those found 250 miles northwest of Chihuahua, they never planned or constructed those at Gran Quivira.

History represents that Vasquez de Coronada, finding no gold during his great expedition, returned to Mexico, where he fell into disgrace and died in obscurity.

The Spaniards did not return to colonize the province of New Mexico until the year 1581; and the country could not be considered as conquered until 1595. For eighty-five years after this the colony seems to have prospered and to have grown in power. Towns and villages were built, and valuable mines of gold and silver were found and worked with success. The Catholic clergy were aided in their efforts to convert the Indians to christianity by the government, at whose expense large churches were erected in different parts of the province of New Mexico, corresponding with the *missions*, which were built for the same purpose and at about the same period in the other provinces of Texas and California. It was during this time, doubtless, that the large edifices at Abó, Quarrá, and Gran Quivira were erected. It is more than probable that valuable mines of the precious metals were found in their vicinity, and worked under the direction of the Spaniards by the Indians who had been subjugated; for there is every reason to believe that the mountains east of the Rio Grande are at this day rich in gold and silver.

It appears that during these eighty-five years the Spaniards treated the Indians with the most cruel oppression, until finally the latter revolted against them. The night of the 13th of August, 1680, was the time set throughout all New Mexico, when the Indians should rise and make an indiscriminate massacre of all the Spaniards in the country. This plot was made known to Don Antonio de Otermin, then the governor and military commandant of the province, by two Indian chiefs. Every effort was made for defence and to avert the coming storm, but without success. The Indians rose as agreed upon: after various conflicts, they destroyed great numbers of the inhabitants; and, finally, by the latter end of September of that year, succeeded in driving all the rest, with Governor Otermin included, to El Paso del Norte, entirely beyond the confines of the territory.

We have been informed that there is now a tradition amongst the Indians, that as soon as their forefathers had become successful in expelling the Spaniards, they filled up and concealed all traces of the mines where they had toiled and suffered for so many years; declaring the penalty to be torture and death to any one who should again make known their locality.

Old Mr. Chavis, who overtook us soon after our arrival at Gran Quivira, informed Major Carleton that he had been told, when in his youth, by very old people, that a tribe of Indians once lived here called the *Pueblos* of Quivira; that the Spanish priests came and lived amongst them, in peace and security, for twenty years; that during this period these large churches were erected; and that at the time of the great massacre there were seventy priests and monks residing here—all of whom were butchered excepting two, who contrived to make their escape; that, previous to their massacre, the priests had had intimation of the approaching danger, and had not only buried the immense treasures which had been collected, but had concealed likewise the bells of the churches; that many years afterwards the people of Quivira died off until but few remained; that one of these, a descendant of the chief, knew where the treasures were buried; that the remnant of the tribe afterwards emigrated and joined other Pueblos below El Paso; and that many years ago an old man, one of the last of the tribe, had told in what direction from the church these great treasures had been concealed. So far as the building of the churches and the massacre of the monks and priests are concerned in this account, as well as the final decrease and removal of the people who once lived here, there is no doubt but the story told by Mr. Chavis is, in the main, correct. The account of the depositories of the bells and the treasure is said to have been written down as given from the lips of the last cacique of Quivira, who, at the time he made the disclosure, was living away below Mesilla, on the Mexican side of the river. A copy of this paper has been secured, and is here inserted in the original language, for the benefit of those who may take an interest in such matters.

"En el Semetario de la Parroquia grande en el centro del costado derecho segun la figura numero uno esta una entraña escarbando estan dos campanas tomando la linea de la abertura que dejan las dos campanas se bera al oriente para el callejon que deja la eglesia vieja y el pueblo una lomita a distancia de tres cientas varas mas o menos que no hay otra que forme linea con las campanas debajo de dicha loma hai un sotano de diez o mas varas retacado de piedras el cual tiene el gran tesoro.

"Nombrado por Carlos quinto de la Gran Quivira."*

The grammar of this document is preserved, as in the original. There can be no doubt but the belief that a large amount of gold and silver has been buried here, has for a great number of years been seriously entertained. We find in the cathedral and in the chapel, in every room in the monastery, in every mound of stones in the neighborhood, and in every direction about the ruins, large holes dug, in many places to the depth of ten feet, by those who have come from

* "In the cemetery of the great parish church, in the centre of the right side, according to figure number one, there is a pit, and by digging will be found two bells. By taking the line of the opening left by the two bells, there will be seen to the east, along the lane left by the old church and the town, a hill, at the distance of three hundred yards, more or less, which forms precisely a line with the bells. At the foot of said hill is a cellar of ten yards or more, covered with stones, which contains the great treasure.

"Mentioned by Charles Fifth of Gran Quivira."

time to time to seek for these hidden treasures. Some of these holes look as if they were made more than a century ago, while others appear to be quite recent. Even the ashes of the dead have not been left undisturbed during these explorations. Near the east end of the chapel we saw where the people who had been digging had thrown up a great many human bones, which now lie scattered about. From these we have selected six skulls to send to some one who is skilled in the science of craniology, that he may determine, if possible, to what race of people they once belonged. These skulls are thought to be unusually large.

The ruins of Gran Quivira have hitherto occupied the same position with respect to the boundless prairies which the fabulous island of Atlantis did to the ocean in days of antiquity. No one seemed to know exactly where this city was situated. But the uncertainty of its locality seemed to make no difference in regard to the interest that was felt concerning it; for people would believe in its existence, and receive great pleasure in listening to traditions about its marvellous beauty and magnificence, even when to a reasonable mind those traditions and accounts ran counter to probability.

Men of genius and distinction have taken great pains in following up mazes in the labyrinth of reports concerning it, whether oral or written, and in their glowing descriptions it has appeared almost like a city of enchantment. To them it had paved streets, and fluted columns, and ornate friezes, and sculptured façades; it had the remains of aqueducts and fountains; it had long colonnades, and even barbaric statuary; it had the groined arch, the shouldering buttress, the quaint gargoyle, and everything in outline and in detail that could betoken skill, and taste, and opulence. It was a city, they said, whose inhabitants departed from it so long back in the gloom and mists of the past as to leave in utter obscurity all other records concerning them.

The sphynx, they said, about whose bosom the sands from the Lybian desert had drifted for unknown centuries, was no more of an enigma than this was. Here were palaces and temples, and deserted courts, and long-echoing corridors, and grass-grown streets, and reigning over all a silence so profound as almost to be heard.

Historical societies had taken up these descriptions, and filed them away among their transactions as documents of deep interest. Venerable and learned ethnologists searched in dusty manuscripts and black-letter volumes of antiquity for some authentic account of that race of men who reared and then abandoned such a city. But to this moment their researches have proved fruitless, and the story they seek is still recorded in an unsealed book.

Our business is not that which will permit us to clothe with imaginary grandeur these vestiges of a people whose name has been erased from the book of nations, nor that which will allow us time to indulge in abstruse speculations as to their race or their language. These things belong to the poet and philosopher. With all those pleasant reveries and romantic fancies which these ruins away here on a desert are so wonderfully calculated to awaken we can have nothing to do. We came here to note realities; and now the facts we have seen, the theories we have read which were of value, the traditions we have heard deserving of attention, and the conclusions to which we have come concerning this interesting place, are all written down. All else save the things we saw admits of doubt, and is obscured by so dark a cloud of uncertainty as to leave much ground for new theories, and for, perhaps, infinitely more valuable conclusions.

We found that the Mescalero Apaches, with whom we had some business of interest, had all gone far towards the south. Our guide, who was a captive amongst them for eight months, gave us some information as to their strength in warriors, which is worthy of record. He says they live in small bands, or families, in order to distribute themselves over a greater extent of country for purposes of hunting. When they are engaged in war, or upon any other enterprise of importance, these bands become united. When separated, they are each controlled by a sub-chief; when acting in concert, they choose a head-man to direct affairs for the time being. The following list shows the name of each of these sub-chiefs and the strength of his band in fighting men:

Santos has forty men;
Josecito has nine men;
Barranca has nineteen men;
Negrito has twenty men;
Jose Largo has fifteen men;
La Pluma has thirteen men;
Santana has nineteen men.

Two chiefs who live in the Sacramento mountains, whose names are unknown, have fifty men.

Add to these the ten sub-chiefs, and we have in this tribe two hundred and eight men capable of bearing arms.

They are represented as having many good rifles, and as being most excellent shots. Living in the neighborhood of the great thorougfare that leads from Texas to California, and having mountain fastnesses in which to take refuge when pursued, they are able, and very willing, to do a great deal of mischief.

From Gran Quivira, the northern point of the Sierra Blanca bears by the compass S. 30° E., and is distant about fifty miles.

The highest point of the Sierra de las Gallinas bears E. 5° N., and is distant about fifteen miles.

The peaks known as Las Tetillas bear N. 36° W., and are distant about fifty-five miles.

We left the ruins about three o'clock in the afternoon, and retraced our steps to the Laguna de la Puerta, where we arrived an hour after dark.

THURSDAY, *December* 22, 1853.

To-day we returned to Manzana, over the same track we had made to the Laguna. Here we encountered a snow-storm. This town is so elevated that hardly a cloud passes the mountains that does not shower upon it either rain, snow, or hail. From what we have observed during our second visit to this place, this Botany Bay of New Mexico, we have concluded that our former estimate of the character of the inhabitants was premature and ill-judged; we now believe that there is not one single redeeming trait of disposition or habits to be found within its borders.

FRIDAY, *December* 23, 1853.

Our course to-day was about N. 10° W., and lay along the eastern slopes of the Sierra de la Manzana. We faced a snow-storm for nearly the whole forenoon, and were therefore unable to observe much about the features of the country. Six miles 729 yards from Manzana we passed a small mountain stream running towards the east—a mere brook, that is soon lost in the ground. On this there is a little village called Torreon. Two miles 1,181 yards further north we passed another similar brook, and another small town called Tagique. From this last place, over a rolling, broken, and well timbered country, we marched to a small hamlet called Chilili. This town, like Torreon and Tagique, is situated upon a mere rivulet, running from the mountains to the open plains towards the east. Here we encamped in the snow, and suffered much during the whole night from a cold wind frcm the north.

SATURDAY, *December* 24, 1853.

This morning, before we left camp, an old Mexican brought us some ore, which he said is to be found in great abundance near the Tetilla Peaks, but that it is now covered so deeply in the snow as to be difficult to be procured. We believe the specimen he gave us contains silver. When the snow has melted, it will be worth the trouble, perhaps, to explore these mountains thoroughly, with a view to the discovery of precious metals.

After travelling north for about two miles this morning, we turned off toward the west, by a road that leads to Albuquerque by the Cañon del Infierno. As we ascended the eastern slope of the mountain, we passed through extensive groves of large pine-trees, suitable for boards and other building purposes. The snow was a foot in depth, and the air dry and cold, as in mid-winter in the extreme north. The Cañon del Infierno is 10 miles 562 yards in length. It is very circuitous. The mountains rise abruptly thousands of feet above it on either hand. This makes it a pass of great ruggedness, as well as of a wild and picturesque beauty. Half-way down through it we came to a fine spring of water. The rocks are the same stratified, fossiliferous limestone, which we saw at Los Puertos de Abó. From the mouth of the Cañon del Infierno to Albuquerque, the road descends through an open prairie, entirely destitute of water for the whole distance, which is 20 miles 492 yards.

We arrived at Albuquerque at 8 o'clock in the evening, having marched to-day 36 miles 317 yards.

REPORT

ON THE

FISHES OBSERVED ON THE COASTS OF NEW JERSEY AND LONG ISLAND DURING THE SUMMER OF 1854, BY SPENCER F. BAIRD, ASSISTANT SECRETARY OF THE SMITHSONIAN INSTITUTION.

A period of six weeks spent on the coast of New Jersey, principally at Beesley's point, and Long Island, New York, furnished an opportunity of studying the habits and distribution of the principal species of fishes that are found on that portion of our shores during the summer.

Although many others, doubtless, are to be found in the same region, yet none have been introduced except those which were actually caught and carefully examined. A considerable number of the species whose habits and peculiarities are given at some length, have hitherto had nothing placed on record concerning them; and it is hoped that the present article may be found to contain some interesting information, given here for the first time, in addition to its character as a contribution to our knowledge of the geographical distribution of species.

The difference of the names applied to the same species of fish at various points of our coast, even when these happen to be connected very closely, both commercially and geographically, must strike every one with astonishment.

It is scarcely too much to say that no one species of fish bears the same vernacular appellation from Maine to Maryland, still less to Florida or the coast of Texas. This is probably owing to the fact that our shores have been originally settled by various nations from widely remote parts of Europe, each introducing its peculiar nomenclature, or deriving names from the equally isolated aboriginal tribes with their various languages. Thus the names of blue fish, white fish, perch, black fish, bass, king-fish, porgee, hake, tailor, whiting, horse mackerel, shad, smelt, dog-fish, &c., may apply equally to two or more very different species. Among the synonyms of the species will be found the vernacular equivalents in the regions visited, together with some from other localities. It will be sufficiently evident, therefore, that before any species referred to under a trivial name can be identified, the origin of the fish or that of the writer must be ascertained.

Although most of the facts recorded in the following paper have reference to Great Egg harbor, New Jersey, during a period extending from the middle of July to the end of August, it has been thought not amiss to incorporate the results of a visit to Brooklyn, Riverhead, and Greenport, Long Island, as well as to some points on the Hudson river, in September. Some valuable information was thus obtained tending to illustrate more fully the natural history and distribution of the species found on the New Jersey coast.

And here I take occasion to render an acknowledgement for much kind assistance and important information derived from various gentlemen at the different points of operation. Among these I will particularly mention Messrs. Samuel and Charles Ashmead, at Beesley's point, who devoted all their time to the furtherance of my objects in this exploration. I may also mention Messrs John Stites, Willis Godfrey, Washington Blackman, John Johnson, in fact, most of the residents of Beesley's point. Much benefit was derived at Greenport, Long Island, from the companionship of Mr. E. D. Willard, of the National Hotel, Washington; while to Mr. J. Carson Brevoort, of Bedford, Long Island, well known as the first ichthyologist in New York, and surpassed by no one in his knowledge of our marine species, I am under the greatest obligations. Through the kindness of Mr. John G. Bell, of New York, and Smith Herring, of Piermont, I was enabled to make a complete collection of the fishes of the upper Hackensack and Sparkill.

It must be understood that the present article does not aim at giving a complete account of the species referred to. Such descriptions of color as have been given were in every case taken from the fresh and living fish, the object being to place on record features not usually preserved in alcoholic specimens. Of the species whose colors were known not to fade or alter in spirits no notes of their peculiarities in this respect were taken, while the tints of others were so evanescent as to have escaped or altered before a description could be noted down.

Very little respecting the habits or history of the species has been added from other authors, nor does the nomenclature profess to be at all final as to critical accuracy. To have accomplished this latter object, would have required more time than is at present at my disposal, involving, as it would, the entire revision of American ichthyology generally. The names given are principally those of De Kay in his history of the fishes of New York, and can thus be readily identified.

As will be seen in the course of the article, several of the species collected appear new to science; to these I have been obliged to give names for the sake of proper reference, without at the same time furnishing a complete scientific description. This will, however, be supplied soon through another medium—want of time preventing its being done in season for the present Smithsonian Report. For important assistance in determining the species I am under many obligations to Mr. Girard.

The coast of New Jersey is well known to consist, for most of its extent, of a low beach with sand-hills, separated from the mainland by a wide strip of low meadows filled with small ponds, and intersected by creeks and thoroughfares, which traverse it in every direction. There is no rock or stone of any description, and, consequently, there is a deficiency in the plants and animals which frequent rocky localities. At Beesley's point there is scarcely a pebble of the smallest size to be seen.

The meadows are densely coated with grass, and are covered with water only during unusually high tides.

Beesley's point is situated at the mouth of Egg Harbor river, where it empties into Great Egg Harbor bay. The water is, of course, salt at this point, though somewhat diluted by the volume of fresh water brought down by the river.

The distance from the mouth of the river, or head of the bay, to the inlet on the beach, is about two or three miles; the extreme width about the same, although extending into thoroughfares, through which a boat may be taken to Absecom on the one side, and to Cape May on other, without going outside of the beach. The mouth of the river is occupied by very extensive beds of oysters, which are celebrated for their excellent flavor. The bottom of the bay is in some part hard and shelly, in others sandy, or again, consists of a soft mud; the latter condition prevails near the shore, or wherever the current is of little strength.

There are numerous mud-flats or sand-bars in the bay, some of them bare at low tide, or nearly so, and occupied by various species of water-fowl. These flats, continuing to increase in height, and at length acquire a growth of grass which fixes still more the accumulating mud and sand, so that in time what was formerly a bar becomes an island elevated some feet above the water.

This transition is, in fact, so rapid, that many of the inhabitants now living have known islands several acres in extent to form within their own recollection.

The greater part of the bottom of the bay and of the thoroughfares, generally, is a soft mud, rich in organic matter, and covered with a profuse growth of *Zostera marina* and algæ of various species. Mr. Samuel Ashmead, who has been engaged for some years in studying the sea-weeds of our coast, has found a much greater variety of species at Beesley's point than Professor Harvey allots to the New Jersey coast. The water being generally shallow except in the channels, the sub-marine vegetation can be seen to great advantage, while sailing over the surface. The water becomes very warm during the summer, and supplies all the conditions necessary for the development of young fishes of many species. The young of all the large fish of the bay may thus be found in greater or less numbers along or near the shore.

The ponds in the meadows, like the waters of the bay itself, are generally muddy at the bottom, sometimes bare of vegetation, and sometimes covered with a thick growth. The fishes found in these ponds consist almost entirely of cyprinodonts of various species, with occasional specimens of *Atherina*, small mullet, or sticklebacks. The creeks likewise contain cyprinodonts, generally of different species from those of the ponds, with young fish of various kinds. Crabs and eels are found everywhere.

The line of beach is two or three miles from the mainland, and consists of a clear white sand raised into hills ten to thirty feet high, a few hundred feet from the water's edge. It is in the inlets at the ends of these beaches that the greatest variety of fish is to be found, particularly in the small indentations, protected from the roughness of the waves, and the bottom of which is covered with *Ceramium* or sea-cabbage.

Corson's inlet, frequently mentioned in the following pages, is situated at the southern end of Peck's beach, which begins directly opposite Beesley's point at the entrance to the harbor, and extends to this inlet over a distance of about five miles.

The only fresh water near Beesley's point is Cedar Swamp creek. This stream, rising in a cedar swamp, and flowing with a very sluggish current, (the water of a chocolate color,) is cut off from the tide by a dam at Littleworth, three miles from the point. The bottom is very muddy. But little variety of fresh-water fish is to be found in this stream. Several species of *Esox*, two *Leuciscus*, one eel, three *Pomotis*, one each of *Aphredoderus*, *Labrax*, *Etheostoma*, and *Melanura*, and several cyprinodonts. The species are nearly all different from those found in the interior of Pennsylvania on the same latitude.

Another Cedar Swamp creek occurs on the opposite side of Egg Harbor river, in Atlantic county. In many respects it differs from that first mentioned in being of more rapid current, and the bottom at some distance from the tide-water dam consisting of sand or small pebbles. The water too in small quantity is clear, though where of considerable depth it appears almost black. Fewer species of fish were found here than in the other; the only additional one being the *Catastomus tuberculatus*.

Ludley's Run is a small run crossing the road to Cape May, about eight miles from Beesley's point; fresh at low tide but flooded at high water. The only fish found in it consisted of two cyprinodonts, and the *Gasterosteus quadracus*.

NOTE.—For the sake of avoiding a constant repetition, the initials only of the names of the fins are used. Thus, D. indicates the dorsal fin; C., the caudal; A., the anal; V., the ventral; and P., the pectoral.

LIST OF FISHES.

1. Labrax lineatus, Cuv. and Val.

Rock-Fish—Striped Bass.

Labrax lineatus, Cuv. and Val., Hist. Nat. Poiss. II, 79.—Storer's Report, p. 7.—DeKay, Fauna of New York, Fishes, 7, plate i, fig. 3.

The well known rock-fish, or striped bass, was not caught abundantly during my stay, although occasionally taken in the mouth of the river, and near bluff banks along the thoroughfares. In winter and spring they are captured in considerable numbers in seines, and of a weight extending to twenty or thirty pounds. Individuals of this size are, however, rarely met with. No young ones were seen, as they had not yet returned from the upper portion of the river. At Sing Sing, New York, a few weeks later, several sizes of young were taken.

The rock takes a bait readily, and, from the vigor of its actions, affords fine sport with the rod and reel; the fly is especially adapted to the capture of this species.

As is well known, the rock-fish is the associate of the shad and several species of herring, in a vernal migration from salt water to fresh, for the purpose of depositing their eggs. The development of their young is very rapid, as, when they return to the sea in the fall, they have already attained a length of about four inches; up to a size somewhat greater than this they exhibit decided indications of vertical dark bars, as in the yellow perch, but this fades out in a short time after being taken from the water.

The rock-fish is more abundant in Chesapeake bay and its tributaries than anywhere else to the northward. Here they occur all the year round, and are taken in great numbers. During their migration, they feed voraciously upon the herring bound on the same errand up the fresh water streams. These they ascend to a great height; in the Susquehanna, before the dams were built, reaching the forks at Northumberland, and possibly beyond. The falls of the Potomac offer serious impediments to their passage much above the city of Washington. Arrested in this way, they accumulate in considerable numbers, and afford great sport to the citizens of this place during spring and early summer. The late Mr. Webster was frequently to be seen patiently exercising that skill which made him eminent among the celebrated fishermen of the day.

Owing to its abundance, the rock is the chief staple of the Washington fish-market, where it is to be seen throughout most of the year. It is usually sold at a moderate price, and it is no uncommon thing to have the opportunity of purchasing one of 30 or 40 pounds for 75 cents.

Much interest has been excited in the experiments of Mr. R. L. Pell, of Pelham, Ulster county, New York, in reference to the breeding of rock-fish and shad in fresh waters. I have been kindly furnished by this gentleman with the following communication, which explains his method of stocking fish-ponds.

"I have succeeded in rearing the striped bass, known in our river as the Croton bass, thus: male and female were placed in a small pond, the water of which was salted twice each week until the small fry appeared, when salting ceased. Sixty days after, the old fish languished, and became excessively weak, in which state they continued to exist ten days, when they died. The small fry of both shad and bass grew rapidly, and when six weeks old were placed in a larger pond, and their progeny became fresh-water fish.

"I have a trout pond, which you probably did not see, in which I placed several hundred brook trout, varying from four to twelve inches in length. I was accustomed, for several years, to feed them frequently, and, to my surprise, they became very tame and confiding. On one occasion a large trout followed me around the pond, and so pertinacious was he, that if I suddenly passed around he crossed over; the next day he did the same thing several times, and, finally, I lifted him from the water and discovered a corroded hook in his mouth, after removing which I replaced him in the pond. How can you account for so much instinct in a fish?"

---

2. Labrax mucronatus, Cuv. and Val.

White Perch.

Labrax mucronatus, Cuv. and Val., Hist. Nat. Poiss. II, 86, plate xii.—Storer's Report, 8.—*Labrax rufus*, DeKay, Fauna of New York, Fishes, 9, plate iii, fig, 7.

The white perch was at no time during the summer taken in the bay, although in winter they occur there in great numbers, and are caught in seines, with rock-fish, eels, and flounders, which constitute the principal kinds of that season. They are very common in the Tuckahoe river and Cedar Swamp creek, Cape May county; indeed they exist in almost all the creeks of the salt meadows. The largest were taken in the perfectly fresh water of Cedar Swamp creek, above the tide-water dam, and exceeded a foot in length; very few, however, attain this size.

I found them abundant at Sing Sing, New York, in the brackish waters of Croton river; they are also very common, the year round, about Washington.

By setting a net across the current of a creek, at high tide, a great many white perch can usually be caught. I have seen many bushels taken out when the water was low. Great care must be exercised, however, lest the crabs, which are intercepted at the same time, eat holes in the net while nibbling at the fish gilled in the meshes.

The white perch bites readily at a hook, and is frequently caught in this way in great numbers. The flesh is very insipid and rather tough; in fact, the fish is one of the poorest of all the marine species of our coast.

The yellow perch, *Perca flavescens*, does not appear to occur at Beesley's Point.

---

3. Centropristes nigricans, Cuv. and Val.

Black Bass—Sea-Bass.

Centropristes nigricans, Cuv. and Val. Hist. Nat. Poiss. III, 14. —Storer's Rep. 9.—DeKay, New York Fauna, Fishes, 25, plate ii., fig. 5.

Like the porgee and several other species, the sea-bass or black fish, taken in Great Egg harbor, are of diminutive size, compared with those caught some distance out at sea. I do not remember any exceeding 20 ounces in weight, while most of them were not above half that size. They were seldom taken in large numbers, and in fact were rather difficult to catch at all, owing to their habit of nibbling at the bait without swallowing the hook. A very small hook, with a bait of corresponding proportions, was found to furnish the best mode of capturing them. Where they abounded, however, they generally put a stop to any successful fishing.

The black fish appears to be a summer visitor in Egg harbor, as I could not learn of its capture in winter. They were generally to be found off steep bars near the channels, very rarely near the shore. A few young ones, about an inch long, were captured at Corson's Inlet.

The black fish, as an article of food, may be reckoned among the best of the fishes of the coast. The meat is firm and very white, and the comparative absence of bones renders it possible to eat those of quite a small size.

Few authors, in their description of this fish, mention the broad, vertical, dark bands so conspicuous in the fish when first caught.

Color of young specimens.—Each scale on the body with a yellowish green or greenish white centre, and a border of darker. The sides, between the head and tail, crossed by five or six broad vertical bars of blackish, (constituted by the above mentioned borders,) not, however, obliterating the lighter centres ; the borders of the scales between these bars are olivaceous. Head dark olive, the centres of the scales, the inferior border of the orbit, and several lines radiating from the eye towards the snout, rich green. Lower jaw blue, the extreme tips olive; isthmus inside the mouth and gill-covers, with the branchial arches, yellow, branchiostegal membrane brown. D. with the membrane olive green, brightest towards the edge; between each two adjacent rays of the dorsal are transverse bars of bluish white, and a larger number in the soft portion of this fin. These bars are slightly oblique to the rays, or, when the fin is erect, nearly parallel to the dorsal outline. Extreme margin of D. greenish white, with a narrow border of black on the soft portion ; C. A. V. with membranes dark olive at base, then greenish white, and margined with black, the dark portions occasionally relieved by lighter patches of whitish or olivaceous, especially along the rays. P. olive green. Length 8 inches. August.

4. POMOTIS OBESUS, Girard.

Pomotis obesus, Girard in Proc., Boston Soc. Nat. Hist., V, 1854, 40.

General color dark olive green, with six or eight vertical bars of darker on each side, covering a breadth of three or four scales. The skin at the base of the scales, in the space covered by these vertical bars, shows spots of golden purplish; cheeks with narrow lines and spots of the same and similar spots on the basal portion of the membrane of the vertical fins. A. and V. are glossed with metallic green on the interradial portion. Opercular flaps, rich velvet black, bordered (except behind) with a narrow line of golden purple; a crescent of the same on the basal half, the convexity anterior; opercles metallic green. P. transparent olivaceous. In some specimens a distinct vertical bar passes through the eye. In some, too, there is a shade of violet on each side, above the anal fins.

This species was only found in the Cedar Swamp creeks, Cape May county, and Atlantic county, among the splatterdocks, or in small runs or ditches. They were most abundant in muddy water, though occasionally occurring where it was quite clear. Fins nearly black.

This modestly colored species of sun-fish appears to be confined to the fresh water in the immediate vicinity of our Atlantic coast. I first detected it in the boggy brooks near Framingham, Massachusetts, and have since taken it at other points. It was very abundant in the Sparkill, near Piermont, New York, but does not appear to have been caught by any one but myself. Of its southern range along the coast I cannot speak, although a fish strongly resembling it is contained in a collection recently received from Georgetown, South Carolina.

---

5. POMOTIS CHÆTODON, Baird.

Banded Sun-Fish.

Pomotis chætodon, Baird.—General form sub-circular; greatest depth of body comprised less than twice its length; dorsal and ventral outlines regularly convex; profile descending towards the snout, which is obtuse. The mouth is small; the eye large, its diameter contained but three times in the length of side of head; spinous portion of dorsal extending over a base nearly equal to that of the soft portion, and almost as high; caudal subtruncated posteriorly and largely developed, and extending a little more posteriorly than the caudal; tip of ventrals extending beyond the three anal spines; pectorals rather small, their extremity reaching as far backwards as the ventrals.

D. X. 11; A. III, 12; C. 4 I. 8, 7, I. 3; V. I. 5; P. 10 or 11. Scales quite large; lateral line concurrent with the dorsal outline.

General color dirty white, with clouds of olivaceous; the tints clearer in smaller specimens; sides of abdomen silvery. Six well defined vertical bands of black on each side, covering each a breadth of two or three scales; the first passes through the pupil across the cheeks; the second is posterior to the edge of the preoperculum, but interrupted in the middle so as not to cross the operculum; the third is posterior to the first ray of dorsal; the fourth posterior to the spinous rays of anal; the fifth posterior to the end of the dorsal and anal; the sixth passes across the base of the tail. Between the third and fourth bands are short bars, one proceeding from the dorsal, the other from the ventral outline in the same vertical line, and parallel to the others. This may in fact be described as an additional bar interrupted in the middle.

Fins greenish yellow, with mottlings of dark. Ventrals black centrally, yellow posteriorly, and deep red on the two anterior rays and intermediate membrane. Dorsal with the three anterior rays and their membrane black; the membrane between the third and fourth rays red. Pectoral plain.

In large specimens the tints are darker, and the ground color tinged with olivaceous. The red of the dorsal is not distinct. Length three inches.

Abundant in the muddy water of Cedar Swamp creek, Cape May county, New Jersey.

---

6. Centrarchus pomotis, Baird.

The Bass Sun-Fish.

Centrarchus pomotis, Baird.—General form elongated, subfusiform in profile; upper and lower lines regularly curved. A depression above the eye. Snout very much abbreviated; lower jaw longest. Mouth large; posterior extremity of maxillary extending to the vertical posterior rim of eye. Diameter of the eye contained about four times in the length of the side of head. Head constituting two sevenths of total length. Six rows of scales above the lateral line; twelve rows beneath. Lateral line concurrent with the dorsal outline. Spinous portion of dorsal quite low, and extending over a base twice as long as the soft portion. Caudal rounded posteriorly. Anal extending a little more backwards than dorsal. Five short anal spines. External soft ray of ventrals extending as a filiform appendage beyond the other rays, which do not reach the anterior margin of the anal. Tip of pectorals extending to a vertical which would intersect the vent.

D. XI. 12; A. V. 10; C. 4. I. 7. 6. I. 3; V. I. 5; P. 12 or 14.

Color.—Dark greenish olive, with three or four irregular longitudinal bands of dull greenish yellow, and occasionally cloudy spots of golden green. Sides of the head of this color, with three indistinct bands of dark olive. A dusky spot at the end of operculum. Iris purplish brown; cornea olive green. Fins quite uniform, very dark greenish olive, with darker margins, except the pectorals, which are light olivaceous, and the ventrals, the spinous rays of which are uncolored. Length six inches.

Some specimens may be better described as dark golden green, with longitudinal bands of dark olive, broken up by cloudings of greenish.

This species was only found in muddy water, or where there was considerable cover. They were stirred out from along the banks. I sometimes thought that they lay at times completely embedded in the mud. They were not rare in Cedar Swamp creek, and I caught a few in the Hackensack, Rockland county, New York.

---

7. Aphredoderus sayanus, Lesueur.

Aphredoderus sayanus, Lesueur.—DeKay, New York Fauna, Fishes, 35, plate xxi, fig. 62.

Prevailing color dark olive brown, with occasional obscure dots of lighter. Abdomen and under surface of the throat and head, with the sides of the latter, yellowish, with fine punctations of greenish brown indistinctly visible on the sides. A vertical dark bar beneath the eye. Iris silvery, dotted with black.

D. C. and A. dark olive, with darker margin and base. This character on the tail shows as a vertical bar, parallel to which is another near the base of the tail. P. olive, V. greenish yellow, with cloudings of dusky towards the tip. Lateral line lighter than the ground color.

Largest specimens four and a half inches. Ditches of Cedar Swamp creek, Cape May county.

This species was very abundant in a small branch of Cedar Swamp creek, above Littleworth, where many were taken in a short time.

The size above given is probably a maximum one, as most I have seen from other localities are considerably less. The species is little known to naturalists, although occurring in many streams on the Atlantic coast.

---

8. Sphyræna borealis, DeKay.

Northern Barracuda.

Sphyræna borealis, DeKay, New York Fauna, Fishes, 39, plate lx, fig. 196.

Nothing specially noteworthy was observed as to the habits of this diminutive representative of the ferocious barracuda of Florida. None of the specimens caught, in fact, exceeded four inches in length. They were taken from a small cove at Corson's inlet; a few of them were found among the grass at the mouth of the river.

9. PRIONOTUS PILATUS, Storer.

Flying Fish.

Prionotus pilatus. Storer, Proc. Bost. Soc. Nat. Hist. II, 77; also, Hist. of the Fishes of Mass. 20, plate vi, fig. 1.

Above mottled olive and reddish brown, with three or four large quadrate spots of darker across the back. The reddish brown spots predominate along the lower part of the sides, in some cases almost forming a longitudinal stripe. Abdomen and inferior part of the body generally reddish white. Head reddish brown, cheeks coppery. Branchiostegal membrane and inside of mouth behind, brownish black. Pupil violet; iris olive-green externally, brassy or coppery internally. Anterior dorsal olivaceous dusky at base, with two or more interrupted bars of pale bluish nearly perpendicular to the rays. A distinct dark spot on the membrane, between the fourth and fifth dorsal spines. Posterior dorsal transparent, mottled or coarsely vermiculated with olivaceous. P. very dark olive-green, with reticulations of a lighter color; chalk-white on the posterior edge of the lower surface. A. C. V. with the pectoral processes reddish brown, brightest along the margin; the former white along the base. Length six inches.

This species was very abundant, and frequently taken with the hook, when its disentanglement proved to be a matter of some danger, on account of the spines of the head. In one instance a man was confined to the house for two weeks in consequence of a puncture received in this way.

When caught, this fish commences a loud croaking or barking, the sound apparently produced in the abdominal region. This is so loud and constant that in hauling a large seine the presence in the net of a single specimen of this gurnard, however small, could generally be determined by the peculiar sound emitted. For this reason it is sometimes called pig-fish by the inhabitants.

The pectoral processes are used as organs of progression, the fish dragging itself slowly upon the bottom by their aid, or raising itself up and resting on their tips. In swimming, or resting, the broad pectoral fins are generally spread out horizontally to their fullest extent—presenting a very beautiful and striking appearance, and closely resembling the wings of some butterfly.

The flesh is sweet, white, and palatable, though on account of its comparatively small size this fish is seldom eaten. Specimens caught on the surf or out at sea are usually much larger than those in the bay, sometimes exceeding a foot in length. It is said to be only a summer visitant.

10. Acanthocottus virginianus, Girard.

The common Sculpin.

Acanthocottus virginianus, Girard, Proe. Bost. Soc. Nat. Hist. III, 1850, 187.—*Cottus virginianus*, Storer, Rep.—DeKay, New York Fauna, Fishes, 51, plate v, fig. 13.

A dried specimen of a sculpin was given me by Mr. Ashmead, which, unfortunately, was mislaid and lost. It was taken in the winter, but does not seem to be abundant.

---

11. Boleosoma fusiforme, Girard.

Darter.

Boleosoma fusiforme, Girard, Proc. Bost. Soc. Nat. Hist. V, 41.

The only specimens procured were taken from Cedar Swamp creek, at Littleworth, where it was seen lying motionless at the bottom of the water, darting off swiftly when disturbed.

---

12. Gasterosteus quadracus, Mitch.

Stickleback.

Gasterosteus quadracus, Mitch. Trans. Lit. and Philos. Soc. 430, plate i, fig. 11. DeKay, New York Fauna, Fishes, 67, plate vi, fig. 18.

Reddish olive above; sides with a broad but ill-defined band of mottled dark brown, of irregular outline, extending from the snout to the tail, with finer mottlings of the same above and below. This is sometimes broken up into irregular mottlings of dark and lighter brown, with better defined and larger blotches of darker interspersed.

Region of lateral line generally lighter; lower part of cheeks and under parts yellowish silvery; fins, transparent with dark mottlings on the rays; ventrals red behind the anterior spine.

A few specimens were taken, at intervals, in the salt-ponds in the meadows, or among the grass and sea-cabbage of the bay. They were most abundant in Ludley's run, at the crossing of the Cape May road; where the water is perfectly fresh at low tide, and brackish at high water. Here they kept along and underneath the bank, whence they were dislodged with considerable difficulty. This species was also taken in the brackish waters about Sing Sing, New York.

13. Leiostomus obliquus, DeKay.

The Lafayette.

Leiostomus obliquus, DeKay, New York Fauna, Fishes, 69, plate lx, fig. 195.

The "Cape May Goody" of the Jersey coast, so called from its great abundance at Cape Island, is very rarely taken in winter, and appears to be rather a summer visitor. It makes its appearance, in large numbers, at Cape May, in August; the first run being composed of quite small individuals, and the larger ones succeeding these. They enter the creeks in crowds, and are caught there in company with the white perch. When perfectly fresh they are most delicious—excelled in flavor by no species on the coast. Their usual size in the bay is about six inches, though occasionally caught measuring ten.

This species is somewhat capricious in its visits to the northern shores; intervals of years sometimes intervening between periods of abundance.

From a coincidence of one of these runs and the last visit of General Lafayette to America, they are known by his name about New York.

---

14. Otolithus regalis, Cuv. and Val.

Weak Fish—Squeteague—Blue Fish.

Otolithus regalis, Cuv. and Val., Hist. Nat., Poissons, V, 67.—DeKay, New York Fauna, Fishes, 71, plate viii, fig. 24.

Young.—Back greenish, shading into yellowish silvery, with purple reflections on the side. In some specimens there are indications of subvertical blotches on the sides. None of the spots of the adult are seen until the fish exceeds 4 inches in length. D. and C. dusky; P. V. A. yellow; Iris, silvery. Length, 4 inches.

The adult, when first caught, in addition to the markings which are retained in alcohol, presents all over a rich tint of purplish red, which very soon fades out into a dull silvery.

This species, known as blue fish at Beesley's point, weak fish at New York, shecutts at Greenport, Long Island, and trout in Philadelphia and Baltimore, is the species most abundant of all those considered as game by the fisherman. It makes its appearance early in the spring, and leaves for the sea late in the autumn, attaining its period of greatest abundance towards the end of July. It is very easily captured with almost any bait—clam, soft crab, or pieces of fish. Indeed, some of the best sport I ever witnessed with this fish was had by using the eyes of those already caught as bait.

No species on the coast shows so large a count in a successful day's fishing as the weak fish, it being not uncommon for a single boat of three or four men to take from 150 to 250 in an hour or two. When caught in such numbers, however, the size is not great, perhaps not averaging three-quarters of a pound. The large specimens are generally scattering in their appearance, being seldom taken in numbers. These fish moves about in shoals of greater or less extent, usually swimming pretty near the surface, and requiring for their capture a line leaded very lightly or not at all. They take the bait at a snap, seldom condescending to nibble, thus requiring the line to be kept taut and ready to haul in at a moment's warning. It is, however, only for a short time that they bite voraciously, the run seldom lasting more than one hour.

These fish keep much in the channel ways of the bay and river, when moving, but during ebb-tide, they settle in the deep holes in great numbers, remaining until flood, when they again sally forth. The old stagers are always on the alert to move up to the places of this kind well known to them, and, anchoring their boat, wait patiently for the fish. After passing some time without a nibble, the sport suddenly begins, and, for half an hour to an hour, the excitement of hooking a fish almost the instant the line is dropped, is kept up, when it again as suddenly ceases by the disappearance of the game. The most noted place of this kind about Great Egg harbor is Molasses point, already referred to, where the current is very strong during height of tide, and the great depth of water scarcely extends for one hundred yards.

During the night the weak fish runs much up into the larger creeks of the salt meadows, and, by putting a net across the mouths of these, the weak fish, king fish, and some other species may be penned up and caught in great numbers. In any attempt to retain specimens of moderate size, or, of the small species generally, great annoyance is experienced from the crabs, *(Lupa dicantha,)* which are exceedingly abundant, and, arrested by the same operation, leisurely set themselves to work in catching the fish gilled in the net. In so doing, they cut the meshes very badly, in fact some of my best seines were almost totally ruined by them.

The weak fish appears to require, during the summer, a slight dilution of fresh water in the marine element it inhabits, as it concentrates in large numbers about the mouths of rivers in dry weather.

During the excessive drought of the past summer, it was observed that the weak fish was taken much higher up rivers than ever known before. They disappeared almost entirely from Beesley's point about the middle of August, and could only be heard of towards Tuckahoe and higher up. The fishermen prayed devoutly for rain to weaken the waters of the bay, and bring back the weak fish.

At Sing-Sing, New York, and even much higher up the North river, they were taken in numbers in August and September.

The young weak fish were very abundant along the edges of the bay and in the small creeks, of sizes not exceeding four or five inches. It is quite probably that they spawn early in the season, and that these are the fry of the year. At this time they are broadly banded vertically, and, with their much compressed body, would never be referred to the weak fish but for the two prominent canines of the upper jaw. A few only had the spots of the adult.

As a table fish, this species is very much inferior to almost any other captured on the coast. It looses its rigidity soon after being taken, becoming soft and flabby. It can hardly be used whole a few hours out of the water, and is usually served up cut into short pieces. The flesh, when cooked, is somewhat gelatinous and translucent, very different from the snowy opacity of that of the king fish.

As usual, the fish of this species taken outside in the surf, either with the line or by hauling the net, are much larger than the common run of those in the bay and rivers. The largest I have ever seen weighed about five pounds, though they are said greatly to exceed this occasionally.

When taken, this species makes a peculiar croaking, somewhat like that of *Prionotus*. This is said at times to be heard above water when the fish is at the bottom.

---

15. Corvina argyroleuca, Cuv. and Val.

The Silver Perch.

Corvina argyroleuca, Cuv. and Val., Hist. Nat. Poiss. V, 105.—DeKay, New York Fauna, Fishes, 74, plate xviii, fig. 51.

A single specimen only of the adult fish was taken during my stay at Beesley's point. It was caught in the bay by Captain Townsend Stites, and seemed to be unknown to the fishermen.

The young, however, were very abundant in the grass along the edge of the river, of various sizes, not exceeding three inches. They had no markings of any kind, the sides being of a uniform yellowish white.

It is not unfrequently brought to market in New York, where it is known as silver perch.

---

16. Umbrina alburnus, Cuv. and Val.

The King-Fish.

Umbrina alburnus, Cuv. and Val.—DeKay, New York Fauna, Fishes, 78, plate vii, fig. 20.

This species is known at Beesley's point as the hake, a name derived probably from its possessing one barbel at the chin, in common with the *Phycis americana*, which bears the same appellation with more propriety. About New York it is called king-fish, and its congener at the south is known as whiting. Everywhere it bears the deserved reputation of being one of the finest fish caught, the sheepshead (*Sargus ovis*) scarcely excepted. Of late years this fish appears to have become quite rare about New York, but they are still abundant on the Jersey coast. At Beesley's point they come next in the count of a day's sport to the weak fish, although thirty or forty may be considered as a first rate catch for a single boat and tide.

The king-fish makes its appearance in the bays early in the spring, leaving in the fall, and appears to observe much the same periods with the weak fish. Like this species, it is fond of a slight mixture of fresh water, running up the mouths of rivers and ascending in proportion to the duration of dry weather.

During the past summer several were taken at Sing Sing, New York, where they had previously been unknown.

The young fish were exceedingly abundant in the river at Beesley's point, on sandy bottom, as well as in the surf, hundreds being taken at a single sweep of a small net. The smallest were about an inch long, probably the spawn of the spring. As usual, the largest specimens of the fish were caught with nets in the surf, though none that were seen exceeded fifteen inches in length.

The king-fish keeps much in schools, in or near the bottom where it is sandy or hard, preferring the edge of channels or the vicinity of sand-bars. They keep about oyster beds, and when oysters are being taken up frequently congregate in large numbers about the boats in eager quest of the worms and other minute animals dislodged by the operation. They bite very readily at clams, crabs soft or hard, and at times make little objection to pieces of fish. The best time for capturing them is on the young flood.

Like the weak fish they at times run up the small creeks in the salt meadows at night, and are taken by intercepting their return with the falling tide. This, however, is by no means so common a habit as with the other species.

The eastern range of the king fish is not extended. Dr. Storer records a single specimen only as having been taken in Boston harbor.

---

17. Pogonias fasciatus, Lacép.

The Banded Drum.

Pogonias fasciatus, Lacép., Hist. des Poiss.—DeKay, New York Fauna. Fishes, 81, plate xiv, fig. 40.

Sides yellowish silvery, with six or seven broad, dark, vertical bars between the head and tail. D. and C. dusky towards their borders, the anterior D. quite dark; P. colorless; V. and A. yellow.

The young fish of this species were found very abundantly during August in the small bays along the shore about Beesley's Point. Few were seen in the rivers.

---

18. Lobotes emarginatus, B. and G.

Lobotes emarginatus, B. and G. Body elongated, subfusiform in profile; head subconical, contained a little more than three times in the total length. Posterior extremity of maxillary extending to the vertical line of the anterior rim of pupil; eye circular; its diameter contained about four times in the length of side of head; external soft ray of ventrals continued into a membranous thread extending beyond the other rays, but not reaching the anal fin. Caudal emarginated posteriorly.

D. X. 14; A. III. 8; C. 4, I. 8, 7, I. 3; V. I. 5; P. 15.

Scales well developed; in six rows above lateral line, and fourteen to fifteen below.

General color light olive green, with narrow, well defined longitudinal lines of purplish brown along the sides; one through the centre of each row of scales. These lines, above the lateral line, are parallel to it; below, they are somewhat oblique, ascending behind. A narrow, well defined horizontal line of steel blue passes beneath the eye, tangent to the orbit; a broader one of violet extends through the pupil, parallel to the upper outline of the head.

D. light olive green, the distal half of the spinous portion dull purplish; the membrane elsewhere mottled with purplish brown. C. with rays yellow and red, the membrane mottled with purplish.

A. and V. purplish red anteriorly, yellow behind, the former somewhat mottled. P. greenish yellow. A narrow margin of D. A. and P. pale violet. Length, three inches..

A few specimens were taken, in August, among the grass along the river.

---

19. Pagrus argyrops, Cuv. and Val.

The Big Porgee.

Pagrus argyrops, Cuv. and Val., Hist. Nat. des Poiss. VI, fig. 164.—DeKay, New York Fauna, Fishes, 95, plate ix, fig. 25.

About six vertical broad bars of dark purplish brown on each side between head and tail; the first just anterior to the dorsal fin. The intermediate space, when viewed directly, appears of a brownish olive and greenish white mixed; but, held a little obliquely, this resolves into a silvery tint, with well defined longitudinal lines of purplish, a line for each row of scales, and usually along the adjacent edges. Above the lateral line these lines are oblique, and nearly parallel with the dorsal profile anterior to the D. fin. Head above (excepting a lighter bar beneath the eyes), operculum, and an oblique bar beneath the eye rich purplish brown. Back along the dorsal fin and a space on each side of the nape with reflections of rich metallic green. A dark spot on the base of the pectoral bones. Belly white, closely punctate with dark brown.

D. with the rays silvery, the membrane mixed green and purplish brown, the margin clear dark reddish brown. C. brown at base, then greenish, then violaceous white, and ending in dark purplish brown; these colors in rather ill defined V-shaped bands, parallel with the posterior margin. Extreme tips of caudal lobes of a brighter brown; A. green and purplish brown, bluish towards the edge, which itself is milk white. V. similar. P. transparent, tinged with dusky. Iris dark reddish brown. Length, six inches.

After death, and, indeed, most specimens when fresh caught, exhibit but faint traces of the vertical bars, the sides being silvery, with longitudinal lines of brassy yellow. Iris silvery.

This species is caught with a hook, in water from six to twelve feet deep. They feed on the bottom, and are very destructive to bait, which they nibble off from the large hake and blue fish hooks in a very short time. Few exceeded six inches.

The porgee did not make its appearance in Egg Harbor bay until towards the middle of August, although said to be found at sea at an earlier period. As usual, the specimens were smaller than those taken outside the beach, though exhibiting the same beauty of color. Very few descriptions or figures convey any idea of the variety of delicate tints on this beautiful fish, which fade in a short time after death into a uniform silvery hue.

After the arrival of the porgees in the bay and mouth of the river, they become very troublesome by their great numbers and the destruction of bait caused by their incessant nibbling. A large book will be cleaned entirely in a moment, while all efforts to catch the depredator prove vain. The only way of taking them is to use a fine line, and very small minnow hooks, baited with small bits of clams, fish, or other food. These will be swallowed boldly, and, as they bite voraciously, large numbers can be taken in a short time. It is only necessary to throw the line out to its full extent, and then at once haul it in slowly, during which movement the bait will generally be seized. A single clam, chopped fine, may serve to catch twenty or thirty.

Quite large porgees are taken about Greenport, Long Island, in very great numbers, with seines. The usual ground is on the east side of Shelter island, where a fishing smack will frequently be loaded at a single haul. During the months of August and September these fish constitute the principal stock of those sent to the New York market over the Long Island railroad. The flesh of the porgee is excellent when fresh—scarcely surpassed by that of any other fish on the coast.

Genus EUCINOSTOMUS, B. and G.

Genus *Eucinostomus*, B. and G.—This genus has been established to include a species of the Menid family, possessing the following generic characters: Mouth small and very protractile; when protruded presenting a subconico-tubular appearance; lips thin; palate and tongue toothless; opercular apparatus without either spines or serratures. The second spine of the anal itself is less developed than in the genus *Gerres*, a genus to which the present one bears a close affinity.

20. Eucinostomus argenteus, B. and G.

Eucinostomus argenteus, B. and G.—Mouth very small; when retracted the posterior extremity of maxillary extends slightly beyond the vertical of anterior rim of the eye; base of spinous portion of dorsal equal in length to that of the soft portion; posterior extremity of soft dorsal rays extending a little more backwards than those of the anal fin.

D. IX, 10; A. III, 7 or 8; C. 5, I, 8, 8, I, 4; V. I, 5; P. 13.

Head forming about one fourth of the whole length; eye large, its diameter contained nearly three times in the length of the side of head; scales large; ground color silvery, with transverse fasciæ of a darker hue in immature specimens.

This species was quite abundant in the latter part of August, in the river and small bays. None were taken exceeding three inches in length.

---

21. Cybium maculatum, Cuv. and Val.

The spotted Cybium—Spanish Mackerel.

Cybium maculatum, Cuv. and Val., Hist. Nat. Poiss. XIII, 181.—DeKay, New York Fauna, Fishes, 108, plate lxxiii, fig. 232.

Of this fish but two specimens were taken during my stay at Beesley's point, and the species is scarcely known to the fishermen. It was more abundant at Greenport, Long Island; and in the Peconic bay, towards Riverhead, four hundred were caught at one haul of the seine. The flesh is excellent, having much the flavor of true mackerel, only a little softer and richer.

The fish bears a high price in the New York market, where it has been but recently known. It has been more abundant off our coast generally this season than ever before; and in the lower part of the Potomac, numbers have been taken and salted down. They may frequently be found in this state in the Washington market, and readily recognised by the round yellow spots on the sides, and the size so much larger than that of the common salted mackerel. The posterior portion of the body, to the base of the tail, is slenderer and much more elongated than in the other species.

---

22. Lichia carolina, DeKay.

Lichia carolina, DeKay, New York Fauna, Fishes, 114, plate x, figure 30.

Bright silvery, with bluish reflections on the back and upper part of sides; dorsal transparent, dusky towards the tips of the longest soft rays. C. A. yellowish towards their margin—the latter brightest anteriorly; V. white, tinged with yellow; P. brownish anteriorly. Iris silvery. Length, 5 inches.

This species was very abundant in the edge of the surf on the beach, moving about slowly in small schools. Occasionally they were seen in great numbers in the small slues running up into the beach, where several bushels were frequently taken in a sweep of ten yards with a seine eight feet long. They are most delicious as a pan-fish, and give very little trouble to fit them for cooking, not requiring scaling and scarcely gutting. The only preparation needed is to cut off the head a little obliquely, which will remove all the intestines.

---

23. Lichia spinosa, Baird.

The spinous Dory.

Lichia spinosa, Baird.—*Trachinotus spinosus*, DeKay, New York Fauna, Fishes, 117, plate xix, fig. 53.

Similar in colors to the *L. carolina*. The anterior yellow of the dorsal and anal is, however, brighter—even gamboge yellow; basal half of the anal, dusky; ventrals, chalk white, yellow anteriorly. Length, 2½ inches.

Caught in very small numbers with *L. carolina*.

---

24. Caranx chrysos, Cuv. and Val.

The yellow Caranx—Yellow Mackerel.

Caranx chrysos, Cuv. and Val., Hist. Nat. Poiss. IX, 97.—DeKay, New York Fauna, Fishes, 121, plate xxvii, fig. 85.

Sides bright wax color, becoming olivaceous along the back; a darker tinge of yellow on the cheek and operculum than elsewhere. In some lights there is a violet reflection on the back. A black spot on the upper part of the posterior edge of the operculum. Dorsals, dark olive green, dusky along the margin; C. dark wax yellow at the base, then lighter yellow—the tips blackish brown; A. dark wax yellow, the margin and spinous portion opaque white; V. white, yellowish centrally; P. greenish yellow. Length, 8½ inches.

Only one specimen of this fish was seen during my stay. It was caught in the bay with a hook. A few more were found among the porgees at Greenport, Long Island.

25. Argyreiosus capillaris, DeKay.

The Hair-finned Dory.

Argyreiosus capillaris, DeKay, New York Fauna, Fishes, 125, plate xxvii, fig. 82.

One specimen was taken in August while hauling the seine in the surf.

---

26. Temnodon saltator, Cuv. and Val.

The Blue Fish—Horse-Mackerel—Skip-Jack.

Temnodon saltator, Cuv. and Val., Hist. Nat. des Poiss. IX, 225, plate 260. DeKay, New York Fauna, Fishes, 130, plate xxvi, fig. 81.

The blue fish, or horse-mackerel, as it is called at Beesley's point, arrives in the bay early in the spring, accompanying the weak fish in its migration and preying habitually upon it. It is not usual to take them of large size during the summer; later in the season, however, specimens of two and three pounds are not unfrequently captured. Their usual size in August was from eight to twelve inches. The very young ones were found abundant at Corson's inlet, measuring two or three inches in length. At this age they are much more compressed than afterwards.

The blue fish is one of the most voracious fishes on the coast. It bites readily at any object drawn rapidly through the water, as a bone squid, or metal spoon, minnow, white rag, and, in fact, any conspicuous bait. They are generally caught by trolling on the surface of the water, best by sailing back and forth across a channel way, when the wind and tide are in opposite directions. Unless the line is armed with quill near the hook, or wired for a short distance, it is cut off by the sudden snap of their nipper-like teeth, this species ranking with the shark in the facility with which it takes off the hook.

The blue fish keeps near the surface of the water, and frequently leaps some distance into the air. It preys habitually upon the weak fish, and its ravages among the latter species seem to have diminished greatly its numbers off the coasts of New York and New England. It finds, likewise, an easy prey in the schools of Mossbunkers, among which it is said to commit such havoc that the gulls are attracted far and near in quest of the bits of flesh and mutilated fish which float on the surface.

Such congregations of birds often indicate to the fishermen the presence of blue fish on his grounds.

This species, like the weak fish, runs up the mouths of rivers even to where the water is comparatively fresh. Small ones were very abundant at Sing Sing the past summer, and were caught readily from the rocks or along the wharves. They were known as white fish.

They are taken in large numbers in the Potomac river as far up as Acquia creek, as well as in Philadelphia, where they are called tailors.

---

27. Peprilus triacanthus, Cuv.

Harvest-Fish.

Peprilus triacanthus, Cuv., Règne Anim. 3d ed.—*Rhombus triacanthus*, DeKay, New York Fauna, Fishes, 137, plate xxvi, fig. 80.

Several specimens were taken in a net at Corson's inlet. They were occasionally seen swimming slowly in small schools close to the steep banks of the inlet. The flesh is said to be tolerably well flavored, though less so than that of many other scomberoid species of the Jersey coast.

---

28. Atherinopsis notatus, Girard.

The Silverside—Sand-Smelt.

Atherinopsis notatus, Girard, Proc. Acad. Nat. Sc., Philad. VII, 1854, 198.—*Atherina notata*, Mitch.—DeKay, New York Fauna, Fishes, 141, plate xxvi, fig. 88.

This diminutive species may be said almost to out-number all others on the coast, the cyprinodonts not excepted. It is found quite abuudantly everywhere throughout Egg Harbor bay, though of small size; but it is along the sands of the beach and about the inlets that its vast schools are met with. Here they come in with the rising tide, especially when it flows over an extensive tract of sands bare at low water or with only a few pools. At times the water will appear in a state of constant agitation with the attempts of the fish to keep in the edge of the tide as it rolls on, and bushels can be taken in a short time merely with scoop-nets. Several parties, provided each with a fine meshed seine of twenty or thirty feet in length, could readily fill a wagon in a little while. Although no use is made of these "silver sides" on our coast, except as bait, there is no doubt that, potted and prepared as sardines and anchovies, they would be excellent.

With the exception of *Hydrargira flavula*, which is found in large numbers in the same localities, few other fish are met with in these large schools of atherinas. A few scattered *Cyprinodon ovinus* and small mullets only are to be seen. The maximum size to which the atherina attains is about six inches, although fish of this length are seldom caught in the bay. The flesh is nearly translucent and very sweet; and no preparation being required to fit them for the frying-pan, they might, though comparatively small, be eaten more frequently than they appear to be.

The silver-side, or sand-smelt, as it is called further east, makes an excellent bait for blue fish, weak fish, and, in fact, almost any other species. It must constitute the chief article of food for the larger fish on our coast, as it is found everywhere, even far up the mouths of rivers. It was very abundant at Sing Sing. In fact, I have seldom drawn a net anywhere in salt water or brackish without seeing it. It is a constant associate of the cyprinodonts in the salt ponds and meadows. It bites readily at a hook, although very seldom swallowing the bait owing to the smallness of its mouth.

---

29. Mugil albula, Linn.

The White Mullet.

Mugil albula, L.—DeKay, New York Fauna, Fishes, 146.

Back dark bluish black; sides lustrous silvery; beneath opaque white; a dark bluish black spot on the body, at the base of the pectoral fin; iris silvery, with a yellowish tinge above, as also on the operculum; D. and C. dark bluish on the membrane, especially towards the extremities; P. less strongly marked in the same manner; V. and A. opaque white, the latter with a few brown dots on the rays. Length 4½ inches.

Although small mullets were caught in considerable numbers in the creeks and about the inlets, none of large size were seen. The larger ones do not arrive until September, when they are said to be abundant. They then come close to shore among the grass, and run up the creeks in numbers, even where the water is shallow. When intercepted in a seine they leap over the upper edge with great readiness, one following the other, like a flock of shep. Their maximum size is from eight to ten inches.

This fish becomes extremely fat, so much so as to require no grease in frying. The flesh is said to be very palatable, though rather rich. The large mullets do not remain long in the bay, generally returning to the sea in the fall. A few, however, are said to remain all winter in the salt ponds.

---

30. Gobius alepidotus, Bose.

The variegated Goby.

Gobius alepidotus, Bosc.—DeKay, New York Fauna, Fishes, 160, plate xxiii, fig. 70.

Translucent olive green, with seven or eight vertical lines of lighter along the side; vertical fins, mottled with dusky spots, arranged in series transverse to the rays. Length one inch.

A few specimens only of this rare fish were taken in the grass along the beach of the river.

31. Batrachus variegatus, Les.

Toad-Fish—Oyster-Fish.

Batrachus variegatus, Les., Journ. Acad. Nat. Sc. Philad. III, 398.—DeKay, New York Fauna, Fishes, 171.

Body olivaceous, closely but rather coarsely vermiculated with darker; three or four quadrate spots across and along the back; iris greenish yellow, with four broad double radii of greyish; fins reddish brown towards the borders, their general color light olivaceous; C. and P. with well defined bands of darker, transverse to the rays; D. and A. with similar bands disposed obliquely towards the rays, the angle anterior; a dark spot on the anterior dorsal ; V. and inferior parts of body reddish white—in large specimens, the latter yellowish, with dark blotches. Length six inches.

The toad-fish, or, as it is called at Beesley's point, the oyster-fish, on account of its frequenting the oyster beds, is one of the fishermen's pests, from its great abundance, and pertinacity in taking the hook baited for nobler game. Few fish are more repulsive in appearance than this species, with its large, flattened head, broad mouth, laciniated processes or fringes about the jaw, goggle eyes, and slimy body. It will live a long while out of water, snapping at the finger even when almost dried up. It is capable of inflicting quite a severe bite, and is always handled with a great deal of caution.

The eggs are said to be laid on oyster shells, or between their empty valves, at Beesley's point, in the entire absence of stones or pebbles, which constitute the usual place of deposite. An artificial pile of stone near Chattin's tavern is a favorite locality with them. The eggs are about the size of number 6 shot at first, but enlarge to the bulk of a pea; their color is a bright yellow. The fish watches its nest very vigilantly, and can scarcely be driven away, snapping at the finger or a stick, and when forcibly removed returning with the first opportunity.

The flesh is said, by those who have been able to overcome their aversion to the fish, to be very sweet and palatable.

The toad-fish seldom comes very near shore, few having been taken in the hauling of small seines. I have never seen it up the small creeks.

---

32. Tautoga Americana, Cuv. and Val.

Tautog—The Black Fish.

Tautoga americana, Cuv. and Val., Hist. Nat. des Poiss. XIII, 293.—DeKay, New York Fauna, Fishes, 175, plate xiv, fig. 39.

The tautog, smooth black fish, or chub, as the species is indifferently called, was not abundant at Beesley's point during the past summer, although their number is said to be greater in the fall. They are caught off the steep banks, in the channel-ways and the thoroughfares.

The flesh is not very remarkable for its excellence, being greatly surpassed by several other species.

Owing to the toughness of the skin and the firm adhesion of the scales, it is customary to skin the tautog before cooking, whenever of sufficient size to permit it.

Young fish of this species were taken in considerable numbers in the river and about the inlets, when hauling the nets. Their color was generally of a light olive green.

---

33. Ailurichthys marinus, B. and G.

Sea Cat-Fish.

Ailurichthys marinus, B. and G., Proc. Acad. Nat. Sc. Philad. VI.—*Galeichthys marinus*, De Kay, New York Fauna, Fishes, 178, plate xxxvii, fig. 118.

The sea-cat or channel-cat, was occasionally taken with the hook in the channel of the river. Nothing specially was learned of its habits. The flesh is very indifferent, being coarse and rank, tasting much like that of small sharks.

---

34. Leucosomus americanus, Girard.

Dace.—Wind-Fish—Shiner.

Leucosomus americanus, Girard in Storer, Hist. Fishes of Massach. 117, plate xxi, fig.—*Abramis versicolor*, DeKay, New York Fauna, Fishes, 191, plate xxxii, fig. 103.

This species was very abundant in the fresh waters of Cedar Swamp creek and Cedar creek, two streams emptying into the Egg Harbor river on opposite sides. None were seen excepting in perfectly fresh water above the tide dams. They were in considerable numbers, as being the principal representative of the cyprinoids in the New Jersey streams. This species is found everywhere in the streams of the Atlantic coast to Maine. Nothing of special interest was noted as to its habits.

---

35. Catostomus gibbosus, Les.

The Horned Sucker—Chubsucker.

Catostomus gibbosus, Les.—*Labeo gibbosus*, DeKay, New York Fauna, Fishes, 194, plate xxxii, fig. 101.—*Catostomus tuberculatus*, Les.—DeKay, ibid, 199, plate xxxi, fig. 97.

This was the only sucker found in the Cedar creeks, nor is any other species believed to occur there. It is everywhere constantly associated with the *Leucosomus americanus;* and these, with a small species of *Leuciscus* allied to *L. hudsonius*, constitute almost the only cyprinoids of the fresh waters on our coast. I have seen no other species from New Jersey to Maine in streams emptying directly into the ocean or into brackish waters, except when quite removed from the salt water.

---

36. MELANURA PYGMÆA, Agass.

Mud-Fish.

Melanura pygmæa, Agass.—*Leuciscus pigmaeus*, DeKay, New York Fauna, Fishes, 214, plate xlii, fig. 134.

Only one specimen of this species was obtained, caught in a muddy ditch along side the fresh waters of Cedar Swamp creek. Of the five or six species of this genus indicated by Professor Agassiz, all appear to have the same peculiarity of living almost entirely in mud. A locality, which, with the water perfectly clear, appears destitute of fish will perhaps yield a number of mud-fish on stirring up the mud at the bottom and drawing a seine through it. Ditches in the prairies of Wisconsin, or mere bog-holes apparently affording lodgment to nothing beyond tadpoles, may thus be found filled with melanuras. Their usual associates in such places in the west are *Gasterosteus inconstans*, Kirt.

I found none on Long Island, although they doubtless occur in the muddy streams about Riverhead. Mr. J. C. Brevoort, obtained a single specimen near Bedford, and Dr. Ayres some at Brookhaven. This genus appears to be confined to a few points near brackish and salt waters, and to the vicinity of the great lakes; they are especially abundant on the plateaus dividing the waters of the lakes from those of the Mississippi. I have caught them all around Lakes George and Champlain; on the American shores of all the great lakes except Lake Superior; and on their dividing ridges, as already stated, as far west as the Mississippi, in Wisconsin. They have, however, not yet been detected much south of this region in the interior.

This species of *Melanura* is probably identical with *Leuciscus pygmæus* of DeKay, an unfortunate name, as it belongs to an entirely different family than the Cyprinidae, and attains to a larger size than the rest, much larger than many of the *Leucisci*. Specimens taken in Rockland county, New York, and in the same localities whence Mr. J. G. Bell obtained those sent to Dr. DeKay, measure nearly six inches in length. I procured a large number of them during the past summer.

---

37. FUNDULUS ZEBRA, DeKay.

Fundulus zebra, DeKay, New York Fauna, Fishes, 218.

Above, dark olive green, lighter on the sides; on the throat and belly greenish white; 12 to 15 vertical bands on each side of greenish white, with spots of greenish golden sprinkled in the intervals. Operculum bronzed, iris greenish black, with a narrow golden ring on the inner border; D. and C. dark olive, margined with light grass green, the former with greenish white spots on the posterior half, some of them occasionally confluent; the latter with smaller spots of the same on the membrane, arranged in series transverse to the rays; A. and P. gamboge yellow on the distal half, with black spots posteriorly, the former with some light spots. Length three inches.

Female fishes corresponding to the *F. viridescens* of De Kay, and probably of this species, are uniform olive, with the belly yellowish white. Some specimens have obscure vertical dark lines.

This species is exceedingly abundant in the small creeks of the salt meadows, less numerous in the ponds. They are very active in their movements, darting to cover at the slightest alarm. Like all the other species, they are excessively voracious, and a dead fish of considerable size will be eaten up in a few minutes by the dense crowd of these diminutive scavengers, darting upon it from all points. A clam pounded up and thrown in among them, will in a moment attract many hundreds, and they are frequently taken for bait, by putting the clam into a scoop-net, and withdrawing the net suddenly, with the fish enclosed.

There is no doubt that the various species of cyprinodonts on our coast perform very important services in rapidly removing dead animals, as fishes, crabs, shells, &c., from the water, and thus keeping up the proper equilibrium. This they do to a much greater extent than the crabs, which, however, assist in the labor. Abundant everywhere along the shores and in the creeks and ponds of the meadows, they are always on hand to do their work.

Nothing was observed at Beesley point in regard to the reproductive peculiarities of any of the cyprinodonts, the season of the year not being favorable. It is very probable, however, that most of them are viviparous, like many other species of the family. Like the others, this one is remarkably tenacious of life, resisting successfully long absence from water, even to the extent of considerable desiccation.

A few specimens were caught in the fresh waters of Cedar Swamp creek. They are, however, essentially a salt water species.

---

38. Fundulus diaphanus, Agass.

Hydrargira diaphana, Lesueur.—DeKay, New York Fauna, Fishes, 219.

This species was found abundantly in Ludlum's run, at a point where the water is perfectly fresh at low tide, but becomes brackish during high water. It was also taken in the fresh waters of Cedar Swamp creek. I do not remember to have ever noticed it in perfectly salt water.

39. Fundulus multifasciatus, Cuv.

Fundulus multifasciatus, Cuv. and Val., Hist. Nat. des Poiss. XVIII, 200.—*Hydrargira multifasciata*, Lesueur.—De Kay, New York Fauna, Fishes, 220.

This species was found everywhere associated with *H. flavula*, but in quite limited numbers.

---

40. Hydrargira flavula, Storer.

Hydrargira flavula, Storer.—*Esox flavulus*, Mitch.—*Fundulus fasciatus*, DeKay, New York Fauna, Fishes, 216, plate xxxi, fig. 98.

This species may be called the giant of the northern cyprinodonts, attaining a size only approached by the females of *Fundulus zebra*. As in *F. zebra*. the female is considerably larger than the male. Specimens were taken nearly eight inches in length.

The *H. flavula* is very rarely found in the bays and meadows, the few that occur in such localities being very small, and much scattered. It is along the beach, and about the inlets, that the immense numbers that exist on our coasts can be appreciated. As the tide is rising and flowing over flat sands, or up the narrow shores and channel ways, this species will be seen in dense schools, slowly swimming with the tide, and readily recognised by its large size and the light spot near the dorsal fin.

It generally keeps distinct from the atherinas, which are equally or even more abundant in the same situations. A few *Cyprinodon ovinus* are sometimes seen in company, rarely any other species of the same family.

The sexes of this species are conspicuously different in marking, the male having many broad vertical bands on each side, from head to tail, the female two or three longitudinal ones.

---

41. Hydrargyra luciæ, Baird.

Hydrargira luciæ, Baird.—General form elongated, though of rather short appearance. Head constituting less than one-fourth of total length. Insertion of anal slightly in advance of origin of dorsal, and rather more developed than the latter. Vertrals very small; their extremity reaching the anus. Tail large. D. 8; A. 9; C. 6, I. 8, 7, I. 5; V. 6; P. 15.

Dark olive green above, lower part of sides and beneath rich ochre yellow. Sides with 10 or 12 broad, well defined, vertically disposed dark bars, nearly as large as their inter-spaces, which are of a faint tint of greenish white. All the fins but the dorsal are of a uniform yellowish, lighter than the abdomen. Dorsal, yellow on the terminal half, the basal portions olivaceous, with a large black spot posteriorly, and immediately anterior to it a white one. The dark spot is bordered above and behind by the yellow part mentioned. In one specimen the posterior half of the base of the dorsal fin is dull white, with a large subcircular spot of black in the centre. Length about one inch.

P. similar, the dorsal unspotted, the yellow less intense.

A few specimens only were taken, in a small ditch at Robinson's landing, Peck's beach, opposite Beesley's point.

---

42. Cyprinodon ovinus, Val.

Cyprinodon ovinus, Valene.—*Esox ovinus*, Mitch.—*Lebias ovinus*, DeKay, New York Fauna, Fishes, 215, plate xxvii, fig. 87.

This species was very abundant in the salt ponds, more so than any other; it was seen but rarely in the creeks or in the bays. Specimens were taken of much larger size than the supposed average; and the males, recognised by the black band on the end of the caudal fin, were found to be larger than the females.

---

43. Cyprinodon parvus, B. & G.

Cyprinodon parvus, B. and G.—Form elongated, resembling a diminutive *Leuciscus;* head constituting less than a fourth of the total length; eye quite large and circular, being contained three times in the length of the side of the head; caudal posteriorly rounded.—D. 10; A. 10; C. 5. I. 7. 6. I. 4; V. 6; P. 15. Scales quite large, deeper than long, and disposed in eight longitudinal series upon the line of greatest depth of the body; seven series may be observed upon the peduncle of the tail.

This species was found in the small ponds of the salt meadows, generally in the grass; and owing to their diminutive size the males were not often taken, and, in fact, neither sex was found in anything like the abundance of most other species. The colors during life were very plain, being without any of the peculiar patterns of other species. I observed it, sparingly, in many localities in Long Island, especially at Greenport. It has a close resemblance to the females of *Heterandria.*

---

44. Esox fasciatus, DeKay.

Short-billed Pike.

Esox fasciatus, DeKay, New York Fauna, Fishes, 224, plate xxxiv, fig. 110.

Brownish olivaceous; a longitudinal lighter vertebral stripe. On each side of the body a median longitudinal irregular band of golden, sending off bars transversely above and below, sometimes opposite each other, sometimes alternate, occasionally branching and anastomosing. Beneath greenish or yellowish white. Iris purplish brown, with a golden interior ring.

Dorsal and caudal fins plain olive, tinged with red. A. V. P. pink—this color becoming rather deeper after death. Length, 10 inches. Abundant in Cedar Swamp creek. Specimens of considerably larger size were taken.

---

45. Esox reticulatus, Les.

Pickerel.

Esox reticulatus, Les.—DeKay, New York Fauna, Fishes, 223, plate xxxiv, fig. 107.

Rather rare in Cedar Swamp creek. Associated with *E. fasciatus*.

---

46. Belone truncata, Les.

The Bill-Fish—Sea-Pike—Silver Gar-Fish, &c.

Belone truncata, Lesueur.—DeKay, New York Fauna, Fishes, 227, plate xxxv, fig. 112.

Color.—Back dark green; sides opaque silvery white; beneath dull white—the lines of separation between these colors very distinct; cornea green; iris silvery; fins subtransparent, with fine punctations of greenish on the membrane, much thickest on the D. and C.; length, 8 inches.

The silver gar made its appearance, in August, in considerable numbers, though of quite small size. It was found in the shallow bays and creeks—more abundantly in the slues on the beach, keeping in compact bodies, and swimming slowly along.

This species is fond of running up into fresh water during the summer, and is often taken a considerable distance from the ocean. I have seen them in the village of Riverhead, Long Island; and they are at times quite abundant off the city of Washington. They have been seen at Columbia, Pennsylvania, in the Susquehanna. They sometimes are taken with a hook, although such an occurrence is quite rare. When of large size, their flesh is of excellent flavor.

---

47. Saurus mexicanus, Cuv.

Saurus mexicanus, Cuv., Règne Anim.—(Griff. transl.) X, 431.

A single specimen of this fish was taken in a seine in the river. Although abundant off the southern coast, it is rarely seen so far to the north. Dr. DeKay does not enumerate it among the fishes of New York, yet several have been procured by Mr. Brevoort about Long Island.

---

48. Engraulis vittata, B and G.

The Anchovy.

Engraulis vittata, B and G.—*Engraulis mitchilli*, Cuv. and Val., Hist. Nat. Poiss., XXI.—*Clupea vittata*, Mitch.—DeKay, New York Fauna, Fishes, 254.

It is a little remarkable that no mention of the occurrence of *Engraulis* on the Atlantic coast of the United States, is made by any American writer. The species was long ago described by Dr. Mitchill, so accurately as clearly to indicate this genus; but Dr. DeKay does not appear to have noticed it at all.

The anchovy made its appearance early in August in the shallow waters along the beach, although of very small size. They became subsequently more abundant; and towards the end of the month, while hauling a large net in the surf, many were taken measuring over six inches in length. As the meshes of the net were very large, the greater portion readily escaped; but with a seine properly constructed enough could be readily procured to supply the American market.

I procured several specimens of this fish, in 1847, at the residence of Mr. Audubon, on the Hudson river, above New York.

---

49. Alosa menhaden, Mitch.

The Moss-Bonker—Bony Fish—Hard Head.

Alosa menhaden, Mitch.—Storer, Rep., p. 117.—De Kay, New York Fauna, Fishes, 259, plate xxi, fig. 60.

Back dark green, shading into yellowish, silvery on the sides and beneath. Iris silvery. A rounded dark spot behind the upper part of the operculum, and five or six smaller ones, less distinct, in a longitudinal row behind it, the latter sometimes indistinct. All the spots are on the skin, showing through the transparent scales.

D. and C. yellowish, with a dark margin; the remaining fins colorless.

The moss-bonker is a fish of great economical importance, as much so, perhaps, as any other on our coast. This is not on account of its flesh, which, though sweet, is too full of bones to be generally acceptable; as a manure, however, it replaces all other fertilizers on and near the sea-shore.

The countless schools of moss-bonkers, most of them of vast extent, seen everywhere on the Atlantic coast, represent a species quite equal in numbers to any other of the same size belonging to our fauna.

Every bay and river-mouth along our coast is filled with them during the summer, and they can everywhere be taken with great ease. The schools swim at the surface, their dorsal fins projecting above the water, and keeping it in such agitation as to be readily discernible at a great distance. They are generally followed by blue fish, sharks, and other predacious species, which commit such havoc in their ranks, it is said, that the gulls frequently follow in their wake to feed upon the fragments left floating behind.

The fishermen about Greenport, when in pursuit of moss-bonkers, lie some distance off shore, with two seines joined together, each seine resting on a separate boat, provided with its crew. When a school is seen of sufficient size to warrant the trouble, the joined ends of the nets are dropped into the water, and as the boats separate they make a turn, and thus enclose the fish; the ends of the nets are then taken to the shore, and the net itself drawn up by means of a windlass. Many thousands are taken at a haul, and meet with a ready sale. Quite recently several establishments have been erected on Long Island for the manufacture of oil from the moss-bonker. The fish, as brought in, are chopped up and boiled, and the oil skimmed off; a heavy pressure on the residuum expresses the remaining oil, and what is left is still useful as a manure. The oil finds a ready market. It has been estimated that a single fish will furnish enough oil to saturate a surface of paper eighteen inches square.

Most of these fish, however, are used directly as fertilizers, by being ploughed or hoed in the ground. It is quite customary when planting corn to place a fish in each hill, the result being seen in a very luxuriant growth of the plant.

Besides being taken in the manner just described and by single seines put out from the shore, many are captured in gill-nets set in channels of rivers and other localities frequented by them. Many are taken in this way in the Hudson river and tributaries, as well as elsewhere.

Besides its use as manure, the moss-bonker, from its abundance, is employed to a great extent as bait for other fishes. Chopped up fine, it constitutes a chief bait for eels in eel-pots, and the flesh is very attractive to the blue fish and other species. When used as food, it is usually skinned, to remove the oilier layer of black fat, and the back bone is generally taken out at the same time.

The moss-bonker is much infested by a species of lernaean, which is buried in the skin by its star-shaped processes with a long projecting thread.

The moss-bonker is not much sought after at Beesley's point, nor did I hear of any who made a business of catching them there for manure.

50. Alosa mattowaca, DeKay.

Alosa mattowaca, DeKay, New York Fauna, Fishes, 250, plate xl, fig. 127.—*Clupea mattowaca*, Mitch.

A few specimens were caught in the surf with a large seine.

---

51. Alosa teres, DeKay.

Alosa teres, DeKay, New York Fauna, Fishes, 262, plate xl, fig. 128.

A number of specimens of this rare species were found one day in the edge of the surf along the beach; they seemed to be very weak, and died soon after their capture.

---

52. Chatoessus signifer, DeKay.

Thread-Herring.

Chatoessus signifer, DeKay, New York Fauna, Fishes, 264, plate xli, fig. 132.

A few specimens were taken in a net in the bay. In life the back is bright green; the caudal fin yellow, black at the tip.

---

53. Platessa ocellaris, DeKay.

The long-toothed Flounder.

Platessa ocellaris, DeKay, New York Fauna, Fishes, 300, plate xlvii, fig. 152.

This flounder is caught very abundantly during the summer, especially in the month of July, when it frequently constitutes the chief result of a day's fishing. It is generally found on sandy bottoms, and bites readily at almost any bait. They are sometimes taken in large numbers by means of nets in the deep slues along the beach.

In winter they at times seem to be quite torpid on the shallow grounds, suffering themselves to be taken up with oyster tongs without making any attempt to escape.

---

54. Platessa plana, Storer.

The New York Flat-Fish—Winter Flounder.

Platessa plana, Storer.—DeKay, New York Fauna, Fishes, 295, plate xlviii, fig. 154, and plate xlvix, fig. 158.

A few specimens only of this species were taken in the shores on he beach. It is said to be found abundantly in the bay during winter.

55. Rhombus maculatus, Girard.

The spotted Turbot.

Rhombus maculatus, Girard, in 7th Ann. Rep. Reg. Univ. N. Y., on State Cab., 23.—*Pleuronectes maculatus*, Mitch.—DeKay, New York Fauna, Fishes, 302, plate xlvii, fig. 151.

Taken occasionally of small size in the surf.

---

56. Achirus mollis, Cuv.

The New York Sole.

Achirus mollis, Cuv., Règne Anim., II.—DeKay, New York Fauna, Fishes, 303, plate xlix, fig. 159.

A few specimens were caught in the river by means of seines. The species, though resident, is taken most frequently in early spring. When thrown on the shore it buries itself in the sand, and is out of sight in a few moments. It is familiarly known at Beesley's Point under the name of hog-choker, as when seized by the hogs it doubles itself up, and, filling the æsophagus, obstinately resists by the scabrous nature of its scales all effort on the part of the animal to swallow it.

---

57. Anguilla tenuirostris, DeKay.

Anguilla tenuirostris, DeKay, New York Fauna, Fishes, 300, plate liii, fig. 173.

As might be expected from the vast mud-flats of the bay and its generally muddy bottom, eels are exceedingly abundant about Beesley's point. In passing slowly over the shallow waters near the shore, they will be seen darting out from among the sea-weeds at the bottom every few rods, and may readily be captured by a skillful hand armed with a gig. They can be caught readily, likewise, by means of a hook and line, by bobbing, with eel-pots, and the other devices suitable to the capture of the genus. Night is, of course, the best time for taking them in any way.

In winter they bed in the soft mud, to the depth of about a foot, and are then easily secured by means of a broad gig or spear.

58. Conger occidentalis, DeKay.

The Conger Eel.

Conger occidentalis, DeKay, New York Fauna, Fishes, 314, plate liii, fig. 172.

Clear olive above, shading into silvery on the sides and beneath. Vertical fins thin and transparent, with a narrow and well defined margin of brownish black. Iris, silvery. After death the silvery hue is more predominant.

Only one specimen of this species was taken at Beesley's point. It was captured on the 16th of August at Molasses point, and seemed entirely unknown to the residents.

---

59. Ophidium marginatum, DeKay.

Ophidium marginatum, DeKay, New York, Fauna, Fishes, 315, plate lii, fig. 169.

One specimen was taken during the past winter, and presented by Mr. Chatten.

---

60. Syngnathus viridescens, DeKay.

The Green Pipe-Fish.

Syngnathus viridescens, DeKay, New York Fauna, Fishes, 321, plate liv, fig. 176.

This pipe-fish was very abundant in the sea-weed and grass near the mouths of the inlets, every haul of the net bringing in hundreds. They were of many shades and colors, and of sizes varying from one inch to eight.

---

61. Diodon maculato-striatus, Mitch.

The Spot-Striped Balloon-Fish.

Diodon maculato-striatus, Mitch.—DeKay, New York Fauna, Fishes, 323, plate lvi, fig. 185.

A few specimens were taken in the river.

---

62. Diodon fuliginosus, DeKay.

Diodon fuliginosus, DeKay, New York Fauna, Fishes, 324, plate lv fig. 181.

A few specimens captured in the river by means of a seine.

63. Tetraodon turgidus, Mitch.

Toad-Fish.

Tetraodon turgidus, Mitch.—DeKay, New York Fauna, Fishes, 327, plate lv, fig. 178.

Dark olive green above and on the upper part of the sides, with fine black points intermixed. Abdomen and beneath, pure opaque white. Lower part of sides ochre yellow, with six or seven large vertically oblong and rounded blotches of brown. Above these are occasionally traces of dark mottling; fins pale yellowish. Iris reddish brown, with an inner circle of a coppery or brassy color.

This fish is frequently caught in the bay of Great Egg harbor, while fishing for better species. When drawn up, it immediately inflates its body to a prodigious size by means of short jerking inspirations, the sac becoming distended with air if in the atmosphere, or water, when submerged. By scratching it on the belly or pounding it, it will readily inflate itself several times in succession, and again discharge its load at a single effort through mouth and gills. When inflated and thrown on the water, it will sometimes float to a great distance before collapsing.

The skin around the eye of this species is contractile to such an extent as completely to close up the latter by a kind of puckering.

This fish is most abundant in summer; rarely, if ever, taken during the winter, and only occasionally in early spring.

---

64. Carcharias cæruleus, DeKay.

The small blue Shark.

Carcharias cæruleus, DeKay, New York Fauna, Fishes, 349, plate lxi, fig. 200.

The blue shark was quite abundant in the bay during the summer, and quite a number were captured by various parties. They were taken by means of large shark-hooks baited with eels or other fish, a small keg being used as a float. Several of the boats always carried shark-lines, which were put out when on suitable ground, the buoy being allowed to float off to some distance. On getting a bite the small lines would be taken up, the anchor raised, and every effort made to tire out the shark. Sometimes the fish would be towed to an island and hauled up, or again drawn in to the side of the boat, and killed by means of a harpoon or sword. The largest taken in this way was about nine feet long.

Though sufficiently abundant to be seen any day swimming with their dorsal fins above the surface, no instance was mentioned by the inhabitants of their attacking bathers while in the water.

Small specimens were occasionally taken on hooks baited for other fish.

65. Mustelus—canis, DeKay.

The Hound-Fish—Dog-shark.

Mustelus, Mitch., *canis*, DeKay, New York Fauna, Fishes, 355, plate lxiv, fig. 200.

The little dog-shark was sufficiently abundant to constitute a grievous pest to those who aimed after something more edible. It was no uncommon thing to see from ten to twenty taken in a few hours' fishing. They bite at almost any bait, and their presence is generally fatal to much success among other species. The flesh is not very palatable, having much of the coarse and rank flavor of the sea cat-fish.

---

66. Zygæna tiburo, Val.

Zygæna tiburo, Val.—Yarrell, Brit. Fish., I, 507—*Squalus tiburo*, Linn. Syst. Nat. I, 399, 6.

Only one specimen of this shark was obtained, although several were taken by the fishermen. This one was caught by Mr. Charles Ashmead, in the bay, and measured about eighteen inches. The *Z. malleus* is also said to occur even more abundantly than the present species. I do not find this species recorded hitherto as occurring on the American coast.

---

67. Pastinaca hastata, DeKay.

The Whip Sting-ray.

Pastinaca hastata, DeKay, New York Fauna, Fishes, 373, plate lxv, fig. 214.

This species was found to be abundant in the bay and elsewhere. It was frequently taken with the hook, and every haul of the seine in the surf brought in numbers. The smallest caught were about the size of a breakfast plate, the largest measured about four feet across, with a tail five feet long.

The wounds inflicted by means of the serrated spine on the tail of the sting-ray are justly dreaded by the fishermen, who use the greatest care in handling them. The usual practice is to cut off the tail at once, and thus render the fish *hors du combat.* Instances have been known of this spine being driven through the hand with such violence as to render it necessary to pull it out from the opposite side.

The large ones, when brought in by the seines, are so heavy as materially to impede the hauling of the net. In this case some of the men were in the habit of thrusting the handle of an oar into the orbit, and with this convenient *point d'appui* sliding the monster out upon the bank.

Catalogue of rocks, minerals, and ores, collected during the years 1847 and 1848, on the Geological survey of the United States mineral lands in Michigan, by Dr. C. T. Jackson, United States geologist, and deposited in the Smithsonian Institution.

Progressive No.	No. of specimens.	No. of box.	Description.	Locality.
1	1	1	Cocks' comb sulphate of baryta and dog tooth spar	New York Company, near Agate Harbor
2	2	1	Cocks' comb sulphate of baryta and calc. spar	do.
3	3	1	Cocks' comb sulphate of baryta	do.
4	4	1	Do. do.	do.
5	5	1	Do. do.	do.
6	6	1	Do. do.	do.
7	7	1	Do. do.	do.
8	8	1	Do. do.	do.
9	9	1	Do. do.	do.
10	10	1	Do. do.	do.
11	11	1	Do. do.	do.
12	12	1	Do. do.	do.
13	13	1	Do. do.	do.
14	14	1	Do. do.	do.
15	15	1	Do. do.	do.
16	16	1	Do. do.	do.
17	17	1	Do. do.	do.
18	18	1	Do. do.	do.
19	20	1	Cocks' comb sulphate of baryta, with sulphate of baryta and black sulphuret of copper	do.
20	65	1	Sulphate of baryta and black sulphuret of copper, mixed	do.
21	66	1	Do. do.	do.
22	67	1	Do. do.	do.
23	68	1	Do. do.	do.
24	69	1	Sulphate of baryta containing black sulphuret of copper coated with green carbonate of copper	do.
25	70	1	Do. do. do.	do.
26	71	1	Calc. spar and [illegible] sulphate of baryta	do.
27	25	1	Fine crystals of calc. spar	do.
28	26	1	Calc. spar, six-sided prisms	do.
29	27	1	Calc. spar, scalene dodecahedrons	do.
30	28	1	Geodes of calc. spar	do.

31	29	1	Do.	do.
32	30	1	Crystals of calc. spar	do.
33	31	1	Crystals of calc. spar colored by black sulphuret of copper.	do.
34	32	1	Do. do.	do.
35	33	1	Single crystal of calc. spar.	do.
36	34	1	Fine crystals of calc. spar.	do.
37	35	1	Calc. spar.	do.
38	36	1	Do.	do.
39	37	1	Do.	do.
40	38	1	Do.	do.
41	39	1	Do.	do.
42	40	1	Do.	do.
43	41	1	Do.	do.
44	42	1	Calc. spar colored by black sulphuret of copper.	do.
45	43	1	Do. do.	do.
46	44	1	Yellow dog-tooth spar.	do.
47	46	1	Calc. spar.	do.
48	47	1	Do.	do.
49	48	1	Do.	do.
50	49	1	Do.	do.
51	50	1	Do.	do.
52	51	1	Do.	do.
53	52	1	Black sulphuret of copper and calc. spar colored by black sulphuret of copper.	do.
54	53	1	Black sulphuret of copper on calc. spar.	do.
55	54	1	Black calc. spar colored by black sulphuret of copper	do.
56	55	1	Do. do.	do.
57	56	1	Do. do.	do.
58	57	1	Do. do.	do.
59	58	1	Do. do.	do.
60	59	1	Dog tooth spar and black sulphuret of copper	do.
61	61	1	Do. do.	do.
62	61	1	Blue calc. spar.	do.
63	62	1	Do.	do.
64	63	1	Blue calc. spar and black sulphuret of copper	do.
65	64	1	Do. do.	do.
66	714	7	Calc. spar, six-sided prisms	do.
67	972	10	Vein of [illegible]	do.
68	593	6	[illegible] red feldspar	do.
69	74	1	[illegible] of copper in red amygdaloid.	Eagle Harbor mine.
70	75	1	Do. do. do.	do.
71	76	1	Do. do.	do.

Catalogue of rocks, minerals, and ores, collected by Dr. C. T. Jackson—Continued.

Progressive No.	No. of specimens.	No. of box.	Description.	Locality.
72	77	1	Native copper and black sulphuret of copper in red amygdaloid	Eagle Harbor mine
73	78	1	Veinstone and black sulphuret of copper	do.
74	79	1	Do. do.	do.
75	80	1	Do. do.	do.
76	81	1	Do. do.	do.
77	82	1	Veinstone	do.
78	83	1	Do.	do.
79	321	3	Native copper in laumonite	do.
80	322	3	Do. do.	do.
81	323	3	Do. do.	do.
82	324	3	Do. do.	do.
83	529	5	Native copper in [illegible]	do.
84	531	5	Native copper in [illegible], with calc. spar colored green by carbonate copper	do.
85	534	5	Native copper with [illegible]	do.
86	19	1	Red amygdaloid	do.
87	606	6	Native copper in [illegible]	do.
88	709	7	[illegible], with native copper in crystals of calc. spar, with red feldspar	do.
89	710	7	Massive native copper in [illegible], with laumonite	do.
90	711	7	Do. do. do.	do.
91	712	7	Do. do. do.	do.
92	713	7	Do. do. do.	do.
93	715	7	Dentritic native copper in ve[illegible], with laumonite	do.
94	7[illegible]	7	Do. do. do.	do.
95	717	7	Mass of native copper, with laumonite	do.
96	718	7	Dark red compact sandstone	do.
97	719	7	Trap, [illegible] with sandstone, [illegible] with light green chlorite	do.
98	720	7	Fine-grained [illegible] trap, [illegible] [illegible]ite finely disseminated	Eagle harbor
99	721	7	Trap, containing scattered nodules of chlorite	do.
100	722	7	Do. do.	do.
101	723	7	[illegible], containing [illegible]aloid of chlorite calc. spar and laumonite	do.
102	732	8	Mass of native copper in laumonite	West Vein [illegible]
103	733	8	Do. do. do.	do.
104	734	8	Mass of native copper in chlorite	do.

105	735	8	Do........do..........do	do
106	736	8	Native copper in [illegible]mite	do
107	737	8	Do............do	do
108	738	8	Do............do	do
109	739	8	Do............do	do
110	21	1	Native copper coated with red oxide	Northwest corner of Kewconaw point
111	22	1	Native copper in quartz	do
112	23	1	Native copper in quartz and phrenite, with red oxide	do
113	24	1	Do	do
114	72	1	Do	do
115	73	1	[illegible]te and quartz	do
116	512	5	Native copper in phrenite	do
117	513	5	Do............do	do
118	514	5	Do............do	do
119	515	5	Native copper and calc. spar	do
120	516	5	Native copper in calc. spar	do
121	517	5	Do............do	do
122	518	5	Do............do	do
123	519	5	Mass of native copper	do
124	520	5	Do......do	do
125	521	5	Native copper coated with red oxide, with fine crystals of green carb. copper	do
126	522	5	Native copper in red feldspar	do
127	523	5	Crystals of calc. spar	do
128	524	5	Native silver and copper in [illegible]one, c[illegible] [illegible]ing [illegible]ed [illegible]k quartz ore	do
129	525	5	Native copper in veinstone, [illegible]ing s[illegible] do[illegible]ed [illegible]k quartz ore	do
130	578	6	Mass of native copper coated with red oxide	do
131	331	3	Native copper in veinstone	Northwest corner of Stautenbury vein
132	332	3	Do............do	do
133	333	3	Native copper coated with carbonate copper	do
134	334	3	Native copper and silver in veinstone, with calc. spar	do
135	335	3	Do............do........do..............do	do
136	336	3	Do............do........do..............do	do
137	371	3	Native copper in [illegible]stone	do
138	372	3	Do............do	do
139	507	5	Native copper in phrenite. The surface of copper impressed by phrenite	do
140	348	3	Native copper in [illegible]	do
141	349	3	Do............do	Northwest corner of Hogan's vein
142	350	3	Do............do	do
143	351	3	Native copper and silver, with yellow calc. spar	do
144	352	3	Do............do..............do	do
145	353	3	Native copper and silver	Northwest corner of Kelley's vein

Catalogue of rocks, minerals, and ores, collected by Dr. C. T. Jackson.—Continued.

Progressive No.	No. of specimens.	No. of box.	Description.	Locality.
146	354	3	Ne per in veinstone	Northwest corner of Kelley's vein
147	355	3	Ntive por with phrenite	do.
148	359	3	Ntive per in calc. spar	Northwest corner of Middle vein
149	378	3	Ntive por in phrenite	do.
150	379	3	Ne por in calc. spar	do.
151	360	3	Do. do.	Northwest corner of East vein
152	361	3	Do. do.	do.
153	373	3	Ne pr in ntc	do.
154	374	3	Do. d.	do.
155	375	3	Ne copper in nne, with red oxide	do.
156	376	3	Do. do.	Northw et corner of West vein
157	377	3	Do. do.	d.
158	508	5	Indian er	Northw et corner of Old Inian mine
159	509	5	Do. do.	do.
160	510	5	Do. do.	do.
161	511	5	Do. do.	do.
162	325	3	Light gen s einstone, containing native copper	pr Falls
163	326	3	Do. do. do. do. do.	do.
164	327	3	Alt pr ard red feldspar	d.
165	328	3	Ne per ard sir, with leonhardite	do.
166	329	3	le and d. spar	do.
167	330	3	Red analcime	do.
168	478	4	Do.	do.
169	479	4	ld ile riat d.	do.
170	480	4	Red nd, d. pr, nd r el feldspar	do.
171	481	4	Ne per in ne passing into red analcime	d o.
172	482	4	Ne pr, d. spar, nd red feldspar	do.
173	535	5	Do. do. do.	do.
174	536	5	Cal. spar. nd el feldspar	do.
175	537	5	Arborescent pr	do.
176	538	5	Alt per al with green oate of copper	do.
177	654	7	Ne er in veinstone wth me	do.
178	655	7	Ne per in ne, containing hdrite with analcime and calc. spar	do.

179	656	7	Native [illegible] in veinstone, co[illegible] [illegible] calc. spar with analcime and calc. spar.	do.
180	657	7	Native [illegible] in veinstone, [illegible]ng [illegible] with red analcime	do.
181	658	7	[illegible] and [illegible] feldspar in trap containing chlorite	do.
182	659	7	Do..........do..........do.	do.
183	660	7	Analcime	do.
184	661	7	[illegible] native copper and fine [illegible]als of analcime	do.
185	662	7	Analcime	do.
186	663	7	[illegible] and [illegible] [illegible]	do.
187	664	7	Vein of [illegible] and [illegible] [illegible]te and calc. spar in trap, containing chlorite	do.
188	665	7	[illegible] of [illegible] and [illegible] spar, with red feldspar—arborescent	do.
189	666	7	Red [illegible] in [illegible], [illegible]aining chlorite	do.
190	667	7	Red [illegible] and [illegible]	do.
191	668	7	Red [illegible] and [illegible] [illegible]	do.
192	672	7	Native [illegible] in light colored veinstone, containing phrenite and carb. lime	do.
193	673	7	Do..........do..........do..........do.	do.
194	674	7	Do..........do..........do..........do.	do.
195	675	7	Red [illegible] in li[illegible]t colored veinstone, containing carb. of lime	do.
196	676	7	Native [illegible] in [illegible], containing phrenite and calc. spar	do.
197	677	7	Do..........do..........do..........do.	do.
198	678	7	Do..........do.	do.
199	679	7	Native [illegible] in [illegible], containing [illegible] spar	do.
200	680	7	Native [illegible] in [illegible], [illegible]aining [illegible] spar and green earth	Copper Falls.
201	681	7	Native [illegible] in [illegible], [illegible]aining green earth	do.
202	682	7	[illegible], [illegible], and calc. [illegible]	do.
203	683	7	Native [illegible] in [illegible]hrenite	do.
204	684	7	Native [illegible] and silver in calc. spar, with [illegible]nhardite and green earth	do.
205	685	7	Do..........do..........do..........do.	do.
206	686	7	Do..........do..........do..........do.	do.
207	687	7	Do..........do..........do..........do.	do.
208	688	7	Do..........do..........do..........do.	do.
209	689	7	[illegible] [illegible] [illegible] copper in trap, [illegible]aining chlorite	do.
210	690	7	Trap [illegible] [illegible]n, conta[illegible]ing red fel[illegible] [illegible] crystals of native copper and calc. [illegible]	Copper Falls (bottom of mine).
211	691	7	Do..........do..........do..........do.	do.
212	692	7	Do..........do..........do..........do.	do.
213	693	7	Native [illegible]er in calc. [illegible] and leonhardite	do.
214	694	7	Do..........do.	do.
215	695	7	Do..........do.	do.
216	696	7	Do..........do.	do.
217	697	7	Native [illegible], [illegible]ing the form and angles of calc. spar	do.
218	698	7	[illegible] [illegible]	do.

Catalogue of rocks, minerals, and ores, collected by Dr. C. T. Jackson—Continued.

Progressive No.	No. of specimens.	No. of box.	Description.	Locality.
219	699	7	Ar[illegible] copper	Copper Falls
220	700	7	Do.	do.
221	701	7	[illegible]hardise and calc. spar	do.
222	702	7	Do. do.	do.
223	703	7	Do. do.	do.
224	704	7	Do. do.	do.
225	705	7	Do. do.	do.
226	706	7	Do. do.	do.
227	707	7	Do. do.	do.
228	708	7	Do. do.	do.
229	740	8	Crystalli[illegible] native [illegible] and red feldspar on amygdaloid	do.
230	741	8	[illegible] in [illegible]c. spar, with red feldspar	do.
231	742	8	[illegible] calc. [illegible]	do.
232	743	8	Mass of [illegible] in laumonite	do.
233	744	8	Crystals of [illegible] and calc. spar—modifications of the scalene dodecahedron	do.
234	1024	10	[illegible] (good specimen)	do.
235	1025	10	Do. do.	do.
236	1026	10	Mass of [illegible] and native [illegible]er, showing large crystals of native copper	do.
237	669	7	Fine [illegible] brown [illegible]	Above Copper Falls
238	670	7	Do. do.	do.
239	671	7	Do. do.	do.
240	337	3	[illegible] in [illegible]	Northwestern Company—Slawsen's vein
241	338	3	Do. do.	do.
242	339	3	Do. do.	do.
243	340	3	Do. do.	do.
244	341	3	Do. do.	do.
245	342	3	Do. do.	do.
246	369	3	[illegible]er in veinstone (dark-colored trappose)	do.
247	370	3	Do. do. do.	do.
248	500	5	Do. do. do.	do.
249	501	5	Nat[illegible] [illegible]er in veinstone, light green trappose	do.

250	502	5	Native [illegible] in veinstone, [illegible]	do
251	503	5	Native [illegible] in [illegible] colored [illegible]	do
252	504	5	Native [illegible] in light green [illegible]	do
253	505	5	Native [illegible] in light green veinstone, (from 2d shaft, 7 feet from surface)	do
254	506	5	Native [illegible] in [illegible] with [illegible]nite	do
255	811	8	Mass of [illegible] [illegible] in [illegible]	Northwestern Company, lease 8
256	812	8	[illegible] [illegible] in [illegible] with bl[illegible] green earth and calc. spar	do
257	343	3	[illegible] [illegible] of [illegible] in veinstone	Michigan Company
258	344	3	Do. do	do
259	345	3	Do. do	do
260	346	3	Do. do	do
261	347	3	Do. do	do
262	366	3	[illegible] [illegible]phuret of copper	do
263	367	3	Do.	do
264	368	3	Do.	do
265	356	3	Amygdaloid containing native copper and silver	Eagle river
266	357	3	Do. do	do
267	358	3	Do. do	do
268	362	3	Red feld[illegible] in trap	do
269	380	3	Tabular spar	do
270	381	3	Do.	do
271	382	3	[illegible] of [illegible] [illegible]er	do
272	383	3	Red [illegible] and [illegible]	do
273	384	3	Do. do	do
274	385	3	Do. do	do
275	386	3	Do. do	do
276	387	4	[illegible] rock	do
277	388	4	Do.	do
278	389	4	[illegible]	do
279	390	4	Do.	do
280	391	4	[illegible]par and chlorite	do
281	392	4	Do. do	do
282	393	4	Red feldspar, analcime, and prehnite in amygdaloid, containing chlorite	do
283	[illegible]	4	Do. do do	do
284	395	4	Do. do	do
285	396	4	Do. do	do
286	397	4	Do. do	do
287	398	4	[illegible] fel[illegible] and crystals of [illegible] [illegible] [illegible] [illegible] [illegible] [illegible]	do
288	399	4	[illegible] fel[illegible], [illegible] [illegible], [illegible] with light green [illegible]	do
289	[illegible]00	4	[illegible] fel[illegible], calc. spar, and [illegible] [illegible]ite, [illegible] with light green chlorite	do
290	[illegible]01	4	[illegible] of [illegible]nite and red fel[illegible]	do

Catalogue of rocks, minerals, and ores, collected by Dr. C. T. Jackson—Continued.

Progressive No.	No. of specimens.	No. of box.	Description.	Locality.
291	402	4	Ne er in phrenite	Eagle river.
292	403	4	Ne er il by le	do.
293	404	4	d fel r on trap containing n ds of chlorite	d.
294	405	4	Do. do. d.	d.
295	406	4	Rd fel r and datho le in k green trap	do.
296	407	4	Red fel r al ie , cal with minute crystals of the same	d.
297	408	4	Amygdaloid containing ed feldspar al hite	do.
298	409	4	D do.	do.
299	410	4	al oil ing red , ie , l calc. spar	d.
300	621	6	Amy al oil ing ie lr l n ie er	d.
301	622	6	Do. do.	d.
302	623	6	Amygd ld g ie r al r	d.
303	624	6	Do. do.	d.
304	625	6	Amygdaloid ing ie sil er al er wh ote	do.
305	626	6	s of ie r l z in trap g dlorite	do.
306	627	6	e er s from mining heap)	do.
307	628	6	Do. do.	do.
308	724	8	Ne er in olored amygdal oid containing qrtz	do.
309	725	8	Do. do. do.	do.
310	726	8	Do. do. do.	do.
311	727	8	e silver and copper in dark colored amygdaloid ing quartz	do.
312	728	8	Do. do. do.	do.
313	729	8	Do. do. do.	do.
314	730	8	Do. do. do.	d.
315	731	8	Do. do. d.	d.
316	[illegible]	8	I h r	Eagle river, west vein
317	747	8	Do.	d.
318	748	8	Hone , light, soft variety, she ig stratification	d.
319	749	8	Do. do.	d.
320	750	8	D. do.	d.
321	977	10	Ne er in e, dl e Sor et ?	Eagle , in pit 3, May 28, 1847
322	978	10	Ne er with l spar, dd e r et ?	Eagle river, g S. drift, Nov. 1846
323	979	10	Ntive er with e, old e Superior net ?	Eagle r vein, pit 3, May 28, 1847

324	980	10	Native copper, old Lake Superior cabinet	Eagle river, Winn B, 40 feet deep, Sept., 1846
325	981	10	Native copper in calc. spar, old Lake Superior cabinet	Eagle river, Winn B, 173 feet deep, Nov. 25, 1846
326	982	10	Native [illegible] in dark red trap, thin sheets, old Lake Superior cabinet	Eagle river, Winn B, 1846
327	983	10	Native [illegible] in dark red trap, thin sheets and masses, old Lake Superior cabinet	Eagle river, Drift No. 1, Irish contract
328	984	10	Native [illegible] in dark [illegible] trap, coated with chlorite	Eagle river
329	985	10	Native [illegible] in [illegible], containing chlorite phrenite, the copper im-[illegible] by [illegible]	do.
330	986	10	Native [illegible] in [illegible]loid containing chlorite phrenite, the copper im-[illegible] by [illegible]	do.
331	[illegible]87	10	Gray [illegible], with calc. spar and decomposed green earth, old [illegible]	Eagle river, Winn B, 60 feet deep, from drift 1
332	988	10	Native [illegible] and [illegible] in [illegible], containing chlorite	d[illegible]
333	989	10	Native [illegible] by [illegible]tz	Eagle river, pit No. 2
334	990	10	N[illegible] in [illegible] of native copper	Eagle river, west side of vein
335	991	10	Do. do.	d[illegible]
336	992	10	M[illegible]s of native [illegible], found [illegible] stone hammers	d[illegible]
337	995	10	[illegible] of iron [illegible]	Eagle ri[illegible]r diggings
338	364	3	Amygdaloid, with agates	Fort Wilkins
339	365	3	Do.	d[illegible]
340	589	6	[illegible]t trap	d[illegible]
[illegible]41	594	6	[illegible], containing chalcedony and quartz	d[illegible]
342	595	6	Amygdaloid, containing agates and geodes of quartz	do.
343	483	4	Gr[illegible] silicate of copper	Pittsburg & Boston company
344	484	4	Do.	do.
345	485	4	Do.	do.
346	486	4	Do.	do.
347	[illegible]87	4	Do.	do.
348	488	4	Do.	do.
3[illegible]9	[illegible]89	4	Do.	do.
350	490	5	B[illegible] of manganese	d[illegible]
351	[illegible]91	5	B[illegible] of [illegible], compact and massive	d[illegible]
352	492	5	B[illegible] oxide of [illegible], slicken-sides	d[illegible]
353	493	5	Black oxide of [illegible], compact and massive	d[illegible]
354	[illegible]	5	Do. do.	d[illegible]
355	495	5	B[illegible] oxide of [illegible], with quartz and calc. spar	do.
356	[illegible]	5	Do. do.	d[illegible]
357	[illegible]97	5	Do. do.	do.

Catalogue of rocks, minerals, and ores, collected by Dr. C. T. Jackson—Continued.

Progressive No.	No. of specimens.	No. of box.	Description.	Locality.
358	498	5	Black oxide of manganese, with quartz and calc. spar	Pittsburg & Boston company
359	499	5	Black oxide of manganese, with calc. spar	do.
360	528	5	Massive calc. spar	do.
361	532	5	Do.	do.
362	533	5	Do.	do.
363	604	6	Trap joining sandstone, glazed and striated	do.
364	605	6	Do. do.	do.
365	607	6	Rock colored by green carbonate of copper	Pittsburg & Boston company, southeast [illegible], upper drift
366	608	6	Do. do.	[illegible]
367	609	6	Dark green trap	Pittsburg & Boston company, southeast corner [illegible] of drift four
368	610	6	Do.	do.
369	611	6	Trap containing chlorite	Pittsburg & Boston [illegible], from trail $1\frac{3}{4}$ miles from [illegible]
370	612	6	Dark brown crystalline trap	Pit[illegible] & Boston [illegible], top of hill, No. 6
371	613	6	Do.	Pittsburg & Boston company, [illegible] corner, bottom of [illegible], No. 1
372	614	6	Dark brown trap, containing chlorite	Pittsburg & Boston [illegible], [illegible] of [illegible], No. 3
373	615	6	Rocks containing vein of carbonate of lime	Pit[illegible] & Boston [illegible], lower drift
374	941	9	Compact dark trap, stecken sides	do.
375	950	9	Dark green compact trap (no trace of crystallization)	Pittsburg & Boston company, southeast corner, No. 5
376	951	9	Light gray trap, containing chlorite	do.
377	952	9	Vein of quartz and calc. spar in dark red trap, containing chlorite	Pittsburg & Boston company, southeast corner, lower drift
378	953	9	Trap containing chlorite	Pittsburg & Boston company, from southeast corner $1\frac{3}{4}$ miles
379	968	10	Dark green crystalline trap, feldspar, and hornblende	Pittsburg & Boston company, south of Copper Hill, south side of hill

380	969	10	Dark green crystalline trap, not so crystalline as the preceding	Pittsburg & Boston company, vein wall, near [illegible]mit of hill
381	970	10	Do. do.	d[illegible]
382	971	10	Rock consisting of red feldspar speckled with chlorite	P[illegible]rg & Boston company, south of [illegible] Hill, s[illegible]th side of hill
383	591	6	Altered [illegible] and [illegible], [illegible]	[illegible] [illegible]
384	601	6	Al[illegible] [illegible] from the [illegible] on	[illegible]s point, Copper harbor
385	919	9	Al[illegible] [illegible] s[illegible] with grey [illegible], furrowed and contorted	do.
386	920	9	Do. d[illegible]	do.
387	921	9	Do. do.	do.
388	922	9	Do. d[illegible]	do.
389	923	9	Do. do.	do.
390	908	9	Amygdaloidal trap, amygdules of chlorite, [illegible]c. spar, and red leonhardite	Point west of Porter's island, Copper harbor.
391	909	9	Do d[illegible]	do.
392	910	9	Do. do.	do.
393	911	9	Do. d[illegible]	d[illegible]
394	912	9	Do. do.	d[illegible]
395	913	9	Do. do.	d[illegible]
396	914	9	Do. do.	d[illegible]
397	915	9	Do. d[illegible]	do.
398	916	9	Do. do.	do.
399	917	9	Do. d[illegible]	do.
400	918	9	Do. do.	do.
401	411	4	[illegible] [illegible] [illegible]lc. [illegible]	Cliff mine
402	412	4	Native [illegible] [illegible] with [illegible] oxide in [illegible] with [illegible]	do.
403	413	4	Native [illegible] in [illegible] with [illegible] [illegible] [illegible] quartz	do.
404	1017	10	Native [illegible] [illegible] [illegible] [illegible] rock (old [illegible] Superior cabinet?)	Cliff mine drift of adit. view four feet
405	1016	10	Native sil[illegible] (large pieces) [illegible] [illegible] [illegible] in [illegible] ([illegible]c. spar and green earth)	do.
[illegible]06	1018	10	Mass [illegible] [illegible] [illegible] [illegible] by [illegible] [illegible], with [illegible] [illegible]	do.
407	1019	10	N[illegible] [illegible] piercing large [illegible] of [illegible] [illegible] (junction of silver and copper)	do.
408	1020	10	[illegible] [illegible] [illegible] [illegible] [illegible] of [illegible] copper	d[illegible]
409	1021	10	Drusy [illegible] [illegible] [illegible] [illegible] of [illegible] [illegible] silver	do.
410	1022	10	Drusy [illegible] [illegible] [illegible] [illegible] [illegible] of [illegible]	do.
411	1023	10	Drusy [illegible] reticulated [illegible] [illegible] [illegible] [illegible] of calc. spar	do.
412	1027	10	N[illegible] [illegible] and [illegible] [illegible] of [illegible] oxide	d[illegible]
413	1029	10	Sample of clipping [illegible] [illegible] in [illegible] large [illegible] of [illegible]	do.
414	428	4	[illegible]	Jasper [illegible]
415	429	4	Do.	do.
416	414	4	Breccia of white and green slate	Near J[illegible] point

Catalogue of rocks, minerals, and ores, collected by Dr. C. T. Jackson—Continued.

Progressive No.	No. of specimens.	No. of box.	Description.	Locality.
417	415	4	Breccia of white and green slate	Near [illegible]r point
418	416	4	Do......do......do	do.
419	432	4	Porphyritic trap	d.
420	433	4	Do......do	do.
421	417	4	Scoria from fusion of trap and sandstone, (small round pebbles,)	Boston lo[illegible]ation
422	418	4	Do......do......do	do.
423	419	4	Do......do......do	do.
424	20	4	Altered sl[illegible]e	do.
425	430	4	[illegible]th of trap and sandstone	Bête Gris
426	431	4	Do......do	do.
427	434	4	Dark colored t[illegible]p	do.
428	435	4	[illegible]r trap	do.
429	436	4	S[illegible]d trap, [illegible]ith chlorite in [illegible]al cavity	do.
430	437	4	Amygdal[illegible] trap	do.
431	438	4	Porphyritic trap, [illegible]ing a [illegible]in of calc. spar	do.
432	439	4	[illegible]r, containing veins of [illegible]d feldspar	do.
433	40	4	[illegible]r t[illegible]p	do.
434	441	4	Do... d.	do.
435	442	4	[illegible]r t[illegible]	do.
436	443	4	[illegible]p, containing veins of calc. spar	do.
437	44	6	[illegible]p, containing chlorite	do.
438	586	6	Jasper	do.
439	967	10	[illegible]y [illegible]e, [illegible]ained	Bête Gris bog
440	421	4	[illegible]d and grey [illegible]e	Point south of Bête Gris
441	422	4	[illegible]d [illegible]nd grey [illegible], with interlayers of red chalk	do.
442	423	4	Grey sandstone, containing spheroids of red chalk surrounded by a ring of [illegible]e slate	d.
443	427	4	[illegible]	d.
44	424	4	[illegible]d and grey sandstone	Kew[illegible]enaw [illegible]y
445	425	4	Do......do	do.
446	426	4	[illegible]d [illegible]e	do.
447	837	9	[illegible]e slate, grey, soft	L'Anse
448	838	9	Do......do	do.

49	89	9	Do........d.	do.
50	80	9	Do........do.	do.
51	841	9	Do........do..	do.
452	842	9	Red nd green le nd, surface polished nd gd, ning scattered rys pls of n pyrites pd by carb. of lime	do.
53	43	9	Red nd green le nd, surface pl hd nd grooved, aining scattered rys of pseudomorphs of iron pys pd by carb. of lime	do.
34	844	9	Red nd gn s late, nd, sur fe polis hd.	do.
45	45	9	Red slate	do.
46	46	9	Do.	do.
457	847	9	Do.	do.
58	88	9	Red sl te, ks in splintery fragments.	do.
59	849	9	Red td, h light green slate, surface polished and grooved.	do.
60	50	9	Red d, ig tals of pseudomorphous pyrites replaced by carb. of li, surface pl hd.	do.
61	851	9	ed le, breaks ry on surfa e.	do.
462	852	9	Boul r of red le, th nd ds of grey sandst ne nd black k in ntre	
63	53	9	ed le, th ls of grey le and k k in ent e.	do.
64	54	9	Do.........do.........do.........do.........d.	do.
65	55	9	ed nd grey and .	d.
66	56	9	ld t, green, compact.	d.
67	857	9	Do.........do.	d.
68	58	9	Do.........d.	d.
69	59	9	Alt ed sandstone, containing a vein of quartz, coarse-grained, green.	d.
470	60	9	Do.........d.........do.........do.........do.	d.
471	61	9	Altered le, coarse-grained, green.	d.
472	862	9	Do.........do.........do.	d.
473	94	10	Jasper, for nd from le.	d.
474	95	10	Do.........do.	58, 28, 30, near Bare rock.
475	96	10	Do.........d.	do.
476	97	10	Do.........d.	do.
477	98	10	Do.........d.	do.
178	99	10	Do.........do.	do.
479	960	10	Grey le.	d.
80	961	10	Do.	d.
481	962	10	Red le.	d.
482	63	10	ld red and grey sandstone.	d.
83	64	10	Breccia jd with chlorite.	58, 28, 29, and 30, near Bare rock.
84	65	10	Do.........do.	58, 28, 29, nd 30, near Bare rock (near sketch).
85	66	10	Chl . This appears to be an indurated slate, green-coated chlorite joined th ben.	58, 28, 29, and 30, near Bare rock.

Catalogue of rocks, minerals, and ores, collected by Dr. C. T. Jackson—Continued.

Progressive No.	No. of specimens.	No. of box.	Description.	Locality.
486	445	4	Native copper	Quincy Mining Company
487	446	4	Do	do
488	447	4	Do	do
489	448	4	[illegible] in [illegible]stone	do
490	449	4	Do do	do
491	450	4	[illegible], in [illegible]one, containing prehnite	do
492	451	4	[illegible] in veinstone, [illegible] green earth	d[illegible]
493	452	4	Do do do do do do	do
494	453	4	[illegible] in amygdaloid trap, [illegible] chlorite	do
495	454	4	Do do do d[illegible] do	do
496	455	4	Do do do d[illegible] do	do
497	456	4	Native [illegible] in amygdaloidal trap	do
498	457	4	[illegible] in hard light green veinstone	do
499	458	4	[illegible] trap	do
500	459	4	Amygdaloidal trap, [illegible]ontaining red felds[illegible]	do
501	632	6	Native [illegible] per in dark brown trap, with [illegible]phrenite and green [illegible]arth	do
502	633	6	[illegible] in trap, [illegible] calc. s[illegible] phrenite	do
503	634	6	[illegible] copper in [illegible] with [illegible] spar	do
504	635	6	[illegible]	do
505	636	6	N[illegible] in [illegible] containing [illegible]	do
506	637	6	Do do do	Quincy Mining [illegible]
507	638	6	Native [illegible] in [illegible] quartz, [illegible]ite, and green earth	do
508	639	6	Do do d[illegible] do	do
509	640	6	[illegible] in dark [illegible] trap, [illegible] epidote trap very compact	do
510	641	6	[illegible] in light green [illegible]	do
511	642	6	[illegible] in [illegible] brown trap, showing [illegible]-sides	do
512	460	4	[illegible]	North American Company
513	461	4	[illegible] in [illegible]	do
514	462	4	[illegible] in [illegible], with calc. spar	North American Company, N. C. qr. sec 3.
515	463	4	Do do do	do
516	464	4	Do d[illegible] do	do
517	465	4	Native silver and copper in veinstone, containing green earth	do

518	467	4	Native copper in veinstone, with carbonate of copper	do
519	468	4	Apophyllite and calc. spar	do
520	469	4	Do ....do	do
521	469	4	Do ....do	do
522	470	4	Do ....do	do
523	471	4	Agate and yellow jasper	do
524	652	6	Dark green compact trap, coated with fibrous chlorite, resembling talc	do
525	751	8	Apophyllite and calc. spar	do
526	752	8	Do ....do	do
527	753	8	Do ....do	do
528	754	8	Do ....do	do
529	755	8	Do ....do	do
530	756	8	Apophyllite and calc. spar (acute rhombohedrons)	do
531	757	8	Apophyllite and calc. spar	North American Company, qr. sec 2
532	758	8	Calc. spar acute rhombohedrons	North American Company
533	759	8	Do ....do	do
534	760	8	Do ....do	North American Company, qr. sec. 2
535	761	8	Native copper in veinstone, containing calc. spar and green earth	North American Company
536	762	8	Native copper in veinstone, containing quartzose	do
537	763	8	Native copper in veinstone, containing calc. spar	do
538	764	8	Native silver and copper in veinstone, containing green earth	North American Company, qr. sec. 2
539	765	8	Native copper in dark green veinstone, containing quartz	do ....do
540	766	8	Native copper in veinstone, composed principally of green earth	do ....do
541	772	8	Native copper from bottom of mine, where the vein takes a steeper dip	North American Company
542	863	8	Calc. spar—curved faces, modifications of rhomboid more obtuse than primary (ac. 79.45, ob. 100.15—180.00)	do
543	864	9	Do ....do ....do ....do	do
544	865	9	Do ....do ....do ....do	do
545	866	9	Do ....do ....do ....do	do
546	867	9	Calc. spar—curved faces, modifications of rhomboid more obtuse than primary; surface of crystals frosted with small crystals	do
547	868	9	Calc. spar—curved faces, modifications of rhomboid more obtuse than primary	do
548	869	9	Do ....do ....do ....do	do
549	870	9	Calc. spar and laumonite	do
550	871	9	Rhombohedron of calc. spar with laumonite	do
551	872	9	Crystallized native copper, and native copper in calc. spar	do
552	873	9	Crystals of native copper in calc. spar—octahedron edges parallel, passing to dodecahedron	do
553	874	9	Acute rhombohedrons of calc. spar, containing native copper	do
554	875	9	Mass of native copper impressed by quartz crystals	do

Catalogue of rocks, minerals, and ores, collected during the years 1847 *and* 1848—Continued.

Progressive No.	No. of specimens.	No. of box.	Description.	Locality.
555	876	9	Mass of native copper penetrated by quartz crystals	North American Company
556	877	9	Native copper, coated with green carbonate	do
557	888	9	Mass of native copper penetrated by quartz crystals	North American Mine
558	889	9	Native copper in veinstone, containing calc. spar	do
559	890	9	Native copper in green veinstone, penetrated by quartz crystals	do
560	891	9	Do......do......do	do
561	892	9	Native copper in veinstone, containing chlorite	do
562	893	9	Native copper in dark red veinstone, with apophyllite and calc. spar	do
563	894	9	Native copper in veinstone, containing epidote, with apophyllite and calc. spar	do
564	895	9	Dodecahedral crystals of copper in dark red veinstone, frosted with minute [illegible] of [illegible]	do
565	896	9	Native copper and silver	do
566	897	9	Do......do	do
567	898	9	Native copper in [illegible], with drusy, [illegible], reticulated [illegible]	do
568	899	9	Crystals of native copper, with drusy, [illegible], [illegible] [illegible]	do
569	993	10	Native copper in veinstone, [illegible] with red oxide—old Lake Superior cabinet	North American Mine, vein No. 1, July, '47.
570	994	10	Native copper in vein of prehnite and calc. spar, with red oxide and green carbonate—old Lake Superior cabinet	North American Mine, new vein, Jan., '47.
571	475	4	Native copper in veinstone; a light, ja[illegible] rock, resembling marbling from veins of trap intersecting	Boston and Lake Superior Company
572	476	4	Do......do......do......do	do
573	477	4	Amygdaloid with prehnite	do
574	938	9	Native copper in vein of calc. spar in veinstone, containing green earth and chlorite	do
575	939	9	Do......do......do......do	do
576	940	9	Do......do......do......do	do
577	943	9	[illegible] of altered sandstone (jasper) shaped like the head of an encrinite	Boston and Lake Superior Company, on lake shore.
578	539	5	Gray sulphuret of copper	Bohemian Mine, shaft No. 1
579	540	5	Do......do	do......do
580	541	5	Do......do	Bohemian Mine, shaft No. 1, upper drift
581	542	5	Gray sulphuret of copper (working ore on bank)	Bohemian Mine, shaft No. 1, north drift
582	543	5	Peacock ore	do......do......do

583	544	5	Gray sulphuret of copper	Bohemian Mine, E. and W. view
584	545	5	Do.	Bohemian mine, shaft No. 1
585	546	5	Do.	Bohemian mine, shaft No. 2
586	547	5	Gray sulphuret of copper with calc. spar	do.
587	548	5	Gray sulphuret of copper from new opening 200 feet from top of mountain	Bohemian mine
588	549	5	Do. do.	do.
589	550	5	Do. do.	do.
590	551	5	Do. do.	do.
591	552	5	Gray sulphuret of copper with calc. spar	Bohemian mine, SE. and W. vein
592	553	5	Copper pyrites	do.
593	554	5	Red [illegible] rock containing chlorite	Bohemian mine, [illegible]
594	555	5	Red [illegible] with trace of copper pyrites	Bohemian mine, No 2 [illegible]
595	556	5	Specular iron and green carb. copper in trap	Bohemian mine
596	557	5	Do. do.	do.
597	558	5	Copper pyrites	Lac la Belle Co., E. and W. vein
598	559	5	Gray sulphuret of copper	do.
599	560	5	Do.	do.
600	561	5	Do.	do.
601	562	5	Copper pyrites	do.
602	563	5	Copper pyrites from [illegible] ore on bank	Lac la Belle Co., shaft No. 1, north drift
603	564	5	Gray sulphuret of copper with calc. spar	do.
604	565	5	Do. do.	Lac la Belle Co., vein No. 1, north drift
605	566	5	Do. do.	do.
606	567	5	Gray sulphuret and green carb. of copper	Lac la Belle Co., shaft No. 2, north drift
607	568	5	Do. do.	Lac la Belle Co., Sibley's vein No. 2, N. drift
608	596	6	Trace of gray sulphuret of copper in rock composed of feldspar, carb. of lime, and chlorite	Lac la Belle adit
609	597	6	Do. do. do.	do.
610	598	6	Do. do. do.	do.
611	599	6	Rock containing a little gray sulphuret of copper	Lac la Belle Co., N. and S. vein
612	600	6	Gray sulphuret and green carb. copper	Lac la Belle Co., E. and W. vein
613	924	6	Gray [illegible], [illegible], and green carb. copper	do.
614	925	9	Serpentine and calc. spar, with a little gray sulphuret of copper	do.
615	926	9	Gray sulphuret of copper in [illegible] containing calc. spar	do.
616	927	9	Do. do.	do.
617	928	9	Gray sulphuret of copper in veinstone containing [illegible] and calc. spar	Lac la Belle Co., N. and S. vein
618	929	9	Do. do. do.	do.
619	930	9	Do. do. do.	Lac la Belle [illegible] adit
620	931	9	Gray sulphuret of copper in veinstone containing [illegible] and calc. spar, and [illegible]	do.
621	932	9	Do. do. do.	do.

Catalogue of rocks, minerals, and ores, collected during the years 1847 *and* 1848—Continued.

Progressive No.	No. of specimens.	No. of box.	Description.	Locality.
622	933	9	Gray [illegible] of [illegible] in [illegible] [illegible] [illegible] [illegible] spar, and little laumonite	Lac la Belle Co. adit
623	934	9	Light grayish [illegible] (serpentine and calc. spar) containing a little [illegible] of [illegible]	do.
624	935	9	[illegible] slate [illegible] [illegible]	do.
625	936	9	Trap [illegible] [illegible] of feldspar and chlorite rock in confused masses	do.
626	937	9	Trap [illegible] of [illegible], chlorite, and brown hornblende (?)	do.
627	587	6	[illegible] [illegible] [illegible], feldspar, chlorite, and epidote in which the ore is [illegible]	do.
628	569	5	Trap rock	[illegible] [illegible], Lake Bluff.
629	570	5	[illegible] [illegible] specular i[illegible] with spots of [illegible]	do.
630	571	5	[illegible] [illegible] a little g[illegible] [illegible] [illegible] [illegible] [illegible]. copper	do.
631	572	5	Do. .do.	do.
632	573	5	[illegible] [illegible] a little [illegible] [illegible] of [illegible]per.	do.
633	574	5	[illegible] containing [illegible] of [illegible] [illegible] of [illegible]pper with chlorite	do.
634	575	5	[illegible] [illegible] [illegible] [illegible] [illegible]. copper	do.
635	59	6	[illegible], [illegible] of chl[illegible], [illegible] [illegible] conglomerate	do.
636	602	6	[illegible] [illegible] [illegible] [illegible]	NW. cor. of loc. 17 on train for Lac la Belle.
637	603	6	Do.	do.
68	80	6	Cleaveable jas[illegible]	Mount Haughton
639	581	6	Do.	do.
60	582	6	Uncleaveable [illegible] [illegible] the trap	d.
641	583	6	[illegible] [illegible] [illegible] [illegible] [illegible]	d.
642	616	6	[illegible] [illegible], [illegible]	[illegible] Shore Mining Co., W. the Portage.
643	617	6	[illegible]o.	do.
64	618	6	Do.	d.
645	619	6	Do.	do.
66	620	6	[illegible] [illegible] [illegible]umonite	d.
67	643	6	[illegible] [illegible] in [illegible] fine grained trap containing green earth.	Eagle [illegible], Sheffield and Nott's vein
68	644	6	Do. .do. .do.	do.
69	65	6	Native [illegible] in [illegible] fine grained trap containing calc. spar	d.
650	46	6	N[illegible] [illegible] in [illegible] fine grained trap containing green earth.	d.
651	647	6	N[illegible] [illegible] in [illegible] fine grained trap containing calc. spar	do.

652	648	6	Native silver and copper in dark brown fine grained compact trap containing green earth	do
653	649	6	Light green veinstone, containing no copper, coated with quartz and prehnite, and showing slicken sides	do
654	650	6	Do. do do	do
655	651	6	Do. do do	do
656	745	8	Mass of native copper containing native silver	Forsyth Co's. mine.
657	813	8	Mass of native copper with red oxide and green carbonate	do
658	814	8	Do. do	do
659	815	8	Do. do	Forsyth Co.
660	816	8	Boulder of native copper found by Agendos.	Forsyth Co. loc
661	817	8	Native copper in epidote	do
662	818	8	Native copper in veinstone containing epidote and prehnite	do
663	819	8	Native copper in veinstone containing chlorite and quartz	do
664	820	8	Native copper in veinstone containing prehnite and quartz	do
665	821	8	Native copper in veinstone containing calc. spar, epidote, and chlorite	do
666	822	8	Native copper in veinstone containing calc. spar, quartz, and chlorite	do
667	767	8	Gray sulphuret of copper in porphyritic trap	Pray's lease 101
668	768	8	Do. do	do
669	760	8	Do. do	do
670	770	8	Do. do	Praysville
671	771	8	Gray sulphuret of copper in veinstone containing calc. spar	do
672	790	8	Gray sulphuret of copper in porphyritic trap (bright red crystals of feldspar)	Pray's lease 101
673	791	8	Do. do do	do
674	792	8	Do. do do	do
675	793	8	Do. do do	do
676	794	8	Do. do do	do
677	795	8	Do. do do	do
678	796	8	Do. do do	do
679	797	8	Do. do do	do
680	798	8	Do. do do	do
681	799	8	Gray sulphuret of copper in porphyritic trap containing calc. spar	do
682	800	8	Do. do do	do
683	801	8	Do. do do	do
684	802	8	Do. do do	do
685	803	8	Do. do do	do
686	804	8	Do. do do	Pray's lease 102
687	805	8	Do. do do	do
688	806	8	Do. do do	do
689	807	8	Do. do do	do
690	1010	10	Porphyritic trap containing chlorite and prehnite	Pray's location.

Catalogue of rocks, minerals, and ores, collected during the years 1847 *and* 1848—Continued.

Progressive No.	No. of specimens.	No. of box.	Description.	Locality.
691	1011	10	Gray sulphuret of copper in veinstone containing calc. spar	Pray's location
692	1012	10	Do. do do	do.
693	1013	10	Gray sulphuret of copper and green carb. in porphyritic trap	do.
694	1014	10	Do. do. do	do.
695	808	8	Iron containing a little copper	Pray's furnace.
696	809	8	Black metal vesicular containing [illegible] copper	do.
697	810	8	Do. do.	do.
698	472	4	Native copper in mass of calc. spar	58.32 S. W. $\frac{1}{4}$ sec. 36
699	773	8	Vein of native copper (thick) in prehnite	do. do.
700	774	8	Large mass of native copper from a vein coated with green carb	57.32 S. W. $\frac{1}{4}$ sec. 33
701	775	8	Native copper in epidote with calc. spar and prehnite	[illegible]32 S. W. $\frac{1}{4}$ sec. 33
702	776	8	Native copper in epidote with calc. spar and chlorite	do. do.
703	777	8	Do. do	do. do.
704	778	8	Native copper in epidote with chlorite	do. do.
705	779	8	Native copper in epidote with chlorite, calc. spar, prehnite, and laumonite	do. do.
706	780	8	Native copper in epidote with calc. spar and laumonite	do. do.
707	781	8	[illegible] epidote in calc. spar	57.32 N. W. $\frac{1}{4}$ sec. 11
708	782	8	Do. do.	do. do
709	783	8	Native copper in dark-green trap containing chlorite	do. do.
710	784	8	Native copper with calc. spar and soft, light-green earth	57.32 N. W. $\frac{1}{4}$ sec. 11
711	784	8	Native copper in [illegible] green trap containing chlorite	do. do.
712	786	8	Native copper in veinstone containing massive prehnite and calc. spar	do. do
713	473	4	Calc. spar	do. do.
714	474	4	Calc. spar and prehnite	do. do.
715	787	8	Dark-green compact trap	[illegible] mine
716	828	8	[illegible]ous light-gray crystalline fracture showing metallic copper	do.
717	788	8	Gray sulphuret of copper and dark-green trap	Buffalo Company
718	789	8	Native copper in dark-green trap containing veins of quartz	do.
719	823	8	Gray sulphuret of copper in [illegible]-green veinstone containing chlorite	do.
720	824	8	Do. do. do	do.
721	825	8	[illegible]-red, smooth trap containing chlorite in [illegible] patches	Douglas Houghton mine
722	826	8	Veinstone containing prehnite and calc. spar (no copper)	do. do
723	827	8	Do. do. do	do. do

724	900	9	Native copper in veinstone containing epidote with veins of quartz and calc. spar mixed	do.......do
725	901	9	Do.......do.......do	do.......do
726	902	9	Native copper in epidote with veins of calc. spar	do.......do
727	903	9	Native copper in epidote containing quartz, calc. spar, and laumonite	do.......do
728	904	9	Native copper in epidote traversed by veins of chlorite rock showing slicken sides	do.......do
729	905	9	Native copper in a vein of quartz in chlorite rock	do.......do
730	906	9	Chlorite rock near the mine	do.......do
731	1001	10	Native copper in light-colored veinstone containing prehnite and calc. spar	do.......do
732	1002	10	Do.......do.......do	do.......do
733	1003	10	Do.......do.......do	do.......do
734	1004	10	Trap rock containing large quantity of chlorite	do.......do
735	829	8	Some prehnite in calc. spar (loose)	Albion Company
736	830	8	Do.......do	do.
737	831	8	Calc. spar with leonhardite (called [illegible])	do.
738	832	8	Do.......do	do.
739	833	8	Veinstone containing quartz, prehnite, and calc. spar, with chlorite rock	do.
740	834	8	Calc. spar (veinstone)	do.
741	835	8	Red slate (easily stains)	New York and Michigan Co. Agate harbor.
742	836	8	Veinstone with calc. spar (no copper apparent)	do.......do
743	1007	10	Native copper in veinstone with calc. spar	do.......do
744	1008	10	Do.......do	do.......do
745	1009	10	Native copper in veinstone containing epidote	do.......do
746	946	9	Red porphyry	Massachusetts Company
747	947	9	Porphyritic trap containing large crystals of feldspar and Babingtonite (?)	do.......do
748	948	9	Do.......do.......do	do.......do
749	949	9	Porphyritic trap containing large crystals of feldspar and Babingtonite (?) (more compact than the preceding)	do.......do
750	996	10	Native copper in porphyritic trap containing specular iron	Copper Rock Company
751	997	10	Porphyritic trap—fine crystals of red feldspar	do.......do
752	998	10	Do.......do	do.......do
753	999	10	Native copper in porphyritic trap, containing specular iron quartz and calc. spar	do.......do
754	1000	10	Native copper in veinstone mixed with chlorite	do.......do
755	1005	10	Veinstone having slicken sides apparently talcose light green chlorite rock, mixed with quartz	Trap Rock Company
756	1006	10	Compact trap crystalline	do.
757	363	3	Layer probably formed by fusion of sandstone	Near Little Montreal river, lake shore
758	526	5	Boulder of porphyritic trap	Lake shore
759	527	5	Do	do.
760	653	6	Black iron sand	Lake shore, Keweenaw Point
761	944	9	Breccia	Lake shore, ½ mile W. of Lake Superior Co.

Catalogue of rocks, minerals, and ores, collected during the years 1847 *and* 1848—Continued.

Progressive No.	No. of specimens.	No. of box.	Description.	Locality.
762	945	9	Porphyritic trap	Lake shore, ½ mile E. of Montreal river
763	530	5	Green amygdaloid, colored by chlorite and epidote	Loose
764	576	5	Agate	Near end of Keweena Point
765	577	5	Do	do
766	584	6	Amygdaloid with amygdules of chlorite	Keweenaw Point
767	585	6	Scoria, from fusion of trap and sandstone	do
768	588	6	Compact trap	do
769	590	6	Ripple marks in sandstone	do
770	592	6	Cornelian and calcedony or trap	do
771	907	9	Porphyritic trap (feldspar stained green, resembling epidote)	do
772	942	9	Agate	do
773	629	6	Coarse red sandstone (feldspar and quartz)	4 miles E. of Portage
774	630	6	Do ... do	do
775	631	6	Do ... do	do
776	84	1	Native copper in epidote	Ohio and Isle Royal Co. Epidote I. R.
777	85	1	Do	do ... do
778	86	1	Do	do ... do
779	87	1	Do	do ... do
780	88	1	Do	do ... do
781	89	1	Do	do ... do
782	90	1	Do	do ... do
783	91	1	Do	do ... do
784	92	1	Do	do ... do
785	93	1	Do	do ... do
786	94	1	Do	do ... do
787	95	1	Native copper with datholite	do ... do
788	96	2	Do	do ... do
789	162	2	Mass of native copper	do ... do
790	163	2	Do	do ... do
791	164	2	Native copper in datholite	do ... do
792	165	2	Native copper in veinstone	do ... do
793	225	2	Native copper in epidote rock	do ... do
794	226	2	Do ... do	do ... do

795	227	2	Do.............do	.........do	.do
796	228	2	Do.............do	.........do	.do
797	229	2	Do.............do	.........do	.do
798	202	2	Red calc spar	.........do	.do
799	203	2	Do	.........do	.do
800	211	2	Jasper	Near lake shore.	Epidote I. R.
801	240	2	Epidote rock, 6 feet thick, containing no copper directly beneath the copper-bearing epidote	Ohio and Isle Royal Co.	Epidote I. R.
802	173	2	Native copper in datholite	Ohio and Isle Royal Co.	Datholite I. R.
803	174	2	Native copper in datholite. Direction of vein N. 55 E., dip 51 W	.........do	.do
804	175	2	Native copper in datholite. Direction of vein N. 25 E., dip 55 W	.........do	.do
805	262	2	Native copper in veinstone with datholite. Direction of vein N. 25 E	.........do	.do
806	272	2	Datholite	.........do	.do
807	273	2	Native copper in datholite	.........do	.do
808	97	1	Native copper in veinstone	Ohio and Isle Royal Co.	Rock Harbor. I. R.
809	98	1	Do.............do	.........do	.do
810	99	1	Do.............do	.........do	.do
811	100	1	Do.............do	.........do	.do
812	101	1	Do.............do	.........do	.do
813	102	1	Do.............do	.........do	.do
814	103	1	Do.............do	.........do	.do
815	104	1	Do.............do	.........do	.do
816	105	1	Do.............do	.........do	.do
817	106	1	Do.............do	.........do	.do
818	107	1	Do.............do	.........do	.do
819	108	1	Do.............do	.........do	.do
820	109	1	Native copper in epidote	.........do	.do
821	116	1	Quartz containing native copper	.........do	.do
822	110	1	Quartz and prehnite	.........do	.do
823	111	1	Do.......do	.........do	.do
824	112	1	Do.......do	.........do	.do
825	113	1	Quartz, prehnite and green carb. copper	.........do	.do
826	114	1	Quartz and prehnite with native copper	.........do	.do
827	115	1	Quartz containing native copper	.........do	.do
828	117	2	Quartz, prehnite and green carb. copper	.........do	.do
829	187	2	Trap	.........do	.do
830	189	2	Prehnite	.........do	.do
831	319	3	Crystals of quartz colored by red oxide of copper	.........do	.do
832	221	2	Native copper in indurated slate	Head of Rock Harbor.	I. R.
833	222	2	Do.............do	.........do	
834	223	2	Do.............do	.........do	

Catalogue of rocks, minerals, and ores, collected during the years 1847 *and* 1848—Continued.

Progressive No.	No. of specimens.	No. of box.	Description.	Locality.
835	224	2	Native copper in indurated slate	Head of Rock Harbor. I. R
836	235	2	Native copper in epidote rock containing carb. lime	do
837	236	2	Native copper in epidote rock	do
838	237	2	Do do	Near Rock Harbor
839	238	2	Do do	do
840	239	2	Do do	do
841	263	2	S[illegible]ite of iron	do
842	120	2	Native copper in trap	Scovill's point, I. R
843	121	2	Do do	do
844	122	2	Do do	do
845	123	2	Do do	do
846	124	2	Do do	do
847	125	2	Do do	do
848	126	2	Do do	do
849	127	2	Do do	do
850	128	2	Native copper in veinstone	do
851	129	2	Do do	do
852	130	2	Do do	do
853	131	2	Native copper in veinstone, with specular iron	do
854	132	2	[illegible]c trap, [illegible]ing prehnite	do
855	133	2	Do do	do
856	137	2	Native copper in datholite	do
857	138	2	Native copper in veinstone, with calc. spar	do
858	139	2	Chocolate-colored amygdaloid, with native copper in prehnite	do
859	140	2	Native copper in prehnite	do
860	141	2	Scoria formed by fusion of trap and sandstone	do
861	230	2	Jacksonite and compact a[illegible]le spar	Scovill's point, I. R., on the forefinger 10 rods from the end, just beyond the point.
862	231	2	Do do	
863	232	2	Do do	Scovill's point, I. R
864	233	2	Do do	do
865	264	2	Do do	do
866	265	2	Do do	do

[illegible]	[illegible]	[illegible]	Do. . . . . do	. . . . do
868	267	2	Do. . . . . do	. . . . do
869	268	2	Do. . . . . do	. . . . do
870	134	2	Native copper in veinstone	Scovill's point, J. R., Shaw's location
871	135	2	Do. . . . . do	. . . . do
872	136	2	Do. . . . . do	. . . . do
873	142	2	Native copper in veinstone, containing datholite	65, 35, 27, 4 rods from W. edge
874	143	2	Do. . . . . do. . . . . do	. . . . do
875	144	2	Do. . . . . do. . . . . do	. . . . do
876	145	2	Do. . . . . do. . . . . do	. . . . do
877	179	2	Trap from a vein	65, 35, 27, [illegible]
878	180	2	Veinstone, containing native copper and datholite	65, 35, 27, 4 rods from W. edge
879	182	2	Trap rock	65, 35, 26, and 27
880	204	2	Native copper in datholite	65, 35, 27, 4 rods from W. edge
881	208	2	Trap rock	65, 35, 28, and 33, 10 chs. from sec. corners 28, 29, 32, and 33.
882	245	2	Shot trap from bluff 20 feet high	65, 35, 28, and 29 S. of quarter post.
883	177	2	Amygdaloid trap from a bluff 400 feet high	65, 36, chs. from sec. corners 20, 21, 28, & 29.
884	247	2	Do. . . . . do. . . . . do	. . . . do
885	194	2	Native copper in [illegible]	65, 35, 26, lake shore
886	195	2	Do. . . . . do	. . . . do
887	178	2	Trap rock from a bluff	65, 35, 24.
888	181	2	Do. . . . . do	65, 35, 23, and 24.
889	191	2	Sandstone	65, 35, 25 NW. end of lake
890	192	2	Do.	. . . . do
891	207	2	Trap from a small bluff south of northeast end of lake	65, 35, 22.
892	219	2	Native copper in [illegible]	65, 35, 22 [illegible] of lake
893	220	2	Do. . . . . do	. . . . do
894	244	2	Erratic boulder of granite	65, 35, 21, and 22 NE. end of lake
895	190	2	Trap rock	65, 35, [illegible] corners 15, 16, 21, and 22.
896	197	2	Boulder of granite	65, 35, 20 on a trail 1 mile from N. shore
897	198	2	Trap rock	65, 35, 3.
898	200	2	Do.	65, 35, 3, and 4.
899	199	2	Do.	65, 35, 9, and 10.
900	201	2	Do.	. . . . do
901	205	2	Do.	65, 35, 8, and 9, 10 chs. from sec. corners 4, 5, 8, and 9.
902	206	2	Do.	65, 35, 12.
903	217	2	Quartz	. . . . do
904	218	2	Do.	65, 35, 1[illegible] on lake shore, near NW. cor. sec.
905	316	2	Native copper	65, 35, 4 rods from W. edge

Catalogue of rocks, minerals, and ores, collected during the years 1847 *and* 1848—Continued.

Progressive No.	No. of specimens.	No. of box.	Description.	Locality.
906	166	2	[illegible] per in prehnite	65, 36, 17, lake shore
907	176	2	[illegible] per in [illegible] se veinstone	65, 36, 18, 15 chs. from E. line
908	213	2	Veinstone in trap	65, 36, 17, lake shore, near NE. line
909	241	2	[illegible] [illegible] in prehnite	65, 36, 17, lake shore, near SW. corner
910	242	2	Do. do.	do.
911	243	2	Do. do.	do.
912	246	2	Quartz [illegible]	65, 36, 17, lake shore
913	261	2	[illegible] trap	65, 36, 17, near E. line
914	196	3	[illegible] [illegible] epidote	64, 37, on a [illegible] [illegible] sec's 23 & 24
915	210	2	[illegible] of trap [illegible] sandstone	do.
916	211	2	Do. do.	do.
917	146	2	[illegible] per in veinstone	Whittlesey's Union Co., I. R.
918	148	2	Do. d[illegible]	do.
919	149	2	[illegible] per and [illegible]c. spar	do.
920	150	2	[illegible] per [illegible] [illegible]	do.
921	150	2	Native per in [illegible]	do.
922	151	2	Do do.	do.
923	152	2	Do. do.	do.
924	153	2	M[illegible]ss of [illegible] [illegible]	d[illegible]
925	154	2	Do.	d[illegible]
926	155	2	[illegible] [illegible] in [illegible]olite	d[illegible]
927	156	2	[illegible] per in [illegible]c. [illegible]	d[illegible]
928	157	2	Native per in datholite	d[illegible]
929	158	2	[illegible] [illegible] in [illegible], Lake Shore, [illegible] Union county	d[illegible]
930	159	2	Do. do. do.	d[illegible]
931	160	2	Do. do. do.	d[illegible]
932	161	2	Do. do. do.	do.
933	167	2	[illegible] [illegible] in veinstone, with [illegible]lite	Conglome[illegible] Bay, I. R.
934	168	2	Do. d[illegible] do.	d[illegible]
935	169	2	Do. d[illegible] do.	d[illegible]
936	170	2	Do. do. d[illegible]	d[illegible]
937	171	2	Do. d[illegible] d[illegible]	do.
938	172	2	Do. do. do.	[illegible]o.

939	212	2	V[illegible] trap	do.
940	248	2	V[illegible] amygdaloid	do.
941	249	2	Do.	do.
942	250	2	Do.	do.
943	251	2	Trap rock with quartz and calc. spar, (no copper)	do.
944	252	2	Conglomerate containing [illegible]	do.
945	253	2	Breccia	do.
946	254	2	Scoria	do.
947	255	2	[illegible]al trap containing [illegible]	do.
948	256	2	[illegible] with [illegible] spar	do.
949	257	2	Trap breccia	do.
950	258	2	Jasper [illegible] from [illegible]	do.
951	259	2	Quartziferous porphyry [illegible]	do.
952	260	2	Sandstone showing [illegible] resembling fucoids	do.
953	215	2	[illegible]	Near Conglomerate Bay, I. R.
954	216	2	Do.	do.
955	274	3	Native copper in veinstone	Pittsburg and Isle Royal Company, Todd's Harbor, I. R.
956	275	3	Native copper in [illegible]olite	do.
957	276	3	Native copper in [illegible]	do
958	277	3	Native copper in [illegible]	do.
959	278	3	Native copper in trap with [illegible]olite	do.
960	279	3	Native copper in [illegible]	do.
961	280	3	Native copper in [illegible] with calc. spar	do.
962	281	3	Native copper in [illegible] with calc spar and chocolate colored trap	do.
963	284	3	Crystals of quartz and [illegible]	do.
964	285	3	Quartz and prehnite	do.
965	286	3	Native copper with quartz and hornblende	do.
966	287	3	Native copper in [illegible] spar vein	do.
967	288	3	Do. do.	do.
968	297	3	Native copper in [illegible] with chlorite lining a cavity	do.
969	270	3	Do. do.	Washington Harbor, I. R.
970	289	3	Native copper in [illegible]	Todd's Harbor' I. R.
971	290	3	Veinstone	do.
972	294	3	Native copper in [illegible]nite and calc. spar	[illegible] and Isle Royal Company near [illegible] Landing.
973	298	3	Do.	Small island near Miller's Landing
974	973	10	Amygdaloid, green base, containing amygdules of laumonite and calc. spar	[illegible], Isle Royal
975	974	10	Do. do. do. do.	do.
976	975	10	Amygdaloid, dark red base, containing amygdules of laumonite and calc. spar	do.
977	976	10	Do. do. do. do.	do.

Catalogue of rocks, minerals, and ores, collected during the years 1847 *and* 1848——Continued.

Progressive No.	No. of specimens.	No. of box.	Description.	Locality.
978	183	2	Boulder and [illegible] h[illegible]y	Isle Royal
979	193	2	I[illegible]d green [illegible], [illegible]d by [illegible]rite	
980	209	2	Amy[illegible] [illegible]l t[illegible]p [illegible]g [illegible]e	
981	234	2	[illegible]ck [illegible]e ad [illegible]pt [illegible]e [illegible]r l [illegible]r	N [illegible]r Scovill's point, l [illegible]e shore
982	269	3	Boulder [illegible]ing i[illegible]e [illegible]pr	Isle Royal
983	271	3	Boulder [illegible]ing [illegible]e pr in [illegible]ite with datholite	do
984	282	3	N[illegible]e pr in trap with c [illegible] [illegible]r [illegible]d [illegible]es of datholite	Isle [illegible]l, north shor e
985	283	3	Do. do. do.	do
986	291	3	Native per in veinstone, [illegible]s a nail piercing the rock)	do
987	292	3	Do. do.	do
988	293	3	Do. do.	do
989	295	3	Boulder i[illegible]g i[illegible]e pr in prehnite	Lake [illegible]e
990	296	3	Boul[illegible]r i[illegible]g i[illegible]e pr in prehnite with datholite and calc. spar	do
991	318	3	Native pr in [illegible]e	North [illegible]e
992	302	3	[illegible]d i[illegible]e pr [illegible]d calc. spar	Isle Royal
993	308	3	Native pr in [illegible]in of [illegible]ehnite	do
994	309	3	Do. d	do
995	320	3	Trap [illegible]k with prehnite and quartz in fine crystals	do
996	314	3	N[illegible]e copper	Small i[illegible]ds on north shore
997	315	3	Do.	do
998	299	3	[illegible]e per in prehnite with datholite	[illegible]e sl[illegible]e
999	300	3	[illegible]o. do	d
1000	301	3	Do. do	d
1001	303	3	Native per crystallized with datholite	d
1002	304	3	[illegible]e of [illegible]e	d
1003	305	3	Boulder containing agate and black quartz	d
1004	306	3	Druses of t[illegible]lite, boulder	do
1005	307	3	[illegible]l trap, with native copper in prehnite	do
1006	310	3	Native pr in prehnite	Lake shore, loose
1007	311	3	Do. do.	do
1008	312	3	Do. do.	do
1009	313	3	N[illegible]e pr in prehnite, with datholite	do
1010	317	3	l[illegible]d native copper in prehnite, with quartz	do

1011	118	2	Native silver and blende	British and N. American Co., Prince's Bay.
1012	119	2	Galena amethyst and calc. spar	Prince's vein, Spar island, Canada shore...
1013	184	2	Blende and calc. spar	..........do
1014	185	2	Copper pyrites	..........do
1015	186	2	Peacock ore	..........do
1016	188	2	Copper pyrites, blende, and native silver	Prince's vein, Spar island, Canada shore...

Catalogue of rocks, minerals, ores, and fossils, collected by Dr. John Locke.

Progressive No.	No. of specimens.	No. of box.	Description.	Locality.
1	4	1	Iron pyrites, galena, and calc. spar	Presque Isle
2	5	1	Do..........do	..........do
3	8	1	Do..........do	..........do
4	9	1	Do..........do	..........do
5	10	1	Do..........do	..........do
6	12	1	Do..........do	..........do
7	15	1	Do..........do	..........do
8	32	1	Do..........do	..........do
9	37	1	Do..........do	..........do
10	42	1	Do..........do	..........do
11	48	1	Do..........do	..........do
12	60	1	Do..........do	..........do
13	89	1	Do..........do	..........do
14	250	1	Do..........do	..........do
15	252	1	Iron pyrites, galena, and calc. spar, (iron pyrites encrusting calc. spar)	..........do
16	479	1	Iron pyrites, galena, and calc. spar	..........do
17	13	1	Iron pyrites and (octahedral) galena	..........do
18	31	1	Do..........do	..........do
19	45	1	Iron pyrites and [illegible] galena, covered with minute crystals of pyrites	..........do
20	47	1	Iron pyrites and [illegible] galena	..........do
21	49	1	Iron pyrites, [illegible] galena, and calc. spar	..........do
22	51	1	Iron pyrites and galena	..........do
23	54	1	Do.......do	..........do

Catalogue of rocks, minerals, ores, and fossils, collected by Dr. John Locke.

Progressive No.	No. of specimens.	No. of box.	Description.	Locality.
24	58	1	Iron pyrites and galena, [illegible]al	Presque Isle.
25	59	1	Iron pyrites and galena, [illegible]d	do.
26	61	1	Do. do.	do.
27	62	1	Iron pyrites and galena, octahedral.	do.
28	63	1	Do. do.	do.
29	64	1	Do. do.	do.
30	65	1	Do. do.	do.
31	66	1	Do. do.	do.
32	67	1	Do. do.	do.
33	68	1	Iron pyrites and galena, impressed.	do.
34	70	1	Iron pyrites and galena.	do.
35	76	L 1	Fine iron pyrites and galena, [illegible]rystallized	do.
36	77	" 1	Do. do.	do.
37	78	" 1	Fine particle of iron pyrites and galena, octahedral	do.
38	90	" 1	Fine particle of iron pyrites, a [illegible] [illegible]ent	do.
39	106	" 1	Do. do.	do.
40	494	" 1	Do. do.	do.
41	499	" 1	Do. do.	do.
42	509	" 1	Do. do.	do.
43	614	" 1	Iron pyrites and galena.	do.
44	615	" 1	Do.	do.
45	6	" 1	Crystals of iron pyrites and calc. spar, six sided prisms	do.
46	14	" 1	Do. do.	do.
47	16	" 1	Do. do.	do.
48	17	" 1	[illegible]cent iron pyrites and calc. spar	do.
49	18	" 1	Do.	do.
50	19	" 1	Crystals of iron pyrites and calc. spar, crystallized.	do.
51	20	" 1	Crystals of iron pyrites and calc. spar, in a green rock apparently colored by [illegible]	do.
52	21	" 1	Do. do.	do.
53	22	" 1	Do. do.	do.
54	28	" 1	Do. do.	do.
55	29	" 1	Botryoi[illegible]al iron pyrites and calc. spar	d.

56	35	" 1	Do	d.
57	40	" 1	Do	do.
58	47	" 1	Do	do.
59	55	" 1	Do	d.
60	87	" 1	Do	d.
61	91	" 1	Do	d.
62	101	" 1	Do	do.
63	478½	" 1	Do	do.
64	480	" 1	Cubic iron pyrites and calc. spar, in short prisms	do.
65	502	" 1	Cubic iron pyrites and calc. spar, in yellow silicious rock	do.
66	25	" 1	Cubic galena and calc. spar	do.
67	57	" 1	[illegible] galena and [illegible] [illegible]	do.
68	92	" 1	[illegible] galena and calc. spar (form of galena octahedral)	do.
69	96	" 1	[illegible] galena and calc. spar (surface of galena decrystallized)	do.
70	477	" 1	[illegible] galena and calc. spar [illegible]	do.
71	647	" 1	[illegible] galena and iron pyrites, in [illegible] rock	do.
72	648	" 1	Crystallized galena and iron pyrites, in [illegible] rock	do.
73	23	" 1	Iron pyrites, in green rock	do.
74	24	" 1	Galena and pseudomorphous pyrites taking the form of the pentagonal termination of calc. spar	do.
75	26	" 1	Iron pyrites	do.
76	33	" 1	Galena and calc. spar	do.
77	38	" 1	Iron pyrites, in the rock	do.
78	39	" 1	Do	do.
79	56	" 1	Do	do.
80	74	" 1	Do	do.
81	83	" 1	Iron pyrites, iridescent	do.
82	86	" 1	Do	do.
83	93	" 1	Do	do.
84	251	" 1	Do	do.
85	506	" 1	Iron pyrites and peroxide of iron	d.
86	507	" 1	Do	d.
87	534	" 1	Do	do.
88	617	" 1	Do	do.
89	631	" 1	Do	do.
90	632	" 1	Do	d.
91	633	" 1	Do	do.
92	647	" 1	Do	do.
93	648	" 1	Do	do.
94	27	" 1	Calc. spar, crystallized	do.
95	50	" 1	Calc. spar, six sided prisms	do.

Catalogue of rocks, minerals, ores, and fossils, collected by Dr. John Locke—Continued.

Progressive No.	No. of specimens.	No. of box.	Description.	Locality.
96	105	L 1	Calc. spar, six sided prisms terminated by three pentagonal faces, external layer opaque, interior transparent	Presque Isle do.
97	492	" 1	Dog tooth spar	do.
98	497	" 1	Calc. spar, hexahedral, retained by Dr. J.	do.
99	30	" 1	Galena, dodecahedral	do.
100	36	" 1	Do.	do.
101	41	" 1	Do.	do.
102	43	" 1	Do.	do.
103	44	" 1	Do.	do.
104	69	" 1	Galena, octahedral	do.
105	72	" 1	Do.	do.
106	73	" 1	Do.	do.
107	75	" 1	Galena, dodecahedral	do.
108	80	" 1	Do.	do.
109	81	" 1	Galena and calc. spar	do.
110	82	" 1	Do.	do.
111	84	" 1	Do.	do.
112	85	" 1	Galena, three separate dodecahedral crystals	do.
113	94	" 1	Galena, octahedral	do.
114	95	" 1	Do.	do.
115	97	" 1	Do.	do.
116	98	" 1	Do.	do.
117	103	" 1	Do.	do.
118	115	" 1	Do.	do.
119	116	" 1	Galena, octahedral, passing into dodecahedral	do.
120	117	" 1	Galena, dodecahedral	do.
121	505	" 1	Galena	do.
122	508	" 1	Do.	do.
123	616	" 1	Do.	do.
124	114	" 1	Iron pyrites and asbestos	do.
125	478	" 1	Blende in a vein of quartz, with galena	do.
126	493	" 1	Galena and asbestos	do.
127	495	" 1	Black calc. spar, sulphuret of copper and carb. lime	do.

128	80	" 1	Quartz, dog-tooth spar, iron pyrites and galena	do.
129	498	" 1	Cal. spar, containing pyrites surrounded by [illegible] of gypsum, derived from	
130	99	" 1	decomposition of pyrites	d.
			Decomposed [illegible] vein	d.
131	102	" 1	Vein of [illegible] in [illegible] sandstone	d.
132	119	" 1	Vein of [illegible] jasper in [illegible] rock	do.
133	122	" 1	[illegible] with a [illegible] lustre	do.
134	124	" 1	Small vein of jasper in trap	do.
135	163	" 1	[illegible] breccia	do.
136	164	" 1	[illegible] of [illegible] in trap	do.
137	104	" 1	Drusy quartz	do.
138	110	" 1	Silicious rock	do.
139	113	" 1	Small quartz vein in a ferruginous rock	do.
140	118	" 1	[illegible] rock	do.
141	123	" 1	[illegible] in trap	do.
142	126	" 1	Quartz in brown silicious rock	do.
143	167	" 1	Drusy quartz	do.
144	253	" 1	[illegible] quartz from indurated sandstone	d.
145	1	" 1	Coarse gray sandstone, containing [illegible] of quartz and crystals of feldspar cemented by a greenish paste	
146	2	" 1		do.
			Do.....do.....do.....do	do.
147	3	" 1	Do.....do.....do.....do	do.
148	7	" 1	Veinstone, containing carbonate of [illegible] and a [illegible] chlorite	do.
149	34	" 1	[illegible] of [illegible] rock [illegible] by white veins	do.
150	79	" 1	Veins of [illegible] spar in trap	do.
151	99	" 1	[illegible] of [illegible] sandstone, [illegible] from epidote	do.
152	61	" 1	Red and gray sandstone with [illegible]	do.
153	162	" 1	[illegible] sandstone, containing carb. of lime	do.
154	165	" 1	Gray sandstone, [illegible] with carb. of copper	do.
155	169	" 1	Trap rock, very ferruginous	do.
156	222	" 1	Serpentine	do.
157	501	" 1	Do	do.
158	503	" 1	Do	do.
159	84	" 1	[illegible]	do.
160	500	" 1	Carbonate of lime and iron	do.
161	107	" 1	Slaty red hematite	do.
162	108	" 1	Do	do.
163	109	" 1	Do	do.
164	111	" 1	Do	do.
165	112	" 1	Fragment of a vein of red silicious matter in green altered sandstone	do.
166	121	" 1	Red hematite in a silicious breccia	do.

Catalogue of rocks, minerals, ores, and fossils, collected by Dr. John Locke—Continued.

Progressive No.	No. of specimens.	No. of box.	Description.	Locality.
167	120	L 1	Compact red hematite	Presque Isle
168	163	" 1	Earthy silicious red hematite	do.
169	166	" 1	Pebble of rich red hematite	do.
170	177	" 1	Red [illegible]	do.
171	125	" 1	Yellow epidote rock with coarse veins	do.
172	127	" 1	Black trap	do.
173	128	" 1	Do.	do.
174	129	" 1	Red slate, reticulated with veins of carb. lime	do.
175	130	" 1	Do. do.	do.
176	131	" 1	Altered sandstone, containing pebbles of quartz	do.
177	132	" 1	Do. do.	do.
178	133	" 1	Dark brown sandstone, containing pebbles of quartz	do.
179	134	" 1	Do. do. do.	do.
180	135	" 1	Jaspery red rock, veins of quartz	do.
181	136	" 1	Do. do.	do.
182	137	" 1	Portion of conglomerate indurated, containing porphyry and micaceous sandstone	do.
183	138	" 1	Do. do. do. do.	do.
184	139	" 1	Red sandstone, composed of grains of quartz, peroxide of iron and decomposed feldspar	do.
185	140	" 1	Do. do. do. do.	do.
186	170	" 1	Red slate coated with peroxide of iron and glazed	L' Anse
187	174	" 1	Red slate	do.
188	554	" 1	Do.	do.
189	555	" 1	Red slate coated with peroxide of iron and glazed	do.
190	173	" 1	Gray slate	do.
191	175	" 1	Do.	do.
192	207	" 1	Novaculite, drab colored	do.
193	208	" 1	Do. do.	do.
194	209	" 1	Do. do.	do.
195	210	" 1	Do. do.	do.
196	482	" 1	Novaculite	do.
197	483	" 1	Novaculite slate	do.

198	86	" 1	Novaculite	do.
199	56	" 1	Red [illegible]lk, rat[illegible]er [illegible]	do.
200	171	" 1	Gray [illegible]e	do.
201	84	" 1	[illegible]t quartzy [illegible]e overl[illegible]ying tr[illegible]p	do.
202	488	" 1	[illegible]d [illegible], [illegible]tz [illegible]nd [illegible]d fel[illegible]par	do.
203	172	" 1	[illegible] [illegible]s [illegible]tz	do.
204	481	" 1	[illegible]s [illegible]tz	L'Anse
205	487	" 1	Quartz	do.
206	489	" 1	Do.	do.
207	90	" 1	Do.	do.
208	491	" 1	Q[illegible]tz [illegible]nd [illegible]n	do.
209	176	" 1	Iron ore—peroxide—stratified	Jackson mine
210	178	" 1	Do. do	do.
211	179	" 1	Do. do. (Retained by Dr. J.)	do.
212	96	" 1	Do. do.	do.
213	267	" 1	[illegible]t red [illegible]on ore	[illegible]d Loc.
214	268	" 1	Do. (Retained by Dr. J.)	do.
215	510	" 1	Do.	do.
216	182	" 1	Slaty [illegible]on ore	[illegible]n mine
217	99	" 1	Slaty [illegible]on ore co[illegible]pact	do
218	512	" 1	[illegible]r [illegible]on ore	do.
219	514	" 1	Do. ([illegible]ained by Dr. J.)	do.
220	533	" 1	Do.	do.
221	184	" 1	Red iron o[illegible]e with jaspery [illegible]—curved strata	do.
222	187	" 1	Do. do. do.	do.
223	183	" 1	Red iron ore with j[illegible]pery [illegible]ds	do.
224	511	" 1	Do. do.	do.
225	513	" 1	Do. do.	do.
226	188	" 1	[illegible]ry iron o[illegible]e	do.
227	595	" 1	Bor[illegible] [illegible]is [illegible]on ore	do.
228	180	" 1	Red [illegible]e	do.
229	181	" 1	[illegible]ite sl[illegible]te	do.
230	339	" 3	Purple [illegible]pr[illegible] o[illegible]e. B	[illegible]e mine
231	346	" 3	Do. A	do.
232	349	" 3	Do. A	do.
233	351	" 3	Purple copper ore in quartz C	do.
234	352	" 3	Do. do. C	do.
235	354	" 3	Do. do. A	do.
236	360	" 3	Purple copper ore B	do.
237	364	" 3	Do. A	do.
238	85	" 3	Do. (Retained by Dr. J.) A	do.

Catalogue of rocks, minerals, ores, and fossils, collected by Dr. John Locke—Continued.

Progressive No.	No. of specimens.	No. of box.	Description.		Locality.
239	374	L 3	Purple copper ore	A	Bruce mine
240	376	" 3	Do	A	do
241	387	" 3	Do	A	do
242	388	" 3	Do	A	do
243	394	" 3	Do	A	do
244	397	" 3	Do	A	do
245	403	" 3	Do	B	do
246	407	" 3	Do	B	do
247	408	" 3	Do	A	do
248	410	" 3	Do	A	do
249	411	" 3	Do		do
250	335	" 3	Purple copper pyrites and quartz	B	do
251	336	" 3	Do .... do .... do	B	do
252	341	" 3	Do .... do .... do	B	do
253	340	" 3	Copper pyrites, yellow	C	do
254	342	" 3	[illegible]r pyrites in quartz	C	do
255	343	" 3	Copper [illegible]rites in quartz, with iridescent copper	C	do
256	345	" 3	Copper p[illegible]ites in quartz	C	do
257	353	" 3	Do .... do	C	do
258	355	" 3	Co[illegible]per pyrites		do
259	356	" 3	Do	B	do
260	363	" 3	Do	B	do
261	366	" 3	Do	B	do
262	367	" 3	Do	C	do
263	368	" 3	Do .... (Retained by Dr J.)	B	do
264	370	" 3	Do		do
265	373	" 3	Do	C	do
266	375	" 3	Do	C	do
267	377	" 3	Do	C	do
268	378	" 3	Do	B	do
269	379	" 3	Do	C	do
270	380	" 3	Do		do
271	381	" 3	Do	C	do

272	382	" 3	Do	B	do
273	383	" 3	Do		do
274	384	" 3	Do	C	do
275	385	" 3	Do	C	do
276	386	" 3	Do	B	do
277	389	" 3	Do	B	do
278	390	" 3	Do	C	do
279	391	" 3	Do	B	do
280	392	" 3	Do	B	do
281	393	" 3	Do	C	do
282	401	" 3	Do	B	do
283	405	" 3	Do	A	do
284	409	" 3	Do	C	do
285	414	" 3	Do		do
286	427	" 3	Do	C	do
287	[illegible]26	" 3	Gr[illegible] [illegible]ps in sienite, wall vein	C	do
288	358	" 3	Gray [illegible]pr [illegible]e	A	do
289	359	" 3	Gray [illegible]pr ore—quartz and green carb., (first discovery of the mine,)		do
290	362	" 3	Gray [illegible]pr ore	A	do
291	369	" 3	Do	A	do
292	371	" 3	Gray [illegible]pr ore, coated with green carb	A	do
293	396	" 3	Do ... do		do
294	404	" 3	Gray [illegible]pr [illegible]e	C	do
[illegible]95	413	" 3	Do	C	do
296	594	" 3	Do		do
297	398	" 3	[illegible]e of [illegible]p	C	do
298	348	" 3	Q[illegible]z, with a [illegible]e carb. of copper		do
299	361	" 3	Do ... [illegible]d		do
300	337	" 3	Q[illegible]zifer[illegible]us trap rock gangue		do
301	337½	" 3	[illegible]t of trap dyke in [illegible]p feldspathic [illegible]k		do
302	338	" 3	Trap rock		do
303	344	" 3	T[illegible]p [illegible]k, [illegible]g of [illegible]e [illegible]nd [illegible]r	B	do
304	347	" 3	Trap [illegible]k porphyritic	A	do
305	350	" 3	Do ... do	B	do
306	372	" 3	T[illegible]p [illegible]k	C	do
307	[illegible]06	" 3	Do	B	do
308	415	" 3	T[illegible]p rock, resembling sienite	C	do
309	416	" 3	Trap [illegible]k		do
310	418	" 3	Do	C	do
311	412	" 3	Sienite, [illegible]p[illegible]	C	do
312	417	" 3	Sienite, rhbl[illegible] [illegible]e [illegible]ad feldspar		do

Catalogue of rocks, minerals, ores, and fossils, collected by Dr. John Locke—Continued.

Progressive No.	No. of specimens.	No. of box.	Description.	Locality.
313	420	L 3	Sienite	Bruce mine
314	424	" 3	Do	do.
315	421	" 3	Hornblende rock, consisting of hornblende and feldspar	do.
316	422	" 3	Do ..do ..do	do.
317	423	" 3	Do ..do ..do	do.
318	435	" 3	Hornblende rock	do.
319	425	" 3	Chlorite slate, next to vein, the wall	do.
320	428	" 3	Breccia, jasper and quartz	2 miles west of Bruce mine
321	429	" 3	Do ..do	do.
322	430	" 3	Do ..do	do.
323	431	" 3	Do ..do	do.
324	434	" 3	Jasper breccia	do.
325	433	" 3	Bluff and red jasper in place	do.
326	436	" 3	Trap rock	do.
327	439	" 3	Limestone	do.
328	441	" 3	Do	do.
329	442	" 3	Do	do.
330	440	" 3	Indurated chlorite slate	do.
331	443	" 3	Coarse gray sandstone	Grand Island
332	444	" 3	Do ..do	do.
333	448	" 3	Do ..do	do.
334	445	" 3	Red sandstone	do.
335	453	" 3	Do	do.
336	446	" 3	Red and gray sandstone	do.
337	447	" 3	Do ..do	do.
338	449	" 3	Fine white sandstone	Grand Portal
339	451	" 3	Do ..do	do.
340	452	" 3	Do ..do	do.
341	450	" 3	Coarse sandstone	do.
342	557	" 4	Nodules stained with oxide of iron in white sandstone and nodules of oxide of iron	do.
543	558	" 4	Do ..do ..do ..do	do.
344	559	" 4	Do ..do ..do ..do	do.
345	560	" 4	Do ..do ..do ..do	do.

346	561	" 4	Do..........do..........d..........do	do
347	562	" 4	Do..........do..........d..........do	do
348	563	" 4	Do..........d..........d..........do	do
349	564	" 4	Do..........do..........d..........do	do
350	565	" 4	Do..........do..........d..........do	do
351	566	" 4	Do..........do..........d..........do	do
352	567	" 4	Do..........do..........d..........do	do
353	568	" 4	Do..........do..........d..........do	do
354	569	" 4	Do..........do..........d..........do	do
355	570	" 4	Do..........do..........d..........do	do
356	571	" 4	Do..........do..........d..........do	do
357	572	" 4	Do..........do..........d..........do	do
358	573	" 4	Do..........do..........d..........do	do
359	574	" 4	Do..........do..........d..........do	do
360	575	" 4	Do..........do..........d..........do	do
361	576	" 4	Do..........do..........do..........do	do
362	577	" 4	Do..........do..........do..........do	do
363	578	" 4	Do..........do..........do..........do	do
364	579	" 4	Do..........do..........do..........do	do
365	580	" 4	Do..........do..........do..........do	do
366	581	" 4	Do..........do..........do..........do	do
367	582	" 4	Do..........do..........do..........do	do
368	584	" 4	Nodules of peroxide of iron in white sandstone	do
369	585	" 4	Do..........do..........do	do
370	586	" 4	Do..........do..........do	do
371	587	" 4	Do..........do..........do	do
372	588	" 4	Nodules of peroxide of iron in white sandstone	do
373	589	" 4	Do..........do	
374	590	" 4	Do..........do	
375	591	" 4	Do..........do	
376	592	" 4	Do..........do	
377	583	" 4	Pseudomorphs carbonate of lime in peroxide of iron	
378	627	" 4	Vein of sulphate of baryta in coarse gray sandstone	
379	628	" 4	Do..........do	
380	629	" 4	Do..........do	
381	454	" 3	White sandstone	Portal rock
382	620	" 4	Fine gray sandstone	do
383	455	" 3	Nodule of calcareous rock	Portal cave
384	456	" 3	Fucoides duplexus in white sandstone, (retained by Dr. Jackson,)	Grand Portal cave
385	457	" 3	Do..........do..........do	do
386	458	" 3	Fucoides duplexus in white sandstone	do

Catalogue of rocks, minerals, ores, and fossils, collected by Dr. John Locke—Continued.

Progressive No.	No. of specimens.	No. of box.	Description.	Locality.
387	459	L 3	Fucoides [illegible] in [illegible] [illegible]	Grand Portal cave
388	460	" 3	Do. do	
389	461	" 3	Do. do	
390	462	" 3	[illegible] in white [illegible], (retained by Dr. Jackson,)	
391	463	" 3	[illegible] in white [illegible]	
392	464	" 3	Fucoides [illegible] in white [illegible], (retained by Dr. Jackson,)	
393	465	" 3	Fucoides [illegible] in white sandstone	
394	466	" 3	[illegible] do	
395	467	" 3	Fucoides [illegible] in [illegible] [illegible], [illegible] by Dr. Jackson,)	
396	468	" 3	Fucoides duplexus in [illegible] [illegible]	
397	469	" 3	[illegible] in [illegible] [illegible], (retained by Dr. Jackson,)	
398	470	" 3	[illegible] in [illegible] [illegible]	
399	471	" 3	[illegible] in [illegible] [illegible], (retained by Dr. Jackson,)	do
400	335	" 3	Sandstone [illegible] of [illegible]	[illegible] rocks (probably)
401	646	" 4	[illegible] with [illegible] of [illegible]	do
402	287	" 3	Buff [illegible]	Near head of the rapids of Sault St. Marie.
403	288	" 3	Do	do
404	292	" 3	Do	do
405	294	" 3	Do	do
406	297½	" 3	Do	do
407	299	" 3	Gray sandstone	do
408	289	" 3	Red sandstone, mottled	do
409	290	" 3	Red sandstone	do
410	291	" 3	Do	do
411	295	" 3	Do	do
412	296	" 3	Red sandstone, mottled	do
413	297	" 3	Do. do	do
414	293	" 3	Red sandstone	do
415	298	" 3	Red and gray sandstone, mottled	do
416	300	" 3	Copper pyrites, in quartz	Echo lake
417	301	" 3	Do. do	do
418	302	" 3	Do. do	do
419	303	" 3	Do. do	do

420	304	" 3	Do.........do	d.
421	305	" 3	Do.........do	do.
422	306	" 3	Do.........do	do.
423	307	" 3	Do.........do	do.
424	308	" 3	Do.........do	d.
425	309	" 3	Do.........do	do.
426	310	" 3	Do.........do	do.
427	395	" 3	Do.........do	do.
428	399	" 3	Do.........do	do.
429	402	" 3	Do.........do	do.
430	311	" 3	Bl uish gray mpt limestone	do.
431	312	" 3	Do.........do	do.
432	317	" 3	Li one dd by ter, showing strata	do.
433	318	" 3	Li ne dd by ter, less acted upon	do.
434	319	" 3	Limestone rdd by ter.	do.
435	320	" 3	Do.........do	do.
436	325	" 3	Li one mpt, ted for analysis	do.
437	326	" 3	Li tne dd by ter, showing strata	do.
438	327	" 3	Li tne dd by ter	do.
439	330	" 3	Do.........do	do.
440	332	" 3	Do.........do	do.
441	329	" 3	Li one ing drift scratches	do.
442	313	" 3	Chlorite lte containing pebbles of quartz and feldspar	do.
443	314	" 3	Do.........do.........do.	do.
444	324	" 3	Kle lte containing scattered nodules of feldspar rock	do.
445	328	" 3	Kle slate	do.
446	331	" 3	Silicious indurated slate	do.
447	321	" 3	Tp rock	d.
448	322	" 3	Do.	do.
449	323	" 3	Do.	d.
450	333	" 3	White sandstone from a bul dr	W. mp, August 10
451	334	" 3	White de from a bul dr	Nar mp; August 10
				T. R. S
452	186	" 4	Indurated slate, containing pyrites	48, 25, 2—Cross island
453	255	" 4	Indurated slate	do.
454	216	" 4	Rock composed of feldspar and quartz	do.
455	226	" 4	Rock composed of green feldspar and quartz	do.
456	230	" 4	Quartz	48, 25, 2
457	189	" 4	Green slate, with vein of carb. lime	48, 25, 11, Dead River Falls
458	193	" 4	Do.........do	48, 25, 11
459	194	" 4	Green slate, with vein of magnesian limestone	do.

Catalogue of rocks, minerals, ores, and fossils, collected by Dr. John Locke—Continued.

Progressive No.	No. of specimens.	No. of box.	Description.	Locality.
				T. R. S.
460	243	L 4	Green slate, with ein of carb. li ne	48, 25, 11, Dead River Falls
461	244	" 4	Do.....do	48, 25, 11
462	190	" 4	Magn li tne, pink colored	do
463	191	" 4	Magn li tne, pi rk od, in slate	d
464	192	" 4	Magnesian li tne, pink colored	do
465	262	" 4	aMgn li tne, vein, ; (ad by Dr. J.)	do
466	265	" 4	Mgn li tne, vein	do
467	195	" 4	Fiesh odd fel par nd qartz ok, porphyry (?)	do
468	283	" 4	Be of breecia, ipd fel par ad iron ore	Mth of Dead river
469	197	" 4	Fdh olored lfar nd qartz, fie gid porphyry?	Mle isl d
470	200	" 4	Rock r pd of feldspar nd quartz	do
471	612	" 4	Do.....do	Middle isl d, S. end of island
472	198	" 4	Argill es slate	Mle isl d
473	199	" 4	r Gct slate, ontaining pyrites	do
474	204	" 4	Brown slate	do
475	205	" 4	Altered lte	do
476	206	" 4	dle ate	do
477	261	" 4	Green sl at	do
478	201	" 4	Hornblende slate	do
479	203	" 4	Hornbl de rock ng into ienite, red feldspar	do
480	202	" 4	St, r pd aly of hornblende and a little red feldspar	do
481	203	" 4	Gct blk tap	do
		" 4	Hornblende ok, vin of enite	do
482	254			
483	211	" 4	Calc. spar in indurated sandstone	49, 25, 34, Granite Point
484	263	" 4	Calc. spar in red sandstone	49, 25, 34
485	212	" 4	Light green hornblende rock, a boulder	do
486	214	" 4	Lamellar hornblende rock, a boulder	do
487	215	" 4	Do.....do	do
488	259	" 4	Do.....do	do
489	260	" 4	Do.....do	do
490	219	" 4	Slate rock	do

491	220	" 4	Gh nd ed nodule, from sandstone near the trap	do.
492	242	" 4	Bih ed de	do.
493	249	" 4	Red fel par nd vein of calc spar	do.
494	257	" 4	Red fel dr tall ed	do.
495	217	" 4	Hbl de ck	48, 25, 2, Savine island.
496	221	" 4	Red feldspar, hy	do. do.
497	225	" 4	Porphyry	48, 25, 2.
498	283	" 4	Rock pd of fe par nd t	48, 25, 11, Dead ier
499	223	" 4	Ke suitable for ig pipes, spc. grav. 2.90	Gp River pt fe
500	269	" 4	Do do	do.
501	516	" 4	Do d.	do.
502	224	" 4	Quartz rock	do.
503	609	" 4	Gr tz ck, ttled with d.	do.
504	610	" 4	Gr tz ck, ttled with d, (see No. 560)	do.
505	553	" 4	Krite in d, pd of chlorite nd fr	Carp river.
506	608	" 4	Gt calcifer us sl te, containing iron pys.	do.
507	618	" 4	Gt ble li t, ing iron pys	do.
508	541	" 4	Tp ck, green f, ar de	1 mile N. of Carp river, Lake shore
509	227	" 4	Gr ite tz, (ly d de)	Head of Upper Nubish Rapids
510	228	" 4	Gr pk tz, (ly d dst ne)	do.
511	229	" 4	Do do	do.
512	284	" 4	Gr te tz, (ly al ed sandstone)	Nubish Rapids.
513	286	" 4	Do d.	do.
514	274	" 4	Gr tz, d de	do.
515	275	" 4	Do do	do.
516	276	" 4	Alt ed d, fie ig, compact, large grooves	do.
517	277	" 4	Alt ed d, pt	do.
518	278	" 4	Altered d, p, grooved.	do.
519	279	" 4	Altered d, pt	do.
520	218	" 4	Si te, d th ple	49, 25, 29, near Mount Burt.
521	238	" 4	Do do	do.
522	245	" 4	Do do	do.
523	234	" 4	Si ite, in p.	do.
524	246	" 4	Si ite, se grained	d.
525	247	" 4	Si ite, fie grained	do.
526	248	" 4	Do	do.
527	280	" 4	Si ite, s, pd of large crystals of hornblende and feldspar	do.
528	281	" 4	Trap ck, 20 et yd, ds No. 1	Mount Burt.
529	282	" 4	Tp ck, 20 feet dyke, de No. 2	do.
530	232	" 4	Red porphyry, large ls, red feldspar, and large grains quartz, with carb. li ne tr	49, 25, 29, near Mount Burt.

Catalogue of rocks, minerals, ores, and fossils, collected by Dr. John Locke—Continued.

Progressive No.	No. of specimens.	No. of box.	Description.	Locality.
				T. R. S.
531	236	L 4	Rock composed of feldspar and quartz	49, 25, 29, near Mount Burt
532	264	" 4	Epidote	Near Mt [illegible], on shore
533	270	" 4	Drab [illegible]d novaculite, [illegible]d and comp[illegible]t, superior quality, (retained by Dr. J.)	48, 26, 30, Teal lake
534	272	" 4	Dark [illegible]d novaculite, [illegible]d and [illegible]pact, superior quality, (see 561)	do.
535	530	" 4	White [illegible]ste, [illegible]taining a little carb. lime	Near Tobacco [illegible]r
536	531	" 4	Do do	do.
537	622	" 4	[illegible]e gray san[illegible]de	Near Miners' river
538	626	" 4	Do	do.
539	543	" 4	Q[illegible]z and [illegible]ed feldspar. Standard No. 2.	46, 26, 6
540	542	" 4	Q[illegible]z and [illegible]d feldspar	46, 27, 25, Eskanawby rapids
541	544	" 4	Rock [illegible]pd of [illegible]ble quartz and white feldspar	46, 26, 30, Eskanawby rapids
542	545	" 4	Rock [illegible]pd of [illegible]arge crystals of blue quartz and red feldspar	46, 26, 31, G[illegible]at [illegible]lls of Eskanawby
543	546	" 4	Light-red sandstone	From a point [illegible]st of Train point
544	547	" 4	Do do	[illegible]d.
545	548	" 4	Red and [illegible]e [illegible]done	do.
546	552	" 4	[illegible]e [illegible]d.	[illegible]d.
547	549	" 4	Vein of [illegible]e of baryta in sandstone	do.
548	550	" 4	Do do	do.
549	551	" 4	Do do	do.
550	611	" 4	G[illegible]n [illegible]p rock [illegible]icular covered with fine crystals of epidote	Gros [illegible]
551	635	" 4	T[illegible]p [illegible]k [illegible]g nodules of chlorite and epidote	do
552	640	" 4	[illegible]al [illegible]p	do
553	641	" 4	T[illegible]p [illegible]k [illegible]g leonhardite	do
554	642	" 4	Amygdaloidal [illegible]p amygdules of a bright red mineral (retained for analysis)	do
555	644	" 4	Rock [illegible]pd of feldspar, chlorite, and quartz	do
556	634	" 4	[illegible]in of [illegible]tz.	do
557	638	" 4	[illegible]b. lime with a slight coating of carb. of copper	do
558	639	" 4	[illegible]te	do
559	645	" 4	Epidote and [illegible]d.	do
560	606	" 4	[illegible]i-colored [illegible]e [illegible]e (should follow 504)	Carp [illegible]r post office
561	527	" 4	Novaculite, [illegible]d, yields to knife, good quality (should follow 534)	48, 26, 30, Teal lake
562	520	" 4	Quartz containing sp[illegible]ds of copper pyrites	48, 26, 26

563	521	" 4	Q[illegible]z [illegible]aining [illegible] of [illegible]opper pyrites with chlorite	48, 26, 28 S. E. ¼ sec
564	522	" 4	Q[illegible]z containing [illegible] [illegible]rites	do
565	526	" 4	Chlorite slate	do
566	593	" 4	[illegible]n pyrites in sl[illegible]	do
567	523	" 4	S[illegible]e [illegible]h [illegible]z	48, 26
568	524	" 4	Slate with carb. of lime	48, 26
569	535	" 4	[illegible]t, [illegible]d, [illegible]y, magnetic iron w[illegible]th polarity	48, 26 $\frac{1}{8}$ mile N. of sec 18
570	536	" 4	Do ... do ... do	do
571	537	" 4	Do ... do ... do	do
572	539	" 4	[illegible]t, [illegible]d, [illegible], [illegible]c iron [illegible]h pol[illegible]rity (retained for analysis)	do
573	540	" 4	[illegible]n [illegible]e [illegible]k, [illegible]d [illegible]n N[illegible]. 1	47, 26, 18
574	518	" 4	[illegible]e [illegible]k containing [illegible]b. [illegible]e [illegible]d [illegible]s	
575	525	" 4	[illegible]t [illegible]s [illegible]e containing [illegible]. l[illegible]me	
576	605	" 4	[illegible]s slate	
577	623	" 4	[illegible]r [illegible]s of sulph[illegible]te [illegible]f lime	
578	624	" 4	Do ... do	
579	842	" 4	[illegible]a (fragment) ([illegible]d by Dr. J.)	St. Joseph's
580	650	" 4	A, [illegible]t [illegible]longing to the [illegible]t [illegible]a, at the point A to be glued on	do
581	651	" 2	B, [illegible]t belonging to [illegible]e great [illegible], at [illegible]e [illegible]t B to be glued on	
582	649	Long box.	Great [illegible], 5 feet [illegible], 8 [illegible]es in [illegible]r, joints about three to the [illegible]h, [illegible]g in all [illegible]t 180 [illegible]s. Siphuncle large, well marked, [illegible]d filled [illegible]h [illegible]s, [illegible]e [illegible]wing.) [illegible]r end contracts ab[illegible]y [illegible]n 2 or 3 [illegible]s of [illegible]e [illegible]erminat[illegible]on	
	652 to 841	L 2	All the [illegible]e [illegible]il, [illegible]s [illegible]s	T. RE. G. 42, 4, 17
			Nos. 750, 780, 781, 782, 783, 784, 785, 787, 788, and 789 are missing	
			Nos. 660, 680, 710, 711, 734, 738, 768, 798, 815, and 826 retained for examination and analysis of limestone	

Catalogue of rocks, minerals, &c., collected by J. W. Foster.

Progressive No.	No. of specimens.	No. of box.	Description.	Locality.
1	1	F 1	Ferruginous sandstone, base of silurian	Below Chippewa island, Menomoneek
2	2	" 1	Do. do	do
3	3	" 1	Do. do	do
4	29	W 1	Red [illegible]ziferous porphyry, large crystals of red feldspar, (probably erratic)	do
5	30	F 1	Do. do do	do
6	31	" 1	Do. do do	do
7	27	" 1	[illegible]act trap (marked "Basalt" F.)	½ mile below [illegible] isl'd, Menomoneek.
8	28	" 1	Do. do	do
9	34	" 1	Sienite	1 mile [illegible] Chi[illegible] isl'd, Menomoneek.
10	32	" 1	[illegible] slate with [illegible]	½ mile [illegible] Chi[illegible] isl'd, Menomoneek.
11	33	" 1	[illegible] jasper	do
12	21	" 1	[illegible] gray [illegible]lor	Chip[illegible], [illegible]neek
13	22	" 1	Do. do	do
14	23	" 1	Do. do	do
15	24	" 1	Talcose [illegible], reddish [illegible]	do
16	25	" 1	[illegible] trap, contains pyrites	do
17	26	" 1	Do. do do	do
18	4	" 1	Calcifer[illegible], [illegible]er silurian	33, 28, Caulkin's saw mill, Menomoneek
19	5	" 1	[illegible]	do
20	6	" 1	Sandstone, [illegible] of [illegible]	[illegible]e rapids, Menomoneek
21	7	" 1	[illegible]	do
22	8	" 1	Red sandstone, fine grained [illegible], lower silurian	Grand rapids, [illegible]
23	9	" 1	Do. do do	do
24	10	" 1	Drab col[illegible] magnesian [illegible], [illegible] silurian	do
25	11	" 1	Do. do	do
26	12	" 1	[illegible] brown [illegible], [illegible] silurian	do
27	13	" 1	Do. do	do
28	35	" 1	[illegible]ar quartz, [illegible] to be i[illegible] white sandstone with ripple marks, [illegible]	Twin falls, Menomoneek
29	36	" 1	[illegible]ular limestone	Upper Twin falls, Menomoneek
30	37	" 1	[illegible]ular limestone, containing zoisite (?)	do
31	40	" 1	Do. do	do
32	42	" 1	Do. do	do

33	41	" 1	[illegible] li [illegible] and [illegible], [illegible]taining zoisite (?)	do.
34	38	" 1	[illegible]z, [illegible] [illegible] of [illegible] (?)	do.
35	39	" 1	Do. do	do.
36	43	" 1	Bl[illegible] [illegible] [illegible], ("[illegible] slate" F.)	do.
37	44	" 1	Do. d[illegible]	do.
38	45	" 1	Bl[illegible] gy [illegible]	Below Twin falls, Menomoneek
39	46	" 1	Do.	d[illegible]
40	47	" 1	[illegible] ad chlori[illegible]	Little Bequinnesee falls, Menomoneek
41	49	" 1	[illegible] ad chlori[illegible], vein	d[illegible]
42	48	" 1	[illegible] ad chlori[illegible], containing copper pyrites	d[illegible]
43	50	" 1	[illegible]in of [illegible] in sl[illegible], with octahedral crystals of magnetic iron	d[illegible]
44	51	" 1	Blue argill[illegible] sl[illegible]te, ("roofing slate" F.)	d[illegible]
45	52	" 1	Do. do.	d[illegible]
46	53	" 1	Talcose [illegible]	Big [illegible] falls, Menomoneek
47	54	" 1	Do	do.
48	55	" 1	[illegible] [illegible], [illegible]sist[illegible] of [illegible]tz and mica, gneissoid	do.
49	56	" 1	[illegible] [illegible] in [illegible], with a little serpentine and white magnesian limestone	[illegible]falls, Menomoneek
50	57	" 1	Magnesian [illegible] in [illegible]ntine, veinstone	do.
51	58	" 1	Diall[illegible] [illegible], ("s[illegible]" F.)	do.
52	59	" 1	Do. do	do.
53	60	" 1	Sienite, pr[illegible]cipally [illegible] [illegible]de	do.
54	61	" 1	[illegible] of [illegible] feld[illegible]	do.
55	62	" 1	Do	do.
56	63	" 1	[illegible] with [illegible] of [illegible] pyrites	do.
57	64	" 1	[illegible] with [illegible] [illegible]	$2\frac{1}{2}$ mil[illegible] [illegible] Sturgeon falls, Menomoneek.
58	65	" 1	Do. do.	do.
59	66	" 1	[illegible], (" [illegible]" F.)	Head of [illegible] falls, [illegible]
60	67	" 1	[illegible] [illegible]" F.)	Head isl'd above Pem. falls, [illegible]
61	106	" 1	[illegible] trap (" [illegible] trap" F.)	Quiver falls, [illegible]
62	107	" 1	[illegible], li [illegible]een, ("porphyry" F.)	d[illegible]
63	108	" 1	Do. d[illegible] do	do.
64	14	" 1	Decomposed [illegible] limestone, lower silurian	Near the [illegible]uth of Menomoneek
65	17	" 1	Do. do.	d[illegible]
66	15	" 1	[illegible] li[illegible]nestone, lower silurian	d[illegible]
67	16	" 1	Do. do	d[illegible]
68	18	" 1	Do. d[illegible]	At the m[illegible] of Menomoneek
69	19	" 1	Do. d[illegible]	d[illegible]
70	20	" 1	Brown [illegible] limestone, lower [illegible]; *no* "organic remains"	d[illegible]
71	73	" 1	[illegible] gray [illegible] [illegible], ("marble" F.)	4, 31, 27, [illegible] 28, Machigamig river
72	74	" 1	[illegible] [illegible] [illegible] li[illegible]	d[illegible]
73	68	" 1	[illegible]act [illegible] li[illegible] [illegible] ad pink colored ("marble" F.)	44, 31, 27, M[illegible]igamig river

Catalogue of rocks, minerals, and ores, collected by J. W. Foster—Continued.

Progressive No.	No. of specimens.	No. of box.	Description.	Locality.
74	69	F 1	[illegible]t magnesian limestone, drab and pink colored, ("marble" F.)	44, 31, 27, Machigamig river
75	70	" 1	Do. ... do ... do	d[illegible]
76	72	" 1	[illegible] ... do ... do	d[illegible]
77	71	" 1	Do. ... do ... do	44, 30, 27, Machigamig river
78	77	" 1	[illegible]a slate	[illegible], No. 9
79	78	" 1	Do.	[illegible]g ri[illegible], (Postage No 9)
80	80	" 1	[illegible]a [illegible]late with large crystals of mica, ("granite" F.)	[illegible], [illegible], 3, [illegible]amig river
81	81	" 1	Do. ... do ... do	do
82	82	" 1	G[illegible]nite	42, 30, 33
83	83	" 1	Do.	45, 30, 5
84	79	" 1	Gr[illegible]nite, coarse without, (apparently a boulder.)	46, 29, 30
85	90	" 1	[illegible]t hornblende rock, ("amphibole rock" F.)	46, 29, 31
86	84	" 1	[illegible]a [illegible]te with a little epidote with the iron, ("metamorphic rock" F.)	46, 30, 31
87	85	" 1	[illegible]us specular iron ore with red silicious bands; too silicious for working ores	do
88	86	" 1	Do. ... do ... do	do
89	87	" 1	Do. ... do ... do	do
90	89	" 1	Do. ... do ... do	do
91	88	" 1	Mi[illegible]s [illegible]r iron ore, wavy with nodules of silex; too silicious for working [illegible]	d[illegible]
92	103	" 1	Mi[illegible]s [illegible]ular iron ore, rich and pure	d[illegible]
93	105	" 1	Do.	d[illegible]
94	104	" 1	Mixture of magnetic and specular iron ore, very rich	d[illegible]
95	75	" 1	[illegible]e slate	44, 31, [illegible]amig falls
96	76	" 1	Do.	do
97	91	" 1	[illegible]t [illegible], ("amphibole" F.)	50, 33, [illegible], Fall river
98	92	" 1	[illegible]s slate, ("chlorite rock" F.)	50, 33, [illegible], [illegible]ar S. line of Fall river
99	93	" 1	Do. ... do	do
100	95	" 1	[illegible]c iron ore	48, 30, 20, [illegible]W. ¼ section Sagiaginő
101	94	" 1	Do.	48, 31, 20, [illegible]W. ¼ section Sagiaginő
102	96	" 1	Do.	d[illegible]
103	97	" 1	[illegible]t [illegible]z rock ("amphibole" F.)	48, 31, 17, [illegible]W. ¼ section Sagiaginő
104	98	" 1	[illegible]r quartz rock, ("metamorphic" F.)	do

105	109	W 1	Gray quartz rock, (quartz and feldspar, "metamorphic" F.)	do.
106	99	F 1	Gneissoid granite	48, 31, 17, SW. ¼ section Sagiagino
107	100	" 1	Do.	do.
108	101	" 1	Do.	40, 33, N. part of Sagiagino
109	102	" 1	Hornblende rock, ("sienite" F.)	40, 32

Catalogue of the rocks, minerals, &c., collected on the district between Portage and Montreal river, during the years 1847 *and* 1848, *by J. D. Whitney.*

Progressive No.	No. of specimens.	No. of box.	Description.	Locality.
1	1	W 1	Mixture of [illegible] and a little quartz, very rich in native copper [illegible] through the mass. This [illegible] is [illegible] to yield 60 per cent.	52, 37, 36, Algonquin Mining Company
2	2	" 1	Same as No. 1, but not quite so rich in copper. The mixture has a tendency to [illegible], the copper [illegible] being in [illegible] or [illegible] masses, and a [illegible] with red [illegible]	do.
3	3	" 1	Rock resembling No. 2, but more amygdaloidal, the [illegible] being an [illegible] trap, with [illegible] of quartz. The [illegible] of quartz are [illegible] by a [illegible] of [illegible]. This specimen contains but little copper and that in the quartz amygdules	do.
4	4	" 1	[illegible] of a vein of quartz, 4 inches wide, with [illegible] of [illegible] to trap on the [illegible]. This quartz [illegible] 4 to 5 per cent. of [illegible] copper [illegible] through it in fine [illegible]	51, 37, 16, Douglas Houghton Mining Co.
5	5	" 1	Vein of quartz, colored rose red by [illegible] of copper, metallic copper [illegible] through it in [illegible]. [illegible] copper [illegible] with the quartz	do.
6	6	" 1	Same as No. 5, [illegible] mixed with the quartz	do.
7	7	" 1	Quartz colored by [illegible] of copper, with [illegible] of [illegible] and [illegible] metallic copper. One side of the specimen is covered with crystals of quartz and red feldspar	do.
8	8	" 1	[illegible] red feldspar and quartz in [illegible] and quartz with [illegible] copper	do.
9	9	" 1	Group of [illegible] red feldspar in [illegible] and [illegible] rock containing native copper	do.
10	130	" 1	[illegible] greenstone trap	51, 37, 16, shaft of Douglas Houghton Mining Company

Catalogue of rocks, minerals, and ores, collected by J. D. Whitney.—Continued.

Progressive No.	No. of specimens.	No. of box.	Description.	Locality.
11	10	W 1	A [illegible] of trap [illegible] [illegible] [illegible] into a [illegible] trap. The specimen [illegible] to be [illegible] [illegible] [illegible] [illegible] with a little quartz disseminated [illegible]	51, 37, 16, from a trap bluff
12	11	" 1	[illegible] of [illegible] [illegible] [illegible] [illegible] with No. 12, (13)	50, 39, 16, Minnesota Company
13	12	" 1	[illegible] [illegible] [illegible] of [illegible] [illegible] with [illegible] oxide of iron and [illegible] [illegible]; occurs with [illegible] [illegible] irregularly scattered through it	do.
14	13	" 1	Epidote [illegible] [illegible] [illegible] with [illegible] [illegible]	50, 39, 15, Minnesota Company
15	14	" 1	[illegible], [illegible] with thin [illegible] of copper, principally on faces of joints of [illegible]	do.
16	15	" 1	[illegible] [illegible] [illegible] [illegible] [illegible] an [illegible] [illegible] [illegible]	50, 39, 22, Ontonagon Company
17	16	" 1	[illegible] [illegible] [illegible] [illegible] with [illegible] [illegible]	do. do.
18	17	" 1	[illegible] [illegible] with [illegible] of [illegible] [illegible] [illegible]. spar coated with epidote	50, 39, 16, in bed of brook near cabins
19	18	" 1	Yellow [illegible] [illegible] [illegible] [illegible] [illegible], occurs mixed with epidote and trap, W)	do. do.
20	19	" 1	[illegible] [illegible] [illegible] with [illegible] [illegible] of [illegible]	50, 39, 19, Randolph's
21	20	" 1	[illegible] with [illegible] [illegible] [illegible] [illegible]	50, 39, 31, Ontonagon Co., from drift
22	21	" 1	M [illegible] [illegible], [illegible] [illegible] [illegible], [illegible] filled with [illegible], thin [illegible] of [illegible] [illegible] [illegible] [illegible] the [illegible] surface of [illegible] [illegible] [illegible] of [illegible] [illegible] [illegible] [illegible] of [illegible] scales, tar-[illegible] with [illegible] [illegible] [illegible]	50, 40, 36, Ontonagon Co., from drift
23	22	" 1	R[illegible] [illegible] No. 21 (22) [illegible] [illegible] amygdaloidal	do. do.
24	23	" 1	[illegible] [illegible] of [illegible] [illegible] [illegible] [illegible] [illegible] [illegible] [illegible], resembling old boiler copper	do. do.
25	24	" 1	[illegible] [illegible] [illegible] [illegible] of [illegible], [illegible] [illegible]	do. do.
26	25	" 1	[illegible] [illegible], [illegible] filled with [illegible] epidote	do. do.
27	26	" 1	[illegible] [illegible] [illegible], [illegible] [illegible], [illegible] into small angular fragments, [illegible] a [illegible] to [illegible] [illegible]ure, and has fine specks of [illegible] [illegible] through it; [illegible] of the [illegible] round the mine is of this [illegible], and it [illegible] [illegible] into trap	do. do.
28	27	" 1	Brown jasper	
29	28	" 1	E [illegible] [illegible] [illegible] [illegible] [illegible] [illegible] of [illegible]	35, United States Loc.
30	29	" 1	A [illegible] [illegible] [illegible], [illegible] [illegible] filled with epidote and quartz, principally the	

			former	do.
31	30	" 1	Rock breccia, a mixture of trap rock, epidote, calc. spar, and quartz, in drift	34, United States Loc., near cabin
32	31	" 1	Breccia of trap and sandstone	36, near south line
33	32	" 1	Red porphyry with crystals of red and white feldspar ("quartzose porphyry, base red quartzose rock, crystals of white feldspar sparsely scattered through it," W)	34, Half mile east of western boundary of township High-hill, named by us Porphyry, H. M
34	33	" 1	Gray silicious sulphuret of copper and crystallized sulphate of baryta implanted on it	18, Mendenhall, from shaft
35	34	" 1	Crystallized sulphate of baryta	18, Mendenhall, from shaft, in conglomerate.
36	35	" 1	Missing ("carbonate of lime, six sided prisms and hemitropes of a rare form on a vein of sulphuret of copper," W.)	do. do.
37	36	" 1	Prismatic slate ("black argillaceous sandstone, breaking into rhombohedral fragments," W.)	18, Mendenhall, in bed of brook near cabins.
38	37	" 1	Prismatic slate ("same as No. 36, rhombohedron with very regular sides, natural fracture of sandstone," W.)	do. do.
39	38	" 1	Massive epidote with fine particles of native copper disseminated through it, say 10 to 15 per cent	49, 41, 12, Ohio Trap-rock Co., northwest corner from principal shaft
40	39	" 1	Quartz with native copper	do. do.
41	40	" 1	Epidote with native copper	do. do.
42	41	" 1	Radiated epidote	do. do.
43	42	" 1	Quartz and epidote with incrustation of radiated epidote, native copper in the quartz	do. do.
44	43	" 1	Crystallized quartz and radiated epidote	do. do.
45	44	" 1	Calcareous spar and native copper	do. do.
46	45	" 1	Impure epidote with a small per centage of copper	do. do.
47	46	" 1	Native copper encrusted with earthy matter stained by green carbonate copper.	49, 41, 12, Ohio Trap-rock Co., from vein
48	47	" 1	Radiated epidote in quartz with a small per centage of native copper scattered throughout	11, Boston & Lake Superior Co., 2° on broken shaft
49	48	" 1	Epidote and quartz with native copper	11, American Exploring Co
50	49	" 1	Epidote with copper scattered through the mass in fine particles, per centage small	do.
51	50	" 1	Radiated epidote in quartz with native copper	do.
52	51	" 1	Prehnite calc. spar and quartz	9, American Exploring Co., western location, in bed of brook near cabins
53	52	" 1	Dark slaty sandstone, ripple marked	51, 42, 12, bed of Iron river
54	53	" 1	Red slaty sandstone, overlaid by amygdaloidal trap	16 and 21, on line between 16 and 21, $\frac{3}{4}$ miles west of east corner

Catalogue of rocks, minerals, and ores, collected by J. D. Whitney—Continued.

Progressive No.	No. of specimens.	No. of box.	Description.	Locality.
55	54	W 1	Amygdaloidal trap, characteristic base reddish trap, amygdules filled with chlorite	16 and 21, on back of hill
56	55	" 1	Altered sandstone, or dark brown imperfect jasper, has a trappose structure	51, 42, 16, and 21, position of summit of hill between 53 and 54
57	56	" 1	Bed of chloritic trap, amygdaloidal, amygdules filled with chlorite	27, Union river, Minnesota Co
58	57	" 1	Same rock, but base of amygdaloid more chloritic, native copper in scales on the rock	do.
59	58	" 1	Imperfect elongated crystals of native copper, from drift	do.
60	59	" 1	Amygdaloidal chloritic trap, with fine particles of native copper scattered through it	27, Union river, Minnesota Co., from south drift
61	60	" 1	Same as No. 59, copper seems to be confined to the surface of natural fracture	do. do.
62	61	" 1	Sandstone with coating of native copper, from drift of	Union river, Minnesota Co
63	62	" 1	Slaty sandstone at junction with trap	In bed of Union river, near mine
64	63	" 1	Quartz and calc. spar colored by copper, in trap	do.
65	64	" 1	Quartz and Jacksonite from vein in trap	22, Boston Mining Co
66	65	" 1	Same specimen contains a few fine particles of native copper	do.
67	66	" 1	Polished surface of trap (slicken sides) from shaft of	do.
68	67	" 1	Breccia of sandstone and conglomerate	30 and 19, ½ mile east of western boundary of township
69	68	" 1	Close grained sandstone	do.
70	69	" 1	Quartzose rock, imperfect jasper	do.
71	79	" 1	Amygdaloidal trap rock; amygdules filled with chlorite	30 and 19, bed of Carp river
72	71	" 1	Nodules of rock with red oxide of copper	49, 42, Boyd's location
73	72	" 1	Trap with native copper	do.
74	73	" 1	Trap stained with red oxide of copper, with green carb. of native copper	do.
75	74	" 1	Epidote rock	do.
76	75	" 1	Epidote rock with nodules of quartz and native copper	49, 42
77	76	" 1	Breccia, brown jasper, and epidote, little native copper	49, 42
78	77	" 1	Epidote trap with a little copper	48, 42, 6, Charter Oak Co
79	78	" 1	Epidote trap with small grains of copper	48, 42, 5. do.
80	79	" 1	Trap	48, 42, 6. do.
81	80	" 1	Hornblende rock barely stratified. ("Hornblende and quartz rock," W.)	46, 41, 24

82	81	" 1	Chlorite and red feldspar, forming veins in No. 80	46, 41, 24
83	82	" 1	Mica slate containing small garnets	46, 41, 35
84	83	" 1	[illegible]le [illegible]k	45, 43, 1
85	84	" 1	Fine grained mica slate	do.
86	85	" 1	Thin strata of metallic copper, coated with red oxide in sandstone; "from red oxide vein," W.	51, 43, 14, Isle Royal Co's. location
87	86	" 1	Fragment of one of the rounded masses of sandstone and spar found between trap and sandstone	do.
88	87	" 1	Sandstone breccia with sulphuret of copper and a little carbonate	51, 43, 27, Delavan Co.
89	88	" 1	; [illegible]ed carb. lime in sandstone breccia, with a little sulphuret of copper	do.
90	89	" 1	Amygdaloidal trap; cavities filled with crystallized epidote on the exterior, and quartzose within	do.
91	90	" 1	Breccia composed of jasper in particles in an impure epidote base, with much calc. spar	do.
92	91	" 1	Amygdaloidal trap; cavities filled with a yellow pulverulent substance supposed to be decomposed epidote (?)	51, 43, 32, Croton Co
93	92	" 1	Massive epidote rock	do.
94	93	" 1	Epidote and native copper with some quartz	51, 43, 30, Isle Royal Co
95	94	" 1	Trap with epidote veins; copper in the epidote	
96	95	" 1	Altered sandstone and jasper forming a ledge	51, 43, 32 and 33, ¼ mile past south boundary of township
97	96	" 1	Jasper	do.
98	97	" 1	Red and white quartzose rock	51, 43, 32, near summit of hill
99	98	" 1	Near junction of trap and quartzose rock	do.
100	99	" 1	Jasper and quartz rock	50, 43, 1, [illegible]st corner
101	100	" 1	Brown sandstone	50, 43, 12, 1½ miles south of northern boundary of township on E. R. line
102	101	" 1	Porphyry, feldspar base; red feldspar, crystals, and quartz disseminated through it	49, 43, 33 and 34, on S. boundary
103	102	" 1	A dark mineral like labradorite scattered through the base	do.
104	103	" 1	Brown red porphyry. ("Red porphyritic trap," W)	50, 42, 32, (64 chains)
105	104	" 1	Red porphyritic trap	49, 42, 14, (?)
106	105	" 1	Mixture of trap, epidote, and calc. spar	50, 44, Atlas Mining Co
107	106	" 1	Mixture of trap with very minute particles of copper	do.
108	107	" 1	Mixture of trap with crystallized [illegible]	do.
109	108	" 1	Crystallized quartz, prehnite, and datholite	do.
110	109	" 1	[illegible]ct trap. Bed of Presque Isle river	49, 45, 1 location 149
111	110	" 1	Very fine grained compact trap	Tyler's location
112	111	" 1	Laumonite	do.
113	112	" 1	Quartz, prehnite, and a minute film of sulphuret of copper	do.
114	113	" 1	Greenstone trap, contains fine particles of iron pyrites	47, 45, 19

Catalogue of rocks, minerals, and ores, collected by J. D. Whitney.—Continued.

Progressive No.	No. of specimens.	No. of box.	Description.	Locality.
115	114	W 1	Very fine grained greenstone	49, 46, 9
116	115	" 1	Fine dark argillaceous sandstone, thin layers	Mouth of Black river
117	116	" 1	Soft amygdaloidal white rock; amygdules filled with white feldspar. ("Epidote rock," W.)	32, Black River Mining Co
118	117	" 1	Vein of quartz in trap with a few specks of [illegible] [illegible]ate of [illegible]r	32, bed of Black river at shaft
119	118	" 1	Amygdaloid produced by fusion of trap and sandstone. (Nondescript rock made up of a greenish [illegible], trap, and oxide of iron.)	do.
120	119	" 1	Granite composed mainly of quartz and feldspar; the feldspar largely predominates, and is both white and red, with a few minute specks of black mica and chlorite	47, 46, 31
122	121	" 1	Granite composed principally of greyish green feldspar and quartz	do.
123	122	" 1	Hornblende rock containing minute specks of sulphate of iron	47, 46, 1
124	123	" 1	Do. do.	do.
125	124	" 1	Magnetic oxide of iron in quartz and feldspar, granite	
126	125	" 1	Native copper in bluish green quartzose rock, colored by chlorite	48, 49, loc. of Montreal River Mining Co.
127	126	" 1	Quartzose seam in amygdaloidal trap	48, 49, from a so called vein of this Co.
128	127	" 1	[illegible] gradually passing into trap	
129	128	" 1	Missing	
130	129	" 1	Do.	
131	131	" 1	Large mass of native copper in veinstone, containing calc. spar with chlorite on the border; red feldspar mixed with the copper	No locality given

Catalogue of geological specimens collected by Dr. D. D. OWEN, *and deposited in the Smithsonian Institution by the Commissioner of the Land Office, December,* 1851.

1. Amethystine quartz, Prince's Bay, Lake Superior.
2. Lepidodendron, Muscatine quarries, Iowa.
3. do. do. do.
4. Pecopteris, do. do.
5. Calc. tufa., St. Croix.
6 and 7. Tutenmergel, near Amsterdam, Des Moines R., Iowa.
8 and 9. Lithostrotion ananas, D'Orb., Iowa R., Dev.
10 and 11. Tutenmergel, Keith's Rapids, Des Moines R., Iowa.
12. Plaster stone, 5 miles below Lizard Fork, Des Moines.
13. Cannel coal, Barcroft bank, near Marion, Missouri.
14. Palæotherium Proutii, 2 lower jaw, Bad Lands, Nebraska,
15. Ripple marked sandstone, South shore, Lake Superior.
16. do. do. do.
17. Fossil turtle, Bad Lands, Nebraska.
18. Shell beds of the limestone of the Iowa, Devonian.
19. Calc. spar crystals, Falls St. Croix.
20. Lingula bed, F. 1, b. of report, Falls St. Croix.
21. do. do. do.
22. do. do. do.
23. Marine Mill trilobite grit, 4th trilobite bed of report, St. Croix.
24. Portion of large ammonite, Fox Hills, Nebraska.
25. do. do. do.
26. do. do. do.
27. Third trilobite bed, Mountain Island, Upper Miss.
28. do. do. do.
29. do. near Mouth Miniskah,
30. do. do. do.
31. Cannel coal, on branch of Aux Vasse, Callaway Co., Missouri.
32. Coralline beds of Iowa city, containing Alveolites, Celleporites of D'Orb., Calamapora polymorpha of Goldf., pl. 27, fig. 3.
33. Do., containing Favosites cronigera, D'Orb.
34. Do., containing both corals. Pl. 27, fig. 3.
35. Orthis umbraculum, opposite Iowa Point, Missouri R.
36. Selenite from the upper Carbs. limestone, Indian Creek, Iowa.
37. Leptæna limestone, containing L. planumbona, 3 miles above Savannah, Wisconsin.
38. Do., containing L. sericea.
39.
40. Bituminous limestone, containing Asaphus (Isotelus) megistos of Locke, Otter creek, Turkey R , Iowa.
41. Part of scapula of Palæotherium Proutii, Bad lands.
42. Casts of Leptæna, undet, Falls St. Anthony, F. 3, a of report.
43. Oolitic limestone, Lower Carbs. limestone, Burlington, Iowa.
44. Retepora Archimedes, Keokuck Rapids.
45. Encrinital limestone from the Lower Carb. limestone of Burlingtou, Iowa.
46. Do., containing Pentremites melo.

47. Productal limestone, containing P. Cancrini, 10 miles below Fort Kearney, Missouri river.
48. Spirifer striatus limestone, upper beds of Carb. limestone of Augusta, Iowa.
49. Productus punctatus, Keokuk Rapids, Miss.
50. Do.
51. Do.
52. Do.
53. Fusulina cylindrica in Carboniferous limestone, 10 miles below Fort Kearney, Missonri.
54. Fucoidal beds, Marine Mills, St. Croix, F 1, d, in part.
55. Lithostrotion, probably a var. of basaltica, Sugar creek near the Iowa line.
56. Stromatopora concentrica, Iowa city, Dev.
57. Productal limestone, a few miles above the Racoon Forks on the Des Moines River.
58. Head of femur of Palæotherium Proutii? Bad Lands.
59. Magnesian limestone, with green particles of silicate of iron disseminated, intercalated with the lower sandstones, F. 1, of report. (Lower Silurian date,) Sac Prairie, Wisconsin river.
60. Magnesian limestone, intercalated with F. 1, 14 miles above Sac Prairie.
61. Lower sandstone, F 1 of report. Dalles of the Wisconsin river.
62. Lower sandstone, F 1, (Lower Silurian date,) 7 miles below Helena, Wisconsin river.
63. Magnesio-calcareous bed containing impressions of Orthis intercalated in F 1. Section 5 miles above Plymouth, Wisconsin river, 138 feet above river.
64. Magnesio-calcareous rock, intercalated in F 1, 143 ft. above Wisconsin river, 5 miles above Plymouth. Contains remains of encrinites.
65. Lower sandstone, F 1. Petenwell Peak, 200 ft. above the Wisconsin, (Lower Silurian date.)
66. Do. of Castle Rock, 65 feet above Wisconsin river.
67. Green beds of F 1 d. charged with silicate of iron. Miniskah Pass, Upper Mississippi.
68. Brown magn. calc. bed of F 1 d. Miniskah, Upper Mississippi.
69. Lower sandstone of Petenwell Peak, 80 feet above Wisconsin.
70. Lower sandstone, F 1, 5¾ miles east of Adams, Barraboo river.
71. Quartzite, 5¾ m. e. of Adams, Barraboo river, Wisconsin.
72. Do. gray.
73. Red beds of Lower sandstone, F 1, 1 m. above Fortification Rock, Wisconsin river.
73[1]. Yellowish-red beds of F 1. Castle Rock, 35 feet above the Wisconsin river.
74. Quartzite in F 1, between the Wisconsin river and Adams on the Barraboo.
75. Reddish quartzite 2½ m. e. of Adams, on the Barraboo river, Wisconsin.
76. Light pink quartzite, sec. 34, township 12, R. 6 east of 4th P M, Wisconsin.
77. Gray quartzite, Devil's Lake, Wisconsin

78. Pink quartzite, F 1, Devil's Lake, Wisconsin.
79. Conglomerate of F 1, Devil's Lake, Wisconsin.
80. Obolus beds of F 1, b. Miniskah River.
81. Lower Magnesian Limestone, F 2, 3 miles above Lansing Iowa.
82. Lower Magnesian Limestone, F 2, Cape Winnebago, Upper Mississippi.
83. Red Conglomerate, below Lac Travers, Snake River, Minnesota.
84. Specular Iron, associated with the quartzite, 2½ m. E. of Adams, Barraboo River, Wisconsin.
85. Do. with the milky quartz.
86. Cherty masses, in F 2, b. near Lanzing, Iowa.
87. Cellular quartz, in F 2, b. do. in the lead bearing beds.
88. Rugged cherty beds of Lower Magnesian Limestone, (lead bearing beds,) near the mouth of the Kickapoo, Wisconsin.
89. Lower Magnesian Limestone, F 2, a. Prairie á la Crosse, Wisconsin.
90. Do. 20 feet below the top of section.
91. Crystallizations of hydrate brown oxide of iron, on chest in beds F 2, b. of Lower Magnesian Limestone. Prairie á la Crosse, Wisconsin.
92. Kikapoo Copper ore. Sterling's Diggings.
93. Kikapoo Lead ore, (Galena,) in F 2, b.
94. Coarse green Lingula grit, F 1, c. Lawrence creek, near the St. Croix River.
95. Coarse Lingula grit, F 1, c. Mountain Island, Wisconsin.
96. Amygdaloid asssociated with the trap of Snake River, Minnesota, near Lac Travers.
97. Do.
98. Trap of Snake River, ½ mile below Lac Travers, Minnesota.
99. Do. 2 miles below Lac Travers.
100. Trap of Kettle River, 3 m. above its mouth, Minnesota.
101. Do. 16 miles above its mouth.
102. Greenstone trap from the Range near the Falls of the St. Croix, Minnesota.
103. Porphyritic trap, Falls St. Croix, Minnesota.
104. Obolus grit, F. 1, b., nearly opposite old mouth of Black river, Mississippi river.
105. Slab, full of lingulas, &c., from the Falls St. Croix, F. 1, b.
106. Pebbly sandstone, of F. 1, a. L'Eau Clair.
107. Coarse sandstone, F. 1, a., six miles below the falls of the Chippewa, Wisconsin.
108. Fragmentary and concretionary bed of limestone, above the coralline beds at Iowa city. Dev.
109. Favosites basaltica, Cam. Calamopora of Goldf., pl. 26, fig. 4, from the coralline beds of Iowa city.
110. Do.
111. 5th trilobite of F. 1, near the base of La Grange Mountain, upper Mississippi.
112. 5th trilobite bed of F. 1 of Report, lake St. Croix, Minnesota.
113. Limestone containing Retepora prisca? Fenestela chætetes, &c. Upper carboniferous limestone, near mouth of Missouri.

114. Spirifer limestone, near top of the lower carboniferous series, Keokuk Rapids, Mississippi.

115. Do.

116. Iron stone, similar to the "black band" of the Scotch iron masters, near Bennington, and elsewhere on the Des Moines river.

CATALOGUE
OF
BERLANDIER'S HISTORICAL AND GEOGRAPHICAL MSS.*

In the year 1826 Luis Berlandier, historian, geographer, and naturalist, a native of Switzerland, arrived in Mexico for the purpose of making researches in that republic. He died near Matamoros in 1851. The result of his extensive labors are in manuscripts, now deposited at the Smithsonian Institution, comprising an amount of information of the country west of the Sabine of the highest importance.

The following is a brief catalogue of the MSS.:

Travels in Mexico and Texas, 1826 to 1834, inclusive. Containing notes upon the statistics, early settlements, and Indian tribes between the Sabine and Pacific, &c., &c., &c.—7 vols.

Travels in Mexico, 1828–'30. Comprising interesting notes of the early settlers of Texas, by the Spanish and French; account of the ancient Indian tribes, &c., &c.—3 vols.

Geography and statistics of the republic of Mexico.

History of the Indian tribes that formerly ranged from the Sabine to the gulf of California.—2 vols.

Notes upon the different Indian tribes of the ancient republic.—1 vol.

Vocabularies of different tribes bordering the Rio Grande.—1 vol.

Of the Cotonames, Carrissos.—1 vol.

Of Indians that formerly lived to the northeast of Texas.—1 vol.

Of different tribes in the neighborhood of the missions.—1 vol.

Revolt of the Tepeguanas, 1616.—1 vol.

Indian assassinations of the priests.—1 vol.

Of the Texian Indians. Buit.—1 vol.

Indians of Texas and Coahuila; fertility of their soil, &c.—1 vol.

Medicine of the ancient and modern Indians of Mexico.—1 vol.

Paintings of thirty different Indian tribes.—1 vol.

History of the agriculture of ancient and modern Mexico.—1 vol.

Regulations of the ancient Presidios, 1772.

1.—Travels in Tamaulipas and New Leon, 1844.

2.— " " Tamaulipas, San Luis Potosi, 1846.

3.— " " the country west and south of Matamoros, 1847.

The above vols., 1, 2, 3, of travels, give an interesting history of the country adjacent to the Sierra Madre.

March and espionage of the American army from Corpus Christi till the occupation of Matamoros.—1 vol.

Geographical Gazetteer of the territory lying between the Sabine and Pacific, comprising a history of places, situations, positions, &c., &c.—12 vols.

Geography of ancient and modern Mexico.—1 vol. notes.

---

* See p. 13 of this Report.

Geography of Puebla, Mexico, Mechoacan, Oaxaca. Position of places in the above Archbishoprics.—1 vol. notes.

Diary of the Commission of Limits in Northern Mexico, 1830.—3 vols.

Diary of Gen. Rivera, New Mexico and Texas, 1728.—1 vol.

Com. Limits, Geography and stat. Physiques, &c., &c., by various authors, with notes by Berlandier.—Notes.

Astronomical observations made in Northern Mexico, Texas, &c.—6 volumes.

Dictionary. Geology of the rocks and minerals between the Sabine and Sierra Madre.

Upon the Meteorology of Texas and the valley of the Rio Grande, comprising some important deductions in the science.—15 vols.

Observations, cyanometer, pendelum.—2 vols.

Disquisitions upon the Fevers of the lower Rio Grande, &c., &c., &c.—Notes.

Maps of States accurately and scientifically projected by Berlandier, member of the Geographical Society, viz: Tamaulipas, Vera Cruz, San Luis Potosi, Zacatacas, Juanaxata, Orirava, Tampico and adjacent country. Gulf of Mexico, vicinity of Vera Cruz.

Maps in MSS. of journeys, routes, valleys, defiles, suburbs of towns, villages, &c., &c., of the country lying between the Sabine and Rio Grande and valley of Mexico.

1.—Topography of routes and sections in New Leon, Tamaulipas, San Luis Potosi, made in 1844, with distances.

do. do. from San Luis to Matehuala, distances, &c.

do. do. from Matamoros to Morelos, Guajuco, &c.

2.— do. from Victoria to Tampico, Soto la Mariana Santander.

do. Matehuala to Boquillo, Palo Blanco to Missions.

do. Tampico to the city of Mexico.

do. Tampico to Matamoros, accompanied with notes.

3.—Topography in detail of the route from San Antonia to Laredo, in Tamaulipas, &c., &c.

Of the country between Matamoros, Barreales, Mosquete, Caracol and Anacahuetas, Tamaulipas. Survey of the Rio Grande from the mouth to San Elirario, plans of Presidios, &c., &c. Maps and topography of different portions of the country south of the Rio Grande, between Reynosa and San Fernando. 12 MSS. Tampico and its environs, lower Tamaulipas, San Patricio and Monclova, city and environs of Tampico, plans of Tamaulipas, of different sections of the State, &c., &c., and 13 maps in MSS. Various routes of ancient Texas, giving positions of the Indian tribes that formerly inhabited Missions. Different plans of the State, sections, ancient maps, &c., &c. 25 maps in MSS.

Upper Tamaulipas, Coahuila, N. Leon, with topography in detail of various routes in the centre of the Republic, bars and entrances of the coast south of Brasos Santiago, &c., &c., &c. 23 maps in MMS.

Maps of different portions of the coast between Tampico and River Goasacoalco, 8 MSS.

Department of Orizava, Jalapa, Canton of Cordova, Orirava, Cosamaloapan, plan of Cordova and Birava cities, &c.; of the Isthmus of Tehuantepec; State of Mexico, of the Lakes, Valley, Tenango, Queretaro. The Huasteca, San Luis, routes through the Sierra Madre east and north, valley of Vernallo, Mateuala to the north and east, &c., &c., 16 MSS.

Topography in detail, of the country lying between San Luis and San Fernando, Gulf coast, &c., &c., 6 MSS.

CIRCULAR.

[See page 23 of this report.]

SMITHSONIAN INSTITUTION,
Washington, March 22, 1855.

Nearly five years have elapsed since the publication of a report on the Public Libraries in the United States by the Smithsonian Institution. This report contained all the information respecting American Libraries which could be collected at that time; but great changes have taken place in the Libraries then in existence, numerous others have since been established, and a new and enlarged edition of the work, it is believed, will supply a want much felt. The following circular has therefore been prepared for the purpose of collecting information relative to Libraries, and it is particularly desired that the answers be transmitted without delay to this Institution. As some of the questions may relate to points which have not heretofore received your attention, it is suggested that the replies be now forwarded to those only which can be answered at once, and that the other blanks be filled up and returned, when the materials can be collected.

It is a part of the original plan of the Smithsonian Institution to render it a centre of bibliographical knowledge, and for this purpose it is deemed highly desirable to collect cataloges of all the libraries in the country. The student can then learn where to find any particular book by addressing the Smithsonian Institution.

It is suggested that catalogues of all libraries be printed, in order that they may be rendered more generally useful, and it is earnestly requested that copies of these be sent to the Smithsonian Institution.

A duplicate circular is enclosed, which you are requested to fill up at the end of the present year.

A copy of the Report will be sent to every Library in the United States, and another also to the individual furnishing information.

JOSEPH HENRY,
Secretary Smithsonian Institution.

SMITHSONIAN REPORT ON PUBLIC LIBRARIES IN THE UNITED STATES.

Please return this paper with the answers to the Smithsonian Institution, Washington, D. C.

1. Name of Library.
2. Locality.
3. Name and address of the Librarian?
4. Officers employed, and their salaries?
5. When founded, and by whom.
6. How supported and governed.

7. Receipts from all sources during 1854, $
8. Expenditures during 1854 for Books, $
    " " Binding,
    " " Periodicals,
    Salaries,
    " " Incidentals,
9. Who are entitled to use the Library?
10. On what terms?
11. Is it a reference or a Lending Library?
    Special, or Miscellaneous?
12. Are the books arranged on the shelves by subjects?
    If not, what is the arrangement?
13. How many days and hours is the Library open?
14. How many *volumes* were lent during 1854?
15. How many *persons* have borrowed books during 1854?
16. What number of volumes in the Library are in the English language?—French?—
    German?—Spanish?—Other Modern Languages?—Latin?—Greek?—Hebrew?—Oriental?—
17. What is the date of the last printed Catalogue?
    Cost of its publication, size, and number printed?
18. What system of classification is adopted in the construction of the Catalogue?
19. If possible, state what number of books have been read during 1854, in the different classes of literature—how many works of theology, law, medicine, fiction, &c.—and what particular books have been most called for.
20. On the 1st of January, 1855, how many books, &c., in the Library?

	Books.	Pamphlets.	Manuscripts.	Maps.	Music.	Engravings.	Specimens of fine arts.	Other articles, as coins, medals, &c.	Total.
Purchases.......									
Donations.......									
Exchanges.......									
Total........									

21. What collections of Natural History are connected in any way with the Library?
22. What is the nature and extent of these collections?
23. What other Natural History collections, public or private, are found in your neighborhood, and what is their character?
24. Have any regular publications of Memoirs, Transactions, Proceedings, &c., been made by any Institution or Society with which the Library is connected, and of what character and extent?
25. Please send copies of your Catalogue, Charter, Rules and Regulations, &c., and any information respecting the history or condi-

tion of the Library which you desire to be included in the Report; also a list of all Reviews, Magazines, and Newspapers taken regularly in your library or reading-room.

Copyright Laws, &c., relating to the Smithsonian Institution.

CIRCULAR.

SMITHSONIAN INSTITUTION, *Washington*, 1855.

SIR: Your attention is respectfully called to the fact that an act of Congress of August 10th, 1846, requires you to send to the library of the Smithsonian Institution a copy of any "*book, map, chart, musical composition, print, cut, or engraving*," which shall be copyrighted by you. The following is the law on the subject:

"*An act to establish the 'Smithsonian Institution,' &c.*

"SEC. 10. *And be it further enacted*, That the author or proprietor of any book, map, chart, musical composition, print, cut, or engraving, for which a copyright shall be secured under the existing acts of Congress, or those which shall hereafter be enacted respecting copyrights, shall, within three months from the publication of said book, map, chart, musical composition, print, cut, or engraving, deliver, or cause to be delivered, one copy of the same to the librarian of the Smithsonian Institution, and one copy to the librarian of the Congress Library, for the use of the said libraries.

"Approved August 10, 1846."

An act of Congress passed at its last session, and approved March 3d, 1855, contains the following section:

"SEC. 5. *And be it further enacted*, That all books, maps, and charts, or other publications entered for copyright, and which, under the act of August 10th, 1846, are required to be deposited in the Library of Congress, and in the Smithsonian Institution, may be sent through the mail free of postage, under such regulations as the Postmaster General may prescribe.'

"Approved March 3, 1855.

The following instructions have just been issued by the Postmaster General in reference to these acts:

"No. 35. Copyright books, charts, &c., [see law annexed,] required to be delivered to the Library of Congress or Smithsonian Institution, and which are entitled to pass free in the mail, should be superscribed 'Copyright for Congress Library,' or 'Smithsonian Institution,' as the case may be."

These provisions will enable you to send all your copyright publications to the Institution free of charge, and you are requested to forward them by mail, in the manner indicated.

Please inform us by letter when any articles are sent, and enclose a postage stamp if you wish a certificate of deposit to be returned.

Very respectfully, your obedient servant,

JOSEPH HENRY,
Secretary Smithsonian Institution.

CONTENTS.

REPORTS OF THE SECRETARY.

Page.
Letter from the Secretary to Hon. Linn Boyd 3
Letter from the Chancellor and Secretary to Congress 4
Officers and Regents of the Institution 5
Members ex-officio of the Institution 6
Honorary Members of the Institution 6
Report of the Secretary for 1854 7
Report of Professor S. F. Baird, Assistant Secretary 31
Donations to the Museum 42
List of Meteorological Stations and Observers 47
Meteorological Observers. New York system 51
Alphabetical List of Meteorological Observers 52

REPORTS OF COMMITTEES TO THE BOARD.

Report of the Executive Committee for 1854 57
General Statement of Expenditures 60
Fund Account 62
Report of the Building Committee for 1854 69

BOARD OF REGENTS.

Journal of the Board of Regents 72

EXPLORATIONS.

Report on American Explorations in 1853 and 1854. By S. F. Baird 79

LECTURES.

Lectures 98
"The Camel." By Hon. George P. Marsh 98
"On the Nature and Cure of the Bite of Serpents, and the Wounds of Poisoned Arrows." By Dr. D. Brainard 123
"The Zone of small Planets between Mars and Jupiter." By Professor E. Loomis 137
"The American Fire-Alarm Telegraph." By Dr. W. F. Channing 147
"The Union." By Professor Henry Reed 156
"Meteorology" By R. Russell, Esq. 181
Appendix to Mr. Russell's Lectures. By the Secretary of the Institution . 215

CORRESPONDENCE—PHYSICAL SCIENCE.

Page.

On Mr. John Wise's Observations and Inferences respecting the Phenomena of a Thunder Storm to which he was exposed during an Aerial Voyage, made by means of a Balloon, June 3, 1852, from Portsmouth, Ohio. By Dr. ROBERT HARE 224

The Climate of San Francisco. By Dr. H. GIBBONS 231

Meteorological Observations at Sacramento, California. By THOMAS M. LOGAN, M. D. 259

Meteorological Observations at Sacramento, California. By F. W. HATCH, M. D. 263

Remarks contributing to the Physical Geography of the North American Continent. By JULIUS FROEBEL 272

CORRESPONDENCE—NATURAL HISTORY.

Natural History of Beaver Islands, Michigan. By JAMES J. STRANG 282

Habits of the Black Bass of the Ohio (*Grystes fasciatus*). By JOHN EOFF 289

Natural History of the Country about Fort Ripley, Minnesota. By J. F. HEAD, Surgeon U. S. A 291

Habits of the Gopher of Illinois (*Geomys bursarius*). By J. B. PARVIN 293

Habits of a species of Salamander (*Amblystoma opacum*). By Rev. CHAS. MANN... 294

On the *Amblystoma luridum*, a Salamander inhabiting Wisconsin. By P. R. HOY.. 295

MISCELLANEOUS.

Diary of an Excursion to the Ruins of Abõ, Quarrã, and Gran Quivira, in New Mexico, under the command of Major JAMES HENRY CARLETON, U. S. A. 296

Report on the Fishes observed on the coasts of New Jersey and Long Island during the summer of 1854. By S. F. BAIRD 317

Catalogue of Rocks, Minerals, and Ores collected during the years 1847 and 1848, on the Geological Survey of the United States Mineral Lands in Michigan. By Dr. CHARLES T. JACKSON 338

Catalogue of Rocks, Minerals, Ores, and Fossils collected by Dr. JOHN LOCKE..... 367

Catalogue of Rocks, Minerals, &c., collected by J. W. FOSTER 384

Catalogue of Rocks, Minerals, &c., collected by J. D. WHITNEY 387

Catalogue of Geological Specimens, collected by Dr. D. D. OWEN 393

Catalogue of the Berlandier Collection of Manuscripts, Maps, &c 396

Circular sent for information respecting Libraries 398

Circular to Publishers respecting Copyrights 400

INDEX.

	Page.
Abbott, Dr. R. V., Table of Rain by	245,247
Aberdeen	212,213
Abiquiu	85,276
Abispah river	83,85
Aboriginal remains, attention directed to	11
Abó, Ruins of	300
Abramis versicolor	341
Absorption, Level of	226
Absorption, Magendie's Experiments on	129
Abstinence of Camel	109
Acacia	118
Academy of Natural Sciences	35,42
Academy of Natural Sciences, Cal., Magnetic Instruments for	16
Academy of Sciences at Paris, Memoir on Poisons	126
Acanthocottus virginianus (*common Sculpin*)	328
Achievements of Man	98
Achirus mollis (*New York sole*)	350
Achromatic Microscope, Description of	26
Ackley, Dr	38
Acquia Madre	277
Adams, J. Quincy, Language of, respecting Will of Smithson	7
Adams, Professor C. B	94
Adaptation of Camel to climate and soil of the United States	116
Additions to the Library during 1854	24
Additions to Library by Exchange	20
Addresses of Congress to Canada	173
Addresses of packages	32,33
Addresses to Canada, printed in French	174
Admission of packages for Smithsonian Institution duty free	21
Advance, Brig	92
Advantages of Camels in security against stampedes	121
Advantages of Fire-Alarm Telegraph	153
Advantage of greater range of vision on the Camel than the Horse	121
Advantages of introducing the Camel in America	116
Advantages of the Camel for Military Purposes	120
Aeronaut, Safety of, in Thunder Storm	224
Africa	38,45
Africa, Exploration of	92
Africa, Whirlwinds i	187
Agassiz, Prof	42
Agassiz, Prof , Species of Fish described by	342
Age attained by the Camel	113
Agents for distributing Volumes	36

Page.
Aghouat, Gen........ 109
Agriculture, connected with Rain........ 243
Aguachas, Las........ 304
Agua de Juan Lujan........ 299
Aid afforded Lieut. Strain by English party........ 93
Aid furnished Exploring Expeditions by Smithsonian Institution........ 79
Ailurichthys marinus (*Catfish*)........ 340,341
Air, Composition of........ 182,193
Airy, Prof........ 181
Alabama........38,43,46,49
Alabama, Direction of Thunder Clouds in........ 200
Alama de Parras........ 87
Alarm Bell tolled by Lightning........ 155
Albany........ 35
Albino Blackbird........ 38
Albino female of Agelaius Phœniceus........ 45
Albuquerque........37,83,275,316
Albuquerque, Expedition from........ 296
Albuquerque to Zuñi, Road from........ 276
Alcohol in Cases of Serpent Bite........ 132
Alcohol no security against effects of Venom of the Rattlesnake........ 132
Alcohol, use of in Treatment of Serpent Bite........ 136
Aleppo, Turcoman Camel procured from........ 121
Alexander, Capt. B. S........ 69,70
Alexander, Prof. S. A., Photographs of Eclipse by........ 17
Alexander VI........ 159
Alexdretta........ 121
Algeria, Army of Occupation in........ 119
Algeria, Camel used in, by French........ 113
Algeria, Camels suffer from sting of insect in........ 120
Algeria, Dromedaries should be brought from........ 122
Algeria, Performance of Camels in........ 105
Algiers, Winter too severe for Arabian Camel........ 118
Alkalies in Cases of Serpent Bite........ 132
Alleghany Black Snake........ 44
Alleviation of feelings of hostility between Dutch and English........ 175
Alligators........ 39
Aloe, said not to be touched by the Camel........ 108
Alosa Mattowaca........ 349
Alosa menhaden (*Moss Bonker, Bony Fish, Hard Head*)........ 347
Alosa Teres........ 349
Alphabetical list of Meteorological Observers........ 51
Alps........ 274
Alum used for Serpent Poison........ 133
Alvord, Major B., memoir by, on Tangencies of Circles and Spheres........ 13
Amazon........ 127
Amazon Valley, Exploration of........ 93
Amboyna, Massacre of English Traders at........ 175
Amblystoma luridum (*salamander*)........ 295
Amblystoma opacum........ 45,294
Ambroise Parē, the most distinguished surgeon of the 16th century........ 123
American Academy, Appleton Bequest to........ 18

Page.
American Academy of Arts and Sciences 35
American Antiquities, Account of History of.......... 10
American Antiquities, History of, by S. F. Haven.......... 11
American Association for the Advancement of Education, meeting of.......... 28
American Association for the Advancement of Science, meeting of.......... 28,35
American Astronomers, Triumphs of.......... 145
American Colonization Society 94
American Ethnological Society.......... 35
American Fire-Alarm Telegraph, Lecture on 147
American Fur Company 81
American Institute 35
American Institutions, Packages sent from.......... 35
American Journal of Science 35
American Method of Recording Astronomical Observations.......... 145
America, not an Englishman in, in 1664 164
American Oriental Society.......... 35
American Philosophical Society 35,202
American Societies, Packages for 35
American State Paper, the oldest 159
Ames, A. H.......... 89
Ammonia favors Action of Serpent Poison.......... 132
Amount expended on Library 22
Anahuac, Plateau of.......... 277
Analogy between Municipal Telegraph and Nervous Organization of Individual... 153
Analysis of Air 182
Analysis of Woorara.......... 127,128
Anatomy of the Camel.......... 103,106
Anchovy 347
Ancient Peruvian Vase.......... 39
Anderson, S. C.......... 43
Andes 90,227,273
Andrews, Prof. E. B.......... 42
Anemometer.......... 219
Anglo-Saxon, Title not expressive.......... 157
Anguilla tenuirostris 350
Animals exempted from Climatic Laws.......... 100
Animals, Existence of, perpetuated by Man 99
Animal Substances enter into Composition of Woorara 128
Ann Arbor 87
Annals and Magazine of Natural History.......... 127
Annales de Chimie, Analysis of Woorara in.......... 127
Annual Report of Secretary presented.......... 77
Answer to Difficulties in the way of Introducing the Camel.......... 121
Antelopes, Flock of 298
Antidote to Poisons.......... 135
Antidote to Venom of Rattlesnake hitherto unknown.......... 131
Antioch 111
Antiquarian Society.......... 35
Antilles.......... 198
Antiquities 10, 39, 45
Antisel Dr.......... 84

	Page.
Antiseptic Properties of Iodine	135
Anton Chico	83,300
Antonio de Otermin	312
Aoonakara river	83
Apache Indians	296
Aphredoderus sayanus	326
Apparatus by which Serpent inflicts a Wound	124,125
Apparatus, Cabinet of, collected	9
Appendix to Mr. Russell's Lectures	215
Appendix to the Report of the Regents	79
Appendix to the Report of the Secretary	31
Appleton Bequest	18
Appleton, D., & Co	96
Apple-trees at Manzana	303
Appropriation by Congress for Explorations	89
Appropriation by Congress to introduce Camels	121
Appropriations for 1855	68
Aqueduct at Gran Quivira	309
Aqua Ammonia applied to Cases of Serpent Bite	132
Arabian Camel, Information respecting Military Qualities and Hygiene of	121
Arabian Dromedaries	110
Arabian Poem older than Mohammed	104
Arabia, Whirlwinds in	187
Arab, has remained immutable	101
Arab, opinion of, respecting origin of Camel	114
Arabs habitually travel by night	115
Arab's regard for Dromedary and Horse	115
Arabia Petræa, Ascent of Caravan in	105
Arabia Petræa, Journey in	107
Aransas	46
Arctic Expedition	91
Argentine Confederation	90
Argyreiosus capillaris (*Hair-finned Dory*)	337
Aridity of Mediterranean Shores	189
Aristotle	182
Aristotle, Passage of, respecting Camel	102
Arkansas	37, 45
Arkansas, Fall of Rain at, during 1850	244
Arkansas River	83, 85
Army of 15,000 men transported solely by Camels	119
Armstrong, Robert	94, 95
Arnold, quotation from, on Centralization and Active Life	160
Arrangement of Smithsonian Building	70
Arroyo de la Cienega	304
Arsenic used for Serpent Bite	131
Artesian Borings	85
Ascension	90
Ashmead, Charles	*337
Ashmead, Charles, Thanks to	317
Ashmead, Samuel, Thanks to	317
Ashmead, Samuel, Sea-Weeds found by	319

	Page.
Ash, Wonderful Properties of	133
Asia Minor	111
Asiatics, Use made of Camel in War by	118
Association of Medical Superintendents of Hospitals for the Insane, meeting of	28
Astaci	39
Asteroids all of diminutive size	143
Asteroids, Discovery of	138, 139
Asteroid Orbits distinguished from all others	144
Asteroids, Relationship between	143
Asteroids, Cause of	141
Astraca, Orbit of	141, 144
Astronomers, Association of, to discover Planet	137
Astrology, Doctrines of, respecting Poisons	128
Astronomical Discoveries in America	145
Astronomical Expedition to Chile	96
Astronomical Journal	35
Astronomical Journals, only two in existence	18
Astronomical Journal, Observations of Eclipse published in	17
Astronomical Positions of Mexican States incorrect	279
Atherina	319
Atherinopsis notatus (*Silverside, Sand-Smelt*)	338
Atlanta, Classic Fable of	131
Atlantic and Pacific Junction Company	93
Atlantic Ocean, Depths of	91
Atmospheric Currents	190
Atmospheric Pressure at Greenwich	218
Atmospheric Pressure at Philadelphia	222
Atmosphere, Pressure of	182
Atomic Constitution of Mixed Gases	193
Atwater's Researches	11
Audubon, Mr	347
Auguste, Tension Tables of	267
Aulick, Com. J	39, 42
Auriferous Deposits of Vermont	39, 43
Aurora Boreal Coruscations	227
Aurora Borealis, Explanations of	13
Aurora Borealis, History of Exhibitions of	12
Aurora Borealis, Memoir on, by Prof. D. Olmsted	12
Aurora Borealis, Notices of, by Peter Force	13
Aurora not seen at San Francisco	253, 258
Austin, Joseph B	38, 42
Ayres, Dr	342
Azow, Sea of	122
Aztecs, Suppositions respecting	311
Bache, Professor A. D., Commission on Building Material	18
Bache, Professor, Observations by	215
Bache, Professor, Proposition by, relative to Bibliography	22
Bache, Professor A. D	95, 96
Bactrian Camel, obtained at Odessa	122
Bactrian Camel, Superior for Transportation	11[illegible]

Page.
Baffin's Bay 92
Bagdad to Damascus, Mails carried by Dromedary from, in seven days 111
Baird, Mr., Encampment near Residence of 296
Baird's Lake 88
Baird, S. F 16, 31, 38, 42, 79, 87, 94, 317
Balloon Ascent by John Wise 224
Balloon Ascent by Mr. Walsh 196
Banded Drum-Fish 332
Banded Sun-Fish 324
Baptist Mission, Kansas 86
Barker, Dr. S. W 38, 43
Barometer at Bombay 220
Barometer, Cause of Fall in Tropical Storms 210
Barometer, Cause of Fluctuation 204
Barometer, During Storm of 12th 210
Barometer, Fluctuations of, from 7th to 16th November, 1854 .... 207, 209, 210
Barometer, invention of 182
Barometer, two Maxima and Minima of 218
Barometer, Variations of 218
Barometrical Observations at Sacramento, California 264
Barnacle, Growth and Ravages of, and Protection against 39, 45
Barnard, Major J. G 39, 43
Baron de Zach 137
Barranca, Indian Chief 315
Bartlett, Jno. Russell 96
Bartlett, Professor, Photographs of Eclipse by 17
Barry, Rev. A. C 16, 37, 38, 43, 87
Basrah 111
Bashee Islands 89
Bass of Beaver Islands 287
Bass Sun-Fish 325
Batrachus variegatus (*Toad-Fish, Oyster-Fish*) 340
Batoseãgachic, Rich Mining Place 278
Batrachia 43
Battery Employed in Boston Fire-Alarm Telegraph 154
Bay of Monterey 84
Bay of San Francisco 242
Beale, Lieutenant E. F 85, 96
Bear creek 88
Beaumont, Elie de 274
Beaver Islands, Michigan, Natural History of 282
Beckwith, Lieutenant E. G 37, 82, 96
Beckwith's Cut 86
Bedouin Arab, the only Race that retains Original Mode of Life 101
Beesley's Point, New Jersey 16, 42, 43, 88, 317, 318
Bejuco de Menacure 127
Belcourt, Rev. S. A., Dictionary of Chippewa Language by 14
Belfast 212
Belgium 39, 44
Bell, Jno. G 88, 318, 342

Page.
Bell on City Hall, Boston, struck by Telegraphic Operator in New York.......... 150
Belone truncata (*Bill-Fish, Sea-Pike, Silver Gar-fish*).......................... 346
Beloochistan, Food of Camels in....................................... 108
Benicia.. 84
Benjamin, Park, Lectures by.. 28
Ben Moor Mountains 276
Bennett, Mr.. 93
Benton, Lieut. J. G. 39, 43
Bergen, Norway, Temperature in 195
Berghaus, Estimate of Number of Camels by............................ 118
Bergmann 110, 111, 117, 122
Berlandier, Luis, Account of....................................... 15, 87
Berlandier Collection, Catalogue of.................................. 396
Berryman, Lieut. O. H.. 91
Berlin Almanac.. 137
Berlin Maps...139, 140
Bermudas, to be Admitted into the Confederation 174
Bernard, Mr., Opinions of, respecting Poisons............................ 126
Berthoud, Dr. E. L.. 39, 43
Bessarabia 111
Bessarabia, Age of Camel, in 113
Bessarabia, Camel abounds in 101
Behring's Straits...79, 89, 96
Bibliographical Centre at the Institution............................... 22
Bibliography, Works on, collected 22
Bidwell's Bar 86
Bigelow, Dr. J. M.. 83, 84
Big Plover.. 88
Big Porgee.. 333
Big Witchita... 86
Billeton Passage.. 90
Bill-Fish.. 346
Bill Williams's Fork 84
Biographer of the English Chief Justices................................ 161
Birds... 43
Birds of Beaver Islands 282
Birds of Minnesota.. 291
Birds, North American.. 42
Birds received.. 37
Bird Skins... 46
Bitter Root River.. 81
Bite of Serpents, Nature and Cure of 123
Black Bass... 323
Black Bass of the Ohio, Habits of 289
Black Fish... 340
Blackfoot Pass 81, 82
Blackfoot River 81
Blackman, Washington, Thanks to 318
Black Massassauga 38
Blake, William P.. 84
Blank Forms for Meteorological Observations, &c., furnished 20

Page.
Blodget, Lorin, Report of Executive Committee relative to........................ 74
Blodget, Lorin, Communication and Bill from........................ 77
Blood Globules........................ 129
Blue Fish........................ 329
Blue Shark........................ 352
Board of Regents, Proceedings of........................ 72
Bodega, California........................ 45
Bode, Professor, Law of........................ 137
Boggs, W. B........................ 89
Bokham........................ 114
Bokhara, Camel used for Military Purposes in........................ 118
Boleosoma fusiforme (*Darter*)........................ 328
Bolson de Mapimi........................ 87, 277
Bombay, Meteorological Tables for........................215, 219, 220
Boneset, used for Serpent Poison........................ 133
Bony Fish........................ 347
Booghdee, the cross between Bactrian and Arabian Camel........................ 103
Books read in the Smithsonian Library........................ 21
Boonville, Missouri........................ 88
Boporah, Liberia........................ 93
Borgia, Name of, infamous........................ 159
Bossange, Hector, Distribution of Matter by........................ 32
Boston........................ 35, 36
Boston, Appropriation from, for Telegraph........................ 151
Boston, Fire-Alarm Telegraph introduced into........................ 150
Boston, Visits of Dickinson and Reed to........................ 169
Boston Society of Natural History........................ 35
Botanic Garden........................ 35
Botany Bay of New Mexico........................ 316
Boundary Survey of United States and Mexico........................ 80
Bourbon County, Kentucky........................ 43
Boussingault, Analysis of Woorara by........................ 127
Bowditch Library........................ 35
Bowman, J. Soulé........................38, 43, 86
Bowman, S. M........................ 86
Brainard, Dr. David, Lecture by........................ 123
Brandon, Vermont........................ 39
Brazil........................ 38
Brazos........................37, 46, 85
Brazos, Exploration of the........................ 86
Brevoort, J. Carson........................38, 318, 342
Brevoort, C. C........................ 43
Brewer, Dr. T. M........................38, 42, 43
Brewster, Sir David........................ 181
Breda, Result of Treaty of........................ 175
Bridger, Mr. J. L........................38, 39, 43
Bridgewater, Vermont........................ 39
Bristol, Vessels from........................ 159
British Association for the Advancement of Science........................ 188
British Association, commendation of Astronomical Journal by........................ 18
British Practitioners' use of Arsenic........................ 131

Page.
British Provinces, Efforts to obtain co-operation of, with the Thirteen Colonies 172, 173
British Rule repugnant to Dutch 175
Brooke, Lieut. J. M. 89
Brooklyn, New York 42, 317
Brown Coal Beds of Vermont 39, 43
Brownsville 86
Brussels, Belgium 212, 213
Buckland, D. 39, 43
Buckhardt 111
Buenos Ayres 90
Building, Amount expended on 70
Building, cause of Delay in completing 27
Building Committee, Authority to use Funds on deposit 76
Building Committee, Report of 69
Building Committee, Jno. T. Towers elected to 76
Building, Description of 27, 69
Building Materials collected in Europe 44
Building Materials, Commission on 18
Building Material, Specimens of, from Europe 39
Buist, Dr., Observations by 215
Bureau of Yards and Docks 39
Burke, Speech on Conciliation with America 165
Button Snake-Root, used for Serpent Poison 133
Burlington, Vermont, has smallest annual Fall of Rain 244
Burnett, Dr. J. W., Observations on Blood-Globules, by 130
Cabot, commission to 159
Cabot's Voyages, result of 163
Cacique of Quivira, statement by, respecting Treasure in New Mexico 313
Cactus consumed by Camel 108
Cadot's Pass 82
Cairo 110, 111
Cajava 119
Cajon Pass 84
Calcasieu, Louisiana 46
Caledonia bay 93
Caliente Pass 84
California Academy of Natural Sciences, instruments for 16
California 37, 38, 39, 46, 51, 83, 84, 87
California, general remarks on Climate of 231
　　Winds of 197, 236
　　Sea-breeze of 240
　　Rain, Storms, Clouds, and Mists of 243, 248
　　Review of Weather for 1853 251
　　　　of Weather for February, 1854 254
　　　　of Weather for 1854 255
Calliope, Orbit of 144
Calmucks 117, 122
Calvert county, Maryland 44
Camel, lecture on, 98; as an animal of war, 116; age of, 113; accounts of the power of, 117; Arabian, indifferent to heat, 115; appropriate home of, 100; advan-

Page.

Camel—continued—
tages of for military purposes, 120 ; anatomical differences between the Arabian and Bactrian, 102 ; appropriation by Congress to introduce, 121 ; burden of, 111; best place to procure them for the United States, 122 ; bad swimmer, 106 ; civilized life prejudicial to, 106 ; caravans cross glaciers, 117 ; color of, 114 ; domesticated in Tuscany, 108 ; detects water at great distance, 109 ; difficulties in introduction of, 121 ; endures privation from food, 107 ; effects of introduction of, among the Indians, 120 ; foot of, 105 ; fords rivers, 106 ; free from disease, 120 ; favorite food of, 107 ; feeding at temperature of 25° below zero, 118 ; fleece of some species equal to the wool of Cashmere goat, 114 ; finest and fleetest Arabian will not bear winter climate of Algiers, 118 ; growls of the, 115 ; hair shawls, 114 ; height of, 113 ; harness of, 112 ; instances of fleetness, 110 ; in some parts of the East employed as a beast of draught, 111 ; longevity of, greatest in the cold and damp Russian provinces, 117 ; milk of, 114 ; milked without halting, 120 ; method of securing at night, 121 ; most valuable in winter in the Crimea, 117 ; moisture of our climate unfavorable to, 117 ; most important peculiarity of, 106 ; not fed ordinarily, 107 ; nostrils of, slit by Bedouins, 104 ; nomade in his habits, 101 ; never feeds at night, 115 ; numbers of, 118 ; not as patient as represented, 115 ; practicability and advantages of introducing into America, 116 ; performance of, in Algeria, &c., 105 ; price of, 120 ; preferred to horses by the Calmucks, 117 ; period of gestation of, 120 ; paroxysms of, calmed, 115 ; power of, to abstain from water, 109 ; quantity of food required by, 108 ; rate of travel of, 110 ; security of seat on, 120 ; skeleton of, not found in the catacombs, 102 ; special properties of different varieties, 117 ; surpasses all domestic quadrupeds in speed and endurance, 110 ; species of, 101 ; used to carry sacred veil to Mecca, 115 ; transportation of an army by, 119 ; travels with security over snow and mud, 106 ; training of, 113 ; used in war, 118 ; utility of, 114 ; used by Napoleon, 118 ; used in military service, 113 ; weight of, 113.

Camelus bactrianus 101
Camelus dromas 102
Camelus dromedarius 101
"Camel's temper," proverbial expression 115
Camels, food prepared and cooked on the backs of 120
Camels in General Aghouat's Expedition did not drink from February to May...... 109
Camels of the Sultan of Morocco 115
Cameron, Gilbert 69, 74, 77
Campbell, Albert H 83
Campbell, General Robert B 37
Campbell, Hugh 83, 84
Campbell, Lord, Observations of 161
Camp Far West, Rain at 245, 247
Camp Shawnee Reservation 83
Cambridge 35
Cambridge Observatory 145
Camp Yuma 37, 84
Canada 35, 47
Canada, embassy from Congress to 174
Canada, efforts to obtain co-operation of, with thirteen colonies 173
Canada, expedition under Montgomery to 174
Canada, transfer of, from French to British dominion 174
Canada, Thunder-storm in 201

Page.
Cañada de las Uvas 84
Canadian river 83
Canal at Isthmus of Darien impracticable........ 93
Canary islands 198
Canoe from Madagascar........ 43
Cañon del Infierno........ 316
"Cape May Goody"........ 329
Cape of Good Hope........ 89
Cape Palmas........ 45, 94
Caranx chrysos (*Yellow Caranx, Yellow Mackerel*) 336
Caravan, day's journey, length of........ 110
Carboniferous Fossils........ 39
Carbuccia 103, 105, 107, 108, 109, 111, 112, 114, 115, 118, 120, 121
Carcharias cœruleus (*small Blue Shark*) 352
Carimata passage........ 90
Carleton, Major James Henry, Excursion in New Mexico by........ 296
Carlisle, Pennsylvania........ 38, 45
Caroline islands 89
Carol, Rev. John, mission to Canada of........ 174
Carp lake........ 88
Carrol, Charles, mission to Canada of........ 174
Carson's Valley........ 87
Casa Colorada........297, 298
Casa de Montezuma 311
Casas Grandes, seen along Gila river........ 311
Cascade range........ 81, 82
Cascade mountains 279, 280
Casey, Captain........ 39, 43
Cashmere Goat........ 114
Cassidy, Mr........ 97
Castañeda's History 306, 310, 311, 312
Catalogue of geological specimens collected by J. W. Foster........ 384
Catalogue of geological specimens collected by Dr. Charles T. Jackson........ *338
Catalogue of geological specimens collected by Dr. John Locke........ 367
Catalogue of geological specimens collected by D. D. Owen........ 393
Catalogue of geological specimens collected by J. D. Whitney........ 387
Catalogue of Berlandier collection........ 396
Catalogues of Stars 145
Catalogues of Libraries collected........ 22
Catastornus gibbosus (*Horned Sucker, Chub-sucker*) 341
Catacombs, skeleton of Camel not found in the........ 102
Cat-Fish........ 340
Catharine de' Medici........ 123
Catholic Clergy in New Mexico........303, 312
Caucasus, Hills in........ 274
Cause of Westerly Winds at San Francisco 243
Cause of West Winds being cold 196
Caustic Potash in cases of serpent bite 132
Cavalry, introduction of, in France........ 122
Cavia australis........ 91
Cedar Swamp creek 319, 322

Page.
Centralization 160
Centrarchus pomotis (*Bass Sun-Fish*) 325
Century of American colonization 166
Centropristes nigricans (*Black Bass*) 323
Ceramium, or Sea-cabbage 319
Ceres, discovery of the planet 138
Cervus dama 38, 45
Cette, Harbor of, frozen 260
Ceylon, Palm-leaf from 42
Chacornac, of Paris, Asteroids discovered by 139
Chaldean Shepherds, Planets known to 137
Chamouni, Temperature in 195
Chandler, Lieut 297
Channing, Dr. W. F., Lecture by 147
Chapparal Cock 44
Character of Inhabitants of New Mexico 298
Charles Fifth of Gran Quivira 313
Charles IX, Times of 123
Charleston College, S. C. 43
Charleston, Wind at 188
Charleston, spoken of as "The Distant Shore" 169
Charleston, S. C. 36
Chase, Rev. Benjamin 38, 43
Chase, Samuel, Mission to Canada of 174
Chatten, Capt 43
Chattin's Tavern 340
Chatoessus signifer (*Thread Herring*) 349
Chavis, Mr 297, 313
Chelonians, from Nebraska 82
Chelonura serpentina 39
Chemistry, Lectures on, by Dr. Smith 29
Chenay, Tornado of 229
Cherokees, Treatment of Serpent Poison by 133
Cherry-Tree in Norway near Ice 195
Chesney, Col 111, 120
Cheviot Hills 171
Chicago, Ill 36
Chief Justiciar, an Office introduced into England by William the Conqueror 161
Chihuahua 38, 45, 278
Chile, Astronomical Expedition to 96
Chilili 316
Chimère, French Steamer 93
China Seas 79, 89, 96
Chinese Tartary, Camel in, used for Saddle or Burden 112
Chippewa Language, Dictionary of 14
Chlorine, Effect of, on Poisons 135
Choate, Rufus, re-elected Regent 72
Choate, Rufus, Resignation as Regent 76
Choate, Rufus, Statement relative to Paper by Mr. Jewett, by 75
Church at Abó 300
Church at Quarrá 302
Church, Prof. A. E., Examiner of Major Alvord's Memoir 14

Page.
Ciboleta Mountains........ 298
Cincinnati........ 36
Circular for Information on Libraries........ 23, 398
Circular to Publishers respecting Copyrights........ 400
Civilization, changes, forms, products, and habits of Vegetables and Animals........ 99
Civilization, Demands of........ 99
Civilization, Science the Instrument of........ 147
Civilized and Savage Life........ 99
Circuit, necessary for Electrical Conduction in the Telegraph........ 149
Clapperton and Denham........ 105, 106, 107, 109, 114, 118, 120
Clarke county, Virginia........ 45
Clarke's Fork........ 81
Clavigero, Opinion of, respecting Aztecs........ 312
Clear and Cloudy Days at San Francisco........ 244
Cleveland, Ohio........ 36, 38, 44
Climate, Difference of, between Eastern and Western Continent........ 117
Climate of California, in Summer........ 242
Influence of, on Health........ 242
Climate of San Francisco, by Dr. H. Gibbons........ 231
Climate of San Francisco during 1854........ 255
Climates, Camel adapted to different........ 115
Clouds at Philadelphia........ 223
Clouds at Sacramento, California........ 268
Close-Roll of the 24th of Elizabeth........ 164
Clouds, Formation of........ 197, 217
"Cloud Cap" described by Mr. Wise........ 227, 228, 229
Cloudiness of the Air at Greenwich........ 217
Clouds, Direction of, during Rains........ 249, 250
Clouds, Mists, Rain, Storms, at San Francisco........ 243, 248
Clupea mattowaca........ 349
Coagulation of the Blood produced by Viper Poison........ 129
Coahuila........ 87, 277
Coast Range of Sonora and Sinaloa........ 279
Coast Survey........ 36, 66, 96
Coast Winds at California........ 238
Cœur d'Alène........ 81
Coffin, Prof. J. H........ 17, 20, 186, 188, 190, 201, 202
Coincidence of Explanation of Storms between Mr. Russell and Prof. Mitchell........ 199
Colcasieu, Louisiana........ 38
Coleoptera........ 42
Coldest Month in California........ 257, 258
Coldest Month of the Year........ 233
Coldest Period of the Day........ 215
Collections Received for Museum........ 37
Colleges........ 36
Collins, Lieut. Napoleon........ 89
Colonial Combination........ 174
Colonization of the French in Canada........ 165
Colonization, Schemes of, in the 16th Century........ 164
Colorado River........ 37,83,84,85,94
Columbia, Pennsylvania........ 44,346
Columbia River........ 81

Page.
Columbus, Discoveries before........ 158
Columbus, Discovery of America by 158,159
Columbus, Ohio........ 35
Comanches 86
Combination of Principles of Centralization and Local Independence........ 160
Comets, Discovery of........ 145
Commerce between England and America, Beginning of........ 163
Commerce between Russia and China carried on by means of Camels........ 118
Commission on testing Building Materials........ 18
Commissioner of Indian Affairs........ 36
Committee appointed to attend Committee of House of Representatives........ 77
Committee of Conference with Establishment........ 74,78
Committee of Finance appointed 77
Committee of House of Representatives appointed to investigate Affairs of the Institution........ 77
Common Sculpin........ 328
Communication between Regents and Establishment........ 73,78
Communication from G. Cameron........ 74,77
Communication from Hon. C. W. Upham 76
Communication from J. M. Stanley........ 77
Communication from L. Blodget........ 75,77
Communication relative to Geographical Gazette........ 77
Communications to be addressed to "Secretary of the Institution."........ 20
Conclusions of Mr. Frœbel........ 281
Concordia, Lake 43
Condamine 127
Condensation, Level of........ 226
Confederacy, Character and Duration of the First........ 176
Confederacy, the First in America 176
Conger Eel 351
Conger occidentalis (*Conger Eel*) 351
Congress, Appropriation by, for Surveys........ 80
Congress, Appropriation by, for Introducing the Camel 121
Congress, first object of, to obtain Colonial Redress........ 173
Congress of 1774........ 169
Congress Library........ 23,36
Conia Digitaline destroys Action of the Heart........ 129
Connecticut........ 47
Connexion of different Ranges of Mountains........ 275
Constantinople, Rain at........ 189
Constitution, Adoption of........ 170
Constitution of United States, Primary Purpose of........ 157
Contents of Ninth Annual Report........ 401
"Continental," use of the Term Explained........ 173
Contra Costa, Winds at........ 243
Conventional Lines running East and West........ 171
Cooachotope Pass 83,85
Cooke's Route........ 275,279
Co-operation and not Monopoly, Maxim of Institution........ 19
Cooper, Dr. J. G........ 82
Cooper, Schooner Fennimore........ 89

Page.
Copal inclosing Insect and Lizard 44
Coppermine Mountains 276
Copyright Law, Operation of.... 24
Copyright Laws and Instructions 400
Copyright Publications sent free of Postage to the Institution.... 24, 400
Copyright Receipts.... 23
Coral Seas.... 89
Corare, Description of 127
Corcoran and Riggs.... 57,65,66
Cordilleras 91,273
Cornwall 162
Coronado, Francisco Vasquez de.... 306,310,312
Correspondence of the Institution, Character of 14
Correspondence on Natural History 282
Correspondence, Resolution of Board respecting.... 78
Corson's Inlet.... 319
Corvina argyroleuca (*Silver Perch*).... 331
Corypha umbracaulifera.... 42
Cotheal, Messrs.... 39,43
Cotton Regions, none in Europe.... 189
Cotton, Seeds of, from Madagascar.... 43
Cottus virginianus.... 328
Couch, Lieut. D. N.... 15,86,87
Count Cypriani 87
Crabs 330
Creed, Unanimity in, required in Confederacy.... 176
Cretaceous formation of Texas.... 280
Cretaceous Strata 281
Crimea, Age of Camel in the.... 113
Crimea, Camel abounds in.... 101
Cromarty Coast.... 187
Cromwell and Leverett, interview between.... 171
Cromwell's Plan for Securing Conquest of Jamaica.... 171
Crotalophorus massasauga.... 38,44
Crotalophorus tergeminus.... 44
Crotalus, or Rattlesnake.... 124
Crotalus durissus.... 38
Crotalus tergeminus 38
Crustaceans.... 44
Cuba, Land and Sea Breezes in.... 187,190
Cuba, Northers at.... 203
Cucurbitaceous plants.... 99
Cullen, Dr.... 93
Cumberland, Rain at.... 197
Cumbre Pass.... 91
Cunningham, John P.... 43
Cunningham, William 39
Cupping glasses, use of in cases of Serpent Bite.... 132

Page.
Curare, description of........ 127
Cure of the Bite of Serpents........ 123
Currents at the Surface of the Earth and above it........ 186
Curves of temperature and pressure........ 206
Curve of temperature and pressure for Milwaukie, Wisconsin........ 206
Curve of temperature and pressure for New Wied, Texas........ 206
Curve of temperature and pressure for Steuben, Maine........ 207
Curve of temperature and pressure for Tuscaloosa, Alabama........ 206
Customs, great variety of, in England........ 161
Catostomus tuberculatus........ 341
Cutts, R. D........ 38,43,97
Cuvier, Conjecture of........ 106
Cyane, sloop-of-war........ 93
Cybium maculatum (*Spotted Cybium, Spanish Mackerel*)........ 335
Cypriani, Count........ 87
Cyprinodon ovinus........ 344,345
Cyprinodon parvus........ 345
Cyprinodonts........ 319
Dace........ 341
Dallas, George M........ 62,63
Dalles........ 81,82
Dalton, John, the Father of Meteorology........ 183
Dalton, John, on Fluctuations of Barometer........ 204
Dalton's Conditions of Atmospheric Equilibrium........ 185
Dalton's Explanation of the existence of Water in the Air........ 190
Dalton's Experiments on Vapor........ 192
Dalton's Observations........ 226,230
Dalton's Tables of Force of Vapor........ 267
Dalton's Theory of Constitution of Gases........ 193
Damascus........ 111
Dane county, Wisconsin........ 43
Daniel, Mrs. M. E........ 38,43
Daniel's Hygrometer........ 267
Darien Ship Canal Expedition........ 93,96
Darter........ 328
Date-Palm, Arab's opinion of Origin of........ 114
Davenport, Dr........ 87
Davis, Lieut. Alonzo B........ 89
"Dead Man's Journey"........ 276
Declaration of Independence........ 170
Deer........ 38,45,99,100
DeKay, Nomenclature of........ 318
Delaware........ 48
Delaware Creek........ 85
Delaware River, Settlement on........ 175
De le Condamine, Account of Woorara by........ 127
Deloul, species of Camel........ 113
Denham and Clapperton........ 105,106,107,109,114,118,120
Denig, Edward T........ 43

Page.
Deposites of Specimens of Natural History......44,45,4
Depths of Atlantic ocean, Soundings of...... 91
Derby, H. W...... 36
Desert, home of the Camel...... 101
Desert, north of the Lower Colorado, lowest spot of the American Continent...... 281
Desert of Gabi...... 118
Desert, six days' journey in width, without any vegetation...... 107
Deserts, few portions of without shrubs...... 10
Deserts, nature of Soil of...... 104
Detroit, Michigan...... 35, 87
Detroit river...... 87
Dew, law of formation of...... 194
Dew point at Greenwich...... 215
Dew point, explanation of...... 216
Dew point, Russell's rule for ascertaining...... 221
Diablo, Mount...... 251
Dia-magnetism, Explanation of...... 17
Dia-magnetism, Ruhmkorff's apparatus...... 17
Diary of an Excursion in New Mexico, by Major J. H. Carleton...... 296
Dickinson, Jno., Visit to Boston of...... 169
Dictionary of Chippewa Language...... 14
Diffendorfer, Dr...... 85
Difference between climate of Eastern and Western continents...... 117
Diodon fuliginosus...... 351
Diodon maculato-striatus (*Spot-Striped Balloon-Fish*)...... 351
Discovery of the Asteroids...... 138, 139
Dissenting Colonists of Rhode Island Refused Admission into Confederacy...... 176
Distribution of Collections...... 41
Distribution of Duplicate Specimens in Natural History made...... 25
Division of Longitudinal Basin of American Continent by Depression of Soil...... 281
Dix, W. G., Lectures by...... 28
Dodgeville, Wisconsin...... 88
Dog-shark...... *337
Dolphin, Brig...... 91, 95
Domestic Animals of Beaver Islands...... 282
Doña Ana......84,96,297
Donations to Museum during 1854...... 42
Donelson, Lieut...... 81,82
Donné, found Iodine to counteract Strychnia...... 135
Doty, Mr...... 81
Douglas, Stephen A., Resolution of, respecting Correspondence...... 78
Dromedary Corps in Algeria...... 109
Dromedary Corps Practicable...... 116
Dromedary, Description of...... 102
Dromedary, Johnson's Story of...... 110
Dromedary, not a Camel with two Humps...... 102
Dromedary, Performance of a...... 122
Dromedary Regiment of Napoleon...... 119
Dromedary should be brought from Algeria...... 122

Page.
Drought, caused by Westerly Winds.......... 196
Dryer, T. J.......... 43
Dry Lagoon of Cooke's Route.......... 280
Dryness, Maximum and Minimum.......... 217
Dryness at Greenwich.......... 216
Dryness at Philadelphia.......... 221
Dutch Dominion favorable to Colonial Combination.......... 176
Dutch West India Company, Grant to.......... 175
Durango.......... 87,277
Dwight, President..........186,196,197,200,201
Eagle Pass.......... 37
Ear of Corn from Talcahuana, Peru.......... 43
Earthquake Shocks in California.......... 258
Earth not yet Subdued by Man.......... 98
East Indies, Method of Preparing Poison in.......... 127
East and West Floridas to be Admitted into the Confederation.......... 174
Eastman, Capt. S.......... 95
East Troy, Wisconsin.......... 88
Eaton, Prof., Associated with Mr. Spencer.......... 26
Eccentricity of the Planetary Orbits.......... 142
Eckels, J.......... 43
Eclipse of Sun, May 26, 1854, Account of.......... 17
Edgecombe County, N. C.......... 43
Edgeworth, A. E.......... 38,43
Edrisi, Camels Fed with Dried Fish, according to.......... 107
Edward I, Life Saved by his Wife.......... 132
Edwards, Dr. L. A.......... 37,43
Effects of Serpent Bite.......... 126
Effect of Poisons referred to Sympathy.......... 128
Effects of Wounds of Poisoned Arrow identical with those of the Bite of Serpents. 128
Efficient Action Secured by Harmony of Views and Unity of Purpose.......... 30
Effigy Mounds of Wisconsin.......... 10
Eterretninger om Marokos.......... 115
Eggs of American Birds.......... 42
Egypt, Irrigation Required in.......... 189
Egyptologists, Opinion of, respecting the Camel.......... 102
Elaps fulvus.......... 43
Elaphas canadensis.......... 38, 45
Elasticity of Steam.......... 192
Eleanor, Wife of Edward I, Saved his Life from Wound of a Poisoned Dagger.... 132
Electricity, Agent in Generation of Storms.......... 225
Electricity, Experiments of Professor Henry in.......... 153
Electro-Magnetic Escapement.......... 152
Electric Telegraph described.......... 148
Electric Telegraph, introduction of.......... 148
Elephantiasis, in Many Cases Remote Effect of Serpent Bite.......... 126
Elie de Beaumont.......... 274
Elizabeth, Queen.......... 164

Page.
Elizabeth, Queen, Dedication of the Fairy Queen to ... 165
Elk ... 45
El Paso del Norte ... 37, 80, 84, 85, 275, 278, 298, 312
Elyria, O ... 87
Embarrass River ... 88
Embassy to Canada from Congress ... 174
Emory, Major W. H ... 37, 80
Endicott, Governor, Leveret's Dispatch to ... 171
Engelman, Dr. George ... 36, 38, 43
England, Annual Fall of Rain in ... 197
England and Holland, War between ... 175
England, great Variety of Customs in ... 161
England, Hills in ... 274
English colonization in America ... 166
English, Delay of, in colonizing America ... 163
English Expedition to Isthmus of Darien ... 93
English Party, Rescue of Lieut. Strain by ... 93
English Race, Title of, to America ... 159
English Writers attribute Poison of Woorara to Strychnine ... 137
English, W. H., Resolution of, to appoint a Committee on Finance ... 77
Engraulis vittata (*Anchovy*) ... 347
Engravings, Collection of ... 27
Entomology ... 42
Entomology of Minnesota ... 292
Eoff, John, Habits of Black Bass, by ... 289
Equivalents of Mountains ... 274
Erman ... 112, 118
Ervendburg, Dr. L. C ... 39, 43
Eryngium aquaticum, or Button-Snake Root ... 133
Escapement, Electro-Magnetic ... 152
Esox fasciatus (*Short-Billed Pike*) ... 43, 345
Esox flavulus ... 344
Esox ovinus ... 345
Esox reticulatus (*Pickerel*) ... 346
Espiègle, Brig ... 93
Espy, Professor ... 194, 196, 197, 198, 200
Espy, Professor, his Explanation of Fall of Barometer ... 210
Espy's Explanation of Oscillations of the Barometer ... 218
Espy, Professor, Hypothesis of ... 228, 229
Espy, Professor, Line of Minimum Pressure traced by ... 205
Espy's Meteorological Report, Hare's Queries on ... 203
Espy, Professor, his Services in Meteorology ... 181
Espy's Theory founded on Dalton's Observations ... 226
Estanque at Gran Quivira ... 308
Estimates for Building exceeded ... 71
Estimate of Appropriations for 1855 ... 74
Estufas at Gran Quivira ... 308
Ethnology, Attention especially paid to ... 11

Page.
Eucinostomus argenteus........ 335
Eucinostomus, genus........ 334
Eupatorium perfoliatum, or Boneset........ 133
Europe, Packages from, for American Societies........ 35
Europe, no Cotton or Sugar Regions in........ 189
Europe, Peculiarities of Weather and Storms of........ 210
Europe, Public Buildings in........ 39
Eutænia........ 45
Evans, Dr. J........ 38, 39,
Evans, Dr. J........ 43, 44, 82
Evaporation........ 194
Exceptions to Rule of Rise of Temperature with Rise of Barometer........ 208
Exchanges, Account of System of........ 20, 31
"Excito-Motory" System of Fire-Alarm Telegraph........ 153
Executive Committee, Estimates by........ 74
Executive Committee, Report of........ 57
Expansion of Air causes Cold........ 196, 197
Expansion of the Republic........ 163
Expedition to the Arctic........ 91
Expedition to the Euphrates........ 120
Expedition to the Isthmus of Darien........ 93
Expenditure on Library........ 22
Expenditures during 1854........ 57, 58
Experiments for testing Building Materials........ 18
Experiments in Algeria on Camel........ 119
Experiments in Stereotyping........ 23
Experiment of introducing Camel should be tried on a large scale........ 121
Experiments on Serpent Poison........ 133, 134
Experiments with Rattlesnakes........ 132
Exploration in Western Missouri and Kanzas........ 88
Explorations by Dr. Hoy, Mr. Barry, and Professor Baird........ 15
Exploration by Herndon and Gibbon........ 93
Exploration by Thomas H. Scrope........ 93
Exploration of Behring's Straits........ 89
Exploration of China Seas........ 89
Exploration of Coast of Western Africa........ 92
Exploration of Northern Wisconsin........ 88
Exploration of the Parana........ 90
Exploration of the Red River........ 94
Exploration of the Valley of the Amazon........ 93
Exploration of the Zuñi and Colorado Rivers........ 94
Explorations, Government........ 94
Explorations, Report on........ 79
Extracts from Scientific Correspondence........ 224
Fabulous Stories respecting Ruins of Gran Quivira........ 314
Fairy Queen, Dedication of........ 165
Fallow Deer........ 45
Falls of the Missouri........ 81
Fangs or teeth of Rattlesnake described........ 125

Page.
Faraday.......... 227
Farancia abacurus.......... 43
Farmer, M. G., Invention by.......... 150,152
Farmer's Protected Grove's Battery.......... 154
Father Huc.......... 106,107
Father Huc.......... 112
Father Huc.......... 114,115
Father Huc.......... 117
Father Huc.......... 121
February, 1854, Weather of San Francisco during.......... 254
Federal Republic, Development of.......... 162
Ferguson, Asteroids discovered by.......... 139
Fertility of United States, Cause of.......... 189
Finance, Committee of.......... 78
Financial System, good Results of.......... 9
Fins, Abbreviations of Names of.......... 320
Fire-Alarm Telegraph, Lecture on.......... 147
Fire-Alarm Telegraph, Construction of by M. G. Farmer.......... 151
Fire-Alarm Telegraph contains elements of a perfect Police System.......... 155
Fire-Alarm Telegraph, Experiments to test.......... 151
Fire-Alarm Telegraph, First Experiment with.......... 150
Fire-Alarm Telegraph, First Notice of.......... 150
Fire-Alarm Telegraph, Method of Action.......... 152
Fire-Alarm Telegraph, System of Organization.......... 151
Fire in London in 1666.......... 168
Fires in Cities.......... 150
Fishes.......... 38,42,43,44,45,46
Fishes Collected in the Lake Basin.......... 87
Fishes of Beaver Islands.......... 282
Fishes of Long Island.......... 317
Fish of Minnesota.......... 292
Fishes of New Jersey, Report on.......... 317
Fishes of the Ohio.......... 87
Fishes, Vernacular Appellations of different.......... 317
Flathead Lake.......... 81
Flathead Village.......... 82
Fleece of Camel Equal to Wool of Cashmere Goat.......... 114
Flight of Birds, Legend respecting.......... 159
Flood in Eastern Pennsylvania.......... 246
Flora, Orbit of.......... 142
Florida.......... 37, 49
Florida, Temperature at.......... 209
Flügel, Dr. J. G., Distribution of matter by.......... 32
Flügel, Dr. J. G., Thanks to.......... 36
Fluctuations of Temperature.......... 235
Flying Fish.......... 327
Fœtus of Right Whale.......... 45
Fog at Sacramento, California.......... 268
Foospinney River.......... 81

Page.
Fond du Lac........ 88
Fontana attributes Death from Serpent Poison to effect on Blood........ 129, 130
Fontana's Experiments........ 131
Force of the Winds at California........ 238
Force of Vapor at Philadelphia........ 222
Force of Wind at Philadelphia........ 223
Force, Peter, Series of Notices of Aurora by........ 13
Forde, Mr........ 93
Foreign Elements in the Union........ 175
Foreign Exchanges, Statistics of........ 31, 32
Foreman, Dr., left the Institution for Patent Office........ 23
Forshay, Professor........ 39
Fortuna, Orbit of........ 141
Fort Atkinson........ 45, 85
Fort Belknap........ 86
Fort Benton........ 37, 81, 82
Fort Boisē........ 82
Fort Brown, prevailing Winds at........ 190
Fort Colville........ 81
Fort Hall........ 81
Fort Kearney........ 86
Fort Laramie........ 86, 87
Fort Leavenworth........ 81
Fort Massachusetts........ 37, 83
Fort Morgan........ 46
Fort Ripley, Natural History of country about........ 291
Fort Smith........ 37, 45, 83
Fort Towson........ 37, 43
Fort Webster........ 84, 277
Fort Union, Nebraska........ 43, 81, 82
Fort Vancouver........ 81
Fort Yuma........ 80, 279
Fossil Bone, from North Carolina........ 45
Fossil Mammals from Nebraska........ 82
Fossil Wood........ 39, 44
Fossils........ 39, 43, 44, 45
Foster, J. W., Catalogue of minerals, &c., collected by........ 384
Foxes........ 38
Fox, Rev. Charles........ 38, 44, 87
Fox river........ 88
Franklin, Benjamin, Character and influence of........ 170
Franklin, Benjamin, Mission to Canada of........ 174
Franklin, Benjamin, Postmaster General........ 169
Franklin, Benjamin, Scheme of Confederation of........ 173
Franklin, Benjamin, Travels of........ 169
Franklin Institute........ 35
Franklin, Sir John........ 92, 96
Framingham, Massachusetts, Fishes at........ 324
Fraser........ 103, 116

Page.

Fraxinus, or common Ash........ 133
Fredericksburg, Virginia........ 44
Frémont, Col. J. C........ 83, 85, 89, 96
French Canadians read little........ 174
French Expedition to Isthmus of Darien........ 93
French naturalist, observations by, on Mountain Ranges........ 171
Fulton........ 148
Fund Account of the Institution........ 62
Fundulus diaphanus........ 343
Fundulus fasciatus........ 344
Fundulus multifasciatus........ 344
Fundulus zebra........ 342
Frenchmen and Englishmen, characteristic Difference between........ 161
Freshets........ 246
Frœbel, Dr. Julius........ 39
Frœbel, Julius, Physical Geography by........ 272
Frogs, Account of........ 40
Frost in July in New England........ 197
Frosts in Latitude 13° North........ 118
Fry, an American Hunter at Manzana........ 304
Gadsden Purchase........ 281
Galeichthys marinus........ 341
Gallery of Art........ 9,26
Garden Key, Florida........ 37
Garner, G. G........ 83,84
Garrard, Lieutenant........ 85
Gases, Diffusive Velocity of........ 193
Gases, Mechanism of........ 183
Gases, Properties of........ 184
Gases, Specific Gravity of........ 193
Gasparis of Naples, Asteroids discovered by........ 139,140
Gasper........ 90
Gasterosteus inconstans........ 342
Gasterosteus quadracus (*Stickleback*)........ 328
Gauss, Prof........ 138
Gaza, Theodore........ 102
General Catalogue of Libraries........ 22
General Remarks on Fishes of Beaver Islands........ 287
General Statement of Expenditures........ 60
General View of Receipts and Expenditures, 1854........ 57
Genoa, Harbor of, frozen........ 260
Geococcyx mexicanus........ 44
Geographical and Commercial Gazette, Communication relative to........ 77
Geographical Distribution of the Camel........ 101, 102
Geographical Knowledge of California........ 272
Geography, Science of........ 273
Geological Character of California........ 280
Geological and Statistical Society........ 35
Geological Survey of California........ 35

Page.
Geological Survey of Pennsylvania........ 35
Geological Survey of United States in Michigan........ *338
Geologists, Question raised by, respecting Mountains........ 274
Geology, well established fact of........ 274
Geometry, Contribution to........ 14
Geomys bursarius (*Gopher*), Habits of........ 293
George II........ 166
Georgetown........ 36
Georgetown College........ 36
Georgetown, S. C., Fish from........ 324
Georgia........ 49
Georgia, Settlement of........ 166
Germany........ 45
Germany, Opinion in, respecting Planets........ 137
Gessner, Error respecting Dromedary exposed by........ 102
Gestation of the Camel........ 120
Gibbes, Professor L. R., Examiner of Major Alvord's Memoir........ 13
Gibbon, Lieutenant Lardner........ 93, 95
Gibbons, Dr. Henry, on the Climate of San Francisco........ 231
Gila River........ 84, 276
Gila, Valley of the........ 280
Gilbert, Sir Humphrey........ 164
Gilliss, Lieutenant J. M........ 39, 40, 44, 66, 90, 96
Girard, C........ 40, 94, 318
Girard, Charles, Catalogue of Exchanges by........ 21
Girard College, Prof. Bache's Observations at........ 215
Gisborne, Mr........ 93
Glaishier, Observations by........ 215
Gloucester county, Virginia........ 45
Gobius alepidotus (*Variegated Goby*)........ 339
Godfrey, Willis, Thanks to........ 318
Goldsmith of Paris, Asteroids discovered by........ 139
Goodfellow, Henry........ 92
Gookin, Captain........ 172
Gopher of Illinois, Habits of the........ 293
Gorgona Pass........ 84
Goudot, M., opinion of, respecting Poisons........ 127
Gould, Dr. B. A., Astronomical Journal........ 17, 18
Gourard's paper on Dromedary regiment........ 119, 121
Government Expeditions sending Collections........ 37
Government reports of Explorations........ 94
Graham, Asteroids discovered by........ 139
Granada, Temperature in........ 195
Grand Duke of Tuscany, working Camels on farm of........ 108
Grand River........ 83
Gran Quivira, Excursion to........ 296
Gran Quivira, Ruins of........ 307
Grapes ripen near glaciers in Switzerland........ 195

Page.
Gray, A. B. 96
Great Britain, Barometer in 208
Great Britain and Ireland 33
Great Britain, Sovereign of, from Holland 175
Great Egg Harbor, Fishes at 317
Great Egg Harbor river 88
Great Salt Lake 83, 87
Greece, Mountains in 274
Green Creek 88
Green, James; Meteorological Instruments by 19
Green Pipe-Fish 351
Greenport, Fishes at 317
Greenport, Long Island 16, 42, 88
Green River 83
Greenwich, Observations at 215, 216, 217, 218, 219
Greenwich Observatory 145
Gregg, Mr., on the Ruins of New Mexico 309
Greiner, John 44
Grinnan, Dr. A. M. 44
Grinnell Expedition 92, 96
Grinnell Expedition, instruments furnished to 16
Grosse Isle, Michigan 38
Grove's Battery 154
Growth of the American Union during the Colonial Period, Lecture on 156
Grystus fasciatus, (Black Bass,) habits of 289
Guadalupe Mountains 84
Guadalupe Pass 279
Guatemala, Mountains of 273
Guaymas, Railroad from El Paso to 278
Guiana 45, 46
Guiana, Belief respecting Animal Poisons in 126
Guiana, Prevailing Winds at 190
Gulf of Mexico 38
Gulf of Venice frozen 260
Gunnison, Captain 80, 82, 83, 85, 86
Gustavus Adolphus, Settlement by Subjects of 175
Guzman, Lake 280
Hackensack, Fishes of the 88, 318
Hackley, Prof. C. W., Lectures by 28
Hair-finned Dory 337
Hake from New York 43
Hall of Museum, Description of 41
Hallowell, Benj., Lectures by 28
Hallowell, Dr. Edward 94
Hamlet, Description of Thunderstorm in 199
Hamlet, Effects of poison described in 130
Hampshire County, Virginia 44
Hancock, Steamer John 89
Hard Head 347

Page.
Harding, Asteroids Discovered by 138,139
Hare, Dr. Robert, Apparatus presented by 69
Hare, Dr. Robert, Queries and Strictures by 203
Hare, Dr. Robert, his Remarks on Wise's Observations 224
Hares 38
Harlan, General 103,106,120
Harris, J. O. 38,44
Harper and Brothers 96
Harpers' Magazine 96
Harvard University 35
Harvest-Fish 338
Harvey, Prof., Seaweeds of New Jersey 319
Hatch, F. W., Meteorological Observations at Sacramento, California, by 263
Haven, S. F., Paper on Antiquities by 10
Hawley, Gideon, re-elected Regent 72
Hayes, Dr. J. J. 92
Head, J. F., Natural History of Country about Fort Ripley, by 291
Health promoted by Climate of California 242
Heap, G. H. 85,87,96
Heart, General, active Explorer 11
Heat in the Atmosphere increased by Moisture 195
Heerman, Dr. A. L. 84
Hedjin, a Dromedary of the Upper Nile 114
Heligoland, Denmark 212
Helsten, Cornwall 212,213
Hencke of Driesen, Discovery of Asteroids by 139
Henderson, Dr. 44
Henry III. of France, Times of 123
Henry, Dr. T. C. 85
Henry, Prof. Joseph, Electrical Experiments of 153
Henry, Prof., Fact stated to Mr. Russell by 199
Henry, Prof., Suggestions respecting Lecture-Room 71
Henry, Prof., Lectures at Princeton 62
Hereford, Dr. 44
Hereford, Mrs. Mary 44
Herring, Habits of, Manner of Catching, &c 286
Herndon, Lieut. Wm. Lewis 93,95
Herring, Smith 318
Heterandria 345
Heteron niger 43
Herschel, study of Saturn by 145
Herschel's Measurements of Ceres 138
Highfield, Nottingham 211
Hilgard, J. E., Magnetic Instrument by 16
Hilliard, H. W 62,63
Hillsgate River 81
Hind, of London, Asteroids discovered by 139
Hindostan, Observations in 186
Historical Society of Massachusetts, Appleton Bequest to 18

Page.
History, Sacred and Profane 156
Hitchcock, President.... 94
Hog Choker (*Achirus mollis*).... 350
Holkham, Norfolk.... 212
Holland, Claim of to Territory in America.... 175
Holland gave sovereign to Great Britain.... 175
Hollins, Captain.... 93
Holmes, Prof.... 38
Holston River, Tennessee.... 45
Homans, T. L.... 82
"Home," applied to Mother Country.... 168
Home, Sir Everard, his Description of Stomach of Camel.... 107
Honduras, Mountains of.... 273
Hong Kong.... 89
Honorary Members of the Institution.... 6
Hood, Mount, Oregon.... 43
Höst 101, 115
Hound Fish.... *337
House of Representatives, Special Committee of.... 76
Hoy, Dr. P. R.... 15, 37, 38, 44, 87, 88, 295
Huerfano River 83, 85
Hudson River, Fishes and Crustacea from 16, 88
Hudson River, Settlement on.... 175
Hudson's Bay Company.... 81
Hudson's Voyage.... 175
Humboldt.... 101, 187
Humboldt, Account of Manufacture of Woorara by 127
Humboldt, Squall Described by.... 198, 200
Humboldt, Voyage of, to South America.... 128, 198
Humboldt River.... 86
Humidity of the Air at Greenwich 217
Humidity of the Air, Means of ascertaining.... 217
Humming Bird.... 45
Hump of Camel, Test of Condition of the Animal.... 103
Hunt, Rev. Thomas R.... 44
Hurricanes of West Indies.... 187, 198, 199
Hurricane on the Charles and Savannah Rivers.... 209
Hutchinson's History.... 172, 176
Hutton, N. H.... 83, 84
Hydrargira diaphana.... 343
Hydrargira flavula.... 344
Hydrargira luciæ.... 344
Hydrargira Multifasciata.... 344
Hydrophobia, Indian Remedies for 133
Hygeia, Orbit of.... 142, 144
Hygrometers, Principle on which formed.... 194
Ibrahim Pasha 111
Ice, performs part of an Electric.... 227
Ichthyology.... 318
Illinois.... 37, 38, 39, 44, 45, 50
Illinois Hospital, Case of Serpent Bite in 126

Page.
Illinois, Thunder Storm in 201
Impatiens, or Jewel Weed, used for Serpent Poison........ 133
Important to select Proper Season for Importation of the Camel........ 120
Importation of Turkeys into England from America........ 163
Improvements in Plan of Building........ 71
Increase of the Museum during 1854........ 36
Independent Tartary, Camel is used for Saddle or Burden 112
Indiana........ 50
Indianapolis, Snow at........ 208
Indiana, Thunder Storm in........ 201
Indian Corn 99
Indian Corn, best Region for, in Europe 189
Indian Gallery, Proposition to dispose of........ 77
Indianola........ 83
Indian Portraits, Stanley Collection of........ 26
Indian Relics 39, 43
Indian Tribes, Schoolcraft on 95
Indians on the Rio Grande, Poisoned Arrows by........ 127
Indians in California, Poisoned Arrows by 127
Indians use Venom of Serpents on Arrows 126
Indian Warriors in New Mexico........ 315
Indians, Plot of New Mexican........ 312
Indian Tribes in Texas, Lands donated to 86
Indians, Habits of resemble those of the Nomade Arabs........ 120
Indians, Remedies for Serpent Poison used by.. 133
Influence of Race 159
Influence of Seasons on Vegetation 235
Infusorial Earth of Monterey 39, 43
Inglis, Mr., Travels in Spain........ 195
Inoculation in case of Poisons 135
Inorganic nature, Conquest of, has been chief object of Man........ 99
Insects........39, 44, 46
Instructions for observing Eclipse published 17
Instruments constructed in London for the Institution........ 16
Instruments for Meteorological Observation not furnished........ 20
Intercourse between Colonies limited........ 169
Intercommunication, facilities of........ 168
Intoxication does not prevent effects of Rattlesnake Venom 132
Introduction of camel desireable for the fleece alone........ 114
Invertebrata, received 38
Invertebrates 38, 42, 46
Investigations in Laboratory........ 18
Investigations in State Records........ 164
Iodide of potassium, use of, in Serpent Poison 132, 133
Iodine, effect of, on Poisons 135
Iodine, solution of, only substance capable of neutralizing Venom of the Serpent or Woorara........132, 133
Iowa, Thunder storm in........ 201
Iowa........ 50

Page.
Ireland, Admission of, into Confederation........ 173
Ireland, Address from Congress to........ 173
Ireland, no Self-reliance felt in........ 161
Iris, Orbit of........ 144
Island of Juan Fernandez........ 45
Isthmus of Darien........ 273
Isthmus of Darien, Expedition to the........ 93
Isthmus of Panama........ 43
Italian Manners introduced into France........ 123
Italian Perfumers, Method of, to convey Poisons........ 123
Italy, Summers of........ 189
Ives, Lieutenant J. C........ 83
Jackson, Dr. C. T., Catalogue of Minerals, &c., collected by........ *338
Jacob's Hardships from Drought and Frost........ 195
Jalisco........ 278
Jamaica, Cromwell's Plan to secure Conquest of........ 171, 172
James I........ 166
James II........ 176
Jamestown, Building of........ 166
Japan........ 90
Japan Expedition........ 91, 96
Jarvis, John........ 45
Jàrvis, Mr., Experiments by, on Teredo, Barnacle, &c........ 39
Jeddo Bay........ 91
Jefferson Fork of Missouri River........ 81
Jersey Coast........ 37
Jewel Weed, used for Serpent Poison........ 133
Jewett, Proctor, and Worthington........ 36
Jewett, C. C., Notices of Libraries........ 23
Jewett, C. C., Memorial from, withdrawn........ 75
Jillson, Professor, Catalogue of Library of Congress........ 23
Josē Largo, Indian Chief........ 315
Johnson, Dr. George, Statement of, respecting Poisons........ 127
Johnson, Professor........ 38
Johnson, Captain, Ruins visited by........ 311
Johnson, John, Thanks to........ 318
Johnson's Story of the Dromedary........ 110
Jornada del Muerto, or " Dead Man's Journey "........ 276
Josecito, Indian Chief........ 315
Journal of Proceedings of the Board........ 72
Juno, Discovery of the Planet........ 138
Juno, Orbit of........ 141
Jupiter, Planets between Mars and........ 137
Jupiter, Orbit of........ 143
Kalispe Lake........ 81
Kamschatka........ 118
Kane, Dr........ 91
Kansas........ 86
Kansas, Exploration in, by Dr. Hoy........ 15, 88
Kansas River........ 83, 296
Keleoliess, Fife........ 211, 213

Page.
Kendal, Mean Annual Range of Barometer at 204
Kennerly, Dr. C. B. R..... 83
Kennedy, Hon. John P., Secretary of Navy..... 89
Kennedy, Storeship John P..... 89
Kennicott, R. W.....37,38,44
Kent..... 162
Kentucky 43
Kepler 137
Kern, E. M..... 89
Kern, R. N..... 82, 83
Kew Gardens..... 196
Key West, Florida 38, 45
Khiva..... 118
Khorasan..... 116
Kiachta 118
King, Captain 188
King of Denmark, Astronomical Journal published by..... 18
King, Dr. W. S..... 44
King-Fish 331
Kirgh ses, One-humped Camel found in the 101
Kirtland, C. F..... 44
Kirtland, Dr. J. P.....38, 44, 87
Kooskooskie River 81
Labeo gibbosus..... 341
Laboratory of the Institution, Investigations in 15,18
Laborde..... 110
Labrax lineatus (*Rockfish—Striped Bass*) 321
Labrax mucronatus (*White Perch*)..... 322
Labrax rufus..... 322
Lac-qui-Parle 45
Ladrone Islands 89
Lafayette-Fish..... 329
Laguna 83, 300
Laguna de la Puerta.....305, 315
Laguna de Santa Maria..... 276
Lake Butte des Morts..... 88
Lake Champlain 87
Lake Guzman, Level of..... 280
Lake Santa Maria, Level of 280
Lake Shad..... 287
Lake Winnebago..... 88
Lambert, G 39, 44
Lammont, Robert, of California..... 247
Land Breezes 187
Land Shells..... 45
Land Winds and Sea Winds in California..... 237
Lander, Mr..... 96
Langton, W. F 39, 44
La Place, Theory of..... 144
La Plata..... 37
La Pluma, Indian Chief..... 315

	Page.
Las Vegas, road from	275
Laval's Observations on Barometer	204
Law of Decrease of Magnetical Intensity	90
Law of Decrease of Temperature for Increase in Height	185
Law of Density and Elasticity of Gases	184
Layard	120
Layard's Researches	113
Leaf of Talipot Palm from Ceylon	39, 42
Lear, O. H. P	38, 44
Lebias ovinus	345
Le Conte, Dr. J. L	42, 44
Lecture Room, description of	27, 70
Lectures	98, 137, 147, 156, 181
Lectures, during 1853–4	28
Lee, Lieutenant S P	91, 95
Leiostomus obliquus (*Lafayette Fish*)	329
Leipsic	36
Lemonweir River	88
Leptophis ostivus	44
Lepus artemisia	45
Leroux's Route	275
Letter from Secretary of War on Pacific Railroad	95
Letter of the Secretary to the Speaker of the House	3
Leucosomus americanus (*Dace, Wind-fish, Shiner*)	341
Leuciscus pygmæus	342
Level of Absorption and Condensation	226
Leveret and Cromwell, Interview between	171
Leveret's Despatch to Governor Endicott	172
Leverrier, M	143, 145
Lewis's Fork	81
Lexington, Mo	88
Lexington, Storeship	91
Liatris, species of, used for Serpent Poison	133
Liberia	92
Liberty County, Ga	44
Library, Amount expended on	22
Library, Difficulty in	21
Library of Congress, Catalogue of	23
Library, Statistics of	21, 24
Library, Value of Books in	9
Libraries in the United States, Account of New Edition of	23
Libraries, Circular sent to	398
Lichia carolina	335
Lichia pinosas (*Spinous Dory*)	336
Liebig's Explanation of the Action of Poisons	129
Ligatures, Beneficial in cases of Serpent Bite	132
Light house Board	35
Lightning at San Francisco	258

Page.
Lightning Catchers 154
Lightning, Protection from, to the City of Boston 154
Limestone in New Mexico 316
Lineback, J. C 38, 44
Line of the Nodes 141
Ling, or Lawyers, of Beaver Islands 287
Lippincott, Grambo & Co 36, 96
Lisbon and Washington Winters compared 196
List of Meteorological Stations and Observers 47
Little Colorado 83
Little Lagoon, Mud Deposites of 281
Little Plover 88
Little Salmon river 81
Little Salt lake 85
Little Salt settlement 85
Little Waupacca 88
Littleworth 320
Liverpool, Lancashire 211, 213
Lizard enclosed in Copal 44
Lizards received 38
Llano Estacado 83, 85
Lobotes Emarginatus 332
Locke, Dr. John, Catalogue of Minerals, &c., collected by 367
Local Independence, Principle of 160
Logan, Thomas M., Meteorological Observations by 259
Lombardy, Fertility of, owing to melting snow 189
London 33, 36
London Company, Grant of Land to 166
London Society of Arts, Models, &c., from 26
Long Island 43
Long Island, Fishes of 317
Longitudinal Basin of American Continent 281
Long-toothed Flounder 349
Loomis, Professor Elias, Lecture by 137
Loomis, Professor, Storms described by 202, 203
Lord, John, Memorial, &c., from 76
Loretto 93
Los Angelos 84, 85, 256, 276
Los Puertos de Abó 316
Loss by Fire in Boston under Telegraph Fire-Alarm System 155
Loudoun, Lord 169
Louisiana 37, 38, 39, 46, 49
Louisiana, Direction of Thunder Clouds in 200
Louisiana Gulf-coast 97
Lowest Spot on American Continent 281
Leuciscus 345
Ludley's Run 320
Lupa Dicantha 330
Lutetia, Orbit of 141

Page.
Luther of Bilk, Asteroids discovered by 139
Luxor, Head of Camel on Obelisk at 102
Lyon's Travels 106, 113, 114, 118
Lynch, Lieutenant W. F 92, 95
Lynxes 38
Lynx rufus 38, 44
Macedonia, Sloop-of-war 91
Macfeely, Lieutenant 81
Mackinac Trout 284
Mack, R. C 44
Madagascar Canoe 43
Madison, Va 44
Madison, Wis 35, 87, 88, 208
Magendie's Experiments on Absorption 129
Magnetic Apparatus lent to Arctic Expedition 92
Magnetic Instruments, Account of 16
Magnetic Observatory 16
Magnetism, Ruhmkorff's Apparatus 17
Mahafa 119
Maherry of the Desert 103, 114
Maine 47
Mamelukes 111
Mammalia 45, 291
Mammalia, North European 42
Mammalia of Minnesota 291
Mammals 37, 43, 44, 46
Mann, George 45
Mann, Rev. C 45
Mann, Rev. Chas., on habits of a Salamander 294
Mann, William 45
Mansfield, Colonel J. K 39, 45
Mansfield, Ohio 44
Manure, Fish for 347
Manzana 315
Manzana, Character of inhabitants 303
Manzana, description of town 302
Manzana Mountains 275
Manzana, Spanish name for apple 303
Map of Earth-works to be published 11
Map of Eclipse published 17
Map of Solar Eclipses by Professor Coffin 17
Maps of Mexico, misconstruction of 278
Maps to Report on Pacific Railroad 96
Marias Pass 82
Marcy, Captain R. B 85, 86, 94
Marcou, Jules 83
Marengo County, Alabama 43
Maricopa Village 84
Marine Infusoria 79

	Page.
Marion County, Missouri	44
Marriotte	184
Mars and Jupiter, Planets between	137
Marseilles, Barometrical Observations at	204
Marseilles, Harbor of, frozen over	260
Marshall, Lieutenant	85
Marsh, Hon. George P., donation from	45
Marsh, Hon. G. P., Lecture on the Camel	98
Marsh, Hon. G. P., Remarks respecting rain at Constantinople	189
Marryatt, Captain, Description of Hurricane by	199
Marth, Asteroids discovered by	139
Maryland	48
Marysville, California	43, 86
Massachusetts	47
Massachusetts, aid from, to sufferers at the London fire, 1666	169
Massacre of English Traders at Amboyna	175
Massacre of Spaniards in New Mexico	312, 313
Massacre of St. Bartholomew	123
Massilia, orbit of	141, 144
Mastodon Teeth	43
Mastodon Bones	39
Matamoras	87
Matates, from Gran Quivira	308, 311
Materials for the Union	167
Matter, Composition and Nature of	183
Maury, Lieutenant M. F.	38, 45, 91, 181
Mauvaises Terres	82
Mayer, Brantz, Memoir by, on Mitla remains	12
Mazatlan	277
McClellan, Captain George B.	81, 82, 94, 95
McDonald, M.	44
McNair, J. C.	38, 44
MacRae, Lieutenant	44, 90, 91
Meacham, Jas., motion to admit Reporters	72
Meacham, Jas., Report of, on Distribution of Income presented	77
Meacham, Jas., Resolution on Library	73
Meacham, Jas., Resolution on Library Committee	73
Mean Temperature calculated by table	234
Mean Diurnal Variation of Temperature at Greenwich	215
— of the weight of water in a cubic foot of air at Greenwich	215
— of the dew-point at Greenwich	216
— of dryness at Greenwich	216
— of the humidity of the air at Greenwich	217
— of the cloudiness of the air at Greenwich	217
— of the weight of a cubic foot of air at Greenwich	217
— of atmospheric pressure at Greenwich	218
— of the pressure of the wind at Greenwich	219
— of temperature at Bombay	219
— of tension of vapor at Bombay	219

Page.
Mean Diurnal Variation of the barometer at Bombay.......... 220
of the temperature of the air at Philadelphia.......... 220
of the dew-point at Philadelphia.......... 221
of dryness at Philadelphia.......... 221
of the calculated force of vapor at Philadelphia.......... 222
of atmospheric pressure at Philadelphia.......... 222
of the force of wind at Philadelphia 223
of the sky covered by clouds at Philadelphia.......... 223
Mecca, Sacred Veil carried to by the Camel 115
Mechanics' Institute, Chicago 36
Mechanics' Institute, Lectures for.......... 28
Medicinal Plants, discovered by Neapolitan Naturalist 170
Medicine River.......... 81
Meeting of the Board of Regents January 3, 1855 72
January 12, 1855 72
January 13, 1855 74
January 15, 1855 75
January 27, 1855 76
February 10, 1855 77
February 17, 1855 77
February 24, 1855 77
Mehemet Ali.......... 111
Meigs, Captain M. C., Specimens of Building Material selected by 18
Melanura Pygmæa, (*Mud-Fish*).......... 342
Members *ex officio* of the Institute.......... 6
Memorial from C. C. Jewett withdrawn.......... 75
Memorial from John Lord.......... 76
Mendoza 90
Menopoma.......... 45
Meridional Instruments, introduction of 145
Mesa de los Tumanes 304
Mesa de Paja 187
Mesas of Sandstone in New Mexico.......... 299
Mescalero Apaches 304
Metis, Orbit of 141
Meteorological Instruments cannot be furnished.......... 20
Meteorological Materials, Description of 20
Meteorological Observations at Sacramento, Cal.......... 259, 260, 261
Meteorological Reductions by Prof. Coffin 20
Meteorological Stations and Observers 47
Meteorological System of New York University.......... 51
Meteorological Tables .... 189, 209, 210, 211, 212, 213, 215, 216, 217, 218, 219, 220, 221, 222, 223, 232, 233, 234, 235, 236, 237, 238, 239, 240, 241, 244, 245, 247, 249, 250, 251, 252, 253, 254, 255, 256, 257, 258, 259, 261, 264, 265, 266, 267, 268, 269, 270, 271.
Meteorology 19, 47, 181, 224, 231, 259, 263
Meteorology, Russell's Lectures on 181
Meteorite, remarkable one presented by Lieutenant Couch 15
Meteorites, Analysis of, by Dr. Smith 18

Page.
Meteors at San Francisco in 1853 253
Metropolitan Mechanics' Institute, School of Design.... 26
Mexican Boundary Commission 37, 80, 96
Mexico.... 38, 45
Mexico, Exploration of, by Lieutenant Couch.... 15, 86
Mexico, separated from rest of North America by an Ocean 280
Mezquit Trees 118, 281
Michigan 50
Michigan, Minerals from.... *338
Michigan State Agricultural Society 35
Michigan, Zoology of.... 38
Michler, Lieutenant.... 80
Michoacan 278
Microscope, Fontana claimed Invention of.... 130
Microscope made by Mr. Spencer, Account of.... 26
Microscopic Shells.... 97
Milianeh, Expedition to 105
Milk of the Camel.... 114
Milk River 81
Miller, Hugh.... 187
Millsburg.... 93
Milwaukie, Wis 87
Milwaukie, Wis., Curve of Temperature and Pressure for 206
Mimbres.. 276
Mineral Acids in cases of Serpent Bite.... 132
Mineral Lands in Michigan *338
Minerals received 39, 45
Minerals, Investigations relative to, by Dr. Smith.... 18
Minerals received 39
Mining connected with Rain 243
Ministre des Ponts et Chaussées.... 161
Minnesota.... 38, 39, 45, 51
Minnesota Historial Society.... 66
Minnesota, Natural History of.... 291
Minnesota, Mines in California.... 44
Minutoli.... 102
Mirage 186
Miscellaneous Correspondence on Natural History.... 282
Missionaries in South America, Account of Poison by 127
Missionary to East Indies, Account of Poison by.... 127
Mission of Man.... 98
Missions in New Mexico.... 312
Mississippi....38, 39, 46, 49
Mississippi, Steamer 91
Missouri....37, 38, 44, 50
Missouri, Exploration in, by Dr. Hoy.... 15
Missouri River 81, 82
Mists, Rain, Storms, Clouds, at San Francisco.... 243, 248
Misty Weather, Table of at San Francisco.... 249

Page.

Mitchill, Doctor, Fish Described by 347
Mitchell, Professor, Explanation of Storms by 199, 213
Mitla, Mexico, Ancient Remains at 11
Mobile, Alabama 45, 46
Model of Madagascar Canoe 43
Mode of Life of Indians modified by Introduction of the Camel 120
Models Presented by Professor Wilson 26
Mogador 111
Mohammed, Tradition relative to 115
Mohave River 37, 84, 85
Moisture in Air Increases Heat 195
Moisture of Atmosphere Unfavorable to Camel 117
Moisture, Time of Maximum 216
Molasses, Investigations Respecting, by Dr. Smith 18
Molasses Point 330
Möllhausen, H. B. 83
Monge, General Marcy, Remarks of Respecting Cavalry 122
Mons 39
Monrovia 93
Monterey 39, 43, 45, 87
Montgomery's Expedition to Canada 174
Montreal 87
Moore, W. E. 45
Morfit, Doctor J. C., Experiments with Rattlesnakes 132
Mormon Settlements 85
Morris, Captain 83
Morris, Professor O. W. 45
Morocco 101, 111
Morocco, Sultan of 115
Morrow, Doctor James 91
Morton, Remark Respecting the Work of 9
Mosquitia, Mountains of 273
Mosquitos in Minnesota 293
Moss Bunker, Great use for Manure 347
Motion of the Nodes of the Planets 142
Motor Function of Electricity 153
Mountain Camel, Reason why so called 117
Mountain Ranges, Influence of upon Civilization 170, 171
Mountains between El Paso and California 276
Mountains, Character of, West of Pecos River 277
Mountains, Relations between 274
Mount Ararat, Annual Sermon Preached at 115
Mount Diablo 251
Moyle, Mr., Fact stated by, Respecting Snow 213
Mud Fish 342
Mugil Albula, (*White Mullet*) 339
Mules in Captain Stansbury's Expedition, travelled two Days without Food or Water 109
Mullen, Lieutenant 81

	Page.
Municipal Telegraph	149
Museum, Additions to	25
Museum, Character and Value of	9
Museum, Donations to during 1854	42
Museum, Object of	25
Music Copyrights	23
Mustelus Canis, (*Hound Fish, Dog Shark*)	*337
My School and Schoolmasters, Hugh Miller's Work	187
Names of Fishes, Great Diversity in	317
Napoleon, Camels employed by	118
National Institute	36
Natural History Apparatus, best ever taken to Sea	89
Natural History, Correspondence on	282
Natural History of Beaver Islands, Mich	282
Natural History of the Country about Fort Ripley	291
Natural History, Specimens Collected by Lieutenant Couch	15
Natural History Society	35
"Nature and Course of Storms," by Mr. Thom	190
Nature and Cure of the Bite of Serpents	123
Nautical Almanac	17, 35
National Observatory	35, 36, 145
Navajo Country, Ruins in	311
Naval Astronomical Expedition to Chile	90, 96
Neapolitan Naturalists, Medicinal Plants discovered by	170
Newberry, Dr. J. S	38, 45
Nebraska	51, 82
Nebular Hypothesis	144
Nedjd, fine Camels from	113
Negabad, Pass of	105
Negrito, Indian Chief	315
Neighbors, Major	86
Neosho	85
Nerodia Erythrogaster	43
Nettle used by Cherokees for Serpent Poison	133
New England	166
New England Confederacy	170, 176
New England, Dwight's History of	196
New England, Thunder Storm in	201
New Hampshire	47
New Haven	35
New Haven, Storm in 1809 at	200
New Jersey	38, 39, 48, 88
New Jersey, Description of Coast of	318
New Jersey, Exploration on Coast of, by Professor Baird	16
New Jersey, Fishes of	317
New Jersey Zinc Company	39
New Leon	87
New Mexico	38, 39, 44, 45, 46
New Mexico, Character of Inhabitants of	298, 303

Page.
New Mexico, Gregg's Description of Ruins in ... 309
New Mexico, Major Carleton's Excursion in ... 296
New Mexico, Report of Surveys in ... 96
New Mexico, Mountains in ... 277
New Orleans ... 35, 36, 46
New Orleans Academy of Natural Sciences ... 35
New Orleans, Shell Road at ... 299
Nez Perces Trail ... 81
New River, Periodical Filling and Drying of ... 281
New Species of Mammals, &c ... 94, 95
New Wied, Texas, Curve of Temperature and Pressure for ... 206
New Wied, Texas, Temperature at ... 208
New York ... 35, 36, 38, 47, 48
New York Flatfish ... 349
New York Lyceum of Natural History ... 35
New York Solefish ... 350
New York State Library ... 35
New York, Temperature at ... 209
New York, Thunder Storm in ... 201
New York University, Meteorological System ... 51
Nicaragua, Volcanic Cones of ... 273
Nicotine destroys Action of the Heart ... 129
Niebuhr ... 162
Ninth Annual Session of the Board of Regents ... 72
Nishnei Novgorod ... 114
Nitrate of Silver in cases of Serpent Bite ... 132, 135
Norfolk ... 89
Norman, B. M ... 36
Norman Conquests ... 161
North Britain, Summer Sea-breeze of ... 187
North Briton ... 162
North Carolina ... 38, 39, 49
Northern Barracuda ... 326
Northern Route to the Pacific ... 80
Northern Wisconsin, Exploration of ... 88
Northers, Description of ... 203
Northers in New Mexico ... 306
Northman, America not Meant for the Home of ... 158
Norway, Temperature in ... 195
Norway, West Winds of ... 197
Notices of Public Libraries in the United States (new edition) ... 23, 398
Nova Scotia ... 47
Nova Scotia to be Admitted into the Confederation ... 174
Nuevo Leon ... 277
Oases of the Desert without the Camel ... 101
Observations at the Smithsonian Institution ... 205
Observatory, National ... 35
Observatory of Chile ... 35
Observatory in Washington, Catalogues of Stars made at ... 145

Page.
Ocean, Depths of........ 91
Officers of the Institution........ 5
Oglethorpe's Settlement of Georgia........ 166
Ohio........ 38, 49, 50
Ohio Board of Agriculture........ 35
Ohio, Thunder Storm in........ 201
Oil in cases of Serpent Bite........ 132
Ojibwas, Facts Respecting Language of........ 14
Olbers, Astronomical Discoveries by........ 138, 139, 140, 141
Olmsted, Prof. D , Memoir by, on Aurora Borealis........ 12
Olympia........ 81, 82
Oology, Work on, by Dr. Brewer........ 42
Opal of Mexico........ 39, 45
Ophibolus Getulus........ 43
Ophidium Marginatum........ 43, 351
Opium acts on the Brain........ 129
Opium given to Camels by Belooches........ 108
Orange Trees........ 196
Orange and Banana in Region of Pine-Trees........ 278
Orbits of the Planets........ 140, 141
Ore from Tetilla Peaks, New Mexico........ 316
Oregon, Winds at........ 197
Orenburg........ 118
Orfila, Poisons Described by........ 135
Organic Nature not fully developed by Man........ 98
Orography........ 273, 281
Ortyx Virginianus........ 43
Osage........ 85
Oshkosh, Wisconsin........ 88
Osler's Self-registering Anemometer........ 219
Ostrich called by Arabs the Camel Bird........ 103
Otolithus Regalis, (*Weak-fish*)........ 329
Ottawa, Illinois........ 44
Owen, Dr. D. D........ 38, 43
Owen, Dr. D. D., Catalogue of Geological Specimens collected by........ 393
Owen, Prof. R........ 45
Oxford, Mississippi, Temperature at........ 208
Oyster Fish........ 340
Oysters at Beesley's Point........ 319
Pacific Railroad........ 37, 80, 95
Pacific Railroad, Advantages of Pass of Abó for........ 300
Pacific Railroad, Line traced by Nature........ 281
Pacific Railroad Reports........ 96
Packages from American Institutions for Distribution abroad........ 35
Packages sent abroad........ 32, 33
Packages received from Europe for American Societies........ 35
Pack-Saddle for Camel described........ 112
Page, Lieutenant Thomas J........ 37, 90
Pagrus Argyrops, (*Big Porgee*)........ 333

Page.
Pah Utahs, Destruction of Gunnison's Party by.......... 83
Pallas, Accounts of Power of Camel, by.......... 117
Pallas, Discovery of the Planet.......... 138
Pallas, Orbit of.......... 144
Palestine.......... 45
Palestine, Early and Latter Rains of.......... 246
Palestine, no Rain in Summer in.......... 189
Palmas, Cape.......... 93
Palm Leaf from Ceylon.......... 42
Palmyra, Wisconsin.......... 88
Panama.......... 39, 44
Para.......... 93
Para, Reptiles from.......... 42
Paraguay.......... 51, 90
Parana River.......... 90
Paré, Ambroise, Opinion of, respecting Influence of the Stars on Action of Poisons... 128
Paris.......... 36, 204, 212, 213
Paris, Mean Annual Range of Barometer at.......... 204
Parke, Lieutenant J. G.......... 37, 38, 80, 84, 96
Parliamentary Aid to Georgia.......... 166
Parowan.......... 85
Parras.......... 87
Parson, General, active Explorer.......... 11
Parvin, J. B., on the Habits of the Gopher.......... 293
Pascal, Discovery by.......... 182
Passes through the Mountains.......... 299
Pass of Abó, Advantages of.......... 300
Pastinaca Hastata, (*Whip Stingray*).......... *337
Pattenger.......... 108
Patent Office Report, Meteorological Table in.......... 244
Patent Office Report, Notes Respecting Camel in.......... 103, 106
Paths in the Deserts worn by Caravans.......... 104
Patrapawlowsk.......... 118
Pearce, James A., Estimate of Appropriations by.......... 74
Pearce, James A., Report from, on L. Blodget.......... 74
Pearce, James A., Resolution approving Removal of Mr. Jewett.......... 75
Pearce, James A., Resolution to appoint a Committee to attend meetings of House Committee.......... 77
Pearce, James A., Resolution on Conference with Establishment.......... 73
Pearce, James A., Resolutions on Income.......... 73
Peck's Beach.......... 319
Pecos River.......... 85 277
Peculiarities of the Orbits of Asteroids.......... 143, 144
Pell, R. L., Experiments on Breeding of Rockfish in Fresh Water.......... 321
Felouze, Mr., Opinion of, Respecting Poisons.......... 126
Peltier, Report on Tornado of Chenay.......... 229
Pennsylvania.......... 44, 48
Pennsylvania, Thunder-Storm in.......... 201
Penrose, William M.......... 38, 45

Page
Peprilus Tricanthus, (*Harvest-fish*) 333
Perch of Beaver Islands 287
Perry, Commodore M. C 90, 91, 96
Persia, Camel used for Military Purposes in 118
Puruvian Amazon 93
Peruvian Vase 39, 43
"Peter Simple," Hurricane Described in 199
Peters, J. H 82
Petrapawlowsk 118, 122
Phelps, Mr 190, 200
Phenomena in Desert of Colorado 281
Philadelphia 35, 36
Philadelphia, average Temperature of 233
Philadelphia, Clear Days at 248
Philadelphia College of Pharmacy 35
Philadelphia, Meteorological Tables at 215, 220, 221, 222, 223
Philadelphia, Winds at 238
Photographic Views of Eclipse 17
Phrynosoma 44
Physical Character of America no Impediment to Union 170
Physical Geography of the North American Continent 272
Physical Law of Civilization 171
Phycis Americana 331
Piazzi 137, 138, 139
Pickerel 346
Piermont, New York 88
Pietro Della Valle 105
Pigeons, Experiments with, on Serpent Poison 134
Pig Fish 327
Pike and Pickerel of Beaver Islands 283
Pilgrims to Mount Ararat 115
Pillichody, Charles 45
Pimas Village 96, 276
Pima Villages 84
Pine River 88
Pisa, Weight of Camels at 113
Pityophis 45
Placer Mountains 275
Planets known to the Ancients 137
Plan of Treatment for Serpent Bite and Poisoned Arrows 135
Plantago used for Serpent Poison 133
Plants 39, 43
Plants, Seeds of, from Texas 44
Plants used for Serpent Poison 133
Platessa Ocellaris, (*Long-toothed Flounder*) 349
Platessa Plana, (*New York Flat-fish, Winter Flounder*) 349
Pleuronectes Maculatus 350
Plan adopted in accordance with Will of Smithson 9
Plan adopted to carry out Intentions of Smithson 8, 9

Page.
Plan to make General Catalogue of Libraries 22
Plinii, Hist. Nat 107
Plover Portage 88
Plymouth Company, Grant of Land to 166
Plymouth Governor, Despatch to 176
Plymouth, Sloop-of-War 91
Poem Older than Mohammed 104
Pogonias Fasciatus, (*Banded Drum*) 332
Point of Difference between Climate of Eastern and Western Continents 117
Poison, Action of 129
Poison by Serpent Bite, Treatment of 131
Poison, Cause o the Effects of 130
Poisonous Substances, Nature of, and Means of Detecting 123
Poisons conveyed by Italian Perfumers 123
Poisons deprived of their Bitter Taste by Perfumers, &c 123
Poisons, Effect of, referred to Sympathy 128
Poisons, Knowledge of, introduced into France 123
Poisons, Manner in which they Act 128
Poisoned Arrows, Method of Preparing, in South America 127
Poisoned Arrows, Treatment for Wounds from 135
Poisoned Arrows, Wounds of 123
Poisoning, Means of avoiding, by Paré 123
Poison of Serpents acts on the Brain 129
Poison of Serpents, Treatment of, by Indians 133
Poison used by Indians on Arrows, the Venom of Serpents 126
Poland, Ohio 87
Police System of Boston by Fire-Alarm Telegraph 155
Pomotis Chætodon (*Banded Sunfish*) 324
Pomotus Obesus 324
Pope, Captain J 37, 80, 85, 96
Pope Clement, Poisoning of, by Vapors of a Torch 123
Popular Belief erroneous respecting properties of common Ash Tree 133
Porphyritic Mountains 280
Porpoise, Brig 89
Port Huron 87
Portillo Pass 91
Portsmouth, O., Balloon Ascension from 224
Portsmouth, Va 45
Portugal, Climate of 196
Portugal, Maritime Adventure in 158
Potomac river suited to Bass 290
Post, New York Evening, S. Thayer, of 72
Potts, John 38, 45
Poultney, Iowa, Temperature at 208
Powhatan, Steamer 91
Power of Bactrian Camel 117
Practicability of introducing the Camel into the United States 116
Practical Results and Abstract Researches 131
Prairie Rattle-snake 38

Page.

Precious Opal from Mexico........ 45
Preevoort, Captain........ 93
Premiums not necessary........ 10
President of the United States........ 36
Presidio del Norte........ 45, 277
Preston, Texas........ 37, 84
Pressure of the Wind at Greenwich........ 219
Pretat's Accounts of Dromedary Regiment........ 119
Priestly........ 182
Prince George County, Md........ 44
Prince Henry, Voyages planned by........ 158
Prince of Orange........ 176
Principle on which Iodine acts on Poison........ 135
Prionotus Pilatus (*Flying-fish*)........ 327
Private Explorations, Results from........ 37
Private Reports of Explorations........ 96
Probable discoveiy of New Planets........ 145
Proofs of Divine Creator........ 100
Preposition to buy Stanley's Indian Gallery declined........ 77
Providential Government of the World........ 162
Prussian Government, action of, relative to Exchanges........ 21
Prussic Acid, Antidote to........ 135
Psychrometrical Observations at Sacramento, Cal........ 267, 269, 270, 271
Pteropus........ 45
Publications during 1854, quarto and octavo........ 31
Public Buildings in Europe........ 39
Publishers, Copyright Circular to........ 400
Pueblo of Zuñi........ 83
Pueblos of Quivira........ 313
Puerco river........ 300
Puerto del las Limpias........ 277
Puerto del Paisano........ 277
Puertos de Abó........ 299
Puget's Sound........ 82
Pulse........ 99
Pun in a Despatch from Plymouth Agent........ 176
Puryear, Hon. R. C., Member of Investigating Committee of the House of Representatives........ 77
Putnam, George P., & Co........ 36, 66
Putnam, G. P........ 66
Putrefactive Poisons........ 135
Pyrenees........ 171, 274
Quadrupeds........ 42
Quantity of Food required by the Camel........ 108
Quantity of Water required to make an Inch of Rain........ 246
Quarrá, Excursion to........ 296
Quarrá, Ruins of........ 302
Quebec........ 87
Quebec, to be admitted into the Confederation........ 174

Page.
Quebec, Winds at 213
Queen Eleanor, Wife of Edward I., Historical allusion to 132
Querechos, Manners and Customs of.... 310
Queries and Strictures, by Dr. Hare 203
Quincy's Visit to Southern Colonies.... 169
Racine, Wisconsin 87
Radiation.... 194
Rafar Palm.... 43
Railroad from El Paso to Guaymas.... 278
Railroad to Pacific....37, 80, 96, 281, 300
Railroad to Pacific, Line traced by Nature 281
Railroads, Invention and Introduction of.... 148
Rain, Amount of, from air over one spot.... 198
Rain, Annual Quantity on Atlantic and Pacific.... 244
Rain at Sacramento, California.... 268
Rain, Fall of, during 1854, in California.... 258
Rain, Quantity of, to Produce Floods.... 248
Rain, Qantity of Water to make an Inch of 246
Rain, Storms, Clouds, and Mists, at San Francisco.... 243, 248
Rain, Usual quantity of in Atlantic States 245
Rainy Seasons in California 246
Rainy Winter of 1849–'50, at San Francisco.... 245, 246
Raleigh, Sir Walter....127, 164, 166
Randall, Doctor A., of California, Liberality of.... 16
Rattle of Rattlesnake Carved on Temples in Central America.... 124
Rattlesnake, Description of.... 124
Rattlesnake, Dr. Brainard's Experiments with 132
Rattlesnake Weeds or Roots.... 133
Rattlesnakes Presented to Museum.... 38
Ray's teeth.... 42
Reading, a Rare Accomplishment with the French Canadians.... 174
Reading-room, Character of.... 22
Receipt of Books by Exchange.... 33
Receipts during 1854.... 57
Reed, Joseph, Visit to Boston of.... 169
Reed, Professor Henry, Lectures by 156
Re-election of Regents.... 72
Redfield Theory.... 228, 229
Red River 86, 94
Red Shale 44
Reduction of Meteorological Observations.... 19, 20
Regents of the Institution 5
Regents, Re-election of Rufus Choate and Gideon Hawley as.... 72
Register used in Fire-Alarm Telegraph.... 151
Remarkable Brown Coal-beds of Vermont.... 39
Remarkable Fact in History of Mankind 171
Remarks contributing to the Physical Geography of N. American Continent, by J. Froebel 272
Remedies for Poisoning.... 124
Removal of Mr. Jewett.... 75

Page.
Rennele's Estimate of Speed of Camel 110
Reporters not to attend Meetings of Board.... 72
Report of Coast Survey 95
Report of Executive Committee on L. Blodget.... 74
Report of the Assistant Secretary 31
Report on American Explorations, in 1853 and 1854 79
Report of the Building Committee.... 69
Reports of Explorations, published in 1853-'54 94
Report of the Executive Committee.... 57
Report on Estimates of Executive Committee adopted.... 76
Report on the Fishes of New Jersey, by S. F. Baird.... 317
Report of Mr. Meacham, on Distribution of Income, presented 77
Report of Secretary for 1854.... 7
Report of Secretary presented.... 77
Report of Special Committee on Communication between Board and Establishment 78
Reports on Vertebrata of Exploring Expeditions.... 40
Representation from Board requested to attend Special Committee of House of Representatives 76
Reptiles received 38, 39, 43, 44, 45, 46
Reptiles of Minnesota.... 292
Requirements of the act of Congress complied with.... 8
Researches.... 15
Research stimulated by Institution 9
Rescue, Brig.... 92
Resolutions approving Removal of Mr. Jewett 75
Resolution giving authority to Building Committee to use Funds on Deposit.... 76
Resolution to appoint Committee of Finance.... 77
Resolution to appoint Committee to confer with Committee of Establishment.... 73
Resolution to appoint "Library Committee".... 73
Resolution to appoint Committee to meet Committee of House of Representatives. 77
Resolutions on Distribution of Income.... 73
Resolutions on Income Appropriated to Library.... 73
Resolution of House of Representatives on Resignation of Mr. Choate.... 76
Resolution of Mr. Douglas, Relative to Correspondence.... 78
Resolutions of Select Committee, on Distribution of Income adopted.... 73
Results of Plan.... 8
Review of Weather at San Francisco for 1853.... 251
Resolution of 1688, Influence of, in Producing the Union.... 176
Revue Orientale.... 122
Rhees, William J., Collection of Materials for Notices of Libraries by.... 23
Rhees, William J., succeeded Dr. Foreman.... 23
Rhode Island.... 47
Rhode Island Colonists, Refused Admission into Confederacy.... 176
Rhombus Maculatus, (*Spotted Turbot*).... 350
Richland City.... 88
Riggs, Alfred C.... 38, 39, 45
Riley saw Camels fed with Charcoal.... 107
Ringgold, Captain C.... 89, 90, 96
Rings of Rattlesnake.... 124

Page.
Rio de los Mimbres 276
Rio de Papigóchic, or Conception 278
Rio del Fuerte 278
Rio de Santa Maria 280
Rio Grande, Collections from the 37
Rio Grande, Division of Rocky Mountains at 275
Rio Grande, Features of 296
Rio Grande, Level of, at El Paso 280
Rio Mimbres 280
Rio Yaqui 278
Ritter 100, 102, 103, 111, 114, 120
Rivers, Influence of, upon Civilization 170
Rivers in Mexico 278
River Head, L. I 16, 42, 88, 317
Rives, John C., Stereotype Process adopted by 23
Roads in New Mexico 299
Roanoke, N. C 45
Robinson, Estimate of Speed of Camel 110
Robinson's Landing 345
Rochester, Wis 88
Rochester, N. Y., Temperature at 201
Rock-fish 321
Rocky Mountains 39, 81, 82, 196, 197
Rocky Mountains, Divides into two Ranges 275
Rocky Mountains, Southern Extremity of, defined 277
Rocky Mountain Passes, not more rugged or steeper than those of Arabia and Tartary 117
Rodgers, Lieutenant John 89, 90
Rogers, Hon. Sion H 45
Rogers, Jeremiah 39, 45
Rolando, Lieutenant 89
Romans, use of Camels in War by 118
Rome, View of History of 156
Route Proposed for Pacific Railroad 300
Roulin, Analysis of Woorara by 127
Royal Society, Books distributed by 33
Ruhmkorff, Apparatus for Dia-Magnetism 17
Ruins of Abó, Description of 300
Ruins of Gran Quivira 307
Ruins of New Mexico 309
Ruins of Quarrá 302
Russell, John 36
Russell, Robert, First Lecture on Meteorology 181
Second Lecture on Meteorology 192
Third Lecture on Meteorology 202
Appendix to Lectures by 215
Russell's Rule for ascertaining Dew Point 194, 221
Russell mentions Abstinence of Camel for Fifteen Days 109

Page.
Russia, Mean Annual Range of Barometer at 204
Russian Expedition against Khiva and Bokhara 118
Russian Provinces, Longevity of Camel in 117
Rutherford 182
Sacramento, Cal., Hatch's Meteorological Observations at 263
Sacramento, Cal., Logan's Meteorological Observations at 259, 260, 261
Sacramento City, great Rain at 251
Sacramento River 246
Safety of Aeronaut in Thunder Storm 224
Salada, La 299
Salamander 45, 294, 295
Salamander of Wisconsin, Description of 295
Salem, N. C 44
Salem, Snow fell in July, 1804 197
Salinas River 84
Salt Lake 37
Salt Lake City 43, 83, 86
Salt Lake near Manzana 303
Sampson Fox 37, 44
San Antonio 43, 83, 84
San Antonio de Bejar 277
San Bernardino Chain 278
San Carlos, Narrows and Rapids of 279, 280
Sand Creek, Va., Expedition to 289
Sandia Peak 298
Sandilla Mountains 275
San Diego 44, 45, 84, 256
San Diego, Rain at 256
Sand Smelt 338
Sandwich Manse, Orkney 211, 213
Sandy Hill Fork 83
San Francisco 35, 37, 84, 86
San Francisco County, Cal., Birds from 43
San Francisco, Climate of 231, 255
San Francisco Mountains 37, 83
Sangre del Christo 83
San Joaquin 84
San José, Winds at 243
San Juan River 276
San Luis Potosi 83, 277
San Salvador, Volcanic Coves of 273
Santa Anna, Concession by 278
Santa Anna, Indian Chief 315
Santa Barbara 276
Santa Cruz 188
Santa Fé 44, 45, 275
Santa Maria, Laguna de 276, 280
Santiago, Chile 35
Santos, Indian Chief 315

	Page.
Saratoga, Sloop-of-war	91
Saratoga	201
Sargus Ovis	331
Satow, Germany	39, 45
Saturn, Orbit of	143
Saturn, American Discoveries respecting	146
Sanrus Mexicanus	346
Savages possess Art of Poisoning unknown to Civilized Man	124
Savannah, Temperature at	209
Sawkins, J. G., Description of Ruins at Mitla, by	11
Saxon Characteristics	161, 163
"Saxondom"	157
Saxton, Lieutenant	81, 82
Scalops Breweri	45
Scandinavian Discoveries	158
Scandinavian Alps	171
Scenery in New Mexico	293
Scheel, Dr.	82
Schomburgk, Sir R	45
Schomburgk, Sir Robert, Statement of, respecting Poisons	126, 127
Schoolcraft, H. R.	95, 96
School of Design, Models lent to	26
Schuchart, Mr	280
Science the great Instrument of Civilization	147
Scientific Correspondence	224
Scorpions	44
Scorpion, Schooner	93
Scrope, Thomas H.	93
Scotland, Land and Sea Breezes in	187
Scotland, Winds in	211
Scotophis Alleghaniensis	44
Scripture, Law of Temperature alluded to in	195
Scrophularia, Used for Serpent Poison	133
Sculpin	328
Scutellaria, Used for Serpent Poison	133
Seaton, W. W.	62, 63, 65, 67
Sea Bass	323
Sea-Breezes in Europe.	187
Sea-Breeze in California.	240
Sea Catfish	341
Sea Pike	346
Sea Water, Use of by Camels	100
Secretary of the Navy	89, 93
Secretary of War	80, 95
Secretary, Annual Report of, Presented to the Board	77
Secretary of the Institution, Appendix to Mr. Russell's Lectures, by	215
Sedimentary Rocks of Texas	280
Seeds of Silk Cotton	43
Seeds of Texas Plants	44

	Page.
Sergeant, J. D	38, 45
Sermon at Mount Ararat	115
Serpents, Nature and Cure of the Bite of	123
Serpents Furnished with Poison	124
Serpents, Treatment for Bite of	135
Settlements by Dutch and Swedes	175
Seven Planets only Supposed to Exist	137
Seven Rivers	297
Seventeenth Century, that of Colonization	167
Seventh Volume Smithsonian Contributions	10
Sevier Lake	83
Sevier River	83
Shakspeare, Description of Thunder-Storms, by	199
Shakspeare's Account of the Killing of the King, in Hamlet	150
Sharks	352
Shark's Teeth	39, 42, 43
Shawnee Reservation	83
Sheboygan, Wisconsin	88
Shecutts	329
Sheet Lightning	225, 227
Shells	45
Shelter Island	334
Shepard, Professor C. U	94
Sherburne, Mr	83
Shiel	182
Shiner	341
Ship Canal Expedition	93
Ship of the Desert	100
Shippen, William, Experiments by	18
Shirley, General	169
Shirley's Packet	94
Shoalwater Bay	82
Shooting-Stars in California	258
Short-Billed Pike	345
Shrew Skin	44
Shriver, Mr. William, Introduction of Bass into the Potomac, by	290
Shriver, David	290
Shumard, Dr. B. F	82, 94
Shumard, Dr. George G	45, 85, 86, 94, 95
Siberia, Camel in, used for Saddle or Burden	112
Siberia, Bactrian Camel indifferent to the Cold of	115
Sickness of Whites at Liberia	93
Sidney, Sir Philip, Character and Enterprises of	164, 165
Sienitic Mountains	280
Sierras	87, 227
Sierra Blanca	276, 297, 315
Sierra de las Gallinas	306, 315
Sierra de la Manzana	299, 316
Sierra del Palo Duro	299

Page.
Sierra de los Mimbres........ 276
Sierra Madre, Remarks respecting........ 273
Sierra Madre, Erroneous Idea entertained of........ 277
Sierra Nevada........ 84
Signal Circuits and Boxes........ 151
Silliman's Journal........ 229
Silliman's Journal, Explanation of Storms in........ 199
Silk, Cotton Seeds of........ 43
Silver Garfish........ 346
Silverside........ 338
Silver Perch........ 331
Simms, W. Gilmore, Lectures by........ 28
Simonton, J. W........ 72
Simpson, Captain........ 83
Sinaloa, Coast Range of........ 279
Singer, Lieutenant........ 93
Sing Sing, New York........ 42, 88
Sing Sing, White Perch at........ 322
Siskowit, Habits........ 283
Sitgreaves, Captain........ 83, 89, 94
Sixteenth Century, State of Society in........ 123
Size of the Camel........ 113
Sizzi, an Astronomer of Florence........ 137
Skin of Sperm Whale........ 45
Sky covered by Clouds at Philadelphia........ 223
Smith, Captain E. K........ 45
Smith, Commodore........ 39, 45
Smith, J. Lawrence, Investigations by, in Laboratory........ 18
Smith, Dr. J. Lawrence, Lectures by........ 28, 29
Smithson, James, Proceeds of Bequest of........ 62
Smithson, James, Personal Effects of........ 70
Smithson, James, Analysis of Specimens of Meteorites belonging to Cabinet of........ 18
Smithsonian Bequest........ 57
Smithsonian Contributions, Distribution of Volume VI........ 36
Smith's Sound........ 92
Snakes........ 38
Snapping Turtle........ 39
Snow, Effects of........ 246
Societies meeting in Smithsonian Building........ 27
Society in the Sixteenth Century........ 123
Society of Arts, London, Models, &c., from........ 26
Socorro Mountains........ 276, 298
Soft and Salt Water........ 188
Solar Eclipse of May 26, 1854, Account of........ 17
Solar Eclipse of November 30, 1853........ 91
Solar Eclipses, Map of, by Professor Coffin........ 17
Solar System more Complex than supposed........ 140
Solfatara, on Northern Side of Lower Colorado........ 281
Solinus, Mistranslation by........ 102

Page.
Solution of Iodine Prevents or Retards Death from Serpent Bite.................. 133
Sonora..80, 83, 278, 279
Sontag, Augustus.. 92
Sooloo Sea.. 90
Sorex Dekayi.. 38, 44
South America... 33
South America, Humboldt's Voyage to.................................. 198
South America, Method of Preparing Poisoned Arrows in................ 127
Southampton, Storeship... 91
South Carolina...38, 43, 49
Southerly Winds prevail more in Summer than in Winter................ 202
South Pass... 87
Spain, Maritime Adventure in... 158
Spain, Summers of.. 189
Spanish Expeditions to New Mexico.................................... 306, 312
Spanish Mackerel... 335
Spanish Trail.. 83, 276
Sparkill, Fishes of the.. 88, 318
Spawning Grounds in the Lakes.. 288
Special Locality of Little Planetary Bodies.......................... 143
Special Committee of House of Representatives........................ 76
Species of Camel... 101
Species of Animals Suited to Man as a Migratory Animal............... 99, 100
Specific Gravity of Gases.. 193
Specimens Illustrating Experiments on Growth of Teredo and Barnacle, &c....... 45
Spencer, Mr., Microscope by.. 26
Spenser's Allusion in the "Fairie Queen" to Virginia................. 165
Sphyræna Borealis, (*Northern Barracuda*)............................ 326
Spinous Dory... 336
Spot Striped Balloon Fish.. 351
Spotted Turbot... 350
Spotted Cybium... 335
Springbrook.. 88
Squails, Cause of.. 198
Squalus Tiburo... *337
Squeteague... 329
Stampedes, Security against, by using Camels......................... 121
Stanley, J. M., Communication from................................... 77
Stanley, J. M., Indian Collection by................................. 26
Stansbury, Captain... 83
Stansbury's Mules Travelled Two Days without Food or Water........... 109
Stars, Catalogues of... 145
State Department... 36
State Libraries.. 36
State Records in England, Recent Investigations in................... 164
Statistics of Library for 1854....................................... 21
St. Aubin, Jersey.. 212, 213
St. Augustine, Florida... 45
St. Bartholomew, Massacre of... 123

	Page.
Steam	183, 192
Steamboat, Introduction of	148
Steele, Dr. Thomas R.	38, 45, 94
Steilacoom	82
Stereotyping, Experiments in	22
Sternothærus	43
Steuben, Maine, Temperature at	207, 209
Stevens, Dr. R. P.	39, 45
Stevens, Governor I. I.	37, 80, 95, 96
Stevens, Henry, Books distributed by	33
Stevens, Lieutenant H. R.	89
Stickleback	328
Stites, Captain Townsend	331
Stites, John, Thanks to	318
Stimpson, Wm.	89
St. John found Camel at Oasis of Jupiter Ammon	102
St. John's to be Admitted into the Confederation	174
St. Lawrence, Winds on	213
St. Louis, Missouri	36, 43, 81
St. Louis, Missouri, Temperature at	208
St. Mary's Mission	81
Stocking Fish-ponds, Pell's Method of	321
Stomach of the Camel	106, 107
Stone in New Mexico	299
Stoneman, Lieutenant	84
Storer, Dr. D. H.	42, 332
Storer, F. H.	89
Storm in Europe, Example of, by Mr. Russell	211
Storm of November 12, 1854	208
Storms in New Mexico	297
Storms of February, 1842	202
Storms, Peculiarities of, in Europe	210
Storms, Rain, Clouds, and Mists at San Francisco	243, 248
St. Paul's	81
St. Paul's River, Africa	93
St. Pilen, Barometrical Observations at	204
Strabo	102
Strain, Lieutenant	93, 96
Straits of Sunda	90
Strang. J. J., Natural History of Beaver Islands by	282
Striped Bass	321
Strychnos Toxifera	127
Strychnia acts upon Spinal Marrow	129
Strychnia counteracted by Iodine	135
Strychnine, Poison of Woorara attributed to	127
Strychnine. Effects of	128
St. Simon's Bay	89
Stuart, Frederick D	89
Sturgeon, Habits, Manner of Catching	283

Page.
Sturgis, Lieutenant S. D. 296
Sturm, F 42
Suckers, Habits, Qualities, Method of Catching, &c 286
Suckley, Dr 81, 82
Suez to Cairo, Eighty-four Miles 110
Sugar Regions, None in Europe 189
Sulphate of Alumine or Alum used for Serpent Poison 133
Sulphuret of Iron 44
Sultan of Morocco's Camels 115
Summary of Means of Temperature for San Francisco, December, 1850, to Janary, 1852 232
Summer Climate of California 241
Summers of Spain, Italy, &c 189
Summerville, North Carolina 44
Sunfish of Beaver Islands 287
Supply, Store-ship 91
Surface Wind at rest at night 190
Surgeon General U. S. A., Remarks on Natural History, communicated by 291
Surgeon, most distinguished of the 16th century 123
Surinam 38, 46
Survey of Routes to Pacific 80
Surveying Parties, Order and Organization of 80
Susquehanna, Steamer 91
Sutter Lake, California, frozen over 260
Sweden, mean annual Range of Barometer at 204
Sweden, West Winds of 197
Swedish Academy of Sciences 42
Switzerland, Temperature in 195
Sykes, Colonel 186
Syngnathus Viridescens, (*Green Pipe-fish*) 351
Synopsis of Wise's Observations on Aerial Voyage 225
Syria 45
Syria, age of Camel in 113
Szabo, Mr 97
Table for calculating Mean Temperature 234
Table-lands in Mexico 280
Tachtirawan, or litter borne by Camels 119
Taflin, Captain 85
Tagique 316
Tailors, Temnodon Saltator, known as 338
Talcahuana 39, 43
Talipot tree 39, 42
Tamaulipas 87
Tangencies of Circles and Spheres, a Memoir on 13
Tanjore Pill, Arsenic in the form of 131
Taos 85
Tartary 121
Tautoga Americana, (*Tautog*, *Black-fish*) 340
Tartary, Camels used for military purposes in 118

Page.
Tartary, one-humped Camel found in........ 101
Tavernier........ 103
Taylor, Hon. N. G., member of Investigating Committee of House of Representatives. 77
Tejon Pass........ 37, 84, 85
Telegraph, Fire-Alarm........ 147
Telegraph for Cities described........ 150
Telegraph, differences between common and the municipal........ 149
Telescope, first imported into the United States........ 145
Temperature at Bombay........ 219
Temperature of San Francisco in 1853........ 253
Temperature at Philadelphia........ 220
Temperature on East Coast contrasted with that on the West of the Mississippi........ 209
Temperature at Greenwich........ 215
Temperature of United States west of the Mississippi adapted to Camel........ 116
Temperature of California........ 231
Temperature and Pressure Curves........ 206
Temnodon Saltator, (*Blue-fish, Horse Mackerel, Skip Jack*)........ 337
Tendency to local self-government........ 160
Tennessee........ 38, 45, 49
Tension of Vapor at Bombay........ 219
Teredo, Growth and Ravages of, and Protection against........ 39, 45
Tertiary Fossils........ 43
Terrestrial Magnetism........ 16
Terra del Fugo........ 273
Tetillas, Las........ 299, 302, 315
Tetraodon Turgidus (*Toad-fish*)........ 352
Texans, Visit of, to Gran Quivira........ 304
Teton river........ 81
Texas........ 38, 39, 44, 46, 49
Texas, Surveys in........ 86
Texas Plants, Seeds of........ 44
Teyas, Manners and Customs of the........ 310
Thalia, Orbit of........ 144
Thayer, S........ 72
Thermometrical Observations at Sacramento, California........ 265, 266
Themis, Orbit of........ 142, 144
Thermometrograph, Observations with........ 267
Theories respecting Action of Poisons........ 129
Theory of Olbers respecting Asteroids........ 138, 141
Theory of Gradual Condensation........ 144
Thirty-eighth Parallel, Pacific Railroad Route on........ 82
Thirty-fifth Parallel, Survey of Route to Pacific on the........ 83
Thirty-second Parallel, Survey of Railroad Route on the........ 84
Thom, Mr........ 190
Thornbury, N. C., Temperature at........ 209
Thomas, Professor W. H. B........ 38, 45
Thread Herring........ 349
Three great Slopes of Table-land........ 280
Thunder-clouds coming together........ 226, 228, 229

Page.
Thunder only heard twice in San Francisco, in 1853 253
Thunder in California 258
Thunder-storms less grand in Europe than America.... 199
Thunder-storms 197, 198, 225
Thunder-storms have two plates of clouds.... 225
Thunder-storm, Phenomena of, during aerial voyage.... 224
Thuringian Forest.... 274
Tibboo Maberry.... 114
Tiennas, Description of.... 127
Times, New York Daily, J. W. Simonton, editor of.... 72
Timkowski.... 117, 118
Timber in New Mexico.... 290
Tinkham, Mr.... 81
Toad-fish.... 340, 352
Toads, North American, Account of.... 40
Topographical Maps, necessity of.... 272
Torreon 304, 316
Torrey, Dr. J 94
Toricelli.... 182, 184
Tornado of Chenay.... 229
Tortillas.... 308, 311
Totten, General, Resolution relative to Building.... 76
Totten, General, Commission on Building Material.... 18
Towers, John T., elected Member of Building Committee.... 76
Toxicology, Principle of, well established.... 135
Trachytic mountains 280
Trachinotus Spinosus.... 336
Trade Winds, Origin of.... 186
Tradition respecting Mines in New Mexico.... 312, 313
Training of the Camel.... 113
Translation of Spanish Account of Treasure.... 313
Transactions of the American Philosophical Society.... 202
Travel, Rate of, by Camel.... 110
Traveller in California, Account of Poison by.... 127
Travelling with Camels.... 116
Treasurer, Statement of Finances to Board.... 74
Treasures supposed to be in New Mexico.... 304
Treatment of Poisoning by Serpent Bite and Woorara.... 130
Treatment of Serpent Bite in different Countries.... 131
Treatment for Serpent Bite and Poisoned Arrows.... 135
Trebizond.... 121
Trentera.... 84
Trincheres Pass.... 83
Trial by Jury.... 159
Trichomycterus.... 91
Trinity River, Thunder Storm at.... 256
Trinidad 38, 45
Tropical Countries have most Rains.... 244
Trout from New York.... 43

	Page.
Trout, Method of Catching, Snatching, &c.	284
Trowbridge, Lieutenant W. P.	37, 38, 45, 97
Truckee River	86
Tuckahoe River, White Perch in	322
Tucker, Beverley	95
Tudor Kings, nothing achieved by	163
Tueson	37, 84
Tulare	84
Tuley, Colonel Joseph	38, 45
Tumanes, La Mesa de los	304
Tuni	37
Turcoman Camel very powerful	113
Turcoman Camel obtained at Aleppo	121
Turcomans	111
Turkeys first imported into England	163
Turner, Professor W. W.	95
Turtles	38
Tuscany, Camels domesticated in	108
Tuscany	121
Two Maxima and Minima of Barometer	218
Tuscaloosa, Alabama, Curve of Temperature and Pressure for	206
Umbrina Alburnus, (*King Fish*)	331
Unanimity in Religious Creed required by Confederacy	176
Uncompagre River	83
Unfavorable Condition of Climate of Western Continent to the Camel	117
Uniformity in Lower Orders of Creation	162
Uniform Temperature of California	233
Union County, Arkansas, Fall of Rain at	244
Unexpended Income on hand	9
United States Military Academy, West Point	35
United States Patent Office	35, 36
United States and Mexican Boundary Survey	80
United States Agricultural Society, Meeting of	27
United States Naval Astronomical Expedition	36
Union, The, Lectures on	156
Union, The, how formed	158
United Colonies of New England	176
University System of New York	51
Uppernavik	92
Upham, Charles W., Communication from	76
Upham, Charles W., Chairman of House Investigating Committee	77
Uranus, Discovery of	137
Uspallata Pass	90, 91
Utah, Heavy Storm of Rain and Hail in	256
Utility of the Camel	114
Valley of the Lower Danube has Summer Rains	117
Valverde	276
Valencia	297
Van Dieman's Land	89

	Page.
Vandalia, Sloop-of-war	91
Variation of Temperature at California	242
Variegated Goby	339
Vegas of Santa Clara	85
Venom of Serpents used by Indians on Arrows	126
Venom of the Rattlesnake	125
Venom of Serpents used by Man	124
Venom of Serpents cannot be distinguished by Chemical Tests from Saliva	124
Vera Cruz	277
Vera Cruz, Northers at	203
Vermont	47
Vermont, Auriferous Deposits of	39, 43
Vermont, remarkable Brown Coal-beds of	39
Versailles, France	212
Vesta, Discovery of	139
Vertebrata, Reports on	40
Vincennes, Sloop	89
Virago, British Steamer	93
Virginia	38, 48, 49
Virginia, Arrival of First Colony in	166
Virginia, Title to an Indefinite Region of America	164
Virginia, Mentioned on first page of "The Fairy Queen"	165
Volney	189
Volney, Explanation of Snow Storm by	199
Volume V, Distribution of	36
Vortisch, Reverend L	39, 45
Voyages Planned by Prince Henry	158
Vulpes Fulvus	38, 44
Wade, Major, Testing Machine invented by	18
Wahsatch Pass	83
Wailes, Colonel B. L. C	38, 46
Wales	162
Walla-Walla	81
Walker's Pass	84
Walsh, Mr., Balloon Ascent by	196, 204
Wanderings in South America, by Charles Waterton	128
Warmest Month in California	257
Warmest Month of the Year	233
War Department	86
Warner's Ranch	84
War, use made of the Camel in	118
Washington	35, 36
Washington and Lisbon, Winters Compared	196
Washington, Direction of Thunder-clouds at	200
Washington, Mississippi	46
Washington Monument Society	64
Washington, Roch-fish Chief Staple of	321
Washington, Temperature at	209
Washington Territory	81, 82

Page.
Washington, Travels of.... 169
"Water-meter" described.... 152
Waterton, Charles, Statement by, respecting Woorara.... 128
Water-Witch, Steamer.... 90
Waupacca river.... 88
Weak fish.... 329
Weather of February, 1854, at San Francisco.... 254
Weather of San Francisco for 1853.... 251
Weather, Peculiarities of, in Europe.... 210
Webb, Dr. T. H.... 38, 46
Webster, Daniel, a celebrated Fisherman.... 321
Weight of a Cubic Foot of Air at Greenwich.... 217
Weight of Boxes sent abroad.... 32, 33
Weight of Cubic Foot of Steam calculated.... 192
Weight of the Camel.... 113
Weight of Water in a Cubic Foot of Air at Greenwich.... 215
Wells, Hon. Daniel, Member of the Investigating Committee of the House of Representatives.... 77
Westerly Wind, cause of cold.... 196
Western Africa, Exploration of.... 92
Western Missouri, Exploration in.... 88
West India Islands, Hurricanes in.... 187
West India Islands to be admitted into Confederation with the Thirteen Colonies.. 174
West Indies, Hurricanes of.... 198, 199
West Point.... 35
Westport.... 85, 87
West Winds preponderate at California.... 240
Whale, Fœtus of.... 38
Whipple, Lieutenant A. W.... 37, 80, 83, 86, 96
Whipple's Route to Pacific.... 300
Whip-sting ray.... *337
Whirlwinds in Arabia and Africa.... 187
Whitaker, Professor J., Lectures by.... 27, 28
White, Mr.... 83
White-fish at Sing Sing.... 337
White-fish, Method of Catching, Habits, &c.... 285
White Mullet.... 339
White Perch.... 323
White Zinc Paint.... 39
Whitney, J. D., Catalogue of Minerals, &c., collected by.... 387
Wild Animals of Beaver Islands.... 282
Wildcats.... 38, 44
Wild Pigeon, Flights of.... 99
Wild Rose Pass, Wild and Romantic Scenery at.... 277
Willard, E. D., Thanks to.... 318
William the Conqueror.... 161
Williamson, Lieutenant R. S.... 37, 80, 84, 96
Wilkes, Captain.... 89
Wilmington, Delaware, Fall of Rain at.... 244

	Page.
Wilson, Professor, Models, &c., Presented by	26
Wind at Greenwich	219
Wind at Sacramento, California	268, 269, 270, 271
Wind, Direction of, during Rains	249
Wind-fish	341
Wind, Force of, at Philadelphia	223
Winds and Currents of the Ocean	91
Winds at Philadelphia	238
Winds, Course of	186
Winds, Cause of Coldness of Westerly	196
Winds, Direction of, in United States	189
Winds during Storm of November 12	210
Winds in Scotland	211
Winds in Winter in United States	196
Winds of California	236
Winds, Reductions by Professor Coffin	189
Winds, Relation of, to Elevation of Barometer, the Temperature and Humidity	263
Winter Flounder	349
Winter of 1849–'50 in San Francisco	245
Winters, Cause of Cold, in United States	196
Wisconsin	37, 38, 43, 44, 50, 51
Wisconsin, Explorations of	16, 88
Wisconsin State Agricultural Society	35
Wise, John, Balloon Ascension by	224
Wise, John, Dr. Hare's Remarks on Aerial Voyage of	224, 230
Wiswall to Hinckly	176
Witte, Hon. W. H., Member of Special Committee of House of Representatives	76
Wolf River	88
Wollaston	138
Wolves	38
Woodhouse, Dr.	94
Wool of Cashmere Goat	114
Woorara, Description of	127, 128, 129
Woorara, innocuous when Swallowed	128
Woorara, Opinions respecting Poison of	127
Woorara, Poison of, does not depend on Strychnine	128
Woorara, Quantity of, required to cause Death	134
Woorara, Treatment of Poisoning by	130
Worcester, Mass	35
Work done in the Museum	40
Wounds of Poisoned Arrows	123, 135
Wright, Charles	89
Wright, Lieutenant H. G	37, 38, 46
Wurdemam, Gustavus	37, 38, 39, 46, 97
Wyman, Dr. J	38, 46, 64, 65
Yellow Caranx	336
Yellow Creek, Ohio	44
Yellow Mackerel	336
Yellow River	88

Page.
Yellow Stone River 81, 82
Yond, Rev. Thomas, Description of Woorara by 127
Young Men's Christian Association, Lectures for 28
Zanzibar Copal 44
Zeuglodon 44
Zone of Small Planets between Mars and Jupiter 137
Zoology of Michigan 38
Zostera Marina 319
Zuñi 94, 300
Zygaena Mallens *337
Zygaena Tiburo *337

Lightning Source UK Ltd.
Milton Keynes UK
UKHW02f1818210818
327592UK00012B/496/P

9 780282 883713